THE SYMPHONIC REPERTOIRE

Published with the generous support of the Allen
Whitehill Clowes Charitable Foundation

*THE SYMPHONIC REPERTOIRE
VOLUME III PART B:
THE EUROPEAN SYMPHONY FROM
CA. 1800 TO CA. 1930: GREAT BRITAIN,
RUSSIA, AND FRANCE*

A. Peter Brown (1943–2003)

THE SYMPHONIC REPERTOIRE

VOLUME III PART B

The European Symphony from ca. 1800 to ca. 1930: Great Britain, Russia, and France

A. PETER BROWN

WITH BRIAN HART

INDIANA UNIVERSITY PRESS
BLOOMINGTON AND INDIANAPOLIS

This book is a publication of
Indiana University Press
601 North Morton Street
Bloomington, IN 47404-3797 USA

http://iupress.indiana.edu

Telephone orders   800-842-6796
Fax orders   812-855-7931
Orders by e-mail   iuporder@indiana.edu

Library of Congress Cataloging-in-Publication Data

Brown, A. Peter; with Brian Hart
    The European symphony from ca. 1800 to ca. 1930 :
Great Britain, Russia, and France / A. Peter Brown.
        p.   cm. — (The symphonic repertoire ; v. 3B)
        Includes bibliographical references (p.   ) and index.
        ISBN 978-0-253-34897-5 (cl : alk. paper)

ML1255.B87   2008 vol. 3B
784.2'184s—dc21
[784.2'184'0943]   98-26549

I   2   3   4   5   13   12   11   10   09   08

To all of the conductors, musicians, mentors, colleagues, and academic scholars who fueled A. Peter Brown's lifelong interest in the symphonic repertoire and its performance

Contents

Contents

Contents

Plates

Tables

Preface to the Series

A SURPRISING ASPECT OF THE twentieth-century musical historiography is that some of the central repertoires of Western art music remain unexplored in broad-based treatments; the exceptions are Donald J. Grout's *A Short History of Opera* (1947), William S. Newman's *History of the Sonata Idea* (1959–1969, 3 vols.), and, most recently, Howard Smither's *History of the Oratorio* (1977–2000, 4 vols.). Except for Newman's efforts for the sonata, the large instrumental genres such as the string quartet and symphony, which form the core of the canon, have received the least attention. The reasons for this neglect have been practical: much of the music for large ensembles was disseminated in parts rather than scores during the eighteenth century, and many of the scores published during the nineteenth century have deteriorated to brittleness. Fortunately, within the 1980s and 1990s a sufficient number of the more obscure symphonies has been made available in editions and reprints so that a measured and reasonable overview can be constructed.

The last comprehensive effort by one scholar to deal with the symphony appeared in 1921, when the Swiss musicologist Karl Nef published his *Geschichte der Sinfonie und Suite,* of which something less than two-thirds of the tome is devoted to the symphony, and because of space limitations, Nef's tale is often reduced to the naming of composers and titles. Only two types of treatments have seen publication since Nef's book: the symposium with a series of different authors writing sections in their fields of specialization (e.g., the volumes edited by Ralph Hill [1949], Robert Simpson [1966–1967], Ursula von Rauchhaupt [1973], and Robert Layton [1995]), and the textbook meant for collegiate students (e.g., Homer Ulrich [1952], Louise Cuyler [1973], Roland Nadeau [1974], Preston Stedman [1979], and D. Kern Holoman [1997]). In addition, there are compendiums of program notes and the like by such writers as Donald L. Ferguson (1954), Alfred Frankenstein (1966), Edward O. D. Downes (1976), and Ethan Mordden (1980). In this latter category belongs the most distinguished contribution: Donald Francis Tovey's program notes for the concerts of the Edinburgh Reid Orchestra, collected in six volumes as *Essays in Musical Analysis.*

The series of volumes offered here does not belong exclusively to any of the above genres, but incorporates elements from all of them. It is not a history in the narrative sense, since it does not attempt to place a large number of symphonies under a covering hypothesis. And yet, it uses historical suppositions to explain interrelationships among works of composers known to each other and belonging to the same traditions of training and milieu. It is not a textbook, for it attempts to deal with the repertoire in greater detail. And the discussions, while adaptable as program notes, go beyond the usual requirements of the form.

Titling the series *The Symphonic Repertoire* raises the question as to what constitutes "the repertoire" or symphonic canon today. Fifty or a hundred years ago, it could be defined as those works which were repeatedly programmed decade after decade in the major cities of Europe and the Americas. Today, there is also the "technological canon," which is represented by a series of symphonies heard on orchestral programs in scattered locations, but not a part of every orchestra's repertoire.

This other canon is heard by an audience larger in scope than the four to six thousand listeners who might attend an orchestral concert during a given week in New York, London, or Vienna. Its dissemination is through radio broadcasts, long-playing records, tapes, and compact discs. Two examples might be cited. First, the Danish symphonist Carl Nielsen has always been a major force in his country, not as a "Nationalist," but as a "national" composer. While his six symphonies loom large on the Danish landscape, they are only occasionally heard in live performances outside of Scandinavia. Yet, as of this writing (2003), there exist at least four complete sets on compact disc recorded by orchestras and conductors of different backgrounds and temperaments. Secondly, there is Gustav Mahler, who prophetically said, "My time will come." In the 1950s and 1960s, Mahler's works were an anathema to some audiences. When Fritz Reiner conducted the Fourth Symphony and *Das Lied von der Erde* in Chicago, it was reported that a substantial number of the old-line subscribers left at the intermission. During the same period, the Mahler revival was beginning with a series of recordings by the New York Philharmonic under Leonard Bernstein. The availability of these big and tightly formed symphonies for repeated hearings in brash interpretations led to their canonic status in the concert hall, which today is buttressed by a large contingent of passionate advocates. The present status of Mahler's symphonies reveals the impact of recordings on the concert-hall repertoire.

While it is impossible to deal with all of the symphonies heard in the concert hall and on compact disc, these volumes attempt to cover a significant fraction of the repertoire. Though the organization of the series is chronological, the individual books are being published in an order that reflects the present state of research. The author began with Volumes II and IV, on the Viennese symphony; this book, Volume III, is devoted to other European developments from *ca.* 1800 to *ca.* 1930; Volume I, which will discuss the eighteenth century in Europe and England, will appear next.

At the pinnacle of the repertoire are the symphonies written by composers whose central areas of activity were in the old Austrian lands. The first flowering occurred at the end of the eighteenth and in the first three decades of the nineteenth century with Haydn, Mozart, Beethoven, and Schubert. Beginning in the 1780s, Haydn's and Mozart's symphonies were repeatedly heard in concerts throughout Europe and England, and Beethoven's symphonies achieved a revered status almost immediately. Schubert's symphonies, however, went into hibernation until mid-century, when his last two, the "Unfinished" (D.759) and the "Great" (D.944), were revived respectively in Vienna (1865) and Leipzig (1839); his earlier symphonies, except for No. 6, first received public hearings at the Crystal Palace in London through the efforts of Sir George Grove and the conductor August Manns. With these four composers this repertoire of more than 175 symphonies constitutes the domain of the second in the series of five volumes, *The First Golden Age of the Viennese Symphony,* though the first to appear.

After nearly a half century in hibernation, the sleeping Viennese giant awoke to what some viewed as a reincarnation of Beethoven's symphonic language with the first hearing, in Vienna, of Brahms's Symphony No. 1, which was performed on December 17, 1876, at the concerts of the Gesellschaft der Musikfreunde under the direction of the composer. A year later his Second Symphony was premiered at the Philharmonic Concerts. Even though Bruckner had composed some gigantic symphonies prior to Brahms's first contribution, their impact was diminished until the composer's authoritative texts were made available after World War II. Bruckner, like Brahms, received recognition in some Viennese quarters and was disdained in others. Antonín Dvořák, though often viewed as a nationalist composer, was in his symphonic writing—except for the third movements—a musician whose primary heritage was Beethoven, Schubert, and Brahms. It was Brahms who aided the younger composer with letters of support for monetary stipends from the Austrian government. Mahler was seemingly ambivalent toward Brahms as a symphonist; as a conductor, Mahler programmed Brahms's orchestral works with retouchings of the orchestration. For both Bruckner and Mahler, the symphony constituted the heart of their output; for Brahms and Dvořák, it occupied something less than a central place. Yet, for all of them, the central figure of the past remained Beethoven. These composers, together with the conservative Hungarian Karl Goldmark and the more idiosyncratic symphonic works of Schoenberg, Berg, and Webern, among others, constitute Volume IV: *The Second Golden Age of the Viennese Symphony.*

Volume III covers the European symphony from *ca.* 1830 to *ca.* 1930. The composers considered are either outgrowths of the old-line Classicism or essentially Romantics in their musical language. Beethoven, for many of these composers, must have conjured up feelings of ambivalence. On the one hand, they recognized his hegemony; on the other hand, it was artistically a futile pursuit to be a clone of such a powerful figure. In short, they suffered anxieties aggravated by an influence from which they could not escape. Nearly every composer dealt with in this volume showed signs of Beethoven's powerful precedents by either direct modeling, by taking over some aspects while rejecting others (e.g., Mendelssohn's Symphony No. 4 and Beethoven's Symphony No. 7, or Berlioz's *Harold in Italy* and Beethoven's Symphonies Nos. 7 and 9), or by total rejection. Alternative exemplars for the composers of the Leipzig/Berlin group were the Schubert of the "Great" C Major Symphony D.944 as well as the works of Mendelssohn and Schumann. A number of composers from all over Europe and England, such as Sterndale Bennett, Franz Berwald, Niels Gade, Edvard Grieg, and Johan Svendsen, spent time in Leipzig and/or Berlin. Outside of the Viennese circles, they were, except for Schumann, a somewhat less powerful force in symphonic writing. Another significant circle—for want of a better designation—might be called the "New Germans," even though the strongest practitioners of this aesthetic were the Frenchman Hector Berlioz and the Hungarian Franz Liszt, leaving only Richard Wagner, Richard Strauss, and perhaps Joachim Raff as bona fide "New Germans." Wagner found the symphony after Beethoven a spent genre and believed that its true successor was the music drama. As a result, Wagner composed but one symphony in 1832 heavily modeled on Beethoven long before he came to his self-serving conclusion. For Strauss, the term *symphony* became a convenient tag for an expanded symphonic poem.

Volume I, *The Eighteenth-Century Symphony,* will consider the form before and contemporary with Haydn and Mozart. It will commence with a discussion of the special historiographic problems of the era: precursors of the genre, symphony types, and performing environments. Several generations of symphonic activity will be considered according to cultural areas, with the highlighting of individual accomplishments and regional traits. Among composers active during the early and mid-century phase, the most important were Giovanni Battista Sammartini, Johann Stamitz, Matthias Georg Monn, Georg Christoph Wagenseil, C. P. E. Bach, William Boyce, and Louis-Gabriel Guillemain. For Haydn's and Mozart's generation, special attention will be given to the leading composers in Italy, Spain, Germany, England, Scandinavia, and France; and to Austrians such as Florian Leopold Gassmann, Johann Vanhal, Karl Ditters von Dittersdorf, and Leopold Mozart.

Volume V, *The Symphony in Europe and the Americas in the Twentieth Century,* will deal with the "afterlife" of the genre as seen in works by European composers who have continued in or reformulated the tradition; by American composers who in Leonard Bernstein's words have pursued the "great American Symphony"; and by Latin American composers who have attempted to incorporate their own regional idioms into the symphony tradition. It will be a symposium with contributions on the symphonic repertoire for various regions and national groups.

Among my professional colleagues and friends, I am particularly indebted to those who in the past have undertaken large projects of a similar nature and by doing so have encouraged me directly or indirectly in this effort. Jan LaRue, H. C. Robbins Landon, William S. Newman, and Howard Smither have shown how one might proceed. In particular, the ideas of Jan LaRue and, I hope, some of his analytical acumen, are written all over these pages. To all these scholars, I offer my sincerest acknowledgment.

Preface to Volume III

THE SYMPHONIES DISCUSSED IN THIS VOLUME are by composers who remained mainly outside of the Viennese sphere during the nineteenth and early twentieth centuries. After the deaths of Beethoven and Schubert, the epicenter of symphonic writing during the next two generations moved from Vienna to Leipzig, where all of the stimulants were present to encourage writing for the orchestra: an established ensemble, the Gewandhaus Orchestra; music publishers willing to invest in orchestral music; a critical establishment; and a conservatory that attracted students from North America, England, and Europe.

Though in Volume IV we dealt with the strong divisions within the critical community, here in Volume III the stylistic divisions are stronger. On the conservative side of the Germanic symphony, we have Weber, Wagner (as a symphonist), Spohr, Mendelssohn, and Schumann, and the Northern or Nordic composers. Virtually all these composers had connections to Leipzig either through the Gewandhaus or the Conservatory. In contrast, we have the *avant-garde* consisting of Berlioz, Liszt, Raff, and Richard Strauss. What distinguishes them from the conservatives is the use of programmatic titles, a more colorful exploitation of orchestral resources, and unusual approaches to the cycle's construction. To refer to this group, as well as some other composers who associated themselves with Liszt and Wagner and their philosophical/aesthetic leanings, as the "New German School" is misleading. After all, it could be convincingly argued that Berlioz, a Frenchman, was the first of the *avant-garde* composers. Furthermore, Berlioz had a profound effect on Liszt, an ardent Hungarian, and Richard Wagner, who of course would not acknowledge that a Frenchman could have stimulated or affected his thinking. Raff was Swiss, though his outlook indicated by the program for his First Symphony makes him an ardent national for the formation of a greater German nation (i.e., Austria, German-speaking Switzerland, and Germany). This leaves only Richard Strauss, a second- or third-generation practitioner and the only symphonic master to follow in Wagner's footsteps as a composer of opera. With Franz Brendel, the editor of the *Neue Zeitschrift für Musik* beginning in 1844 and a teacher of music history at the Leipzig Conservatory, the concept had a vociferous advocate. However, the above named *avant-garde* symphonists had no connections with the Conservatory, but did with the Gewandhaus, where Berlioz and Liszt on a few occasions presented their own works outside of the regular subscription series. This segregation was not practiced with Raff, whose works were admitted to the regular series.

Unlike Volumes II and IV, which dealt with the two Viennese Golden Ages of the symphony (*ca.* 1758–1828 and 1876–1930), the existing literature on the composers dealt with in Volume III is less evenly distributed, with some composers remaining hardly explored. In the case of some of the Nordic countries and Russia, the literature is often in languages unconquered by this author and many other musicologists. Even with the acceptance of nineteenth-century studies as musicologically viable, the symphonies of Spohr, Berwald, Lindblad, Svendsen, Frøhlich, J. P. E. Hartmann, Gade, Raff, Potter, Stanford, Parry, Rimsky-Korsakov, Borodin, Balakirev, Kalinnikov, and many of the French symphonists dealt with (in the chapter contributed by Brian Hart) have elicited minimal interest. In addition, scores for many of these pieces are not easily available except in the appropriate national libraries. Thus, in a number of instances, this is the first time some of this music has been written about. Throughout the odyssey of writing this volume, I was impressed with the quality of many of these works.

In *toto* Volume III deals with some 170 symphonies, providing background, compositional context, descriptions of the music itself, and reviews contemporary with early performances. Some may wish to quibble with my choice of repertoire; in my view the composers chosen are either representative of their geographic area and/or have composed works of exceptional merit. One could make cases that Burgmüller, Cowen, Kalliwoda, Melartin, Norman, Ries, Anton Rubinstein, and the Wranitzky brothers should be included. However, the volume is already long and not a great deal would be gained by their inclusion. It has been our intent to cover the entire output for each composer discussed and we come close to accomplishing this goal.

Many of the points made in the text require reinforcement by the music itself. While many musical and schematic examples are provided, it is impossible to illustrate in musical examples every movement of each symphony discussed. We provide measure numbers even though most scores from the time have none; our numbering system includes both first and second endings. If numbers are provided in a score we adopt them regardless of their policy with regard to endings.

Economic constraints made it impossible to present all the documents cited in both their original languages and English. Since the original versions are available in most research collections, I give these texts only in translation. In the case of symphonic themes associated with a poetic text, both the original and its translation are presented side by side. For translations from German, I am indebted to Gesa Kordes. Translations of French texts were provided by Austin Caswell and Brian Hart. Lynn Sargeant took responsibility for all Russian translations. Other translations are taken from available published sources as cited.

The abbreviations for the bibliographic references are based on the system designed by William S. Newman in his *History of the Sonata Idea.* The bibliography lists only the books, articles, and editions cited. Notes identify sources of quotations and new ideas. Further materials are cited in the bibliographic overview found at the end of each chapter.

One cannot prepare a work of this sort without the help, encouragement, and assistance of many people and institutions. For financial aid and personal support, I am first of all indebted to my wife, Carol Vanderbilt Brown, who in a real way has allowed me to pursue my research programs and has underwritten these pursuits with her full-time employment as a business professor in the management of information systems. At Indiana University, the Office of Research and Graduate Development has supported this volume and the larger project at crucial points in its progress. David Fenske, Michael Fling, and David Lasocki of the music library of Indiana University have aided with searches and the ordering of material. I am particularly grateful to David Lasocki, who on many occasions has provided instant bibliographic help and has expeditiously procured materials from other libraries. Without the assistance of libraries and librarians in Sweden, Denmark, England, and Germany, one could not have even thought about a project of this sort.

For research assistance including bibliographic work, proofreading, and checking, I thank my assistants: Brian Hart, Gesa Kordes, David Lieberman, Luiz Lopes, James Rodgers, Dawn Reindl, Amy Bland, and Tong Cheng. Anouska Antunez and Bethany Kissell gave the entire text an unusually careful reading; any remaining errors are entirely my responsibility. My friend and colleague Austin Caswell read, from the viewpoint of a proclaimed generalist, those parts about which I was not certain, while Theodore Albrecht carefully read the penultimate version. Natalia Minibayeva provided invaluable help with the Russian chapter.

A special acknowledgment goes to Yvonne Gray, the musicology department secretary of the last twenty years, who has entered and word-processed this study many times over. Working from my yellow legal pads with scratchings from no. 2 pencils, she has produced copy with unusual accuracy and efficiency, and has turned my messy tables, schematic diagrams, notes, and bibliographies into formats of unusual clarity. Ms. Gray not only does everything with professional pride but has also saved me from embarrassment by pointing out my inconsistencies and redundancies and by correcting my German.

This book is primarily a synthesis of ideas I have accumulated over the past thirty years from classes I have taken and taught, from the many books and articles I have perused and absorbed, and from conversations I have had with colleagues. As a result, I have certainly appropriated work and original ideas from other scholars without realizing that I have done so. To those who have claims to material not acknowledged, I offer my apologies and hope for your understanding.

Bloomington, Indiana   A. Peter Brown
January 2003

Postscript

A. Peter Brown passed away on March 10, 2003, after a relatively short battle with an aggressive cancer. At the time of his death, all of Volume III had been written, revised, and revised again over a seven-year period. The musical examples and plates had also been selected and the captions prepared. Unlike the previously published volumes of this series (Volumes II and IV), which had been all his own work, however, Peter had asked a former Indiana University Ph.D. student, Brian Hart, to write the chapter on the French symphony. A few months before his death, Peter had also asked Lynn Sargeant to collaborate on the collection and translation of reviews for many premiere performances of Russian composers' symphonies that up to then had not been published in English.

Following his death, it was decided to publish Volume III in two physical parts; Part A includes Peter's Chapters I–XIII, which are divided into three sections: the German Classic / Romantic Symphony, the Symphony in Northern Europe, and the Avant Garde / New School Symphonists. Part B includes Peter's Chapters XIV and XV on the Symphony in Great Britain from Potter to Elgar and the Russian Symphony, as well as Chapter XVI on the French Symphony by Brian Hart.

As Peter states in his Preface to Volume III, several doctoral students in musicology at Indiana University continued to assist him with text and table standardizations and bibliographic searches. One of these students, Bethany Kissell, has continued to work with me in following up on any remaining handwritten suggestions that Peter had made in the margins of the chapter copies as well as responding to queries raised by Ted Albrecht, who once again read the entire volume for Indiana University Press, and other copyeditors. More recently, Bethany has helped with various proofreading tasks, including the software transcriptions of the musical examples for Part A by other graduate students. Without Bethany's research skills and dedication, the remaining tasks would have been much more arduous and the delays incurred in bringing this volume into production would have been considerably longer. I am greatly indebted to her for her perseverance, commitment, and friendship.

I also wish to acknowledge the ongoing assistance of Yvonne Gray, who as the longtime secretary for the musicology and music theory departments (and family friend) has been the word processor extraordinaire for not only Volume III, but also Volume II (which Peter saw in print) and Volume IV (which had not yet appeared before his death, but for which he had seen the proofs). Rika Asai has expertly overseen the software transcriptions of the musical examples for Part B. Katie Lundeen and Kunio Hara have diligently developed the indices for both Parts A and B. Finally, Malcolm Brown, who was the musicology department chair when Peter was hired by Indiana University in 1974, also helped me answer questions about the Russian symphony chapter and helped me to identify plates for that chapter in Part B.

I am also grateful to the various music and general editors at Indiana University Press who worked with Peter, and, lately, with myself, over more than a decade to help make his Symphonic Repertoire Series a reality.

Finally, I owe a great debt to one of Peter's first Ph.D. students, Mary Sue Morrow, and to my own faculty mentor at Vassar College in the 1960s, Bathia Churgin, for their enthusiastic agreement to develop Volume I for this series, based on Peter's table of contents for this book. It was a delight to witness the collaborative efforts of many of the more than eighteen contributors to Volume I as they met for a multi-day symposium on the Indiana University campus in November 2005 to share their ideas about the beginnings of this genre. I am grateful to the current dean of IU's School of Music, Gwyn Richards, and the members of the musicology department for their continued endorsement of Peter's final scholarly contributions.

Volume III is therefore dedicated to all those who today share Peter's passion for scholarship and live performances of the symphonic repertoire, as well as to all those who fueled his own intellect during his lifetime. Those of us closest to him take great comfort in the fact that his ideas about the symphony in Germany, the Nordic countries, Great Britain, and Russia from 1800 to 1930 can be read, and no doubt in some cases be debated, by other scholars, conductors, performers, and listeners.

Bloomington, Indiana   Carol Vanderbilt Brown
March 2006

Acknowledgments

In addition to those persons acknowledged in the Preface and Postscript, we are grateful to the following institutions, persons, and publishers who responded to queries and provided permissions to use and reproduce materials.

Bibliothèque nationale de France (Paris)
British Library (London)
Carlo Caballero (University of Colorado–Boulder)
The Elgar Birthplace Museum
Catrina Flint de Médicis (Montreal)
André Gedalge (Paris)
Andreas Giger (Louisiana State University)
Edwin F. Kalmus & Co.
National Portrait Gallery (London)
Novello & Company Ltd.
Editions Salabert
Stainer & Bell Ltd.
Stanford Archive, University of Newcastle upon Tyne Library
Michael Strasser (Baldwin-Wallace College)

Abbreviations

A	part form refrains
adum.	Adumbrate, etc.
ambig.	ambiguous
Anh.	Anhang (Appendix)
aug.	augmentation
B	part form episodes
b.	before
Bclar.	Bass clarinet
BD	Bass drum
Bssn.	Bassoon
Btpt.	Bass trumpet
Btrom.	Bass trombone
BWV	Bach Werk Verzeichnis
ca.	circa
cad.	cadence
cb.	Contrabass
Cbells	Cow bells
Cbssn.	Contrabassoon
CE	Collected edition
Chiappari	Chiappari/LISZT CATALOGO
Clar.	Clarinet
cont.	continuation
cresc.	*crescendo*
ctrpt.	counterpoint
Cym.	Cymbals
D.	Deutsch/SCHUBERT VERZEICHNIS
DC	Deceptive cadence
Dev.	Development section
dim.	*diminuendo*
dolciss.	*dolcissimo*
dom.	dominant
EH	English Horn
espr.	espressive
Expos.	exposition
ext.	extension
F	Fast movement in a cycle
facs.	facsimile
FBSW	Franz Berwald Sämtliche Werke
Flt.	Flute
FMB-LA	Felix Mendelssohn-Bartholdy
FMS	Free Music School (St. Petersburg)

FS	Fugal subject
GA	Gesamtausgabe
GP	Grand Pause
Hob.	Hoboken's Catalogue of Haydn's Work
Hol.	Holoman's Catalogue of Berlioz's Works
Hr.	Horn
Instr.	instrument/instrumental, etc.
Intro.	introduction
J.	Jahns's Catalogue of Weber's Works
JSW	Jean Sibelius Sämtliche Werke
K.	Köchel/K^1, K^3, K^6
K	closing material
Lp	Luftpause
m. (mm.)	measure(s)
Mand.	Mandoline
mid.	middle
mod.	modulatory (modulation)
ms.	manuscript
mvt.	movement
N	new material
NBE	New Berlioz Edition
Neap.	Neapolitan sonority
NMA	Neue Mozart Ausgabe (New Mozart Edition). See Mozart/NMA
O	introduction/introductory material
P	primary material in the tonic key
Perc.	percussion
Perf.	performed
Phryg	Phrygian
Picc.	Piccolo
Pno.	Piano
Ps.	Psalms
Raabe	Catalogue in Raabe/LISZT
Recap.	recapitulation
retrans.	retransition
rev.	revised, revision
rhy.	rhythm
RMS	Russian Music Society
RWSW	Richard Wagner Sämtliche Werke
S	Slow movement in a cycle
S	secondary material presented initially in a related key or the solo section in a concerto-like piece
sc	scale passage
SD	Snare Drum
Searle	Searle/LISZT
SR	surface rhythm
Strgs.	Strings
SWV	Spohr Werkverzeichnis, see Göthel/SWV
syncop	syncopation

T	transition material usually of a modulatory nature
Tamb.	Tambourine
Timp.	Timpani
Tpt.	Trumpet
trans.	Transition of a smaller-dimension level than a *T*
Tri.	Triangle
Trom.	Trombone
TrV	Trenner/STRAUSS WERKVERZEICHNIS
Va.	Viola
Var.	variation
Vc.	Violoncello
Vn.	Violin
Vs.	Verse
WO/WoO	Werke ohne Opuszahl (Works without opus designations)
Ww.	Woodwinds
WWV	Wagner Werke-Verzeichnis

ORCHESTRAL INSTRUMENTATION

Full	1 or 2 Flt., 2 Ob., 2 Clar., 2 Bssn., 2 Hr., 2 Tpt., Timp., and Strgs.
Grand	2 Flt., 2 Ob., 2 Clar., 2 Bssn., 4 Hr., 2 Tpt., 3 Trom., Timp., and Strgs.

The analytical symbols *K, N, P, R, S,* and *T* used for movements in sonata form derive from the system developed in LaRue/GUIDELINES. Letters preceded by Arabic numerals define constituent parts of a function (e.g., *1P, 2P*). Lower-case letters *a, b, c, d,* etc., following upper-case letters indicate phrases or smaller-dimension portions of a function; while *x, y, z* following *a, b, c, d,* etc., identify a still smaller component. Thus, the initial motive of the beginning of a primary section of an exposition would be *Pax*; the second idea of the second phrase of the second motive of the secondary area would be *2Sby*. Parentheses are for derivations: *S(P)* means that the secondary area derives from the primary material. Superscript numerals signal variants: e.g., *Pa^t* indicates a variant of *Pa*. The superscript *k* (e.g., *P^k*) means that a closing function is present at the end of the main function. *I/1P* and similar designations indicate that *1P* material from the first movement is used in a subsequent movement.

For forms other than sonata form, the standard upper- and lower-case letters are used (e.g., Rondo: *A–B–A–C–A*).

When necessary, the dimensions (i.e., number of measures) of each part, section, etc., are given in Arabic numerals directly below the analytical symbols.

In the schematic examples, the morphological structure of a phrase, statement, section, etc., is indicated as follows:

2 + 2   Balanced or connected phrase remaining within a tonal orbit
4 × 2   Sequence of two repetitions of a four-measure unit. Read as: 4 measures times two.

The strength and nature of a cadence may be indicated as:

AIS	Authentic Imperfect Strong	DC	Deceptive Cadence
APS	Authentic Perfect Strong	HC	Half Cadence

Finally, tonal changes are pointed out by Roman numerals; a jagged line (⋙) signals tonal instability, while a horizontal arrow (→) identifies an area of stability or a destination. An arrow pointing downward (↓) indicates a structural downbeat. In the diagrams and tables the major mode is assumed, so that only the minor mode is indicated; i.e., "C" means C major.

Identification of the Works

Identifying the symphonies discussed in this volume is less problematic since the composers in the nineteenth century composed fewer works and kept closer tabs on them. Beginning with Beethoven, composers and publishers generally assigned a "chronological" number to symphonies. Later bibliographers and musicologists, in some cases, provided thematic and non-thematic catalogues. In identifying the works in Volume III Part B, we may use any one of these types of identifying numbers:

Potter: Chronological number from autographs and dates
Bennett: Chronological number, Williamson catalogue numbers, and Opus numbers
Stanford: Symphony number, Opus number, and Title
Parry: Symphony number and Title
Elgar: Symphony number and Opus number
Glinka: Title
Rimsky-Korsakov: Symphony number and Opus number
Borodin: Symphony number
Tchaikovsky: Symphony number and Opus number
Balakirev: Symphony number
Kalinnikov: Symphony number
Rachmaninoff: Symphony number and Opus number
Gounod: Symphony number
Bizet: Title
Saint-Saëns: Symphony number, Opus number, and Title
Lalo: Title
Franck: Title
Chausson: Title
Dukas: Title
d'Indy: Symphony number and Title
Ropartz: Symphony number
Tournemire: Symphony number and Title
Dubois: Title
Widor: Title
Gedalge: Symphony number
Magnard: Symphony number

Other composer's works are identified by the standard or the only existing catalogs, which are found in the list of abbreviations and with full citations in the Bibliographies of Works Cited in this and the other volumes.

Section Four
The British Symphony

CHAPTER FOURTEEN

The Symphony in Great Britain:
From Potter to Elgar

The Symphonic Milieu from *ca.* 1800 to *ca.* 1850

AT THE END OF THE eighteenth century, London possessed an active musical life in the private salons and in public concerts. The public concerts benefited from London's large population and the importation of musicians from the continent for whom England's political stability and economic prosperity were attractive. The results of wealth and stability drew musicians not only from France, but also from the Germanic lands and Italy. In 1791, the *Public Advertiser* was able to announce concerts and operatic performances for every night of the week encompassing repertoires from new works by Haydn to the Concerts of Ancient Music, which revered earlier music from the Elizabethan madrigalists up to music only two decades old. In addition, there were the concerts given at the pleasure gardens, such as Vauxhall, whose programs also included symphonies.

However, after Haydn's second sojourn to London and with his final return to Vienna, concert life to some degree declined. In part the downturn was because of the inability of the impresarios to attract musicians of comparable talent and reputation (e.g., Beethoven) to London, but perhaps more importantly it was because of the stiff competition among the various concert organizations during the 1780s and 1790s for a finite number of subscribers who had the financial means to buy a series. The result was a dearth of public and formal concerts with less programming of orchestral music. During the post-Haydn era such a situation discouraged the composition of symphonies.

This situation caused some of the major players active in the various late-eighteenth-century concert series to gather together to improve London's musical climate nearly two decades after Haydn's departure. On January 24, 1813, Philip Antony Corri, the son of the famed music publisher; Johann Baptist Cramer, the internationally respected pianist and teacher; and the violinist Henry Dance convened a meeting of eminent musicians to organize regular concerts of orchestral and other instrumental music. The result was The Philharmonic Society, which included the violinists Johann Peter Salomon and Giovanni Battista Viotti, the flutist Andrew Ashe, and the pianist Muzio Clementi:

> The want of encouragement, which has for many years past been experienced by that species of music which called forth the efforts, and displayed the genius of the greatest masters, and the almost utter neglect into which instrumental pieces in general have fallen, have long been sources of regret to the real amateur and to the well-educated professor: a regret which, though it has hitherto proved unavailing, has not extinguished the hope that persevering exertions may yet restore to the world those compositions which have excited so much delight, and rekindle in the public mind that taste for excellence in instrumental music which has so long remained in a latent state. In order to effect this

desirable purpose, several members of the musical profession have associated themselves, under the title of THE PHILHARMONIC SOCIETY, the object of which is to promote the performance, in the most perfect manner possible, of the best and most approved instrumental music, consisting of Full Pieces, Concertantes for not less than three principal instruments, Sestetts, Quintetts, and Trios; excluding Concertos, Solos and Duets; and requiring that vocal music, when introduced, shall have full orchestral accompaniments, and shall be subjected to the same restrictions.[1]

The restrictions on settings and genres were soon to be changed; vocal solos and duets were introduced in 1816, and concertos joined the repertoire beginning in 1819.[2] Other rules of the Society concerned administrative matters, such as the number of members, associate members, and directors, and the details of tickets and subscriptions. The first concert took place at the old Argyll Rooms on March 8, 1813; to older members it might almost have seemed like a trip back in time, for J. P. Salomon was the leader of the violins and Muzio Clementi presided at the fortepiano. The program, too, was reminiscent of the concerts during the 1790s, except for the absence of concertos and vocal solos.

PART I

OVERTURE, "Anacréon"	*Cherubini*
QUARTETT for two Violins, Viola and Violoncello	*Mozart*
F. CRAMER, MORALT, SHERRINGTON, and R. LINDLEY.	
VOCAL QUARTETT and CHORUS, "Nell' orror"	*Sacchini*
MRS. MORALT, WM. HAWES, P. A. CORRI, and KELLNER.	
SERENADE for Wind Instruments	*Mozart*
MAHON, OLIVER, HOLMES, J. TULLY and the two PETRIDES.	
SYMPHONY	*Beethoven*

PART II

SYMPHONY	*Haydn*
CHORUS, "Placido e' il mar" (Idomeneo)	*Mozart*
MRS. MORALT, MISS HUGHES, P. A. CORRI, C. SMITH, &c.	
QUINTETT for two Violins, Viola and two Violoncellos	*Boccherini*
SALOMON, CUDMORE, SHERRINGTON, R. LINDLEY and C. ASHLEY.	
CHACONNE, JOMELLE and MARCH [*sic*]	*Haydn*
Leader, MR. SALOMON. Pianoforte, MR. CLEMENTI.[3]	

Unfortunately, the works themselves cannot always be identified. But what makes this program distinctive from those of the 1790s is that only two works date from the last decade (Cherubini's overture to *Anacréon* of 1803 and the Beethoven Symphony); all the rest date from eighteen or more years earlier. A distinction between the policies of the Philharmonic Society and the Concerts of Ancient Music seems almost gone as both organizations virtually ignore new music.

Looking at the other works on the program, the String Quartet is certainly one of Mozart's quartets composed during his residence in Vienna after 1781, the Sacchini cannot be further identified for now, the Mozart wind Serenade is probably the sextet version of K.375, and the Mozart vocal quartet is from *Idomeneo*. The Boccherini could be any one among many of his cello quintets. The symphonies by Haydn and Beethoven cannot be identified, even though the latter could only be one of Beethoven's first four symphonies. The Haydn Chaccone, Jomelle, and March is in all likelihood a botched printer's job; Ehrlich unscrambles it as a Chaconne by Jomelli and a March by Haydn.[4]

During the first half of the nineteenth century, from the first decade of the Society's existence through 1852, the emphasis was on symphonic music stemming from the pens of Austro/German composers. Taking Myles Birket Foster's statistics by decade, the dominance of the Austro/German flank is overwhelming.[5] French and English symphonies are almost ignored. Foster's figures do not take into consideration repetitions, so works from the first decade (1813–1822) may have been also programmed in the second decade, but are not tabulated.

	1813–1822	1823–1832	1833–1842	1843–1852
Austro/German	66	6	23	2
French	3	—	3	—
English	5	2	2	1

Besides Haydn and Mozart, the main composers during the first half of the nineteenth century who were considered by the English to be exemplars of symphonic writing were Beethoven, Mendelssohn, and Spohr. All three held a special relationship with the Philharmonic Society.

From the very first Philharmonic concert, Beethoven's symphonies had a presence.[6] Though Beethoven never traveled to England, the Philharmonic Society maintained contact with the eccentric and revered composer through Ignaz Moscheles, Charles Neate, and Cipriani Potter, all of whom had friendly contacts with him during their stays in Vienna. During Beethoven's final illness, the Society sent him £100 "to be applied to his comforts and necessities."[7] Beethoven replied, giving thanks, supplying metronome markings for the Ninth Symphony, and implying that the Tenth Symphony would be for the Society. However, in March of 1825 when the Ninth Symphony was first performed in London, the Philharmonic Society billed it falsely as "composed expressly for this Society."[8]

Both Spohr and Mendelssohn were frequent participants in the concerts of the Society and became favored guests. Spohr contributed as composer, violin soloist, and conductor. For many years he was regarded in England as the first to conduct in the modern manner with a baton, a claim that today cannot be supported.[9] Among the more than ninety works by Spohr programmed between 1820 and 1896, the Society claimed rightly or wrongly some precedence for their performances of nine works (see Table XIV/1).[10]

For all the prestige and admiration Spohr was able to muster, neither his music nor his musical personality could compete with that of Felix Mendelssohn. Even though the number of Mendelssohn works programmed by the Society was about one-third fewer than those by Spohr, Mendelssohn had a greater impact on English music and musical life, one that was comparable to that of Handel and Haydn. Part of this luster stems from Mendelssohn's first appearance at these concerts on May 25, 1829, when the nineteen-year-old composer conducted his C Minor Symphony. Though the concert was erroneously billed as its "first performance," Mendelssohn did dedicate the work to the Society. Additionally, unlike Beethoven, Mendelssohn projected the image of an ideal young man: talented, accomplished, proper, and unspoiled. Witness the letter he sent to the Society:

> I deeply feel the honour of which the Philharmonic Society has deemed me worthy, in performing a Symphony of my composition at the last concert, an honour which I can never forget.

TABLE XIV/1
Philharmonic Society's Claims for Works by Spohr

| Work | Philharmonic Society | | Other Early Performances |
	Date	Claims	
Symphony No. 2 in D Minor Opus 49	April 10, 1820	Specially Composed Premiere	
Overture in F WoO1	March 21, 1821	Specially Composed Premiere	Leipzig, Gewandhaus, November 29, 1819
Overture to *Der Alchymist* WoO57	June 6, 1831	Premiere	Kassel, July 28, 1830
Symphony No. 4 Opus 86 "The Consecration of Sound"	February 23, 1835	Premiere	Kassel, November 4, 1832
Symphony No. 5 in C Minor Opus 102	March 9, 1840	Premiere	Vienna, March 1, 1838
Symphony No. 6 in G Major Opus 116 "Historical" Symphony	April 6, 1840	Specially Composed Premiere	
Symphony No. 7 in C Major Opus 121 "Earthly and Divine in Human Life"	May 30, 1842	English Premiere	
Concertante for String Quartet and Orchestra Opus 131	June 1, 1846	Premiere	Leipzig, Gewandhaus, February 12, 1846
Symphony No. 8 in G Major Opus 137	May 1, 1848	Specially Composed Premiere	Kassel, December 22, 1847

Sources: Foster/PHILHARMONIC SOCIETY LONDON, Elkin/ROYAL PHILHARMONIC, Göthel/SWV, Ehrlich/PHIHARMONIC SOCIETY LONDON.

> I know that my success, obtained through the brilliant execution of the orchestra, is due much less to my talent than to the indulgence shown to my youth; but, encouraged by a reception so flattering, I shall labour to justify the hopes entertained of me, to which I undoubtedly owe the kind feeling shown to me.[11]

It was no wonder that he was soon inducted into the Philharmonic Society as an honorary member.

The works by Mendelssohn deemed as having a special connection with the Philharmonic Society are given in Table XIV/2. Again, the Society makes some claims that cannot be supported by the historical record. Symphony No. 1 was first heard in Leipzig in 1827. For Symphony No. 4, the claims are valid except that Mendelssohn was unsatisfied and began working on a revision soon after the London performance.[12] Other claims can be evaluated from the data given in the table.

That both Spohr and Mendelssohn had a special and mutual relationship with the English gentried class and that they appeared just prior to the beginning of Victoria's reign resulted from not only the nature of their music, but also their personalities, which were consonant with the age. If Beethoven had come to England, his music would no doubt have continued to elicit deep admiration, but one might doubt if the man himself could have found a comparable niche in early-nineteenth-century English society.

Other Germans who wrote symphonies and gained a hearing at the Philharmonic concerts were Joseph Wölfl (1813 with an 1815 repetition), Andreas Romberg (1813 and 1826),

Sigismund Neukomm (1831), Ignaz Moscheles (1832), and Ludwig W. Maurer (1835). However, next to the Viennese triumvirate, Mendelssohn, and Spohr, the most significant German composer of symphonies active in London was Ferdinand Ries (1784–1838), a student of and amanuensis to Beethoven during the first years of the nineteenth century (see Table XIV/3).

Ries arrived in London in 1813 and soon established himself as an active member of the Philharmonic Society. During the next eight years, Ries composed a series of piano works geared to appeal to English tastes for private consumption and had a series of symphonies played at the Philharmonic concerts. He appeared seven times as piano soloist and conducted twelve times in English fashion while presiding at the fortepiano, and his symphonies were programmed a total of twelve times. Nicholas Slonimsky's appraisal of Ries's work seems appropriate: "His music reflects the spirit and technique, if not the genius, of Beethoven's style."[13]

Ries experienced considerable success in London not only at the Philharmonic Concerts, but also as a piano teacher and salon performer. However, Ries apparently believed his compositions were not programmed often enough by the Philharmonic Society, even though

TABLE XIV/2
Philharmonic Society's Claims for Works by Mendelssohn

| Work | Philharmonic Society | | Other Early Performances |
	Date	Claims	
Symphony No. 1(13 [14]) in C Minor Opus 11	May 25, 1829	Premiere	Berlin, November 14, 1824
Piano Concerto No. 1 in G Minor Opus 25	May 28, 1832	English Premiere	Munich, October 17, 1831
Symphony No. 4[16] in A Major Opus 90 "Italian"	May 13, 1833	Specially Composed Premiere	
Trumpet Overture in C Opus 101	June 10, 1833	Specially Composed Premiere	Berlin, April 18, 1828; rev. version: Düsseldorf, May 26, 1833
The Beautiful Melusine Overture Opus 32	April 7, 1834	Premiere	
Scena: Ah! Ritorna (Infelice) Opus 94	May 19, 1834	Specially Composed Premiere	Rev. version: Leipzig, February 9, 1843
Calm Sea and Prosperous Voyage Overture Opus 27	February 22, 1836	Premiere	Berlin, September 8, 1832
Symphony No. 3[18] in A Minor "Scottish" Opus 56	June 13, 1842	English Premiere	Leipzig, Gewandhaus, March 3, 1842
A Midsummer Night's Dream Incidental Music Opus 61	May 27, 1844	English Premiere	Potsdam, October 14, 1843
To the Sons of Art (*Festgesang: An die Künstler*) Soloists, Chorus, and Brass, Opus 68	April 10, 1848	English Premiere	Cologne, June 1846

Sources: Foster/PHILHARMONIC SOCIETY LONDON, Elkin/ROYAL PHILHARMONIC, Grove/MENDELSSOHN, Dörffel/GEWANDHAUS, Ehrlich/ PHILHARMONIC SOCIETY LONDON.

TABLE XIV/3
The Symphonies of Ferdinand Ries

Title	Date	Identification
Symphony No. 1 in D Major	1809	Opus 23 (1811) Bonn: Simrock
Symphony No. 5 in D Minor	1813	Opus 112 (1823) Leipzig: Breitkopf & Härtel
Symphony No. 2 in C Minor	1814	Opus 80 (1818) Bonn: Simrock
Symphony No. 3 in E-flat Major	1816	Opus 90 (1825) Bonn: Simrock
Symphony No. 4 in F Major	1818	Opus 110 (1823) Leipzig: Breitkopf & Härtel
Symphony in E-flat Major	1822	WoO 30
Symphony No. 6 in D Major	1822 (rev. 1826)	Opus 146 (1827) Leipzig: Peters
Symphony No. 7 in A Minor	1835	Opus 181

next to Haydn, Mozart, and Beethoven he was the most frequently heard composer of symphonic works. Ries left London in July 1824 and returned to Germany; his remuneration in London made it unnecessary for him to seek a permanent post or to accept other less than appealing offers. Nevertheless, his years in London marked the apex of his career, and after 1830 his position in the musical world deteriorated; his music had become unfashionable, and he was unable to adjust his style to current tastes.

The prominence afforded to the symphonies of Haydn, Mozart, Beethoven, and Ferdinand Ries during the first decade on the programs of the Philharmonic Society certainly had the same effect as the lack of venues prior to 1813; it discouraged the composition of symphonies by native composers. While other venues certainly existed, such as the Society for British Musicians, the histories of these musical organizations still need to be culled from the pages of British periodicals.

The Society of British Musicians was founded in 1834 for "the advancement of native talent in composition and performance."[14] It continued until 1865 when internal squabbles among its members doomed the organization. The Society held readings of new works as well as concerts; at its full flowering it had some 350 subscribers. Around 1835, Thomas Attwood wrote to Mendelssohn about the new society, but it was not until June 15, 1844, that Mendelssohn, during his eighth English sojourn, attended one of their meetings "to hear the works of some of its members. Compositions by the following gentlemen were performed much to the satisfaction of the distinguished guest: [W. M.] Rooke, [Cipriani] Potter, [William] Horsley, [E. J.] Westrop, [James] Calkin, and [George] Macfarren."[15] Among others to this short list should be added William Sterndale Bennett, who in Attwood's opinion "stands pre-eminent."[16] No doubt the Society for British Musicians was established as a corrective to the programming of both the Concerts of Ancient Music and the Philharmonic Society.

Nevertheless, the Philharmonic Society did make efforts to commission new works. For example, in December of 1814, Cherubini received a commission amounting to

£200. In 1815, the Society purchased three overtures from Beethoven: *The Ruins of Athens, King Stephen,* and *Nameday.* In addition, £200 were set aside for the reading of new music composed in England as a kind of audition for inclusion on the subscription series. The results, however, hardly propagated the composition of symphonies by English composers.

A second effort of the Philharmonic Society to encourage and train native talent was the establishment of a counterpart to the Royal Academy of Art. A committee was appointed at the General Meeting that took place on January 16, 1822. When the committee reported on July 8, a group of men led by the later Lord John Fane Burghersh, the eleventh Earl of Westmoreland, had met to supersede any action by the musicians of the Philharmonic Society. Within two months, this group from the gentry and noble classes had secured financial support, and in November a building was taken over for the Academy. Though many members of the Academy's faculty were from the Philharmonic Society, as an entity it had no administrative power within the new institution. While this structure had the advantage of some financial security, the board from the aristocracy, under the iron hand of Lord Burghersh, directed day-to-day operations.[17] The first principal was William Crotch, who served until his retirement a decade later. His pupil Cipriani Potter, who remained in the position until July 1859, succeeded him in 1832. Since the Academy offered courses in composition, had an orchestra available for readings, and provided lessons in the applied areas, it laid another foundation for a potential flowering of English symphonic composition.

The effect of all this activity was at best mixed and can be seen in Table XIV/4. Discounting the three symphonies by Lord Burghersh—two are undated—and the one symphony movement (*ca.* 1834) by Samuel Sebastian Wesley, whose training was mainly private and in the cathedrals, all the other symphonies are by composers who were at one time either teachers or students at the Royal Academy of Music: Cipriani Potter, William Sterndale Bennett, and George Macfarren. However, the effect of the Academy must have been minimal, for only a small fraction of the composers trained there contributed to the genre. If the Academy propagated symphonic composition, one would expect an increase in the number of symphonies after *ca.* 1826. Instead, beginning in 1837 and lasting until 1863, except for the two symphonies by George Macfarren and one each by John Barnett (1802–1890) and Henry Leslie (1822–1896), no native English composer was contributing to the genre. While Table XIV/4 could certainly be missing symphonies from this period, it is unlikely that the overall impression would appreciably change. Nevertheless, it is certain that during the first half of the nineteenth century the major symphonists were the trio of men closely associated with the English Royal Academy of Music. None of these composers could be considered as having produced works that are part of the symphonic repertoire, for with a few exceptions they have not been revived by the early music movement or recorded. However, they form an essential track for the English symphony during the so-called English Musical Renaissance that flowered during the last third of the century.

As has been demonstrated in our discussion of the repertoire of the Philharmonic Society, there were two dominating forces: the three composers of Viennese Classicism (Haydn, Mozart, and Beethoven) and the two composers of German bourgeois sensibility (Spohr and Mendelssohn). Since the symphonies of Macfarren are the least known, we will concentrate on those by Cipriani Potter, whose efforts often demonstrate direct links to the Classical Viennese tradition, and William Sterndale Bennett, whose symphonic temperament aligns with the Mendelssohnian aesthetic.

TABLE XIV/4
Symphonies by British Composers from *ca.* 1815 to 1912

1815	
1816	
1817	Lord Burghersh, Symphony No. 1.
1818	
1819	*Potter, Sym. No. 1 G Minor.*
1820	
1821	*Potter, Sym. No. 2 B-flat Major.*
1822	
1823	
1824	
1825	
1826	*Potter, Sym. No. 6 C Minor, Sym. No. 7 F Major.*
1827	
1828	*Potter, Sym. No. 8 E-flat Major*; Macfarren, Sym. No. 1 C Major.
1829	
1830	
1831	Macfarren, Sym. No. 2 D Minor.
1832	*Potter, Sym. No. 10 G Minor*; *Bennett, Sym. No. 1 E-flat Major*; Macfarren, Sym. No. 3 E Minor; S. Wesley, Sym.
1833	*Potter, Sym. No. 11 D Major*; *Bennett, Sym. No. 2 D Minor*; Macfarren, Sym. No. 4 F Minor, Sym. No. 5 A Minor.
1834	*Potter, Sym. No. 12 C Minor, No. 15[14] D Major*; *Bennett, Sym. No. 3 A Major.*
1835	*Bennett, Sym. No. 5 G Minor.*
1836	Macfarren, Sym. No. 6 B-flat Major.
1837	Barnett, Sym. (composed while a student in Europe).
1838	
1839	
1840	Macfarren, Sym. No. 7 C-sharp Minor.
1841	
1842	
1843	
1844	
1845	Macfarren, Sym. No. 8 D Major.
1846	
1847	Leslie, Sym. F Major.
1848	
1849	
1850	
1851	
1852	
1853-1863	
1864	*Bennett, Sym. No. 8 G Minor Op. 43 (first version)*; Barnett, Sym. A Minor.
1865	
1866	Sullivan, Sym. No. 1 E Major "Irish."
1867	*Bennett, Sym. No. 8 G Minor Op. 43 (second version).*
1868	A Holmes, Sym. "The Youth of Shakespeare."
1869	Wingham, Sym. No. 1 D Minor; Cowen Sym. No. 1 C Minor.
1870	
1871	Gadsby, Sym. (No. 2?).
1872	Cowen, Sym. No. 2 F Minor; Wingham, Sym. No. 2 B-flat Major; H. Holmes, Sym. No. 1 A Major.
1873	Wingham, Sym. No. 3 E Minor.
1874	Benedict, Sym. No. 1 G Major; Macfarren, Sym. No. 9 E Minor; Prout, Sym. No. 1 C Major.
1875	*Stanford, Sym. No. 1 B-flat Major*; A. Holmes, Symphonie Dramatique No. 1 E Major "Jeanne d'Arc" (comp. 1867?); Benedict; Sym. No. 2 C Major.
1876	Davenport, Sym. No. 1 D Minor.
1877	Prout, Sym. No. 2 G Minor.
1878	

	TABLE XIV/4 *(continued)*
1879	
1880	Cowen, Sym. No. 3 C Minor "Scandinavian."
1881	Leslie, Sym. in D Minor "Chivalry."
1882	*Stanford, Sym. No. 2 D Minor "Elegiac"*; *Parry Sym. No. 1 G Major.*
1883	*Parry, Sym. No. 2 F Major "Cambridge" or "University"*; Wingham Sym. No. 4 D Major.
1884	Cowen, Sym. No. 4 B-flat Minor "Welsh."
1885	Prout, Sym. No. 3 F Major.
1886	
1887	*Stanford, Sym. No. 3 F Minor "Irish"*; Cowen, Sym. No. 5 F Major; Prout, Sym. No. 4 D Major; H. Holmes, Sym. "Boscastle."
1888	Gadsby, Sym. D Major "Festal."
1889	*Stanford, Sym. No. 4 F Major "English"*; *Parry, Sym. No. 3 C Major, Sym. No. 4 E Minor (Version 1)*; Cliffe, Sym. No. 1 C Minor.
1890	German, Sym. No. 1 (or 2) E Major.
1891	
1892	Cusins, Sym. C Major; Cliffe, Sym. No. 2 E Minor.
1893	German, Sym. No. 2.
1894	*Stanford, Sym. No. 5 D Major "L'allegro ed penseroso"*; Bridge, Sym. F Major.
1895	Davies, Sym. No. 1 D Major.
1896	Coleridge-Taylor, Sym. A Minor.
1897	Cowen, Sym. No. 6 E Major "Idyllic."
1898	McEwen, Sym. No. 1 A Minor.
1899	Wallace, Sym. "The Creation"; Bell, Sym. No. 1 "Walt Whitman."
1900	Holst, Cotswolds Sym. F; Scott, Sym. No. 1.
1901	
1902	Scott, Sym. No. 2.
1903	
1904	
ca. 1905	*Stanford, Sym. No. 6 E-flat Major.*
1906	
1907	
1908	*Elgar, Sym. No. 1 A-flat Major.*
1909	
1910	*Parry, Sym. No. 4 E Minor (Version 2) "Finding the Way."*
1911	*Stanford, Sym. No. 7 D Minor*; McEwen, Sym. No. 2 C-sharp Minor "Solway"; *Elgar, Sym. No. 2 E-flat Major.*
1912	*Parry, Sym. No. 5 B Minor (Symphonic Fantasia).*

Cipriani Potter

INTRODUCTION

Though unknown today, Cipriani Potter (1792–1871) was a seminal figure for the nineteenth-century symphony in England and in the direction of British musical institutions: he was not only principal of the Royal Academy of Music for nearly four decades, he was also an active member of the Royal Philharmonic Society from 1815 until his death.[18] Potter's principal teachers were Joseph Wölfl (1773–1812), himself a student of Leopold Mozart and Michael Haydn in Salzburg, and William Crotch, the one-time famed child prodigy, painter, and composer. Wölfl was completely a musician of his time, while Crotch was an advocate of the so-called ancient style; thus, Potter received a balanced musical education with teachers who embraced two opposite points of view. Potter was also an accomplished pianist and appeared some eleven times as a soloist at the Philharmonic concerts over a twenty-year period from 1816 to 1836. Potter's specialty was Mozart and his edition of the complete piano works (1836–1849?) was a significant factor in the English reception of the Austrian composer (Plate B1).

From the end of 1817 to the spring of 1819, Potter went to the continent (Austria and Italy), where he was on friendly terms with Beethoven, who wrote to Ferdinand Ries on

March 5, 1818: "Botter [*sic*] has visited me a few times. He seems to be a good fellow and has talent for composition."[19] Potter recorded his encounters with Beethoven for the *Musical World* in 1835, where he writes of his personality and deafness, and makes incisive observations about his style.[20] This association with Beethoven enhanced the Englishman's reputation throughout his life. After Potter's return to London before the end of 1819, his First Symphony was completed. In May of the following year, he led from the keyboard his first Philharmonic Society Concert, whose major orchestral offerings were Mozart's E-flat Symphony K.543, Beethoven's *Prometheus* Overture, a D Major Symphony by Haydn (likely No. 93, 96, 101, or 104), and once again Cherubini's *Anacréon* Overture. Also included was Beethoven's Septet Opus 20, one of Potter's favorite works.

By 1825, Potter's reputation was such that he was included in John Sainsbury's *Dictionary of Musicians*.[21] After assuming the principalship of the Royal Academy, Potter's career was devoted to teaching composition, piano, and orchestral practice; to administering the Academy and the Philharmonic Society; and to composing in a variety of genres. Potter never completely retired from music; in July 1871 he played in the first English performance of Brahms's *German Requiem* just three months before his death and just shy of his seventy-ninth birthday.

Though Potter was primarily a pianist, he was also a master of writing for the early-nineteenth-century orchestra. Indicative of this is an incomplete series of articles that appeared in the *Musical World* in 1836 entitled "Companion to the Orchestra; or, Hints on Instrumentation." Unfortunately, only four articles appeared which cover the four principal string instruments. Potter introduced the series with the following paragraph:

> It is proposed to give an analysis of the different instruments composing an orchestra, describing the peculiarities and genius of them individually, and collectively, as applied to the formation of an orchestra; their relative situations, with the mode of treatment of them, appropriated to the various styles of composition: this idea has originated from the following observations, viz: the increased cultivation of the science of music in this country: the number of its professors (many of whom are excellent musicians), almost every town of consideration possessing an orchestra of its own, and in some places even a Philharmonic Society; consequently, the resident professor, if not possessing imaginative powers for composition, may wish to arrange certain works for an orchestra, to add instrumental parts to vocal compositions, not to be procured in this form; from these considerations, it was thought the following remarks would not be unacceptable; at the same time it is necessary to observe here, that it would be a presumption to attempt to give general rules for instrumentation, or to endeavour even to limit the powers of the respective instruments in an orchestra, since the capabilities and genius of each become more and more developed every day, and to so astonishing an extent, as to render it impossible to form an idea of the degree of perfection to which they may arrive.[22]

Potter continues to discuss balance of winds to strings for certain repertoires, how to orchestrate the strings when dealing with voices, the requisite characteristics of the leader (concertmaster), voice crossings, the character of the various instruments, and so forth. Potter's remarks are certainly not as significant as Berlioz's later articles, which he culled into his book on orchestration, but they are above all practical observations that aim directly at the author's audience. This little treatise is of particular importance for it is the only material we have that indicates something of Potter the teacher, an activity for which he was revered.

Except for the dissertation by Philip Peter (1972), there exists no comprehensive attempt to deal with Potter as a person and musician. Peter does not make any effort to analyze or discuss the music; he does provide a thematic catalogue and commentaries that deal with all the essential bibliographic problems.

Since not a single symphony by Potter was published during his lifetime and only one of these works (No. 10) has been offered in a modern edition, our approach will assume that more of the symphonies will become more easily accessible. All of the sources are available in what appear to be for the most part autograph scores, many of which belong to the Royal Philharmonic Society and were deposited in the British Library in 1914.

Current research suggests that Potter composed fifteen symphonies, of which six appear to be lost (Table XIV/5). The dating of the extant symphonies is not problematic; the autographs are each dated either on the title page or at the end. Four or five of these works were first programmed at the Royal Philharmonic Society's concerts; three were possibly heard in the Society's trial sessions; and two were known to be used at Potter's own benefit concerts. Interestingly, Potter seemingly used two different systems for numbering these works; besides the traditional approach of a consecutive listing by chronology, Potter also numbered them by key so that the two symphonies in G minor and the four in D major are also identified as Nos. 1, 2, 3, 4 in D major and Nos. 1 and 2 in G minor. Such a system could also have been applied to the two symphonies in C minor, but apparently was not.

All of the symphonies are in four movements, except for No. 2, and two place the Scherzo in second position, a cyclic order not uncommon during the eighteenth century. Only four symphonies commence with a slow introduction including—contrary to Haydn's typical practice—one in the minor mode. Note the variety of instrumentation: most are for grand orchestra, some less two horns, and one is for a full Classical complement plus a bass trombone, a scoring probably more frequent during the first half of the nineteenth century than one might think.[23] Also note the divided violas in five of the symphonies, a scoring that may owe something to Viennese practice.

A curiosity of the scores themselves is that Potter adopts two different score orders without chronological significance: one is based on the Classical model known from the autograph scores of Haydn and Mozart, while the other is closer to the modern approach with woodwinds at the top of the score, followed by brass and timpani, and the strings at the bottom. Table XIV/6 tabulates these two approaches. Curious are the two manuscript sources for the first movement of Symphony No. 1, one of which uses the older model, and the other the more modern one. One can explain this by the 1826 revision. However, the last three extant symphonies (Nos. 11, 12, and 15[14]) dating from 1833–1834 return to the older practice. Perhaps there were practical reasons for these different orders. Nevertheless, one must admit that having the treble strings at the very top, during an era when the strings were almost totally responsible for the most important material, makes good sense.

SYMPHONY NO. 1 IN G MINOR

The sources for Potter's Symphony No. 1 are one autograph for the first movement alone and another that has a complete four-movement cycle. The single movement carries the date of 1819; the complete cycle has no date and is in a different hand with the first movement revised. This, of course, opens the possibility that the first movement's origin is much earlier than the remaining three movements. Whether the revisions to the first movement were a result of a hearing in 1824 or earlier cannot be determined; by 1824, however, Potter may have revised the first movement, and he may have completed the remainder of the cycle for the 1824 trials, but waited until July 1826 for a formal concert performance. All our remarks are based on the complete and revised version.

By 1819 and certainly by 1824, the key of G minor had achieved a distinctive tradition

TABLE XIV/5

The Symphonies of Cipriani Potter

Key	Date	Title	Movements	Instrumentation	Comments
G Minor [No. 1]	December 1819–[1826?]	Symphony No. 1	1. Allegro con spirito ¢ (392 m.) 2. Andantino quasi allegretto 3/4 (146 m.) G major 3. Tempo di Menuetto 3/4 and Trio (87 m.) 4. Allegro non tanto 6/8 (242 m.)	Grand minus 2 Hr.	Possible first performance: Royal Philharmonic Society 1824 trials(?) of first movement. Complete symphony: Royal Philharmonic Society, May 29, 1826.
B-flat Major	January 1821	Symphony [No. 2]	1. Allegro 4/4 (331 m.) 2. Andante ¢ (141 m.) F major 3. Vivace 6/8 (524 m.)	Full plus 1 Trom.	First confirmed performance: Potter's Benefit, June 6, 1839.
One in D Major [No. 1]		Symphonies Nos. 3–5			Lost
C Minor	January 1826	Symphony No. 6	1. Allegro con fuoco ¢ (351 m.) 2. Scherzo: Allegro con spirito 3/4 (152 m.?) 3. Andante 2/4 (178 m.?) A-flat major 4. Allegro 4/4—Presto 2/4 (275 m.)	Grand plus 1 Va.	No known performance. Parts prepared in 1847. Score seems left in an unfinished state since the cuts in the second and third mvts. are not always clear or, as they stand, viable. Perhaps these were resolved in the extant parts.
F Major	November 1826	Symphony No. 7	1. Allegro con fuoco 4/4 (378 m.) 2. Andantino grazioso 4/4 (180 m.) B-flat major 3. Menuetto: Allegro non tanto F major and Trio B-flat major 3/4 (156 m.) 4. Finale: Allegro assai 6/8 (616 m.)	Grand plus 1 Va., minus 2 Hr.	Possible first performance: Royal Philharmonic Society on January 22, 1827(?) trials.
E-flat Major	November 1828	Symphony No. 8	1. Maestoso 4/4—Allegro non tanto 3/4 (380 m.) 2. Andante con moto ma sostenuto 2/4 A-flat major (151 m.) 3. Scherzo: Allegro vivace 3/4 (171 m.) 4. Finale: Allegro vivace ¢ (450 m.)	Grand plus 1 Va., minus 2 Hr.	First performance: Royal Philharmonic Society trial in late 1828 or early 1829 and at Potter's Benefit, June 8, 1846.

TABLE XIV/5 (*continued*)

Key	Date	Title	Movements	Instrumentation	Comments
D Major?	1829	Symphony No. 9			Lost. See Peter/POTTER, p. 262.
G Minor [No. 2]	1832	Symphony No. 10	1. Allegro con fuoco 3/4 (528 m.) 2. Andante con moto ¢ (177 m.) D minor 3. Scherzo: Vivace 3/4 B-flat major and Trio E-flat major (224 m.) 4. Finale: Allegro assai 2/4 (354 m.)	Grand plus 1 Va. minus 2 Hr.	First performance: Royal Philharmonic Society trial on January 13, 1833; first public performance on May 27, 1833. "This symphony was composed expressly for the concerts of the Philharmonic Society." Conducted by Richard Wagner on May 28, 1855 at the Philharmonic.
D Major [No. 2]	November 1833	Symphony No. 11	1. Introduzione: Moderato assai 4/4—Allegro vivace ¢ (490 m.) 2. Scherzo: Allegro moderato 3/4 B minor and Trio B major (140 m.) 3. Andante ¢ G major (161 m.) 4. Finale: Vivace 2/4 (359 m.)	Grand plus 1 Va.	First performance: Royal Philharmonic Society, March 21, 1836.
C Minor	November 1834	Symphony No. 12	1. Moderato ¢—Allegro assai 3/4 (388 m.) 2. Andante con moto quasi allegretto ¢ E-flat major (128 m.) 3. Scherzo: Allegro con brio 3/4 C minor and trio C major (95 m.) 4. Allegro molto ¢ (234 m.)	Grand plus 1 Va., minus 2 Hr.	First performance: Royal Philharmonic Society, June 8, 1835(?). Textual condition of autograph seems to indicate the work was never brought to a satisfactory completion.
D Major [No. 3]	b. 1833	Symphony No. 13			Lost
A Minor		Symphony No. 14			Lost. Played at the Royal Philharmonic Society concerts on May 27, 1833 and June 8, 1835(?). Not listed in Peter/POTTER.
D Major [No. 4]	November 24, 1834	Symphony No. 15 [14]	1. Moderato assai 4/4—Allegro 4/4 (251 m.) 2. Andante 6/8 (95 m.) F major 3. Scherzo: Allegro 3/4 (130 m.) D minor 4. Finale: Presto 6/8 (429 m.)	Grand minus 2 Hr.	First performance: Potter's Benefit Concert in 1835(?). Listed in Peter/POTTER as Symphony No. 14.

TABLE XIV/6
Score Order in Potter's Symphony Autographs

Sym. No. 1/1	*Sym. No. 1/1-4*	*Sym. No. 2*	*Sym. No. 6*
Vln. 1	Flt.	Vln. 1	Flt.
Vln. 2	Ob.	Vln. 2	Ob.
Va. 1 + 2	Clar. B-flat	Va.	Clar. B-flat
Flt.	Bssn.	Flt.	Bssn.
Ob.	Hr. G	Ob.	2 Hr. E-flat
Clar. B-flat	Tpt. C	Clar. B-flat	2 Hr. C
Bssn.	Timp.	Bssn.	2 Tpt. C
Hr. G	3 Trom.	Hr. B-flat Basso	Timp.
Tpt. C	Vln. 1	Tpt. B-flat	3 Trom.
Timp.	Vln. 2	Timp.	Vln. 1
1 Trom.	Va.	1 Trom.	Vln. 2
Vc.	Vc.	CB.	Va. 1 + 2
CB.	CB.		Vc.
			CB.

Sym. No. 7	*Sym. No. 8*	*Sym. No. 10*	*Sym. No. 11*
Flt.	Flt.	Flt.	Vln. 1
Ob.	Ob.	Ob.	Vln. 2
Clar. B-flat	Clar. B-flat	Clar. B-flat	Va. 1 + 2
Bssn.	Bssn.	Bssn.	Flt.
Hr. F	Hr. E-flat	Hr. G	Ob.
Tpt. F	Tpt. E-flat	Tpt. C	Clar.
Timp.	Timp.	Timp.	Bssn.
3 Trom.	3 Trom.	3 Trom.	Hr. 3 + 4 A
Vln. 1	Vln. 1	Vln. 1	Hr. 1 + 2 D
Vln. 2	Vln. 2	Vln. 2	2 Tpt. D
Va. 1 + 2	Va. 1 + 2	Va. 1 + 2	Timp.
Bassi (Vc. + CB.)	Vc.	Vc.	3 Trom.
	CB.	CB.	Vc.
			CB.

Sym. No. 12	*Sym. No. 15[14]*
Vln. 1	Vln. 1
Vln. 2	Vln. 2
Va. 1 + 2	Va.
Flt.	Flt.
Ob.	Ob.
Clar. B-flat	Clar. A
Bssn.	Bssn.
Hr. C	Hr. D
Tpt. C	Tpt. D
3 Trom.	Timp.
Timp.	3 Trom.
Vc.	Vc.
CB.	CB.

N.B. Winds in pairs unless otherwise indicated.

resulting from a series of works by the primary composers of Viennese Classicism: Mozart wrote two symphonies in this key (K.183/173dB and K.550), a striking string quintet (K.516), and a piano quartet (K.478); and Haydn wrote two agitated symphonies (Hob.I:39 and 83), the String Quartet Opus 74/3, a piano sonata (Hob.XVI:44), and two piano trios (Hob.XV:1 and 19). Beethoven's works in this key are less striking: the Piano Sonata Opus 49/1, the Cello Sonata Opus 5/2, the Fantasia Opus 77, and the Allegretto WoO 61a. Potter certainly knew K.550 and K.478 as well as the later Haydn pieces; K.550 was a favorite at the concerts of the

EXAMPLE XIV/1   Potter. Symphony No. 1/1, mm.1–9.

Royal Philharmonic Society. One can hypothesize that Potter's First Symphony has some direct connections with K.550 as well as K.551, the "Jupiter" Symphony, and that its Finale exudes, in the minor mode, something of Haydn's *contredanse*/jig-like last movements of the London Symphonies. In addition, there are passages that evoke Beethoven.

Whereas Mozart's G Minor Symphony K.550/1 begins with a thoroughly modern *1P,* Potter's begins with one that is old fashioned with its diminished seventh and diminished fifth (Example XIV/1), more related to Mozart's Serenade in C Minor K.388 and the C Minor Piano Concerto K.491. *2P* (m.12) with an initial leap of an augmented octave also reminds one of Mozart's intervallic inclinations. After the model of Beethoven's Symphony No. 3/1, *1T* (m.30) is introduced by a *crescendo* to *ff* and related to *1P. S* also reminds one of Beethoven with a fabric not unlike *S* in the *Coriolan Overture* and a theme reminiscent of the "Pathétique" Sonata. And as was so common, one of the *K* themes relates to *P.* As might be expected from such a derivative statement, the exposition is repeated. Rather than ending in the expected common B-flat major, Potter decisively articulates D minor at the exposition's end.

The development, which matches the exposition in length, is strong both thematically and tonally. Potter treats his themes in the order of their expository presentation, but in the process reduces *1P* to its essential motives, uses it in a contrapuntal texture, and inverts *1Pax. S* is stated in E-flat and is expanded by repeating its expository extension, which leads to *1Pax* and a chromatically descending retransition (m.226). The inversion of *1Pax* and this last portion recall the parallel passages in Mozart's K.550/1. Tonally, Potter's plan is also strong, beginning with measured changes that lead to accelerations in surface activity. *S* provides an oasis, while its extension and the return to *P* motives achieve previous activity levels.

Except for the tonal change for *S* to the tonic minor, the recapitulation is essentially a replay of the exposition. A brief coda (m.381) recalls a contrapuntal episode from the development in the mode of closure. Though a highly derivative piece, this first movement reveals a skilled composer of the sonata style. The main differences between this version and the presumed earlier one are a thinning of the orchestration in certain passages so that the winds are strategically held in reserve and the elimination of the "Silence" bars between the end of *T* and the beginning of *S* in the exposition and recapitulation, which thereby eliminates some rather ineffective dead time.

Potter composes the second movement in a not so slow tempo (Andantino quasi Allegretto 3/4); places it in the tonic major key; eliminates the heavy brass, timpani, and clarinets; and shapes it as a rondo.

$\boxed{A}$	$\boxed{B}$	$\boxed{A}$ Variation	$\boxed{C}$	$\boxed{A}$ /Coda
G major	G minor	G major	B-flat modulatory	G major
m.1	41	83	91	129

One of its more distinctive aspects is that a sixteenth-note figure presented first in *B* recurs in the subsequent *A* and *C*, a type of a larger-level formal continuity practiced by Mozart in K.551/2 and by Beethoven in Opus 13/2 and Opus 18/1/2; these and other pieces decisively affected the shape of nineteenth-century slow movements. Such continuity is underlined here by a reluctance to bring the episodes and refrain to full closure. This is most readily apparent with the varied repetition of *A* (m.83), which almost melds into the second episode.

Though the piece is in many ways indebted to Mozart and Beethoven, its character recalls Haydn: the triple-meter refrain, the opening scored for strings, the sostenuto marking, and the hymn-like impression recalls the triple-meter slow movements of some favorite Haydn symphonies in England, such as Nos. 75/2 and 98/2. Potter was too young to have encountered these pieces in the 1790s, but he may well have become familiar with them in various arrangements. Indeed, its reduced scoring without clarinets results in something approaching the sound of Haydn's Symphony No. 98/2.

Tempo di Menuetto marks the third movement, and again the clarinets are tacet (cf. Mozart's revised Viennese version of the "Haffner" Symphony K.385/3), even though all of the heavy brass, including the trombones, have returned. Potter's style is that of the old-fashioned aristocratic Minuet saturated with dotted rhythms encapsulated in binary forms. One might expect in a minor-mode cycle the main part to be in the minor mode, as is the case with Haydn, Mozart, and Beethoven, and a turn to the major for the Trio, where it forms a bright patch within the cycle (e.g., K.550/3); instead, Potter places both in the major. Nevertheless, in the Trio's epilogue he does adopt the corresponding passage in Mozart's G Minor Symphony K.550, which features sinewy chromaticism, smooth rhythms, and the timbre of woodwinds with horns.

For the Finale, Potter combines the character of a Haydn Finale (i.e., a *contredanse* or jig) with a Mozartean rondo (i.e., *A–B–A–C(A)–B–A*). The heavy scoring with trombones seems to be incongruous for the former, while the main characteristic of the latter is the elimination of the *A* return after *C* (m.106), since *C* concentrates on the development of *A* material and *A* is further developed by expansion after the two statements of *B* (mm.48 and 184). Its other departure from the norm is the beginning in the minor mode with *A*'s return (m.90) occurring in the major. Potter's brief coda (m.208) deals with motives that can be viewed as coming from both the refrain and episodes. By using this sort of Finale, Potter is rejecting the culminating Finales found in some of Haydn's symphonies (e.g., Nos. 95, 101, 103), Mozart's K.550 and 551, and Beethoven's Nos. 2, 3, and 5.

In his so-called Symphony No. 1, Potter can be viewed as taking a middle-of-the-road stance between the more revolutionary aspects of Haydn, Mozart, and Beethoven, and the more conservative preferences of his potential audience for the Royal Philharmonic Society. Potter possesses in this work all of the technical facility any commentator could hope for, whether it be in thematic development, textural variety, tonal control, or rhythmic drive. What he lacks is the ability to harness these attributes in a powerful and original way.

This, probably Potter's First Symphony, was seemingly first heard at the Philharmonic Society on May 29, 1826. *The Harmonicon* published the following review:

> The Symphony chosen for the opening of this concert is, in our opinion, by far the ablest composition that Mr. Cipriani Potter has produced: it not only shews the thorough knowledge of harmony—of the characters of the different instruments, and of their combined use in the orchestra, that he has always evinced, but it also displays

invention, the want of which is so oppressively felt in nineteen out of twenty of those things called *new,* that are annually brought forward, in various shapes, and immediately consigned to oblivion. The present work is in the usual number of movements; the Minuet and trio have the most novelty; herein are some unexpected, excellent effects. There are likewise passages of considerable originality in both the first and last movements, but the finale would be improved by abridgment. The whole met with great applause.[24]

SYMPHONY [NO. 2] IN B-FLAT MAJOR

Potter's Second Symphony may in reality be his first completed work in the genre if movements two through four of Symphony No. 1 were composed after early 1821. It has the distinction of having three movements without a Minuet or Scherzo. This concision is somewhat compensated for by the length of the Finale, which is considerably longer than that of Symphony No. 1 (242 mm. vs. 524 mm.), while the first two movements are of a comparable length. Symphony No. 2 is the leanest scored of all Potter symphonies; of the trombones only the bass trombone remains. It functions to further bolster the bass line. Such parts demand that the bass trombone be able to blend within the orchestra.

The B-flat Major Symphony's first movement takes a totally different stance from that of the parallel G minor movement. Whereas the G minor movement presented a series of discrete thematic statements with some motivic interrelationships, Symphony No. 2/1 is thematically a more minimalist effort. *P* and *S,* though contrasting, are both motivically structured with *P* using motivic repetition and sequence to build the phrase. *S* relates to *P* by a rhythmic similarity. Thus, all the material of the exposition relates in one way or another to the opening two measures:

‖ :	*P*	*P^k(Pax)*	*T(Pax)*	*S(P)*	trans. *(Pax)*	*S(P)*	exp.	*Sax*	exp.	*Pax*	*1K(Pax)*	*2K(Pax)*	: ‖
	B-flat		mod.	F	mod.	F	mod.				F		
	m.1	15	23	34	43	53	62		82		94	114	

Such intensity over a single motive recalls the first movement of Beethoven's Symphony No. 5, and also Haydn's compositional credo of taking an idea and developing it. However, Potter's response to Beethoven is without any of the *brio* of his mentor and friend; rather, the movement possesses a Scherzo-like character.

If the exposition is concerned with motivic elaboration, the development places more emphasis on rhythmic control as well as contrapuntal and tonal development. Beginning with *S,* Potter slows its surface rhythm. This is the beginning of a long-term gradual increase of activity through counterpoint (m.138), the return of *Pax* (m.153), then *P^k* (m.165) with its sixteenth-note response to *Pax.* A slowing of the surface activity and two sequences—the first downward through thirds, the second downward through fifths—mark the retransition. Here, too, one can observe a favorite Beethovenian gesture: the regular alternation of *forte* and *piano* in a statement/response syntax. A measure of silence precedes the recapitulation, which closely follows the exposition; Potter seems to have been unable until his late symphonies to exploit the recapitulation as both a reprise and a furthering of the theme's potential. It concludes with a brief coda based on the rhythm of *Pax.*

From every perspective, the Andante is one of the highlights of Potter's symphonic efforts. Not only does it possess attractive melodies, but Potter presents them in a form that fits none of the standard shapes, yet unfolds in a convincing manner. Table XIV/7 attempts to provide an outline of the piece using sonata form as its basis. Here, however, the tonal scheme is mirrored with the exposition taking the usual tonic/dominant scheme and the recapitulation reversing this scheme from dominant to tonic. The most notable thematic manipulation is the transformation of *P* (Example XIV/2) from a lyric beginning to a marcato march (cf. mm.1 and 35). The development is atrophied to a ten-measure transition. In contrast to his first movements, Potter subtly alters his recapitulation by changing phrase lengths in *P, T,* and *S,* adding new material between *T(Pa)* and *S,* and appending an evocative coda with two swells and a final phrase that dies away. Though the level of accomplishment is not to be immediately duplicated, this work reveals Potter at his very best.

The Finale is another 6/8 piece in *contredanse*/jig style reminiscent of Haydn. However, the drive of compound meter is broken by three episodes (mm.150, 221, 437) in 2/4 that serve to slow the surface from triple to duple subdivisions. Though cast in a full sonata form, Potter departs from the expected expository plan. *P* is cast in two parts: *1P* is a jig beginning with two pick-ups (cf. Haydn Symphony No. 98/1) followed by *2P* (m.36), another jig of a more lyrical character. That *2P* is heard twice, first carried by the strings in the tonic and then repeated by the woodwinds on the dominant, leads one to believe that this is *S.* However, an extended *T* based on *1P* leads to the actual *S* (m.97), which has a slower surface and is mainly scored for the winds. *S* is followed by a further expansion on *Pax,* the 2/4 episode, and the return to 6/8 for *K.*

Except for the 2/4 episode, the development concentrates on *1P* beginning with a deceptive resolution that takes us from the dominant of B-flat to G minor, A minor, C major, and then D and B-flat. Surprisingly, this leads to D-flat, C, and then an enharmonic transfer (mm.272–73) back to D. With a second deceptive resolution the dominant of D resolves to B-flat for another regular recapitulation. The structural use of the deceptive resolution also articulates the beginning of the coda (m.472) as B-flat's dominant shockingly resolves to G-flat, which eventually returns to a dominant pedal over a chromatic rise. This gesture distinctly recalls the ending of Haydn's "The Heavens are Telling" from *The Creation* and the coda to Beethoven's Symphony No. 2/1.

More than Symphony No. 1, Symphony No. 2 is a thorough and convincing imitation of a late Classical symphony, not unlike Schubert's Symphony No. 5 in B-flat D.485.

TABLE XIV/7
Potter. Symphony No. 2/2: Structure

Exposition												False Development		
Pa	a¹	b	b¹	a		T(P)	S(Pb)	Pax			K(Pax)	Pax		T(P)
4	4	4	4	4		11	3	2+2+2			1×4+2	4		6
									ff					
F							C				C	C minor		A minor
m.1						21	28	35			44	50		54

Recapitulation													
Pa	a	a²	b	b²	T(Pax)	N extension				S	Pa	Pb	Pa
4	4	4	4	4	4	2	2	3	1	4	3		
											ff	*f* *p* *f* *pp* *calando*	
C										F	F		
60		68	72		80	84				92	99	108	131

EXAMPLE XIV/2   Potter. Symphony No. 2/2, mm.1–8, 35–41. British Library Loan 4/377.

The intensive development in the first movement, the wonderfully flexible approach to form and syntax in the Andante, and the Haydnesque Finale with its structural use of the deceptive cadence almost make one think this to be a studied effort. But it is more than a study since the material is treated with a skill that could only belong to an experienced professional. Like the First Symphony, the Second would have captured the attention of his audience, for it is both old fashioned and up to date with some unexpected items mixed into the brew. Potter did not regard his Second Symphony as a work to be suppressed for any of the above reasons; he apparently used it for the benefit concert on June 6, 1839, some eighteen years after its completion.

Philip Peter surmises that because of the series numbered Symphonies Nos. 6, 7, and 8, Nos. 3, 4, and 5 are now lost along with several later symphonic efforts.[25]

SYMPHONY NO. 6 IN C MINOR

By 1826, the key of C minor must have, like that of G minor, evoked a tradition. The implications of the power of Beethoven's Opus 67 and his other works in this key in the non-symphonic genres invoke the tragic and the *pathétique*. The Beethovenian C minor tradition presented a dilemma to any composer using this key; either he could attempt to write a powerful work that might be compared to Beethoven's or compose a piece that could not possibly recall the "great mogul." Spohr in his two symphonies in C minor, one of which was his Fifth, seems to have ignored the implications of Beethoven's C Minor Symphony. To some degree, Potter adopted a similar stance in his two C minor symphonies; however, his efforts are saturated in seriousness and his Beethovenian references are subtle. It was not until the last quarter of the century that symphonies by Brahms, Bruckner, and Mahler challenged Beethoven's C minor rhetoric.

Potter's cycle has none of the drama and connected movements of Beethoven's Opus 67. Indeed, the only cyclic similarity is that Potter's slow movement is in the same key as Beethoven's, A-flat major, and is juxtaposed with C minor even though Potter's Andante is in third rather than second position. This A-flat major movement, as we shall see, does hold some other similarities with Opus 67/2. Otherwise, Potter's tonal scheme results in a lyric cycle. Rather than Beethoven's long-term dramatic strategy of moving from the minor to the major mode, Potter's first and final movements each turn from the minor to the tonic major before their conclusion; in addition, the Scherzo is in C minor, but the Trio, as might be expected, turns to the major.

Symphony No. 6 has a first movement that is structured unlike any of Potter's earlier ones. Though the exposition is repeated, in the second part the recapitulation does not return with *P* in the tonic, but rather with *S* scored for the full band *fortissimo* (m.230) instead of the strings marked *piano* as in its first appearance. This C major *fortissimo* moment (Example XIV/3) seems poorly prepared; it is preceded by a *diminuendo* and the two pick-ups for the gavotte theme are ambiguously articulated and thinly scored, essentially beginning *S* on the downbeat. In less than thirty measures, the coda arrives (m.259) with new material and *1P* (m.278) touching on the subdominant, then modulating, and finally establishing the tonic major (m.326). Thus, in the larger perspective, the recapitulation may be viewed as either substantially cut or reversed.

The exposition itself is well within normal practice. Potter effectively divides *1P* into *a* and *b*, but does not stabilize its components with a repetition. *1Pa* is for strings in octaves, while *b* is for winds providing a deep Mozartean contrast (Example XIV/4). A grand pause sets up a nervous *2P*, where the string/woodwind dialogue comes at one-measure rather than three-measure intervals. An extension culminates in a heavily articulated half cadence. *1P* (m.25) reappears in the bass with a treble counterpoint operating in contrary motion. One might think this to be the beginning of *T*, except Potter concludes this statement with a decisive cadence in C minor. *T* (m.44) takes up a Beethovenian dialogue of *fortissimo/tutti* versus *pianissimo/*reduced scoring. The contrasting *S* (m.78) employs a singing Allegro texture, and the three members of *K* (mm.99, 107, 118) deal with now-agitated material, *2P*, and *1P* in turn.

Potter's development section (m.128) deals almost exclusively with material from *1P* and *2P;* an obvious justification for beginning the reprise with *S*. Most remarkable is the modula-

EXAMPLE XIV/3   Potter. Symphony No. 6/1, mm.226–37. British Library Ms. Add. 31, 783.

tory plan. It begins in A-flat and moves toward its relative minor of F. Potter then descends by fifths:

A-flat ⟶ D-flat ⟶ (G-flat) ⟶ C-flat/B ⟶ G-flat (F-sharp) ⟶ C-flat/B
m.128   164   166   182   191

A rising sequence (m.194) moves to the dominant of C (m.206), which ultimately confirms C major with *S* (m.230) for the recapitulation. Though belonging more to the classical *Sturm und Drang* style than to Beethoven's reformulation of this idiom, this first movement does

EXAMPLE XIV/3 (*continued*)

possess some Beethovenian aspects: the most distant tonal points (mm.166 and 191) coordinate with the most complete reduction of the thematic material, and mm.13f, 44f, 98f, and 111f from the exposition remind one of the *Coriolan Overture* Opus 62.

Potter's second movement Scherzo, marked Allegro con spirito, is another movement filled with dotted rhythms that might make one think that the quarter note warrants the beat, but in fact this C minor piece works rather well with one beat to the bar. However, Potter must have realized that the surface rhythms imposed some restrictions on the tempo, for the Trio pushes the tempo to Più Presto, which can be well tolerated by its smoother rhythms.

To some degree the opening of the Andante 2/4, in addition to its key, also reminds one of the slow movement of Beethoven's Fifth Symphony. Both movements at the beginning

EXAMPLE XIV/4   Potter. Symphony No. 6/1, mm.1–20. British Library Ms. Add. 31, 783.

provide a relaxation of tension with leisurely surface activity for sonorous strings and extended cadential repetitions in the woodwinds as well as in the string/wind dialogues. Notice too the layering of surface rhythms, which provides a rich sonority that also recalls the corresponding Beethoven movement. What Potter does avoid are any *tutti* passages where the trumpet takes the lead; this would have immediately revealed his partially veiled model. Cast in an alternating part form (*A–B–A–B–A*) in the key of A-flat, the two episodes are in F and D-flat major, a pair of descending thirds that move the orchestra into the less comfortable keys of more than four flats but also enrich the string sonorities by making the use of open strings almost an impossibility.

For the first time in these works, Potter offers a Finale that does not immediately bring to mind the Finales of Haydn's two sets of symphonies for London. The Allegro begins in common time with a compact sonata form; i.e., at the end of the exposition (m.66) *P* returns

EXAMPLE XIV/4   *(continued)*

in the tonic like a false repeat of the exposition only to divert in tonal activity for a short development section, followed by a retransition and a recapitulation. This first section accounts for 177 bars. For section two, the meter changes to 2/4 and the tempo to Presto forming a coda of 98 measures in C major that begins with a diminution of *P*. Since every measure is filled with sixteenth notes, Potter has provided a *perpetuum mobile* that brings this predominantly serious piece to a jocular end. The symphony ends not in the world of Beethoven's Fifth, but rather that of Beethoven's Fourth.

Potter's Sixth is a symphony astride two centuries which is indicated by the two styles of the Finale; the first style looks forward as it gives the last movement the same aesthetic weight as the first movement of the cycle, the second looks backward to the eighteenth century in

EXAMPLE XIV/4   *(continued)*

that it again recaptures Haydn's idiom. Despite the presence of trombones, the orchestration still depends heavily on Classical practice, particularly if one considers that by the end of 1825, Carl Maria von Weber had created some of his most important works with striking orchestrations, which Potter must have heard.

SYMPHONY NO. 7 IN F MAJOR

The double personality of Symphony No. 6 is less obvious in Symphony No. 7. There are four movements in the traditional order with a Minuet and Trio, rather than a Scherzo, in third instead of in second place. Potter's key scheme is about as conservative as can be with only two keys used at the cyclic dimension: F for the first, Minuet, and last movements, and the subdominant B-flat for the Andante and Trio of the Minuet. Like its predecessor, No. 7

EXAMPLE XIV/5   Potter. Symphony No. 7/1, mm.1–22.

is a thoroughly skilled piece leaving no want of technique. Why it did not gain a public hearing at the concerts of the Philharmonic Society remains unknown.

Its first movement maintains the proper large-scale form with a coordinated recapitulation of *P* and the tonic key, concluding with an effective coda. Again, Potter uses the grand pause to articulate points of structure; here, the "Silence" occurs between *T* and *S*. As seen in No. 6, Potter's strength is revealed in his departure from the expected tonal plans. Here, he does not wait until *T* or the development section, but diverts within *1P*, where after the establishment of F major Potter suddenly takes us to D-flat (m.7) by way of B-flat minor and ends *2P* with a full tonic close (Example XIV/5). *1T* begins as if it could be *S*, while *2T* comes after the cadence in the dominant. Potter now modulates further, concluding on a dominant seventh of C. *S* (m.58) features a wind/string dialogue, as *1T* did, which is considerably extended and ends with the full band. *1K* (m.93) also commences in the same way, and this fabric continues into *2K* (m.113). Since *1T*, *S*, and *1K* all begin with the same type of gesture, the grand pause before *S* gains a particular structural significance.

EXAMPLE XIV/5 *(continued)*

Rather than concentrating on one motif in the development section, Potter uses most of the thematic material but scrambles its presentation:

1P	*1T ext.*	*S*	*2T*	*2P*	retrans.
F minor	D-flat	D	D minor	A-flat	dominant pedal
m.120	132	153	167	175	184

Between *1P* and *1T,* Potter articulates F-sharp minor (m.128) as an enharmonic relation to D-flat, which leads eventually to D. This move is a natural outgrowth of the parallel tonal event in *P* of the exposition.

Unfortunately, the exposition's treatment of *P* is replayed in the recapitulation; one could not imagine Haydn, Mozart, or Beethoven passing up such an opportunity for a new tonal move that would aim, at least temporarily, in a new direction. The rest of the recapitulation follows the exposition except for the expected tonal adjustment. In the coda (m.317), Potter manipulates material from the first part of the exposition (*1P, 2P, 1T*) into a collage, which forms something quite different from their original presentations.

EXAMPLE XIV/5   *(continued)*

The Andantino Grazioso immediately recalls Symphony No. 2/2 in its gradual and beautifully calculated entry of the strings; if anything, No. 7/2 is a refinement over what was admired in the earlier slow movement. In addition, both movements depart from formal conventions. In No. 2/2, the conventions of sonata form were toyed with; in No. 7/2 it is the rondo. Here, the first episode (*B*) is heard twice in the two most likely keys: first (m.25) in B-flat's relative minor of G and then in its subdominant, E-flat (m.71). While the G minor portion of the first episode is extended and modulatory, also a departure from normal procedure, the E-flat version is almost like a retransition except that it is the subdominant rather than the dominant that prevails. Oddly, it is the return of the refrain (*A*, m.88) that is undergirded by a dominant pedal and whose fluid part-writing is reformulated. Potter's second episode, *C* (m.131), begins as if it were the first; it presents a new tune. After eight bars, *C* takes on its more usual modulatory character as it finds its way to B major (m.149)

as part of an intensive development of the *A* material (m.144f). *C*'s final portion (m.159) is undergirded by a tonic pedal before a Più lento coda (m.170) brings back *A* in a becalmed form.

Potter's third movement, Menuetto: Allegro non tanto, is treated more like one of his full sonata forms with a repeat of its expository part, but no repetition of the second half. Its B-flat Trio features blocks of string and woodwind choirs, *sans* oboe, perhaps an echo of Mozart's E-flat Symphony K.543. Potter treats the second strain (m.101) as another opportunity for tonal exploration; it touches on D-flat, G-flat, and C-flat before sliding back to B-flat for the recapitulation (m.133).

The Finale, Allegro assai 6/8, returns to the *contredanse* idiom of the first two symphonies. The opening, with its almost ostinato bass and somewhat improvisatory treble, does something more than invoke the *contredanse* idiom; it imitates it. After twenty-one measures, the oboes and bassoons take up the ostinato with a drone in the flutes and clarinets freeing all the strings for thematic participation. *T* (m.54), colored by the diminished-seventh sound, completely breaks from the *contredanse* idiom as do the subsequent distant harmonies whose only purpose is to land us in the dominant for *S* (m.128) where another jig is now offered by the woodwinds. *K* shockingly shifts to the Neapolitan's dominant (m.167).

The development is in two stretches: the first is concerned entirely with *P* (m.197), the second with *S* (m.260), which is followed by a retransition. Beginning with *P* in the dominant and as heard in the beginning, Potter explores mostly the key of D in both its major and minor modes. *S* tonally moves further afield: the enharmonic relationship and distant key of B/C-flat is reached (m.260). Potter now deals with both *S* and aspects of its texture, which is brought into greater prominence so that the long-note accompaniment to *S* in the exposition also becomes a response to the same material in the development (see m.299f). Thus, *x/y* becomes *x+y*. Again the retransition (m.345) is identified with a dominant pedal, but this time it ceases (m.359) just before the recapitulation (m.368), which is, surprisingly, less regular than in the earlier movements. In the area between *T* (m.425) and *S* (m.470), some thirty measures are deleted, and a coda (m.551) of sixty-six measures brings the movement to an energetic close.

To say that Potter's Seventh is a fine example of a normative symphony by this composer should not be misconstrued. Not a single symphony by Potter reveals anything but a composer completely in control of his materials, one who has the skills and technique to use his ideas to fine effect. Also revealed here is that Potter is not an innovator who goes beyond acceptable boundaries; yet, at the same time, he is not reluctant to use surprising harmonies and dissonances.

SYMPHONY NO. 8 IN E-FLAT MAJOR

Potter's Eighth Symphony separates itself from all of his previous symphonies in that it is the first to commence with a slow introduction. But this is no brief *exordium* since it is on a scale comparable to Mozart's "Prague" Symphony K.504 and Beethoven's Symphony No. 7 Opus 92 and conveys a seriousness reminiscent of K.504 and the overture to *The Magic Flute,* K.620. Not only does this piece exude something of *The Magic Flute*'s character, it also is in the same key and uses a thematic turn in its Allegro whose source cannot be mistaken, even though Potter's Allegro is in triple rather than duple meter. This latter aspect also recalls the cycle to Mozart's Symphony No. 39 in E-flat K.543, as does the main body of the first movement and the inclusion of a 2/4 Moderato con moto ma sostenuto slow movement in A-flat major with much of the ambiance of Mozart's Andante con moto. Potter knew this Mozart symphony well from its frequent performances at the Philharmonic Concerts. The prominence offered the clarinets in Potter's Eighth, though oboes are not absent from the scoring, also recalls K.543. If the first two movements are Mozartean, the Finale seems to owe something to Haydn's Symphonies Nos. 95 and 103. Of all Potter's symphonies to date, this one is the most obviously derivative.

The Maestoso introduction is a triple statement/response shape.

A	*B*		*A*	*B*		*A*	*B*
E-flat	C minor		mod.	B-flat minor mod.		G	G
m.1	8		19	27		31	37

The solemnity of this introduction is underlined by its "ombra" topic, emphasis on the minor mode, and its ending on the dominant of C minor, which sets up a bifocal relationship to the E-flat major Allegro.

In the recapitulation of Symphony No. 7/4, Potter made a cut of about thirty measures of expository material during T; in Symphony No. 8 the surgery is more radical with an exposition of 189 measures and a recapitulation of 97 measures from its beginning to the coda (m.341). A large portion of the difference is a result of cutting material associated with *Pb* not only in *P*, but also in the various *T* areas based on it (see Table XIV/8). In this instance, there is a logic to Potter's excisions in the recapitulation because *Pb* and its *Magic Flute* motive is given prominence in the exposition and development sections. Thus, for the first time in his symphonies, Potter displays a larger awareness of thematic distribution. A precedent with which Potter was familiar is Haydn's Symphony No. 104/1, where the employment of two *P* motives is divided so that one is emphasized in the exposition and the other in the development/recapitulation.[26]

Though the content is Mozartean, the conduct of this material in the exposition and development is more like Haydn. That much of the material of the exposition is related immediately brings to mind Haydn (see Table XIV/8), as does the motivic development, which concentrates on only material from *Pb*. The tightened presentation of expository material in the recapitulation, apart from the relative importance of the *Magic Flute* motive, is a Haydn-like approach in that only the essentials return.

Potter's version of K.543/2 for the slow movement is more conservative. Instead of making various allowances for Mozart's aberrations of sonata structure in K.543, including a return of significant material a tritone away, Potter presents his structure very much like his own previous practices in first movements with clear functions, a repeat of the exposition, a development with some of the characteristics already observed in the first movements, a recapitulation similar to but not an exact expository replay, and a coda undergirded by a tonic pedal.

Perhaps the most remarkable aspect of the Andante is the suppleness of the melodic material orchestrated in a series of solo and section colors. Notice at the beginning the pairs of solo woodwinds in dialogue with the string choir and the deft writing for solo clarinet and bassoon at the beginning of *T* (m.13; Example XIV/6). This striking beginning is coloristically elaborated at the start of the recapitulation as the cello adds a new voice to the clarinet duo. Almost every measure is effectively orchestrated, another example of Potter's particular skill in this department (i.e., to modestly demonstrate his mastery without ostentation).

Only slightly ostentatious is the beginning of the Scherzo announced by the brass followed

TABLE XIV/8

Potter. Symphony No. 8/i: Structure

Allegro non tanto

Exposition

||: Pa	b	a	a	ext.	b	1T(Pb)	2T(Pb)	lead-in	S	3T	4T(Pb)
E-flat									B-flat		
m.43	47	51	55		63	75	105	122	126	157	163

Development

1K	2K	:|| Pb	Pb plus new ctrpt. mod.	𝄐 V₇/E-flat
		G minor		
175	185	190	222	243

Recapitulation

Pa	1T	lead-in	S
E-flat			
244	256	282	286

Coda

4T (Pb)	Pb	Pa	Pa ||
		dom. pedal	
306	319	330	341

EXAMPLE XIV/6   Potter. Symphony No. 8/2, mm.1–17. British Library Ms. Add. 31, 783.

by an almost *tutti* fermata. The Trio features the horns in A-flat, though Potter does not specify if *alto* or *basso* crooks are to be used. In Italian operatic usage *basso* would be assumed, but in orchestral works, the *alto* crook is perhaps more often expected (see Berlioz "Queen Mab" Scherzo). However, the character of the Trio could point to the *basso* color. Since Potter was probably there for the third reading by the Philharmonic Society in late 1828/1829 and conducted his own benefit in 1846, such specificity in the score was not necessary. As in Symphony No. 7/3, the key of the Trio is the same as the slow movement resulting in a two-key cycle. Notice that the *da capo* of the Scherzo is marked senza replica, indicating that by the end of 1828 *da capo* repeats were still expected.

The Finale, like the first movement, has most of its themes deriving from the opening material; *T* (m.38), *S* (m.76), and *2K* (m.147) owe something to *P.* Two elements of *P* become of particular importance: the initial four measures (*1P*) reminiscent of Haydn's Symphony

EXAMPLE XIV/6 *(continued)*

No. 95/4 and the motive (*2Px*) | ♪ ♩ ♩ ♩ | ∘ | that recalls Haydn's Symphony No. 103/4. A chromatic lead-in takes us to *S,* which is initiated by the motive with three pick-ups; unlike Haydn, however, it is not presented in a driven context, but in one where the energy is completely relaxed as the accompanying surface rhythms are now at their slowest. With *S*'s repetition, the eighth-note accompaniment momentarily drives the theme forward. *1K* (m.111) has all the energy of *P* and *T,* but diverts (m.129) to a developmental passage. Then *2K* reconfirms its closing function with a vengeance. This gesture of interrupting *K* is also one used effectively by Haydn (see Opus 74/3/4 and Opus 76/3/1). Characteristically, Potter ends this section with a bar of "Silence."

In the development, *1P* is now altered to modulate, and Potter moves expeditiously to distant keys, though this time without any enharmonicism. Potter then combines polyphonically *1P* and *2P* (m.176), as ideas from both are treated to thematic reduction during which

35

a climax is reached. A final section returns to the development's opening, builds to a second momentary peak, and then quiets for a *pianissimo* recapitulation. Otherwise, the recapitulation again closely follows the exposition. Potter's coda (m.384) concentrates on *2P*. The subdominant (A-flat) is immediately touched on (m.386), then to G-flat (m.408) before the return to the dominant in preparation for the final section (m.432), which pounds out *1P* and *2P* in the tonic.

Despite the transparency of the musical models for Potter's Symphony No. 8, one has to admit that he is able to unleash these materials in a different way. Whether they be Mozart's or Haydn's materials and procedures, Potter has his own musical discourse that cannot be confused with his mentors' works. And again, Potter's formidable musical skills and techniques are always in evidence. Still, in terms of the Philharmonic Society, this symphony seems to have achieved only a trial reading in late 1828 or early 1829. Perhaps its derivative aspects were recognized by the learned musicians of the orchestra and the directors of the Society. It was apparently not until Potter's benefit concert in 1846 that it received a formal public hearing. The critic for *The Athenaeum* who heard the 1846 rendition did not take well to Potter's effort:

> *Mr. Cipriani Potter* gave his annual concert on Monday,—with a new Symphony in E flat. Now, our respect is great for the professor who, in these days, has patience to turn aside from more frivolous and profitable tasks, to write symphonies. But to every piece of music there must be two consenting parties; and, in this case, we have respect for the audience also,—who sat through a work so long and so totally unrelieved by any character of interest. Mr. Potter may be credited with a singular notion, as having written a part for *fagotto obbligato* to his slow movement; but the ear longed in vain for a passage of melody, or a flash of originality, in the grouping of the instruments.[27]

According to Philip Peter's reckoning, sometime between Symphonies No. 8 and No. 10, Potter composed a symphony no longer extant.[28] From a notice in the *Harmonicon*, a Symphony in D Major is cited as being played for Potter's benefit concert in 1829.[29] Since there are no known earlier works in this key, one must be missing. However, this hypothesis does not account for the existence of more than one work in D major among the lost Symphonies Nos. 3–5.

SYMPHONY NO. 10 IN G MINOR

On the title page to Symphony No. 10, Potter wrote: "This symphony was composed expressly for the concerts of this Society. . . . 1832 London." Such was the result of a commission approved by the Society on November 5, 1832.[30] Subsequently, it had one trial in January 1833 and was first publicly performed on May 27, 1833, at the Society's concerts. In addition, this, his second Symphony in G Minor, was probably subsequently programmed at further Philharmonic concerts and for the composer's benefit on June 14, 1843. It was also arranged for piano four-hands in 1832 by the composer and probably published, even though only one copy of the print survives in a private collection. The Tenth is the only Potter symphony to have appeared in a critical edition.[31]

The cycle of Symphony No. 10 is somewhat different in its tonal layout from Potter's previous symphonies. Though, as expected, the first and last movements are in G minor, the Andante is in D minor and the Scherzo in B-flat major with a Trio in E-flat, the key of the first movement's *S*. Additionally, the Andante slow movement has F major and A minor as its secondary tonal areas for *S* in the exposition. Perhaps Potter was aiming for some new, if not striking, tonal juxtapositions. Still, Potter writes four discrete movements without any attempt toward movement linkage or thematic recall.

As for the large-scale form of the opening Allegro, Potter for the first time dispenses with any repeat of the exposition. The omission of the repeat still results, even taking into account the repeats in the previous first movements, in the longest opening movement by Potter to date. Nevertheless, this is not a sprawling piece for it is motivically generated and tightly composed.

The beginning reminds one of Haydn's Symphony No. 78/1 (Example XIV/7): the triple meter, octave sonority, statement/response layout, and motivic orientation. Also, both movements subject the opening to a less gruff transformation: Haydn with the strings, Potter with the woodwinds. Additionally, the motivic imitation of *Pax* of Haydn's mm.9–14 is taken up later in Potter's piece. Symphony No. 78 has a long English history, for Haydn sold it to the publisher William Forster in 1784; Potter therefore probably encountered Haydn's C Minor Symphony many years before he composed his own G Minor Symphony.

P ends with a two-measure "Silence" followed by what here is designated as two *T* themes (mm.46, 76) based on *Pa+b* and *Pc* beginning in E-flat major. However, when *S* begins (m.114), it too is in E-flat rather than the expected key of B-flat major or D minor. Since *P* concludes (mm.42–43) on the dominant of G minor, one does not expect C minor or its bifocal alternative of E-flat major; one might hear *T* (m.46) as *S* (m.114), particularly since in minor-mode movements *S* often appears rather early. The issue of where the second subject begins in this movement points to a significant structural ambiguity. However, with *T*, the question is: Could this be *S*? With *S*, the reply is: This must be *S*!

B-flat major is not only absent in the exposition, it is also avoided during Potter's long (135 mm.) development section (m.148), which begins in C minor, but centers on D with some attention paid to G minor. D is articulated by a striking *fortissimo* augmented-sixth chord (m.160) that undergirds *Pay* and *z*. When this striking moment returns (m.247), the augmented sixth resolves to G minor even though it will not be until m.283 that the recapitulation occurs again *fortissimo* now reinforced by a *tutti* downbeat. Not only does Potter take peculiar paths tonally in the development section, he also concentrates on *P* elements, which received intensive attention in the exposition with *T* and the extension of *S*.

The tonal make-up of the exposition makes for a rather normal, yet somewhat peculiar, recapitulation with regard to mode that continues to raise doubts concerning the location of *T* and to a lesser degree *S*.

Exposition		
P	T	S
G minor	E-flat major	E-flat major
m.1	46	114

Recapitulation		
P	T	S
G minor	G major-minor	G minor
m.283	328	390

That *T* begins in G major, the normal key for *S* in the recapitulation, lends credence to the assertion in the exposition that *T* could very well be *S*. By changing the exposition's E-flat *S* to G minor in the recapitulation seems in this context somewhat ambiguous.

Perhaps the only Beethovenian echo is found in the coda (m.470), where thematic

EXAMPLE XIV/7 Potter. Symphony No. 10/1, mm.1–20. © 2001 by Stainer & Bell Ltd, *Musica Britannica* volume 77, edited by Julian Rushton; reprinted with permission.

development continues as *Pax* and *Paz* expand by sequences that lead to reiterated cadences. However, in contrast to Beethoven, its fifty-eight measures hardly balance out or complete a task from earlier in the movement. Potter certainly has exhausted *P*'s possibilities, but has not led us to hearing it from a new perspective.

Potter's Andante con moto ¢ commences with another carefully textured and orchestrated beginning (Example XIV/8): first violins alone; a sextet of clarinets, bassoons, and horns; and a duet with bassoons, violas, cellos, and basses. Indeed, throughout the exposition, Potter is constantly shifting sonorities and colors so that none are duplicated until the recapitulation of this sonatina form. Another issue concerning the beginning is its tonal ambiguity. In the opening two measures, D minor is expected, but Potter fails to sharpen the leading tone of C. Within two measures, the winds cadence in F. However, with the next string and bassoon entry, the pitch C-sharp is established as the leading tone so that there is no doubt that D is the tonic, which is confirmed by the cadence in m.14. *S* (m.68) is also somewhat ambiguous by beginning in F major and then cadencing in A minor (m.79). The recapitulation (m.89) erases the ambiguity of D and F by the repeated C-sharp prior to *P*'s restatement with the C-natural, and *S* (m.139) does not emphasize any key other than D. In the coda (m.158), Potter replays *P* with a solo violin, but this time with C-sharp at the end of the second measure, which provides a long-term resolution to *P*'s ambiguity. Even though C-natural does return in the subdominant nudges of the following passage, C-sharp reasserts itself again for the conclusion. Symphony No. 10/2 is Potter's first effort in which a long-range tonal strategy is carefully presented and resolved.

After a Scherzo with Trio in *da capo* form, but in B-flat, the relative major previously so carefully avoided, Potter embarks upon another *contredanse* Finale that begins in the minor mode; here, *P* is labeled scherzando and leggiero, which seems to contradict the usual associations of the minor mode as tending more toward the serious and ponderous. After the double bar (m.101), the strings are urged to play *P* con energia. Also adding to the bustle is the orchestration of *S* (m.45), which has accompanying multiple stops in the strings with melodies and countermelodies in the woodwinds. *S,* this time in the expected key of B-flat, again has the slowest surface in the movement, which is overtaken by sixteenths in the strings (m.61). Suddenly the music becomes subdued and sustained with a deceptive shift to G-flat major (m.77). It returns enharmonically to the dominant of G (m.91) for *K* and the repeat of the exposition.

The development (m.101) also begins on G, but immediately leaves this anchoring tonality only to later gain some moments of stability with a dominant pedal on E-flat (m.141). This resolves bi-focally to C, which sets off another spate of activity. But modulatory activity and the sheer surface drive of the themes themselves are not Potter's only means of revving up the excitement. Others are the dialogue between treble and bass at one-measure intervals (m.126), the chromatically descending counterpoint to *P* motives (m.130), the systematic motivic play moving downward through the strings (m.133), the passing of motives through the woodwinds at two- or one-measure intervals (m.150), and a one-measure wind/string dialogue (m.159). A retransition (m.182) barely allows room to catch a breath before the recapitulation (m.197), which again closely follows the exposition. After two measures of "Silenzio" (m.315), the coda begins with material from *K* (see m.96) and the retransition. It then builds to the final cadences. This Finale is the most driven among Potter's symphonies; the character indications accompanying some of the themes are completely appropriate, but it is con energia that seems to apply to the entire movement.

From the Finale alone, one can well understand why this symphony among Potter's

EXAMPLE XIV/8   Potter. Symphony No. 10/2, mm.1–14. © 2001 by Stainer & Bell Ltd, *Musica Britannica* volume 77, edited by Julian Rushton; reprinted with permission.

some fifteen works in this genre was probably the most frequently heard. The first movement is among his most intense developments of an opening idea and ranks among his best opening pieces. The Andante displays all the care and effectiveness of his earlier slow movements and additionally works through the resolution of a tonal/modal problem presented by the opening measures of *P* and *S*. And the Scherzo with Trio fulfills its function as a divertissement to the other, weightier movements. In sum, this is Potter's most convincing symphonic statement.

A critic for *The Harmonicon,* though he heard the man of genius in every movement, had a few reservations:

> Mr. Potter's symphony is not only the best composition that has yet proceeded from his pen, but a work that will give him an honourable place in the temple of fame,—a work, that the oftener it is heard the better it will be understood, and the more it will be liked; for not only the experienced master, but the man of genius, is evinced in every movement. It consists of an allegro con fuoco, in G minor, strikingly original; a very melodious and effective andante in D minor; a bold scherzo in G minor [*sic*], and trio in E flat; and a finale in G minor. The only point in this symphony that seems to us liable to objection, is, that all the movements, except a short trio, are in the minor key [*sic*], and this three times the same; thus a want of contrast is felt at the beginning and ending of each, though in the modulations the major third is sufficiently often introduced to afford the necessary relief.[32]

When Richard Wagner conducted the piece in London in 1855, he remembered Potter:

> I also made the acquaintance of a rather old-fashioned but very amiable composer named Potter, one of whose symphonies I was obliged to conduct. This work pleased me by its unassuming dimensions and its clean contrapuntal working, and was all the more enjoyable in that its composer, an elderly but sociable eccentric, clung to me with almost fearful modesty. I virtually had to compel him to let me play the Andante of his symphony in the right tempo, thus proving that it was really rather pretty and interesting, whereas he had so little faith in his own work that he believed only the adoption of an unduly rapid tempo could overcome the danger of its causing boredom. When I earned him an ovation by taking this Andante in my tempo, he literally beamed with gratitude and joy.[33]

Concerning this same performance, *The Musical World* reported,

> Mr. Potter's fine symphony—composed many years ago for the Philharmonic Society, and of which we have frequently spoken—was well played. Herr Wagner took great pains with it.

However, they found Wagner's rendition of Mendelssohn's "Italian" Symphony "unworthy."[34]

SYMPHONY NO. 11 IN D MAJOR

No doubt the reception of Symphony No. 10 led Potter within the next two years to compose four or five new symphonies. Three of these are in D major (one is lost), and one or two are in the minor mode. For Symphony No. 11, as well as the last of Potter's contributions to the genre, we have "Analytical and Historical Programme" notes by Potter's friend and colleague George A. Macfarren. The notes for Symphony No. 11 (also known as No. 2 of the D major series) were prepared for a posthumous performance by the Philharmonic Society on March 20, 1872, in tribute to the composer, a long-time active member, who died on September 26, 1871.[35]

Symphony No. 8 was the first of Potter's symphonies to have a slow introduction; beginning with No. 11, the three remaining and extant symphonies are all prefaced by a Moderato *exordium*. Again, the introduction is a serious and grand gesture (52 mm.) made up of a series of *tutti* acclamations (*A*) followed by quiet responses (*B*).

Moderato								Allegro vivace
A	*B*	*A*	*B*	*A*	*B*	*A*	*B*	
V		VII^{o7}		VII^{o7}		V_2^4	V	
D octaves $\rightarrow$	D	E	$\rightarrow$ C $\rightarrow$ D	A	$\rightarrow$ D	G	$\rightarrow$ D $\rightarrow$	D
m.1	3	14	16	28	30	48	50	53

Notice that harmonically and structurally, this is a true *exordium* as the composer poses a series of assertions of which only the first and last fit the key of D major. This series of improper juxtapositions only serves to highlight the intended tonic and make its ultimate resolution with the Allegro vivace stronger than it would have been if preceded by a series of only D resolving chords. Potter again uses the appellation con energia to underline the rhetorical stance.

The Allegro vivace proper presents a rather normal layout for a Potter exposition with all the functions present and a grand pause, this time situated at the end of *P*. Perhaps somewhat different from its predecessor is a slightly greater emphasis on closing functions, which occur at the end of *T* (*T^k*, m.107) and three *K* themes (mm.154, 164, 170). Again, Potter reuses *P* material in the subsequent functions except for *S* (m.126), which has its expected double statement and lyric character. The development (m.174) concentrates on but two motives *Pax* and *2Ta*, the two most pliable ideas: the first is based on an arpeggio and the second on a descending sweep of sixteenth notes. Potter again subjects his material to many of the same techniques we have observed earlier, including the reduction of a theme or motive down to its smallest identifiable unit. If anything, the tonal plan is somewhat less adventurous than what we have previously observed by avoiding enharmonic areas and otherwise seeming more predictable. Nevertheless, Macfarren remarked in his description of Symphony No. 14(15) that it is this "portion of the piece [development] wherein always the greatest musicianship, and often the greatest imagination, are evinced in the unraveling of new effects, and sometimes even of new ideas, out of the elements presented in the foregoing [exposition]."[36] However, while this development section is certainly a strong "unraveling" of the ideas, it is not Potter's best effort.

It is in the recapitulation (m.261) that the composer departs most remarkably from his usual reprise of the exposition (Table XIV/9). First, Potter states *P* and then treats it to further development, a practice frequently encountered in many sonata-form movements, but not often exploited by this composer. Second, *1K* now concludes *P*. And third, *1T(P)*, *T^k*, and *3K* are excluded. Notice that at the end of *2K* two fermatas on the dominant seventh of G and D dramatically interrupt the momentum in a Beethovenian manner. The result of all these changes is that the recapitulation, despite all of the exclusions, is still sixteen measures longer than the exposition, not including the ninety-five-bar coda that surprisingly reprises *S* and again recalls the two main motives upon which Potter concentrates in the development section. Some of these exclusions are a result of cuts, but this does not include changing the order of presentation. Once again, Potter produces a skillful and

TABLE XIV/9
Potter. Symphony No. 11/1: Structure

Exposition

‖: P	GP	1T(P)	2T	T^k	lead-in	S exp.	1K	2K	3K :‖
m.53		65	87	107	126		154	164	170

Recapitulation — *Coda*

P	dev. exp.	1K	2T	lead-in	S	exp.	1K	2K	⌢ ⌢	S
261		289	295	311	322		372	382		395

	Più Presto
2Tay + 1Pax	1Pax + cadences
417	449

effective movement that is preceded by a striking *exordium* and concluded with an exciting coda.

Returning to second position in the cycle is the Scherzo, which Macfarren notes has a "two-fold character" in that the bass has "a separate accent from the other instruments" and has an "independent prominence almost throughout."[37] Macfarren also notes Potter's use of invertible counterpoint for the main theme of the Scherzo. He finds the Trio to be "specially happy in the quaintness of its first phrase, which is enhanced by being without harmony [Violin 1], and by the rare instrumental combination [Violin, Horns, and Trumpets] that accompanies the sequel." Also reclled is that Potter eliminated the coda based on the Trio, even though it is not crossed out in the autograph: "This one might regret as a point lost, but for reverence for the self-judgment and the unsparing self-criticism of a writer who could both originate and improve."[38] However, the coda ends with a quiet fermata scored for trumpets, horns, and cellos and is marked Segue Andante. Whether this would still hold when the movement ends with the Scherzo proper cannot be determined. If so, then this is among Potter's rare efforts in these works to link movements by a run-on from one movement to the next.

The Andante is another one of Potter's sensitively presented slow movements in an alternating part form (*A–B–A1–B1–A²*[Coda]) with *A* in G major and *B* in C major. Each return is treated in Haydn's manner as a variation. The structure of the first part of each first strain is of symmetrical four-measure lengths and repeated, while the second strain contains irregular lengths. *A¹* follows without the repeat within *A,* but treats the varied surface embellishments to triplets and sixteenths, thereby abandoning the monolithic variation rhythms found in many variation sets. *B¹* has varied phrase lengths when compared to *A* and comes to an abrupt early end, thereby making way for the return of *A²* as the coda. Here, only the first eight measures are preserved before the remainder of the coda presents further expansions and contractions of the phrases. Macfarren called the coda a "peroration" where he states in reference to the opening material:

> [T]he last but one bar of this extract [m.7] is charmingly extended with imitations by the viola first [m.131] and then by the flute [m.132], so as to swell the strain into ten instead of eight bars and the same pleasant device is repeated [m.142] when the phrase recurs in

the key of G at the same period of the second strain [m.136]; thus, the coda is an ampli-
fication of the theme itself, not an addition to it,—the filling out or ripening of the idea,
rather than its ornamentation with surrounding leaves.[39]

For the year 1833, the end of the movement is rather daring as the orchestration thins to
chamber music proportions with a final pizzicato and then a final quiet chord from the flute,
oboes, and horns as they *diminuendo* to nothing (Example XIV/9).

Macfarren writes that had the Finale been composed by someone else that "Potter would
have called it 'a bit of fun,' and the definition may be applied in recollection of him by anyone who knew his quick, vivacious, active, untiring manner."[40] In many respects, this Vivace
Finale is a major-mode replay of Symphony No. 10/4 with, except for *S*, its almost *perpetuum
mobile*, unbounded energy, and rapid-fire color changes. Perhaps the most distinctive aspect
of Symphony No. 11 is the eight-measure introduction that anticipates *1P*. This passage as a
concept is expanded upon throughout much of the development section (m.165) so that it
serves as a long preparation for the recapitulation. Otherwise, this sonata-form Finale is not
unlike Potter's previous efforts. Its Più Presto coda only serves to intensify the energy already
present in the main part.

From our perspective, it is the first movement and the third movement Andante that
point to a new freedom in Potter's handling of syntax and form. Both reveal a flexibility particularly in structural sections that reprise previous ones with changes in the order of presentation and in the length of subphrases and phrases. The sort of freedom displayed in the recapitulation of the first movement and the alterations in the repetitions within the third
movement again point to an awareness of a composer like Joseph Haydn, who was expert in
these sorts of changes. George Macfarren saw this symphony as an example indicative of Potter's accomplishments:

> The Symphony [No. 11] is notable for contrapuntal ingenuity, for conciseness and per-
> spicuity of plan, and for clearness and vigour of orchestration. It worthily represents the
> composer, and must place him on a high level in the esteem of anyone unacquainted
> with his numerous other works.[41]

A critic for the *Musical World* in 1836 remarked on its skillful orchestration and the "energy
and brilliancy of effect."[42] The critic for *The Athenaeum* found, on the contrary, it to be "one
of the dreariest of his works, and with so many better compositions in store, we regret that it
should have been selected."[43]

SYMPHONY NO. 12 IN C MINOR

Potter completed his Symphony No. 11 on November 2, 1833; one year and six days later, he
finished his Symphony No. 12, his second in C minor, a key whose striking tradition has
already been discussed in the introductory remarks to Symphony No. 6 (1826). Like its
chronological neighbors, Symphony No. 12 begins with a slow introduction, but one somewhat more concise than Nos. 8 and 11. Distinctive is that a minor-mode symphony has a slow
introduction at all; not one of the minor-mode symphonies by Haydn, Mozart, or Beethoven
has a musical preface, but Schubert's Symphony No. 4 in C minor D.417, which Potter certainly did not know, does. Often slow introductions to major-mode pieces are in the minor;
Potter's slow introduction to the C Minor No. 12 is in the major. Rather than the usual darkness to light analogy for minor to major, Potter here suggests a light to dark relationship.

Both the introduction and the body of the Allegro are considerably shorter than their
two predecessors: No. 10/1—no introduction 528 mm., No. 11/1—introduction plus Allegro:

EXAMPLE XIV/9 Potter. Symphony No. 11/3, mm.128–45, 157–61. British Library Loan 4/379.

EXAMPLE XIV/9   (*continued*)

TABLE XIV/10

Potter, Symphony No. 12/i: Structure

Exposition

1P	2P	3P	1T(2P)	1S	2S	1K(1P)	2K(2P)
C minor	major			E-flat			
m.35	63	81	92	111	126	143	155

Development [*Recapitulation?*]

1P	3P	3P	3P	1Px	1S	2S	3P	3P/1T version	lead-in
E-flat	F minor		D-flat		D	D → A-flat →		C	
							pp	*ff*	
160	184	188	198	209	226	238	252	265	288

Recapitulation

1S	2S	1K(1P)	1K ext./2K(2P)	*Coda* 3P	3P	2P plus cadences
C major	minor	minor				
291	306	323	331	365	379	388

490 mm., and No.12/1—introduction plus Allegro: 388 mm. Symphony No. 12 has an introduction of only thirty-four measures, which in the context of Haydn is still rather long. Potter begins his Moderato ¢ with string flourishes and a *tutti* signal (mm.1–2). The flourish returns (m.8), but the *tutti* response waits for twenty-three measures (mm.30–31), after which a quiet epilogue leads to the Allegro (Table XIV/10). In between, Potter presents lyric material that hints at modulation, but no other key than C is asserted.

Like the earlier G Minor Symphony (No. 10), there is no repetition of the exposition, even though the C minor Allegro is 354 mm. compared to that of No. 10, which is nearly two hundred bars longer. Additionally, like Symphony No. 6, also in C minor, there is no strong recapitulation consisting of a return to *P* and the tonic key simultaneously. In fact, Symphony No. 6 had a strong *fortissimo* return of *S* in C major, but in No. 12 *S*, which is the first convincing tonic return, remains in the expected quiet character of this function. One may argue that since *1P* also commences quietly, it makes little structural difference whether *1P* or *S* introduces the tonic in the reprise. But one may also wish to propose the tonic and *forte* return of *3P* (m.265) as the reprise. Why an ambiguous recapitulation occurs only in Potter's two C minor first movements has no explanation. *1P* is given much space in the development section, but this is also true of *3P* and *S*.

The quiet and often unagitated nature of the exposition sets this movement apart from the usual *Sturm und Drang* associations; only about one-fifth of the exposition has a dynamic of *forte* or louder. Indeed, also conspicuous by its almost total absence is the pulsating and syncopated background so often found in minor-mode movements. All that remains from the *Sturm und Drang* tradition is a dark coloring. Again, the exposition consists of related material. This time, in addition to the reuse of stretches of the themes in different functions as happens with *1T(2P)*, *1K(1P)*, and *2K(2P)*, Potter also takes motives from one theme and embeds them within another as happens in the initial statements of *1P*, *2P*, and *3P*. They, in turn, less obviously pollinate *S*. One peculiarity is that *2Px* occurs first in its major mode form then in *3P*, and finally in *S* in the minor mode. At the end of *1P*, the *x* motive is also inverted (m.57).

With the exposition's last cadence in the key of E-flat major, the development section (m.160) begins. *1P* is then taken up in E-flat and then in F minor (m.184). This continues with *3P* (m.198) in D-flat and *1Px* in F minor (m.209). A half-step rise leads to the dominant of D and *1S* in that key (m.226), and then in A-flat (m.240) using *2S* as a counterpoint. *3P* (m.265), with little tonal preparation, arrives in the tonic *fortissimo*, a possible recapitulatory moment followed by *S*, which we believe to be the real reprise. But notice what takes place before m.265; in m.252 the horn plays *3P pianissimo* in C with A-flat as the root of the chord (Example XIV/10). This recalls the famous passage prior to the recapitulation in Beethoven's Symphony No. 3/1; the second horn quietly enters in what seemingly is a mistaken entry. If this is in fact the case, then in Potter's mind, *3P* (m.265) is arguably the recapitulation. While one cannot completely settle where the recapitulatory articulation occurs, one can state that after *S*, Potter expands the last part by bringing back *1P* as *1K* (m.323) and eventually *3P* again (m.365) and *2P* (m.379) before the final cadences. This allows one to say that essentially all of the thematic material of the exposition has, in some form or another, been recapitulated.

Apparently the Andante con moto caused Potter a number of problems during the process of revision. Such revisions offered in previous movements have always been absolutely clear in the boundaries of any cuts and any changes in materials and orchestration. One has the distinct impression that when Potter set this piece in full score, he was not yet ready to do so, since there are many places where one cannot determine the composer's intent (Plate B2).

EXAMPLE XIV/10   Potter. Symphony No. 12/1, mm.248–68.

One can surmise from the score, however, that this piece would not have staked any new ground among Potter's slow movements and probably would have had much in common with Symphonies Nos. 10/2 and 11/3. Though there are a couple of revisions in the Finale, in both this movement and the Scherzo, the composer's text is absolutely clear. The unusually brief Scherzo follows the expected pattern; the Scherzo itself is in the minor and the Trio in the major with emphasis on woodwind and horn timbres.

Potter's Finale also does not call for the expository repeat and is his only last movement that begins to approach a march-like character. The exposition is divided into three clear sections of which the first and third use basically the same closing material:

P	*P*	*Pᵏ*	*T(P)*	*S*	*S*	*S* (trans.)	*K(Pᵏ)*
m.1	17	24	32	63	71	83	94

EXAMPLE XIV/10   (*continued*)

Notable here is the transformation of *S* from its lyric first two statements to a marcato/ militaristic character, thereby unifying *S* with the affect of *P* and *T.* The development section (m.109) is, after Potter's cuts, among his shortest (37 m.) and its beginning is not well defined. Potter begins with *S* in the tonic and continues with *P* and *S* motives in sequence. Potter also strips the recapitulation down to *P,* the *tutti* of m.17, and *P^k*, disposes of much of *T,* and presents in full the triple statement of *S* (m.168). The coda (m.199) deals with *P_{ay}* and contains a final proclamation of *P.*

After the skills and expression displayed in Symphonies Nos. 10 and 11, Symphony No. 12 leaves one somewhat disappointed. Evidence from the holograph seems to support a hypothesis that Potter too may have been unhappy with the final product with the numerous cuts found throughout and in particular the state in which the slow movement was left. My guess is that No. 12 was never performed due to the state of the score, the fact that there are seemingly no orchestral parts, and the peculiar situation that No. 12 was finished on November 8, 1834, and No. 15[14] in D Major was finished sixteen days later on November 24. To complete two symphonies in the same month given the performance

EXAMPLE XIV/10   (*continued*)

opportunities London offered in 1834 makes no practical sense. Philip Peter believes Symphony No. 12 might have been performed by the Philharmonic Society on June 8, 1835,[44] but I would think that this would be either the lost Symphonies Nos. 13 and 14 or even Symphony No. 15.

SYMPHONY NO. 15[14] IN D MAJOR

That Symphony No. 15 would wait sixteen years for its first performance as Philip Peter suggests in his thematic catalogue is contradicted by George Macfarren's "Programme Note." Macfarren states that it was probably first performed at the author's 1835 benefit concert, was definitely heard at the Society of British Musicians on January 25, 1836, was played at the Philharmonic Concerts on March 21, 1836, and was in the future "several times repeated."[45] Potter also chose it for his benefit concert (June 13, 1844), as noted in the *Musical World* on June 20, 1844.

George Macfarren describes Potter's Moderato assai introduction in an almost rhetorical fashion:

> The interest of the Introduction lies mainly in the novel changes of key that intersperse it, and in the broadly contrasted orchestration that colours them. It seems as though the artist herein collected his forces before entering upon a task of love, rather preparing himself for the development and his auditors for the reception of his chief idea, then forestalling its announcement by fragmentary allusions.[46]

Macfarren's comments, when looking at the music, seem exaggerated and perhaps more applicable to the rather extraordinary introduction of Symphony No. 11 discussed above. In Symphony No. 15, the tonal play seems rather conservative only extending away from the tonic by secondary dominants. No doubt, it does display a variety of timbres in various combinations that marks Potter's orchestral style. Obviously, Macfarren does not favor an introduction that adumbrates the expository material of the Allegro.

Two new aspects observed in this Allegro's exposition are the introduction of *1S* (m.71) by a bold *tutti forte* beginning and the use of bi-modality, here found in *2S* (m.80), which is repeated (m.89) in the minor mode. In a less striking way, a minor/major duality is also found in *1K/2K* (mm.101/104). Otherwise, the exposition follows Potter's earlier first movements with several *P* ideas, the repetition of *S,* and a pair of closing themes of which *2K* (m.104) is based on *P.* The development (m.114) momentarily remains in D, but then assumes E-flat (m.121f), and by means of *1T* moves to *1P* in B major (m.136). *1T* (m.139) again intervenes, and now *1P* is reduced motivically for the retransition. It is no wonder Macfarren referred to the "intricacies" of this again relatively short central section.[47] The recapitulation's most striking change is the bi-modal treatment of *1P* (m.157). A brief coda (m.225) takes material from *T, P,* and *S* as the Allegro heads for closure.

For the first time in Potter's symphonies, the slow movement reveals an effort to connect the ending of the Allegro to the following piece; the first measures of the Andante move from D to F major as the horn presents *P.* The horn solos in this movement are virtuosic, requiring probably a valve horn and a technique of a Chopinesque agility, as the beat has quintuple subdivisions (Example XIV/11). One of the major complaints about the orchestra for the Philharmonic Concerts was that the horn playing left much to be desired; such complaints lasted up to the end of the century when it was said that the conductor Hans Richter, himself a horn player, had a profound impact in improving horn playing in England.[48] That no other symphony by Potter contains any horn writing that approaches these demands suggests that a particular player was in London at the time of its composition.

This pastorale 6/8 Andante returns to a sonata structure that again emphasizes continuity by reusing *P* material in *T,* by suppressing closing functions, and by the increasing density of small notes as the piece unfolds. The latter reminds one of the slow movement to Mozart's "Jupiter" Symphony K.551/2 since much of this activity is confined to the development and recapitulation. After the *P* (m.4), *T(P,* m.16), and *S* (m.31) exposition, the development devotes itself to *P/T.* Most notable is the passage just before the recapitulation as Potter's bass line rises chromatically to D-flat (m.58), the dominant's Neapolitan, over which *P* (m.60) is played in F minor with a descending chromatic bass as the horn takes up *P* in major for the recapitulation (m.62). Macfarren heard this passage as a "signal incident" and that the

EXAMPLE XIV/11   Potter. Symphony No. 15/2, mm.1–15. British Library Loan 4/376.

EXAMPLE XIV/11   (*continued*)

recapitulation has "the better effect for this delay."[49] The passage is also another display of Potter's bi-modal interests; at the larger level the entire development changes its signature to four flats. After a tightened recapitulation, the coda (m.88) contains one last statement of *Pa* whose end is passed through strings and winds; in the final measures the main line passes from solo violin, to horn, bassoon, and flute, who provides the final *calando* to this pastoral piece.

Within the context of the first and second movements' bi-modal aspects, the Scherzo with its D minor main section and D major Trio becomes a significant factor, even though such modal changes are rather common in these movements. This time, Potter provides a four-bar transition between Scherzo and Trio consisting of repeating the tonic in octaves throughout the orchestra; it reminds one of a similar link in Haydn's Symphony No. 99/3. None of this was noticed by Macfarren, who was taken with the tonal shift in the second strain of the Scherzo:

> A capital conceit in the Second Part that strangely startles while it infinitely diverts one, is the sudden tangent from the approached key of D minor into the key of D-flat, by the enharmonic change of the unisonous G-sharp into A-flat [mm.40–44], which former is the supposed course to A—the dominant of the key which so abruptly vanishes. This key of D minor slips out of hearing but for a moment, however, and its re-entry [m.49], with all its tonal rights and dignities in the harmonic notes of the trumpets, makes another as novel effect as that of its disappearance.[50]

As has been shown several times, enharmonic approaches and departures are a central aspect of Potter's language.

The Finale, a Presto 6/8, again recalls Haydn. After an introductory call to attention ($Ox+y+x$), IP (m.13), a tantalizing jig for the flute, enters only to be rudely interrupted by Ox (m.30), which is again answered by Oy. This sets off a transition passage that cadences in F-sharp (mm.64–65) and leads to S (m.98), which surprisingly at this date begins not in major, but minor. K is dispensed with and the development (m.130) is announced by a shocking deceptive cadence (mm.128–29) that launches the keys of F major/D minor with P. But Potter soon concerns himself with Ox and y, again making the development both thematically and harmonically a big structural upbeat to the recapitulation (m.260) and the return of P (m.272). After a compressed recapitulation, the coda (m.366) plays on the introductory motives, sometimes expanding them and sometimes offering new responses, thereby placing the listener in the position of expecting either closure or a final return of P. Only the former expectation is fulfilled.

Macfarren's enthusiasm for this Finale is rightfully overflowing. He characterizes the introduction as a "rattling commencement to a movement that is brimful of animation"; S is "wild as it is vigorous." As for the movement as a whole, he writes that it

> has so strong an individuality, that it separates itself from other music in the memory, and stands forward as a pleasant recollection after many years. Its ceaseless vivacity, its admirable continuity, and, above all, its strong but unstrained individuality mark the hand of a master, and render it a worthy conclusion to an excellent work.[51]

The *Musical World* in 1844 found this symphony to be "one of the most brilliant and striking" of Potter's symphonies.[52] Six years later, *The Athenaeum's* critic found the performance admirable, but the work itself "not exciting."[53] The *Musical World* in 1850 was even more positive than in 1844:

It is always a pleasure to hear a work of importance from the pen of a native composer, and more especially when such distinguished talent is displayed as in the symphony of Mr. Cipriani Potter, which, if we are not mistaken, was written many years ago for the concerts of the Society of British Musicians. Mr. Potter, whose early genius for composition attracted the notice of the great Beethoven, is one of the very few in whom the veneration for art is so firmly rooted that composition becomes a labour of love, zealously pursued in the face of unceasing opposition and disappointment. The symphonies, concertos, sonatas, quartets, and other works of magnitude which Mr. Potter has produced, are more numerous and of a higher order of merit than is generally imagined, and it reflects no credit on the professed lovers of music in this country that they are so little known. The symphony in D is a favourable example of Mr. Potter's style. The writing is masterly, the forms of each movement are closely allied to the models left us by the great masters, and the method of orchestration betrays not only consummate knowledge of the characters of instruments and the effects of combination, but fancy and taste of a rare order. The first movement, a spirited *allegro,* has much of the feeling of Haydn, so far as the themes are concerned, but their lengthened development and the varied treatment of the orchestra, bear the incontestable stamp of a modern hand. The slow movement, an *andante,* full of genial melody, is remarkable for ingenious employment of the wind band; the first theme is a solo for the horn, admirably written for that instrument; the second, a pretty pastoral phrase, contrasts with it in the happiest manner. The *scherzo* strongly recals [sic] the early style of Beethoven, although the subject is quite original; the *trio,* a melody of expressive simplicity, in the major key, affords an agreeable relief, and a good effect is produced by shortening the *scherzo* in the *reprise.* The *finale,* a *presto,* vigorous and animated, is sustained to the end with undiminished power. In the second part there is abundant evidence of contrapuntal skill, both in the arrangement of the episode and the working of the principal theme. The whole movement is remarkable for clear and brilliant orchestration. The symphony was played to perfection, and the *scherzo* encored. It is due to Mr. Costa to acknowledge the evident pains he took in directing the performance of this work of an English composer, the warm reception accorded to which will doubtlessly encourage the directors to make other steps in the same direction.[54]

CONCLUSION

What is presumably Potter's last symphony reveals that in 1834 he was still composing in a style very much the same as that observed in his earliest contributions to the genre, i.e., something between late Haydn and middle-period Beethoven. Thus, Potter belongs to a camp that also might include Ferdinand Ries, the Wranitzky brothers, and, in Potter's more progressive moments, Louis Spohr. His stylistic ideals were no doubt Haydn and Mozart; in our descriptive survey, we have noted a number of reminiscences that come from specific passages. Though Potter knew and admired Beethoven and though we have cited some parallels, they are more generalized ones. The other force in English orchestral music was Felix Mendelssohn; in Potter's symphonies of the 1830s, it is as if Mendelssohn was never a factor in English musical life. Still, Potter was revered in his time; the *Musical World* noted,

> Mr. Potter is one of the most accomplished musicians of the age—the father of our instrumental music, and the master of almost every British artist of eminence. We cannot wonder, then, at the attention and applause bestowed on his compositions and his playing, both of which are of the highest order.[55]

William Sterndale Bennett
INTRODUCTION

As can be concluded from our quotations from Macfarren and others, Potter from a young age was admired as a teacher and composer. As principal of the Royal Academy of Music, he had a hand in the musical education of every important British musician who was registered there from 1832 to 1859. But if Potter was a transmitter of the Viennese classics, there was another English musician, Sir William Sterndale Bennett (1816–1875), who, though educated from the age of ten at the Academy, promulgated the musical tenets of contemporary German composers. Bennett continued his studies not in Vienna, but in the then current Continental hothouse of musical activity in Leipzig, where his works were given accolades by both Mendelssohn and Schumann.

Bennett seems to have done everything in England that Potter did: he was both conductor of the Philharmonic Concerts (1856–1866) and principal of the Royal Academy (1866–1875). In addition, Bennett was a tireless teacher, often beginning instruction early in the day and extending into the late evening (Plate B3). Such a schedule interfered with his productivity as a composer, particularly in the larger genres. Indeed, there were some years when Bennett's compositional output was at best meager and sometimes restricted to a single piece.

With the appearance of the thematic catalogue of Bennett's musical works by Rosemary Williamson in 1996, it became possible to construct a more accurate view of Bennett as a symphonic composer.[56] Among Bennett's major orchestral works were piano concertos, overtures, and symphonies. Table XIV/11 provides a summary, based on Williamson, of Bennett's symphonies in chronological order. Even though Bennett was Potter's junior by twenty-four years, both composers center their main orchestral activity in the 1830s, and both composers cease symphonic composition during the same decade. After a break of twenty years, Bennett wrote one additional symphony (No. 8), his only symphony to achieve publication and to bear an opus number (Opus 43). Additionally, three documented works are lost and two others remain unavailable but in private hands, *WO* 20 and 23. This leaves only three available and extant works as well as comments from an important secondary source about *WO* 20 and 23.

SYMPHONY NO. 1 IN E-FLAT MAJOR *WO* 20
AND SYMPHONY NO. 2 IN D MINOR *WO* 23

The Bennett scholar Nicholas Temperley has pointed out that *WO* 20 was composed under the tutelage of William Crotch in 1832 and that *WO* 23 (1832–1833) was a product of the period when Bennett was studying with Cipriani Potter; both men made their mark on these two symphonies. William Crotch (1775–1847) was in some respects an advocate of the ancient style with its imitations of earlier musical idioms, in particular those of Handel. A symphony of Crotch's was programmed by the Philharmonic Society during the 1814 season, and he appeared as conductor at several of their concerts. Crotch's stylistic leanings are to be found in the introduction to Bennett's Symphony No. 1 *WO* 20. It begins in the *stile antico,* a gesture perhaps only duplicated in the 1782 Symphony in C-sharp minor (VB 140) and its C Minor revision from 1783(?) by the Swedish composer Joseph Martin Kraus (1756–1792). The slow introduction was to be reused forty years later for the opening of his full anthem "In Thee, O Lord, have I put my trust" (*WO* 84).[57] The main body of the first movement is a sonata form whose *S,* according to Temperley, is an "unconscious reminiscence" of Weber's *Oberon.* Temperley also finds the elaboration of the themes in the development "somewhat aimless and lacking in clear design." A Lento slow movement follows, whose theme has an "original chromatic twist." Following the Minuet and Trio, the Finale, after a lively beginning,

TABLE XIV/II
The Symphonies of William Sterndale Bennett

Williamson No.	Key	Date	Title	Movements	Instrumentation	Comments
WO 20	E-flat Major	1832	Symphony No.1	1. Lento—Allegro vivace 4/4 (308 m.) 2. Lento 2/4 (74 m.) B-flat major 3. Minuetto 3/4 (47 m.) E-flat major Trio 3/4 (24 m.) B-flat major 4. Finale 2/4 (304 m.)	Full	Score in private collection; unavailable for study and not published. First performance: Royal Academy of Music on June 16, 1832.
WO 23	D Minor	1832–33	Symphony No. 2	1. Larghetto 4/4—Allegro assai 4/4 (474 m.) D minor/major 2. [Andante] 3/8 (112 m.) A major 3. Minuetto 3/4 (69 m.) D major Trio 3/4 (42 m.) B-flat major (+ Coda 22 m.) 4. Finale 4/4 (474 m.) D minor	Full plus 1 Trom.	Score in private collection; unavailable for study and not published. No known performances.
U3	[D Minor?]	1833	Symphony No. 3		[Full plus 1 Trom.]	Lost. Overture in D Minor WO 24 may have been the opening mvt. of this abandoned work.
WO 28	A Major	1833–34	Symphony No. 4	1. Allegro spiritoso ¢ (631 m.) 2. Minuetto: Presto 3/4 (139 m.) A major Trio 3/4 (114 m.) G major Coda 3/4 (4 m.) 3. Andante espressivo 2/4 (228 m.) D major 4. Finale 4/4 (272 m.)	Full plus 1 Trom.	First performance: Society of British Musicians on January 5, 1835. Ed. by Temperley in Brook/ SYMPHONY E VII
WO 31	G minor	1835–36	Symphony No. 5	1. Allegro con brio 4/4 (316 m.) 2. Scherzo: Allegro vivo 3/4 (305 m.) 3. Andante con moto 12/8 (81 m.) B-flat major 4. Finale: Presto con fuoco 3/4 (290 m.)	Full plus 1 Trom.	First performance: Society of British Musicians on February 8, 1836. Ed. by Temperley in Brook/ SYMPHONY E VII. Finale based on Opus 11/6, the Sixth Study "in the Form of a Capriccio," See Temperley, p. xxvii.

TABLE XIV/II (*continued*)

Williamson No.	Key	Date	Title	Movements	Instrumentation	Comments
U7	B Minor	1836–37	Symphony No. 6			Lost. A first movement was reportedly completed during Sterndale Bennett's trip to Germany.
U10	—	1838–40	Symphony No. 7			Lost. Worked on during Sterndale Bennett's second stay in Germany. See letter of December 29, 1838. Planned for the 1839–40 season of the London Philharmonic Society.
Opus 43	G Minor	1863–64 1867	Symphony No. 8	1. Allegro moderato 4/4 (312 m.) 2. Introduzione al Minuetto: Maestoso 4/4 Minuetto 3/4 B-flat major Trio: Pomposo 3/4 (131 m.) E-flat major 3. Romanza: Larghetto cantabile 3/4 (126 m.) D major 4. Intermezzo: Tempo di minuetto 3/4 (13 m.) G minor Rondo Finale: Presto ¢ (218 m.)	Grand less 2 Hr.	First performance of original version (1863–64), i.e., without the Romanza: London Philharmonic Society on June 27, 1864. With Romanza: London Philharmonic Society on July 1, 1867. Score and parts pub. Leipzig: Kistner, 1872 as Opus 43. Ed. by Temperley in Brook/ SYMPHONY E VII. Mvt. 2 originated in the Cambridge Installation Ode Opus 41. See Temperley, p. xxviii. Mvt. 3 was from the song "Tell me where, ye summer breezes" *WO* 65 from 1861/1866.

59

has an *S* that also suggests Weber. Scored for a full Classical orchestra—pairs of woodwinds, brass (horns and trumpets), timpani, and strings—its cycle is tonally conservative only using the tonic and dominant keys.[58]

This Symphony in E-flat reveals the precocity of the fifteen-year-old Bennett. Crotch arranged for a performance by the orchestra of the Royal Academy on June 16, 1832, in the Hanover Square Rooms some two months after its completion. According to the Academy's report: "Bennett has composed a Symphony, performed at the last concert, which does him the greatest credit."[59]

Bennett's Symphony No. 2 (1832–1833) comes from the time of studies with Potter. As we have seen, Potter was strongly affected by the music of Haydn, Mozart, and early Beethoven. To some degree, this is now also the case with Bennett's Second Symphony, as there are references and allusions to these composers. According to Williamson, the slow movement was composed first, followed by the Finale, and then the first movement. The place of the Minuet and Trio in this scheme is unknown; the autograph is not dated. Such an order of composition may suggest that *WO* 23 had its origins as a composition exercise for Potter, who seems to have lavished special care in composing his slow movements. Additionally, the orchestration adds one trombone to the full Classical complement as Potter had done is his Second Symphony of 1821. It has been pointed out that the cycle has a peculiar use of major and minor modes in the outer movements. The slow introduction is in D minor as is the Finale, whereas the first movement's Allegro assai is in D major, just where one might expect the minor mode in a D minor cycle. This too may have been a result of Potter's interest in bi-modal possibilities.

Temperley detects in the introductory Larghetto something of the Mozart *Don Giovanni* Overture; for the Allegro he hears aspects of Haydn's Symphonies Nos. 95 and 104; and the development at times recalls Mozart's D Minor Piano Concerto K.466, a work that Bennett knew and had performed at the Philharmonic Concerts by Mendelssohn on May 13, 1833. The second movement heard, marked Legato, has a theme derived from Beethoven's Symphony No. 2/2 and the *Andante favori* for piano; its predominant character belongs to the pastoral. The Finale is overall Mozartean. Mozart was a model for not only Potter: Bennett at an early age admired Mozart's mastery of "broad rhythm," his "control," his "seriousness," and the fact that he "never seemed to make a mistake" except that of "overseriousness."[60]

Bennett's so-called lost Symphony No. 3 (U3), also in D minor, from 1833 may be a bibliographic mirage. Some believe that all that survives is the Overture in D Minor *WO* 24, which may have been the first movement of this intended symphony, according to the composer's son and biographer.[61] Temperley rejects J. R. Sterndale Bennett's hypothesis; he believes the symphony left unaccounted for is the Symphony in B Minor U7 of 1836–1837. However, if Symphonies No. 4 (*WO* 28) and No. 5 (*WO* 31) carry authentic numbers, there must be another symphony prior to 1834, and the B Minor Symphony clearly postdates Nos. 4 and 5. Thus, we conclude that either U3 or some other lost symphony exists between *WO* 23 and *WO* 28.

SYMPHONY NO. 4 IN A MAJOR *WO* 28

Bennett's A Major Symphony was begun during his Christmas break from the Royal Academy in 1833, continued in February 1834, and completed sometime during the same year. The only known performance was for the Society of British Musicians on January 5, 1835. The models for this symphony were again Mozart, Beethoven, and Mendelssohn. But for anyone who has looked at the symphonies of Cipriani Potter, his influence is also striking; indeed, several aspects come from Haydn, Mozart, and Beethoven; these may come second-hand by way of Potter. Temperley's detection of Mendelssohn as a model is important; Mendelssohn was for Bennett, like for Niels Gade and other mid-century composers, a guiding force.

Bennett's cycle is notable for its key scheme. While the two outer movements are in the tonic A major and the third movement Andante in the subdominant, the Minuet proper is in A and ends on F-sharp, but its Trio is in G. It is the F-sharp that serves as a common-tone link to the opening of the Andante. Thus, there is an internal indication that the second and third movements should be performed without a break. Additionally, for a cycle in A major the expected bright orchestral sonorities colored by horns using the A crook are now replaced by horns in E and D, which give forth a mellower timbre. Those expecting the brilliant colors of Beethoven's Symphony No. 7 or Mendelssohn's Symphony No. 4 will be disappointed. Both the Beethoven and Mendelssohn require horns with control of the upper register in a wide range of dynamics; perhaps horn playing in London was not yet ready for near clarino writing.

According to George Macfarren, when Potter took over at the Royal Academy of Music, he changed the emphasis of compositional studies to principles of musical form and orchestration.[62] Potter's own symphonies reveal his mastery of these two aspects. Therefore, to anyone looking at Sterndale Bennett's first movement, one can easily see Potter's own approach to musical structure. Both composers repeat the exposition and both define the usual expository functions with unusual clarity. *S* for both composers was usually a deeply contrasting moment which, as seen in Bennett's Fourth, also follows Potter in its double statement (mm.107, 133) and in its transformation (m.149). Temperley complains that *S* is "too languid,"[63] but one might say that Bennett is slightly exaggerating what Potter had done with some consistency. As in the Potter model, there are also two *K* themes, the second of which is based on *P* and *S*.

Potter at times extended *K* into the development section as Bennett does here. Bennett also demonstrates Potter's skill at both the tonal and thematic aspects of development. After heading toward F, Bennett does a bi-focal turnaround to D as the closing to *P* (m.237). This is contrapuntally elaborated and then again combined with *S* (m.254). The latter gives a double impression; the slowness of *S* and the speed of *P* occur simultaneously over a lengthy stretch. Bennett then cadences in the expected key of the relative minor (F-sharp, m.261). A series of descending lines often by thirds leads to an E pedal and the retransition (m.293), which culminates in the slowest motion of the movement. This provides a stark juxtaposition as *P* enters for the recapitulation (m.313).

As Potter did until his last several symphonies, Bennett's recapitulation, except for the tonal adjustment, brings back all the material of the exposition. However, Bennett's exposition, except for *2K* (*P* and *S*), does not reuse materials previously stated in earlier functions. The coda takes eighty measures and in its use of themes parallels the development section.

Though there are some bold and brash moments in this Allegro spiritoso ¢ (e.g., *2Pk* [m.37]), the *S* transformation (m.149) and *1K*(*P*+*S*) (m.189) are more introspective than what is usually associated with the bright key of A major. The beginnings of *P* and *S* reflect a certain reticence, but without diffidence. This is in its own way an accomplished piece, which makes it all the more unfortunate that the first pair of symphonies are not available for us to see first-hand how Sterndale Bennett came this far.

In second position is the "Minuetto," in reality a Scherzo; Potter in his symphonies twice places the dance piece after the first movement. Bennett's Minuetto is blatantly modeled on Beethoven's Second Symphony; he begins with Beethoven's fifth bar and from there elaborates further. The Trio also echoes Beethoven's No. 2 in the initial phrase. Though

Bennett imitates Beethoven's melodies, he makes no attempt to deal with the imbroglios of Beethoven's rhythms. The most striking aspect of this piece is its tonal layout that seemingly has neither a predecessor nor an imitator; not only does the Scherzo proper have a bi-focal ending (A–F-sharp), but the G major Trio has cadences on E and D with a passing allusion to B-flat.

As noted above, the ending on F-sharp is oddly continued at the start of the Andante espressivo, which begins with the common tone within the dominant seventh of G resolving to G, followed by another dominant seventh resolving to D, the key of the third movement. Bennett's *P* (m.5) is striking for its irregular phrases $(4+5+4+8[\text{or } 9])$. While the reiterated upper neighbor in *P* (Example XIV/12) recalls the opening to Beethoven's Symphony No. 6/2 "Pastoral," this impression is supported by the scoring of *S* (m.55), which is initially set for two solo cellos, a distinctive aspect of Beethoven's "By the Brook." A lengthy *T* (m.26) links *P* and *S;* notice that *T* soon becomes the background for the material stated by the woodwinds. This was a technique used with striking success in England by both Mendelssohn and Spohr.[64] After *K* (m.78), which is based on *P,* Bennett bypasses the expository repeat and begins the development (m.90) with *K(P)* in C major, a bi-focal relationship to the dominant conclusion to the exposition. *P* is well worked over and modulates to the expected F-sharp minor (m.118) before moving directly (i.e., without the first four measures) to *P* for the recapitulation (m.130). *T* (m.142) is articulated by a striking deceptive cadence that lands us on the subdominant of F, which ultimately paves the way to *S* (m.174) in the tonic now rescored for horn, bassoons, and cello. After *K* (m.197), the coda (m.203) concerns itself with *Pax* over a tonic pedal. The Andante ends quietly scored for the entire band.

Unlike most of Potter's Finales, Bennett's has none of the Haydn-like qualities of the *contredanse* and gigue; this is a common time last movement without choreographic styles. Temperley, however, finds Haydnesque elements here: the drone(?) and the humor (mm.9–20).[65] *T* (m.23) changes the mood to con fuoco in preparation for the characteristic contrast of *S* (m.41), which Temperley hears as an echo of Mendelssohn's *Hebrides Overture* and complains again of its slow motion.[66] *K* (m.72) renews the surface activity, raises the tessitura, and then diminishes for the repeat of the exposition.

Bennett begins the development section with the restatement of *P* in the tonic, and then in Potterian fashion develops it along with *S* (m.116) in a contrapuntal fabric. Again, the surface activity slows (m.124) and remains almost in a state of suspension for the next thirty bars; this makes for a very long preparation (30 mm.) for the tonic return of *P* (m.154). The recapitulation is slightly expanded in *T* (m.176) and *K* (m.222), and the coda brings back *P* (m.256) with a subdominant leaning so characteristic of the final section in high Classic and early Romantic sonata forms.

From the first and fourth movements of Bennett's Symphony in A Major, it becomes clear that besides themes and keys, the composer also builds his forms out of polarities in rhythmic activity. In the first and last movements, *P, T, K,* and the first part of the development section generate activity, while *S* and the end of the development pare activity down to a suspension of motion. On a larger level, the juxtaposition of activity and rest also invades the two central movements even though one is very fast (Scherzo) and the other relatively slow. Whether Temperley's criticism that Bennett's areas of suspended activity are too long and too slow can be truly tested only when one hears this work in performance. My belief is that the suspensions of activity provide effective counterweights to those more active areas.

Bennett's A Major Symphony is what one might expect of a gifted eighteen-year-old composer with its formal prototypes, themes, and their idealizations. The gift is not in the

EXAMPLE XIV/12   Bennett. Symphony No. 4/2, mm.1–25.

EXAMPLE XIV/12   (*continued*)

themes, keys, or materials, but in the way they are stated and connected. Here, Bennett deserves high marks. That thematic ideas from Beethoven and Mendelssohn are so well absorbed demonstrates how they became Bennett's own.

Bennett's A Major Symphony was heard at the newly formed Society of British Musicians on January 5, 1835, conducted by the composer on a program which also included music by J. B. Calkin, J. H. Griesbach, Charles Lucas, John Macfarren, Catchpole, Thomas Walmisley, John Clifton, and C. Hubert H. Parry. It was reviewed in *The Athenaeum:*

> We have left ourselves but little space to speak of the Fourth Concert of the establish-ment which has given rise to the above remarks. Mr. W.S. Bennett's symphony was the best music performed in the course of the evening: the *allegro,* slow movement, and *scherzo,* had a purpose, originality, and character of their own, with one or two delight-ful melodies introduced, which fully justify our high expectations from the future works of this young writer:—we are beginning to look for his name in the concert bills.[67]

SYMPHONY NO. 5 IN G MINOR WO 31

Encouraged by the success of his Fourth Symphony, Bennett began sketching his Sym-phony No. 5 in March of 1835. He completed the first movement in full score by November 1 and finished the remaining movements of the cycle during early February 1836. Another work from Bennett's student years at the Royal Academy, its composition was affected by his extended vacations between terms: Bennett later told one of his students that "in his own case, the best of his work had been done on the holidays" when he went home to Cam-bridge.[68]

This is the first of two symphonies in G minor by Bennett. The popularity of this key is in part attributable to Mozart's famous Symphony No. 40 K.550, which received many performances at the Philharmonic concerts. But Cipriani Potter also wrote two G minor symphonies, the second of which (No. 10) became highly admired and was heard during three Philharmonic seasons in 1826, 1834, and 1855. No doubt Bennett heard the May 19, 1834, performance of his mentor's newest G Minor symphony. During the time Bennett was composing Symphony No. 5, he was still under the tutelage and certainly the influence of Potter, who was regarded as a direct link to Beethoven. However, it seems far-fetched to propose that Potter's work served as a model for Bennett: in the most basic ways, these works present totally different versions of the G minor *ethos.* Additionally, it should be noted that about the time that Bennett was composing his G Minor Symphony, Potter's style in sonata form was becoming more like Haydn in that his *P, T, S,* and *K* themes were now re-lated to each other and, perhaps as a result, Potter's recapitulations were considerably tight-ened.

Concerning the cycle, Bennett's G Minor Symphony is less adventuresome than what was seen in his previous symphony: only the slow movement changes key to B-flat major. Again Bennett chooses the alternative order with the Scherzo in second position, the Andante con moto third. Bennett's choice of meter is also deserving of notice since three of the movements, the second, third, and fourth, are triple-meter based: 3/4, 12/8, and 3/4. The 12/8 Andante con moto again brings to mind Beethoven's Symphony No. 6/2 "Pastoral" in more ways than a like tempo marking and identical meter. To have two fast 3/4 movements considerably reduces the inherent contrasts embodied in the sym-phonic cycle; essentially Bennett has juxtaposed two Scherzo-like pieces in the minor mode.

EXAMPLE XIV/13   Bennett. Symphony No. 5/1, mm.1–23.

EXAMPLE XIV/13 *(continued)*

The first movement, Allegro con brio, conveys some of the *Sturm und Drang* character often associated with G minor: agitated background rhythms, vigorous themes, and thematic transformations. *P* (Example XIV/13) begins with a tonal ambiguity as the opening chord is a first-inversion E-flat triad. It is not until the end of the second measure that an F-sharp appears to suggest G minor, but the full articulation of the tonic is delayed until m.20 where the fabric resolves to an unmistakable G minor as *P* is elaborated upon for the beginning of *T* (m.20). *T* is more heavily articulated by a deceptive resolution (m.40) that generates further development of *P*. *S* (m.68) is very reminiscent of something Potter might offer at this point with a double statement (mm.68, 77), a transformation from lyric to marcato, and a diminution of the *Sx* motive (m.87). *K* (m.113) further elaborates *P* and cadences in B-flat.

The ambiguous tonal nature of *P* generates the development section; this enables Bennett to begin by outlining the G minor chord, which launches its first part (m.125). Part 2 (m.146) deals with *Sx* but in a context with a very slow and patterned harmonic rhythm that reminds one of Beethoven. Bennett then brings a certain ferocity to this *S* motif as it is repeated as a counterpoint to *P* (m.158). A *diminuendo,* a thinning of the orchestration, and a narrowing of the range leads to the recapitulation, this time articulated by a *tutti* downbeat (m.174). The *P/T* span is considerably altered, and *S* (m.213) returns in the tonic major, a practice of Potter's minor-mode movements. Bennett returns to the minor (m.258), builds to a climax, and then repeats the *Sx* motive (m.274) as in the development section culminating

67

in the return of *P* at the Più stretto (m.290) with *Sx* as a counterpoint. Note the bar marked "Silence" at the end: this is in direct imitation of Potter's scores where "Silence" is often written in empty bars within a movement.

The Scherzo has no Trio. It is a kind of ritornello shape with its refrain occurring in different keys combined with elements of sonata form (Table XIV/12). The refrain (*R*) has a memorability associated with its function, and its octaves recall an often encountered Baroque fabric. One is reminded of Beethoven in the episode (*E*) with its dotted rhythms; both the Seventh and Ninth Symphonies had been heard at the Philharmonic Concerts prior to 1835. Temperley describes *S* (m.65) as a "blazing second subject,"[69] and *K* (m.93) brings back the dotted rhythm in a strong recollection of Beethoven's Symphony No. 9/2. Another Beethovenism is the structural use of Neapolitan harmony in passing during the first episode (m.16) and then structurally at the beginning of the development (m.133). Temperley believes this Scherzo to be "Bennett's best symphonic movement to date."[70]

Bennett's slow movement again brings to mind more than the slow movement of the "Pastoral" Symphony; its two-plus-two-measure upbeat (mm.1–4) returns in various forms before each function of its exposition (Example XIV/14: *1P* [m.5], *2P* [m.15], *T* [m.21], *S* [m.28], *K* [m.32]), which recalls Beethoven's Symphony No. 4/2 with its two-measure upbeat that has a dual function as both a beginning and an ending. While Bennett does not pursue the beginning-as-ending phenomenon as strongly as Beethoven, there is nonetheless a fraternal similarity of the recurring upbeat having larger structural significance. A less apparent model is the slow movement of Mozart's Symphony in E-flat K.543, which has a long-term tritonal relationship of F minor to B major; in Bennett's Symphony No. 5/3, he begins the movement in B-flat major and *T* (m.21) begins in E minor, but unlike Mozart it returns in the recapitulation in B-flat minor (m.62).

Bennett's exposition is unusually uniform with virtually no drop-off in activity for *S;* an eighth-note surface and homophonic texture almost totally characterizes this first section. In contrast, the development (m.37) is saturated with sixteenth notes and polyphony and is also dynamically stronger at its melodic peaks. Indeed, the development breaks the spell of pastoral calm; it portrays the opposite extreme of the blissful pastoral: the storm. The characteristic nature of this Andante precludes its having a coda that, like the first movement, would parallel the development. Instead, Bennett merely extends *K* (m.73) to bring the piece to a satisfying and quiet conclusion.

A Presto con fuoco Finale recaptures some of the agitation associated with G minor. It is based on Bennett's Opus 11, "Six Studies in the Form of Capriccios," the last of which is an Allegro agitato 3/8 in G minor of some two hundred bars. In the adaptation for the symphonic Finale, Bennett increases its size by almost half. Table XIV/13 duplicates and revises Temperley's helpful comparison of the two versions: the first is a relatively simple binary shape and the second a full sonata form Finale on par with the other movements in the cycle.[71] Bennett's orchestration of *S* (m.41) immediately brings to mind Potter's treatment of this area with the mixing of colors and the reorchestration of *S*'s repetition, as does *K* (*P,* m. 76). Nearly all of the development is undergirded by a rising bass line, which for the recapitulation comes to rest not on the tonic, but on the dominant (m.155). Indeed, Bennett avoids a full tonic resolution until the return of *K* (*P,* m.220), which is confirmed many times over in the coda (m.235) where *P,* now in the bass, receives a new countermelody. One is struck by the curious ending of this piece; the strings play G at the end after the winds have concluded; it is almost as if the errant strings needed to resolve their concluding D to G.

TABLE XIV/12
Bennett. Symphony No. 5/2: Structure

Exposition

‖ R	E	R	E	S	K	R ‖
G minor		E-flat		B-flat		B-flat
m.1	16	47	54	65	93	125

Development

R plus S	R
A-flat	D
133	181

Recapitulation

R	E	Silence	S	K	R	Silence	‖
G minor			G		G		
197	212	244	246	272	292	306–7	

Bennett's G Minor Symphony *WO* 31 received two performances at the Society of British Musicians in February 1836 and February 1837. The first was reviewed in *The Athenaeum:*

SOCIETY OF BRITISH MUSICIANS—We cannot regret that this series of Concerts was brought to an end on Monday last. We are sorry, however, that the second season of this Society should close with so little benefit to English music; for we are of opinion that there is no standing still in Art, and that every effort which does not succeed in advancing it, must throw it back. But we have, on former occasions, expressed our dissatisfaction at the mismanagement of these Concerts; we have only therefore now to specify the pieces performed on Monday, by which, to say the truth, our patience was somewhat tried. Mr. W.S. Bennett's Symphony in G minor was clever, as an exercise, and combined some good ideas; but it was wanting in clearness—that first requisite in orchestral music.[72]

Felix Mendelssohn was well taken with the piece, for he wrote to Thomas Attwood from Düsseldorf on May 28, 1836,

I think him the most promising young musician I know, not only in your country but also here, and I am convinced if he does not become a very great musician, it is not God's will, but his own. His Concerto and Symphony are so well written, the thoughts so well developed and so natural, that I was highly gratified when I looked over them yesterday, but when he played this morning his six studies and the sketches, I was quite delighted, and so were all my musical friends who heard him. He told me that you wanted him to stay some time on the continent and with me. I really do think it impossible to give him (advanced as he is in his art) any advice which he was not able to give

EXAMPLE XIV/14   Bennett. Symphony No. 5/3, mm.1–34.

EXAMPLE XIV/14 (*continued*)

EXAMPLE XIV/14 (*continued*)

EXAMPLE XIV/14   (*continued*)

himself as well, and I am sure if he goes on the same way as he did till now, without los-
ing his modesty and zeal, he will always be perfectly right and develop his talents as his
friends and all the friends of music may desire; if however he should like to live on the
continent for a while, and if he should stay at Leipzig, I need not say that I should feel
most happy to spend some time with such a musician as he is, and that at all events
I shall always consider it as my duty to do everything in my power to assist him in his

EXAMPLE XIV/14   (*continued*)

musical projects, and in the course of his career, which promises to be a happy and blissful one.[73]

In October, Mendelssohn urged Bennett to bring the instrumental parts of both the symphony and piano concerto to Leipzig. However, it appears that only the Piano Concerto Opus 9 was heard during the 1837 Gewandhaus season. Dörffel documents no performance of this symphony.[74]

As a result of the enthusiastic reception of *WO* 31, Bennett was encouraged to undertake further symphonic projects. According to his correspondence with J. W. Davison, who was for four decades music critic of *The Times* (London), Bennett reportedly completed the first movement of a Symphony in B Minor (U7) during his stay in Leipzig from 1836 to 1837.[75] No further evidence exists about this piece. A second symphony from this time (U10) was worked on during Bennett's second German sojourn and was planned for the 1839–1840

TABLE XIV/13

Bennett. Comparison of Piano Study Opus 11/6 and Symphony No. 5/4

Structural revision in the *Finale* of Symphony in G Minor

PIANO STUDY, Op. 11, no. 6				SYMPHONY IN G MINOR, Finale			
M.	Part	Unique sections	Sections in common	Unique sections	Part	M.	
0–16	First part		1st subject, g		Exposition	‖:0–16	P
16–40			Transition, g-B♭			16–40	T
41–76		Scherzando, B♭-g^V	2nd subject, B♭	Scherzando, B♭		41–76	S
76–85 →						76–86:‖	K(P) →
				Formal close, B♭	Development	87–98	[Development]
85–98			Scherzando, g^V	Modulatory development, B♭-A♭^V		98–130	
				Return to tonic via German 6th		131–41	
						141–54	
99–112	Second part		1st subject, g		Recap.	155–68	P
113–28			Transition, c^V-g^V			169–83	T
129–64			2nd subject, G			184–219	S
164–75			Scherzando, G-g^VV			219–34	K(P)
175–90 →			1st subject, g		Coda	234–49	
190–201		*Calando* ending		Climax with IV harmony, g		249–84	
				Final ♯ tonic harmony, g		285–92	

Source: Temperley/BENNETT SYMPHONIES, p. xxvii with analytical symbols added in last column

London Philharmonic Society's season. However, while a piano concerto and several overtures by him were programmed during these years, no symphony by Sterndale Bennett was played. It is assumed that U7 and U10 are different works, but there is no evidence to support such; U10 could be the same symphony as U7.

Whether we are dealing with one or two symphonies from 1836–1840, one thing is clear: Bennett was having difficulty bringing to fruition any symphonic cycle. Perhaps the G Minor Symphony *WO* 31 had raised high expectations. Or perhaps there was something else at work here, for the 1840s, as we have noted, was a fallow time for symphonies composed by native English composers. Or was it the composer's grueling teaching schedule? It was to be almost twenty-five years (1863–1864) before Bennett produced a first version of his second symphony in the key of G minor, which did not reach its final form until 1867. It was subsequently published by Kistner of Leipzig as Opus 43, a singular event in Bennett's symphonic output. In our reckoning, it was, depending on how one counts his symphonies, his eighth or maybe only his sixth or seventh symphony.

SYMPHONY NO. 8 IN G MINOR OPUS 43

The symphony known as Opus 43 was conceived in two stages as two finished and complete works. In the 1863–1864 version, it was in three movements: 1. a sonata-form Allegro, 2. Introduzione, Minuetto and Trio, and 3. Intermezzo in Tempo di Minuetto and Rondo Finale. In this original form, Bennett did not wish to even refer to it as a symphony but rather as *Overture-Symphonique* because "it is little more than a long Overture on a Symphony plan."[76] The plan, and the association with the genre of the overture, brings to mind a work by Robert Schumann dating from 1841, the *Overture, Scherzo, and Finale* Opus 52. Both works are essentially symphonies without a slow movement. The second version of 1867 was made at the request of the Philharmonic Society, who thought the work was deserving of a slow movement.

The actual circumstances of the symphony's genesis support our view that Bennett did not write any symphonies after 1840 in part because he was just too busy. Bennett's son provides us with the tale of a symphony written out in a little more than a week before its premiere at the Philharmonic concerts:

As the Philharmonic season advanced, he decided to complete the above-mentioned orchestral work in G minor. The Directors arranged for its performance at the last concert of the year on June 27. In his teaching-book, he accounts for lessons missed during the week before the concert by writing: "This was a bad week, as I wrote the whole of my G minor Symphony in it." This was nearly true as regards music-paper and penmanship, but not so as regards the composition itself. To the first movement he had certainly given much previous thought, and though, towards the end of the time at his disposal, he discarded a very taking second subject in favour of another which he said was "more workable," the movement was complete in his head and already *sketched* on paper, as the subscribed date on the score proves, eight days before the concert. An engagement then took him to Cambridge. On his return, he was met at King's Cross, and he then said that he had just composed a last movement in the train and could write it out when he got home. The rhythm derived from the motion of the train may be fancied when listening to the music, but he said that a rustic fair was in his mind, and that some pathetic bars, in which the oboe is prominent, portrayed a disconsolate maid who had lost her lover in the crowd.[77]

Some of the movements, however, did not originate as pieces for this G minor cycle. Its second movement's Minuet proper first belonged to the *Cambridge Installation Ode* Opus 41 composed for the Duke of Devonshire's elevation to the chancellorship of Cambridge University. Bennett slightly expanded this piece and composed a Trio for the brass section of two trumpets, four horns, and three trombones. The added Romanza slow movement of 1867 is an arrangement of Bennett's song "Tell me where, ye summer breezes" *WO 65* for solo violas and orchestra. Temperley rightly characterized this movement as a song without words and associated it with the last portion of Mendelssohn's "Fantasia on The Last Rose of Summer."[78]

Though certain cyclic connections have been mentioned with regard to Bennett's earlier symphonies, by the 1860s the concept of the symphony as a unified cycle in some way or another had become *de rigueur.* Bennett's response was to take this collection of movements and pull them together with characteristic transitions. An Introduzione al Minuetto in 4/4 of eight measures dissipates to some degree the mood of the first movement with a gesture that paves the way for an aristocratic dance and provides a tonal bridge from G minor to B-flat major. The thirteen-measure Intermezzo, a Tempo di Minuetto coming before the Finale, recalls the end of the Minuet, which this time culminates in a Grave *tutti* fanfare on the dominant. Here, except for a tonal connection, the Intermezzo hardly prepares for the Rondo Finale. What it does is provide a way out of the central portion of the cycle consisting of two triple-meter movements in moderate tempos. Another connection, which comes only with the 1867 version, is that both the first and third movements contain instrumental recitatives, a striking gesture in symphony writing even after the Finale of Beethoven's Symphony No. 9/4.

Bennett's first movement both in the general and the particular again recalls Mendelssohn: the scoring and mood of *1P* (m.1) (Example XIV/15) could well have been written by the German composer, as could *2P* (m.17) and the animato *3P* (m.39). *T* (m.47) is Mendelssohnian in animation, and the beginning of the development section (m.140) with its pizzicato theme that turns into an accompaniment for *2P* is a direct imitation of Mendelssohn's Symphony No. 1(13[14])/1 in C Minor, which made a splash when first heard at the Philharmonic Concerts in 1829. Bennett dubbed *1P* as the "waves of life" theme, and it serves as a recurring motif; it is hinted at in *T,* and, as might be expected, returns more blatantly in *2K* (m.111). *K* is a lengthy statement (45 m.) almost equal in size to *P;* its opening *1K* in B-flat (m.94) some might wish to consider *S; 2K* (*P,* m.111) turns to the related key's subdominant minor, which underlines impending closure by the strong B-flat cadences and full scoring of *3K* (m.128). This does not obliterate the importance of *1S* (m.75), which has a recitative response (*2S,* m.81) that sets it apart from the other expository functions.

The Mendelssohnian beginning to the development (m.140) turns again to E-flat minor (see *2K*) and then with the entry of *2P* (m.145) edges toward D-flat, A-flat, and B-flat minor. A C minor cadence articulates a second section (m.159) beginning with *1P* and concluding with *1K* (m.167) in A-flat which leads to D major and the retransition (m.173). Bennett's recapitulation provides a strong return to G minor and *P, T, S,* and *K.* However, beginning with *T* (m.204) some unexpected tonal changes occur. As might be expected, *T* sets up D major, which serves as the dominant for *S*'s G minor (m.220), but the recitative of *2S* occurs in the same tonal orbit as in the exposition (m.226). *1K* (m.238) acts as if it were to cadence in G, but deceptively moves to E-flat, the dominant of the Neapolitan. *2K* (m.255) heads to C minor on the way to the strong tonic assertion of *3K* (m.268). Closure is further underlined by another appearance of *1K* (m.276) and *3K*

EXAMPLE XIV/15   Bennett. Symphony No. 8/1, mm.1–23.

EXAMPLE XIV/15 (*continued*)

(m.281) outlining the diminished seventh. A coda (m.290) recalls the Mendelssohnian beginning to the development now in E-flat major. A half-step slip to the dominant D lands us on G minor for *2P* (m.301). The *calando* allows the "waves of life" motive (*1P,* m.309) to be heard once more before the movement's almost withdrawn *pianissimo* and pizzicato end.

A certain reticence dominates the first movement's expression. This is not to say that the piece is lacking in boldness. Rather, it is another attempt to compose a symphony without the baggage of the heroic. Such an effort in this symphonic direction was somewhat tardy by the 1860s, that is, after Mendelssohn and Schumann had shown alternatives to Beethoven's symphonic idiom.

The Minuetto by its very presence conveys something of a Classical restraint; it hardly exceeds a *piano* dynamic even though it is rather fully scored. Peculiar is the structure of the Minuet proper with three repeated strains, each ending in B-flat followed by a four-measure close: ‖: *a* :‖: *a¹* :‖: *b a²* :‖ *k* ‖. The reprise after the Trio eliminates the third set of repeats and lengthens *k*. Compare this to the earlier *Cambridge Installation Ode* version; it eliminates the first *k* and then repeats the Minuet without *a* and adds *k* to the end. Bennett's Trio reverses the traditional qualities of the Minuet and Trio; here, the Trio is scored for brass with bold dynamics, while the Minuet stresses restraint. Sterndale Bennett said: "It will surprise the audience to find that there is a full brass band in the orchestra."[79] And one might add that this occurs after a first movement and Minuet proper with minimal brass involvement.

Romanza normally refers to a lyric instrumental piece or a vocal piece in strophic form, often of a pastoral orientation.[80] Bennett combines both of these types with a touch of the operatic. Bennett's song upon which this movement is based had a pastoral text concerning warm summer breezes. In the orchestral version, the introduction has a pulsating triplet background, swells and *diminuendos,* and overall quiet dynamics. The violas take the melody through two strophes (mm.8 and 35), followed by a dramatic orchestral interlude that builds to a *fortissimo* juxtaposed to a delicato recitative (m.72). This gradually returns to a lyric idiom for the third strophe (m.101) ending with a plagal cadence and another *calando* close.

The central protagonist in this movement is the viola, an instrument whose image was hardly one of an ardent lyricist. This deprived member of the string section had virtually no original soloistic literature. Berlioz to some extent changed this with the solo viola part in *Harold in Italy,* but here the viola is still a reluctant protagonist, who all but disappears in the Finale. Bennett's piece is not for solo viola, but a section of them displaying their collective virtuosity and timbre. He also published this piece in a version for solo viola and piano dedicated to the principal violist of the Philharmonic Society, Richard Blagrove. Few viola players take advantage of this solo piece.

Some critics wondered about the advisability of adding this slow movement into the already established cycle of an Allegro, Minuet, and Finale. Two critics or a critic who wrote for both the *Pall Mall Gazette* and the *Musical World* observed that the Romanza,

> intrinsically charming no doubt, has, nevertheless, the fault of being in the same measure as its immediate predecessor . . . [and] is as brief in duration as its companion, and a want of something longer and more carefully developed is felt. . . . Still, we are of the opinion that the third movement must be reconsidered.[81]

> The new movement is graceful, melodious, and full of delicate touches; but it is not equal to any of its companions; nor, we think, is it sufficiently important as to plan for the place it occupies . . . and fails to produce the desired contrast.[82]

After a recall of the Tempo di Minuetto for something less than thirteen measures, Sterndale Bennett embarks upon a Rondo Finale. One may outline its larger shape as follows:

A	B	A	C(B)	A	B	A
G minor	B-flat	G minor	mod.	G minor	G major	G minor
m.14	53	93	119	151	166	198

The above makes this look like a normal rondo except perhaps for the second episode's (*C*) relationship to the first (*B*). However, this is not the case, particularly with regard to the refrain. Rondo refrains tend to be closed and clearly shaped and the first theme tends to begin with an upbeat. Returns of the refrain, though abbreviated, retain something of its shape and remain closed. None of this is true here. The first statement of the refrain is open-ended and begins on a downbeat. At m.93, the refrain begins, fails to find closure, and then expands by developmental means (m.101). The third statement of *A* (m.151) is more developmental as the theme, considerably altered, is divided among various wind instruments and leads rather quickly to *B*. *A*'s final statement (m.198) begins with m.34, i.e., the second part of the refrain, making its aural identification less immediate. *A* is not a particularly assertive idea as it begins *pianissimo*. *B* is also *pianissimo,* and is characterized as delicato and ends with a passage (m.84) that Temperley calls almost atonal.[83] *C* begins in a tonal ambiguity (G minor/E-flat), confirms E-flat (m.123), then moves quickly to A-flat, C minor, and then to D major, which prepares the way back to the tonic.

Haydn was a master of the symphonic rondo Finale, particularly in his transitions and retransitions with their repeated head motives that tease the listener into desiring a return of the refrain. Bennett does a somewhat different take on this trick with the repetition of a motive from the previous rather than the upcoming section. The result is that one believes that the opening of the episode is to return for a formal rounding rather than a return of the refrain.

Bennett portrayed this Finale as a rustic fair which no doubt is the reason for the mixture of arco and pizzicato writing in the refrain, as well as pizzicatos with *sforzandos* on the weakest beat of an *alla breve* measure (Example XIV/16). In the first episode (*B*), the "disconsolate maid who had lost her lover in the crowd"[84] bemoans her situation in the sigh and wails of the oboe. No doubt the delicato motive with which *B* begins must also have an extra-musical connotation. Other possible pantomimic moments include the timbral and motivic dialogues that occur at various places in the Finale (mm.47–52, 89–91, 115–16, 127–31, 133–38, 159–62).

Bennett's second G Minor Symphony in its two versions probably obtained more performances than any of his other public works. It was heard not only in English venues in Manchester (1875) and in London at the Crystal Palace (1870, 1875) and the Philharmonic Concerts (1864, 1865, 1867, 1869, 1872), but also in Leipzig at the Gewandhaus (1865) and in New York at the Summer Garden Concerts (1875).[85] This indicates that Bennett's somewhat introverted style appealed to more than an English public. Cipriani Potter wrote in the composer's album after the premiere of the 1864 version:

> I must congratulate you on your transcendent success last Monday, not more than you deserved. I was perfectly charmed with your Symphony, for the beauty of *Composition*

EXAMPLE XIV/16   Bennett. Symphony No. 8/4, mm.14–22 [mm.1–9 of Rondo Finale].

as well as the truly happy *instrumentation*. I thought it went admirably; no doubt we shall hear it again early next season with another movement.[86]

The Leipzig performance was enthusiastically applauded at the Gewandhaus and received notices in both the *Allgemeine Musikalische Zeitung* and the *Neue Zeitschrift für Musik*:

Bennett's composition distinguished itself advantageously with its beautiful sonorous effects, lovely motives, witty treatment of themes, and clear formal organization; otherwise, it did not demonstrate any new aspects of this well-known, recently somewhat neglected composer, who received at his appearance a friendly greeting from the audience, in memory of times past. The Minuet made the strongest impact with its charming main theme and the piquant trio for brass. The first movement also made quite a pleasant impression with its pretty contrasts, although its main theme displays a certain lack of rhythmic energy. The finale satisfied us the least, [since] its motives and phrases seemed to lack close coherence. The lack of an adagio might have prompted the composer to avoid the title "symphony" for the entire [work]. We do not know why an adagio was not composed or left out.[87]

The abovementioned novelty was a symphony (Allegro, Minuet, and Rondo Finale) by W. Sterndale Bennett. It is an unpretentious, light, pleasing [piece of] music that does credit to an Englishman and presents in every respect a perhaps not original, yet experienced and clever composer; however, he is unable—especially in the third movement—to steer clear of trivialities. The second movement was the most attractive. The composer, who conducted his work himself, encountered enthusiastic applause.[88]

Among the English performances, the review in the *Musical World* was the most positive:

Here was an ample and varied programme of itself; but yet another piece materially added to its attraction. This was the new symphony in G minor, written expressly for the Philharmonic Concerts by their excellent conductor, Professor Sterndale Bennett, and produced near the end of last season. Received with enthusiasm on the first occasion, it was still more enthusiastically appreciated now. In the interval between the two Philharmonic performances the symphony in G minor had been adopted by the celebrated Gewandhaus Concerts in Leipsic, where its composer, more than 20 years ago, used to play, to conduct when Mendelssohn played, and to hear his own overtures and other works performed so often and with such applause. A composition so original, so fresh, spontaneous, and full of genuine musical beauty, could hardly fail to please an assembly of connoisseurs like the subscribers to the Gewandhaus; and their quondam English favourite, now of mature age, could not have revisited them, after a lengthened absence, with more honorable credentials—with a more convincing proof, indeed, that the Cambridge Musical Professor and "Doctor in Music" was the same Sterndale Bennett whom their illustrious Mendelssohn loved so well, and about whose music their intellectual Robert Schumann wrote in such eloquent and thoughtful terms. The Leipsic amateurs and the Leipsic press were loud and unanimous in praise of the symphony. They only echoed, however, the opinion of London judges, which was last night even more emphatically expressed than before. The work gains much by closer acquaintance. The character of the *allegro serioso,* the opening movement, is only so far not symphonic inasmuch as the customary elaborations of the second part, or "free *fantasia,*" as the Germans sometimes call it, is replaced by a wholly independent episode. This episode, nevertheless, reappearing unexpectedly near the end, at once vindicates its own importance and makes clear the design of the composer. The movement abounds in melody, has quite a romantic tone, and is instrumented with a master hand from one end to the other. The succeeding movement, a *minuetto* with *trio* in the old established form, is as perfect in its way as it is entirely unpretending. The two sections are contrasted with great felicity, the brass instruments in the *trio* giving a wonderful brightness of colouring after the quiet repose of the *minuetto.* The *rondo finale* is fully as original, fully as spirited, and fully as interesting as either of its precursors. The leading themes are not merely striking, but effectively opposed to each other; and the movement is conducted with a vigour and animation that never flag. The *finale,* in short, has only one fault, and that fault is its somewhat disproportionate brevity. If ever Professor Bennett can be induced to develop it, and, further, to compose a slow movement for the symphony, he will bestow still higher importance upon a work which, as it stands, is a credit to himself and an honor to the English school.

The execution on Monday night was satisfactory in all respects. The members of the band played as if they loved as well as esteemed their conductor, and the result was all that could have been wished. The applause at the conclusion of every moment was such as is rarely elicited by any performance at the Philharmonic Concerts, where the habitual frequenters are by no means easily roused. Professor Bennett must have felt quite as much gratified as his audience were delighted.[89]

Already, both Potter and this reviewer were awaiting a slow movement to complete what they regarded as an unfinished symphony.

We have already cited comments on the 1867 version with their qualifications concerning the movement so earnestly desired. Perhaps Bennett had it right the first time, since the addition of the Larghetto was only undertaken at the urging of the directors of the Philharmonic Society. Still, in 1876 the curmudgeonly Bernard Shaw referred to it as "beautiful and original."[90]

CONCLUSION

W. Sterndale Bennett was not a composer who pursued the symphony as a genre to be conquered except perhaps during the 1830s when he composed or worked on as many as seven symphonies. Later, he was to compose only one further work, a second symphony in the key of G minor. His two works in G minor (*WO* 31 and Opus 43) are his most effective, even though their characters are quite different from each other; the former belongs more to the *Sturm und Drang* idiom, while the latter belongs more to the introverted reflective style so frequently found during the nineteenth century. Even in a key like A major, Bennett does not follow its brilliant timbral possibilities, but instead tends toward a less boisterous approach. If Bennett had been a symphonist in central Germany during his lifetime, he probably would not have gained notice in this survey. But the fact that he came from an environment with only three significant native symphonists before 1850, Cipriani Potter, George Macfarren, and himself, demands that he be given attention because of his importance to the English symphony. His Opus 43 was the first nineteenth-century symphony by a native English composer to be published.

But where does Bennett belong in the constellation of nineteenth-century symphonists? His symphonic personality belongs to an English tradition from Viennese Classicism promulgated by Potter and to the Leipzig School whose dominating protagonists were Mendelssohn and Schumann, men whom Bennett knew on both a friendly and a professional basis. But even Schumann may have been too radical a composer for Bennett's tastes; Bennett was not an admirer of Schumann's music.[91] His musical relationship to Louis Spohr seems to be even less significant. The European composer who seems to most closely parallel Bennett's career and musical personality is the Dane Niels Gade. Both men, even in their latest symphonies, reveal a sympathetic connection to Mendelssohn's style at a time when the new music was no longer following this path. Perhaps the finest general characterization of Bennett's musical personality comes from Schumann himself, who tellingly takes on the persona of the introverted Eusebius in an 1837 essay:

> The first thing that strikes every one in the character of his compositions is their remarkable family resemblance to those of Mendelssohn. The same beauty of form, poetic depth yet clearness, and ideal purity, the same outwardly satisfying impression,—but with a difference. The difference is still more observable in their playing than in their compositions. The Englishman's playing is perhaps more tender, more careful in detail; that of Mendelssohn is broader, more energetic. The former bestows fine shading on the

lightest thing, the latter pours a novel force into the most powerful passages; one over-powers us with the transfigured expression of a single form, the other showers forth hundreds of angelic heads, as in a heaven of Raphael. Something of the same kind occurs in their compositions. If Mendelssohn produces, in fantastic sketches, the whole wild faërie of a "[Mid]Summer Night's Dream," Bennett in his music evokes the charming figures of the "Merry Wives of Windsor"; one spreads out before us the broad, deep, slumbering surface of the sea, the other lingers beside a balmy lake, on which the beams of the moon are trembling.[92]

The Symphonic Milieu from *ca.* 1850 to 1912

During the first half of the nineteenth century, English composers who wanted to write symphonies were hardly encouraged by opportunities to hear their works. Essentially there were only two venues: the Royal Philharmonic Society of London and the Society of British Musicians (1834–1865). The former was hardly hospitable to English symphonists; during its first fifty years only Potter, Bennett, and Macfarren of the significant native composers received repeated hearings. The Philharmonic Society seems to have been more taken with Germanic orchestral music above all and much of this was rooted in Viennese Classicism. In a sense, the Society of British Musicians was founded to fill this void and encourage native composers by providing a series of concerts where their works could be heard publicly. Though several symphonies by Potter, Macfarren, and Bennett were heard and reviewed, the Society of British Musicians during its some thirty years of existence did not stimulate the composition of symphonies by other native British composers.

Turning back to Table XIV/4, it appears that Bennett's Symphony No. 8 Opus 43 spawned a series of native symphonies after a fallow period from 1848 to 1864. Even in the decade previous to this time, if it were not for George Macfarren and Henry Leslie, this fallow period would have started in 1836. Except for Bennett's G Minor Symphony, the Philharmonic Society contributed very little or nothing to an English flowering of the symphony. Some of this may have to do with the conductor of the Philharmonic Concerts from 1846 to 1854, Michael Costa, who programmed few works by native English composers. Around mid-century and later, new venues and societies came into existence.

In 1852, the *New* Philharmonic Society was established. It courted not the exclusive families of the old Philharmonic Society, but the favor of the general public. Its purpose was to present "more perfect performances than have, hitherto, been attained" and to bring the music of contemporary and British composers before the public.[93] In addition, a number of prominent Continental composers accepted honorary membership in the new Society including Berlioz, Rossini, and Spohr. Remember that Spohr also had close ties to the old Philharmonic Society. Originally, the New Philharmonic Society gave their concerts in Exeter Hall, but four years later moved to the smaller Hanover Square Rooms, making it necessary to raise ticket prices and thereby excluding a portion of their audience. Since the Society was governed and operated by wealthy amateurs, a group assembled by the conductor and educator Henry Wylde (1822–1890), at times chaos occurred. For example, when Berlioz tried to program parts of his *Roméo et Juliette,* he found the wrong voices engaged and mix-ups with regard to what language was to be used. Besides Berlioz, Spohr and Lindpainter also conducted concerts. Wylde became sole conductor in 1858; as a result, a number of members split with the Society, weakening its effectiveness. Nevertheless, the programs of the New Philharmonic Society were more adventuresome and more carefully prepared. Their first concert consisted of Mozart's "Jupiter" Symphony K.551, a selection from Gluck's *Iphigénie en Tauride,* Beethoven's Triple Concerto Opus 56, Weber's *Oberon* Overture, and excerpts from Berlioz's *Roméo et Juliette.*[94]

Perhaps the most important of these new venues and societies were the Crystal Palace Saturday Concerts under the direction of August Manns, who in collaboration with George Grove established in 1856 London's most adventuresome series of concerts. Even though it was still oriented toward German music from the continent, works by native English composers, including symphonies, came to be performed. So together with European symphonies by Schubert, Raff, Brahms, and Dvořák, among others, symphonies by Sullivan, Gadsby, Holmes, Wingham, Cowen, Prout, and others were heard under the direction of its Teutonic conductor, August Manns. George Grove, secretary of the Crystal Palace association and an advocate for Continental music, also understood the need for the performance of major works by native composers that were not oratorios. Established in 1856 and continuing until the end of the century, the Crystal Palace Orchestra could render new works quite effectively; it was the only fully established, permanent, and completely disciplined orchestra active in London. The audience at the Crystal Palace was more of a middle- and working-class group taken into the world of culture by the Victorian belief in "progress" through education and experience.

Other concert series of importance also tried to appeal to something more than members of the upper- and upper-middle classes. In 1858 and lasting until 1898 were the Popular Concerts at St. James's Hall, one of the largest London concert venues at the time, holding more than 2,100 listeners. These events were strategically planned to educate their audiences in a wide range of repertoire discussed in analytical program notes and to present chamber ensembles and soloists of stellar repute such as Grieg, Paderewski, Anton Rubinstein, Clara Schumann, Hans von Bülow, and Joseph Joachim, among others. Besides the Continental repertoire, one could also hear works by native musicians such as Sterndale Bennett, C. Hubert H. Parry, Charles Stanford, and A. C. MacKenzie.

Beginning in 1838 were the less formal concert events known as Promenades, which began at the Lyceum and were in imitation of a Parisian series founded by Philippe Musard. However, it was not until 1893 that the Queen's Hall Orchestra under Henry Wood provided the series with a stability that continues until today. The repertoire for these concerts was unusually catholic, including the high Romantics, English composers, as well as trivial music and music from the turn-of-the-century *avant-garde.* With later financial problems, a group of players splintered from the Queen's Hall Orchestra to form the London Symphony Orchestra in 1904, a long-lasting experiment in musicians' self-governance and a new chapter in British orchestral management.

In addition, there were concerts organized by conductors such as the great Hans Richter, who, after the end of his Continental career, was the music director of the Hallé Orchestra in Manchester (1899–1911) and also, to the consternation of his Manchester employers, conducted at the same time in London not the Hallé Orchestra, but one of his own assemblage for the "Richter Concerts." Later, Thomas Beecham was to do much the same thing, but without invoking his name as he took over and sponsored the Philharmonic Society and established the London Philharmonic and, past the scope of this survey, the Royal Philharmonic Orchestra.

Richter, Beecham, Manns, and Wood were all conductors of superb abilities, broad tastes, and unquestioned musicianship. In Volume IV of this survey, Hans Richter is recognized as a conductor who premiered many works by Brahms, Bruckner, Goldmark, and other composers who entered the canon. He continued to do the same during the last decade of his career in England as he conducted new works by C. Hubert H. Parry, Charles Stanford, other

English composers, and presented to the world Elgar's Symphony No. 1, which was perhaps the most widely admired new symphony in musical history when it was first heard in 1908.

Musical life in England during the second half of the nineteenth century was not restricted to Manchester and London. Apart from the music in the college chapels, there were also active concert-giving organizations in the university towns of Oxford and Cambridge. It was, however, the Cambridge University Musical Society (CUMS) that toward the end of the century came to be of particular significance for the symphony in England. In March of 1877, the CUMS gave the first English performance of Brahms's Symphony No. 1, conducted by Joseph Joachim. This was an important date for the English symphony, for Brahms the symphonist provided a model for both Charles Stanford, the director of the CUMS, and C. Hubert H. Parry, his Oxford rival and contemporary. While both composers used extramusical aspects in their symphonies, both wrote symphonies that did not in the main try to portray specific aspects, but only characteristic ones in much the same way as Beethoven did in his symphonies. And both composers essentially heard and treated the orchestra in Brahmsian terms. Brahms never came to Cambridge to receive a doctorate, but other composers did. Antonín Dvořák received his degree in June 1891 and conducted his Symphony No. 8 in one of its early performances. In June of 1893, Camille Saint-Saëns, Max Bruch, Pyotr Il'yich Tchaikovsky, and Arrigo Boito all came to receive the terminal degree *honoris causa*. Charles Stanford was responsible for the CUMS achieving such a level of prestige so that its concerts attracted as much attention as any musical event in London.

Our discussion of the English symphony from mid-century to the First World War will center on three figures: Charles Villiers Stanford (1852–1924), C. Hubert H. Parry (1848–1918), and Edward Elgar (1857–1934). But as can be seen from Table XIV/4, there are a host of symphonies composed in England after Bennett's final Symphony in G Minor Opus 43 (1864, 1867). First, we will briefly survey this repertoire by composer according to the occurrence of their first symphony on the list. Many of these works are to us merely titles, some are probably lost, while others may reside today in the collections of educational and concert institutions with which these composers and their works were associated.

Barnett is a name that represents an important family of gifted musicians. John Francis Barnett (1837–1916) studied at the Royal Academy. His Symphony in A Minor was first heard at the Musical Society of London on June 15, 1864. He is perhaps best known for his completion of the draft for Schubert's Symphony in E D.729, whose autograph was owned by Sir George Grove and was heard at the Crystal Palace in 1883. Unfortunately, it only survives in a four-hand piano arrangement. John Barnett (1802–1890), John Francis Barnett's uncle, also wrote a symphony in 1837 while in Europe when he was a pupil of Franz Xaver Schnyder von Wartensee in Frankfurt. No performances of the work are known. His reputation was built upon his work as a composer and conductor for the theater.

Sir Arthur Sullivan (1842–1900) also studied at the Royal Academy and is best known for his collaborations with W. S. Gilbert. Many of his friends and colleagues regretted his contemporary popularity as a stage composer, since in their judgment his more important compositions had been overshadowed. In addition, the time that these operettas took away from Sullivan's pursuit of symphonic composition left him with the completion of but one symphonic work, a Symphony in E Major first heard at the Crystal Palace on March 10, 1866. Known as his "Irish" Symphony, it continues in the characteristic tradition of Mendelssohn's "Italian" and "Scottish" Symphonies and no doubt fostered other works of like and similar titles by Cowen, Stanford, and later Hamilton Harty (1926).

One of the most important British symphonists was the pianist, conductor, and composer Sir Frederic Cowen (1852–1935). He wrote six symphonies:

1869	Symphony No. 1 in C Minor
1872	Symphony No. 2 in F Minor
1880	Symphony No. 3 "Scandinavian" in C Minor
1884	Symphony No. 4 "Welsh" in B-flat Minor
1887	Symphony No. 5 in F Major
1897	Symphony No. 6 "Idyllic" in E Major

As can be seen, Nos. 3, 4, and 6 are characteristic pieces with Nos. 3 and 4 concentrating on geographic/cultural entities. His "Scandinavian" Symphony came to be one of the most widely performed symphonies of its time. It was first heard at St. James's Hall on December 18, 1880, conducted by the composer. Later performances were in Vienna, Paris, the United States, and Australia. According to Fuller-Maitland: "As a work of one who never had a lesson in orchestration it is a very remarkable feat, local colour is used with admirable felicity, and there is little wonder that it soon became popular."[95]

Henry Gadsby (1842–1897) was organist and teacher of theory at Queen's College and the Guildhall School. Largely self-taught, he composed a significant amount of Anglican church music and three symphonies: No. 1 in C, No. 2 in A—excerpts heard at the Crystal Palace in 1871—and No. 3 in D "Festal" played at the Crystal Palace on November 3, 1888.

Thomas Wingham (1846–1893) studied at the Royal Academy of Music, where he concentrated on piano and composition with Sterndale Bennett. He composed a number of works for the Roman liturgy. His orchestral output includes six concert overtures and four symphonies:

1869	Symphony No. 1 in D Minor	Royal Academy
1872	Symphony No. 2 in B-flat Major	Crystal Palace, March 23
1873	Symphony No. 3 in E Minor	Alexandra Palace
1883	Symphony No. 4 in D Major	?

His third symphony has a choral Finale.

The Holmes family seems to constitute an English musical dynasty. Three members of the family wrote symphonies: William Henry Holmes (1812–1885), Alfred Holmes (1837–1876), and his brother Henry Holmes (1839–1905). William Henry studied at the Royal Academy during its first year, took medals in both piano and composition, and was a student of Croft and Potter. According to *Grove 2,* he composed symphonies. Alfred Holmes and his brother Henry were both violin prodigies and were also choristers at the Oratory. In 1855, the brothers toured the continent, visiting Belgium and Germany as well as Austria, Sweden, and Denmark. By 1864 Alfred had settled in Paris and in 1867 his Symphony "Jeanne d'Arc" for soloists, chorus, and orchestra was heard in St. Petersburg; it was revived at the Crystal Palace on February 27, 1875. This work appears to be a *symphonie dramatique* after the concept of Berlioz's *Roméo et Juliette.* His later symphonies also carried titles: "Robin Hood," "The Siege of Paris," "Charles XII," and *Romeo and Juliet.* He died in Paris. Henry returned to London and composed four symphonies: No. 1 in A was heard at the Crystal Palace on February 24, 1872, and another, titled "Boscastle," was heard in London in 1887. After a scandal of morals at the Royal College of Music in 1894, he left for San Francisco, where he lived out his remaining years.

Francis William Davenport (1847–1925) was educated at Oxford and composed two symphonies, in D minor and C major. His D Minor Symphony took first prize in the Alexandra Palace competition in 1876; Stanford received the second prize. His Second Symphony cannot be traced beyond the information in *Grove 2.* He taught at the Royal Academy of Music from 1879 and published several pedagogical treatises on harmony, counterpoint, and the piano.

Sir Julius Benedict (1804–1885), the famed London operatic and orchestral conductor, wrote two symphonies, both of which were heard at the Crystal Palace. Ebenezer Prout (1835–1909), the music theorist, editor, pedagogue, and critic, composed four symphonies: Symphony No. 1 in C (1874), No. 2 in G Minor (1877), No. 3 in F Opus 22 (1885), and No. 4 of unknown date and key. According to Slonimsky, he was "a competent composer of useless works."[96] Henry David Leslie (1822–1896), mainly a conductor of amateur choral societies, wrote a Symphony in F (1847), perhaps composed for the Amateur Music Society of which he was the honorary secretary. Frederick Cliffe (1857–1931), a violoncellist and keyboardist, produced two symphonies: Symphony No. 1 in C Minor Opus 1, rejected by the Leeds Festival but performed at the Crystal Palace on April 20, 1889, and Symphony No. 2 in E Minor, heard at the Leeds Festival in 1892. Robin H. Legge considered his Opus 1 to be a "fine symphony."[97] Edward German (1862–1936), an organist, violinist, and conductor, composed mainly music for the theater. His Symphony No. 1 in E Minor premiered at St. James's Hall on July 16, 1887, and Symphony No. 2 in A Minor debuted at the Norwich Festival in 1893. William George Cusins (1833–1893), though a conductor of the Philharmonic Society from 1867 to 1883, produced but one symphony (in C Major, 1892), as did Joseph Cox Bridge (1853–1929), an organist at the Chester Cathedral, a Symphony in F Major in 1894. Henry Walford Davies (1869–1941), a student of Stanford's, best known for his anthems, wrote a D Major Symphony heard at the Crystal Palace on October 19, 1895, and later a pedagogical work in 1927, "A Children's Symphony," for school use. Only one symphony came from the pen of the Black-English composer, Samuel Coleridge-Taylor (1875–1912): his Symphony in A Minor (1896). Three symphonies, one in A minor (1892–1898), another, "Solway," from 1911 in C-sharp minor, plus one more, came from the Scottish composer John McEwen (1868–1948). William Wallace (1860–1940) specialized in symphonic poems, but also wrote a symphony, "The Creation," in 1899. William Henry Bell (1873–1946) wrote four symphonies: a First Symphony, "Walt Whitman" (1899), followed by two symphonies many years later (a Second Symphony in 1917–1918 and a Third in 1918–1919), "A South African Symphony" (1927), and a Fifth Symphony in F Minor (1932). His "Walt Whitman" Symphony was heard at the Crystal Palace on March 10, 1900. In 1912, Bell moved to Capetown, thereby disengaging himself from the London musical scene. The English impressionist Cyril Scott (1879–1970) had his First Symphony played at Darmstadt (1900), and his Second (1903) was heard at the Promenade Concerts. A Sinfonietta for Strings (1962) exemplifies Scott's constant productivity over a long creative life.

In contrast to the first half of the nineteenth century, the period after 1864 up to the Great War was one in which every important British composer tried his hand at writing one or more symphonies. The fruits of the Royal Academy and the new Royal College (established 1852) were now ripening to make England a center of symphonic as well as choral writing. Even at the end of the century the ghosts of Cipriani Potter and Sterndale Bennett seemed to hover over their students and their students' students. In the next generation, another pedagogical tree will emanate from the Royal College of Music and the personalities of Charles Stanford and C. Hubert H. Parry. Now there was a reasonable chance that new and accomplished symphonies would be performed, whether it be at the various London venues now so rich and richly varied, in the secondary centers like Manchester or Liverpool, at the regional festivals such as Birmingham and Norwich, or at the Cambridge University Musical Society.

Charles Villiers Stanford

INTRODUCTION

Charles Villiers Stanford (1852–1924) was born in Dublin and studied there at St. Patrick's Cathedral and the Royal Irish Academy of Music. In 1862, he went to London for further instruction and then entered Queens College of Cambridge University where he was awarded the B.A. in 1874. After a two-year pilgrimage to Leipzig and Berlin for further work, he returned to Cambridge, where in 1877 he received the M.A. He later held appointments, both in conducting and teaching composition, at Cambridge and at the Royal College of Music. During his Cambridge appointment, the activities of the Cambridge University Musical Society came to be a significant force in British musical life. His reputation at both institutions was as a compelling leader and a perceptive—if idiosyncratic—teacher who had a lasting impact upon his students.[98] In his activities as a composer, he bordered on being an Irish nationalist: he collected and wrote about Irish folk music and incorporated it into his compositions, such as his six *Irish Rhapsodies,* the *Irish Concertino,* his well-known Third Symphony, "Irish," and his opera *Shamus O'Brien* (1896).

Considering his activities as a pedagogue and a conductor, Stanford was prolific as a composer (Plate B4). He turned out numerous songs, anthems, and services, nine operas, three piano concertos, two violin concertos, four violin sonatas, three piano trios, eight string quartets, two string quintets, a series of large choral/orchestral works, and some overtures. In this context, his seven symphonies listed in Table XIV/14 do not loom as a central genre except in the realm of his instrumental music, where they are only exceeded in number by the string quartets. Like so many English composers of his generation, vocal genres dominate his output.

Stanford's ability to be so active and so productive can be attributed to his assiduousness and his highly developed technique. One could say that, like Richard Strauss, for Stanford composing was a natural and daily act. Not a day went by when he did not devote some time to composition. His ability to assess a situation and solve compositional problems was legendary. Those who studied with him often remarked on his ability to look at their work, root out the problems, and make suggestions as to how to rectify the situation. And all this could take place within a few minutes. It was said that his own work as a composer was almost spontaneous and without struggle or the need for sketches. Such an all-encompassing technical facility, however, can lead to works that are too formulaic and superficial. While Stanford was not totally immune to this charge, the superficiality and a certain crassness as found in the symphonies of Joachim Raff cannot be attributed to Stanford's works, where fine taste and conciseness always prevailed.

Stanford's symphonies are each essentially made up of four discrete movements, except for No. 7 where the third movement combines the functions of two: slow movement and Finale. Four of the seven imply some sort of extra-musical associations. No. 2, the "Elegiac" after Tennyson, and No. 5, "L'Allegro ed il Pensieroso [*sic*]" after Milton, are essentially characteristic pieces whose extra-musical aspects fit rather well into traditional symphonic four-movement cycles. No. 3, the "Irish," uses a formula adopted by Continental composers to further their nationalistic desires: traditional dances of a given area and the quotation and/or imitation of folk materials. Symphony No. 6, written "in honor of the life-work of a great artist: George Frederick Watts," cannot be explicated, since we do not know firsthand if this piece was to be a kind of "pictures at an exhibition" or if it is a tribute to the artist without any direct associations to his work. That leaves three works without any apparent background: the prize Symphony No. 1, Symphony No. 4, and the pithy Symphony No. 7, which lasts *ca.* twenty-eight minutes.

TABLE XIV/14

The Symphonies of Charles Villiers Stanford

Opus	Key	Date	Title	Movements	Instrumentation	Comments
—	B-flat Major	1876	Symphony No. 1	1. Larghetto 4/4 Allegro vivace 3/4 (868 m.) 2. Scherzo and 2 Trios: In Ländler tempo—Presto—Poco più lento 3/4 (426 m.) G minor 3. Andante tranquillo 4/4 (164 m.) E-flat major 4. Finale: Allegro molto ¢ (512 m.)	Grand	Awarded second prize in competition for British symphony composers sponsored by the Alexandra Palace. Dedicated "to his friend Arthur Duke Coleridge." First performance(?): March 8, 1879 at the Crystal Palace, conducted by Manns.
—	D Minor	Summer 1879	Symphony No. 2	1. Allegro appassionato 6/8 (335 m.) 2. Lento espressivo 4/4 (136 m.) F major 3. Scherzo: Allegro con fuoco 6/8 (199 m.) D minor/major 4. Adagio 4/4—Allegro moderato 4/4 Allegro molto ma non presto ¢ (328 m.) D major	Grand	"Elegiac" after Tennyson's "In Memoriam." First performance: March 7, 1882 at Cambridge by the University Musical Society, conducted by the composer.
28	F Minor	1887	Symphony No. 3	1. Allegro moderato 4/4 (359 m.) 2. Allegro molto vivace 9/8 (245 m.) D minor 3. Andante con moto 3/4 (231 m.) B-flat 4. Allegro moderato, ma con fuoco 4/4 (373 m.) F minor/major	Grand	"Irish" First performance: June 27, 1887 in London conducted by Richter. Published in London: Novello, 1887. Contains quotations of Irish folksongs: "Remember the glories of Brian the Brave" (mvt. 4), "Let Erin remember the days of old" (mvt. 4), and a motive from "The Lament of the Sons of Usnach" (mvt. 3).
31	F Major	Summer 1888	Symphony No. 4	1. Allegro vivace e giojoso 3/4 (444 m.) 2. Intermezzo: Allegretto agitato (ma moderato in tempo)—Tranquillo ma l'istesso tempo 2/4/6/8 (237 m.) A minor 3. Andante molto moderato 4/4 (203 m.) D minor 4. Finale: Allegro non troppo—Maestoso ¢ (417 m.)	Grand	First performance: January 14, 1889 in Berlin, conducted by the composer. Published in London: Novello, 1890.

TABLE XIV/14 (*continued*)

Opus	Key	Date	Title	Movements	Instrumentation	Comments
56	D Major	1894	Symphony No. 5	1. Allegro moderato 4/4 (278 m.) D major 2. Allegretto grazioso 6/8—Più mosso (Quasi Presto) 2/4 (336 m.) G major 3. Andante molto tranquillo 4/4 (151 m.) B-flat major 4. Allegro molto 4/4/3/4 (610 m.)	Grand plus organ	"L'Allegro ed il Pensieroso[*sic*]" after Milton. First performance: March 20, 1895 in London, conducted by the composer. Published in London: Stainer & Bell, 1923.
94	E-flat Major	1905	Symphony No. 6	1. Allegro con brio 6/8 (440 m.) 2. Adagio e molto espressivo 4/4 (159 m.) B major 3. Presto 3/4 (384 m.) 4/4 C minor 4. Poco Allegro Moderato e Maestoso 4/4 (262 m.)	Grand plus EH, Tuba, and Harp.	"In honor of the life-work of a great artist: George Frederick Watts" First performance: January 18, 1906 by the London Symphony Orchestra, conducted by the composer.
124	D Minor	1911	Symphony No. 7	1. Allegro 4/4 (222 m.) 2. Tempo di Minuetto: Allegretto molto moderato 3/4 (178 m.) B-flat major 3. Variations and Finale: Andante 4/4/3/4—Allegro giusto 4/4—Poco più lento 4/4/3/2—Allegro maestoso ¢ (356 m.)	Grand	First performance: February 22, 1912 in London, conducted by the composer for the centenary of the Philharmonic Society. Published in London: Stainer & Bell, 1912. New ed. Chichester: Chiltern, 1992.

The overall impression of these works is that they belong to the Brahmsian tradition, a composer whose music Stanford came to respect before he left Dublin for London. Similarities can be found in the traditional movement layout, the approach to the orchestra and its dark coloring, the use of cross rhythms in triple and compound meters, and the Classical formal structures and developmental procedures. Though Stanford was familiar with what was going on with the new music during the last quarter of the nineteenth century, he referred to many of these new works as "modern ugliness."[99]

SYMPHONY NO. 1 IN B-FLAT MAJOR

Stanford's First (1876) was a prize-winning symphony and provided the composer with a recognition he had previously not experienced. Stanford was awarded second place in a competition for "the best two Orchestral Symphonies to be written by British composers" sponsored by the Alexandra Palace to celebrate its reopening. The judges were George A. Macfarren and Joseph Joachim. Of the thirty-eight or, as some sources report, forty-six entries, the first-prize winner for £20 was F. W. Davenport (1847–1925), and Stanford received £5 plus a performance by the Alexandra Palace Orchestra under the direction of Thomas Henry Weist-Hill (1828–1891). One might question the fairness of the award to Davenport; Macfarren was not only his teacher, but also his father-in-law. Nevertheless, it was Stanford who became a significant composer, while Davenport became merely a blip in the history of British music.

One cannot assert that this B-flat Symphony is indebted to Brahms's symphonies since it is unlikely for Stanford to have heard or seen Brahms's First Symphony; its English premiere took place in Cambridge on March 8, 1877. Nevertheless, Stanford did know Brahms's earlier work and, of course, knew the main sources of Brahms's style: the symphonies of Beethoven and Schumann. Even a casual hearing of Stanford's Symphony No. 1 reveals that Beethoven's "Eroica" Symphony, perhaps his Seventh Symphony, and Schumann's First and Fourth Symphonies were in Stanford's head when he composed the first and last movements.

Stanford begins with a big (80 mm.) introduction of alternating sections that immediately brings to mind the parallel shape of Beethoven's Symphony No. 7/1. But unlike the Beethoven example and Schumann's Symphony No. 1/1, this time there are two transitions (mm.46, 57) to the Allegro, each of which has an accelerando. The beginning of the second transition (m.57) returns to the first tempo at its beginning, which in turn is almost proportional to the Allegro: Larghetto 4/4: ♩=80 → Allegro vivace 3/4 ♩.=84. The Allegro vivace 3/4 exposition seems to owe a great deal to Beethoven's "Eroica"; there are three statements of an arpeggiated *P* (mm.81, 97, 141); the first is undergirded by pulsating eighths, the second is followed by a development and a *crescendo* to *fortissimo* for the third statement of *P. T* (m.199) also recalls Beethoven's Third as the material cascades through the woodwinds (Example XIV/17). *S* (m.219) departs from the Beethoven model to adopt a textbook secondary theme with its multiple lyrical statements (mm.219, 231, 267), the first introduced by the viola. Departing somewhat from the tradition of *K* in Potter and Bennett, all of the closing material (m.295) is based on *P*. Originally Stanford's intent was to repeat the exposition; later he cancelled the first ending.

The development (m.335) begins with *T*, but diverts to *P* (m.370) treated to expansive sequences that parallel the first section of the "Eroica"'s development. *P* (m.438) is then answered by *S* (m.450). During this stretch, both *P* and *S* are heard in their original forms and in inversion. By doing this, Stanford reveals a relationship between the contrasting *P* and *S* themes. Tonally, the development transfers from the dominant to subdominant (m.334f) and then in broad expanses moves upward to D (m. 402) for a *fortissimo* statement of *P*. Stanford's response to this is a faster-moving section as the bass descends (m.419), finding its way

EXAMPLE XIV/17 Stanford. Symphony No. 1/1, mm.198–218.

to a long section on the dominant of C (m.446), the submediant, which often serves as a central tonality in Classical developments. From here, Stanford reaches the dominant of B-flat (m.497) for the *fortissimo* and *tutti* recapitulation, a Beethoven fingerprint, with *P* in the bass (m.521) (cf. Beethoven's Symphony No. 8/1).

Though the recapitulation is only twenty-two bars shorter than the exposition and brings back all of the essential themes, it is reformulated. With *P* entering *fortissimo,* Stanford has essentially started the recapitulation with the exposition's third statement of *P* (m.141). After a lengthy resumption of developmental procedures, a typical post-*P* maneuver in the Classical form, *K* appears (m. 688), followed by *T* (m.728), which takes us to the più animato coda (m.753). Here, Stanford begins with a dominant pedal over which *P* is further worked over. It is not until near the movement's close that a perfect tonic resolution takes place (m.851), but it is followed by two plagal endings that quickly turn to three authentic resolutions to bring the movement to a close. The end with its brilliant writing for brass recalls another triple-meter first movement of an E-flat symphony: Schumann's Symphony No. 3 "Rhenish."

Stanford's first movement is overall a strong piece of writing for a First Symphony by a twenty-three-year-old composer. It reveals a sure sense of how to handle the orchestra and a sure sense of shape bolstered by memorable and appealing thematic material. If one were to note the weaknesses, they occur not so much in *P* and *S,* but in the more transitory sections. The double transition to the first movement allegro, particularly in its second part (m.57), does not quite work, even though it was an imaginative effort to modulate from a common-time Larghetto to an Allegro vivace in triple meter. And one might too have reservations about the lead-in to *P*'s third statement (m.141) and the retransition to the recapitulation.

As Potter and Bennett sometimes did, Stanford places the dance movement in second position. Though labeled a Scherzo, its first G minor strains are "In Ländler Tempo," the first Trio is a G minor Presto 2/4 in a *contredanse* idiom, and the second Trio is in B-flat and slightly slower with three strains. After a reprise of the Ländler section, the coda (m.408) is the movement's slowest moment. None of this sounds like an Irish composer writing for a potential London audience, but rather a Czech or German trying to delight listeners in Prague, Vienna, or possibly Berlin. One here thinks of Dvořák's *Slavonic Dances,* except again Stanford could not have known these to be famous pieces. On the other hand, the strong Central-East European orientation of the English audience, whose tastes were guided by Germanic or foreign conductors active in London such as August Manns, makes this idiom no less appealing; when Manns conducted Dvořák's *Slavonic Dances* Opus 46 at the Crystal Palace in 1879, they were received with enthusiasm. One can almost be sure the same sort of reception greeted Stanford's Scherzo two years prior to the London hearing of Dvořák's Opus 46.

The Andante tranquillo was the sort of movement that both Stanford and Parry were experts at composing. Their wide experience as choristers and their writing vocal and choral music perfected a skill in turning out euphonious pieces, whether it be for chorus or orchestra alone. An affect of tranquillo is underlined by the con sordino coloring in the string choir. Stanford's *A* material (m.1) (Example XIV/18) is perfectly molded with its carefully controlled peaks and valleys. After the strings, the winds (m.18) take over for a different block of timbre. A third portion of *A* (m.37) uses soloistic colors accompanied by a walking bass, then the strings and winds combine for a climactic moment before unraveling to solo wind colors for closure. *B* (m.66) makes a daring move to E major, E-flat's Neapolitan. A fugue-like beginning never fully materializes and the fabric changes to an atmospheric homophony supported by a B-flat pedal, which forms the backdrop for a marcato, chorale-like statement

EXAMPLE XIV/18   Stanford. Symphony No. 1/3, mm.1–8.

in the horns. A cadenza-like clarinet passage leads to the return of *A* (m.105) in the winds, which this time is deftly embroidered by the strings. Only the first part returns before the coda (m.122) commences; *A* is interspersed with cadenzas for solo violin. Stanford's line reaches a climax (m.140) and then gradually disintegrates as the end approaches. Even in this early symphony, Stanford offers a thoroughly affecting composition almost without any echoes of Beethoven, Mendelssohn, or Schumann and with none of the awkward moments observed in the opening movement.

In the Finale, echoes of Schumann seem to predominate in the exposition from the first measure (Example XIV/19); the introduction corresponds unmistakably to the introduction of Schumann's Symphony No. 1/4. Stanford's *P* (m.9) also reminds one of Schumann with its full sonorities of the sort found in many of the piano works (e.g., *Carnival* Opus 9, *Symphonic Etudes* Opus 13). *T* (m.60) corresponds to Schumann's First Symphony's *2P* (m.30) in its orchestration, while *S* (m.92) has one of those quasi-canonic beginnings for which Schumann was also known. Stanford's development begins with an octave sonority sustained by a fermata that immediately recalls the same structural spot in the first and last movements of Schumann's Symphony No. 4. The Finale concludes with a Schumannesque accelerando (Symphony No. 1/4) and a timpani solo as found at the end of Schumann's Second Symphony. Why Stanford let stand a series of obvious references to a composer who was perhaps the most revered symphonist between Beethoven and Brahms is difficult to understand. But maybe it explains why Stanford, if not for reasons of nepotism, received second rather than first prize.

Except for the heavy borrowing from Schumann, on its own this is an effective Finale. Its *P* (m.9) has an energy thoroughly appropriate to its function; it is weighty enough in its own right, yet jovial in a distinctive way, without any reminiscence of the Classical *contredanse*. *Pᵏ* (m.45) builds on this by intensifying *P*'s driving rhythms. *T* (m.60) has more pointed timbres in contrast to the massive sounds of *P*, while *S* with its lyric line and rescored repetitions matches those in Potter and Bennett. *K* (m.139) brings back *P* in more contrapuntal garb. As in the first movement, Stanford at first indicated a repeat of the exposition, but then decided against a rehearing.

The development begins with a transition (cf. mm.154 and 161) that takes us to B major (m.162) and a fugato based on *P* (m.174). This disintegrates from what seems to be four-part to two-part imitative polyphony (m.206) undercut by uniform rhythmic values, and then to almost pure homophony. A second part concentrates on *S* (m.240) and almost immediately

EXAMPLE XIV/19   Stanford. Symphony No. 1/4, mm.1–24.

EXAMPLE XIV/19   (*continued*)

returns to B-flat (m.252) over a dominant pedal which culminates in the introduction's return and *P* for the recapitulation (m.293). Like many of the English symphonies so far examined, the recapitulation closely follows the exposition: *T* (m.344) is slightly abbreviated and *K* is eliminated to make way for the coda (m.406). The latter begins with a deceptive resolution to A-flat in octaves (another Schumann echo?) and continues with music that is rhythmically energized and accelerated, and is in its own way brilliantly scored.

After the presumed but undocumented Alexandra Palace performance in 1877, there was also a second rendition reported at the Crystal Palace on March 8, 1879, probably conducted by August Manns. One assumes this because Stanford's autograph score contains some conductorial markings in German. Concerning the reception of Stanford's First Symphony, the following notices were published in the *Musical Times* and *The Athenaeum:*

> The novelty at the concert on the 8th was the production of Mr. C. Villiers Stanford's Symphony in B flat. This work gained the second of the two prizes offered about three years since at the Alexandra Palace, when the first prize was carried off by Mr. F.W. Davenport. We are by no means disposed to rank the present among Mr. Stanford's most successful efforts; indeed we consider both his "Forty-sixth Psalm" and his "Festival Overture," written for Gloucester, far superior to it. That the work shows the hand of a trained musician need hardly be said; but the ideas are in parts too trivial for symphonic treatment; and there is a tendency to diffuseness which impairs the effect that the work might otherwise produce. The finale we consider the most successful movement; and it is only fair to Mr. Stanford to say that the orchestra is throughout treated skillfully, and sometimes with great felicity.[100]

> Now that the B flat has been heard, it is once more seen how difficult it is for musicians to write to order; the old remark is confirmed that there is little or no vitality in occasional music. The most ardent admirer of Mr. Stanford must have been pained, but certainly not surprised, at the solemn silence which succeeded the close of each of the four movements, for, except from a very few hearers, there was little or no applause. The main defects of the symphony are its inordinate length and its consequent over-elaboration. The *larghetto,* leading to the *allegro vivace* of No. 1, with some passages *obbligato* for the wood instruments, followed by the *scherzo,* No. 2, in G minor, with two trios in fast and slow time, the *andante tranquillo* in E flat, No. 3, were somniferous in their effect. The attention, however, was aroused a little by some display of vigour in the *finale allegro molto,* but it was not sufficiently startling to remove the evident conviction of the audience that the whole work, whilst it indicated here and there a knowledge of orchestration, was deficient in breadth and power. That Mr. Stanford, who is an Irishman, should be so impressed with the melodies of his own country as to reproduce them involuntarily is no doubt not surprising. The greatest composers will be at times carried away by a national impulse; but, strange to say, a Scotch subject had evidently haunted Mr. Stanford and the tune, "The Campbells are coming," mentioned aloud by some amateurs, is the source of the prominent *motif* in the *allegro.* Mr. Stanford has studied at Leipzig, where the tendencies of the German music of the present period is excess of modulation and to the abuse of iteration of the themes have influenced him. After all, it is much to be regretted that our young composers should waste their strength in essaying the symphony; in less ambitious productions they could win enough fame.[101]

It has been more than one hundred twenty years since this symphony was first heard. As a First Symphony, it is a distinguished beginning but not one that can compare to those by, for example, Carl Nielsen and Jean Sibelius. Nielsen's First is highly dependent on Brahms, but mostly in general ways. Today, with repeated hearings of the so-called standard repertoire, the kind of borrowing that Stanford commits would be heard by any sophisticated listener as a form of plagiarism. Therefore, Stanford's First Symphony would be an unlikely candidate for revival. From an academic viewpoint, it tells us something about the sources of Stanford's symphonic style, which are more fully concealed in the originality of the later symphonies.

SYMPHONY NO. 2 "ELEGIAC" IN D MINOR

In the intervening years between the First and Second Symphonies, Stanford wrote relatively few works that would prepare him to write another symphony more individual in its profile; apart from songs and choral music, there is a Sonata for Cello and Piano Opus 9, a Sonata for Piano and Violin Opus 11, and a Quartet for Piano and Strings Opus 15. The only big orchestral piece was the five-movement Serenade for Full Orchestra Opus 18 composed for the Birmingham Festival of 1881. This array of works, however, should not deceive for Stanford's Second Symphony (1882) represents a breakthrough, which to some degree is also evident in his Opus 18.

The title "Elegiac Symphony" is written on the first page of the manuscript without number or tonality together with four verses of section seventy from Alfred, Lord Tennyson's deeply admired and lengthy poem "In Memoriam":

> I cannot see the features right
>> When on the gloom I strive to paint
>> The face I know; the hues are faint
> And mix with hallow masks of night;
>
> Cloud-towers by ghostly masons wrought,
>> A gulf that ever shuts and gapes,
>> A hand that points, and pallid shapes
> In shadowy thoroughfares of thought;
>
> And crowds that stream from yawning doors,
>> And shoals of pucker'd faces drive;
>> Dark bulks that tumble half alive,
> And lazy lengths on boundless shores;
>
> Till all at once beyond the will
>> I hear a wizard music roll,
>> And thro' a lattice on the soul
> Looks thy fair face and makes it still.

The relationship of these four verses to Stanford's symphony is not at all clear. Are the four verses individually a reflection of each of the four movements? Or is it a general setting of the mood for the entire symphony? Are there passages in the symphony that correlate with some of these lines? None of these questions have been pursued, nor is there any way of finding an answer. A critic for the *Musical Times* and later J. A. Fuller-Maitland take the first line of the poem "I cannot see the features right" as a motto and a "key to the whole composition." Fuller-Maitland goes on to say, "There are some striking phrases on the brass instruments which recur at various points in the work, and the last movement, in which the face of the departed friend seems at last to be recognised, is ushered in by an introduction which gathers up the main themes of the preceding movements."[102]

There may be other clues to the meaning of this symphony in D minor in its musical allusions. On March 8, 1877, the Cambridge University Musical Society gave the first English performance of Brahms's Symphony No. 1 in C minor under the direction of Joseph

Joachim. While it is difficult to cite passages from the Brahms in Stanford's work, one can note some more general aspects. First is the general tragic mood that both works have in common. The first movement Allegro appassionato 6/8 recalls the Brahms in its treatment of the compound meter with cross rhythms. The last movement begins, for example, with a substantial slow introduction and ends with a coda (m.269) beginning in 6/4 / ₵ and contains a chorale that parallels Brahms's Finale. There are also allusions to several other works: in the Finale's slow introduction, the opening certainly recalls Schumann's overture to Byron's *Manfred,* and there is also an allusion to Wagner's *Siegfried* and *Götterdämmerung;* the horns proclaim a motif associated with Siegfried himself. In addition, *P* (m.43) of the Finale presents a timbre and tessitura that belongs to the celestial style as described by Berlioz. One critic of an early performance also heard Beethoven's Symphony No. 9/1 in the coda of the first movement—particularly in the ostinato (m.291), a technique which Beethoven also used in the codas of Symphony No. 7/1 and 7/4. In the Scherzo the dotted rhythms reveal another reminiscence of No. 9 as well as the Violoncello and Piano Sonata in A Major Opus 69. To this, one can add the rising chromatic line so prominent in the "Eroica" Symphony; it is compounded at the end of Stanford's Scherzo, which parallels the coda to Beethoven's third movement. The progress of the cycle from minor to major in a dramatic sense is characteristic of the two most famous C minor symphonies: Beethoven No. 5 and Brahms No. 1; Stanford, however, uses this device in a less dramatic manner. All these allusions bring to mind concepts that are congruent with the implications of Tennyson's poem: the heroic, the tragic, the celestial, and the progression from darkness to light.

Unlike the earlier English symphonies we have examined, Stanford's D Minor Symphony is the first to explicitly bring back material from a previous movement in the Finale's introduction and coda. After the opening *Manfred* motif (m.1), *P* of the first movement is recalled (m.2), then the main Scherzo theme (m.5) and its Trio material (m.8). The *Manfred* motif again is heard (m.12), and *I/P* is then developed by sequence and motivic reduction. Then again the Scherzo theme (m.18) is also developed as the tempo accelerates from its agitato start to the beginning of the Allegro, which proclaims the Siegfried theme in anticipation of the Finale's exposition. Another return is the chorale from the end of the third movement (m.179) in the Finale's coda (m.291). That Stanford restricts most of the cyclic recalls to the slow introduction of the last movement, rather than integrating them into the Allegro, also again brings to mind such models as Beethoven's Symphony No. 9/4.

Stanford's first movement is a wonderful piece of writing, reflecting the kind of metric flexibility in compound meters for which Brahms is so well known. Stanford does not so much emphasize the changes between 6/8 and its hemiolic equivalent 3/4, but treats them more subtly as passages can be read in either accentual configuration. This is true of *P* (m.14), *T* (m.36), *S* (m.56), and *K* (m.77) (Example XIV/20). Compared to Stanford's First Symphony, Symphony No. 2 is a tight piece of writing with an exposition of little more than eighty measures. Even *S* is not allowed the usual reorchestrated repetition that was so much a part of the practice in symphonies by Potter and Bennett. Instead, *S* is followed by an expansion before *K* is articulated. Even with the expository repeat, Symphony No. 2 is about half the length of the First Symphony's exposition with its repeat cancelled.

The development begins with material from the slow introduction minus *P*'s anticipatory motive. When *P* does appear (m.109), it now becomes a basso ostinato that Stanford treats carefully with regard to pitch; it moves upward in modules of diminishing size, thereby affecting a striking acceleration:

Px ———————————————————————————————————————→								
2×2	2×2	2×2	2×2	2×2	1	1	1	1
C		C-sharp		D	F	G	A	B
m.109		117		125	129	130	131	132

A *fortissimo tutti* climax (m.137) brings this portion to an end. Part two (m.144) works over *T* in further sequences undergirded by an ostinato. This texture is then inverted (m.154). More and more *T* comes to dominate the fabric culminating with a return to *P* (m.177) and another *fortissimo,* this time articulating the beginning of part three (m.183). Here the climax is sustained as the line peaks and builds (m.208). An assumptive switch in the bass to A as a dominant resolves to D minor and the recapitulation (m.222).

The exposition is further tightened in the recapitulation as each section is shortened. The coda (m.291) is built on another ostinato, but this time its repetitions remain on the same pitch as it circles D minor. Stanford intensifies the repeated shape by changing the bowings from one bow on a two-measure stretch |♩♪♩♩♪|♩♪♩♩♪| to one bow per three-eighth-note modules ♩♪♩♩♪♩♩♪♩♩♪. As the bass resolves deceptively (A–B-flat, m.307), another ostinato, with similar shape, moves into the treble and *crescendos* to another peak (m.321). It *crescendos* further to a *subito pianissimo* three times, followed by another *crescendo,* and then the movement ends quietly. In a sense, this is a Victorian response to the first movement of Brahms's C Minor Symphony; Stanford's is less intense and shorter, but nearly as skillful and in some ways as satisfying as the Brahms first movement.

To follow this first movement with the Scherzo, as Stanford did in his First Symphony, would be counterproductive; it would be too close to the compound meter and would not provide the proper respite from the activity of the first movement. Stanford's Lento espressivo in F major is another euphonious slow movement featuring, until its final portion, a Brahmsian richness in the orchestral sonorities; it serves as an appropriate foil to the first movement.

A two-measure upbeat for violas and cellos leads to the violins taking the theme (*A*) accompanied by a sustained background for clarinets and bassoons. The theme is repeated (m.11) with a background for violas and cellos. In *T* (m.18) solo wind colors are heard for

EXAMPLE XIV/20   Stanford. Symphony No. 2/1, Themes.

the first time as the tonality moves from F to C major. The episode (*B*, m.37) allows the violas to take the lead, which brings to mind the added movement to Bennett's last G Minor Symphony. Its repetition (m.45) is given to the clarinets with bassoons, flutes, and oboes joining in. The retransition (m.64) recalls a similar passage in the First Symphony as solo lines turn the orchestra into a chamber ensemble. *A*'s reprise (m.78) is carefully embroidered with sixteenth notes, sometimes added to the melody, sometimes to the accompaniment. In any case, the timbres as well as the embroidery provide a variation. At the end of the reprise, the tempo accelerates, the range peaks, the bass becomes more polaric to the melody, and the dynamic reaches *fortissimo* (m.111). The coda (m.119) takes up the material of the episode in an almost introverted way; except for an exclamation by the cello (m.129), the ending remains in its sentiment quiet and private with a distant fanfare for the horn and a *tutti pianissimo*.

The horn sound at the end of the slow movement comes to the fore at the beginning of the Scherzo with a *forte* rout that anticipates the Siegfried-like call in the Finale. Stanford for the rest of the Scherzo proper captures an almost Mendelssohnian mood: *pianissimo*, staccato, and a nimble surface. Otherwise, the movement only slightly departs from the normal large-scale ternary shape:

Scherzo Exposition	Development	Recapitulation		Trio		retrans.	Scherzo Exposition dal segno	Coda
P— T—S/K		*P—tutti*	*	*a*	*a* ‖:	:‖		
							(mm.8–48)	
m.7 25 35	53	79		94	105		143	148

Here the *da capo* consists of only the exposition before commencing the coda (m.148), which, as already mentioned, is an intensification of Beethoven's Symphony No. 3/3. But accompanying this is a persistent dotted rhythm (♩♩♩ ♩♩♩) that has a mesmerizing effect upon the listener just as it does in Beethoven's Symphonies No. 7/1 and No. 9/2. The two entries of the chorale (mm.179, 187) calm the surface in preparation for an introverted close.

Of special note is the orchestration, with its orientation toward choirs and at times the rapid dialogue among them. Of particular interest is the timpani, which participates in a dialogue with the *pianissimo* strings; only rarely, however, does the timpani rise to the dynamic level experienced in Beethoven's Symphony No. 9/2. To believe that Stanford's movement was significantly influenced by No. 9/2 is more difficult to support when one looks beyond a few not-so-telling characteristics.

After the impressive slow introduction with its combination of allusion, quotation, and reprise of motives from earlier movements as described above, Stanford begins the exposition with a celestial *P* (m.43). This affect is underlined by the absence of the orchestral bass instruments until *T(P*, m.64), where the theme appears in the bass and is imitated by the violins. This repetition of *P* as *T, tutti* and *fortissimo* with a more marked articulation, is a tradition that begins with Beethoven's Symphony No. 3/1. In contrast to Beethoven's Symphony No. 3/1, Stanford has both an elaborate modulatory plan, going beyond the necessary move from D to F major, and an intensive development of *P*. *S* (m.92) has the expected double statement, reduced orchestration, and tranquillo character. Notice its syntactical similarity to *S* of Brahms's Symphony No. 1/4: the second measure (m.93) is a variation and diminution of the first measure. Stanford's expansion continues to reveal its kinship with Brahms. *1K* (m.129) recalls the *Manfred* motive of the slow introduction, while *2K* (m.137) strongly asserts the dominant in this three-key (D major, F major, A major) exposition.

Without a repeat of the exposition, the development (m.150) is introduced by a reference to *S* and then proceeds with *T(P)* in the tonic (m.154), raising the expectation for an expository repeat. Instead, the expansion of *P* found in *T* is elaborated upon by moving to G-flat (m.168) and then after the beginning of the retransition to B major (m.187) and its satellite keys on the way to D major for a *fortissimo/tutti* recapitulation (m.204) beginning with *T(P)*. This already eliminates a large chunk of the exposition, but *S* (m.223) does return and is soon followed, without *K*, by the coda (m.269) marked Allegro molto ma non presto ¢. On the way to the Presto, Brahms's No. 1/4 is momentarily invoked (mm.259–264, cf. Brahms mm.279–290). The chorale comes twice (Example XIV/21), the second of which leads to the final cadences. Of the four movements of Stanford's Second Symphony, only the Finale ends on a note of triumph; movements one to three, as in Brahms's First, end quietly on a note of tragic resignation.

The "Elegiac" Symphony No. 2 is worthy of revival. With a committed interpreter, one could imagine its entrance into the repertoire. It deserves a frequency of performance comparable to the First Symphony of Sibelius. In contrast to Stanford's First Symphony, the references to other works seem less immediately obvious and better integrated into the total work, thereby not disturbing the composition's integrity. The "Elegiac" was first heard at the Cambridge University's Music Society conducted by the composer in March 1882. In 1883, the Gloucester Festival programmed the new symphony, but a critic complained that it could not be heard because of the din of the latecomers.[103] Fortunately, the listeners in Cambridge were more attentive to a long program that also included the Brahms Violin Concerto, Joachim's Theme and Variations in E Minor, Beethoven's *Coriolan Overture,* and Wagner's "Siegfried Idyll," all of which were being heard together with Stanford's piece for the first time at the CUMS. Reviews appeared in both *The Athenaeum* and the *Musical Times:*

> Three years ago a Symphony in B flat by Mr. Villiers Stanford was performed at the Crystal Palace, and those who were present on that occasion and who also heard the new Symphony in D minor on Tuesday, will agree with us that the progress made by the composer is really surprising. The later work, which was written in the summer of 1880, is, if we may be pardoned the expression, a head and shoulders taller than its companion. The ideas are more dignified, and the treatment altogether broader, freer, and more in the style of a master. Still, extraneous influence is not altogether absent, Beethoven being the composer who seems to have been most prominently in Mr. Stanford's mind. Thus, near the close of the first movement (a movement remarkable for vigorous, scholarly writing, and also for its attractive second subject) there is a passage recalling one in the corresponding portion of Beethoven's Ninth Symphony. In the charmingly melodious *lento espressivo* in F the influence of the Bonn master is absent; but in the *scherzo* another reminiscence of number nine occurs, and also one from the Piano and Cello Sonata in A. The *finale* in the tonic major is elaborate, and its merits cannot be accurately gauged from one hearing. But here, as in all the movements, the themes are developed with great skill, and the orchestration is exceedingly rich and varied. In short, the symphony is not only a clever but an interesting work, and it should find a place in one of the multitudinous orchestral concerts in London which are to be given this season.[104]

The second part of the Concert consisted solely of a new work by Mr. C. Villiers Stanford. The title "Elegiac Symphony" is accounted for by the fact that the lines in Tennyson's "In Memoriam" which begin, "I cannot see the features right," are appended to

EXAMPLE XIV/21 Stanford. Symphony No. 2/4, mm.287–307.

the work by way of motto. Yet the new Symphony in no way deserves the now some-what opprobrious name of programme-music, for realism of representation is neither intended nor attempted; merely the general feeling of the short poem being reflected in the musical composition. We may perhaps be permitted to see in the first three move-ments the variety of conflicting images that at first distract the poet's memory, and ulti-mately give place to the true presentment of the "fair face" of the departed friend, this last being figured forth in the final movement of the work, which is full of a serene calm-ness and solemnity. The first movement has for its first subject an impetuous theme in 6–8 time, given out by the strings, in marked contrast to which is a phrase that is heard on the brass instruments several times in the course of the movement, one of a number of phrases set in the same way, and of the same solemn kind, that appear at intervals throughout the

EXAMPLE XIV/21 *(continued)*

whole Symphony, giving it a peculiarly grave character. The slow movement is well worked out on a suave and flowing theme of great beauty. The Scherzo is full of spirit and energy, and contains a noticeable rhythmic figure on the drums, which is persistently adhered to even through the trio. At the close of the movement the introduction of another of the phrases above referred to leads us to expect a second trio, but the Scherzo stops immediately after the phrase has been heard. The Allegro of the last movement is ushered in by a long and elaborate introduction, based for the most part upon reminiscences of the three earlier movements, and having a somewhat turbulent and unsatisfied character. A broad phrase for the trumpets immediately precedes the very unpretentious

EXAMPLE XIV/21   (*continued*)

entry of the first subject proper, which is given out by the flute alone against sustained tremolo passages in the violins. By this method of treatment the most important subject of the movement is hardly given due prominence. This, however, is but a slight defect in an earnest and noble composition. Both the principal themes of the finale are calm and serene in character, but in other respects are in contrast to one another; the coda, *presto,* in 6–8 time, is very energetic and original, and the whole is brought to a solemn and most impressive conclusion by the last of the phrases we have mentioned before, a short choral-like strain of great beauty. The whole Symphony is by far the most important orchestral work by Mr. Stanford that has hitherto been heard.[105]

After these few performances, the "Elegiac" Symphony in D Minor passed from view. In part, this happened because only its composer had a score, and it was never published. To this day, Symphony No. 2 only survives in a fair copy, not in the composer's hand, in the Pendlebury Library in Cambridge. That such a careful source exists may suggest that Stanford was seriously considering publishing his symphony and using this copy for the engraver.

Some years were again to pass before Stanford embarked on another symphony. In the meantime, he again concentrated on choral works and songs as well as theater music, tackling only a few big cyclic instrumental works: a Piano Sonata Opus 20 (*ca.* 1884) and a Quintet for Piano and Strings Opus 25 (1887).

SYMPHONY NO. 3 "IRISH" IN F MINOR OPUS 28

Stanford's Third Symphony was his first public musical exploration of his Irish identity. A list of such works that either incorporate Irish materials into art music or collect and edit the tunes themselves makes one conclude that as Stanford matured, he became more interested in preserving his Irish heritage. Stanford collected, edited, and arranged national songs both independently as well as in collaboration with others. In 1915, Stanford published an article "Some Thoughts Concerning Folk-Song and Nationality" in the *Musical Quarterly* in which he discusses not only Irish music but also music from other areas, revealing for its time only a mild chauvinism, which perhaps is better characterized as a partiality.[106]

When the Third Symphony was published by Novello in 1887, it was prefaced by a brief note in Latin (see Plate B5a), translated below:

> Ipse fave clemens patriae
> patriamque canenti,
> Phoebe, coronata qui canis
> ipse lyra.
>
> Be thou gracious to my country,
> and to me who sing of my country,
> Phoebus, who thyself singest with the
> crowned lyre.

The reference to Phoebus and the crowned lyre refers to singing with the Irish national instrument, the harp, one of whose constructive characteristics is the presence on the royal coat of arms. In connection with this Symphony in F Minor, Stanford no doubt was thinking of the third movement, which is marked by extensive sections for the harp and the quotation of "Lament of the Sons of Usnach" as an accompaniment. Other quotations appear in the Finale (see composer's note in Plate B5b): "Remember the Glories of Brian the Brave," also known as "Molly McAlpin," and "Let Erin Remember the Days of Old." The dance movement is an Irish jig.[107] Other portions incorporate pentatonic and modal materials providing a style outside of what was then the mainstream of French/Germanic art music.

Nevertheless, Stanford's Third Symphony belongs just as much to the mainstream as do the "Italian" and "Scotch" Symphonies of Mendelssohn with their pentatonic and modal touches and their use of national dances. But Mendelssohn, unlike Stanford, does not take over folk materials and turn them into inspirational declarations or poignant slow movements; instead, he composes pieces that have come to be stylistically associated with a location. Like Mendelssohn, Stanford retains the four-movement cycle, but does not make it cyclic, composes in the forms expected, and treats them in a conservative way. For Mendelssohn, it is the "character" of the music that holds the cycle together as a unified entity; the same is true of Stanford's "Irish" Symphony. Perhaps the only specific gestures of cyclic unity in Stanford's "Irish" is the appearance of an incipient chorale at the end of

EXAMPLE XIV/22   Stanford. Symphony No. 3/1, Themes.

the first movement (*Pᵏ*, m.339) and at the close of the jig movement whose implications are only fully realized in the chorale on "Let Erin Remember the Days of Old" near the Finale's end (m.313).

The first movement begins straight away. Notice its quasi-modal quality, a result of the failure to raise the leading tone, and the interrelationships among the various thematic ideas. The former lends to the movement a national flavor; the latter recalls how totally Stanford had absorbed the subtle use of motive and intervals so characteristic of Brahms's writing. Example XIV/22 reveals some of these generative aspects. All of *P* (m.1) is clothed in the dark colors of octave strings and subdued chordal winds. *P* and *T* (m.42) are both concluded by a similar closing idea (m.33 and 55). A brief link (m.62) leads to *1S* (m.68), *2S* (m.79), and the two *K* ideas (mm.87 and 96), which are related in different ways to *2S*. Stanford again returns to repeating the exposition.

After a transition, the development gets underway (m.118) with material that is both vaguely familiar and new as it is made up of ideas and affects from the exposition. As these materials evolve, they weave a new fabric that culminates in the homophonic coming together with *Pᵏ* (m.136) in D major, G major, then C major before finally cadencing in A minor (m.153). The next portion (m.154) plays on the half step, as Brahms might have done, by isolating the interval and then restoring *1S,* which Stanford works over in the next section

EXAMPLE XIV/23   Stanford. Symphony No. 3/2, mm.1–12 (Strings only).

(m.183) on the dominant of A major. A retransition (m.203) on C-sharp, the enharmonic Neapolitan of the dominant, slips down to C-natural for the recapitulation (m.209) as the dominant undergirds the beginning of the return. This does not resolve to F minor until P^k (m.227), providing an effect in its *pianissimo* and *tutti* scoring quite different from the bare-bones octaves of the exposition's beginning. The recapitulation closely follows the exposition. A rather long transition (m.304) takes us to the coda proper (m.323) based on *1S* (m.324) and P^k (m.339). *Forte* is built up to four times before ending with another *tutti pianissimo*.

Concerning the traditional Irish genre to which the second movement belongs, we turn to Stanford's own discussion:

> It is not always easy to differentiate between Irish jigs and marches. The character of the music itself is the only safe guide. The jig rhythm is always in a 6/8 rapid tempo, and often infinite, i.e., devoid of any ending, and perpetually repeating itself. The hop-jig is similar to it, but in 9/8 time.[108]

Other characteristics that underline its Irish folk quality is the big upbeat with a fermata, the pizzicato accompaniment perhaps in imitation of a harp supporting a fiddler, the so-called Irish cadence with its three-repeated pitches on the tonic, and, except for the fermata, the almost perpetual motion (Example XIV/23). The Trio changes to 3/2 l'istesso tempo ♩=♩. with the triplets of the hop-jig changing to duplets. As it progresses this middle section (m.87), featuring the winds, becomes invaded by the Irish cadence now treated as an ostinato first in the strings and later in the timpani. In a way, this ostinato serves as a very long anticipation of the hop-jig's return (m.127). Stanford casts the movement in a large ternary form departing from the Classical model in that the first strain is repeated in the jig, the second strain in the Trio, and there are no repeats in the reprise. As in Symphony No. 2/3, the timpani is given a prominent role; here, the movement ends with a brash solo. Some might hear the concluding plagal cadence in relation to P^k of the first movement.

Stanford's slow movement has been characterized by John F. Porte as "one of the most poignantly expressive things Stanford ever composed. . . . The whole of this movement is music of the soul. It throbs throughout with deep emotion that grows in places to a heart-shaking sadness."[109] It was not so much the expressive aspects of the movement that gained comment early on, but the quotation from the "Lament of the Sons of Usnach" which is almost identical to the Phrygian opening of Brahms's Symphony No. 4/2. In these pages, Stanford's strong Brahmsian orientation has been noted. But here the controversy, if indeed there ever was one, is somewhat pointless because Brahms uses this motive as the introduction and the main thematic idea, while Stanford uses it as an accompaniment that emerges from the background only momentarily. Otherwise, the two movements are so different in character and realization that to make comparisons between them on the basis of a single identical motive would be a fruitless pursuit.

In this movement, Stanford combines elements of traditional aspects of folk with symphonic idioms. At the beginning comes the ricercare/toccata as the balladeer warms up on the harp with four, five, six, and seven subdivisions of the quarter note. The warm-up continues in the winds culminating with a cadenza for the flute (an Irish penny whistle?). The introduction begins again, and the main section (*A,* m.26) commences with the following shape:

| *a* | *k* | *a* | *k* | *k* + expansion | *a* + expansion |
| m.26 | 31 | 36 | 40 | 42 | 55 |

The two irregular strophes at the start give a nod to the folk aspects at least as perceived by a composer of Germanic art music. What follows beginning with m.42 and again at m.55 are expansions of a developmental sort also clearly belonging to Germanic art music. With *B* (m.66) comes the quotation from the "Lament of the Sons of Usnach" in the violas as the woodwinds play a new theme in D major (Example XIV/24), which takes a dark turn to D minor (m.75). *B* begins like *A* with two strophes, one each in major and minor, after which the fabric becomes developmental, which is quickly terminated by *A*'s return with two more strophes (mm.92 and 100). The close (*k*) becomes expanded in the second strophe and begins to modulate (to A-flat and D-flat), thereby infecting the folk material with symphonic means. Such a stance is continued in *C* (m.122), which has all the attributes of a learned composition: motivic development, polyphony, modulation, and the assemblage of complex fabrics. *A* (m.165) returns again in two strophes (mm.165, 173), but this time its presentation has lost much of its initial simplicity as the texture is thickly layered. A bar of silence (m.192) gives pause to these turns of events, and *B* (m.193) is again heard first in minor and then in major, the modal reverse of its previous presentations, and in something approaching a reprise of its simple fabric. The listener is returned to the folk idiom as the balladeer recapitulates the opening ricercare/toccata idiom. The movement concludes quietly with a plagal cadence and the warm colors characteristic of Brahms. This Andante serves as an emblem of Stanford's different musical inclinations: a composer steeped in Irish folk music, tempered by his scholarly tendencies and the traditions of an essentially conservative Germanic composer, who could not escape from the expected symphonic forms, procedures, and timbres.

EXAMPLE XIV/24 Stanford. Symphony No. 3/3, mm.66–76.

If the Andante reveals several of Stanford's musical proclivities somewhat compartmentalized, the Finale synthesizes with telling effect the national tunes with conservative Germanic tendencies. Though the two tunes quoted here are strongly profiled Irish creations, they gain full status as sonata form themes: "Remember the Glories of Brian the Brave" or "Molly McAlpin" is the generator of the introduction and becomes *P* (m.15), while "Let Erin Remember the Days of Old" is saved for the coda (m.313) and becomes a memorable chorale peroration for the entire symphony. Stanford's Finale is not a rondo, as J. F. Porte believes,[110] but a full-fledged sonata form without the expository repeat.

Stanford's treatment of "Remember the Glories" is rather special as it appears in three evolving stages: as the introduction where it is altered and fragmented, as *P* (m.15) where it is more fully realized, and as *2P* (m.32) where it is stated in its original and clearest form as a march with the woodwinds taking the lead. *2P* is stated twice, the second time as a triumphant *fortissimo tutti* (m.54) that in traditional fashion becomes *T* (m.61) (Example XIV/25). *S* is a Brahmsian statement in imitation of Symphony No. 1/4–*P* and No. 2/4–*S* with their stirring G-string theme here marked *con largezza* and *sonore* and immediately repeated by the woodwind choir in the tertian key of A-flat. *K* (m.112) brings back *2P* in the major as Stanford allows the tune to disintegrate back to its introductory form at the development's start (m.130). Thus, in a way, the exposition has a loose palindromic form:

Exposition						Development	
O	1P	2P	T	S	K(2P →)	1P	O

Since the expository repeat is absent, the development's *O* begins in the tonic. Within a few measures, Stanford takes us to F-sharp (m.137) and A minor (m.146) for an exploration of *S*. Unexpectedly, we find ourselves in A major for the introduction of "Let Erin Remember" (*N*) played quietly by the brass choir (m.162). A retransition ensues with *1P* (m.202) in G minor/B-flat, which finds its way to F minor (m.222), where the declaration of *2P fortissimo* by the full band (m.230) articulates the recapitulation. *S* (m.255) returns in D-flat making for a full axial third relationship of *S* to the tonic: F to A-flat in the exposition, F to D-flat in the recapitulation. Suddenly, "Let Erin Remember" (*N*) appears in the march topic of *2P* and indeed becomes confused with it. Just as suddenly, the surface rhythm stagnates (m.311), and *N* returns (m.313) to its chorale style interspersed with the major mode version of *2P* (m.320), which eventually is also augmented into a chorale presentation (m.351). For the end, through dynamics, orchestration, and thematic transformation, Stanford creates a stirring conclusion so that it becomes irrelevant whether "Remember the Glories" or "Let Erin Remember" arouses any national response, because the music transcends these quotations regardless of the listener's location.

There may be a certain irony to all this, but it was Stanford's "Irish" Symphony—a national and perhaps provincial work—that solidified his international reputation. It was first heard at the Hans Richter Concerts in London on June 27, 1887. Subsequently, it was performed in various venues throughout Great Britain, in Amsterdam, in Berlin and Hamburg under Hans von Bülow, in New York under Gustav Mahler (1910), and most distantly in Melbourne. A sampling of critical reactions in London follows. After the premiere *The Times* (London) reported:

> Mr. Stanford's new symphony, played under Herr Richter's leadership, is the third English work of that class which the great conductor has introduced to a London audience in the course of one month, and, like its predecessors, may be accepted as another and

EXAMPLE XIV/25   Stanford. Symphony No. 3/4, mm.52–61.

EXAMPLE XIV/25 *(continued)*

conclusive proof, if proof were needed, that our native school is progressing with rapid strides and in various directions. Mr. Stanford has denominated his symphony the "Irish," and in a Latin motto prefixed to the score calls upon Phoe bus for help in his patriotic endeavour of doing justice to the melodies of his native land. Even without this indication the most casual listener would observe that the rhythm and the type of melody prevailing throughout belong to the Green Island. On the subject of national music, which plays so important a part in modern art, much may be said. Various composers have applied various methods of giving local colour to their work; Liszt in his Hungarian rhapsodies copies the melodies of the people; Dvorak avoids doing so, but imitates the peculiarities of Bohemian fiddlers and popular minstrels instead. Mr. Stanford combines both these methods. There are a good many Irish melodies actually embodied in his music, and in addition to this he introduces the peculiar tonalities and scales which are in many respects akin to Greek modes and offer welcome material to ethnological students bent upon demonstrating the affinity between Celtic and Eastern races. The result is an extremely pleasing and in many respects remarkable work, which was acclaimed with enthusiasm by audience, and will no doubt materially enhance its composer's reputation. The first movement, *allegro moderato,* is essentially of a flowing, one might almost say lyrical, character. Here melodiousness of a high type is combined with scholarship and ingenuity of device, and the instrumentation adds considerably to the effect of the materials presented, the entire symphony, indeed, marking in this respect a considerable advance upon Mr. Stanford's previous efforts. The second movement, which takes the place of the *scherzo,* is cast in the form of a so-called hop-jig, and in accordance with that name is full of life and bustle, the suave melody of the trio bringing welcome relief. But the gem of the symphony is undoubtedly the slow movement, the dreamy melancholy of which conveys an intense poetic impression. Here the local colour is laid on with the hand of a master. A prelude for the harp in combination with the flute leads to a beautiful "lament," the melody of which is all the more remarkable for its broad development, because it springs from a simple germ of only four notes. The final *allegro* is the least flowing and the most laboured of the four movements, although here the composer embodies two old Irish melodies—a fact which should give pause to those who think that it is easier to borrow a tune and treat it artistically than to invent one. A masterly performance was an almost foregone conclusion in the circumstances, Herr Richter never conducting with more care and energy than where the production of an English work is concerned.[111]

The *Musical Times* missed the premiere under Richter, but commented on the rendition for the Novello Oratorio concerts:

The third Concert of the season, given on the 15th ult., had a mixed programme, comprising three works very far removed from each other in character. Of these, one—Mendelssohn's Psalm 114—has long ranked among the classics of sacred music, and needs no further discussion. Another—J. F. Barnett's "Ancient Mariner"—represents a type of Cantata in the Mendelssohn school, which was much in vogue twenty years ago; while the third—Stanford's "Irish" Symphony—illustrates the present strong tendency towards the utilisation of national melodic forms for purposes of high class music. The Concert, therefore, had no ordinary interest for intelligent amateurs, many of whom attended it. Professor Stanford's Symphony was taken first of the three, and enjoyed the benefit of a good performance under the composer's direction. So much has been said of late in this and other journals regarding the increased attention paid to national characteristics in music, that we shall not now trouble the reader with renewed discussion of that very interesting topic. But we may express gratification that a leading British musician has given a practical proof of the importance it assumes in his view, and that his national Symphony has so far won a frank and undoubted success. By the way, the two best symphonies of the young English school are both based upon local characteristics. We refer, of course, to the "Scandinavian" of Mr. Cowen and that at present under notice. The fact has a significance not to be overlooked or put aside. Professor Stanford was greatly favoured by the decided character and powerful charm of Irish melody. Indeed, he found the most potent of all musical forces ready to his hand, and he cannot be blamed if, in addition to inventing themes, Irish in form and spirit, he adopted two examples that have long been traditional in his native land. These occur in the *Finale,* where amateurs delightedly recognise "Remember the glories of Brian the brave" and the grand strains of "Let Erin remember the days of old." The second movement, or *Scherzo,* is Irish to the core, thanks to the hop-jig tune forming its principal feature; while the slow movement derives its national character from a harp prelude, and the reiteration of a single short phrase known as the "Lament of the sons of Usnach." As for the opening *Allegro,* the scale largely employed serves, in conjunction with other devices, to make that movement scarcely less national than its companions. Professor Stanford, it is clear from the foregoing, has not carried out his idea in a half-hearted way. The Symphony is distinctly what it pretends to be, and for all its shaping and elaboration according to classic models, cannot be regarded as other than it is. We need scarcely add that it abounds in thematic beauty, or that the composer has worked up his charming materials to excellent purpose, adding to melodic interest that which arises from skilful development and tasteful colouring. We make bold to predict unusual favour for the "Irish" Symphony; encouraged thereto by the enthusiasm it created in St. James's Hall, where all seemed pleased with it.[112]

Negative reactions to Stanford's "Irish" were few, but among them was George Bernard Shaw, who, being the "perfect Wagnerite," could not look always positively at a work called a symphony. Shaw wrote at least two columns with comments on the "Irish" Symphony. The first of these appeared without attribution in the *Pall Mall Gazette* on May 15, 1888:

> As for Mr Villiers Stanford's Irish symphony, it is only an additional proof that the symphony, as a musical form, is stone dead. Some such structure as that used by Liszt in his symphonic poems would have admirably suited Mr Stanford's fantasia on Irish airs. The effect of mechanically forcing it into symphony form has been to make it diffuse and pedantic. Since Bach's death, the rule as to fugue has been "First learn to write one, and then don't." It is time, and has been ever since Beethoven's death, to extend the rule to the symphony.[113]

A longer and certainly excessive tirade was published in *The World* on May 10, 1893, from which we provide only a selection:

> But in the recent cases where the so-called folk music is written by a composer born of the folk himself, and especially of the Celtic folk, with its intense national sentiment, there is the most violent repugnance between the popular music and the sonata form. The Irish Symphony, composed by an Irishman, is a record of fearful conflict between the aboriginal Celt and the Professor. The *scherzo* is not a *scherzo* at all, but a shindy, expending its force in riotous dancing. However hopelessly an English orchestra may fail to catch the wild nuances of the Irish fiddler, it cannot altogether drown the "hurroosh" with which Stanford the Celt drags Stanford the Professor into the orgy. Again, in the slow movement the emotional development is such as would not be possible in an English or German symphony. At first it is slow, plaintive, passionately sad about nothing.
>
> According to all classic precedent, it should end in hopeless gloom, in healing resignation, or in pathetic sentiment. What it does end in is blue murder, the Professor this time aiding and abetting the transition with all his contrapuntal might. In the last movement

the rival Stanfords agree to a compromise which does not work. The essence of the sonata form is the development of themes; and even in a rondo a theme that will not develop will not fit the form. Now the greatest folk songs are final developments themselves: they cannot be carried any further. You cannot develop God Save the Queen, though you may, like Beethoven, write some interesting but retrograde variations on it. Neither can you develop Let Erin remember. You might, of course, develop it inversely, debasing it touch by touch until you had the Marseillaise in all its vulgarity; and the doing of this might be instructive, though it would not be symphony writing. But no forward development is possible.

Yet in the last movement of the Irish Symphony, Stanford the Celt, wishing to rejoice in Molly Macalpine (Remember the glories) and The Red Fox (Let Erin remember), insisted that if Stanford the Professor wanted to develop themes, he should develop these two. The Professor succumbed to the shillelagh of his double, but, finding development impossible, got out of the difficulty by breaking Molly up into fragments, exhibiting these fantastically, and then putting them together again. This process is not in the least like the true sonata development. It would not work at all with The Red Fox, which comes in as a flagrant patch upon the rondo—for the perfect tune that is one moment a war song, and the next, without the alteration of a single note, the saddest of patriotic reveries "on Lough Neagh's bank where the fisherman strays in the clear cold eve's declining," flatly refuses to merge itself into any sonata movement, and loftily asserts itself in right of ancient descent as entitled to walk before any symphony that ever a professor penned.

It is only in the second subject of this movement, an original theme of the composer's own minting, that the form and the material really combine chemically into sonata. And this satisfactory result is presently upset by the digression to the utterly incompatible aim of the composer to display the charms of his native folk music. In the first movement the sonata writer keeps to his point better: there are no national airs lifted bodily into it. Nevertheless the first movement does not convince me that Professor Stanford's talent is a symphonic talent any more than Meyerbeer's was.[114]

SYMPHONY NO. 4 IN F MAJOR OPUS 31

The tremendous success of his Third Symphony, particularly in Berlin, resulted in Stanford working on his Symphony No. 4 (1888), which was separated from No. 3 by only two *opera:* the incidental music to *Oedipus Tyrannus* (Cambridge, 1887) and a set of lyrics "A Child's Garland of Songs," with texts by Robert Louis Stevenson. One piece from *Oedipus Tyrannus* was taken into the second movement of the symphony. Its premiere was at a concert of the Berlin Philharmonic on January 14, 1889, conducted by the composer; the program was made up exclusively of music by Stanford including the Prelude to *Oedipus*, a new Suite for Violin and Orchestra (Joseph Joachim was the soloist), the ballad "La belle dame sans merci," and two Irish folksongs (in the latter three works the singer was Rudolf von Milde). In England, the first performance was a month later at the Crystal Palace on February 23, 1889, conducted by the ubiquitous August Manns.

As with Symphony No. 2, which was prefaced by lines from Tennyson's *In Memoriam*, and Symphony No. 3 with Latin lines by Stanford, Symphony No. 4 has a couplet motto at its beginning:

Thro' Youth to Strife
Thro' Death to Life

Such a motto represents an archetype found in the symphonic genre such as Beethoven's Symphony No. 5 or Mahler's Symphony No. 1. Indeed, the normal symphonic cycle, particularly those that begin in the minor and end in the major mode, can fit this motto with ease. Since the middle two movements often change places, death can be either a mournful slow movement or a macabre Scherzo. Any Allegro movement of the right character can easily represent youth or life.

Stanford's Symphony lays out its cycle as follows: 1. Allegro giojoso, 2. Intermezzo e Trio, 3. Recitativo-Andante maestoso, and 4. Finale: Allegro. Since the main part of the Intermezzo was from the *Oedipus* music, where Stanford tried to capture the increasing afflictions to the family of Oedipus, there can be no question that this movement, despite its hymn-like Trio, portrays strife. The generally optimistic first movement certainly fulfills the mood of youthful aspirations. As for the slow movement, it is an operatic *scena* for orchestra with a lengthy beginning in the style of a recitative followed by a deeply serious aria with passages of celestial music (mm.94, 173). The Finale has the required *joie de vivre*.

In the view of the annotator for the Crystal Palace premiere, the Finale does not measure up to the motto's requirements:

> [T]he composer seems to have contented himself with depicting the happiness of freedom from this world's cares rather than to have attempted the impossible task of representing the state of life after death, as the motto would lead one to expect.[115]

But one might suspect that some of what the annotator expects could have already been captured in the slow movement's celestial music, which the second time anticipates the Finale's *P* theme (m.173), leaving the Finale as a continued revelation of one person's desire for the heavenly life. J. F. Porte views the motto and the symphony as autobiographical.[116] However, it should be remembered that this motto generates not a programmatic piece in the narrative sense, but a characteristic one requiring only a general capturing of an affect with the rest to be filled out by the listener. In the end, not too much should be made of the motto; according to J. A. Fuller-Maitland, it was dropped two years after the symphony's first performance.[117]

Like his earlier symphonies, Symphony No. 4/1 is not without reminiscences of earlier composers; again, Stanford's models are Beethoven and Brahms. The triple-meter first movement with its *P* that initially outlines the tonic triad almost immediately brings to mind Beethoven's Symphony No. 3/1 "Eroica" and Brahms's Symphony No. 2/1. Other passages support the general impression that Stanford had these two pieces in his mind. From Beethoven, the *T(P)* *fortissimo* restatement in the exposition (m.31) can be traced to the "Eroica," the *fortissimo* recapitulation of quieter expository material is found in a number of Beethoven symphony movements, and the indications "Ritmo di tre battute" (m.367) and "quattre battute" (m.385) are again markers of Beethoven's Symphony No. 9/2. Some may also wish to connect the opening of the third movement with its recitative to Symphony No. 9/4, but Stanford's recitative gives a totally different impression; it is more like something out of an Italian opera. As for Brahms, connections are not only made to the shape of *P* but also to the warm scoring of *S* (m.54). Also reminiscent of Brahms's No. 2/1 (m.183) is the beginning of the development (m.124) with the quasi-canonic treatment of *P* with trombone scoring (m.124, see Brahms No. 2/1 m.224), the lengthy undulating horn solo (m. 178, see Brahms No. 2/1 m.455), and the calm and graceful allusions to *P* (m.367, see Brahms No. 2/1 m.477). Additionally, the Intermezzo second movement, which replaces the Scherzo, is a hallmark of Brahms's third movements, and aspects of its texture and fabric also recall the German composer. Finally, the Trio with its duple meter and chorale-like material recalls a work that played a role in Stanford's Symphony No. 1: Schumann's Symphony No. 2/2. In the Finale, the alteration of the *P* material from quadruple subdivisions of the beat to triple ones also recalls the end of Schumann's Symphony No. 2/4, which in turn, because the triplet quarter notes occur in the coda, forms a parallel with the coda of Brahms's Symphony No. 1/4. Yet, as in Stanford's Symphonies Nos. 1 and 2, the allusions found in his Symphony No. 4 transcend their sources and become an integral part of the composer's own idiom.

The Allegro vivace e giojoso's exposition is organized in a traditional fashion with a repeat of the section, a triple statement of *P* with the third statement introducing *T* (m.31), a double statement of *S* (m.54) with varied orchestration, and two *K* themes (m.97) with the first one related to *P.* The course of the tonality as it moves from F to C for *S* requires notice; Stanford first moves toward G (m.31), then B-flat minor (m.35), and declares B minor (m.41). The key now slips, after a grand pause, to the dominant of C in preparation for *S* (m.54). After *S,* another area of transition takes us to A-flat major/F minor for the beginning of *K* by means of another series of declarative chords (mm.99–102) that return us again to the tonic for the exposition's repetition.

After an epilogue (m.113) to the exposition, the development proper commences (m.124) with the trombones intoning *Px* canonically against which the basses play a version of *Sx*. This is answered by *Py* in the clarinet, and the entire passage is repeated. *Px* is also contrapuntally combined with *Py* (m.140) as the entire *P* becomes a counterpoint to itself. This culminates in a massive homophonic *fortissimo* (m.153), based on a rhythm from the seventh bar of *P,* that enharmonically modulates from A minor to E-flat. This slips down to D for an exploration of *S* (m.170) concentrating on extending its concluding motive (*Sy*), which Stanford stretches out to some twenty measures with fragments of *Sx* intervening. *Sx* leads to a section in C-sharp minor (m.199) again treating *Sx* and *y,* which turns to D-flat (m.219) and *Px*'s return (m.231). Surprisingly this section in D-flat becomes the retransition as D-flat slips down to C, the dominant of F (Example XIV/26). Within a single beat a *fortissimo* recapitulation (m.247) is upon us. This sudden shift from D-flat to the tonic is one of the few miscalculations in all of Stanford's symphonies; it is only magnified by the occurrence of *Pxm* and *n* simultaneously. Why this otherwise leisurely development section is marred by a hasty conclusion is inexplicable.

The recapitulation is unlike any of Stanford's previous symphonies in that it is reformulated and its tonal scheme is somewhat unusual: *S* returns first in A (m.297) and then in F major (m.315). Furthermore, *P* and *S* are treated to further development (mm.280, 348, 356, 367, 385). The sections meant to be beat as three- and four-measure groups (mm.367, 385) may seem to defeat an accelerando in the phrase rhythm, but the four-measure groups are in reality two-measure modules so that the music moves from three (9/4 bars) to two 3/4 bars (equaling 6/4 bars) and culminates with five measures of 4/4 (♩=♩) before returning to 3/4. At this point, Stanford employs an acceleration with one-bar units that pushes to the final cadence.

The first movement would have given Bernard Shaw all the ammunition he would have needed against academic composers. Excepting one miscalculation, Stanford produces a piece that displays all kinds of technical facility in counterpoint, in the handling of pace, and in its effective, though not flashy, orchestration. It lacks what his "Irish" Symphony had in abundance: distinctive themes.

The Intermezzo clearly also belongs to Stanford's Brahmsian streak. Its counterpart is Brahms's Symphony No. 1/3: both have a similar metric plan with a section of simple duple meter contrasted by one in duple-compound time with some mixtures of simple and compound duple meters occurring simultaneously. Immediately, one is struck by the relationship

EXAMPLE XIV/26   Stanford. Symphony No. 4/1, mm.239–54.

EXAMPLE XIV/26   (*continued*)

of the opening theme to *I/Sy,* one of the most Brahmsian gestures of the first movement. Unlike the counterpoint in Brahms's symphony, Stanford's opening section unfolds by increasing the complexity of the fabric through rhythm. Thus, the first large portion of this Intermezzo progresses from essentially pure compound meter (mm.1–50), to simple duple and compound operating simultaneously (mm.51–77), followed by the layering of simple duple eighths and sixteenths with sextuplet sixteenths and simple triplet subdivisions (mm.78–101). In contrast, the Trio is introduced by a sudden simplification of texture going on into the Trio proper, which has a hymn-like fabric. The return of the opening section moves from the rhythmic equivalent of mm.1–50 to 78–101. Stanford's coda (m.219) returns to the relative simplicity of the opening with an almost compound presentation; it combines the opening of the main section and the introduction to the Trio. Notice the movement's unusual tonal plan: A minor–A-flat–A minor. The tempo marking, Allegretto agitato, reflects its intended character, though one could argue whether the music itself is convincingly agitated.

A serious posture is immediately established for the Andante (Example XIV/27) by the *pianissimo* invocation in D minor of the horns and trombones, a timbre of the funereal. This gesture becomes an *exordium* to the recitative that builds its declarative statements into polyphony. Stanford's musical conversation becomes more animated and builds to a *tutti/fortissimo* climax of the invocation. At the end of the recitative, the conversation slows and becomes hushed. The Più Andante is an aria that is bifurcated between the D minor of the funereal and the D major of the celestial. The former with the accompanying strings imitates the muted roll of the drum and centers on the darker orchestral timbres. This builds to the climax/refrain. The latter stresses the sound of the harp and the higher winds; its melody derives from the recitative. This, too, leads to the climax/refrain. The D-minor material returns (m.132), becomes more funereal, and again builds to the climax/refrain. New celestial music is heard (m.173) and the Finale's theme is adumbrated. This leads again to a climax based on the invocation, which withdraws to a quiet conclusion.

While not as immediately appealing as the slow movement of the "Irish" Symphony, this is Stanford's most substantial and original slow movement. Here, he does not accept a traditional presentation of his themes in ternary, rondo, or sonata form. Instead, he adapts an operatic *scena* in an original way for orchestra. A polyphonic recitative is probably a rare encounter in opera and is not known in the instrumental styles during the nineteenth century. The interactions of recitative, refrains, aria strophes, climactic passages, and characteristic styles make for a special experience. It is the apex of the cycle as the protagonist vacillates between the anguish of death and the promise of life, a conflict fully resolved in the Finale, but not at its very beginning.

Stanford starts the Finale with three defiant chords on G minor, D minor, and C major, ending after a few flourishes with B-flat, a supertonic seventh, and a dominant six-five chord to which the timpani responds with the root played *fortissimo*. *P* (m.14), with a folk-like character, commences a sonata-form or rondo movement (see Table XIV/15). The crux of the distinction here rests on the return of *P/A* at m.141. Prior to this occurs a normal exposition with a double statement of *P/A* (mm.14, 34), followed by a *T* (m.47), a double statement of *S/B* (mm.80, 89), and a relatively weak *K* (m.101). At this point, *K* is considerably expanded into a section that could be heard as the beginning of the development, but then *P/A* returns briefly in the tonic (m.141). This can either be heard as the refrain's return in a rondo or as a false return of *P* that in the last quarter of the nineteenth century often occurs when there is no expository repeat. A big expansion or a second development follows (m.159); within the rondo scheme, this would be the developmental second episode, *C.* However, this section is too long for one of those post-expository developments that often occur after *P*'s recapitulatory

EXAMPLE XIV/27   Stanford. Symphony No. 4/3, mm.1–13.

return. Now *S/B* (m.316) returns not in the tonic, but the Neapolitan (D-flat), followed by *K* (m.337) in the tonic. That *S/B* never returns in the home key is very unusual for either structure. Indeed, the presence of *K* in both the exposition (m.101) and recapitulation might speak against the rondo. One sure function is that of the coda (m.358) with the temporary metric change from ¢ to 3/2. Here, Stanford builds a peroration based on *P/A* first by metric elongation, then by extremes of dynamic and range, and finally by a learned working out as *P/A* is simultaneously heard in imitation with its inversion (m.363) over a dominant pedal.

TABLE XIV/15
Stanford. Symphony No. 4/4: Structure

Sonata or Rondo Form

Allegro non troppo ¢

Introduction	*Exposition*						
O	P	P	T	S	S ext.	⌒	K
	A		T	B			
mod.	F major			C major			C major
m.1	14	34	47	80	89		101

Development 1	*Recapitulation*		*Development 2*				
K	P		T		P		S
	A		C		A	T	B
retrans.							
C major	F major		mod.		F major		D-flat
127	141		159		262	281	316

Poco Tranquillo	Animato 3/2 ¢		Maestoso e sostenuto	
	Coda		*Introduction*	
K	P		O	
	A			
dominant mod.	dominant		F major	
pedal	pedal			
337	358	363	375	

The return of introductory material (m.375) is followed by an area of tonal stability with a tonic pedal leading to the final cadences.

After performances in Berlin and in London at the Crystal Palace in early 1889, the new symphony was given notice in both German and British musical journals from which some excerpts follow:

> The principal feature of last night's Concert was an unpublished Symphony, the latest work of the composer. The subjects, which are well defined, have been worked out with extraordinary skill, and the whole effect of this very remarkable piece of writing is clear and sonorous. . . . It is difficult to say which is the most successful movement, for the style of the Symphony is even and well sustained throughout, but we should be inclined to distinguish more particularly the second and third, on account of the greater warmth of feeling by which they are characterised.[118]

> The principal work performed was Mr. Stanford's new Symphony in F major. All four parts compel the attention of the hearer to the development of the themes and the gracefulness of the melody, but the first and fourth are especially remarkable for these qualities. Few composers attain such delicacy and transparency of instrumentation.[119]

Professor Stanford's new Symphony, which was performed for the first time in this country at the Concert of the 23rd ult., fully justified the high praise bestowed upon it by the Berlin press. It is not only exceedingly interesting as a piece of scholarly workmanship; it is also full of fresh and genial thoughts. The *Intermezzo,* already known as an *Entr'acte* to the composer's "Oedipus" music, is thoroughly graceful and attractive; but it is in the slow movement that the composer has put forth his whole strength. We have not space to do more than indicate the singularly effective introduction of the second subject, in which the harp accompaniment plays a most prominent part, and the impressive climax in which the movement culminates. The *Finale* is a most spirited movement, in which one can hear the instruments, as though endowed with human voices, for ever reiterating the word "Freiheit." The first principal subject is a fine and original tune, a fact on which we lay the more stress because the second subject of the first movement is practically indistinguishable from the theme of the first of Brahms's *Liebeslieder* (first series). The performance was on the whole excellent, though the *Intermezzo* was taken too slow and the *Finale* somewhat hurried. In conclusion, we have no hesitation in pronouncing this Symphony to contain the best and maturest work which Professor Stanford has yet done. It exhibits the qualities of head and heart in completer equipoise than is to be met with in any of his previous compositions.[120]

After its initial performances, Stanford's Fourth did not receive, like the "Irish" Symphony, repeated hearings. Despite its skill and drive, and a piece rich in the execution of its ideas, this was not enough to engage the interest of the conductors. Perhaps the reason why lies with the ideas themselves. By 1890, Brahms was the composer of currency, and his symphonies had reached canonic status in the ears of the English audiences. Stanford's indebtedness to the German master that was noted in the last review, particularly in the first two movements, would also have been recognized by conductors and audiences. In an era where originality was valued, such a work could not easily enter the repertoire.

A half-dozen years were to pass before Stanford embarked on another symphony in 1894–1895. In the meantime, some twenty-five *opera* appeared, including chamber music (a piano trio, a cello sonata, two string quartets, etc.), the *Festival Overture* Opus 33, and some incidental music. Most of Stanford's efforts were devoted to song, church music, and oratorios/cantatas for the regional choral festivals.

SYMPHONY NO. 5 "L'ALLEGRO ED IL PENSIEROSO [*SIC*]"
IN D MAJOR OPUS 56

Stanford's Fifth Symphony was commissioned by the Philharmonic Society of London for its 1895 concerts at which it was first heard on March 20. It came in the second part of a program that included two blockbusters: Tchaikovsky's First Piano Concerto and Beethoven's *scena* "Ah! perfido" as well as a Cherubini overture (*Les deux journées*) and a Chopin Scherzo (Opus 39). Considering that prior to this commission the Society had only performed Stanford's "Irish" Symphony, the request comes as something of a surprise. However, another symphony (No. 7) was later to be commissioned by the Philharmonic for its centenary season in 1912.

The Fifth's cyclic structure is centered around lines from Milton's poems *L'Allegro* and *Il Penseroso,* which are attached to each movement (see Table XIV/16). The first two movements—an Allegro and the dance movement—represent *L'Allegro*'s lines of happiness and jollity, while the second part—Andante molto and an Allegro Finale—represent "il pensieroso [*sic*]," the thoughtful and spiritual. Though the plan of movement tempos is the same as observed in

TABLE XIV/16
Milton's *L'Allegro* and *Il Penseroso*:
Sections Quoted in Stanford's Symphony No. 5

L'Allegro
1st Movement: Allegro moderato

1	Hence, loathed Melancholy,		25	Haste thee, Nymph, and bring with thee
	Of Cerberus and blackest midnight born			Jest, and youthful jollity,
	In Stygian cave forlorn			Quips and cranks and wanton wiles,
	'Mongst horrid shapes, and shrieks and sighs unholy			Nods and Becks and wreathed smiles,
5	Find out some uncouth cell.			Such as hang on Hebe's cheek,
	When brooding Darkness spreads his jealous wings,		30	And love to live in dimple sleek;
	And the night-raven sings;			Sport that wrinkled care derides,
	There under ebon shades and low-browed rocks,			And Laughter holding both his sides,
	As ragged as thy locks			Come and trip it as you go,
10	In dark Cimmerian desert even dwell.			On the light fantastic toe;
	But come thou Goddes fait and free,		35	And in thy right hand lead with thee
	In heaven yclept Euphrosyne,			The mountain-nymph, sweet liberty;
	And by man, heart-easing Mirth;			And if I give thee honour due,
	. . . .			Mirth, admit me of thy crew.
				. . . .

2nd Movement: Allegro grazioso

53	Oft listening how the hounds and horn			When the merry bells ring round,
	Cheerly rouse the slumbering morn,			And the jocund rebecks sound
55	From the side of some hoar hill,		95	To many a youth and many a maid,
	Through the high wood echoing shrill.			Dancing in the chequer'd shade;
	. . . .			And young and old come forth to play
	While the ploughman, near at hand,			On a sun-shine holy-day,
	Whistles o'er the furrow'd land,			Till the live-long day-light fail:
65	And the milkmaid singeth blithe,		100	Then to the spicy nut-brown ale,
	And the mower whets his scythe,			With stories told of many a feat
	And every shepherd tells his tale			How faery Mab the the junkets eat;
	Under the hawthorn in the dale.			. . . .
	. . . .		151	These delights if though canst give,
91	Sometimes with secure delight			Mirth, with thee I mean to live.
	The upland hamlets will invite,			

Il Pensieroso [sic]
3rd Movement: Andante molto tranquillo

11	But hail, thou goddess sage and holy,		51	But first, and chiefest, with thee bring
	Hail, divinest Melancholy!			Him that yon soars on golden wing
	Whose saintly visage is too bright			Guiding the fiery-wheeled throne,
	To hit the sense of human sight,			The cherub Contemplation;
15	And therefore to our weaker view		55	And the mute Silence hist along,
	O'erlaid with black, staid Wisdom's hue;			'Less Philomel will deign a song
	. . . .			In her sweetest saddest plight,
31	Come, pensive nun, devout and pure,			. . . .
	Sober, steadfast, and demure,		61	Sweet bird, that shunn'st the noise of folly,
	All in a robe of darkest grain			Most musical, most melancholy!
	Flowing with majestic train,			Thee, channtress, oft the woods among
35	And sable stole of cypress lawn			I woo, to hear thy even-song;
	Over thy decent shoulders drawn:		65	And missing thee, I walk unseen
	Come, but keep thy wonted state,			On the dry smooth shaven green,
	With even step, and musing gait,			To behold the wandering Moon
	And looks commercing with the skies,		68	Riding near her highest noon,
40	Thy rapt soul sitting in thine eyes:			. . . .
	. . . .			

	TABLE XIV/16 (*continued*)			

4th Movement: Allegro molto

73	Oft, on a plat of rising ground		155	But let my due feet never fail
75	I hear the far-off curfew sound			To walk the studious cloister's pale,
	Over some wide-water'd shore,			And love the high-embowed roof,
	Swinging slow with sullen roar:			With antique pillars massy proof,
	. . . .			And storied windows richly dight
97	Sometime let gorgeus Tragedy		160	Casting a dim religious light:
	In scepter'd pall come sweeping by			There let the pealing organ blow
	Presenting Thebes, or Pelops' time,			To the full-voiced quire below.
100	Or the tale of Troy divine;			In service high and anthems clear,
	. . . .			As may with sweetness, through mine ear,
151	And, as I wake, sweet music breathe		165	Dissolve me into ecstasies,
	Above, about, or underneath,			And bring all Heaven before mine eyes.
	Sent by some spirit to mortals good,			. . . .
	Or the unseen Genius of the wood.			

Symphony No. 4, here the poetic program also divides the cycle into parts, a concept used previously by Spohr, Raff, Mahler, and certainly others. But the extra-musical aspects of this piece is unlike Symphony No. 4's relationship to its motto in that Stanford writes something more than a series of characteristic pieces; he actually paints some of the images put forth in Milton's lines: the brooding of the very beginning, the imitation of laughter, the hunt, the Queen Mab–like atmosphere, another song of the nightingale, and at the end of the piece the addition of the organ to the orchestra. These events and others will be cited as each movement is observed from the extra-musical and structural viewpoints.

Apart from the unity offered by the program, thematic material also recurs in various movements, making Stanford's Fifth his most cyclically conceived symphony to date. Though the second movement seems immune to any reminiscences of previous thematic material, the Andante third movement recalls the first movement within its middle section (m.69), its coda anticipates the beginning of the Finale, and the end of the Finale recalls the beginning of the third movement. Thus, as appropriate, "il pensieroso" is given the most careful thematic consideration. If the programmatic aspect unifies two juxtaposed pairs, the tonal scheme, as expected, provides cyclic coherence with the first and last movements in the same key and the two central movements in the subdominant and the relative major of its minor (G/B-flat).

The first movement contains two oddities in the context of Stanford's symphonies: the introduction begins in the tempo of the Allegro followed by a Più lento (m.21) and a return to *tempo primo* (m.30) before the exposition (m.38). Otherwise, the exposition is presented without peculiarity except for a central motive labeled *l* (m.66)

1P	2P	T	l	S	1K	2K
D —————————→				A —————————→		
m.39	49	54	66	72	86	96

for its obvious imitation of laughter in the Milton text.

The introduction and the exposition seem to take in the entire text that accompanies the first movement. We propose the following correspondences of measures to line numbers:

Stanford		Milton			
					Introduction
m.1		line 1	Allegro moderato	D minor	*1-O*
m.10		line 4			
m.22		line 7	Più lento		*2-O*
m.30		line 11	Tempo 1	D major	
					Exposition
m.39		line 25			*P*
m.66		line 32			
m.72		line 33		A major	*S*
m.82		line 38			

Nevertheless, whether one agrees with the specificity of the above parallels, the fact that one can find correspondences underlines an important change in Stanford's approach to the extra-musical.[121] While one can certainly boil the exposition down to two characteristic styles, darkness and mirth, there seems to be something more operating here.

Stanford's development section (m.102) begins with *P* in E minor, which is expanded and modulates to the dominant of C major (m.126) and a leggiero theme that is both new (*N*) and still has much in common with *S*. *S* follows in augmentation (m.137) as the background retains its rhythmic bustle and the tonality moves toward and establishes B minor. A tranquillo epilogue (m.154) suddenly allows the surface to slow as *1K* is quietly presented in augmentation. B minor slips to C major (m.159), and the surface rhythm and tempo both accelerate to Più lento and then Tempo 1. Finally, the dominant of D is established for the recapitulation (m.190).

As has been the case with the previous two first movements, Stanford tightens the recapitulation. This time he begins with *2P*, cuts *T*, restates *1* (m.206), which now ends with a fermata over the bar line, and moves directly to *S* (m.211) and the two *K* themes (mm.226, 236). The coda (m.242), Più lento, reprises a part of the introduction, and after the Tempo 1 is reached, *N* is heard in the tonic. Mirthful music takes over, the tempo accelerates, and the movement ends with a burst of laughter.

The relationship of the dance-like second movement to the text is more obvious as Stanford conjures up the musical codes for the pastoral in the Allegretto grazioso: the drone, the horns playing intervals of their natural state (thirds, sixths, and fifths), the emphasis on woodwind colors, the rhythms of the siciliano, and the strong, if not all-pervading, diatonicism. One can, however, also find more specific similarities between music and text:

Stanford		Milton			
m.1	*A*	lines 53–56	Allegretto grazioso 6/8	G major	
m.14		lines 63–64			
m.30		line 65			
m.53		line 66		G → D	
m.95		line 67		G → D	
				G	
m.116	*B*	lines 91–94	Più mosso 2/4 (Quasi Presto)	E-flat major	
m.163		line 96			

A is then recapitulated (m.196) followed by a Prestissimo 2/4 (m.296), which perhaps takes in lines 100–102, certainly lines 150–51, and contains material from *A* and *B*. As can be seen, the shape of this movement is that traditionally associated with the symphonic dance movement: *A–B–A*–Coda. *B* (Example XIV/28), with its fleet scales and lightness of timbre and fugal textures, recalls not the Mendelssohnian idiom, but more that of Berlioz in his famous evocation of Queen Mab in the Scherzo from his *Roméo et Juliette* Symphony. Perhaps its most

EXAMPLE XIV/28   Stanford. Symphony No. 5/2, mm.116–39. © 1923 by Stainer & Bell Ltd.

EXAMPLE XIV/28   (*continued*)

striking aspect is the juxtaposition of the fantastic in the nineteenth-century sense with the learned style.

The texts Stanford quotes at the beginning of the third movement commence with the eleventh line of Milton's *Il Penseroso*, an invocation to melancholy, followed by couplets concerning a "pensive" nun (lines 31–40), and Philomel, the famed avian singer, better known as the nightingale (lines 51–57, 61–66). The Andante is in a sonata form and similar to the first movement in that most of the parallels to the poetic lines occur in the exposition; here they extend into the central development section (m.53).

A five-measure introduction begins with full string sonorities and modal materials. The introduction and *P* (m.6) follow the verse's three couplets as the range of the materials reflects the "too bright . . . saintly visage" by beginning with a''' in the first violins. *P*'s beginning in its dark G-string theme (sonore) accounts for lines 14–16 about the darkening of light so that it can come within the realm of human vision. *P*'s brightness increases as it unfolds but never achieves the height of its beginning. There is essentially no *T* as the putative dominant key is only hinted at (mm.23–24) but then the expected *S* (m.26) is heard in the tonic. Here, Stanford paints the scene of the nun in her dark robe: he begins with the violas and cellos arpeggiating the harmonies supported by bass pizzicatos as the clarinet and bassoon carry the melody which rises, and the violins joined by the flutes carry the line to its highest peak c'''' as the movement reaches a climax, perhaps analogous to the spiritual achievements of the contemplative life. A brief, darkly hued *K* (m.49) serves more as a transition to the middle/development section (m.53); it represents lines 51–57 and 61–68 concerning the nightingale. Stanford paints this with an agitated background as the flute and clarinet imitate bird song. The sonority builds to a brief interruption by a first-movement motive (I, m.30; IV, mm.69–72) after which the avian music resumes (m.79); this builds and then diminishes on the way to the transition and an abbreviated reprise (m.95). *P* is followed by *K* inverted (m.116) and in diminution. Then *S* (m.119), also in diminution and inversion, ushers in the coda. Measures 127ff, given its position, may very well be another adumbration of the Finale's opening. One then detects the first Brahmsian echo (m.134). Specifically, Brahms's Symphony No. 3/2 has a similar ending with the mixture of dark horns and trombones against celestial strings, a juxtaposition that gathers together the two governing concepts of this Andante: worldly darkness and contemplative celestial light.

The Finale is substantially different from the previous movements in that its overall shape is a sonata form preceded by an introduction and concluded with a coda. The relationship here between the music and Milton's verses is mixed as the introduction and coda rather clearly paint the text, while the exposition's relationship to the text is not clear. Stanford's introduction (mm.1–8) imitates bells and within the exposition another passage (m.33) seems to represent "Over some wide-water'd shore." For the next explicit portrayal of the text one must wait until the entry of the organ (m.459), which remains a significant sonority for the remainder of the movement. After the organ entrance, lines 162–66 may be reflected in m.575 to the end as the music dissolves to one note in the trumpet from which a final climax is built and withdrawn in the quiet final chords. Notice that the material beginning with m.584 seems to be an altered version of the invocation hailing "divinest melancholy."

The exposition is all of the same dark and subdued timbre and strikingly undifferentiated in surface structure. Because of the nature of the bass line one expects the piece at any moment to become a passacaglia, a ground, or some similar type. But this never happens in the *P* (m.9)—*T* (m.55)—*S* (m.123)—*K* (m.159) exposition; one must wait until the development (m.199), which is paradoxically an ostinato with permutations. One wonders if the scholarly side of Professor Stanford is coming to the fore; was he paying tribute to the leading composer of "grounds," the English master, Henry Purcell (1659–1695)?

The development begins (m.199) quietly as a regular ostinato with three statements, then the pattern begins to change but still maintains its identity as each measure of the four-bar module maintains its shape despite pitch changes. Like Purcell's concept, the ostinato phrase does not coordinate with phrase ends and beginnings in the upper voices; however, Stanford never achieves the imaginative levels that Purcell revealed in this procedure. By m.247, the ostinato migrates into the treble as the bass momentarily comes close to that of *P.* The surface has quickened as quarters become eighths, a *crescendo* occurs, and the sonority thickens as the woodwinds and horns add a new layer in 6/8 while the heavy brass and strings remain in 3/4. This leads to a dominant-seventh of C in the strings, while woodwinds, horns, and trumpets emphasize D. Four bars of this bitonal approach resolve to D and the *fortissimo/tutti* recapitulation (m.279).

The recapitulation is about thirty measures shorter than the exposition, but it still adds new material before, within, and after *T* (m.328). *S* (m.383), except for the key, remains very close to its expository counterpart, but *P* is considerably shortened, and *K* is expanded by two times to accommodate the entry of the organ. Stanford's unusual tonal preparation for *P*'s return and its brevity in the recapitulation may perhaps explain *P*'s reappearance at the start of the coda (m.539). However, one might expect the preparation to be that of the dominant of D. Instead, Stanford sets up a bifocal situation in the retransition by a D and F major preparation with the E half-diminished chord resolving to D minor (mm.538–39) for a maestoso declaration. The final section transfers to D major (m.584) and concludes with celestial music.

Stanford's Fifth Symphony is an extraordinary piece both for its inherent merits and for its place in Stanford's evolution as a composer. In Stanford's symphonic output, it is his most original symphony; it is almost impossible to cite thematic, textural, sonorous, or structural aspects from his favorite models. Indeed, there is only one passage at the end of the third movement that echoes Brahms, and this allusion would probably be missed by many sophisticated listeners. Together with Symphony No. 7, Symphony No. 5 is Stanford's most accomplished work. That it is an organ symphony immediately brings to mind the Saint-Saëns Symphony No. 3 (1886), a work that gained a following in England where it was first performed in 1886 and repeated with the composer conducting at the Philharmonic Concerts of June 1895 and certainly on other occasions. But the similarities between Saint-Saëns's wonderfully lyric and bombastic piece and Stanford's more restrained and reflective cycle are insignificant. One could even program both on the same evening with only the most superficial of parallels drawn and without any sense of duplication.

Reviews from the Philharmonic premiere of Stanford's Fifth appeared in both *The Athenaeum* and the *Musical Times,* as follows:

> It would not be fair or reasonable to offer dogmatic opinions on such an ambitious and elaborate work as Prof. Villiers Stanford's new symphony "L'Allegro ed il Pensieroso," which was produced by the Philharmonic Society on Wednesday evening, after a first hearing; but if initial impressions may be trusted, the composer has surpassed all his previous efforts in this direction, not excluding the beautiful "Irish" Symphony. Of course, Prof. Stanford has taken Milton's poem as his source of inspiration, but there are no grounds of comparison between his symphony and the choral settings of Handel and Dr. Hubert Parry. The first movement, after a grave introduction, is appropriately bright and genial, and the second is delightfully pastoral. The slow movement, illustrative of the lines commencing "But hail! thou goddess sage and holy," is the most difficult to grasp on first acquaintance. The *finale,* with a happy introduction of the organ towards the close, is at once fresh and impressive. So much for the present on a work which most certainly does honour to its composer and to British musical art generally.[122]

> Professor Stanford's new Symphony is not a thing to be judged off-hand, and while, so to speak, it is flying past the observer. Besides, it would be a poor compliment to speak with an air of authority after one glance at a work upon which an eminent musician has exhausted the resources of his art. "L'Allegro ed il Pensieroso" must be heard again, and studied on paper, if haply that is possible, before such an attitude can safely be assumed by critics, unless, indeed, they wish to pass as mere recorders of impressions. But, while reserving definite opinions regarding the Symphony as a whole, we may say that a large part of it appealed to one's sense of satisfaction, by the charm and propriety of the themes, and their skilful as well as picturesque treatment. Everywhere could be seen the deft hand of the practised musician, going straight to the point and working out results with ease and certainty. Our feeling is that the Symphony will largely improve upon acquaintance and take its place among Mr. Stanford's best works.[123]

It is unfortunate that the critics did not have opportunities to hear this symphony for further comment. Unlike the Third and Fourth Symphonies, which were published with some dispatch by Novello, the Fifth Symphony was published in 1923 by Stainer & Bell, underwritten by the Carnegie United Kingdom Trust, which was publishing the Carnegie Collection of British Music for the advancement of music in the British Isles. The Trust evaluated Stanford's symphony:

> A work written in 1894 of remarkable freshness and individuality. It should be enjoyed not only for its intrinsic merits but because it represents a phase of British music of which the composer was a pioneer.[124]

Its merits were certainly recognized then and should be recognized today. It is a British symphony worthy of revival and should find a place at least on the edge of the repertoire.

A decade was to pass before Stanford finished his Sixth Symphony. This decade saw the production of some thirty-eight works including all the other important instrumental genres—concertos, string quartet, violin sonata, *Irish Rhapsodies,* string quintets—as well as liturgical works, oratorios, collections of Irish national songs, and his opera that became something of a hit, *Shamus O'Brien* (1896).

SYMPHONY NO. 6 IN E-FLAT MAJOR OPUS 94

The Sixth Symphony is directly titled as such on the autograph. For its first performance, however, a subheading was added: "In honour of the life-work of a great artist: George Frederick Watts." It has been assumed, apparently based on statements by the composer, that the music of this symphony was inspired by various creations of Watts, considered by some to be the English Michelangelo. According to J.A. Fuller-Maitland,

> The music seems to represent four phases of the painter's art, and there is a Death theme that is easily recognisable; the slow movement has a very important part for *cor anglais* (is this representative of Love?) and the scherzo struck one hearer as suggesting the charming picture "Good luck to your fishing," while the finale might be taken as the musical picture of the equestrian statue in Kensington Gardens ["Physical Energy"].[125]

Lewis Foreman states that these citations from Fuller-Maitland originated with Stanford and that the paintings and statue established the character of a given movement.[126] He further expands on Fuller-Maitland by specifying that "Good Luck to your Fishing" is a whimsical vignette of an angling cupid found in the Trio of the Scherzo. Other Watts pictures cited by Stanford were "Love and Life" and "Love and Death." Foreman also claims that the opening of the slow movement is a "Love" theme and that there is a "Death" theme of a dirge-like character that appears first in the opening movement as a "third" subject (m.159?). More accurately, this is at best a new theme (*N*) in the development that serves as a response to a motive derived from *S*. According to Foreman, the "Love" theme rises while the "Death" idea descends.[127] However, the only themes designated by a special characteristic marking are: II/mm.48, 147 teneramente, and IV/m.227 solenne. The indications "Love" and "Death" are not inscribed at any place in the autograph. Perhaps these commentaries were derived from the program notes of the London Symphony Orchestra, but this material has not been seen.

There is, however, apart from the Watts pictures and statue cited by Stanford, another poetic or extra-musical element that comes at the end of the symphony where an apotheosis of sorts occurs beginning with the section marked solenne (m.227). Here, something approaching the opening of the second movement returns in imitation, rises to a celestial climax, and then diminishes in power as a clear recollection of the "Love" theme is heard in alternation with IV/*P*. The Symphony ends quietly with a pizzicato stroke in the strings that articulates the final chord in the winds with its swell and a *diminuendo*. This ending again recalls the quiet close to Brahms's Symphony No. 3/4.

How strongly the cyclic concept operates in Symphony No. 6 depends on what constitutes a theme and how closely it must follow something presented earlier. For this commentator, it must be more than a rising or descending melody; it must be an immediate aural recognition of something heard earlier in the cycle. Nevertheless, the opening theme of the slow movement becomes a rather prominently recalled idea in the Finale particularly in transitory areas and near the end of the piece. In its original statement, the intervals rise and then fall within a two-measure statement. Quite clearly this falling line in II/mm.1–2 is rather

EXAMPLE XIV/29   Stanford. Symphony No. 6/1, mm.1–23. Stanford Archive, University of Newcastle upon Tyne Library; used by kind permission of the Royal School of Music.

different from I/m.159 where the descending line moves entirely by step rather than several different intervals.

Stanford also has his last two movements flowing continuously. This is achieved by a l'istesso tempo in that four measures of the Scherzo equal four beats of the 4/4 transition that takes us to the Finale. Additionally, the second movement is in B major and the C minor Scherzo begins not on C, but on B-natural and eventually finds the way to its tonic. Having the slow movement in B major (C-flat) is not uncommon in a cycle whose tonic is E-flat. Haydn used this enharmonic relation (Hob.XV:29, 31) and most notably so did Beethoven in his "Emperor" Piano Concerto. Its effect is to move from one musical realm to a strikingly new one.

EXAMPLE XIV/29 (*continued*)

Stanford's first movement is an invigorating affair marked Allegro con brio 6/8 with materials that fulfill its appellation. Much of this comes from its descending syncopated *P* (m.1) that finds its first cadence (mm.21–22) with a powerful downbeat articulating both the end of *P* and the beginning of *T* (Example XIV/29). *1T* (m.22) is a short development of *P*, while *2T* (m.72), whose nineteen measures one might consider as too long for its function, provides both a lead-in and an adumbration of *S* (m.91). Nevertheless, the tonal plan of this expansive *T* does reflect moves one might expect in a development section: to the parallel minor of E-flat (m.33), a descent of the bass line from m.35 to m.43 that takes us toward G-flat (m.48), then toward the dominant of B-flat (m.65), which is diverted from the resolution (mm.69–71) and finally resolves with a full cadence (mm.90–91). Compared to *T, S* (m.91) occupies only thirty-two bars, and since *T* has already foreshadowed its content, its definition is through tonality. *K* takes precedent one step further as it is based on both *P*'s syncopations and motives from *S* and ends with a cadence (mm.142–43) as powerful as that at the end of *P.*

Stanford moves directly to the development (m.144). Beginning with *P* in the dominant,

EXAMPLE XIV/29   (*continued*)

the tonality moves upward through fifths: B-flat, F (m.151), C (m.159), G (m.170). Now the bass moves upward in groups of four notes: mm.171, 176, 181, 183. Then the bass moves downward (m.184) to the dominant of the relative minor (m.189) and from there to another descent (m.197). Through this entire swath, material from *S* is worked over. The texture thins for a new lead-in to *S*, but when *S* arrives over the dominant of C (m.225) the full resolution anticipated from the lead-in never occurs. The bass again begins its descent (m.245), the harmonic rhythm slows, the solo violinist takes the lead, and *circulatios* rise to the tonic of E-flat with another powerful cadence that again defines the formal boundaries (Example XIV/30).

The recapitulation (m.282) is almost Classical: *P* is mostly left intact, *1T* is done away with, *2T* (m.303) remains, *S* (m.325) is greatly expanded, and *K* is excluded. One might think that all the emphasis on *2T* and *S*, since these two elements have been treated so thoroughly, might be counterproductive in the recapitulation. But such emphasis certainly remains effective

EXAMPLE XIV/29 *(continued)*

in performance. Another big tonic cadence (mm.397–98) defines the coda and brings back *P*, which leads to a series of powerful cadences bringing this Allegro con brio to an assertive and exciting conclusion.

By any measure this is one of Stanford's most effective and rhythmically active first movements. One might think that for a composer so taken with Brahms a movement in 6/8 would be loaded with hemiola; however, Stanford has not a single triple subdivision of the measure. There are only duple divisions of the beat and syncopations crossing over the bar line. Stanford also resists being taken in by two other powerful first movements in 6/8, Beethoven's Symphony No. 7 and Mendelssohn's Symphony No. 4 "Italian"; not a single passage even vaguely brings them to mind.

EXAMPLE XIV/30 Stanford. Symphony No. 6/1, mm.257–82. Stanford Archive, University of Newcastle upon Tyne Library; used by kind permission of the Royal School of Music.

As noted, the Adagio is in B major, clearly setting it apart from the first movement. Cast in a free ternary form, its most striking aspect is its internal tonal scheme.

A				B				retrans.	A	
a	b	a	k	Aa	b	a	b		a	k
B ————————————————→				V/C	F	V/D	B-flat ————————→		B	
m.1	27	36	48	58	76	84	95	111	124	147

EXAMPLE XIV/30 (*continued*)

Notice the progression of B to C and B-flat to B; this maintains the half-step upward slip and then repeats it down a half step to return to the tonic at the end. Buried within this plan is a measure of thematic development in *Ab* and in *B* where *Aa* is worked over in sequences and in inversion.

The *Aa* material is the so-called "Love" motive. According to Foreman, one critic found this theme comparable to Watts's female figures with their "ample dignity."[128] It is concluded with a tag (mm.10–12), which with its five-fold repetition, its short-long rhythmic pattern,

EXAMPLE XIV/30 (*continued*)

and its rising minor thirds and perfect fifths remind one of an open Irish cadence. As Sidney Waddington said of Stanford's speech: it was an "Irish brogue crafted onto a Cambridge idiom."[129] One might also say the same of this theme with its perfect syntactical presentation combined with an Irish musical idiom.

One is struck by both the subtleties of the details and the overall beauty this movement possesses. Right at the start (Example XIV/31), Stanford's orchestral mastery is revealed by the use of the English horn rendering a melody of close intervals accompanied by lower strings

EXAMPLE XIV/30   (*continued*)

with the timpani intoning a funeral march rhythm followed by the entry of flutes, clarinets, and bassoons with the arpeggiating harp to punctuate the end of the first subphrase (m.4). At the larger level, the refrain is carefully laid out with changing blocks of sound:

EH	Upper W.W.	Strgs.	EH	*Tutti*	W.W.	EH	W.W.
Lower Strgs.	Violins		Strgs.		Hrn.	Strgs.	Strgs.
m.1	13	27	36	44	48	50	52

EXAMPLE XIV/30   (*continued*)

EXAMPLE XIV/31   Stanford. Symphony No. 6/2, mm.1–12. Stanford Archive, University of Newcastle upon Tyne Library; used by kind permission of the Royal School of Music.

But notice how the rhythm of timbre changes as the movement begins in large groupings, then diminishes down to two-measure units becoming a prime source of motion in this Adagio molto. In *B* (m.58), the color changes less regularly at the start, but by m.76 the timbre modules are larger, then diminish in size and again broaden in preparation for the movement's climax (m.122). The above description provides only the shell of Stanford's multifaceted control.

Though not indicated as such, the Presto 3/4 is a Scherzo with an unmarked Trio (m.123). But unlike the usual form, both the material of the Scherzo and the Trio return abbreviated in the tonic, so that one might, since there are no binary repeats, hear this as a sonatina shape:

Scherzo	Trio	Scherzo	Trio
P	*S*	*P*	*S*
C minor	A-flat	C minor/major ⟶	
m.1	124	242	306

EXAMPLE XIV/31 (*continued*)

In *S,* one is reminded of the Scherzo/Trio to Beethoven's Symphony No. 2/3 in its sense of movement, but, as noted earlier, in this symphony such allusions are rare, and when they do occur, are far removed from the putative model.

The end of the Scherzo moves directly to a transition section (m.1) that combines the pace and material of the Scherzo, introduces *P* of the upcoming Allegro in augmentation, greets the Finale with distant fanfares, and gathers these increasing sonorities with a *crescendo* to *fortissimo* (m.29) that leads to the Finale proper (m.35). The layout is formally close to Stanford's other later expositions in that its material is homogeneous, the exposition is not repeated, and, as in the first movement, *T* is in two parts (mm.60, 80) and accounts for a large portion of the exposition. However, here *S* is obviated by a brief *S/K(P,* m.110). Perhaps the most notable aspect of this Finale's material is its *Pomp and Circumstance March* idiom which manifested itself in Parry's and many of Elgar's works and spread to Stanford, Walton, and many others. It became an emblem of English national music throughout the world, characterized by a boisterous pesante first section and a lyric Trio scored initially for quiet strings in their darker range, often with horns doubling the melody followed by a *tutti forte* repetition. Stanford only incorporates the boisterous pesante portion of the style.

Rather than concentrating on *S* for the development section (m.122), after the bass rises from B-flat to D, a fugato based on *P* commences (m.127). It is followed by a lyric interlude (m.148) related to II/*Aa* in which its elements are treated rather freely. The retransition (m.163) continues with II/*Aa* less dissembled over a D pedal that moves downward to C and then to B-flat for the recapitulation (m.176). Again, the reprise is under-articulated and is tightened (exposition: 121 mm.; recapitulation: 50 mm.), but with the essence of all its functions. The coda to this movement and to the entire symphony marked *solenne* has already been described. In its own quiet way, the ending provides an effectively introspective and moving conclusion to this fine work.

According to the singer and his biographer Harry Plunket Greene, Stanford reportedly stated that the Sixth was his own favorite among his symphonies.[130] It was first heard in a performance by the London Symphony Orchestra conducted by the composer on January 18, 1906. The reception was favorable as the following reviews from the *Musical Times* and *The Athenaeum* indicate:

> The programme of the fourth concert at Queen's Hall on January 18 included Sir Charles Stanford's new Symphony in E flat (Op. 94), written "in honour of the life-work of a great artist, George Frederick Watts"; and it was performed for the first time under the direction of the composer. According to the analyst the work has no programme, and should be listened to simply as music. The composer, however, mentally worked to Watts' fine piece of sculpture called "Physical energy," and to his two pictures, "Love and Life," and "Love and Death"; but so clear is the form of the various movements, so straightforward the developments of the thematic material, that the work may be fully appreciated quite apart from the source or sources whence the composer sought inspiration. There are many modern works in which the form is so absolutely determined by what is known as the "poetic basis," that knowledge more or less of the latter is indispensable. In the case of the symphony under notice such knowledge, however, is decidedly interesting. In the opening *Allegro* the syncopations of the principal theme seem to betoken rugged strength, a salient quality of the great painter's personality, while the phrase for trombones which follows the melodious second theme is naturally associated with Death. The slow movement is based on a flowing theme, the *Scherzo* is full of rhythmical life, while the *Finale*—if not perhaps the strongest of the four movements—has many points of interest. Throughout the work the scoring is admirable. At the close of the performance Sir Charles was recalled several times to the platform.[131]

> One thing strikes us particularly in the music: the absence of anything sensational or extravagant. Much modern music produces an immediate effect by means of strange rhythms, strong colouring, and striking contrasts; yet when one comes to study the scores the actual musical substance often proves to be very slight. In the symphony under notice all the interest created is produced by natural, not artificial means. The workmanship is sound, and there is organic development; the orchestral colouring, too, is of the best. We must frankly say that the impression produced on us was not strong, because, in spite of all the skill displayed, the thematic material of the first and last movements did not strike us as very original; but possibly familiarity with the work might modify our opinion. We listen again and again to the symphonies of the classical masters, and we find that each fresh hearing seems to reveal new and unexpected beauties. With our native composers years may—do, in fact, in many cases—elapse before a second hearing of their works is granted. How, then, can they be properly appreciated, properly judged?

The slow movement of Sir Charles's symphony seems to us the most poetical, and the Scherzo the most piquant. The performance was good, though the composer did not display quite his usual firmness and energy.[132]

Stanford's E-flat Symphony, even though given the Opus number of 94, was never published and thus like so many works could only with persistence and difficulty enter the repertoire of conductors, who needed to receive the performance materials directly from the composer. Apart from the London Symphony Orchestra premiere on January 18, 1906, its only follow-up performance was a year later in Bournemouth. After this, the score seems to have rested in the composer's collection and in two additional manuscript copies reportedly at Stainer & Bell in London.[133]

The fate of Stanford's Sixth seems to have nothing to do with either the quality of the symphony or its reception, but with the availability of the music. For example, in J. F. Porte's monograph on Stanford with thumbnail overviews of each work, he can only say of the Sixth that it was not published. Together with the Fifth Symphony, this work deserves a place on the edge of the repertoire. This is music lively, reserved, and profound representing something emotionally opposite of Gustav Mahler's approach to the genre. Still audiences will certainly respond and not be disappointed by Stanford's E-flat Symphony, particularly if it is taken on its own terms.

In the six-year interval between the Sixth and Stanford's Seventh Symphony, his output was again much the same, with a variety of works in various genres and settings ranging from large-scale vocal works to a Nonet for Winds and Strings and songs for voice and piano as well as solo works for organ and piano. If one sensed with the Fifth and Sixth Symphonies a refusal to compose works of unusual length for a large orchestra, such an idea is further confirmed by the Seventh.

SYMPHONY NO. 7 IN D MINOR OPUS 124

Stanford composed the Seventh (1911) in response to a commission from the Royal Philharmonic Society as one of a series of works that celebrated their centenary; other composers receiving commissions included Elgar, Parry, Cowen, Mackenzie, German, and Davies. It differs from Stanford's earlier symphonies in that there are no extra-musical connotations to be dealt with; its orchestra is slightly smaller; its length is shorter—according to the composer it lasts but twenty-five minutes; and its expression is at times austere in ways that conjure up the Sibelius of the Third Symphony. Also like Stanford's Third, and in the tradition of Beethoven's Seventh and Eighth symphonies, there is no true slow movement.[134]

Most striking is that Stanford has departed in other ways that affect the most basic aspects of the symphonic cycle. Sonata form, though present, is really only operative in the first movement and here in a very compact rendering. Movements two and three are variation-based structures: the second is a Tempo di Minuetto with variations that destroy the strophe of the theme, while the third movement is a theme also followed by a series of five variations that run directly into the Finale, whose opening is based on the third movement's materials. One thus thinks the beginning of the last movement to be a sixth variation. Within the Finale, there also occurs a recapitulation of *II/P* (m.224). One might ask why Stanford after six symphonies without a variation movement would compose two such pieces adjacent to each other. Perhaps he was affected by two British sets of orchestral variations: Parry's *Symphonic Variations* of 1897 and Elgar's *Enigma Variations* of 1899. In addition, considering the profound effect Brahms had on Stanford, the so-called *Haydn Variations* and Symphony No. 4/4 must have had some impact.

Stanford's first movement is about fifty percent shorter than that of the Sixth. Yet all the expository functions are formally present, the development is strong but only fifty-three measures in length, and the recapitulation acts very much like that of its predecessors, with judicious exclusions and a coda. There is no room for an introduction here; Stanford commences *P* softly and dolce with a lean texture and modal inflections. *P*'s single big period (21 m.) is heard but once, then the Più animato *T* (m.22) changes to a more aggressive character with a Brahmsian touch. *S* still preserves its double statement (mm.42, 50), but its character is close to *P*. Stanford's orchestration of *S* (Example XIV/32), however, is more colorful in a Sibelian sense with layers of activity buttressed by strumming cellos and the upper strings exchanging triplet arpeggios. The oboe takes the lead, while other winds sustain the harmonic rhythm. With *S*'s repetition, the strings and winds exchange roles with the violins taking over the melody, which peaks both in range and dynamics, but only at *forte* minus the heavy brass. *K* (m.65) repeats the end of *S*, has a molto tranquillo lyric statement, and quietly disintegrates melodically.

The development (m.76) returns to *T*, the exposition's most aggressive music. It becomes tranquillized and turns to *S* (m.109). *T* is undergirded by a rising bass over some twenty bars, while *S* establishes A-flat, a tritone to the tonic, and then heads toward D and the recapitulation (m.129). Here, Stanford makes an unprecedented move among his own symphonies: *P* itself does not return, and after two measures, which match the beginning of the piece and turn to the tonic major, a new melody appears that preserves only *P*'s character. This event is partially resolved later in the Finale. A portion of *1T* (m.150) is merged with elements of *P*, but its more aggressive character is now toned down. *S* (m.158) comes back with only the background's surface rhythm accelerated. At this point, the recapitulation takes another path moving toward a pair of climaxes on E-flat and A major (mm.173, 176). During the ensuing passage, the character of *P* again returns and one almost believes that *P*, absent at the recapitulation, is about to be heard (m.184). Instead, the end of *K* is restated (m.185). Stanford's coda (m.188) begins with a tonic pedal and a turn to D minor. At this point, Stanford fulfills some tasks left incomplete by the recapitulation, the reprise of *T* (m.200) and the first measures of *P*, but now the latter is marked by introverted cadences as the music becomes becalmed and the movement ends quietly.

Stanford's second movement Tempo di Minuetto (Allegretto molto moderato) comes close to a neo-Classical idiom in its restraint (e.g., the trombones are *tacet* and the dynamics never exceed *forte*). However, its harmonic language and chromaticism make it a piece of its time. Given the Minuet character of the opening, one expects not a series of variations but a Trio; one is even initially inclined to accept the first variation (m.46) as the middle portion of the Minuet proper. The layout of the movement (Table XIV/17) reveals that each variation maintains the small ternary structure of the theme, but not its exact number of bars. Notice that after two non-strophic but rather straightforward variations, Variation 3 changes the meter to 3/8 for the episode, while Variation 4 does another take on the changing meter as *a* and *b* are in 2/4 and the return to *a* changes to 6/8. A six-measure coda recalls the Minuet's opening phrase.

Among Stanford's middle movements, this piece comes closest to the Intermezzo in Symphony No. 4/2 and the Allegretto grazioso of Symphony No. 5/2. All of these pieces have something of Brahms's symphonic third movements, excepting his Symphony No. 4/3. Indeed, one might find a similarity between No. 7/2 and Brahms's Symphony No. 2/3 with their incorporation of changing meters and initial Minuet styles. However, Brahms's Symphony No. 2/3 is a much more complex entity, not only in its shape, but also in its tempos,

EXAMPLE XIV/32 Stanford. Symphony No. 7/1, mm.42–53.

EXAMPLE XIV/32   (*continued*)

TABLE XIV/17
Stanford. Symphony No. 7/2: Structure

Tempo di Minuetto (Allegro molto moderato)

			a	*b*	*a*
m.1 [Minuet]	3/4	*Theme*	13	20	12
46 [Trio]	3/4	*Variation 1*	*a*	*b*	*a*
			12	13	14
85	6/8	*Variation 2*	*a*	*b*	*a*
			11	16	8
120	3/4	*Variation 3*	*a*	3/8 = *b*	3/4 = *a*
			6	11	7
144	2/4	*Variation 4*	*a*	*b*	6/8 = *a*
			16	5	8
173	3/4	*Coda* Tempo del Minuetto			
		6			

meters, and character. Another movement with whose variations one might want to compare it is Mahler's Symphony No. 4/3, which also has changing meters. Like Brahms, Mahler's sections are more strongly distinguished in the depth of their contrasts, whereas Stanford's movement is more restrained in character and content. Whether Stanford knew Mahler's work is certainly open to question, but without doubt the Brahms No. 2, as we have already discussed, was, prior to Stanford's No. 7, a repertoire piece. Nevertheless, in the context of this restrained Seventh Symphony, this movement in the tempo of a Minuet seems to be an entirely appropriate solution.

The joining of the last two movements among Stanford's symphonies first occurred in the Sixth, where the Scherzo's material continues into the 4/4 transition and the Finale. Here, the second set of variations in this cycle continues into the Finale, where P (m.138) is another treatment of the third movement's theme. Stanford, however, conceives of this or wishes us to conceive of it as a single gesture: "Variations and Finale."

The Andante consists of a theme and five variations. Compared to the previous movement, these variations are less tightly controlled and less likely to have a single figuration throughout a given variation. Table XIV/18 reveals the shape of the set. Notice that the theme and fifth variation are strophic and the first variation is nearly so. Variations 2, 3, and 4 are much expanded with 2 and 3 between themselves nearly strophic. Thus, a symmetrical shape informs these variations with the theme and last strophic variation framing the middle variations of expanded non-strophic structures. However, the key of this almost strophic variation prevents it from supplying a tonal frame, and its lengthy continuation as a transition to the Finale weakens a strophic perception.

What is striking about the theme marked *teneramente* is its simplicity; its rhythm contains only quarter and eighth notes, the melody has only a few accidentals, and its texture is that of a chorale. Such a posture is very advantageous in a variation movement because it leaves open many options for alteration. Though Variation 1 has nearly the same phrase lengths, Stanford still maintains the eighth note as the shortest duration, but now there are more of them. Also, the texture is more polyphonic, the range expanded, and the dynamics are stronger as more instruments are involved. Though there is more chromaticism than in the theme, it is not until the second variation that chromaticism begins to generate modulatory activity with an enharmonic shift from D-flat to E by means of A-flat/G-sharp (mm.29–33). In fact, the variation is markedly transitory/developmental with its rising and falling bass line. Here, the climax expands to a *tutti/forte* and then dies away to *pianissimo* with horn sixths and thirds in the minor mode. Stanford's molto tranquillo third variation in B-flat intensifies the triplet surface rhythms, but has less modulatory activity and ranges in dynamics from *pianissimo* to *mezzo piano*. Variation 4 (Example XIV/33) has still less activity and projects the movement's *fortissimo* climax in the key of G-flat, the Neapolitan of the main key of F and the enharmonic pivot to the F-sharp minor fifth variation, the only variation of the series to depart from the 4/4 measure of the theme to simple triple meter.

One can also project upon this movement aspects of a sonata form. The Theme and Variation 1, which remain in the tonic, are the P; the tonal instability of Variation 2 is a kind of T; Variation 3 beginning in the subdominant and marked tranquillo is almost an embodiment of S, and Variations 4 and 5 and the latter variation's continuation are a development section, although less of a development than found in Variation 2. Perhaps the beginning of the Finale in D major based on the theme could be heard as a recapitulation, even though it appears in the new tonic as a structural downbeat.

Marked Allegro giusto, the Finale's P (m.138) emerges as a hymn based on the opening

TABLE XIV/18
Stanford. Symphony No. 7/3: Structure

Variations and Finale

Variations—Andante				Exposition
m.1	*Theme* 4/4	5+5+4	F	*p*
15	*Variation 1*	4+4+5	F	
28	*Variation 2*	9+6+8	mod.	*T*
51	*Variation 3*	8+6+8+1	B-flat	*S*
				Development
74	*Variation 4*	6+6+5+8	G-flat	
98	*Variation 5* 3/4	5+5+4	F-sharp minor	
112	transition	4+4+4+3+4+2+4		

Finale—Allegro giusto 4/4			
	Exposition		
138	*P*—Chorale derived from Theme for above	D major	
156	*T (P)*	mod.	
176	*S*	A major	
190	*Development*	F-sharp minor	
208	retransition	A pedal	
224	*Recapitulation 1*	D major	
	I/P		
228		F major	
249	Tranquillo, ma quasi l'istesso tempo	D major	
	P transformed		
264	Animato		
266	*Recapitulation 2*		
	P original character	F-sharp minor	
277	*S*	D → B minor → D	
297	*P developed*		
311	Poco più lento ¢ → 3/2	G-flat/F-sharp → E-flat minor	
323	Allegro maestoso ¢	F → D	
	P	D major	
334	Più mosso ed animato		

of the variation theme in chorale-prelude style; the winds play the chorale phrase by phrase, while the strings provide brief figurative interludes. *T* (m.156) takes the downward motive of the chorale and develops it in both its original form and inversion. After a brief lead-in (m.172), *S* (m.176) is stated, which perhaps is also related to the variation's theme and its third variation (m.51) in the accompanying triplet figuration. A relatively brief development/transition (m.190) of eighteen bars plus a retransition (m.208) takes us not to the chorale *P*, but to *I/P* (m.224) for a cyclic reprise or recapitulation 1. Surprisingly, this does not resolve to D, but slips into F (m.228) and twenty-one bars later finds D (m.249) with a transformation of the Finale's *P*. But when *P* returns (m.266) in its original character and sound (recapitulation 2), it begins in F-sharp minor followed by *S* (m.277) in the tonic. This soon modulates to B minor (m.291), and a further development of *P* (m.297) ensues moving as far afield as G-flat/F-sharp (m.311), E-flat (m.316), and F (m.322) before finding the tonic for its conclusion. In a sense, this Finale reflects the larger action of the variations: a stable beginning of an expository nature followed by a long development with, in this case, a second recapitulation that fails to completely settle in the tonic until the very end.

Stanford's last symphony was something of an experiment in its brevity, some of its structural aspects, and its treatment of tonality. The incorporation of two adjacent variation sets and the very nature of these variations might cause one to raise an eyebrow here or there,

EXAMPLE XIV/33   Stanford. Symphony No. 7/3, mm.73–98.

EXAMPLE XIV/33 *(continued)*

EXAMPLE XIV/33   (*continued*)

but by any measure they are effective pieces. This could also be said of its restrained first movement. It is the Finale that perhaps raises more questions about its tonal and formal plan. Stanford's return to *I/P* is effective, but incomplete because of its tonal placement and its duration. On the one hand, it provides a resolution obviated in the first movement, but on the other hand, if this material is to be brought back, it should find stability in the tonic.

Stanford's new symphony was greeted with respect and veneration after its premiere at the Royal Philharmonic Society of London:

> A new Symphony (No. 7, in D minor) by Sir Charles Stanford, was the most interesting feature of the concert given on February 22. In some respects the character of the Symphony was a surprise because so simple and straightforward a composition was hardly expected in these times, when a new orchestral work is so often a melancholy psychological problem. Whilst listening to Sir Charles Stanford's music one could imagine Mozart benignly approving. The Symphony is in three movements. The first Allegro is a joyous outpouring easy to follow. The second movement—a Minuet and Trio—is in a kind of variation form, and the Finale is also based on variations. As the Symphony is practicable for ordinary resources it will no doubt be often heard. The composer conducted, and was recalled many times.[135]

Though published soon after its first performance, the Seventh seems to have never found the revivals this early critic thought it deserved. Together with Stanford's other symphonies, its fate was one of oblivion.

As he became older, Stanford felt more detached from the music of his day and as a composer felt himself to be an outsider. One could view his Symphony No. 7 as an effort to both experiment and to display the advantages of a conservative stance in the early-twentieth-century symphony.[136] Though the Seventh possesses simplicity and an economy of means, Stanford's requirements for the music he approved of, perhaps the solution he found here, was not totally satisfying to him as a composer. Stanford was to live for another thirteen years; he composed no more symphonies even though he remained active in other genres and as a teacher and conductor. In his later years, Stanford's Victorian optimism was broken by the devastation of the first great European war, a devastation magnified by his happy past associations with German musicians and institutions. The symphony as a genre was by this time one that almost always ended on a note of optimism and triumph; after the war Stanford may have felt that such a positive affect was no longer justified. His orchestral efforts were then directed toward concerted and "Irish"-based works.

CONCLUSION

As with Bennett, in the context of Stanford's total output, the symphony was not a central genre. The areas that occupied him the most were song, liturgical music, oratorio-like pieces, and opera. Today, he is mainly known through his liturgical music, but during his lifetime, it seems that his songs and oratorios established his reputation. Since oratorios based on secular texts and on biblical ones were written for the oratorio societies and regional music festivals, which are no longer flourishing, these works have receded into the past. Since the symphony orchestra remains a viable institution, the orchestral concert is still in need of new and/or unfamiliar repertoire. However, few works from the past have been able to reenter this repertoire; only the symphonies of Gustav Mahler have achieved a posthumous distinction. It is unlikely that Stanford's symphonies will ever achieve such status. Yet among his output there are symphonies that deserve a hearing and even a place in today's symphonic repertoire. The First Symphony, despite all of its energy and skill, is too derivative to be accepted by audiences.

Symphony No. 2, though a decidedly Brahmsian piece with references to Wagner, Schumann, and Beethoven, is in total effect a first-rate symphony in its own right and deserves a hearing. The "Irish" Symphony No. 3, the most popular of Stanford's symphonies, could regain a place in the repertoire on both the appeal of its Irish materials and the skill with which they are absorbed into the symphonic genre. The last movement is strikingly effective and can hold its own against any Finale in other symphonies scored for the normal late-nineteenth-century orchestra. Symphony No. 4 lacks the distinction of its predecessor except for its slow movement, an operatic *scena* for orchestra.

Our enthusiasm for Symphonies Nos. 5 and 6 has already been registered. Both are deeply original in conception and execution and end not with a bang, but with celestial music of a striking kind. Given a sympathetic conductor, both of these works could become viable symphonies in the concert hall. Symphony No. 7 we regard as a failed experiment in writing a short symphony of less than thirty minutes. Though individually the movements are noteworthy, the use of variation form in two adjacent movements and the inability of the Finale in its present form to completely resolve earlier issues of tonality and recapitulation make this a problematical effort.

Even if Stanford's legacy is not to be found in the concert halls, his other symphonic legacy is as a teacher. His students, while not forming a compositional school, all came out of his studio at the Royal College as individuals. Among them was Ralph Vaughan Williams, who with his nine symphonies was perhaps the most important English symphonist.

C. Hubert H. Parry
INTRODUCTION

C. Hubert H. Parry (1848–1918) and Charles Stanford were the leading composers in England during the last quarter of the nineteenth century, before the rise of Edward Elgar as an orchestral composer beginning with the 1899 premiere of the *Enigma Variations*. Both men distinguished themselves from Elgar in that they were academics, who not only composed and conducted but also wrote critical and musicological works. In addition, both also turned out from their posts at Oxford, Cambridge, and the Royal College of Music a cadre of successful students who took up prominent musical positions in England during the first half of the twentieth century.

Hubert Parry, however, in a number of respects was a different sort of mentor than Stanford, both professionally and personally. Whereas Stanford hailed from the Irish Protestant middle class, Parry came from the English gentry with country estates and yachts among other *accoutrements*. Stanford was always committed to music as a profession, though his parents hoped for another livelihood; Parry did not have a full commitment to the art until after he had worked at Lloyd's of London and severed his ties with the firm in 1877. Stanford was a political conservative; Parry was a progressive. Stanford was a man of belief; Parry an agnostic and antagonistic toward church ritual, though this did not deter him from writing works for the Anglican service. Stanford was a tough autocratic teacher, who at times frightened his students but gained their respect; Parry was a teacher both respected and loved by those under his tutelage. Parry was a successful administrator, who succeeded Grove as the director of the Royal College of Music; Stanford continued as composition teacher and conductor of the College's orchestra and operatic performances. And for both, the symphony was not a central genre to their activities as composers: Stanford composed only seven symphonies, while Parry wrote but five including his *Symphonic Fantasia* of 1912.

Though both men were much taken with the music of Brahms, their approach to composition was totally different. Stanford reportedly wrote into the full score without the benefit of sketches and, if this is not legend, the only revisions were those indicated in the autograph scores and these mostly consisted of cuts to tighten the form. Parry, on the other hand, was constantly involved in revision of works already heard in public performance (see Table XIV/19). Symphony No. 2 exists in three versions (1883, 1887, 1895), Symphony No. 3 in three versions (1889, 1895, 1902), and Symphony No. 4 in at least two versions (1889, 1910). This Brucknerian attitude would only have irritated the anti-academic and anti-symphonic George Bernard Shaw, who had given Parry a notorious review of his oratorio *Job*.[137]

Parry's five symphonies span a period from 1882 to 1912, placing his symphonic efforts into approximately the same time frame as those of Stanford (1875 to 1911). The first efforts of both Parry and Stanford reveal the influence of Robert Schumann's symphonic works. Both composers completed their final symphonies for the Philharmonic Society's centenary, and both wrote them in reaction to the progressive tendencies of the first decade of the new century and in opposition to the expanded orchestra required for a number of these compositions, especially those by Mahler and Richard Strauss.

Stanford's symphonies took on extra-musical aspects from literature, art, and national Irish sources; Parry's topics are in a sense more wide-ranging. Symphony No. 2, known as the "Cambridge" or "University," traces the life of an undergraduate's student years. Symphony No. 4, in its second (1910) version "Finding the Way," deals with discovering the meaning of life. Some of the individual thematic ideas are connected with philosophical concepts such as "man's questioning and destiny."[138] Parry's Fifth has no overriding title; the movements are labeled Stress, Love, Play, and Now, which deal with seemingly unconnected aspects of life. In Nos. 4 and 5, Parry adopts something akin to Wagnerian leitmotifs, as individual thematic ideas receive labels such as brooding thought, tragedy, and so on.[139] Dibble views the extra-musical aspects in Nos. 4 and 5 to be an effort to "imbue instrumental music with the spirit of his ethical choral works."[140] Regardless of Parry's goal, the result for the audience must have been confusion and bewilderment by being asked to connect philosophical and moral abstractions with music that had no characteristic traditions with such concepts.

SYMPHONY NO. 1 IN G MAJOR

On March 8, 1877, Brahms's First Symphony was heard for the first time in England, but Parry missed this performance at the Cambridge University Musical Society. When Parry finally heard Brahms's C Minor Symphony on April 13, 1878, in London, he was somewhat disappointed, especially since Grove's assessment had raised his expectations:

> He does not seem quite at his ease in the orchestration and there are many bits which don't come out at all, and the work doesn't seem to me to hang well together, and what is most curious of all there are some decided reminiscences in it, especially in the last movement.[141]

This dissatisfaction apparently was not a conclusive judgment, for when he heard the Brahms No. 1 in November 1880 he judged it as "altogether much finer than his second."[142] One month later, Parry began composing his own First Symphony.

If Brahms provided a stimulus, it was not necessarily his works that served as dominating models for Parry. Though by 1880 there were a number of British symphonies heard in London which might have served as models, Parry seems to have adhered to the older Germanic exemplars from the continent he may have heard at the Richter concerts as well as at the Crystal Palace under Manns.[143] Such works included symphonies by Schubert, Schumann, Mendelssohn, Raff, Brahms, and others. Though parts of Parry's First Symphony remind one of Dvořák, it is unlikely that his symphonies had any effect on the budding

TABLE XIV/19

The Symphonies of C. Hubert H. Parry

Key	Date	Title	Movements	Instrumentation	Comments
G Major	1880–82	Symphony No. 1	1. Con fuoco 3/4 (531 m.) 2. Andante (quasi Adagio) 4/4 (121 m.) E-flat major 3. Presto 3/4 (504 m.) C minor 4. Allegretto; molto vivace 2/4 (573 m.)	Grand	"Dedicated to my dearest little wife." First performance: Birmingham Festival, August 31, 1882, conducted by the composer.
F Major	1883 rev. 1887 and 1895	Symphony No. 2	1. Andante sostenuto 4/4—Allegro moderato 6/8 (363 m.) F minor/major 2. Scherzo: Molto vivace 2/4 (490 m.) D minor 3. Andante 4/4 (105 m.) B-flat major 4. Allegro vivace 3/4 (489 m.)	Grand	The "Cambridge" or "University" First performances: June 12, 1883, Cambridge, conducted by Stanford; June 6, 1887, London, conducted by Richter; mvts. 1 & 4 recomposed; May 30, 1895, London, conducted by the composer, in further revision.
C Major	1889 rev. 1895 and 1902	Symphony No. 3	1. Allegro energico 2/4 (369 m.) 2. Andante sostenuto 6/8 (123 m.) A minor 3. Allegro molto Scherzoso 3/4 (271 m.) F major 4. Moderato 4/4 (185 m.)	Grand. Trom. added for 1895 version.	"English" First performances: May 23, 1889, London, conducted by the composer; January 30, 1895, Leeds, conducted by the composer; December 18, 1902, Bournemouth, conducted by the composer? Published in London: Novello, 1907.
E Minor	1889 rev. 1910	Symphony No. 4	1. Con fuoco 3/4 (612 m.) 2. Molto Adagio 4/4 (77 m.) C major 3. Allegretto 3/8 (536 m.) E major 4. Spiritoso 3/4 (260 m.) E major		"Finding the Way" 1. Looking for It; 2. Thinking on It; 3. Playing on It; 4. Girt for it First performances: July 1, 1889, London, conducted by Richter; February 10, 1910, London, conducted by the composer. Published in London: Novello, 1921 (prepared for publication by Emily Daymond).
B Minor	1912	Symphony No. 5	1. Slow 4/4—Allegro (143 m.) 2. Lento 3/4 (108 m.) D major 3. Vivace 6/8 (286 m.) G major 4. Moderato 4/4 (222 m.) B major	Grand plus EH, Bclar., Cbssn., Tuba, 2 Harps.	"Symphonic Fantasia: A Symphony in Four Linked Movements" 1. Stress; 2. Love; 3. Play; 4. Now! First performance: December 5, 1912, London, conducted by the composer. Published in London: Goodwin & Tabb, 1922.

English composer. Rather, it was probably Dvořák's first set of *Slavonic Dances* Opus 46 that captured Parry's imagination for the main material of the Finale. There is nothing of Raff, but much of Schumann in the first movement.

Whereas Stanford in his early symphonies seemed to have no interest in thematic connections among the four movements, Parry in his First Symphony makes striking use of the first movement's *P*, adapted in the third and final movements to each of their meters and character (Example XIV/34). In the Scherzo, the response (m.130) to its antecedent phrase (m.121) begins with *I/1P*, but it has a different continuation and its character is changed from the con fuoco of the symphony's opening to *dolce cantabile*. For the Finale, the relationship to *I/1P* is more subtly realized in that *S* (m.103) begins like *I/1P*, now altered to fit duple meter. In the coda (m.459), *I/1P* (m.525), still in duple meter, adjusts the first three measures of the 3/4 first movement opening into duple meter, then repeats this a third higher before continuing with the next subphrase of *I/1P*. Thus, in this First Symphony, Parry presents not the simplest form of cyclic recall (i.e., blatant repetition), but one that evolves from the gradual unfolding of *S* to which the return of *I/1P* is a natural consequence. Additionally, one also might notice the timbral similarity of the final cadence in the first and last movements (I, m.523; IV, m.562). Furthermore, Parry's cyclic key scheme for the two middle movements moves to the flattened sixth (E-flat major) for the Andante and then to its relative minor or the tonic's subdominant minor (C minor) for the Scherzo. A common tone of G provides the link from the key of the first movement to the Andante.

Parry begins the first movement straight away with neither an introduction nor a *tutti* hammerstroke. His theme is full of brio and immediately brings to mind *P* of Schumann's "Rhenish" Symphony No. 3. But an effective *1P* (m.1) needs more than a memorable melody; an underlying rhythmic drive and plan are also needed. Schumann achieves this by the pulsating eighth-note accompaniment and by the use of hemiola in opposition to a normal 3/4 acceleration. In addition, Schumann's *tutti* orchestration and subtle polyphony are more effective. Parry's failure to use wholesale doubling of his melody by the winds results in an anemic presentation particularly by m.17. *2P* (m.25) might be regarded as a *T* due to its cancellation of F-sharp, but a G pedal sustains the tonic and only moves in preparation for the return of *1P* (m.45) almost *tutti* and *fortissimo*. Again, the melody is scored for flutes, oboes, and first violin. At its melodic peak (m.53) only the first violins carry the melody, while seconds, violas, and the first clarinet play a new counterpoint. Perhaps it was this sort of passage that bothered August Manns when he wrote to George Grove that a "little less 'polyphony'" would be an improvement.[144] This big ternary *P* is followed by *1T* (m.57), which continues *P* by winding down from its climax. *2T* (m.71) entrusts the violas with the lead as counterpoints occur in the clarinet and the other string lines. The music calms in preparation for the D major *S* (m.91) with the typical double statement scored first for winds and then strings with a flute embellishing the first violins. A lengthy extension is marked by more polyphony, thick orchestration, and dense chromaticism. *1K* (m.129) over an A pedal, the dominant's dominant, is purged of its chromaticism, but not its polyphony in a *tutti/fortissimo* context. Again, the chromaticism thickens only to be again purged at the start of *2K* (m.156). An epilogue (m.177) based on *S* is heard over the dominant of G leading not to an expository repeat, but the development section (m.190).

The exposition presents several attractive themes that have something of the compelling nature of Schumann's impassioned melodies. At times this material is presented effectively in larger spans. However, Parry's first movement exposition, for all its attributes, never quite matches the music that has overtaken his own imagination. Parry's orchestration is at times also highly effective, but his anemic *tuttis* detract from the exposition's overall impact.

EXAMPLE XIV/34   Parry. Symphony No. 1/1, mm.1–12; /3, mm.130–38; /4, mm.103–20, 525–33.

The development continues the epilogue, which is assertively broken by the appearance of *1P* in the subdominant (C major, m.207). Parry sequences on a motive from mm.5–6 that leads to *1P* on C major's subdominant (F major, m.230). This time the chromaticism thickens, and the material is incrementally reduced down to the motive of m.2, which is expanded by sequence over a long stretch (mm.257–75). Its rhythmic pattern continues and hooks on to *S* (m.311), first in its epilogue form and then *S* (m.319) in the major of G's relative minor. A rhythm common to both *2P* and *S* is reshaped melodically and leads to *1P*'s return in the tonic, but now *piano* and scored for strings. Is this meant to be the recapitulation, whose *piano* return seems to be an imitation of the first movement of Schubert's "Great" C Major Symphony D.944/1? After *2P* (m.383), *1P* (m.399) again returns *tutti/fortissimo* distracted by filigree in the second violins and violas. *1T* is eliminated, and *2T* (m.420) leads quietly to *S* (m.441) and *K* (mm.479 and 499). The coda features *1P* (m.503) in its least encumbered form, even though this *tutti* presentation could be more effectively scored.

Parry's deficiency in scoring his heroic *1P* in the first movement has no parallel in the Andante (quasi Adagio), where the orchestration is consistently effective in supporting the character of its themes. And it is the character of the themes that distinguishes this piece with its chamber-music introduction that leads to a completely effective Schumannesque *P* for strings (m.4). *S* (m.26) is an animated recitative mostly featuring a string/wind dialogue. Because of the nature of *S* and the minimization of *T* (mm.18–26), one is likely to initially believe that this is a refrain and episode of a rondo. However, when *P* is heard in G-flat (m.51), turns strongly developmental, and eventually combines elements of *P* and *S* (m.62), one's perception is rapidly changed. For the recapitulation, *P* and *S* are tightened (50 mm. vs. 27 mm.). One's initial impression of its structure is reinforced by the coda (m.112), which brings back *P* as a final statement of the refrain.

Manns also complained that "a little more 'placido' in the midst of the ceaseless *Sturm und Drang* would be improvements at least to my enjoyment of such genuinely enthusiastical flow of high-souled aspirations."[145] No doubt this complaint applies together with that of too much "polyphony" to this slow movement. Its first three measures with unaccompanied solos for the horn and clarinets set up an expectation of a calming pastoral affect as does the initial measures of *P* for strings (Example XIV/35). But soon it rises to an impassioned climax (m.12), quiets down, and then rises again (m.21) and quiets before the poco più moto of *S*. At this point one might expect Manns's "placido," but instead *Sturm und Drang* is served up in an almost improvisatory manner. Here too, Parry's orchestral treatment was, in Manns's words, "awfully difficult to master" with its fussy rhythms and fragments of melody treated polyphonically. No doubt when Parry complained of the orchestra not concentrating in reading his symphony, they must have been bewildered by the material of *S*. In the development section, the difficulties presented by *S* are only compounded. Nevertheless, the Andante is a masterful and original slow movement that quickly makes one forget the occasional inadequacies of the first movement.

It has been observed that Parry's Scherzo also owes something to Robert Schumann because of the two Trios, a characteristic of four of Parry's symphonic Scherzos. While such an assertion is true, Parry also inserts a development section:

Presto ⟶		Meno mosso	Tempo 1 ⟶			Meno mosso	Tempo 1 ⟶	
Intro.	*Scherzo*	*Trio 1*	*Development*	retrans.	*Scherzo*	*Trio 2*	*Scherzo*	*Coda*
C minor		E-flat	C minor mod.		C minor	A-flat	C minor	
m.1	10	121	200	266	286	310	392	462

The Scherzo begins in an almost macabre fashion: pizzicato cellos and basses responded to by clarinet and bassoons. This becomes an accompaniment for the theme of the Scherzo proper introduced by the violas and then taken up by the violins. This material bears some relationship to *II/2P* and *I/S,* but it is not strong enough to be readily identified. A second portion (m.27) has a basso ostinato, which leads to the dominant A-flat (m.47) followed by a lengthy lead-in to a reprise of the Scherzo's beginning (m.94). A return to the introduction both rounds off the Scherzo and provides a lead-in to an adumbration of the first Trio (m.121):

a	b (*II/1P*)	a	b (*II/1P*)	a		
Hrns.	Strgs. W.W.			b (*II/1P*)		ext.
F	E-flat	F	F	F(B$_\flat$ pedal)		
m.121	130	140	153	171		181

The passage for a quartet of horns (*a*) brings to mind Weber's *Der Freischütz* or passages for horns and bassoons in Mendelssohn's "Italian" and Schubert's "Unfinished" Symphonies. This produces a pastoral foil for the movement's macabre aspects. The development (m.200) is a fugato on the main theme of the Scherzo. After an exposition, Parry treats the subject to a tight stretto at one- and two-measure entries (m.232) and then essentially repeats the beginning of this section with a dominant pedal as a retransition. Thus, Parry's Scherzo reprise

EXAMPLE XIV/35 Parry. Symphony No. 1/2, mm.1–13.

merely states its main theme followed by a transition before embarking on the second Trio (m.310). One could probably connect the second Trio's theme again to *I/S,* but only the connoisseur would possibly make a connection. A lengthier version of the Scherzo proper (m.392) ends with a "Slavonic" flourish.

Perhaps this flourish prepares for the somewhat Dvořákian Finale as heard by Bernard Benoliel; in contrast, Jeremy Dibble hears something of Schumann's Symphony No. 4/4.[146] Both commentaries could be effectively argued; like the first movement's allusions to Schumann's "Rhenish" Symphony, the Finale's relationship to Schumann's Symphony No. 4 in D Minor is easily identifiable, but still Parry has made his own imprint with his use of these materials. As for the Dvořákian aspect, Benoliel describes it in the opening of the Finale as

> a vigorous tune . . . , it is amusing to hear it anglicized as Parry moulds it through a finely proportioned, thematically inventive movement.[147]

Additionally, Benoliel hears *S* as a successor to the "great tune in the first movement of Parry's Piano Quartet." To our ears, Parry's *S* (m.103), together with some of its accompanying figuration, is a strictly Brahmsian affair in the tradition of the German composer's *P* from Symphony No. 1/4 and *S* from Symphony No. 2/4 with their dark, thick string sound delivering a majestic melody. Also paralleling Brahms is Parry's double statement of this material with the first scored for strings, the second for woodwinds. As we have already noted, however, *S* evolves into *I/1P* during the course of Parry's Finale so that regardless of its ancestors it belongs to this movement and this symphony.

The structure of this Finale as it unfolds, like that of the Andante, sends mixed signals of whether it will become a sonata or rondo. After hearing the opening section equivalent to an exposition one is almost certain that it is a rondo: *A/P* is a closed form followed almost without transition by *B/S* (m.103) and then *K* (*A/P,* m.189), which though in the related key duplicates the clarinet scoring of the opening. Thus, most listeners are prone to hear this as an *A–B–A,* since melody and timbre often take precedence for listeners over key. The development/*C* section falls into two parts: fugato on *A/P* beginning in C major (m.211) followed by *B/S* in D-flat (m.263), the most distant key from the tonic. The recapitulation brings back *A/P* in G major (m.309), but *B/S* reappears in B-flat, the relative major of G minor (m.405). *K*(*A/P*) does not reappear; it is replaced by *I/P* in the tonic key (m.525) for an appropriate peroration for both the Finale and the symphony as a whole.

Manns called this First Symphony in G Major "a very remarkable work."[148] While Manns certainly had his reservations about Parry's composition, one could not argue persuasively that his assessment is off the mark. Critical opinion of the first performance in Birmingham on August 21, 1882, was more than encouraging. Reviews appeared in both *The Athenaeum* and the *Musical Times,* as follows:

> Mr. Hubert Parry, whose Symphony in G opened the second part, is one of the most earnest musicians whom we have among us. Whatever he writes is characterized by loftiness of aim and by a devotion to art for its own sake which it is to be wished were more frequently to be met with. His works, therefore, will always appeal rather to the cultivated musician than to the general public. His style resembles that of Brahms more nearly than that of any other composer; there is a similar vein of deep thought and of contrapuntal ingenuity, occasionally with a slight tendency towards obscurity, which is to be found in the German master. It is therefore with much pleasure that we are able to say that in his new symphony we find a distinct advance towards clearness of expression as compared with his earlier works. There are passages in the symphony, more particularly

in the slow movement and the *finale,* which require more than one hearing for their due appreciation; but in general there is little difficulty in following the train of the composer's thought. His ideas are often full of charm, their treatment is musicianly, and the orchestration well balanced and effective. The symphony was received with a warmth which agreeably surprised us, and which said not a little for the good taste of the Birmingham audience. The remainder of the programme requires no detailed notice.[149]

The second part of the Concert began with Mr. C. Hubert Parry's new Symphony, conducted by the composer. This work, although undoubtedly reflective of the modern school of writing, differs not in its construction from the established models. Opening with a well-marked theme in G major, carefully and appropriately harmonised, an effectively contrasted subject, commenced by the wind instruments, appears in due course, the development of these movements proving that, although the composer has reverently studied in the good school of writing, he has dared to think for himself. The Andante in E flat has an attractive theme, with a well-contrasted second subject, the dialogue passages for strings and wind being an especial feature in the movement, which, although amply worked out, wearies not by its length. The Scherzo contains much clever writing. By the introduction of two Trios it is, perhaps, somewhat unduly prolonged; but the themes are interesting, and the continuity of thought is unbroken throughout. The Finale is an elaborate movement, requiring for the due comprehension of all its details more than a single hearing; but it may be mentioned that the introduction of the principal subject of the first movement has the effect of establishing a link which much enhances the interest of the work. Every movement of the Symphony was warmly received, and the composer was loudly applauded on his retirement from the orchestra.[150]

In April 1883, Manns conducted the symphony at the Crystal Palace. By this time, Parry had nearly completed his Symphony No. 2, commissioned by the Cambridge University Musical Society for its concert on June 12.

SYMPHONY NO. 2 "CAMBRIDGE" OR "UNIVERSITY" IN F MAJOR

Parry's Second Symphony was the first of his symphonies to have been treated to extensive revisions. Parry's first version from 1883 was written with difficulty; an enlarged version of the Finale was composed at the request of Stanford. In 1887, the first movement and Finale were recomposed, and there were further changes in the middle two movements; this version was conducted by Richter on June 6. Some critics considered this version a new work.[151] Eight years later, further changes were made in the Finale; it was given more substance for a performance conducted by the composer at the Philharmonic Concerts on May 30, 1895. In 1906, the Second was published by Novello with, no doubt, some further alterations. Our discussion is based on this final version.

For the 1887 version conducted by Richter, the analytical notes contained a program that explains its alternate subtitle, "University" Symphony:

In the introduction we are brought face to face with the novel sensations and high aspirations which an undergraduate feels on reflecting that from lately being a mere school-*boy* he has suddenly become a university *man,* and are further furnished with some premonitions of his character. The *allegro,* which immediately follows, might be regarded as descriptive of the jollity of university life: health, high spirits, happiness in making new friends, and some prefiguration of that which *must* come—the dawn of love. In the *scherzo* we realize all the jollification of a home scene: rustic merry-making at a harvest festival during the long vacation; with (in the trio) not a little serious flirtation in a corner. The slow movement reveals to us our hero's first passion and ardent love-making; its anxieties as well as its happier phases. In the *finale* we are alive to his delight at having taken his degree, his grand resolves for the future, and determination to make his way in the world.[152]

That Parry did not reveal the piece's extra-musical aspects for the premiere at Cambridge may have been because he believed that a program about undergraduate student life and the progress from boyhood to manhood would not have been taken seriously in an academic setting where he had been given an honorary doctorate.

As in the case of Stanford's Symphonies Nos. 4 and 5, the extra-musical aspects fit into the traditional four-movement layout with the reversal of the slow movement and the Scherzo. Thus, Parry gives us a serious introduction in the minor mode that effectively returns at the movement's end, followed by a gigue-like piece with Wagnerian overtones. Indeed, the Allegro perhaps connects our undergraduate with the character of Siegfried in the third and fourth music dramas in Wagner's *Nibelungen* tetralogy. The Scherzo represents vacation time at home between terms, and like Symphony No. 1/4 this piece in simple duple meter seems to owe something to Dvořák's *Slavonic Dances* Opus. 46. Love scene or not, the slow movement, which uses the material that framed the first movement, is again an especially effective piece where every element seems perfectly placed. Even after several rewrites, the Finale still does not seem to strike the right affect for the positive sentiments of its program.

Parry had heard about Wagner from the English Wagnerian Edward Dannreuther and later visited Bayreuth. Though in our view the First Symphony has nothing of Wagner, in the Second Symphony Parry uses his brass instruments more forcefully, which together with the themes they play are unmistakably of Wagnerian derivation. Parry, however, never became a Wagnerite for he maintained his deep admiration for Brahms. Indeed, when Stanford played at the piano the first movement, in our view the most Wagnerian, for George Grove, the piece seemed Brahmsian. On February 28, 1883, Grove wrote to Parry,

> I long to hear it again for it has left the impression on my mind of a really original, great, and most interesting work. Except a Brahmsy bit (and they were reminiscences of the composer and not of passages) once or twice nothing *reminded* me of anything else— but, as in the finale of the other Symphony, I felt its kinship to the greatest; and again [Beethoven's?] No. 7 seemed to stand by as if to *welcome it into the family.*[153]

No doubt Grove's connection with Beethoven's Seventh Symphony centers on their same meters and similar rhythmic motives. Otherwise, Parry's and Beethoven's movements hold little in common. Jeremy Dibble, however, also hears the Scherzo movement in D minor as "the most Brahmsian-sounding movement." But he hears the slow movement as more Dvořákian than Brahmsian, drawing a parallel with the former's Fifth Symphony's slow movement. Of course, the opening of the Finale and its *K* (m.115) is indubitably Brahmsian with its G-string melody for the violins, even though this movement lacks the tightness of presentation so characteristic of this Teutonic composer.[154]

As for the cycle itself, Parry makes use of several ideas heard in the first movement in both the third and fourth movements. The slow introduction serves as the main idea for the opening and closing sections of the slow third movement. Thus, although its role in the slow movement is different from that of the first movement, in both it functions as a frame to a substantial central section. This relationship of first movement introduction to the slow piece was one previously used by Joseph Haydn in the slow introductions to Symphonies Nos. 84 and 86, which are related to the openings of the slow movements. Given Parry's knowledge of the symphonic repertoire, it is very likely that he was familiar at least with Haydn's "Paris" Symphonies. Parry's other cyclic first movement theme is *1P,* which, in its Siegfried garb with the brass instruments, reappears toward the end (m.191) of the development and in the coda (m.437) of the Finale.

Grove found the introduction "lovely" and its connection to the Allegro as being "most happy—close and yet quite unforced."[155] Parry's lushest symphonic utterance, it reveals his increased acumen for the symphonic gesture. Here, he demonstrates a sophisticated contrapuntal unfolding in four parts, a sophisticated sense of timbre in the way he uses the octave tuning in the timpani, and an effective way of filling in the sonority as the woodwinds play a simplified version of the opening motive. All this and more gathers for a wonderfully wrought climax (m.12) (Example XIV/36). A second section (m.16) is in part based on an inversion of the opening motive, which builds to a second climax (m.24) and quickly dissipates for the Allegro's beginning. Both portions of the introduction return in the first movement: the first as a slow conclusion after the business of the Allegro is tended to, and the second becomes *S* (m.71).

Parry's Allegro is in the best sense a thoroughly academic sonata form in that every textbook requirement is fulfilled. But this is vital music and not dry academicism. *P* (m.30) both dances and soars, then its cadence (m.41) articulates *1T(P)*. The various parts of *T* fulfill expectations: *1T* is saturated with sixteenths and *2T* with a sequence. *3T* (m.53) begins to set up the new key, departs from it, and then establishes it. *S* (m.71) is presented with a counterpoint in the cellos and bassoon that derives from the introduction's opening motive and in proper form is continued (m.80) in a new orchestration with the cellos now taking the lead. A lengthy expansion (m.91) acts more and more like *T* (mm.103, 123) until *K* (m.135) firmly anchors the related key. Reminiscent of Potter, a "silent" measure (m.144) separates the exposition from the development.

Parry's development is also a Classical example except that *P* (m.145) serves as an introduction to a lengthy section based on *S* (m.151) marked *tranquillo* and *cantabile*. Above two long pedals on A and F, *S* is reduced down to its opening descending interval, then treated in diminution as *P* is played against it in augmentation (m.185). Now the third measure of *S* or the first measure of *P* is worked over (m.197) in diminutive states; this culminates in the arrival of the recapitulation (m.209). Except for the elimination of *K,* the recapitulation parallels the exposition. The coda (m.329) commences with a tonic pedal undergirding *P* and then *S* (m.340). Parry slows the background activity in preparation for the abbreviated return of the introduction (m.355) undergirded by a tonic pedal that continues to the end.

Parry's Scherzo this time is in 2/4, but it begins in a way close to the parallel movement in Symphony No. 1. Rather than organizing the first part in a sonata or binary form, Parry uses as his model Beethoven's Symphony No. 6/3 where he presents a series of *contredanses:* mm.5, 45, 89, and then a reprise of the first dance (m.107) all glued together by their quasi-Slavonic character and the key of D minor. Poco più mosso (m.172) marks the Trio. Even though its beat is faster, the surface fulfills our expectations in its lower level of activity, cantabile character, and drone bass. With the return to the Scherzo proper the four dance sections are repeated (mm.289, 329, 373, 391). The remaining measures reprise the Trio (m.451), and, after two measures of silence (mm.478–79), the Presto coda, a penultimate measure of silence, and a cadence conclude the movement. Such an ending brings to mind Beethoven's Symphony No. 9/2. Nevertheless, except for its length, this piece could well find a place among Dvořák's *Slavonic Dances.*

EXAMPLE XIV/36   Parry. Symphony No. 2/1, mm.1–14.

Parry changes the character of the third movement from that of the slow introduction to the first movement by accelerating the tempo from ♩=60 to ♩=70, by changing the mode from F minor to B-flat major, and by eliminating the pedal from the fabric. In particular, the absence of the timpani makes the sound initially less foreboding. After the initial statement, which modulates to the dominant, Parry slides into D-flat major (Example XIV/37) where the music becomes menacing with timpani rolls, viola shakes, and the horn

EXAMPLE XIV/36   (*continued*)

EXAMPLE XIV/36   (*continued*)

and trombone punctuations. Tonally, Parry moves further afield, sliding into B-flat minor (m.22), E-flat minor (m.25), and C minor (m.28), which begins the middle section of mainly new material. Here high drama prevails with double-dotted rhythms, *tutti* scoring, *fortissimo* dynamics, extremes of the high ranges, and tonal instability. A transition (m.42) of a funereal character with dark timbres, pulsating timpani, and descending woodwinds leads back to the opening section (m.54) but in G-flat (m.72) before finding the complete stability of B-flat major (m.80). The coda (m.93) vacillates between B-flat and G-flat with the timpani insisting on B-flat. At the final chord, the drum sustains not the tonic, but the dominant.

Parry offers here something again that is an amalgam of sonata and ternary forms:

Exposition ——→ Development ————————————→ Recapitulation   Coda

| A | | B | | A | | A | | A |

B-flat → F   D-flat → C   mod.   F pedal   unstable   G-flat   B-flat   B-flat/G-flat   B-flat
m.1   17   18   28   43   54   72   80   93

Only the larger sonata-form outline is clearly present. That the development contains both contrasting material as well as *A* in a less than stable presentation does not seem to belong to a textbook ternary concept. The retransition (m.43) that precedes *A* (m.54) is merely a ruse to make us think this could be a simple *A–B–A*, but with *A*'s thematic and tonal behavior this is certainly not an option. Though not what we might expect of an "academic" composer, it passes the test of being more than a musically viable effort; it is perhaps the finest of Parry's symphonic slow movements.

Some commentators have dubbed the Finale a "broad sonata rondo," but it is nothing of the sort; the return of *A/P* after *B/S* (m.65) does not occur. The return of *A/P* is prepared for (m.109) only to end with *K* (m.115) and a double statement of *B/S* that sounds Brahmsian. Instead, the Allegro vivace is a sonata form without the expository repeat. The development (m.145) begins with a pedal undergirding *1P* (cf. the first movement) and leads to the dominant of D-flat. D-flat enharmonically transfers to E major for tonal explorations on the sharp side of the spectrum coordinated with the entrance of *1/P* (m.185). At this point, Parry repeats a technique found in Symphony No. 1 by suggesting a relationship between some of his thematic ideas; in this case, the rhythmic similarity of *1/P* and *IV/1P* are juxtaposed for the listener to make a connection. Material from the start of the development returns (m.234), this time together with *1/P.* An A pedal in the violins (m.249) leads directly to the recapitulation (m.269) with a weak common-tone articulation further sapped by a second-inversion tonic chord. Parry somewhat expands the recapitulation by mainly lengthening *S* (m.332). The coda (m.437) further juxtaposes *1/P* and *IV/1P*; at the end *1/P* reigns triumphant.

Regardless of its formal niceties and the clever thematic sleight of hand between *1/P* and *IV/1P,* this Finale is the only movement of the cycle that is inadequate to its task. Part of this has to do with the thematic content, which is hardly memorable. Several commentators have noted that *1P* and *K* are treated to the same sonority so effectively used by Brahms in the main theme of his Symphony No. 1/4 and the *S* of Symphony No. 2/4. But in both cases, Brahms's themes come after sections of instability, and the strong character for these themes represents arrival and release; in Parry, the themes are merely dressed in Brahms's clothes,

EXAMPLE XIV/37   Parry. Symphony No. 2/3, mm.18–22.

without their larger context. In other words, Parry's Finale is merely a collection of themes in the right order to present something resembling sonata form. But Parry has forgotten the innate drama of this formal stereotype.

The defects of the Finale have perhaps been the main reason why Parry's Symphony No. 2 has left the repertoire and why its restoration seems unlikely. Obviously, how to end this symphony became something of an impossible task; it underwent at least three revisions. Parry met success with a compelling first movement, an immediately appealing Scherzo, and a slow movement in which the composer reveals his ability to sustain and control his materials in a manner comparable to the most striking nineteenth-century examples. The best one can say about the Finale is that perhaps Parry was thinking in terms of an eighteenth-century fourth movement, which was more a *lieto* conclusion rather than an edifying one. Perhaps the problem was in Parry's program for the Finale, which is difficult to musically distinguish from that of the first movement. Parry fails to evince anything of the heroic or triumphant that by the last half of the nineteenth century became a Finale requirement.

The "Cambridge" or "University" Symphony in a sense had several premieres with its different versions. The first version to be performed was heard at the Cambridge University Musical Society in 1883. Critics for both the *Musical Times* and *The Athenaeum* filed their reactions:

> Dr. Parry's Symphony No. 2, in F, produced at the Cambridge Concert on the 12th ult., will, in the general opinion of English critics, more than confirm the position he had attained as a composer by his "Prometheus Unbound," and his Symphony No. 1, in G. His last work is written in accordance with ordinary models. Its familiar form being easily followed, it will get the cheap credit of clearness of outline; a quality always welcome, and in immature composers a sign of progress. In Dr. Parry's case, it is simply a sign that he, like many others, finds it easier to work in old grooves, or that as a newly installed professor at the Royal College of Music he is desirous of setting a wholesome example of reverence. Beyond the mere schematic form, there is nothing archaic in Dr. Parry's new Symphony. Indeed, if in following the propensity we have just impugned, we wanted to find fault at all, we should say it erred in being too faithful a representative of the music of the day. Its over-elaboration is fortunately mellowed by strains in themselves captivating, and by an instrumentation which has colour and warmth, if at times a little laboured and artificial. The Symphony commences with a short Introduction, Andante sostenuto, in F minor. This is followed by a Moderato in the major, a Scherzo in the relative minor, and a Trio in D major. The slow movement is in B flat, and the final movement, an Allegro moderato, is in the normal key and in 3–4 measure. In the last coda group the strings introduce a melody, simply harmonised and, like the subject of the Trio, of a very engaging vein. The annotator of the printed programme refers to it as derived from the principal subject; and in reference to other instances he justly calls attention to the unusual skill and lavishness with which the composer has utilised all his thematic material in producing a general unity of effect. At the conclusion of the Symphony Dr. Parry was called for and received long and hearty applause.[156]

As "G." [Grove] well puts it in his description of the work, "It is pleasant to notice what a strong attraction this great style of composition exercises on composers when they first begin to practise it." It is even more satisfactory when the second effort is an advance on the first, which may fairly be said to be the case in the present instance. An elaborate analysis without illustrations in music type would be unintelligible, and a few remarks on the salient features of each movement will be sufficient. The first section, *moderato,* is prefaced by an *andante sostenuto* in the tonic minor based on an expressive and well-defined figure. The themes of the principal movement are exceedingly melodious; and though we may take exception to some portions of the development as giving the impression of unrest, the general effect is undeniably pleasing. The *scherzo* in D minor, with trio in D major, is somewhat grotesque, thanks in a measure to the orchestration, in which the reed wind plays an important part. The slow movement, *larghetto,* in B flat may be considered the gem of the work, the principal melody being really beautiful, and the general manner calm and dignified with one or two outbursts of passion. The *finale, allegro moderato,* is less rich in subject matter and more involved in style. It was, therefore, less easy to follow at a first hearing, but the elaborate and protracted *coda* created a marked effect. Speaking of the work as a whole, it may be said that the points of superiority over the Birmingham Symphony in G lie in the greater beauty of the themes and the advance towards distinctness of outline. These are important matters, and Mr. Parry may, therefore, be congratulated on his progress. The reception of the new symphony was most encouraging, and at the close the composer was cheered with enthusiasm.[157]

For the 1887 version, the reactions in these two periodicals were quite different. The *Musical Times* saw it as a sign of Dr. Parry's "progress," praising his "fertility of idea, uncommon mastery of orchestral detail," and "a knowledge of how to obtain noble effects of figure and colour." This piece's weakness is a "tendency towards diffuseness."[158] The writer for *The Athenaeum,* however, was this time less positive; he was confused by the relationship of the program to the music and wrote that "from an artistic point of view [it was] a mistake." He found the "two middle movements the best" and the outer pieces "less spontaneous."[159]

Six years separated the first version of the Second Symphony from that of the Third. Besides being occupied with his administrative and teaching duties at the Royal College of Music, Parry composed mainly a series of vocal works both small and large. Among the former are two sets of *English Lyrics* and the *Four Sonnets of Shakespeare.* The latter includes "The Glories of Our Blood and State," Milton's Ode at a Solemn Music "Blest Pair of Sirens," and the oratorio *Judith.* The instrumental works include a Piano Trio, a Theme and Nineteen Variations for Piano, and a Violin Sonata. It was after the Violin Sonata that the Third and Fourth Symphonies were completed in 1889, forming a chronological pair to Symphonies Nos. 1 and 2.

SYMPHONY NO. 3 "ENGLISH" IN C MAJOR

The Third Symphony was the result of a request from the Philharmonic Society of London for a short symphony. Parry responded that he had "a short and very slight symphony all but finished."[160] He also offered as a possibility the Second Symphony, since it had not been heard at the Philharmonic concerts. But to Parry's chagrin, the directors decided on the new work. The composer wrote,

> It is quite a small and unimposing kind of symphony, in the plain key of C major and consists of an opening Allegro, a slow movement in A minor, Scherzo in F, and a set of variations. I suppose it must be announced as a Symphony—Sinfonietta looks too affected. The announcement might perhaps give it as a "Short Symphony."[161]

This "Symphony for Small Orchestra" was thoroughly revised in January 1889 and first heard on May 23, conducted by the composer. This version was without trombones, which were added in 1894–1895 for a performance at the Leeds Subscription Concerts on January 30 with the Scottish Orchestra. In addition, in 1894–1895 the Finale's Variations 2 and 3 were replaced.

Parry further revised the first movement for a Bournemouth rendition on December 18, 1902.[162] Presumably, this was the version published in 1907 by Novello, and this is the version upon which our discussion is based.

How Symphony No. 3 gained its appellation "English" is somewhat of a mystery, as it contains nothing of English folksong or anything indebted to it. In 1934 Fuller-Maitland stated: "The markedly English character of Parry's third symphony . . . struck every hearer, and the name 'English Symphony' has stuck to it ever since."[163] The earliest record, however, comes from the program notes for the Philharmonic Society which were subsequently taken up in a review in *The Athenaeum,* where its critic wrote that "its proper title would be the 'English' Symphony" and goes on to say that "Dr. Parry has given the themes a national colouring with intent."[164]

When Parry described his Symphony No. 3 as "quite small and unimposing" one would think that its total length would be considerably shorter than No. 2, but in fact No. 3 is only about three minutes shorter. Whereas large-scale cyclic considerations were a factor in Nos. 1 and 2, in Symphony No. 3 there are virtually no thematic connections, whether obvious or hidden, and no transitions between movements. The only remaining connection was one observed in Symphony No. 1; i.e., the similar sonorities of the final cadences of the first and last movements. In No. 3, this is even more marked by the alternation of multiple stops with a unison middle C in both movements (I/m.359, IV/m.180). Furthermore, while the first movement is in sonata form and the second movement an Andante in ternary form, the third movement Scherzo reverts to the Classical layout of Scherzo–Trio–Scherzo with coda, and the Finale is, like that of Symphony No. 2, a rather casual affair, but this time Moderato in tempo and in variation form. The fact that a non-sonata structure is used may explain why material from previous movements does not reappear in the Finale; it would be both intrusive and artificial.

Parry's first movement is almost stereotypical for the English symphony as it has been viewed here. The exposition begins straight away. *1P* (m.1) and *2P* (m.23) are unusually diatonic for Parry. Such diatonicism only returns for the recapitulation of *1Pc* (m.203) and at the end of the coda (m.351). *1T* (m.31) continues the material of *2P,* while *2T* (m.46) begins to move further from the tonic toward B major (m.53) which slips into C for *S* (m.61). After *S*'s double statement in the dominant, it is taken further afield to A with G major becoming reestablished for *K* (m.110), whose descending diatonic bass provides a strong sense of direction.

This directional use of a strong descending line is also characteristic of the main thematic material of the exposition. This is particularly true of *1P* and *2P* even though their rhythmic profiles are decidedly different. As might be expected of its function, the prominence of the downward line is diminished in *2T. S,* however, strengthens the direction, and *K* presents the descent shorn of any embellishments (Example XIV/38). Perhaps this sense of destination was what caused commentators to think of this piece as particularly "English," together with the largamente for *2P* and the animando for *K* which pulls and pushes the main tempo, and the rich string sound of *P* and the *S* repetition (m.77) scored for first and second violins in octaves.

The development section (m.137) is organized first around ascending fifths and then a chromatic descent in the bass on a repeated figure:

G	D	A	F	B-flat	E-flat	A-flat	B	B-flat	A	A-flat	G	G-flat	F
m.137	141	145	153	155	156	157	161	165	169	171	173	175	177

EXAMPLE XIV/38   Parry. Symphony No. 3/1, mm.107–19.

EXAMPLE XIV/38   (*continued*)

A slip upward to G, which becomes a pedal (m.179), sets up a retransition. Thematically the development first dissects *1P* using each of its subphrases and then moves *1P* into the bass. *S* is now combined with *1Px* (m.161) and the chromatically descending bass.

As seen in Symphony Nos. 1 and 2, Parry seems to avoid making the recapitulation a strong articulation. In Symphony No. 3, the recapitulation is incrementally defined: *1Pa* together with *Sa* is strongly anticipated over a dominant pedal (m.179), but does not reappear anchored in the tonic; *1Pc* (m.203) further sustains the dominant, and *2P* (m.211), though the strongest articulation, also avoids any root-position resolution. In fact, the strength of *2P* as an articulatory force stems not from any harmonic articulation, but from the tempo change (largamente), the rich string timbre, and the simple memorability of the melody. Indeed, one must wait until m.351 for a full and strong authentic cadence in the tonic, which is further articulated before the movement ends eighteen measures later.

Between *2P* (m.211) and m.351, Parry avoids a full commitment to C major. By doing so, he provides a momentum to the structure that would have been weakened by a series of strong C major cadences. Apart from the tonic and dominant keys, the other tonality given identity is E minor, the relative minor of G major, which replaces the exposition's reference to B minor (m.53) before the appearance of *S*. The recapitulation is somewhat abbreviated mainly at the start; the reduction is more than compensated for in the coda (m.309), which concentrates on *P* material. Here, a C pedal (m.317) in the timpani struggles against an A-flat root, but this slips to A minor (m.329) and then back to A-flat (m.335). Finally, C major, swept clean of any non-diatonic intrusions (m.351), allows the Allegro to conclude.

Though Parry disparaged this symphony in his description of it to the Philharmonic Society, its first movement is something considerably more than a solid accomplishment. It reveals Parry's mastery of long-range tonal control, different types of thematic development, and of directionalized themes in different expressive idioms. Though some have pointed to the first movement as having influence on the type of quasi-patriotic gesture (see the *2P* "largamente") for which Elgar became so well known, such writing certainly finds its origin in the symphonies of Brahms.

The Andante 6/8 with its anacrustic and dotted rhythms imparts something of the pastoral idiom in much the same way as do Mozart's symphonic slow movements in 6/8 from the 1780s (K.425, K.504, and K.550). Again, Parry offers a form somewhere between ternary and sonata form. In this case, the development presents new material surrounded by an exposition and recapitulation. This central section (development/*B*, m.45) begins and ends with strong hemiolas that, together with the agitato climax (mm.54–55), attempt to destroy the pastoral calmness of the first section. However, the Andante's most striking structural aspect is the opening, which itself acts like a frame/refrain (see Table XIV/20) resulting from its *P* and *K(P)* functions and the unusual qualities of the theme itself, with its hauntingly voiced initial A minor chord together with pizzicato cellos and basses. Notice also that *T* (m.13) is eliminated from the recapitulation, but commences the coda (m.110). This time it is undergirded by a persistent tonic pedal that attempts almost in vain to bring stability to material previously associated with a modulatory role. Scholarly evaluations of this movement have been positive: Benoliel considers the Andante to be "the heart of the symphony,"[165] and for Dibble it "stands out as a real gem."[166]

However, the Scherzo serves as a point of contention for these same two Parry *aficionados*: Dibble damns it as "dull," but Benoliel takes this judgment to task by pointing out that Vaughan Williams chose to quote from this theme for the ritornello in the *Concerto Accademico* of 1924.[167] Compared to the parallel movements in Symphonies Nos. 1 and 2, this is a neo-Classic effort perhaps in imitation of Schubert, whose early symphonies had recently

---

TABLE XIV/20
Parry. Symphony No. 3/2: Structure

Andante sostenuto 6/8

Exposition/ A

P "frame"	T	S	K(P) "frame"
	Poco animando		
A minor	mod. → G pedal	C major	
m.1	13	25	41

più animato

Development/ B

N		retrans. "frame"
mod. ————→ D minor		D minor
45	55	65

a tempo

Recapitulation/ A   Coda

P "frame"	S	K(P) "frame"	T
A minor	A major	F major	A pedal
67	77	99	110

---

gained revivals at the Crystal Palace. The central problem of this movement is not a question of dullness, but one of an English composer attempting to compose in an idiom that is foreign both in time and place. This attempt, with an added coda that follows in the tradition of Mendelssohn's "Italian" Symphony by bringing back material from both the main section and the Trio, is clearly not successful. It lacks the lilt of the Schubertian idiom, the distinctively memorable melodies, the telling use of harmony and tonality, and the effect of asymmetrical phrases; thus, its presentation is too predictable. In the end, we have a movement that is neither Parry nor Schubert. No doubt this is the weakest link in the cycle.

Again, Parry to some degree withdraws from the so-called problem of the Finale by composing a piece in common time moderato in tempo, but maestoso in outlook and using variation form. It is almost as if Parry had imposed upon himself the Classical restrictions of the form as practiced by Mozart, Haydn, and often Brahms: mostly strophic structures, harmonic repetitiveness, and the imposition of a single tonality. Indeed, the theme because of its syntactical simplicity further restricts his options; it consists of two four-bar phrases repeated. Strangely, however, whereas the previous movement was something of a failure, this one in spite of its restrictions is a success. The overall layout of the variations is given in Table XIV/21.

As can be seen up to m.149, Parry presents us with a dozen essentially strophic variations. Sometimes both the repeats are there, sometime they may be written out, sometimes there is

TABLE XIV/21

Parry. Symphony No. 3/4: Structure

	Part 1	
m.1	*Theme* ‖ : 4 : ‖ : 4 : ‖	♩ ♪
11	*Variation 1* ‖ 4+4 ‖	♩ ♪
19	*Variation 2* ‖ : 4 : ‖ 5 ‖ animato	♪ ♩
29	*Variation 3* ‖ : 4 : ‖ 5 ‖	♪ ♩
38	*Variation 4* ‖ 4 ‖ : 4 : ‖	♪
46	*Variation 5* ‖ 8 ‖ : 4 : ‖ animato	♪
59	*Variation 6* ‖ : 4 : ‖ : 4 : ‖ con fuoco	♪
	Part 2	
67	*Variation 7* ‖ 8 ‖ 8 ‖ poco meno mosso	♩ ♪
85	*Variation 8* ‖ 8 ‖ 8 ‖ a tempo	♪
101	*Variation 9* ‖ 8 ‖ 8 ‖	♩ ♪
117	*Variation 10* ‖ 4+4 ‖	♪
	Part 3	
125	*Variation 11* ‖ 4 ‖ 4+4 ‖ allargando	♪
137	*Variation 12* ‖ 4 ‖ 4+4 ‖	♪
149	*Variation 13* ‖ 7 ‖ a tempo	♪
156	*Variation 14* ‖ 13 ‖	♪
169	*Coda* 4+4 9 Tempo del Tema cadences	♪ ♩

a repeat to one-half of the strophe, but not to the other. In this way, Parry avoids the inevitability of the regular phrase structure by paradoxically destroying it in a way that at the same time preserves it. Only Variations 2 and 3 elongate the second half of the strophe by one bar. Of course, these shapes are underlined by the repeating harmonic structure. When we come to m.149 (Variation 13) the strophe is now but seven bars with two of these in 2/4 rather than 4/4, and at m.156 (Variation 14) the strophe is now extended to thirteen bars. When Parry destroys the strophic shape he also varies to a considerable degree the harmonic vocabulary. In the Theme and Variations 1 through 12, the basic vocabulary remains tonic to dominant and mediant to tonic. With Variations 13 and 14 the harmonic vocabulary is almost developmental. This makes the return to the theme (m.169) and its harmonic vocabulary recapitulatory.

The rhythmic plan of the set is also mainly Classical. The Theme through Variation 6 is an incremental acceleration of surface rhythm and of tempo. Tempo increases occur at Variations 2 and 5, both marked *animato,* and at Variation 6, marked *con fuoco.* Variation 7 slows in both tempo and surface for another acceleration lasting through Variation 10. Surprisingly, the remainder of the movement except for Variation 14 remains in the same tempo and surface.

This provides a kind of stability and majesty to these mainly moderato variations. Parry's rhythmic plan is at times reinforced by the strength of the instrumentation. Variations 5 and 6, except for the absence of the trombones, are at times *tutti* scorings. Indeed, the trombones are held in reserve until Variation 14 (m.156) and the coda. One could say that the most prominent scoring is one that combines the richest of Brahmsian colors: violins using their G- and D-string sonorities, horns, and perhaps also clarinets and bassoons. These instruments themselves suggest a timbre appropriate to the moderato tempo. Occasionally, the Brahmsian element comes close to parody. While none of Brahms's *Haydn Variations* Opus 56a are models, one passage in its Finale (m.381f) seems to have inspired Parry's Variations 2, 5, and 9.

This Finale was a brave experiment, even considering Brahms's Symphony No. 4/4; Parry ends his symphony with a variation set that never approaches a truly fast tempo, displays no virtuosity, and makes no attempt at a heroic or tragic climax. At the same time, this Finale is one that is thoroughly satisfying. Though one is reluctant to invoke the Zeitgeist, Symphony No. 3/4 conveys something of the self-satisfaction that a nation like Great Britain must have felt during the last two decades of the century. It was no longer necessary to speak of superiority, but only to enjoy it. The stronger side of the Victorian and post-Victorian mood was embodied in the music of Edward Elgar. But we must remember that Elgar was to establish himself as an orchestral composer with the *Enigma Variations* in 1899, the five *Pomp and Circumstance Marches* from 1901 to 1907 and 1930, and the Symphony No. 1 (1908). One might posit that Parry's Third and Fourth Symphonies had a profound effect on Elgar's later work.[168]

Of the reviews, we quote but two from the 1889 premiere. The first appeared in *The Star* written by George Bernard Shaw, who again had no use for attempts to revive what he believed to be a dead genre:

> After the Figaro came a new symphony by Mr C. Hubert H. Parry. And here I protest against the cruelty of these professional exercises in four mortal movements. I respect Mr Parry; I enjoy his musical essays; I appreciate his liberal views; I know the kindly feelings his pupils at the Royal College have for him. If he would only be content with an overture, I should praise it to the skies sincerely; for I like to hear just one specimen of shipshape professional composition in sonata form occasionally. But I really cannot stand four large doses of it in succession—*Allegro con spirito,* in C; *Andante sostenuto,* in A minor; *Allegro scherzoso* (*scherzoso* indeed!) in F; and *Moderato,* with variations (two repeats in each)—twelve [*sic*] variations, as I am a living man! I hate to be told that "the figure in the first bar should be observed on account of the prominence to which it is destined in the working out." That is exactly why it should *not* be observed by anybody who can get comfortably to sleep like the man who sat next to me, or the man who has a Standard to read, like the lady two bars in front of me—I mean two benches. Mr Joseph Bennet, the programist, says of the symphony:—"It has been described by the composer as a 'little' work; *and amateurs may remember that Beethoven used the German equivalent of the same term in connection with his No.8.*" I leave the world to contemplate those words in silence: no comment of mine shall disturb its inexpressible thoughts.[169]

In contrast, the critic for *The Athenaeum* took both the symphony and Parry more seriously:

> The important alteration of style which has been noticeable in Dr. Hubert Parry's recent works is conspicuous in the Symphony in C, which was produced at the Philharmonic Concert on Thursday last week. It is scarcely correct to describe it as written for

small orchestra, as the score contains the full modern complement of instruments save trombones [*sic*]. Though not so designated by the composer, its proper title would be the "English" Symphony. There can be as little doubt that Dr. Parry has given the themes a national colouring with intent as that he designedly imitated the style of Handel in his air "God breaketh the battle" in his oratorio "Judith." In the first movement we are conscious of a sense of brightness and vigour, but, with the exception of the second subject, the thematic material is not remarkable. The slow movement, *andante sostenuto* in A minor, appeared at a first hearing the weakest portion of the work. There is still a suggestion of Handelian or old English melody, but it is too long drawn out to be in keeping with the rest of the symphony, though the delicate and piquant scoring deserves praise. In the third movement, *allegro scherzoso,* we return to the frank, animated style of the first section; and the same ingenuous, unaffected manner is preserved in the theme with variations, which forms the *finale.* As the variations are twelve [*sic*] in number some contrast in the tonality would have been effective, but on the whole the composer has managed to avoid monotony, and the general conciseness of his symphony and the interest of the structural details prevent a sense of weariness. The audience found no difficulty in following the music, loud applause after each movement and two recalls at the close testifying to the general appreciation of the work. Dr. Hubert Parry has now conquered the tendency that was at first observable in his music to follow subserviently the lines of the modern German school, and he will do well to remain, at any rate for the present, in the path he is pursuing with so much success.[170]

SYMPHONY NO. 4 "FINDING THE WAY" IN E MINOR

For Parry, 1889 saw the premieres of not only the Third Symphony but also the Fourth, within six weeks of each other; Parry conducted No. 3 at the Philharmonic Society on May 23 and Richter conducted No. 4 on July 1 at his own series in London. Parry was unhappy with the Fourth Symphony; he was only pleased with the Scherzo and thought the first and final movements needed reworking. Another performance in 1904 at Bournemouth convinced him that the symphony could not stand in its original state. However, the task of revision was postponed and then finally mostly completed in 1910.[171] In February, the composer conducted it at Queen's Hall. Our discussion is based on the 1921 Novello publication prepared posthumously by Parry's amanuensis Emily Daymond, which included further revisions from after 1910.

In the revised version of 1910, Parry attached to it a program, "Finding the Way," of a quasi-autobiographical nature. Each movement was given a title: 1) Looking for It; 2) Thinking on It; 3) Playing on It; and 4) Girt for It. In addition, the themes of the individual movements are labeled in an almost leitmotific sense (Example XIV/39). Jeremy Dibble, as mentioned above, views this as a symphonic manifestation of Parry's ethical cantatas.[172] Thus, the moral and philosophical nature of these labels must have again been bewildering to the listener reading the now requisite "notes on the programme." Parry said that he "didn't think they understood much of any of it."[173] What is one to make of *I/1P,* "man's rejoicing in the consciousness of effectual forces working within him," or of the three-theme exposition of the Finale: *P* (m.1)—"man guided for life's challenges"; *1S* (mm.38, 62)—"regret at having to forego domestic comfort"; and *2S* (m.46)—"domestic intimacy," each in a different key (E major, C-sharp minor, and G major)?

An Intermezzo linking movements one and two (cf. Bennett's Symphony No. 8 in G Minor Opus 43) was dropped in 1910 and even the Scherzo, the movement that in 1889 Parry thought came off the best, was replaced. The new movement was described in the *Musical*

EXAMPLE XIV/39 Parry. Symphony No. 4/1, Themes with Program.

1st Mvt. "Looking for It"

2nd Mvt. "Thinking on It"

1st Mvt. "Looking for It"
Man rejoicing in the consciousness of effectual forces working within him

The Questions (mm. 56–58), Destiny (mm. 59–61)

Were it not better done as others use,
To sport with Amaryllis in the shade,
Or with the tangles of Neaera's hair?
Fame is the spur that the clear spirit doth raise
(The last infirmity of noble mind)
To scorn delights, and live laborious days;
(Milton. "Lycidas.")

Distaste, discontent, nausea, distress

2nd Mvt. "Thinking on It"

EXAMPLE XIV/39 (*continued*)

"*The mental vitality that throbs within, like the unceasing pulse of the physical being, rebels against the idea of extinction; the self cries out against the shortness of the spell of individual consciousness poised betwixt two abysses.*"

3rd Mvt. "Playing on It"
4th Mvt. "Girt for It"
Man girded for the challenges of life

Man's sense of regret

as he is impelled to forgo the comforts of domestic intimacy

Dedication

4th Mvt. "Girt for It"

Times as "an *al fresco fête* in the olden time—a coquettish dance of lords and ladies, interrupted by a song."[174] This gives some idea of how the conception of the Symphony in E Minor changed from the 1889 to the 1910 version and later revisions. Dibble reports that as late as 1918, Parry was still trying out portions of the middle two movements with the Royal College of Music Orchestra.[175]

Both musically and philosophically, the 1910 version with later revisions perhaps should be regarded as a new work based on some of the thematic material of 1889. This is because the first movement was completely recast, the linking Intermezzo was eliminated and replaced by a slow movement directly after the first Allegro, there was a completely new Scherzo, and in the Finale only *1P* (m.1) was retained.

It is not surprising that Parry's Symphony No. 4 is the most Brahmsian of all his symphonies. Not only does it share a No. 4 and the somewhat unusual key of E minor, it also makes use of Brahmsian sonorities in the first two movements. The opening of the first movement, even before one goes beyond the first measure, is already imprinted with a Brahms *tutti* sonority that continues with each repetition of *1P* (Example XIV/40); notice the vast spaces between the pitches (e.g., compare with the opening hammerstrokes of Brahms's *Tragic Overture* [1881]). Parry's quiet conclusion of this movement recalls Brahms's Symphony No. 3/1. The opening of the Molto Adagio, again with its warm G- and D-string timbres, also brings to mind Brahms. Movement three is almost a blatant parody of a Dvořák dance movement; perhaps its closest parallel is the Czech composer's *Scherzo Capriccioso* (1883–1884). The Finale is another example of a Brahms model, a ceremonial march, which is an element that can first be seen in Parry's 1879 Piano Quartet in A-flat.

The opening sonority of the first movement and the theme (*1P*) that travels with it (Example XIV/40) serve as pillars for the structure. As seen in Table XIV/22, Parry does not articulate the shape with binary repeats and at no point does *1P* return in its opening harmonic configuration; only at the coda (m.524) is the tonic articulated in the major mode, but this lasts only one beat before it is destroyed by a dissonance, which momentarily recalls the diminished-seventh sonority of G that marked its entrance at m.361. Both the memorability of *1P* and its failure to resolve in its original form opposes a sonata form. We have labeled *1P*'s return at m.329 as a recapitulation, but only *1S* (m.445) returns in the tonic during this stretch. Indeed, it is not until the coda that the major mode dominates the tonal landscape and brings back *P* (mm.524, 583) and *S* (mm.568, 599) in the home key. Rather than an arguable sonata structure, perhaps a more accurate description of the movement is two statements of a thematic *gestalt* of *P–T–S* and three abbreviated statements of *P–S*, where the two principal themes return in the tonic during the final two stretches.

In the opening expository presentation, as well as in the subsequent sections, sonata-form functions are clearly present. *1P* and *2P* (m.17) form a large, if open, period. *1T* (m.33), based on *P*, follows in the thematic layout that was observed in Beethoven's "Eroica" first movement, except here *1T* does not begin in the tonic. *2T* (m.57) does exactly as expected with its series of less than stable statements, while *S* (m.130) enters in a correct key (G major). As for the second section, it would be difficult to argue that it is more developmental than the first section or that section three (recapitulation [?]) is any more stable than section 2. Both stability and tranquility are established with the coda's double recapitulation.

If Parry's audience was confused by the extra-musical designations of his themes within the traditions of characteristic styles, it was with good reason. While all opening themes provide the "impulse" of the work, the idea of a man rejoicing "in the consciousness of effectual forces from within him"[176] seems at odds with the minor mode, the open fabric, and the

EXAMPLE XIV/40   Parry. Symphony No. 4/1, mm.1–15. © by Novello & Company Ltd.
International copyright secured. All Rights Reserved. Reprinted by permission.

EXAMPLE XIV/40   (*continued*)

TABLE XIV/22
Parry. Symphony No. 4/1: Structure

Con fuoco
Exposition ①

1P	2P	1T(1P)	2T	GP	2T	1S	2S
E minor	B minor	D-flat	F mod.		F mod.	G	G mod.
m.1	17	33	57	103	105	130	162

Development ② *Recapitulation (?)* ③

1P	1P	1S	2S	1P	2P	1T(1P)	2P
G minor	B-flat	D-flat	A	C	D	G	E
200	224	264	288	329	345	361	392

Coda ④   *tranquillo meno mosso* ⑤

1S	2S	1P		1S	1P	1S
E	A-flat	E major	B pedal	E	E	E
445	477	524	561	568	583	599

stark impression of *1P*. And how does *2P* (m.17) represent ideas about man's questioning and destiny when it is a lush consequent to *1P* over a dominant pedal? *1S* (m.130) in Parry's program is elucidated by lines (67–72) from Milton's *Lycidas:*

> Were it not better done as others use,
> To sport with Amaryllis in the shade,
> Or with the tangles of Neaera's hair?
> Fame is the spur that the clear spirit doth raise
> (That last infirmity of noble mind)
> To scorn delights, and live laborious days;

1S (m.130) is typical of its function: lyrical, quiet, and with solo colors in a related key. While one could say that it is pastoral in topic, as are the first three lines from Milton, such is not particularly convincing. As for the last three lines, how this has any relation to the music seems beyond the most imaginative of interpreters. *2S* (m.162) reflects "distaste, discontent, nausea, and distress,"[177] but here the music is not all that different from *1S*.

In the Adagio "Thinking on It," this appellation is at least not contrary to what is presented musically for *P*. However, *P^k* (m.19) text-paints in part its accompanying explanation, "death":

> The mental vitality that throbs within, like the uneasing pulse of physical being rebels against the idea of extinction; the self cries out against the shortness of the spell of individual consciousness poised betwixt two abysses.[178]

Here, P^k with its pizzicato bass (4/4 ♩♩ 𝄽 ♪ 𝄽 ♪ 𝄽 ♪) and its subsequent more agitated form (♫ ♫ ♫ ♫ ♫) in *S* could represent "the uneasing pulse," and the growing "appassionata" represent "the uneasing pulse," and the growing "appassionata" line (m.29) "the self cries out." For the coda (m.70), the death theme (P^k) returns *pianissimo* after which *P* (m.74), "vibrating in the memory," diminishes away.[179] One is struck that in such a serious movement dealing with death and contemplation, the major mode predominates, forming another odd juxtaposition of topic and mode.

As for the shape of this wonderfully reflective movement, Parry casts it in something of a sonatina shape. *P* (mm.1–2) is a closed form articulated with its own closing section, but overlaps into *S* (m.22), which moves into B-flat minor (m.26) and from there slips into D-flat (m.27) and to the movement's central climax (mm.35–37) when pitch and dynamics reach their high point, *P*'s reprise is reorchestrated and much more agitated as the surface moves from ♪ to ♪ to ♫. Here *P* attempts to recapture some of the climactic power of *S*, but even with its increased agitation cannot match the dynamic and pitch peaks of the central section. P^k is for now deleted as the demarcation between *P* and *S* is less well defined. *S* repeats its climax (mm.65–68) without the intensification of surface experienced in *P*, and the coda takes up P^k concluding with *P* as the horn recalls *S* (m.75). Parry's treatment of the larger shape is nearly flawless. Perhaps the recapitulatory *S* could have been intensified by continuing the increased surface activity from *P* at least through the *S* climax; instead Parry opts to make the larger recapitulatory gesture a single and more gradual intensification using different means in *P* and *S*.

Perhaps the movement that best fulfills the nature of its title, "Playing on It," is the third movement Scherzo, although not formally designated as such by Parry. There can be little doubt that Dvořák was the inspiration for this newly written movement: the plethora of different themes with a folk-like character, the colorful but not ostentatious orchestration, and the sure sense of metric shifts. Another aspect, the teasing lead-in to the next section, recalls Haydn. Unlike Dvořák and Haydn, Parry does not use central and east European folk materials; some of his themes (mm.11, 33, 77) instead sound like stylizations of English folksongs, which, at the time this movement was composed, were being studied, collected, and published by Cecil Sharp, Ralph Vaughan Williams, and others.[180] In fact, these materials could substitute for the tunes in a piece like that of *The English Folksong Suite* by Parry's student, Ralph Vaughan Williams. It should not be surprising that national elements should be revealed in the dance movement; the Minuet/Scherzo was particularly exploited in this way by Haydn, Svendsen, Dvořák, and many others in the history of the symphony. The main criticism that could be leveled at Parry's movement is that he uses too many different tunes so that the Scherzo becomes more of a potpourri rather than a symphonic movement.

This patchwork is the most noticeable in the opening section where three discrete themes are presented, each of which is preceded by an introduction/transition, thereby underlining their independence from each other (Example XIV/41). The introduction and transitions motivically anticipate the beginning of the theme (m.3), close the previous section (m.30, 69), or combine these two procedures (m.121). What is particularly noteworthy is that most of these transitions involve changes of tempo, which in turn make the structure more sectional. In contrast to the first movement, the Scherzo, after an ambiguous beginning, settles into G major (m.11) with excursions into the dominant and the dominant's Neapolitan before a strong tonic conclusion.

The Trio (m.181), though also not identified as such, uses a different approach, one commonly found among the national schools: the repetition of the theme that is varied by means other than embellishing the melody. Thus, the hunting theme (m.181) is stated five times

EXAMPLE XIV/41 Parry. Symphony No. 4/3, mm.1–18. © by Novello & Company Ltd. International copyright secured. All Rights Reserved. Reprinted by permission.

EXAMPLE XIV/41 (*continued*)

TABLE XIV/23
Parry. Symphony No. 4/3: Structure

Scherzo
*Allegretto 3/8
E minor/ambig

Tempo	Vivace				dolce grazioso		Vivacissimo		*Trio*				Animado	
Section	Intro.	A	trans.	B	trans.	C	trans.	A	C/B	D	D^1	D^2	D^3	D^4	trans.
Key		G		D		E-flat →		G	G	C					
m.	1	11	29	33	69	77	121	137	160	181	197	213	233	247	255

Scherzo
Tempo 1

Tempo	Tempo 1		Animando		dolce grazioso		Animando Vivace		*Trio*	Animado		*Coda* Vivace
Section	A	trans.	B	DC	C	trans.	A	DC	D	D	trans.	
Key	G		B		B-flat		G		E-flat	G-sharp/A-flat		G-B-flat-G
m.	263	279	286	318	326	368	392	436	448	488		504

*only structural tempos are included
DC = deceptive cadence

with changes in fabric and orchestration, the last of which is animando and curtailed for the transition to the reprise of the Scherzo proper. The reprise (m.263) differs from the opening in its new key plan as seen in Table XIV/23. Noteworthy are the two deceptive cadences (mm.318, 436), which shock since they were not present in the expository statement. In the first instance, it sets up theme *C* in B-flat and in the second leads the way to an abbreviated reprise of the Trio (m.436) in E-flat and G-sharp/A-flat. A series of changing tempos beginning with m.368, called "banter" by Parry, eventually brings the movement to an unexpectedly quiet close.[181]

Although the third movement had some music that Parry's audience might have found vaguely familiar, the model for the Finale would have been clear: a series of themes evokes the *nobilmente* of the ceremonial march for the "land of hope and glory," an Empire of such breadth not duplicated in history (Example XIV/42). Its affect is indicated by the spiritoso that heads the movement and the sostenutos that occur during the course of the piece. The view that the Finale evoked something of English patriotic fervor is to some degree supported by Parry's commentary in the themes: *1P/1A* (m.1)—"man guided for life's challenges," *1S/1B* (m.38)—"regret at having to forego comforts of domestic intimacy," *2S/2B* (m.46)—"comforts of domestic intimacy," and *N* (m.130)—"dedication."[182] Considering that Parry was a member of Britain's upper crust, both in terms of wealth and education, these designations can be regarded as sacrifices that might have to be endured for the preservation of the Empire.

Thus, the form of the Finale can either be viewed from its content of a ceremonial march with Trios or as something of a sonata form. Concerning the latter, we have a full exposition less the *K* function; *1T* (m.28) is based on *1P*; and *S* forms a ternary shape: *1S* (m.38), *2S* (m.46), and *1S* (m.62). The development begins with *1P* (m.76), is interrupted by *N* (m.130) *meno mosso tranquillo*, and eventually leads to the recapitulation (m.192) of *P* and *T*. *S* is bypassed for a grandioso rendition of *N* (m.226), a subdued reference to *1/1P* (m.247), and a heroic conclusion. Since *S* has a closed form (ternary), new material occurs in the development, and the recapitulation excludes *S,* the piece fits almost as well, if not better, into a march with two Trios followed by a coda:

March	*Trio 1*			*March*	*Trio 2*	*March*	*Coda*
	a		*b a*				Trio 2—apotheosis and cadences
E	C-sharp		G C-sharp	C-sharp	C	E	mod. → E
m.1	38			76	130	192	222

Regardless of one's inclination towards a sonata or a march type shape, the most problematic for either is the key scheme: the tonal plan within Trio 1 or *S*, the march return (*1P*) in a key other than the tonic (C-sharp), and the key of Trio 2 in C major within an E major movement.

Finally, this movement has one significant miscalculation and because it occurs at the very end of the piece, it could be considered a rationale for not programming the symphony. Beginning with the Trio 2 apotheosis, the coda is organized around slow and fast tempos:

Slow	*Fast*	*Slow*		*Fast*	*Slow*
Trio 2	March	Trio 2	*1/1P*	(*1Py*)	
Apotheosis		Apotheosis			
mod.	E	mod.		E	E
m.222	228	236	247	252	259

EXAMPLE XIV/42   Parry. Symphony No. 4/4, mm.1–10. © by Novello & Company Ltd. International copyright secured. All Rights Reserved. Reprinted by permission.

EXAMPLE XIV/42   (*continued*)

Three bars from the end, the forward thrust of *1Py* stops (Example XIV/43) as the orchestra plays six hammerstrokes on an E major chord, then is silent for three beats, and the horns play a slowly descending tetrachord that comes to rest on the fifth degree of the final E-major triad. The rests combined with the retard deflate the ending. One solution is to move the horn entrance back one bar and ignore the ritardando, thereby allowing the music to maintain its momentum.

Though known as Parry's Fourth Symphony, the work remained in progress until the end of his life. Despite its one flaw at the end, this Symphony in E Minor should be regarded as the composer's capital achievement. Both technically and expressively the cycle transcends its Brahmsian recollections, and therefore is worthy of revival. In the hands of a conductor as committed to this piece as one might be to those other E minor symphonies by Brahms, Tchaikovsky, Dvořák, and Sibelius, audiences would discover Parry worthy of their attention.

The 1889 version received notice in *The Athenaeum*, the *Monthly Musical Record*, and the *Musical Times. The Athenaeum* provided the most detailed reaction:

> The Symphony in E Minor by Dr. Hubert Parry, which was performed for the first time on Monday evening, was, it appears, composed expressly for the Richter Concerts at the request of the Viennese conductor. It was undertaken after the production of "Judith" at the Birmingham Festival, and this probably accounts for the striking resemblance between the introduction to the oratorio and the first movement of the symphony. The two open with short energetic phrases with syncopations and sequences, and in both the rugged commencement is succeeded by a second strain of a more gentle and flowing character. Resemblance ceases, however, in the working out, which contains some very clever writing, and, speaking generally, the movement is excellent, though perhaps a little too restless, the music constantly surging onward with a degree of force that renders a full comprehension of the ideas most difficult to gain at a first hearing. The slow movement in C major is full of deep expression without the least trace of sentimentality. It might be termed a song of mourning, but the grief is that which a strong virile nature might feel, the music in this respect having something in common with the second movement of the "Eroica" Symphony though otherwise the two are utterly unlike each other. The succeeding section, *allegro scherzoso,* in A minor, is very slightly suggestive of an old-fashioned dance, but the details are full of touches such as could only have proceeded from a modern composer. It is, at any rate, a charming movement, and at first acquaintance the most pleasing portion of the symphony. The *finale* is even more vigorous than the first movement, and the energy increases as the end is approached. It will be as well to defer passing critical judgment on this part of the work until another occasion. There need be no hesitation, however, in saying that the symphony as a whole is quite worthy of the composer, and we are inclined to place it first among his efforts of this kind, though it may not be so genial and engaging as his "English" Symphony, produced a few weeks ago.[183]

The *Monthly Musical Record* found the first two movements superior to the lengthy Allegretto and the "diffuse finale with its marked reminiscences from [Wagner's] . . . Kaisermarsch," while the *Musical Times* found this symphony "more elaborate and ambitious than the so-called 'English' Symphony" and the Finale "triumphant in tone" but "more restless than the first movement."[184] When the revised version was heard in 1910 the *Musical Times* and *The Athenaeum* provided brief but positive paragraphs:

> Parry's Symphony is, as revised, a large and important work. It has a sort of moral programme as a basis. The first movement is headed "Looking for it," the second movement

EXAMPLE XIV/43 Parry. Symphony No. 4/4, mm.251–60. © by Novello & Company Ltd. International copyright secured. All Rights Reserved. Reprinted by permission.

EXAMPLE XIV/43 (*continued*)

(an Adagio) has "Thinking about it" as a motto, the Scherzo illustrates "Playing on it," and the brisk Finale "Girt for it." There is much to admire in the work. It displays considerable strength and vivacity, and the slow movement has much beauty. It may be hoped that the whole symphony may soon be heard again before an audience not previously tired out.[185]

It is a stately work, and in form and phraseology it virtually follows the lines of the great classical symphonists, who, by the way, in their day acted in like manner. Modern methods, however, are not to be condemned; but to rising composers who, by merely imitating the bold experiments of gifted men trying to open up new paths, lose all regard for the past, Sir Hubert sets a fine example of respect and restraint.[186]

Between the first version of Symphony No. 4 (1889) and Symphony No. 5 (1912) Parry penned another work that is symphonic in conception: *Symphonic Variations for Full Orchestra* (1897), also known, according to *Grove 2,* as *Characteristic Variations.* Perhaps his only orchestral work to find an occasional performance after Parry's death, such luminaries as Joseph Joachim, Hans Richter, Sir Adrian Boult, Donald Francis Tovey, and others were to conduct the *Variations* and, in the case of Boult, to record it. In a 1904 letter to Richter, Parry explained its symphonic dimension in that the variations were grouped in a cyclic fashion that reflected a symphonic order and a tonally closed totality with the middle movements in other keys:

1. *Maestoso energico* 4/4 E minor and major
   Theme and Variations 1–11
2. *Allegro scherzando* C major
   Variations 13–18
3. *Largo appassionato* A minor
   Variations 19–22
4. *Vivace* E minor [rechte major]
   Variations 24–27[187]

This approach, with some reservations, was retained by Tovey when he wrote the essay for the performance of the variations by the Reid Orchestra of Edinburgh.[188]

Given the date and key of the *Symphonic Variations,* one wonders if at one point it was not considered as a possible Finale to the Fourth Symphony, also in E minor. Since a set of variations also closed Symphony No. 3 that was very close in concept and affect to the E Minor Variations, such speculation is not beyond consideration. Indeed, the concept of a symphonic variation Finale in E minor also has a precedent with Brahms, one so strong that it might have caused Parry to see the E minor variations as uncomfortably close to the Brahms, which also has a central section that in a sense is a slow movement. At the end of the "slow movement," Parry also has a chorale for horns (m.190), which suggests one of the slow 3/2 variations in the Brahms (e.g., m.113). Interestingly, both sets are headed with the appellation "energico."

Otherwise, between 1889 and 1912, Parry turned out mostly vocal music: songs, odes, oratorios, and settings of liturgical texts. Several more volumes were added to the "English Lyrics." Among the orchestral works, besides the *Variations,* there were overtures and incidental music for plays given at Cambridge and Oxford. Among the bigger cyclic pieces were a Piano Trio in G, Lady Radnor's Suite for Strings, and various sets for violin and piano.

SYMPHONY NO. 5 "SYMPHONIC FANTASIA" IN B MINOR

There were two symphonies that no doubt affected Parry's conception of his Fifth Symphony: Schumann's Symphony No. 4 in D Minor and Stanford's Symphony No. 7 in D Minor. Schumann's D Minor provided a model and a title: both Schumann's and Parry's works were titled *Fantasia* and promulgate the concept of four movements thematically interrelated and played without pause. Stanford's Symphony No. 7 was commissioned, as was Parry's, for the centenary of the Royal Philharmonic Society. Since Stanford's Symphony was heard by Parry at its premiere on February 22, 1912, Parry had every opportunity to be affected by it; he did not begin work on his commission until September 3 for its premiere on December 5. Parry wrote in his diary that Stanford's Seventh was "mild, conventional [and] Mendelssohnic—But not so interesting as Mendelssohn."[189] Such an evaluation was no doubt damning, since the ghost of Mendelssohn was as strong in late-nineteenth-century England as Handel had been at the end of the eighteenth. To say this of Stanford's work was to label it as reactionary, perhaps a reflection of Stanford's conservative political tendencies in contrast to Parry's more progressive ones and to the problems Stanford had caused Parry as director of the Royal College of Music. Indeed, there is little, if anything, that reminds one of Mendelssohn and whatever there is (e.g., the chorale) can also be found in Parry's Fifth. In some respects, Stanford's Symphony No. 7 is more progressive than Parry's. One suspects, though, that Stanford's Seventh had a strong effect on Parry, since it lasted not much longer than twenty-five minutes—about the duration of the "Symphonic Fantasia"—and brought back *II/1P* material in a recapitulatory fashion in the Finale. If Schumann's D Minor Symphony served as a conceptual model, Stanford's served as a specific challenge.

The formal similarities to Schumann are blatant (Table XIV/24). After a slow introduction, the exposition is complete, the development (m.76) ample, and the recapitulation essentially done away with in favor of a coda (m.126). In Schumann, the coda is based on new material first presented in the development, but in Parry it is the second idea of the introduction that returns in the tonic. As in the Schumann, the slow movement is in ternary form with the *B* (m.31) section based on *II/1–O*, and the Trio of the Scherzo is also based on this same material. A transition takes us from a slow introduction to the Finale, which is based on *II/1–O* in an antithesis of Schumann's affect; rather than transforming from the mysterious to the heroic, Parry composes chamber music with solo strings and woodwinds that seems almost improvisatory. As in Schumann, another complete exposition (m.14), development (m.98), and a coda (m.158) constitute the Finale. The content, however, is quite different, but no less affecting.

As in his Fourth Symphony, Parry again composes what one might call an ethical or philosophical symphony with titles to the movements and sometimes nebulous leitmotivic names to the themes (Example XIV/44). These associations, however, are less baffling than those found in the Fourth Symphony because at least the middle two movements deal with activities that have strong musical associations, "Love" and "Play," and while "Stress" can certainly be elicited in music, the title "Now" for the Finale seems not to possess any past musical associations. In the program note, Parry labeled the themes with such titles as "brooding thought," "tragedy," "wrestling thought," and others. While some of these also have musical associations, such as "suffering and distress" with its chromatically falling lines that are like extended "sighs," others, such as "content and hopefulness," are more difficult, particularly since the Finale's *K* theme is obviously related to the "wrestling thought" of the first movement's *P*. The critic for the *Musical Times* seems on target when he writes "we found the music itself more eloquent that [*sic*] explanations of its purport."[190]

TABLE XIV/24

Parry. Symphony No. 5: Structure of Cycle

	1ˢᵗ Movement: Slow—Allegro 4/4		
	Slow		
m.1	*1-O*		D major/B minor
8	*2-O*		
	Allegro		
	Exposition		
20	*P*		B minor
32	*T*		
56	*S*		D major
64	*K*		
	Development		
76	*S*		D/B/modulatory
110	*K*		F-sharp pedal
	Coda		
126	*2-O*		B minor
134	trans.		
	2ⁿᵈ Movement: Lento 3/4		
1	*A*		D major
31	*B (I/1-O)*		F major/D minor
79	*A*		D major
97	trans.		
	3ʳᵈ Movement: Vivace 6/8		
1	*[Scherzo] 6/8 (I/2-O)*		D/B vs. G/E
101	*[Trio] 2/4 (I/1-O)*		C major
181	*[Scherzo] 6/8 (I/2-O)*		D/B vs. G/E
277	trans.		
	4ᵗʰ Movement: Moderato 4/4		
1	*I/1-O*		
	Exposition		
14	*P (I/P)*		B major
23	*1T*		
31	*S (I/2-O)*		D major
51	*2T*		
82	*K*		B major
	Development		
98			
100	*N and I/2-O*		B-flat—F pedal—E-flat pedal
125	*I/2-O*		E-flat minor—B minor
149	*I/1-O*		
	Coda		
158	*I/2-O*		B major

Though Parry titled the work as in B minor for its early performances, the music itself is less explicit about its home key. Indeed, the symphony begins melodically in D major with a B minor chord and persists in this ambiguity for some time. Such a perception is underlined by *S* (m.56), which at one point hints at the dominant of D, but also D itself as well as F-sharp. *K* (m.64) further reconfirms D. Thus, we have an exposition to a first movement of a piece putatively in B minor that spends little time articulating this key. It is not until after the modulatory development (m.76) that the retransition (m.110) establishes the dominant of B minor and clearly resolves to a tonic pedal (m.126) for a short coda. Parry now reestablishes D for the slow movement which begins with a lengthy tonic pedal, while its central section vacillates between F and D before the reprise. The Scherzo is mainly in G major, E minor, and C major with more ambiguity in the opening bars. Is it B minor or D major?

EXAMPLE XIV/44   Parry. Symphony No. 5, Themes.

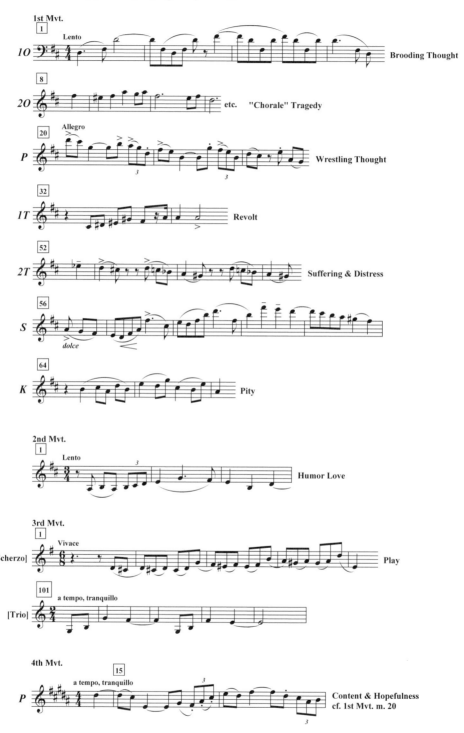

Indeed, it would be difficult to justify what turns out to be G major, which itself is made bifocal by its relative minor of E. It is not until the Finale that B major/minor convincingly reigns. In contradiction to the first movement, the exposition now articulates B over D. Still, in the exposition, there are relatively lengthy passages of modulatory activity, making it like a development section. Parry's development is short, the recapitulation is eliminated, and during the coda B major reestablishes itself. Thus, the key of B is "in process" over the approximately twenty-five-minute length of this symphony.

In the introduction to "Stress," Parry states two ideas: *1–O* described as a "rocking" motive, which the composer dubbed "brooding thought," followed by *2–O* "tragedy" (m.15), a quasi-chorale-like phrase. With the Allegro, *P* (m.20), "wrestling thought," appears undergirded by a subdominant pedal; *T* (m.32) begins on F-sharp with the motive of "revolt" and ends in "suffering and distress" (m.52); *S* (m.56), without an appellation, touches on the relative major before moving afield; and *K* (m.66) with its continuation of "pity" brings the exposition to a close. Parry's development section (m.76) concentrates on the motive of "suffering and distress." Its descending line is extended against a sequentially rising bass, then treated in diminution against an ornamented version close to its original duration. This builds to a wrenching climax and a *luftpause* followed by "pity" (m.110) and the brief coda or recapitulation of *2–O*, "tragedy," firmly entrenched in the tonic and ending with "suffering and distress" (m.134).

"Love" is another expert slow movement from Parry's pen. Each of the three eight-measure statements of the theme is treated as a canon, the first two over a D pedal, the third with an accelerating harmonic rhythm followed by a closing (m.25) that slows the action again with a D pedal. This, the first part of a ternary form, is vintage Parry with its expressive line and rich timbres here further darkened in the first phrase by the bass clarinet. Each repetition increases the size of the orchestra and raises the tessitura by an octave forming a long-term *crescendo,* but with only a single measure of *fortissimo* (m.21) before unwinding to a quiet conclusion. *B* (m.31), based on *I/1–O* ("brooding thought"), is more active than *A* and is in a much more agitated version than its original first-movement statement. Indeed, every aspect has more activity as the piece moves toward two climaxes (mm.55 and 66), the second concluding with a *feroce* recitative. A retransition (m.71) anticipates *A*'s return. *A* (m.79) now has only two statements; the second (m.87) is close to the original third statement somewhat elongated for the transition to the Scherzo. Notice that near the end (m.100f), Parry offers something approaching *Klangfarbenmelodie* as subtle changes of color form the line. In September 1912, Schoenberg's *Five Pieces for Orchestra* was heard in London with its third movement of subtly shifting colors. While Parry did not experience the piece firsthand on that occasion, he may very well have heard about it. Parry did hear Schoenberg's Opus 16 in 1914; his reaction was not favorable.[191]

When Parry accused Stanford of being Mendelssohnic, he might have looked again at his own Scherzo, whose fabric and articulation recalls more of Mendelssohn than of Berlioz. Nevertheless, it is articulation that shapes the rhythm of this metrically shifting piece with hints of hemiola, compound duple, and syncopation, and later an unexpected shift to 2/4 as part of a larger transition to the Trio (m.101). The relationship of this material to *I/2–O* is almost Brahmsian in its use of the first four intervals (cf. Brahms Symphony No. 2) and in its reduction down to half-steps. The Trio is based on *I/1–O* with its tonal ambiguity now gone as C major becomes strongly articulated. If the Scherzo proper has something of the fantastic, the Trio has something of the pastoral with its thirds, sixths, and open fourths and fifths in the horns and woodwinds. C major, which is unrelated to the remainder of the cycle, underlines the pastoral interlude as separate from the otherwise burdensome affects of this symphony.

At the introduction to the Finale, both the change of mode to B major and the entry of the harp suggest, together with the transformation of *I/1–O* and *II/P*, a celestial affect. *II/P* is now transformed in *IV/P* (m.14) from "brooding thought" to "content and hopefulness." *S* (m.31) bears a similar relationship to *II/2–O* in that it is an inverted transformation of the first movement's presentation. After a short, but very Brahmsian, development (m.98), including an E-flat minor appearance of *I/2–O* (m.125) as a chorale and then a working over of its head motif (m.137) in B minor, the coda (m.158) turns to B major and a tranquillo affect as *I/2–O* becomes a chorale peroration (m.158) concluding in a triumphant transformation (Example XIV/45).

Despite its strong modeling on Schumann's Symphony No. 4, Parry's Symphony No. 5 is, perhaps next to Elgar's Symphony No. 1, one of the finest English symphonies of its time. Unlike Parry's other symphonies, it has no weak links and because of its brevity, there is no padding. It came to be one of the composer's most widely performed works in England. After its premiere on December 5, 1912, the next year heard three performances: at the concerts of Balfour Gardiner, at Bournemouth (April 17), and under Henry Wood at the Queen's Hall (November 1). In 1980, Sir Adrian Boult recorded it. Though its language is that of high Romanticism, it is a deeply affecting work that goes far beyond Parry's other symphonies in coherence and originality. Parry's Fifth is a work truly deserving revival.

Early reviews appeared in the *Musical Times* and *The Athenaeum:*

> The new Symphony made a great impression. It was felt to be a work of deep thought and earnest self-expression. . . . In the account of the work, presumably written by the composer, given in the programme, it is well stated that "the sphere of music is the expression of feelings, moods, impulses, and emotions; so mere words will not cover what it means." Suggestions, however, are offered to follow the intentions of the composer in dealing with external ideas. We regret we are compelled to postpone a full consideration of this work. It must suffice just now to give briefly some general impressions. First, we would say that we found the music itself more eloquent that [*sic*] the explanations of its purport. The first movement has great breadth and gravity; the second movement introduces a charming theme delicately treated; the third movement ("Play"), a sort of Scherzo, is one of the most delightful and joyous things the composer has ever written, and the last movement makes a fitting climax and peroration to the whole scheme.[192]

> A new symphony in B minor, by Sir Hubert Parry, was the chief feature in the programme of the third concert of the "Royal" Philharmonic Society on Thursday evening in last week. That Symphony is not only new in the ordinary sense, but also a departure from the usual classical lines. The composer had already prepared us for some change, for in his book "Style in Musical Art" he declared that "one of the drawbacks of sonata forms is that they are too limited"; that "they tend to emphasize the formal at the expense of the spiritual." Liszt was of the same opinion, and created the "symphonic poem," or rather developed a plan partially adopted by Beethoven in his later pianoforte sonatas. Sir Hubert's new work is a symphonic poem, but—to quote again from his book—without "a superficial suggestion of externals such as we find in Liszt and Berlioz and the earlier programme composers." His four movements are linked together, and the principal themes, bearing titles, appear, in various transformations, in all the sections. The practical acknowledgement by so able a writer and composer as Sir Hubert that old forms "are not in keeping with modern views of the function and powers of music," will do great good. It will help to dispel the notion that "sonata forms" alone are legitimate.

EXAMPLE XIV/45   Parry. Symphony No. 5/4, mm.213–22.

EXAMPLE XIV/45   (*continued*)

In this new Symphony the harmonies, phraseology, orchestration, and conciseness of the various sections are at variance with the methods of many modern composers. Thus, though the form is modern, the atmosphere is still classical. The work was given under the direction of the composer.[193]

CONCLUSION: PARRY'S SYMPHONIES AND HIS SYMPHONY
ARTICLE IN *GROVE'S DICTIONARY*

Like his contemporary Stanford, Parry began his career as a symphonist strongly under the influence of Robert Schumann and later took the mantle of Johannes Brahms and Antonín Dvořák. But Parry, while perhaps reaching greater heights than Stanford, was less able to turn out one masterly movement after another. After the heavily influenced First Symphony, Parry struggles with the Finale problem. Symphony No. 2 has a Finale that even after revisions handicaps any performance of an otherwise fine work. Symphony No. 3 does have a Finale of unusual form and affect that almost works for its cycle, but it is preceded by a Scherzo that engenders little interest except as an English recycling of Schubert. With Symphony No. 4, Parry reaches a new stage in the composition of cycles with ethical/philosophical programs, but it took him a series of revisions lasting to his death in order to get it as close to right as his life span allowed. And still its Finale has a weak conclusion. With his Fifth Symphony, Parry achieves an originality of content, a musical coherence, and an eloquent expression in a conception based on Robert Schumann's Symphony No. 4.

Parry was a prolific composer but, unlike Stanford, his work as a teacher was not only in composition but also in music history. Additionally, he was an administrator who succeeded George Grove as the director of the Royal College of Music. Composition was something often apart from his main activities at the College and at Oxford.

Parry's duties as an assistant editor of the first edition of *Grove's Dictionary of Music and Musicians* developed the musicological side of his talents. One of the articles he wrote for *Grove* was on the symphony, which was perhaps one of the first articles of its type to view the genre from a comprehensive stylistic and historical view. Parry's historical model was that of evolution in a Darwinian sense; he often writes of the "progress" of the genre. Further, this article was probably begun *ca.* 1875, which was about seven years before Parry began his own First Symphony. Thus, all of Parry's symphonies were composed after his study of the genre up to 1875, beginning with the early opera overture and progressing through Brahms's Symphony No. 2.

In pursuing his study of the early symphony, Parry visited libraries at Oxford, Cambridge, and the British Museum. Considering the non-existence of serious study of this music and the lack of editions in score, Parry's knowledge of the early repertoire is extraordinary. He studied the use of the term "sinfonia" in early-seventeenth-century music and, from later in that century, also surveyed examples from the overtures of Lully as well as those of Alessandro Scarlatti, Leonardo Vinci, David Perez, Niccolò Piccini, Niccolò Jommelli, Antonio Sacchini, and Baldassare Galuppi. And, of course, he also deals with the other related genres, such as the concerto. Composers that Parry gives special attention to are J. C. Bach, C. F. Abel, C. P. E. Bach, and Johann Stamitz, the latter before Riemann issued his editions and declarations. The fact that Parry's discussion of Joseph Haydn's symphonies seems dated is because so few of his works were then available in score or in parts outside of Austria. Mozart's last symphonies and Haydn's "London" Symphonies are given rather detailed treatment, as are those of Beethoven. Notice that Parry gives almost as much space to Louis Spohr, Felix Mendelssohn, and, of course, Robert Schumann. Serious discussion is also given to Hector Berlioz, Franz Liszt, Joachim Raff, and Anton Rubinstein. He ends with Brahms: "the greatest representative of the highest art in the department of [the] Symphony."[194] While today we might regard some of his concepts as dated, his symphony article still resonates as first-rate scholarship.

Edward Elgar
INTRODUCTION

Parry's article on the symphony did not mention Edward Elgar; at the time it was written, Elgar had not yet made his mark as a musician. However, he had read Parry's contributions to the first edition of *Grove,* and his clear discussions were of help to the largely self-taught young musician.[195] Elgar had neither a conservatory nor a university education; from the age of sixteen he was essentially a freelance musician; he played violin and organ and did some conducting and teaching. Thus, Elgar's orientation as a musician was decidedly different from Parry and Stanford. He learned his craft by going directly to the scores of others. Elgar's counterpart in this respect was George Grove, whose life in music was without any formal training.[196] Grove, however, was a man of London, whereas Elgar could not make much headway professionally in the capital city. Elgar moved to London in March 1890, but found himself somewhat uncomfortable in its environment and returned to provincial life in June 1891.

As a man of the provinces, initially without an academic appointment, Elgar was able to achieve recognition and strike a sympathetic tone that came to be synonymous with England as a national musical entity. Elgar achieved the status of a national composer not through folk-songs or dances, but through the *nobilmente* character of his music. At the heart of this style are the marches he composed—the five of the *Pomp and Circumstance* series, the *Coronation March* (1911), and the *Empire March* (1924)—as well as passages from the *Enigma Variations,* the two completed symphonies, and certainly other instrumental and vocal works.

Though Elgar had composed a series of cantatas and oratorios, it was not until June 19, 1899, that he achieved his first success in instrumental music with the so-called *Enigma Variations,* conducted in London by Hans Richter. While the *Variations* had extra-musical aspects that drew attention to them, it was the music itself that made them so successful. Nothing in English orchestral music up to this time could match its skilled invention, originality, melodic transformations, and handling of the orchestra, which in its own idiosyncratic way established Elgar as the master among his English contemporaries and a certain match for the most acknowledged orchestrator among the Germans, Richard Strauss. Both Strauss's *Don Quixote* and Elgar's *Enigma* are trail-blazing works making the orchestral variations by Parry and Stanford pale by comparison. Elgar was forty-two when he achieved public recognition as a composer of tremendous gifts. England was to wait with anticipation almost ten more years for Elgar's First Symphony.

Elgar's first involvement with the symphonic genre took place during his boyhood and was discussed by the composer in a lecture he gave in 1905 at the University of Birmingham as the Richard Peyton Professor. He remarks that the first works he studied at *ca.* the age of sixteen were the Beethoven symphonies and Mozart's Symphony in G Minor K.550:

> In studying scores the first which came into my hands were the Beethoven symphonies. Anyone can have them now, but they were difficult for a boy to get in Worcester thirty years ago. I, however, managed to get two or three, and I remember distinctly the day I was able to buy the Pastoral Symphony. I stuffed my pockets with bread and cheese and went out into the fields to study it. That was what I always did.

I once ruled a score for the same instruments and with the same number of bars as Mozart's G minor Symphony, and in that framework I wrote a Symphony, following as far as possible the same outline in the themes and the same modulation. I did this on my own initiative, as I was groping in the dark after light, but looking back after thirty years I don't know any discipline from which I learned so much.[197]

The anticipation of a symphony by Elgar and his intimidation by the tradition of the genre could only be matched by the long wait for the Symphony in C Minor by Johannes Brahms. Elgar had said,

I hold that the Symphony without a programme is the highest development of art. Views to the contrary are, we shall often find, held by those to whom the joy of music came late in life or who would deny to musicians that peculiar gift, which is their own, a musical ear, or an ear for music. I use, as you notice, a very old-fashioned expression, but we all know what it conveys: a love of music for its own sake.

It seems to me that because the greatest genius of our days, Richard Strauss, recognises the Symphonic Poem as a fit vehicle for his splendid achievements, some writers are inclined to be positive that the symphony is dead. Perhaps the form is somewhat battered by the ill-usage of some of its admirers, although some modern Symphonies still testify to its vitality; but when the looked-for genius comes, it may be absolutely revived.[198]

Elgar's editor at Novello's was August Johannes Jaeger, the famed Nimrod of the *Variations,* who placed a notice in the March 1899 *Musical Times:*

Mr. Edward Elgar has several interesting compositions "on the stocks." Chief among them is the new symphony for the Worcester Festival, which is to bear the title "Gordon." As in the case of Beethoven's No. 3, Mr. Elgar has selected a great hero for his theme, though one of a very different type from that of the "Eroica." The extraordinary career of General Gordon—his military achievements, his unbounded energy, his self-sacrifice, his resolution, his deep religious fervour—offers to a composer of Mr. Elgar's temperament a magnificent subject, and affords full scope for the exercise of his genius; moreover, it is a subject that appeals to the sympathies of all true-hearted Englishmen.[199]

General Charles Gordon, a figure who Elgar deeply admired and in the view of some had achieved a form of sainthood, was killed in the Battle of Khartoum. He became a national British hero with the formation of Gordon Boys Clubs and the circulation of copies of Cardinal Newman's *The Dream of Gerontius* with Gordon's annotations, a copy of which was owned by Elgar.[200]

However, Jaeger's notice was certainly without foundation, for on October 20, 1898, Elgar complained,

"Gordon" sym. I like this idee but my dear man *why* should I try?? I can't see—I have to earn money somehow & it's *no good* trying this sort of thing even for a "living wage" & your firm wouldn't give 5£ for it—I tell you I am sick of it all: why can't I be encouraged to do decent stuff & not hounded into triviality.[201]

After much ballyhoo of competing conductors and organizations jockeying for position—which included the Three Choirs Festival and the 1904 Elgar Festival in London (three days at Covent Garden devoted entirely to Elgar's music); Hans Richter and Felix Weingartner; and others—in the end the idea of a "Gordon" Symphony never went very far. When Elgar was in the throes of completing his A-flat Major Symphony he was explicit that this symphony was not the long-awaited "Gordon" Symphony and that the only extra-musical aspect was "a wide experience of human life with a great charity (love) and a *massive* hope in the future."[202]

After the spate of reports concerning the "Gordon Symphony," Elgar completed two works in the genre and began a third (See Table XIV/25). His First Symphony was created when he was fifty-one and had already established his reputation. By this time Parry, Stanford, and Cowen had completed nearly all their symphonies; Parry and Stanford were to compose one more each. Elgar's Second Symphony was to come three years later and was officially dedicated to the late King Edward VII. It was also prefaced by lines from Percy Bysshe Shelley's *Invocation.* This and other factors have led to searches for extra-musical meaning in this work. Some have also thought that the First Symphony, because of its dramatic juxtapositions of character and key, also contains some sort of narrative even though Elgar denied such associations. His Third Symphony in C minor was commissioned by the BBC, and Elgar worked on it almost up to his death in 1934. Very little of it was left in a performable state (Plate B6). However, Elgar left behind a number of sketches which have been "reconstructed" by Anthony Payne. This effort was premiered by the BBC Symphony Orchestra, fulfilling a commission left unfinished from sixty-five years earlier.

SYMPHONY NO. 1 IN A-FLAT MAJOR OPUS 55

Stanford, Parry, and probably Cowen represented the finest English symphonists after Bennett's ill-fated Symphony in G Minor Opus 43. They had more performances than any other symphonists of English birth and training. However, nothing prepared the English musical establishment and the public for the triumph Sir Edward Elgar was to experience. Not even the success of the *Enigma Variations* and the *Five Sea Pictures* in 1899, and *The Dream of Gerontius* as well as other oratorio-like works after 1902, could match the reception of the long-awaited First Symphony in 1908. Hans Richter, to whom the symphony was dedicated and who conducted the first performance in Manchester with the Hallé Orchestra, declared it to be "the greatest symphony of modern times *and not only in this country.*"[203] These were words from a conductor who during his years in Vienna had premiered more symphonies that had entered the canon prior to the First World War than anyone else.[204] The London premiere of the First Symphony hosted every important British musician as well as Gabriel Fauré; one can only wonder what the introspective French composer thought. In the first year after its premiere, about one hundred performances were given not only in England but also on the continent, in Australia, and in America. It was published by Novello in the same year it was premiered (1908), which guaranteed further renditions. In England the piece gained something of a cult following. One wonders if there might be some significance to its opus number of 55, the same number used for Beethoven's "Eroica" Symphony.

Though it was denied that there was any extra-musical aspect to Elgar's Opus 55, on January 6, 1918, Landon Ronald conducted the symphony at which Lady Elgar was present and took the work as dealing with the "particular" synthesized with the "universal":

> The great tune so majestic and beautiful [Introduction]. Then the wild underspirits and vain things conquered by it [first movement proper]. Then the pagan tune absolutely a picture of the Huns and the great struggle [second movement] ending in absolute triumphant victory for the great rights of humanity. So wonderful and uplifting [third movement and Finale].[205]

On the next day Ronald told Lady Elgar that after the slow movement he always wanted to cross himself. Regarding what seems to be the Trio (m.130) of the Scherzo/march, Lady Elgar

TABLE XIV/25
The Symphonies of Edward Elgar

Opus	Key	Date	Title	Movements	Instrumentation	Comments
55	A-flat	1907–8	Symphony No.1	1. Andante. Nobilmente e semplice 4/4—Allegro 2/2 (631 m.) 2. Allegro molto 1/2 (463 m.) F-sharp minor 3. Adagio 4/8 (124 m.) D 4. Lento 4/4—Allegro 2/2 (426 m.) D minor—A-flat	Grand plus Flt. (Picc.), EH, Bclar., Cbssn., Tpt., Tuba, 2 Harps, and BD, SD, Cym.	Dedicated to Hans Richter "True artist and true friend." First performance: December 3, 1908, Hallé Orchestra, Hans Richter conducting.
63	E-flat	1910–11	Symphony No. 2	1. Allegro vivace e nobilmente 12/8 (343 m.) 2. Larghetto 4/4 (176 m.) C minor 3. Rondo: Presto 3/8 (606 m.) C major 4. Moderato e mestoso 3/4 (356 m.)	Grand plus Flt. (Picc.), EH, Bclar., Cbssn., Tpt., Tuba, 2 Harps, and BD, SD, Cym., and Tambourine	Dedicated to the memory of "His late Majesty King Edward VII." First performance: May 24, 1911, Queen's Hall Orchestra, the composer conducting. Motto: "Rarely, rarely comest thou, Spirit of Delight" (Shelley).
88	C Minor	1932–33	Symphony No. 3	1. Allegro molto maestoso 12/8(4/4) (276 m.) 2. Scherzo: Allegretto 3/4 (216 m.) A minor 3. Adagio solenne 4/4 (161 m.) C major 4. Allegro 4/4 (330 m.) C major	Grand plus Flt. (Picc.), EH, Bclar., Cbssn., Tpt., Tuba, 2 Harps, and BD, SD, Cym., Tri., Tambourine, Tam-tam	Reconstruction by Anthony Payne. First performance: February 15, 1998, BBC Symphony Orchestra, Andrew Davis conducting.

wrote on August 2, 1907, "E. wrote *lovely* river piece. You cd. hear the wind in the rushes by the water."[206] Later in early 1909, Elgar told the London Symphony Orchestra of this passage: "play it like something we hear down by the river."[207] If this symphony has any narrative, it is a heroic one, not unlike Beethoven's Symphony No. 5, following the archetype of struggle to triumph.

Unlike many of the English symphonies surveyed in this chapter, Elgar's First is an effort to bring unity to the cycle in a manner that reminds one of Schumann in his Second, Third, and Fourth Symphonies. The theme of the first movement's introduction is referred to by almost every commentator as the motto; Michael Kennedy prefers to call it the *idée fixe*.[208] This motto plays a rather prominent role in the first and last movements and is also heard in movements two and three. Apart from undergoing a number of transformations spanning from the *misterioso* to the triumphant, Elgar applies to it on two occasions a sense of distance or perspective by having only the last desks of the violins and violas playing it *piano* (I/m.542, IV/m.197). Elgar remarked of this effect,

> I have employed the *last desks* of the strings to get a soft diffused sound: the listener need not be bothered to know *where* it comes from—the effect is of course widely different from that obtained from the *first desk soli:* in the latter case you perceive what is there—in the former you don't perceive that something is not there—which is what I want.[209]

This use of separation, particularly if the violins are divided to the left and right of the conductor with the violas on the inner right and the cellos on the inner left, makes for a new wrinkle on the Berliozian concept of music and space. Since the motto is one of the most memorable themes in all symphonic music, it easily operates on the level of the cycle, but also within the first and last movements as structural pillars.

Such an observation of a double thematic function at the cyclic and movement level can also be applied to its tonalities (Example XIV/46). The principal key of the cycle is A-flat, which begins and closes the first movement and then closes the Finale. The bulk of the first movement's main sonata structure has as its tonic the most distant key from A-flat: D minor. Elgar's Finale begins with its slow introduction in D minor and finds its way to A-flat for the coda (m.352). F-sharp minor is the key of the second movement and D major that of the third. Thus, F-sharp serves as a long-term transition to D major. Perhaps it might be more correct to view this as a symphony in D that begins and ends in A-flat. According to Adrian Boult, this tonal peculiarity was because of a bet placed with Elgar that one could not produce a symphony in two keys.[210] Yet when listening to this expansive work of more than fifty minutes, until the motto returns in A-flat, the work cannot end. Part of this phenomenon is a result of the imprintability of I/1–0 on the listener and its ability to also convey the sense of tonality to both the trained musician and the casual listener (Example XIV/47).

Additionally, the middle two movements not only enhance the anchoring of D as the most articulated key, if not the most strongly articulated key; they are also thematically made of the same pitch materials (See Example XIV/48). The transformation from a perpetual motion theme in the second to an Adagio theme in the third movement constitutes a musical miracle. One wonders if Elgar was trying to duplicate a thematic similarity that had initially bypassed him in the Brahms Third Symphony, a work he deeply admired. The extraordinary aspect of the relationship of the two middle movements is that the artifice is seldom detected because it seems so correct as both a scherzo-like theme and as an inspired Adagio theme. It was Hans Richter who remarked of the slow movement: "Ah! this is a *real* Adagio—such an Adagio as Beethove' would 'ave writ."[211]

Elgar begins the A-flat major introduction with a double and symmetrical statement of

EXAMPLE XIV/46 Elgar. Symphony No. 1, Cyclic Key Scheme.

EXAMPLE XIV/47 Elgar. Symphony No. 1/1, mm. 1–9.

EXAMPLE XIV/48 Elgar. Symphony No. 1/2, mm. 1–4 and /3, mm. 1–4.

the motto (mm.1, 26). The first time is quietly scored for woodwinds and lower strings; the second, *tutti* and *fortissimo*, lumbers along like a Trio out of the *Pomp and Circumstance Marches*. There is nothing symphonic here, just two strophes rudimentarily connected and concluding with a sustained A-flat tonic that takes us to the Allegro almost firmly in D minor. Elgar's motto (*M*) comes back before the development (m.202), before the recapitulation (m.359), before the coda (m.542), and at the end (m.611). In many ways, the motto comes to represent the stability that a refrain offers.

M	Exposition	*M*	Development	*M*	Recapitulation	*M*(Coda)	*M*
m.1	51	202	214	359	382	542	611

The exposition uses many traditional aspects. Well-defined functions are in evidence: *P* (m.51), *1T* (m.92), *2T* (m.104), *S* (m.114), and *K* (m.150). Since *P* already has some of the storminess often associated with *T*, Elgar needs to intensify *T*'s lack of stability, which is accomplished by suddenly changing from 2/2 to 6/4 with hemiola as well as by using more regular rhythms. *S* in F major presents the most serene music of the exposition, while *K* has some of the instability of *T*. *K*'s agitation and muscularity in G minor and other keys is again underlined by hemiolas and syncopations. This is in part allowable because of the motto's return (m.202) in the stable key of C major with that reassuring melody. Not only is the A-flat/D minor juxtaposition striking, but so is the key plan of the exposition. While the *P/S* relationship from D minor to F major seems orthodox, once one adds the other articulated keys of G minor for *K* and C major for the motto, Elgar has come close to a four-key exposition. Two of the most stable of these keys, F and C, could be regarded in Brahmsian fashion as having an axial relationship to the introduction's A-flat.

Much of Elgar's exposition, except for *S* and the motto, acts more like a traditional development section in its thematic treatment, rhythmic agitation, and stormy character. Elgar deflects much of this by devoting large chunks of the development section (m.214) to new material (*N*). After two stretches, the first dealing with the rhythm of *P* (m.214) and the second with *K* (m.230), at m.264 *N* is introduced, a theme that in its nature and treatment defies the image of Elgar the late Romantic in favor of Elgar the progressive. *P* (m.214) is a fairly normal Brahmsian presentation with duplets and triplets heard simultaneously centering around G and B minor. *1K* (m.230) begins ambiguously tonal with *K* treated to invertible counterpoint. To this Elgar adds a new swirling motif that will gain further prominence as the fabric increases in density. *N*, what Elgar called a "restless, enquiring, and exploring" motive,[212] is remarkable for its intervallic spans of almost or little more than an octave. After a section in the neighborhood of B minor, *N* is heard again (m.332) with material from *K*, the motto returns (m.359), and a retransition (m.370) based on the opening section of the development leads to a recapitulation (m.382) with *P* in D minor.

Apart from small alterations as the recapitulation unfolds, notable is the addition of the swirling motive to *1T* (m.417), the varied and developed *K* (m.504), and the overall key scheme in relation to the exposition:

	P	*T*	*S*	*K*	*M*
Exposition:	D minor	mod.	F major	G minor	C major
Recapitulation:	D minor	mod.	A-flat major	D minor	A-flat

The composer noted about the beginning of the recapitulation: "As [the treble] gives a feeling of A minor + [the bass] of G maj:—I have a *nice sub-acid feeling* when they come together."[213] Otherwise, Elgar here promotes no regular pattern of new keys, which is evident in *1T* (m.417) transposed down a whole step and *2T* (m.429) transposed up a minor third leading to *S* in A-flat. That *S* returns in A-flat rather than D major certainly emphasizes the dual importance of A-flat and D minor to the cycle. As frequently found in Beethoven and the post-Beethoven sonata forms, the coda (m.542) complements the development but here in a more relaxed tempo; after the motto (m. 542), *P*'s rhythm (m.565) is presented in a pure and stabilized form, *N* (m. 585) returns undergirded by an A-flat pedal, *K* (m.601), now più lento, has the added swirls, and for the quiet close (m.611) the motto and *K* combine contrapuntally. After the storminess of substantial sections of the Allegro, a quiet reflective ending seems in order.

The dance movement, as so frequently occurs in the English symphony, moves to second place. Though absent of any triple meter, it maintains a choreographic stance throughout with the broken *perpetuum mobile* (m.1), a march (m.42), and the pastoral "river" music (m.130).[214] Though not of the length of a Mahlerian movement, it does possess something of a Mahlerian spirit and a sense of expanded form. As for the spirit, the pastoral river music sounds like something that could belong to Mahler's Symphony No. 3 and its orchestration seems like vintage Mahler. Like Mahler's use of naïve material, *B* seems to evoke a childhood memory of playing by the river. Indeed, the march too seems Mahlerian. But all this is speculation without foundation: Elgar did not own any Mahler scores[215] nor do we know of any Mahler symphony performances he could have heard.

The form of Symphony No. 1/2 is outlined in Table XIV/26. With the expectations of a main section with Trio, one can easily become confused in terms of formal dimensions. After the opening *A–a* section with transition, one would expect *b* (m.42) in the dominant to be the Trio. Though beginning quietly, the middle section soon becomes a boisterous march after which *Aa* returns in the tonic. *B* (m.130) appears in B-flat followed by an abbreviated return of *Aa* with a new counterpoint. At this point, one might expect the movement to conclude, except Elgar continues to repeat his material with *Aa* and *b* combined polyphonically (m.257) and *Aa* (m.356) with its counterpoint. In the coda (m.373), Elgar seems to begin the process again, except this time *Aa* appears in F minor, the *B* section follows (m.386), and concludes with *Ab* in augmentation (m.430) in F-sharp. Its key scheme of F-sharp and C-sharp minor for *A* and B-flat for *B* seems to present the same sort of tonal dichotomy found in the first movement. That the coda begins in F at a slower tempo seems to be a concession to B-flat. However, Elgar refuses to conclude in F, preferring the prevailing tonic of F-sharp. The movement ends by sustaining F-sharp mixed with D major moving directly into the D major Adagio.

The first two movements present a series of stark contrasts of keys, affects—nobilmente, stormy, march, pastoral—and orchestration from simple *tutti* formations to fabrics that rival those of the high German Romanticists, the French Impressionists, and the neo-Classicists. While the Adagio preserves the complex fabrics of the first two movements with regard to orchestration, its texture is more melody oriented and its affect more of one mood. This lends to the slow movement a kind of stability not present in the first two pieces of the cycle. But it is not only in context that this Adagio is a potent force; in isolation it is also a quietly sublime statement. In this survey of the English symphony, one thing that does stand out are the slow movements; going back to Haydn, it was not the first or last, but the second movements that made the strongest impact on his English audience and to which the word "sublime" was often applied.

TABLE XIV/26
Elgar. Symphony No. 1/2: Structure

Allegro molto 1/2

Introduction	$\boxed{A}$ a	a	trans.	b		trans.	a	trans.	$\boxed{B}$
	Perpetual motion			March					River Music
F-sharp minor				C-sharp minor			F-sharp minor $\longrightarrow$ B-flat		
m.1	5		26	42	74		102	118	130

$\boxed{A}$ a	trans.	b	b	$\boxed{B}$		$\boxed{A}$ a
new ctrpt.		March		River Music		
F-sharp minor		F-sharp minor		B-flat		F-sharp
204	216	232	257	281		356

Coda $\boxed{A}$ a	$\boxed{B}$	M	$\boxed{A}$ b	M	‖ attacca
	River Music		augmented		
F minor			F-sharp minor	D F-sharp	
373	386	402	430	442	

M = motto

Elgar designs the Adagio along the traditional lines of sonata form: *P* (m.1) is in D major and *S* (m.33) in A major with two *T* sections (m.17 and m.24). The middle section essentially brings back the *T* themes transposed up a third and a fourth respectively leading to a recapitulatory *P* and *S*—the former in D, the latter beginning in C-sharp (m.82) and moving enharmonically to F minor (m.84). In the Classical tradition, the coda (m.96) makes allusions to the subdominant before carrying this to completion with a plagal cadence.

In a movement of this sort in a slow tempo listeners rarely turn their attention to form, but instead to content. Apart from the already discussed derivation of the material, perhaps what is most striking is the length and seamlessness of the opening theme; *P* is sixteen measures of 4/8 time with the tempo ♪=50. Elgar carefully controls nearly every aspect of this theme's *a* (m.1) and *b* (m.10) to make them into a single span of music in which range, dynamics, and orchestration converge. *Pa* encompasses a range from d' to g-sharp" in which the line incrementally rises and more rapidly falls almost back to the tonic. Dynamics reinforce this by reaching their climax with g-sharp", but then returning to *pianissimo* more rapidly than the line falls. Elgar's orchestration in this passage centers on the strings with the winds adding a background of changing timbres. Notice that this background might consist of one to four or five voices, but expands as the g-sharp" and *forte* are approached and realized. *Pb* deepens the action observed in *Pa:* the range is increased, the dynamics widened, the climax more sustained, and the orchestration increased. In addition, for *Pb* the tempo broadens to *largamente* and the melody is marked *sonore.* One could make many of these same points for subsequent passages in this most accomplished movement.

In addition, *S* (m.33) is provided with an atmospherically articulated countermelody that alludes to the motto. Perhaps the best example of Elgar's special filigree orchestration is *1T* (m.46): many of the motives played as a line in one instrument are motivically divided among various woodwind instruments, sometimes with additional embellishments. In the coda (m.96), much of this activity becomes streamlined so that the last measures are an unadorned homophony that diminishes into nothingness. Elgar's melody for this coda comes from a 1904 sketch labeled from *Hamlet:* "The rest is silence."[216]

The last chord of the Adagio can almost move directly into the Finale. The interlude quality of the slow movement as something apart from the main affect of the symphony is underlined by the Finale's beginning, which gives the impression of taking up somewhere in the middle of the first movement; it begins with *I/N* introduced in the first movement's development section. However, now *I/N* is merely played in the distance by the last desks of violas and cellos. This is interspersed in fuller scorings with various transformations of the motto as a march (m.6) both bowed and pizzicato as well as in a more cantabile articulation. In a letter to Ernest Newman, Elgar drew attention to mm.10–11, a "romantico" theme that comes back transformed in the coda.[217] Elgar's Allegro begins with a *P/A* theme (m.37) not all that different from I/*Pa* with its dotted rhythms. *S/B* (m.68) comes upon us with dispatch, and here Elgar falls into a rare moment as he recalls the *S* from the Finale of Brahms's Symphony No. 3 with its lyrical quarter-note triplets over duplet quarters. The exposition concludes with the motto as *K* (m.97) in its march-like guise; in five four-measure groups, it gathers strength beginning *piano* for woodwinds and strings and ending *tutti* and *fortissimo.*

At this point, one is primed for a sonata structure to move on directly to a development, but the return of *P/A* in the tonic might signal a rondo, a sonata structure with a false repeat, or a full sonata form with expository repeat. Elgar essentially takes the first option. After *P/A* (m.117) in D minor and an expansion upon it, a fugato (m.137) on the motto, also presented in inversion, is boldly begun by the brass. By m.150 the motto is alternating with *P/A* and *O* in diminution mixed with syncopation. Another fugal exposition begins as before (m.172) but is interrupted by *S* (m.179), which Elgar might have described as E-flat in the treble and C minor in the bass. The motto scored for the last desks only is heard again beginning in E-flat minor (m.197). This time it introduces a lyric version of its fraternal twin (m.206) as the second part of the second episode (*2C*). The almost celestial character of this stretch becomes something more than the connecting tissue of a retransition leading to a recapitulation of *P/A* (m.248), but in A-flat's relative minor of F. *S/B* (m.281) this time begins in C-flat followed by the "romantico" theme (m.297) in a new state, and the march version of the motto (m.309) in its *K* function ending in F minor (m.328). The "romantico" theme is now metamorphosed into a "heroic" sostenuto character (m.328) and then stated in free diminution (m.339). Elgar's coda (m.352) marked Grandioso (an intensification of nobilmente?) brings back both the motto, *S* (m.404), and closes with the first phrase of the motto (m.418).

The coda's fabric (Example XIV/49) is the most complex moment in the entire symphony. The motto is only played by the oboes, English horn, bassoon, horns, the third trumpet, and the last desk of the violins, violas, and cello—hardly the sonority of a late Romantic peroration. Elgar surrounds this leading line with chordal outlines sometimes moving in contrary motion to each other, while the contrabassoon, first and second trumpets, second and third trombones, tuba, timpani, and contrabasses support the hemiola of the 6/4 measures, causing bursts of color upon the musical canvas. This fabric is contrasted with an almost chorale presentation of the motto mostly for the *tutti* orchestra in block harmonies.

EXAMPLE XIV/49   Elgar. Symphony No. 1/4, mm.352–63.

EXAMPLE XIV/49　　(*continued*)

Elgar returns to a more complex fabric for the end, but does not use his brass and timpani to full advantage, nor does he allow all of the instruments to play at once until the final chord. But even here the piccolo and harp remain silent. Nevertheless, this is a wonderfully effective conclusion, perhaps suggesting that less is more.

Elgar's Finale in a distant way reminds one of the parallel movement in the First Symphony of Johannes Brahms: the symmetricality of the introduction and coda surrounding a central section in a sonata-rondo-like form. However, the Brahmsian influence seems to be limited to form; the content of the two works is decidedly different. Other Brahmsian aspects are the already mentioned *S* distantly deriving from the Brahms's Third Finale and the use of bi-tonal presentation of *S* in the Finale's recapitulation. A more general aspect is that for both composers one can argue effectively that there are reminiscences of one theme in another, which provide unity to a cycle or, more often, unity to a movement.

We have already remarked about the extraordinary reception that Elgar's Symphony No. 1 received from audiences in Manchester and London. The press was also positive, but at the same time expressed minor reservations. We quote from reviews that appeared in *The Athenaeum*, the *Musical Times,* and *The Times* of London, respectively:

> The production of Sir Edward Elgar's Symphony in A flat, Op. 55, under the direction of Dr. Hans Richter at the Free Trade Hall, Manchester, on Thursday evening, was a genuine success. Great expectations had been raised, and they have been fully realized. The composer has attempted the highest form of instrumental music, and has convincingly proved that great thoughts can still be expressed and developed in it. All that is needed is a composer who has something to say and knows how to say it. Sir Edward has practically followed classical lines, but the contents are thoroughly modern. Although the workmanship is clever and complex, it is always clear, for the themes are not only striking, but in some form or other are ever kept in mind; moreover the orchestration is remarkably rich and vivid in the Allegro. After the first noble theme there is storm and stress alternating with quiet passages. A second Allegro, a kind of Scherzo, is instinct with life and colour. The Adagio is based on a broad heavenly theme, and the treatment of it is full of beauty and tenderness, while the Finale brings the work to a triumphant close. The rendering of the work was superb. There was an immense audience. Sir Edward Elgar was called to the platform after the Adagio, and twice at the close.[218]

The effect of the music upon the two audiences was an interesting study. Both the Free Trade Hall at Manchester and the Queen's Hall in London appeared to be quite full with expectant and attentive audiences, but a difference of attitude could not be ignored. To the Londoners the fact that Elgar had written a Symphony which Richter had declared to be a masterpiece, as well as the news of the effect of its production in the North, was sufficient to make excitement run high and to ensure an immediate triumph, which was emphasized by the magnificent playing of the London Symphony Orchestra. At the end of each movement the composer was called to the platform and enthusiastically applauded. But at Manchester there was more reserve. Through a period of fifty years the Hallé concerts have been pioneers of musical taste in the North of England, and many important works, including Berlioz's "Faust," have there received their first English hearing. It was an open question, therefore, whether the concert of December 3 would prove specially memorable. It was most interesting to watch the somewhat formal appreciation which followed the first movement ripen into enthusiasm as the work progressed. There could be no doubt that it was the slow movement which struck home and called forth the most sympathetic response, but lovely as this is with its pure melody and its delicate colouring, there are more robust features in the two large movements which will make a stronger appeal as the work becomes better known. Even the London performance, which was for us a second hearing, attracted interest and admiration more to the vivid and moving drama of the first movement than to the placid mood of the *adagio* or even the *Nobilmente* theme. At the end of the first performance the wholehearted applause and the double call of the composer to the platform showed that Manchester realized that another important musical event had been added to the long list which the Hallé concerts can boast.[219]

The first London performance of the symphony by Sir Edward Elgar, about which so very much has been heard both before and after its production last week at Manchester, took place at the Queen's Hall last night with all the success that was to be expected. Perhaps the enthusiasm might have been even greater than it was if the *réclame* had been rather less; but the composer was recalled at the end of each movement, and several times at the end of the work, so that the feeling of disappointment which many people experienced made no effect upon the success, nor is it likely to diminish the size of the audience when the work is repeated at a special extra concert on the afternoon of the 19th inst., again with Dr. Richter as conductor. A feeling of disappointment, it may be said, is entirely out of place, for the symphony seems, on a first hearing, to be by far the most important work of the composer, inasmuch as it is altogether on a larger scale than the variations or the other orchestral works. It is very long and throughout its colouring is of the richest, though, as in some of the composer's other things, a little relief from the constant wealth of sonorities would occasionally be most welcome. So much for the "colouring," which contains happy touches of instrumentation too numerous to mention; the matter of the symphony has been so minutely analysed that we can all form our own opinion as to its being a piece of "programme" or of "absolute" music according to the preferences of each.[220]

In addition, the *Musical Times* underlined the importance of the work itself by printing in the December 1908 issue a detailed program-note-like analysis with eleven musical examples prior to the premiere in Manchester on December 3, 1908.[221] This was possible because a miniature score had been published prior to the first performance.

Three years were to lapse before English audiences could confront Elgar's next symphony. In the meantime, he composed some songs and small choral works and three instrumental pieces: an *Elegy* for string orchestra, the Violin Concerto in B Minor, and a *Romance* for Bassoon and Orchestra. The *Elegy* was for a memorial concert of the Worshipful Company of Musicians, the Violin Concerto was for Fritz Kreisler who played it in November 1910 with the Philharmonic Society, and the *Romance* was for the principal bassoonist of the London Symphony Orchestra and an amateur orchestra in Herefordshire. Symphony No. 2 Opus 63 was first heard in London under Elgar's baton on May 24, 1911.

SYMPHONY NO. 2 IN E-FLAT MAJOR OPUS 63

With the reception of the First Symphony standing as one of the extraordinary moments in the history of English music, the Second Symphony could not possibly rise to an audience's expectations. Not only was the Queen's Hall not filled on May 24, 1911, but Elgar, who conducted, felt the reception was less than the level of enthusiasm he expected.[222] However, as pointed out by the critic and Schubert scholar Richard Capell, who was present, the hall was not filled for two reasons that had little to do with Elgar's Second Symphony: the tickets were more expensive and the program, as part of a London Music Festival, consisted of three other premieres: Granville Bantock's *Dante and Beatrice,* Walford Davies's little suite entitled *Parthenia,* and Percy Pitts's *English Rhapsody.*[223] One other circumstance may have also contributed— its public dedication was to the late King Edward VII when the English were about ready to celebrate the coronation of King George V.

Symphony No. 2 lacks the memorable motto theme that echoes throughout the First Symphony. Some analysts have argued that a motto also occurs in Symphony No. 2 (Plate B7), but it lacks the transparency and identity of its predecessor. Whereas any extra-musical associations for the First Symphony were discouraged by Elgar, a number of factors encourage one to speculate as to the Second Symphony's meanings. First is the dedication to the late monarch and, as a result, do the movements reflect anything of the person or the reaction to his death? Some note that the piece is in E-flat and that this key brings to mind the "Eroica" Symphony and the memory of a great man.[224] In addition, the slow movement can be, as is the case in the "Eroica," considered a funereal piece.[225] However, Elgar denied the funereal nature of the Larghetto.[226] One can also consider the lines from Shelley's *Invocation,* which Elgar wrote on the score:

> Rarely, rarely, comest thou,
> Spirit of Delight!

Does this mean that other portions of this eight-stanza poem are relevant to movements or passages? According to Elgar: "To get near the mood of the Symphony, the whole of Shelley's poem may be read, but the music does not illustrate the whole of the poem, neither does the poem entirely elucidate the music"[227] (see Table XIV/27).

It can also be asked what role quotation and allusion play in this piece to Elgar's earlier works and to compositions by others. Does the fact Elgar told Mrs. Alice Stuart-Wortley, affectionately addressed as "Windflower," that the symphony was "your symphony" have real significance?[228] What about the "Spirit of Delight!" motive coming after an allusion of the "sei euch vertraut" music from Walther's Prize Song from *Die Meistersinger*? What of the "Hans himself" motive in the Finale (Example XIV/50)? Does this refer to the conductor Hans Richter, to the Meistersinger Hans Sachs, or to both? Such questions lead to a number of possible or even multilayered interpretations.

In a well-argued though speculative article, Allen Gimbel puts forth both evidence and some possible conclusions one might draw. Among his conclusions are that the Symphony No. 2 was intended for Alice Stuart-Wortley and is a veiled expression of Elgar's infatuation with her, an attraction that would and could go no further; this is immediately made clear in the opening when measures of the "Spirit of Delight!" motive combine with Walther's Prize Song. One might read this as Spirit of Delight (=Alice Stuart-Wortley) together with Walther's text. Additionally, Elgar spoke of a feminine voice in the oboe at I/m.157 and II/m.96, which may very well again be a reference to Stuart-Wortley.[229] Gimbel concludes concerning this and other points:

> The *Preislied* thus has an intimate connection with Elgar's Second Symphony, whether as a symbol of artistic independence [the concept of rules], as an homage to two departed Wagnerians [Alfred E. Rodewald and Hans Richter], or as a love letter to Mrs. Stuart-Wortley.[230]

Elgar wove into his Second Symphony a tapestry of quotation and allusion, together with the association of musical motives written into the sketch books and those discussed in the composer's letters. Among these associations are:

TABLE XIV/27

Shelley's *Invocation* as quoted in Elgar's Symphony No. 2

I	V
Rarely, rarely, comest thou,	I love all that thou lovest,
Spirit of Delight!	Spirit of Delight!
Wherefore hast thou left me now	The fresh Earth in new leaves dressed,
Many a day and night?	And the starry night;
Many a weary night and day	Autumn evening, and the morn
'Tis since thou art fled away.	When the golden mists are born.
II	VI
How shall ever one like me	I love snow, and all the forms
Win thee back again?	Of the radiant frost;
With the joyous and the free	I love waves, and winds, and storms,
Thou wilt scoff at pain.	Everything almost
Spirit false! Thou hast forgot	Which is Nature's, and may be
All but those who need thee not.	Untainted by man's misery.
III	VII
As a lizard with the shade	I love tranquil solitude,
Of a trembling leaf,	And such society
Thou with sorrow art dismayed;	As is quiet, wise, and good;
Even the sighs of grief	Between thee and me
Reproach thee, that thou art not near,	What difference? But thou dost possess
And reproach thou wilt not hear.	The things I seek, not love them less.
IV	VIII
Let me set my mournful ditty	I love Love—though he has wings,
To a merry measure;	And like light can flee.
Thou wilt never come for pity,	But above all other things,
Thou wilt come for pleasure;	Spirit, I love thee—
Pity then will cut away	Thou art love and life! Oh, come,
Those cruel wings, and thou wilt stay.	Make once more my heart thy home.

EXAMPLE XIV/50   Elgar. Symphony No. 2/1, mm.1–3 and /4, mm.35–39.

I/m.148 "Ghost" Episode—"a sort of malign influence wandering thro' the summer
   night in the garden"

II/m.1—Interior of St. Mark's Cathedral in Venice

II/m.167—"Like a Woman Dropping a Flower on the Man's Grave"

III/m.1—Lively Piazza outside of St. Mark's

III/m.390—Following lines from Tennyson's *Maud* for the Symphony's climax:

> Dead, long dead,
> Long dead!
> And my heart is a handful of dust,
> And the wheels go over my head,
> And my bones are shaken with pain,
> For into a shallow grave they are thrust,
> Only a yard beneath the street,
> And the hoofs of the horses beat, beat,
> The hoofs of the horses beat,
> Beat into my scalp and my brain.

Later, Elgar characterized this passage as follows:

> Now, gentlemen, at this point I want you to imagine that my music represents a man in a high fever. Some of you may know that dreadful beating that goes on in the brain—it seems to drive out every coherent thought. This hammering must gradually overwhelm everything. Percussion, you must give me all you are worth! I want you gradually to drown the rest of the orchestra.[231]

> IV/m.35—"Hans himself"
> IV/m.165—"Braut's bit" perhaps also associated with Mrs. Stuart-Wortley
> IV/m.195—"Art made tongue-tied by authority" from Shakespeare's Sonnet No. 66[232]

While Symphony No. 2 does not have the compelling recurring theme of Symphony No. 1, it does have thematic recurrence in later movements of ideas first heard in the opening piece. In the Larghetto, just before the coda (m.169), the clarinet plays the motive from the Prize Song (m.163) as a counterpoint to T (m.165). The Prize Song motif's afterthought also returns near the close of the Finale (m.334), forming a kind of rhyme scheme with the opening of the first movement and the close of the second. The other recurrence is of $2N$ of the first movement (mm.148, 170), the so-called "Ghost Episode," coming back in the third-movement rondo (mm.342, 370, 382, 390), the first time considered with the refrain. This combination of $I/2N$ followed by A leads to the third-movement climax of the entire cycle (m.390). In addition, as the climax winds down, $I/1N$ is also heard (m.399). That $I/2N$ and $I/1N$ come in the middle of the rondo lends to it a different kind of reminiscence than the bringing back of P quietly near the close of the second and fourth movements. What Elgar accomplishes here is in its own way more subtle and sophisticated than the more blatant use of cyclic thematicism of the First Symphony. Not only are the thematic connections more allusive, but other means of connection are either absent or underplayed. There are no movements that run on from one into another. Most striking is the simplicity of the key scheme with the outer movements in E-flat, but the two central movements in C minor and C major. A final peculiarity is the meters Elgar chose for the cycle: 12/8, 4/4, 3/8, and 3/4. Thus, the emphasis is on triple meter, either simple or compound, except in the slow movement where triple subdivisions are present, but suppressed and limited to a couple of isolated passages.

The first movement carries the adjectival hallmark of Elgar's style: Allegro vivace e nobilmente. The big introduction is here replaced by a dominant upbeat that immediately resolves to the tonic and P. Pa consists of two motives (see Example XIV/50): x, the Prize Song quotation, and y, the "Spirit of Delight," marked con ardore; Pb (m.9) has been associated with the Dies Irae and the judgment motive from *The Dream of Gerontius*, even though it has a rhythmic swing inappropriate to these affects. A lengthy T (m.13) continues out of P and works up to a climax (m.40) that is almost breathless and reminds one of Act II of Wagner's

Tristan und Isolde. A quick wind-down leads to a theme beginning in G major/minor (m.47), which gains stability through two variations (mm.51, 56); here, this is considered *1S* though Elgar himself placed *S* at m.64, our *2S*. Tonally and in other ways, *2S* is no more stabilized than *1S*, which returns after *2S* (m.76). The tonal ambiguity of *S* continues with *1K*. This builds to a secondary climax (m.116); it quickly unwinds and resolves with *2K* (m.121) undergirded by a dominant pedal; here, stability is finally achieved. Essentially, the exposition consists of, after its opening, two climaxes that are built in a Tristanesque manner by using every musical resource: dynamics, range, orchestration, tempo, surface activity, chromatic density, and harmonic rhythm.

The development section (m.132) in traditional manner begins in the dominant but leans toward G. However, except for *P* in the episode at m.148, the development uses new material (*1N*) in a modulatory context, which for its time sounds more like a symphonic poem rather than a symphony first movement. Elgar's modulations are effected by a bass line that mostly descends mainly by step and half-step. At m.148, Elgar combines *1N*, a second new idea *2N*, and *P* in a section he referred to as the "Ghost Episode." Evocatively scored (Example XIV/51) for an almost *tutti* orchestra less the trumpets, Elgar uses the horns and trombones con sordino; the harps, flutes, and second violas with figurative colors; and the basses playing a reiterating rhythm. Melodic tasks are left to the violins, first violas, and the cellos. A foreboding atmosphere is underlined by the timpani and bass drum sustaining a quiet pedal. The affect of the exposition returns for the retransition (m.183), which builds to a multi-faceted climax that culminates in a *luftpause* and a *fortissimo* recapitulation (m.215). In this passage, the portion beginning at m.208 places the Prize Song motive in a mainly tritone context, which recalls the chain of thirds in the parallel passage in Brahms's Symphony No. 4/1 (mm.227f). Except for the retransition, the development does not present a stormy struggle of themes and keys, but rather a subdued interlude that does everything to underline a relaxed atmosphere with lower dynamics, slower and slowing tempos, more transparent orchestrations, more deliberate harmonic rhythms, and less intense surface rhythmic activities. Thus, the recapitulation begins as the culmination of another climax. Elgar's use of a *luftpause* at the development/recapitulation juncture brings to mind the similarity functioning *luftpause* in Mahler's Symphony No. 1/4 (mm.374–75).

The length of the recapitulation and coda almost matches that of the exposition; in effect Elgar cuts material from the *P/T* and *1S* repetition but mainly makes up for it in the brief coda (m.330). Again, Elgar's most interesting departure from recapitulatory practice is in the key scheme when compared to the exposition:

	P	*T*	*1S*	*2S*	*1S*	*1K*		*2K*
Exposition	E-flat	mod.	G	B-flat/G	B-flat		$\longrightarrow$	
	m.1	13	47	64	76	86		121
Recapitulation	E-flat	out	F	F	out	A-flat/D-flat		E-flat
	m.215		238	255		268		310

Here, Elgar's concept of the recapitulation is mainly thematic, an observation supported by his own placement of *S* in the exposition. One could, however, argue that the weak articulations of A-flat prepare for E-flat's return with *2K*. The subdominant pressure certainly prepares for the final plagal cadence (mm.339–40). Otherwise, the coda (m.330) builds to a final climax with dispatch in little more than a dozen measures.

In the case of the first movement, the thematic references and associations certainly

EXAMPLE XIV/51   Elgar. Symphony No. 2/1, mm.148–53.

EXAMPLE XIV/51 (*continued*)

suggest that the composer had an infatuation with Mrs. Alice Stuart-Wortley. This is also supported by the passionate music that Elgar produced for the first movement con ardore and the structure of the first movement with its multiple passionate climaxes in the exposition and recapitulation that bring to mind Act II of *Tristan und Isolde*. The respite supplied in the development/central section perhaps also owes something to *Tristan* Act II. And all this appears to be hidden behind a dedication to the memory of Edward VII. Thus, in the first movement, Elgar maintains his public persona with the dedication of a work perhaps otherwise meant to convey the most private of post-Victorian thoughts.

The second movement Larghetto in the key of C minor has some funereal undertones that certainly bring to mind the second movement marcia funebre of Beethoven's "Eroica" Symphony. Indeed, several observers have referred to Elgar's slow movement as a funeral march, including Elgar's wife, Charles Sanford Terry, and Tovey in his *Essays in Musical Analysis*.[233] Elgar was no doubt familiar with the tradition of the funereal from a number of different but interrelated traditions; in addition to the "Eroica," which Elgar knew thoroughly, he also later orchestrated the funeral march from Chopin's B-flat Minor Sonata Opus 35 and had a thorough knowledge of tragic Italian opera, whose librettos demanded moments of a funereal character. It is the latter tradition that Elgar seems to follow in Symphony No. 2/2.

Elgar placed the middle two movements in Venice, the second movement's opening material evoking the interior of St. Mark's Cathedral.[234] After this introduction, the funeral march commences (m.8). Its dark colors, slow-moving melody, and pulsating timpani remind one of Verdian funereal evocations such as found near the end of *La Traviata*. When this passage returns at the recapitulation (m.96), its character is intensified as bassoons and contrabasses take up the timpani's rhythm to which the upper strings, harps, and brass respond. To all this is added an oboe solo (molto rubato, quasi ad lib) mourning in a more individualized manner. Elgar's main melodic line begins with the Prize Song's initial intervals. Other funereal associations are found in *T* (mm.29, 89, 165), which is nothing more than an embellished sigh, and just before the return of introductory material at the end, which Elgar compared to "a woman dropping a flower on the man's grave" (m.167).[235] Other portions also bring to mind Italian opera. Elgar was an admirer of Puccini, with a particular attraction to *Tosca*.[236] *1S* (mm.36, 115), *2S* (mm.52, 127), and *2K* (mm.70, 146) in their melodic gestures and orchestration contain something of Puccini's musical personality.

1K (m.58), distantly derived from *P*, is thoroughly Elgarian (Example XIV/52): the nearly *tutti* sonority at a low dynamic level, the lines doubled at octaves, the daunting virtuoso passages to be rendered unobtrusively by the strings, the almost bar-by-bar changes in orchestration, and the differentiated vertical dynamics. The constant coloristic changes in the background and melody almost result in a *klangfarbenmelodie*. Thus, an essentially slow piece gains momentum in these dozen or so bars that prepare for closure.

Elgar presents all these materials in what is essentially a large exposition and recapitulation linked only by a transition and framed by the music associated with the interior of St. Mark's.

Exposition

O		P	T	1S	2S	1K	2K	T			
C minor				F		D	F				
m.1		8	29	36	52	58	70	89			

Recapitulation

P	1S	2S	1K	2K	I/P	T	P	O
C minor	E-flat		C	E-flat	C			
96	115	127	134	146	163	165	169	173

EXAMPLE XIV/52   Elgar. Symphony No. 2/2, mm.58–63.

EXAMPLE XIV/52   (*continued*)

Apart from the Elgarian changes in the recapitulation, where C minor and E-flat major seem to be interchangeable, there are other aspects deserving of notice. *2K* (m.146) builds in seven bars to a powerful climax (m.153) from which the entire movement unwinds to a quiet close, prepared for with an allusion to the Prize Song (m.163), to the sighing *T* (m.165), the flower-dropping motif (m.167), and the marcia funebre (m.169). The piece closes with a return to the introductory material capped with a celestial sonority that underlines the spirit of St. Mark's interior.

In many respects, this Larghetto is the most successful piece in the cycle. Every gesture is carefully and successfully calculated. Elgar colors his materials with a constantly changing orchestral background and foreground. The materials themselves are tellingly shaped, forming longer-term lines. Rhythms are controlled to achieve their climax with *1K* (m.58) and relax with a nobilmente *2K* (m.70) and a further slowing at *T* (m.89) in preparation for *P*'s reprise (m.96), which itself is enhanced by a faster surface. Elgar again slows for *2S* (m.127), then accelerates for the movement's climax (m.153), and concludes quietly.

If the Larghetto paints something of the interior of St. Mark's, the third movement attempts to capture something of the "lively Piazza" outside the cathedral with an untitled Scherzo, a Presto Rondo in 3/8.[237] Of central interest here is the juxtaposition on a large scale of various rhythmic gestures, which together with tonality are primary in defining the formal functions. However, this movement's tonalities are less defining than its rhythmic aspects; Elgar uses only C minor and major as well as its dominant and C minor's relative major. Since the dominant is absent from the second episode, a sonata-rondo is outside of its tonal structure. Only in the developmental second episode does he move toward D major/B minor, the two tonalities that surround C. Except for the climax, much of this movement is less than satisfying. Despite its rhythmic contrasts, contrapuntal artifices, and functional orchestration, Elgar never brings these elements to bear upon a convincingly coherent larger statement. Instead, the movement is perceived as a series of discrete sections somewhat weakly connected. While one can hear each of the separate sections as artfully constructed, when brought together they lack the coherence to make a movement of real consequence.

The refrain of the rondo is marked by rhythmic dissonance with hemiola and syncopation, the first episode (m.43) by metric and rhythmic consonance, and the second episode (m.218) by combining some of the dissonance of the refrain with a quadruple subdivision of the three-eight bar. The refrain's second return (m.342) combines *A* with material of *I/2N*. Ultimately, *I/2N* takes over and is then again combined with *A* (m.390) so that one quadruple meter bar operates simultaneously with four three-eight measures. For Elgar, this section brought to mind lines from Tennyson's *Maud* with its beating of horses' hoofs into "my scalp and my brain."[238] On a purely musical level, this passage also brings to mind Berlioz's combination of two tempos and meters such as is found in the third movement of *Harold in Italy*. This is but one instance of Berlioz's importance to the formation of Elgar's musical language.

Jerrold Northrop Moore hears this stretch, which Elgar characterized as a "man in a high fever," as the "most ferocious climax of the entire symphony."[239] *B* (m.408) follows, but this time beginning diffidently until m.424 when it bursts in *fortissimo*. *A* (m.476) is followed by the coda (m.555). In these final two sections, Elgar intensifies his materials with chromaticism, counterpoint, and greater thematic and textural density.

A special characteristic of the refrain is its kaleidoscopic orchestration. Considering its rapid tempo, Elgar orchestrates it to exploit flashes of color. As the strings form the basic melodic line, the woodwinds duck in and out of the fabric. With each return, Elgar alters the orchestration at an almost microscopic level. In contrast, the first episode is dominated by string and wind colors changing at the subphrase and phrase levels, emphasizing its already noted rhythmic/metric stability. At the climax (m.396), the dimension of activity coheres massively with its extended pedal pulsating in the percussion.

Elgar's Finale, though more continuous and less differentiated thematically than the Scherzo, also suffers from the same affliction: the themes do not seem to belong to the same gesture. Much of this material dates back to the composer's stay in Italy for the winter of 1903–1904.[240] *P* (m.1), marked *con dignita*, derives from a tune heard from an Italian shepherd's pipe that was also used for the concert overture *In the South* dating back to December 1903.[241] *S* (m.35) comes from sometime before October 27, 1905, with the exclamation "Hans himself." The exposition concludes with the end of *S* marked *grandioso* (m.67) and *nobilmente* for *K* (m.71). Despite the appeal of these discrete themes on their own terms, they tend to expand by *Fortspinnung*, which reduces their developmental potential, rather than by adding phrase and subphrase groups. *P* and *T* use a form of developmental variation as their initial one-measure module is repeated with different pitch configurations. *S* and *K* use much the same means of expansion.

As a result, the development (m.105) spends somewhat less time with *P* than one might expect and then only as a counterpoint to *S* or new material. Its first part concentrates on *S* and defines itself with a new counterpoint, a sudden acceleration in surface activity with virtuosic demands on the strings, and an unexpected D-major beginning. Part two (m.139), marked *con fuoco*, begins in B minor and combines elements from *P*, *S*, and a new theme contrapuntally. The mood becomes quieter (m.147) as *P* and *S* continue to spar, first undergirded by a pedal point and then by a descending bass that leads to part three (m.165). Here, Elgar introduces a new theme labeled in the sketches as "Braut's bit," which holds something in common with *P* of Brahms's Symphony No. 3/1. It also becomes a counterpoint to Elgar's *P*. Though this section continues the B minor key of part two, it finds its way to C minor (m.195), which slips down to the dominant of E-flat for the recapitulation. Elgar associated the C minor material (m.195) with a line from the above-quoted Shakespeare Sonnet No. 66.[242]

Though the recapitulation's *P* (m.210) begins quietly as in the exposition, it is more developmental as it moves toward D-flat, but then deflects back to E-flat for *S* (m.237) and *K* (m.275). Elgar strengthens the orchestration of *S*, builds to the movement's climax (m.258), and continues to present *K* in a strengthened form. After all these Elgarian gestures of nobility and triumph, the music becomes more subdued for the coda (m.312), prepared for by a calmer character leading to the *più tranquillo*. This coda contains the sound of celestial music (m.319), *I/1P* (m.333), and a final mellow *crescendo* to *fortissimo* before the final chord diminishes to *pianissimo*. Elgar's ending was probably an anti-climax for his audience, which was so acclimated to the composer of the First Symphony, the ceremonial marches, and the *Enigma Variations*. But perhaps the entire Finale was something of a letdown with its casual and quiet opening and subdued close.

Even though Elgar himself was disappointed with the reception of his Second Symphony, the critics for *The Athenaeum*, *The Times* of London, and the *Musical Times* were all enthusiastic:

> On Wednesday evening was produced, under the direction of the composer, Sir Edward Elgar's Second Symphony in E flat. His first achieved success; and as regards the first, second, and last movements of the present work, we believe that success has been more than maintained. There is wonderful life and energy, combined with great dignity, in the opening movement; and the workmanship and scoring are deeply interesting. The joy of the Shelley motto at the head of the score, "Rarely, rarely comest thou, spirit of

delight," seems particularly to apply to this Allegro. Ecstatic joy is expressed in the principal theme, while in the secondary one that mood is of a quieter kind. The Funeral March suggested by the second movement may be explained by the dedication of the work to King Edward VII. After the introductory bars there enters a theme of rare simplicity, yet most impressive, and it is enhanced by the sable-coloured accompaniment. Later there is a second one of imposing character, and richly scored. The quaint, plaintive coda is very striking.

A change comes over the spirit of the music in the next movement, entitled a Rondo, and marked presto. With its syncopated rhythm and rapid tempo, the opening section has a disturbing effect. The composer must have worked to some picture in his mind, but no clue is given. There is much skilful writing in it, but inspiration is less strong than in what preceded. In the Finale the composer again gives us some of his best music. One great feature of this Symphony is the general clearness of the form, although there are many noteworthy details which cannot be grasped at a first hearing; moreover there are no sensational, extravagant effects. The performance by the Queen's Hall Orchestra was admirable.[243]

The new Symphony by Sir Edward Elgar, which was the main attraction of the Festival yesterday, may at once be said confidently to be a great deal better than his first, and two of its movements undoubtedly reach very near the level of the Variations and the Violin Concerto—that is to say, they touch the composer's highest mark. It is a great though subsidiary advantage that it is much shorter than its predecessor, only exceeding the ordinary symphonic length by a very few minutes.

The first movement, an allegro vivace in E flat, has such an abundance of thematic material that it is impossible to do all the subjects full justice or indeed to develop them with any degree of thoroughness. Groups of themes occupy the place held in the classical days by single germs; beautiful as many of them are, we would fain hear more of them, but there is not time, and they pass singly or in combinations in too swift a procession.

The slow movement is open to no such objection as this, for it flows along in most expressive fashion and is wrought to a splendid climax of melodic and harmonic richness. The third movement, called a "rondo," reminds the hearer of Berlioz's "Queen Mab" Scherzo, and has remarkably effective moments, and one very strenuous climax, in which the very noisy tambourine could with advantage have been spared; the finest movement is the finale, the themes of which are finely kept together by a figure of unusual rhythm, appearing for the most part as an accompaniment, but possessing great originality and charm.

The whole is of course richly scored; it is satisfactory to find that all the effects (many of which succeed marvelously well) are made with the ample means at the disposal of the ordinary conductor. To the student of orchestration the work is a rich storehouse of devices, which will soon be imitated, we doubt not, by the younger composers. The work was received with much favour, though with rather less enthusiasm than usual, and the composer, who conducted it, was repeatedly called at the close.[244]

Owing to the late period of the month in which the London Musical Festival fell, we are able to deal with it here no further than the concert of Wednesday evening, May 24, at which Elgar's new Symphony in E flat was performed for the first time. As this was fully analysed in our columns last month, detailed description of its contents is unnecessary here. It fully bore out the anticipation that, as a whole, it would prove brighter and less strenuous in character than its predecessors. In the new work the emotion runs more placidly and evenly, though there are many moments of intense feeling and one or two tornado-like outbursts. While never ceasing to bear Elgar's characteristic signature, the music takes us into fields of thought that the composer has not touched upon before. This is especially so in the extremely fanciful Scherzo and the solemn slow movement. The Symphony generally suggests a mind that has lived through many illusions and disappointments, and found the deeper peace of things. There is an exquisite refinement in the exhilaration of the first and last movements, and a peculiar nobility in the thematic fragment, derived from one of the motives of the opening Allegro, that is so frequently used as a kind of philosophic summing-up of all that has gone before. The orchestration presents many new and interesting features. The Symphony received an extremely good first performance, though certain of the details of the score may be expected to come out more clearly later on. It was enthusiastically received, the composer being frequently recalled.[245]

Nearly ninety years later, this observer finds that the Elgar Second begins as a work nearly as strong as his Opus 55, but after its second movement, certainly one of the composer's finest creations, the quality declines. Unlike his First Symphony, where both the movements and the cycle cohere and every gesture seems inevitable, the Second Symphony's Scherzo and Finale are more like a collage of materials arbitrarily placed into the same environment. On October 25, 1910, Elgar wrote to Alice Stuart-Wortley expressing reservations about his new symphony: "I have also been making a little progress with Symphony No. 2 and am sitting at my table weaving strange and wonderful memories into very poor music, I fear."[246] Though Elgar is perhaps too self-critical, his Second pales when compared to his First, but still maintains a strong position in the history of the English symphony, second only to his earlier exploration of the genre.

SYMPHONY NO. 3 IN C MINOR (FRAGMENT)

Two decades were to elapse before Elgar considered writing a third contribution to "the highest development of art." Its composition was at the urgings of George Bernard Shaw. Perhaps there is something ironic about Shaw's urgings upon his friend Sir Edward, given that Shaw as a music critic had expressed great disdain for the genre in the works of Stanford and Parry. The correspondence from Shaw and others, reproduced below, urges England's great national composer to produce another symphony, which Elgar attempted over a period of twenty-one months beginning in January 1932 and lasting until a major physical setback in October 1933.[247]

January 7, 1932: Shaw wrote to Elgar,

Why don't you make the BBC order a new Symphony? It can afford it. (Moore/ELGAR, p. 795)

June 29, 1932: Shaw also wrote to Elgar six months later:

Why not a Financial Symphony? Allegro: Impending Disaster. Lento mesto: Stony Broke. Scherzo: Light Heart and Empty Pocket. All° con brio: Clouds Clearing. (p. 796)

July 1, 1932: Elgar sent Shaw's message written on a postcard to Fred Gaisberg of H.M.V. with the following message:

Perhaps H.M.V. would like to commission (say £5,000) for such a symphony as G.B.S. suggests: the p.c. [postcard] is worth more than my music! (p. 796)

August 4, 1932: Walter Legge, also of H.M.V., writes to Sir Edward:

I hope you will forgive me for writing to you on this topic, but I have heard, on what I believe to be very reliable authority, that you have practically completed a third symphony. Is there any truth in this rumor? If you could tell me, I should be delighted to make use of the information, not only in "The Voice," but in the general press. Moreover, our mutual friend, Ernest Newman, is very anxious to know whether there is any truth in the news, which I passed on to him for what it is worth. (p. 803)

August 5, 1932: Elgar replies:

Many thanks for your letter: there is nothing to say about the mythical Symphony for some time,—probably a long time,—possibly no time,—never. (p. 803)

September 1932: At the Worcester Festival Elgar spoke of the "written" Symphony No. 3 but said "no one wanted his music now." *Daily Mail* urges the performance of Elgar's Symphony No. 3 (pp. 803–04).

September 30, 1932: George Bernard Shaw wrote to Sir John Reith of the BBC,

May I make a suggestion?

In 1823 the London Philharmonic Society passed a resolution to offer Beethoven £50 for the MS of a symphony. He accepted, and sent the Society the MS of the Ninth Symphony. In 1827 the Society sent him £100. He was dying; and he said "God bless the Philharmonic Society and the whole English nation."

This is by far the most creditable incident in English history.

Now the only composer today who is comparable to Beethoven is Elgar. Everybody seems to assume either that Elgar can live on air, or that he is so rich and successful that he can afford to write symphonies and conduct festivals for nothing. As a matter of fact his financial position is a very difficult one, making it impossible for him to give time enough to such heavy jobs as the completion of a symphony; and consequently here we have the case of a British composer who has written two great symphonies, which place England at the head of the world in this top department of instrumental music, unable to complete and score a third. I know that he has the material for the first movement ready, because he has played it to me on his piano.

Well, why should not the BBC, with its millions, do for Elgar what the old Philharmonic did for Beethoven. You could bring the Third Symphony into existence and obtain the performing right for the BBC for, say, ten years, for a few thousand pounds. The kudos would be stupendous and the value for the money ample; in fact if Elgar were a good man of business instead of a great artist, who throws his commercial opportunities about *en grand seigneur,* he would open his mouth much wider.

He does not know that I am meddling in his affairs and yours in this manner; and I have not the faintest notion of what sum he would jump at; but I do know that he has still a lot of stuff in him that could be released if he could sit down to it without risking his livelihood.

Think it over when you have a spare moment. (p. 804)

October 13, 1932: Elgar writes to his biographer Basil Maine,

I fear there is nothing to say in regard to the new Symphony or anything else: things take shape without my knowing it—I am only the lead pencil & cannot foresee. (p. 805)

During November 1932: A formal offer from the BBC is tendered (p. 805).

December 14, 1932: The commission is made public (p. 806).

February 5, 1933: W. H. Reed plays through sketches on the violin with Elgar at the piano (p. 807).

February 20, 1933: Elgar writes to Sir John Reith,

I am hoping to begin "scoring" the work very shortly: I am satisfied with the progress made with the "sketch" & I hope that the "fabric" of the music is as good as anything I have done—but naturally there are moments when one feels uncertain: however I am doing the best that I can & up to the present the symphony is the *strongest* thing I have put on paper. (p. 809)

April 21, 1933: The BBC inquires,

We have carefully considered the question of your new symphony which you are writing and the best place to put it in our big series of concerts commencing next autumn. The series opens on 18th October and we should very much like to play your symphony at that opening concert.

I wonder if you could yet tell me whether it will be finished in time? Obviously parts and score would have to be ready by the end of September at the latest so that the fullest rehearsal and preparation could be given. At the same time, you might let me know whether you would like to honour us by conducting the work yourself.

I am sorry to worry you about it so early, but you will understand that our arrangements have to be made a long way in advance. (p. 809)

April 24, 1933: Elgar responds,

Many thanks for your letter: I fear we must not announce the first performance of the Symphony until everything is printed, and, as you say, the "material" wd. have to be ready for rehearsals in September: too much depends on the "reading" of proofs & printing generally for me to be able to say "yes."

I am as forward with the work as I hoped to be &, if nothing untoward occurs, shd. be able to begin to "feed" the publishers with M.S. shortly. In the meantime I think no announcement or reference need be made: As to conducting—we will "wait & see." (p. 810)

April 25, 1933: Another epistle from the BBC:

I quite understand the difficulties and dangers and certainly we must not make any announcement until we are quite sure. At the same time, such an important event in music must receive every advance notice possible, and I have been wondering whether you could tell us just a little more. Would it be possible to say now that the work would definitely be ready for our May Festival in 1934? It would be a magnificent time to produce it and it would give us plenty of time to get everything ship-shape before any announcement were made.

I know how you must dislike committing yourself, but this strikes me that it might be far enough ahead for you to say "Yes" and everything will be clear for rehearsal and performance before May of next year. (p. 810)

April 27, 1933: Elgar writes to the BBC,

I like your idea to announce the Symphony for the May Festival of 1934: that wd. give us all full time for preparation in all departments, printing, rehearsals, etc. So if you like to proceed pray do so: you do not worry me! So if there is anything else to ask or answer be sure to write. . . .

Symphony in C minor
I.   Allegro
II. Allegretto
III. Adagio
IV. Allegro

Now the trouble is that I have not decided finally the positions of II & III that is to say III might follow I. (pp. 810–11)

On the same day Sir John Reith was told by Elgar,

This is only to say that as far as an artist can feel satisfied with his work,—and no real artist can ever feel that,—the thing goes on happily. I have, with the invaluable aid of Mr. W.H. Reed, played through portions of the MS. & he is delighted: I can say no more now but you have been so really kind in the whole matter that I felt I should like to send you this note.

I presume it will be correct for me to send my MS—(which will be delivered in portions) *direct* to the publishers. . . . (p. 811)

July 27, 1933: the G.B. Shaws came to tea and Elgar and Reed played a "great deal" of the Symphony (p. 814).

August 27, 1933: From the diary of Fred Gaisberg of H.M.V.:

Tea in the Music Room—Elgar in fine humour. Started by playing me bits of his opera—a bass aria, a love duet, and other bits. He then started on his IIIrd. The opening a great broad burst *animato* gradually resolving into a fine broad melody for strings. This is fine. 2nd movement is slow & tender in true Elgar form. The 3rd movement is an ingenious Scherzo, well designed: a delicate, feathery short section of 32nds contrasted with a moderate, sober section. 4th movement is a spirited tempo with full resources, developed at some length.

The whole work strikes me as youthful and fresh—100% Elgar without a trace of decay. He makes not the smallest attempt to bring in any modernity. It is built on true classic lines and in a purely Elgar mould, as the IVth Brahms is purely Brahms. The work is complete as far as structure & design and scoring is well advanced [*sic*]. In his own mind he is enthusiastically satisfied with it and says it is his best work. He pretends he does not want to complete and surrender his baby. His secretary Miss Clifford says he has not done much recently on the Sym. and seems to prefer to work on his opera. . . . (p. 816)

October 7, 1933: Elgar's health has had a setback and he writes to Sir John Reith:

I have to go to a nursing home today for a sudden operation (gastric); this upsets all plans. I am extremely sorry to have to tell you that everything is held up for the present. I am not at all sure how things will turn out and have made arrangements that in case the Symphony does not materialise the sums you have paid on account shall be returned. This catastrophe came without the slightest warning as I was in the midst of scoring the work.

Perhaps it will not be necessary to refer publicly to the Symphony in any way at present; we will wait and see what happens to me.

I have written to no-one else on the subject. (p. 818)

It turned out that Elgar had inoperable intestinal cancer and was experiencing severe pain. With insensitivity, the staff from the BBC thought that one solution to relieving Elgar's pain, so that he could complete the symphony, would be to cut his spinal cord, but he refused the suggestion and then remarked:

> If I can't complete the Third Symphony, somebody will complete it—or write a better one—in fifty or five hundred years. Viewed from the point where I am now, on the brink of eternity, that's a mere moment in time.[248]

On February 23, 1934, Elgar died, leaving the various movements and passages of the Third Symphony in different states of the compositional process. In the months preceding his death, Elgar's documented wishes about the completion of the symphony were somewhat contradictory.

Sometime during the month of November 1933, Eric Fenby—Delius's one time amanuensis—wrote to Elgar offering his services to aid with the symphony, but his offer was not accepted.[249] On November 23, 1933, W. H. Reed visited Elgar and reported the composer's anguish over the thought of someone else completing it:

> Then it was evident that he was trying very hard to speak; and gradually and at long intervals the words came from him. "I want you . . . to do something for me . . . the symphony all bits and pieces . . . no one would understand . . . no one . . . no one." A look of great anguish came over his face as he said this, and his voice died away from exhaustion.
>
> Leaning over him, I said, "What can I do for you? Try to tell me. I will do anything for you; you know that."
>
> Again a long silence; but a more peaceful expression came back into his face, and before long he drew me down again and said, "Don't let anyone tinker with it . . . no one could understand . . . no one must tinker with it."
>
> I assured him that no one would ever tamper with it in any way . . .
>
> A little while later he said in a whisper and with great emotion, "I think you had better burn it."
>
> I exchanged glances with his daughter, who was now sitting at the opposite side of the bed; and I saw that she looked, as I am sure I did, a little startled at this suggestion. Then I felt that it was only a suggestion and not really a request; so I leaned over him and said, "I don't think it is necessary to burn it: it would be awful to do that. But Carice and I will remember that no one is to try to put it together. No one shall ever tinker with it: we promise you that."
>
> Hearing this, he seemed to grow more peaceful. His strugglings and efforts to speak ceased; he lay there with his eyes open, watching us . . .[250]

However, on December 22, 1933, Elgar dictated a message to Ernest Newman to accompany some additional passages:

> With this I send the opening four bars (introductory) of the slow movement. I am fond enough to believe that the first two bars (with the F# in the bass) open some vast bronze doors into something strangely unfamiliar. I also have added the four final bars of this movement. I think and hope you may like the unresolved *estinto* of the viola solo.[251]

Although Elgar's contradictory remarks about the completion of his Third Symphony cannot be explained, six months after Elgar's death, the task of finishing the sketches into a completed symphony was seen as an impossibility by George Bernard Shaw. He wrote to W. H. Reed on August 17, 1834:

All the great symphonies after Beethoven are as expressionist as Wagner's music-dramas, even when, as in the Symphonies of Brahms and Elgar, the skeleton of the old pattern is still discernible. All possibility of reconstruction from fragments or completion from beginnings is gone.

Consequently, though Elgar left some sketches of a third symphony and was actually at work on it when he died, no completion or reconstruction is possible: the symphony, like Beethoven's tenth, died with the composer.[252]

Indeed, one month earlier, on July 20, 1934, Elgar's daughter Carice had signed an agreement with the BBC. It reserved the copyright for the family but gave the sketches to the BBC, which agreed that the manuscript would not be published and that no one should finish or complete Elgar's final magnum opus.[253] In 1935 Reed published some of the material in facsimile in the BBC house organ, *The Listener.*[254] In his 1936 memoir, *Elgar as I Knew Him,* Reed also published a large portion of, but not all of, the sketches.

In 1968, the BBC presented a broadcast that dealt with the materials of Elgar's Third. Up to that point in time, it was generally considered that Reed had included all of the extant sketches.[255] However, Roger Fiske, a British musicologist, assembled the sketches for the 1968 broadcast using not only Reed's memoir, but also some materials not included in the memoir. In the early 1970s the English composer Anthony Payne took an interest in Elgar's Third and intermittently studied the sketches. Two decades later, in November 1993, the BBC decided to produce another program on the unfinished Elgar Symphony in C Minor and engaged Payne to bring some of the sketches into a performable state. By Christmas the Scherzo was finished and by February 23, 1994, the Adagio was also completed, before the BBC began talks with Elgar's descendants. However, their feelings remained negative with regard to the project until two years later when the whole Elgar clan came to an agreement in June 1996 that Payne's project could go forward.[256]

The first performance of Elgar's Third Symphony in C Minor "elaborated by Anthony Payne" was given by the orchestra of the BBC, the symphony's original commissioners, conducted by Sir Andrew Davis on February 15, 1998, at the Royal Festival Hall in London. A recording of the "elaboration" was released along with explanations concerning the state of the sketches. In addition, Payne wrote a short book on the history of the sketches and his work on them, and the score has been published by Boosey & Hawkes.[257] Payne's effort received a great deal of publicity via news releases and a website. Within a year of its first performance, it was heard again in London as well as in Birmingham, Glasgow, Aberdeen, Philadelphia, Edinburgh, Manchester, Chicago, Washington, and New York, conducted by Andrew Davis, Leonard Slatkin, and Mark Elder, among others.[258]

As has been our policy with Cooke/Mahler Symphony No. 10 (in Volume 4 of this series), the Cooper/Beethoven 10, and the various Schubert completions of Brian Newbould (both in Volume 2 of this series), we will not discuss the Payne elaboration here in any detail. Although side-stepping again the direct discussion of whether anyone can, or has the right to, complete posthumously an unfinished symphony, there are two matters to comment on with regard to Elgar's Symphony No. 3: Is the material Elgar left us worthy of completion? How much of the final product sounds like real Elgar?

Our answer to both questions is contrary to commonly held opinions. In the few passages scored for full orchestra, the Elgar sketches are weak shadows of his previous two symphonies; given the quality and nature of these materials, Payne's efforts do not sound like viable Elgar. Considering that, outside of England, Elgar's First and Second are not often heard, performances of the "elaboration" of Elgar's sketches for his Third Symphony have only taken away opportunities to hear two works that are inherently some of the finest symphonies from the first two decades of the twentieth century. Unfortunately, Elgar's music does not attract the international devotion that Mahler's symphonies have had since the 1960s. Thus, an Elgar Third will probably not be able to sustain an interest much beyond its initial reception.

CONCLUSION

Though Elgar wrote fewer symphonies than Potter, Bennett, Stanford, and Parry, his two completed symphonies are among the only English works prior to the First World War to establish a permanent place in the repertoire. Of these composers, only Elgar never saw the inside of a classroom in Oxford, Cambridge, London, or Leipzig. Perhaps this lack of contact with the English and European musical establishments allowed him to develop a musical language of a particular individuality. While some critics have heard a distinctive English voice in Parry's "English" Symphony (No. 2), it was Elgar who was able, both in his vocal and orchestral music, to capture a sentiment that all English citizens came to recognize as distinctively theirs. The appellation "nobilmente e semplice" was at the core of the spirit of his music. Often these words were enhanced by music of majestic simplicity and deep melodic richness frequently accompanied by a walking bass. That Elgar became a national composer or even a nationalistic composer without reverting to incorporating folksong speaks to the special character of his music.

Perhaps the most surprising aspect of Elgar's two completed symphonies are their layers of meaning, gained from a study of his sketchbooks. Often Elgar would use themes written down many years earlier that are labeled with specific associations or might gain extra-musical associations by a thematic relationship of an almost leitmotivic nature to Elgar's oratorios. However, there exists a tendency in Elgar criticism in the latter instance to take meaning as merely coincidental or otherwise weak resemblances. The prime example is, of course, the misunderstood Symphony No. 2, which though dedicated to the memory of King Edward VII, has stronger associations with Elgar's infatuation with his "Windflower" Alice Stuart-Wortley. This interpretation tends to be supported by its leitmotivic associations.

In both works, Elgar adheres to the tradition of the four-movement structure. For each, he brings back thematic material in successive movements. However, in the First Symphony, Elgar forges a highly coherent and hierarchical relationship, while in Symphony No. 2, the thematic recurrences are more casual, with most of them returning at the ends of the various movements. In other ways, the cycle of Symphony No. 2 is less dramatic in its focus. In the First Symphony Elgar delivers a cycle that clearly culminates in the Finale. On the other hand, Elgar's Second places its weight in the first two movements as the Finale is a less intense piece that ends in calm resignation. The coherence of the cycle in Symphony No. 1 also extends to the strong sense of sweep in the opening and final movements. The result is that the First Symphony is a dramatic and heroic piece of deep affect; the second takes a more pastoral stance.

Apart from his compelling themes, Elgar's handling of the orchestra reveals him to be among the finest orchestrators; he ranks as an equal with Nikolai Rimsky-Korsakov—though less exotically colorful—Richard Strauss, Gustav Mahler, and Maurice Ravel. Particularly characteristic is his kaleidoscopic treatment of the predominantly *tutti* passages where instrumental colors come in and out at a relatively small dimension, as in the ending to the First Symphony and the third movement of Symphony No 2. Another distinctive practice is the statement of a significant thematic idea by the last stands of strings within a fairly full sonority, providing a sense of space and distance, which is a variant on a Berliozian concept. Also striking are the scorings of his *nobilmente* themes for strings in their warmest registers, often doubled by the mellowest of brass colors. Like Mahler, Elgar separates strands in his fabrics by assigning lines to various strata, but also adopts the Straussian practice of doubling lines in different registers. At times, orchestration defines the character of a theme and a structural section. Though one is reluctant to speak of weaknesses in Elgar's orchestration, sometimes his kaleidoscopic *tuttis* result in a less than powerful climax or conclusion.

Elgar's two completed symphonies are, outside of England, some of the most ignored great works of the repertoire. Both of them, despite some weaknesses, are masterworks. Elgar had a sure sense of form, a melodic gift equal to any of his contemporaries, a high level of orchestral control, and an ability to develop, transform, and vary his materials to fine overall effect. For many years audiences outside of England heard Elgar's music as pompous and, to those more politically minded, as possessing the character of post-Victorian English imperialism. Whether these perceptions are justified or even relevant should be questioned, since the totality of the music's affect transcends any of its weaknesses.

Conclusion: The British Symphony

In Victorian and post-Victorian England, the symphony came to be a significant genre and a test of supreme accomplishment for native composers. English composers saw a need to pursue it as part of a validation process to prove that indeed England was capable of producing a composer comparable to the great German symphonists: Haydn, Mozart, Beethoven, Schubert, Schumann, Mendelssohn, and Brahms. As a result, the composers of British birth or residence are to some degree clones of one or more of the Germans. As we have seen, Potter's models were Haydn, Mozart, and Beethoven; for Bennett it was Mendelssohn; and for Stanford and Parry it was Schumann and Brahms. No doubt these same composers must also have been models, on some level, for the other British symphonists listed in Table XIV/4.

Still, there are many composers active as symphonists in England that need to be studied to fill in the significant lacunae that remain, such as the efforts of Cowen, Barnett, the Holmes brothers, Prout, Davenport, Cusins, German, and Holst, among others. Only a few of their works were published; many others only exist in manuscript scores and/or parts; and a number are probably no longer extant. Hence, many of these symphonies are only known from listings in the early editions of *Grove's Dictionary of Music and Musicians*. Even the scores of the symphonies of Bennett, Stanford, and Parry are not easy to obtain. Only Elgar's orchestral output is easily accessible today and ready for performance.

Nevertheless, the composers surveyed here have all proven themselves to be symphonists worthy of exploration and, as has been indicated above, worthy of revival. In every case, they are technically secure and capable of composing first-rate symphonies, though not with consistency. Except for Elgar, they also all were gifted teachers, in their own ways, who produced through the Royal Academy and the Royal College of Music students well grounded in the Germanic symphonic tradition.

Indeed, it was the German symphony that provided a hindrance for the composition of distinctively English symphonies. Granted, here were attempts to adapt the Germanic symphonic form by filling it with content from native sources in the folk music of the British Isles or with extra-musical British trappings (e.g., "Irish" and "Welsh" symphonies or Holmes's "The Youth of Shakespeare" and Leslie's "Chivalry" Symphony). Yet it was not until Elgar's two symphonies that one could sense and identify a distinctively English idiom that settled once and for all the question of whether the English were a creative musical people. Elgar's breakthrough provided an impetus to the flourishing of a British school of composers in the twentieth century that could claim at least equality, and perhaps even superiority, to the various

Continental composers and schools. One need only mention Vaughan Williams, Tippett, Britten, and Maxwell Davies to support a convincing argument.

Bibliographic Overview

The nineteenth century in England was regarded as a special time in its musical history since it was during this period that the nation emerged as musically creative. In addition to Fuller-Maitland's book on English music in the nineteenth-century, other histories by Frank Howes and Peter Pirie designate the time after mid-century as an "English musical renaissance." This renaissance included not only composers acknowledged both at home and abroad, but an intensification of musical life that included participatory music making, the rise of orchestral concerts, and native musical journalism. All this as well as the continued cultivation of opera fostered also the publication of Sainsbury's *Dictionary* early in the century (1824) and at the century's end Grove's *Dictionary of Music and Musicians* (1879–1889).

Grove was behind more than the *Dictionary;* as mentioned previously, he was also secretary of the Crystal Palace, which promulgated an active musical life and established the first permanent orchestra in London, as thoroughly documented by Michael Musgrave and by Grove himself in his catalogue of repertoire [Grove]/CRYSTAL PALACE CATALOGUE. If the orchestra at the Crystal Palace provided some of the most interesting programs, the most prestigious series was offered by the Philharmonic Society, whose activities are documented in three books by Foster, Elkin, and Ehrlich. Concerts by the Palace's and the Philharmonic Society's orchestras as well as other more *ad hoc* groups were reviewed in the *Harmonicon* (*HARM*), *Musical World* (*MW*), *Musical Times* (*MT*), and the intellectual community's weekly, *The Athenaeum,* in addition to the daily press. There were also memoirs by Cowen, Davison, Macfarren, several by Stanford, and certainly others that document both public and private musical activities. Perhaps the most thoroughly documented musical events were the concerts of the Cambridge University Musical Society in Norris/STANFORD, which contains much more than its title promises, as does Jeremy Dibble's seminal article on Perry, Stanford, and the British symphony.

Very little work has been done on Cipriani Potter and practically none of his orchestral music is available in modern editions, though one symphony has appeared in *Musica Britannica* edited by Julian Rushton. Macfarren/POTTER was the first survey of the man and his work by one who knew this doyen of British music. Philip Peter's 1972 dissertation provides much valuable information not otherwise available, but does not deal with the music itself as a stylistic entity. William Sterndale Bennett has received more attention thanks to the early biography by J. R. Sterndale Bennett published in 1907. This work can now be supplemented by Rosemary Williamson's fine thematic catalogue. The ongoing work of Nicholas Temperley, including his edition of the symphonies, makes Bennett less of an obscurity than Potter. Other useful studies are Stanford's tribute, and Bush/BENNETT.

Though both Potter and Bennett dominated activities at the Royal Academy and at the Philharmonic Society, the next generation dominated by Stanford and Parry was equally, if not more, active in a variety of musical enterprises. Books and articles on Stanford by Dunhill, Greene, and Porte as well as recollections by his students (Pupils/STANFORD) for many years filled the lacunae of the deserved full life and works. Now there are two big biographies by Rodmell and Dibble, which unfortunately appeared too late to be incorporated into this chapter. Norris/STANFORD, however, remains a major achievement that cannot be ignored. Hudson has provided a revised non-thematic catalogue that tends to the bibliographic problems.

Parry has been treated to three full-scale works. Graves/PARRY appeared first (in 1926) in two volumes but leaves a lot of questions unanswered and borders on hagiography; Smith/ PARRY (1926) is a review of Graves's work but suffers from its dated sexist attitudes. Dibble/ PARRY is a first-rate life and works in almost every respect, and Benoliel/PARRY is a series of essays on various aspects partially written as a response to Dibble's book. Hadow/PARRY is a posthumous tribute to the composer. There is also a book that deals with Parry and Stanford in tandem by Fuller-Maitland. Dibble's article PARRY & ELGAR clarifies the relationship of these two composers from totally different backgrounds.

If the literature on Potter, Bennett, Stanford, and Parry seems sparse, that on Elgar is abundant; probably the literature on the *Enigma Variations* alone comes close to the amount for Bennett, Parry, or Stanford. Before Elgar's death, seven monographs of his life and/or works had appeared, and they continued to appear to the end of the twentieth century. Among the most important are the ones by Maine, Reed, McVeagh, Young, Kennedy, and most recently the capital achievements of the books by Jerrold Northrop Moore. In addition, Elgar's letters are now in the process of publication. Anderson/ELGAR MANUSCRIPT provides insight into the composer's working methods and the interpretation of his compositions. Cox/ ELGAR SYMPHONIES, Kennedy/ELGAR ORCHESTRAL, and Hepokoski/ELGAR [SYM-PHONIES] are useful surveys. Despite its popularity, apart from reviews and press introductions, Symphony No. 1 has generated few specialized studies. Symphony No. 2, however, has had essays by Tovey, Kent, and Gimbel. The third symphony has recently, due to the completion by Payne, received a great deal of attention including Payne/ELGAR 3 and the above-mentioned website. At the time of writing, there had not yet been any scholarly studies evaluating the completion of the work by Payne and the work itself.

PLATE B2 A&B Cipriani Potter, Symphony No. 12 in C Minor, first two pages of autograph of second movement Andante con moto quasi Allegretto. British Library.

PLATE B4 Group photograph of some leading British composers taken at the Bournemouth Festival in 1910. From left to right: Edward Elgar, Dan Godfrey, C. Hubert H. Parry, Alexander Campbell Mackenzie, Edward German, and Charles Villiers Stanford. Courtesy of The Elgar Birthplace Museum.

PLATE B5 A&B Charles Villiers Stanford, Symphony No. 3 in F Minor "The Irish," Opus 94, title page and Note by composer for first edition by Novello, Ewer and Co. British Library.

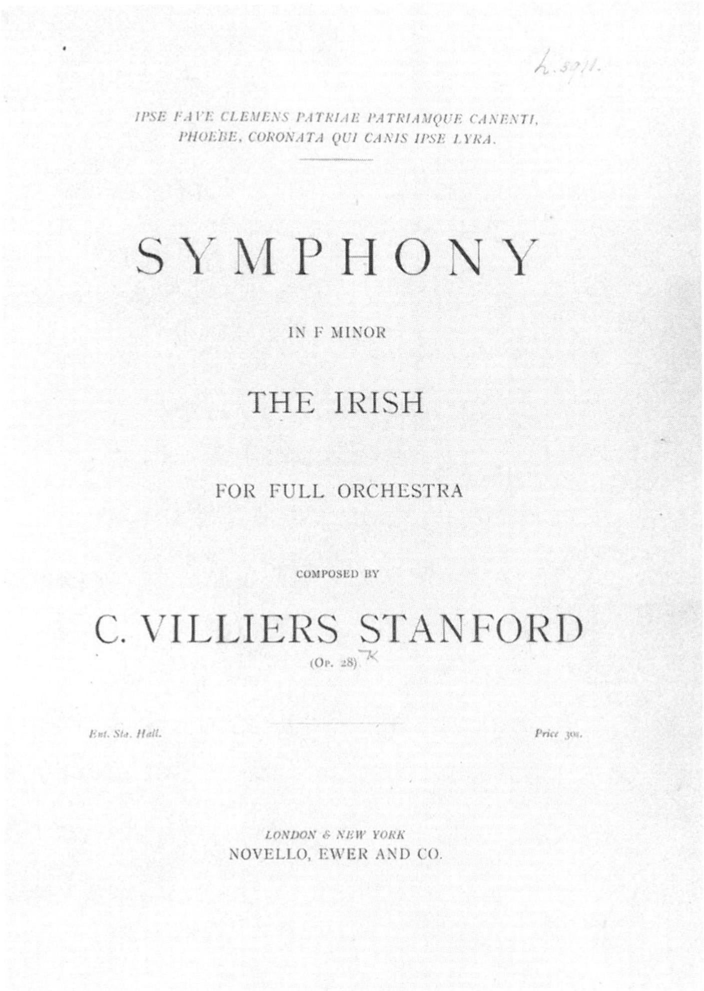

h. 5911.

IPSE FAVE CLEMENS PATRIAE PATRIAMQUE CANENTI,
PHOEBE, CORONATA QUI CANIS IPSE LYRA.

SYMPHONY

IN F MINOR

THE IRISH

FOR FULL ORCHESTRA

COMPOSED BY

C. VILLIERS STANFORD

(Op. 28)

Ent. Sta. Hall.   *Price 30s.*

LONDON & NEW YORK
NOVELLO, EWER AND CO.

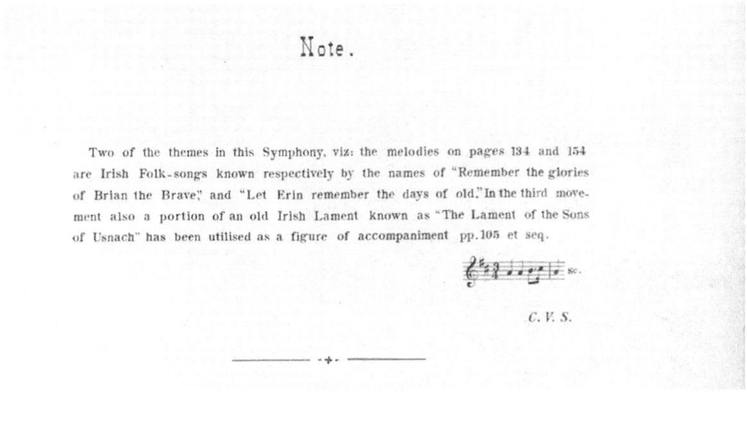

Note.

Two of the themes in this Symphony, viz: the melodies on pages 134 and 154 are Irish Folk-songs known respectively by the names of "Remember the glories of Brian the Brave," and "Let Erin remember the days of old." In the third movement also a portion of an old Irish Lament known as "The Lament of the Sons of Usnach" has been utilised as a figure of accompaniment pp. 105 et seq.

C. V. S.

PLATE B6 Edward Elgar, Symphony No. 3 in C Minor, autograph to the beginning of the first movement. British Library.

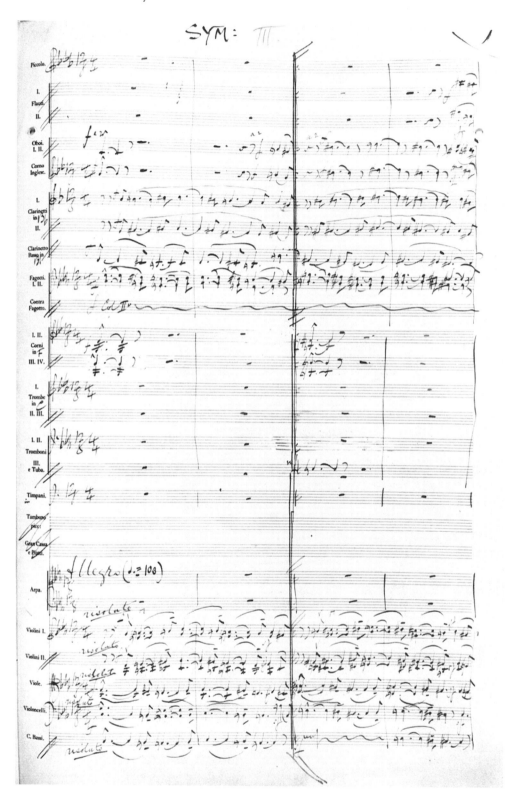

PLATE B7 Edward Elgar, Symphony No. 2, sketch to the opening of the first movement with its poetic motto. Courtesy of The Elgar Birthplace Museum.

PLATE B8 Mily Alekseyevich Balakirev, photograph portrait from 1893. Dedication in Balakirev's hand: "Sincere congratulations to Vladimir Vasilievich Stasov 10 June 1893." Balakirev was the leader of the *kuchka* (the "mighty handful"), a name introduced by Stasov.

PLATE B9 Nikolay Rimsky-Korsakov, photograph portrait from 1906–1907.

PLATE B11 Aleksandr Profir'yevich Borodin, photograph portrait by K. A. Shapiro, St. Petersburg, 1877.

PLATE B12 Pyotr Il'yich Tchaikovsky and his favorite nephew Vladimir L'vovich Davidov (1871–1906), photographed at the spa in Vichy, France, 1892. Davidov was the dedicatee of his Symphony No. 6 "Pathétique" in B Minor.

PLATE B14 Serge Vasil'yevich Rachmaninoff, photograph portrait from 1928. As a professional musician, Rachmaninoff was a triple threat: a piano virtuoso, a striking conductor, and a composer.

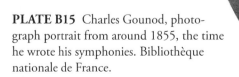

PLATE B15 Charles Gounod, photograph portrait from around 1855, the time he wrote his symphonies. Bibliothèque nationale de France.

PLATE B16 Georges Bizet, photograph portrait from about the time he returned from Rome in 1860. Bibliothèque nationale de France.

PLATE B17 Georges Bizet, Symphony in C Major (1855), first page of autograph. Bibliothèque nationale de France.

PLATE B18 Camille Saint-Saëns, photograph portrait from 1883, shortly before he composed the "Organ" Symphony. Bibliothèque nationale de France.

PLATE B19 "M. Édouard Colonne lets a pianissimo slip by": caricature by Charles Léandre in *Le Rire,* December 7, 1895. Bibliothèque nationale de France.

PLATE B21 César Franck, photograph portrait. Bibliothèque nationale de France.

PLATE B20 "M. Lamoureux lets out a fortissimo": caricature by Charles Léandre in *Le Rire,* December 7, 1895. Bibliothèque nationale de France.

PLATE B22 Ernest Chausson, souvenir post-card with photograph. Bibliothèque nationale de France.

PLATE B24 Vincent d'Indy, photograph portrait. Bibliothèque nationale de France.

PLATE B23 Paul Dukas, photograph portrait from the time he wrote the Symphony in C Major. Bibliothèque nationale de France.

6 mars 1904

NOUVEAU-THÉATRE
15, Rue Blanche, 15

❦❦❦❦❦❦❦❦❦❦❦❦❦❦❦

23ᵉ Année   Saison 1903–1904

ASSOCIATION
DES

Concerts Lamoureux

VINGTIÈME CONCERT
(Série B)
Dimanche 6 Mars 1904, à 3 heures

PAR MESURE D'ORDRE

Le Public est prévenu que la circulation dans la Salle sera rigoureusement interdite pendant l'exécution des morceaux

PROGRAMME

1. **OUVERTURE DE GWENDOLINE.** . E. CHABRIER

Gwendoline, opéra en trois actes, poème de M. Catulle MENDÈS, musique de M. E. Emmanuel CHABRIER, a été conçu et écrit dans l'esprit de la nouvelle école dramatique musicale.

L'action se passe sur la côte de la Grande-Bretagne, fin du VIIᵉ siècle.

2. DEUXIÈME SYMPHONIE *(si ♭)* . . . . Vincent d'Indy

En quatre Parties :

1º Introduction et 1ᵉʳ mouvement (très vif).
2º Modérément lent.
3º Intermède. (Modéré et très animé).
4º Introduction, Fugue et Final (assez vif).

« *Deuxième Audition* ».

Cette symphonie (œuvre 57), une des plus récentes productions de l'auteur, a été composée en 1902 et 1903.

Vincent d'Indy l'a écrite à l'intention de l'orchestre de l'Association des Concerts Lamoureux, à qui il en a, d'ailleurs, réservé la première exécution.

3. CONCERTO en sol majeur · · · · · · · Mozart

pour Violon et Orchestre.

M. Henri MARTEAU

4. TROIS POÈMES MARITIMES. . . Georges Hue

I. Mer grise.
II. Mer païenne.   } Paroles d'André Lebey.
III. Mer sauvage.

(Première Audition).

Mˡˡᵉ Suzanne CESBRON.

MER GRISE

La mer immensément soupire dans la nuit
A travers le silence éveillé par les palmes,
La mer immensément déroule une onde calme
Où baigne le sillon d'une lune aux tons gris.

La mer immensément étale du mystère
Où l'ondulation des voiles et des ailes
Fait vivre le silence où l'ombre jusqu'au ciel
Recule l'horizon dont s'agrandit la terre.

PLATE B26 Joseph-Guy Ropartz (seated), Albéric Magnard (standing left), Eugène Ysaÿe (standing right), photographed in 1903. Bibliothèque nationale de France.

PLATE B27 André Gedalge photographed at his workdesk, with photograph of his teacher, Ernest Guiraud, on the mantle. Private collection of André Gedalge, the composer's grandson, Paris.

PLATE B28 Albéric Magnard, Symphony No. 4 in C-Sharp Minor, autograph of opening bars from 1911–1913. Bibliothèque nationale de France.

Section Five
The Russian Symphony

CHAPTER FIFTEEN

The Symphony in Russia:
From Glinka to Rachmaninoff

In Collaboration with Lynn Sargeant

The Symphonic Milieu

Symphonies were not propagated in either St. Petersburg or Moscow until after the mid-nineteenth century. Whereas in Vienna it was the ghosts of Haydn, Mozart, and Beethoven that suppressed symphonic interests, in Russia it was a musical environment not conducive to symphonic efforts. Even with well-trained native composers, the relative lack of venues (societies and concert series) likely discouraged most potential Russian symphonists.[1]

Instead, musical life continued to focus on Italian opera, as it had since the reign of Catherine the Great (1762–1796). Composers such as Baldassare Galuppi (1706–1785), Tommasso Traëtta (1727–1779), Giovanni Paisiello (1740–1816), Giuseppe Sarti (1729–1802), Vincente Martín y Soler (1754–1806), Domenico Cimarosa (1749–1801), and others had been employed at the court at various times during Catherine's reign.[2] Since many of these composers had one-time connections with the Imperial Theaters in Vienna, one suspects that the Russian ambassador to the Imperial Court played a role in their recruitment. However, French was the dominant language at the Russian Court, and it is also known that in 1764 Catherine brought a French troupe to the capital, which performed works by François-André Danican Philidor (1726–1795), Egidio Duni (1708–1775), and Pierre-Alexandre Monsigny (1729–1817), among others.[3] During the first half of the nineteenth century, most public concerts were held during the Lenten season, when the theaters were closed.

In 1860 a Russian Theater was established. It staged homegrown opera by composers such as Mikhail Glinka (1804–1857), César Cui (1835–1918), Modest Musorgsky (1839–1881), and Nikolay Rimsky-Korsakov (1844–1908), as well as foreign works.[4] However, operas by Russian composers constituted only a small part of the total repertoire through the mid-nineteenth century, even in the Russian Theater. This favoring of foreign works eventually resulted in the growth of a national consciousness and specific initiatives to propagate native musical works during the second half of the century. Most notably, in St. Petersburg there were diametrically different efforts led by two rivals: Anton Rubinstein (1829–1894) and Mily Balakirev (1837–1910).[5]

Anton Rubinstein came from a family of Jewish merchants who were baptized into the Orthodox faith. His early piano studies were with his mother and Alexander Villoing, who took him to Paris at the age of ten where he had encounters with both Chopin and Liszt. Rubinstein started his professional career with an extended concert tour that covered England and much of northern Europe. He returned home in 1843 and the following year went to Berlin with his brother Nikolay, also a pianist of prodigious abilities, for composition studies with Siegfried Dehn (1799–1858). In 1848 Anton took up residence in St. Petersburg, where he found a patron in the Grand Duchess Elena Pavlovna. After composing three Russian operas before the age of twenty-five (1852–1853), he embarked on another tour, promoting himself as both a pianist and a composer of international rank. During his travels, he came to realize that St. Petersburg could not compete in the musical marketplace of Europe without establishing a regular concert series and a conservatory to train professional performers and composers.

By 1858, at the age of thirty, Anton Rubinstein assumed the leadership of the court concerts for the Grand Duchess. With her patronage and the assistance of several other leading figures in St. Petersburg musical life, he founded the Russian Musical Society (RMS) in 1859. A focal point of the RMS's activities in its early years was its ten-concert orchestral season; in 1860 chamber-music concerts were also sponsored. In 1862 Rubinstein founded the St. Petersburg Conservatory, which to this day remains one of Russia's premier institutions of musical education. Thus, within just a few years, through political connections, personal ambition, and prodigious abilities, Rubinstein had established himself as the most important and powerful musician in Russia.[6]

Though today Anton Rubinstein is remembered as a first-rate pianist and for his influential role in Russia's musical development, during his lifetime he was also regarded in many quarters as an accomplished composer of operas, orchestral music, chamber music, songs, piano music, and choral works.

Rubinstein composed a total of six symphonies, which were heard throughout Europe and Russia:

No. 1 in F Major Opus 40	1850
No. 2 "Ocean" in C Major Opus 42	1851, rev. 1863, 1880
No. 3 in A Major Opus 56	1854–1855
No. 4 "Dramatic" in D Minor Opus 95	1874
No. 5 "Russian" in G Minor Opus 107	1880
No. 6 in A Minor Opus 111	1886

During his lifetime, Symphony No. 2 (Opus 42) became a repertoire piece, and its two revisions expanded the number of movements from the standard four to seven. Symphony No. 5 was his only symphony to incorporate Russian folk music; like his other symphonies, however, the work belongs to the Central European tradition with strong ties to Mendelssohn and Schumann.

Of course power and influence can breed jealousy, criticism, and competition. In the case of Rubinstein, his nemesis was Mily Balakirev (Plate B8) and the circle of composers that surrounded him, which the critic Vladimir Stasov (1824–1906) was to dub *moguchaya kuchka* or the *Mighty Handful*.[7] As the undisputed leader of the *kuchka*, Balakirev was an overbearing mentor and teacher, perhaps only matched in the history of music to date by Arnold Schoenberg.[8]

Balakirev took up residence in St. Petersburg in 1855. During the following year, before he had turned twenty, he encountered César Cui, an amateur composer and civil engineer whose music criticism became part of an ongoing effort to reduce Rubinstein's power and prestige. In 1857, Modest Musorgsky, a product of landed wealth whose devaluation forced him into civil service, came under Balakirev's spell. In 1861, Balakirev met the young naval cadet Nikolay Rimsky-Korsakov, who joined the group. In 1862, the doctor of medicine, chemist, and university professor Aleksandr Borodin (1833–1887) completed the five recognized as the "mighty handful." Vladimir Stasov should also technically be considered a part of this circle, since his writings supported many of Balakirev's central tenets. In contrast, the composer and critic Aleksandr Serov (1820–1871) also subscribed to many of the *kuchka*'s ideas in his writings, but maintained an independence from Balakirev. Following the success of his operas *Judith* (1863) and *Rogneda* (1865), Serov was distanced further from the group and, like Rubinstein, became a rival to Balakirev's ambitions.[9]

The *kuchka*'s main agenda was the propagation of indigenous Russian art music: music by Russian composers using Russian/Slavic folk music and topics. However, there were also other agendas, such as the advocacy of modernism as represented by Schumann, Berlioz, and Liszt. But perhaps it was not what the *kuchka* advocated that unified them, but what they were opposed to, which included German music; Italian opera; the music of Bach, Haydn, Mozart, early Beethoven, and Mendelssohn; conservatory training with its pedantic emphasis on harmony, counterpoint, and technical analysis; as well as absolute music and the aesthetic ideas of Eduard Hanslick. For the *kuchka,* the systematic study of music theory, for example, was replaced by a study of the "acceptable" classics in discussions led by Balakirev himself. Balakirev's authoritarianism thus replaced the authority of systematic theory.

These agendas and beliefs served in part as a basis for the *kuchka*'s attacks on Anton Rubinstein. Though they acknowledged his accomplishments as a pianist, Rubinstein was considered at best a mediocre conductor, a conservative in his choice of repertoire, a pedant in his advocacy of professional education for musicians, and, as a composer, not worthy of acknowledgment.

While we cannot comment on Rubinstein as a conductor, we do know something of the RMS repertoire during the first year of his tenure. Included on the first ten programs were works by Gluck, Mozart, Haydn, Beethoven, von Weber, Schubert, Hiller, Spohr, Liszt, Berlioz, and Wagner. In addition, each concert contained one work by a Russian.[10] Although in later seasons the Russian component diminished, the argument that these were conservative and not varied programs, despite their heavy Germanic orientation, appears unjustifiable.

Further, depriving the *kuchka* of conservatory training that Balakirev would have characterized as pedantry was in almost all cases detrimental to their own development as composers. According to Tchaikovsky, in a letter to Madame Nadezhda von Meck dated December 1877 (January 1878), Rimsky-Korsakov was the one exception:

> The young Petersburg composers are very gifted, but they are all impregnated with the most horrible presumptuousness and a purely amateur conviction of their superiority to all other musicians in the universe. The one exception, in later days, has been Rimsky-Korsakov. He was also an "auto-didact" like the rest, but recently he has undergone a complete change. By nature he is very earnest, honourable, and conscientious. As a very young man he dropped into a set which first solemnly assured him he was a genius, and then proceeded to convince him that he had no need to study, that academics were destructive to all inspiration and dried up creative activity. At first he believed all this. His earliest compositions bear the stamp of striking ability and a lack of theoretical training. The circle to which he belonged was a mutual admiration society. Each member was striving to imitate the work of another, after proclaiming it as something very wonderful. Consequently the whole set suffered from one-sidedness, lack of individuality, and mannerisms. Rimsky-Korsakov is the only one among them who discovered, five years ago, that the doctrines preached by this circle had no sound basis, that their mockery of the schools and the classical masters, their denial of authority and of the masterpieces, was nothing but ignorance. I possess a letter dating from that time which moved me very deeply. Rimsky-Korsakov was overcome by despair when he realised how many unprofitable years he had wasted, and that he was following a road which led nowhere. He began to study with such zeal that the theory of the school soon became to him an

indispensable atmosphere. During one summer he achieved innumerable exercises in counterpoint and sixty-four fugues, ten of which he sent me for inspection. From contempt for the schools, Rimsky-Korsakov suddenly went over to the cult of musical technique. Shortly after this appeared his symphony and also his quartet. Both works are full of obscurities and—as you will justly observe—bear the stamp of dry pedantry. At present he appears to be passing through a crisis, and it is hard to predict how it will end. Either he will turn out a great master, or be lost in contrapuntal intricacies.

C. Cui is a gifted amateur. His music is not original, but graceful and elegant; it is too coquettish—"made up"—so to speak. At first it pleases, but soon satiates us. That is because Cui's specialty is not music, but fortification, upon which he has to give a number of lectures in the various military schools in St. Petersburg. He himself once told me he could only compose by picking out his melodies and harmonies as he sat at the piano. When he hit upon some pretty idea, he worked it up in every detail, and this process was very lengthy, so that his opera *Ratcliff*, for instance, took him ten years to complete. But, as I have said, we cannot deny that he has talent of a kind—and at least taste and instinct.

Borodin—aged fifty—Professor of Chemistry at the Academy of Medicine, also possesses talent, a very great talent, which however has come to nothing for the want of teaching, and because blind fate has led him into the science laboratories instead of a vital musical existence. He has not as much taste as Cui, and his technique is so poor that he cannot write a bar without assistance.

With regard to Moussorgsky, as you very justly remark he is "used up." His gifts are perhaps the most remarkable of all, but his nature is narrow and he has no aspirations towards self-perfection. He has been too easily led away by the absurd theories of his set and the belief in his own genius. Besides which his nature is not of the finest quality, and he likes what is coarse, unpolished, and ugly. He is the exact opposite of the distinguished and elegant Cui.

Moussorgsky plays with his lack of polish—and even seems proud of his want of skill, writing just as it comes to him, believing blindly in the infallibility of his genius. As a matter of fact his very original talent flashes forth now and again.

Balakirev is the greatest personality of the entire circle. . . . In spite of his great gifts, he has done a great deal of harm. For instance, he it was who ruined Korsakov's early career by assuring him he had no need to study. He is the inventor of all the theories of this remarkable circle which unites so many undeveloped, falsely developed, or prematurely decayed, talents.[11]

Rimsky-Korsakov echoed Tchaikovsky's views in a letter he wrote to Semyon Kruglikov in November 1880:

> One can learn by oneself; sometimes one needs advice, but one has also to learn, that is, one must not neglect harmony and counterpoint and the development of a good technique and a clean leading subject. All of us, myself and Borodin and Balakirev, but especially Cui and Moussorgsky, neglected this. I consider that I caught myself in time and made myself get down to work. Owing to such deficiencies in technique Balakirev writes little; Borodin, with difficulty; Cui, sloppily; Moussorgsky, messily and often nonsensically; and all this constitutes the very regrettable specialty of the Russian school.[12]

Nevertheless, Balakirev did actively encourage the members of his circle to compose symphonies, and all of the members of the *kuchka* worked on symphonic compositions during the 1860s. Rimsky-Korsakov began his Symphony No. 1 in 1861, completing the original version in 1865. Borodin, the amateur among the group, began his Symphony No. 1 in 1862 and completed it in 1867. Musorgsky planned a Symphony in D during 1861, but never completed it.[13] Not even César Cui completely escaped Balakirev's urgings, but he never made substantial progress. Balakirev himself composed the first movement of his Symphony No. 1 in C major in 1864, but the remaining movements and his Second Symphony were only completed in the last decade of the nineteenth century and first decade of the twentieth century, and were ultimately anachronistic. In the end, the members of the *kuchka* only completed some eight symphonies.

There is also a certain irony to these symphonic efforts. By 1860 the symphony had become a symbolic means for comparison with the achievements of Haydn, Mozart, Beethoven, Schubert, Mendelssohn, and Schumann—i.e., the main representatives of the great Germanic symphonists up to mid-century. The conservatories in Paris, Leipzig, Berlin, and Vienna either required or encouraged their composition students to test their mettle at the end of their studies with the completion of a symphony movement or an entire cycle. Composing in the symphonic genre gave these students an opportunity to display their abilities in thematic presentation and development, tonal manipulation, counterpoint, orchestration, and form. Yet in the view of Balakirev, all of these skills were indicative of the pedantry the conservatory propagated. Thus, one could argue that Balakirev was contradicting his own philosophical and aesthetic beliefs, and acknowledging German superiority, by encouraging his mentees to compose in this genre. Alternatively, one could argue that Balakirev was following a long tradition of Russian musical thought and criticism that focused on the progressive, i.e., Romantic music, as represented not just by Schumann but also by Berlioz and Liszt.

Despite the dominance of Rubinstein in St. Petersburg, Balakirev was able, through determined efforts, to find a post as orchestra conductor for the Free Music School. Established in 1862 as an educational institution that focused on choral singing, its director was Gavriil Lomakin (1812–1885), who was reputed to have been "the most distinguished choral conductor in mid-nineteenth-century Russia."[14] By 1867, Balakirev had become the director of the Free Music School and, more surprisingly, with Rubinstein's resignation from the Royal Music Society, Balakirev also became the conductor of the RMS concert series. Thus, Balakirev found himself in a different position of influence: the proverbial outsider had become an insider. He could therefore either decide to propagate the music and aesthetic stances of his circle to the exclusion of the RMS audience's preferences, or he could soften his beliefs about the historically more distant composers (i.e., Haydn, Mozart, and early Beethoven) as well as the central European/Germanic repertoire. Balakirev chose the former, and by 1869 he had been relieved of his RMS post. This also resulted in Balakirev's withdrawal from musical life for the next twelve years.[15]

Table XV/1 provides a list of symphonies composed by significant Russian composers, beginning with the early efforts of Glinka, from *ca.* 1824 until 1918, the year after the Bolshevik Revolution. The cutoff date for this chapter was selected for both political and musical reasons. Politically, the October Revolution was the beginning of new relationships between the arts and the state, while musically Russia was also coming to the end of an era. César Cui, the last surviving member of the *kuchka,* died in 1918 and other composers also left Russia about this time: Rachmaninoff, Nikolay and Aleksander Tcherepnin, Stravinsky, and Prokofiev—who did not return to his homeland until 1936.

The works in italics in Table XV/1 will be the focus of this chapter. We begin with the influential orchestral pieces by Glinka, and then discuss the symphony works by two major

TABLE XV/1

Symphonies by Significant Russian Composers from *ca.* 1824 to 1918

ca. 1824	*Glinka, Sym. B-flat* (incomplete).
1834	*Glinka, Sym. On Two Russian Themes* (incomplete).
1850	A. Rubinstein, Sym. No. 1 F Opus 40.
1851	A. Rubinstein, Sym. No. 2 C Opus 42 "Ocean" (rev. 1863, 1880).
1855	A. Rubinstein, Sym. No. 3 A Opus 56.
1864	*Balakirev, Sym. No. 1 C.*
1865	*Rimsky-Korsakov, Sym. No. 1 E-flat Minor Opus 1 (rev. 1884).*
1866	*Balakirev, Sym. No. 1/1; Tchaikovsky, Sym. No. 1 G Minor Opus 13 "Winter Daydreams" (rev. 1874).*
1867	*Borodin, Sym. No. 1 E-flat.*
1868	*Rimsky-Korsakov, Sym. No. 2 Opus 9 Antar.*
1872	*Tchaikovsky, Sym. No. 2 C Minor Opus 17 "Little Russian" (rev. 1879–80).*
1873	*Rimsky-Korsakov, Sym. No. 3 C Opus 32 (rev. 1886).*
1874	A. Rubinstein, Sym. No. 4 D Minor Opus 95 "Dramatic"; Taneyev, Sym. No. 1 E Minor.
1875	*Tchaikovsky, Sym. No. 3 D Opus 29 "Polish."*
1876	*Borodin, Sym. No. 2 B Minor.*
1877	*Tchaikovsky, Sym. No. 4 F Minor Opus 36.*
1878	Taneyev, Sym. No. 2 B-flat Minor.
1880	A. Rubinstein, Sym. No. 5 G Minor Opus 107 "Russian."
1882	Glazunov, Sym. No. 1 E Opus 5 "Slavyanskaya" (rev. 1885, 1929).
1883	Arensky, Sym. No. 1 B Minor Opus 4.
1884	Taneyev, Sym. No. 3 D Minor.
1885	*Tchaikovsky, Manfred Symphony Opus 58.*
1886	A. Rubinstein, Sym. No. 6 A Minor Opus 111; Glazunov, Sym. No. 2 F-sharp Minor Opus 16.
1887	*Borodin, Sym. No. 3 A Minor;* Lyapunov, Sym. No. 1 B Minor Opus 12.
1888	*Rimsky-Korsakov, Sheherazade Opus 35; Tchaikovsky, Sym. No. 5 E Minor Opus 64.*
1889	Arensky, Sym. No. 2 A Opus 22.
1890	Glazunov, Sym. No. 3 D Opus 33.
1891	Rachmaninoff, Sym. in D Minor (incomplete)
1893	*Tchaikovsky, Sym. No. 6 B Minor Opus 74 Pathétique;* Glazunov, Sym. No. 4 E-flat Opus 48.
1894	Grechaninov, Sym. No. 1 B Minor Opus 6.
1895	*Kalinnikov, Sym. No. 1 G Minor;* Glazunov, Sym. No. 5 B-flat Opus 55; *Rachmaninoff, Sym. No. 1 D Minor Opus 13.*
1896	Glazunov, Sym. No. 6 C Minor Opus 58.
1897	*Kalinnikov, Sym. No. 2 A; Balakirev, Sym. No. 1/1-4 C.*
1898	Taneyev, Sym. No. 4 (pub. as No. 1) C Minor Opus 12.
1900	Skryabin, Sym. No. 1 E Opus 26; Glier, Sym. No. 1 E-flat Opus 8.
1901	Skryabin, Sym. No. 2 C Opus 29.
1902	Glazunov, Sym. No. 7 F Opus 77 "Pastoral'naya."
1904	Skryabin, Sym. No. 3 C Opus 43 "Le poème divin."
1906	Glazunov, Sym. No. 8 E-flat Opus 83.
1907	Stravinsky, Sym. E-flat Opus 1; *Rachmaninoff, Sym. No. 2 E Minor Opus 27.*
1908	*Balakirev, Sym. No. 2 D Minor;* Glier, Sym. No. 2 C Minor Opus 25; Myaskovsky, Sym. No. 1 C Minor Opus 3.
1909	Grechaninov, Sym. No. 2 A Opus 27 "Pastoral'naya."
1910	Glazunov, Sym. No. 9 in D (incomplete).
1911	Glier, Sym. No. 3 Opus 42 "Il'ya Muromets"; Myaskovsky, Sym. No. 2 C-sharp Minor Opus 11.
1914	Myaskovsky, Sym. No. 3 A Minor Opus 15.
1917	Lyapunov, Sym. No. 2 B-flat Minor Opus 66.
1918	Myaskovsky, Sym. No. 4 E Minor Opus 17

composers from the Balakirev circle, Rimsky-Korsakov and Borodin; the most important Russian symphony composer, Tchaikovsky, who also had some important associations with Balakirev; Balakirev himself; Vasily Kalinnikov (1866–1901); and, finally, the symphonies of Serge Rachmaninoff (1873–1943).

As seen from the works not in italics in Table XV/1, this selection bypasses a number of other symphonists whose works have a place in Russian symphony orchestra concerts, notably Aleksandr Skryabin (1871/72–1915), Sergey Taneyev (1856–1915), Aleksandr Glazunov (1865–1936), Anton Arensky (1861–1906), Sergey Lyapunov (1859–1924), Aleksandr Grechaninov (1864–1956), and Reyngol'd Glier (1875–1956). At the time of writing, the works of Nikolay Myaskovsky (1881–1950), a composer of twenty-seven symphonies, together with those by Igor Stravinsky (1882–1971) and others of their generation, are slated to be included in the fifth volume of *The Symphonic Repertoire* series.

The Seeds of the Russian Symphony: Mikhail Glinka

Central to Balakirev's musical beliefs were the works of Mikhail Glinka. In Balakirev's selective view, Glinka was the ideal Russian composer, as evidenced by his operas *A Life for the Tsar* (1836) and *Ruslan and Lyudmila* (1842) and the orchestral piece *Kamarinskaya* (1848). In fact, *Kamarinskaya* served as a model for Balakirev's own *Overture on the Themes of Three Russian Songs* (1858, revised 1881) and to a lesser degree its sequel, the *Second Overture on Russian Themes* (1864), known in its revised form as *Russia* (1884).

Tchaikovsky also greatly admired Glinka's little orchestral piece, though he had mixed feelings about Glinka overall. As he wrote in his diary on June 27/July 9, 1888, *Kamarinskaya* was a seed ("acorn") for other Russian symphonic works:

> *Kamarinskaya* is also a work of remarkable inspiration. Without intending to compose anything beyond a simple, humorous trifle, he has left us a little masterpiece, every bar of which is the outcome of enormous creative power. Half a century has passed since then, and many Russian symphonic works have been composed; we may even speak of a symphonic school. Well? The germ of all this lied in *Kamarinskaya*, as the oak tree lies in the acorn. For long years to come Russian composers will drink at this source, for it will need much time and much strength to exhaust its wealth of inspiration. Yes! Glinka was a true creative genius![16]

The piece itself is based on two Russian folksongs, one a Wedding Song (*A*) and the other a Dance Song (*B*) that alternate in the following larger structure:

Introduction	*A*	*T*	*B*	*A*	*T*	*B*	*Coda (B)*
D minor	F	D minor	D	F	D Minor-B-flat	B-flat/D	D
m.1	11	35	54	182	144	173	302

Of more significance is its smaller-dimension structure, which is based on a type of variation practice frequently encountered in symphonic renderings of national folk tunes: the melody is repeated many times as an unadulterated *cantus firmus* while its harmonies, texture, timbre, or other aspects of its environment change with each repetition. Such an approach to variation is not special to Glinka, for such a procedure is to be found, among other places, in Haydn's famous variations on *Gott erhalte Franz den Kaiser* from his String Quartet Opus 76/3/2. The Wedding Song is heard a total of six times with the changing background, while the Dance Song grows out of a three-measure ostinato heard more than sixty times. For Glinka, the Wedding Song, after a presentation in octaves, is formalized by counterpoint. In contrast, the Dance Song is reminiscent of a *contredanse* with the sounds of folk fiddling (N.B. the use of open harmonies and bariolage [e.g., mm.114f]).[17]

If *Kamarinskaya* represents what Balakirev considered Glinka to be—a nationalist composer who created a special way of treating folk material—then his famous overture to *Ruslan and Lyudmila* is a piece in the Germanic tradition: a potpourri of themes from the opera encased in an academic sonata form. *P* (m.1) comes from the opera's final scene of rejoicing, *S* (m.81) from Ruslan's second act aria.[18] *T* (m.57) is based on *P.* The development (m.120) is compact, but still displays Glinka's deep command of its techniques. The recapitulation commences with *2P* (m.237) followed by *T* and *S*. All this material falls within the major/minor system; it is not until the coda (m.349) that a more exotic whole-tone scale (m.357) is heard in the trombones before *1P* (m.386) returns for the final bars. Also notable is the treatment of the orchestra: the brilliant violin writing, the soloistic moments for the timpani, the snatches of woodwind colors, the warmth of *S* scored for cellos and repeated by the full orchestra, and the horn dissonances with timpani in the retransition. Few composers during the first half of the nineteenth century could consolidate their forces for such a compact and stunning piece of writing.

The dichotomy between *Kamarinskaya* and the *Ruslan and Lyudmila* Overture certainly underlines that Glinka was at times looking west and at other times looking east. Of Glinka's four major completed orchestral works, three are on Spanish subjects:

Capriccio brilliante on the Jota aragonesa (First Spanish Overture)—1845
Recuerdos de Castilla (Recollections of Castille)—1848
Recollection of a Summer Night in Madrid: Fantasia for Orchestra (Second Spanish Overture)—1851

In addition, there is a *Polonaise* [on a Spanish bolero theme] from 1855. Indeed, if one surveys Glinka's total output, except for the stage works and songs, it would be difficult to know that he was Russian; one might be more inclined to think he was a Spanish or Polish composer.[19]

As shown above in Table XV/1, Glinka did begin two symphonies: one in B-flat from *ca.* 1824 and a second on two Russian themes a decade later. However, he apparently made little effort to bring these two works to completion.

Nikolay Rimsky-Korsakov
INTRODUCTION

Based on their initial titles, Rimsky-Korsakov (1844–1908) (Plate B9) wrote either two or three symphonies (see Table XV/2): the total is two if one counts only Nos. 1 and 3, for which the composer never changed his mind about their genre. For Symphony No. 2, the programmatic *Antar* Symphony with a Berliozian *idée fixe,* Rimsky-Korsakov had misgivings about whether or not it was a symphony. He retitled it as a symphonic suite in 1897, despite the fact that it is a cyclic work, a conventional marker for the symphonic genre. On the other hand, if one considers *Antar* to be an actual symphony, then Rimsky-Korsakov's other symphonic suite, *Sheherazade,* also belongs to the genre, and thus it is included as well in Table XV/2.

Both Nos. 1 and 3 are pieces of absolute music, without obvious cyclicism, and are coloristically heavier and darker than *Antar* and *Sheherazade.* Additionally, the two latter suites/symphonies incorporate melodies that in the West would be considered Oriental[20] and use different tempos within a movement as a prime contributor to their shape. What separates *Antar* from the other three cycles is that it has not a single standard symphonic structure. Thus, there is something of a bifurcation in Rimsky's concept of the genre: Nos. 1 and 3 belong to the Schumann tradition both coloristically and thematically, while the two suites seem more indebted to the Berliozian concept as found in the *Symphonie fantastique* and *Harold in Italy.*

TABLE XV/2
The Symphonies of Nikolay Rimsky-Korsakov

Opus	Key	Dates	Title	Movements	Instrumentation	Comments
1	E-Flat minor E minor	1861–1865 rev. 1884	Symphony No. 1	1884 version 1. Largo assai—Allegro 2/2 (324 m.) E minor 2. Andante tranquillo 3/4 (141 m.) C major 3. Scherzo: Vivace 3/8—Trio 2/4 (534 m.) E minor 4. Allegro assai 3/4 (397 m.) E major	Grand plus Harp	First performance: St. Petersburg on December 19/31, 1865, conducted by Mily Balakirev at the Free Music School; revised version: St. Petersburg on December 4/16, 1885, conducted by Georgy D. Dyvtsh. 1884 version published in St. Petersburg: Bessel, 1885.
9		1868 rev. 1875 rev. 1897	Symphony No. 2 Symphonic Suite *Antar*	1897 version 1. Largo 4/4—Allegro giocoso 3/4—Largo 4/4—Allegretto vivace 6/8—Adagio 4/4—Allegretto vivace 6/8—Largo 4/4 (287 m.) 2. Allegro 2/2 (242 m.) D minor 3. Allegro risoluto alla Marcia 4/4 (164 m.) D major 4. Allegretto vivace 6/8/2/4 (210 m)	Grand plus Flt., EH, Cym., BD, Tam-tam, Tri., Tamb, Harp	"Antar" 1. The Fairy promises Antar the joys of life. 2. The joy of vengeance. 3. The joy of power. 4. The joy of love and death. Dedicated to Cesár Cui. Note: for the 1897 version its genre was changed from Symphony to Symphonic Suite. First performance: St. Petersburg on March 10/22, 1869, conducted by Mily Balakirev. Published in St. Petersburg: Bessel, 1880 (1875 version) and 1913 (1897 version).
32	C major	1866–1873 rev. 1886	Symphony No. 3	1886 version 1. Moderato assai—Allegro 3/4 (663 m.) 2. Scherzo: Vivo 5/4—[Trio?]: Moderato 3/4 E-flat major—B major(?) (396 m.) 3. Andante 6/8 Animato assai (160 m.) *attacca:* 4. Allegro con spirito—Animato 2/2 (312 m.)	Grand plus Picc.	First performance: St. Petersburg on February 18/March 2, 1876, conducted by the composer; revised version: St. Petersburg on October 29/November 10, 1886, conducted by the composer. 1886 version published in Leipzig: Belyayev, 1888.
35	E major	1888	Symphonic Suite *Sheherazade*	1. Largo e maestoso 2/2—Lento 4/4—Allegro non troppo 6/4 (236 m.) 2. Lento 4/4—Andantino 3/8 (473 m.) B minor 3. Andantino quasi allegretto 6/8 (209 m.) G major 4. Allegro molto 6/8—Lento 4/4—Vivo 2/8 (6/16 /3/8)—Allegro non troppo e maestoso 6/4 (665 m.) E minor/major	Grand plus Picc., EH, Tuba, Cym., Tri., BD, SD, Tamb., Tam-tam, Harp, Vin. Solo	"Sheherazade after a Thousand and One Nights." 1. The Sea and Sinbad's Ship; 2. The Story of the Prince Kalandar; 3. The Young Prince and Princess; 4. Festival in Baghdad. The Ship Breaks Up against a Cliff Surmounted by a Bronze Horseman. Conclusion. Dedicated to Vladimir Stasov. First performance: St. Petersburg on October 28/November 9, 1888 conducted by the composer. Published in Leipzig: Belyayev, 1889.

However, Berlioz never distanced a symphony so far from the tradition as Rimsky-Korsakov did in *Antar.*

A second important characteristic of Rimsky-Korsakov's symphonic works is that, except for *Sheherazade,* each comes down to us in more than one version. Apart from being a perfectionist of sorts, Rimsky-Korsakov also made changes for practical reasons. For example, he reduced the orchestral size for *Antar,* thereby making it suitable for more orchestras. He also brought his works up to date with regard to his current tastes and preferences, and Symphonies Nos. 1 and 3 were revised with such motivations. For each symphony we focus our discussion on the final version, addressing the earlier versions in a more cursory fashion.[21]

SYMPHONY NO. 1 IN E-FLAT MINOR/E MINOR OPUS 1

Rimsky-Korsakov began his Symphony No. 1 in 1861 under the direction of his piano teacher Fyodor Andreevich Kanille, to whom it is dedicated. Kanille then directed his pupil to Balakirev. During his later years, Rimsky reflected on Balakirev's insufficient guidance in helping him compose his first symphony:

Of all his pupil-friends I was the youngest, being only seventeen years old. What did I need? A piano technique, the technique of harmony and counterpoint, and an idea of musical forms. Balakirev should have made me sit down at the piano and learn to play well. That was so easy for him, as I worshipped him and obeyed his advice in everything. But he did not do it; declaring from the outset that I was no pianist, he gave up the whole thing as altogether unnecessary. He should have given me a few lessons in harmony and counterpoint, should have made me write a few fugues and explained the grammar of musical forms to me. He could not do it, as he had not studied systematically himself and considered it unnecessary; hence also he did not tell me to study under someone else. Having made me write a symphony after our first meeting, he cut me off from preparatory work and the acquisition of a technique. And I, who did not know the names of all intervals and chords, to whom harmony meant but the far-famed prohibition of parallel octaves and fifths, who had no idea as to what double counterpoint was, or the meaning of cadence, thesis and antithesis, and period, I set out to compose a symphony. Schumann's *Manfred Overture* and Third Symphony, Glinka's *Prince Kholmsky* and *Jota Aragonesa,* and Balakirev's *King Lear*—these were the models I followed in writing the symphony; copied, thanks to my powers of observation and imitation. As for orchestration, the perusal of Berlioz's *Traité d'Instrumentation* and of some Glinka scores gave me a little fragmentary information. I had no idea of trumpets and French horns and would get confused between writing for natural-scale and chromatic-scale instruments. But Balakirev himself had not known these instruments and became acquainted with them only through Berlioz. The bow instruments, too, were an absolute muddle to me; the movements of the bow, the strokes, were completely unknown to me—I indicated interminable legatos, impossible of execution. I had a very vague notion of the execution of double notes and chords, blindly following Berlioz's table, in case of emergency. But Balakirev himself did not know this chapter, having the most confused notion of violin-playing and positions. I felt that I was ignorant of many things, but was convinced that Balakirev knew everything in the world, and he cleverly concealed from me and the others the insufficiency of his information. But in orchestral colouring and combination of instruments he was a good practical hand, and his counsels were invaluable to me.[22]

The slow movement was apparently composed while Rimsky was on naval duty during a stopover in England in 1863—a result of Balakirev's insistent letters. Balakirev conducted the premiere in December 1865 at a concert of the Free Music School.

The 1865 version immediately reveals the musical naiveté of both composer and mentor. First, its key of E-flat minor was practically unheard of in the annals of symphonic composition because of its difficulty for the strings and the dark coloration such a tonality lends to the string choir. Secondly, the *kuchka*'s understanding of the orchestra and orchestration came not from any first-hand experience either in an orchestra or with the instruments themselves, but from studying scores and Berlioz's *Treatise on Orchestration* published in 1843. Much had changed in the more than twenty years since its publication, including the horn which now was commonly outfitted with valves; by placing the four horns in three different keys, the young composer was aping Berlioz's idiosyncratic solution for avoiding stopped notes as suggested in the *Treatise* and practiced in the *Symphonie fantastique.* In addition, the string players would be further confused by the lengthy slurs of the introduction that could probably not be sustained by a single stroke of the bow. In the 1884 revision, the composer rectified these and other problems.

The 1865 cycle placed the Scherzo in second position and the slow movement third, but this is in reverse to what was regarded as the nineteenth-century norm. The result is an increase in contrast by following the opening Allegro with a change of character, tempo, and key, in this case the dominant's Neapolitan. Rimsky also altered some of the themes and made the transitions more convincing. The deepest alterations are made in the Finale; the tentativity of the 1865 version is swept away for an appropriately assertive and at times colorful conclusion. Certainly the 1884 revision in E minor is anachronistic for Rimsky's current style. If nothing else, Rimsky's earlier effort became viable.

In his memoir, the composer acknowledged his models to be Schumann, Glinka, and Balakirev himself. He specifically cites not only Schumann's *Manfred Overture* but also Schumann's Second and Fourth Symphonies. These were works that he could have come to know from four-hand piano renditions at meetings of the Balakirev circle. The Schumann gestures are most prominent in the first movement. For example, the influence of the *Manfred Overture* has been described by Griffiths as follows: "both works open in protean gloom, from which the tentative strains of the main subject of the following Allegro emerges."[23] In the 1884 revision, one can hear the introduction to Schumann's Fourth Symphony in both the basic line and the anticipation of the Allegro's main theme. *P* is also reminiscent of Schumann's Finale; they both use the same rhythmic motive. Measures 116f come from Schumann's first movement development section (mm.121f). The Scherzo's Trio recalls Schumann's Symphony No. 2/2, while the Finale's theme immediately reminds one of the "Rhenish" Symphony's first movement *P.*

Glinka's influence has been described by Richard Taruskin: the first movement's coda parallels the closing section to the overture to *A Life for the Tsar;* the Scherzo's "playful ostinato" (m.437) that brings it to an end comes from the last entr'acte to the forgotten play *Prince Kholmsky.*[24] As for material from Balakirev, we cannot cite any specific references, but it is certain that he closely supervised the symphony's composition. Rimsky also acknowledged that the Finale owed something to a now lost fragment of a symphonic Allegro attempted by Cui.[25]

In the expected *kuchkist* practice, Rimsky-Korsakov utilizes Russian folksongs. The first movement *P* alludes to the well-known tune "Down by the River Volga" (mm.62f). For the slow movement, Balakirev provided his young charge with a melody belonging to a series of tunes known as "On the Tatar Captivity." The thematic treatment recalls Glinka's "acorn"

Kamarinskaya and one of its many "oaks," Balakirev's *Overture on the Themes of Three Russian Songs.*

For the first movement of the 1884 version, Rimsky-Korsakov combines the enthusiasm of his youth with the perspective of an academic's view of the late-nineteenth-century symphonic tradition. The larger shape is one in the post-Mendelssohn/Schumann mold that owes something to Beethoven: a dark, slow introduction with an accelerando into the Allegro, a formally correct sonata-form movement with the exposition repeated in the 1884 version, a development that displays some of the composer's contrapuntal skills, a proper recapitulation now with *S* (m.234) building to a *fortissimo* climax, and a coda (m.256) with accelerations. Tonally, there are several departures from Classical expectations: the exposition states *S* (m.68) not in E minor's relative major, but in its dominant, B minor. Rather than being encircled by fifths, the development emphasizes thirds in relation to the tonic with pedals and tonal areas on G and C and passes through G minor, A-flat (G-sharp), and E-flat. The dominant is held in reserve until the last part for a fugato on *S* (m.167), a contrapuntal version of *P* (m.184), and the retransition. Rimsky's coda (m.256) properly turns to the major mode and at the beginning is built on an ostinato (cf. Beethoven Symphonies Nos. 7/1 and 4, 8/1, and 9/1 and 4), and then has a passage of sequenced suspensions (m.274) that vaguely recalls Schumann, but without his powerful brass coloration. Another ostinato commences the second quickening of the tempo, and concludes with the *P* motive from "Down by the River Volga."

Apart from the formal and tonal treatment, perhaps the most academic aspect of this first movement is the prominence of four- and eight-measure phrases, though the development is less squarely conceived. Griffiths judges that this aspect negatively impacts the symphony as a whole.[26] However, Rimsky-Korsakov compensates for such regularity in his control of the surface rhythm. Not only is the rhythm often lively eighth notes in an *alla breve* meter, but the exploitation of anacrustic rhythms also constantly drives the activity forward. Looking next at *T* (m.58), nearly every bar is upbeat oriented and at times the upbeats are of multiple lengths (mm.62ff) (Example XV/1). *S* (m.68) does not let up on this agitated background of eighths, which accelerate to triplets for *S*'s repetition.

Although the first movement reveals Rimsky-Korsakov in 1865 as capable of executing a symphonic first movement with some success, it is the slow movement with its Russian theme that allies him more closely with the Balakirev circle. The young naval cadet had some difficulty completing this symphony because of his trepidation over creating a lyric piece. He wrote in his memoir:

> My attempts to write an Adagio met with no success, and it was useless to hope for any: in those days one was somehow ashamed to write a cantabile melody; the fear of dropping into the commonplace precluded any kind of sincerity.[27]

Balakirev's letters of encouragement and his contribution of a Russian theme broke Rimsky-Korsakov's reluctance. Characteristically, Balakirev made some suggestions in writing, which the dutiful student adopted, and Balakirev considered the slow movement to be the best movement of the cycle.

Though this movement is in a compact sonata form, the structure has been adapted to the tonal characteristics of the Tatar melody (Example XV/2). Notice how easily the melody moves modally from one area of tonicization to another: from G to C to E and back to G, C, and finally G. All these changes are controlled by the range of the melody and, except for the last, without the use of any pitch alteration. C is given some emphasis by the pedal and the

EXAMPLE XV/1   Rimsky-Korsakov. Symphony No. 1/1 (1884 Version), mm.58–65. Courtesy of Edwin F. Kalmus & Co.

two chords used in the first phrase: C major and its dominant seventh, though the dominant seventh is never sounded in root position. The tonal quality of the melody allows the slip to the dominant to occur almost imperceptibly. In the 1865 version, C major is given more emphasis by expanding the second full bar and the eleventh bar to four-quarters. In 1884, the tonal result is less certain. *S* (m.21) is made of the same material as *P,* but it is structured somewhat differently; in *Kamarinskaya* fashion, its environment is elaborated with counterpoint, and tonally the dominant G veers toward E-flat as a G pedal counters this activity. Notice the end of the exposition with its typically Rimsky-Korsakov color not of 1865, but of the 1870s and 1880s (Example XV/3).

The development (m.56) is cast in an almost Beethovenian mold as a descending bass and then a descending sequence on *P* is undergirded with a dominant pedal, funereally intoned

EXAMPLE XV/1 *(continued)*

EXAMPLE XV/2 Rimsky-Korsakov. Symphony No. 1/2 (1884 Version), mm.1–19. Courtesy of Edwin F. Kalmus & Co.

EXAMPLE XV/3   Rimsky-Korsakov. Symphony No. 1/2, mm.42–55. Courtesy of Edwin F. Kalmus & Co.

by the timpani's triplet rhythm. Again, there is a striking moment of 1870s/1880s Korsakov color: tremolos played *sul ponticello* (m.80). In the context of the tonal plan, the recapitulation (m.105) sneaks in with the ninth measure of the theme not undergirded by a tonic pedal, but one on the mediant and/or the dominant. Another move toward E-flat with a C pedal makes one wonder if this is not the natural minor of C. The coda also has a C pedal, but the tune is in A-flat or maybe F minor. A plagal cadence (mm.136–37) with a minor subdominant is followed by an augmented sixth, which resolves irregularly. Is there something of the extra-musical in this piece with its pounding timpani followed by the unmistakable celestial close? Perhaps the song's text, if recoverable, might offer an applicable narrative to this piece.

The third movement has the Classical shape of Scherzo–Trio–Scherzo. The Scherzo itself is in 3/8 time, which was used by several Russian symphonists, no doubt a product of Berlioz's "Queen Mab" Scherzo from *Roméo et Juliette;* it became something of a sensation in Russia in performances under the composer's baton. Rimsky's Trio in 2/4 time hails from Schumann's Symphony No. 2/2; both are 2/4 chorales exchanged between strings and winds and treated to *cantus firmus* variations—the Schumann is one of many pieces of Western European art music using this often claimed Slavic technique. In the 1884 version, the composer

EXAMPLE XV/3   *(continued)*

adds harmonics to the string color. Though delightful in and of itself, it was another anachronism to the composer's orchestral lexicon of the 1860s. This Scherzo together with the slow movement are the symphony's most striking utterances.

Almost immediately, one becomes aware that the Finale is a child of the first movement of Schumann's "Rhenish" Symphony. What is most surprising is that Rimsky, when revising the Finale in 1884, makes it even more Schumannesque than the 1865 version. While there are allusions to the "Rhenish" in the exposition, it is not until the *K* section (m.92) that the rhythmic tattoo of the Schumann first movement (3/4 ♩ ♪♪♪ ♩ ♪) is given special prominence; it is almost as if the 1884 Rimsky-Korsakov were proclaiming: "This is my model." Like the "Rhenish," the Finale is otherwise a sonata form without an expository repeat.

P is shaped with that continually popular "Eroica" model; several *P* themes (mm.1, 16, 24) are stated with *2P* undergirded by a dominant pedal in preparation for a *crescendo* to *1P*'s repetition in the tonic as *1T* (m.36). As in the Schumann "Rhenish," the *T* (*2T*, m.44) anticipates the material of *S* (m.60). *S* begins as a lyric utterance, but then is transformed to risoluto and becomes a fugato (m.68). *K* (m.92) continues the transformed state of *S*, but with a Schumannesque cadence (mm.96–100) and a *diminuendo* to the beginning of the development (m.120).

The development begins with a lengthy rising sequence consisting of the Schumann rhythmic motive in alternation with the lyric *S*. Then *P* (m.168) is taken up in a scherzando transformation as a fugato that quickly dissipates, but then builds to a climax (m.202) that combines *1P* with the Schumann tattoo and a dominant pedal as *2P* (m.219) and *3P* (m.228) lead to the recapitulation (m.239). Both *P* and *S* (m.254) are tightened and are given in a tonally more stable form. The close of the recapitulation leads to a passage from the beginning of the development. An acceleration (m.342) and a dominant pedal mark the coda, which combines elements from both *P* and *S* (see m.360f). Since one is so conscious of Schumann's ghost in this movement, one can easily lose track of a significant relationship of contour and accent between *1P* and *S* that lends to the thematic material a unity that lurks just beneath the surface.

Though this symphony is not what one might expect from the composer of the better-known *Capriccio Espagnol, Russian Easter Overture,* and *Sheherazade,* its 1884 revision remains an attractive addition to the repertoire, particularly for amateur orchestras that do not have the resources either in instrumentation or in personnel to perform any of his more popular works. This evaluation does not imply that in purely musical terms this piece is unworthy of concentrated listening, even though its two versions are both anachronistic: in its original 1865 version it belongs to the generation of the late 1840s and early 1850s, and in its revision of 1884 it represents the 1850s from the perspective of a mature composer now in total control of his Opus 1.

César Cui attended the first performance on December 19/31, 1865, and published in the *St. Petersburg Gazette* a decidedly pro–Rimsky-Korsakov essay:

> During all the time when I have found myself writing about happenings in the musical life of St. Petersburg, I have never before taken up my pen with such pleasure as today. For today is my quite enviable lot to be writing about a young Russian composer, a beginner, who has made his first appearance before the public [on December 19, 1865] with an extremely talented composition, the *first Russian symphony.* The public listened to the symphony with increasing interest and after the Andante and the final loud applause was supplemented by the usual calls for the composer. And when the composer came on to the platform, an officer in the navy, a young man of about twenty-two, everyone who responded to his youth, talent and artistry, everyone who believed in his great future among us, everyone, finally, who does not need to have an authoritative name (often that of some mediocrity) to go into raptures over a fine composition—everyone stood as one man, and the sound of a loud, unanimous salutation to the young composer filled the hall of the City Council.
>
> Perhaps I too will be allowed to salute the composer at the start of his career and tell him how much we expect from him and what great hopes we place on him. I do not know how his career will take shape, I do not know to what extent the circumstances of life will promote the development of his talent; but it is certain that at the present time his talent is already extremely remarkable; it is certain that in any of life's sorrows and in all difficult circumstances he will find solace and support in his art and in sacred and unsullied service to music. Let Mr. Korsakov not forget that we too are in need of such

solace and support, let him strengthen his talent by continual musical labours and bestow upon us more often moments of pleasure such as we experienced while listening to his symphony.

It is fascinating to follow the growth of a young talent through his compositions, to follow him as we grow more self-reliant with each step that he takes, and thus to form an opinion of the direction in which his taste is moving, which composers he liked and what music he has been studying. Mr. Rimsky-Korsakov's symphony represents an interesting case-study of this sort. . . .

Mr. Korsakov's music is distinguished in general by simplicity, healthiness, power, ease of invention, the free flow and profound growth of thought, and by variety. If this music has to be compared with something, then it most resembles that of Glinka, which has the same qualities in the highest degree. It is precisely the complete absence of morbidity, over-refinement and a forced quality in the composition which compel me to have high hopes for Mr. Rimsky-Korsakov's future, who right from his first work to be performed in public seems to be a fully-fledged composer. This symphony is very good, by even the strictest criteria; but if one takes into consideration that it is the first work of a young man of twenty-two, then one has to admit that *not a single* composer has had such a beginning. The symphony is orchestrated unpretentiously, without superfluous orchestral colouring, and quite meticulously, but the Andante is scored with wonderful elegance, taste and knowledge of the character of orchestral instruments. It was performed with Mr. Balakirev's customary mastery and fire; if one wanted to carp at any price about the performance, then the only thing one could say was that the two wind chords which end the first limb of the scherzo were a little late. I cannot help returning by way of conclusion to the truly joyful impression made on the public by the appearance of a new Russian composer in the person of Mr. Rimsky-Korsakov, cannot help again foretelling a great future for him if the circumstances of his life turn out favorably for his further musical development.[28]

Both the critic Cui and Balakirev referred to the work as not only Rimsky-Korsakov's First Symphony, but also the "first Russian symphony," knowing full well that Rubinstein had completed three symphonies during the previous decade (including his famous Symphony No. 2 "Ocean"). One can interpret this label in two different ways: 1) They considered these works to be not true Russian symphonies but rather works in the German tradition, or 2) Rubinstein was not considered to be a Russian, even though baptized into the Orthodox faith, because he was a Jew. The second interpretation is supported by the antisemitic correspondence from members of the Balakirev circle.

The excerpt quoted above is also full of ironies, particularly in the final paragraph, for Rimsky-Korsakov was to become one of the most "over-refined" orchestrators by the end of the nineteenth century, writing what Cui would certainly consider to be "pretentious" orchestrations.

Between the First (1865) and Second Symphonies (1868), Rimsky-Korsakov worked on a series of orchestral pieces: a *Fantasia on Serbian Themes* (Opus 6) in 1867, an *Overture on Russian Themes* (Opus 28) in 1866 (revised 1879–1880), the musical picture *Sadko* (Opus 5) in 1867 (revised 1869, 1891–1892), and an incomplete Symphony in B Minor (1866–1869). Each of these completed works would have been ideologically proper for the goals of the *kuchka* with their use of Slavic music and extra-musical content. The same could be said of the Second Symphony *Antar* Opus 9, which again demonstrates ideological solidarity among the members of the Balakirev circle toward the end of the 1860s.

SYMPHONY NO. 2/SYMPHONIC SUITE *ANTAR* OPUS 9

At the urgings of Balakirev and Musorgsky, Rimsky-Korsakov used an Arabian story by Osip Ivanovich Senkovsky (1800–1858) for Symphony No. 2. Arabian melodies from Salvador Daniel's *Album de chansons arabes, mauresques et kabyles* (1863) and Aleksandr Khristianovich's *Esquisse historique de la musique arabe* were incorporated into the music, perhaps with the goading of Aleksandr Borodin, who owned a copy of Daniel's book. According to the composer, the 6/8 melody in F-sharp major in the first movement (m.136) and the 4/4 A major melody in the third movement (m.224) come from Daniel's book. The "love music" of the Finale (m.15) came from the Khristianovich collection in a form harmonized by Aleksandr Dargomïzhsky, which Rimsky-Korsakov retained.[29] Rimsky also admitted that the *idée fixe*, the theme representing Antar himself, was influenced by "certain phrases" of *William Ratcliff*, an opera by César Cui.[30]

As was the case with virtually all of Rimsky-Korsakov's major works, Opus 9 went through a series of versions:

1868	Symphony No. 2. The original version conducted by Balakirev in March 1869 at St. Petersburg. CE Vol.17A.
1875	Symphony No. 2. Instrumentation reduced from 1868 version. Performed by the RMS, conducted by the composer 10/22 January 1876. Published by Bessel in 1880. Not in CE.
1897	Symphonic Suite. Definitive final version. New key for second movement. Published by Bessel in 1913. CE Vol.17A.
1903	Compromise version of 1880 published version with 1897 revisions that could be incorporated onto the 1880 plates. Published by Bessel in 1903. CE Vol.17B.[31]

Thus, the 1897 version is the last authentic text sanctioned by the composer. Many conductors have used the 1903 edition, which is a conflation of a version the composer had rejected (1875) with one he deemed definitive. (It is unfortunate that the collected edition failed to provide an edition of the 1875 version, while providing a text of the 1903 print.) Throughout this discussion, unless otherwise indicated, we refer to the 1897 version.

Though the composer originally designated his Opus 9 as his Second Symphony, after he had later taken up a professorship at the St. Petersburg Conservatory he changed its genre to Suite:

> I named this work (rather unfortunately, too) my *Second Symphony;* many years later I renamed it a *Symphonic Suite.* The term "suite" was then unfamiliar to our circle in general, nor was it in vogue in the musical literature of western Europe. Still, I was wrong in calling *Antar* a symphony. My *Antar* was a poem, suite, fairy-tale, story, or anything you like, but not a symphony. Its structure in four separate movements was all that made it approach a symphony. Berlioz's *Harold en Italie* and *Épisode de la vie d'un artiste* [*Symphonie fantastique*] are incontestable symphonies, despite being program music. The symphonic development of the themes and the sonata form of the first movements of these works remove all doubt as to incongruity between their content and the requirements of symphonic form.[32]

Rimsky-Korsakov goes on to discuss the nature of the individual movements and how they are not academically symphonic. By doing so, he departed from the *kuchka* ideology and embraced the pedantic and conservative Germanic idea of the symphony genre.

Certainly, the cycle is symphonic in concept. The *idée fixe* (Example XV/4) is heard in some form or another in all four movements. Though the cyclic key plan is not closed, i.e.,

EXAMPLE XV/4   Rimsky-Korsakov. Symphony No. 2/1, mm.26–37.

the Finale does not conclude in the key of the first movement, it does consist of related keys: F-sharp minor, D minor (originally C-sharp minor), D major, and D-flat major. In the earlier 1868 version, the second movement would have been heard as a sort of dominant to the first movement's F-sharp minor mode. By changing the second movement to D minor the two middle movements have the same tonic and the Finale remains in the real dominant of F-sharp, i.e., D-flat/C-sharp major. In addition, the Finale also relates back to the first movement by bringing back some of its thematic styles and allusions.

Compared to the First Symphony, the Symphony No. 2/Symphonic Suite *Antar* Opus 9 is marked by its evocative and brilliant orchestration. Though this skill had been building in the three intervening orchestral works (Opera 28, 6, and 5), in Opus 9 the contrast is especially striking. One can turn to almost any page of the score and find something worthy of comment. At the beginning, the fourth horn becomes the second bassoon of the 1868 version, but the passage that follows for low strings and timpani is also distinctive. The beginning of the Allegro (m.42) calls for flute, 2 horns, harp, and first violins, with shifts in both textural function and color. Even the *tutti* scorings in the third movement march are marked by a number of timbral shifts to which a battery of four percussionists (triangle, tambourine, cymbals, and bass drum) contribute. By way of illustration, mm.36–38 in the third movement (Example XV/5) combines percussion with four different levels of activity. Though the page looks heavily scored, the horn has no problem projecting its *dolce* solo. To those who know Rimsky-Korsakov based on his works commonly played today, the orchestration of the *Antar* Symphony/Suite will be recognizable as that of the composer.

In the view of the composer, besides cyclic practice and orchestration, it was the extra-musical aspect of the piece that ultimately governed the shape of the movements and the coherence of this cycle. For movements one and four, a narrative is provided that is to a large degree followed in the music. Movements two and three are described by single sentences that evoke two contrasting characteristic styles: vengeance and power. Table XV/3 provides a translation of the program found in the collected edition prefacing the 1903 publication. To this, we have added measure numbers for the movements that portray a narrative.

Rimsky described the first movement in *My Musical Life:*

The first movement of *Antar* is a free musical delineation of the consecutive episodes of the story, save that they are musically unified by the ever recurring theme of Antar himself. It has no thematic development whatever—only variations and paraphrases. In general the music of the introduction (the desert, Antar, and the episode of the gazelle), enfolding, as it were, the scherzo-like F-sharp major part in 6/8—again, forming as it does the conclusion of the first movement—gives the latter a rounded structure, with suggestions of an incomplete tripartite form.[33]

EXAMPLE XV/5 Rimsky-Korsakov. Symphony No. 2/3, mm.36–38. Courtesy of Edwin F. Kalmus & Co.

TABLE XV/3
Rimsky-Korsakov. Symphony No. 2/ Symphonic Suite *Antar:* Program

1ˢᵗ Movement

Beautiful was the desert of Sham [m.1]; beautiful were the ruins of Palmira, a town, built by evil spirits, but Antar [m.26], pride of the desert, did not fear them and proudly stood amidst the ruined city. Antar has left people for ever and has sworn to hate them, since they rewarded his good will with evil. . . .

All at once a gazelle appeared [m.42], light-footed and beautiful; Antar was about to catch it, when suddenly a terrible storm arose high above and the air was darkened by a black shadow [m.72]; a monstrous bird was pursuing the gazelle. In a moment Antar changed his mind. He plunged his lance into the monster, which flew away with a shriek [m.101]; almost immediately the gazelle disappeared too. Antar [m.118], left alone among the ruins, thinking about what had happened, soon fell asleep. . . .

He saw himself in a palace [m.122], where a crowd of slave girls attended him and delighted his ear. It was the abode of Princess Palmira, the peri Gyul' Nazar. The peri was that very gazelle, whom he had saved from the pursuit of the evil spirit. In gratitude the Peri [m.236] promised Antar [m.242] the three great delights of life, and when Antar decided to experience them, the vision disappeared and he found himself again amongst the ruins [m.264].

2ⁿᵈ Movement

The first delight given to Antar by the Princess Palmyra was the joy of vengeance.

3ʳᵈ Movement

The second delight was the joy of power.

4ᵗʰ Movement

Again Antar [m.1] found himself in the ruins of Palmira; the third and final delight was the joy of love [m.15]. Antar begged the Peri [m.76] to take his life away as soon as she notices in him the slightest sign of cooling and she swore to do this.

When one day, after long mutual happiness, the Peri noticed that he was absent-minded and was gazing thoughtfully into the distance [m.167], she straightaway guessed the reason; then she passionately embraced Antar, her ardour flew like a spark to his heart . . . and the Peri with a final kiss [m.190] joined Antar's soul with her own and he fell asleep forever on her bosom.

Source of translation: Seaman/RIMSKY GUIDE, pp. 14–5.

Table XV/4 represents something of the structure of the opening piece. Formally, the beginning almost slips into a standard shape with its antecedent/consequent structure and the return of *b* after *c*. With the appearance of the Gazelle (m.42), this potential shape is broken. According to Richard Taruskin, among Rimsky-Korsakov's debts to Liszt is the very opening where Rimsky-Korsakov lifts a characteristic chord progression out of Liszt's *Prometheus*. Here, two minor triads with roots a major third apart are linked with a half-step (semitone) progression by contrary motion in the outer voices and a common tone in the middle.[34] To consider this 121-measure stretch as an introduction to the first movement—as does Rimsky—is over-extending the concept. The one alternative would be to consider this more as a prologue to the entire cycle, an idea that certainly has viability since it introduces the main characters and sets up the conflict between the Gazelle and the monster. To do this, Rimsky taps characteristic styles from operatic practice to further his narrative: the stark colors of *a* and the slightly warmer timbres of *b* provide a deep contrast to *c*, the *Antar* theme and the *idée fixe*. Its *dolce* marking and viola, cello, and English horn scoring accompanied by clarinets, bassoons, horns, and basses recall an operatic cavatina sung by a heroic tenor.

In Rimsky's words, the main portion of the movement is "scherzo-like." Here he is not

TABLE XV/4
Rimsky-Korsakov. Symphony No. 2/ Symphonic Suite *Antar*/1:
Structure and Program

m.1	*Largo 4/4 ♩ = 66*	F-sharp minor
	a b "Desert"	
13	*a¹ b¹*	A-sharp minor
26	*Idée fixe/*"Antar" theme	
	c b	
42	*Allegro 3/4 ♩ = 160* "Episode of Gazelle"	D minor
	d	
72	e	
88	f "Great Noise"	
101	"Antar Strikes Monster"	
102	"Loud Cry"	
106		
117	*Largo 4/4 Idée fixe/*"Antar" theme "Antar Alone" *c*	F-sharp minor
122	*Allegretto 6/8 ♪ = 84* "Antar's Dream"	F-sharp major
	Introduction *h* anticipated (m.136)	
142	*g h* (m.150) *i* (m.154)	
174	*h*	E-flat/D-sharp
178	*Idée fixe/*"Antar" theme *c* plus *i* as counterpoint	F-Sharp major
192	*i*	
212		D major
216	*Idée fixe/*"Antar" theme *c* plus *i* as counterpoint	
	Adagio 4/4 ♩ = 66 Harp Cadenza	V of B minor
236	*In tempo* "Fairy/Gazelle"	B minor
246	*Allegretto 6/8 ♪ = 84* "Dream Continues"	B major
264	*Largo 4/4* "Antar Awakes"	F-sharp minor
	a b	
277	*Idée fixe/*"Antar" theme	
	c	

referring to the Beethovenian concept with its often unexpected paths, but to a certain flirtatious playfulness that is often marked by the word *dolce*. When he speaks of the absence of thematic development and its replacement with "only variations and paraphrases," he is loosely following the approach of Glinka's *Kamarinskaya,* as the four or so motives of the character Antar, marked *g, h, i,* and *c,* are clothed in various textures and timbres while the melody itself remains pure. The key scheme emphasizes tertian relationships as well as that of the dominant. Though we have marked the keys by their approximations of major or minor modes, they should be thought of as loosely modal. To emphasize this trait, these melodies are often accompanied by easily shifting pedals and drones. In practically every respect, this first movement represents a *kuchka* ideal: narratively programmatic, anti-sonata form, and use of melodies from the Orient treated non-developmentally. Though Rimsky here has not invented a new approach, he has brought polish and sophistication to the *Antar* Symphony/Suite's first movement.

Rimsky describes his second movement as follows:

The second movement ("Joy of Revenge"), in structure, brings more to mind the sonata form; yet it is built upon a single fundamental theme of Antar himself and upon the introductory phrase of threatening character. The first subject is in reality a development of these motives: Antar's theme and the introductory phrase. There is no subsidiary

TABLE XV/5

Rimsky-Korsakov. Symphony No. 2/ Symphonic Suite *Antar*/2: Structure

		Key	Rimsky–Korsakov
Part 1			*Exposition*
	Allegro 2/2 ♩= 84		*Allegro 2/2* ♩= 84
m.1	*a*—phrase of threatening character	D minor	*p*
17	*b* fanfare		
25	*a*	F-sharp	
42	*b*		
47	*Idée fixe*/"Antar" theme *c* developed with counterpoint	A minor	*S*
			Development
			S
91	*Meno mosso*		
	Idée fixe/"Antar" theme *c* transformed in brass		
	Tempo I		
101	Part 2		
	a	F minor	
106	*b¹*		
124	*d*		
134	*b¹*		
148	Dies Irae *e* developed as ostinato		
160	*d*		
168	*Idée fixe*/"Antar" theme *c* Augmentation		
			Recapitulation
222	*Idée fixe*/"Antar" theme *c* dolce e lamentoso	D minor	*S*

subject—its place is taken by the same theme of Antar in its original complete form (trombones in A minor). Then follows the development of the same material, omitting only the moment of the return to the first subject. This leads directly to Antar's complete theme (trombones in C-sharp minor), which serves as subsidiary subject. Then follows a coda on the introductory phrase and a soothing conclusion, again on Antar's principal theme.[35]

It seems that the composer is again stretching credibility when he tries to mold this movement into a sonata form: it is more convincing as a two-part large-dimension structure (see first column of Table XV/5) with part two commencing with the same material as the beginning. Granted, there is the introduction of motives *d* and *e* with its allusion to the Dies Irae in part two, and there is much thematic development in both parts. However, many composers, among them Haydn, Mozart, and Beethoven, used thematic development in expositions, recapitulations, and codas. It is also difficult to accept the *idée fixe* as *S*, since we have heard it so frequently, and it also comes to a larger function in the cycle. Furthermore, A minor is hardly heard as a secondary key area, even if it is in a way D minor's dominant.

It is not the form that is so important, but rather Rimsky's use of characteristic styles that could be construed as portraying vengeance. The two middle movements in a more general sense portray a battle followed by a march for the victors, Antar and his troops. The agitation at the start belongs to the traditions of storm music, but since the audience has been by the program primed for vengeance and the agitation is followed by dissonant fanfares, one knows that the music has a meaning beyond a brewing storm. The Antar theme, as we have noted, spends practically no time as an expository function, but is constantly undergoing development and transformation. Against its first movement context as a *dolce* theme, its ferocity in this movement is very striking (Example XV/6); the scorings for brass, the use of modulation, and its contrapuntal treatment contribute to this character. At the end of the first part (m.91), one is struck not only by the scoring for brass, but also by the *crescendo* and *diminuendo,* which imparts an anger to Antar's theme. Finally, there is the allusion—we refrain from calling it a quotation—to the Dies Irae (m.148), a chant seemingly close to the heart of Russian composers, which itself imparts the concept of horror.

In the first movement, Antar is portrayed as protective and sensitive. In the second movement, he takes on another character, but at the end (m.222) his theme is marked *dolce e lamentoso.* Only in the context of the first pair of movements can this moment be considered a recapitulation.

Rimsky wrote of the third movement:

> The third movement ("Joy of Power") is a species of triumphal march (B minor–D major), with a subsidiary Oriental cantabile melody and a conclusion on Antar's theme. Then follows a sort of middle part and light development of the two principal subjects; return to the principal subject of the march; transition to Antar's concluding theme, and a coda built on the subsidiary Oriental subject. The conclusion is a diverging passage of chords on an ascending eight-step scale (tone, semitone, tome, semitone, etc.), which I had once before used in *Sadko.*[36]

This movement is at once the most traditional symphonic piece, but at the same time fulfills the ideals of the *kuchka.* First, it has a very traditional shape for a march, i.e. March–Trio–March–Trio–March. Even though its phrase lengths are irregular in the first March $(7+5+7+5)$, the phrases in subsequent presentations are all of even lengths. The *idée fixe* comes after the first Trio and the last March just before the coda. This brings to mind the central movement of Berlioz's *Symphonie fantastique,* where the *idée fixe* is situated at similar structural points. As for the ideals of the *kuchka,* the March melody has its own vaguely oriental quality, but the Trio tune is a lush melody from Daniel's collection owned by Borodin. Indeed, the Trio sounds like something Borodin might have composed for his opera *Prince Igor* or his Second Symphony. In addition, the mosaic structure, i.e. in the opening March $a+a+a+a,$ is perfect for applying variations to the background. Such a structure is also prominent in the Trio.

Rimsky took particular pride in the harmonies on the ascending eight-tone scale (T [tone]–ST [semitone]–T–ST–T–ST–T–ST), today known as the octatonic scale, which spread from Rimsky-Korsakov to his students and became a fingerprint of the Russian idiom.[37] One might say of this movement the same thing the composer himself said about *Capriccio Espagnol,* where his intention "was to glitter with dazzling orchestra colour."[38] This was not to be Rimsky-Korsakov's only brilliantly colored march; he also produced one for his opera *The Golden Cockerel.*

With the Finale, we return to the more narrative shaping found in the first movement, but here long sections are devoted to characteristic love music. Of the Finale, the composer commented,

> The fourth movement ("Joy of Love"), after a brief introduction borrowed from the first movement (Antar reappears amid the ruins of Palmyra), is an Adagio. It is built in the main on the cantabile Arab subject (which Dargomïzhsky had given me) and its development, together with the phrase of the peri Gül Nazar and Antar's principal theme. In form it is a variety of simple rondo with one subject and subsidiary phrases (which are

EXAMPLE XV/6   Rimsky-Korsakov. Symphony No. 2/2, mm.52–61. Courtesy of Edwin F. Kalmus & Co.

EXAMPLE XV/6 (*continued*)

episodic and enter, now here, now there, into a passage-like working out), with a long coda on Antar's and Gül Nzar's themes.[39]

One certainly can find a sort of loose rondo on a larger scale as the composer seems to imply (see Table XV/6), but only a thematic one, the way in which Rimsky-Korsakov probably defined it, rather than one where tonality receives primacy. Additionally, the refrain—the music of the Fairy and of Love marked andante amoroso in the 1903 score—is constantly evolving as the piece unfolds so that its Arabian style with decorating arabesques is the essential characteristic. The recurring episode is easily identified by the death rhythm (6/8 ♪♪ 𝄾 ♪ ♪♪ ♪♪ 𝄾 ♪ ♪♪ | ♪♪) and the *idée fixe*/Antar theme, and secondarily by its key of A major in its first statement. Not unexpected is the importance of the orchestra as a structural factor; after the introduction there are two waves of sound (mm.15f and 76f) and the beginning of a third (m.156), which culminates not in *tutti* statements, but with a celestial version of the Arabian style undergirded by a dominant pedal that concludes the final statement of the *idée fixe*/Antar theme.

What is so striking about this Finale is the amoroso music, which dominates the movement and moves the *idée fixe*/Antar theme to a secondary role. Previously, it was the Antar theme that came to prominence because of its cantabile nature and often sensuous orchestration; now this role is taken by the Fairy and Love music (Example XV/7) with the Antar theme at times seamlessly integrated within this refrain. Though Rimsky supplies a list of musical sources for the *Antar* Symphony/Suite from Liszt and Wagner to Glinka and the *kuchka*, he interestingly omits Berlioz.[40] Berlioz provides a conceptual model for this Finale in his Love Scene for *Roméo et Juliette*, which Rimsky-Korsakov must have known from the 1867–1868 season in St. Petersburg, when Berlioz conducted excerpts from his Shakespearean Third Symphony. Indeed, the *dolce* attitude in the Berlioz and Rimsky-Korsakov love scenes

---

TABLE XV/6
Rimsky-Korsakov. Symphony No. 2/ Symphonic Suite *Antar*/4:
Structure and Program

	Allegretto 6/8 ♪ = 84	
m.1	Introduction: Reprise of I/m.122	G → C
15	*Adagio 2/4 ♩ = 58* [1903: Andante amoroso]	G-flat
37	A Fairy Music	
54		A
76	1B Pledge to take life away, death rhythm	A
100		B-flat minor
104	2B *Idée fixe*/"Antar" theme	
126	A	
152	2B ending	D-flat
156		
166	*Coda*	
	2B *Idée fixe*/"Antar" theme in broken phrases, death rhythm	
190	A as celestial music with final kiss and embrace	

EXAMPLE XV/7   Rimsky-Korsakov. Symphony No. 2/4, mm.15–48. Courtesy of Edwin
F. Kalmus & Co.

EXAMPLE XV/7 *(continued)*

provides quite a different perspective from that of Act II of Wagner's *Tristan und Isolde,* which, if known to Rimsky, was certainly rejected.

A review of the first performance on March 22, 1869, of the first version conducted by Balakirev at the Free Music School concerts was, as usual, written by an insider: the *kuchka's* Aleksandr Borodin. His essay, in contrast to César Cui's for Symphony No. 1, is a more balanced appraisal. Excerpts follow:

> The main interest in this concert was concentrated, without any doubt, on Mr. Rimsky-Korsakov's new, second symphony, *Antar.* This symphony is a work remarkable

both for the novelty and beauty of its music and for the astounding brilliance and colourfulness of its orchestration. It belongs as regards form to be the kind of symphonic compositions created by Berlioz. That is, it is a symphony in several movements written on a definite subject with the division into movements and the construction of each of them determined not by the conventional framework of the sonata but exclusively by the contents of the subject itself. . . .

All four movements have a completely oriental colouring in both harmonization and orchestration. With regard to orchestration *Antar* is positively one of the most perfect and most distinctive works in contemporary music. It is impossible to enumerate all the astounding orchestral effects with which every movement of the composition is filled to overflowing, and there are very few places, which are orchestrated in an ugly way (for example at one movement in the second movement the horns are so used, and so on). And how new and colourful all this is! How much fantasy of the most capricious and sumptuous kind!

There is not even a suspicion of anything routine or ordinary anywhere in the whole symphony. *Antar* in general is new evidence of the unwontedly powerful creative talent of Mr. Rimsky-Korsakov, whose work as a composer represents an extremely gratifying occurrence in our musical world. In speaking of this symphony's virtues I must also indicate its weak sides, One can level at the composer the reproach that the theme representing Antar himself is not entirely original; that in the third movement there is insufficient vastness and grandeur; that in the fourth movement the music is in places rather cold; that the symphony offends rather by the variety of elements in the details; but the last circumstance finds partial justification in the subject itself.[41]

Other performances of the first version, in 1871 and 1872, also garnered critical praise and served as excuses to celebrate the youth and energy of Russian music:

However, on December 18, I witnessed a real triumph of a composer—the triumph so much more delightful for it fell to the lot of one of our domestic musicians. On that day, a concert of the Free School was held; the symphony of N.A.Rimsky-Korsakov *Antar* was performed. . . . *Antar* belongs to the realm of "program music"; and, since the content of the program here is not lyrical or philosophical, as in Liszt's "symphonic poems," but narrative and descriptive, *Antar* . . . comes closest to the program symphonies of Berlioz. . . . However, Mr. Rimsky-Korsakov's music doesn't bear [much] resemblance to Berlioz's; one can see that our gifted symphonist has been shaped by a completely different trend of musical thoughts and moods. In *Antar*, as well as in other orchestral works of Mr. Rimsky-Korsakov, and in his romances, there can be [seen a] scrupulous study of Glinka (mainly "Ruslan and Lyudmila"), Schumann, and Liszt: Mr. Rimsky-Korsakov has wonderfully mastered Russian folk tunes, which Glinka demonstrated in his most mature works. . . . Lovingly, he develops the poetry of the Orient, the poetry that, since the days of Pushkin and Lermontov, has so frequently and so efficiently cast its charming light on our literature, and that, since Glinka's time has illuminated our music also. . . . Mr. Rimsky-Korsakov approaches the *program, or expressive* aspect of music very clearly and cleverly, choosing for reproduction various moments of the story and different features of poetic pictures,—such rhythms, harmonies and instruments, that—with the aid of this kind of program, he vividly awakens the image of these moments and features in the audience. More than once in my critical analysis, I've had an occasion to point out, that this *expressive* capacity of music is not as strong, as it is usually thought to be; that music, by its very nature, is much closer to architecture, than it is to poetry;

and that to ascribe to it a definite content (even if only on equal terms with painting) is to mistake the reveries of one's imagination for an empiric fact. I shall not conceal that the talented and beautiful work of our young symphonist—despite all its merits—hasn't shaken my views on that subject. I'll repeat again: Mr. Rimsky-Korsakov has fulfilled his poetic program with great understanding; I'll say even more: the harmonic and instrumental aspects of his characteristics reveal much graceful taste and brilliant capacity for color. However, even with such a happy approach to the solution of his task, he didn't manage to avoid means of expression that had been used before him [by other composers] to convey absolutely different moods and images. . . . May the reader not think that, while pointing out the commonalities Mr. Rimsky-Korsakov shares with some other composers, I wish to reproach him for lack of originality. There is hardly one musician in whose compositions there aren't unintentional reminiscences and borrowings from his predecessors. Composers that relying exclusively on what is *their own,* must, probably, produce very little. . . . If we notice a similar phenomenon in case of the creator of *Antar,* it only proves that he works as a real artist, devoting himself directly to his task; . . . it is neither a tendency to imitate, not musical plagiarism; it is just a characteristic feature of artists—to unite and form schools, where separate individuals resemble each other in both common spirit, and particularities of technique—that is the reason of those frequent occasions, when one artist reproduces another's thought, or motif. . . . Whatever the shortcomings of the school, to which *Antar* belongs, it constitutes a talented and brilliant sample thereof; and at the concert of December 19, it was greeted with lasting, loud applause. The composer was summoned twice: I've never witnessed such sympathy to Russian symphonic music on the part of the masses. Speaking in pure musical terms, *Antar* strikes us with its appealing, graceful nature and its rich color, lavished all over with inexhaustible luxury. The warm, passionate tone of the newest harmony prevails in Mr. Rimsky-Korsakov's music; the fresh, wild charm of a folk tune, a technique which he uses frequently and successfully,—these luxurious colors of the modern orchestra affect you very differently than it would have with the cold, pseudo-classical harmony and elegant, a-la salon, melody of French composers. . . . What a young passion, what an ingenuous and rapturous power there is in our music! And what an old-man's experience, what knowledge of its craft and its audience—but also what a cold, business-like calculation—there is in the music of the French![42]

César Cui reviewed an 1872 performance of the work. With predictable and undisguised enthusiasm he noted not only the strengths of the composition but also the increasing sympathy with which it was being heard by the public:

The task of *Antar* is poetic, exceptionally musical, and quite befitting the characteristics of Mr. Rimsky-Korsakov's talent; therefore it comes as no surprise that this symphony has come out as a wonderful, remarkable work. The first movement is one of the most perfect examples of descriptive music, with variety a faithful color. Suffice it to recall the depiction of the dreary desert—these despondent, dead chords; the grandiose running of the gazelle; the heavy flight of the monstrous bird, expressed by the original, sinister harmonies; finally, the ravishing dances in Peri's palace—dances full of languor, beauty, and gracefulness. If you analyze the music of this movement regardless of the program, it might seem somewhat variegated. But if you consider it as musical realization of this program, it satisfies the most refined, the most rigorous aesthetic demands quite well. The form of the second movement, as the program requires, is much smoother: this part is not descriptive; it expresses Antar's psychological state. The music of this movement is powerful; it's full of indomitable energy and unbridles fierceness. Strong and new instrumentation (the unprecedented usage of horns) imparts to it a shade of blood. The third movement—march and dances—although weaker in terms of music, is still beautiful: its themes are good [and] it is decorated with great taste. . . . The fourth movement is very appealing and enthralling; its ending is extremely poetic, yet this movement is somewhat cold, although some passion can be felt in this music, it is not enough to express the raptures of Antar and Peri's love. It should be also added that the whole symphony is imbued with Oriental character, to which a significant contribution is made by the three original Arabic themes, employed by Mr. Rimsky-Korsakov. . . . In spite of the variety of the tasks that each separate movement of the symphony has, in its entirety the symphony doesn't lack unity, for the theme of Antar proper is kept throughout all its movements. This multiple repetition of the same theme doesn't lead to monotony, since the very same theme is differently harmonized and orchestrated every time, in accordance with the mode of Antar's spirit, which changes its image beyond recognition. *Antar* is orchestrated amazingly well. Mr. Korsakov, even in our time of generally good orchestration, is remarkable for his talent and creativity in this respect. He creates new effects, and prodigious combinations of instruments that are always extremely successful. . . .

Antar was performed with great success. . . . If one compares this enthusiastic welcome with the cold reception of *Antar* when it was performed for the first time a couple of years ago, one cannot but rejoice at both the developing musical understanding of our concert audience, the established reputation of Mr. Korsakov, and the rapidly growing number of adherents of lively, modern music; those, who are not blinded by dull, obsolete classicism.[43]

The premiere of the 1875 version also attracted the attention of the press. The critic Rostislav (F. Tolstoy) assessed both the revised symphony and program music in general in the pages of the *Moscow Gazette* (*Moskovskie vedomosti*):

This symphony belongs to so-called *program* music, the beginning of which lies, as I already stated previously, with the humorous escapades of Beethoven in the Pastorale symphony. It is well known that in that unique poetic symphony every movement bears its own designation: "Au bord d'un ruisseau, l'orage," and so on. One may depict by sound the general outline of the babbling of a brook or a thunderstorm, or the merry making of the common people, but in the end, in scenes by the brook the great composer took it into his head to depict not only the trill of the nightingale but also the cry of the cuckoo and the quail. . . . And so this humoristic episode gave birth to program music. Berlioz, Wagner, and Liszt began to accompany their compositions with extensive texts in which they described in detail what exactly they intended to depict in sound. So, for example, in one of Wagner's programs it states: A knight gallops on a *white* horse, which has in its saddle-bow straps a dead enemy. The galloping of the horse, perhaps, may be depicted by imitative sounds, but it is not possible, of course, to define the color of its coat. In a word, the humoristic episode of the great symphonist gave birth to a whole school of program music, to which belongs, incidentally, the symphony *Antar,* a composition by our countryman Mr. Rimsky-Korsakov, which was written by him, if I am not mistaken, some six years ago.

An oriental tale of Senkovsky serves as the theme for the symphony, and in what words its contents are laid out in the program: . . . The first moment, that is the desert solitude of Antar, the composer expressed with a fairly developed, melancholy melody.

Here there appears, however, a short, four-bar phrase which serves as a sketch of Antar himself and which appears in all four movements of the symphony, changing, as G*** expresses it, its character and harmonization in accordance with the psychological mood of the hero. The running of the gazelle is depicted by racing triplets, the flight of the monstrous bird—by a dark and fanciful harmonization, the blow of the spear—by a sharp crash of brass cymbals (an effect beloved by Franz Liszt), the dream of Antar—by long drawn-out sounds. The visions during the dream, that is, the halls of the queen of the Palmirs and the dances and singing of her servants, are expressed by a graceful melody in dance rhythm. This first movement is varied and picturesque, but due to a lack of unity, not entirely artistic. In the other three movements, the composer strives to depict, as declared in the program, three of the great delights of life: revenge, the joy of power, and the sweetness of love. It seems to me that only the last feeling may be liable, more or less, to expression in sound; but no musical nuances can depict sufficiently clearly the difference between the joy of vengeance and that of power. And, really, the entire difference between the character of the music of the second and third movements consists of the fact that in the second [movement] Antar's principal theme is loudly played by the trombones, but in the third [movement] it is heard as a festive march. In my opinion, the most successful movement of the symphony is the fourth, in which the *sweetness of love* is depicted. Here the orchestration (a la Berlioz) achieves a high degree of vividness. The opening of this movement is entrusted exclusively to wind instruments. The languid cooing of the clarinets, the delicate sound of the flutes, the sympathy of the English horn and perfect use of the bassoons depicts voluptuousness and languor better than ever before. It is fitting to note that the primary, somewhat coarse theme for Antar is entrusted here to the flutes, as if in proof that the soul of Antar has overflowed with tenderness and emotion. In general, the symphony of Mr. Rimsky-Korsakov is a work talented to the highest degree, one which, in my opinion, is not at all in need of the detailed commentary of the program. All of these gazelles, monstrous birds, the joy of vengeance and power, in no way elucidate the thought of the composer. In an aesthetically satisfying musical work one ought to grant full freedom to the imagination of the audience, "Il ne faut pas mettre les points sur les I" [One must not dot every I] say the French, and especially one should not *overemphasize* musical intentions. It's impossible to set off by sounds the difference between the *joy of vengeance* and the *joy of power* and the misfortune is not great if the listener perceives the *galloping gazelle* as a galloping horse.[44]

Rimsky-Korsakov's *Antar* Symphony/Suite is the first fully polished and original symphony to emanate from the Balakirev circle. And there was not to be another Russian symphony like it, except for that other symphonic suite by Rimsky-Korsakov, *Sheherazade* Opus 35. This is not to say that except for his own Opus 35, *Antar* has no progeny. First, *Antar* seems to be the earliest Russian symphony to conclude with a slow movement. However, few would trace this practice to Rimsky-Korsakov; most would instead think of Tchaikovsky's Symphony No. 6 "Pathétique" (1893). Second, there are even stronger reasons to believe that the *Antar* cycle affected Tchaikovsky's "Pathétique," since the third movement of *Antar* is also a triumphal march.

SYMPHONY NO. 3 IN C MAJOR OPUS 32

If *Antar* is not a symphony but a suite, then Rimsky-Korsakov's Symphony No. 3 in C major Opus 32 is in reality his second contribution to the genre. Be that as it may, the composition of Opus 32 began as early as 1866 with the Scherzo followed in 1870 with a Trio. The bulk of the cycle dates from 1873 when the first, second, and fourth pieces were composed. The Scherzo and its Trio were certainly not originally considered for a C major symphony, since the Scherzo itself is in E-flat and the Trio in G-flat major in the 1873 original. Rimsky almost admits this by saying that he took these from his portfolio.[45] Some critics consider this second movement to be the most fetching of the cycle. The movements dating from 1873 were not written without some difficulty:

> I began writing a Symphony in C major; for its Scherzo I took the E-flat-major Scherzo in 5/4 time which I had in my portfolio and the trio of which I had composed aboard some steamer on one of the Italian lakes during my honeymoon abroad. Work on the first movement of the symphony was slow, however, and beset with difficulties; I strove to crowd in as much counterpoint as possible; but being unskilled in it and hard put to combine the themes and motives, I drained my immediate flow of imagination considerably. The cause of this was, of course, my insufficient technique; yet I was irresistibly drawn to add greater interest to the structural style of my compositions. A similar fate befell the third movement of the symphony—Andante. The Finale presented somewhat less difficulty; but the combination of several subjects at its end proved another stumbling-block. Nevertheless, the sketch of the symphony was ready in the spring and, from the rough draft, we tried it out on the piano at our gatherings.[46]

The Third Symphony was composed during a period when Rimsky was transforming himself from *kuchkist* to an academic. In July 1871, he accepted an appointment at the St. Petersburg Conservatory to become professor of practical composition and instrumentation and to direct the student orchestra. Anyone who had composed as brilliant a work as the *Antar* Symphony/Suite must know what he or she is doing, except Rimsky was an intuitive composer, whose intuition was nothing short of extraordinary. As a result, he began teaching himself all of the pedantic subjects objected to by the *kuchkists:* instrumentation and orchestration, harmony, and counterpoint. This caused something of a musical crisis as technique came to interfere with this intuition and *kuchkist* ideology. The first version of Symphony No. 3 was overburdened by learned counterpoint; one aim of the 1886 revision was to streamline the textures and make the structures more effective.

The first movement in the 1873 version is a generic one with a slow introduction followed by an Allegro; in 1886 the slow introduction returns as part of the coda to give it what Rimsky-Korsakov would have called a rounded form and an ending in C minor. In addition, the 1886 version clarified the recapitulation by presenting *P* in augmentation. The Scherzo and Trio in 1873 are in E-flat and G-flat respectively, while in 1886 they are in E-flat and B major, keys more easily negotiated by the strings. Here, major changes are also made to the already effective orchestration, lending to it a greater brilliance. In both versions, the third movement runs into the Finale without a pause, but both movements are essentially newly composed, even though some of the thematic material remains—the *A* of the third movement and *S* of the fourth. The final result shows that Rimsky was his own severest critic; the 1886 version represents a vast improvement over that of 1873. Unless specified otherwise, all further comments relate to the 1886 revision.

An issue confronting the post-*Antar* Rimsky-Korsakov was what constitutes a symphony. Now the academic, burdened with tradition, saw not Symphony No. 2 as a proper symphony, but instead reverted to his Leipzig-styled Symphony No. 1. Thus, Symphony No. 3 holds more in common with No. 1 than with No. 2, even though Richard Taruskin finds in

No. 3 a synthesis of the tonal symmetries of No. 2 with the formal plan of No. 1.[47] Still, Symphony No. 3 remains anachronistic both in terms of Rimsky's stylistic development and in the larger history of the late-nineteenth-century European symphony. Indeed, only a few connoisseurs, if given Symphony No. 2 as a benchmark, could hear No. 3 as a product of the same composer. And if asked for a chronology, even connoisseurs would place No. 3 after No. 1, followed by No. 2.

In Rimsky's now conservative view of the symphony, cyclicism is not a central factor. Even if Schumann and Berlioz were his models, he does not even begin to approach their cyclic practices in his Symphony No. 3 nor his own cyclicism in the *Antar* Symphony/Suite and later in *Sheherazade*. In the two versions of No. 3, the movement key plans are mainly based on thirds:

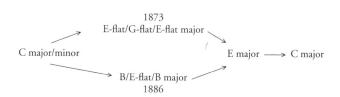

As can be seen, the 1873 version is more strongly third based, but in 1886 Rimsky-Korsakov chooses a most distant key from C major: B major. One might guess that the key of the Scherzo was changed for practical reasons since G-flat is not an idiomatic orchestral key, whereas B major is much more accommodating. Apart from tonality, there are only two attempts at cyclic unity. Movements three and four are played without pause and the main thematic material of the Andante becomes connecting tissue, which generates *P* of the Finale.[48]

This emphasis on third relationships also extends to the keys used in the 1886 first movement: in the exposition *S* is in E major, while for the recapitulation *S* returns not in C major, but in A-flat. Oddly, the coda (m.585) concludes this piece in C minor. Also peculiar is the coda's tempo sequence: the tempo becomes faster only to return to the slow introduction before the Allegro returns for the final cadence as *P* is stated pizzicato. This gesture is almost without precedent; the closest parallel is Haydn's Symphony No. 103/1, where the slow introduction returns near the end of the movement and the fast tempo resumes for the final cadences.

The lengthy slow introduction (49 mm.) presents a nine-measure subject followed by three variations. In contrast to Rimsky's other variations, these are freer, more developmental, and not constricted by melodic purity in an environment of changes in the other elements favored by the *kuchka*. Rather, Rimsky uses the opening motive as an articulator of the phrase's beginnings (mm.10, 20, 28), after which a variety of responses are composed including the inversion of the head motive itself (m.20) and a transformation (m.28). All this seems Haydn-like, while the motive, which generates *P* of the exposition, is reminiscent of Beethoven's Symphony No. 8/1. The final variant (m.28) generates a Schumann-like transition to the exposition.

The exposition starts with a stretch that reminds one of the first movement of Beethoven Symphony No. 3: *P, PU* plus extension and lead-in, and *1T* restating *P* as a culminating gesture. *2T* (m.101) is remarkable for its change of meter from 3/4 to 2/4 and its rising chromatic bass; *3T* (m.103), also derived from *P,* complements this with a descending bass and a return to triple meter. The bass finds rest on the dominant of E in preparation for *S* (m.148), which in typical late-nineteenth-century fashion relaxes the speed and surface activity and returns to tempo for *K* (m.191).

As was the case with Symphony No. 1, the development section at the beginning recalls Schumann's Symphony No. 3/1, even more so than the 1873 version. As in *T* of the exposition, much of the modulatory activity is affected by descending bass lines, enharmonicism, and a half-step slip. In Classical fashion, Rimsky concentrates on *P* material and a new rhythmic motive (♩ ♩ ♪ | ♩ ♩ ♪) through the retransition. Since *P* has certainly been exhausted in its present form, at the recapitulation (m.427) *P* is transformed in a heroic environment and presented in augmentation as the meter broadens to 3/2. Except for its already-discussed key scheme and a shift to the Neapolitan, the recapitulation is rather regular. *K* is excluded in favor of the coda.

Except for the key scheme and the changes in the recapitulation—*S* returns in A-flat—this first movement is highly derivative, almost to the point that one might wish to whisper neo-Classicism. Passages are reminiscent of Haydn, Beethoven, and Schumann. The second movement Scherzo, written before the other movements, is in the traditional Scherzo-Trio-Scherzo shape, but uses keys distant from C major. Otherwise, the Scherzo itself is for its time unique: it is in 5/4 meter conducted as one to the bar. After the Trio in the traditional 3/4, the return to the Scherzo is written out with variances: a new counterpoint to the 5/4 subject is in *alla breve,* which itself is treated imitatively (m.342), and the 3/4 music of the Trio becomes a counterpoint to the 5/4 subject (m.382) during the coda. While this contrapuntal combining of themes echoes Berlioz, despite the 5/4 meter, one hears the Scherzo proper as decidedly Mendelssohnian. This experiment in metric manipulation and the change to 2/4 in the first movement must have opened the ears of Rimsky's composition student Igor Stravinsky to the possibilities of rhythmic and metric play. This play with rhythm and meter was also characteristic of the *kuchka:* Rimsky-Korsakov used it himself in both the first and slow movements of the 1865 version of Symphony No. 1, and Borodin used it in the slow movement of his Second Symphony and the first movement of his Third Symphony.

With its emphasis on wind colors and 6/8 meter, the Andante projects a pastoral character. It is laid out in a slightly irregular rondo form that again emphasizes tertian relationships:

Intro.	*A*	*B*	*A*	*C*	*B'*	*A*	Coda/trans.
E major	⟶	G	E major	E ⟶ C modulatory	E major	⟶	C
m. 1	13	35	51	77	107	115 143	153

Developmental elements are hinted at in *B* and fully exploited in the agitated music of *C,* which recalls the same section in the third movement of Berlioz's *Symphonie fantastique.* By leaving out *A* after *C,* Rimsky allows the climax of *C* to gradually wind down to the animation level of *B* and the calm *A* and coda before the tempo begins to pick up for the transition for the *attacca* to the Finale. This slow movement is among the symphony's strongest sections, but the transition to the Finale is somewhat awkward. Although its figuration anticipates the Finale's *P,* the motive that comes on an upbeat in the Finale occurs on an accented beat in the transition. Thus, the request for an *attacca subito* is stalled because the conductor

EXAMPLE XV/8   Rimsky-Korsakov. Symphony No. 3/3, mm.153–60 and /4, m.1.

must provide an upbeat for the Allegro con spirito of the Finale (Example XV/8). With his own experience as both a composer and a conductor, Rimsky-Korsakov should have been aware of this uncomfortable moment, but this may have been what he wanted, since the 1873 version contains the same sort of problematic passage and in the 1886 version a 2/4 measure is inserted into this *alla breve* movement just before the recapitulation.

Rimsky's key plan for the Finale furthers the prominent use of tertian relationships in the first and third movements. Here, the tonal plan extends the tertian relations even to the development and the coda. In the exposition, the two secondary keys are A minor (m.50) and E minor (m.78), and for the recapitulation, these keys are now E-flat (m.158) and A major (m.174). In the development, C (m.86), E (m.114), and A-flat major (m.125) are articulated. As Taruskin points out, the expository keys are the normal diatonic mediants, in the development they are major thirds, and for the recapitulation minor thirds (C, E-flat, A).[49] In addition, the coda momentarily struggles with A minor (mm.262–64, 267–68) before re-entrenching C major (mm.270–71). Certainly, these are significant observations and some of these keys provide local tonal color, but in the larger plan of the movement one does not sense any musical or dramatic significance.

Rimsky-Korsakov's themes in the Finale seem too cluttered with motivic repetition (Example XV/9): *Pa* consists of four repetitions within six measures, and *Pb* (m.7) twelve

EXAMPLE XV/8 *(continued)*

EXAMPLE XV/8   (*continued*)

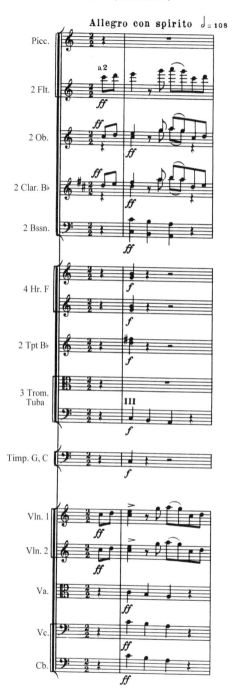

EXAMPLE XV/9   Rimsky-Korsakov. Symphony No. 3/4, mm.1–16 (strings only).

repetitions in six measures before there is a four-measure unit of new material prefacing the contrapuntal combination of *Pa* and *Pb* (m.18). *T* (m.32) also derives from *P* and begins with a series of two-measure repetitions, which eventually expand to larger phrases in preparation for *S* (m.50). Though *S* provides some relief from small module thinking, with its complete repetition (m.70), material from *T* is in the accompaniment. *K* (m.78) returns to measure and half-measure thinking. At this point, one might hope for new material in the development section, but the composer insists on additional development of *P*?

One may wish to attribute the development's brevity to the nature of the exposition, but Rimsky-Korsakov provides us with a recapitulation where its last part is considerably expanded (exposition—83 mm., recapitulation—128 mm.). The coda reminds one again of both Schumann (m.270) and then of Beethoven (m.298).

Symphony No. 3 is indicative of the ravages that the study of technique had on Rimsky-Korsakov, whose own intuition had created something as polished as the *Antar* Symphony/Suite. Having struggled both with its original composition and then revision, Rimsky's academic concept of the symphony was not adaptable to his innate creative abilities; the dark orchestral timbres of Schumann did not bring out the best in a composer able to conjure up brilliant sounds, driving rhythms, and sensual melodies. The completion of the 1873 version was the end of his orchestral writing for some six years; in 1879 he composed *Skazka* (*A Fairy Tale*). Then in 1887–1888 came the three orchestral pieces for which he remains best known. They used idioms where Rimsky-Korsakov would not be inhibited by academicism and tradition: the capriccio, the symphonic suite, and a festive overture.

The reception of Symphony No. 3 was mixed. Among the composer's friends, Aleksandr Borodin sardonically described it as "Ein grosse Symphonie in C." Tchaikovsky wrote a more favorable review and sent a copy of it to the composer, with the following letter:

> Your [Third] Symphony has been performed here. I listened to it carefully at the three rehearsals and at the concert itself and came to the conclusions which I have expressed frankly in the enclosed extract from my review. Forgive me for crawling to you with my candid comments: I do it out of sincere affection for you and your works and I feel the need to tell you what my impressions are. I personally am in raptures over the first two movements.[50]

The review itself appeared on January 3, 1875:

> Now I will turn to a short examination of the new symphony by Rimsky-Korsakov. . . . The general impression given by this composition may be characterized as follows: the predomination of technique over the quality of thought, and inadequacy of inspiration and impulse, in exchange for a manufactured character and diversity of artistic details, approaching excess.
>
> This symphony is cultivated and cared for with a love that recalls that masterly love which supposes that the essence of upbringing consists of the warmth of the hothouse. . . . Rimsky-Korsakov finds himself, apparently, in a transitional stage; he is looking for his bearings, he is vacillating between an inclination to novelty . . . and a secret sympathy for antiquated, archaic musical forms. This is a philistine, a conservative at heart, once attracted to freethinking but who is now making a timid retreat. As a result of this lack of sincerity, the spontaneity of artistic conception of Rimsky-Korsakov has degenerated into aridity, coldness, emptiness. . . . This is why one cannot be surprised that the public did not accept the Korsakov's symphony very sympathetically.

As far as the experts, they were unable to not be fascinated by the charming details which caress the ear with the combinations of sound that cover the score of our symphonist. From behind the masks of philistine and innovator, which the author dons in turn, . . . continually seeps through a strong, and talented in the highest degree, a lithely graceful creative individuality. When Rimsky-Korsakov . . . comes at last to the firmly established stage of his development, he will certainly make of himself the major symphonist of our time. . . . This will be musical eclecticism in the best sense of the word, in the sense of Glinka, who united in himself strict, organic classical forms and methods with dazzling beauty in exposition, which is an integral quality of the new school. But this is in the future, and meanwhile we heard a symphony with two movements that, despite the above mentioned inadequacy—an excessive diversity in details—convey to the connoisseur an abundant source of musical delight. These two movements are the first ones, the Allegro and the Scherzo.

In the Allegro, Rimsky-Korsakov displays significant mastery of form, a surprising knowledge of the orchestra and an ability for contrapuntal development of themes, which cannot but be the envy of any who pursue a symphonic career. I will not say that I particularly liked the themes of this part of the composition, but by means of the most diverse illustrations, the author is able to give to them an interest that never weakens even for a moment. In places, Rimsky-Korsakov gives to his orchestra a purely magical sonority. As an example, I point to the episode in the introduction where the flutes in the low register play a phrase in unison, in counterpoint to excerpts of the main theme, which is entrusted to the violins and violas; or I might recall that spot heard in the symphony where the clarinet repeats a one measure scrap of a phrase fourteen times in a row, at the same time that the violins with strong, abrupt bow strokes play an expansion of the original theme. This is strikingly original, new, and fantastic.

The pearl of the symphony is the scherzo; here the talent of Mr. Korsakov, uninhibited by a destructive reflex, unrestrained by a deliberately premeditated pursuit of two rabbits, appeared in all of its might. An original five-four rhythm, on which the effectiveness of this movement of the composition is based, incessantly joins in battle against a rhythm of an opposing character. . . . If one adds to this the Rimsky-Korsakov's unusual mastery of instrumentation, the lightness and roundedness of the harmonic outlines of his music, then in sum one receives a work that is unusually sweet and original.

In the other movements there is nothing except traces of diligent, skilled, and painstakingly produced technical work. Both the Andante and the finale in particular . . . suffer from aridity, from an icy coldness, and in places from an oversalting, if one may express it that way, with heaps of dramatic effects, which merge into an undefined mass of expressionless sounds.[51]

Despite the composer's efforts to revise the symphony, reception to it remained decidedly lukewarm. A performance in 1886 resulted in the following dismissive review by the often acerbic Mikhail Ivanov in the popular musical magazine, *Nuvellist:*

The subscription concerts of the "moguchaia kuchka" concluded rather sadly both in their artistic and in their material respects: their organizer . . . suffered significant losses due to the fact that the audience at these concerts was small. But the material losses of the affair are not particularly important. . . . All of the new works turned out to be either lacking in substance—even according to the opinions of the newspapers, who are of like minds with this party of musicians—or of little substance. . . . The symphony of Mr. Korsakov, like all warmed-over dishes, brought little success to the author: if in its original conception a piece is organically weak, than no reworking will help, as was the case here. The symphony, in which Mr. Korsakov strives to stand on the ground of the European symphony, which he had up to now avoided, does not possess any particular musical interest; it is a mediocre symphony, although individual sections remind [one] that Mr. Korsakov is a superb orchestrator.[52]

SYMPHONIC SUITE SHEHERAZADE IN E MAJOR OPUS 35

Certainly, if Rimsky-Korsakov had not gotten himself in a quandary over what constituted a symphony, he would have retained the title for *Antar* and probably would have called *Sheherazade* Opus 35 a symphony rather than a symphonic suite (Plate B10). After all, *Sheherazade* is more of a traditional symphony than *Antar:* it is tonally unified in that the Finale begins and ends in the key of the first movement (E major/minor), the two central movements are in closely related keys (B minor and G major), and the movement sequence is F-Scherzo-S-F. In addition, there are recurring themes: the first movement's opening theme *P* returns at the end of the Finale and the violin cadenzas of the first movement come back in all of the subsequent movements. *P* also recurs in transformations in the second and final movements. Indeed, these themes represent *Sheherazade* and the Sultan Shakhriar; they are double *idées fixes* in the Berliozian sense, though Berlioz never used this device to represent more than one personage in his first two symphonies. Furthermore, the movement forms are more traditionally symphonic than those of the *Antar* Symphony: an introduction and large binary structure with coda that recalls an eighteenth-century overture form, i.e., without a development section; a dance movement in ternary form with the middle section (*B*) like a development and the outer portions (*A*) treated to variations; a slow movement (andantino quasi allegretto) shaped somewhere between ternary and sonata form; and a Finale in sonata form without recapitulation, but with a coda (cf. Schumann's Symphony No. 4/1 and 4).

Like so many symphonists who wrote characteristic or programmatic pieces, Rimsky had reservations about retaining titles and narratives. Originally, Rimsky was going to merely label the movements with loose generic titles: Prelude, Ballade, Adagio [*sic*], and Finale. Then, with urging from Anatoly Lyadov (1855–1914) to provide further direction for the listener, in the autograph the following was inscribed:

> Sultan Shakhriar, convinced of the perfidy and faithlessness of women, has vowed to execute each of his wives after the first night [the words "On the next day after the wedding" are crossed out in the autograph]; but the Sultana Sheherazade saved her life by the fact that she was able to occupy him with her stories, which she told him over 1001 nights, so that, roused by curiosity Shakhriar continually put off her execution and finally completely abandoned his intention. Many wonders Sheherazade told him of Sinbad's voyages at sea, of the wandering Kalender princes, of the knights turned into stone, of the great bird Rul, of the evil geniis, of the pleasures and amusements of the eastern rulers, of the ship dashed to pieces on the magnetic rock with the bronze horseman and much else, quoting the verses of poets and the words of songs, weaving story into story and tale into tale.[53]

Early on an even less specific outline appeared in the printed editions:

PROGRAM

The Sultan Shakhriar, convinced of the perfidy and faithlessness of women, vowed to execute each of his wives after the first night. But the Sultana Sheherazade saved her own life by interesting him in the tales she told him through 1001 nights. Impelled by curiosity, the Sultan continually put off her execution, and at last entirely abandoned his sanguinary resolve. Many marvels did Sheherazade relate to him, citing the verses of poets and the words of songs, weaving tale into tale and story into story.

I. The sea and Sinbad's ship.
II. The story of the Prince Kalandar.
III. The young Prince and young Princess.
IV. Festival in Baghdad. The Sea. The ship breaks up against a cliff surmounted by a bronze horseman. Conclusion.[54]

Rimsky was unhappy with these somewhat vague suggestions because they stimulated listeners to look further at the music for a more specific narrative:

In composing *Sheherazade* I meant these hints to direct but slightly the hearer's fancy on the path which my own fancy had traveled, and to leave more minute and particular conceptions to the will and mood of each. All I had desired was that the hearer, if he liked my piece as *symphonic music,* should carry away the impression that it is beyond doubt an Oriental narrative of some numerous and varied fairy-tale wonders and not merely four pieces played one after the other and composed on the basis of themes common to all the four movements. Why then, if that be so, does my suite bear the name, precisely, of *Sheherazade?* Because this name and the title *The Arabian Nights* connote in everybody's mind the East and fairy-tale wonders; besides, certain details of the musical exposition hint at the fact that all of these are various tales of some one person (who happens to be Scheherazada) entertaining therewith her stern husband.[55]

Ultimately, the composer wished to have no programmatic or even generic hints as to what the piece was all about. Perhaps in retrospect, Rimsky would have settled, as Tchaikovsky was to do, with the simple title "Symphonic Suite."

As in many of Rimsky's other works, excluding Symphonies Nos. 1 and 3, *Sheherazade* is a brilliant work for orchestra that espouses many different textures and timbres and a brazen display of virtuosity throughout the ensemble. This the composer achieves not with an orchestra of Wagnerian proportion, but with one of normal size and instrumentation for the time: piccolo, pairs of flutes, oboes (the second doubles English horn), clarinets and bassoons, a quartet of horns, a pair of trumpets, a trio of trombones, tuba, timpani, a battery of percussion (triangle, tambourine, side drum, cymbals, bass drum, and tam-tam), harp, and strings. From the start of this piece, Rimsky's mosaic melodic style enhances the kaleidoscope of colors:

1. The bold *pesante* statement of the Sultan's theme (m.1)
2. The high woodwind chords (m.8), which Rimsky admitted he took from Mendelssohn's *A Midsummer Night's Dream* Overture
3. The solo violin accompanied by the harp (m.14) representing Sheherazade.

In the second movement, after the *exordium* cadenza for solo violin and harp, Rimsky scores the theme for bassoon and a quartet of four solo string basses *con sordino,* and subsequently scores every variation differently, which brings to mind the scorings in the second movement of Berlioz's *Symphonie fantastique*. Or one can cite the central section of the third movement, with its clever use of percussion and the flute (m.79), which takes over the function of the snare drum from the previous phrase. In the Finale, Rimsky combines his kaleidoscopic colors with driving surface rhythms for one of the most brilliant pieces in the entire history of orchestral writing.

That the central key of the cycle, E minor/major, was no accident for this composer is a certainty; like his countryman, Skryabin, he believed in the association of color and key. For Rimsky, E major was dark blue and both the first and last movements of *Sheherazade* are sea pieces. Rimsky told his Boswell, Vasiliy Vasil'evich Yastrebtsev, that the Allegro paints "the sea—with white-crested waves."[56] In fact, the background is almost *Augenmusik* as its figures surge up and down.

After the episodic slow introduction, the expository *P* (m.20) begins with the opening material of the introduction transformed from its almost ferocious character to a lyric statement. Over more than twenty bars, it builds to a *forte* restatement à la the "Eroica" Symphony as *1T* (m.46). *2T* begins in C major with an unusually tranquil statement (m.70) followed by *3T* (m.76), a *dolce* restatement of *P* with a new consequent (m.78). *3T* sequences downward through thirds to B major and *1S* (m.94), which is based on the second introductory theme. The latter, decorated with triplet roulades both here and in the introduction, is at least from a western perspective characteristic of Arabic melody. *2S* (m.102) is another decorated version of *1S* with its descending outline in double augmentation. *K* (m.114), in Classical fashion, is based on *P*. Notice that again, Rimsky uses a three-key exposition: E to C to B. Since there is no development section proper, the exposition turns back toward the tonic for its resolution at the recapitulation (m.123), where *P* is restated *tutti* and *fortissimo*. This reprise differs from the exposition in several important respects: *P* contains a small section that acts developmentally (m.135) and remains throughout a powerful statement; *1T* is essentially eliminated; *2T* is restated in the tonic (m.149) as is *1S* (m.173); *2S* veers toward C major but is restated in E (m.185); and the coda (m.206) focuses on *3Ta* and *2T*, thereby bringing the movement to a quiet close. Unlike Symphony No. 3/i, here, the composer seems completely at ease with both the idiom and form he has chosen to pursue. Rather than an artificial conception of what a symphony movement ought to be, Rimsky-Korsakov lets the content determine its destiny.

Movement two, "the story of the Prince Kalandar," begins with the violin invocation/cadenza of the first movement; with this repetition it not only is the voice of Sheherazade but becomes a series of rhetorical phrases common to the telling of a tale (e.g., "Once upon a time"). In contrast to the first movement, the second, despite its use of variations, has more of a narrative structure. In the opening theme with three variations, each part is assigned a distinct character (see Table XV/7).

The exposition is peculiarly formed: *P* (m.5) comprises a lyric theme with three variations, a *T* (m.86), and a declamatory *K*, (m.104) consisting of material based on the Sultan's theme now having taken on a fanfare-like transformation con forza within a *senza misura* environment. This overall concept of *P* variations and dwarfed other functions recalls the Finale to Beethoven's "Eroica." The variations themselves concentrate on leaving the melody unadulterated in good *kuchka* fashion. Rimsky's intensive development section (m.120) certainly underlines his credentials as a composer well informed in the ways of western European music. In the first part, he concentrates on the fanfare theme interrupted by *senza misura* sections marked recitative. A second section (m.173), Vivace scherzando 3/8, is another debt that the composers of the *kuchka* owe to Berlioz's "Queen Mab" Scherzo. At times in this brief passage, one almost thinks that Rimsky has equaled if not exceeded Berlioz's exemplar

TABLE XV/7

Rimsky-Korsakov. *Sheherazade/2*: Structure

m.1	*Introduction—Lento 4/4—Recitative*
	I/Ob
5	*Exposition*
	[A] Andantino 3/8 ♪ =112 Capriccioso, quasi recitando
	P Theme dolce espressivo
26	*P¹* Variation 1 dolce ed espressivo assai
48	*P²* Variation 2 poco più mosso ♪ = 144 grazioso
71	*P³* Variation 3 a tempo (un poco più animato)
85	*T*
104	*K* Allegro molto 2/4 ♩ = 144—Fanfare *I/Oa*
108	Molto Moderato 3/2 Recitative—Fanfare *I/Oa*
110	Tempo giusto—Allegro molto 2/4—Fanfare *I/Oa*
118	Molto Moderato 3/2 Recitative—Fanfare *I/Oa*
120	[B] *Development—Part 1*
	Allegro molto 2/4 ♩ = 144—Fanfare *I/Oa*
162	Moderato assai 4/4 ♩ = 72—Recitative *I/Ob*
165	A tempo giusto Allegro molto 2/4 ♩ = 144—Fanfare *I/Oa*
173	*Development—Part 2*
	Vivace Scherzando 3/8 ♪ = 132 *I/Oa*
229	2/4 ♩ = ♩. → ♩ = 144 *I/Oa*
322	Moderato assai 4/4 ♩ = 72
328	Allegro molto ed animato ♩ = 152
348	*Recapitulation*
	[A] Con moto 3/8 ♪ = ♩
	P⁴ Variation 4
373	*P⁵* Variation 5 ♪ = 152, ♪ = 144, ♪ = 152, ♪ = 126
424	*P⁶* Variation 6 Poco meno mosso ♪ = 112, ♪ = 100
436	*T*
449	*Coda* ♪ = 112 Accelerando a poco a poco
467	Animato ♪ = 144

of fantastic orchestration. Section one (m.229) resumes and again its energy is broken by the *senza misura* section. However, this time the unmeasured music of the recitative becomes measured (m.329) and serves as the retransition. As in the Beethoven Finale, after a development consisting of freer thematic treatments, Rimsky returns to stricter variations for the recapitulation (m.348). Here the approach to the new tempo is deft; the triplet roulades in the woodwinds are transferred at the same speed to the viola and cello accompaniment of the now fourth variation. Two further variations, five and six (mm.373, 424), are marked by less stable tempos and are followed by *T* (m.437) and an accelerating coda (m.449). This movement, together with the Finale, is representative of Rimsky-Korsakov at his very best. Although his formal model appears to be Beethoven's "Eroica" Finale, he is able to adapt it to his own purposes in a convincing way so that one is unlikely to recognize his borrowing. Still, a significant dichotomy governs this movement: the contrasts of sections that are strictly conceived versus those that are *senza misura* and improvisatory. Whether this was innovative or not, Rimsky-Korsakov's central achievement here was the transition from one rhythmic style to another, which in this movement has a deftness that remains unmatched.

The slow movement, "The Young Prince and Young Princess," is laid out in another synthesis of part form and sonata concepts (see Table XV/8), in one of the composer's most integrated thematic efforts. It is almost as if he had been studying works by Joseph Haydn. *S* is

---

TABLE XV/8

Rimsky-Korsakov. *Sheherazade*/3: Structure

	Andantino quasi Allegretto 6/8 ♩.=52	
m.1	$\boxed{A}$ *Exposition*	
	P	G
21	*T*	
25	*S(P)*	D
45	*T*	
49	*Development*	B-flat—mod.
	P	
69	$\boxed{B}$ *Pocchissimo più mosso ♩.=63*	B-flat—G minor
71	⌈ *a*	
91	⌊ *b*	F
95	⌈ *a*	F minor/major
99	⌊ *b*	
103	⌈ *c(a)*	B-flat
115	⊢ *a passionato*	D
119	⌊ *b* with *K(A)*	D as V/G
127	$\boxed{A}$ *Recapitulation*—Come prima	
	P	G—C
142	*Lento 4/4 Recitative I/Oa*	E minor
146	*Tempo 1 6/8*	
	S(P)	G
162	*T*	
166	*S(P)*	E-flat
174	$\boxed{B}$ *Pocchissimo più animato*	
	a'	G
188	*Coda*	
	P cantabile	G (D pedal)
		(G pedal)
205	*I/Oa scherzando*	G

based on *P,* and even the sections, here designated as *I/Oa,* seem also to be a descendant of *P.* After a Haydn-like exposition, Rimsky begins a section (m.49) that seems like a development. However, after twenty measures, he changes his mind and inserts something that acts more like an episode of a part form with its own internal structure and decided change of character from the sensual lyricism of the exposition to a more scherzando-like mood. Its thematic materials also derive from *P.* The recapitulation is altered: the first *T* is replaced by *I/Oa* (m.142), the key scheme is changed from the exposition's G–D–B-flat to G–C–E–G–E-flat–G, which in turn is balanced by a coda (m.188) solidly entrenched in G major.

Yet despite the skill and cleverness displayed in the structure, both in terms of layout and tonal manipulations, what dominates one's perception of this piece is not the programmatic possibilities, but in more absolute terms the sheer beauty of the melodies and the way that, in contrast to Symphony No. 3/4, Rimsky-Korsakov builds his phrases with a minimum of material without trying the listener's toleration of repetition. In this case, the melodic materials have a sensuality that is supported by their timbres. Examples include the opening that would instinctively be played on the A string but is here designated "sul D," which richens and darkens the sound; the importance given to the cello as a conveyer of the main material;

EXAMPLE XV/10   Rimsky-Korsakov. *Sheherazade*/4, mm.105–13.

and the request to add an occasional glissando when the melody leaps up a seventh rather than down a second (e.g., m.42). Add to this the use of the clarinet for both its timbre and agility, the richness of the voicing for the brass section tintinnabulation by the percussion and multiple-stop strummed pizzicatos (Example XV/10). Furthermore, Rimsky uses his forces sparingly; the number of measures of *tutti* scoring is no more than 15 in a piece of some 210 bars. Finally, rhythm is used both strategically and coloristically. Notice at the start of the piece, there is relatively little activity. In *S(P,* m.25) the rhythmic activity is only so slightly increased (see violin 2 and viola). The development both embellishes the melody and adds thirty-second-note decorative runs; when the function changes to an episode (m.69), the tempo quickens and the percussion adds surface vitality and color. By m.107, the movement has reached its maximum level of rhythmic activity. From this point on, Rimsky alternates stretches of activity with repose, knowing that a gradual *diminuendo* of activity might both fulfill expectations and test the listener's patience.

Fast rhythmic activity, the fastest of the cycle, and quick changes of timbre mark the main part of the Finale, "Festival at Baghdad," which is characterized by a bacchanal in small bars, 3/16 and 3/8. It is preceded by an introduction dealing with *I/Oa* and *I/Ob* and concluded with a stormy reprise of the first movement's sea music (m.586) that leads to the destruction of Sinbad's ship. This final section also contains the *I/Ob* fanfare (m.261), *I/1P* (m.269), *I/2 Ta* (m.635), *I/Oa* (m.641), *I/Ob* in a docile transformation (m.645), ending with the famed Mendelssohnian colors and the violin, harp, and woodwinds providing *Midsummer Night's* sounds (m.655). As for the bacchanal itself, it is cast in a sonata form whose exposition consists of *P* (m.30) with a single variation (m.70); three *T* themes (mm.85, 105, 118), of which *2 T* is an adaptation of *III/A;* and *S* (m.142), which incorporates *III/B. K* (m.174) is perpetually in motion and heightens the excitement of what has come before. Again, Rimsky provides a three-key exposition with *S* beginning in A and *K* in C-sharp. The development works over all of the previous material except for *II/Ob.* As noted earlier, the composer obviates any bacchanal recapitulation, but its coda (m.496) reprises *P* at a still faster pace, states it on the dominant, and places the melody in the bass.

One could certainly argue that the return of *I/P* (m.586) is the recapitulation. Though this is a powerful thematic return, Rimsky-Korsakov delays the tonal return until after Sinbad's ship has been destroyed (m.623) (Example XV/11), signaled by the first and only sounding of the tam-tam, and the resolution of the dominant pedal to tonic (m.633) underlined by the reprise of *I/2T.* It is not only the chords at the end, but also the lead-in to these chords that again allude to Mendelssohn's overture to *A Midsummer Night's Dream;* in both pieces the hyperactive rhythmic drive of the movement reaches a state of repose.

Sheherazade is often heard even today as a blockbuster piece. Yet not one of its movements ends fast and loud. Nevertheless, it is a virtuoso piece, a veritable concerto for orchestra; every instrument is exposed in a technically impressive way. Rimsky-Korsakov also filled this work with one appealing melody after another, whether they be diatonic or modal, western or eastern, with lively and driving or relaxed rhythms, and all with a sheen of orchestral sound. Add to this touches of the exotic and the use of characteristic styles to give some credibility to its extramusical associations. The end result is one of the most appealing and popular works of western art music. Because of its popularity, it is often viewed as not being profound, but merely a cold and calculated work by a superb craftsman. Nevertheless, it is still one of the finest works in the orchestral repertoire and ought to be openly regarded as such. It remains Rimsky-Korsakov's orchestral masterwork and is just as deserving of a place in the repertoire as any big cyclic piece by a German or French composer.

EXAMPLE XV/11   Rimsky-Korsakov. *Sheherazade*/4, mm.621–34.

EXAMPLE XV/11   (*continued*)

EXAMPLE XV/11   (*continued*)

Early reviews, however, were somewhat mixed. *Nuvellist* greeted *Sheherazade* with cautious enthusiasm, despite its broader disappointment with the "Russian Symphony Concert" series in which it premiered:

> The first "Russian" [?] concert took place in the empty hall of the Noble's Assembly, among "their own" public, where each knows the other. . . . Besides the work of Mr. Rimsky-Korsakov, his students and a few of his likeminded fellows, it would be vain to search for other authors. And so, unfortunately, all of these composers possess very intimate similarities, so one may image what kind of monotonous impression one carries away from these concerts, even if one finds very gifted works in the program. In the first concert attention was attracted by a new suite (in four movements) by Rimsky-Korsakov, "Sheherazade." In this half-programmatic work, the author has given freedom not so much to his fantasies as to his truly rare ability to play with orchestral coloration. It would be vain to search for greater diversity of orchestral effects, or greater unexpectedness in them, among any other Russian composer. Mr. Korsakov possesses in this respect also great daring, allowing himself to utilize effects which others fail to notice: he is in perfect command of the string quartet—that basis for the orchestra—with him virtuoso effects in the individual instruments are met at every step, this trumpet or horn with mute, that highest flageolet-like sound of the violin, that large-scale bassoon solo, employed with great bravery. In "Sheherazade" he needs, of course, oriental motives and these are dressed up in brilliant colors. The three last movements of the suite are [particularly] musically interesting (the first is rather ordinary). . . . Nonetheless, the character of all the movements is identical and one consequence of this is an unintentional monotony: each individual movement is more or less interesting but taken together they are deprived of an impression of strength.[57]

Cui, although presenting a more detailed critique, shared many of the same opinions as the previous reviewer:

> It is apparent that the new symphonic suite of Mr. Korsakov is a programmatic work, but with a quite undefined program. It is an aural illustration of oriental tales, but what kind of tales, what their contents are, is not known; every listener may give complete freedom to his or her own imagination. I have more than once had occasion to write in opposition to detailed programs, in which facts play an important role, programs that are not suitable, that are not in accordance with the goals of music. But here, it seems to me, that Mr. Korsakov has gone to the other extreme, and that some slight general direction would have served as a useful guideline for listeners. . . .
>
> The first movement of *Sheherazade* serves as an introduction. In it the author apparently sketches the relations of the sultan to his wives in general and to Sheherazade in particular. Two themes serve as the material for this: one masculine, which consists of the stern procession of the basses, the second feminine, not lacking in a certain playfulness, entrusted to solo violin. . . . After the exposition of the two themes, there follows a development primarily of the first, the severe one, which is harmonized in a very beautiful manner, and in its logical development acquires significant strength. Then the tales begin. The first, a type of scherzo, begins with a sweet little theme in 3/4 of a semipastoral character. This is followed by interesting variations, among which several Russian turns of phrase are encountered. The variations are interrupted by the tremolo of violins, recitative phrases of the orchestra, and

fanfares, more exactly bellicose summons. In general, *Sheherazade* is full of caprices and surprises. This is understandable: otherwise the sultana would not be able to sustain continued interest of her spouse. Besides the ones pointed out above (tremolo, recitative, fanfares), among the surprises of the second movement one should ascribe changes of meter and curious eastern flourishes, constructed on uniformly repeating pizzicato chords, in which the flourish remains the same, but the chords change, creating a beautiful harmonic alternation. Among the inadequacies of this movement one must consider a certain lengthiness, which results from the quite frequent repetition.

The third movement Andante is weaker than the two previous ones, despite an attempt at a broader melodiousness: it represents only a beautiful eastern commonplace; in addition something in the first theme recalls the oriental Andante of Borodin, but the second theme is a somewhat altered [version] of the Persian chorus from *Ruslan.* Mr. Korsakov is quite partial to this theme: it is found in *Antar,* we also meet it in the last movement of *Sheherazade.* In the movements under scrutiny there are also reminders of Balakirev's *Tamara,* once again almost inescapable given the common deflection of our composers to the east. The first half of the last movement (the finale) presents only aural interest, an interest of timbres, primarily of the percussion; once in a while a successful little theme is glimpsed briefly, something in the nature of an oriental tarantella. But the second half of the finale, the return to the themes of the sultan and sultana is superb. The sultan appears in a grandiose form, the sultana in a soft one, it all ends in beautiful tranquility. On the whole, *Sheherazade* is an interesting, colorful, characteristic, effective work; but its interest is fleeting because it is based on a mosaic quality, on surprises, on lighting effects of aural colors, and not on the strength and depth of a defined mood. There is nothing to say about the masterly, brilliant instrumentation of *Sheherazade.* The new symphonic suite of Mr. Korsakov, after *Sadko, Antar,* and especially after his *Tales (Skazki),* definitely shows that his talent is most of all drawn to musical landscape, to sound painting; that the task he loves most is not the expression of feelings and heartfelt moods, but playing with the sounds and colors of the orchestra. Mr. Korsakov has fulfilled his most recent mission masterfully, with striking virtuosity, and no one has the right to force his own goals on the composer.[58]

CONCLUSION

Rimsky-Korsakov was a reluctant symphonist. His first, a Germanic symphony, would never have been completed were it not for Mily Balakirev's postal urgings. Symphony No. 2 *Antar* was withdrawn as a symphony in all likelihood because it did not conform to what a *kuchkist* of conservative leanings thought a symphony should be. Symphony No. 3, which exists in two versions, returns to the Schumannesque symphony with its dark and thick orchestrations. Here, the composer was ready to write an academic piece to demonstrate that he was capable of doing something equal to a graduate of a conservatory: the form shapes the content. In contrast, then, to Rimsky's *Antar* and *Sheherazade,* which are examples of content shaping the form in the best sense, Symphonies Nos. 1 and 3 tell us something of Rimsky's uncertainties concerning his own musical languages.

It is regrettable that Rimsky wrote virtually no significant orchestral pieces after completing the *Capriccio Espagnol, Sheherazade,* and the *Russian Easter Overture.* Instead, he turned from writing fantastic orchestral pieces to composing fantastic operas, which are unfortunately all but ignored outside of Russia.

Aleksandr Borodin

INTRODUCTION

In addition to Rimsky-Korsakov, only two other *kuchkists* completed symphonies: Aleksandr Borodin (1833–1887) and the leader of the group, Mily Balakirev. Though an immensely talented composer, Borodin remained an amateur because of his devotion to his profession as a physician, chemist, and as a research and university classroom professor (Plate B11). His accomplishments as a scientist were nearly as significant as his activities as a composer.

Born in 1833 in St. Petersburg, Borodin received his M.D. at the age of twenty-three; two years later he presented his first scientific paper; and in May of 1858 he received his Ph.D. in chemistry. Over the next several years he did post-doctoral work in laboratories in western Europe, before returning to St. Petersburg in September of 1862. In the subsequent years, he maintained a research laboratory and lectured at several institutions, and was promoted to professor at the Medical-Surgical Academy in April 1864.

Although his academic obligations resulted in his musical pursuits receding into the background, in the autumn of 1862 Borodin joined Balakirev's circle, and it was Balakirev who persuaded him (as he had Rimsky-Korsakov) to begin working on a symphony. Borodin began his Symphony No. 1 that same year, but due to his heavy academic obligations, the work was not completed until 1867 (Table XV/9). The composer lived next to his research laboratory, and Rimsky-Korsakov recalled how his scientific and musical endeavors became intertwined:

> I became a frequent visitor at Borodin's, often staying overnight as well. We discussed music a great deal; he played his projected works and showed me the sketches of the symphony. He was better informed than I on the practical side of orchestration as he played the cello, oboe, and flute. Borodin was an exceedingly cordial and cultured man, pleasant and oddly witty to talk with. On visiting him I often found him working in the laboratory which adjoined his apartment. When he sat over his retorts filled with some colourless gas and distilled it by means of a tube from one vessel into another, I used to tell him that he was "transfusing emptiness into vacancy." Having finished his work, he would go with me to his apartment, where we began musical operations or conversations, in the midst of which he used to jump up, run back to the laboratory to see whether anything had either burned or boiled over; meanwhile he filled the corridor with incredible sequences from successions of ninths and sevenths. Then he would come back, and we proceeded with the music or the interrupted conversation.[59]

SYMPHONY NO. 1 IN E-FLAT MAJOR

From Borodin's widow and other sources, we can partially document the chronology of his composition of Symphony No. 1 in E-flat Major during the five or more years of its gestation:

December 1862	First movement sketched.
May 1863	Finale sketched.
Summer 1864	Scherzo composed.
Summer 1865	Central section of Andante composed.
May 1866	Completion of Finale.
Early 1867	Symphony completed.

TABLE XV/9

The Symphonies of Aleksandr Borodin

Key	Dates	Title	Movements	Instrumentation	Comments
E-flat major	1862–1867	Symphony No. 1	1. Adagio—Allegro 3/4—Andantino 3/2 (548 m.) E-flat minor—major 2. Scherzo: Prestissimo 3/8 Trio: Allegro 3/4/4/4 (507 m.) 3. Andante 3/4 (99 m.) D major 4. Allegro molto vivo ¢ (451 m.)	Grand	First performance: St. Petersburg, Russian Music Society on January 4/16, 1869, conducted by Mily Balakirev. Published in St. Petersburg: Bessel, 1882.
B minor	1869–1876 rev. 1879	Symphony No. 2	1. Allegro ¢ (325 m.) 2. Scherzo 1/1—Allegretto 6/4 (409 m.) F major—D minor 3. Andante 4/4/3/4 (127 m.) D-flat major 4. Allegro 3/4 (280 m.) B major	Grand plus 2 Picc., Flt., Tuba	First performance: St. Petersburg, Russian Music Society on February 26/March 10, 1877, conducted by Eduard Nápravnik. Prepared for publication by Rimsky–Korsakov and Glazunov. Published in St. Petersburg: Bessel, 1887.
A minor	1882, 1886–1887	Symphony No. 3	1. Moderato assai 2/2 (313 m.) 2. Scherzo: Vivo 5/8— Trio: Moderato 3/4 (344 m.) D major	Grand	First performance: Borodin Memorial Concert on October 24/ November 5, 1887, conducted by Rimsky–Korsakov. Two mvts. completed by Glazunov from sketches and hearing Borodin play excerpts. Published in Leipzig: Belyayev, 1888.

March 1868	RMS reading under Balakirev; many errors found in parts.
January 4/16, 1869	First performance: RMS conducted by Balakirev.
1875	Piano duet arrangement published.
1882	Full score published by Bessel.

The two main sources for the above datings are Dianin's book (Dianin/BORODIN), in part based on the widow's testimony as told to Stasov during her final illness in 1886, and the *New Grove* (*NG*) article by Gerald Abraham and David Lloyd-Jones, which claims that Dianin's dates are somewhat early.[60]

The process of composition was also presumably held up by Borodin's consultations with Balakirev, who claims to have micromanaged the composer's work. According to Balakirev's letter to Stasov: "Every bar he wrote was submitted to me for criticism and this succeeded in developing a critical feeling for his art, which in the end determined his musical taste and sympathies."[61] Although the self-witness may have been prone to exaggeration to ensure his own place in history, testimonies from some of the other members of the *kuchka* suggest that such critiques were a part of the process, and also included input from the other members of the circle.

Borodin's cycle displays no interest in unification beyond that of the tonic key, which dominates three of the movements: the first, the second movement Scherzo, and the Finale. However, the Trio begins in B major, a not totally unused key for ternary movements in E-flat (e.g., it was used by Haydn and can be found in Beethoven's Piano Concerto No. 5 and Rimsky-Korsakov's Symphony No. 3). The striking tonal juxtaposition, however, is in the Andante, which occurs not in a related key, but in D major with its central part slipping down to D-flat and then returning to D for the conclusion. Such a half-step juxtaposition between movements was also exploited in an earlier version of Borodin's Symphony No. 2/1–2, where the first movement ends with B-natural and the second begins with C.

Borodin's Symphony No. 1/1 is framed by its slow introduction. While such is not to be found in the symphonies of Haydn and Mozart that Borodin could have known, it seems that he used Haydn's models where the Allegro's beginning does not mark a structural downbeat but rather a continuation of the introduction's transition. Borodin stalls the structural downbeat for twenty-six measures, and *1P* enters at m.56. At this point, Borodin begins to treat his first movement in a way that breaks the bounds of tradition (see Table XV/10). One can view the piece from two different perspectives. The first is an irregular sonata structure with two development sections separated by a recapitulation, a concept no doubt suggested to Borodin by Beethoven's Symphony No. 5/1. The second is conceptually different: the slow introduction/*exordium* and a postlude/*conclusio* frames the central Allegro. Since the introduction/*exordium* presents the essential material of the Allegro first in the tonic and then the subdominant, in reality, this is the exposition followed by an Allegro that transforms and develops this material. The final Andantino 3/2 provides the recapitulation with one statement of *P* in the tonic.

While one might consider this an idiosyncratic view of the first movement, this perspective can be discredited if one considers Borodin's approach to tonality. What defines his exposition is Tovey's distinction of being in or on a key. At only a few points in the Allegro does Borodin establish a key with an authentic-strong-perfect cadence. Bar 56, the beginning of the Allegro's *P* theme, is one, and *P*'s repetition is another (m.66). Perhaps m.225 is another one, but this occurs in a developmental environment. The recapitulatory resolution is imperfect (m.301), but *P*'s repeat here retains its perfect cadence. Borodin keeps in

TABLE XV/10

Borodin. Symphony No. 1/1: Structure

[Exposition]
Adagio 3/4
Introduction

Oax y z m	Oax' y z m	trans.				
E-flat minor	A-flat minor	D pedal	B-flat pedal			
m.1	8	18				

[Development]
Allegro 3/4
Exposition

trans. cont'd	ay z n y ext.	cadence	trans.
29			54

1P(O)ax y x	2P	T	S/K			
E-flat minor	A pedal		B-flat pedal			
56	91	115	131			

Development 1

	1P	1P	1P
G minor	descending bass B-flat		A
		E pedal	
152	154		166

	Meno mosso		Tempo 1			
1P	S/K	Py	Py+z	T	2P as retrans.	
E pedal As V of A	A-flat	E-flat				
170	204	213	225	233	260	

Recapitulation

1P	1P	2P
V₇/E-flat	E-flat	E-flat/A-flat
293	303	338

305

TABLE XV/10 (*continued*)

			Development 2							*Animato assai*
	T	*S*	*Px*	*S*	*Px*	*y*	*Px*	*y*	*Px* rhythm	*Coda*
G → G-flat			C pedal	C				B-flat pedal		m
		D → E-flat	A-flat							G pedal
	364	379	410	420				456	468	484

[*Recapitulation*]
Andantino 3/2

Px	*y*	*z*
E-flat pedal		
E-flat		
514		

reserve his structural cadence (m.532) for the postlude/*conclusio*. At this point, E-flat is sustained to the end—first with a pedal and then with an almost diatonically pure melody. Borodin, having already established his tonic with seventeen more long measures to the end, underlines closure by using the celestial style, the idealized ending in programmatic pieces, which here is used in an absolute context. These final measures with their use of a pedal are indicative of Borodin's use of sustained tones as a substitute for cadential tonal articulations.

Borodin's first movement treatment of tonality does not get in the way of propelling the structure forward. Like Rimsky-Korsakov, Borodin drives his music by the use of surface rhythms, which provide identity to his themes in much the same way as Beethoven does in his Symphony No. 3/1. One cannot imagine in 3/4 time rhythms more driving and indeed almost jazzy as that found in *1P* and *2P*:

Hemiolas or syncopations are characteristic of almost all of the themes lending both a metric dissonance and a forward thrust.

Often Borodin's rhythm is just as important, if not more so, than tonality in defining the structure. The lively rhythms of *P* give way to the more *dolce T* (m.115) and *S/K* (m.131). Only with the beginning of the development proper (m.152) is a high level of activity revived. The development is shaped somewhat differently; rather than high activity becoming calmed, this sequence is countered with an invigoration that leads to the recapitulation (m.301). The second development (m.410) enhances its surface activity with a tempo acceleration near its end. This underlines a wonderful sense of relief and fulfillment when the postlude/*conclusio* presents *P* in augmentation and in a *dolce* character.

Borodin was to develop his own sure sense of the orchestra as revealed in Symphony No. 2, but in Symphony No. 1, he did not always feel at ease nor did he write in a way that showed an understanding of the instruments within an orchestral context. The first movement, which is among the most difficult technically, at times leaves something to be desired in both voice-leading and orchestration. In *T* (m.115), the tenths with the bass in octaves and the simultaneous thirds between the second violin and viola is not as effectively presented as it could have been. The same is true in m.514, the first measure of the final Andantino, where the two bassoons enter simultaneously with an unprepared minor seventh.

The second movement Scherzo seems to be a more musically polished effort, perhaps because it had a model in Berlioz's "Queen Mab" Scherzo: both are Prestissimo 3/8 pieces marked *pianissimo* and leggiero requiring both pizzicato and off-the-string bowing, and *divisi* writing. Borodin's orchestration, however, uses the heavy brass, which Berlioz resisted throughout, and is less evocative particularly in the Trio, which uses choir-oriented groupings. Apart from having chosen a radical model, Borodin's Trio is in two respects notable: its key scheme and its use of meter. We have already mentioned that this Trio begins in a modal-flavored B major; however, the composer follows this with F-sharp, D-flat, and A before returning to B via F-sharp. Dianin hears this as Russian folk material, or perhaps folk-derived music.[62] Such a designation is reinforced by changing meters: 3/4, 4/4, and 2/4 are mixed together into 7/4 and 5/4 units. These mixed meters were no doubt inspired by the 1864 version of the slow movement of Rimsky-Korsakov's Symphony No. 1, which was based on a Russian folksong given to him by Balakirev. For the coda (m.627), Berlioz also seems to be the model, but this time it is his coda to the Ball Scene in the *Symphonie fantastique* with its descending bass line. Unfortunately, Borodin does not exploit this device to an exciting end as does Berlioz. Also Berliozian are some details of the orchestration. For example, the sequence from the bottom of the strings to the top is capped by a *fortissimo* outburst in the winds (mm.89–97), followed by *piano* dissonances in the flutes and clarinets. At the larger dimension, Borodin stays well within the traditional bounds: a large Scherzo–Trio–Scherzo layout, with the Scherzo proper in sonata form and the Trio more relaxed both in its surface rhythms and tempo.

The slow movement echoes the oriental interests of the *kuchka;* they would rather look east than west even though they could never escape from the latter. Here, it is the introduction of the English horn into the orchestra, whose darker quality seemed more Eastern to Russian composers than did the regular oboe. Additionally, Borodin creates melodies containing thirty-second-note *arabesques,* and other twists as ornaments. *A* is soloistically scored: first for the cellos accompanied by woodwinds, then the English horn and flute ending with a cadenza for the former. *B* (m.34) follows much the same pattern of colors, but builds to a climax and the return of *A* (m.69). One wonders if this passage was not one that Balakirev helped Borodin mold. Its layout is very close to the introduction to the *S* in Tchaikovsky's *Romeo and Juliet* Overture-Fantasy, for which Balakirev also played a mentoring role. *A*'s return is a striking *tutti* orchestration: the treble woodwinds play the melody, while bassoons, horns, and strings sustain the background (Example XV/12). The voicings are controlled so that the range of the wind melody falls between the pitches allotted to the accompaniment. This allows the woodwinds to sing through the sonority with ease. English horn and clarinets are featured over a tonic pedal in the coda (m.85), which closes with another celestial gesture, perhaps a reminiscence of the first movement's final bars. Except for the already discussed tonal outline (D–D-flat–D), this piece represents the early Borodin at his very best: a beautifully shaped melody seasoned with oriental touches effectively orchestrated. This Andante is in effect an accomplished study for Borodin's slow movement in his Symphony No. 2.

Borodin's Finale is another derivative piece; the Scherzo owes to Berlioz, but the Finale is indebted to Robert Schumann. From the very first measure's rhythm, the Schumann of Symphony No. 4/4 is recalled. After a double statement of *Pa* (m.9), its treatment in *1T* (*P,* m.17) follows that of Schumann as the motive is passed from one instrument to another. *2T* (m.39) is marked by a dominant pedal with the main material given to the trombones. *S* (m.54) is in G-flat, and *K* (m.80), derived from *S,* settles in B-flat. The development (m.99) begins with *Pa* and *S* on the subdominant and then takes the *Pa* rhythm in an ostinato as the trombones sound a series of fifths. *P* (m.137) is then heard in D-flat over an A-flat pedal. Beginning in m.150, the Schumann sources are compounded as *P* is presented with the chords of Schumann No. 4/1 (mm.121f). After all this concentration on *P, S* (m.182) is introduced in the same way as Schumann does in Symphony No. 1/1 (m.77). *P* returns and begins a long retransition animated by syncopations culminating with *P* stated *fortississimo* (Example XV/13) by the full band in augmentation (m.264). All this recalls the climactic chorale transformation in the coda of Schumann's Symphony No. 3/5 "Rhenish" (m.255). *T* (m.296) and *S* (m.336) in A-flat follow in time. As in the first movement a short second development (m.357) follows that ends with *S* and *K* occurring in the tonic, *tutti* and *fortissimo* (m.406).

Abraham complains that this is second-rate music, saying that it "opens with a vigorous theme" with the "mood of boisterous high spirits which so often disguises [its] weaknesses."

EXAMPLE XV/12 Borodin. Symphony No. 1/3, mm.67–74. Courtesy of Edwin F. Kalmus & Co.

He finds the recapitulation's beginning "slightly vulgar." To the contrary, our impression is that this is a successful conclusion to the symphony and, by Germanic symphonic standards, it is the strongest movement of the cycle. Perhaps Borodin needed models like Schumann's symphonies in order to instill some discipline, in contrast to the more enthusiastic and more originally conceived first movement. In this Finale, the use of tonality is more coherent and even strategic (e.g., the various presentations of *S*) and the orchestral writing is less problematic. In the end, we have exactly what one might expect in a First Symphony written by an immensely talented amateur; it contains both deeply original as well as derivative gestures.

EXAMPLE XV/12   *(continued)*

Its first performance in January of 1869 received mixed notices, one of which follows:

As Robert Schumann has it in his notes, there are talents that act freely only when they feel themselves to be under a higher talent; this can apply to Mr. Borodin. Those parts of his symphony where he imitates his favorite patterns are successful, but whenever he crosses the limits of his talents and solicits originality, he lapses into ugliness.

The most successful movements of the symphony are the scherzo and allegro; the former is a talented copy—both conceptually and in orchestration—of the scherzo "Queen Mab" from Berlioz's symphony "Romeo and Juliet"; especially beautiful is the movement in the basses (in diminished fifths, if we are not mistaken). The last allegro, in its rhythmic and harmonic solutions, is completely imbued with Schumann's spirit, the main idea is taken almost in toto out of the latter's D-minor symphony, the only difference being that Schumann has it in a minor key, Mr. Borodin in the major. The other two movements . . . are much weaker than those mentioned above. Despite the symphony's many deficiencies, it is composed very nicely and gives much credit to Mr. Borodin, especially considering the fact that he—to the best of our knowledge—is not a musician by profession.[63]

EXAMPLE XV/13   Borodin. Symphony No. 1/4, mm.259–76. Courtesy of Edwin F. Kalmus & Co.

After he had studied the score several years later, Liszt told Borodin his reactions (as documented by Borodin in a letter from July 1877):

> He [Liszt] told me that he had presented my modulations as models to his students. Pointing out several, he remarked that nothing similar could be found in Beethoven, Bach, or anywhere else, for that matter, and that despite its novelty and originality, the work could not be quibbled with since it was so polished, definite and full of attractive qualities. He regarded the first movement very highly; its pedal points, particularly the one in C, pleased him enormously.

EXAMPLE XV/13 (*continued*)

He said nothing special about the other movements, but gave me some practical advice in case I were to publish a second piano version, namely, that of writing certain passages an octave higher or lower to facilitate reading.[64]

Borodin's indebtedness to Schumann is also highlighted in an emphatically positive review of a performance in 1886, extracts of which follow:

This remarkable piece represents the pinnacle of talent and is the result of inexhaustible inspiration. There is no bad music in it; good music prevails in it to such a degree that it's only possible to point at more or less wonderful moments. As a symphonic composition, it is very successful as well: its form is perfectly consistent; its harmonic quality amazes you by its beauty; and its counterpoint by the adroitness with which Mr. Borodin has mastered it in this symphony. One more outstanding characteristic of this symphony should be pointed out: it is its distinctness and originality, especially considering the period when it was composed (the 1860s). In this respect, out of principle, Mr. Borodin can be reproached for the fact that the first theme of finale has the character of Schumann, whereas both in its further development, and in the remaining three movements, there are no traces of Schumann whatsoever. . . . The instrumentation of the symphony is very colorful and diverse. From the subtlest [pianissimo] to the strong, resonant, but not overdone [fortissimo], everything in it sounds good. In terms of subtlety, the conclusion in the first movement and Andante are especially successful. Nevertheless, in the whole symphony, it is possible to find several isolated bars that, as they say, don't come out well in orchestra.[65]

SYMPHONY NO. 2 IN B MINOR

In contrast, Borodin's Symphony No. 2 in B Minor is at once both skillful and original in its totality. Though this symphony is today rarely heard in concert, during the first half of the twentieth century it was a repertoire piece. In some quarters it was considered to be the greatest of the Russian symphonies, which again raises the controversial question of what makes a symphony Russian. In contrast to the issues raised earlier about the "true Russian" status of symphonic works by Rubinstein, in the case of Borodin's Second, there is no similar controversy: the symphony is both composed by a Russian and uses materials that seem idiomatically Slavic.

Like his Symphony No. 1, Borodin composed his second symphony over a long period, from 1869 to 1876. During this time, Borodin was also occupied with his never-completed opera *Prince Igor,* from whose sketches some of the symphony's themes were taken. According to Gerald Abraham, the themes for the first, third, and fourth movements of the Second Symphony were probably intended for the epilogue of the opera.[66] The lengthy chronology for this work appears to be as follows:

1869	Decides to compose a second symphony after performance of Symphony No. 1.
1871	First movement completed.
October 1871	Finale sketched.
April 1875	Writes that he must finish orchestration of the symphony during the summer.
January 1877	Four-hand arrangement published.
February 26/March 10, 1877	First performance by RMS, conducted by Nápravník.
February 20/March 4, 1879	Revised version, mainly thinning the brass scoring, performed at the Free Music School concerts, conducted by Rimsky-Korsakov.
Before February 15/27, 1887	Further revisions by the composer before his unexpected death on this date.
October 24/November 5, 1887	Revised version by the composer performed at the Borodin Memorial Concert, conducted by Rimsky-Korsakov.
Late 1877	Full score published posthumously by Bessel under the care of Rimsky-Korsakov and Glazunov.

The preparation of the score for posthumous publication by Rimsky-Korsakov and Glazunov has raised questions as to the integrity of its text. This issue arises from Rimsky's and Glazunov's efforts to improve some of the scores of Borodin as well as Musorgsky. Nearly all of the changes between the 1877 and 1879 versions were approved by the composer for the performance conducted by Rimsky-Korsakov, including Balakirev's addition to the beginning of the second movement. The integrity issue concerning the published score, which includes the statement "rédigée par N. Rimsky-Korsakov et A. Glazunov," came to a head in 1924 when the critic M. D. Calvocoressi noticed discrepancies between the four-hand piano transcription of 1877 and the full score of 1887.

An examination of the complete sources, including the published score, reveals that the changes were minimal. Rimsky added the following: "various tempo changes in the first movement and in the Finale certain changes were made to the triangle part." The metronome markings in the published score also are from Rimsky. Since he conducted the work during the composer's lifetime, one is probably safe in assuming that they are authoritative. Other changes include the keys of the clarinet and trumpet parts and various other details. David Lloyd-Jones characterizes the changes as "those of any editor entrusted with the task of seeing a piece of writing through the press."[67]

Vladimir Stasov claimed that Borodin had a tableau in mind for three of the movements: 1) A Gathering of Russian Warriors; 3) Bayan [A Mythic Bard]; and 4) Scene of Heroes Feasting to the Sound of Guslis [a zither-like instrument] Amid the Exultation of a Great Host of People. Stasov called it the "Bogatyrskaya" or "Heroic" Symphony.[68]

Like Symphony No. 1, the cycle for Symphony No. 2 is in four movements with the Scherzo in second place and is mainly unified by the tonality of the first and last movements. The central movements of both symphonies are also in deeply contrasting keys: here, the Scherzo is in F major, with its Trio in D minor, and the following Andante is in D-flat. Symphony No. 2 differs from No. 1 in that the last two movements are to be played without pause. In the revised 1879 version, perhaps this is also true of the first pair of movements: Balakirev suggested the addition of the first four measures of the Scherzo to cover the distance from B minor to F major. Despite the generally low level of overt efforts to unite the cycle (see, however, *I/S* and *II/B*), Borodin's Second Symphony is perceived as a satisfying whole. Whether that unity is something Russian, as Stasov was to believe, merely a result of the deeply contrasting styles of the movements, or a result of the common origin of the potential *Price Igor* materials, Borodin composed a symphony which is as viable as any composed in Russia or anywhere else.

The first movement is a sonata form again shaped by a somewhat unusual key scheme in the recapitulation:

	P	*S*	*K*		*P*	*S*		*K*
Exposition:	B minor	D		*Recapitulation*:	B minor	E-flat	C	B minor
	1	78	93		224	263		283

This time the exposition is textbook normal, but Borodin's treatment of *S* in the recapitulation avoids bringing it back in the tonic or even in closely related keys. Rather, he chooses keys distant from B minor: E-flat, which is more closely related to B major, and C, which is not closely related to either the tonic or the exposition's *S* key.

P (Example XV/14) is a bold declamatory statement that has something of the character

EXAMPLE XV/14   Borodin. Symphony No. 2/1, mm.1–10. Courtesy of Edwin F. Kalmus & Co.

of a recitative. This theme takes on a structural importance beyond what one already expects of *P*. During the course of the exposition, it is developed through augmentation, change of meter from 2/2 to 3/2, and transformation. The augmentation of *P* takes on a larger significance since this slower pace of delivery emphasizes the articulatory strength of the recapitulation (m.224), and at the end (m.313) of the coda (m.289) it is further underlined by double augmentation (m.313), *tutti* scoring, *fortissimo* dynamics, and *peasante* articulations. Though augmentation was used in the recapitulation of Symphony No. 1/4, here it is used on a higher plane. Furthermore, *P* is laid out in two contrasting members *Pa* (m.1) and *Pb* (m.11). *Pa* is heard more frequently while both *Pa* and *Pb* recur as *T* (m.60).

T (m.60) and S (m.78) also follow textbook expectations. *1T* (*Pax*) rises in sequence through the strings, and *2T*(*Pb*) is destabilized by a descending bass, then stalls on D major's dominant for *S*, which is broadened in tempo (Poco meno mosso), in meter from ¢ to 3/2, and surface activity. Rather than the *tutti forza* style of much of *P, S* is *dolce* and scored in the rich baritone range of the orchestra. Notice that *S* is like a grand extension/augmentation of *1T* as *S* takes longer to build to the higher range and fuller sonorities of the orchestra. *K* (m.93) is also based on *P*. However, *K* both picks up the tempo and changes its meter to a mixture of 3/2 and *alla breve* bars that equal two measures of 7/2.

Part one of the development (m.141) begins with *Pa* augmented and is answered by *1T* (m.155). This juxtaposition highlights that *Pa* and *1T* are motivically related (Example XV/15). Part 2 (m.163) accelerates to Animato assai, changes the meter from *alla breve* to 3/2, and uses a driving rhythmic ostinato. *Pa* is subjected to an intensive tonal development and takes on a new physiognomy. *Pb* follows in ¢, and the meter returns to 3/2 with the lyrical *S* (m.192) pitted against an agitated background. *Pax* also returns (m.199) in the same agitated environment. By m.206, the bass, after descending, settles on a dominant pedal in preparation for the recapitulation. Here, *T* is eliminated, and *S* follows almost immediately. A developmental area is interpolated (m.269) that combines *P* and *S* in alternating one-measure units, which overruns into *K(Pa,* m.283). The coda (m.289) pushes the tempo forward culminating in the return of *P* in double augmentation. With these maneuvers, Borodin avoids the one pitfall of placing so much emphasis on *P:* overexposure.

In this first movement, a significant contributing factor to avoiding overexposure is Borodin's expertise in balancing rhythmically active sections with those that are in a state of repose. In the exposition, sections of repose (R) and activity (A) alternate below the level of the function:

Pa	*b*	*a*	*b*	*1T*	*2T(Pb)*	*S*	*1K(P)*	*2K*
R	A	R	A	R	A	R	A	R
1	11	17	37	60	68	78	93	107

The development has lengthy stretches of repose and activity, thereby changing the character of several of the themes. The listener is also drawn to the small-dimension motivic work that dominates Part 2:

Part 1		*Part 2*				
Pa	*1T*	*Pa*	*Pb*	*S*	*P*	*1T*
R ———————→		A ———————————————————————→				
141	155	163	187	193	199	213

In the recapitulation, Borodin presents a significant variant of the exposition by tightening the structure and altering the lengths of the activity levels:

					Coda		
Pa (augmentation)	*Pb*	*S*	*Pa*-developed	*K(Pa)*		*Pa*	
R ———————————→	A	R	A ——————————————————→			R	
224	248	263	269	283	289	313	

For a supposedly dilettante composer who had little training in the academic studies of musical composition, this first movement is a significant accomplishment. Though it has virtually no polyphony, Borodin has sustained this piece with attractive melodies motivically interrelated, a large-scale sense of rhythm, effective orchestration in the revised version, and idiosyncratic use of harmony and modulation, particularly in the recapitulation. This masterly first movement is a considerable advance over that of his First Symphony, whose high originality made it at times less effective.

EXAMPLE XV/15 Borodin. Symphony No. 2/1, mm.141–63. Courtesy of Edwin F. Kalmus & Co.

EXAMPLE XV/15   (*continued*)

Borodin's Scherzo is a striking piece that breaks from the triple meter requisite; the first part is in 1/1 time 𝅝 = 108, i.e., four quarter notes to a bar with a whole note receiving a beat. After the first four bars of introduction, the bulk of the Scherzo proper is a perpetual motion with quarter notes virtually always present in a kaleidoscope of color. One might expect these measures to be arranged in groups of four, but Borodin immediately destroys this expectation. After the opening four-bar chord we are given two five-bar phrases, a four-bar group, then two more five-bar units, etc. *T* (m.37) begins a series of two- and one-bar units (Example XV/16) that take us to *S* (m.55) and the key of D-flat with an A-flat pedal supporting a syncopated theme marked *appassionata ed energico*. *K* (m.69) returns to the tonic for a recapitulation, i.e., without a change of key for *S*. *K* is now extended to provide a transition to the Allegretto 6/4 for the second main theme. Perhaps, this Allegretto is a Russian Barcarolle with its lilting rhythms in compound-duple meter, mild hemiolas, and a melody marked *cantabile e dolce*. Borodin's orchestration of the background is almost *Klangfarben* with harp, triangle, and horns providing a pointilistic accompaniment. The form builds through repetitions of its four-measure theme with changes to its background in good *kuchkist* fashion. Tonally, it moves from D major (m.156) to the distant keys of D-flat (m.166), G-flat (m.174), and B-flat (m.184) before returning to D. A nearly literal repeat of the Scherzo proper ensues and leads to the coda

EXAMPLE XV/16   Borodin. Symphony No. 2/2, mm.37–54. Courtesy of Edwin F. Kalmus & Co.

(m.347), which extends *K.* Rimsky-Korsakov found the Scherzo proper the weak link in the cycle: "the Scherzo . . . is of a character alien to the rest of the symphony."[69] Perhaps its key, a tritone from B minor, colored Rimsky's view; he did not find the D major middle section alien.

According to Stasov, the slow movement was to have depicted the Slavic minstrel Bayan, who accompanied himself on a gusli—a kind of zither—which here is represented by the

EXAMPLE XV/16   (*continued*)

harp. One can well imagine Bayan singing a narrative ballad; as Rimsky-Korsakov later was to do in *Sheherazade,* the movement is framed by a few measures that could represent a common beginning or ending to the telling of a tale (mm.1–4, 121–27). Something similar occurs in Borodin's Symphony No. 1/3, though there the beginning (open fifths) and ending (celestial music) are of different material. Also the two slow movements are laid out in simple part forms; Symphony No. 1/3 is a simple ternary structure, while Symphony No. 2/3 is a more extended piece in something that approaches a rondo:

O	A	B	A	C(A)	B	A	B	A	O
D-flat	⟶	E minor	A-flat	A	D-flat	⟶			
1	5	23	46	80	87	91	101	113	121

What marks the two movements, however, are their beautiful melodies, some of them slightly eastern in orientation, others less characteristically marked. Borodin's climaxes (mm.80 and 91), though *tutti,* are, as in a similarly scored passage in Symphony No. 1/3 (m.69), transparently voiced by leaving gaps of sonority where the melody can reside without interference. Other felicities of scoring are the opening solos for clarinet and horn and the *B* material, which is tossed at one-measure intervals among different wind instruments accompanied by string tremolos. Though a carefully calculated piece of writing, something one could not quite say about Symphony No. 1/3, Symphony No. 2/3 benefits from a certain spontaneity that the music conveys from its seemingly improvised materials. The Andante ends with the second violins sustaining A-flat and D-flat, which is changed enharmonically at the beginning of the Finale to G-sharp and C-sharp, thereby becoming a part of the dominant seventh of B major, a chord prolonged until m.18 of the Finale, where it is finally resolved.

According to Stasov, the Finale is a scene of great celebration, a sense that Borodin conveys by writing Slavic dances: its mixed triple and duple meters, its active surface fired by a syncopation on the downbeat, the addition of percussion including cymbals and triangle, "Turkish" instruments to western ears, as well as a tambourine and bass drum. There are at least three approaches to interpreting the Finale, none of which are mutually exclusive from another: 1) in the western tradition of the symphony, i.e., a movement in one of the standard forms such as rondo or sonata; 2) as a collection of dances, whose presentation approximates sonata principles; and 3) as a programmatic piece following the events given to us by Stasov and elaborated upon in the manner of a Soviet musicologist by Serge Dianin.[70] Table XV/11 attempts to outline these three views.

The sonata-form concept is certainly a viable way of looking at this movement. Virtually all of the textbook elements are here: the expository functions, the larger movement functions, and the key scheme are surprisingly traditional with the tertian relationships reserved for the development section. Dianin's effort to attach a specific program to the movement is acceptable until one comes to the recapitulation, where the musical requirements of the form take precedence. Here, a distinction between narrative/programmatic music and characteristic music seems in order, since the latter can express the essence of a mood or occasion without superimposing a narrative upon a stereotypical form. A third alternative seems to fit with the music and at the same time expresses the character of the movement: a series of dances introduced by one or more recurring vamps. Here we find two dances (Nos. 1 & 3) of high spirits and another (No. 2) that is more lyric.

The first dance, or *P* of the sonata form, is structured more like a folkdance than a primary theme. It is built by the repetition of a 5/4 (3/4+2/4) unit that gains its hyperactivity by kinetic recurrence, and its main method of variation is by repetition at a different octave or by a heterophonic counterpoint (see m.26; cf. cello and oboe). To this brew is then added a sixteenth-note counterpoint (m.30) before returning to the initial statement of *P* (m.39). *S* (m.53), or the second dance, uses the environmental variation of the six-measure theme by changing its accompaniment and orchestration. However, Borodin also takes an essentially triple-meter melody and adds measures of new durations: e.g., m.62 3/4—4 bars, 2/4—1 bar, 3/4—2 bars, 4/4—1 bar. *K* (m.76) uses this same idea, but highlights its function with pedals. The third dance, or *1N* (m.149), makes its first appearance near the end of the development

TABLE XV/II

Borodin. Symphony No. 2/4: Structure, Dances, and Program

Allegro 3/4/2/4/4/4/4 ♩ = 126

					Lento 3/2	Allegro 3/4	Lento 3/2	Allegro		
Introduction	*Exposition*				*Development*					
O(*P* adumbration)	P	T(O)	S	K(S)	*P* augmentation		*P* augmentation	T(O)	P	1N
(B)	B		D	D	C minor		B-flat minor	A-flat	E minor	C
Vamp	Dance 1	Vamp	Dance 2		(interruption)			Vamp	Dances 1+2 (transformed)	Dance 3
Crowd and Heroes Gathering for Feast	Beginning of Feast		Singing and Conversation		Ceremony of Commemoration					
m.1	18	44	53	76	96	98	100	102	118	149

Animato

				Coda			
Recapitulation							
O(*P* adumbration)	P	T(O)	S/K	2N	1N	1N1	O/P
F-sharp pedal	B						
V/B							
Vamp	Dance 1	Vamp	Dance 2	Vamp	Dance 3	Vamp	
Later Portions of Feast				Climax of Celebration			
168	184	201	208	232	251	257	265

and is repeated in the coda (m.251). *IN* grows from a repeated two-measure module sometimes at the same pitch and sometimes in sequence. All of the characteristics cited are common to East European and Russian folk music: multiple repetition of modules of one or two measures; heterophonic counterpoint; environmental variation, mixtures of meters, pedals, and drones; and also the quasi-modal melodies that avoid major- and melodic-minor construction.

Every one of these dances has a pronounced rhythmic drive arising from syncopation and strong anacrustic formations. This is also true of the recurring vamp. Note the rhythmic structure of the first vamp (Example XV/17) which arrives at the first dance after seventeen bars. Combined with the complete cadential resolution (mm.17–18) and the dance's forward thrust, one experiences all the energy needed to render this Finale an appropriate conclusion for this appealing and powerful symphony.

Borodin's Symphony No. 2, as indicated above, went through two revisions after its first public hearing on February 26/March 10, 1877, at the concerts of the Russian Musical Society. A second version was first heard in 1879, the final posthumous version in 1887, with both performances conducted by Rimsky-Korsakov.

The second version received a substantive review by the *kuchka*'s partisan critic, César Cui, who heard a later performance on November 11/23, 1885:

> The Popular Russian Symphony Concert conducted by Dyutsh, which took place on 11/23 November in the Hall of the Assembly of the Nobility, was of the utmost interest on account of its programme, made up exclusively of works by Russian composers, by virtue of the début of a new conductor and of the attempt to keep ticket prices as low as possible with a view to making the concert open to everyone. The works performed were as follows: first, Borodin's Second Symphony.[. . .] It is a capital work of staggering talent and thoroughly typical. Nowhere do the individuality and originality of Borodin reveal themselves in sharper relief than in this symphony; nowhere do his gifts appear with such versatility and diversity or his ideas so distinctively, powerfully and profoundly. In Borodin's Second Symphony it is power which predominates, power which is tough—in short, unconquerable, elemental power. The symphony is permeated by traits of Russian nationality (*simfoniya proniknuta narodnost'yu*), but the nationality of remote times; Rus' is perceptible in this symphony, but primitive pagan Rus'. This symphony might be known as a work concerned with the people's way of life. It is as much a picture of everyday life as the introduction to *Ruslan,* and much of *The Snowmaiden,* especially the scene with the *gusli*-players. This unconquerable, elemental power makes itself felt most in the first Allegro and the finale. Right from the start, the first unison phrase startles the listener with its originality and strength. The latter quality increases and reaches its upper limit after the middle section, at the return of the same phrase augmented twofold, halting on bleak, energy-filled chords. These two movements also contain gentle and beautiful contrasting episodes, but power predominates. This power is not clothed in the balanced, serene forms of western harmonization but manifests itself with rare and harsh originality both in the themes themselves and in their contrapuntal, harmonic, and even orchestral treatment.
>
> This harshness of thought and expression, which is quite unmitigated but at the same is not deprived of colour by conventionally worked-out, custom-hallowed western forms, may prove shocking to many, but everyone must be struck by the force of its boldness and originality. Notwithstanding the resemblance in character between the

EXAMPLE XV/17   Borodin. Symphony No. 2/4, mm.1–17. Courtesy of Edwin F. Kalmus & Co.

EXAMPLE XV/17   (*continued*)

EXAMPLE XV/17 (*continued*)

symphony's first and fourth movements, there is a difference. In the first movement an atmosphere of grandeur is predominant, whereas humour prevails in the last movement. The first movement is like an everyday picture of some solemn ritual; the last movement is a vivid, motley, varied celebration of sparkling gaiety.

The character of the second movement (scherzo) and the third (Andante) changes markedly. The musical themes in these movements are full of fascinating passion (the syncopated theme in the scherzo), or full of appealing simplicity (the trio in the scherzo), or filled with charming poetry (the beginning and ending of the Andante). But the power of real life is not wholly absent from these two movements; it shows through in the angular playfulness of the opening of the scherzo and in the severe progressions in the middle of the Andante. To sum up, Borodin's Second Symphony is one of the most original, most highly talented works in the whole of the symphonic music.[71]

Reviews of the 1887 memorial concert in tribute to Borodin as the scientist/composer, who had died unexpectedly on February 15/27, 1886, made only brief mention of the third version, and instead focused on the first performance of his Third Symphony.

The Second Symphony proved to be Borodin's great work. Whatever Borodin's technical limitations as a composer, they fail to be revealed in this symphony. The power, the playfulness, the lyricism, and the liveliness incorporated into each of the movements make for a compelling gesture. Although today one hears more frequently *In the Steppes of Central Asia* (1880), the overture to *Prince Igor* (reconstructed by Glazunov), and the Polovetsian Dances from the same opera, it is because these are smaller and more colorful pieces, not necessarily works of greater merit.

SYMPHONY NO. 3 IN A MINOR (FRAGMENT)

At the time of his death, Borodin left two major works unfinished: his opera *Prince Igor*, which he had worked on over a period of eighteen years (1869–1887), and his Symphony No. 3 in A minor dating from 1882, with further work during 1886–1887. No doubt his composition of the Third Symphony was in part stimulated by the success of his Symphony No. 2; in particular, a Belgian patroness, the Countess Louise de Merci d'Argenteau, urged him to compose another symphony.

The first two movements—including the Scherzo—were conceptualized first, while movements three and four were worked on in 1886–1887. In February 1887, Borodin wrote to his wife that he had a Third Symphony in "embryonic form," but that he needed time to work on *Prince Igor*. As was often the case, Borodin used sketches, but also did much of his composing in his head. Fortunately, Borodin had played for Glazunov, known for his phenomenal musical memory, both the overture to *Prince Igor* and portions of the new symphony. This, together with the few sketches, enabled Glazunov to assemble the entire overture and the first two movements of the A Minor Symphony. As recalled by Glazunov:

Themes were on hand for all movements. The first was to a large extent incomplete and unnotated. I had managed to memorize the general outline of the work, and several episodes were contained on fragments of paper. I myself composed all the linking episodes as well as the coda, faithfully adhering to Borodin's style throughout, with which I was then intimate.[72]

The Glazunov effort was published in 1888 in both orchestral score and an arrangement for piano four-hands. Unlike the situation with Elgar's Third Symphony as "elaborated" by Anthony Payne some sixty-five years after Elgar's death, here we have a different scenario. Therefore, the reconstruction by Glazunov merits some discussion.

For the second movement, it was Borodin's plan to orchestrate the Scherzo for a String Quartet composed in 1882 and to add to it a Trio from a portion conceived for *Prince Igor* near the end of the first act, the Merchant's report on the defection of Igor's troops. As for the third movement Andante, only two bars are so marked in a sketch. However, we know it was played by Borodin for his friends, the Dobroslavins, and they reported hearing variations on a Russian chant. Aleksandr Dianin, Borodin's lab assistant, heard the composer play the Finale, which was remembered as powerful and "unlike any other Borodin work." The third and forth movements were also played for Boris Asaf'yev and Glazunov. When Asaf'yev asked Glazunov why he had not notated such beautiful music, Glazunov said that at that point he did not find it beautiful.[73]

The first movement Moderato assai, as reconstructed by Glazunov, is a sonata form with a rather short development (52 mm. for a 116-mm. exposition). One must admit that the main thematic ideas *P* (m.1), *T* (m.51), *S* (m.73), and *K* (m.93) are typically quasi-modal and attractive Borodin melodies. It is the connecting tissue and the development section that prove to be less worthy, i.e., those sections to which Glazunov made more substantial contributions. The recapitulation (m.169) closely follows the exposition, and the coda, also restored by Glazunov, is rather effective with its quiet and quasi-celestial conclusion. Though the orchestration is skillful, it lacks some of the luster one came to expect of Borodin after *In the Steppes of Central Asia,* the Polovetsian Dances, and the Second Symphony.

The Scherzo and its Trio do not seem to belong together either as contrasting or undifferentiated statements. The Scherzo proper is another Scherzo in 5/8 meter; Russian ethnologists and ethnomusicologists would claim this to derive from the accents of the Russian language. Here the 5/8 bar is almost consistently a 2/8 plus a 3/8 unit; the only departures are four three-bar statements in 2/4 (Sostenuto e pesante) ♩=72, which interrupts the flow of the ♩♩♩=66 sections, and some brief implications of 3/8 plus 2/8 units (e.g., mm.55–58, 185–87). For the Trio, the tempo slows and the meter is 3/4. The scoring is now reduced with much of the leading material given to the solo clarinet or solo oboe with strings, lending to it more of a chamber-music quality. In its transcription from rejected material for *Prince Igor,* the melody seems to maintain something of a declarative cantabile quality. The return of the Scherzo is abbreviated by roughly one-half (235 mm. versus 124 mm.) including the closing.

Neither of these movements reveals any of the interest found in the parallel pieces of the First and Second Symphonies; the creation of themes, while central to symphonic success, is not the only requirement. Also required is the connection and elaboration of the material, which can only be satisfactorily accomplished by the creator of the themes. Other works completed by Glazunov and Rimsky-Korsakov had more of Musorgsky and Borodin in them than this Third Symphony. The so-called Borodin Symphony No. 3 therefore contains, at most, themes by Borodin.

This raises the question: Do we need to hear Beethoven's No. 10, Schubert's No. 7, or Mahler's No. 10 even if the completions cannot possibly reflect the style and intent of the composer? Of these, only Schubert's No. 7—where the composer has accounted for every measure if not every harmony, counterpoint, and texture—seems to ring true in Brian Newbould's realization, in that it actually sounds like Schubert. In contrast, Borodin's Third Symphony is a weak realization that does not reflect its composer's gifts. It is only of peripheral importance to an understanding of Borodin and of no significance to the development of the symphonic tradition in Russia or Europe.

Borodin's so-called Symphony No. 3 was first heard at the memorial concert for the composer on October 24/November 5, 1887, conducted by Rimsky-Korsakov. Besides the Third Symphony, the concert included the first performances of the "March of the Polovtsy" from *Prince Igor* orchestrated by Rimsky and the *Prince Igor* Overture as realized by Glazunov. The reception of this concert with posthumous realizations by the self-appointed executors of his musical estate was critiqued by Cui in the pages of the *Musical Review*:

> The uncompleted 3rd Symphony of Borodin consists of two parts—the first allegro and scherzo. The first allegro is a Russian folk pastoral—soft, beautiful, appealing, and rich in content. It may be somewhat sketchy, underdeveloped, but even in this form it makes the most gratifying impression with its clarity, abundance of thought, and folk spirit. It was notated by Mr. Glazunov from memory after the death of the author, who repeatedly played it to his friends. The broadly developed scherzo is absolutely complete. Its first part is in 5/4, and its thematic phrases fit into this original rhythm in a most natural way. The general character of scherzo is brisk, joyful, harmonically and rhythmically capricious, and, once again, pure folk in spirit. The 5/4 rhythm is periodically interrupted . . . by phrases of great power and energy. . . . The trio . . . is very melodious and makes the playful, provoking and humorous character of the first part even more visible. This scherzo was written down by Borodin, but not orchestrated, and was initially meant for a string quartet.[74]

The reviewer for *Nuvellist* was much less charitable:

> Works until now unknown to the public, both early and new ones, were played, specifically—the overture to the opera *Prince Igor,* two movements from the unfinished 3rd symphony (A minor), the "Polovetsian March" (from the opera) and two romances. As far as the two first works, they were transcribed, as the [concert] poster announced, from memory (?!) by Glazunov, who heard the late Borodin play them and this surely explains the uncoordinated scraps of which they consist: [among Borodin's papers] there remained only a manuscript of the second movement of the symphony, the remainder he had not yet written down. Apparently, he played the overture and first movement of the symphony for friends in the nature of an improvisation, each time changing them and varying the details. You can imagine what emerged from such things, transcribed by another musician from memory![75]

CONCLUSION

Borodin's symphonies do not seem to have generated any models, or progeny, except in a general way. While Rimsky-Korsakov had, together with Balakirev, injected an Eastern element into Russian orchestral music in works like Rimsky-Korsakov's *Sheherazade* and Balakirev's *Tamara,* Borodin seems, unlike his two colleagues, to have fully absorbed these elements into his musical language with a naturalness not present in other Russian composers. Borodin's First Symphony reveals less of this accomplishment, with its orientation toward Berlioz and Schumann, particularly in the Scherzo and Finale. It is in the Second Symphony where Borodin finds his stride. Here, every element seems to be Borodin, because he has so fully absorbed outside influences to make them his own. The themes of his incomplete Symphony No. 3 reveal a similar integration, but because of the embryonic state of this symphony at the time of the composer's death, it remains only a work-in-progress—despite Glazunov's efforts to realize it in his colleague's language.

Borodin's total musical output was relatively slim and much of what we know of him today was filtered through Rimsky-Korsakov and Glazunov. However, those works fully realized by the composer, *In the Steppes of Central Asia* and the first two symphonies, reveal a potential that was not fully developed because of Borodin's devotion to chemistry and medicine.

We turn next to one of the composers that Balakirev mentored but who was not a member of the *kuchka,* Pyotr Il'yich Tchaikovsky, who became something of a model for Balakirev's later symphonies. Tchaikovsy is undoubtedly the most important, and the only universally recognized, nineteenth-century composer of the Russian symphonic fraternity.

Pyotr Il'yich Tchaikovsky
INTRODUCTION

If one takes into account his activities up to his twenty-third year, with eight years of study at the School of Jurisprudence, five years as a clerk at the Ministry of Justice in St. Petersburg, and studying music in his spare time, one can easily see Pyotr Il'yich Tchaikovsky (1840–1893) as a potential member of the *kuchka* coming under the spell of Balakirev. Despite his overly sensitive personality, however, Tchaikovsky was able to maintain his independence. He attended the conservatory in St. Petersburg and became a technically accomplished composer after nearly four years of study. Following his graduation, he took a post in January 1866 at the newly established conservatory in Moscow. Similar to Rimsky-Korsakov, Tchaikovsky was thus able to establish himself as a professional Russian composer—a rare breed in the land of the tsars. And Balakirev did in fact have an influence on Tchaikovsky's composition of two important later works: 1) the *Romeo and Juliet* Overture-Fantasy (1870), for which the *kuchka*'s mentor and teacher suggested the topic and criticized the result, and (2) the *Manfred* Symphony Opus 58 (1885), for which Balakirev gave Tchaikovsky the scenario that had been originally intended for Berlioz.[76]

Though Tchaikovsky's enumerated symphonies end with No. 6, by some reckonings he actually wrote eight symphonies (see Table XV/12). One of these two additional works, the *Manfred* Symphony, chronologically falls between Symphonies Nos. 4 and 5 and was published as an explicitly characteristic/programmatic piece, which may account for why the composer did not number it along with his other symphonies. In addition, an E-flat Major Symphony was worked on from 1891 to 1892; it has been given the number seven, even though chronologically it falls between Symphonies Nos. 5 and 6. The materials for No. 7 were adapted by Tchaikosvky for his one-movement Piano Concerto No. 3 Opus 75 (1893) and for the Andante and Finale for piano and orchestra Opus 79 (1893); the latter was orchestrated by the composer's student Sergey Ivanovich Taneyev (1856–1915). Some fifty years later, the Soviet composer Semyon Bogatyrev reconstructed a version of the uncompleted Symphony No. 7, which was first performed by the Moscow Philharmonic on February 7, 1957, conducted by M. Terian. It made a temporary splash in the West with performances and a recording by Eugene Ormandy and the Philadelphia Orchestra in 1962;[77] a Russian recording led by Gennady Rozhdestvensky with the Moscow Radio Symphony Orchestra was released in 1977.[78] Thus, Tchaikovsky actually composed seven symphonies, and worked on an eighth (No. 7), which he ultimately abandoned.

TABLE XV/12

The Symphonies of Pyotr Il'yich Tchaikovsky

Opus	Key	Dates	Title	Movements	Instrumentation	Comments
13	G minor	1866 rev. 1874	Symphony No. 1	1. Allegro tranquillo 2/4 (723m.) 2. Adagio cantabile ma non tanto 4/4 (168 m.) E-flat major 3. Scherzo: Allegro scherzando giocoso 3/8 (441 m.) C minor. 4. Finale: Andante lugubre 4/4—Allegro moderato ¢ (610 m.) G minor—major	Grand plus Picc., Tuba, Cym., BD	"Winter Daydreams": 1. Reveries of a Winter Journey. 2. Land of Desolation—Land of Mists." Mvt. 2 uses material from overtures to *The Storm*. Mvt. 3 transcribed from the Scherzo to a C-sharp Minor Piano Sonata (1865). Mvt. 4 based on a folk song "The Gardens Bloomed." Dedicated to Nikolay Rubinstein. First performance of entire cycle: Moscow, Russian Musical Society on February 3/15, 1868, conducted by Nikolay Rubinstein; revised version: Moscow, Musical Society on November 19/December 1, 1883, conducted by Max Erdmannsdörfer. Published in Moscow: Jürgenson, 1875.
17	C minor	1872 rev. 1879–1880	Symphony No. 2	1. Andante sostenuto 4/4—Allegro vivo ¢ (369 m.) 2. Andantino marziale, quasi moderato 4/4 (179 m.) E-flat major 3. Scherzo: Allegro molto vivace 3/8 and Trio: 3/8 (482 m.) C minor 4. Finale: Moderato assai—Allegro vivo 2/4 (847 m.) C major	Grand plus Picc., Tuba, Cym., BD, Tam-tam	"Little Russian (=Ukraine)" uses Ukranian folk songs in the first, second, and final mvts. Mvt. 2 uses a wedding march from his destroyed opera *Undine* (1869). Dedicated to Imperial Russian Society of Music, Moscow. First performance: Moscow, Russian Musical Society on January 26/February 7, 1873, conducted by Nikolay Rubinstein; revised version: St. Petersburg on January 31/February 12, 1881, conducted by Karl Zike. Published in St. Petersburg; Bessal, 1881.
29	D major	1875	Symphony No. 3	1. Introduzione: Moderato assai (Tempo di marcia funebre)—Allegro brillante 4/4 (472 m.) D minor—major 2. Alla tedesca: Allegro moderato e semplice and Trio 3/4 (289 m.) B-flat major 3. Andante elegiaco 3/4 (182 m.) D minor 4. Scherzo and Trio: Allegro vivo 2/4 (439 m.) B minor 5. Finale: Allegro con fuoco (tempo di polacca) 3/4 (350 m.) D major	Grand plus Picc., Tuba	"Polish" Trio of mvt. 4 based on material from an 1872 cantata commemorating the bicentennial of Peter the Great's birth. Dedicated to V.S. Shilovsky. First performance: Moscow on November 7/19, 1875, conducted by Nikolay Rubinstein. Published in Moscow: Jürgenson, 1877.

TABLE XV/12 (continued)

Opus	Key	Dates	Title	Movements	Instrumentation	Comments
36	F minor	1877	Symphony No. 4	1. Andante sostenuto 3/4—Moderato con anima (In movimento di Valse) (423 m.) 2. Andantino in modo di canzone 2/4 (404 m.) B-flat minor 3. Scherzo: Pizzicato ostinato 2/4 (414 m.) F major 4. Finale: Allegro con fuoco 4/4 (293 m.) F major	Grand plus Picc., Tuba, Tri., Cym., Tam-tam	Dedicated "A mon meilleur ami" [Madame von Meck]. Originally programmatic: see later to von Meck (February 17/March 1, 1878). First performance: Moscow on February 10/22, 1878, conducted by Nikolay Rubinstein. Published in Moscow: Jürgenson, 1880.
58	B minor	1885	*Manfred* Symphony	1. Lento lugubre—Moderato con moto 4/4—Andante 3/4 (338 m.) A—B minor 2. Vivace con spirito and Trio 2/4 (555 m.) B minor/D major 3. Andante con moto = Poco più animato 6/8 (282 m.) G major 4. Allegro con fuoco 4/4—Adagio ma a tempo rubato 3/4 (491 m.) B minor	Grand plus Flt./Picc., EH, Bclar., Bssn., 2 Cornets, Tuba, Cym., BD, Tam-tam, Tri., Bell, Tamb., 2 Harps	"Symphony in 4 Tableaux after the dramatic poem by Byron" 1. Manfred wanders in the Alps. 2. The Alpine Fairy appears. 3. Pastorale. 4. The subterranean palace of Arimanes. Infernal Orgy. Appearance on Manfred in the middle of the bacchanal. Evocation and appearance of the shade of Astarte. He is pardoned. Manfred's death. Dedicated to Mily Balakirev. First performance: Moscow on March 11/23, 1886, conducted by Max Edmannsdöfer. Published in Moscow: Jürgenson, 1886.
64	E minor	1888	Symphony No. 5	1. Andante 4/4—Allegro con anima 6/8 (542 m.) 2. Andante cantabile, con alcuna licenza 12/8 (184 m.) D major 3. Valse: Allegro moderato 3/4 (266 m.) A major 4. Finale: Andante maestoso 4/4—Allegro vivace ¢ (565 m.) E major	Grand plus Flt./Picc., Tuba	Dedicated to Théodore Avé-Lallement. First performance: St. Petersburg on November 5/17, 1888, conducted by the composer. Published in Moscow: Jürgenson, 1888.
—	E flat	1891–1892	Symphony [No. 7]			Unfinished. Reconstructed by Semën Bogatyrev from sketches and fragments and Mvts. 1, 2, and 4 in version for Piano Concertos (Opus 75 and 79), mvt. 3 as Scherzo-Fantasie Opus 72/10 (Moscow, 1961).
74	B minor	1893	Symphony No. 6	1. Adagio—Allegro non troppo 4/4 (354 m.) B minor—major 2. Allegro con grazia 5/4 (178 m.) D major 3. Allegro molto vivace 4/4 (12/8) (347 m.) G major 4. Finale: Adagio lamentoso 3/4 (171 m.)	Grand plus Flt./Picc., Cym., BD, Tam-tam	"Pathétique" Dedicated to Vladimir Davidov. First performance: St. Petersburg on October 16/28, 1893, conducted by the composer. Published in Moscow: Jürgenson, 1894.

SYMPHONY NO. 1 "WINTER DAYDREAMS" IN G MINOR OPUS 13

Tchaikovsky's Symphony No. 1 in G Minor Opus 13 was the composer's first major effort after his appointment in January 1866 as professor of harmony at the Moscow Conservatory. After conducting Tchaikovsky's Overture in F at the Moscow concerts of the RMS on March 4/16, 1866, Nikolay Rubinstein reportedly encouraged the young composer to try his hand at a symphony. Since his prior orchestral pieces had been single-movement works, often scored for a small orchestra, Tchaikovsky probably also felt some obligation to legitimize his Moscow appointment with a symphony. However, working in such a large and prestigious form for the first time apparently caused Pyotr Il'yich much angst that resulted in insomnia and something that approached a nervous breakdown.

Later in his lifetime, the composer acknowledged that the composition of Symphony No. 1 was the most difficult task of his career. In part, the birth pangs of the First Symphony were intensified by a searing review by César Cui[79] of his graduation cantata for soloists, chorus, and orchestra, on Schiller's *An die Freude,* a setting that immediately invited negative comparisons with the Finale of Beethoven's Ninth. Despite the state of his mental health, Tchaikovsky persevered so that by early June 1866 he was in the throes of orchestrating his sketches. A nearly finished symphony was shown to his conservatory teachers, Anton Rubinstein and Nikolay Zaremba, who were critical of his efforts, and Tchaikovsky revised his Opus 13 during the fall term. In November, A. Rubinstein and Zaremba approved new versions of the slow movement and Scherzo, and on December 10/22, 1866, the Scherzo was heard at an RMS concert in Moscow conducted by Anton's brother, Nikolay Rubinstein. The initial reception was cool, but on February 11/23, 1867, the two middle movements were heard in St. Petersburg with approbation. After further revisions, the entire symphony was first performed in Moscow, with Nikolay Rubinstein conducting, on February 3/15, 1868, and was warmly received. Nevertheless, Tchaikovsky undertook further revisions before its publication in 1875. It is this published version that is the basis for the discussion that follows.

The symphony carries the title "Winter Daydreams" and the first two movements are entitled "Reveries of a Winter Journey" and "Land of Desolation—Land of Mists." Some have questioned the legitimacy of these titles, since they reveal no obvious programmatic aspects of the music itself. But if one moves from programmaticism to characteristic styles that could be associated with the titles, one is less prone to dismissing the titles completely. Certainly, the opening passage of the first movement evokes a dream-like atmosphere with the low dynamic, minor mode, stagnant harmonic rhythm, the undulating pitches of the tonic chord in the first and second violins, the high tessitura, and the bare octaves of the melodic flute and bassoon (Example XV/18). Indeed, at times Tchaikovsky invokes the Mendelssohn of the *Fingal's Cave* or *Hebrides Overture* and of the *A Midsummer Night's Dream* music— certainly music of mists and dreams. As for the slow movement, the strings are *con sordino* throughout, a sound that evokes the funereal, which in turn is related to the desolate. In addition, the viola melody at m.46 is marked piangendo (lamenting), which also can be related to desolation. Perhaps the "Land of Mists" is related to the return of undulating figures in the violins (m.64) that are related to the opening of the first movement. While these elements certainly capture an atmosphere or character, they do not underline a narrative that makes a piece programmatic.

Concerning this movement, David Brown has written,

The relevance of the title Tchaikovsky gave to this second movement is badly compromised by the very first eight bars, for they had already done service to open the second

EXAMPLE XV/18   Tchaikovsky. Symphony No. 1/1, mm. 1–25.

subject of *The Storm,* where they had embodied Katerina's "yearnings for true happiness and love"—though it must be conceded that their character is considerably changed by now being scored for strings alone, and played adagio instead of allegro.[80]

However, it seems to this observer that nothing has been compromised, for the character of the music fits the context and the nature of the movement's title. Even if one knew *The Storm* and remembered the theme as *S* of this work, it would be no more disturbing to the listener than Mahler's reuse of thematic material in different contexts in his Fourth and Fifth Symphonies.

Since Tchaikovsky provided no hints as to his thinking behind movements three and four, one can only speculate. The content of the Scherzo is a transcription, transposed down a half step, of the same movement from the C-sharp Minor Piano Sonata Opus 80 (1865). For the Trio, Tchaikovsky composed a new waltz, no doubt under the influence of Berlioz's Ball movement from the *Symphonie fantastique*. After a brief upbeat for winds, the sound of *divisi* violins captures something of a dream-like atmosphere, which is subsequently repeated by the woodwinds. Overall, the Scherzo proper recalls the parallel movement from Mendelssohn's *A Midsummer Night's Dream*. For its type, the waltz itself is unusually reticent and subdued; it never exceeds *mezzo forte* and the melody never finds the kind of abandon associated with Berlioz or Johann Strauss Jr. This positions the waltz as part of a dream, with some distance from reality. Like Mendelssohn's Symphony No. 4/3 "Italian," the final section (m.394) combines elements from the two previous contrasting sections, while the final portion (m.422), except for the last two chords, again invokes the Scherzo in *A Midsummer Night's Dream*. Alternatively, one can merely regard the Scherzo as an intermezzo to the events of the surrounding movements.

The main clue to an interpretation of the Finale is the introductory Andante lugubre (gloomy), which quotes from the Russian folksong "The Gardens Bloomed" and makes for a transition from G minor to G major and the exposition at the Allegro maestoso ¢ (m.65). The folksong returns for *S* (m.126), the Andante lugubre returns (m.359) in the recapitulation in place of *S* and *K*, and a coda (m.415) culminates in a chorale (m.431) that begins like *S*. Here, it appears that the Finale represents the change in the season from the depression of winter to the exhilaration of spring. During the course of this transition, winter returns for an extended episode only to be overtaken with lasting force by spring.

The only other coherent cyclic force is that of tonality; Tchaikovsky does not repeat themes from one movement to the next, nor does he connect two or more movements together. The two outer movements both begin in G minor, but the Finale spends most of its time in, and ends in, the major. Tchaikovsky places the third-movement Scherzo in C minor and the slow second movement in E-flat major, i.e., the tonic's subdominant and its relative major. In addition, Tchaikovsky holds his heavy brass in reserve for the Finale to underline the transfer to the major mode. Notice that the slow movement is in second place and the Scherzo in third place; this was the norm for the German symphony of the nineteenth century, but contrary to the practices of the *kuchka* and other Russians, who often reversed this movement order.

That Tchaikovsky agonized over the composition of his First Symphony is evident from the unfolding of the opening exposition, which reveals a thorough study of the symphonic tradition, even though the composer has chosen a more introspective approach. After a four-bar introduction, Tchaikovsky lays out his two *P* themes with unusual care. *1P* (m.5) (see Example XV/18) contains the seed (m.22) for *2P* (m.40) (Example XV/19), which naturally invites their rehearing. But the composer varies each repetition by changes in the three-phrase lengths:

m.5	*1P*		*1P* (*2P* adumbration)		
	4 + 8 + 3		4 + 4 + 3 + 3 + 4 + 2		
m.40	*2P*				
	4 + 3 + 3 + 3 + 3 + 2				
m.68	*1P*	*2P*	*1P*	*2P*	trans.
	3 + 3	6 + 4	3 + 3	7 + 4	5

EXAMPLE XV/19   Tchaikovsky. Symphony No. 1/1, mm.38–49.

  This material also serves as the basis for *1T*(*2P*, m.106) and *2T*(*1P*, m.117). During the course of *P* and *T*, G minor leans toward B-flat (m.68), B major (m.84), and then slips back toward G minor for *T*, which can easily slip toward D major for *S*. *S* (m.138), though contrasting with *P*, has a similar contour. *1K* (m.190) reminds one of Mendelssohn's overture to *A Midsummer Night's Dream,* while *2K* (m.251) serves as a transition to the development. Here too, Tchaikovsky breaks with textbook form by inserting B-flat major (m.205) into a closing, whose principal key is not the relative major, but the dominant.

The development section (m.271) concentrates almost entirely on the leanest of resources: thematically *1P* and *2K* and tonally B minor and a fifth away on either side, F-sharp minor and E major. After a climax with *1P* (m.340) over a rising chromatic bass, a three-measure grand pause clears the air and prepares for the retransition (m.386), certainly one of the more arresting moments in the Allegro. Here, Tchaikovsky begins by destabilizing the meter, then introduces a potent half-step dissonance (m.407), and finally accelerates the surface as everything stabilizes for the reorchestrated recapitulation of *P* (m.432). Tchaikovsky changes the background to triplets, which accelerate to sixteenths with *1P*'s second statement (m.462). *S* (m.523) is shortened, and *1K* is excluded, while *2K* (m.562) is slightly expanded. In the coda (m.592), Professor Tchaikovsky almost reveals himself as *S* becomes the accompaniment to *2P* and then *2P* momentarily becomes the subject of a fugato (m.625), which dissipates within eighteen bars. This builds to a climax on *2T* (*1P,* m.670). The music of *1P* (m.700) and *2P* (m.709) are now reheard in their original coloring (cf. m.5), finishing a task avoided at the recapitulation; this brings the movement to a tranquil close.

Some critics have argued that Tchaikovsky was not capable of composing a symphonic movement. Because of his lyrical gifts, his thematic material has been viewed as not well suited to development; a thematic quality such as found in Beethoven's symphonies does not exist in Tchaikovsky's. However, contrary to these arguments, this first movement is both lyrically memorable and developmentally strong. In addition, it is structurally strong—even though there are weaknesses at the junctures between *T* and *S* and just before the retransition. Overall, however, the stitching seems not too obvious, and perhaps even an effective part of the design.

One may describe the Adagio as a part form. However, the manner in which Tchaikovsky treats tonality and function of some of the sections makes it a very free adaptation of academic practice (Table XV/13). Indeed, in many respects, it is more like a sonata structure with a reversed recapitulation. The opening stretch clearly consists of two themes, *1A/1P* and *2A/2P/T,* both in the tonic with the second settling on C minor supported in fine Russian fashion by an extended pedal (mm.32–44). Since this first part is left open tonally and a second key is rather well established, a sonata label seems more plausible than that of a part form even though there is no clear *S* or *K*. Its central section (mm.44–124) acts more like a sonata development than a developmental episode of a part form: it is extended to more than twice the length of the exposition; it deals with *A/P* material; and it is tightly organized in terms of tonal activity as it consists of major and minor tertian relationships on either side of the subdominant and the tonic, a pattern that derives from the exposition's tonal plan. The recapitulation (m.125) is reversed and it is unusual: *2A/2P/T* moves again to C minor before returning to E-flat for *1A/1P,* which possesses the atmosphere of a coda.

Besides its structure, the Adagio is also remarkable for its use of dynamics both locally to bring out a line in the texture and structurally to build a climax. For the former, there are the *mezzo forte* viola and flute lines (m.46) accompanied by a *piano* background or, more striking, the *fortissimo* horn line (m.125) accompanied by a *pianissimo* background. Note that the latter prepares for the climax of the entire movement (m.140), where the entire band builds to *fortissimo*. In some quarters, Tchaikovsky has been accused of excess and bombast with regard to dynamics and scoring; here, however, we have a carefully calibrated use of these elements for an unusually effective result.

As in the first movement, the professorial Tchaikovsky also emerges in the Adagio. *1P/1A* displays careful and at times beautiful part writing. At m.54, *2A/2P/T* breaks into a canon

TABLE XV/13
Tchaikovsky. Symphony No. 1/2: Structure

Adagio cantabile ma non tanto 4/4 — Pochissimo più mosso — a tempo

Exposition | **Development**

1P	2P/T		2P/T	piangendo			2P/T		trans.
1 [A]	2 [A]		B(2A)			3	2A		
p	pp		p/mf	mf	pp		p/mf		p
E-flat	E-flat	C minor	A-flat	B/C-flat			A-flat	F minor	
m.1	23	32	44	54	58		64	68	85

Pochissimo più mosso — Marcato la melodia con moto espressione

Recapitulation | **Coda**

2P/T anticipation	2P/T		2P/T				1P
B	B(2A)	3	2 [A]				1 [A]
pp	mf		ff/pp		ff climax	f>p	pp
	E-flat	G-flat	E-flat	C minor			E-flat
90	104	116	125	134	140	146	157

at the octave in the distant key of B major, which continues for only four measures. This momentary canon returns (m.90) in anticipation of *B/2A/2P*, but this time in a sequential pattern of imitation. Even during the *B/2A/2P* restatement (m.104), the initial motif is treated in imitation, but it never fulfills one's expectation for a complete canonic statement of this theme.

The Piano Sonata version of the Scherzo proper was the first of these movements to have been composed. For the orchestral version, Tchaikovsky made only a few changes: he added the four-bar introduction and extended by a couple of bars the retransition. His replacement of the original Trio by a waltz sets an important precedent for Tchaikovsky's symphonies; a waltz is also to be found in Symphonies Nos. 3/2, 4/1, 5/3, and perhaps 6/2, which has a 5/4 meter (and will be examined later).

For 1866, the shape of the Scherzo seems somewhat conservative with the exposition and the development/recapitulation enclosed by repeats. Twelve measures provide a transition from Scherzo to the Trio's waltz. Here, the stitches are quite audible, and the transition seems rather superfluous; one could just as effectively begin with the waltz (m.118) straight away. Tchaikovsky casts his waltz in a standard sonata structure whose development is notable for its increasing chromaticism before returning to the purely diatonic version (m.202) at the recapitulation. If the transition to the waltz was completely inadequate, the retransition to the Scherzo is effective and refined. Beginning with m.250, Tchaikovsky quickens the surface to sixteenths and provides a pedal. This leads to music of a more scherzo-like character (m.266), the introduction of the Scherzo's theme (m.282), a pause, a snippet of the waltz (m.287), material from the Scherzo's introduction (m.290), and the reprise (m.294), where Tchaikovsky provides additional activity and different orchestrations. A timpani solo marks the coda (m.394) while it plays the head motif of the Scherzo as the strings play material from the waltz. After an authentic cadence (mm.436–37), Tchaikovsky substitutes the chord of deception, A-flat, for the dominant in the last four bars.

Though some have heard Russian-like folk materials in the earlier movements (e.g., the slow movement's *2P*), it is not until the Finale (Table XV/14) that folk materials are quoted, rather than suggested. The treatment of this folksong "The Gardens Bloomed" again fits well into Glinka's, and the *kuchka*'s, way of treating folksong to variation by changing its surroundings. In the *minore* introduction of the Finale, the folksong (m.17) receives one of these variations (m.25), while in the *maggiore S* (m.126) there are two variations (mm.142, 160). When only the prelude to the theme returns in E minor (m.359) in the midst of the recapitulation as a substitute for *S,* the listener might very well be disappointed. It was probably Tchaikovsky's intent that expectations be delayed until the chorale (m.431), which begins like *S,* but this does not quite work as a peroration—in part, because the strings continue to play the figuration from the end of the retransition. Though this gesture was intended to enhance the climax, it seems to be in the way of the chorale's melody; at times it is above the chorale and at other times it forms a dissonance with it.

Unfortunately, this is not the only miscalculation in the Finale. In both the first and second movements, Tchaikovsky presents moments of fugato and canonic textures that never come to fruition. In the Finale, fugatos are found in *T(P,* m.90) and in the development section on *S* (m.181) and *P* (m.213). And while here they have come to fruition, these sections do not seem to totally fit their context. In the case of *T(P)*, the countersubjects seem more like something out of counterpoint exercises: scales, tetrachords, and suspensions with sequences. Additionally, *P* is built out of small repeated motives. Much the same problems affect the *S* fugato at the beginning of the development and the one based on material from *P.* Note that the latter is a five-bar subject of which the fifth measure is a diminution of the previous two-measure pairs. While fugues and like textures can be effectively used to increase the activity level, here the counterpoint seems static.

Looking at the overall shape of the movement as outlined in Table XV/14, it begins with a prelude based on the Russian folksong, a statement and variation on the song, and a postlude that parallels the prelude. All this is in the minor mode, with the dark color of the bassoons and other woodwinds in their low range, and a descending chromatic bass. An unusually long transition takes us to the exposition (m.66), which is a textbook example, except for the absence of *K.* Though less than persuasive, the development section does all the right things: it modulates, develops themes, and uses more counterpoint than the exposition. Somewhat curious is the B pedal that leads to the G major recapitulation. As we have noted, the recapitulation after *P* (m.283) and *T* (m.206) is surprisingly reformulated with an introductory reprise (m.359) in E minor, followed by a long retransition to the coda with a chorale.

One is tempted to speculate about the tradition from which this movement emanates. Haydn's Symphony No. 103/1, Beethoven's Symphony No. 5/3–4, Schubert's Symphony in C D.944/1, and Schumann's Symphony No. 3/5 all hold similarities with Tchaikovsky's Finale. One might also speculate about a North German Baroque tradition since the introduction is like a choral prelude; the main body incorporates fugal textures and artifices; and the coda includes a chorale for a peroration. In this context, one is reminded of Mendelssohn's "Reformation" Symphony. However, of this list, the only pieces we can be absolutely certain that

TABLE XV/14

Tchaikovsky. Symphony No. 1/4: Structure

Introduction / Exposition

Andante lugubre 4/4 Introduction				Allegro moderato	Allegro maestoso ¢ Exposition					
Prelude (1-O)	1-O	Var.	Postlude (1-O)		P	T(P) fugato	trans.	S(1-O)	Var. 1	Var. 2
G minor chromatic bass				G major						
m.1	17	25	34	47	66	90	124	126	142	160

Development

S fugato	P	P fugato		
F-sharp minor	E minor	G major	stretto	pedal B
181	201	213	258	263

Recapitulation

P	T(P)	trans.
G	G minor	
283	306	343

Coda

Andante lugubre 4/4 Introduction		Allegro vivo ¢ Coda			
Prelude	retrans. (cf. 1/retrans.)		Chorale(S)	P	Più moto
E minor			G		
359	371	415	431	459	467

Tchaikovsky knew were the Beethoven and Schumann symphonies. Despite its weaknesses, this Finale provides a rousing conclusion to a mostly effective symphonic work.

Though this was Tchaikovsky's First Symphony, it could hardly be characterized as an immature work. It also contains all the markers of the other six completed cycles: the lyricism of both the fast and slow movements, the use of a waltz as part of the dance movement, the sure sense of the orchestra and its resources, an ability to manipulate form in the service of content, and the happy collocation of musical structure and content with the extra-musical inferences of characteristic styles.

During Tchaikovsky's lifetime, the "Winter Daydreams" Symphony was performed only a few times. Still, the composer held a special affection for the work. On October 17/29, 1883, he wrote to the conductor and his friend Karl Albrecht, "Despite all its glaring deficiencies, I have a soft spot for it, for it is a sin of my sweet youth."[81] To his patroness Nadezhda von Meck, the composer called the symphony "immature," but that "it is essentially better and richer in content than many other more mature works."[82]

When Nikolay Rubinstein conducted the entire symphony at a RMS concert in Moscow on February 3/15, 1868, Nikolay Kashkin noted that "the symphony met with a warm public reception which even surpassed our expectations."[83] "Winter Daydreams" was not heard in St. Petersburg until October 22/November 3, 1886, almost two decades later, and the reception in the press was appropriately subdued, as represented by the following notice:

> The "Winter Daydreams" symphony by Tchaikovsky is one of his early and almost one of his first orchestral works; it was written by an extremely likeable and talented composer, twenty-one years ago (in 1865). At present, when Tchaikovsky has already introduced so many brilliant and superb compositions into the symphonic literature, his first symphony seems to us, relatively speaking, thin and weak, although one can find in it more than a few very beautiful episodes. In the sense of thematic development of motives, and their conception in general, the symphony testifies, however, about the fact that it came from the hand of a master, who, twenty years ago, already possessed all the qualities necessary for the creation of music in a purely symphonic style. Of course, there is no need to point out that Tchaikovsky in his first symphony cannot be compared to Tchaikovsky in his later works. In the first symphony—this is a beginning composer with wonderful instincts, who has much promise; in later compositions—this is a composer who is fully mature and established and who has justified brilliantly all hopes. The best part of the "Winter Daydreams" symphony is undoubtedly the first—Allegro tranquille. The Scherzo would be significantly more beautiful and likeable if its waltz-like trio were not so impoverished in its design. The second movement—Adagio cantabile, is sweet but somewhat monotonous. The last, fourth movement of the symphony is mediocre in design, but superbly developed; in particular, a masterly constructed fugato . . . stands out. In general, this symphony makes a pleasant impression; its freshness, naturalness, simplicity, and wonderful sonority win over listeners.[84]

Roughly six years separate the completion of the First and Second Symphonies, but only a few other orchestral works were composed by Tchaikovsky in the interim, namely the *Festival Overture on the Danish National Anthem* (1866), written to celebrate the marriage of the Tsarevich and Princess Dagmar of Denmark on their visit to Moscow; the symphonic fantasia *Fatum* (1868); and the famous *Romeo and Juliet* (1869), which underwent further revisions in 1870 and 1880. In fact, vocal music of all types, rather than orchestral music, was at the center of Tchaikovsky's activities at this time, including work on three operas: *The Voyevoda* (1867–1868), *Undine* (1869), and *The Oprichnik* (1870–1872). Only the last of these is completely extant; except for materials used in other works, the music for the first two operas was destroyed. However, one of these excerpted materials, the Wedding March from *Undine*, has survived as the second movement of the Second Symphony.

SYMPHONY NO. 2 "LITTLE RUSSIAN" IN C MINOR OPUS 17

Symphony No. 2 in C Minor Opus 17 has a somewhat elaborate history, as outlined below:

June 1872	Begins work on Symphony No. 2.
November 2/14, 1872	About to finish sketches.
November 15/27, 1872	Begins orchestration.
December 1872/January 1873	Plays Finale for gathering at Rimsky-Korsakov's apartment in St. Petersburg to great approval.
January 26/February 7, 1873	Premiere at 7th RMS Concert in Moscow, conducted by Nikolay Rubinstein; Tchaikovsky writes to Stasov expressing his dissatisfaction with the first three movements.
February 23/March 7, 1873	First hearing in St. Petersburg at RMS Concert, conducted by Eduard Nápravník.
March 27/April 8, 1873	Repeated at 10th RMS Concert in Moscow.
1874	Publication by Bessel in St. Petersburg of four-hand piano arrangement.
November 1879	Requests Bessel to return full score.
December 3/15, 1879	Writes to Madame von Meck of intent to revise "immature, mediocre symphony" while in Rome.
January 4/16, 1880	Letter to Taneyev about revisions to first, Scherzo, and last movements. Writes of difficulty in dealing with Bessel about publication of symphony in either version.
January 11/23, 1880	Writes to publisher Jürgenson about how he plans to prevent Bessel from publishing symphony.
1880	Bessel publishes second version in score, parts, and four-hand arrangement.
January 31/February 12, 1881	New version heard at 10th RMS Concert in Moscow, K. K. Zike conducting.
November 21/December 3, 1881	New version heard at RMS Concert in St. Petersburg, conducted by Zike.

The symphony came to be known as the "Little Russian," not through any efforts of the composer, but from his colleague at the Moscow Conservatory and critic Nikolay Kashkin. "Little Russian" refers to the Tsarist name for the Ukraine where the folksongs quoted seem to have originated.

The revisions undertaken by Tchaikovsky substantially affected all of the original movements. The introduction and coda to the opening movement were left intact, but the central Allegro was completely rewritten. According to Tchaikovsky, "the movement is now short, concise, and not difficult. If anything deserves the epithet *impossible,* it was the first movement in its original form. My God, how different and noisy and disconnected and obscure it was!"[85] The second movement was rescored. As for the Scherzo, according to Abraham, the composer "altered the character of the scherzo, while preserving the original harmonic basis and scoring." Tchaikovsky referred to it as "radically revised."[86] Concerning the Finale, the composer commented, "I've made an enormous cut: directly after the long pedal before the recapitulation of the first theme after the development, I've gone straight into the second [theme]."[87]

Despite Tchaikovsky's obvious preference for the 1880 revisions, Nikolay Kashkin and Tchaikovsky's student and successor at the Moscow Conservatory, Sergey Taneyev, continued to prefer the original version of 1872. As Taneyev wrote to Tchaikovsky's brother Modest on December 15/27, 1898, after the composer's death,

> My God, what a difference! How good the old *Allegro* is, despite some imperfections—rambling modulations, which could be dispensed with, a beautiful first theme, a melodious, graceful sound. How weak by comparison with this is the new *Allegro*! A poor first theme consisting of a three-note motive many times repeated, a still less interesting second theme [i.e. bar 102] worked in as countermelody to a snatch of the original first theme, a little bit of the original *Allegro* artificially stuck into the new one as a pretext for keeping fragments of the original development section: all this is manufactured, in no definite mood, laboured. It seems to me that in some future concert you ought to let people hear the real Second Symphony, in its original form. . . . The only things lacking are the parts for bass drum and cymbals in the finale. But it would be very easy to put them in from the printed score—the finale, except for one big cut, remains in its original form. When I see you I will play both versions and you will probably agree with me about the superiority of the first.[88]

This first version of the work was preserved in parts in the Library of the Moscow Conservatory. It was not published in full score until 1954, when it appeared as part of the Tchaikovsky Complete Works. In our discussion, we will concentrate on the 1880 version, since, despite reservations by Taneyev and Kashkin, it was the version preferred by the composer.

It has been said that of all Tchaikovsky's works, the Second Symphony was the most saturated in national materials and in techniques associated with Glinka and the *kuchka*. Quotations from identified folksongs are found in three of the movements: the frame to the first movement uses a Ukrainian version of "Down by the Mother Volga," which is also dealt with in the development section; the second movement uses "Spin, O My Spinner" in the episode; and in the Finale "The Crane" is the principal material. As for its compositional techniques, in contrast to the First Symphony where variations with a theme subjected to a changing environment are not widely used, in the Second Symphony this favored practice of the *kuchka* is extensively employed whenever folk materials are expanded upon. Whether this change in approach was a result of Tchaikovsky's interaction with Balakirev in 1869–1870 concerning *Romeo and Juliet* seems unlikely since this overture-fantasy is perhaps the one work of Tchaikovsky without any connection to *kuchka* ideals or any form of musical nationalism.

It is the combination of folk music and *kuchka* techniques that provides coherence to the cycle; again the composer lays out the cycle without any connected movements and without reusing themes in subsequent movements. Only tonality remains as the central means of coherence. Here the approach is often reminiscent of the First Symphony: a minor-mode first movement, a major-mode Finale, and the middle two movements explore a minor key and its relative major. However, this time *tutti* scoring is used in both first and last movements with the heavy brass left silent in the March and Scherzo. Unlike Symphony No. 1, there is no true slow movement in Symphony No. 2.

Tchaikovsky's first movement begins with a big introduction on the same scale as that of Beethoven's Symphony No. 7/1 and Schubert's "Great" C Major Symphony D.944/1, and by this time period (1872), he certainly knew both of these works. The slow introduction to Schubert's D.944/1 seems closest to Tchaikovsky's No. 2 with its synthesis of sonata form with variations.[89] Like Schubert, Tchaikovsky begins with the solo horn unaccompanied, followed by variations (mm.9, 16), a developmental area (m.22) that also incorporates another variation (m.28), and a recapitulation (m.48). Additionally, both composers incorporate the introductory material into the Allegro, though Tchaikovsky restricts his to the development section, and both bring back the introductory theme at the movement's end—Schubert in a triumphal transformation, Tchaikovsky more in its original state. Though the Schubert model seems more than plausible, the musical result is vintage Tchaikovsky: the melancholy theme from Russian folk music, the nature of the variations—concentrating more on the background instead of changing the melody—and the textures themselves with pizzicato accompaniments (m.9), agitated syncopations (m.16), and swirls of thirty-second notes (mm.23, 42). At the end (m.350), the horn plays its theme to the pizzicato accompaniment of the first variation, which concludes with a not fully closed cadence.

If the introduction could be seen as a *kuchka* approach to variation, the main body of the movement could only be viewed as a central European sonata form. From the introduction, the horns hold through the dominant (cf. Beethoven Piano Concerto No. 5/3) into the beginning of the Allegro for seven bars. This undermines the beginning of the exposition, which is not secure until m.61 (Example XV/20), when the strings play a motivically structured theme. *P* expands by a *fortspinnung*-like process that requires *T* to find the relative major of C minor for *S* (m.87). *1S* is simply built on a lyrical idea and its diminution (m.92). *2S* (m.102) adds a striking lyric outburst as a counterpoint to *1S*. A transition (m.112) develops *1Sx* to a *tutti* climax. *K* (m.138), based on *P*, now is placed a half-bar later, and *S* reappears in diminution (m.146). Such an expository plan is almost Classical in its layout and in its adaptation of themes to different functions. *K* runs into the development (m.150) articulated by an unprepared transfer to the relative major's subdominant. Like taking a page from the development of Symphony No. 1/4, Tchaikovsky introduces a fugato (m.160) that uses elements from *1S*—in both its original state and in diminution—and the introduction. Again, the fugato is not particularly effective: the voices are not clearly established, *1Sx* is tossed from one instrument to another and is used in its diminutive and original form. The introductory theme is heard in stretto and the development proceeds to *K* (m.191) in C minor, which is juxtaposed with A-flat (m.195), then creeps upward chromatically to F-flat/E (m.202), heads toward the tonic, and reaches the movement's climax with *P* (m.215) played *fortissimo, tutti,* and held back in tempo. This, however, is not the recapitulatory resolution, as a dominant pedal undergirds this moment, a parallel to the first measures of the Allegro (mm.54–60). Now the tempo is recovered, the dominant pedal ceases, and the strings play *P* in its original setting for the recapitulation (m.221), which closely follows the exposition. Tchaikovsky's coda (m.304) proceeds as if it were another development, builds to a climax (m.340), quiets to *pianissimo,* and ends with the solo horn's restatement of "Down by the Mother Volga."

The Andantino marziale is the Wedding March from Act III of Tchaikovsky's aborted opera *Undine,* which he worked on from January to July 1869. Whether Tchaikovsky literally lifted the March from the opera, transposed it to fit the C minor cycle, or even revised it in other ways has not been documented. Such a movement belongs to a tradition that goes back

EXAMPLE XV/20   Tchaikovsky. Symphony No. 2/1, mm.54–66.

to the second movements of Beethoven's Third and Seventh Symphonies, extends to Tchaikovsky's Sixth Symphony, and includes movements by Mendelssohn, Spohr, Raff, Mahler, Rimsky-Korsakov, and certainly others. That this march lacks the joyful or celebratory affect of other wedding Marches perhaps foreshadows the ill fate of the character Undine.

Tchaikovsky's second movement takes the large three-part form of March–Trio–March upon which is superimposed a *crescendo* in the reprise of the March (m.109) and a *diminuendo* with thematic disintegration in the coda (m.157). Variation principles operate within the March, and on a smaller level in the Trio, as shown in Table XV/15. One should not be surprised by these small-dimension environmental variations in the Trio since they are on the Russian folksong "Spin, O My Spinner." The March from *Undine* thus helps integrate the cycle, as folk materials are also used in the first and last movements.

To compare this movement to the slow movement of the First Symphony, as David Brown does, seems inappropriate, since they belong to totally different types.[90] The first symphony's Adagio is a carefully wrought lyric-dramatic piece, whereas this March, though skillfully put together, lacks the depth of its predecessor; it was not intended to have the same affect. David Brown also argues that the central section of the March does not have the level of imaginative treatment that Glinka would have provided. But this argument ignores the fact that Tchaikovsky chose to use a movement from his portfolio, rather than a newly composed one. During his 1879–1880 revisions, Tchaikovsky had the opportunity to replace this movement, but chose to keep it; thus, it must have more than adequately provided what the composer felt the cycle needed.

In the original version, Tchaikovsky's Scherzo was a more daring piece with its *col legno* bowings. This sort of experimentation highlights the fascination Russian composers had with the Scherzo in general, often composing Scherzo movements as pieces independent of a cycle, with metric and other peculiarities. The 1880 version of the "Little Russian" Symphony's Scherzo uses 3/8 for the Scherzo proper and 2/8 for its Trio (3/8 ♩.=2/8 ♪). The change

---

TABLE XV/15
Tchaikovsky. Symphony No. 2/2: Structure

March					Trio					
[A] a	b	a¹		trans.	[B]					
pp	*p*				*p–mf*		*pp*	*mf f*	*p*	*cresc.* *f dim.*
		Var. 1			Theme	Var. 1	Var. 2	Var. 3	Var. 4	Var. 5
E-flat	G	E-flat			B-flat					
m.1	19	43		51	53	61	69	77	85	97

March				Coda	
[A] a²	b	a¹		[A] +	[B]
p cresc. ff mf	*p*	*p*		*pp*	*ppp*
Var. 2		Var. 1			
E-flat	G	E-flat			
109	125	149		157	

to duple meter in the Trio brings to mind the parallel movement in Robert Schumann's Symphony No. 1/3 "Spring." As for the Scherzo itself, its ancestors could be Berlioz's "Queen Mab" Scherzo and Borodin's Symphony No. 1/2. Since in comparison to "Queen Mab," Tchaikovsky's Scherzo has too much of this world in its timbres and sonorities, perhaps Borodin's Scherzo is a better possibility.

The coda sounds the 3/8 and 2/8 meters simultaneously, a trick probably taken from Berlioz, known in Russia for his *Harold in Italy,* although Rimsky-Korsakov also employed a combination of different meters in his Scherzo for Symphony No. 3. David Brown astutely notes the metric irregularities that occur in the gatherings of individual measures within Tchaikovsky's Scherzo proper:

> The scherzo of the First Quartet had shown Tchaikovsky avoiding this pitfall by exploiting simple metrical switches within regular phrase lengths to vitalise the rhythmic life, and the process is carried further in the Second Symphony's scherzo, where a far wider variety of metrical irregularities provide constant foreground dislocations against the regular background of three- or six-bar phrases.[91]

The Scherzo form is traditional: a sonata form enclosed in two sets of repeats. The Trio is almost as traditionally ordered, but more of a *kuchka* variation due to the small measures and the subsequent brevity of each unit:

a	a¹	b	b¹	a	a¹	a²
	ctrpt.		ctrpt.		ctrpt.	dialogue/retrans.
E-flat		mod.		E-flat	F-sharp →	G as V/C
155	179	203	215	227	239	257

The Scherzos to the First and Second Symphonies are both fine examples of their genre. Whereas the First Symphony Scherzo has more than a hint of Mendelssohn, the Second Symphony seems less Mendelssohnian, with a stronger linkage to emerging Russian practices and, of course, Berlioz and Schumann.

Unlike Symphony No. 1/4, the Finale to Symphony No. 2 more than takes up the function of its task. Here is a rousing piece without any of the miscalculations observed in the previous Finale. It is also a movement that elicited the enthusiasm of both the *kuchka* as well as less nationalistic factions: its *P* theme comes from a well-known Ukrainian song, "The Crane," and it combines *kuchka* variations with European sonata form. In addition, *S* is often inappropriately described as having a rumba rhythm; however, whether heard in Havana, New York, Paris, Moscow, or St. Petersburg, it has the same captivating effect.

The opening slow introduction might remind some of the "Great Gate of Kiev" from Musorgsky's *Pictures at an Exhibition,* except this mighty Finale to *Pictures* (1874) had not yet been composed; perhaps, instead, Musorgsky was influenced by Tchaikovsky's "Little Russian" Finale (Example XV/21). A precedent for these mighty chords in C major would be Beethoven's acoustical-testing hammerstrokes at the start of *The Consecration of the House Overture* Opus 124.[92] The Allegro vivo presents an unusual combination of variation, rondo, and sonata principles. Indeed, one is almost certain when hearing this piece for the first time that it is a theme with variations, then a rondo with varied refrains, and then a sonata form as the exposition unfolds.

Something of this can be seen in Table XV/16. Within *P, Pb* is almost obliterated by the statement and eight variations of *Pa.* However, if *Pb* is taken into consideration, one might

TABLE XV/16
Tchaikovsky. Symphony No. 2/4: Structure

Moderato assai — Introduction | Allegro Vivo — Exposition

Theme	P anticipated	Pa	a	a	b	a	b	a	a	a	a	1T(P) a	2T	3T
Variation			Var. 1	Var. 2		Var. 3		Var. 4	Var. 5	Var. 6	Var. 7	Var. 8		
Key	C major	C										E/G	(A)	C
m.	1	25	33	41	49	57	65	73	81	89	97	106	114	126

Theme	4T	a	4T		S	a	a	a	a	1K(P)a	a	a
Variation		Var. 9	Var. 10				Var. 1	Var. 2	ext.	Var. 11	Var. 12	Var. 13
Key	C	whole-tone ostinato	C	whole-tone ostinato	A-flat					A-flat/F		
m.	134	142	180	188	204	212	220	228	236	254	262	270

Development

Theme	2K(P ext.) a	a ext.	Pa	S	Pa	S	Pa / S	S	Pa / S
Variation	Var. 14	Var. 15							
Key			D-flat	D	E-flat	B	D / G	C	E
m.	278	294	326	342	358	374	398	406	414

TABLE XV/16 (continued)

Recapitulation

S	*Pa* S rhy.	*Pa* S rhy.	ext.	*Pa* S	*Pa*	*Pa*	*Pa*	*Pa*	S ⌐a a⌐a
D	G	A		A		dom. pedal ⟶			C · Var. 1
422	430	438		462	470	478	494	514	530

⌐a a	ext.	*1K(P)a* Var. 11	*a* Var. 12	*a* Var. 13	*2K(P* ext.) *a* Var. 14	*a* Var. 15	new ext.
Var. 2		C/A minor			C	C	C
546		564	572	580	588	604	612

Presto Coda *Pa*/1K	*Pa*	Cadences
653	693	

349

EXAMPLE XV/21   Tchaikovsky. Symphony No. 2/4, mm.1–24.

be more inclined to hear *P* as a rondo refrain. *1T* (m.106) is essentially another *Pa* variation, except that it now tonally tends toward E minor/G major, while *2T* (m.114) seems to be heading to A minor, but *3T* (m.126) heads back to C major and another variation of *Pa* (m.134). *4T* (m.142) also, after a whole-tone-scale ostinato, heads back to C major and another variation (m.180). With the return of *4T* (m.188) the whole-tone tetrachord (C–B-flat–A-flat–G-Flat) becomes a vehicle for introducing *S;* its key is A-flat and its melody

EXAMPLE XV/21   (*continued*)

begins with the first three pitches of the tetrachord breaking from the whole-tone pattern with its fourth pitch, G-natural. *S* (m.204) also is treated to variations, but at the dimension of sixteen rather than eight measures, which further contributes to its more tranquil surface. At m.254, *K*(*P*) resumes variations on *Pa*, now in the tonal neighborhood of A-flat.

For the development section (m.326), Tchaikovsky juxtaposes *Pa* and *S*—activity and relaxation—and also combines *P* and *S* contrapuntally, a more effective move than the attempt to write a fugato on the expository motives in the first movement. The key plan seems effective on a small level with groups of three tonal areas strongly connected by half steps (mm.326–358) and descending fifths (mm.398–406). As expected in a late-eighteenth/early-nineteenth-century development, Tchaikovsky comes to rest on the submediant (m.462), which deflects to a dominant pedal (m.478) that does not resolve to *P*—as Tchaikovsky did in the original version—but to *S* (m.514). Given the shape of the exposition with some sixteen statements of *Pa* in both *P* and *K*, this was a brilliant solution, particularly since the development toward its end heightened the level of activity and stated *Pa* on the tonic with a dominant pedal (m.494). *K* (m.564) presents five varied statements of *Pa* that, except for key, duplicate those of the exposition. In the passage prior to m.612 and at the start of the coda (m.653) the relative tonal purity and the stability found in *S* and *K* is sullied. The remaining task is to firmly establish C major and bring the movement to a certain conclusion, which Tchaikovsky does by making the melodic materials completely diatonic and moving from altered to pure chords. While this strategy is a simple one, Tchaikovsky plays it out on a small scale within a part of the Finale rather than across a large swath of the movement.

Though one may consider this Finale weak from a musical-intellectual viewpoint, and therefore dismiss the movement and perhaps the entire symphony as not equal to the rigor found in Brahms and other German symphonists, the Finale and the symphony as a whole are marked by an energy that few other composers could even begin to muster. Much of this stems from Tchaikovsky's ability to manipulate rhythm in all of its manifestations—phrase, surface, timbral, and harmonic rhythms—to build a completely effective edifice. If the Finale of the First Symphony left something to be desired, the Finale of the Second Symphony may very well be the composer's most successful symphonic conclusion with the exception of the Finale of the Sixth Symphony. Certainly, the Finale to No. 3 is not as effective, and those to Nos. 4 and 5 some critics have found overplayed: the end of the Finale for the Fourth Symphony is disturbingly frenetic, while the Finale for the Fifth has been criticized as lacking the right triumphal transformation of its recurring cyclic theme. In contrast, Symphony No. 2/4 does not overplay its hand.

The reception of the "Little Russian" Symphony was almost always favorable from both audiences and critics. What follows are comments by Herman Laroche, one of the most important and knowledgeable Russian critics of the late nineteenth century, from the first performance of the 1872–1873 version in Moscow:

> I see Mr. Tchaikovsky's Second Symphony as a new and indeed gigantic step forward. It is a long time since I encountered a work with so powerful a thematic development of ideas, such well motivated and artistically considered contrasts. I was struck by these very qualities in the first Allegro, with its pathetic and sorrowful character. In this Allegro three basic ideas—the main and secondary sections of the Allegro itself and the theme borrowed from the slow introduction—are grouped together, alternate, combine by means of counterpoint—first two ideas and finally all three ideas together—with a freedom and nobility, with perpetual harmony and with an inspired brimfulness of life such as show that the artist has reached a level of art rare in our day and age. Were I not

afraid to take a sacred name in vain, I would say that in the strength and elegance with which Mr Tchaikovsky plays with his themes and makes them serve his own purposes there is something reminiscent of Mozart, something which brings to mind the Symphony in B-flat minor [G Minor] or the big Symphony in C major [K551, the "Jupiter"] by the greatest of composers. Naturally, my comparison holds only for the mastery of counterpoint, a field in which Mozart shone. As far as content is concerned, there cannot fail to be a gulf between the harmonious reconciliation and the ideal objectivity which emanate from every page of Mozart, and the wretched disillusionment of the nineteenth century, an expression of which we find in Mr. Tchaikovsky's Allegro, among other places. But in the works of our gifted compatriot disillusionment does not turn into antipathetic morbidity; for this he has a too sensitive and keen symphony with the wholesome and majestic simplicity of our folksong.

Tchaikovsky has turned to Russian songs in many of his compositions, working on and varying them with a skilled touch. The Scherzo à la russe for piano, the Andante of his String Quartet, and many numbers from the opera *The Voyevoda* contain good evidence not only of Mr. Tchaikovsky's subtle and refined understanding of the spirit of these songs, but also of his talent for variation form. Both these qualities can be observed in the new symphony, but in a much higher state of evolution. The introduction to the symphony is based on a beautiful, peaceful, and flowing melody in the style of our drawn-out [*protyazhnïye*] folksongs. The composer has borrowed a folksong directly for the theme of the finale, this time one of an animated and lively nature. The theme of the introduction is developed by the composer in a series of magnificent variations, some of which are simply startling in the beauty of their orchestration; but far more remarkable and developed are the themes of the finale. As I have already pointed out, it leaves one with an impression of gaiety and even joviality. What is more, with its dance-like rhythm the theme belongs to the same category as *Kamarinskaya* and even the main themes of the finales of Beethoven's Seventh and Eighth Symphonies. The first phases of Tchiakovsky's development of the theme do not destroy its light and unruly character, but in the middle section of the finale the theme suddenly takes on a new and grand meaning, Repeated in various keys in the upper registers of the string instruments, the theme is accompanied here by powerful exclamations from trumpets and trombones in alternation, coming in with long dissonances. No description could adequately convey the harmonic beauty and stupendous tragedy of this section. At this point it is not so much the skilled and unexpected harmonic combination, which in any case is remarkable, but rather the very contrast between the tragic strength and the carefree joy of the first pages of the finale which has such an effect on the listener. Thus sometimes in life brief Bacchic rejoicing gives way to the blows of a menacing, inexorable fate. . . .

Despite the outstanding beauties of the remaining movements of the symphony, in my opinion the bold and stately finale decidedly outshines them all. This point is of particular interest since, in the majority of symphonies, the richest content is concentrated in the first movement (of course there are notable exceptions to this, such as Beethoven's Fifth and Eighth Symphonies and Mozart's big Symphony in C major [K.551]), and the finale is weaker; thus, as a result, the progression normally considered necessary for artistic works is not present. The absence of this progression can be observed in highly celebrated compositions which are regarded, and rightly so, as models. This can be explained by the fact that we treat movements of symphonies as separate entities. It might also, perhaps, be partly due to the fact that after the powerful, stupendous impressions made by the first movement or movements of a symphony the listener needs some moral relaxation.

However, I must confess that the continual growth of ideas and effects right up to the very end of the symphony seems to be more worthy of a monumental work. I am glad to see in Mr. Tchaikovsky's piece the preponderance of the finale over the excellent first movement.[93]

Performances of Tchaikovsky's Symphony No. 2 are much less common than his more favored Fourth, Fifth, and Sixth Symphonies. However, this is a piece that deserves to be in the repertoire of orchestras not only in Russia, but also in Europe, England, and North America. Its materials are attractive, its energy is invigorating, and its control of form—generally thought to be one of Tchaikovsky's weaknesses—is thoroughly convincing.

The time span between beginning the first version of the Second Symphony (1872) and the Third Symphony (1875) was three years. During this time Tchaikovsky was again occupied with vocal and chamber music, as well as an opera *Vakula the Smith,* and perhaps the beginnings of *Swan Lake.* As for orchestral works, the interim between the two symphonies was fallow: a Serenade for Nikolay Rubinstein on his nameday (1872) and *The Tempest,* another symphonic fantasy after a Shakespeare play. Instead, his most significant composition during this time period was his First Piano Concerto, which was Tchaikovsky's first encounter with the concerto genre and potentially temperamental dedicatees.

SYMPHONY NO. 3 "POLISH" IN D MAJOR OPUS 29

Symphony No. 3 in D Major Opus 29 is the least documented of the Tchaikovsky symphonies—in part because it caused little difficulty in its composition, but also because it was not revisited for revisions. Its history is outlined below:

June 5/17, 1875	Begins sketching at estate of Vladimir Shilovsky and finishes by end of June. Moves on to estate of N.D. Kondratiev in Nizy, Ukraine.
July 8/20, 1875	Begins scoring.
July 9/21, 1875	Finishes scoring Finale (fifth mvt.).
July 13/25, 1875	Finishes scoring fourth mvt. Moves on to Verboka, residence of brother-in-law.
July 26/August 7, 1875	Finishes scoring first mvt.
July 28/August 9, 1875	Finishes scoring second mvt.
July 31/August 12, 1875	Finishes scoring third mvt.
August 14/26, 1875	Writes to Taneyev that he has finished the symphony.
November 7/19, 1875	Premiere at First Concert of RMS—Moscow, Nikolay Rubinstein conducting.
January 24/February 5, 1876	Performed at RMS Concert—St. Petersburg, Eduard Nápravník conducting.

The Third Symphony came to be known as the "Polish" because of its Polacca Finale. This title has no authentic authorization; it originated from a performance at London's Crystal Palace and was probably called such by Sir August Manns, the music director of the Palace's orchestra.

There are two larger aspects that distinguish the Third Symphony from all of Tchaikovsky's others: it is the only one in a major key and it is the only one to expand the four-movement layout to five. As for the latter, three precedents with which Tchaikovsky was familiar have been suggested as models: Beethoven's Symphony No. 6 "Pastoral," Berlioz's *Symphonie fantastique,* and Schumann's Symphony No. 3 "Rhenish." However, it seems to this observer that in movement layout, these works are only superficially similar to each other and to the Tchaikovsky Third. As can be seen in Table XV/17, Symphony No. 3 has a symmetrical layout: a central Andante is surrounded by two dance movements, which are framed by two fast movements at the beginning and end. Such a plan seems more reminiscent of Mozart's five-movement divertimento cycles with two Minuet movements surrounding a central slow movement. Tchaikovsky was taken with Mozart's music—witness his later *Mozartiana Suite* Opus 61—and thus Mozart seems a more viable conceptual model than the commonly cited Beethoven, Berlioz, and Schumann cycles.

Tchaikovsky's cycle is notable for its characteristic music, perhaps here more defined than in any of his other symphonic cycles. The first movement pits a dark funeral march as an introduction against an Allegro brillante. The Alla tedesca second movement is a very Tchaikovskian Ländler, more grazioso than most German dances. For the Andante elegiaco, Tchaikovsky draws on the central movement of the *Symphonie fantastique,* while the Scherzo—at least in its outer portions—has the élan of Mendelssohn supported by its minor mode. The Polacca was a dance not infrequently found at the end of cyclic compositions particularly in concertos and the like during the first half of the nineteenth century. Certainly, these materials provide a variety of styles; however, they do not add up to a convincing larger unit. Such coherence is again the province of tonality as the first, third, and fifth movements are anchored to D major and minor. The second movement is tonally odd in that it begins in C minor, a distant key to D major/minor, but it ends in B-flat. Its central section is in G minor, B-flat's relative minor, which in turn has a subdominant relationship to D. The fourth movement is directly related to D, since B minor is its close relative and D major is the key of the central section.

The Introduzione, apart from the marcia funebre tempo and character, is laid out in a manner similar to the introduction to Symphony No. 2/1: an eight-bar theme is followed by three variations, then an accelerando in which motives from the theme are developed and lead directly into the Allegro brillante. Unlike Symphony No. 2/1, Symphony No. 3/1 is not built from a cantabile folksong, but rather from a series of motives separated by rests over a pedal. Each variation (mm.9, 17, 25) fills in the motivic interstices with different material as the theme again remains unadulterated. At the poco più mosso (m.34), a single motive from the theme is developed until the Allegro. P (m.80) is a D major march of triumph, a foil to the marcia funebre. $2P$ (m.96) acts almost as if it were T with its motivic play and sequences. This leads not to S, but to a repetition of $1P$ (m.127), which within six measures (mm.137–43) transports us to B minor and $1S$ (m.143); this theme melodically recalls P from the first movement of Schumann's Piano Concerto, but its rhythmic accompaniment (♩♪♪♩♩♩♩) seems mildly Slavic. $2S$ (m.162) is similar to $1S$ of Symphony No. 2 and leads directly to $1K$ (m.174) and $2K$ (m.198) as a third expository key, A Major, is established.

Again, Tchaikovsky becomes irritatingly professorial in the development section (m.208) by applying more contrapuntal artifices to his themes than in Symphonies Nos. 1/4 and 2/1 (see Table XV/18). Here, he exploits his themes with imitation, counterpoint with two different themes, stretto, diminution, augmentation, and double diminution. Overall, the writing of contrapuntal textures is more successful than his earlier attempts in part because Tchaikovsky at no point leads us to expect a full fugal exposition, and the tonal sequence seems more cogent. Where the development becomes awkward is at what should be its climactic point (m.289), a moment coming just before the recapitulation where $1Py$ is subjected simultaneously to diminution, double diminution, and imitation in a blatantly artificial manner. In m.292, it becomes clear that Tchaikovsky was accelerating $1Py$ to sixteenths in

TABLE XV/17
Tchaikovsky. Symphony No. 3: Cyclic Plan

Introduzione e Allegro Moderato assai: Tempo di marcia funebre 4/4—Allegro brillante 4/4	Alla Tedesca: Allegro moderato e semplice	Andante elegiaco 3/4	Scherzo: Allegro vivo 2/4	Finale: Allegro con fuoco (tempo di polacca) 3/4
	Trio: L'istesso tempo		Trio: L'istesso tempo 2/4	
Sonata Form	A—B—A	A—B—A—B—A	A—B—A	A—B—A—C—A—Coda
D Minor—D Major	C Minor G Minor C Minor → B-flat Major B-flat Major	D Minor	B Minor D Major B Minor	D Major

TABLE XV/18
Tchaikovsky. Symphony No. 3/1: Development Section

Development 2K imitation	1P imitation	2K+1Px imitation	1S+1P counterpoint	1Py imitation stretto	1Py	1S+1P	1Py	1Py
m.208	212	220	225	229	233	239	243	247

1Py diminution imitation	1Py normal imitation	1P normal augmentation counter subject	1Py stretto augmentation	1P normal augmentation	1Px normal augmentation stretto	1Py normal diminution imitation
251	255	260	270	275	281	285

1Py diminution double diminution imitation	2P retrans.	*Recapitulation* 1P
289	292	308

357

order to form a bridge to *2P* for the retransition. Unfortunately, the passage does not meet expectations, for in mm.289–91 one becomes distracted by an overabundance of activity.

The recapitulation (m.308) is only minimally reorganized: the repetition of *1P* after *2P* (m.324) is eliminated and goes directly to *1S* (m.342) transposed down a fifth to E minor, setting in motion a destination of D major for *K*. However, Tchaikovsky does not take the easiest route; he sets up a lengthy B-flat pedal that slips down to A for *1K*. Finally, Tchaikovsky exploits the scale of *P* for the coda (m.421), using it for an old-fashioned Italian overture *crescendo* that reaches a Tchaikovskian frenzy and substitutes the flattened sixth for the dominant in the cadences (m.450f).

Tchaikovsky remarked in a letter to Rimsky-Korsakov on November 12/24, 1875, that Symphony No. 3 "doesn't present any particularly successful ideas—but technically it's a step forward."[94] This remark seems particularly pointed at the first movement. *1P* and *2P* serve their functions quite well, though their affect could be more potent; *S* is too reminiscent of Schumann, and *K* also lacks distinction. In the development, one's attention is entirely drawn to the techniques of thematic manipulation; perhaps this time the composer has overplayed his hand to the point of miscalculating the climax. However, in contrast to Symphonies Nos. 1 and 2, the execution is more successful.

Several commentators find the central movements the more attractive ones. The Alla tedesca's most striking trait, already mentioned, is that it begins in one key and concludes in another. Both melancholy and expressively restricted, at no point does the waltz reach a state of abandon. Tchaikovsky ups the surface activity from eighths to triplets for the *B* section, which has a touch of a Mendelssohnian Scherzo. As so many examples, when *A* resumes (m.154), the triplets of *B* continue through the return. However, unlike other movements that continue the more active surface throughout the return, Tchaikovsky resumes the opening values after eight bars (mm.154–61). In the coda (m.250), Tchaikovsky goes up and down through the woodwinds ending with quiet solos for clarinet and then, one of Tchaikovsky's favored instruments, the bassoon. Edward Garden believes the movement is based on Glinka's *Valse-Fantasie in B Minor* for piano that is also known from an 1856 orchestration. One might also think of this movement as a precursor to Symphony No. 5/3: their character, expression, and execution hold much in common.

Andante elegiaco heads the central slow piece; it is perhaps the composer's most affective symphonic slow movement to date. Cast in a Schubertian rondo,

the opening refrain itself acts like the beginning of a *scena* featuring solo winds. After an introduction scored for woodwinds alone, a more *parlando* section (*b*) for solo bassoon and horn accompanied by pizzicato strings leads to an orchestral interlude (*c*) and a return to the bassoon/horn dialogue. *B* (m.35) is dominated by string sound with woodwind support (Example XV/22). Notice the flutes at the very bottom of their register, which adds a patina to the low range of the molto espressivo violin melody. At the end of this section, *Aa* and *Ac* return followed by a full return of *Aa* with an extension leading to *B*'s reprise now embellished with an ostinato triplet rhythm from *Ab*. Here in this *B* (m.104) Tchaikovsky discovers one

EXAMPLE XV/22   Tchaikovsky. Symphony No. 3/3, mm.35–40.

of his hallmark lyrical textures: the melody dominates in one choir as the other choir pulsates in the background; then the roles are reversed (m.114). Typically, after the melodic climax is reached, the accompaniment calms and *A* returns, here with *c* (m.148) and closing with *b* (m.171) again colored by bassoon and horn.

Commentators such as David Brown hear something of Berlioz's *Symphonie fantastique*'s central slow movement in this piece.[95] The opening is reminiscent of Berlioz's melodic beginning, while the bassoon and horn dialogue recalls the English horn's conversation with a distant oboe. If a reinterpretation of Berlioz's opening was indeed Tchaikovsky's intent, he has demonstrated an unusual transmission of one composer's ideas to another. Otherwise, Tchaikovsky appears to go his own way. Though his opening implies the potential for a narrative, he does not oblige us except with his special lyrical gifts.

Thus far, no movement in this symphony displays the orchestra as an ensemble of virtuosos; this lacuna is filled by the Scherzo as figures of sixteenth notes are rapidly exchanged among different instruments. Though no instrument is heard for more than a measure of Allegro vivo 2/4, when all of the parts are together, Tchaikovsky has given us a *perpetuum mobile* with a kaleidoscope of timbres. It is not until m.44 that the timbral rhythm slows only to resume its pace after sixteen measures, and then slow again (m.69). It does not, however, resume its most colorful exchanges; the dialogue is now between wind and string choirs. At m.109, the composer introduces a new disposition: the exchange of primary figuration among the strings, while woodwinds sustain the second quarter, and the trombone renders something that sounds like a chorale. Only when the trombone concludes its melody do the kaleidoscopic colors in sixteenths return. This is another display of Tchaikovsky's striking mastery of the orchestra prior to his last three symphonies.

The Trio is based on material from Tchaikovsky's 1872 occasional cantata for the opening of the Polytechnic Exhibition in Moscow, which also celebrated the bicentennial of Peter the Great's birth. It is built almost entirely from a woodwind/string dialogue over a D pedal in the horns that is sustained for more than a hundred measures. After a wash of D-major color in the strings (m.237), the horns intrude with F-sharp, which when left to itself becomes the dominant of B minor for the Scherzo's reprise. The coda (m.396) recapitulates *in nuce* material from both Trio and Scherzo, the former now with an F-sharp dominant pedal for its eventual resolution to B.

Balakirev admired this movement and considered it to be among Tchaikovsky's best efforts; Edward Garden called it a gem; and this writer is inclined to agree. It is therefore doubly unfortunate that it is surrounded in its cycle by pieces that are less than the composer's very best efforts. Since the Third Symphony is rarely played today, the masterly Scherzo is virtually lost to the modern audience. However, given the deft nature of the piece and its bald virtuosity, it is the perfect first orchestral encore, because it asks for less than the *tutti* band and emphasizes dynamic restraint.

The thoroughly successful Finale for even the original version of the Second Symphony seems not to have been a breakthrough, as the issue of an effective symphonic Finale again raises its head in Symphony No. 3/5. The problem is not that this Finale is a vigorous triple-meter dance movement in rondo form, as this is a viable option for a Finale during the last quarter of the nineteenth century. In this case, though, Tchaikovsky seems unable to leave well enough alone. Specifically, in the coda he feels it necessary to introduce a chorale (m.255) that is a quasi-transformation of the first episode (m.66). Indeed, the first time the episode is heard, one almost knows that it will be repeated in *tutti fortissimo* triumphal garb before the movement can conclude. With this ending, however, too much is made of a not-so-worthy thematic statement. Nevertheless, the coda does function as a part of the movement's larger tonal resolution by presenting the first episode unequivocally in the tonic key. Besides the solemnity of the chorale transformation, Tchaikovsky still includes a fugato (m.178) based on the refrain as a developmental episode during its third and penultimate presentation. After the critical success of the Second Symphony, one might assume that such a validation could have been omitted by an established composer.

Except for the fugato and chorale, the rondo form is a textbook case. Even the key scheme uses the most closely related tonalities:

A	*T*	*B*	*A*	*C*	*A*		Coda: *B*		*A*	
a b a					*a b* Fugato *a*		Chorale		*a a*	
D		A	D	B minor	D		D			
1	35	66	111	118	158	178 223	255		274	302

At first hearing, Tchaikovsky seems to use the Classical model for the length of the refrains: the first return (m.111) only recapitulates the opening phrase. However, the second restatement (m.158), where some trimming might also be in order, is nearly three times the length of the first refrain. The refrain is heard yet one more time (m.274) in the coda at its strongest dynamic.

After the opening refrain, *T* (m.35) seems to be breaking into a fugato, but this merely becomes imitative motivic play based on *Aa* that reduces down to *circulatio* figures (mm.50, 58). In this context of surface sixteenths, one might expect this acceleration to continue into *B,* but instead the chorale is accompanied by triplets; they provide a certain gravitas to this theme played in octaves by the woodwinds and horns. At the same time the descending bass line provides a forward direction. After *Aa* (m.111), *C* (m.118), which often takes a developmental stance, is somewhat modulatory, but does not have much in the line of motivic play. An essentially new theme is presented as follows:

a	*a*	*a¹*	*a²*	*a*	retrans.
B minor		D	F-sharp minor → A → A-sharp	B minor	Bass: B – B-flat – A
118	124	130	136	143	149

For a rondo movement, this second episode is essentially expository right down to its basically rounded binary layout: written-out repeat of *a* altered at the end, a quasi-developmental section in terms of tonal activity based on *a* (m.130ff), and a recapitulation (m.143) with a retransition back to the refrain (m.158).

The third refrain (m.158) with its embedded fugato requires comment. At its beginning, it fulfills the requirements of return: theme and tonic key. However, unlike the two previous refrains that are both closed, this refrain extends the movement with an open structure by adding the fugato (m.178), and the *a* that follows (m.223) is undergirded by a dominant pedal, which prepares for the coda with the triumphant chorale of *B* (m.255) and the final statement of *Aa* (m.274).

That both performances in Moscow and St. Petersburg occurred soon after its completion, and the score and parts were published with some dispatch, was indicative of Tchaikovsky's growing stature in Russian musical life. The reception by the audiences was full of warmth. The reviews, while positive overall, were more discriminating, such as found in Laroche's typically detailed and informed critique on the pages of the newspaper *Golos:*

> Tchaikovsky goes further and further ahead. In his new symphony the art of form and contrapuntal development stands above [that achieved] in his earlier compositions; in particular the first allegro in its middle section is executed with superb imitation, energy, and impetuosity which does not allow the listener's interest to slacken. However, the contrapuntal style predominates in the entire work, although, on the other hand, in it there is not that clumsiness, that excessive richness of dense harmonies with which the previous C-minor symphony sinned. One may only reproach the newest work of Mr. Tchaikovsky in abuse of the pedal: for example the entire slow introduction of the first movement—a colossal pedal on *a;* the allegro scarcely has begun and we once again enter an enormous pedal on *e* and so on. But, having made this proviso, I should repeat that all the same the new score of Mr. Tchaikovsky displays a deep and refined art. The grouping of ideas, the succession of contrasting motives one after the other displays an unusually adroit hand and elegant taste. To this one must add the melodic charm of the ideas themselves. In this regard only the finale (the fifth movement) suffers from a certain aridity that in significant measure is concealed by a bold and brilliant technique. In each of the remaining movements you will find a melody, the lush and intimate beauty of which is fully worthy of the name of the composer. I note in particular the minor key episode (oboe) in the first movement and the second (major) key theme [of the] *andante.*

Speaking generally, with regard to the strength and significance of its content, the diverse richness of form, its noble style, imprinted with an independent, individual creativity, and the rare perfection of technique, the symphony of Mr. Tchaikovsky is one of the major musical events of the last ten years not only [in Russia] but in the whole of Europe, and if it were to be performed in one of the musical centers of Germany then it would establish this Russian artist on equal level with the most illustrious symphonic composers of our day.[96]

Nikolay Solov'ev, writing in *Novoe vremia,* held similarly mixed views on the new work:

Last Saturday, in the fifth and, unfortunately, last of its symphonic concerts, the Russian Musical Society familiarized the public with the new, third symphony of Tchaikovsky. . . . The symphony . . . was received extremely cordially and the composer was called back [to the stage] several times. This sympathy is easily understandable; Tchaikovsky, both in his previous compositions and in this symphony rouses [the public] with a lively rhythmic system, attractive melodies, and the brilliance and subtlety of his orchestration. In comparison with the last orchestra work by Tchaikovsky that was performed last winter in one of the concerts of the R[ussian] M[usical] Society, music to Shakespeare's the Tempest, the third symphony is less interesting; it does not reveal new aspects of Tchaikovsky's talent and even suffers from routine, which has unfortunately arisen quickly in Tchaikovsky although he is still a young composer, an original routine, but routine nonetheless. Despite this, the new symphony by Tchaikovsky was heard with pleasure, thanks to his dexterity which is apparent in his use of form, and in thematic development and orchestration; in general, one can see in this symphony a master who fully commands musical technique.[97]

When it was first heard in New York on February 8, 1879, the critic for the *New York Times* was even more restrained in his praise for the work:

Tschaikowsky's Symphony in D No. 3 was the most noticeable feature of the programme. The Philharmonic Society produced it at this concert for the first time in the United States, and it is certainly worthy of the consideration of all thoughtful lovers of music. It is written in five movements, and it is an elaborate and novel composition, which it is hardly fair to characterize at a first hearing. The second movement is beautifully written, and was performed with the utmost finish of an orchestra of accomplished musicians. The movement is peculiar, the instrumentation full of original merit, and it was played on both occasions with the traditional skill of the Philharmonic Society. Of the other movements of the symphony, the allegro con fuoco was the most marked feature. It sounds like Wagner, and, without reflection on the composer, may be said to be in the nature of plagiarism in the finale. The symphony is of decided merit, and cannot fail to command the respect and attention of all who hear it. The difficulties it presents seem almost insurmountable to the average listener.[98]

However Tchaikovsky interpreted the reviews, they did not discourage him from pursuing another symphony and other orchestral works over the following two years. Specifically, *Swan Lake* was completed; a *Sérénade mélancolique* (1875) and *Valse-scherzo* (1877), both for violin and orchestra, served as studies for the 1878 Violin Concerto; the *Variations on a Rococo Theme for Cello and Orchestra* (1876) revealed the neo-Classical side of the composer; *Francesca da Rimini* (1977) was a successor to *Romeo and Juliet* and *The Tempest;* and the *Slavonic March* (1876) underlined the composer's national side. Additionally, there was a

String Quartet (1876) and the set of piano pieces titled *The Seasons* (1876). In other words, during this time period Tchaikovsky concentrated on orchestral music that reveals many sides of his musical personality, although today he is often unfairly characterized as one-dimensional: dramatically lyrical.

SYMPHONY NO. 4 IN F MINOR OPUS 36

Though the time span between the completion of the Third and Fourth Symphonies was only slightly greater than two years, this was a period of *Sturm und Drang* in Tchaikovsky's life and a time of crucial change in his symphonic style. The Fourth Symphony was a work of special importance, for together with his First Piano Concerto and *Romeo and Juliet,* it would establish Tchaikovsky as a composer whose reputation was, without dispute, international.

With regard to his personal life, three situations are of particular importance: 1) the beginning of his correspondence with Nadezhda von Meck in December 1876, who in the following October offered him a yearly stipend of 6,000 rubles; 2) his ill-fated marriage in July 1877 to Antonina Ivanovna Milyukova—Tchaikovsky, a homosexual, found any sort of meaningful relationship with this woman impossible; and 3) the growing grind of his duties at the Moscow Conservatory, from which he resigned in late 1878. The latter two items have been viewed as primary causes for sending Tchaikovsky, a depressive neurotic, into a near breakdown. That is, although today we might view depression at the root of Tchaikovsky's mental health problems and correctable with proper treatment, the traditional view has been that the circumstances of the time caused his collapse.

The interactions between Tchaikovsky's personal life and his music during this period are difficult to deny. According to the composer, his work on the opera based on Pushkin's *Eugene Onegin* was central in his failure to reject the infatuated Antonina Ivanovna. With regard to his Symphony No. 4 in F Minor Opus 36 one also cannot ignore his explanations of the narrative. This work's program is a personal portrait; to dismiss the program is to lessen one's understanding of the work itself, and certainly Tchaikovsky did not fabricate an explanation to respond to Madame von Meck's query. In his letter of February 17/March 1, 1878, he began his explanation of the program with a lengthy discussion of the relationship between the act of composition and extra-musical matters:

> You ask if in composing this symphony I had a special programme in view. To such questions regarding my symphonic works I generally answer: nothing of the kind. In reality it is very difficult to answer this question. How [to] interpret those vague feelings which pass through one during the composition of an instrumental work, without reference to any definite subject? It is a purely lyrical process. A kind of musical shriving of the soul, in which there is an encrustation of material which flows forth again in notes, just as the lyrical poet pours himself out in verse. The difference consists in the fact that music possesses far richer means of expression, and is a more subtle medium in which to translate the thousand shifting moments in the mood of a soul. Generally speaking, the germ of a future composition comes suddenly and unexpectedly. If the soil is ready—that is to say, if the disposition for work is there—it takes root with extraordinary force and rapidity, shoots up through the earth, puts forth branches, leaves, and, finally, blossoms. I cannot define the creative process in any other way than by this simile. The great difficulty is that the germ must appear at a favourable moment, the rest goes of itself. It would be vain to try to put into words that immeasurable sense of bliss which comes over me [when] directly a new idea awakens in me and begins to assume a definite form. I forget

everything and behave like a madman. Everything within me starts pulsing and quivering; hardly have I begun the sketch ere one thought follows another. In the midst of this magic process it frequently happens that some external interruption wakes me from my somnambulistic state: a ring at the bell, the entrance of my servant, the striking of the clock, reminding me that it is time to leave off. Dreadful, indeed, are such interruptions. Sometimes they break the thread of inspiration for a considerable time, so that I have to seek it again—often in vain. In such cases cool headwork and technical knowledge have to come to my aid. Even in the works of the greatest master we find such moments, when the organic sequence fails and a skilful join has to be made, so that the parts appear as a completely welded whole. But it cannot be avoided. If that condition of mind and soul, which we call *inspiration,* lasted long without interruption, no artist could survive it. The strings would break and the instrument be shattered into fragments. It is already a great thing if the main ideas and general outline of a work come without any racking of brains, as the result of that supernatural and inexplicable force we call inspiration.[99]

Table XV/19 provides the complete program for Symphony No. 4 that the composer sent to von Meck. Though this program provides a central unifying theme to the symphony, it should also be noted that this is Tchaikovsky's first symphony in which a musical theme blatantly recurs in more than one movement: the opening fanfare not only delineates structural points in the first movement, it also interrupts the festivities of the Finale. Like a Wagnerian opera, the material of the fanfare thus becomes a leitmotif. Here it is Fate, a concept derived, according to the composer, from Beethoven's Symphony No. 5/1.

Perhaps the most significant aspect of this leitmotif is that the fanfare is in the minor mode. Prior to the invention of valves for the brass, minor-mode fanfares were an impossibility. In terms of the history of the symphony, the only other instance of a prominent minor-mode fanfare is later found in Mahler's Symphony No. 5/1, which begins with a marcia funebre. Prior to the invention of valves, the brass managed the funereal affect by using mutes. That Tchaikovsky's fanfare is without mutes, *minore,* and *fortissimo,* no doubt startled or, at the least, left his audience in a state of bewilderment. Its reappearance in the Finale as a foreign element was more baffling, particularly if one was not aware of the movement's programmatic aspects. Others have reported hearing the opening themes of each movement as interrelated, but this seems more coincidental than significant: descending from tonic to dominant or a perfect fourth is hardly a distinctive gesture, much less a unifying one.

The other striking peculiarity of the Fourth Symphony is the cycle's proportions and weight. It is the first movement that is the weightiest and longest piece. For example, the timings for the 1959 recording by Pierre Monteux with the Boston Symphony Orchestra are as follows:

1.	2.	3.	4.
17:27	8:10	5:13	8:40

Notice that the first movement is longer than the second and fourth movements together, and these are not unusually short pieces. It is almost as if the real business of the symphony occurs in the first movement; that is, except for the fanfare's intrusion in the Finale, the remaining pieces are divertissements.

This interpretation is to some degree confirmed by the key scheme of the cycle: only the

---

TABLE XV/19
Tchaikovsky. Symphony No. 4: Program

The introduction is the germ, the leading idea of the whole work.

This is fate, that inevitable force which checks our aspirations towards happiness ere they reach the goal, which watches jealously lest our peace and bliss should be complete and cloudless—a force which, like the sword of Damocles, hangs perpetually over our heads and is always embittering the soul. This force is inescapable and invincible. There is no other course but to submit and inwardly lament.

The sense of hopeless despair grows stronger and more poignant. Is it not better to turn from reality and lose ourselves in dreams?

O joy! A sweet and tender dream enfolds me. A bright and serene presence leads me on.

How fair! How remotely now is heard the first theme of the Allegro! Deeper and deeper the soul is sunk in dreams. All that was dark and joyless is forgotten. Here is happiness!
It is but a dream, Fate awakens us roughly.

So all in life is but a continual alternation between grim truth and fleeting dreams of happiness. There is no haven. The waves drive us hither and thither, until the sea engulfs us. This is, approximately, the programme of the first movement.

  The second movement expresses another phase of suffering. Now it is the melancholy which steals over us when at evening we sit indoors alone, weary of work, while the book we have picked up for relaxation slips unheeded from our fingers. A long procession of old memories goes by. How sad to think how much us already *past and gone*! And yet these recollections of youth are sweet. We regret the past, although we have neither courage nor desire to start a new life. We are rather weary of existence. We would fain rest awhile and look back, recalling many things. There are moments when young blood pulsed warm through our veins and life gave all we asked. There were also moments of sorrow, irreparable loss. All this has receded so far into the past. How sad, yet sweet to lose ourselves therein!

  In the third movement no definite feelings find expression. Here we have only capricious arabesques, intangible forms, which come into a man's head when he has been drinking wine and his nerves are rather excited. His mood is neither joyful nor sad. He thinks of nothing in particular. His fancy is free to follow its own flight, and it designs the strangest patterns. Suddenly memory calls up the picture of a tipsy peasant and a street song. From afar come the sounds of a military band. These are the kind of confused images which pass through our brains as we fall asleep. They have no connection with actuality, but are simply wild, strange, and bizarre.

  The fourth movement. If you can find no reasons for happiness in yourself, look at others. Go to the people. See how they can enjoy life and give themselves up entirely to festivity. A rustic holiday is depicted. Hardly have we had time to forget ourselves in the spectacle of other people's pleasure, when indefatigable Fate reminds us once more of its presence. Others pay no heed to us. They do not spare us a glance, nor stop to observe that we are lonely and sad. How merry, how glad they all are! All their feelings are so inconsequent, so simple. And will you still say that all the world is immersed in sorrow? Happiness does exist, simple and unspoilt. Be glad in others' gladness. This makes life possible.

Source : Tchaikovsky/LIFE & LETTERS

---

first movement remains in F minor. Otherwise, the canzona of the second movement is in B-flat minor, but with a central section in F major; the third movement Scherzo has a section in F-sharp minor, but otherwise remains in the major (F and D-flat); and the Finale, except for Fate's intrusion, remains primarily in the major mode. Furthermore, none of the principal keys touched on within the first movement play a vital role in the succeeding pieces. Thus, the key scheme actually somewhat segregates the first movement from the remainder of the cycle.

  Though Symphony No. 3/2 begins in one key and ends in another, Tchaikovsky's earlier tonal excursions are relatively mild compared to the idiosyncratic key scheme that dominates the first movement of Symphony No. 4 (Table XV/20). Here, with a few possible

TABLE XV/20

Tchaikovsky. Symphony No. 4/I: Structure

Section / Tempo	Label	Key	Dynamic	m.
Introduction — Andante sostenuto 3/4	Fanfare/Motto	F minor	ff	m.1
Exposition — Moderato con anima 9/8	1P	F minor	ff	28
	2P/T		p cresc. ff	53
	1P	(A minor)		70
	1P	F minor	ff	92
	T		mf dolce	104
Moderato assai, quasi Andante	1S	A-flat minor		116
	1S / 2S			122
	K(S) anticipated			128
[Development] — Ben sostenuto / Il tempo precedente	Fanfare/Motto — 1K (S+P)	B/C-flat	pp cresc.	134
	2K		fff	161
	2K			169
	trans.			189
	(B)		fff	193
Development Part 1	1N (1P)	B-A-G	p cresc.	201
	1P	C		218
	1N	F		224
	1P	F		231
Part 2	2N (P)	descending bass		237
Part 3	Fanfare/Motto — 1N	C	fff	253
		D-flat		263
retrans.	1N			273
Recapitulation — Moderato assai, quasi Andante	1P	D	fff	284
	1S / 2S	D	pp cresc.	295
Ben sostenuto il tempo precedente	1K (S+P) Fanfare/Motto	F major	fff	313
			fff	355
Coda — Molto più mosso	(D-flat pedal)		p	365
	‖: :‖		p cresc. ff	381
Più mosso. Allegro vivo 3/4	1P	F minor	fff	402
	Cadences			412

reinterpretations, the key rises in a series of minor thirds: *P* (m.28) in F minor, *S* (m.116) in A-flat minor, *K* (m.134) in B/C-flat, then the modulatory development, *P* (m.284) in D minor for the recapitulation, and the return of *K* (m.313) in F minor. The recapitulation (m.284) in Beethovenian fashion begins at a strong dynamic level and *tutti*, unlike its initial statement scored for *piano* strings; this more extreme recapitulatory dynamic and *tutti* scoring in part compensates for its non-tonic tonality. As seen in this passage, dynamics function structurally throughout the movement. Most characteristic is the *piano-crescendo-fortissimo* or *fortississimo* sequence; such swells dominate *P, S,* and *K,* as well as the development and coda. In addition, each function is underlined by its own tempo.

Some may wish to hear the recapitulation as not beginning in D minor with *P* (m.284). Since *P* eventually returns in F minor (m.402), some may instead see an extended development and a recapitulation that begins with *K* (m.313), followed by the fanfare/motto (m.355) and the coda (m.365) with its repeated buildup to the *fortissimo* tonic *P* return (m.402). However, if one adopts the latter view, the result is a recapitulation of the Berliozian type in a reversed order. Rather, to this writer, the recapitulation is convincingly articulated in D, even more so than *1P* in F minor (m.231), which occurs in the middle of the development.

One may also view such a disposition of resources as counter to Tchaikovsky's desire to deal with his structural fault lines by concealing the transitions or, as he would say, "the stitching." To a large degree, the transitions, or lack of them, are compensated for by a dominating musical style, the waltz: *P, S,* and *K* are all waltzes in one form or another even though the characteristic accompaniment ($\flat$ ♪ ♪) is never present. Instead, Tchaikovsky concentrates on characteristic rhythms in the melody in much the same way as Ravel was to do some forty-three years later for *La Valse.* At the same time, Tchaikovsky's accompaniments counter the implications of the melody: in *P* (m.28) the characteristic accompaniment is misplaced in the measure, then other non-waltz accompaniments are used, and the misplaced waltz background returns at the end (m.104) for *T. S* (m.116) uses the characteristic accompaniment, but here the second beat, certainly more important than the third, is missing. For *K* (m.134), it is almost as if Tchaikovsky is reviewing his thematic material as *P* and *S* are juxtaposed. *2K* (m.169), a heroic theme for the horns, is not beholden to the waltz even though its background continues with the rhythm of *P.* This moment reminds one of Berlioz's *Symphonie fantastique's* ball scene, as the waltz material recedes into the background and the *idée fixe* comes to dominate in the episode.

Tchaikovsky organizes his development in three stages. After the fanfare interruption, the first part (m.201) concentrates on new material derived from both the fanfare and *P* as well as direct *1P* quotations, which Tchaikovsky sets out in five-, six-, and even seven-measure groups. Part 2 uses new material (*2N*) again derived from *P,* which gains its sense of movement from a combination of anacrustic melodic gestures and a descending bass that extends over sixteen measures. In Part 3, the fanfare enters first in C (m.253) and then in D for the recapitulation of *1P* (m.284).

One of the most skillful passages is that of the coda (m.365), where Tchaikovsky reveals his genius for musical movement. Here, he begins with a new idea in the woodwinds as the strings quietly play the rhythm of *P.* The potential for motion resides in the D-flat pedal, which after nine measures begins to move downward to F in four-measure units, returns to D-flat, and moves downward, again to set up an ostinato for the Molto più mosso in two-bar units. The ostinato begins to disintegrate just before the passage is repeated and leads to *P* in a climactic statement where all the energy gradually built up from the beginning of the coda dissipates. This descending bass has its genesis in the development section where a descending bass is introduced against the rhythm of *P.* The implications of this passage are only fully realized near the end of the movement.

The first movement of the Fourth was a breakthrough within Tchaikovsky's symphonic output. In this opening movement the composer bypassed some of the artificialities that the professorial composer previously thought had to be included in a legitimate symphony: counterpoint, fugato textures, and chorale transformations. This is not to say that this movement does not display contrapuntal passages, but they are so well integrated that one does not notice them as separate entities. Additionally, Tchaikovsky creates a unique approach to the tonal outline for sonata form: for the first time he uses a motto theme as a structural and dramatic entity. Tchaikovsky accused himself of composing weak transitions and padding. In this movement, transitions are minimally used as the themes are joined by their characteristic similarities. Despite its length, there also seems to be not a bar that could be removed. Though this is his first symphonic movement to be associated with a program that contributed to an understanding of its musical content, it is also his first movement whose own musical integrity is unassailable.

Although the first movement has virtually no *kuchka* characteristics, the second movement, marked "in modo di canzona," returns to *kuchka* variations, but within a context of traditional musical part forms. Compared to the Finale of Symphony No. 2, the structure of Symphony No. 4/2 remains closer to a traditional form, in this case a ternary structure. The canzona *A* (Example XV/23) is cast in two bar forms (*a a b*); this allows for one thematic statement and three variations in which *a* remains unadulterated. Each statement of *Aa* is assigned to different instruments, and Tchaikovsky begins with the simplest of textures: solo oboe with strumming strings. The second hearing (*Aa¹*) is given to the cellos with the winds providing sustained support. *Ab* (m.42) has something of a processional character; it adumbrates the rather different march of *B. Aa²* (m.77) is assigned to the bassoon and viola as the violins and cellos toss sixteenth-note figures among themselves, while *Aa³* (m.85) gives the melody to violins and violas as a solo flute and clarinet supply the sixteenth-note counterpoint. The march of *Ab* returns (m.98) and provides a transition to *B.* This is certainly not a weak transition as one march-like passage flows into the next (*B*), and the anticipation of *B* (m.118) seems to be a natural metamorphosis of *Ab.* If *A* is an introspective, intimate, and quiet song, *B* builds to an impassioned Tchaikovskian climax underlined by dynamics, increasing forces, higher tessitura, and effective counterpoints in this somewhat learned march. Then the dynamics decrease, the instrumentation is reduced, the tessitura lowered, and the counterpoints brushed aside in preparation for the canzona's return. *Aa⁴* (m.199) assigns the unadulterated melody to the first violins with pizzicato accompaniment and pointillistic colors added with figures in the solo woodwinds for a continuous sixteen-measure statement. *Ab* is abbreviated, and for the coda (m.334) is combined with *Aa* fragments exchanged among the woodwinds and strings. The bassoon takes up *Aa* (m.374) in its entirety and then horns and woodwinds imitate tolling bells amongst fragments from *Aa* (Example XV/24). The ending recalls Berlioz's slow movement from *Harold in Italy,* where this effect is more potently executed.

The relationship of program and music is again rather explicit. The canzona of *Aa* and the impassioned march of *Ab* represent "melancholy" and a "long procession of old memories." *B* elicits the "moments when young blood pulsed warm through our veins and life gave all we asked." The final section, *A*'s reprise, where the theme is broken into fragments, turns "melancholy" into "sorrow and loss." The tolling of bells (m.292) seems an appropriate musical conclusion to Tchaikovsky's description.

The relationship of program to music is more transparent in the third movement

EXAMPLE XV/23   Tchaikovsky. Symphony No. 4/2, mm.1–9.

Scherzo: Pizzicato Ostinato. As Tchaikovsky writes, "no definite feelings find expression." Instead, the protagonist goes on an excursion through an episode of stream of consciousness, which brings forth three images: tipsy peasants, a street song, and a military band. The first is captured through pizzicato strings and off-beat rhythmic figures that are capable of temporarily destroying the duple meter; the second is sung by a windband of nine players with all kinds of arabesques; and the third is a brass band with timpani playing a clipped march. The retransition (m.185) back to the opening (m.218) mixes material and styles from all three

EXAMPLE XV/24   Tchaikovsky. Symphony No. 4/2, mm.390–404.

sections, after which the pizzicato section resumes, then the mixtures of styles and timbres return, and the movement comes to a quiet close.

Particular notice should be taken of the key plan. Remembering that the first movement's tonal order consisted of a series of minor thirds for that tragic utterance, the third movement uses all major keys, a major third on either side of the tonic. This movement is, in a sense, the tonal and affective opposite of the first movement. Here, too, the keys are color associated: F major for the pizzicato strings, A major for the woodwinds, and D-flat/C-sharp major for the brass. Indeed, in the last section of the Scherzo colors, keys, and themes at times become confused as the woodwinds play the pizzicato theme in F major, the strings answer in D-flat/C-sharp, and later the strings and woodwinds are in F, but now the brass answer in D-flat/C-sharp before the movement closes in F (Example XV/25).

Such a piece in 1877 must have been, in the true meaning of the word, unique. The stringing together of three dances for a Scherzo was already done by Beethoven in Symphony No. 6/3, but the concept of using blocks of timbres with different instrumental choirs was very special. Even after more than a century, the movement still possesses a certain magic that captures an audience in hushed silence as the strings strum their last *pianissimo* notes. In many performances, the *tutti fortissimo* of the Finale immediately follows, intruding on the quiet conclusion.

Tchaikovsky underlines the extra-musical aspects of the Scherzo as explicated in his program by the use of characteristic styles; the same is true of the Finale, which depicts a festival with our protagonist finding himself outside the circle of celebration. To depict the turnaround in the mood of the outside world versus the mood of the protagonist, Tchaikovsky uses the major mode, adds cymbals, bass drum, and triangle to the percussion, calls for a fast tempo that becomes faster, and floods the surface with sixteenth notes. In addition, Tchaikovsky incorporates a Russian folk song "In the Field There Stood a Birch Tree." Its text and music were first published in a collection of Russian folksongs in 1806 brought together by Nikolay L'vov and Johann Pratsch. The song was both well known to the Russian populace at large and to composers of art music; Balakirev, Fomin, Glinka, Grechaninov, and Khandoshkin each used it in instrumental or vocal works.[100] As in the first movement, the fanfare/motto reappears (m.199) and functions as a structural interruption. It also appears in a somewhat disguised fashion in *Ak;* in m.53 a *minore* motif from the fanfare/motto infects the celebratory music (see also m.140). Even in the raptures of celebration, our protagonist cannot escape fate.

Claims for the form of the movement have included variation, sonata form, and rondo. Variation practice certainly plays a rich role in the unfolding of this Finale (see Table XV/21). One could argue that *Aa* is varied upon repetition, in that *Aa¹* and *a²* have accelerations in their background surface rhythm from whole note, to eighths notes, to triplets. And because of the long-range ramifications, it becomes a variation whose process is structurally significant. A more localized use of the *kuchka* variation occurs in *B* and *C(B)* with a total of four variations (mm.68, 76, 84, 157) and perhaps more if one counts this material's appearance as *Ab* (mm.9, 268). Additionally, at the end of *C, Ba* is treated to developmental tactics (m.173).

Hans Keller has posited that the Finale is a sonata form. Since his approach is idiosyncratic, we quote his description and add measure numbers in brackets:

The ternary structures of the middle movements are more immediately comprehensible, though no less inventive and characteristic. But the structure of the finale is less simple than it has seemed to all commentators I have come across. In the textbooks, that is to

EXAMPLE XV/25 Tchaikovsky. Symphony No. 4/3, mm.395–414.

TABLE XV/21

Tchaikovsky. Symphony No. 4/4: Structure

Allegro Con fuoco

[A]	a	a	b	a¹	c	k	[B] (Ab)	a	a¹	a²	a³	trans. (Ab)	[A]	a¹	a¹	c	k	[C]	(B)a	a⁴	trans./ext.
							Theme	Var. 1	Var. 2	Var. 3										Var. 4	
	F			A minor C major			B-flat minor					G-flat mod.		F					D minor mod.		
m.1	5		9	30	38	47	60	68	76	84		92		119	123	127	136		149	157	173

Andante 3/4

Tempo I 4/4

[Fanfare/Motto]	[A] c¹		a²	c	b	Coda
	trans.					
F minor	F major C pedal					F major
199	223		249	257	268	277

373

say, the movement is described as "a set of free variations" upon a Russian folksong, *In the fields there stood a birch-tree*. In reality, it is not a variation movement at all, but another of Tchaikovsky's intriguing sonata structures. As in the first movement, a decisive contrasting stage—this time the thematic second subject itself—is anticipated [m.9] by the middle section of the preceding stage—here the first subject: after a mere eight bars of the first subject in the tonic major, which has been the key of the scherzo, Tchaikovsky jumps upon us with the folksong in A minor [m.9] which, after the first subject has been resumed, turns into the second subject [m.60]. It is a tune which confines itself to the first five notes of the diatonic scale, like the "Joy" theme from Beethoven's Ninth: one was chosen, the other composed as the simplest possible thematic basis. At the second-subject stage proper, it is treated as an *ostinato* climax in B flat (the subdominant) minor, the key of the slow movement; and in the recapitulation it returns, modified, in D minor [m.149], the tonic's relative minor—as did the thematic recapitulation of the first movement. The symphony's motto/theme finally comes back [m.199] between the end of the recapitulation and the coda [m.223] as, again, it did in the opening movement. This is indeed an ideal spot for such a free insertion: in the background, there hovers the idea of the cadenza which, in the first movement of a classical concerto, unfolds precisely at this formal juncture.[101]

Keller rightly would like to hear m.60 as *S,* but he does not notice the closed *A/P* section, which is more characteristic of a rondo refrain. Keller also does not account for the return of *A/P* (m.119), though this could be dismissed as a false and partial repeat of the exposition. His desire to place the recapitulation at m.149 with the music of *B/S* in D minor is a misguided effort to unify the tonal functions between the first movement and Finale, since the first movement does have an arguable recapitulation in this key. His observation about the conclusion and the return of the fanfare/motto is insightful, though its return after being absent in the second and third movements and for most of the Finale is meant to be disruptive on a scale not encountered with the entrance of a Classical concerto cadenza.

The most accurate way of describing this movement is certainly from the view of a Classical rondo form: it has a closed refrain (*A*); the first episode (*B*) has contrasting material with *kuchka* variations; the refrain returns in the tonic and again is closed; and the second episode (*C*) begins in the relative minor with a further variation, but then becomes developmental as often happens in the Classical rondo. After the dramatic interruption of the motto and a long preparation with a dominant pedal, *Aa* returns as the refrain followed by the frenetic coda (m.277). The main peculiarity is the appearance of the episode's main material (*B*) within the opening refrain (*Ab*), but this is compensated for by its absence in the refrain's first return and its relocation to the end of the refrain's final statement. In the latter, its function becomes ambiguous: is it a part of the refrain or the episode?

It appears that in this Finale, Tchaikovsky was trying to recapture something of the success of Symphony No. 2/4, which featured another folksong, "The Crane." In the earlier example, the *kuchka* variations were buried into a sonata form, and at times the variation aspects seemed to overwhelm the sonata structure. In Symphony No. 4/4, the variations are subsumed to the rondo structure as an embellishment. Seemingly the Finale's only flaw, apart from its lack of comparability to the first movement, is one of Tchaikovsky's central deficiencies: the rhetoric of closure is exaggerated.

The Fourth Symphony is a rather remarkable work for its individuality, particularly if compared to the bland Symphony No. 3. In his latest symphony, Tchaikovsky was able to coalesce several tendencies of the earlier works and bring to bear some practices not previously adopted. With Symphony No. 3, Tchaikovsky learned that he could not create a symphony with neutral thematic material that was easily adaptable to thematic and tonal development. Such an act might further his technical arsenal, but Tchaikovsky was not a symphonist in the mold of Beethoven, like Brahms and Bruckner; his *forte* was the lyrical expanse. To remove this from his symphonic vocabulary was to obliterate his greatest strength. Nevertheless, in Symphony No. 4, Tchaikovsky combined both lyricism and dramatic developments in the first and last movements, composed a cantabile of irresistible appeal in the slow movement, and provided a panoply of keys, colors, and characteristic styles in the Scherzo. While commentators have, with great effort, found melodies derived from Bizet's *Carmen*, Wagner's *Ring* Cycle, and even Delibes's *Sylvia*[102]—a work Tchaikovsky could not have been influenced by while working on the Fourth Symphony—in the end his music does not sound like Bizet or Wagner, but only like Tchaikovsky. Additionally, here a motto theme, a programmatic explanation, and a Russian folksong were brought together in one large musical canvas. Though his orchestra was essentially the same as that for Symphony No. 3, again there are elements of virtuoso display, the juxtaposition of instrumental families, and an expanded dynamic range by combining strong dynamics with powerful orchestral sonorities. Though musical form was not considered one of Tchaikovsky's strengths, here the structures are at once traditional, original, and effective.

Nikolay Rubinstein conducted the premiere in Moscow at the RMS concert on February 10/22, 1878. Tchaikovsky was in Florence at the time and his patron and dedicatee of the Fourth Symphony, Madame von Meck, had attended the premiere and wired the composer a message. On February 12/24, 1878, Tchaikovsky wrote this response to his patron:

> Early yesterday came your telegram, dear friend. It gave me inexpressible pleasure. I was more than anxious to know how you liked the Symphony. Probably you would have given me some friendly sign of your sympathy, even if you had not cared much about it. From the warm tone of your telegram, however, I see that you are satisfied, on the whole, with the work which was written for you. In my heart of hearts I feel sure it is the best thing I have done so far. It seems rather strange that not one of my friends in Moscow has thought it worthwhile to give me any news on the Symphony, although I sent off the score nearly six weeks ago. At the same time as your telegram I received one signed by Rubinstein and all the others. But it only stated the fact that the work had been very well performed. Not a word as to its merits; perhaps that is intended to be understood. Thank you for your news of the success of "my favorite child," and the cordial words of your telegram. My thoughts were in the concert-room. I calculated the moment when the opening phrase would be heard, and endeavoured, by following every detail, to realize the effect of my music upon the public. The first movement (the most complicated, but also the best) is probably far too long, and would not be completely understood at the first hearing. The other movements are simple. . . .[103]

In fact, Nikolay Rubinstein's performance left something to be desired; it needed more rehearsal, livelier tempos, and a better appreciation for its effective orchestral writing. Even though today the Tchaikovsky Fourth practically plays itself in the hands of a skilled conductor and professional orchestra, in 1878 this was a new and difficult work to prepare, which required more than a couple of rehearsals. Eduard Nápravník conducted the first hearing at St. Petersburg in November of that year, and this time the reception was very favorable indeed. Hermann Laroche, for example, praised the new work lavishly in the pages of the popular newspaper *Golos* (The Voice):

Last Saturday we heard the Fourth symphony of P. I. Tchaikovsky (in the key of F minor). Enormous in scope, the symphony in its conception is one of those courageous, exceptional attempts which composers so enthusiastically set about when they begin to tire of praise for more or less ordinary works. Having said "ordinary" I do not want however to say "banal." Tchaikovsky has never written tritely, and in our time no one loves the beaten track; even the Italians have abandoned it. But the three previous symphonies of Mr. Tchaikovsky did not represent such a striking departure from the ordinary, such unprecedented innovations as this one, and the sympathy with which the public met the ideas of the composer on this occasion, despite their unusual casing, gratifyingly testifies to this. The main thing that startled me in the new score was the intention of the author to seize a much broader area than the usual symphonic one, to liberate itself, if one may put it this way, from the official "high style," in which symphonic composers write, to combine in it a tragic accent with a light-hearted rhythm of a balletic "figure"; not to *combine* simultaneously, of course, but in consecutive movements of the symphony or even in consecutive sections of a single movement. This aspiration came out most strongly in the first movement. The terrible trumpet call of the introduction . . . the pathetic complaint of the first theme and its ornate development (in character rather close to "Tristan and Isolde"), connected with the second theme which not only does not have a threatening or complaining character but rather a flittery and bouncy one. . . . A humoristic character predominates in the second movement (andantino in modo di canzone), especially in the affected clumsiness of accents in the repeated chords in the string quartet; the scherzo is light and fantastic in the main section (pizzicato in the strings), the cheerful and dance-like in the first trio (brass alone), and on the whole has the character of a joke, which becomes particularly elegant and witty in the conclusion, where the themes of the scherzo and both trios are effectively interwoven. After this, the final with its terrifying fortissimo roar belongs on the whole to the realm of the serious, although even here there is an admixture of whimsy (a folk dance theme). In this finale there are grandiose features: the energy and aspiration of the first theme illuminates the listener with its unusual brilliance. But an improbable uproar and fuss of instrumentation . . . extends like a pall over all that is good in it. I knew even without the Fourth Symphony that Tchaikovsky, if he takes it into his head, might cause a sensation in the orchestra no less than another composer. . . . I am prepared to add that this ability has value, if it is carefully saved for one or two decisive blows, inflicted at an exceptional moment. But, for all my love of the works of the most preeminent of Russian composers, I am unable not to openly express myself regarding this inclination which threatens with him to turn into an organic defect, into a disease of the ear. Squandering beautiful harmonic and contrapuntal details, Tchaikovsky continually either drowns them out or distracts attention away from them by an unimaginable abuse of the bass drum and the cymbals. A Schumannist and Glinkist in the musical content of his compositions, Tchaikovsky in his orchestration more readily amounts to a mixture of Litolff and the newest Parisians and moreover he has become enamored of the *worst* side of Litolff.

The most important movement of the symphony remains, all the same, the first. I spoke of the bounding character of the second theme, but must add that this musical grasshopper in no way is unharmonious with the majestic and terrible figures that surround it. The merger of diverse characters that are extremely distant from each other is accomplished in this allegro (or more exactly Moderato con anima) by a not only brave but also successful hand. The trumpet motif of the introduction from time to time appears amidst the harmonic progressions based on the theme "moderato" and every time in such unexpected, effective, and beautiful corners (if one may express it this way), that for these combinations alone one can identify the author as a first-class master of harmonic technique and sonata form. If I primarily liked the "moderato," the audience was brought to frenzied rapture by the zesty scherzo, by the truly charming mischief of the subtle and clever artist.[104]

The critic for the popular musical magazine *Nuvellist*, Mikhail Ivanov, provided a similarly positive, if more succinct, assessment of the new work:

Each of the last three symphonic [concerts] of the Musical society—the fourth, fifth, and sixth—presented a new work by a Russian composer: "The Procession of Dionysus" of Famintsyn, the Fourth Symphony of Tchaikovsky, and in the last of these even two [new works]: an overture by Zike to Schiller's "Bride of Messina" and the Fourth Concerto for cello by Davidov. . . .

Nearly all of the new Russian musical works performed proved to be gifted, to the great satisfaction of their listeners. In first place one must put the symphony by Tchaikovsky. This talented composer, who has now completely recovered from his ill health and has taken up residence in Florence, has proved once again with his new symphony that his gifts are continually developing, continually moving ahead. In this new symphony, at every step, on every page . . . the ever-increasing proof of his talent shines through. The symphony is written in standard form, from which the composer does not deviate: the form is actually quite classical. (For all of that, the composer took great freedom in the conception of the spirit and direction of the symphony.) For example, the second theme of the first movement of Tchaikovsky's new work with its cheerful dancelike character (a kind of mazurka) sharply contrasts with the passionate, melancholy mood of the first theme. This confrontation of two themes of heterogeneous character produces a very poignant impression; in addition it provides the occasion for many witty technical details. For the scherzo the composer found a very interesting sonority. The entire first part consists of a sustained pizzicato in all the string instruments; this contrasts perfectly to the trio, which employs a sonority first of woodwinds alone and subsequently with the addition of brass instruments. In the finale, a theme [based on] a folk song is beautifully developed; this finale would create a stronger impression if it was not a bit too short. In the orchestration of the finale, Tchaikovsky, in general inclined to orchestral thunder, does not stint on the brass and percussion; in general all the finales of his symphonies and operas suffer from similar inadequacies.[105]

Certainly, the opinion that may have mattered the most to the composer was that of Sergey Taneyev, his pupil and successor as professor of harmony at the Moscow Conservatory. Tchaikovsky sent a score to Taneyev, and on March 18/30, 1878, Taneyev obliged him with his own candid review:

The first movement of your Fourth Symphony is disproportionately long in comparison with the others; it seems to me a symphonic poem, to which the three other movements are added fortuitously. The fanfare for trumpets in the introduction, which is repeated in other places, the frequent change of *tempo* in the tributary themes—all this makes me think that a programme is being treated here. Otherwise this movement pleases me. But the rhythm ♪ ♫ appears too often and becomes wearisome.

The Andante is charming (the middle does not particularly please me). The Scherzo is exquisite, and goes splendidly. The Trio I cannot bear: it sounds like a ballet movement.

Nicholas Grigorievich (Rubinstein) likes the Finale best, but I do not altogether agree with him. The variations on a folksong do not strike me as very important or interesting.

In my opinion the Symphony has one defect, to which I shall never be reconciled: in every movement there are phrases which sound like ballet music: the middle section of the Andante, the Trio of the Scherzo, and a kind of march in the Finale. Hearing the Symphony, my inner eye sees involuntarily "our *prima ballerina,*" which puts me out of humour and spoils my pleasure in the many beauties of the work.

This is my candid opinion. Perhaps I have expressed it somewhat freely, but do not be hurt. It is not surprising that the Symphony does not entirely please me. Had you not sent *Eugene Onegin* at the same time, perhaps it might have satisfied me. It is your own fault. Why have you composed such an opera, which had no parallel in the world? *Onegin* has given me such pleasure that I cannot find words to express it. A splendid opera! And yet you say you want to give up composing, You have never done so well. Rejoice that you have attained such perfection, and profit by it.[106]

Taneyev's remarks about the balletic nature of the Fourth caused Tchaikovsky to respond at length. His entire defense follows:

I have read your letter with the greatest pleasure and interest. . . . You need not be afraid that your criticism of my Fourth Symphony is too severe. You have simply given me your frank opinion, for which I am grateful. I want these kinds of opinions, not choruses of praise. At the same time many things in your letter astonished me. I have no idea what you consider "ballet music," or why you should object to it. Do you regard every melody in a lively dance-rhythm as "ballet music"? In that case how can you reconcile yourself to the majority of Beethoven's symphonies, for in them you will find similar melodies on every page? Or do you mean to say that the Trio of my Scherzo is in the style of Minkus, Gerber, or Pugni? It does not, to my mind, deserve such criticism. I never can understand why "ballet music" should be used as a contemptuous epithet. The music of a ballet is not invariably bad, there are good works of this class—Délibes' *Sylvia,* for instance. And when the music is good, what difference does it make whether the Sobiesichanskaya dances to it or not? I can only say that certain portions of my Symphony do not please you because *they recall the ballet,* not because they are intrinsically bad. You may be right, but I do not see why dance tunes should not be employed episodically in a symphony, even with the avowed intention of giving a touch of coarse humour. Again I appeal to Beethoven, who frequently had resource to similar effects. I must add that I have racked my brains in vain to recall in what part of the Allegro you can possibly have discovered "ballet music." It remains an enigma. With all that you say as to my Symphony having a programme, I am quite in agreement. But I do not see why this should be a mistake. I am far more afraid of the contrary; I do not wish any symphonic work to emanate from me which has nothing to express, and consists merely of harmonies and a purposeless design of rhythms and modulations. Of course, my Symphony is programme music, but it would be impossible to give the programme in words; it would appear ludicrous and only raise a smile. Ought not this to be the case with a symphony which is the most lyrical of all musical forms? Ought it not to express all those things for which words cannot be found, which nevertheless arise in the heart and clamour for expression? Besides, I must tell you that in my simplicity I imagined the plan of my Symphony to be so obvious that everyone would understand its meaning, or at least its leading ideas, without any definite programme. Pray do not imagine I want to swagger before you with profound emotions and lofty ideas. Throughout the work I have made no effort to express any new thought. In reality my work is a reflection of Beethoven's Fifth Symphony; I have not copied his musical contents, only borrowed the central idea. What kind of programme has this Fifth Symphony, do you think? Not only has it a programme, but it is so clear that there cannot be the smallest difference of opinion as to what it means. Much the same lies at the root of my Symphony, and if you have failed to grasp it, it simply proves that I am no Beethoven—on which point I have no doubt whatever. Let me add that there is not a single bar in this Fourth Symphony of mine which I have not truly felt, and which is not an echo of my most intimate spiritual life. The only exception occurs perhaps in the middle section of the first movement, in which there are some forced passages, some things which are laboured and artificial. I know you will laugh as you read these lines. You are a sceptic and a mocking-bird. In spite of your great love of music you do not seem to believe that a man can compose from his inner impulses. Wait awhile, you too will join the ranks![107]

Despite the breakthrough achieved in the Fourth Symphony, eight years were to pass before another big symphonic work was to be undertaken. In the meantime, the important compositions brought to completion were *Eugene Onegin* (1878), the Violin Concerto (1878), the Orchestral Suite No. 1 (1879), the Piano Concerto No. 2 (1880), the String Serenade (1880), *The Maid of Orleans* (1882), *Mazeppa* (1883), the Orchestral Suites Nos. 2 (1883) and 3 (1884), and in 1885 the *Manfred* Symphony. It should be noted that the Serenade for Strings and the Orchestral Suites were in a sense surrogates for symphonic composition, where the composer felt less constricted by tradition. Indeed, it has been demonstrated that the first of these suites, Opus 43, "shares more than mere historical proximity [with Symphony No. 4]. The two in fact reveal a complex system of interconnections."[108]

MANFRED SYMPHONY OPUS 58

With the unnumbered *Manfred* Symphony Opus 58 the characters of Mily Balakirev and Vladimir Stasov return to the narrative of the Russian symphony. In the winter of 1867–1868, Hector Berlioz was engaged to conduct the concerts of the RMS in St. Petersburg; among the works he conducted was *Harold in Italy,* a symphony that apparently held great appeal for Balakirev, Stasov, and the members of the *kuchka.* Here was a superb composition by a gifted composer, an *avant-garde* work, and a composition from the pen of a non-German composer. As a result, Stasov formulated an outline for a work like *Harold* based on Lord Byron's *Manfred,* which he gave to Balakirev, suggesting that he compose a symphony to this outline. Balakirev decided he was not up to the task, but retained the outline and forwarded it in September 1868 to Berlioz, who was terminally ill. For fourteen years the program seemed to be forgotten. However, on September 1/13, 1881, Tchaikovsky resumed his contact with Balakirev concerning the publication of a new edition of *Romeo and Juliet* that contained the earlier-intended dedication to the *kuchka's* mentor. One year passed before Balakirev answered Tchaikovsky's epistle; on September 28/October 10, 1882, he thanked the composer for the score and brought up the subject of an outline for a symphony:

> I should be glad to see you, and I should like to communicate to you the programme of a symphony which you'd carry out splendidly. . . . Your apogee is reached in your two symphonic poems—*The Tempest* and *Francesca da Rimini,* particularly the latter. . . . It seems to me that in the subject I've prepared for you, you would do at least as well as in these pieces of yours, for I trust I well understand where your real forte lies.[109]

Tchaikovsky did not wish to meet Balakirev in person so he asked him to mail the program, which Balakirev did on October 28/November 9, 1882. At no point does Balakirev attribute authorship to Stasov and he adds his own commentary about how the music ought to be composed (Table XV/22).

Tchaikovsky's reply (November 12/24) was negatively neutral to the proposal; he needed to read Byron's *Manfred* before he could make a decision. However, Tchaikovsky went on to say he was disappointed with the outline, since it seemed more directed toward an imitation of Berlioz rather than a work suited to himself. "It leaves me absolutely cold. . . . Such writing [forced in the style of Berlioz] doesn't attract me in the least." He concludes:

> I by no means think that the programme music *à la Berlioz* is in general a false form of art, but only mention the fact that I myself have done nothing significant in this direction.
>
> It may well be that *Schumann* is to blame for the hopeless coldness I feel toward your programme. I am extremely fond of his "Manfred," and am so accustomed to connect Byron's "Manfred" in one indivisible conception with Schumann's "Manfred," that I don't know how to approach the subject so as to evoke from it other music than Schumann has provided for it. . . .
>
> But all the same, I will read "Manfred."[110]

The project again lay dormant until October 1884 when Tchaikovsky went to St. Petersburg for the premiere of *Eugene Onegin* at the Imperial Opera. There he saw and held discussions with Balakirev that included again the *Manfred* Symphony. Balakirev supplied Tchaikovsky with Stasov's own copy of the program and more suggestions of his own (see Table XV/22). By October 31/November 12 Tchaikovsky was ready to purchase a copy of Byron's *Manfred* and even sounded enthusiastically committed to the project: "I assure you that *at all costs,* I will employ all my powers to carry out your wish."[111] On November 17/29, Tchaikovsky was even more positive, saying that the symphony will be "written no later than summer."[112] The chronology of Tchaikovsky's work on *Manfred* begins in the spring:

April 1885	Skecthes begun.
May 13/25, 1885	Sketches completed.
June 12/24, 1885	First movement fully scored.
July 22/August 3, 1885	Scherzo (second movement) fully scored.
September 11/23, 1885	Slow movement fully scored.
September 12/24, 1885	Finale fully scored [finalized ten days later].
September 13/25, 1885	Writes to Balakirev, "I have fulfilled your wish."
March 11/23, 1886	Premiere at the Moscow RMS, Max Erdmannsdörfer conducting.

Manfred is set apart from Tchaikovsky's other symphonies in that it is without a number. As we have also seen in the symphonies of Rimsky-Korsakov, the professional and professorial Russian composers had a tendency to view the symphony, despite Balakirev, as a part of the Germanic symphonic tradition, which emphasized absolute music. *Manfred* in a number of respects counters this Germanic heritage: it is programmatic in the first movement and Finale, characteristic in the second and third movements; sonata form is absent from the cycle; an *idée fixe* is used and other themes also return in subsequent movements; and one might argue that it is a cycle of symphonic poems rather than a symphonic cycle, for example, something not unlike Smetana's *Má Vlast*. On the other hand, the first and last movements end in the same key and the central movements are in more closely related keys to the tonic than in some

---

TABLE XV/22

Stasov/Balakirev/Tchaikovsky: Plans for *Manfred*

1.

Balakirev (1882)	Balakirev (1884)	Tchaikovsky (1885)
F-sharp Minor	B-flat Minor	B Minor

Helpful Materials according to Balakirev: Tchaikovsky–*Francesca da Rimini*, Liszt–*Hamlet*, Berlioz–*Harold in Italy* Finale, Chopin–Preludes in E minor, E-flat Minor, C-sharp Minor [No. 25].

1885 Program: Manfred wanders in the Alps. Weary of the fatal questions of existence, tormented by hopeless long-ings and the memory of past crimes, he suffers cruel spiritual pangs. He has plunged into the occult sciences and commands the mighty powers of darkness, but neither they nor anything in this world can give him the forgetfulness to which alone he vainly aspires. The memory of the lost Astarte, one passionately loved by him, gnaws at his heart, and there is neither limit nor end to Manfred's despair.

2.

A Major (slow movement)	G-flat Major (slow movement)	B Minor (Scherzo)

Helpful Materials: Berlioz–*Symphonie fantastique* Adagio

1885 Program: (Scherzo) The Alpine Fairy [Byron's Witch of the Alps] appears before Manfred in the spray of a waterfall.

3.

D Major (Scherzo)	D Major (Scherzo)	G Major (slow movement)

Helpful Materials: Berlioz–"Queen Mab" Scherzo from *Roméo et Juliette*, Tchaikovsky–Scherzo from Symphony No. 3

1885 Program: (slow movement) Pastorale—The simple, free, and peaceful life of the mountain people.

4.

F-sharp Minor	B-flat Minor/Major	B Minor/Major

Helpful Materials: Same as first movement.

1885 Program: The subterranean palace of Arimanes. Infernal orgy. Appearance of Manfred in the middle of the bacchanal. Evocation and appearance of the shade of Astarte. He is pardoned. Manfred's death.

Translation: Warrack/TCHAIKOVSKY and Warrack/MANFRED LINER NOTES

---

of Tchaikovsky's other symphonies; there are four movements, and their tempo sequence is comparable to that of a standard *kuchka* symphony with the Scherzo in second place.

Central to the cogency of this cyclic piece is Byron's dramatic poem *Manfred,* written in 1817, that came to be a marker of English romantic literature. Byron described the poem to his publisher:

> I forgot to mention to you—that a kind of poem in dialogue (in blank verse) or drama—from which "the Incantation" is an extract—begun last summer in Switzerland is finished—it is in three acts—but of a very wild—metaphysical—and inexplicable kind.—Almost all the persons—but two or three—are Spirits of the earth & air—or the waters—the scene is in the Alps—the hero a kind of magician who is tormented by a species of remorse—the cause of which is left half unexplained—he wanders about in-voking these spirits—which appear to him—& are of no use—he at last goes to the very abode of the Evil principle in propria persona—to evocate a ghost—which appears—& gives him an ambiguous & disagreeable answer—& in the 3d. act he is found by his

attendants dying in a tower—where he studied his art.—You may perceive by this out-line that I have no great opinion of this piece of phantasy—but I have at least rendered it *quite impossible* for the stage—for which my intercourse with D[rury] Lane had given me the greatest contempt.[113]

What this description or the Stasov/Balakirev program does not deal with explicitly is the reason for Manfred's brooding: Astarte was his sister with whom he had an incestuous rela-tionship. *Manfred* may well have appealed to Tchaikovsky for at least two reasons: his sym-pathies for wronged women and his own burden of sexual guilt. As with any program or op-eratic libretto, the Stasov/Balakirev effort could account for only some of the characters (Manfred, Astarte, and the Witch [Fairy] of the Alps) and a few of the incidents.

Two of Tchaikovsky's fears about undertaking this topic were Schumann's precedent and how Berlioz's concept of the dramatic symphony might affect him. The Schumann problem may have been alleviated by the difference of genre; Schumann composed inciden-tal music for the dramatic poem, which Byron had written so that it was "quite impossible for the stage."[114] Tchaikovsky was to compose a symphony. Berlioz was thus a factor that Tchaikovsky could not shake: the *idée fixe* represented Manfred in all the movements; the Scherzo recaptured some of the atmosphere of "Queen Mab"; and the "Pastorale" has re-minded some of the "Scene in the Country" from the *Symphonie fantastique.* Several of these works were recommended as models by Balakirev to the composer (see above Table XV/22). However, the most significant Berliozian aspect was Tchaikovsky's orchestra and his ap-proach to it. Among the other symphonies, this is his largest orchestra (an asterisk marks those instruments not employed in the other symphonies): three flutes (the third doubles on piccolo), two oboes, *English horn, two clarinets, *bass clarinet, three bassoons, four horns, two trumpets, *two cornets, three trombones, tuba, timpani (three drums), cymbals, bass drum, *tambourine, triangle, bells, tam-tam, two harps, and strings. Tchaikovsky also makes specific Berliozian requests of the instruments: horns are asked to put their bells in the air, bowings are indicated in the string parts, strings are instructed to use the entire bow, the bass drum and cymbals are requested to use timpani sticks, and the bell is specified backstage. Perhaps more characteristic of Tchaikovsky are extremes of dynamics from *ffff* to *ppppp*; though such extreme markings are not found in Berlioz—his range is from *ppp* to *ff*—he achieved much the same by using a larger orchestra and selectively reduced scorings.

The first movement (Table XV/23) is not governed by a standard form: there is no expo-sition either tonally or thematically. While there are passages of development, there is no functional development section. There is a reprise, but it only involves the *idée fixe* (*1Aa*) rep-resenting *Manfred* (Example XV/26). As outlined, it is closer to a ternary structure. Notice that section *2A* is heard but once and that this is the closest the movement comes to having a development section. Since the form of the first movement is so untraditional, one would at-tribute this to the program. However, this is difficult to pin down except in the most general way: *A* deals with the "torments" of Manfred, *B* with Manfred's "memory of the beautiful Astarte," and the return of portions of *1A* with the intensification of the torments of *A* as the "tortures of [his] grievous despair." In a way, the first movement follows in the tradition of Liszt's *Faust* Symphony in three character pictures, except here Manfred is delineated, and then Astarte is seen through Manfred's eyes. The two main characters are strongly drawn: Manfred's music is in the minor mode, given to strong outbursts and *crescendos* of sound and surface rhythm, and predominantly colored by darker orchestrations; Astarte is characterized by the major mode, more contained dynamics, delicate orchestrations, calmer rhythms, and muted but brighter timbres. If Tchaikovsky had followed with an explication for this movement

TABLE XV/23
Tchaikovsky, *Manfred* Symphony/I: Structure

System 1A — Lento lugubre 4/4

Measure	m.1	15	38	59	78	80	82	84	86	92	95	98
Tempo	Lento lugubre 4/4				poco animando	Più mosso						
Motif	a	b	c			a	b	a	b	b	a	ay
Articulation											diminution	tutta la forza
Dynamics	ff		p cresc. f ff	mod.	mod. / ff fff	fff						
Key	A/E minor		C minor	C-sharp minor		B minor						

System 2A — Moderato con moto 4/4

Measure	111	120	130	144	150	154	159	171	180	192	203
Tempo	Moderato con moto 4/4					Moderato assai		Andante 3/4	Largo stringendo	Andante	Largo
Motif	a	b d	b/d	b/d	b	c		B	a b	a¹ b	b
Description		synthesis	synthesis	canon	diminution	ext.			dolce		
Dynamics	p	mod.	mod.						p cresc. f	mp	p
Key	E minor	G major / E minor				B/E minor	B/E minor	D major	B minor / D major	D major	E minor

System 3

Measure	213	260	272	289	314	324	328
Tempo	Andante	Poco Più animato / Tempo 1 (Andante)	Allegro non troppo	Andante con duolo 3/4	Più animato	Andante non tanto	Poco più animato
Motif	c	a	d	1A a	c¹		a
Expression	dolce	rit.		dolente e appassionato			
Dynamics	p / mod.	cresc.	fff / dim.	fff	fff		
Key		E minor		B minor / B pedal	B minor		

383

EXAMPLE XV/26   Tchaikovsky. *Manfred* Symphony/1, mm.1–22. Courtesy of Edwin F. Kalmus & Co.

EXAMPLE XV/26   *(continued)*

as he had for Symphony No. 4/1, where each theme was given a meaning, we could account for each of its constituent parts. But Tchaikovsky was ill at ease about the details of program music, even when a work was clearly extra-musical.

At the smaller level, Tchaikovsky sets up a structure in the first part (*1A*): *b* becomes a response/refrain to *a,* and *c* functions as something of a transition. Again, Tchaikovsky displays his unerring sense of pace: up through measure 79 the statements are expansive, the tonality

EXAMPLE XV/26   (*continued*)

EXAMPLE XV/26   (*continued*)

more uncertain, the surface rhythm and the tempo quicken, the dynamics strengthen, and the harmony becomes less stable and more active, which by the end of the section stabilizes the key of B minor (m.80), the tonality in which the movement will end. At this point, *a* and *b* are stated in alternating two-measure units; *a* is heard in diminution ending *tutti la forza*. Since it takes seventy-nine measures to reach the home key of the movement, one might conceptualize this opening as a massive introduction ending at the structural downbeat (m.80), but this is only realized after the downbeat occurs and during the previous section one considers it expository. *1A* ends with a weakly voiced E minor chord that perhaps clarifies the tonality at the movement's beginning and sets up the beginning of *2A* (m.111).

If *1A* was ambiguously expository, *2A* is quasi-developmental. *2Ab* is restated in the opening tonic (E minor) followed by a new theme (*Ad*) atmospherically scored for horn solo (m.120). Tchaikovsky's response is to embed *d* into *b* (Example XV/27). This is treated in canon (m.144), then in diminution (m.150) over a descending bass. Tchaikovsky concludes with chromatic basso ostinatos (m.156) that are darkly punctuated (m.163). *B* returns to the breadth of the movement's opening with two complementary *a b* statements, each spanning twenty-one bars. Spun from a single motive, *c* spans over forty-five bars in modulatory sequences that culminate in *B*'s climax with the *a* return (m.260). *1A* returns (m.289) and remains in B minor.

Tchaikovsky became more disenchanted about his *Manfred* Symphony as time passed, but he always thought that the first movement was an estimable accomplishment. While Tchaikovsky was often his own toughest critic, his positive feelings about this movement are confirmed by the ultimate test of listening.[115] Despite its slow tempo and a tendency to overstate its themes in full orchestrations and lengthy sections of strong dynamics, Tchaikovsky meets the challenge of composing a slow first movement outside of the sonata form tradition without loss of interest. Within the larger view of the cycle, it is an effective prelude to the three pieces that follow.

Lord Byron provides the following commentary to the vision of the witch of the Alps in the waterfall, the concern of the second movement:

> Manfred takes some of the water in the palm of his hand and flings it into the air, muttering the adjuration. After a pause, the witch (fairy) of the Alps rises beneath the arch of the sunbow of the torrent.[116]

One is not surprised that Tchaikovsky tries to capture the droplets and mists spread by the Alpine waterfall in delicate music not unlike that which Berlioz used to depict Queen Mab. However, it is only in the fiber of the music that one might detect Berlioz, for the weave and the texture are completely Tchaikovsky's. A simple ternary form, it is only the movement's *A* portion in B minor that attempts to illustrate the waterfall. The Alpine Witch (Fairy) appears in the Trio (*B*) with her distinctive lyric melody at first accompanied by a pair of harps. The melody is then subjected to a series of *kuchka* variations. In this Trio, Tchaikovsky seems to have been influenced by Borodin's music, particularly the slow movement of the B Minor Symphony No. 2/3 and certain passages from *Prince Igor*. The orchestration at times reminds one of the Russian master of the orchestra, Rimsky-Korsakov. Of special note is the transition out of the Trio and back into the Scherzo proper; here, Tchaikovsky incrementally moves away from Trio material as the colors and figures of the Scherzo proper come to predominate.

The *idée fixe* makes three appearances: the first (m.252) is in the middle of the Trio as a counterpoint to the Witch's (Fairy's) tune; the second (m.334) occurs at the end of the Trio as a climax to the entire Scherzo; and the third in the coda (m.513) with its evocative

EXAMPLE XV/27   Tchaikovsky. *Manfred* Symphony/1, mm.111–29. Courtesy of Edwin F. Kalmus & Co.

orchestration for English horn, two harps, and violins *divisi* migrating to their high registers for the close. These three statements in a way specifically summarize Tchaikovsky's progress as a composer since his early symphonies: the integration of counterpoint into the structure of the piece, the ability to transform themes into different roles, and the expansion of Tchaikovsky's imagination as an orchestrator.

As in the Scherzo to Symphony No. 3, that of the *Manfred* Symphony is a piece intended for a virtuoso orchestra that has not only the fingers, but also a strong sense of ensemble. Both Symphony No. 3/4 and this piece were first performed by the RMS Moscow orchestra under Nikolay Rubinstein and Max Erdmannsdörfer, respectively, and Tchaikovsky knew exactly what he could expect from the Moscow ensemble. In the *Manfred* Symphony Scherzo, the demands are even greater than in Symphony No. 3/4. At the very start the themes are situated so that they begin on the second eighth of the 2/4 bar when they seem to belong on the beat. In addition, there are sections that demand dovetailing between two woodwinds or first and second violins with sextuplet sixteenths. At other times, there is no dovetailing, just the juxtaposition of blocks of color (m.220) as an accompaniment.

There was one Russian composer whose attention was drawn to this piece: Rimsky-Korsakov. He told his Boswell, V. V. Yastrebtsev, in early December 1896 that he did not like *Manfred* very much "except for certain marvelous passages in the first and third movements and the coda of the second movement. To Rimsky, the Scherzo seems insufficiently ethereal and poetic, particularly the Trio, despite the violin solo and even the harp."[117] Whatever his reservations, Rimsky's most famous piece, "The Flight of the Bumble Bee," from his 1900 opera *The Tale of Tsar Saltan,* certainly owes something to Tchaikovsky's Scherzo (cf. the sextuplet figures).

If any movement might evoke Berlioz's *Harold in Italy,* it would be that the third movement of *Manfred* seems to be a slower version of the "Serenade of a Mountaineer. . . ." Berlioz's music seems to evoke more successfully a pastoral atmosphere; in Tchaikovsky's movement, the "simple, free, and peaceful life of the mountaineers" seems to become too complicated in form and texture. And while a storm seems to be a vital part of the pastoral landscape, the stormy appearance of the motto seems too dramatic and disrupting unless it can be justified by the program, which here it is not. This is not to say that Tchaikovsky's piece does not evoke the pastoral. Rather, one could persuasively argue that in the second movement of Symphony No. 4, the simplicity of the *A* section is more pastoral in character. Nevertheless, in *Manfred* the Pastorale is still deeply etched: the six-eight meter, the lilting melodies, the drones and pedals, the melodies for oboe and horn, and the imitations of natural sounds overtake its complexities.

The Pastorale's form (Table XV/24), a rondo, is not structured in its most straightforward way with the refrain's arrival always easily recognized. *A* at its beginning is made up of three different components (*a, b, c*), any one of which can signal the refrain's return, either in the tonic key of G major or in the key in which it was originally stated (*b* in B minor, *c* in E minor). Already in the opening statement played by the most pastoral of instruments, the oboe, the background becomes too thick for the nature of the theme. *Ab,* though undergirded by a B pedal, further questions the pastoral idiom with its contrapuntal texture among the violins and cellos. The strongest evocation of the pastoral occurs in *Ac;* a sustained A-minor chord supports a haunting but simple horn melody. *Aa*'s return is reorchestrated with cello and horn countermelodies and triplet thirty-seconds in the first violins, a seeming reference to the previous movement. This variation, though the melody is left intact, also seems far removed from the *kuchka* approach. Subsequent returns of *A* material, except for m.194 and at the very end (m.277), bring back material other than *Aa:* at m.89 *Ab* now in G

TABLE XV/24
Tchaikovsky. *Manfred* Symphony/3: Structure

System 1

Andante con moto 6/8						Più animato			Animando	Più mosso	
[A] a	b	c	a¹ (II reference)	[B]	[A] b	[C] a	a¹	a²			
G	B	E minor	G		G	E minor			E-flat	G pedal	C pedal
m.1	20	37	48	75	89	108	116	124	131	137	149

System 2

			Più mosso		Tempo 1 *Coda* sounds of nature	Meno mosso
trans. striking of bells 8x	[A] c retrans.	[A] a2	(II reference?)	[A] c inverted as ostinato		
C pedal	E minor				G pedal	C pedal
153	183	194	210	224	242	260	270

System 3

[A] a fragment
G
277

major, m.183 *Ac* but functioning again as a retransition to *Aa,* and at m.242 *Ac* is camouflaged by inversion and becomes an ostinato.

As for the episodes, the transition (m.64) to *B* (m.75) imitates bird sounds over a bassoon drone, while *B* itself (m.75) has more agitated sounds from nature, which are becalmed with the *Ab* return (m.89). *C* is in three strophes (mm.108, 116, 124) in E minor. Matters then turn more developmental as the tempo quickens, building to a climactic statement of the Manfred theme (m.153), and the sounding of the church bell eight times signals midnight. Tchaikovsky's coda (m.260) is undergirded by a tonic pedal. It begins with the transition (cf. m.64) of bird sounds and rustlings in the underbrush, continues with a quickening and slowing of the background surface rhythm, and concludes leisurely. Such an approach to the coda of a pastoral slow movement reminds one of Beethoven's Symphony No. 6/2.

Though in many respects this is a compelling piece of writing, it does not present a consistently credible pastoral idiom, because it is overwhelmed by the composer's gift for melodic beauty and his interest in the dramatic gesture, which is antithetic to the very essence of the pastoral concept. Furthermore, in an effort to demonstrate his now prodigious technique, Tchaikovsky has placed in a secondary role those aspects that should establish this movement's primary character.

The Finale's program (see Table XV/22) is not consistent with the last scene of Byron's *Manfred.* In the Stasov/Balakirev version, the central musical event is the bacchanal; there is no mention of this carousing dance or any hint of anything like it in Byron. Instead, the final scene of Act II is dark, mysterious, and subdued. Astarte informs Manfred that tomorrow he will die. In Act III, Manfred dies without wanting the comfort of religious consolation. As in the first movement, the Finale does not conform to any standard musical structure; it follows more or less the Stasov/Balakirev program. Therefore, the Finale divides into three sections: 1) the bacchanal in the palace of Arimanes (m.1), 2) the appearance of Astarte's ghost (m.303), and 3) the death of Manfred (m.394). Sections two and three have a dual function: to fulfill the requirements of the Finale's program and to provide a recapitulation of material from the first movement.

The palace scene is based upon two themes (Example XV/28): one that represents the Palace of Arimanes (*A,* m.1) and the other the bacchanal (*B,* m.81). Both are based on a chain of like thematic modules—*a, a¹, a², a³,* etc.—with mainly *kuchka* variations and an occasional developmental expansion for the palace theme. The bacchanal is built out of ten- and twelve-measure chains, which in turn are built from mostly two-measure modules of like material. This lends to the music a degree of almost mesmerizing energy, a form of larger-scale kinetic recurrence usually associated with motives rather than modules. After this orgiastic scene, perhaps derived by Stasov/Balakirev from Berlioz's *Harold* Finale, Manfred's *idée fixe* appears (m.147) to announce his presence in the Palace. A contemplative Lento (m.161) *a–a,* each ending with snarls from the brass, turns to *I/Ab,* also in a double statement, which diminishes into silence.

Tchaikovsky now provides a fugato (m.206); as we saw in the early symphonies, fugatos always were the low points in the composer's structure. While the fugato here does not represent the high point of the movement or the cycle, neither does it reveal a noticeably weak link. The entries are not predictable and the countersubjects come across as more than viable. The appearance of the bacchanal as both an episode (m.237) and as a countersubject (m.245) is precisely what Balakirev must have disdained: learned counterpoint as taught at the conservatories where two themes are first treated independently and then brought together in contrapuntal combination. After building to another climax, the activity again slows and the dynamics diminish. *I/Aa,* Manfred's motto (m.282), now alternates with a

EXAMPLE XV/28 Tchaikovsky. *Manfred* Symphony/4, mm.1–4, 81–85. Courtesy of Edwin F. Kalmus & Co.

EXAMPLE XV/28 (*continued*)

fragment of the bacchanal: Manfred has invoked the ghost of Astarte to mark the beginning of part two.

In contrast to the presentation in the first movement, Astarte's music is now marked by the addition of two harps, the muted horn, and by the violins and violas *divisi* in their high register (m.304). Collectively, this scoring is an evocation of the celestial sound and concludes with Manfred's motto or *idée fixe* (m.375). Note that this ends with a burst of percussion, including the tam-tam, the sign of death.

Part three (m.394) represents the demise of Manfred. The Andante con duolo from the first movement (m.289) is recapitulated and builds to a new climax, which is the transformation of the Palace theme into a chorale (m.448) played by the organ (a suggestion of Balakirev's), the woodwinds, and horn. At the end of the phrase, the violins rise through the C major chord to celestial heights. The chorale/celestial gesture is twice repeated. At m.472 the Dies Irae is heard in the bass (m.472) and then becomes an ostinato (m.481). The last four bars evoke Wagner's last stage piece, the music drama *Parsifal*. While Tchaikovsky did not hold *Parsifal* in high regard, such would not prevent him from pilfering one of its gestures.

Some have thought that the Finale is the weakest link in this symphonic cycle. However, when considered along with the preceding movements, one might argue that this Finale is a more convincing ending for this symphonic cycle than the Finales to his previous four symphonies, with the possible exception of Symphony No. 2 "Little Russian." Though, without question, the Palace and bacchanal music repetitiveness can become tiresome, the remainder of the Finale is effective both as a conclusion to this movement and to the cycle as a whole. In contrast, the Finales to Symphonies Nos. 3 and 4 leave the listener bewildered by fugatos, chorales, and an almost uncontrolled energy. Even with their repeated cadences, the listener is left unsatisfied. The conclusion to *Manfred* ends quietly, slowly, tragically, and with a satisfaction absent from Tchaikovsky's previous symphonies. Perhaps Tchaikovsky discovered that a slow and quiet ending was more effective for his musical language, a gesture that was fully, perhaps too fully, realized in his Sixth Symphony.

The *Manfred* Symphony, though composed between Symphonies Nos. 4 and 5, has never been regarded as a symphony in the same sense as the numbered ones. As a result, it remains on the periphery of the symphonic repertoire. Conductors who have this work in their repertoire are few, and one would imagine that the piece requires more rehearsal than Tchaikovsky's other works because it is virtually unknown to most orchestras. Nevertheless, the *Manfred* of Tchaikovsky is deserving of a place in the minds and ears of listeners. Just as Liszt's *Faust* and *Dante* Symphonies are reputed masterpieces, so should the *Manfred* Symphony be regarded. Like the Liszt works, it has its weaknesses, but these are easily compensated for by its strengths.

Early Russian performances received strong but mixed notices, such as Laroche's review of the St. Petersburg premiere, in which he expressed his doubts about program music:

> As a symphony in several movements and at the same time a programmatic "symphonic poem," "Manfred" represents a seeming similarity with the "Faust-Symphonie" of Liszt, all the more because the poems which inspired both composers have much in common if not in their plots then in their mood and basic ideas; one may find traces of Lisztian influence in the frequent unisons and fermatas. But these are insignificant details which are completely absorbed by the original elements of the whole. The new Manfred is from head to heels Tchaikovsky. This circumstance at time even hinders it from being Manfred. Such at any rate is my first impression; but, to this point, I have carried away something similar to this impression every time a new programmatic composition of our celebrated countryman has appeared. Whether Dante, or Shakespeare, or Byron inspires his musical invention—the means of expression employed by Tchaikovsky are *not those* to which we are accustomed. The criteria we have for this are fully palpable, when we are familiar with the means he employs, but we are accustomed to giving them another interpretation. When in a symphonic poem there is a depiction of Faustian spiritual disorder

and criminal remorse, but as decoration—of alpine nature, I hear a charmingly idle, broad melody of purely Russian manner, in my imagination arises [an image] of the steppe of the Volga region, flooded by sunlight, and I enjoy it more the less I recall the program.[118]

The reviewer for *Nuvellist,* V. Baskin, is sympathetic to program music but finds Tchaikovsky's symphony somewhat lacking in comparison to Schumann's *Manfred:*

> Symphonic concerts are continuing every week. The fourth concert was devoted to Mendelssohn and the fifth to Russian composers. Tchaikovsky's "Manfred" symphony appeared on the program of the latter. . . .
> "Manfred" is the work of an excellent symphonist, [sparkling] with bright colors but not free from heaviness and a tiresome length, which at times diminished the impression [made by] other, more poetic pages of the symphony. The second movement is the best of all . . . where a fabulous coloring is produced by the orchestra. Also good is the first movement, despite its fragmented [nature]: in particular, the suffering of Manfred is well portrayed. This suffering theme, as well as Astart's theme, is repeated in the fourth movement, the beginning of which strongly reminds one of pages of the finales of Mr. Tchaikovsky's symphonies. The third movement—the "free and easy life" of the highlanders—seems weaker. Manfred's theme, carried throughout the entire symphony, ties it all together into a single, mournful mood. It is interesting to compare the work of our composer to the well-known "Manfred" of Schumann, which so exactly and deeply fulfills the very same task, although through simpler means than those which Tchaikovsky pursues.[119]

This ambivalence of conductors and audiences to the *Manfred* Symphony was also felt by its composer. At times, he thought the work was a success, and at other times he detested it. Some of Tchaikovsky's own comments follow:

September 27/October 9, 1885—To Madame von Meck:
> My *Manfred* will be played once or twice, and then disappear; with the exception of a few people who attend symphony concerts, no one will hear it.[120]

October 9/21, 1885—To Peter I. Jürgenson:
> I am not in a position to spend an incredible amount of trouble on a work that I regard as one of my very best.[121]

April 9, 1886—To Yuliya Shpazhinskaya:
> I will give you my impressions from hearing *Manfred* at rehearsals (I did not hear it at the concert, i.e. I heard it from a distance). In actual performance there can be no doubt that the first movement is the best. The Scherzo was played at a very quick tempo and I was not disappointed when I heard it (which is often the case with me), but, unless I am mistaken, it is written in such a difficult and impractical way that probably no orchestra will want to play it or be able to, apart from here in Moscow where the players are in general very well disposed towards me. The Andante doesn't sound bad. The *Finale* [is much better] in performance; from *the audience's* point of view it is the most successful movement. I had the general impression that even the Moscow public, which is particularly kindly towards me, *did not like Manfred.* On the other hand, the players grew more and more enthusiastic at every rehearsal and at the final rehearsal they tapped loud and long with their bows and instruments after

each movement. Of my closest friends, some are solidly behind *Manfred,* others do not like it and maintain that I am not *myself* in this work, that I am hiding behind some sort of façade. My own view is that it is my best orchestral work, but that its difficulty, its impracticality, and its complexity will condemn it to *failure and neglect.*[122]

September 21, 1888—To Grand Duke Konstantin Romanov:

So far as *Manfred* is concerned, I can say, with no pretence at being modest, that I find the work disgusting and loathe it heartily, *with the sole exception of the first movement.* However, I intend in the near future to destroy the other three movements entirely—their music is of little value (the Finale in particular is appalling)—and out of the whole great symphony, which is quite impossibly prolix, I will make a *Symphonische Dichtung.* Then, I am sure, my *Manfred* will have the capacity to please; it was inevitable that it would be like this: I enjoyed writing the first movement, but the other three are the fruit of an exertion which, I recollect, made me feel very ill for a time.[123]

In the end, Tchaikovsky thought that only the first movement was worthy of preservation. However, he apparently never attempted to destroy any of the other movements.

SYMPHONY NO. 5 IN E MINOR OPUS 64

Three years separate the Fifth Symphony from the *Manfred* Symphony of 1885. This was another fallow period in Tchaikovsky's life as a composer, but not because of neurotic afflictions. Rather, Tchaikovsky toured as a conductor to Berlin, Leipzig, Hamburg, Prague, Paris, London, and also worked in the opera pit in St. Petersburg, where he was considered an effective interpreter of his own music. The big work of this interim was his opera *The Sorceress,* which he worked on from mid-1885 to its first performance in October 1887. Practically everything else Tchaikovsky composed during this time were small pieces or collections of small pieces: the eighteen songs of Opera 60 (1886) and 63 (1887), *The Mozartiana Suite* Opus 61 (1887), the *Pezzo Capriccioso* for Cello and Orchestra Opus 62 (1887), and the *Jurists' March* (1885). After a preoccupation with conducting his own music, Tchaikovsky had problems returning to the routine required for the larger works. The pangs of giving birth to the Symphony No. 5 in E Minor Opus 64 led to a slow beginning, so much so that Tchaikovsky feared that he had written himself out, but eventually he began to make steady progress:

May 15/27, 1888—To his brother Modest Tchaikovsky:

I have not yet begun to work, excepting of some corrections. To speak frankly, I feel as yet no impulse for creative work. . . . Still I am hoping gradually to collect material for a symphony.[124]

May 19/31, 1888—To Modest Tchaikovsky:

Now, little by little, with difficulty, I am beginning to squeeze the symphony from my benumbed brain.[125]

May 30/June 11, 1888—To Grand Duke Konstantin Romanov:

At the present time, I am intending to write a symphony; however, if it turns out that I have energy to burn and a subject occurs to me, then maybe I will write an opera.[126]

June 7/19, 1888—To Eduard Nápravník:

> I am working quite assiduously on a symphony, which, if I am not mistaken, will be as good as my previous ones.[127]

June 10/22, 1888—To Madame von Meck:

> Have I already told you that I intend to write a symphony? The beginning was difficult; inspiration seems to have come. We shall see![128]

June 11/23, 1888—To Grand Duke Konstantin Romanov:

> At the present time, I am working quite diligently on the composition of a symphony without a programme; by the end of the summer, I hope to finish it.[129]

June 17/29, 1888—To Mikhail Ippolitov-Ivanov:

> I am writing a symphony; have already finished the sketches and will soon start the instrumentation.[130]

June 22/July 4, 1888—Sketches finished.

July 25/August 6, 1888—To Madame von Meck:

> Half of the Symphony is re-orchestrated.[131]

August 14/26, 1888—To Madame von Meck:

> Symphony finished.[132]

October 1888—Score published by Jürgenson.

November 5/17, 1888—Premiere with St. Petersburg Philharmonic, Tchaikovsky conducting.

It has generally been taken for granted, particularly in the English-speaking world, that the Fifth Symphony is a programmatic work. This belief is based on an 1887–1888 Tchaikovsky Notebook in the Tchaikovsky Museum in Klin. The passage in question was discovered and first translated into English by Nicolas Slonimsky for the Boston Symphony Orchestra Program Book in 1937:

> Program of the First Movement of the Symphony: Introduction. Complete resignation before Fate, or, which is the same, before the inscrutable predestination of Providence. Allegro (I) Murmurs, doubts, plaints, reproaches against X X X [three crosses in the original]. (II) Shall I throw myself in the embraces of Faith??? [three question marks in the original]. [On the corner of the leaf] a wonderful programme, if I could only carry it out.[133]

Donald C. Seibert has demonstrated that the application of this program to the Fifth Symphony is contradicted by the letter quoted above (June 11/23, 1888) from Tchaikovsky to the Grand Duke Konstantin. He traces the history of the idea from 1902 when Ernest Newman set forth a program for Opus 64, to the citations of the Tchaikovsky Notebook Program in 1935 and its English translation, and to the growth of the idea in English writings, including some widely read scholarly publications on Tchaikovsky's music up to the publication of Seibert's article in 1990. Seibert demonstrates that Opus 64 does not fit the program and reveals how this has impacted critical evaluation of the Fifth Symphony. His arguments are thoroughly persuasive: the Fifth is simply not a programmatic work.[134]

To debunk the Fifth as programmatic, however, does not obviate the fact that it is a self-contained musical drama. A good deal of this long-term dramatic tension is achieved through the continued transformation of the introductory motto material (*O*) to the first movement (Example XV/29), where it is first treated as a *marcia funebre* underlined by its minor mode, dark timbres, regular rhythmic movement, and strong subdominant minor coloring. Some Russophiles claim the opening of the motto derives from Glinka's *A Life for the Tsar* with the text "Do not turn to sorrow."[135] In the slow movement, this motto becomes a military march that interrupts two times (mm.99, 158) otherwise passionate music. It is transformed into a waltz for the coda (m.241) of the third movement; its placement at the end recalls the fourth movement of Berlioz's *Symphonie fantastique*. For the Finale, it takes on a thematic role, where it is heard in the major mode as a ceremonial march in the introduction and as a blazing triumphal march (m.472) in the coda. Additionally, the march returns as something approaching battle music as *1K* (m.172) in the key of C major and in an anticipatory development (m.426) just prior to the blazing triumphal transformation. The *coup de*

EXAMPLE XV/29   Tchaikovsky. Symphony No. 5/1, mm.1–20.

grâce, however, is the surprising return of *I/1P* tutti *ƒƒƒƒ* in E major, which brings the symphony to a plagal close.

Whatever the motto in the abstract might mean, if anything at all, the narrative of the Fifth of Tchaikovsky is not unlike the Fifth of Beethoven: from darkness to light, despair to joy, defeat to triumph. Tchaikovsky underlines this archetypical narrative by moving on the largest scale from the minor to the major mode and from dark to bright timbres.

The cycle is also a coherent tonal structure. The strong plagal orientation of *O* and *I/1P* is to some degree fulfilled by the A major key of the third movement waltz. The key of the slow movement, which begins on the dominant of E minor, is in D major; it interlocks with the key of *I/1S* (m.162) and *I/K(P/1S,* m.194); D is also used for *1S* (m.128) of the Finale. Since D is a rather remote key to E, its main link is through B, the dominant of E and the relative minor of D, as outlined in the first movement's exposition. The dominant's dominant of the first movement also serves as the secondary key in the Andante second movement and the third movement. Finally, D is a secondary expository key (m.128) of the Finale before turning to C major for *2S* (m.148) and *K* (m.172).

Unlike the Fourth Symphony, the Fifth has a balanced cycle. As pointed out earlier, the Fourth places all of its weight in the first movement, with the remaining three pieces each less than half the length of the first. No. 5, however, has three movements nearly equal in length with only the waltz less than half the length of any of the other three. In this scheme, some might find that the center of gravity exists not in the first movement, but in the second with its impassioned subjects (mm.9, 24, and 45). Additionally, the Fifth's Finale fulfills nearly every demand of the late-nineteenth-century concept, while many might agree that the Fourth Symphony's last movement falls short as a conclusion to its big first movement.

After beginning the Symphony with the motto in three stark strophes scored for the darkest of orchestra timbres and for Tchaikovsky with a restricted (*pp* to *ƒ*) dynamic range, the Allegro con anima begins with *1P* (m.42), which is prepared for with four measures of alternating tonic/subdominant chords. This relationship was also highlighted in the slow introduction (mm.1, 3, 21) and establishes an important progression that generates some local as well as long-range gestures. Even the pick-up to *1P* (Example XV/30) underlines this; it is part of a subdominant rather than dominant sonority. *P*'s repetition (m.58) is decorated in *kuchka* fashion and extended. The extension builds to a *fortissimo* repeat of *1P* (m.100) that in Beethovenian "Eroica" fashion marks the beginning of *1T.* *2T* (m.116) is a sweeping lyric statement in two parts (mm.116, 128) followed by a varied repetition: *a–b–a–c.* *1S* (m.154) unfolds at a faster tempo and with smaller modules: *a* and *b,* with each pair consisting of four measures heard four times. *2S* (m.170) has two twelve-measure statements, the second of which leads to *K* (m.194). *K* is constructed of material from *1P* and *1S* in a series of four-measure units. Thus, in terms of the phrase rhythm from *2T* through *K,* Tchaikovsky alternates sections of fairly rapid change with broader statements.

This control of the phrase rhythms continues into the development section (m.214). *1S* is stated in two-measure modules, then in one-measure statements (m.226) as it decorates two-measure statements of *P,* and finally in half-measure gestures (m.255) marked by *1Pax* and a climax. *1Pax* recedes into an accompaniment to the broader eight-measure statement of *1T* (m.269) punctuated by *1S* (mm.272, 276). *1P* (m.277) and *1S* (m.297) now begin a buildup to another climax (m.309) which quiets for the recapitulation (m.321).

Tchaikovsky's choice of tonal areas for the exposition is somewhat unusual. The now almost normal three-key areas are used, with a clear E minor for both introduction and *P,*

EXAMPLE XV/30   Tchaikovsky. Symphony No. 5/1, mm.42–45.

B minor rather strongly articulated for *2T* (m.116), and *S* and *K* in D major. B minor serves as a bridge between the remote relationships of E minor and D major through their respective dominant and relative major relationships. As for the development, the tonal action is not unusual for the time: it begins in the key in which the exposition ends and has two descending bass patterns (mm.226, 235), which push the activity forward. *Pax* (m.255) begins on A major, which also descends chromatically to B-flat, as E-flat's dominant, then descends again (m.277), finally coming to rest mostly in G minor and thus finally F major. The V$_7$ of E-flat (m.269) is only two simple alterations from the home key: change B-flat to B-natural (m.319) and respell E-flat as D-sharp and suddenly we are in E minor for the recapitulatory moments of *P*'s returns (mm.321, 337).

Except for the tightening of *P*, including the exclusion of *1T(P)*, the recapitulation thematically runs its course, and the key scheme of E–B–D turns to E–C-sharp–E. As seen previously in Tchaikovsky, the coda commences like the development, but now in E, and then instead of developing *Pax, P* enters in the woodwinds and is then imitated by the strings as it builds to a *fff* climax (m.503). The unwinding of this climax over a two-measure basso ostinato is highly effective. The ostinato is disrupted (m.535) and the very end of the movement is particularly remarkable; after the strong orientation of the ostinato to dominant-tonic, it is deceived with a less-than-clear resolution. The movement concludes with an unusually voiced tonic chord (Example XV/31) as both bassoons play their low resonating B against a rumbling E and G in the cellos, and E in the timpani and basses. The result of this ending is an ambiguity that is something less than conclusive.

In this description of the first movement, a great deal of emphasis has been placed on Tchaikovsky's masterly manipulation of phrase rhythm. In addition, Tchaikovsky also displays a striking ability to manipulate the surface activity, particularly with the treatment of the compound duple meter (6/8), which allows the sorts of things that Brahms does in similar metric situations. Tchaikovsky knew Brahms's music and thought it to be cold; he believed himself to be a finer composer.[136] Tchaikovsky also knew Brahms's First Symphony from its transcription for piano four-hands, but whether he would imitate it is unknown. However, Tchaikovsky was apparently very much taken with another work known for its manipulations of triple meter: Robert Schumann's Symphony No. 3/1 "Rhenish."

In Tchaikovsky's first movement, there are a number of passages that incorporate cross rhythms. At the beginning, *P* (m.42), from its articulations, could be easily inferred as 3/4 rather than 6/8 (see Example XV/30), though its accompaniment is a straight duple meter. As the exposition unfolds, Tchaikovsky juxtaposes *P* in its implied triple meter with passages strongly duple (mm.80–86). Another example is the famous cross rhythms that lead

EXAMPLE XV/31   Tchaikovsky. Symphony No. 5/1, mm.527–42.

into *P*'s *fortississimo* restatement as *T* (mm.96–103). In addition, there is the lead-in to *K* (mm.186–94) with its notes tied over the bar line. Notice that except for *P* itself, Tchaikovsky treats these passages as rhythmic dissonances that provide transitions to material that is metrically stable.

Though many critics have disparaged the first movement as inferior to that of the Fourth Symphony, it is a capital accomplishment. In the entire first movement, there is not a single miscalculation affecting its orchestration, structure, and thematic material. Like most of Tchaikovsky's efforts, it requires an interpreter unwilling to overplay its potential for rubato and for breath-taking climaxes. The shape of this first movement has strong Classical proportions that, if maintained, allow the music to speak for itself.

The first movement's ambiguous ending is taken up as a point of beginning for the Andante: the first movement ends *on* E, the second movement begins on its minor dominant B and transits to D major, which brings to mind the tonal plan of the first movement's exposition. The horn solo in D major (Example XV/32) is marked by not only its melodic appeal, but also by a plethora of expressive markings that affect the dynamic of practically every note, the rubato of every phrase, and the overall character—dolce con molto espressivo. Tchaikovsky, it is claimed, wrote the following over this famous horn aria: "O que je t'aime! O, mon amie! [Oh, how I love you! Oh, my friend!]" Added to this famous passage is a counter melody (*Ab*) for the clarinet in its dark and brooding *chalumeau* register. Though introduced as a closing to the horn solo, *Ab* (m.24) takes on an importance as the piece progresses that supersedes *Aa* in sheer power. With the *Aa* return in the cellos (m.33), it is altered and decorated by counter lines in the woodwinds and horn. An outgrowth of the horn solo becomes a transition to *Ab* (m.45) now in D major rather than F-sharp;

EXAMPLE XV/32 Tchaikovsky. Symphony No. 5/2, mm.8–28.

armed with the tonic key, *Ab* now assumes greater prominence than *Aa*. The changes in dynamics (*p* to *fff*), the rubato indications, and the markings of character—con noblezza (m.45) and con desiderio (m.51)—result in a powerful, expressive effect.

B (m.66) turns to the key of F-sharp, which was already anticipated in the first appearance of *Ab* (m.24). It begins as an interlude to the passionate music of *A*; markings are now less detailed and the melody somewhat cooler. *Bax* (m.75) is used as a transition over a descending bass as the sonority and dynamics build for the first *fortissimo* return of the motto (m.99) over a G pedal. At the end, the orchestra's dominant-seventh chords of D, separated

EXAMPLE XV/32 *(continued)*

by rests, test the resonating acoustics of the hall. The pizzicatos (m.108) seem to be echoes of the acoustic chords, but become an accompaniment to *Aa*'s return (m.112). *Aa* is now heard twice (mm.112, 128) without change, except for its scoring and accelerating surface rhythm and tempo. A powerful transition leads to *Ab* (m.142) followed by the motto (*O*), *tutti* and reorchestrated. A subdued version of *Ab* forms the coda (m.170) as the movement ends peacefully.

The shape of the Andante is a ternary form but one with a strong binary orientation (Table XV/25). Its ternary structure is obvious: *A* (m.1)–*B* (m.66)–*A* (m.112), but the strength of a binary layout diminishes the importance of *B*, except to solidly establish another key. The strong two-part layout emphasizes larger aspects: *Introduction–A–B–Motto, Introduction–A–Motto–Coda. B* is further weakened by the fact that its key, F-sharp, has already been introduced by *Ab* (m.24) and it is absent from the last part of the movement. In addition, the second part—except for the motto—is entirely in D.

It is generally acknowledged that with the exception of the Finale to Symphony No. 6, the second movement of the Fifth is Tchaikovsky's most substantial slow symphonic piece. It is the aesthetic equal of any of Tchaikovsky's first movements in the range and control of its expression. Some commentators even believe it to be the center of gravity for the entire Fifth Symphony. If Tchaikovsky was a composer whose sense of strong transitions left something to be desired, here is a convincing example to the contrary, particularly with regard to the constituent parts of *A*. Perhaps this movement, more than any other, is illustrative of Tchaikovsky's concept of the symphony as "the most lyrical of musical forms,"[137] and also as the most cogently dramatic.

Again, Tchaikovsky includes, like in Symphony No. 3/2, a melancholy and somewhat introverted waltz in the cycle. David Brown hears the waltz as something that "haunted the first movement and lingered a little into the second." This justification of the waltz concept, being present in the previous movements, was also taken up previously by Edward Garden.[138] In contrast, this writer hears in the first and second movements nothing more than compound triple meter. In fact, the lack of a waltz accompaniment, plus the existence of cross rhythms atypical for waltz melodies (e.g., the duple subdivisions of the three-eighth unit in the slow movement), suggest that this idea is no more than wishful organic thinking.

The melody of the waltz proper was derived from a popular song Tchaikovsky had heard in Florence during his 1878 trip. He wrote to his patroness von Meck of this experience:

> I wrote to you from Florence about the boy whom I heard in the street one evening and whose wonderful voice so touched me. A couple of days ago to my indescribable joy I found this boy again; he sang "Perche tradir mi, perche lasciar mi" to me again and I simply fainted with delight. I can't remember when such a simple folk-song ever reduced me to such a state. This time he taught me a new local song, which was so attractive that I am going to try to find him again and make him sing it several times over so that I can write down the words and the melody. It goes more or less like this (someone called Pimpinella is singing—what that means I don't know but I am determined to find out).[139]

This melody was used in its entirety for Tchaikovsky's song "Pimpinella" from his Opus 38 (1878).

The melancholy side of this waltz starkly contrasts it with the more glittering piece from Berlioz's *Symphonie fantastique,* yet it appears that the Berlioz had some impact on Tchaikovsky's movement. We have already noted the placement of the motto (*O*) at the end, but Tchaikovsky's orchestration bears some similarities. In the opening accompaniment, the traditional waltz background with strings on the second beat and winds on the third is duplicated with a slightly different distribution in harps and winds (cf. Berlioz m.94), and note more generally the constantly shifting timbres and fabric with each repetition of the waltz theme. Completely Tchaikovsky's own is the bassoon solo (m.57). By placement, it should indicate closure; instead, the syncopations give another impression as they tumble directly into the middle section of the Trio in F-sharp minor (m.73).

TABLE XV/25
Tchaikovsky. Symphony No. 5/2: Structure

Andante cantabile con alcuna licenza 12/8

Introduction	A — a	b	a¹	trans.	b		trans.	Poco meno
	dolce con molto espress.	Con moto dolce espr.	Tempo 1	Poco più animato	Tempo 1 con noblezza	Poco più mosso	Poco animato	
p			mf	f ff	p	cresc. poco a poco	[dim.]	p
V/E minor	D	F-sharp	D	mod.	D	D		
m.1	9	24	33	39	45	52	59	61

Moderato con anima 4/4   Tempo Precedente

B		Motto	Tempo 1 1 12/8/8/4/4	A — a²	a³		trans.
	stringendo		Introduction (New)	molto espr.	cantabile	Più mosso	un poco più animato
mf	f cresc.	ff	mf	mf cresc. f ff	f		f
F-sharp	V/D	V/D	V/D	D	D		
66	96	99	108	112	128		134

Andante mosso

b				Allegro non troppo		Tempo 1
con anima	con dediderio e passione	con tutta forza		Motto	ritenuto	Coda Ab
						dolciss.
ff	ff	ffff	ffff	fff	pp	ppp
D	D			VII⁷/A	D	D
142	146	149	153	158	166	170

With the *spiccato assai* bowing on sixteenth notes tossed from one string instrument to another and then into the winds, some consider this portion to be a Scherzo. Together with the coloristic and constantly shifting orchestration, this is a persuasive view of the section's character. Whereas in the main waltz section the sound changed mainly at the level of the phrase, in the middle section the orchestration is constantly changing. In Example XV/33 notice what takes place in just the opening four bars: m.73—bassoon below strings; m.74—addition of second horn and second clarinet, deletion of some strings; m.75—oboes, first clarinet, and first horn added; m.76—second bassoon added to activate second beat and together with timpani create a cadential overlap. The waltz returns (m.145) in the oboe as some of the other instruments continue the figures of the Scherzo, but this ceases with the phrase repetition (m.153). This time the bassoon melody (m.198) extends on to a real closing (m.214) that cadences in F (mm.222–23) with—has the former professor forgotten?—parallel octaves. The closing is repeated again with the flawed F cadence followed immediately by a turnaround to A major and the motto theme (m.241) again darkly scored for clarinet, bassoons, and strings. The closing is now heard in the proper home key followed by the cadences for the full orchestra (i.e., without trombones and tuba). The ending no doubt prepares for the major-mode opening of the Finale and produces another subdominant relationship.

The Finale's major-mode opening (see Table XV/26) with the motto is not a burst of light, but rather that of a solemn processional. As with so many themes by Russian composers, it remains constant for the repetition, while its environment changes. The introduction builds to a climax, withdraws from it, and makes its way to the exposition. Notice the destination of the *crescendo;* it does not culminate in the processional melody, but rather its

EXAMPLE XV/33   Tchaikovsky. Symphony No. 5/3, mm.73–78.

TABLE XV/26

Tchaikovsky. Symphony No. 5/4: Structure

Andante maestoso 4/4

Introduction: | Motto |

Allegro vivace ¢

Exposition

	Oa	a¹	b	c	a²	a³	b¹	c¹	ext.	1Pa	a¹	b	a	1T	a	b	a	b	2T
						mf	p	cresc.	f ff	f p pp	f			mf			p		mf < ff
	E major						G pedal			E minor		C pedal				E pedal			A pedal
m.1	9		16	20	24		32	39	43 46	48	58	70	74	82			98		106

Development

trans.	1S	2S(1S)	1K (Motto)	2K(P)	1P	1S/1P
ff	mf	mf	ff	ff	ff	fff
D	C	C	C	F	F	B/F-sharp	E-flat minor
122	128	148	172	202	218	234	250

TABLE XV/26 (*continued*)

Group 1 — retrans. (*1Ptcx*)

	266	296	304	312	324	340	348	361	364	368
Tempo / Section		Poco più animato; *Recapitulation*; *1Pa* in bass	*1Pa*							
Dynamics	*ff dim.*	*pp* / *ff*	*fff*	*ff*	*mf*	*p cresc. mf*	*ff*			*fff*
Key		E minor			E minor					
Pedal / Harmony				C pedal		E pedal	A pedal	B pedal	C-sharp pedal	
Theme				*1Pb*	*1T* ⌐*a b*	*a b*⌐ *2T*				

Group 2 — trans.

	372	378	398	426	436	463	469	472	490	504	528	546
Tempo / Section				Poco meno mosso *O*	Molto vivace			Moderato assai e molto maestoso 4/4 *O*; largamente marciale, energico, con tutta forza		Presto ¢ *Pa/Ta S*		Molto meno mosso 6/4 *II/P*
Dynamics	*ff dim.*	*mf*	*mf cresc.*	*fff*				*fff*		*p cresc.*	*fff*	*ffff*
Key	F-sharp	E major	E major		E minor			E major		IV/E		
Pedal / Harmony				B pedal		B pedal —→						
Other			*1S* / *2S*				Half Cadence			*S*		

$\overline{b^1 \quad c^1}$ component. The climax of $\overline{a \qquad d^1}$ is held in reserve for the movement's and the symphony's coda. Tchaikovsky's exposition is a three-key affair: E minor (m.58), D major (m.128), and more importantly C major (m.148), which embraces *2S(1S,* m.148), *1K* (motto, m.172), and *2K(P,* m.202). Here, Tchaikovsky presents a series of contrasting and active ideas: *P* drives relentlessly to the downbeat with often a long anacrusis; *1T* is also anacrustic, but at the dimension of the beat; and *2T* contains three-measure up-beats and a single-measure arrival. Underneath these functions are active surface and harmonic rhythms that both stall, often with pedals, and then drive forward. *1S* (m.128) is mostly a downbeat theme as is its related *2S* (m.148) and *1K* (m.172), a reincarnation of the motto. *2K(P,* m.202) returns to the up-beat orientation of its source.

Though the introduction is marked Andante maestoso, which clearly spells out its character, the Allegro has virtually no indications until *2K* (m.202), where the violin parts are marked "feroce"—perhaps another indication of a military character, which certainly fits some, if not much, of this exposition.

The development is about half the length of the exposition. It first presents *P* (m.218) in F, then *1S* (m.234), accompanied by material from *P,* hovers between B and F-sharp before making its way to E-flat minor (m.250). After the mostly sustained high dynamics and the repeated requests for heavy bowings (marcatissimo), the pace slows, the dynamics diminish, and the tonality moves toward the subdominant (A) as a signal way to return to the tonic and the recapitulation (m.296). However, m.296 is not a fully convincing moment, since *P* is now in the bass and the treble carries a memorable countersubject. Measure 304 places *P* back in the top and increases the dynamic from *ff* to *fff*, but the *tutti* scoring is still not congruent with the beginning. Measure 312 is the most convincing recapitulatory moment, even though it tends more toward C major rather than E minor, because it is the only presentation that duplicates exactly *Pb* of the exposition.

The key scheme of the recapitulation collapses the three keys of the exposition to two: E minor and F-sharp for *1S* (m.378), while its related counterpart *2S* (m.398) returns to E major. Additionally, *2T* in the exposition had two rather lengthy pedals on E and A; in the recapitulation pedals occur on E, A, B, and C-sharp. The latter two pitches become part of an undulating ostinato that again undergirds the start of *1S* (m.378) and continues into *2S* (m.398). In order to make the coda more effective, *K* is bypassed and replaced by the poco meno mosso (m.426) and molto vivace (m.436) that takes up *Ob* and *Oc* of the motto with a dominant pedal. The passage culminates with the notorious half cadence (m.469)—perhaps Tchaikovsky's one major miscalculation. Rather than hearing it as a dominant, audiences inevitably think that the symphony has concluded, because of its strong rhetoric of closure, and begin to applaud. However, the composer must resolve two more issues: the complete establishment of E major and the statement of the motto in this key in a thoroughly triumphant transformation: *fff* marciale, energico, *con tutta forza* (m.472). Tchaikovsky then combines *Pa* with *Ta* (m.504) and restates *S* (m.518) in a Presto tempo. A sudden molto meno mosso 6/4 (m.546) presents *I/P fff* clothed in the major mode and the undeniable rhetoric of closure. With this, the drama of the motto is resolved and *I/P* is transformed from melancholy to triumph.

British musicologists, no doubt influenced by Tovey's essay and by the now-debunked program to the Fifth Symphony, have found the Finale wanting. Since the problem of the program has already been dealt with, here we need only discuss Tovey's remarks about "the problems of getting up any sense of movement in a finale at all":

> I am afraid that my *locus classicus* for impotence in that matter is the finale of Tchaikovsky's Fifth Symphony. If the composer had intended to produce the nightmare

sensation, or the Alice-and-Red-Queen sensation, of running faster and faster while remaining rooted to the spot, he might have been said to have achieved his aim here; but the melancholy fact remains that this finale resembles all other compositions in which the vitally necessary problem of movement has simply not occurred to the composer at all. I have been generously praised for my defence of Bruckner, whose popularity, now at best-seller height in Germany and Austria, has not yet begun in England; and, that being so, nobody has objected to my saying frankly that you must not expect Bruckner to make a finale "go." But the popular Tchaikovsky is in [*sic*] worse case than Bruckner, for he evidently expects his finales to "go," and neither the naïve listener, nor the still more naïve *Heibrau,* can at this time of day be helped by an analysis that leaves it to him to discover the fact that Tchaikovsky's finale wants to go and cannot.[140]

Tovey as a critic primarily focused on tonality, whereas Tchaikovsky tended to place emphasis on a myriad of elements to effect and support his musical arguments. While one could accept Tovey's observation if it were applied to the Finale of the Fourth Symphony, to say this of the Fifth seems completely out of place. Perhaps the Fifth is harmonically and tonally static at times, but this does not mean it moves faster and faster but goes virtually nowhere. (Is Tovey's reference to the final Presto?) Indeed, not every work that a critic encounters needs to be judged in comparison to Beethoven; many composers took their symphonies and their overall style in another direction, and they were not necessarily suffering from a Bloomian anxiety over influence (Bloom/ANXIETY INFLUENCE). Tchaikovsky seems to have been one of these composers. Nevertheless, this observer does not find the Fifth's Finale lacking at all. Nor does it suffer from the "finale problem," as Friedrich Blume would characterize it.[141] Instead, it is a completely effective conclusion.

In toto, Tchaikovsky's Fifth Symphony is more of a natural outgrowth of the *Manfred* Symphony than his Fourth Symphony. Whereas in Symphony No. 4, the fate fanfare/motto only recurs in its original form in the Finale, in Symphony No. 5 the motto theme, as in *Manfred,* returns in every movement of the cycle and is a natural part of the structure in the first and last movements; in the second movement its dramatic interruption is comparable to the fanfare's reappearance in the Finale of Symphony No. 4; and in the waltz, it is appended at the end. The difference between *Manfred* and Symphony No. 5 is one of genre; *Manfred* is governed more by the program, whereas the Fifth's forms and cyclic layout are governed more by a century of accumulated symphonic tradition. Essentially, the Fifth transfers the cyclic practices of the *Manfred* Symphony into a framework less at odds with the concept of the symphony as an absolute genre.

Tovey also takes to task both the symphony and its composer with faint praise and disdain. Concerning Tchaikovsky, he writes,

At the time of Brahms's death in 1897, Tchaikovsky was at the height of his popularity, and his own recent death was shrouded in tragic mystery. Even the "Brahminen" were remarkably timid in their obituary estimate of Brahms, and it was the correct thing to say that his symphonies were eclipsed by Tchaikovsky's. Of course they were, for they were not light music; and with this awful statement I have perhaps more than redressed the balance that I find myself to have disturbed by my high and sincere praise of Tchaikovsky's Pathetic Symphony. Now that my analyses have been collected in book form, the limitations of a counsel for the defence become manifest. The reader, no longer so conscious of the needs of the concert-goer, is apt to assume that I am still talking of the highest classical values, when I am merely stating the legitimate case for other music which is conspicuously the best of its kind. I have said nothing in praise of the Pathetic Symphony which I wish to retract. Nor have I given any grounds for supposing that I think its forms more than successful according to their lights. But I should not have helped the listener by introducing what I take to be Tchaikovsky's best work with an air of damaging patronage. If in 1907 a programme writer had dared to insinuate that Tchaikovsky was primarily a writer of light music and that his tragedy was melodrama, the only effect would have been to excite the exultant fury of the "Brahminen" against the numerically overwhelming opposition of all more persuasive and popular critics. The controversy would have soared to the Empyrean of that region which the Germans have somehow failed to designate by the name of *Heibrau,* and everybody would have been made uncomfortable; though not nearly so uncomfortable as Brahms and Tchaikovsky would have been in the presence of each other.[142]

And about the Fifth Symphony itself, Tovey writes,

> My own conclusion about Tchaikovsky's Fifth Symphony is that great injustice to its intentions results from regarding it as in any way foreshadowing the Pathetic Symphony. Like all Tchaikovsky's works, it is highly coloured; and a critic who should call it restrained would be in evident medical need of restraint himself; but the first three movements are in well-proportioned orthodox form, and my general impression of this symphony is that from first to last Tchaikovsky, though I have never been able to impute to him a sense of humour, is thoroughly enjoying himself. And I don't see why we shouldn't enjoy him too.[143]

Tchaikovsky himself came to have doubts about his Fifth, just as he had about his other symphonies. However, the case of the Fifth is somewhat different because Tchaikovsky conducted it on several occasions and the reception by the audience was overwhelmingly positive. On December 2/14, 1888, he wrote to Madame von Meck,

> After playing my new symphony twice in Petersburg and once in Prague I have become convinced that this symphony is unsuccessful. There is something repellant about it, a certain patchiness, insincerity, and artifice. All this the public instinctively recognizes. It was quite clear to me that the ovations which I received were directed at my previous activities but that the symphony itself was incapable of attracting or, at least, pleasing them. The realization of all this causes me a keen, tormenting feeling of discontent with myself. Have I really already, as they say, written myself out, and am I now only able to repeat and imitate my old former style? Last night I looked through the Fourth Symphony, *ours!* What a difference, how much loftier and better it is! Yes, this is all most, most distressing![144]

In contrast, a year earlier after conducting his Fifth in Hamburg on January 19/31, 1888, he had expressed more positive feelings about this symphony:

> I decided to play the Fifth Symphony in Hamburg. Each time through the players liked it better and better; at the final rehearsal there was a great show of enthusiasm, a flourish from the orchestra, and so on. The concert, too, went off excellently. The best thing is that I no longer find the symphony horrible and have started liking it again.[145]

The critical opinions of the press were mixed. The reviewer for *Nuvellist* found it lacking, when compared to earlier symphonies by the composer:

At the musical society we heard new compositions by Russian composers Tchaikovsky (the Fifth Symphony and the *Hamlet* Overture) and Shchurovsky (two excerpts from the opera "Bogdan Khmel'nitsky").... As far as the compositions of Tchaikovsky, he always attracts attention. The symphony lacks the merits of the second and fourth symphonies of the same composer: there is notable repetition in it of things already said by Mr. Tchaikovsky. Its character is dramatic. The two first movements make the greatest impression ... their themes are very beautiful and developed with complete mastery. The Scherzo is a kind of graceful waltz—a form beloved by Tchaikovsky. The Finale lacks sufficient [internal] bonds even in the character of its themes: in the beginning a quite protestant choral is audible, to which is joined a theme in the Russian style. The instrumentation is brilliant, but massive, due to the predominance of winds.[146]

César Cui, writing in the *Musical Review,* was even more critical of the finale:

The concert of the Philharmonic Society, which consisted of works by P. I. Tchaikovsky under his personal direction, was rich in important new works: performed for the first time were the most recent, fifth symphony in E-minor by Tchaikovsky, his second piano concerto and an overture-fantasia by Laroche, arranged by Tchaikovsky.

One might think that in his new symphony Tchaikovksy looked on sound not as a means but as a goal, for which music serves only as a pretext, given the degree to which aural interest predominates over musical interest. But even in this case Tchaikovsky is only half successful in fulfilling his mission, because if we frequently hear in the symphony new aural effects and new combinations of instruments, then equally often we hear clumsy instrumentation, with a heavy predominance of brass, which drown out all the other instruments. With regard to the musical side of the symphony, this can be reduced to the following characteristic features: in the symphony there are three waltzes.... God forbid that I regard waltzes disrespectfully: as much talent and feeling may be displayed in them as in any other form, but all the same the form of the waltz is narrow and superficial, and to introduce the waltz into a symphony is just as disrespectful to the latter as to introduce some parvenu to a venerable aristocratic circle. The place for the waltz is in a suite, not in the symphony, which preserves always the strict and serious order of its form.—As if in [counterweight] to the three waltzes, there are three funereal episodes in the symphony.... In the first movement there is much pointless repetition, some of which amounts to simple repetition of the very same chords.—the third movement of the symphony—a waltz—is more successful than the others; it is only a leftover snapshot of the typical waltzes of Tchaikovsky, but it is simpler and shorter than the other movements and is easier to listen to. The finale distinguishes itself with its vulgarity and blather. Vulgarity, for example, in the episode in which the brass strike chords on every quarter note, appropriate for the trio from the march from Faust, in which the same device was used.... And among all these cheerless sounds of the finale appears, but then vanishes, one lovely phrase, which recalls Rimsky-Korsakov. On the whole, the symphony distinguishes itself by its lack of ideas, its routine, the predominance of sound over music, as was already noted, and is listened to with difficulty....[147]

Both the Fifth and the Sixth Symphonies belong to Tchaikovsky's late phase, which begins *ca.* 1885, according to David Brown and Edwin Evans, or *ca.* 1888, according to Edward Garden.[148] Between these two almost-landmark works, Tchaikovsky produced the *Hamlet* Overture-Fantasy Opus 67 (1888), *The Sleeping Beauty* ballet Opus 66 (1889), the opera *The*

Queen of Spades (1890), his string sextet *Souvenir de Florence* Opus 70 (1890), incidental music to *Hamlet* Opus 67a (1891), the opera *Iolanta* (1891), *The Nutcracker* ballet (1891–1892), and worked on an E-flat Symphony, which ultimately became the Piano Concerto No. 3. The Sixth Symphony, known as the "Pathétique," was the last work Tchaikovsky completed.

SYMPHONY NO. 6 "PATHÉTIQUE" IN B MINOR OPUS 74

The Symphony No. 6 in B Minor Opus 74 "Pathétique" was composed over seven months in 1893, interrupted by periods from five weeks to two months:

February 4/16, 1893	Beginning of sketching.
February 9/21, 1893	First movement sketched.
February 10/22, 1893	Letter to brother Anatoly saying he was completely absorbed by symphony.
February 11/23, 1893	Letter to Vladimir "Bob" Davidov:

I must tell you how happy I am about my work. As you know, I destroyed a Symphony which I had partly composed and orchestrated in the autumn. I did wisely, for it contained little that was really fine—an empty pattern of sounds without any inspiration. Just as I was starting on my journey (the visit to Paris in December, 1892) the idea came to me for a new Symphony. This time with a programme; but a programme of a kind which remains an enigma to all—let them guess it who can. The work will be entitled "A Programme Symphony" (No. 6). This programme is penetrated by subjective sentiment. During my journey, while composing it in my mind, I frequently shed tears. Now I am home again I have settled down to sketch out the work, and it goes with such ardour that in less than four days I have complete the first movement, while the rest of the Symphony is clearly outlined in my head. There will be much that is novel as regards form in this work. For instance, the Finale will not be a great Allegro, but an Adagio of considerable dimensions. You cannot imagine what joy I feel at the conviction that my day is not yet over, and that I may still accomplish much. Perhaps I may be mistaken, but it does not seem likely. Do not speak of this to anyone but Modeste.[149]

Work interrupted in order to fulfill conducting engagements.

March 19/31, 1893	Resumes work on symphony.
March 24/April 5, 1893	Sketches finished.

Work interrupted for travels and touring as conductor.

July 20/August 5, 1893	Orchestration commences.
July 22/August 3, 1893	Letter to Modest Tchaikovsky about orchestration:

I am up to my eyes in the Symphony. The further I go, the more difficult the orchestration becomes. Twenty years ago I should have rushed it through without a second thought, and it would have turned out all right. Now I am turning coward, and have lost my self-confidence. I have been sitting all day over two pages, yet they will not come out as I wish. In spite of this, the work makes progress, and I should not have done so much anywhere else but at home.[150]

August 3/15, 1893	Letter to Vladimir "Bob" Davidov about composition:

The Symphony which I intended to dedicate to you—although I have now changed my mind—is progressing. I am very well pleased with its contents, but not quite so satisfied with the orchestration. It does not realize my dreams. To me, it will seem quite natural, and not in the least astonishing, if this Symphony meets with abuse, or scant appreciation at first. I certainly regard it as quite the best—and especially the "most sincere"—of all my works. I love it as I never loved any one of my musical offspring before.[151]

August 12/24, 1893	Orchestration finished.
August 20/September 1, 1893	Score sent to his publisher Jürgenson.
October 9/21, 1893	Meeting with Nikolay Kashkin. Told him about reservations concerning cycle of Symphony No. 6:

He had to catch the night rail to Petersburg, where he was going to conduct his Sixth Symphony, which was still unknown to me. He said he had no doubt as to the first three movements, but the last was still a problem, and perhaps after the performance in Petersburg he should destroy the Finale and replace it by another.[152]

October 16/28, 1892	First performance St. Petersburg.
October 17/29, 1893	Program Symphony as a title rejected as was "Tragic." Modest then suggests "Pathétique," which was enthusiastically endorsed by his brother.
October 18/30, 1893	Dedication to Davidov communicated to Jürgenson with following remark:

Be so kind as to put on the title page what stands below.
To Vladimir Lvovich
Davidov
(No. 6)
Composed by P.T.

I hope it is not too late.[153]

October 21/November 2, 1893	Tchaikovsky dies.
November 6/18, 1893	Second St. Petersburg performance conducted by Nápravník.
1894	Published by Jürgenson.

Originally, the Sixth Symphony was simply designated as "Program Symphony," but the program was not to be revealed. It was only between the first performance at St. Petersburg and the mailing of the score to his publisher Jürgenson that "Pathétique" was placed on the title page together with the dedication to Tchaikovsky's nephew Vladimir "Bob" Davidov (Plate B12). On the very next day, Tchaikovsky wrote to Jürgenson requesting the title be withdrawn. This combination of the mysterious extra-musical associations; the affect of the symphony as a whole, and in particular the opening and concluding movements; and the dedication to Tchaikovsky's nephew for whom he had had a homoerotic attraction since 1884, has provided grist for the so-called new musicologists. However, the actual evidence for any specific programmatic interpretation of Symphony No. 6 is rather thin.

Some have attempted to connect an 1892 program, which has sometimes been associated with the aborted E-flat Symphony (No. 7), as relevant to Symphony No. 6. But Symphony No. 6 is separated from this program by perhaps two years and if indeed this were to be the program for the Sixth Symphony, there would be no reason to keep it a "secret" one:

> The ultimate essence of the plan of the symphony is LIFE. First part—all impulsive passion, confidence, thirst for activity. Must be short. (Finale DEATH—result of collapse.)
>
> Second part love; third disappointments; fourth ends dying away (also short).[154]

In addition, attempts to connect this program with the B Minor Symphony are not particularly gratifying. It is difficult to argue that the symphony is about "Life" since both its first and last movements are concerned with musical figures and the minor mode that focus one's thoughts on death. In the first movement there is the descending chromatic tetrachord (m.1), which, together with its dark colors, is an undisputed signal of mourning or death. There is also a fanfare (m.67), the eschatological call to judgment. The quotation from the Russian Orthodox Requiem having the text "With thy Saints, O Christ, give peace to the soul of thy servant" is not about life, but the soul in the afterlife; this is played by three trombones and at the beginning with the trumpet in the low register, a sound associated also with the funereal. Additionally, this passage has sighs and shrieks that bring to mind Slavic mourning. Furthermore, S is scored for strings *con sordini,* a color also associated with mourning, here putting a veil on the sonority of the *teneramente* melody's first presentation. Additionally, does the music underline "all impulsive passion, confidence, thirst for activity"? The "all impulsive passion" seems rather subdued, particularly by Tchaikovskian standards. The last portion of the first movement (m.305) begins *con dolcezza* with an agitated background for S before freeing itself from this mood, but then it returns to it (m.326) with murmurs of the distant timpani. The coda (m.335) is the spiritual apotheosis: the major-mode rising chorale in the winds and the descending pizzicato scales in the strings ending with timpani, a trio of trombones, and tuba. In our interpretation, this could be the elevation of the soul and the descent of the body into its grave.

Further, if the second movement is about love, this is certainly a very cool version, particularly if compared to the slow movement of Symphony No. 5. Certainly the Scherzo/March also cannot be about disappointment. The Finale slow movement is again about death, which is signaled by the striking of the tam-tam. However, as the program implies, the music dies away at the end. Thus, the program is really only convincing with regard to the Finale. One can only conclude that the program's connection to the plan of the Symphony No. 6 is, at best, only marginal.

The title "Pathétique" fits the music perfectly as a work of art that arouses feelings of pity, sorrow, sympathy, and compassion. In this context, the Tchaikovsky Sixth becomes a characteristic symphony and one can read the central two movements as intermezzi or recollections of the past.

The death theme has also been pursued by Henry Zajaczkowski, especially in regard to the Finale. Zajaczkowski demonstrates, by way of Gerald Abraham's work, an association with the divided melody between first and second violins in its aural realization, and passages about death in *Eugene Onegin* and *The Queen of Spades.*[155] Zajaczkowski also demonstrates correspondences between Bizet's *Carmen* and the S theme of the first movement of the "Pathétique," and pursues this topic further using Freudian-derived methods and interpretations. The correspondences themselves require either distortions of one or the other themes or accepting as significant what are rather common activities of tonal music. However, that which cannot be tested by an aural correspondence is, in our view, musically irrelevant. More relevant would be comments about more observable characteristics, descending lines, and dark colors, which bring this movement into line with the content and affect of the first movement.

Perhaps a stronger point of reference for clues to the program of the "Pathétique" Symphony is its musical similarities with Spohr's Fourth Symphony "The Consecration of Sound." Spohr's third movement is mainly a Tempo di Marcia, and the Finale is mainly a triple-meter slow movement whose principal theme has a striking similarity to S of Tchaikovsky's Finale. Spohr's last movement consists of funeral music followed by material similar to Tchaikovsky's S, which is titled in Spohr's movement "Trost in Thränen" (Comfort in Tears). This affect rings true for Tchaikovsky's Finale as does the chorale "Lasst uns den Leib begraben" (We lay the Body in the Grave), which Spohr also uses in his Finale. Both Finales end *pianissimo* or quieter (*pppp*).[156]

In terms of biography, the "death" interpretation of the Sixth could be associated with the death and terminal illnesses of the composer's sister Aleksandra in 1891 and the serious illnesses and anticipated deaths of his friends Alexey Apukhtin, Karl Albrecht, Konstantin Shilovsky, Vladimir Shilovsky, and Nikolay Zverev. Tchaikovsky himself was obsessed with death, and these illnesses and deaths could only have heightened it.

The only biographical discussion of the "Pathétique" from an authoritative source is a letter from Modest Tchaikovsky to the Pressburg city archivist Johan Batka (1845–1917) dating from April 1907:

> You ask me for an explanation of the "Pathétique"—but unfortunately, dear friend, I will never be able to impart it to you in the way that my brother had it in his head. He took the secret with him to the grave. If, however, you would like to hear the program that I developed for myself and that, after all the things I have found out about it from my brother, seems to me to contain the most likely interpretation, I will write it down as follows:
>
> The first part depicts his life, that mixture of pain, suffering, and the irresistible yearning for great and noble [qualities]; on the one hand, struggles and mortal dread; on the other hand, divine delights and heavenly love of all the beautiful, true, and good in everything that eternity promises us of heavenly grace. Since my brother was throughout most of his life a decided optimist, he ended this first movement with the recurrence of this second topic.
>
> In my opinion, the second movement depicts the fleeting delights of his life—delights that cannot be compared to the common pleasures of other people and are therefore expressed in the entirely uncommon five-four meter.
>
> The third movement describes the history of his musical development. It was nothing but a flirtation, a kind of pass-time, and a game at the beginning of his life—until the age of twenty—, but then he becomes more and more serious and finally ends covered in glory. This is expressed by the triumphal march at the end.
>
> The final movement presents the state of his soul during the last years of his life—the bitter disappointment and the deep pain of having to recognize that even his artistic fame is transitory and unable to soothe his horror of the eternal void, the same void which threatens to devour everything that he loved and considered all his life to be eternal and lasting, inexorably and for ever.
>
> Of this entire explanation I can only confirm the meaning of the last part with documents. My brother talked about all this several times in his letters.[157]

Modest offers little here that could not be ascertained from the character and our historical knowledge of the work. Still, it confirms how "secret" the program really was; Tchaikovsky did not relate it in detail even to his closest confidant.

Another interpretation of the Sixth centers around its dedicatee, Vladimir "Bob" Davidov, the son of Tchaikovsky's sister Aleksandra, for whom the composer possessed a passionate obsession. In the view of some critics and musicologists, the "Pathétique" is about the relationship of the composer with his nephew. The nature of this relationship is not entirely clear and it cannot be confirmed if Tchaikovsky's interests were reciprocated. Nevertheless, a leading advocate of a strong interaction between Tchaikovsky's homosexuality and his music is Timothy Jackson. In his monograph on the Sixth, Jackson views the "Pathétique" to be Tchaikovsky's Eros Symphony:

> In the last decades of the nineteenth century and the first of the twentieth century, artists, writers, and composers began to address "difficult" issues with a directness that was essentially new. Although Tchaikovsky referred to the program of the *Pathétique* (his own title) as "secret," in fact its homo-erotic content was made as explicit as possible by the dedication to Bob, and by many other purely musical factors; and this programmatic substance was tactfully recognized (like the composer's homosexuality itself) by Tchaikovsky's immediate circle and widely suspected by the broader public. During approximately two years of gestation (1891–93), this "not-so-secret" program of the Sixth Symphony evolved into an erotic drama of doomed homosexual love richly adorned with intertextual references to opera, specifically to Wagner's *Tristan,* Bizet's *Carmen,* and Tchaikovsky's own operas, especially the last two, *The Queen of Spades* (1890) and *Iolanta* (1891), and a number of earlier works including the Overture *Romeo and Juliet* in its various incarnations (1869, 1879, and 1880), and ballet *Swan Lake* (1875–76).[158]

Jackson's monograph is richly layered, dealing with "Pathétique" metaphors for sexuality and race; gambling and destiny; the "not-so-secret" program; the relationship to the Six Romances Opus 73; and "deconstructing homosexual grande passion pathétique." But perhaps this rich layering and broad context, both historical and contemporary, is the central problem of such an interpretation: it deals with concepts for which we possess little or no evidence of their direct relationship to Tchaikovsky and the music of Symphony No. 6.

Again, the title, the dedication, the composer's homosexuality, the so-called program, the composer's neuroses, and the composer's death within days of the "Pathétique" Symphony's first hearing under the composer's baton do present an inviting series of circumstances. But these circumstances need to be tested against the existing documentation, and the hypotheses based on these circumstances require their own corroboration.

At the very center of distinction for the Sixth Symphony is the make-up of the cycle which, in addition to Spohr's Fourth Symphony, is also reminiscent of Rimsky-Korsakov's *Antar* Symphony/Suite. If we look at the "Pathétique's" layout, what is immediately noticeable is the slow movement at the end and a movement in third position that combines aspects of a Scherzo, March, and Finale. In fact, the rhetoric of ending is so strong in Tchaikovsky's third-movement Allegro that, similar to before the end of Symphony No. 5/4, the audience will burst into spontaneous applause. Indeed, when he was in Cambridge, Tchaikovsky told a friend of Charles Stanford that his original intent was to conclude the Sixth with what became the third movement.[159]

There is a larger ramification for concluding the symphony with a slow movement that ends quietly: it provides a solution to the problem of writing an effective Finale that counterbalances the first movement. In the Sixth, both first and final movements end quietly and slowly, resulting in a sort of poetic parallel only matched in the Fourth Symphony of Spohr and the Third Symphony of Brahms. This is the most satisfying of the composer's symphonic conclusions. Its only parallel is the end of the *Manfred* Symphony, except that the introspective conclusion here comes after a first movement with a lengthy slow coda/recapitulation. From another perspective, the slow last movement of Symphony No. 6 can be viewed as a significant afterthought to the third movement with its heroic close.

It is the tonal plan of the cycle that solidifies the slow final movement as the close. Both first and last movements end in B, the first movement in B major, the last in B minor, an exact reversal of expectations. The Symphony commences in E minor, which recalls the subdominant prominence in Symphony No. 5. The first and second movements interlock tonally: D major is the secondary key of the first movement, and is the only structural key of the following Allegro con grazia. Indeed, the middle section of the first movement is undergirded by a D pedal, which strongly counters its B minor tonality. The third movement Scherzo/March is in G with a secondary key of E; G is a third below B as D is a third above, and E is the key at the symphony's beginning. The Finale returns to the B/D axis of the first movement. Thus, this is the composer's most tightly knit cyclic tonal plan.

Paradoxically, the first movement (Table XV/27) is both structurally tight in its main thematic statements and elaborations (*P* [m.20] and *T* [m.31]) and at the same time prolix in the constant expansion of the form by the addition of new material. If indeed this movement is a programmatic one, its narrative is probably explicated by the six episodes of new material (*N*) that appear after the exposition. The opening swath of material from the beginning up to *S* (m.90) is an expository section preceded by an introduction that is almost Brahmsian in its manner of evolving out of the opening material. The slow introduction, composed after the rest of the movement, both adumbrates *P*—but in the subdominant—and sets in no uncertain terms the character of the following Allegro. *P* (m.20) is presented in two parallel statements, here labeled as *P* and *1T(P)* in m.31, the second of which seamlessly expands to a series of *T* themes that are alike enough to provide a continuity of thought, yet different enough to be distinct from one another. All are marked by lively sixteenths and are mostly in the minor mode. Though distinctly Tchaikovskian, this sort of sound recalls Mendelssohn. *5T* (m.68) to some extent breaks this spell with the trumpet fanfares. *S* (m.90) is a different sort of theme that is not savored for its developmental possibilities, but for its melodic beauty. Tchaikovsky's treatment of it is not to tear it apart; he keeps the melody unadulterated and treats it to *kuchka* variations.

After the serenity of *S* (m.90) and *K* (m.142) in D major, the dramatic shock of *1N* (m.161), *fortissimo, tutti,* and in the key of A/C minor destroys everything the melodies of *S* and *K* might represent. However, this passage is merely an *exordium* to the feroce fugato that follows based on *P*. Though previously we have complained about the ineffectiveness of Tchaikovsky's symphonic fugatos, this one is effective both dramatically and musically. It leads to *2N* (m.186), an episodic dialogue of strings and winds; *3N* (m.190), an apotheosis of the descending lines first heard in the slow introduction; and *4N* (m.202), the Requiem chorale, properly set for the brass with appropriate wailing figures.

A lengthy descent brings us to an Allegro replay of the introduction (m.229), which builds to a *fff* recapitulation (m.245), restated with a string/wind dialogue and then in an intensified rendition in E-flat minor (m.263). *3N* (m.267) returns in polyphony and is inverted over a dominant pedal that continues into *5N* (m.277) and the end of the exposition's first part, which in this recapitulation is fully reformulated. Except for the first statement of *P* in the home key, the recapitulation acts more like a development by using and further working

TABLE XV/27
Tchaikovsky. Symphony No. 6/1: Structure

Introduction (Adagio 4/4) / Exposition (Allegro non troppo)

	Adagio 4/4 Introduction			Allegro non troppo Exposition					Un poco animando				Andante	Moderato mosso	
Theme	Oa	a¹	a-trans.	P	1T(P)	2T	3T	4T	5T/3T Fanfare	4T	5T/3T Fanfare	trans.	1S teneramente molto cantabile con espanzione	2S/2T	2S/2T
Key	E minor			B minor		D	C-sharp	D-sharp	D-sharp	D-sharp	D-sharp	V/D	D major		
Dynamic				p											
m.	m.1	7	12	20	31	43	51	63	68	63	68	86	90	101	109

Development (Andante 12/8 4/4 — Adagio mosso / Allegro vivo)

	Adagio mosso			Allegro vivo Development				
Theme	1S	1K	2K(1S) dolce possible	1N	P-fugato feroce	2N	3N marcatissimo	4N (Requiem Chorale)
Key	D major	IV/D	D	C minor	D minor	D major	E-flat	D minor mod.
Dynamic				ff	ff		fff	
m.	130	142	154	161	171	186	190	202

Recapitulation / Coda

	Recapitulation							Coda			
Theme	O/retrans.	P	P dev.	P dev.	3N	5N		1S con dolcezza	1S con tenerezza	6N (Chorale) cantabile	morendo
Key	B minor	B minor	B minor	E-flat minor		B	B	B major	B major	B major	
Dynamic	p pp cresc.	fff	ff pp cresc.	ff	fff pesante F-sharp pedal	fff	ffff dim.	p cresc. fff	ppp		
m.	224	245	249 259	263	267	277	299	305	326	335	351

over new material first introduced in the development section proper. *S* (m.305), *con dolcezza,* is now presented in a less serene environment, with rising agitated scales in the lower strings. In its ***fff*** repetition, the chromatic destabilizers become ornamental and this extraordinary melody (*1S*) almost disappears in a passage that *crescendos* to ***pp*** and *diminuendos* to ***pppp***. The coda (m.335) presents a new chorale (*6N*) that rises and then descends through the wind band.

In this first movement, Tchaikovsky has essentially reformulated the late-nineteenth-century textbook form. The exposition only fulfills this ideal in its different key areas and with deep contrasts, including a change in tempo. A lengthy section of the exposition is developmental, while the development section introduces four new ideas and its key scheme violates a basic principle by using keys already given their due in the exposition. In the recapitulation, Tchaikovsky emphasizes further development of *P,* a theme structured almost ideally for this purpose, and *3N* (m.267); then he introduces *5N* (m.277) and concludes the movement with another chorale-like melody (*6N*). A good deal of this reassignment of large-scale functions is generated by the introduction and the exposition, which concentrates on the presentation and evolution of *P* in a developmental cast. This in turn restricts what one can do with this material in the development; before the retransition Tchaikovsky devotes but fifteen measures of a high-tension *fortissimo* "feroce" fugato to *P.* In a sense, the reformulated start of the recapitulation is only a logical extension of this passage.

As seen in Symphonies Nos. 4 and 5, dynamics play a structural role. In this first movement, however, the dynamics themselves call for a wider range and distinctions that may be impossible for any performer to convey: ***ffff*** (m.299) to ***pppppp*** (m.160). In the case of the former, it should be noted that although this dynamic is called for, Tchaikovsky does not score this moment for *tutti* orchestra nor does he use all of the brass instruments capable of contributing to this climax. The ***pppppp*** marking comes just before the development, as the bassoon carries the clarinet melody into a lower range. Some conductors rescore this bassoon passage for bass clarinet; the quiet entry would place the solo bassoon louder than the solo clarinet, while the bass clarinet can achieve a better timbral blend and a dynamic distinction. However, Tchaikovsky knew the capabilities of the bass clarinet and used it in the *Manfred* Symphony, which suggests he must have thought the bassoon scoring was better. On the other hand, had he lived to conduct the Sixth with different orchestras in different venues, he might have changed his mind.

The first movement is thought by many critics and commentators to be Tchaikovsky's finest sonata-form movement, despite the fact that it is a break from tradition. Its success can be attributed to the realization that, for the first time, this composer has not filled a sonata form with music, but allowed the content and the program(?) to manipulate the structure. For a composer like Tchaikovsky, who possessed both dramatic and lyric gifts, the old mold extracted from Haydn, Mozart, and Beethoven did not suit his compositional temperament. Having found a solution to this situation, his death within a week of the premiere of the "Pathétique" is a tragedy expressed within the symphony under discussion.

Modern commentaries nearly uniformly refer to the Sixth Symphony's second movement as a waltz in 5/4 time:

> 1949—Cooper: "a kind of *valse macabre.*"[160]
>
> 1966—Keller: "Is there a more original transformation of scherzo function, a more breath-taking contrast, than ultimate metamorphosis of the Tchaikovsky waltz that is the second movement in 5/4 time?"[161]
>
> 1969—Warrack: "by a stroke of genius it is in 5/4, a broken-backed waltz, limping yet graceful."[162]

1973—Garden: "the lovely five-four 'Valse.' "[163]

1980—Brown (*NG*): "one of the middle movements is a waltz, this time given a curious but charming limp by being written in 5/4."[164]

1996—Kohlhase: "the 5/4 waltz of the 'Pathétique.' "[165]

1997—Kraus: "he cleverly subtracts one beat from every other measure of a waltz to produce 5/4 meter."[166]

On the surface, a 5/4 waltz seems ridiculous; since the meter is the primary determinant of a dance style, can one imagine a 3/4 gallop or a 4/4 sarabande? However, Tchaikovsky did compose a movement in his *Eighteen Pieces for Piano* Opus 72 called "waltz" in 5/8 meter which dates (April 17/29, 1893) from the time he was also working on the "Pathétique" Symphony. Of the above writers, only Kohlhase mentions Opus 72 as a parallel. It should also be noted that quintuple meter in Scherzo movements has some precedents in Russian symphonies: the Rimsky-Korsakov Symphony No. 3 (1866–1873) and the Borodin Symphony No. 3 (1882, 1886–1887).

Whereas the Rimsky-Korsakov treats the 5/4 meter as one beat to the bar and combines it with a 3/4 meter running simultaneously, the Borodin uses 5/8 in 2+3 disposition with a few pairs of 2/4 bars interpolated. Tchaikovsky's handling of the 5/4 meter is somewhat more complicated in the changing relationship of the melody to the accompaniment. The melody is usually cast as 2+3, but the accompaniment might be 3+2. For example, take the opening eight-bar phrase:

melody:	2+3	2+3	2+3	2+3	2+3	2+3	2+2+1	5(2+3)
accompaniment:	3+2	2+3	3+2	2+3	3+2	3+2	2+3	3+2

The above example is fairly easy to illustrate because it is relatively simple, but consider m.17 (Example XV/34): the strings have the melody 2+3 beats, the clarinets and horns divide the bar 3+2, and the timpani and basses can be read as 2½+2½ (♩ ♫ ♩ ♩). Consider also m.25: here there are several possibilities for subdividing the string parts.

The middle section, here not labeled as the Trio, is marked *con dolcezza e flèbile* (with sweetness and mournfully). Though in B minor, the pedal D that engulfs every bar of the Trio considerably obscures B minor as a decisive key and makes it something of an inflection. The pounding out of every quarter note in the timpani, the contrabass, and bassoons seems to be an imitation of heartbeats. How the beginning Allegro con grazia mixes with the Trio may be difficult to rationalize; the conductor Arthur Nikisch explained the movement as "a smile through tears" in relationship to the first movement. But did the tears reappear in the central section with its sighing motives?

At the larger level, this second movement's form conforms to what one might expect of a Scherzo movement: use of binary structures with repeat bars, elimination of repeats for the reprise (m.96), and a well-defined closing area at the end of the first main section (mm.48 and 144). Somewhat surprising, considering the small-dimension attention to rhythm, is the unrelenting sameness of the phrase rhythms; every phrase is an eight-bar group.

For the coda (m.152), Tchaikovsky takes a page out of Berlioz's *Symphonie fantastique* waltz coda: the descending scales in the winds countered by rising scales in the strings also rhyme with the first movement's coda. To this brew, Tchaikovsky adds the D pedal from the middle section. Materials from both the first and second sections are combined for the coda's conclusion, which, like the first and last movements, ends quietly.

EXAMPLE XV/34 Tchaikovsky. Symphony No. 6/2, mm.17–26.

If the second movement was considered by Tchaikovsky to be its Scherzo and has a heritage in movements by Rimsky-Korsakov and Borodin, the third movement mixes Scherzo qualities from Berlioz's "Queen Mab" Scherzo and Borodin's First Symphony with its diametrical opposition, a march, which was a style Tchaikovsky had previously used in Symphony No. 2/2 and Symphony No. 4/2 and 3. The theme of the march itself is not original with Tchaikovsky; it is derived from Joachim Raff's Finale to Symphony No. 3/3 "Im Walde." However, the imagination that Tchaikovsky applies to it outstrips Raff's portrayal of the entry and exit of the Wild Hunter, Frau Holle, and Wotan from the forest. There is no reason to believe that Raff's narrative has any relevance to tapping into the secret program of the "Pathétique."

This piece is cast into a large binary structure ($\overline{A\ B}\ \overline{A\ B}$), each part of which begins in a Scherzo style in 12/8 time (mm.1 and 139) and concludes with a march in 4/4 time (mm.71 and 229). As expected, tonally the first part is open (G major to E major), the second part closed (G to G). The oddity here is that the march material of the second part of each section is thematically adumbrated in the Scherzo's first part. This is reminiscent of Symphony No. 4/4 where the material of *B* was first heard within *A*. But this is not the only way that the various sections are held together. At the largest level the use of the orchestra and dynamics create an overall *crescendo* that allows the movement to culminate at its very end. In the first $\overline{A\ B}$ pair (mm.1–138), the maximum sound is an orchestra virtually bereft of the heavy brass and percussion at the *ff* dynamic; the second $\overline{A\ B}$ pair plus coda (mm.139–347) increases the dynamic target to *ffff* and uses a full complement of brass with piccolo, bass drum, and cymbals for a rousing end.

More than the dynamics, it is the brilliant orchestration that sets this movement apart from the darker hues of the surrounding pieces. In the Scherzo portions, Tchaikovsky divides his strings and sets off a dialogue between strings and woodwinds. Additionally, he introduces the march motive (*Bx*), which moves from oboes to trombones and on to other instruments as the strings, oblivious to the march, continue the Scherzo material, now seasoned with pizzicatos descending through the fabric. Similar activities continue throughout the Scherzo sections. Because of the melodic nature of the march theme rather than the purely coloristic one of the Scherzo, the orchestration in *B* changes at the phrase level rather than at the measure level or smaller. With *A*'s reprise (m.139), everything is inflated, even at the very start where the quiet *divisi* first violins and violas are now *tutti* strings. The responses in the winds are also fuller, culminating with an A pedal over which *Bx* (m.197) is quietly tossed from one instrument to another. A searing *crescendo* over a now chromatically rising bass brings us to the movement's first *fff* for the *tutti* orchestra, less the battery. Whirls of sixteenths, sextuplets, and thirty-seconds tossed between strings and winds drive into *B*'s reprise (m.229); the Scherzo has now been totally rejected as only 4/4 meter and duple subdivisions dominate and the dynamics of *fff* and *ff* are sustained to the very end.

One might expect Tovey to claim that the build-up to the end is again like running in place. Instead, Tovey has another complaint:

> The triumph is brilliant but, perhaps in consequence of the way in which it was approached, not without a certain fierceness in its tone. At all events it would, if translated into literature, be the triumph of the real hero not the story. He might share in it at the time, but his heart will be in the mood of Tchaikovsky's finale.[167]

For one reason or another, Tovey had difficulty coming to terms with the music of Tchaikovsky, even when it was incontestably first-rate.

A significant interpretive question in live performances for the juncture of the third and fourth movements is the duration of the pause between them. To go directly from one movement to the other limits the reflexive applause. But one suspects, from contemporary reports, that in Tchaikovsky's time applause between the movements of a cyclic work was not improper; indeed a lack of any demonstration was more likely a signal of disapproval. Nevertheless, due to the combination of a Scherzo with a march, the audience perceives it as a Finale—rendering the first three movements as a cyclic unit, followed by a significant afterthought, the Adagio lamentoso. Already, Tchaikovsky has presented two movements, the first and third, that could function as centers of gravity; to present an additional high-powered movement would have completely saturated the listener in the emotional drama of the cycle.

Instead, Tchaikovsky inculcates this slow Finale with a simplicity that only magnifies its expression. Cast in a large binary form, Tchaikovsky rearranges its contents to establish a balance between *P* and *S* (see Table XV/28). In the exposition, *P* is heard twice and *S* four times ending with a closing; in the recapitulation, *P* is heard in two big statements, while *S* is relegated to the coda. Unlike the first movement with its deep contrasts between *P* and *S,* here the two themes are united by a downward trajectory that at times descends through the orchestra: for example, mm.30–36 in the bassoons and m.148 to the end where the descent does not recover. As in the first movement, dynamics, orchestration, and tempo again decisively shape the piece; the dynamics build and retreat, the orchestration spans from luminous *tutti* to dark bass colors, and the tempos accelerate and slow down, often in coordination with the changing sound. The result is a first part that builds to an overwhelming climax (mm.71–80) using these elements plus range and surface accelerations. Part two does much the same thing, reaching its climax earlier in the section (mm.116–33), but with an ending that literally dies away.

The *Pa* material has been notable for the division of the melodic pitches between the first and second violins, resulting in a theme that looks different than it sounds (Example XV/35). Such a disposition of the notes is maintained throughout the exposition each time *Pa* is heard (mm.1, 3, 20, 22); however, in the recapitulation, all of the melodic notes are given to the first violin. In modern performances, one does not experience this passage in the same way as at the end of the nineteenth century; today's ideal is a homogeneous string sound often enhanced by seating all of the violins to the left of the conductor, whereas in the late nineteenth century the two sections of violins were antiphonally split on the conductor's left and right. Tchaikovsky intended the listener to hear the difference in the two presentations and since one disposition occurs in the exposition and the other in the recapitulation, they probably have a structural and perhaps an extra-musical significance. Such playing with sonority and note exchange occurred earlier (e.g., Symphony No. 5/1, where the horns exchanged octaves [mm.182ff]), but this seems to be the first time it occurs in the melodic line.

Clear *T* sections here are almost non-existent; in contrast to the first movement, Tchaikovsky seemingly desires to focus here on the lyric aspects of *S*. Compared to *P,* *S* is strangely diatonic, perhaps to underline its indicated character *con levezza e devozione* (with gentleness and devotion) and for the trombones *con sentimento* (with delicate feeling). Except for its anacrustic nature and melodic imitation, *S* is almost static, a sensation underlined by the dominant pedal that only moves at the end of each phrase when the tempo accelerates and at the end of *S,* which continues the acceleration into the climax of *K* (mm.71–81). At this point, one would expect the return of *P;* instead, *Sa* fragments are repeated as a retransition. This serves as a recovery period after the dramatic ending to *S* and *K* and demonstrates by juxtaposition the relationship of *S* to *P.*

In the recapitulation (m.90), Tchaikovsky considerably raises the temperature: the

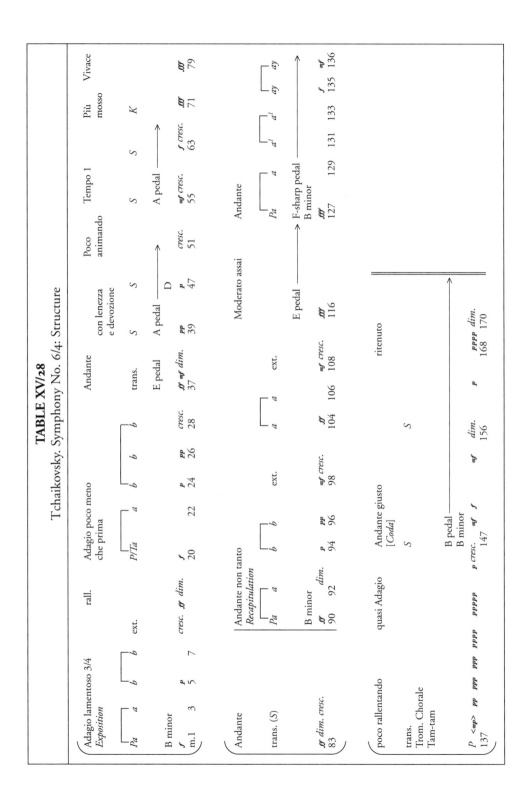

TABLE XV/28

Tchaikovsky. Symphony No. 6/4: Structure

EXAMPLE XV/35   Tchaikovsky. Symphony No. 6/4, mm.1–4 (strings only).

dynamics are increased a notch or two, the highest peak of pitch is achieved (m.115) for the entire symphony, and the dominant pedal (m.126) takes on a nasty sound as the horns stop the dominant pitch *fortissimo* in an especially difficult range. After *P* disintegrates down to *Pay* (mm.135–36) comes the sound of death with a quartet of trombones, a tuba, and a tam-tam *ad libitum*—the instruments of the funereal. Thomas Kohlhase draws a not unconvincing parallel of Liszt's introduction to his Variations on the Basso Continuo of the first movement of the cantata "Weinen, Klagen, Sorgen, Zagen" (1863, published 1865) and the Crucifixus from the B Minor Mass of Sebastian Bach. But as Kohlhase points out, we cannot establish if Tchaikovsky knew or could have known Liszt's piece.[168] Nevertheless, a rhetorical connection exists among the passages. Although the brass quartet sound with dominating trombones also occurred in the opening movement, here (Example XV/36) the redemptive aspects of the first movement are missing as it is followed by *S* (m.148), which descends into the lowest instruments over the pulsating pedal. At the end, only *divisi* cellos and basses remain as the pizzicato heartbeats slow and then stop while the sound dies away to nothingness. The sound of this ending is particularly striking, even though Tchaikovsky did something similar at the end of Symphony No. 5/1.

Tchaikovsky conducted the first performance at St. Petersburg in October 1893. While the native composer, who had already achieved greatness, was warmly greeted with a standing ovation, the critical response to the Sixth was mixed and listeners did not know what to think of this strange piece. The reviewer for the St. Petersburg-based newspaper *Novoe vremia* refers to the influence of "foreign countries":

Mr. Tchaikovsky appeared with his new symphony (B minor) in the first symphonic congress [i.e., the first symphony concert of the season], whose program he also conducted. Without striving to attract attention through intentional originality and artificiality of outward constitution, our composer impresses with the sincerity and warmth exuding from most of his works that are not written on a specific program. Even in places where he yields to a certain tendency he is unable to dissociate himself from his mental physiognomy and brings in some of [the qualities] that are his alone and distinguish him personally. The new symphony was undoubtedly written under the influence

EXAMPLE XV/36   Tchaikovsky. Symphony No. 6/4, mm.147–71.

EXAMPLE XV/36   (*continued*)

of a journey through foreign countries; it contains much sagacity, inventiveness in the use of orchestral colors, grace (especially in the two middle movements), elegance; but with regard to inspiration it recedes behind his other symphonies. It is hardly necessary to discuss the treatment of the orchestra; in this area Mr. Tchaikovsky has long occupied the first place among contemporary composers. If one were to reproach the composer with anything, it would be certain tedious passages in the first and last movement. The new work of the composer of *Onegin* was taken in with great interest by the audience, and the orchestra greeted him with a triple flourish.[169]

Herman Laroche's review in *Teatral'naia gazeta* was more enthusiastic, and far more detailed:

The major work of the first concert of the Russian Musical Society . . . under the direction of P. I. Tchaikovsky, was the new symphony of the conductor. . . . This summer I had the opportunity to express my views on the symphonic music of Petr Tchaikovsky . . . and here I will repeat in brief that, in my opinion, his talent manifests itself most forcefully in absolute music, in music without a program or poetic titles, that, on the contrary, programs and poetic titles inhibit him and quite often they compel him to verge on imitativeness. For this reason, I place his symphonies much above his symphonic poems, although in every one of the poems I recognize individual sections or movements that are full of inspiration and artistry. It is no wonder that I went to encounter this new symphony already inclined to like it, if only because it was simply No. 6. . . . Has my liking for the work been sustained over three recent hearings (in two rehearsals and in concert)? In part it has even increased, but in part it has decreased. In the new work, it is necessary to make a distinction between the material and the form of that material, that is the melodies and the development of the counterpoint, which is always magnificent. As far as melody is concerned, in Tchaikovsky in recent years there has opened up some kind of special richness, some kind of inexhaustible abundance and passionate fascination [in his] themes, and the new symphony in this regard can properly be attached to this period. The contrapuntal treatment, for its part, shines with compressed energy and true beauty . . . in the contrapuntal sections of the . . . symphony the fate of the theme constantly "intrigues" you, and interest never weakens. The form, however, is somewhat enigmatic. "The Secondary Part," that is the second theme of the first allegro, has the character of a modest, independent andante, brought to a conclusion and unusually firmly prevented from continuation with the help of a repeated cadence; after it comes some kind of dramatic seething, like those rhythmic and orchestral devices with which popular unrest, running crowds, and so on, are depicted in operas. Then the so-called "development," that is the contrapuntal elaboration of the middle section of the allegro. This secondary part is more in an operatic style than in a symphonic one. I must add that in my personal impression, in the third part of the allegro elements alien to each other converge and blend together comparatively easily, perhaps because we have already heard the themes. All of this leaves an impression of something alluring and of rare beauty, but which goes beyond symphonic boundaries. The concluding (fourth) movement of the symphony is similar, an adagio in place of the usual allegro or presto, that begins with a smooth melody in the major and concludes in the minor, with a muffled morendo in the very lowest register of the orchestra, as if to convey something happening on stage, for example the slow extinguishing of the life of the hero; it is exactly the same here, for all the unusual beauty of the melody, it feels operatic, not symphonic, in character. One cannot say the same about the two middle movements of the symphony, which, in my view (for all the beauty of the first and final movements), are the pearls of the score. In them, music lives on its own means and provides a completely aesthetic impression, not confusing the listener with ideas about [artistic] fields that merge with it or are adjacent to it. The second movement is a type of intermezzo in 5/4 . . . which is based on a graceful and charming theme (constructed on the ascending major scale) and which once again captivates with the inexhaustible resourcefulness and diversity of the contrapuntal accompaniment. The third movement belongs to the type of quick scherzo so beloved in our age, the main themes of which rush past and are glimpsed only pianissimo and spiccato in the string quintet, the first example of which, if I am not mistaken, Beethoven gave in his Eroica symphony. But here we have a completely new, or, more precisely, completely new and indivisibly original form of this widespread type. The quick, light theme of the scherzo combines with the theme of a carefree and foppish march . . . in further development, lively, bold, and brave, the march becomes ever more solid and strong, it becomes more predominant, and finally, having completely suppressed the flimsy opening theme, roars in a magnificent fortissimo. . . . I cannot recall even one out of my favorite compositions by Tchaikovsky that united in a greater degree the originality of an idea and the artistic fulfillment [of it], the dexterity of a master and the inspiration of a creator, and I suppose that the time is not far off when the public, which has been regarding the new score as a whole, and the scherzo within it, respectfully but with restraint, will comprehend its beauty and place it among the most valuable pages [written by] the composer.[170]

Tchaikovsky's untimely death lent new poignancy to the symphony. Not surprisingly, reviews of the new work at the concert devoted to the composer's memory later that year were quite positive. V. Baskin, reviewing the performance for *Nuvellist,* commented on the public's growing understanding of the symphony:

Of the two symphonic [concerts] the first took place under the direction of P. I. Tchaikovsky, and the second in his memory, under the direction of Napravnik. Tchaikovsky performed his sixth symphony (for the first time), entitled "Pathetique." . . . Nápraník included in his program, which consisted exclusively of works by Tchaikovsky, the aforementioned symphony and "Romeo and Juliet." The new symphony, Tchaikovsky's swan song, was not completely understood the first time by the audience . . . ; the interpretation, which the director of the Russian opera [Napravnik] gave it in many ways, assisted in its comprehension. It is very curious both in terms of its material, that is, its melodies, and in its development. In it, Tchaikovsky deviated from the generally accepted form; the last movement, for example, is an Adagio Lamentoso instead of the usual Allegro or Presto; in the middle of the second movement there is something like an Intermezzo and Scherzo with unusual (for a symphony) tempos . . . and the third movement, which begins with a fast scherzo, is gradually transformed into a march, which [grows] into a grandiose fortissimo. After this, as if for contrast, begins the Adagio Lamentoso, which belongs among the best pages of Tchaikovsky's creative work, as if to say to the listener that after a happy life begins a dismal and inevitable end. . . . This Adagio concludes with a remarkable morendo by the entire orchestra.[171]

The dean of Viennese music critics, Eduard Hanslick, was astonishingly agreeable in his commentary:

The *Symphonie Pathétique* has a special place among the compositions of Tchaikovsky in that there is no trace of national Russian colour. What lamentably trivial Cossack cheer we had to suffer in the Finale of his Serenade, opus 48, in his Violin Concerto, in his

D major Quartet, or in the third movement of his Suite, opus 54! There is nothing of this kind in the symphony, whose character is downright West European and reveals a nobler mind and a more heart-felt interest. The first and the last movements particularly, which I consider by far the best, contain episodes of touching emotion and pure beauty. In the second movement, there is nothing extraordinary except the loathsome five-four time; the third, brilliant and animated in the larger first part, loses, towards the end, all sense of what the normal ear can tolerate in the way of noise and length. Liszt and Rubinstein have not been without influence on it. At any rate, we thank Hans Richter for having made us acquainted with this original and intelligent composition which, despite unbeautiful, purely operatic characteristics and a merciless length, has made a strong impression.[172]

However, Gustav Mahler heard the "Pathétique" conducted by Nikisch in Berlin during 1901. His view was negative, at least according to the report from Natalie Bauer-Lechner:

Coming from the Berlin Philharmonic concert, Mahler was discussing Tchaikovsky's *Pathétique* with Guido Adler. He called it a shallow, superficial, distressingly homophonic work—no better than salon music. Adler, who was quite satisfied with it and found its colour-effects especially delightful, protested. "Even colouring" replied Mahler "should not really be the sort of thing he gives us here. His is fake, sand thrown in one's eyes! If you look more closely, there is precious little there. These rising and falling arpeggios, these meaningless sequences of chords, can't disguise the fundamental lack of invention and the emptiness. If you make a coloured dot spin round an axis, it appears to be magnified into a shimmering circle. But the moment it comes to rest, it's the same old dot, which wouldn't tempt even the cat to play."[173]

The Sixth was a path-breaking work in the history of the symphony, not only because of its cycle that concludes with a slow movement, but also because this is a symphony almost unrelenting in its pathos. The slow movement Finale provided an important precedent, which was taken up by a number of composers during the twentieth century: a symphonic work that did not express darkness to light, defeat to triumph, or just plain joy. After all, and certainly in Tchaikovsky's view, life was not a completely positive experience. What Tchaikovsky produced was an alternative to Beethoven, Schumann, and Brahms in a work that could be viewed as "anti-Beethoven Symphony No. 9." Hence, Tchaikovsky's Symphony No. 6 is an alternative solution, dominated by an unknown program, though certainly saturated with the tragic muse.

CONCLUSION

Tchaikovsky's importance as a late-nineteenth-century symphonist has been consistently undervalued. Of his seven complete symphonies, only one, No. 3, is perhaps not worthy of entering the repertoire. As the composer acknowledged, it was something of an experiment in which he attempted to create themes for their developmental possibilities, rather than play to his own strength as the creator of memorable melodies. While Nos. 4 and 5 are certainly estimable contributions, it was not until Symphony No. 6 that Tchaikovsky found a complete convergence of form, style, and content.

Symphonies Nos. 4–6 already have a place in the repertoire and, even given changes in taste, will no doubt remain. However, it is Symphonies Nos. 1 and 2 that should be heard more often. In Symphony No. 1, Tchaikovsky is a less extreme composer in expression and dynamics; the result is a work replete with wonderful melodies and highly skilled orchestrations. At times there are echoes of Mendelssohn's overture to *A Midsummer Night's Dream* and *Hebrides Overture,* but even these already have Tchaikovsky's imprint. Symphony No. 2 "Little Russian" demonstrated that Tchaikovsky was capable of being a nationalistic composer in the element of the *kuchka,* both in the use of folksong and in its formal elaborations.

Tchaikovsky envisioned *Manfred* as a special sort of symphony made of narrative and characteristic movements. It is a bold work in the style of Nos. 4–6, but with deeper cyclic interrelationships and no movements in sonata form. Its Finale, with the slow and quiet conclusion, is a precursor to Symphony No. 6/4. As with all of his later symphonies, *Manfred* has a highly personal element; Tchaikovsky could easily see himself as having some things in common with Byron's hero.

The under-valuation of the seven symphonies can be traced to a series of British critics. Among the earliest of these were Tovey and Gerald Abraham, who could only view a successful symphonic creation as one stemming from German composers like Beethoven or Brahms. Composers who belonged to a more lyrically inspired group, such as Schubert, Mendelssohn, Schumann, Borodin, Dvořák, and Tchaikovsky, did not have the inherent make-up to be aesthetically viable symphonists and therefore were viewed as either not successful or inferior. Yet every symphonist and every symphony, including those by Tchaikovsky, deserves to be judged on their own formulation of the genre and their success in achieving a synthesis of content and form. The ghost of Beethoven, one suspects, had a greater presence for critics and musicologists than for many nineteenth-century composers.

In 2002, the year of this writing, Tchaikovsky is the only nineteenth-century Russian symphonist to remain in the canon. Symphonies by Rimsky-Korsakov, Borodin, Balakirev, Kalinnikov, and Rachmaninoff (except for No. 2) are rarely heard on orchestral programs outside of Russia. And these are only the first line of possibilities; what about Anton Rubinstein, Taneyev, Glazunov, Arensky, Lyapunov, and Grechaninov? One might even argue that Tchaikovsky's place in the symphonic repertoire is today challenged by the contributions of Shostakovich and Prokofiev.

Mily Balakirev

INTRODUCTION

As discussed in the opening pages of this chapter, Mily Balakirev's position in the history of the Russian symphony is a crucial one—not so much for his own symphonic compositions, but for serving as mentor and teacher to the other four members of the *kuchka* (Borodin, Cui, Musorgsky, Rimsky-Korsakov) and encouraging them all to compose symphonies during the late 1850s and 1860s. Rimsky-Korsakov and Borodin succeeded, but Musorgsky and Cui were not suited to the genre, lacking the wherewithal to compose in an extended instrumental form. Balakirev also maintained relationships with other Russian and Slavic composers, including Tchaikovsky; for the latter, Balakirev became a mentor of sorts during the composition of the *Romeo and Juliet* Overture-Fantasy and the *Manfred* Symphony.

Apart from his roles as mentor and teacher to his charges, Balakirev himself was active as a pianist and conductor during the 1860s and 1870s. With all these activities, Balakirev's own output as a composer was severely limited, particularly in the larger forms. Some of these works were planned and partially composed in the 1860s, but completed many years later: the E-flat Piano Concerto (1861–1862, 1906–1909), Symphony No. 1 in C major (1864–1866, 1893–1897), the symphonic poem *Tamara* (1867–1882). In addition, the 1857 *Overture on a Spanish March Theme* was revised in 1886, the 1858 *Overture on Three Russian Themes* was rewritten in 1881, and the 1864 *Second Overture on Russian Themes* was reworked in 1884. His Symphony No. 2 in D Minor (1900–1908) also includes a movement conceived around 1864. There is a certain irony in Balakirev's failure to compose a complete symphony of his own during the 1860s, as he was nagging and cajoling the other members of the *kuchka* to do what he himself was unable to accomplish.

Despite the fact that during the 1860s Balakirev was an advocate of a national style clothed in modern dress—one of his central arguments against Anton Rubinstein was that he was essentially a conservative German and not a Russian composer—Balakirev's two completed symphonies (see Table XV/29) are anachronisms: rather conservative in their language and derivative by the time they were completed. Symphony No. 1 was composed in two stages, separated by some thirty years, yet it is difficult to ascertain aurally which portions were written earlier and which portions came later. Symphony No. 2 also seems to be stylistically unified; the earlier composed second movement is not at stylistic odds with the rest of the cycle. While both cycles use Slavic folk materials, they are in a style of the 1860s, far from the modern idioms that such melodies began to generate in the works of Kodály, Bartók, and Janáček.

SYMPHONY NO. 1 IN C MAJOR

In Symphony No. 1 in C Major, except for the tonality of the first and final movements and the *attacca* of the third movement to the Finale, there is nothing more that holds the cycle together as is standard with *kuchka* symphonic cycles; the Scherzo is in second position and the slow movement third. As for the keys of these internal pieces, the Scherzo is in A minor with D minor for the Trio, and D-flat major is used for the slow movement. Though one cannot avoid commenting about how these keys relate to C major—as the relative minor, supertonic minor, and Neapolitan—Balakirev had an absolute interest in these keys isolated from their context. For Balakirev, the keys of D and D-flat as well as B minor and B-flat minor appears to have had some sort of mystical association, and he is known to have told Tchaikovsky that a C-sharp (D-flat) minor piano concerto was in his future; it is also worth noting that Rimsky-Korsakov's First Symphony, composed under Balakirev's tutelage, was originally in the impractical key of E-flat minor.

Balakirev's overall approach to the first movement, however, is rather different from that of any other Russian composer; it is the most distant work from the textbook version of sonata form we have encountered in this survey. Perhaps its closest model is the first movement of Schumann's Symphony No. 4, which has no recapitulation, but moves directly from the development section to the coda. Also like the Schumann is the adumbration of thematic material of the exposition in the slow introduction. However, Schumann's example becomes exaggerated in the hands of Balakirev. In the introduction, both *P* and *S* are adumbrated (mm.1 and 5), and the tonic and dominant keys are presented, but the introduction then moves to the Neapolitan (m.18). Already in the introduction, Balakirev also begins to transform and develop his two themes. Indeed, once *P* (m.26) and *S* (m.62) are presented in the Allegro (Example XV/37), these two ideas undergo a myriad of developments and transformations. The course of this movement's unfolding is like a big improvisation, a skill for which the composer, according to Rimsky-Korsakov, had a prodigious gift.[174] The layout of the movement (Table XV/30) has a definable exposition that moves from tonic (m.26) to dominant (m.62), but then finds E-flat (m.151) and ends in the tonic. While this first section is not concluded with anything that functions as a *K,* the second part (m.190) is defined by a change of meter to ¢ from 2/4 ($\decrescendo = \decrescendo$). It is approximately at this point that Gerald Abraham believes the 1860s segment of the first movement ends and the composition of the 1890s

TABLE XV/29

The Symphonies of Mily Balakirev

Key	Dates	Title	Movements	Instrumentation	Comments
C	1864–1866, 1893–1897	Symphony No. 1	1. Largo 4/4/8/8—Allegro vivo 2/4/¢ (551 m.) 2. Scherzo: Vivo—Poco meno mosso 3/4 (456 m.) A/D minor 3. Andante 12/8 (168 m) D-flat major *attacca* 4. Finale: Allegro moderato 2/4 (595 m.)	Grand plus Flt./ Picc., EH, Clar., Tuba, Tri., Cym., BD, and Harp	The first mvt. dates from 1864–66; the remainder from 1893–97. Finale's *thème russe:* "Sharlatarla from Partarla." First performance: St. Petersburg, Free Music School concert on April 11/23, 1898, conducted by the composer. Published in Leipzig: Belyayev, 1899.
D minor	1900–1908	Symphony No. 2	1. Allegro ma non troppo 6/8 (384 m.) 2. Scherzo alla Cosacca: Allegro non troppo, ma con fuoco ed energico 2/4 (397 m.) B minor 3. Romanza: Andante 3/4 (183 m.) F major 4. Finale: Tempo di Polacca 3/4 (281 m.)	Grand plus Flt./ Picc., EH, Clar., Tuba, Tri., Tamb., Cym., BD, and Harp	The second mvt., which dates from *ca.* 1864, quotes a *thème russe.* "The snow is melting," and was originally intended for Symphony No. 1. First performance: St. Petersburg, Free Music School concert on April 10/23, 1909, conducted by Sergey Lyapunov. Published in Leipzig: Belyayev, 1908.

EXAMPLE XV/37   Balakirev. Symphony No. 1/1, mm.26–39, 62–78.

EXAMPLE XV/37 (*continued*)

EXAMPLE XV/37   (*continued*)

TABLE XV/30
Balakirev. Symphony No. 1/1: Structure

Largo 4/4
Introduction

Oa (P)	Ob (S)	Oa	Oa	Oa	ext.
C	G		D-flat		
m.1	5	9	13	18	20

Allegro vivo 2/4
Part 1
Exposition

Pa	T (Pa)	1S	ext.	1S	2S (P)		P
C	G		D pedal			E-flat	augmented
26	46	62	86	106	124	151	167

Alla breve
Part 2
Exposition 2 or Development 1

P	P	P	P	P	P
C, G pedal		E-flat	diminuted		augmented
					B
190	192	227	239	255	271

Part 3
Development 1 or 2

1K	P	2K (P)		S/P	S	S	S
		diminuted	B	augmented mod.	F-sharp pedal		E
291	309	318	330	334	350	368	

Part 4
[Recapitulation?]

1K Fugato	P	P	P	2K (P)	P	S
E → A V/C minor	G pedal →	augmented				augmented, C pedal
384	400	409	417	433	449	466

Più animato
Coda

P	P	S	P	S
G pedal	diminuted, C		Chorale	Fanfares, Cadences
495	499	504	528	540

begins.[175] Balakirev's imagination in handling the themes cannot be faulted. However, this constant development of materials, even in the exposition, reminds us of a composer for whom the Russian mentor had no admiration whatsoever, Joseph Haydn.

One cannot be certain of the function of the second section (m.190), because it is not a logical sonata-form successor to the exposition. That it begins in the tonic and then moves to E-flat recalls the previous section, and the occurrence of a *K*-like function (m.291) in a third key, B major, reminds one of an exposition. However, *P* is developed, diminuted, augmented, and transformed, and none of these reworkings are duplications of anything that was heard in the exposition or previously in this second part. On the other hand, added to the materials of *P* are two *K* themes (mm.291, 318) over a pedal on the leading tone, the second of which relates to *P,* a gesture that seems almost expository. Whether the primary function of this second part is expository or developmental cannot be pigeonholed.

If part two is expository, then part three is a development; if part two is developmental, the next section is a second development. Here, the main efforts are devoted to *S* (mm.324–83), with *P* used as a counterpoint and at the end treated to augmentation (m.417). Otherwise, its main event is a fugato-like presentation of *1K* (m.384), a surprising gesture for a composer so opposed to the learned matters taught at the conservatory. *1K* now is followed by *P* (m.417) in augmentation and *2K*(*P,* m.433). The end of *1K* and *P* (m.417) is underlined by a dominant pedal, which signals something like a retransition, but it ceases before the appearance of *2K*(*P*).

If there is a recapitulation perhaps it starts at m.449, but this is hardly an articulatory event; *P* is undergirded by the dominant and is not presented in its original 1860s form. *S* reappears in augmentation over a tonic pedal. The coda (m.499) in Leipzig style increases the tempo (Più animato) and presents a rehearing of *P* and *S* (m.504). The movement ends with *P* augmented as a chorale (m.528) in the winds (cf. Schumann Symphony No. 3/5) and concludes perfunctorily with brass fanfares.

The stylistic position of this first movement parallels the ambivalence of the *kuchka* itself; they proclaimed that they were the banner carriers for a national Russian music, yet they were still dependent on the practices of Western European art music. Though Balakirev, to a large degree, threw off the shackles of Germanic sonata form in this movement, he still could not avoid the Germanic practices of thematic function and elaboration through development, transformation, and the use of contrapuntal devices. No doubt this is an experimental piece; it is unfortunate that the first movement was not finished in the 1860s, as it could have served as a formal alternative to German symphonic practices for Russian composers.

Scherzos were a specialty of the *kuchka;* often they were the movements held in portfolios for future use and they took on a distinctive cast (e.g., the symphonic Scherzos by Borodin and Rimsky-Korsakov). Balakirev originally conceived the Scherzo alla Cosacca in the 1860s for his First Symphony. In the end, the Scherzo alla Cosacca found its way into the Second Symphony. The replacement Scherzo for the First Symphony has a strong Slavic flavor; it also recalls Anton Bruckner. However, to attribute a Brucknerian influence upon Balakirev is impossible to support; it is almost certain that Balakirev could never have heard any of Bruckner's symphonies, and it is only slightly more likely that a score could have passed through his hands.

As in the first movement, Balakirev manages his materials in the Scherzo in an imaginative way both thematically and orchestrally. *P* (Example XV/38) (m.5) is one of those daemonic Scherzo themes known not only from Balakirev, but also from Beethoven's Symphony No. 9/2. Its repetition (m.21) adds snippets of individual woodwind colors, and when it

EXAMPLE XV/38   Balakirev. Symphony No. 1/2, mm.1–37.

returns after *S* in m.85, it has become a whirling waltz. *S* (m.38) sounds like something Borodin could have written—not only in its contour, but also in its scoring for English horn, as the accompaniment continues the eighth-note motion from *P*. For the closing (m.110), Balakirev combines *P* and *S* contrapuntally, a learned gesture extolled no doubt by the conservatory crowd. Though a thematic sonata form of sorts, Balakirev never establishes a secondary key area basic to this structure.

EXAMPLE XV/38   (*continued*)

The more relaxed Trio in D Minor is, according to Edward Garden, "tinged with a bitter-sweetness."[176] It is expanded in *kuchka* style with environmental variations. After a literal repeat of the opening section, the coda is based on the Trio material now in the tempo of the Scherzo. Of structural significance are the tessitura and the dynamics, which begin *forte* in the bass of the orchestra with a mesmerizing rhythmic ostinato. The bass drops out, the sonorities incrementally move higher and higher, and the dynamics become softer until the movement ends with *divisi* violins, piccolo, and a triangle—*à la* Berlioz's "Queen Mab"—*ppp*.

When Balakirev composed his Andante in 12/8 time, beginning with a transition from the A major ending of the Scherzo to the D-flat of the Andante, he must have been thinking of the slow movement of Tchaikovsky's Symphony No. 5. In the Tchaikovsky, the horn solo is a higher accomplishment than Balakirev's clarinet cantilena: the Balakirev melody (Example XV/39) given to the solo clarinet is less memorable, too short in duration, rhythmically uninteresting, and harmonically colorless. It is not that the Borodin-like melody lacks simple beauty, but that such simplicity cannot be subjected to the seven repetitions it receives during the course of the movement.

The overall shape is a part form of unusual proportions and tonal relationships (Table XV/31). After an expansive *A* (m.7), *B* (m.33) lasts for only eight measures in E major followed by a return to *A* (m.41) but in the key of B. *C* (m.49) transfers to C-sharp minor and *A* returns in E (m.67) followed by two statements of *Ab* in A and A-flat major before returning to *C*, which is now in B minor (m.117) before *A* returns in D-flat (m.135). Thus, while the formal plan is *A–B–A–C–A–C–A*, the tonal plan is D-flat at the beginning and end; up a minor third to E, then up to B and C-sharp minor, up a third back to E with A and A-flat/G-sharp moving back to D-flat, then up to B minor and back to D-flat. A half-step slip downward to C sets up the beginning of the Finale. Balakirev here maximizes some of his favorite keys—D-flat/C-sharp and B minor—and centers the remaining relationships as thirds on either side of the tonic. That *A* operates in two different keys, D-flat and E, must be an effort to add some variety to its repetitions in addition to the diversity provided by its orchestrations.

Compared to its putative model of the Tchaikovsky Symphony No. 5/2, the Balakirev is almost introverted: the dynamic range is limited from *pp* to *ff* with only a few measures reaching the maximum, the scoring of the *tutti* with the heavy brass is used very sparingly, and there are no dramatic or surprising intrusions. It is almost as if Balakirev were composing a utopian pastoral piece without a disturbing moment. As utopia must be, this piece remains somewhat dull despite its beauties. Perhaps when Gerald Abraham refers to this Andante's "languorous nature," he has captured its true character.[177]

Up to this point in the cycle, we have not encountered any identified Russian folk music. This is not to say that some of the material in the Scherzo and the Andante could not owe something to a folk idiom (e.g., the Scherzo's main theme, the modal theme of the Trio, and the refrain of the Andante). However, when we come to the Finale, there are identifiable folk-song materials coming from partially traceable sources: the opening music (Example XV/40) marked *thème russe* is the song "Sharlatarla from Partarla" from Rimsky-Korsakov's *Hundred Russian Folk-Songs* (No. 40) transmitted to Rimsky by his uncle Pyotr Petrovich.[178] The second theme was to have been "We Sowed the Millet" from Balakirev's *Forty Russian Folk-Songs* (No. 8), but it was replaced by a song of oriental origin that Balakirev heard sung on the Finnish Railway by an elderly blind man accompanying himself on an out-of-tune primitive harp.[179] To Western European ears, the latter song has the character of a Saltarello/Tarantella. A third Russian folksong (m.194) is "There Is a Little Tree on the Hill";

EXAMPLE XV/39   Balakirev. Symphony No. 1/3, mm.7–16.

TABLE XV/31

Balakirev. Symphony No. 1/3: Structure

Introduction [A] *a b a*   [B]   [A] *a*   [C] *a*   *a*   [A] *a b b*   [A] *a*

D-flat ⟶

m.1 7 9 17 25   E   A   B   C-sharp minor   E   A   A-flat   D-flat
                      33   41   49   67   81 89   101   109

[C] *a a*   [A] *b*   *a*   *a*

B minor   D-flat   cadenza   cadenza   Attacca il finale
125   135   149   155   159   160   V₇/C
                                                                          168–69

EXAMPLE XV/40 Balakirev. Symphony No. 1/4, mm.1–12, 122–31, 194–209.

it comes from Balakirev's second collection of *Thirty Folk-Songs* (No. 22). The Finale ends with another national style, that of a Polacca (m.663), based on the opening *thème russe.* Thus, in the end, the material of the Finale is not so much Russian, but rather a pan-national conglomeration of Slavic materials and styles.

Otherwise, the Finale is another sonata-form piece not unlike that of the first movement: its key scheme is unusual (C–D–F-sharp–D), the themes are treated in many different ways but here there is less emphasis on transformation, and the moment of recapitulation is not designed to be a major event for it begins with *S* (m.588) rather than *P.* Though in sonata form, the nature of its thematic materials, which Western Europeans might have heard as a series of *contredanses,* suggests an expectation of a part-form of some sort. This may account for the unusually large shape of the exposition with the return of the Tarantella-like theme after "There is a Little Tree" (m.247). Notice that the exposition has a series of pedals; while this is certainly characteristic of the *kuchka,* it also underlines its peasant-dance orientation.

What makes this movement so exciting is not only the themes themselves, but also that they are so amenable to thematic development and contrapuntal combination. In part, this has to do with their immediate memorability, their internal repetitive schemes, and the simplicity of their harmonic plans. Thus, these materials do not require a brilliant contrapuntalist to bring them into polyphony with each other or a master of thematic development to juxtapose one with another. Even though the key scheme of the exposition is unusual, compared to the first movement, here there is less thematic development. In the development section proper, the bold juxtapositions of theme and sound make for a driven, and thoroughly convincing, symphonic experience.

Without any preparation, the Finale begins straight away with *P,* which is expanded by a combination of *kuchka* variations and thematic development. A move toward F-sharp minor and an F-sharp pedal (m.86) provides the beginning of the transition to *S* (m.122) in D major based on *Pax* (m.98). *S* (m.122) seems, at least before the movement is over, to owe something to Rimsky-Korsakov's *Sheherazade* Finale with its rapidly tongued notes in the winds and later scoring with percussion accentuation. As has been pointed out by Abraham and Garden, *1K* (m.190) is distinctive for its placement of accents on the weak beats both within the measure and the phrase.[180] *T* (m.222) takes us to *S,* now functioning as *2K* (m.247) in D major with a rollicking *tutti* scoring including a battery of percussion: tambourine, snare drum, cymbals, and bass drum. After this climax, the music relaxes momentarily in preparation for the development section.

Balakirev begins the development (m.312) with *P* in B-flat. By using an almost identical scoring (m.316) with the movement's beginning, one thinks this to be either a repeat of the exposition or a reprise of the refrain. These impressions are almost immediately dispelled with the entry of the woodwinds repeating in sequence *Pay.* This process is repeated in E-flat (m.334), then in E (m.352), and in A (m.376) over an E pedal where *P* and *S* are juxtaposed. A *tutti* dialogue of *P* between treble and bass instruments in A-flat undergirded by a C pedal ensues (m.400). The texture suddenly thins for a transition on *Pax* that leads to *S* (m.436), now juxtaposed with *1K* (m.444). Balakirev then uses *S* (m.468) as a fugato subject over a G pedal (mm.468–537).

This lengthy pedal eventually leads to a recapitulatory *P* in the tonic (m.542). In the meantime, *P* and *S* are combined contrapuntally (m.507); although not a great feat of learnedness, it is a highly effective move. If m.542 is not the most convincing recapitulation, the reprise of *S* in the tonic (m.588) *tutti* and *fortissimo* certainly is. *1K* follows (m.611) over a tonic pedal with a strengthened lean on the subdominant. Now *S* and *1K* combine (m.647) in counterpoint over a tonic pedal. After the combining of *P* and *S,* such a move raises expectations for another feat of contrapuntal mastery: the combination of *P, S,* and *1K.* This never happens: *S* is combinable with almost anything, but *P* and *1K* cannot be so easily mixed together contrapuntally. *P* has yet to be recapitulated in the tonic; however, it is only heard once more—in the coda (m.663), transformed into a Polacca (Example XV/41). The symphony ends with a heterophonic cadence (mm.688–91) between timpani and strings.

The First Symphony received a strong and respectful review in the leading Russian musical journal, *Russkaia muzykal'naia gazeta.* The premiere performance was clearly received by the public as an opportunity to celebrate Balakirev's contributions to Russian music:

> An utterly exceptional and almost unexpected concert was the marvelous conclusion to the desolate spring musical season. On the 11th of April, in the Hall of the Nobles Assembly, the "Free Music School" gave its concert. A symphony by M. A. Balakirev, which was recently completed by him and which is the first of his works in the form of a classical symphony, was performed for the first time. Its performance occupied the second half of the concert, which garnered a continuous ovation, fully worthy of this remarkable Russian musical figure. . . .
>
> Even prior to the beginning of the first movement, a noisy ovation began aimed at the composer, to whom were presented: an address, a whole series of laurel wreaths and two silver wreaths, and, finally, an original copy of the hands of Franz Liszt. . . .
>
> As regards the new symphony, it also undoubtedly had major interest and success, such that its scherzo was repeated. The symphony was written over the course of four years (1894–1897); such slow, measured creative productivity does not tell in the style of

EXAMPLE XV/41   Balakirev. Symphony No. 1/4, mm.663–71.

the symphony. In general there is no integrity, quite often it comes across as a mosaic; technically almost everything grows [one out of another], but "melos" does not flow smoothly or naturally. This is no uniform, mighty ingot, here there is more the appearance of creativity, of the sumptuous art of sound than the intrinsically passionate inspiration with which breathe so many great creations of Glinka (to whom M. Balakirev, with respect to his creative work, tries to attach himself), even those such as Capriccio brilliante [on the Jota aragonesa], which was written on already prepared and available motives. But, nonetheless, the symphony of Balakirev is a fine, noble work, full of beauty,

EXAMPLE XV/41   *(continued)*

elegance, and talent. Of the four movements, (Introduction, Allegro—Scherzo—Andante, and Finale), the finest of all are the two middle movements, which are the most successful with regard to the originality of their inspiration and even their integrity. The main theme of the Allegro (1st movement) is very similar to the well-known theme of Ivan the Terrible in Rimsky-Korsakov's *Pskovitianka* [*The Maid of Pskov*]. . . . The first and last movements of the symphony are diverse and long-winded, but this does not prevent them from being sumptuous and richly orchestrated pieces. The audience can celebrate a new and excellent Russian symphony.[181]

Though on a different level artistically, the Balakirev First, like the Tchaikovsky Sixth, reveals an original adaptation of the symphonic tradition to fit Balakirev's temperament. Unlike Tchaikovsky, Balakirev retains the cyclic layout, but on the movement level goes his own way in terms of where and how certain events take place, such as pedals, modulations, and thematic development. Balakirev cannot resist his tendency to develop an idea immediately after its presentation. Modulation can occur at virtually any point in the movement, as do pedals; in the normal sonata structure the former would usually be confined to T and development sections proper, the latter mainly to closing functions. While the first and last movements are strong arguments for Balakirev's approach, the Scherzo is possessed by an inner driving force only exceeded by the parallel movements in Beethoven's Symphony No. 9/2 and in the symphonies of Anton Bruckner. The slow movement leaves something to be desired, but its banalities only become apparent with repeated hearings.

Balakirev's First is deserving of a place on the edge of the symphonic repertoire. In the twentieth century, its attributes have been musically extolled by Sir Thomas Beecham, who was able to exploit both the charms and the profundities of this work. Though Balakirev may not use the orchestra as skillfully as Rimsky-Korsakov, and the work may not have the power of expression found in Mahler, it is still worth hearing for its use of folk idioms in artistic clothing.

SYMPHONY NO. 2 IN D MINOR

It took over thirty years for Balakirev to complete his First Symphony, but only seven and a half years to complete his Second. It has been said that during the first decade of the new century, a Third Symphony was also taking shape in his mind.

Balakirev's Symphony No. 2 is organized very much like his First Symphony. The cycle places the Scherzo in second position, and the piece itself incorporates a Russian dance type, as Balakirev inferred with its title: Scherzo alla Cosacca. As noted earlier, the original plan was to use this piece in the First Symphony, but Balakirev had a change of heart. The third movement is now called Romanza, a title certainly not inappropriate for the parallel movement of the First Symphony. And this time, the entire Finale is a Tempo di Polacca, rather than just the coda as in the First Symphony. For the beginning of the twentieth century, the key plan is conservative, with minor third relationships to D minor: the Scherzo is in B minor and the Romanza in F major. Connected movements are again not a part of this cycle. Balakirev does, however, have one thematic interconnection: P of the third movement reappears as the second episode of the Finale, but in a Polacca transformation. Both Abraham and Garden believe the slow movement is the weak link, and Garden thinks the intrusion of the Romanza's P fatally weakens the Finale.[182] While we agree that the third movement is weak, when this material is performed in a faster tempo its effect is less toxic.

In Symphony No. 2, the use of folksong is limited to two quotations. In the Scherzo's Trio, a tune from Rimsky-Korsakov's *One Hundred Russian Folk-Songs* is used: "The Snow Is Melting" (No.33). The first episode in the Finale quotes "We Have in Our Garden" from the same collection (No. 31). That both folksongs are used as secondary materials, and in the Scherzo's Trio, where they would be traditionally expected, gives less prominence to the symphony's ethnicity and Balakirev's once blatant nationalism. But perhaps this shortcoming is made up for by the Scherzo's characteristic dance. Because of the prominence given to the Finale's Polacca, the overall emphasis, however, is more Slavic rather than purely Russian. After all, while Balakirev's allegiances were predominantly Russian, he was much taken with the broader Slavic ethnic heritage in Poland, Bohemia, and the Caucasus.

Balakirev's first movement in 6/8 meter reminds one of the main body of Tchaikovsky's Symphony No. 5/1. This reminiscence extends not only to the similarity of their *P* themes (Example XV/42), but also their scoring; Tchaikovsky sets the theme for clarinet solo, Balakirev for one clarinet with cellos. Woodwind roulades and their scoring also have parallels in the Tchaikovsky. But, in the end, Balakirev is unable to accomplish the orchestral polish that seemed almost instinctive to his slightly younger contemporary. For example, the joint between *1S* (m.42) and *2S* (m.77), with the flutes overlapping the violins by one note, is a crudity Tchaikovsky would never have perpetrated, not even in his earliest works for orchestra.

What separates this sonata-form movement from the two in the First Symphony is the strong structural downbeat at the recapitulation provided by the repeat of the two pairs of hammerstrokes that introduce *P*. These are not ordinary hammerstrokes, for the first cadence is in B-flat minor, the second in D minor—certainly an unusual way to begin a D minor symphony. This tonal dichotomy remains until the recapitulation and returns again eight measures from the end, where the ultimate response is a *fortissimo* confirmation of D minor. Still, Balakirev voices his last two measures to make this cadence weaker than the one in B-flat. All of this results in one's perception of a form somewhat out of joint.

On the other hand, these cadences—juxtaposing the relative major and its related minor—frame and support the structure and allow the exposition to depart from closely related keys:

Intro.	*P*	*T(P)*	*1Sa*	*b*	*a*	*2S*	*K(1S)*
B-flat/D minor	D minor		D-flat	F-sharp minor (G-flat)	D-flat	B-flat minor	D-flat
1	5	29	41	59	69	77	93

The development section (m.111) explores no tonality not already experienced in the exposition, while the recapitulation and coda, except for the framing introductory chords, remain solidly in D minor. Thus, the larger tonal plan is one from exploration to stability.

P (m.5) is marked by a melody, striking for its hemiolas; the interlude for the winds and the *forte* repetition belong more to the standard symphonic presentation first heard in Beethoven's Symphony No. 3/1. In Balakirev, *T* moves to D-flat (m.29), repeats the wind interlude (m.33), and presents *1S* (m.41) in the winds, another theme that recalls Borodin. Striking is its scoring with tambourine, triangle, and harp. In contrast to *P*, this time the strings provide the interludes. *2S* (m.77) has more of a Tchaikovskian scoring: strings, addition of winds, and a buildup to the first *tutti* and the hammerstrokes for *K(1S)* (m.93), where the *tutti* sonorities remind one of Russia's first great symphonic composer. The scoring thins and the dynamics soften for the transition (*Kaz*) to the development section, which is to play a significant role in the development proper. Unlike Symphony No. 1/1, this time the exposition acts more like a traditional opening to a symphony movement: despite the unusual tonal outline, Balakirev resists his tendency toward immediate development of his themes. Here, repetitions and rescorings dominate.

Balakirev begins his development with *1Sax* (m.111) combined with the descending transitory motive (*Kaz*). Surprisingly, *P* (m.137) returns in the tonic and alternates with *Kaz*, then the two combine in rudimentary polyphony (m.173) culminating with *P* (m.185) *tutti* and

EXAMPLE XV/42   Balakirev. Symphony No. 2/1, mm.1–19.

EXAMPLE XV/42 (*continued*)

fortissimo in A. *Kaz* (m.193) again provides the transition, this time back to the tonic's related major, the introductory hammerstrokes, and *P* (m.213) for the recapitulation. For a composer so prone to improvisatory abandon, the regularity of the recapitulation is hardly what one would expect. At its end (m.319), Balakirev continues into the beginning of the development for eighteen measures, then changes direction and tempo (Poco più animato) as *P* and *K(1S)* materials fill out the form, concluding with the hammerstrokes.

In contrast to Symphony No. 1/1, this first movement is a more tightly conceived and disciplined piece. At no point does the structure seem padded, nor does it lose sight of its local and ultimate goals. Both tonally and thematically, the materials are organized into a logical and effective presentation.

It is generally agreed that the high point of the cycle is the Scherzo alla Cosacca. Balakirev gives some indication of the character of the piece from its heading: Allegro non troppo, ma con fuoco ed energico. Rather than a sonata form, the opening section has no development; it is a binary/sonatina piece connected to the recapitulation by the introductory material. The Trio section (m.193) treats the *thème russe* to *kuchka* variations that are quietly interrupted by the introductory material (m.286), leading to the abbreviated reprise of the Scherzo proper. Besides the introduction and *P* (m.306), Balakirev also recapitulates the *thème russe* in the tonic, and the introductory refrain as a coda (m.382).

The main portion of the Scherzo proper is notable for its projection of the folk-like materials (Example XV/43). First the oboes play *P* in parallel fourths (m.9), then the clarinets in octaves (m.17). Finally, it is played in an octave canon in two pairs, one beat apart (m.25), first by woodwinds and strings and then *tutti* with woodwinds opposing strings as the brass and percussion provide punctuation. This latter gesture borders on chaos, but it is also one of Balakirev's most brilliant and original orchestral moments. *S/K* (m.49) brings some order to the riotous canon before the return to *P* in the orchestral bass (m.73). However, order is not to prevail; *P* begins canonically at the third a bar apart (m.125), then the entire orchestra plays the tune (m.133). One might think this to be the end of a sequence of presentations. Instead, Balakirev returns to the octave canon one beat apart (m.141), first for woodwinds and strings, and then in the *tutti* setting followed by *S/K* (m.165)—a reprise of the dance's most brilliant passage thus far. After the variations of the *thème russe*, the Cossack dance returns—first with all parts coordinating (m.306) and then in canonic formations (m.322)—leaving the most brilliant repetition for the very end.

The Romanza third movement has been the most severely criticized of Balakirev's symphony movements.[183] The charge that the piece is banal is certainly true; not one of the themes is memorable, nor is there anything else in the orchestration, texture, dynamics, or structure that lends distinction to the piece. Abraham criticizes it for being weak, but also for being "quite out of place in a symphony predominantly epic and heroic in character."[184] Additionally, the material is not presented in a coherent way. At the very start, it sounds like Balakirev is commencing with an introduction (m.1) followed by *P* (m.19) in two parallel statements. *T* (m.34), however, is a small rondo (*a–b–a–b–a*) giving the structural impression of a thematic statement rather than a transition. Such an impression is further supported by *T^k* (m.60), which brings closure rather than continuation. *S/K* (m.66) is devoid of either melodic or harmonic interest and leads to the introduction (m.84), bypassing what was thought to be *P*, and moving directly to *T* (m.100), which unfolds nearly exactly as it did previously, concluding with *T^k* (m.126) and *S/K* (m.131) in the tonic key. The introduction reappears (m.150), and *P* (m.168) returns for the coda. This combination of undistinguished themes, presented in a way that confuses their function, results in a less-than-optimal experience.

EXAMPLE XV/43   Balakirev. Symphony No. 2/2, mm.9–33.

Both Abraham and Garden have some positive views of the Polacca Finale. Garden thinks it to be "a superb Polonaise . . . charged with rhythmic vitality. Both themes . . . are epic and heroic." He goes on to extol this movement as better than the Polonaises in *Boris Godunov* and *Eugene Onegin.*[185] Abraham had said much the same thing some thirty years earlier, except he, in contrast to Garden, failed to condemn the Romanza's return within the Finale. A strong advocate for Chopin, Balakirev knew Chopin's Polonaises as well as those by Musorgsky and Tchaikovsky, among others. However, Balakirev does not call this Finale a Polonaise, but a Polacca, which can be taken as a generic name.

Balakirev's Finale begins with a fanfare that points toward the heroic and imperial nature of the dance, but after this point the weakness of this piece becomes apparent. The refrain theme is essentially one with an upbeat, whereas downbeat themes are characteristic of a Polonaise. The normal background rhythm (♪♩♩ ♩ ♩ ♩) also occurs in only two measures, beginning at m.51, and weak phrase endings are not a prominent feature of the dance. Certainly, the *thème russe,* used as the first episode (*B*), does not conform to the dance style, especially with the tambourine rhythm (♪♩♩♩ ♩ , ♪) that accompanies it. This is a piece in

EXAMPLE XV/43 (*continued*)

the tempo of a Polacca, but this does not immediately qualify it to be a Polonaise; *B* is a Russian folksong, but *A* certainly could be a generic Polish dance.

The formal unfolding of the movement places more and more emphasis on the episodes (Table XV/32). Indeed, in the second half, *A* only appears in the coda (m.241) as *B,* the *thème russe,* alternates with *C* and concludes the movement. In addition, the *thème russe* is scored much louder and fuller; at one point the trumpet blares out this theme *fortissimo* near the top of its range (m.212). In contrast, the scoring of the refrain is never so assertive; the trumpets provide the introductory fanfares and then change into a supporting role. Perhaps there is a nationalistic agenda to the way these two themes are treated by Balakirev, but until we have some specific evidence apart from the composer's known national interests, such must remain mere speculation.

EXAMPLE XV/43   (*continued*)

The Second Symphony was relatively well received, although the generation gap between Balakirev and his audience (and critics) is evident in this review from *Russkie vedomosti* of a presumably "unofficial" first performance in March 1909:

> The first concert of the "Circle of Lovers of Russian Music" took place on the 17th of March. . . . On the evening's program there appeared symphonic works exclusively, at the head of which stood the second symphony of Balakirev, which was performed for the first time. This symphony is dedicated to the "precious memory of A[leksandr] D[mitrievich] Ulybyshev," the author of a well-known French book on Mozart that appeared 66 years ago. And how strangely moving it is to recall that the same artist, who now releases a new symphony, was in a close, personal relationship with leading figures

EXAMPLE XV/43   *(continued)*

of an epoch that is removed from us by a good two generations. . . . Such a relationship connected Balakirev with Glinka, who highly valued the talent of the then young composer and even called him his successor. And, truthfully, the creativity of Balakirev much resembles that of Glinka. The same striving toward a purity of style, the smallest details painstakingly finished; the same absence of all exaggeration or chaos; the same creative connection with folk tunes, whether Russian, Czech, Spanish, or Oriental; the same monographic style of orchestration. All that is lacking is Glinka-style spontaneity, power, and integrity.

On the other hand, in its more complex and, especially, in its "programmatic" elements, the music of Balakirev reveals the influence of Berlioz, and also Schumann, and also of the symphonic Liszt, whom Glinka did not know at all. Moreover, Balakirev did not write opera like Glinka, but devoted his efforts to the orchestra, the piano, and the romance.

TABLE XV/32
Balakirev. Symphony No. 2/4: Structure

Tempo di Polacca

Introduction	[A] a	b	a	b	[B]			*Introduction*	[A]
V/D minor	D minor				D-flat	E minor	D-flat	V/D minor	D minor
m.1	5	29	33	49	57	82	90	107	111

Poco più mosso

[C] a	a	a	[B]	[C]	*Coda* [A]	[B]
(III/SK)				(III/SK)		
B-flat			D major		D major	B-flat → D
135	169	178	190	220	241	266

459

The new symphony is very much in character for the 73-year-old composer. As always with Balakirev, its themes are for the most part short, but [illegible]. These themes are developed diversely and freshly, while, with regard to form, the strength of the composer is proclaimed not so much in the grandiose integrity of broad [illegible] as in the details of his variations style. Harmonic, rhythmic, and orchestral devices are well-aimed and effective. Each of these separately rarely presents anything unusual, but in lively, organic combination they gain a completely new, combined strength that is very characteristic for the distinctive individuality of the composer, who is free from fiery surges and inclined to studiousness.

The first movement of the symphony, original in its modulation scheme, has a somewhat Oriental character, which unintentionally recalls Balakirev's *Tamara,* with which there are here more than a few points of contact both in the themes and in their development. The second movement is the interesting, lively "Scherzo alla cosacca," in which, however, there is little that is specifically "cossack" or, in general, scherzo-like. The trio of the scherzo is the realm of the winds and is constructed on a Russian theme. The third movement is a romance; where the strings rule; the melody is melodious, well proportioned, and beautiful, but with a Balakirevan coolness. In the brilliant finale, with its clearly expressed Polonaise character, the best episodes of all are those based on the development of a folk tune that has been employed more than once already in Russian music. More colorless are those episodes of the finale that are associated with a theme borrowed from the romance. On the whole, the symphony is a very beautiful composition, not always strong, but interesting throughout. Well-performed under the direction of Mr. Kuper, it was, to all appearances, enjoyed by the audience.[186]

Russkaia muzykal'naia gazeta reported on the Free Music School premiere in April 1909 with more enthusiasm:

> After an interval of many years, the Free Music School has [once again] declared its existence. And it declared itself in an exceptional manner, arranging a symphonic concert on the 10th of April in the Nobles' Assembly. The program was Russian—Balakirev, Lyapunov, and Rimsky-Korsakov—and largely fresh, including excerpts from the music to *King Lear,* the new, second symphony by Balakirev, and the *Ukrainian Rhapsody* of Lyapunov. . . .
>
> Besides the appearance of Mr. Lyapunov, most attention at the concert was focused on the new (D-minor) symphony of Balakirev. Inferior in terms of the beauty and freshness of the music and symphonic development to the first symphony of the venerable composer, the D-minor symphony of Balakirev all the same is an interesting and important work: it might even be deemed a symphonic suite, because except for the first movement, which is the most interesting and developed in terms of its symphonism, [the symphony] consists of a scherzo "alla cosacca," a romance, and a Polish finale. Both themes of the first allegro are elegant and colorful, although rather cold; the second of these, as so often with Balakirev, has an Eastern character. The development of this movement is clear and quite beautiful. The completely original "Cossack" scherzo has a bright theme (2/4) that, in a second, broader development, [also] serves as the melodic basis for the trio of the scherzo (in 3/4).
>
> In contrast to the audience, which compelled [the orchestra] to repeat the romance (3rd movement), we like the latter less, precisely for its archaism, if one can express it this way. But it is planned beautifully and with humor. In it, as in the scherzo, there is something sweet, simple, cast in the classical traditions of Glinka. In the brilliant and interesting

"Polish" [movement] (finale, tempo di Pollacca), the tune of the folk song "Kak u nas v sadochke" is more successfully employed. Less interesting are the episodes in which the theme of the preceding romance is recalled. The symphony was well-conducted by Mr. Lyapunov and its reception by the public was very impressive and hearty.[187]

Balakirev's Symphony No. 2 is an uneven accomplishment. It begins with a rather derivative first movement, which a modern audience would hear as owing something to Tchaikovsky's Symphony No. 5/1. At the same time, its adaptation of sonata form as a tonal structure owes nothing to his highly successful contemporary. The second movement Cossack dance is a brilliant and effective piece of writing that embodies within it all of the *kuchka* ideals in terms of materials and their treatment. All comments and impressions of the Romanza are that it leaves something to be desired; both its content and form are wanting memorability and clarity. Though both Garden and Abraham admire the Finale, this writer finds it, in comparison to Symphony No. 1/4, a much less successful conclusion to the cycle.

Symphony No. 2 seems to be more of a piece conceived at the keyboard rather than for the orchestra. Some passages are too fussy in their detailed figuration to sound idiomatic for a large ensemble, e.g., the *A* theme of the Finale, the viola figuration (I/m.113), and the unlinked violin figures (I/m.14). Others do not sound well because Balakirev lacks an idiomatic knowledge of the individual instruments, e.g., the exposed English horn writing at the bottom of its range requiring a split-second response (I/m.14–17) and the tambourine rhythm (I/m.34) that in this tempo will lack clarity.

CONCLUSION

Perhaps a wider survey of the Russian symphony during the first two decades of the twentieth century will discover that Balakirev's two examples were influential. However, this seems to be unlikely: by the time both were completed, they were setting forth ideals that by 1900 were irrelevant. Certainly the most fascinating issue is not whom Balakirev might have influenced with his two completed symphonies, but the cross-influences here. The mentor seems to have been affected by those he mentored; Borodin, Rimsky-Korsakov, and Tchaikovsky all seem to have contributed to Balakirev's symphonic style. Or was it Balakirev we were hearing in the works of these three composers? If Balakirev had finished both of his symphonies during the 1860s, then such a question, which has no answer, would not need to be posed.

Vasily Sergeyevich Kalinnikov
INTRODUCTION

Vasily Sergeyevich Kalinnikov (1866–1900/1901) (Plate B13) was born in Voina, where he was the son of a musically talented police officer. He attended the seminary at Oryol, where he led the choir while still in his teens. In 1884, Kalinnikov departed for Moscow to further his musical education and enrolled at the Conservatory, but could not continue for financial reasons. He became a bassoonist, played violin, and worked as a copyist to sustain himself; his studies were continued at the Philharmonic Music School in Moscow. In 1893, Kalinnikov was appointed conductor at the Italian Theater. Due to tuberculosis, he moved to the Crimea for relief and died at the age of thirty-four in Yalta.[188]

Kalinnikov's standing in the West, and to a lesser degree in Russia, is almost entirely based on his two symphonies (see Table XV/33). While the First Symphony was heard outside of Russia in Vienna, Berlin, Paris, and New York early on, the Second Symphony was less highly regarded.

TABLE XV/33

The Symphonies of Vasily Kalinnikov

Key	Dates	Title	Movements	Instrumentation	Comments
G minor	1894–1895	Symphony No. 1	1. Allegro moderato ¢ (454 m.) 2. Andante commodamente 3/4 (138 m.) E-flat major 3. Scherzo: Allegro non troppo 3/4—moderato assai 2/4 (462 m.) C major—A minor 4. Finale: Allegro moderato ¢ 3/2 (484 m.) G major	Grand plus Picc., Tuba, Harp, Tri.	Dedicated to S.N. Kruglikov. First performance: Kiev, Russian Musical Society on February 8/20, 1897, conducted by Aleksandr Vinogradsky. Published in Moscow: Jürgenson, 1900.
A major	1895–1897	Symphony No. 2	1. Moderato—Allegro non troppo 2/4 (505 m.) 2. Andante cantabile 3/4 (132 m.) F-sharp minor 3. Allegro scherzando 3/8—2/4 (744 m.) D major 4. Andante cantabile 3/4—Allegro vivo 2/4 (682 m.)	Grand plus Picc., Tuba, Harp	Dedicated to Aleksandr Vinogradsky. First performance: Kiev, Russian Musical Society on February 28/March 12, 1898, conducted by Aleksandr Vinogradsky. Published in Moscow: Jürgenson, 1901.

SYMPHONY NO. 1 IN G MINOR

Unlike Balakirev, whose two symphonies placed minimal importance on thematic recurrence, Kalinnikov's Symphony No. 1 brings back some of the principal themes in the final movement heroically transformed, not unlike what César Franck had done in his D Minor Symphony (1889). That Kalinnikov had heard this later-to-be-famous cyclic symphony, or had seen the music, is probably beyond the realm of possibility. It is more likely that a work like the Tchaikovsky Symphony No. 5 (1888) was the model, which brings back both the motto theme and *I/P* in the Finale's coda. Thus, in the Kalinnikov G Minor Symphony the Finale recapitulates *I/P* as an introduction (m.1), as well as *I/S* (m.148), and both *III/A* and themes from the Scherzo's Trio (mm.200, 208) return in heroic garb for the coda (mm.363, 400, and 449). In addition, the *S* of the Finale (m.37) is similar to that of the first movement (m.45).

Otherwise, the cycle presents a series of not-unexpected gestures. Tonally, it begins on D minor and ends in G major; it must be admitted that the G minor first movement is not particularly dark in the affect of its materials, but the Finale in its culmination is about as heroic and triumphant as a Finale could possibly be. Kalinnikov places the Andante in E-flat major, the Scherzo in C major, and its Trio in the relative minor. The Andante connects to the first movement in that it ends on G octaves and the slow movement commences with a figure undulating between G and E-flats. A similar gesture, though less convincing, connects the Andante to the Scherzo; the Andante ends with G in the top, and the Scherzo begins with an ornamental G that slides to C. Such tonal connections do not exist between the Scherzo and Finale; perhaps they are not necessary since the Finale has cyclic recapitulatory functions.

Kalinnikov opens the first movement with a melancholy theme (*Pa*) that could well be a folksong with its minor thirds, non-leading tone sevenths, and octave sonority moving from G to D (Example XV/44). A contrasting response (*Pb*, m.4) commencing with a 3/2 bar leads to a repeat of *Pa* and *b* a fourth higher on C and an additional statement of *Pa* (m.15) in F. *1T* (m.27) cadences in C-sharp, and its sequences operate not by fourths or fifths but by thirds (mm.27, 29, 31). *2T(P)* is not only based on *P*, but at this point *P* is transformed from a melancholy theme to one more assertive and dramatic (m.36). A short lead-in takes us to *S* (m.45), a seductive *dolce* melody in F-sharp played by violas, cellos, and horn, which is repeated in a different environment (m.61) (Example XV/45). *K* (m.77) is made from *1T* and *P*. The larger tonal plan moves from G minor, back to F-sharp, then to B-flat, and back toward G minor, the latter for the repeat of the exposition.

After a restatement of *S* (m.119) and *3K* (m.125), the development proper begins (m.138) with *Pax* in E-flat minor and concluding in D (m.160). *Pax* is combined with *Tx*, and then the *S* interlude arrives accompanied by *T* (m.178). *Pax* (m.192) becomes manipulated partly by inversion (m.192) against the rhythm of *T*, which brings the development to its first climax (m.203) on the dominant of G minor. As a transition to its second part, *P* is inverted and resolves to the dominant of E for part two marked by a fugato (m.213), whose subject is a synthesis of *P* and *T*. *K* (m.229) serves as a homophonic episode and then the fugato resumes (m.244). Another episode (m.260) of new material builds to the second climax (m.290). A retransition with *Pax,* mostly inverted and at a low dynamic, leads to the recapitulation (m.308). The development section is both intensive and obsessive in that it relentlessly deals with *P*; *S* is only allotted a single thirteen-measure passage.

In the recapitulation, Kalinnikov reorchestrates *P*, re-presents *1T* (m.330) and *2T* (m.339), has a new transition (m.345), states *S* (m.348), presents *1K* in augmentation (m.380) with *T* before combining it with *S* (m.392), and further develops *Pax* (m.403), which builds

EXAMPLE XV/44   Kalinnikov. Symphony No. 1/1, mm.1–8. Courtesy of Edwin F. Kalmus & Co.

to a climax. *S* and *3K* (m.415) lower the temperature, but *T* rapidly builds to another climax. The coda (m.438) restates *P*, first quietly, then *fortissimo* as *Paz* forms plagal cadences.

In many ways, this is a wonderful example of a lyric first movement. It is filled with two winning themes, *P* and *S*, which once heard are not easily forgotten, and at the same time *P* is so structured that it is easily dissected and developed. To be sure, *S* can become tiresome if one repeatedly listens to this movement; it is built from four two-measure units that could benefit from more variety of surface activity. The development section is nearly two hundred measures long, i.e., twice the duration of the exposition. One's impression, besides its tendency toward prolixity, is that Kalinnikov must have been a first-rate improvisator with a sure sense of tonal planning.

One could understate the case for the orchestration of the first movement since it is thoroughly effective without being ostentatious. The orchestration of the opening of the second movement (Example XV/46) is also not ostentatious, but at the same time rather extraordinary. First violins are *con sordini* with legato undulations between G and E-flat, which are doubled by the harp. The harpist's left hand plays a series of open fifths, which are doubled by changing wind colors for each chord. Added to this wash of colors is the movement's principal theme (*A*) played by the English horn—the Russian composer's "oriental" sound—doubled by the violas; *A* is then repeated (m.18) for clarinet and cellos. Kalinnikov's melody, like *P* and *S* of the first movement, makes an immediate and lasting impression.

EXAMPLE XV/45 Kalinnikov. Symphony No. 1/1, mm.45–52. Courtesy of Edwin F. Kalmus & Co.

EXAMPLE XV/46   Kalinnikov. Symphony No. 1/2, mm.1–17. Courtesy of Edwin F. Kalmus & Co.

Though the composer's penchant for lyricism frequently associates him with Tchaikovsky, melodies of this sort with such a scoring are more reminiscent of Borodin's Symphony No. 2/3 and his musical picture *In the Steppes of Central Asia*.

The middle section (*B*, m.30) combines episodic materials with variations of the *A* theme. It commences with a new theme in G-sharp (A-flat) minor of a quasi-oriental nature, scored for oboe. The strings respond (m.38) and the oboe (m.46) concludes the paragraph, but the phrase is unexpectedly extended and begins to build toward a climax that is scuttled. *A* (m.66) is now restated by the horn in A major with a clarinet counterpoint, then by violins with the countermelody in the flutes. Now the texture and dynamics build (m.81) to a climax (m.85), then *A* is heard in G-sharp. Each repetition of the *A* material within *B* is a *kuchka* variation. *A* (m.105) returns in its original key and colors, and the dynamics diminish for a quiet close. This movement is skillfully put together with but one miscalculation: near the beginning of *B* (mm.38–45) the violins soar into their highest register. Such a passage might have been more effectively placed toward the end of this central section.

Kalinnikov's Scherzo proper is the most straightforward portion of the symphony; its key scheme is unremarkable, and its thematic material has little of the distinctive melodies that were poured into the first two movements. For the central section (Trio), the triple-meter Allegro and C major change to a duple-meter Moderato and A minor for another excursion *à la* Borodin into an oriental style, with flexes, swirls, and repeated figures undergirded by a pedal/drone. The return of the Trio's opening is given a *kuchka* treatment that connects directly with the Scherzo's return. Notice at the end of this final section how the dominant chord is avoided and replaced by a supertonic seventh and a flattened submediant.

As noted above, the Finale has a distinct dual purpose: it serves as a musical entity unto itself and as an effective summary in a heroic/triumphant character of themes heard in the previous three movements through thematic transformation. Its shape is that of a big rondo, as outlined in Table XV/34. Nearly every theme from a previous movement is recast in character except for material from the first movement (*P* and *S*); they appear but once and remain in their original minor mode. In terms of the transformations from the second and third movements, those from the second movement (*II/A*) are vital to the Finale's drama, while those from the Scherzo are more ornamental and could be easily overlooked. Additionally, of the material new in the Finale, the refrain (*A*) undergoes augmentation in the third episode and remains augmented for *A*'s return in G major (m.328). No doubt this slowing of the pace is in preparation for *II/A*, with the head motif of *IV/A* retaining the pace as an accompanying ostinato. Also of note is the treatment of *B;* it undergoes no metamorphosis and is not heard in the tonic, but is presented again in its original key. However, this has no structural significance, since it returns within the second episode rather than near the movement's end.

The chief weakness of this Finale is its tendency to overindulge its rhetoric. Instead of hearing *A* and *II/A* once in augmentation, Kalinnikov provides two statements: the first in a non-tonic tonality, the second in the home key. On the other hand, it is this rhetoric combined with the lyricism of *B* and *I/S* that allows this movement to take wing. Certainly, music of a heroic and a triumphant character no doubt had political overtones in a country ruled by an old-fashioned imperial regime.

One might assume that the reason Kalinnikov's Symphony No. 1 has not received its due was that it was first performed by the Russian Musical Society in Kiev in 1897, and therefore did not receive proper public notice. However, the symphony was reviewed in journals widely circulated throughout the empire; was published by the Moscow house of Jürgenson; and was heard throughout the West, conducted by such luminaries as Walter Damrosch,

TABLE XV/34
Kalinnikov. Symphony No. 1/4: Structure

Allegro moderato ¢   Allegro resoluto
Introduction

I/P	trans. (A)	[A]	[B]	trans.1	[A]	[C]	(B)	(B)
G minor	G major	G major	D major		G major	E-flat	E minor	B minor
m.1	7	17	37	63	75	87	97	113

Meno mosso   a tempo

trans. (A)	I/S			[A]	trans. 2	[B]
	B					
	D major	G minor	C minor	G major		E major
	128	144	148	162	175	182

retrans. (A)		[D]	trans.1	[B]		V/E	retrans. (A)		[B]	trans. (A)	L' istesso tempo 3/2
	A pedal	A augmentation		B-flat major	C major			D pedal	augmentation	[A] augmentation	Coda
										II/A	II/A
		D major					G major		G major	G major	A as ostinato
											E-flat
211	223	237	249	261	279	296	304	312	328		361

Allegro con brio ¢

N	III/Trio			Maestoso 3/2	III/Trio (Trpts.)	Cadences
				III/A	(A ostinato)	
				[A] as ostinato		
G major	G major	V/E		G pedal / G		
389	400	434		443	449	

Sergey Koussevitzky, Artur Rodzinski, and Arturo Toscanini during the first half of the twentieth century. On the other hand, Rimsky-Korsakov had a negative reaction when he read through the score; there were numerous errors, and Rimsky thought that Kalinnikov lacked the proper musical training, though he did admit to the younger composer's talent.[189] Sergey Prokofiev also took umbrage when, after he played for Walter Damrosch his own Symphony No. 1 "Classical," Damrosch remarked: "Delightful—just like Kalinnikov." Even though Damrosch meant it as a compliment, Prokofiev was insulted.[190]

The reaction of the critical community to the Kiev and Moscow premieres was generally positive. The leading Russian music journal, *Russkaia muzykal'naia gazeta,* published a detailed review of the Kiev premiere based on an original review published in *Teatral'naia gazeta:*

> On the 8th of February, the fourth symphony concert of the Kiev branch of the Imperial Russian Musical Society took place, the program of which was devoted to Russian composers. The main number was the Symphony in G-minor by the young composer Mr. Kalinnikov. *Zh[izn] and I[skusstva]* provides the following information about the young Russian composer:
>
> "He was born in 1866 in Orlov province, received his musical education in the conservatory [music school] of the Moscow Philharmonic Society, which he completed in 1892 with the title of free artist. The G-minor symphony was begun in 1893 [*sic*] and completed in 1895. Prior to the symphony, an orchestral suite, which was performed at one of the symphonic concerts of the Moscow Philharmonic Society, a ballad for women's choir with orchestra, several overtures, romance, and piano pieces were written."
>
> The musical critic of the same magazine reports that the symphony of Mr. V. Kalinnikov made an enchanting impression on the large audience in attendance. The charm of it lies in the fact that the composer laid the foundation of his symphony in a folk song, which he was able to elevate to a high degree of artistry. Possessing a perfect grasp of form and being a true master of the orchestra, he uses these means in order to bring forth the beauty of folk music. The music of Mr. V. Kalinnikov is an expression of his subjective feelings. The best part is the first section (Allegro Moderato), which presents a poetic picture in the highest degree, the whole of which precipitates the artistic treatment of the folk motif, which unites and illuminates this charming picture. The 3rd movement (Scherzo) comes in second for its virtues, it is imbued with a kind of cheerful but naive mood, which is expressed by a modal motif. . . . In third place [we] may place the Andante commodamente in which you are astonished over the artistry of the composer in executing complete artistic effects by the application of wandering perfect fifths, if one can express oneself so, in the accompaniment. But as with all effects, so these push somewhat into the background the ideal features of the musical work. Finally, the fourth movement (Finale) is a conclusive summary of everything experienced before and, as such, further strengthens the marvelous impression that the first movement made on the soul of the listener. With the exception of a few rhythmical fluctuations and the fact that the harp was completely out of tune, the symphony of this young, talented, Moscow composer came off splendidly under the direction of Mr. Vinogradsky, who, apparently, put his whole heart into the performance.[191]

The Moscow premiere the following year also attracted the attention, and inspired the delight, of Ivan Lipaev, who reviewed the performance for *Russkaia muzykal'naia gazeta:*

Oh, how many cheerful feeling the G-minor first symphony of Vas. S. Kalinnikov inspired in my heart when it was played in the third symphonic concert of the [Moscow Philharmonic Society]! Among the dull, mystically structured, technically tangled works of recent times, the symphony of Mr. Kalinnikov is a ray of sunshine! It is simple, transparent, naive, captivating and delicately poetical, femininely soft and comforting. Take the first Allegro of the first movement. What a light, melancholy theme, how intimate and Russian, melodious and distinct. And it simply is covered in harmonic charms, it is revived by rhythm now in driving syncopation, now in variations of meter. And the secondary part is terrific! Lively, contrasting, it spills out without restraint, without strain, it infects and fascinates with its cheerful mood. The main theme, then, serves as the basis for a fugue, which is adroitly developed and lively in its instrumentation. But among the general animation of all that precedes it, the fugue seems conventional. One must note that the elaboration of the first movement is positively gifted. Everything here is justified, superbly distributed among the various instruments, modulations are subtle and do not shock by their suddenness. . . . The coda of the first movement is not as much to my liking: it is banal in its last chords, and only banal, although it is very bravura. The second movement may be called not only sweet, but surprisingly poetic, a fragrant spring gust.

The picturesqueness of it is delightful. A . . . canvas of scarcely audible muted violins, supported by the harp, creates an enchanting sound painting. Here pours out a beautiful, warm, radiant, and passionate theme in the English horn and the violas, with quiet harmonic accompaniment. It whispers of love, of the happiness of the Russian woman, of the dreamy and sweetly anticipated moment of happiness. . . . This [theme] and the other one embrace each other to the universal rejoicing of the orchestra, which cedes the weary cadence to the horns, after which once again in the violins and the harp there appears the previous figure of thirds, which falls off in pianissimo. In a word, this movement [recalls] memories of the distant past, awakens them. It recalls by its aural construction the manner of Borodin. The Scherzo is a stream of an exultant, clamorous, cheerful mental world. In the beginning, even might and force can be heard, suggested by unisons. The trio is distinguished by its 2/4 meter, so coquettish and affected in the clarinet and so melancholy in the oboe. Distinct boundaries impart much variety to the trio and rivet the listeners' attention. The conclusion of the Scherzo is strong and inspiring. Here, as in the first two movements, Mr. Kalinnikov evidently sketched everything with one stroke of the pen. And this is why, it seems to me, there is a wholeness of spirit in his symphony, very precious, not only in the young, but also in composers who have already acquired a name. All of the prominent, notable moments in the previous [movements], pass by in the final movement of the symphony. This immediately imparts to it a unity in content. Similar reminders, of course, are no rarity, but if they are opportune they lead to appropriate goals. The composer has achieved this: In the finale, he underscores his talent. Everything in this movement lives, now gentle, humble, now impetuous and ungovernable. It concludes the symphony supremely skillfully. And when you then give a report on it, you unintentionally wish every success for its young composer. Mr. Kalinnikov's symphony [premiered] to an enormous furor in Kiev under the direction of Mr. Vinogradsky, drawing to itself the sympathy of local music lovers. And here [in Moscow] conspicuous attention was paid to it, and to Mr. Zumpe, who conducted it, goes the credit for the dissemination of such a marvelous work.[192]

SYMPHONY NO. 2 IN A MAJOR

That Kalinnikov's First Symphony was so positively received—at its premiere in Kiev two movements were encored—must have stimulated the composer to almost immediately begin working on another symphony. Symphony No. 2 is also in the lyric/heroic mode of the First Symphony, but here with a strong dose of the pastoral. In comparing the two symphonies, the composer and Russian critic Boris Asaf'yev (1884–1949) remarked:

> Very promising were the lyrical symphonies of the talented V. Kalinnikov who died so early (G minor and A minor). In them a further assimilation of the influences of Borodin and Tchaikovsky seemed possible. The charm of the first symphony of Kalinnikov lies in its intimate profusely poured out melodies. The second symphony has a greater sweep, but we already feel a want of broad and deep breathing—the scope of the intentions surpasses the actual powers, and the symphony lacks freshness and naturalness (as compared with the first).[193]

This writer takes exception to Asaf'yev's appraisal of the Second Symphony. Granted its thematic materials do not have the immediate appeal of those found in the First Symphony, but they seem to wear somewhat better. In his Second Symphony, Kalinnikov manipulates his materials with greater assurance. Whether the "scope of the intentions surpasses the actual powers" cannot be ascertained since we have no knowledge as to what Kalinnikov hoped to accomplish in composing his Symphony No. 2. However, Asaf'yev's preference for the First Symphony may have had overtones of socialist realism; Symphony No. 2 has less of the heroic and triumphant, but displays more of the composer's acumen.

Though in the First Symphony Kalinnikov treats the larger form of the cycle as thematically and characteristically culminating in the Finale, the Second Symphony takes the introduction to the first movement as the kernel from which some of the themes for each of the movements derive. As can be seen in Example XV/47, *1P* of the first movement shares its opening with the introduction (*O*) and then goes its own way; *A* of the second movement (*II/A*) is also generated from the opening, but here the process and character is completely different from *I/1P* as each subphrase is derivative of the introduction's first seven pitches; the theme of the Scherzo's Trio derives from *II/P_{ay}*, but also foreshadows the principal material of the Finale (m.19); and the Finale's introduction uses *II/A* as a generator, and the Allegro vivo's *A* evolves out of *I/1P*. In addition, at the end of the cycle (m.601), the *P* of the first movement combines with that of the Finale. Similar to the First Symphony, at this point in the structure Kalinnikov becomes a little long-winded not only with his themes' repetitions, but also with a lengthy swath of A major.

In the first movement, Kalinnikov again presents an unusual key scheme: *S* (m.73) appears in B-flat minor, i.e., a half-step above the tonic of A, while in the recapitulation *S* (m.349) appears not in the tonic but in the supertonic of B minor. Although an unusual key scheme is one of the similarities with the G Minor Symphony's first movement, the contrasts are much more striking. At the core of the differences are the slow introduction and the character of *P*. Rather than another melancholy theme, *P* in the Second Symphony is a lyric *contredanse* in the major mode. And since so much of the Second Symphony's materials derive from the introduction and *P*, this characteristic style colors our view of the entire cycle. The first movement's three *T* themes (mm.60, 64, 70) continue in this mood until *3T* darkens the timbre and mode. A more melancholy *S* (m.73) is heard twice and its minor mode is underlined at first by the scoring of the melody for violas and cellos; for the second statement oboes and clarinets are added. *1K(2T*, m.98) and *2K* (m.102) return to the *contredanse* idiom and bring the exposition to closure.

EXAMPLE XV/47 Kalinnikov. Symphony No. 2/1, mm.1–6, 18–24, 55–57; /2, mm.1–4; /3, mm.268–73; /4, mm.1–4, 19–22. Courtesy of Edwin F. Kalmus & Co.

A juxtaposition of *P* (m.130) and *S* (m.141) at the start of the development makes one think that the entire section will be one of high contrasts. Instead, *S* intrudes into what will become *P* territory only one more time (m.229) (cf. Symphony No. 1/1). First, *P* (m.159) moves sequentially and then serves as a fugato subject (m.187) with a brief stretto (m.212) before dissipating into *Sax* in imitation (m.229). The rhythm of *Pax* (m.237) spawns a restatement of *P* (m.245) over a dominant pedal and a statement of the introductory material in tempo (m.253), stretched over a greater span of time. A passage of mysterious chords— perhaps a reminiscence of Beethoven No. 5/1—leads back to the quiet lyric *contredanse* and the recapitulation (m.295).

Kalinnikov's restatement of *1P* with a decorating flute immediately echoes something Haydn might do. What follows for the most part repeats the exposition. The coda is about the size of the recapitulation; it serves as another development, builds to a climax (m.483), and tends to some unfinished business with *S* (m.488). Its climax is an unexpected shift to F major (Example XV/48) for the tutti *fff* orchestra (m.482). This sudden disruption quickly calms, shifts to an E pedal, and *S* is finally heard in the tonic, clearing

EXAMPLE XV/48   Kalinnikov. Symphony No. 2/1, mm.471–84. Courtesy of Edwin F. Kalmus & Co.

the way for the movement's tonal conclusion with a plagal ending that neatly emerges out of *P.*

We have already commented about how *A* of the Andante cantabile emerges out of *I/1P.* Otherwise, this opening recalls Borodin: the harp with strings perhaps imitating gusli (Russian zithers) and the cantilena played by the English horn (Example XV/49). The entry of the oboe, echoing the English horn, is reminiscent of "Scene in the Country" from Berlioz's *Symphonie fantastique.* As in Kalinnikov's Symphony No. 1/2, *1B* (m.25) also begins with the

EXAMPLE XV/48   *(continued)*

violins in their high register. While the beginning of *1B* acts like an episode, the introduction of *A* (m.47) in C major and *D* (m.74) set in full sonorities and *2B* (m.54) are somewhat developmental. The second statement of *A* in the episode soon gives way to the return of *1B* (m.79). The retransition (m.92) distantly recalls that of the first movement with its emphasis on chord and color. This time the oboe takes over *A*'s return (m.98), then clarinet, cellos, and finally the English horn return to the melody. Another plagal cadence (mm.129–30) and celestial arpeggios bring closure. Together with the slow movement of the Tchaikovsky Symphony No. 5, Kalinnikov's Symphony No. 2/2 must rank among the most affecting slow movements to come from the pen of a Russian composer. Carefully shaped by its serene *A* theme, *B*

EXAMPLE XV/49 Kalinnikov. Symphony No. 2/2, mm.1–23. Courtesy of Edwin F. Kalmus & Co.

EXAMPLE XV/49 *(continued)*

increases its temperature only to return to *A*, which unwinds further into the lower-middle range of the orchestra. While certainly lacking the passion of the Tchaikovsky, Kalinnikov here fully realizes a pastoral character.

The 3/8 meter signature brings to mind Allegro Scherzos by Borodin, Tchaikovsky, and probably its origin for the Russian tradition: the "Queen Mab" Scherzo of Berlioz's *Roméo et Juliette*. However, Kalinnikov's movement is not a light-touch piece; it is marked by the refrain's bold statement within the rondo form of the Scherzo proper and vivid cross-rhythms reminiscent of Chabrier's 1883 rhapsody *España*. *P* is another theme capable of different roles as refrain, a strong delineator of form, and the subject of a fugato (m.94). Additionally, it easily dissects for developmental/transitional purposes. A change of meter as well as the material itself prepares one for a return to the *contredanse* world of the first movement. However, Kalinnikov returns not to the *contredanse* style, but to its melodic shape (*I/1Pay*) and the personality of folk music: its almost improvisatory nature, modalism, support of the melody with pedal points and ostinatos, endless repetitions, and *kuchka* variations all point to an attempt to capture something outside the realm of high Germanic art music. Like the Scherzo proper, the Trio also uses a refrain. Notice Kalinnikov's sleight-of-hand move as *IV/A* occurs prematurely in the Trio (mm.300–304) as a counterpoint to its main theme. As seen in Symphony No. 1/3, while an accomplished effort, the Scherzo is the least interesting piece in the cycle.

Kalinnikov creates for his Finale (Table XV/35) a special sort of tonal structure. It is framed by A major: the Andante cantabile introduction is a metamorphosis of the slow movement's theme, which derives from the first movement, and it closes with material from the first movement's introduction and Allegro. In between comes another *contredanse* (Allegro

TABLE XV/35
Kalinnikov. Symphony No. 2/4: Structure

Andante cantabile 3/4 *Introduction* *III/A*	Allegro vivo 2/4 lead-in		[A]			[1B]	ext.	[2B]
		C pedal		F pedal	A pedal			
A major	F major		F major			D major		
m.1	19	35	58	77	81	85		163

		[A]	trans.	[1C]	[2C]	[1C]	retrans.	[A]
A pedal	C pedal						C pedal	
		F major		C major				F major
182	211	234	244	261	290	352	377	400

trans.	*1N*	*2N*	*3N*	*Ax*	L'istesso tempo 2/2 *Coda: I/O* and *II/1P*
		B pedal	B-flat pedal ———→ A pedal		
mod.	D major mod.	E major	E-flat		A major
410	433	449	542	588	601 682 ‖

vivo 2/4) whose governing tonality is F major, the key of the first movement's climax. Indeed, the entire tonal plan of this middle section is governed by F major and its related tonalities: D major and C major. Note that except for the two A pedals up to m.410, one would have no reason to believe, but for one's tonal memory, that A major was the tonic key surrounding a *contredanse* in F major.

Where Kalinnikov runs into difficulty is with reestablishing A major as the tonic. Essentially, there are two solutions: a dramatic tonal move that suddenly shifts the key from F to A major, or a passage of some length that incrementally obliterates F major in favor of A. The former solution seems counter to the character of this Finale and the sort of tonal moves the composer has favored in the previous movements. The second solution was the one pursued. The danger here is a dragging out of this transfer, and Kalinnikov certainly falls into this trap. A second problem with this lengthy tonal transition is whether to thematically integrate it with the refrains and episodes. Kalinnikov chooses instead to use what is essentially new material for a stretch of some two hundred measures. In terms of the total length of the movement, almost a third of the piece is devoted to this transition. It is almost as if one is listening to another movement added to the rondo. Perhaps Kalinnikov's model was Schumann's Symphony No. 2/4, a movement in two almost self-contained parts. Nevertheless, this flaw in Kalinnikov's Second Symphony is not a fatal one, but certainly one that gives this work less of a chance for the revival it deserves.

The first performance in Kiev warranted a small notice in the provincial section of *Russkaia muzykal'naia gazeta:*

> On the 28th of February, in a special symphonic concert of the local branch of the Imperial Russian Musical Society, the *second* symphony of the talented V. Kalinnikov was performed. A Russian mentality is notable in the symphony and it is full of interest and charm, despite a certain monotony and the lengthiness of its movements. It is dedicated to the marvelous Kievan director, A.N. Vinogradsky, by whom it was splendidly conducted.[194]

The Moscow premiere attracted the attention of Ivan Lipaev, who praised the work in his usual breathless style:

> The most prominent, artistically significant event in the life of Moscow was the performance in the eighth symphonic [concert] of the new, second A-Major symphony by Vas. Kalinnikov. It was first performed under Vinogradsky in Kiev and only now, after some time, has it appeared in Moscow. Mr. Kalinnikov is a great, promising talent—we were convinced of this by the first symphony and the entr'acte to "Tsar Boris"; the second symphony, for this reason, has been awaited with impatience. And it does not disappoint, but, on the contrary, inspires confidence in the real talent of its author. The form of the symphony is ordinary and minutely laid out. In the first movement, one encounters two themes, primary and secondary. The first is compact, warm, suitable for development; the second is charming in its broadness and melodiousness, particularly attractive in the cellos and horns. But the main thing is, and this is an important peculiarity, the themes are not contrived, they are the fruit of an unrestrained, unpremeditated creativity. From this derives their sincerity and spontaneity, which is reflected fully both in the counterpoint and in the instrumentation. Both in the first and in the second case we are struck by a so-called local or national color, which flows from something integral, imbibed with mother's milk. And like a subtle shroud, this coloring covers the entire symphony. The composer, apparently, cannot free himself from it even in the scherzo, even in its first half, with its broad Liszt-like intervals. But I will speak of the Andante. Here, as in all of the movements, Mr. Kalinnikov engages the main theme first, which turns out to be very opportune, intertwining it with a sense of artistic proportion, tactically not constraining the fantasy. Here he uses the English horn, the phrases of which are arpeggiated lightly by the harp; this magician-instrument concludes the Andante. In it lies something poetic, a narrative which leaves the listener in a contemplative mood, as if from an ancient lay (bylina), a gripping idea which carries one away to distant ages. If a report on the particularities of the application of aural material here is needed, then I would say that, on average, for the space of fifty bars, there is unnecessary ballast, although little noticed because of the thin orchestration. Partly, I already mentioned, the scherzo is playful, brilliantly daring, especially where little scales in the clarinet and piccolo pour forth, now above, now below. The scherzo is impetuous, ardent, passionate, when a group of brass takes up the leading melody, before the trio, but stopping as if with respect before the pastorale in 2/4, which is invested with a generally Slavic character, and then boldly, with a despairing whistle, it strains toward the concluding chord.
>
> The Andante of the last movement is short, sweet, and contrasts superbly with the Allegro Vivo, which at first seems as if it is curtly searching in anxiety for a familiar place,

but which then flows right up until the end. In this movement, the composer condensed and gathered with a strong hand all the power of paintstrokes and paints, which are torn off and mended in a broad, mighty, free, and smooth movement of the theme, which has flown by through the entire work. On account of the clarity of ideas, mood, and picturesqueness [in his work], Mr. Kalinnikov bears a resemblance to Borodin, because of the subtlety, lightness, transparency, and, so to speak, simplicity of his instrumental structures, the exposition of everything [bears a resemblance] to Glinka. An invigorating, cheerful feeling never abandons the composer, he never mourns with furrowed brow, but like a true artist only pauses in contemplation, and this rare cheerfulness in Mr. Kalinnikov astonishes and captivates. Cheerfulness and sincerity are his companions; they agitate the masses and they speak for a strong talent. The success of the symphony was colossal, the likeable composer was the recipient of the most enthusiastic ovations.[195]

Kalinnikov's Symphony No. 2 falls into that often-encountered category of the genre that has been termed heroic pastoral. Its emphasis on the *contredanse* in the first and last movements and the major mode serve as a point of unity under this rubric. The emphasis on the woodwind colors—the oboe and English horn in the slow movement and the central section of the Scherzo, where other woodwind colors come into prominence—underlines the cycle's pastoral character. As expected, the heroic is stressed at the conclusion of the first and last movements. It is also clear that Kalinnikov has made a concentrated effort to compose a unified piece not by consistently using thematic quotation, but by aurally detectable thematic derivation. Combined with his ability to compose winning melodies, the Second Symphony, despite its formal miscalculations, is *in toto* a substantial achievement.

CONCLUSION

Nearly every commentary on Kalinnikov mentions his premature death at the age of thirty-four and his unrealized potential. Given his musical education, he must have been an observational learner, i.e., from hearing a work or reading a score, he was able to learn how to manipulate the musical elements for his own ends. His greatest gift was in his ability to compose melodies that have an immediate impact; this is particularly true of his *S/B* themes and his slow movements. Contrast this with many other second-rank composers who were unable to compose memorable melodies. Kalinnikov also demonstrates a special knack for transforming and developing his materials, for his sense of rhythmic control at all levels, and for his telling use of harmony and tonality in ways that are out of the ordinary. Kalinnikov was also a master of orchestration, not in the ostentatious manner of Rimsky-Korsakov, but more in the maner of Tchaikovsky, where there are no miscalculations of timbre and balance. Also like Tchaikovsky, one of Kalinnikov's weaknesses was in his forms. Whereas Tchaikovsky admitted his shortcoming at the structural seams between functions, Kalinnikov's were at a movement's conclusion, which could become prolix and thematically empty. All this makes one believe the frequent assertion that his deep potential had not been fully realized by the time of his death.

There is no reason that Kalinnikov's two symphonies should not find a place in the repertoire. Another performance of a Tchaikovsky symphony would not be missed if in lieu of one by Kalinnikov. Although it could be claimed that these symphonies lack the depth of a Tchaikovsky cycle, Kalinnikov still has all the élan any audience might require.

Serge Rachmaninoff

INTRODUCTION

Of the Russian composers considered here, only two were triple threats as composer, pianist, and conductor: Mily Balakirev and Serge Rachmaninoff. Unlike Balakirev, Rachmaninoff achieved international recognition in all three areas (Plate B14). Yet when asked his profession on a tax form, Rachmaninoff reportedly wrote "composer."[196] During his lifetime Rachmaninoff produced music in every imaginable genre: opera, piano music, chamber music, choral music, song, symphonic poem, concerto, and other like pieces, as well as three completed symphonies and two other related pieces: the choral symphony *The Bells* Opus 35 (1913) after Edgar Allan Poe and the *Symphonic Dances* Opus 45 (1940). Since *The Bells* is a choral symphony, in the same sense as Vaughan Williams's *A Sea Symphony*, and not a work of the symphonic tradition, it will not be a part of our discussion. The *Symphonic Dances* will also not be discussed as they are essentially a suite of pieces with little resemblance to Rachmaninoff's own concept of the symphony.

Of the three completed symphonies (see Table XV/36), each has an individual character: the First is a brutally macabre piece of high originality, the Second is a continuation of the Tchaikovskian symphonic lyric tradition, and the Third embeds modernism within an essentially late- or post-Romantic style, not unlike Prokofiev but less tart. Yet among Rachmaninoff's compositions, the symphonies were of secondary significance: the number of performances pale when compared to the four piano concertos. Even Symphony No. 2, the most frequently programmed of the three, probably does not even begin to approach the number of hearings received by the Second and Third Piano Concertos and the *Rhapsody on a Theme by Paganini*.

Rachmaninoff's work in symphonic idioms prior to his Symphony No. 1 was limited to a handful of compositions, which in different ways show the impact of various Russian and European composers. His Scherzo movement in D minor from 1888 reveals Mendelssohn's *A Midsummer Night's Dream* Scherzo to have been its model. Three years later, he worked on a symphony first movement also in the key of D minor. However, there is no evidence that the Scherzo and the symphony movement were in any way connected into a larger cyclic plan. His next major orchestral works were two movements, now lost, on Byron's *Manfred* (1890); his Piano Concerto No. 1 (1890–1891), which underwent revisions in 1917; and two symphonic poems: *Prince Rostislav* (1891) after A. K. Tolstoy, and *The Rock* (1893) after Chekhov's *On the Road* (even though at the beginning of the score are lines from Lermontov's poem *The Rock*). These were followed by the *Caprice bohémien* or the *Capriccio on Gypsy Themes* (1892), which is thematically related to his opera on a gypsy topic *Aleko*. No doubt the *Caprice bohémien* was inspired by Rimsky-Korsakov's brilliant composition for the orchestra, the *Capriccio Espagnol*. It was not until three years later that Rachmaninoff completed his first symphony.[197]

SYMPHONY NO. 1 IN D MINOR OPUS 13

The Symphony No. 1 from 1895 was personally and musically a pivotal work among the composer's *oeuvre*. Unfortunately, its first performance was on March 15/27, 1897, at one of the publisher Belyayev's Russian Symphony Concerts conducted by Glazunov, who was reportedly in a near-drunken state.[198] The concert was such a disaster that Rachmaninoff's first completed symphonic effort could not be heard in a favorable light. Apparently, the combination of this performance, the reviews, and the composer's personal disappointment with his own work sent him into a prolonged state of depression and he could no longer compose. For three years, Rachmaninoff was unproductive as a composer. But during the beginning of this period he concentrated on conducting at the Moscow Private Russian

TABLE XV/36

The Symphonies of Serge Rachmaninoff

Opus	Key	Dates	Title	Movements	Instrumentation	Comments
—	D minor	1891	Symphony			Only first mvt. completed.
13	D minor	1895	Symphony No. 1	1. Grave—Allegro ma non troppo 4/4 (339 m.) 2. Allegro animato 3/4 (9/8) (506 m.) F major 3. Larghetto 3/4 (159 m.) B-flat major 4. Allegro con fuoco 4/4 (466 m.)	Grand plus Picc., Tuba, Tri., Tamb., SD, Cym., BD, Tam-tam	Motto at head of score: "Vengeance is mine; I will repay, saith the Lord" (Romans 12:19), a phrase also used by Tolstoy at the beginning of *Anna Karenina.* First performance: St. Petersburg Conservatory, Russian Symphony Concert on March 15/27, 1897, conducted by Aleksandr Glazunov. Published in Moscow and Leningrad: State Music Publishers, 1947.
27	E minor	1906–1907	Symphony No. 2	1. Largo 4/4—Allegro moderato ¢ (568 m.) 2. Allegro molto ¢ (532 m.) A minor 3. Adagio 4/4 (170 m.) A major 4. Allegro vivace ¢ (572 m.) E major	Grand plus Flt., EH, Bclar, Tpt., Tuba, Cym., BD, Glockenspiel, SD	Dedicated to Sergey Taneyev. First performance: St. Petersburg, Mariinsky Theater on January 26/February 7, 1908, conducted by the composer. Published in Moscow: Gutheil, 1908.
44	A minor	1935–1936 rev. 1938	Symphony No. 3	1. Lento—Allegro moderato 4/4 (318 m.) 2. Adagio ma non troppo—Allegro vivace 3/4 (281 m.) C-sharp minor/F minor 3. Allegro 4/4 (376 m.)	Grand plus Picc., EH, Bclar, Cbssn., Contralto Tpt., Tuba, Xylophone, Tri., SD, BD, Cym., Tamb., Celesta, Harp	First performance: Philadelphia Orchestra on November 6, 1936, conducted by Leopold Stokowski. Published in New York: Edition Tair, 1937.

Opera (1897–1898). In 1900, he undertook hypnotic therapy with Dr. Nikolay Duhl; by the summer he was again composing; and before the end of 1900 he wrote and performed his most popular work, the Second Piano Concerto.

Lore has it that Symphony No. 1 is programmatic. Such a hypothesis has been incrementally erected from a set of circumstances that surround the piece. At the end of the now-lost score was reportedly inserted "Vengeance is mine, I will repay saith the Lord" from Romans 12:19; this same quotation prefaces Tolstoy's *Anna Karenina.* Rachmaninoff dedicated the symphony to A.L., who was Anna Aleksandrovna Lodizhenskaya. A woman of gypsy background, she was married to a man beyond her years: Pyotr Lodizhensky, to whom Rachmaninoff's *Caprice bohémien* was dedicated. He also dedicated a song to A.L. (Opus 4/1) with the text "Oh no, I beg you, forsake me not!" The *Anna Karenina* quotation, the dedications, and the belief that Rachmaninoff was quite taken with A.L. have thus led to the belief that there is a direct personal parallel between the plot of *Anna Karenina* and the D Minor Symphony. This hypothesis has been supported by Boris Nikitin and, in part, by Bertensson and Leyda, but has been doubted by others.[199] Patrick Piggott, for example, states that the piece should not be "an excuse for romantic fantasies."[200] Based on the present evidence, David Cannata also doubts that there is justification for such a hypothesis. He points out that the quotation from Romans comes at the end of the score and considers this problematic; it could just as well have been an afterthought rather than an inspiration. Cannata believes the composer's own recollections, as recorded by Oskar von Rieseman, support his doubts:

> I imagined that there was nothing that I could not do and had great hopes for the future. It was in the confidence bred of this feeling that I composed my First Symphony in D Minor, and the ease with which I worked encouraged my pride and self-esteem.[201]

Because of its dramatic nature, the Rachmaninoff First almost seems to require a narrative. However, until some real evidence surfaces, one must resist ascribing to the music what the critic might wish it to possess.

The source for the claim that the themes of the First Symphony are based on, or derive from, the chants of the *Oktoechos* has authentic support from Rachmaninoff himself, who told Rieseman: "I had a very high opinion of my work [Symphony No. 1], which was built on themes from the *Oktoechos*—the choir book with the chants of the Russian Church Service—in all its eight keys. I was convinced that here I had discovered and opened up entirely new paths in music."[202] However, until evidence of parallel passages is presented, one must be somewhat skeptical of the Symphony's thematic derivations. This is also true of the Dies Irae quotations, which often are approximations or allusions rather than an exact rendering of the chant itself.

The primary musical stimulus for this First Symphony was the music of Tchaikovsky. After the composer's death, Rachmaninoff dedicated to Tchaikovsky's memory his *Piano Trio élégiaque* (1892). There are two direct sources among the works of Tchaikovsky that had a primary influence: the *Manfred* Symphony Opus 58 and the Symphony No. 6 "Pathétique." The influence of the *Manfred* Symphony is seen in certain aspects of Rachmaninoff's Finale: the rather special form which seems to not completely belong to any established tradition, and the parallel incorporation of a dance that seems like a stereotypical bacchanal (m.29). There is also a dynamic boldness often underlined by the heavy brass so characteristic of Tchaikovsky's Opus 58 and the "Pathétique" Symphony. However, the "Pathétique" references are decidedly more concrete: in the first movement, 1) the subdominant emphasis in the introduction (mm.5–6), 2) the derivation of P (m.7) from the themes in the introduction,

3) the strong development of *P* in *T* (m.26), 4) the rising melodic line in the transition (mm.81–85) leading to *1S,* and 5) the crashing hammerstroke (m.111) to introduce the development followed by a fugato; in the Finale, 6) the scherzando/march mixtures, 7) the strike of the tam-tam (IV/m.462), and 8) the slow ending with dynamic extremes. Additionally, the processional music for the entry of the nobles in Rimsky-Korsakov's *Mlada* seems to have impacted the beginning of Rachmaninoff's Finale.

The cycle of Opus 13 is a tightly knit affair, unified by themes first stated in the slow introduction that recur in subsequent movements. In addition, themes in earlier movements are also taken up in later ones. The introductory ideas (*Oax* and *y*) are incorporated into *P* and *T* and at various other places in the first movement. *I/Oax* begins the second movement Scherzo, and *I/2S* (m.3) serves as the first principal idea; both of these recur throughout. At the end (m.496), an allusion to the Dies Irae is introduced. The Larghetto begins with *I/Oax,* and a motive from the Scherzo (m.5), which in turn is related to *I/2S*, is also heard again. The Finale also announces *I/Oax* at the beginning before embarking on an exposition. In the episodic part of its development section (mm.145–324), materials from previous movements are again prominent. *I/Oax* and *y* become almost a motto as they are repeated eight times at the symphony's conclusion.

Tonally, the cycle, unlike those of the previous *kuchka* generation, uses only closely related keys at the movement level: the Scherzo is in the relative major of F and the slow movement is in F major's subdominant. While tonality and thematic recurrence play significant roles in giving coherence to the cycle, it is the almost consistently stark and dark character that first impresses the listener. In this way, the work is rather atypical for one familiar with the Second Symphony and Second and Third Piano Concertos; there is only one warm and soaring lyric theme and that is *S* (m.73) of the Finale. Thus, it is in character more like Tchaikovsky's *Manfred,* a work that Rachmaninoff admired. In contrast, the *S* materials of the two outer movements and some non-primary material in the two inner-movements of the Pathétique result in a less gloomy character.

The introduction presents the motto themes (Example XV/50) of the cycle (*Oax* and *y*) with a subdominant emphasis, but also a gravitation toward the subdominant's relative major of B-flat in its first subphrase. Of particular note is m.6 where the G major chord slips to minor and then plagally resolves to D. This reminds one of a motif that Mahler used first in Symphony No. 2/1, the so-called *Totenfeier* movement (mm.439–40), and later fully exploited in Symphony No. 6 as a motto. However, since Mahler's Symphony No. 2 was first performed in December 1895, it is highly unlikely that the similarities to this motif are anything more than coincidental.

Rachmaninoff constructs his *P* (m.7) from the two elements of the motto into an antecedent/consequent presentation: *Pa* begins with *Oax* and *y;* then *Pb,* with a repetition of *P* followed by *Pk* (m.22). *T* (m.27) continues the character of *Pb*, develops it together with *Oay* over a long stretch that emphasizes the subdominant, and comes to rest in this key for *1S* (m.87) after the "Pathétique" transition. During its course, *1S* nudges toward B-flat, but *2S* (m.99), which consists of only three 7/4 measures, turns back toward G minor. *2Sx* will become one of the important recurring themes in the symphony (Example XV/51). In the ears of some critics, it is this theme that makes for a direct connection with Lodizhenskaya, as it has been said to be based on a "gypsy" scale. *K* (m.102) passionately bursts in B-flat major and diminishes to three quiet statements of *Oay*.

A startling *fff* hammerstroke and a modified statement of *Oax* articulate the development, which continues with a fugato in "Pathétique" fashion. Unlike the fugatos in

EXAMPLE XV/50   Rachmaninoff. Symphony No. 1/1, mm.1–7.

Tchaikovsky's early symphonies, this one is neither pedantic nor ineffective. Its subject is the motto (*Oay*), and like the introduction, it has a strong subdominant flavor both in the subject and in its points of imitation. This fugato dissipates under the power of Tchaikovskian hammerstrokes, leading to other forms of development. *Oay* is taken up (m.138) against scales belonging to G major. Something resembling the Dies Irae (m.146) is given in the trombones, against which are the scales in the woodwinds and a diminution of *Oay* to sixteenths in the second violins. This builds to a B-minor maestoso climax (m.174) and a march

EXAMPLE XV/51   Rachmaninoff. Symphony No. 1/i, mm.99–101.

(m.190). A retransition rewrites the introduction (m.201), now in tempo, and the recapitulation comes upon us before expected. Compared to the exposition, Rachmaninoff's recapitulation eliminates almost the entirety of *T*, leaving only the transitory measures before *1S* (m.251), *2S* (m.263), and *K* (m.269) appear. Articulated like the beginning of the development, the coda (m.277) touches on the Neapolitan and then returns to D minor. For the final sections, *Oay* is further developed, and both tempo and meter contribute to an accelerated end by diminishing the size of the bar line from 6/4 to 2/4. One could postulate that the differences between the exposition/recapitulation and development/coda in this movement are mainly ones of degree. That is, the exposition/recapitulation are developmental, and the development/coda are only more so.

In this same sense, one could argue that the second movement is merely a continuation of the first movement's developmental aspects, but from the perspective of a Scherzo—though not labeled as such in the score. This second movement is outwardly a big ternary structure: *A* (m.1)–*B* (m.184)–*A* (m.341), using F major for the outer portions and D minor for the central portion with a significant section in B-flat major (m.228). Since the main thematic material of *A* (Example XV/52) derives from *Oax* and *I/2S*, in the reprise of *A* the material is inverted, which, because of its identity and simplicity, hardly affects the structural downbeats at m.341 and m.437. Such actions contribute to the constant evolution of the material. Another way in which the reprise of the first *A* becomes more developmental is in the synthesis, vertically and horizontally, of different thematic ideas. In this way, the overall ternary scheme becomes, on the large scale, somewhat modified:

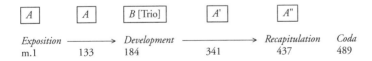

While the above plays against the tonal articulations, it does reflect to some degree the kind of thematic action that transpires. The coda (m.489) alludes to the Dies Irae as well as *Oax* before ending with the super-soft dynamic of ***pppp***. Given the reference to the Dies Irae, together with the orchestration, the mutes, and the other thematic statements, this Scherzo moves into the realm of the macabre. If the Russian audience had problems with the first movement, the Scherzo would certainly have caused more confusion, since on first hearing it

485

EXAMPLE XV/52   Rachmaninoff. Symphony No. 1/2, mm.1–10.

is difficult to parse its shape. The expectations of binary structures are here tossed to the wind.

Expectations for a lyrical slow movement with some attractive and captivating themes are also tossed to the wind. At several points Rachmaninoff leads the listener to believe that a sustained lyric utterance is about to occur (see mm.10, 28), but it never happens. At the start, one is not entirely certain if this is a new movement; it begins with material prominent in the Scherzo: *Oax* and *I/2S*. Another ternary shape, now in B-flat, is open-ended at the conclusion of *A* (m.59), but closed (m.113) in E-flat for *B* (m.60), and has another varied *A* (m.114). *A* is often scored as if it were chamber music with solo winds and somewhat diffident writing for strings. In contrast, *B* is more fully scored and develops the motto (*Oax*) in a dramatic way with snarling *con sordino* horns and dynamics alternating from *mf* to *ff* (see Tchaikovsky's Symphony No. 6/4, m.126). After this series of dramatic declarations, a second part (m.82) returns to the chamber style of *A* with a new, agitated background figure that seems almost oblivious to the bar line. Hints of *A* (m.95) prepare the way for a return (m.100) that in scoring and texture is more complex than its first presentation; this runs into *I/2S* (m.110). A second presentation of *A* (m.114) has a still more complex texture with five different layers, two of which are contrapuntal. *A* builds to a climax over a tonic pedal (m.126): the first violins and flutes play *A*, oboes, violas, and horns take up *Oay*, the second violins play the agitated background figure, and the low brass sustain the harmonies. This music quiets into the chamber style for the coda (m.142) and another subdued ending, with the clarinet playing the agitated figure that finally settles into the *I/2S* (m.154) motive for the conclusion.

One could view the Finale as a "correction" to the functional scrambling of the third and fourth movements of Tchaikovsky's Symphony No. 6 "Pathétique." Here, the Scherzo/march is placed in fourth position, and Rachmaninoff underlines its relationship to the Tchaikovsky by the similarity of the bacchanal music (Example XV/53) to the third-movement themes in the "Pathétique." However, the structure of Rachmaninoff's Finale as noted above reminds one of Tchaikovsky's *Manfred* Finale in its dynamics and structural freedom, even though the Rachmaninoff Finale (Table XV/37) holds a number of traits belonging to sonata form. Rachmaninoff begins with a rather traditional exposition consisting of a *P* (m.11), three *T* themes (mm.28, 51, 59), an *S* (m.73), and a *K* (m.103), which conform reasonably closely to the expected functions. Again, the introductory measures deal with the motto (*Oax*), and the post-*K* materials bring back *Oay* and *II/Ac* (mm.123 and 131). The central development section is in two parts. The first (m.145) is what one might call episodic; it deals with new material and motives from *II/Ac* and *I/2S*. Part two (m.325) is more traditional, taking up material from the exposition. One could also hear part two as a recapitulation of the motto (m.325), the march/*P* (m.352), and the bacchanal/*3T* (m.367) on the dominant. *S* (m.389) returns in D major, and then the bacchanal/*3T* (m.401) is interrupted by a pause punctuated with a funereal strike on the tam-tam. The coda (m.441) attempts to solidly secure D as the tonic, but first it must pass through the dominant (A). However, as the first movement's introduction begins on the subdominant of D minor, so ends the Finale's coda, but with four strong reiterations of dominant to tonic pitches in the strings and the timpani. The D major chords of the final five measures attempt to further obliterate the subdominant minor.

Rachmaninoff's First Symphony is an interesting accomplishment from a number of angles. It reveals the effect that the works of Tchaikovsky had on the most gifted Russian composer of the next generation. Yet the work is like no other Russian symphony up to its time in the force and darkness of its expression. The cycle is also among the most complete attempts to compose a thematically organic symphony with regard to every movement of the cycle, rather than focusing on the Finale. Finally, from the perspective of the beginning of the twenty-first century, it is not the sort of brutal work one might expect from its melancholic composer.

Regardless of how one evaluates the accomplishments of the First Symphony, its historical significance for the composer, as noted above, was profound. César Cui's review perhaps reveals that a musical rivalry still existed between the ideals of the now defunct *kuchka* and the conservatory trained, as well as between composers from Moscow and St. Petersburg, where this Muscovite composer had his symphony premiered:

> If there were a conservatory in Hell, and if one of its talented students was to compose a symphony based on the story of the Seven Plagues of Egypt, and if he had written one

EXAMPLE XV/53   Rachmaninoff. Symphony No. 1/4, mm.59–68.

TABLE XV/37
Rachmaninoff. Symphony No. 1/4: Structure

Allegro con fuoco 4/4 ♩=152

Introduction		Exposition	Moto primo		Con moto		Con anima	Più vivo	
Motto (*Oax*)	Fanfare	Marziale March/*P*	Motto/*1T* with echo	Marcato/*2T*	Baccahanal/*3T* Scherzando	trans.	*S*	*K*	*Oay*
ff		*fff*	*f*	*ff*	*mf*		*ff*	*f fff*	
D major A pedal m.1			G-sharp		A major		A major E pedal	A major E pedal	
7	9 11	28	51	59	71	73	103	123

Allegro mosso 3/4 Development—Part 1

II/Ac	trans.	N/II/Ac		Più vivo 3/4				Con moto 3/4	Più vivo
						I/2S/II/Ac		N/II/Ac	
	pp < f								
A major		G-sharp pedal ornamented	G-sharp pedal C-sharp pedal				G-sharp pedal C-sharp pedal ornamented		G-sharp pedal
131	135	145	178	205	208		224	244	260

TABLE XV/37 (continued)

Meno mosso. Commodo 3/4		Allegro con fuoco 4/4 Development—Part 2				Con moto	[Recapitulation]
II/Ac	trans.	March/Motto (Oax)	March Scherzando	March/P	Bacchanal/3T Scherzando		S
					mf	*ff*	*p cresc. fff*
C-sharp pedal	A minor	A minor	A pedal	A minor/ major		G pedal	D major G→A pedal
272	321	325	336	*ff* 352	367	376	389

Bacchanal/3T	Con moto	Presto		Largo 4/4 Coda	Grave 4/4	Con moto
			Tam-tam	Oax+Oax		Oax
ff	*ff*	*fff*			*fff*	*fff*
A pedal —————→		D major —————→		A:V/D	D minor D pedal —————→	IV/D minor
401	409	415	440	441	449	457

490

similar to Rachmaninoff's, he would have brilliantly accomplished his task and would have delighted the inhabitants of Hell.[203]

To us, this music leaves an evil impression with its broken rhythms, obscurity and vagueness of form, meaningless repetition of the same short tricks, the nasal sound of the orchestra, the stained crash of the brass, and above all its sickly perverse harmonization and quasi-melodic outlines, the complete absence of simplicity and naturalness, the complete absence of themes.[204]

Though most of the reviews were negative, the review by Nikolay Findeyzen in the April 1897 *Russian Musical Gazette* found more potential in the twenty-four-year-old composer's first symphony:

On the 15th and 22nd of March, the last two Russian symphony concerts [of the season] were held. The first of these was the least successful of the season. The focus was on the D-minor symphony by Rachmaninoff, which was not quite successfully conveyed and thus largely incomprehensible and unappreciated by the audience. The work, which contains several new impulses, attempts to find new colors, new themes, and new images, and all of this creates an impression of something that is understated and unsettled. But I am refraining from expressing my definitive opinion, as the majority of critics have done, otherwise the history of Tchaikovsky's Fifth Symphony may easily repeat itself, [a work] which only recently (thanks to Nikisch) was "revealed" to us and which everyone now admires as a work that is new, wonderful, and beautiful. It's true—the beauty of the whole and of the individual parts of Mr. Rachmaninoff's entire symphony cannot be denied, but several pages seem close to mediocre. The first section, and in particular the furious finale, with its concluding Largo—this finale one of the cleverest critics somehow took for some kind of representation of war or of the devil knows what (however, I hesitate to agree with this interpretation as the same critic once proclaimed a parade-ground march to be one of the most brilliant works of Beethoven)—both contain much that is beautiful, new, and even inspiring. This symphony is the work of a not yet fully formed musician; It's true, [however], some kind of musical Poprishchin, or maybe some kind of Brahms, may [yet] emerge from him.[205]

The infamous premiere was to be the only performance of the First Symphony during Rachmaninoff's lifetime. When he left Russia in December 1917, the score was left behind and later misplaced. Whatever intentions Rachmaninoff had for revising it were now an impossibility and reconstruction was certainly unlikely. It was not until the 1940s that the orchestral parts were rediscovered at the St. Petersburg Conservatory and a score was made. Symphony No. 1 was played for the second time on October 17, 1945, in Moscow with Aleksandr Gauk conducting the USSR State Symphony Orchestra; it was subsequently published in 1947.

In contrast, the reception by modern British critics in particular was something more than favorable. Robert Simpson, who was one of England's important composers and one of its leading critics, wrote:

As a piece of symphonic composition the D minor is much superior to the other two: as an artistic whole, created naturally and without strain, it leaves little to be desired. It does not, like the E minor symphony (No. 2) and the piano concertos, try to inflate a lyrical theme into a forced final climax, and the *dénouement* of its finale is as overwhelmingly powerful as it is economical. It never lapses into facile sentiment as does the slow movement of

No. 2; its *Larghetto* is spare and original, and intensely felt. The structure of the work as a whole cannot be faulted.[206]

David Brown concurred with Simpson, and Patrick Piggott found it "interesting and romantic."[207]

While the Rachmaninoff First Symphony may not quite measure up to Simpson's evaluation, it is certainly worthy of an occasional performance. Particularly effective would be to juxtapose it with the Second or Third Piano Concerto or the *Rhapsody on a Theme of Paganini*. Then the audience could not only hear the piece itself, but also the different direction that Rachmaninoff pursued as composer after the First Symphony's underappreciated initial reception.

Twelve years were to separate the composition of the First Symphony from the completion of the Second. In the interim, Rachmaninoff finished only one major orchestral work: the pivotal Piano Concerto No. 2 in C minor. He also tried his hand at another symphony in 1897 that never advanced beyond some sketches. Instead, his major compositional preoccupation was with operas: *Francesca da Rimini* (1905), *The Miserly Knight* (1906), and *Salammbô* (1906). In addition, there were songs and piano music. As a result of the success of the Piano Concerto No. 2, Rachmaninoff became something of a celebrity in Russia, but the political situation there was not calm enough for sustained creative work. Rachmaninoff resigned his Bol'shoy conducting post in 1906 and left for Italy with his family. A brief return to his homeland to tend to his daughter's health was followed by a residence in Dresden, where he could compose without distraction. It was in the Saxon capital that the Second Symphony (1906–1907) was completed.

SYMPHONY NO. 2 IN E MINOR OPUS 27

Unlike the First Symphony, the Symphony No. 2, written in Dresden, was not directly modeled on any Tchaikovsky symphony. Nevertheless, the Second Symphony did follow the Tchaikovskian concept of a genre that was essentially lyric. This is also post-Tchaikovskian music on an expanded scale; whereas the last three symphonies of Tchaikovsky run *ca.* 45 minutes each, the Rachmaninoff Symphony No. 2, without cuts, lasts *ca.* 65 minutes. One also wonders if in addition to the music of his Russian compatriot, there is not something of a Brucknerian, as opposed to a Beethovenian, pace in this symphony. What is certain is that because of its size and pace, it has been subjected, like Bruckner's efforts, to cuts. Some of these cuts emanate from the composer and other cuts, without authorization, from various conductors; the length of the work has been reduced by as much as twenty minutes.

Rachmaninoff's tonal plan for the cycle is unusual for its simplicity; the two central movements are in the subdominant. Additionally, the first half of the cycle is in the minor mode, and the last two movements are in the major. Furthermore, both central movements are ternary structures, while the two outer pieces are traditional sonata and rondo forms. An effort to unify the cycle, in contrast to Symphony No. 1, is mainly located in the Finale. It recapitulates themes from the first and third movements: *III/Aa* (mm.159, 196) and *I/Oy* in transformation (m.262) are incorporated in an effective and integrated manner. On the other hand, Rachmaninoff's use of material from the introduction of the first and third movements in an Adagio interlude (m.244–49) that separates the two parts of the Finale's second episode (*C*) is both ineffective and artificial. There is also a possible allusion to *II/P* in the Finale (m.41, 471).

Some have dubbed the material at the opening of the first movement as a motto theme,

EXAMPLE XV/54   Rachmaninoff. Symphony No. 2/1, mm.154–59 and /3, mm.1–3.

making the point that it recurs in all of the movements. The problem with this motto, particularly if compared to that of the First Symphony, is one of identity; in the earlier work, the so-called motto theme has a strong identity, whereas the materials presented in the introduction to Symphony No. 2/1 have a diminished personality. The whole question of convincing thematic repetition, for example, can be addressed by the relationship of *I/2S* to the opening of the third movement (Example XV/54). Do these ideas have a significant relationship specific to Symphony No. 2, or is this just a characteristic of the soaring lyric themes that mark Rachmaninoff's style?

Something of the expansiveness of the symphony as a whole is captured within the sixty-eight measures of the Largo introduction. Here Rachmaninoff takes some rather unpromising material and is able to effectively stretch it over a lengthy expanse. This is achieved by small-dimension sequences at the start, the increasing intricacy of the texture, the expansion of the orchestral fabric, and the rising tessitura which at the peak is countered by a descending bass (m.45). Once this climax is achieved the metric unit expands from 4/4 to 6/4 for two bars as it all unwinds back to something reminiscent of the introduction's beginning. By using these rather standard Tchaikovskian techniques in the introduction, Rachmaninoff is able to make a single large gesture out of several small motives.

At first glance the Allegro is, for 1907, a rather old-fashioned approach to sonata form. *S* (m.134) and *K* (m.173) occur in the relative major, and the exposition is marked by a repeat; after the development, *S* and *K* are recapitulated in the tonic, and the movement concludes with a coda (m.504). In terms of the way the themes themselves function, they are almost Classical: the agitated *P* material, the still more active *T* (m.114), the lyrical *S* themes—*1S* (m.134) built from small antecedent/consequent units, *2S* (m.154) has a contrasting long-line lyricism—and *K* (m.173) is undergirded by dominant and tonic pedals of the relative major. Yet the content is thoroughly Romantic; indeed, few would even notice its classical or textbook structure since otherwise the content dominates. Contributing to this perception of its style is that this exposition can also be related to the multi-faceted larger *crescendo/decrescendo* structure of the introduction. Comparable units with swells are formed by *P–T–1S* and *2S–1K–2K* combined.

For the development section (m.199), Rachmaninoff devotes his efforts to the introductory *Oa* and *b,* which also intersect with *1P.* This material, together with pedal points, modulations, and ostinatos, constitutes the main stuff of the development. Part one opens on the dominant of E minor with an ostinato in the violas, over which the solo violin plays *Oa* in augmentation. From this, the tempo quickens (m.211), a new ostinato derives directly from

Oa, and the tonality moves toward D minor (m.215). Rachmaninoff now compounds the first ostinato in imitation (cello, first violin) with *Oa* on A minor (m.218). This turns toward its relative major (C, m.233). Another tempo acceleration follows the same process, except now the orchestration is nearly *tutti,* the dynamic has swelled to *ff,* and the tonality slips onto the dominant of B minor (m.243). This first part now begins to find its end: the orchestration thins and the dynamics become softer as the *Oa* motive is transformed among the two violin parts.

Part two commences in a slower tempo (Meno mosso) as the brass intones *Ob* (m.272) over an F-sharp pedal. The pedal slips to D-sharp/E-flat (m.279), and the violas and other instruments simultaneously promote their own pedal (C). E-flat minor triumphs as the accompaniment to *1P* (m.289) becomes an ostinato in the cellos and clarinets; the viola presents its own version of this idea. The dynamics increase and simultaneously the tempo quickens (m.297) as we are offered new versions of *Oa* over a more chromatic bass that comes to rest on A. This deceptively resolves to B-flat (m.337), which becomes the dominant of E-flat minor and leads to the development's final climax. The retransition (m.345) features wind proclamations and a descending bass that leads to the dominant of E minor for the recapitulation (m.361) as the brass continue their proclamations through *P.*

The recapitulation is about as long as the exposition, even though *P* is extensively cut: *T* (m.377), *S* (m.425), and *K* (m.474) are each expanded. Rachmaninoff begins the coda (m.504) by recalling the development section with its motives, ostinatos, modulatory activities, and two waves of *crescendos* (mm.504–20, 521–31). Unexpectedly, the music takes a new turn to a march (m.532), which is smothered by *Oa*'s return (m.552) in the final climax.

This hint of a march prepares for the beginning of the second movement, a *marcato* *A* theme in A minor. *B* (m.85) is another gushy lyric Rachmaninoff statement, this time in C major and a slower tempo. These two themes form something of an exposition followed almost directly by a recapitulation of *A* (m.133), which is left open for a sort of Trio (m.189). A crashing chord introduces a fugato, the only direct reminiscence in this work to Tchaikovsky's "Pathétique" Symphony which so dominated Rachmaninoff's First Symphony. The fugato has one exposition and an episode; it dissipates into another march (m.241) against the fugato's figuration. The march swells and quiets as the marchers move into the distance. With the reentry of the fugato subject (m.288) one thinks another fugal exposition is occurring, but this only leads to the return of *A* (m.308) and *B* (m.390), another retransition (m.414), and *A*'s final statement (m.438). A coda (m.496) is built on *1/Ob* alternating with other elements from *P* and the Trio.

Some critics think this movement is the composer's most energized effort. While this is certainly true of *A,* the composer could not resist breaking this mood with *B* and the almost funereal material taken from *Ob.* Nevertheless, after the eighteen or so minutes of the first movement, the nine and a half driven minutes of the Scherzo seem almost laconic. The Scherzo of Symphony No. 1 is certainly more intellectually realized, but the *joie de vivre* absent in No. 1 is here in abundance. This is perhaps the composer's finest symphonic movement; its materials are memorable, and in this context its terse shape is particularly effective.

Whatever the high memorability quotient for the Scherzo might be, it is certainly exceeded by the opening (*Aa*) of the third-movement Adagio. That the two central movements of the cycle are in the same key, and that the Scherzo is tonally closed, allows the Adagio to begin *in medias res* with Rachmaninoff's most passionate melody (Example XV/55).

EXAMPLE XV/55   Rachmaninoff. Symphony No. 2/3, mm.1–4.

Surprisingly, it lasts but four measures; yet it possesses the quick swell to the peak, followed by a descending sequence ending where it began, a gesture so typical of this composer. Its initial brevity limits its structural importance, but each appearance is comparable to a sudden flash of light that lengthens and strengthens as the movement unfolds (Table XV/38).

Perhaps the most fascinating aspect of Rachmaninoff's presentation of his melodies is their contrapuntal textures. When *Ab* is presented for the first time (m.6), nearly every conductor focuses all the attention on the clarinet line. However, one should also notice the effective part-writing that takes place in the violas and cellos marked *pp* and *dolce* (Example XV/56). These voices should not be inaudible, and careful targeting of certain portions of these parts would make *Ab* a much more interesting experience. In addition to this free counterpoint, Rachmaninoff also is able to combine *Aa* and *Ab* as counterpoints to each other (mm.109, 132), making them something more than just ravishing melodies.

More than anything else, *B* (m.49) seems to function as a lengthy preparation for the return of *Aa* in *B*'s key of C major. Of special interest here is the passage beginning in m.61 with the inexorable buildup to *fortissimo* and *Aa*'s return (m.87). In this case, Rachmaninoff reveals unusual care in his treatment of the incrementally rising line; the pullbacks at mm.61, 67, and 71; the rise from b″ to g‴, and then to c″″ (m.87) for the climax; and a rapid unwinding of pitch together with dynamics, orchestration, and sound. The calculated approach to achieving a potent climax is certainly vindicated. Although *Aa* is to return two more times (mm.95 and 140), these are merely afterthoughts to mm.61–87. Thus, we have an unusual ternary form that does not attempt in its episode to present distinctive new themes, but to present some rather mundane ideas that underscore *Aa*'s eventual arrival (mm.83, 87).

Ba also makes use of *I/Oa*, but it is more identifiable as a continuation of the material used in *T* (m.41). The latter is unusually compact and marked by a descending bass that comes to rest on its new tonic of C major. Its other marker is the descent and rise of the *I/Oa* motives through the strings. *I/Oa* is also prominent in the coda (m.155); here *I/Oa* and its inversion in augmentation operate against each other contrapuntally. A quiet conclusion parallels the end of the previous movement.

If the two central movements form a decided tonal unit in A minor and major, the beginning of the Finale pounds on the dominant of E major, followed by a cadence to define the old tonal realm. As in Classical and early-Romantic symphonies, this Finale has a strong flavor in its refrain. Given the triplet subdivisions of the *alla breve* meter and its driving rhythms and tempo, one is inclined to hear it as a Tarantella or Saltarello. Rachmaninoff's use of an Italian dance flies in the face of viewing him, quite incorrectly we believe, as a nationalist composer. Like Mendelssohn, Rachmaninoff spent some time in Italy during 1906. Whether Rachmaninoff had in mind Mendelssohn's Symphony No. 4/4 we cannot be certain, except to note that Rachmaninoff's second episode is another sweeping lyrical theme totally foreign to any Mendelssohnian model.

This Finale is cast in a rondo form, but one whose key scheme is less conservative than the first movement (Table XV/39). Notice *B* (m.53) sounds in G-sharp minor with only a tertian relationship in E major, which strikes one as an almost Balakirevian key with its large number of sharps. The big theme of *1C* (m.131), after a pedal on A, resolves to D major—the flattened leading tone—for more than one hundred bars. When *B* returns (m.387) it is in the dominant, but *1C* is recapitulated (m.503) in the tonic, giving it a tonal priority normally reserved for *B*. *2C* (m.250), coming after the Adagio interlude, acts like a real development section beginning in G minor.

2C begins with *A,* but after about ten measures this material begins to diminish in

TABLE XV/38

Rachmaninoff. Symphony No. 2/3: Structure

	Adagio				Poco più mosso	Tempo 1					
	A a	b	c	a	T(I/Oa)	B a (I/Oa)	b	a¹	b¹	A a	GP
	cresc. f dim.	pp		mf cresc.	ff	mf	mf	p	mf	p cresc.	ff	ff dim.	
	A major				Bass: E-D-C♮	C major					C major
	m.1	6	29	37	41	49	53	59	61	83	87

	Tempo 1			A a		Tempo 1 Coda T(I/Oa)
	A a	a b	a b	A a		Coda T(I/Oa)
	mf	p	pp cresc.	ff dim.	p	p mf dim. pp
	C major	A major		A major	F-sharp minor	A major
	95	109	132	140	147	155

497

EXAMPLE XV/56   Rachmaninoff. Symphony No. 2/3, mm.6–14.

TABLE XV/39

Rachmaninoff. Symphony No. 2/4: Structure

Allegro vivace ¢
Introduction

[A]	1T(II/A)	[B]	retrans.	[A]	2T	1C [a]	[b]	retrans.	[a]	[b]
V/E	E major	G-sharp minor		E	A pedal	D pedal / D				D pedal
m.1	5 · 41	53		81	121	131				

Adagio — *Tempo precedente*

III/ [A] and I/Oa · [K]	[2C] – *Development*	[A]	1T(II/A)	[B]	[A]
D (K) · D	G minor	E	E	B	E
210 · 244	250	339	375	387	415

Più mosso

	[1C]	[A]
B pedal	E pedal / E	C/E → E
463	503	553

499

importance as other motives come into prominence: a descending scale (m.262) and *II/Oa* (m.280) in diminution. As Patrick Piggott points out, the descending scales accumulate as the section progresses; he compares this to the sounding of bells "as if a thousand bell-towers were ringing out a clamorous celebration."[208] This is particularly true of the second part (m.302), which acts like a long retransition with a pedal on F and not the dominant B-natural (Example XV/57). Rachmaninoff returns to E major by a simple bass line descent to B-natural (mm.337–38) that resolves immediately to E. What is most striking about this passage is the wash of color this accumulation of descending scales establishes. Here the surface rhythm acceleration of the scales from quarter notes to triplets is combined with a *crescendo* in sound both dynamically and orchestrally for a striking effect. Additionally, Rachmaninoff has these scales descending simultaneously at different rates of speed, culminating (m.327) with syncopations, quarters, and eighths. The latter is pushed to triplets for the final four measures before the recapitulation of *A* (m.339).

The second part of the second episode (*2C*) is not the only portion of this movement remarkable for its orchestration; the first part of this episode (*1C*) is also notable. Here Rachmaninoff gives his big tune in octaves to all of the strings except the basses, while the woodwinds and brass pound out or sustain its harmonies and the basses maintain the pedal. Something like this occurs in the piano concertos where the soloist plays the background and the strings take up the big central tune. Its origins are probably to be found in the opening to Tchaikovsky's B-flat Minor Piano Concerto. However, Rachmaninoff uses this disposition not as a non-repeated introduction but as a significant structural entity when it assumes the tonic key (m.503) near the Finale's conclusion. Indeed, this is not the only moment that reminds us of Rachmaninoff's piano concertos; there is also the march-like theme of *1T* (m.41) and the virtuosity of the refrain. Lastly, the Finale, instead of ending with a single long or short note, concludes with a rhythmic activation on the final chord (♩ ♩ ♩♩♩ | ♩) that also brings to mind the distinctive endings of the Second and Third Piano Concertos.

One of the central performance problems of Opus 27 is whether any of the authentic cuts should be observed. The original published score by Gutheil/Breitkopf from August 1908, available in a reprint from Kalmus, apparently contains no cuts, but cuts found in sources having various levels of authenticity are identified by Threfall and Norris and by Cannata. Threfall and Norris cite cuts "probably originally stemming from the composer himself."[209] Cannata, however, distinguishes between authentic excisions in the orchestral parts and the score. Either the rehearsal markings in the Kalmus reprint differ from those of Rachmaninoff's conducting score or these require some notational revisions to make them viable.[210] Our view is that no cuts should be made, since they do not improve the structure or one's aural perception. Recapitulatory cuts seem outright structurally harmful. In general, we find these excisions self-defeating; they result in a less coherent piece. Rachmaninoff's first thoughts for Symphony No. 2 are the best ones.

The Moscow premiere was enthusiastically greeted by the critic Iurii Engel:

> Having spent a year and a half abroad, S. V. Rachmaninoff reappeared before the Moscow public as a composer, a conductor, and a piano-player. In the fifth philharmonic concert (on February 2) he conducted his new, second symphony (E minor), and performed his second piano concerto. One may regret that the rest of the program—sung by Madam Nezhdanova—has not been composed of Rachmaninoff's works as well; had it been so, the whole evening would have acquired a more wholesome character.

EXAMPLE XV/57 Rachmaninoff. Symphony No. 2/4, mm.302–38.

As to Rachmaninoff, he deserves such a special "Rachmaninovian" concert. Despite the fact that he is only 34 years old, he is one of the most remarkable figures in the contemporary Russian musical world. He's a worthy successor to Tchaikovsky, if not by the significance of his talent (that would be a premature statement), then by his concentration, candor, subjectivity, and fine Europeanism. He is a successor, and not an imitator, for Rachmaninoff has an individuality of his own. Its features—in a bright, if somewhat one-sided manner—were already perceptible in the early works of Rachmaninoff. Since then, they have been expanding, growing, and maturing, along with the development of the composer's talent. One can judge this growth by, successively, "Francesca," "Spring," the cello sonata, and, finally, the now-performed, second piano concerto—(the best piano concerto since Tchaikovsky's concerto in B-minor)—that have every chance to become classics of the kind. But the most impressive confirmation of that was Rachmaninoff's new symphony in E minor.

EXAMPLE XV/57   (*continued*)

    I'm taking liberty in stating this, as I heard it only once and am not familiar with the score (the symphony was performed from the manuscript). Although, at the first hearing, the complicated texture of the symphony often gives you only a glimpse at the details promising you a lot of new sensations, once you familiarize yourself with them more closely, the main impression is already definite and strong the first time. Having heard four parts of the symphony with unremitting attention, you are surprised to notice that your watch's hand moved 65 minutes forward. For a wider audience it may be slightly long. . . . But how fresh it is! How beautiful!

    The prevailing mood of the symphony is serious and passionate, which is so typical of Rachmaninoff's works. His music is, truly, the language of spirit: candid, confident, not stilted, without hollow repetitions. Elegiac tone, so strong in Rachmaninoff's music, is strong in this symphony as well, but the broad lyrical scale doesn't exclude here either tragic feeling or fancy; either a joke or courageous vigor. In the profoundly refined accents of Rachmaninoff's music you can, sometimes, feel some suffering quality, but this acute sickly minor is not elevated to the status of the crown of creation. It leads to a whole specter of different feelings, diverse as life itself; and the symphony ends in the

EXAMPLE XV/57 (*continued*)

major. It is not the initial, immutable light of Mozart's or Rimsky-Korsakov's major; it is a light breaking through the dusk; it is enlightenment.

Major also predominated in the second movement (Allegro molto), which is substituted for a scherzo. This part enchants you with boundless richness of contrasts, both in its thematic development, and in its instrumentation—like a chameleon that constantly changes its colors—yet always transparent and wholesome. A charming episode forms here . . . a fugato in the strings, which consequently creates the background for the return of the previous theme. One is tempted to say that this part of the symphony is the best of all, but upon recalling the rest, one starts hesitating. What a strength there is in the first, diverse-yet-complete, movement, despite the fact that its two major themes, unlike the classical pattern, scarcely contrast with each other! How broad is the heartfelt melody sung by

EXAMPLE XV/57   (*continued*)

violins and cellos reigning here, as well as in the third movement (Adagio), and, virtually, everywhere else in the whole symphony! It is a kind of *stringed* symphony. However, with all that, the color of the strings is being perpetually refreshed by means of various other instruments joining the stringed ones. In general, in Rachmaninoff's orchestration there is much that is individual and fresh, which imparts a new charm to his symphony, one that is complete in its form; mature in its content; and independent, in spite of an obvious link in the sources of Rachmaninoff's works to the music of Tchaikovsky and Wagner.

EXAMPLE XV/57 (*continued*)

EXAMPLE XV/57   (*continued*)

The performance of the symphony was marvelous—with such temper, and, at the same time, with the confident self-discipline, that is so characteristic of Rachmaninoff's artistic persona. There were neither superfluous gestures on the part of the conductor, nor unnecessary nervousness in the orchestra; everything was alive and in the right place. This impression, perhaps, was reinforced by the fact that Rachmaninoff was performing his own piece. But Moscow has long known what a superb conductor Rachmaninoff can be.[211]

Except perhaps for some prolixity, the Rachmaninoff Symphony No. 2 has everything in place: the orchestration, like Tchaikovsky's, is totally effective but without ostentation, and the part writing and textures, while essentially homophonic, are the work of a skilled contrapuntalist. One might claim that these represent aspects to which the *kuchka* had been opposed. And even more disconcerting, music like this had made Rachmaninoff universally recognized as a Russian composer. Together with the last three Tchaikovsky symphonies and the Borodin Symphony No. 2, the Rachmaninoff Second Symphony belongs to a group of essentially lyric works that contain big cantabile melodies that are also somberly heroic. In many quarters outside of the academy, the Rachmaninoff No. 2 and the Tchaikovsky Nos. 4–6 today remain as close as any Russian symphony to approaching popularity. Within the academy, some regard these pieces as beneath contempt, perhaps because of their immediate appeal. Nevertheless, the Rachmaninoff Symphony No. 2 is a display of technique almost unrivaled in late-nineteenth-century symphonic writing. At the same time, it contains a potent expressive component appreciated by the musically less sophisticated.

Rachmaninoff remarked that he did not much like composing symphonies.[212] And indeed, he wrote only one more after a break of almost three decades. In the meantime, he was pursuing his career as a pianist, and he came to be recognized as one of the greatest virtuosos of all time. Rachmaninoff was compared with Franz Liszt and, like Liszt, he cultivated an adoring international audience. Though the composer's output was limited during these years, some of the works are among Rachmaninoff's most enduring: Piano Concerto No. 3 Opus 30 (1909), *The Isle of the Dead* Opus 29 (1909), the two sets of *Etudes-Tableaux* Opus 33 and 39 (1911, 1916–1917), the *Variations on a Theme of Corelli* Opus 42 (1931), and the *Rhapsody on a Theme of Paganini* Opus 43 (1934). In addition, Rachmaninoff transcribed a number of works for piano solo to use as recital encores, such as the Scherzo from Mendelssohn's *A Midsummer Night's Dream* and Kreisler's *Liebeslied*.

SYMPHONY NO. 3 IN A MINOR OPUS 44

During the almost thirty years between Symphonies No. 2 and No. 3, Rachmaninoff's style underwent a decided change from a late Romantic language to one more in line with contemporary styles, though still conservative. To his audience, he was the composer of the Second and Third Piano Concertos and the Second Symphony. The *Rhapsody on a Theme of Paganini* Opus 43 (1934) partakes of this new style just as does the Third Symphony, but in the *Rhapsody* one's attention is centered not so much on its style, but on the soloist and the eighteenth variation in the high Romantic idiom. The Third Symphony has none of these compensatory attributes except for a somewhat lyrical *S* theme in the first and third movements. And it has never had the popularity afforded to its predecessor.

Symphony No. 3, unlike Symphonies Nos. 1 and 2, is only in three movements. As was the case in Berwald's Symphony No. 3 and Franck's Symphony in D Minor, the central movement combines elements of a slow movement with that of a Scherzo. Rachmaninoff anchors

EXAMPLE XV/58   Rachmaninoff. Symphony No. 3/1, mm.1–4.

the central movement in C-sharp major, the major third above A minor, but unusually in the major mode; this was just another variant of available tertian relationships. In this movement, the minor mode, however, initiates the piece. As in the other Rachmaninoff symphonies, a motto theme is the strongest unifying factor. This motto commences the first movement and recurs there toward the end of the development (m.204), at the beginning of the recapitulation (m.230), and concludes the coda (m.315). The motto also begins and ends the second movement. In addition, *I/2T* is heard in the Scherzo section (m.207). As for the Finale, the motto returns in the development (m.85) and in the coda (m.321).

Though formally predictable, Rachmaninoff's first movement is a wonderful piece of writing rich in content and bedecked with effective orchestrations. Right at the start, the *pianissimo* motto played in unison by a solo clarinet, a stopped (not muted) solo horn, and a solo cello *con sordino* provides a special collective color (Example XV/58). Only four bars long, this introductory gesture is easily imprintable on the mind of the listener. It establishes a tonality on A, but without asserting the key of A minor; this task is completed in its Allegro answer, where A minor is stabilized but then withdrawn. Again, the exposition (m.12) is enclosed with repeats, though the actual repeat seems to be optional. It was omitted in a recording by the composer and in Eugene Ormandy's recording that was supervised by Rachmaninoff. One suspects, however, that the repeat was omitted because of the limitations of 78 rpm discs upon which these recordings were first made available. Since the material of the exposition is not well known to most audiences, the repeat should be preserved.

By the beginning of *1P,* A in its various modal forms is established as a tonic. Characteristic of both *P* themes (mm.12, 21) are their lyricism, though here without any grand Romantic gestures, and their mixing of 2/4 and 3/4 time. *1T* (m.31) is laid out in *a–b–a–b* structure, something more reminiscent of a Classic *P* layout, with both a surface and tempo acceleration culminating in *2T* (m.41), *3T* (m.43) returns to the opening pace with *3T* (m.43), and a pedal on the dominant of the dominant prepares for *S* in the standard dominant key. Though *S* is closer to the Romantic side of the composer than *P,* it too is reined in by quiet dynamics ranging from *pp* to *mf*. Even upon repetition where the orchestration is enriched, Rachmaninoff holds the expression in check. At *S^k* (*1S,* m.77) where the dynamic increases to *f,* the character changes from *dolce cantabile* to *marcato*. *1K* (m.84), also based on *S,* increases the dynamic to *ff,* but even here Rachmaninoff seems to avoid a climactic grand gesture.

Rachmaninoff again clearly organizes his development section. Part one begins with *1P* (m.103) with an agitated accompaniment alternating with new material (*N,* m.109), which is characterized by a sighing motive. After a repetition, material derived from *2P* (m.130), now in E-flat, almost breaks into the big lyric gesture, but dissipates with a motive from *1P* (m.136). Part two (m.143) increases the tempo and exploits a triplet ostinato that is intruded upon by *N*. Whereas part one was anchored in E-flat, part two is modulatory, and during its course *N* comes to dominate the activity. Part three (m.165) alternates *1P* and *1Ta* in a texture that approaches polyphony and continues the modulatory stance of part two. Whereas the first section of part three is anchored in 4/4, the second section (m.181) combines elements of *1Tb* and *2P* in triple meter before returning to 4/4 (m.188) for a motivic dialogue. *1Sy* (m.194) turns into something of an ostinato; it settles on a G-sharp pedal (m.200), and hammerstrokes bring section three to a close. The G-sharp pedal continues into the retransition (m.204), which is framed by the motto theme: first *marcato* in the brass and second (m.230) as an echo by the stopped horn. In between, the melody in the strings derives from the stacked thirds of *2S* (m.70). G-sharp resolves to A for the recapitulation (m.236).

Here Rachmaninoff states *P*, cuts *T* to a minimum, and recapitulates *S* (m.256) in A-flat and *K* (m.294) in D-flat. It is the coda's duty to reestablish the tonic key, which is accomplished by an A pedal under $S^k(1S)$ (m.297) and a tonic/dominant ostinato under the motto. One more statement, this time in a stark orchestration, brings the movement to a quiet close. Given the variety of rhythmic values in the exposition, the recapitulation and coda are streamlined with almost entirely quarter- and eighth-note motion. Thus, the final sections of the first movement search for a rhythmic as well as a tonal stability.

As in the Second Symphony's first movement, that of the Third Symphony is constructed along Classic lines. There is a proper exposition, a full development, and a slightly quirky recapitulation and coda. Considering that Rachmaninoff in his Symphony No. 2 was a composer deeply committed to late Romantic gestures, the expressive levels of Symphony No. 3 approach both a restrained neo-Classicism as well as a confined late Romanticism. Regardless of how one wishes to pigeonhole this movement, it is a fine accomplishment in the wider perspective of symphonic first movements.

The middle movement, as noted above, is a synthesis of slow movement and Scherzo. Unlike earlier instances of such syntheses, Rachmaninoff does not use a ternary structure of slow movement–Scherzo–slow movement. Instead, the relationship is more complex (Table XV/40). Framed by the motto, the slow movement is shaped like an independent Schubertian rondo. Then comes the second episode (*C*, m.89)—the Scherzo—which internally is a loose ternary form. By means of *T* (m.253), the slow movement material returns in reverse order: *B* (m.260), *A* (m.265), and then the motto (m.280).

The most fascinating passages are the *T* functions (mm.26, 85, 253). Each time Rachmaninoff reconstitutes this material for each of its functions: to *B* twice and once to *C*. The first passage to *B* (m.31) establishes the distinctive profile of *T*: quintuple sixteenths outlining the C-sharp major arpeggio in the violins (Example XV/59). At the moment when the harp joins the arpeggio (m.29) with normal sixteenths, for one measure there is a form of heterophony before the flute undertakes *Ba* (mm.30–31). In the passage to the Scherzo (*C*), the quintuplets now outlining C major accelerate and move in sequence by enharmonic modulation (D-flat/C-sharp) to the dominant of D for the Allegro vivace. For the third passage, again now in C-sharp, the shape of the original arpeggio is modified to fit into the cantabile transition (mm.257–58) to *B* (m.260), which itself blends into *A* (m.265). All three of these passages seem like improvisations made to fit each of their destinations.

In fact, the spirit of improvisation dominates this piece. Rachmaninoff's opening passage for solo horn and harp echoes the opening of Borodin's Symphony No. 2 slow movement, where it is said to represent a minstrel's song. Even *Aa* (m.10), *Ab* (m.16), and *B* convey with their sequences much the same ambience, though the increasing textural complexity steals from their improvisatory simplicity. In contrast, the Scherzo's middle seems improvisatory in that it freely unfolds from its opening motives.

What marks this movement is the deftness and élan of Rachmaninoff's treatment of the

TABLE XV/40
Rachmaninoff. Symphony No. 3/2: Structure

Adagio ma non troppo 3/4

Motto	A a	b		T	B a	a	Development	A a		B a
C-sharp		F-sharp	C-sharp		F-sharp		B-flat pedal / E-flat minor	E-flat minor	A-flat	C-sharp minor
m.1	10	16	20	26	31	36	40	49	56	60

[Scherzo] Allegro vivace 3/4

	4/4	3/4						4/4	mixed meters
a	A a	T		C a		b			
modulatory	C			D		C pedal	F minor	C pedal	C-sharp minor
68	82	84	85	89		105	119	135	155

Tempo come prima 3/4 — Adagio 4/4

		4/4			3/4	¢	Tempo come prima 3/4			Adagio 4/4
retrans.	b	II/2T			[a]		T	B a	A a	Motto
	G-sharp pedal→A→C	C pedal	C	G pedal	C pedal			C-sharp	C-sharp pedal	C-sharp
160	163	169 171 191	207	214	218 222	237		253 260	265 275	279

EXAMPLE XV/59   Rachmaninoff. Symphony No. 3/2, mm.26–31.

orchestra. He is certainly no pianist turned orchestral composer, but rather an accomplished master of the orchestra's potential. Witness the following passages (Example XV/60): the re-orchestrations of *A* and *B* materials, particularly mm.59–67 where the flute, celesta, and harp provide a wash of arpeggiated color to which is added subdivided violins and a soft roll on the cymbal. In the Scherzo section, one almost has the impression that Rachmaninoff has learned something from Schoenberg's *Variations for Orchestra* Opus 31 (1928), particularly in the use of *Klangfarben*. For example, in the Rachmaninoff, mm.101–04 depend almost entirely on pointillistic color.

EXAMPLE XV/60   Rachmaninoff. Symphony No. 3/2, mm.59–67.

EXAMPLE XV/60   (*continued*)

EXAMPLE XV/60 *(continued)*

Again, this is a marvelous piece of work that reveals Rachmaninoff as a composer of his time. Those expecting another slow movement like the Second Piano Concerto and the Second Symphony will be disappointed; rather than striking melodies, the composer reveals his multifaceted abilities as orchestrator, improvisator, and manipulator of texture, melody, and harmony. Here, no one element stands out, as did melody in the earlier works.

Rachmaninoff's Finale is like Symphony No. 2/4, a concerto movement in its virtuoso stance. Up to S (m.51), sixteenth notes drive the Allegro tempo as do the kaleidoscopic changes in orchestration, the interpolation of smaller 2/4 and 3/4 measures into the 4/4 landscape, and the anacrustic motives. Even though the tempo itself is only $\downarrow = 112$, due to all of these activities it seems much faster. After P (m.2), P^k (m.19), and three T themes (mm.23, 28, 41), many of the same observations concerning the first movement's S could be made for the meno mosso S (m.51) of the Finale. Even K (m.67) is again merely a continuation of S. This time, however, the three keys of this exposition are hardly what one might find in a textbook prescription: P is in A major, S in C-sharp minor, and $K(S)$ in E-flat major undergirded by a tonic pedal. In contrast to P through T, S through K is an isle of relaxation; the tempo is slower, and no value faster than an eighth note is to be heard. A bassoon cadenza (mm.72–84) serves as a link to the development (m.85), which commences with a *tutti fortissimo* statement of the motto in C major, a decided transformation from its previous presentations. But this is a false start as the cadenza motive returns, leading to a fast-paced ($\downarrow = 138$) fugato based on P in triple meter with occasional 2/4 compressions. Perhaps this is another echo of Tchaikovsky's Symphony No. 6/1.

The fugato itself (m.95) is one of Rachmaninoff's lengthier explorations of this polyphonic procedure. It goes beyond a single exposition and episode, as seen in Symphony No. 1/2, for a total of three expositions (mm.95, 120, 135) and three episodes (mm.112, 128, 143). Rachmaninoff continues the third episode for forty-two measures, making one believe that we have returned to normal developmental procedures, but then the subject returns (m.195). One might think that another exposition is in the process of unfolding, but that expectation remains unfulfilled as the subject is never countered and disintegrates into a "bluesy" transition (m.210) (Example XV/61). Rachmaninoff was present in New York's Aeolian Hall when Gershwin's *Rhapsody in Blue* was first heard (February 12, 1924), and it may well have impacted the composer in this passage and in his *Rhapsody on a Theme of Paganini*.[213]

A final portion (m.222) takes up what many commentators believe is another Rachmaninoff reference to the Dies Irae. It first appeared in m.139 for but a moment; in m.222 this four-note motive takes on a life of its own. Whether this is considered to be an allusion to the Dies Irae is open to question. The chant incipit consists of a minor second descent, a minor second ascent, and a minor third descent, whereas Rachmaninoff's motive consists of a major second descent and ascent followed by a minor third descent. Of the three intervals, then, two do not match. Perhaps Rachmaninoff was captivated by the shape; in our view, when he does quote the Dies Irae motive unaltered, there is no question what he is doing. Nevertheless, this motive participates in a build-up to a big E-major cadence (mm.245–46), which directly moves to A major and the recapitulation (m.247).

As in the first movement's recapitulation, the T materials are erased, and P moves almost directly into S with only ten measures of new material (N, mm.273–82) separating them. N and S are in E-flat, while $K(S$, m.295) slips up to E major (m.295). The purported Dies Irae motive returns (m.299), sinisterly sounded by the stopped horn. At the start of the coda (m.307), it is now played with the unaltered intervals, but few listeners would hear it as such in this context. Three tempo accelerations (Allegretto [m.321], Allegro [m.347], Allegro vivace [m.354]) with material from P (m.321) and the Dies Irae (m.354) bring the movement to an exciting end with a clipped and activated conclusion typical of Rachmaninoff.

EXAMPLE XV/61 Rachmaninoff. Symphony No. 3/3, mm.210–21.

This third movement fulfills all of the requirements of a late-nineteenth-century Finale: brilliance through virtuosity, lyric contrasts, return of the motto in new guises, and the resolution to the major in a minor mode cycle. Rachmaninoff's fugue in the development section only serves to highlight the virtuosic demands on the orchestra. This movement's weakness is in the *S* and *K* materials, which do not measure up to the parallel functions in the first movement. However, their lack of distinction serve to highlight the more dexterous passages of *P* through *T,* the development section, and the coda.

While the Rachmaninoff Third Symphony is not at the center of the symphonic repertoire, it is deserving of a status held by the *Rhapsody on a Theme of Paganini* with which it

EXAMPLE XV/61   (*continued*)

has many similarities. Its thematic materials, their working out, the variety found in the orchestration, and the handling of the fabrics and textures make for a symphony of no mean accomplishment. That Rachmaninoff in his basically conservative style took elements not only from his compositional mentor Tchaikovsky but also from composers as disparate as Schoenberg and Gershwin, and absorbed them into a personal style, speaks to the fact that Rachmaninoff was not an anachronism but a composer of his time. Indeed, the problem of the Third Symphony centers around its reception; it was too Romantic for connoisseurs, but not Romantic enough for aficionados of the Second Symphony and other works from the first decade of the twentieth century. Rachmaninoff wrote of its first performance with the Philadelphia Orchestra on November 6, 1936, Leopold Stokowski conducting, that both the audience and the critics "responded sourly." However, he went on to say that he was "firmly convinced that this is a good work."[214]

Reviews from the *New York Times* by Olin Downes, the *New York Sun* by W. J. Henderson, and the *Philadelphia Inquirer* by Linton Martin provide a sampling of opinions:

> The première of this symphony had been eagerly awaited. Mr. Rachmaninoff has been too inactive of late years as a composer to satisfy the public. But he was never a man to truckle to popular wish, or the artist to allow himself to be hurried with an important work. After a long silence, if we accept the recent Rhapsody in the form of variations on the theme of a Paganini Caprice for piano and orchestra, he completed the symphony heard last night. It was finished last spring in Switzerland. It is in three extensive movements, and bears no label other than Third Symphony. It is in the key of A minor. As for the rest, the music speaks for itself.
>
> What does it say? Mr. Rachmaninoff would never explain. His work is done with the last note of the scoring and some find his personal reticence reflected in his art, which is prevailingly somber in tone and passionately introspective.
>
> The outward characteristics of Rachmaninoff's style are evident in the work heard on this occasion. There are the broad, curving Slavic melodies, which can say so much with a simple instrumentation confined principally to the choir of strings. There are the throbbing rhythms; the relapses, at one moment, to a point when the whole orchestra seems to lie supine and without strength, only to rise with fresh accumulation of force and to shake with fury. There is the impression of frustrated strength, which gathers, to crash helplessly against some obstacle. There are wildly exultant passages, set off with brilliant instrumentation. Most of the rhythms and themes are fundamentally of a racial quality.
>
> It cannot be said, however, that in these pages Mr. Rachmaninoff says things which are new, even though his idiom is more his own than ever before, and free of the indebtedness it once had to Tchaikovsky. Nor is it easy to avoid the impression, at a first hearing of this work of a certain diffuseness. There is a tendency to overelaboration of detail, and to unnecessary extensions, so that the last movement, in particular, appears too long.
>
> Would not a pair of shears benefit the proportions of this work? Its sincerity and personal accent, the substance of the technic and the skill in orchestration, commanded the admiration of the audience, if not its unqualified enthusiasm.[215]

> In placing the heaviest and most important course at the end of the feast Mr. Stokowski followed an example set by other conductors, who manifestly prefer to consult what they believe to be their artistic ideals rather than the receptive capacities of their auditors. Mr. Rachmaninoff's third symphony was lately produced in Philadelphia and gave rise to the inevitable differences of opinion. Doubtless there will be further arguments pro and con, which will accomplish nothing, since time and repetition will make clear the message of the work and determine its position in the musical cosmos.
>
> It was begun in the spring of 1933 and completed in Switzerland last August. It is in three movements and lasts forty minutes, a tidy period for the coda of a generous concert. It has been described as prodigal in the sweeping cantabile phrases full of brooding and marked by the stress familiar to lovers of Rachmaninoff's symphonic compositions. "Somber, lyrical, defiant" are adjectives which have been applied to it. The symphony is likely to be crushed under the weight of the ponderous epithets piled upon its back. The simple truth is that it is neither so wide as a church door nor so deep as a well, but it will suffice. It is the creation of a genial mind laboring in a field well known and loved by it,

but not seeking now to raise the fruits of heroic proportions. There are strong moments, but the final effect is of much songful utterance punctuated by vigorous exclamation, all tending to court receptivity without too much searching analysis.

In structure the work follows the modern developments of the classic form. The first movement is orthodox in its initial statement of two contrasting chief subjects. They are contrasted in the customary way, in temper and tonality. But the working out section pays only polite respect to tradition. Modern composers do not fence off their sections with double bars as the fathers did, and they do not cross the bridge when they come to it, for usually there is no bridge. The development of themes immediately follows their statement and this is Rachmaninoff's method. The cantabile theme of the first movement is especially attractive in its lyric and plaintive character and the leading subject has virility and possibilities which are not neglected later. In fact, we suspect, after this insufficient first hearing, that there is more organic unity in this symphony through consanguinity of themes than is instantly discernible.

The slow movement sings itself into our knowledge graciously and has the old-fashioned middle section of sharply rhythmic figuration to serve as an incidental scherzo. This movement is firmly outlined and admirably filled in. It listens extremely well at a first performance. The finale is not so easy to grasp and will have to be heard more than once to be properly assimilated. It sounds episodic, but possibly its exclamatory style of many parts and the abrupt marking off of paragraphs are superficial mannerisms which obscure better things beneath the surface. There is an excellently written fugato which seemed to us to have no clearly defined objective. But let us wait. There is much good music in the movement and an external appearance of urge. The work was spendidly performed by the Philadelphians and conducted (from the score) by Mr. Stokowski with complete mastery.[216]

Leopold Stokowski made musical history with his first appearance of the Philadelphia Orchestra season at the concert in the Academy yesterday by presenting three world premieres on an all-Russian program.

Two of them were magnificent orchestral arrangements of his own. The third was the Third Symphony, in A minor, by Serge Rachmaninoff, heard for the first time anywhere on this occasion, and thus constituting the "news" if not necessarily the most engrossing musical interest of the concert.

With the illustrious and almost legendary Leopold acting as musical mountain guide, some Parnassian peaks of symphonic splendor were scaled during the afternoon. The musical metaphor must be somewhat scrambled geographically, because if Parnassus belongs in Greece, it became nothing less than a Himalayan height, and the tonal territory traversed was entirely Russian. Anyway, the audience obviously enjoyed its excursion into the rarefied and exhilarating atmosphere, judging by the applause, and Rachmaninoff himself, as the only living Russian of the three distinguished composers represented, joined in it for Stokowski's magnificent performance of his symphony, finally appearing on the stage to take several bows before the audience permitted him to depart and the orchestra to "break."

Characteristic of Composer

Of the Rachmaninoff Third Symphony it may be said, first of all, that it is thoroughly characteristic of its composer. In musical thought and expression it bears conspicuously closer relationship to the imperial past than to the puny present. Written in three movements its thematic material is developed in highly original and even irregular manner and is of varying vitality in inspiration, though its qualities and construction are such that what it has to say manifestly cannot be entirely apprehended on the strength of a single hearing.[217]

Although the uncharitable coverage of the performance in the *New York Times* helps clarify what the composer meant by the new symphony's "sour" reception, an even harsher verdict was provided by Edwin H. Schloss, music critic of the *Philadelphia Record*:

> The new Rachmaninoff symphony was a disappointment at least to one member of the audience. There are echoes of the composer's earlier lyric spaciousness of style, but sterility seems largely written in the pages of the new score, which is the first symphony written in thirty years by the distinguished Russian. The concert carried this moral: That Serge Rachmaninoff did not have another symphony in him.[218]

The first European performance, in London in 1937, received an equally unfavorable review in the pages of the *Musical Times*:

> At the Philharmonic concert on November 18 Sir Thomas Beecham conducted the first performance in Europe of Rachmaninoff's third Symphony (in A minor, Op. 44). Whether the work was disappointing or not depended on the degree of optimism with which one entered the hall. The man who composed the third Piano Concerto in 1909 and is no further than Op. 44 in 1937 could hardly have written himself out; on the other hand, a life-long failure to think of inspired and clinching ideas is unlikely to repair itself after the age of sixty. In the event it was this second factor that prevailed. The Symphony is made of fine stuff, set down with musicianly accomplishment of the highest order. No one could doubt that this composer had the necessary weight of style and power of continuity for the constructing of large-scale symphonic movements. His Symphony is superior in knowledge of procedure to, say, a symphony by Borodin. But, by the same comparison, it is unilluminated. One of its themes is a beacon or is made to flare up by its treatment. Every good symphony from Haydn to Sibelius has its high lights, its italics, inverted commas, and bits of big type. Rachmaninoff does not bestir himself to search for such things, but goes on thinking well and writing well with a kind of weary disregard for the people who want them—or else a weary acceptance of his inability to think of them. This attitude of negation, or whatever it is, would be all to the good if Rachmaninoff's musical idiom had the subtle intrinsic quality that such aloofness presupposes, but it falls rather flat in combination with an idiom that wants to shape itself into good tunes and fat effects. The first movement completed a spirited course without leaving the impression that anything had happened, though it was always about to. Of the slow movement I can recall no impression whatever. When it woke up into a Scherzo something more than the speed was quickened, the invention of scherzo business being lively and effective; this was the best part of the symphony. The Finale was characterized by the fact that at the moment of crisis it broke out into a fugato. The total effect of the symphony was as if the composer had felt the need to exercise his craft, and not as if he had been urged by the wealth of his ideas.[219]

It was reviews such as these that sealed the fate of the Rachmaninoff Symphony No. 3 into the limbo of only an occasional performance. However, it continues to flourish in recorded performances.

CONCLUSION

After having surveyed the three completed symphonies of Serge Rachmaninoff, one may rightly ask: what constitutes his approach to the genre? For this composer, a summary response is impossible to provide because each of his symphonies is a world unto itself. Symphony No. 1 is an almost brutal piece; Symphony No. 2 is deeply post-Tchaikovskian; and Symphony No. 3 belongs to the non-serial mainstream which *in toto* recalls, in a milder incarnation, his two contemporary Russian symphonists, Prokofiev and Shostakovich. Overall, all three Rachmaninoff symphonies bring to mind Tchaikovsky, particularly his Symphony No. 6 "Pathétique," whether it be in the terrain of the exposition, the use of a fugato in the development, or the complete mastery of the orchestra as an instrument easily negotiated. The other significant thread that runs through these works is an effort to unify the cycle. This is most fully accomplished in Symphony No. 1, where there is an accumulation of motivic returns as the cycle unfolds. Symphony No. 2 is less dogged in this respect, while Symphony No. 3 also has a motto that is reheard at crucial points in each movement.

The issue of Rachmaninoff's Russian-ness has not centered around his adoption of folk materials, but rather around his use of chant from the Russian Orthodox liturgy. Except for the *P* theme of the Piano Concerto No. 3 for which Joseph Yasser has found a similar chant, there have been no parallels drawn between specific Russian chants and the themes in Rachmaninoff's symphonies.[220] For Symphony No. 1, it has repeatedly been pointed out that the themes are based on materials from the *Ocktoekos*. Piggott's explanation is that Rachmaninoff took "small melodic cells . . . and weld[ed] them into themes suitable for symphonic development."[221] Of course, the smaller the motive, the greater is one's chance of finding a similarity. The mottos of the Second and Third Symphonies seem more like something derived from a chant than anything in Symphony No. 1. Yet to say that as a result Rachmaninoff is a nationalist composer is clearly wrong; he was at best a Russian national composer. Some have also claimed that after he left Russia in 1916, Rachmaninoff was less prolific and not as successful. Such is only true if one ignores that he pursued a career as a pianist and that some of his most successful works date from after his departure from Russia: the *Rhapsody on a Theme of Paganini,* the Symphony No. 3, and the *Symphonic Dances.* The viability of Rachmaninoff's symphonies has nothing to do with his, or their, Russian-ness.

Conclusion: What Makes a Symphony Russian?

The question of what makes a Russian symphony has been at the core of critical thinking about the repertoire. A Russian symphony is often judged on its Russian-ness and not accepted solely on the basis of its musical interest. But what is characteristic of a Russian symphony? If one were to say it was centered on its extra-musicality, from our selected survey we would have only *ca.* six works: Borodin's Symphony No. 2, Rimsky-Korsakov's Symphony No. 2 *Antar,* and four symphonies by Tchaikovsky—No. 1 "Winter Daydreams," No. 4 for which a detailed program was provided, the *Manfred* Symphony, and No. 6 "Pathétique." Even the inclusion of Borodin's No. 2 might be questioned, since there is not a strong authentic tradition for its extra-musicality. What is most extraordinary about this short list is that only Borodin No. 2 has a program that might be construed as nationalistic. Thus, the most overt path to a Russian symphony—extra-musicality—was not employed by its native composers.

A second, often-considered central element is the use of folksong. Rimsky-Korsakov, Balakirev, Tchaikovsky, and later Anatoly Lyadov and Sergey Lyapunov collected and published collections of folk music that they had heard. Collections of Russian folksong date back to the eighteenth century with Trutovsky's *Collection* (1776). The most famous is the anthology by Nikolay L'vov and Johann Prach (1790), which went through several editions and provided many folk themes used by Russian composers. Margarita Mazo provides an impressive list of works using material from L'vov and Prach; only the Balakirev Symphony No. 2/4 and Tchaikovsky Symphony No. 4/4 are among the symphonic movements using folk material from this collection.[222] Though materials from other collections were incorporated into symphony movements, this short list is indicative of their relatively minor importance to the propagation of the Russian symphony. Of course, besides the identifiable folksongs, there are also the themes that sound like folk material (modal, small range, distinctive intervallic profiles, unusual metric structures), but cannot be traced to any known source. Perhaps some of these were heard by a composer and used in a symphony or sonata, but never identified as to their source. Other themes may have been intentionally composed in the style of folk music. Even if one includes all of these possibilities, the use of Russian folk or folk-like materials overall is probably rather small in the pre-revolutionary Russian symphony, and mostly restricted to the members of the *kuchka* and Tchaikovsky. In the generation of composers after Tchaikovsky, the issue becomes almost insignificant.

Russian symphonies have been often cited for their skillful and colorful orchestrations. This is particularly true of the works by Borodin, Rimsky-Korsakov, and Tchaikovsky. The origins of this particular aspect go back to the *kuchka* and their study during the 1850s and 1860s of Berlioz's *Treatise on Orchestration* (1843). Since the wind instruments were undergoing significant changes between 1840 and 1860, Berlioz's *Treatise* was in some respects already out of date. Nevertheless, a direct result of studying Berlioz is that some of the Russian orchestral repertoire requires the more colorful supplementary instruments to the contemporary orchestra: the percussion battery, the English horn, the cornet, and the harp. Both the English horn and the harp are often associated with an oriental flavor. Rimsky-Korsakov's subsequent *Principles of Orchestration* (published posthumously in 1913) is at once a complete text and an update to Berlioz.[223]

Particularly characteristic of Russian symphony cycles from the *kuchka* generation is the placement of the Scherzo in second position, probably more a result of an admiration for Robert Schumann's Symphony No. 2 rather than Beethoven's Ninth. What distinctively marks some of these Scherzo movements is a quintuple meter and later changing meters or simultaneous different meters. Only Borodin's Symphony No. 2/2 calls for a 1/1 meter, a movement perhaps better notationally served by reducing its whole notes down to quarters with some use of changing meters. From the next generation, there is the 5/4 movement from Tchaikovsky's Symphony No. 6/2. Mixed meters are also found in the second and third generation of composers, but on a very restricted scale. No doubt this use of changing and unusual meters stimulated Stravinsky to completely revolutionize his own metric treatment.

Balakirev had an obsession with keys of two sharps and five flats and their enharmonic equivalents. To some degree this influenced the choice of cyclic and the internal keys of several other Russian symphonies. The result, though, was to use keys as absolutes rather than coloristically and dramatically. Because of Balakirev's obsession, the Russian symphony had one fewer weapon in its arsenal. Nevertheless, a good part of the tonal color in these works comes at the smaller dimension, and in the "color" of the themes themselves, by using modes—most often the Aeolian, the ambiguity of the major mode and its relative minor, and the old-fashioned bi-modality. Often these qualities result in extensive use of pedals to underline a tonality. For example, the Tchaikovsky Symphony No. 6/2 uses a D pedal to underline the entire Trio, which alternates tonally between D major and B minor. Normally, however, Tchaikovsky is among the least prone of Russian composers to use modality as a significant part of his vocabulary.

In addition to their use of folk materials, then, much more significant is how Russian composers emphasized melody in their symphonic forms. Especially in the works of Tchaikovsky, Kalinnikov, and Rachmaninoff, it is the melodic materials and their presentation that is of primary interest. It is not the unfolding of the material and its thematic development that is remembered, but the themes themselves. Whereas Beethoven's forms depended on the drama he was able to generate, Tchaikovsky and his successors depended primarily on the presentation of the theme itself. In particular, *S* or *B* themes, when combined with a mellow and warm orchestration, are especially affecting. The result was a shift from the primacy of tonality to the primacy of melody. While this has endeared Russian symphonies to audiences, it has caused the academy, until recently, to ignore these symphonies for emphasizing expression over intellect.

Two other thematic approaches were espoused by Balakirev and imposed upon the other members of the *kuchka.* After the statement of the main idea it was immediately treated to development of various sorts, which could be anything from developing variation to thematic transformation. While the result of this could be long range, as in Borodin's Symphony No. 2/1, more often it was a series of localized permutations. The second approach was more significant: the use of variation in the style of Glinka, here called changing background variation, environmental variation, or *cantus firmus* variation. Though not exclusive to the Russian School of composers, they and other nationalistic groups exploited it the most; here, the melody remains unembellished while every other musical element changes. It could be used as a primary generator of a piece as in Glinka's *Kamarinskaya* or as a secondary factor as in the *B* section of Tchaikovsky's Symphony No. 4/4.

For all their rantings about the evils of formal musical education, Balakirev and his circle clearly lost their battle against conservatory training, since the Russian symphony is steeped in the European tradition. The symphonies are almost always in four movements and, but for a few exceptions, in a normal sequence of tempos. Their forms are late-nineteenth-century textbook shapes with sonata and ternary structures dominating. Cyclicism is a significant factor, but not an overwhelming one; often the standard progression from minor to major modes provides the standard narrative from darkness to light, battle to triumph. The major departure is the Tchaikovsky Symphony No. 6 "Pathétique," which remains in the darkness of its concluding slow movement.

Though we have pointed to characteristics of the Russian symphony and have questioned some of the traditional tenets of Russian-ness, none of these traits set these Russian symphonies apart from what was happening in the other Slavic areas or even in Scandinavia. In fact, it was not very different from the practices of Haydn and Beethoven, whose music was saturated with Ländler, *contredanses,* and other local styles. Perhaps a school of Russian symphonists does not exist; they are merely symphonies written by composers of Russian birth who brought into their cycles dances, songs, and tunes absorbed from their musical experiences.

Bibliographic Overview

For the reader who is unable to read Russian, there is a raft of superb literature in English with various viewpoints, much of which is central to an understanding of the Russian symphony. The two pioneers for English readers are Gerald Abraham and Nicolas Slonimsky. In a myriad of articles, essays, and books, Abraham exposed both interested amateurs as well as non-specialist musicologists to the composers and the repertoire. In *Baker's Biographical Dictionary,* Slonimsky provides a thorough coverage of Russian musicians, patrons, publishers, and critics. Here, there is information that can be otherwise found in Russian scores. Abraham seemingly fostered, at least indirectly, an entire group of British Slavic musical scholars including David Brown, Edward Garden, David Lloyd-Jones, and Henry Zajaczkowski. At the time of writing, the most significant contributions to Russian musical studies are the books and articles by Richard Taruskin. Through an incisive critical vision, historical contextualization, and a prodigious knowledge of the music itself, Taruskin has revolutionized one's view of the Russian repertoire, both instrumental and operatic.

Surveys of Russian music have been offered in Leonard/RUSSIAN MUSIC, which is now superseded by Francis Maes/RUSSIAN MUSIC, published in 2002. Abel/SINFONISCHEN RUSSLAND covers the early developments. Greenawalt/RUSSIAN SYMPHONY contains some useful facts on the repertoire as a whole, but fails to deal with any of the critical issues. David Brown's survey (RUSSIA SYMPHONY) provides a fine overview that includes works not discussed here by Anton Rubinstein, Arensky, Tanaeyev, Glazunov, and Skryabin. A few reviews of symphonic works are included in Campbell/RUSSIAN MUSIC 1830–1880. Stasov/ESSAYS provides some of the *kuchka*-oriented views of this famous Russian critic; he dubbed the Balakirev group as the "mighty handful." Taruskin/*KUCHKA* briefly explains the origins and meanings of the term. In the *NG* and *NG2,* the articles on Russia, Moscow, and St. Petersburg (Leningrad in *NG*) provide useful surveys of musical life and institutions. When taken together, the books by Taruskin (DEFINING RUSSIA, MUSORGSKY, and the early portions of STRAVINSKY) are a sophisticated revisionist view of Russian musical history and its styles. Ridenour/19C RUSSIAN MUSIC provides a fine overview of the competing factions headed by Anton Rubinstein and Balakirev. Mazo/LVOV & PRACH is an exemplary commentary on an early collection of Russian folksongs that contains a few symphonic citations. Publication of other folksong collections remains a *desideratum.*

As for individual composers, the first line of information is the *NG* and *Baker's Biographical Dictionary. Baker's* is of particular usefulness because Slonimsky includes dates for the first performances for most of the symphonic works, which are hard to find outside of the literature in the Russian language. Writings on the *kuchka* as a unit are difficult to come by; perhaps the most useful are Rimsky-Korsakov/MUSICAL LIFE and Neef/RUSSISCHEN FÜNF.

Rimsky-Korsakov's life and works are best documented in his MUSICAL LIFE and in the diaries of Yastrebtsev (his Boswell), which are available in an incomplete English translation. These memoirs appear to be some of the most honest and straightforward chronicles of a major composer's education, influences, and points of view. Another primary document is Rimsky's book on orchestration which forms a sequel to Berlioz's *Treatise,* a tract used by the *kuchka.* Seaman/RIMSKY GUIDE, though problematical with regard to the Symphony No. 2 *Antar,* provides the best access to information about this composer, who, together with Tchaikovsky, came to be the most influential of the nineteenth-century Russian composers. Discussions of the cyclic symphonic works are difficult to come by; even *Sheherazade,* his most performed work, is only given particular attention by Abraham/PROGRAMME SCHEHERAZADE and Lloyd James in his preface to the Eulenburg score, reprinted in Field/MUSICIANS GUIDE. Otherwise, Griffith's Ph.D. dissertation (RIMSKY-KORSAKOV) is especially helpful since he covers the works titled symphony in some depth. Yet the most notable source today is Taruskin/RIMSKY-KORSAKOV SYMPHONIES, the incisive liner notes to the Deutsche Grammophon recording. Also relevant to these works is Taruskin/CHERNOMOR, in which he traces back to Schubert the use of certain materials that emerge in Rimsky-Korsakov's and Stravinsky's works.

The instigator of the *kuchka* was Mily Balakirev. Again, the earliest efforts in English to outline his importance and to describe the symphonies are two articles by Gerald Abraham (Abraham/BALAKIREV and Abraham/BALAKIEV'S SYMPHONIES). A comprehensive look at this mysterious figure is supplied by Edward Garden's 1967 monograph, as well as Garden's three subsequent articles on Balakirev: one on his personality and one each on his relationship to Tchaikovsky and Sibelius. Balakirev's main inspiration came from Glinka (see Brown/GLINKA and Glinka/MEMOIRS), whom he regarded as the father of true Russian music; this musical relationship is incisively pursued in Taruskin/ACORN.

There exist two monographs on Borodin by Abraham (1927) and Serge Dianin (1963). Both of these books need to be used with some care—the former because of its date and the latter because of its 1950s Soviet viewpoint. Nevertheless, Dianin remains the leading Russian Borodin scholar, including his editions of the letters and documents. Kuhn/BORODIN provides a basic introduction to the composer with contemporary recollections and Borodin's own critical writings in German translations. David Lloyd-Jones provides the best introduction to the symphonies in his introductions to the Eulenburg miniature scores for Symphonies Nos. 1 and 3, and Abraham offers the same for Symphony No. 2 (see Field/MUSICIANS GUIDE). Older surveys of the symphonies are by Abraham, Foss, and Manduell. Lloyd-Jones/EDITION BORODIN deals specifically with the textual questions of the symphonies.

Not unexpectedly, the Tchaikovsky literature is the largest and the most diverse in approaches and viewpoints; up to the time of writing, Tchaikovsky has been the only Russian composer to attract advocates of the new musicology, mainly because of his supposed neurotic personality and homosexual orientation. The basic reference is Poznansky & Langston/ TCHAIKOVSKY HANDBOOK, which contains a chronology, a catalogue of works, an iconography, the autobiography, a catalogue of letters, and a comprehensive bibliography. The catalogue supersedes VERZEICHNIS TSCHAIKOWSKY from 1973.

The most important biographic work has been done by Alexzander Poznansky (see his TCHAIKOVSKY QUEST and TCHAIKOVSKY RECONSIDERED). Orlova/ TCHAIKOVSKY, while containing valuable material toward a documentary biography, lacks clear bibliographic citations, and Orlova's advocacy of Tchaikovsky's poisoning opens other questions. The latter also mars Brown's *NG* article and the concluding fourth volume of Brown/TCHAIKOVSKY, which is otherwise a capital, though flawed, accomplishment both analytically and contextually. Single-volume surveys of the life and works are Garden/TCHAIKOVSKY and Warrack/TCHAIKOVSKY. Particular note should be made of John Wiley's fine article for *NG2*. Though a complete catalogue of the letters is in the TCHAIKOVSKY HANDBOOK, a number of these are available in translations of varying quality in Tchaikovsky/LIFE & LETTERS, Tchaikovsky/LETTERS FAMILY, and Poznansky's restoration of some previously censored letters. Brown/TCHAIKOVSKY REMEMBERED provides a variety of contemporary observations by friends, critics, and other observers.

Serious studies of Tchaikovsky's style are surprisingly few for a composer of so much popular appeal. An exception is Henry Zajaczkowski, whose monograph and articles fill a significant void. Further stylistic observations can be found in Abraham/MUSIC TCHAIKOVSKY, Kearney/TCHAIKOVSKY WORLD, and in the series *Tschaikowsky Studien* edited and often written by Thomas Kohlhase.

Surveys of the Tchaikovsky symphonies have been published by Cooper, Keller, Kraus, and Warrack. However, except for Blom/EARLY TCHAIKOVSKY SYM and the Preface to the Eulenburg scores republished in Field/MUSICIANS GUIDE by Abraham and Lloyd-Jones, studies of Tchaikovsky's first three symphonies are notably lacking. The same can be said of the *Manfred* Symphony, except for Abraham's preface and for the so-called reconstructed "Seventh Symphony" (see Warrack/TCHAIKOVSKY PIANO CONCERTO 3, SYMPHONY 7 liner notes). In contrast, the literature on Symphonies Nos. 4, 5, and 6 is more plentiful, especially as researchers have taken into consideration possible homosexual aspects within these three works. For Symphony No. 4, Lloyd-Jones provides the main documentary background, but not all of it; Zajaczkowski offers a traditional description, while Dammann takes up its reception. For No. 5 Lloyd-Jones again does the historical/biographical context; Tovey provides an elegant but contentious program note; Kraus traces this E-Minor Symphony's "narrative plot"; while Seibert debunks the myth of its program. For the "Pathétique" Symphony (No. 6), Lloyd-Jones and Tovey provide background and description; Zajaczkowski provides an extramusical biographical reinterpretation; while Abraham deals with the problem of its program. Taruskin takes up Tchaikovsky's homosexuality and the Sixth in a sensitive way, while Jackson/TCHAIKOVSKY 6 goes beyond the scholarly pale in his monograph, providing too many layers to his interpretation without a convincing contextual background.

If the literature on Tchaikovsky in English is expanding, that on Kalinnikov is minuscule but includes an article by Seaman and the usual entries in the standard reference works. The article by Spencer in *NG2* is particularly useful; it contains a relatively large bibliography in Russian.

Like Tchaikovsky, Rachmaninoff has entered the realm of a composer having produced works worthy of modern scholarly exploration (see Palmieri/GUIDE). A thematic catalogue by Threlfall and Norris and dissertations on the symphonies by Cannata and Collins testify to their recent legitimacy. Life and works by Culshaw and Seroff are by authors who knew the composer. The Swans' recollections, published just after his death, are of special value. Norris's book and *NG2* article take into consideration more recent documentation. Besides Cannata and Collins, other literature on the symphonic works are by Hull, Simpson, and Piggott.

Section Six
The French Symphony

By
BRIAN HART

CHAPTER SIXTEEN

The French Symphony After Berlioz: From the Second Empire to the First World War

Brian Hart

Introduction: The Symphony in Mid-Century

IN THE YEARS BETWEEN THE fall of the July Monarchy and the end of the Second Empire (1848–1870), the hegemony of opera dissuaded many French composers from striking too boldly onto the path of symphonic music. Although the extent to which symphonies and other instrumental genres truly suffered neglect remains open to question, composers drawn to abstract music clearly bore a heavy burden.[1] As one indication of the low esteem accorded non-operatic music, nowhere in Paris could one find a hall appropriate for large symphonic concerts. Jules Pasdeloup's Concerts Populaires met in the Cirque Napoléon (later renamed the Cirque d'Hiver), a coliseum normally reserved, as the name suggests, for circuses and other traveling shows; the composer and critic Ernest Reyer observed that in Paris "people solemnly go to hear oratorios and symphonies in a place where they went the day before to see horses gallop, elephants dance, and monkeys grimace."[2] The other major orchestra, the Société des Concerts du Conservatoire, had its own room at the state school; but the small size of the hall, coupled with steep ticket prices and the virtual monopoly renewing subscribers held over them, militated against significant audience growth.

Symphonists also contended with widespread apathy from the public. Berlioz's travails in this regard are well known. Composers of succeeding generations faced similar difficulties, as Camille Saint-Saëns bitterly recounted in 1885:

> It wasn't so long ago—fifteen years perhaps—that a French composer audacious enough to venture onto the terrain of instrumental music had no other means of performing his works than to give a concert himself and invite his friends and the critics. As for the public, the true public, he couldn't even think about them; seeing the name of a composer both French and living printed onto a program had the effect of putting everyone to flight.[3]

When looking back, Saint-Saëns tended to recall suffering more neglect and opposition in his youth than he actually did; he certainly fared better than most of his colleagues. Still, popular antipathy toward the symphony was not a figment of Saint-Saëns's imagination. Léon Kreutzer—himself a symphonist—wrote the following after a performance of the First Symphony of Louis Théodore Gouvy in 1847: "Anyone with a hundredth part of the talent M. Gouvy possesses would have the right to be played at all the lyric theaters, carry the decoration of the Legion of Honor, be a member of the Institut, and earn 30,000F a year; but why the hell does M. Gouvy write symphonies?"[4] Such sentiments remained typical before 1870.

Interest in symphonies grew during the 1850s and 1860s, but audiences gravitated toward works that merged abstract and theatrical elements, such as the "dramatic symphony" (inspired by Berlioz's *Roméo et Juliette*, 1839) and the *ode-symphonie*. The latter, a multi-movement work for orchestra, soloists, and chorus, combined elements of the symphony, symphonic poem, and oratorio. The paradigmatic *ode-symphonie*, Félicien David's *Le Désert* (1844), depicted a caravan in an Arabian desert; this work did much to stimulate French interest in musical exoticism. The popularity of *ode-symphonies* and *symphonies dramatiques* lasted throughout the century: other examples include Ernest Reyer's *Le Sélam* (1846), David's *Christophe Colomb* (1847), Benjamin Godard's *Le Tasse* (1878), Augusta Holmès's *Lutèce* (1878) and *Les Argonautes* (1881), and Cécile Chaminade's *Les Amazones* (1888). When listening to traditional symphonies, audiences preferred canonized masterworks by Haydn, Mozart, Beethoven, and Mendelssohn to new French offerings, no matter how conservative the native works might be; despite the success of *Le Désert,* even David could not convince audiences to listen to his four abstract symphonies. Gouvy concluded that French audiences "understand nothing of the structure, plan, and logical unfolding of a symphony."[5]

The principal orchestra in Paris, the Société des Concerts du Conservatoire, took little interest in symphonies (or anything else) by living French composers; with occasional exceptions, it restricted itself to Classic and early Romantic repertories, especially Beethoven. In the 1850s several concert societies emerged which promoted new French works. Most notable were the Société Sainte-Cécile (1850–1855), led by François Seghers, and Jules Pasdeloup's Société des Jeunes Artistes (1853–1861). Seghers occasionally presented whole concerts of recent compositions; Saint-Saëns's First Symphony figured among his premieres. Pasdeloup's orchestra, made up of students and recent graduates of the Conservatoire, also actively solicited contemporary composers and many of its concerts included at least one piece of new music. Among the symphonists heard at the Jeunes Artistes were Gounod, Saint-Saëns, L.-J.-A. Lefébure-Wély, Gouvy, Jakob Rosenhain, and Henry Litolff.[6] After the demise of Seghers's society, Pasdeloup's became the only one where young French composers had any hope of getting a hearing—a service duly appreciated by the critics:

> If there is a symphonist among our young musicians, or simply one who aspires to be a symphonist, at this time in France only the society directed by M. Pasdeloup can reveal him to us. There, talented composers are assured to find, with all the necessary elements for the performance of their works, no matter how complicated they are, a warm and unbiased welcome.[7]

Unfortunately, both societies came to grief, due in large part to insufficient public interest in new music. Chastened by these failures, orchestras in the 1860s concentrated largely on the classics. Pasdeloup, for example, designed his newly founded Concerts Populaires (1861–1884) to bring the music of Beethoven and other recognized masters to a public much larger than the Société des Concerts du Conservatoire could reach or cared to reach. Mindful of his previous experience, Pasdeloup's support of younger French composers cooled markedly, though it did not disappear. The conductor met his goal: the Concerts Populaires attracted a new audience of lower- and middle-class listeners to "serious" music through affordable prices, a large seating venue (the Cirque d'Hiver accommodated 5,000), and programs of "safe" and digestible works; it remained the primary Parisian outlet for orchestral music until the mid-1870s. So while the public taste for concert music increased, contemporary composers found to their dismay that opportunities to have their own works heard actually declined. In 1864, a critic writing in the journal *L'Art musical* lamented that the rare opportunities to hear French symphonies "proved . . . that the symphony is cultivated among us with much success. If only it could be encouraged a little more than has been done up to now!"[8]

If audiences, and critics to a lesser degree, reacted apathetically to modern symphonic music, the Conservatoire displayed open hostility. The state school officially regarded the symphony as a graduation exercise that students, especially winners of the Prix de Rome, mastered as part of their final progress toward excelling in opera. Writing in 1902, musicologist Julien Tiersot had this to say about the institutional attitude:

> The symphony was considered in France to be a schoolwork exercise, so much so that for a long time the symphony manifested itself only as *envois de Rome* [compositions which winners of the Prix de Rome submitted annually to the Académie des Beaux-Arts during or just after their years as laureates to prove their growing maturity in their art]. A well-written symphony was, it seems, the supreme proof of the talent of the young composers crowned by the Academy. As preparatory work, they had been obliged to write a fugue; the symphony came later, as the definitive crowning. But in the eyes of the judges it undoubtedly had no more importance or a higher artistic meaning.[9]

Many French symphonies of the early and mid-nineteenth century in fact originated as "school symphonies" (*symphonies d'école*), created by following textbook rules. The concept of the symphony as homework assignment helps explain the disdain critics like Kreutzer felt for the genre. It followed that students learned very little about the history and development of the symphony (or of any other genre, including opera). Even after 1870 Conservatoire graduates could remain profoundly innocent in their command of symphonic literature. Vincent d'Indy quoted a Prix de Rome winner who heard the Allegretto of Beethoven's Seventh Symphony and concluded, "Well! now, that's pretty; it must be by Saint-Saëns."[10]

As one would expect, composers of "school symphonies" looked to Classic and early Romantic masters for inspiration; but, given audience preferences for this repertory, it behooved even mature Second Empire composers to write works that reflected the length and style of symphonies by Haydn, Mozart, early Schubert, Weber, and Mendelssohn. More adventurous musicians consulted Beethoven and Schumann as well.[11] The most important symphonists active between 1840 and 1870 were Charles Gounod, Georges Bizet, and Camille Saint-Saëns—in other words, the three composers of the time most celebrated today. The symphonies of Gouvy (1819–1898) and Napoléon-Henri Reber (1807–1880) won the approval of such discriminating contemporaries as Berlioz and Saint-Saëns; the latter regarded Reber as "the first [French symphonist] who completely succeeded in this so very difficult genre; others showed talent, but he demonstrated originality."[12] Besides David and Léfebure-Wély, other symphonists include Édouard Deldevez (whose Symphony No. 3 bears the intriguing title *Symphonie héroi-comique*), J.-B. Weckerlin, Georges Mathias, George Onslow, Georges Pfeiffer, and Louise Farrenc. Farrenc's First and Third Symphonies (1841, 1847) in particular show considerable talent; the Société des Concerts du Conservatoire acknowledged this by premiering the Third in 1849, then an extremely rare honor for a living French composer.[13]

Charles Gounod

Charles Gounod (1818–1893) (Plate B15), the most influential French composer of the mid-nineteenth century, attained the rank of an immortal principally on the basis of his immensely popular opera *Faust* (1859) and, to a lesser extent, *Mireille* (1864) and *Roméo et Juliette* (1867). His oratorios, masses, and other sacred works also received considerable acclaim, though they are rarely heard today. Gounod wrote relatively few instrumental compositions: besides the symphonies, his output includes three string quartets and various pieces for piano, most notably the famous *Funeral March of a Marionette* (1872, orchestrated in 1879).

Gounod's popularity derived from an original operatic style that emphasized tender lyricism, light chromaticism, delicate orchestration, and virtuosic restraint, which distinguished his works from the searing passion and vocal fireworks of Italian opera and orchestral power of German drama. Similarly, his symphonies emphasize charm and tunefulness over rigorous development and make delightful listening (see Table XVI/1).

Gounod's models in the First Symphony are Mozart, Mendelssohn, and Haydn; the Second, a more "symphonic" work in the sense that it conveys an air of serious utterance, looks to Beethoven and possibly Schumann. (French symphonies generally use ordinal numbers and solmization syllables for titles.) The influence of the French lyric tradition remains strong in both works. The sonata forms adhere to "textbook" conventions, occasional surprises notwithstanding; but the Scherzo movements follow a more individual pattern.

SYMPHONY NO. 1 IN D MAJOR

According to his own account, Gounod wrote this symphony in 1854 to ease his dejection over the poor reception of his opera *La Nonne sanglante:* "[Its failure] was rather a grief to me. . . . I solaced my disappointment by writing a symphony for the Société des Jeunes Artistes, which had just been started by Pasdeloup."[14] He described the work as *un vrai enfantillage*—a true work of child's play.[15] This tuneful piece unfolds in a traditional manner with occasional structural anomalies. Consistent with its retrospective cast, the symphony uses a full rather than grand orchestra; also as in earlier times, the strings dominate (particularly the first violins), with woodwinds often limited to solos and support. Most melodies follow stepwise or triadic patterns.

The light and airy first movement (Allegro molto) follows the typical Mozartian approach to sonata form: each function contains numerous discrete themes. Two elements dominate the discourse: *1P* (especially *1Pb,* mm.5–6), which frames the movement and appears throughout the development; and syncopated rhythms and broken lines, as in *2P* (m.7) and the unsyncopated but equally broken *S* (m.81). Tremolos and pedals underlie the texture throughout much of the exposition.

The development concerns itself with *3T, S,* and especially *1Pb.* This section proceeds mostly by sequential repetition; only *1Pb* undergoes motivic fragmentation. While the subdominant, in both major and minor forms, remains the principal key, Gounod also uses the tonic as a major point of arrival (m.135). The climax, based on *1Pb* in D minor, features surface chromaticism in a way that again recalls Mozart (m.194). *1Pb* serves also as the basis for the retransition (m.203).

Since the development relied so heavily on *1P,* the recapitulation begins with *2P* (m.218). Although shortened and laced with short woodwind countermelodies, this section moves normally. The coda (m.288) relies on the same components as the development: *3T, S,* and *1P,* with hints of *2Pa.* A final statement of *1P* closes the movement (m.339).

The Allegretto moderato belongs to the class of solemn processionals familiar from Beethoven's Seventh, Berlioz's *Harold in Italy,* and Mendelssohn's "Italian" Symphony. With the latter it also shares the key (D minor) and general ambiance (light and staccato-articulated); such works as the overture to *A Midsummer Night's Dream,* the *Hebrides Overture,* and the "Italian" Symphony were then favorites in Parisian concert halls. Gounod sets his movement in *A–B–A* form, with *A* as the lyrical processional melody. Near the end of this section, we find one of those piquant turns of harmony so beloved of French composers: a Neapolitan seventh in root position shifts to a first-inversion diminished seventh on the leading tone, causing the bass to slip up a semitone (mm.43–48; Example XVI/1).

B, in the submediant key of B-flat major, begins with two statements of a stepwise melody followed by a fugue based on a transposed and slightly syncopated version of *A*

TABLE XVI/1

The Symphonies of Charles Gounod

No.	Key	Date	Title	Movements	Instrumentation	Comments
1	D Major	1854	Symphony No. 1	1. Allegro molto ¢ (345 m.) 2. Allegretto moderato 2/4 (175 m.) D minor 3. Scherzo and Trio: Non troppo presto 3/4 (124 m.) F major, B-flat major 4. Finale: Adagio C—Allegro vivace ¢ (392 m.)	Full	First performance: Paris, Société des Jeunes Artistes, conducted by Jules Pasdeloup, March 1855. Published in Paris: Colombier, 1855.
2	E-flat Major	1855–56	Symphony No. 2	1. Adagio C—Allegro agitato 3/4 (455 m.) 2. Larghetto (non troppo) C (122 m.) B-flat major 3. Scherzo and Trio: Allegro molto 3/4 (276 m.) G minor/major 4. Finale: Allegro leggiero assai 2/4 (499 m.)	Full plus 2 Hr.	First performance: Paris, Société des Jeunes Artistes, conducted by Jules Pasdeloup, January 1856. Published in Paris: Choudens, 1869 (four-hand piano reduction: Choudens, 1866).
	B-flat Major	1885	Little Symphony	1. Adagio 4/4—Allegretto 4/4 (123 m.) 2. Andante cantabile 3/4 (87 m.) E-flat major 3. Scherzo and Trio: Allegro moderato 6/8 (108 m.) 4. Finale: Allegretto 2/4 (233 m.)	Flt., 2 Ob., 2 Clar., 2 Bssn., 2 Hr.	*Petite Symphonie.* Written for the Société de Musique de Chambre pour Instruments à Vent. Dedicated to Paul Taffanel. Published in Paris: Costallat et Cie., 1904.

EXAMPLE XVI/1   Gounod. Symphony No. 1/2, mm.43–48.

(m.57). The fugue dissolves into unison sixteenth-note runs for full orchestra, leading to a bridge over a dominant pedal (m.117). *A* reappears in the lower strings against a running sixteenth-note motive in the violins and short countermotives in the woodwinds. The coda, like the fugue, is a variant of *A* (m.156).

Although labeled a Scherzo, the third movement is actually a fast Minuet and Trio that would not sound out of place in a symphony by Mozart; the composer acknowledges as much when he inserts the rubric "D.C. il minuetto" at the end of the Trio. The Minuet, in F major, follows an unorthodox form: *a* :||: *b c* :|| instead of the usual *a* :||: *b a* :||. Dotted rhythms predominate, beginning with the stately *a*. After a short excursion in A-flat major, *b* (m.21) repeats *a* in C major, with a lengthy extension; *c* (m.49), which begins in a weak F major, has the same rhythm and contour as *a*. The Minuet ends with a short closing passage featuring a turn figure faintly resembling *I/1Pb* (m.65). The Trio, in B-flat major, is set for winds (especially oboe and bassoon), which carry most of the melody against drones in lower strings and horns, creating the illusion of a bagpipe and a rustic scene.

Gounod reserves the slow introduction for the last movement (Finale: Adagio–Allegro vivace), the weightiest in the symphony. Written in the majestic style of Mozart, though without the latter's typical excursions into *ombra* topics, this section seems more like the beginning of a symphony than the preamble to its end; but it fulfills its purpose of acquainting us with the rhythmic figure that dominates the exposition.

Gounod again follows Mozart's example by using clearly defined functional areas (more so in fact than he did in the first movement), multiple thematic modules for each area except *P*, and a new theme in the development. *P* (m.25) consists of a "galloping" rhythm (*a*) set up in the introduction as well as an extended theme in *Pa* rhythm built upon a pattern of repeated notes (*b*). He tosses in moments of Haydnesque wit by injecting two unexpected diminished seventh harmonies (followed by grand pauses) into the middle of *P*, causing it momentarily to lose its way (mm.38–43).

1T applies *Pa* to triadic arpeggios in the horns, creating a hunting topic (m.52); *2T* (m.78) prepares *S*. The secondary area (in A major) has four themes: *1S*, a cantabile violin melody similar in character to those of the first movement (m.94); *2S* (m.114) and *3S* (m.122), both of which serve cadential functions to *1S*; and *4S*, which converts a running eighth-note pattern from *3S* into a melody (m.132). *K* (m.144) repeats *Pb* sequentially; like several other motives, it is accompanied by a drone.

The development opens with an orchestral unison, and the key shifts to the flattened submediant B-flat major (m.153). A new theme appears in the woodwinds, accompanied in the strings by a rhythmic gesture derived from *Pb;* the theme repeats a step higher. The rhythmic gesture migrates through the strings as C major becomes the dominant of F major. The second section of the development (m.209) reprises *1S* in F major and G major. *Pa* and *1Sa* combine in a sequential pattern that leads to the final section (m.233), which features *1T* in A major, and states *K* over a dominant pedal. Except for ornamental reorchestrations, the recapitulation proceeds normally (m.252). Gounod bypasses *K* and moves directly to the coda (m.364); beginning much like *T*, this final section rounds off the movement with *Pa* and *Pb*.

Pasdeloup's Société des Jeunes Artistes premiered the inner movements in February 1855 and gave a full performance of the symphony the next month. Audiences and critics raved over the new composition. Marie Escudier's review was typical:

> Sunday in the Salle Herz we found the good and true lovers of music. They came to hear the new work by M. Charles Gounod, a musician who will, without any doubt, find his name inscribed in the realm of symphonic music next to those of Haydn, Beethoven, and Mozart, if he continues along this path. . . .
>
> Hearing M. Gounod's score, it seemed to us that we were witnessing an aerial conversation, in which invisible spirits, strangers to the prosaic realities of earth, talked about a thousand joyous things, all stamped with idealism. . . . The last movement admirably concludes this score which—we say it sincerely, with our heart and mind—is one of the most remarkable to appear since Haydn, Mozart, and Beethoven.[16]

Adolphe Adam praised the middle movements in terms that became increasingly common in French critical discourse, especially after 1870: "This new composition should place [Gounod] at the highest level as a symphonist, and it would be a joy and glory for France to be able to oppose such a wise, pure, and inspired music to the ramblings of what one calls the modern German school."[17] Within little more than a year of its premiere, the First Symphony received eight performances in Paris.[18]

SYMPHONY NO. 2 IN E-FLAT MAJOR

Inspired by the success of the First Symphony, Gounod promptly set about composing a sequel: "[The First Symphony] was so well received that I wrote another for the same society.

It too achieved a certain success."[19] The Second Symphony is more elaborate than its predecessor. Whereas the First exudes the tunefulness and charm associated with mid-century French lyric writing, the Second, while not ignoring those qualities, sounds more "developed"—i.e., more "Germanic." Beethoven's "Eroica" Symphony appears to be the model, not least in the choice of key. Here and there one also hears echoes of Mendelssohn and perhaps Schumann. The emphasis upon dotted rhythms and homorhythmic orchestration recalls such works as the latter's "Spring" Symphony, though it is not clear whether in 1855 Gounod was familiar with Schumann's symphonies (he could not have heard them live in Paris, as the symphonies did not appear there in concert until a performance of the "Rhenish" in 1857). As before, though, Gounod creates momentum by repetition and sequence rather than motivic development; he does so in fact almost to excess. The orchestration remains the same, except for two added horns, but it sounds fuller owing to the dense texture. In keeping with the weightier character of the new symphony, Gounod sets the inner sections as true slow and Scherzo movements instead of the light *divertissements* of the earlier work.

By insisting upon an earnest atmosphere and sober working out of themes, the first movement (Adagio–Allegro agitato) somewhat self-consciously betrays its desire to fit into the Germanic tradition. Beethovenian energy permeates the rhythm and dynamics, as in the dotted and double-dotted gestures that figure throughout *P, T,* and *K.*

In its French-Overture style and serious mien, including references to *ombra* topics, the solemn introduction recalls those of notable predecessors such as Mozart's Symphony in E-flat Major (K. 543) and Beethoven's Second Symphony. Even more Beethovenian are passages such as mm.5–9, where the first violins trace a gently descending motive over undulating motions in the lower strings. *P* contains three motives (mm.18, 35, 46). Two elements unite them: the fanfarish double-dotted rhythm of *1Pa* (Example XVI/2) and continuous ascending sequences that extend to a-flat''' by the end of *3P* (m.64). *T* evokes the "Eroica": *1T* (m.66) restates *1P fortissimo* and *2T* (m.78) culminates in a hemiola passage. Consisting again largely of sequences, *T* traverses remote harmonic areas before settling on the secondary dominant; *3T,* for instance, begins with a sudden lurch to an F-sharp-diminished harmony (m.90).

S (m.106), a lyrical melody that abandons dotted rhythm for the first time in the symphony, suggests the world of French ballet, particularly in its lightly textured orchestration. Gounod sets it in the expected B-flat major but, as in the First Symphony, he refers fleetingly to other keys through flavorful turns of harmony. The melody progresses through phrase acceleration, moving from eight-bar to one-bar units; sequential repetitions resume in the latter, reaching to f'''. *1K* (m.138), a variant of *1Pa*, features thick homophonic scoring and a closing hemiola. *2K* combines the rhythmic motion of *1Pa* with the opening gesture of *S* (m.154).

Much larger than its counterpart in the First Symphony, the development (m.168) falls into five sections, all based on *1P* and *S*, especially the combination of *1Pb* and *Sa*. Its sequential repetitions extend into distant tonal regions, including E major. The recapitulation arrives unambiguously with a tutti statement of *1P, fff* (m.288); it then proceeds normally. Like the development, the short coda juxtaposes *1Pb* and *Sa* (m.430).

Gounod sets the Larghetto non troppo in *A–B–A* form in B-flat major. *A* shows the composer's indebtedness to German Romantic lyricism and *B* his affinities with his own theatrical tradition. *1A,* a leisurely and somewhat Schumannesque cantabile, appears twice in the strings (m.7). The three gentle motives of *2A* (m.30) serve a closing function, all reinforcing the tonic.

EXAMPLE XVI/2 Gounod. Symphony No. 2/1, mm.18–34.

B signals a change of mood (m.45): its light-hearted sixteenth-note melody broken by thirty-second rests recalls the kind of theme one might hear in a contemporary *opéra-comique* or post-Rossinian Italian opera. Gounod combines the final segment of *B* with the first section of *2A* (m.72). He reorchestrates the reprise of *1A,* moving the melody to the woodwinds (m.85), and adds a running sixteenth-note commentary in the strings. To *2A* (m.108) he adds the lighter *B* as a countermotive, thus juxtaposing the modules again. The movement ends without a coda.

The Scherzo, in the mediant key of G minor, displays affinities with Mendelssohn's "elfin" music: it is fast (notated 3/4 but better understood as 6/4), light, and moves principally in staccato articulations. As in the First Symphony, Gounod adopts the unusual form *a* :‖: *b c* :‖. *A* consists of a two-part melody: the antecedent phrase moves in a series of dotted-half notes while the consequent forms a descending pattern in faster rhythm. The antecedent repeats a third higher, answered this time by a hunting topic in the woodwinds.

B (m.33) begins like *a* but gives way to a stormy sequential motive whose climax is capped off with a quick chromatic descent. This leads to *c,* a lyrical Mendelssohnian melody (m.97). An extended coda (m.129) brings back the dotted half notes and hunting topic of *a* as well as *c.* The Trio (m.189), in G major, affects a rustic sound: violas sustain a bagpipe-like drone for much of its length, especially the second half. As in the First Symphony, Gounod favors woodwinds over strings, though here he scores the Trio for full ensemble. This time the composer adopts the traditional *a* :‖: *b a* :‖ form.

Following the tempestuous Scherzo, the playful Finale comes as a surprise. Gounod returns to the more easygoing mood of the First Symphony. At the same time, paradoxically, this movement has the most elaborate development of either symphony as well as some surprising turns of key. Three elements appear throughout the movement: the rhythm and contour of *1Pa* (a descending leap followed by a melodic turn, m.1), the ♩♪ ♩♪♪ rhythm of *1Pb* (m.5), and the running sixteenth-note figures at the end of *P^k* (first seen in mm.47–54). *2P* (m.17) and *P^k* (m.33) are based on *1P.* Gounod assigns the whole of *P* to the violins, which play softly throughout; the first *forte* appears only with *1T* (m.55). A mock fanfare briefly replaces the rhythms of *P* but a variant of the *1Pb* rhythm returns whimsically in *2T* (m.67).

S makes a lyrical contrast. *1S* appears innocuously in woodwinds over runs in the strings (m.83), recalling the spirit of the First Symphony, as well as this one's *I/S.* *2S* (m.91) reintroduces the rhythm of *1Pb,* while *3S* continues its thought (m.113). Runs derived from *P^k* appear throughout *S.* A cadential motive closes the area (m.123). *1K* (m.135) is related to *1T,* and *2K* creates a bridge, again with runs in the style of *P^k* (m.147).

The development (m.154) contains two large sections, separated by a grand pause. The first attends wholly to *1P,* especially *1Pa,* which appears unexpectedly in the mediant key of G major, followed by playful sequential repetitions and a bass ascent. Part two consists of three statements of *1S* (m.223), followed by a brief return to *1Pa.* The retransition takes place over a dominant pedal (m.255).

Although Gounod thickens the texture slightly, the recapitulation proceeds as expected, save for a momentary disruption at the start of *1S* when the key shifts abruptly to a very remote B major (m.355). The tonic quickly reasserts itself and the movement continues as if nothing had happened. The recapitulation ends with another grand pause. The coda begins similarly to the development, this time in A-flat major (m.435). *1Pa* and *1Sa* again make up the basic content. Of note is the Schumannesque emphasis on tutti dotted rhythms, just before the entrance of *1Sa* (mm.460–66).

Pasdeloup and his orchestra premiered the Scherzo in April 1855 and the whole symphony in January 1856. It received the same warm reception as its predecessor, especially among conservative critics. Typical is the review of "P.S." (Édouard Monnais), who commended both composer and conductor—the former for avoiding a modern sound in his work and the latter for performing it:

> A new symphony by Gounod was the principal attraction of this concert and, as they say, its *pièce de résistance.* . . . This new symphony, in E-flat major, announces an undeniable progress. It is not only a youthful inspiration, filled to the brim with memories and the study of past masters; it is the work of a master who begins to feel his power and seeks only to be himself. It consists of four movements: an allegro, a larghetto, a scherzo, and a finale. These four movements, broadly treated, developed, and managed with all the resources that imagination borrows from science and from contemplation of the masterpieces of art, forms a whole which is imposing in its totality and charming in its details. . . .
>
> What we praise Gounod for above all is to have the good sense to write symphonies and not wish to go further than Beethoven; to have understood that beyond was the abyss and that it is much better to step back a little and draw near again to Haydn and Mozart—to walk forward and lose oneself in time. Because we don't think it possible to surpass the Symphony in C Minor and the "Pastorale," must we then renounce the symphony? Then we would have to renounce everything, because today there is hardly any virgin ground left in the arts where someone is not exposed to the chance of colliding with Trajan's columns, the cupolas of St. Peter's, the obelisks and the pyramids. When listening to Gounod's symphony, we were more than ever disposed to sing the praises of the Société de Jeunes Artistes, which moreover played it very well. We said to ourselves, "Here is a truly honorable and beautiful work, which would not be known, which perhaps would not even have been born, if the Société de Jeunes Artistes did not exist." Indeed, let us suppose that Gounod had considered offering this score to the venerable Société des Concerts [du Conservatoire], the musical necropolis: God knows with what disdain he would have been received and shown the door![20]

Both symphonies, or portions thereof, appeared frequently in concerts throughout the 1850s and 60s, though their success would be eclipsed three years later when *Faust* premiered. By 1900 they had fallen out of favor: Tiersot classed Gounod's symphonies with those of Félicien David and Henri Reber as representatives of the "fausse direction" that the genre followed in France in the first half of the century—works composed with honorable intentions but totally beholden to the past and ultimately deserving of the "quite justified oblivion" into which they had fallen.[21] In Gounod's case, at least, oblivion is an unjust fate which happily has been reversed today by a proliferation of recordings.

LITTLE SYMPHONY

As his career as a composer of opera and oratorio blossomed, Gounod left the symphony behind; in 1885, however, as a favor to flautist and conductor Paul Taffanel and the Société de Musique de Chambre pour Instruments à Vent, he wrote a *Petite Symphonie* in B-flat major for wind nonet (flute, 2 oboes, 2 clarinets, 2 horns, 2 bassoons). Most characteristics of the earlier symphonies reappear in miniature, as Gounod again produces a tuneful and innocent-sounding score proceeding mostly by sequential repetition.

After a slow introduction, the first movement (Adagio et Allegretto) unfolds in sonata form with simple, folk-like themes that may reflect the influence of *opéra-comique,* although as before this does not preclude excursions to distant keys such as A major. The Andante cantabile, in E-flat major, is essentially an aria for flute in *A–B–A* form. The Scherzo again follows a hunt topic within an unconventional structure (a :||: b :||: c :||); the rustic Trio contains many drones. The Finale (Allegretto) comprises a short introduction and sonata of Mendelssohnian cast. P and S are strongly related: P takes up most of the development, while the recapitulation, to compensate, starts with S. Overall, this seems the weakest movement, somewhat nondescript compared with the others.

Georges Bizet

The death of Georges Bizet (1838–1875) at age thirty-seven deprived the world of a major genius (Plate B16) who achieved full maturity only in his last work, *Carmen* (1875). From the beginning, he set out to find success in opera: when his friend Saint-Saëns suggested that they devote themselves to concert music since the theaters were closed to them, Bizet replied, "That's easy for you to say, [but] I'm not made for the symphony; I need the theater, I can do nothing without it."[22] Bizet underestimated himself, for he had something significant to contribute not only to the symphony (Table XVI/2) but also to the piano (the enchanting *Jeux d'enfants* for piano duet—better known in its shortened version as an orchestral suite—and the *Variations chromatiques* for solo keyboard). In addition, suites from his operas and incidental music (*L'Arlésienne*) remain favorites in the concert hall.

SYMPHONY IN C MAJOR

Bizet wrote his first symphony (Plate B17) at the age of seventeen in 1855, the same year Gounod penned his second symphony. He suppressed the piece and never spoke of it; his widow gave the manuscript to Reynaldo Hahn, who deposited it in the library of the Conservatoire in 1933. D. C. Parker, Bizet's first English-language biographer, brought the symphony to the attention of Felix Weingartner, who conducted the first performance in Basel on February 26, 1935, eighty years after its creation. Gounod served as friend, mentor, and even surrogate father to the young Bizet, who did several transcriptions for the older man, including a four-hand arrangement of the First Symphony.[23] Bizet's motives for writing his own symphony—whether to capitalize on Gounod's success or attempt an *exercice d'école*, perhaps at Gounod's suggestion—remain a mystery, but his reasons for concealing it require little guesswork. Bizet's symphony contains numerous audible resemblances to Gounod's composition, and the young composer most likely thought twice about testing the well-earned reputation of Parisian audiences for seeking out and denouncing perceived points of imitation in new works. It is not known if Gounod ever saw the symphony.

Bizet's score requires the same forces as Gounod's, adding only two extra horns (as did Gounod in his next symphony); it also replicates the earlier work's manner of scoring, in which string and woodwind families remain largely separate. From its opening bars, Bizet proclaims his debts, for his $1P$ is clearly modeled on Gounod's; in addition, both themes appear at the outset, without an introduction (Example XVI/3a-b). Some of the older master's other themes, like $I/3T$ and the extension of I/S, also find resonance in Bizet's first movement. Both composers develop their material by repetition instead of fragmentation, although Bizet relies less heavily on sequence. Thematic affinities also figure in the Finale, as both composers make use of "galloping" motives (two sixteenth notes followed by an eighth), and the melody and pizzicato bass of Bizet's IV/S seem to derive from Gounod's I/S.

Whereas the correspondences in the outer movements mostly concern similarities in thematic material, those in the inner movements are structural, as Bizet copies Gounod's unconventional forms almost exactly. Both second movements follow an *A–B–A* pattern in which *B* consists of a lyrical section followed by a fugue; its subject derives from *A*, the instruments enter in the same order, and the key returns to the tonic before the fugue finishes.

TABLE XVI/2
The Symphonies of Georges Bizet

Key	Date	Title	Movements	Instrumentation	Comments
C Major	1855	Symphony in C Major	1. Allegro vivo ¢ (585 m.) 2. Adagio 9/8 (114 m.) A minor 3. Scherzo and Trio: Allegro vivace 3/4 (269 m.) G major, C major 4. Allegro vivace 2/4 (446 m.)	Full plus 2 Hr.	Written at age 17; modeled on Gounod's First Symphony. Suppressed by the composer. First performance: Basel, conducted by Felix Weingartner on February 26, 1935. Published in Vienna: Universal, 1935.
	1859	Symphony			Began twice; destroyed December 1859.
C Major	1860–68, rev. 1871	Symphony in C Major: *Roma*	1. Andante tranquillo 4/4—Allegro agitato ma non troppo presto 6/8—Andante 4/4 (377 m.) C major/minor 2. Allegretto vivace 3/4 (371 m.) A-flat major 3. Andante molto 4/4 (97 m.) F major 4. Allegro vivacissimo 2/4 (514 m.) C minor/major	Grand plus 2 Harps	Written over a period of years; each movement originally intended to depict a specific Italian city. Described both as a symphony and concert suite. First partial performance (Scherzo only): Paris, Concerts Populaires, conducted by Jules Pasdeloup on January 11, 1863. Second partial performance (the other three movements): Paris, Concerts Populaires, conducted by Jules Pasdeloup on February 28, 1869. First complete performance: Paris, Concerts Populaires, conducted by Jules Pasdeloup on October 31, 1880 (five years after Bizet's death). Published in Paris: Choudens, 1880, under the title *Roma, troisième suite de concert.*

EXAMPLE XVI/3A   Gounod. Symphony No. 1/i, mm. 1–6.

The reprise of *A* is shortened and intensified. Both movements are in a minor key—Gounod's in the parallel, Bizet's the relative—and *B* is in the relative major to *A*. Bizet's Scherzo repeats Gounod's ‖: *a* :‖: *b c* :‖ scheme. The Trio is rustic, with drones, and scored for a trio of woodwinds; it relates melodically to the Scherzo.[24]

As he does with Gounod, Mendelssohn casts a prominent shadow in the second and especially the fourth movements. *IV/P* employs numerous elfin characteristics: light and fleet sixteenth notes, staccato woodwinds, soft dynamics. The sudden changes of mode, the languorous oboe melody of the slow movement, and the rambunctious spirit of the Scherzo suggest the additional influence of Schubert's "Great" C Major Symphony; Bizet had little opportunity to know this work—it appeared only once in a Parisian concert in 1851 (the next performance did not take place until 1873) and he did not own a score—so the resemblance may be fortuitous.[25]

As befits the composer's youth, the Symphony in C Major exudes infectious energy and good spirits: Gounod charms the ear but Bizet excites it. The symphony contains many passages of striking orchestration: first violins tend to dominate, but the young master reserves

EXAMPLE XVI/3B   Bizet. Symphony in C Major/1, mm.1–13.

a number of attractive moments for the woodwinds. Like his mentor, Bizet indulges in un-expected and memorable turns of harmony: the inflections of the relative minors of the dom-inant and tonic in *I/S;* the modal and pseudo-oriental touches in the aforementioned oboe melody; the "bagpipe" drones of the Scherzo; and the unprepared intrusion of a distantly third-related key in *IV/1S.* While doing honor to a composer of any age, this sparkling sym-phony is an especially remarkable effort for a teenager embarking on his first large-scale orchestral work.

In the exposition of the first movement (Allegro vivo), similar gestures unite diverse ideas: *1P, 1T, 3T, S^k,* and *K* all move by triadic leaps and sequential patterns, in staccato artic-ulations and upbeat-oriented rhythms. In addition, *1Pa* closes the *P, T,* and *S* areas. *1P* con-sists of a fast triadic ascent for full orchestra (*a,* mm.1–4) followed by an equally swift descent for the strings (*b,* mm.5–9) and a stepwise one in the woodwinds in a similar rhythm to *a* (*c,* mm.10–17). The fanfarish *2P* (m.33) serves as a dominant prolongation, over which a pattern in the violins climbs sequentially while the phrase rhythm accelerates from two-measure to one-measure units. *1P* returns, extended, as *c* migrates through a series of seventh chords

543

EXAMPLE XVI/3B   (*continued*)

around the circle of fifths before closing in the tonic. Bizet accompanies *c* with a pulsating drum pedal, a gesture which recurs throughout the movement.

Resembling *1P* in rhythm, *1T* (m.86) migrates to the dominant; *2T* (m.101), derived from *2P*, confirms the move. Two more themes reinforce the new key: *3T* (m.113), a close relation of *1P*, and *4T* (m.125), which features another drum pedal. In contrast to the propulsive *P* and *T* areas, *S* offers a lyrical respite—an extended cantabile for oboe with flavorful forays into the relative minor (m.153). *K* returns to the style of *1P* and *1T* (m.225).

The three sections of the development reprise exposition material in new keys. *1Pa* appears in the third-related key of E major (m.245); a horn call ushers in *Sa* in A major; and the whole passage repeats a fourth higher. In the second section, *3T* moves sequentially from the secondary dominant D major to the dominant of F major (m.293). The final section begins with a fuller statement of *S* in F major (m.317) but it is interrupted by *3T*, which leads the harmony back to D major; *2P* confirms that key, maintaining a tonic pedal (m.341). A new motive in the retransition imitates *1Pb* over a pulsating bass and dominant pedal (m.357). Bizet shortens the recapitulation (m.383) by omitting *2T* and *3T* and abbreviating *S*. Like Gounod's symphony, the movement ends by restating *1Pa*.

EXAMPLE XVI/4 Bizet. Symphony in C Major/2, mm.9–14.

As mentioned, the Adagio (A minor) takes its form directly from Gounod's second movement, though Bizet's is more of a true slow movement. In the eight-measure introduction, an upward leap in the woodwinds grows from a third to an octave while the horns and strings produce a chain of sustained chords somewhat reminiscent of the opening of Mendelssohn's *A Midsummer Night's Dream* Overture—a tribute from one precocious seventeen-year-old to another. The upward leap launches a lyrical A-minor melody in a slow 9/8 which demonstrates Bizet's awareness of the vogue for exotic-sounding melodies (m.9; Example XVI/4). Its "orientalisms" include the assignment of the melody to the beguiling timbre of the oboe; a tinge of modality as chromatic motions and reiterations of the dominant degree deceptively suggest a tonic of E with a lowered seventh; and thirty-second turns that faintly suggest the microtonal intonations of a *muezzin*. At times the melody migrates to other woodwinds but always remains in that family; the strings play a strictly accompanimental role, mostly in pizzicato.

As the woodwinds dominated *A*, *B* (m.32) belongs to the strings. The key changes to C major. The section opens with an extended and expressive theme in the violins, rather similar in character to the string melody in the Act III *Entr'acte* of *Carmen*. The range is high, extending to b-flat'''. The subsequent fugue (m.59) demonstrates the risks of following a model too closely: the subject, based on the opening leap of *A*, enters abruptly and somewhat maladroitly; and the ambiance, following Gounod, suggests a processional, which does not fit the mood established by *A* (whereas Gounod's fugue sounds natural in its setting). The key shifts from C major back to A minor. The end of the fugue elides with a reprise of the introduction.

Bizet shortens the repeat of *A* (m.86) but intensifies it slightly by adding sixteenth-note pizzicato descending lines in the violins against the melody. The coda begins with a plaintive chromatic line (m.97); the Mendelssohnian chords return, this time with an oboe descant. The movement closes by reprising the first strain of *A*.

The energetic and effervescent Scherzo (Allegro vivace, G major) recalls Schubert, but an even closer model might be the "Merry Gathering of the Country Folk" from Beethoven's "Pastoral" Symphony: both movements open with descending triadic staccato quarter notes in 3/4 followed by loud dotted halves (later, in Beethoven's case); in addition, both Trios feature drones. So does Gounod's, but overall his authority seems weaker here since Bizet's movement is a true Scherzo and not a Minuet, even though the younger composer once again follows his mentor's idiosyncratic form.

The Scherzo is distinguished by alternations of meter, topics, and phrase lengths. The seven-measure antecedent of *A* suggests a hunt in 6/4 (though notated in 3/4), while the nine-measure consequent implies a march in 3/4. *B* (m.18) pits the woodwinds against the strings in pulsating rhythms not unlike those of the first movement; it features rapid changes of dynamics.

C makes a lyrical contrast in octave violins (m.93); with its long breadth and sudden dynamic interruptions, this theme particularly recalls Schubert's "Great" C Major Symphony.

The Trio evokes Scottish bagpiping by emphasizing open-fifth drones in the middle strings and simple triadic movement (as opposed to a real melody) in the woodwinds. The form again is unusual: ‖: *a* :‖: *a'* :‖. The first section (m.173) is in C major; the greatly expanded *a'* begins in F major and returns to C via a long excursion in E major. At the end Bizet, like Gounod, inserts the instruction, "da capo il Minuetto."

Bizet's Finale (Allegro vivace, C major) has three principal components: *P,* moving in frenetic sixteenth-note rhythms, often on repeated notes; *T,* a "galloping" rhythm, perhaps an inheritance from Gounod's *IV/P;* and *1S,* the theme that dominates the development. Fast reiterations of the dominant degree introduce *P* (m.5), stated by the first violins with occasional contributions from the woodwinds. An elfin theme, it consists mostly of four-bar phrases—another Mendelssohnian characteristic—with occasional breaks.

T, a woodwind theme (m.37), consists of fanfarish dotted rhythms (*Ta*) followed by the "galloping" gesture (*Tb*). Once again, *1S* makes a lyrical contrast: set in the dominant G major, Bizet states it twice in the first violins (the second time an octave higher) with a brief parenthesis in the mediant B-flat major during the second statement (m.89). *2S* recalls *Tb,* while *3S* features antiphonal exchanges between the violins (mm.131, 139). *K* combines the rhythm of *Tb* with the opening gesture of *P* (m.159).

The structure of the development resembles that of the first movement. The first section (m.176) contains partial statements of *P* and *S,* first in E-flat major and B major respectively, then in B major and E major. The next section (m.221) juxtaposes *P* in the strings with *Tb* in the woodwinds as the key moves sequentially from E major to the dominant of D. In the third section, *S* begins in D major (m.251) but changes suddenly to F major. The retransition (m.275) sets up the dominant via *Tb.* Again as in the first movement, the recapitulation is fairly straightforward. Bizet trims *1S* but preserves its mediant change (C major to E-flat major). A slightly extended *K* concludes Bizet's symphony, a fresh and vigorous work that for all its youthful spontaneity shows a composer who has full possession of the language of the Classical symphony but already speaks with a distinctive voice.

SYMPHONY IN C MAJOR: *ROMA*

In subsequent years, Bizet became self-conscious and insecure about his aptitude for creating absolute music. He began and aborted work on a symphony at least twice during his years at the Villa Médicis, where he lived after winning the Prix de Rome in 1857. There survives another symphony, and it has a singularly tortured history. Its genesis dates to 1860 when Bizet, still in the Eternal City, conceived of a musical souvenir of his Italian sojourn, a panoramic overview in symphonic form:

> I have in mind a symphony which I should like to call *Rome, Venice, Florence, and Naples.* That works out wonderfully: Venice will be my andante, Rome my first movement, Florence my scherzo, and Naples my finale. It's a new idea, I think.[26]

Bizet intended to submit the symphony as his third and final *envoi de Rome*—we recall Tiersot's description of the symphony as the culminating exercise for occupants of the Villa Médicis—but the illness and death of his mother in 1861 allowed him to finish only the Scherzo as well as a funeral march which he may or may not have intended as part of the symphony (the theme of the march later found its way into his opera *Les Pêcheurs de perles*). The Académie praised the Scherzo, as did the audience at a private performance at the amateur Cercle de l'Union Artistique, better known as the Jockey Club.[27] A hearing at the Concerts Populaires in 1863 received a much cooler response—Saint-Saëns, who was present, complained that the piece was "badly performed [and] badly listened to, succumbing to general inattention and indifference"[28]—but the critics reacted kindly.

In 1866 Bizet completed his Italian symphony but two years later he changed the first movement from a theme and variations to an *A–B–A,* retaining only *P;* he also revised the slow movement by injecting a theme from the Finale into its center. He became dissatisfied with the last movement but decided not to change it ("The Finale of my symphony is hateful, and I can't face replacing it. What a profession!").[29] Pasdeloup premiered the work in 1869 but without the offending Scherzo; he promised Bizet that as soon as the public embraced the new movements he would "slip in the Scherzo like a letter into the letter-box."[30] To make the work more palatable to his visually minded audience, Pasdeloup entitled it *Fantaisie symphonique, Souvenirs de Rome* and gave each movement an evocative title—*Une chasse dans la forêt d'Ostie, Une procession,* and *Carnaval à Rome,* respectively. It is not known if Bizet participated in this contrivance or if he even approved of it.

The movements received a more agreeable though by no means overwhelming response. Bizet's satisfied reaction says much about the relationship between composer and public in mid-century Paris: "My symphony went very well. First movement: a round of applause, a second round of hisses, third round, a catcall. Andante: a round of applause. Finale: great effect, applause three times repeated, hisses, three or four catcalls. In short, a success."[31] He was not being ironic: as Émile Paladilhe wrote in a letter from the same period, Pasdeloup's audience "is composed of subscribers who want only Classical music and who raise an uproar over every new name"; therefore, "a composer must want to be hissed if he is going to be played by Pasdeloup." For all that, Paladilhe concluded that the benefits of having one's music heard outweighed the disadvantages.[32]

The performance received almost no reviews. Only the *Revue et gazette musicale* took notice, praising the orchestration but finding the ideas derivative:

> In this new work . . . there is a very real talent, undeniable skill, and above all a very lively feeling for orchestration. As for the ideas there is nothing absolutely new about them, although none of them is banal. Nor is the style really personal; M. Bizet still remembers the masters too well.[33]

Bizet made some final revisions in 1871, finally bringing the eleven-year composition of this symphony to an end. Despite efforts to secure another performance, he never heard it again. Under the title *Roma, Symphonie en quatre parties,* Pasdeloup unveiled the complete work—with the Scherzo and without the programmatic titles—in October 1880, five years after Bizet's death. The same year Choudens published the work as *Roma, troisième suite de concert* (the first two being the *L'Arlésienne* suites); he omitted most of the titles but retained *Carnaval* for the Finale. Tiersot concurred with Choudens's nomenclature, describing *Roma* as the first in a distinguished line of picturesque orchestral suites undertaken by French composers who sought to create concert music independent of the theater but free of the formal obligations of the symphony.[34]

Bizet always referred to *Roma* as "ma symphonie," conveniently ignoring its predecessor. Structural anomalies notwithstanding, most notably the absence of any sonata-form movement, *Roma* can comfortably be analyzed as an abstract symphony, as the composer intended. Despite its later date, however, the work pales in comparison to Bizet's adolescent symphony: banal themes—*pace* the *Revue et gazette musicale*—awkward transitions, and rambling constructions, especially in the first movement, offset many excellent moments. As one might expect, given the obvious precedent of the "Italian" Symphony, Mendelssohn exerts a strong influence (again), while Gounod's voice is much less in evidence.

Bizet scored *Roma* for grand orchestra plus two harps. Again C major serves as tonic. The first movement (Andante tranquillo—Allegro agitato ma non troppo presto) opens with a chorale in 4/4 meter: this passage recalls *Tannhäuser*—the tumultuous Paris premiere of which Bizet attended in 1861—but Winton Dean points to *Der Freischütz* and, closer to home, Gounod's *Faust* as the more likely progenitors.[35] The through-composed *B*, Allegro agitato (6/8, C minor, m.59), gives the illusion of an exposition followed by a development. *P* evolves from the opening chorale. This highly dramatic section proceeds as if driven by an unspecified program; instead of the "Italian," Bizet seems here to have in mind the stormier Mendelssohn of the "Scottish" Symphony. Several *T* themes and a lyrical *S* in A-flat major follow. The succeeding "development" ironically contains more thematic fragmentation and manipulation than the true sonata movements of the earlier Symphony in C Major ever do; Bizet also introduces new themes. At the climax, the prevailing diminished harmonies give way to the Neapolitan key of D-flat major, presented in a "celestial" style. The movement closes with a reprise of the chorale in the tonic (m.348). Bizet took pride in the novel form he created: "[It] bears no resemblance to any known first movement. It is new, and I count on a good effect."[36] The score bears out only the first half of his boast: the excessive theatricality, occurring without any evident musical or programmatic justification, vitiates much of the "good effect."

The Allegro vivace is the unfortunate Scherzo of 1863. It falls into regular Scherzo and Trio form in A-flat major, although the Scherzo is through-composed. This vivacious piece opens with a brief fugato, featuring a prominent turn gesture in the subject. Bizet notates the movement in 3/4 but it mostly proceeds in 6/4. Only the second theme breaks the pattern, consisting largely of dotted half notes, many of them on repeated pitches (m.142). The Trio maintains the tonic and meter of the Scherzo; its melody is broad and lyrical, notable especially for its ♩₂♩ rhythms. The turn gesture from the Scherzo dominates the accompaniment.

The Andante molto, an *A–B–A* in F major, opens with a fine theme for the violins. Dean identifies *A* as the melody to an earlier song, "Le Doute," printed posthumously by Choudens; he speculates that the publisher may have added this theme to the movement himself.[37] The melody of *B* (m.37) contrasts sharply; set in C major and 12/8 meter, the most notable feature of this woodwind-and-harp theme is a deceptive cadence on E major. This is the melody Bizet borrowed from the Finale; ironically, it proves more effective here than in its original setting. The composer fools the listener by reprising part of *A* and interrupting it with a second statement of *B*, thus creating a false recapitulation. *A* returns for real afterward, reinforced by a countermotive (m.75). The movement ends abruptly, producing—presumably by accident—a sense of inconclusiveness.

The Finale (Allegro vivacissimo) belongs to the class of splashy, festive conclusions popular in orchestral suites and rhapsodies. Bizet's model seems to be the saltarello of Mendelssohn's "Italian" Symphony. Like the opening movement, the Finale hints at sonata form, but it conforms more to an *A–B–A* structure. In C minor, *A* contains four themes: (1) the saltarello theme; (2) an Italianate folk-like theme; (3) a jaunty motive in G major; and (4) *III/B*, in E-flat major and speeded up to the point of vapidity. *B* (m.228) is built from fragments of the preceding themes, especially the third; it functions somewhat like a development. *A* returns in m.325: Theme 1 is heard in B minor and 2 in D major; Bizet proceeds directly to Theme 4, and the key returns to the C-major tonic. A transition leads to a blustery coda based on Theme 4 which disfigures a mostly engaging and excellently scored movement.

An uneven piece in sum, *Roma* nevertheless contains enough good moments to merit occasional hearings.

Camille Saint-Saëns

Camille Saint-Saëns (1835–1921) (Plate B18) began life as a phenomenally gifted child prodigy who could read, write, and compose by the age of three. By 1846 the ten-year-old was giving public performances of sonatas and concertos of Beethoven, Mozart, and others; at one of these concerts he reportedly offered to play any Beethoven sonata—from memory—as an encore.[38] In his early years he championed Liszt, Berlioz, Schumann, and Wagner at a time when most Frenchmen considered them dangerous subversives. By the 1890s, however, he had become a bitter reactionary, vehemently denouncing the music of Franck, d'Indy, Massenet, and the French Wagnerians. (Although he continued to admire Wagner's music, he feared—not without cause, as it turned out—that the German composer's popularity would smother native talent.) Saint-Saëns's enemies retaliated in kind, dismissing him as a curmudgeonly creator of antiquated music that was all technique and no substance. Debussy, the subject of Saint-Saëns's harshest attacks, avenged himself with this barb: "I detest sentimentality! But I would prefer not to remember that he is named Camille Saint-Saëns!"[39]

Along with Édouard Lalo, Saint-Saëns became the most passionate advocate of symphonic music in France during the period of the Second Empire. Although his personal involvement with the form was relatively short-lived, he completed five symphonies, four of which appeared before he turned twenty-five (Table XVI/3). After 1860, he seems to have lost interest in the genre and concentrated on symphonic poems (against considerable opposition he created the first corpus of such pieces in France), concertos, chamber music, and opera. A quarter-century later, he returned briefly to compose his most famous symphony (the "Organ") and then turned his back on the genre for good.

SYMPHONY IN A MAJOR (RATNER 159)

After initial abortive efforts, Saint-Saëns, like his fellow adolescent Bizet, apparently composed his First Symphony as an *exercice d'école* and then disowned it: written in 1850, the work premiered only in 1974, 124 years later. As one would expect, the symphony abounds in insufficiently digested influences of previous masters and contains numerous weaknesses; but it also possesses considerable charm, especially in the inner movements. Not as finished or ebullient as Bizet's Symphony in C major, it is still a remarkable feat for a fifteen-year-old.

The opening movement (Poco Adagio–Allegro vivace) follows textbook sonata form, as a result of which the ideas—which are not always distinguished and suffer at times from clumsy construction—seem simply to fall into their expected places.[40] A short introduction opens with a motive incorporating *Pa,* followed by an *ombra* section based on an F-major[7] chord voiced to suggest a diminished harmony on A. Most of the first movement derives from *Pa* (m.27), which begins with a transposed but conspicuous woodwind imitation of the famous opening of *IV/P* of Mozart's "Jupiter" Symphony. *T* (m.49) sounds like a second primary theme; based on *Pb,* it converts the descending seventh leap of that motive to fifths and sixths. Saint-Saëns awkwardly tries his hand at Haydnesque wit when he disrupts *S* (m.73) with three progressively shorter grand pauses. *S^k* (m.93) and *K* (m.102), derived from *Pa* and *T* respectively, restore the momentum, asserting E major firmly.

S and *Pa* make up most of the rather overdramatic development. Two statements of *S* (m.125) lead to a turbulent sequential passage that traverses the circle of fifths (m.159). The final section (m.179) prolongs the dominant with repetitions of *Pa* that become increasingly

TABLE XVI/3
The Symphonies of Camille Saint-Saëns

Opus	Ratner	Key	Date	Title	Movements	Instrumentation	Comments
	154	B-flat Major	ca. 1848	Symphony	1. Adagio 2/4—Allegro molto 3/4 (247 m.) 2. Andante 3/4 E-flat major (fragment: 27 m.)	Full	Autograph title, added by the composer as an adult: "Symphonie inachevée (13 ans)" ("Unfinished Symphony, written at age 13"). First movement complete, second movement breaks off after 27 measures. Manuscript at the Bibliothèque Nationale, Paris.
	155	D Major	ca. 1850	Symphony in D Major	1. Andante con moto 4/4—Vivace assai 6/8 (fragment: 195 m.)	Full	Autograph title, added by the composer as an adult: "Symphonie inachevée . . . (probablement écrite vers la 15ᵉ année)" ("Unfinished Symphony . . . probably written about the age of 15.") Fragments break off in the middle of the exposition. Manuscript at the Bibliothèque Nationale, Paris.
	158	A Major	ca. 1850	Symphony in A Major (first movement)	1. Allegro non presto (fragment: 287 m.)	Small orchestra without brass or timpani	Autograph title, added by the composer as an adult: "Premier morceau de la Symphonie en LA [sic] (1ère version)" ("First version of the opening movement of the Symphony in A Major"). Thematic material is unrelated to the final version of the Symphony (see following entry), and the form is much more experimental. Fragments break off in the recapitulation. Manuscript at the Bibliothèque Nationale, Paris.
	159	A Major	1850	Symphony in A Major	1. Poco adagio C—Allegro vivace ¢ (304 m.) 2. Larghetto 3/4 (187 m.) D major 3. Allegro vivace 3/4—Trio 3/4 (94 m.) A major, D major 4. Finale: Allegro molto C (269 m.)	Full	Written at age 15, presumably as a school exercise. First performance: Paris, Orchestre Nationale, conducted by Jean Martinon in 1974. Published in Paris: Editions Françaises de Musique, 1974.
2	161	E-flat Major	1853	Symphony No. 1	1. Adagio—Allegro 4/4 (287 m.) 2. Marche-Scherzo: Allegretto scherzando ¢ (178 m.) G major 3. Adagio 9/8 (165 m.) E major 4. Finale: Allegro maestoso 4/4 (257 m.)	Grand+Picc., EH, Bclar., 2 Saxhorns, 2 Cornets, Timp., Cym., 4 Harps	Dedicated to François Seghers. First performance (presented anonymously): Paris, Société Sainte-Cécile, conducted by François Seghers on December 18, 1853. Published in Paris: Richault, 1855.

TABLE XVI/3 (*continued*)

Opus	Ratner	Key	Date	Title	Movements	Instrumentation	Comments
		C Minor	1854	Symphony	1. Lento assai 2/4	Full?	Fragments consist of an introduction and a portion of the exposition. The thematic material of the introduction later reused in the Fourth Piano Concerto in C Minor, Op. 44. Manuscript at the Bibliothèque Nationale, Paris.
	163	F Major	1856	Symphony in F Major "Urbs Roma"	1. Largo (4/4)—Allegro 6/4 (380 m.) 2. Molto vivace ¢ (400 m.) A minor/major 3. Moderato assai serioso 4/4 (209 m.) F minor 4. Poco Allegretto 3/4 (313 m.)	Full+Picc., 2 Hr.	First prize in composition contest sponsored by Société Sainte-Cécile of Bordeaux, 1857. First performance: Paris, Société des Jeunes Artistes, conducted by Jules Pasdeloup on February 15, 1857. Published in Paris: Editions Françaises de Musique, 1974.
55	164	A Minor	1859	Symphony No. 2	1. Allegro marcato (6/4)—Allegro appassionato ¢ (287 m.) 2. Adagio 3/8 (79 m.) E major 3. Scherzo and Trio: Presto 3/4 (369 m.) A major 4. Prestissimo 6/8 (562 m.) A major	Full+Picc., EH	Dedicated to Jules Pasdeloup. First performance: Paris, Société des Jeunes Artistes, conducted by Jules Pasdeloup on March 25, 1860. Published in Paris: Durand, 1878.
78	176	C Minor	1886	Symphony No. 3	1a. Adagio—Allegro moderato 6/8 (349 m.) 1b. Poco adagio 4/4 (127 m.) D-flat major 2a. Allegro moderato 6/8 (375 m.) 2b. Maestoso 6/4 (296 m.) C major	Grand+Picc., EH, Bclar., Cbssn., Tpt., Timp., Tri., Cym., Organ, Piano	"Organ" Symphony. Published score dedicated "to the memory of Franz Liszt." First performance: London, Orchestra of the Royal Philharmonic Society, conducted by Saint-Saëns on May 19, 1886. Published in Paris: Durand, 1886.

Partially based on Ratner/SAINT-SAËNS, pp. 255–316. Fallon/SYMPHONIES provides details on all these works, including the unfinished symphonies.

assertive and then die down, somewhat in the manner of the "Storm" movement of Beethoven's "Pastoral" Symphony. Saint-Saëns shortens the recapitulation (m.227) by omitting *T* but otherwise it proceeds as expected, save for some passages of quasi-Beethovenian syncopations (e.g., mm.238–43). The coda (m.284) reprises the retransition (based on *Pa*) over a static A-major harmony.

The lyrical theme that dominates the Larghetto (in D major and *A–B–A–C–A* form) is quite attractive, though again the piece suffers from gratuitous histrionics in the contrasting sections. The first violins carry all the principal material until the final section. Saint-Saëns unites the movement through a rhythmic gesture (♩ ♩ ♫) which appears in all sections, including both strains of *A*. The second strain stretches upward and culminates in a precipitous two-octave drop (mm.28–29). *B* (m.47)—notated *minore* as in Classic rondos or variations sets—is an impassioned passage in the tonic minor. *A* returns in D major (m.87; marked *maggiore*), now accompanied with countermotives. A tense mood returns in *C,* sounding all the more exaggerated because its beginning suggests a coda (m.107).[41] The woodwinds present the final statement of *A* (m.157); the texture in that family becomes very busy, like that of a Classic-period wind serenade. The violins take over again in the coda, based on the first strain of *A* (m.179).

The short and charming Scherzo (Allegro vivace, A major) recalls those of Haydn's London Symphonies, e.g., No. 99: both movements open with descending arpeggios in staccato quarter notes. Saint-Saëns reduces his orchestra to strings with flute and oboe soloists. Of special note is an enchanting and innocent-sounding episode for the wind soloists in F major (m.21). The Trio is in D major. While the material in the Scherzo tends downward, it reverses course in the Trio. In the first strain (m.52), the melody moves in dotted half notes. The second strain features hocket-like punctuations of a dominant ninth (m.75).

If the opening movement owed debts to Mozart, the sonata-form Finale (Allegro molto) pays homage to Haydn and Mendelssohn. *P* recalls but does not imitate *II/P* of the former's Symphony No. 102, though Saint-Saëns scores it in elfin orchestration. He maintains the soft and light ambiance until *K* (m.52). The development tends to ramble, courtesy of two new and undistinguished themes: the first derives from *P* (m.78), while the second (m.109) bears no relation to previous material. Only *P* and *T* return in the recapitulation (m.157). The coda (Presto, m.211) reiterates the final cadence with an almost Beethovenian energy but without the master's deftness. Despite the imperfect ending, the movement—and this callow symphony as a whole—remains alluring enough to merit occasional hearings.

SYMPHONY NO. 1 IN E-FLAT MAJOR OPUS 2 (RATNER 161)

Saint-Saëns's first numbered symphony dates from June-July 1853, when the composer was seventeen. He dedicated the work to François Seghers, the conductor of the Société Sainte-Cécile and a personal friend. Concerned that the program committee would balk at accepting a symphony by a little-known French composer—and a teenager at that—Seghers passed it off as the work of an unnamed German. The committee fell for the ruse, and Seghers premiered the still-anonymous work on December 18, 1853, with the following rubric in the concert notes: "The manuscript of this symphony was sent without the name of the composer to the committee which, after careful consideration, has not hesitated to have it performed."[42] Only later did Seghers reveal the composer's identity.

The First Symphony in E-flat major Opus 2 shows a significant improvement in form and orchestration over its predecessor. This time, Saint-Saëns learns not only from Classic and Classic-minded composers like Haydn, Mozart, and Mendelssohn, but from Romantic masters such as Beethoven, Schumann, and Berlioz. The key recalls both Beethoven's "Eroica" and Schumann's "Rhenish" Symphonies; the self-consciously "heroic" style and energetic power further link it to Beethoven, while the ceremonial mood of the first movement, rhapsodic style of the second, dense textures of the Finale, and proliferation of dotted rhythms throughout suggest the influence of Schumann. It is not clear how or when Saint-Saëns came to know the recently composed "Rhenish" Symphony, which did not appear in a Parisian concert until 1857, but the similarities between the two works seem too numerous to be coincidental. Perhaps he had access to a score through Seghers, who championed the German master; at any rate, by the end of the 1850s Saint-Saëns could play piano reductions of all of Schumann's symphonies from memory.[43] He acknowledged his debts when asked to authorize a revival in 1896: "It will be necessary to place in the papers that I wrote this work at the age of 17, which excuses reminiscences of Mendelssohn, Schumann, Félicien David, and also *Faust,* which was not composed until much later."[44] Additionally, the third and fourth movements bear the imprint of Berlioz's melodies and orchestration.

The heterogeneous influences and still-tentative development of Saint-Saëns's own voice militate against the cohesiveness of this otherwise delightful symphony. The second movement could easily serve as an *entr'acte* in a mid-century *opéra-comique* while the Finale splits into two ill-fitting halves: a picturesque march from the world of the *suite d'orchestre,* followed by a fugue. The key scheme is unusual: E-flat major, G major, E major, and E-flat major.

The first movement has the same instrumentation as the "Rhenish" Symphony—full orchestra plus two extra horns—though Saint-Saëns pitches two of the horns in C. Fanfare and military topics dominate the proceedings, in dotted and triplet rhythms. The opening eight measures introduce the central gesture of the movement, a descending motion in double-dotted rhythm. This gesture becomes the defining element of P (m.9), a rather Schumannesque theme for violins in three sections.[45] Pa and Pb are repeated in the clarinet, followed by a new ending, P^k, a series of dotted rhythms over a dominant pedal. T (m.47), which opens similarly to P, features antiphonal sequential repetitions of a scale; insistent dotted rhythms at the end recall the Scherzo of Beethoven's Ninth Symphony. The movement assumes a martial character with the unexpected entry of S (m.59) in the submediant key of C major. Its four sections lie mostly in the woodwinds. Sa is ceremonial, Sb lyrical, and Sc again in majestic dotted rhythms. Sd (m.72) provides a calm closing function both to S and the exposition which, as in the "Rhenish" Symphony, does not repeat.

The development (m.93) is in reality a second traversal of the introduction and exposition in the minor (P and T in G, S in C). Saint-Saëns combines some functionally independent modules: T mixes with the dotted rhythms and ceremonial triplets of Sa, after which the melodies of Sa and Pa join. An extended two-part retransition brings in new material. Beginning in A-flat major, part one features eighth-note arpeggios similar to those of Pc (m.165). Part two (m.173) presents a lyrical variant of Pa without dotted rhythms; the key moves from D-flat major to B-flat major. The texture, which has been thickening throughout part two, becomes more intense in the final section with pervasive dotted rhythms, a chromatic bass ascent, and contrary motion between upper and lower voices (m.193).

The introduction returns once more to open the recapitulation (m.200). As does Beethoven, Saint-Saëns emphasizes the moment of return with full orchestra, *fortissimo. Pa* and *Pb* follow, ending with P^k rescored. Saint-Saëns proceeds directly to S. The coda (m.256) combines the dotted rhythms and ceremonial triplets that have dominated this movement and closes with a final statement of *Pa.* While demonstrating a growing understanding of symphonic procedures, this movement suffers in the end from the fragmentary nature of its themes and from the absence of any true development. Its most distinctive feature, the recall of the introduction in the development and recapitulation, suggests the influence of works like Beethoven's "Pathétique" Sonata.

The second movement, marked Allegretto scherzando, bears the quaint title *Marche-Scherzo.* It actually has little of the march about it; Saint-Saëns saves that topic for the Finale. A lyrical rhapsody somewhat analogous in spirit to the second movement of the "Rhenish," its delicacy and relaxed charm recall most of all the theatrical *entr'acte.* Julien Tiersot, who had high praise for this symphony ("a work perfectly conceived and thought-out, in an excellent style, with a technique already very advanced"), expressed his strongest feelings for this movement, "an excellent model of French symphonic music, and even today one of M. Saint-Saëns's best pages."[46]

Consistent with its rhapsodic nature, the movement adopts no fixed form, though one might see it as a kind of *A–B–A–B* proceeding as follows:

A	*1A* m.1	*2A* 26	*3A* 34	*1A* 49	
B	*1B* 56	*2B(1A)* 70		*3A* 76	*2A* 87
	trans. 98				
A	*1A/2A* 111				
B	*1B* 134			*Coda* (*2A*) 165	

One of Saint-Saëns's most memorable melodies, *1A* appears three times in various woodwinds and strings (Example XVI/5); it begins and ends in G major with the second statement in B-flat major. Soft dynamics, staccato and pizzicato articulations, and grace notes link *2A* to Mendelssohn's elfin style; it moves from G major to A minor. *3A* appears in the flutes, playing mostly in thirds in B minor (m.34); this idea recalls the Nocturne from *A Midsummer Night's Dream.* One restatement of *1A,* an octave higher, closes this section (m.49). *1B* (m.56) closely alternates a dotted-note fanfare with *1Ax;* the key moves from C major to F major. *2B,* a very short motive derived from *1A* (m.70), gives way to rescored versions of *3A* and *2A* in C minor and G minor. A bridge (m.98) reaches a quiet climax on an E-major pedal.

For the return of *A,* Saint-Saëns combines *1A* and *2A* in counterpoint, following the same key scheme as before; the texture soon becomes quite full (m.111). He suppresses *3A* and all of *B* except for *1B* in E-flat major and C major (m.134). The section dissolves with a play on the fanfare rhythm as the key returns for good to G major. The coda (m.165) is largely based on *2A* with wisps of *1Ax* in the woodwinds.

While the first two movements reflect Germanic influence, the Adagio—the movement most admired by the critics—recalls the "Scène d'amour" from Berlioz's *Roméo et Juliette.*

EXAMPLE XVI/5 Saint-Saëns. Symphony No. 1/2, mm.3–10.

Languorous long-breathed melodies with subtle chromatic inflections, set in a gentle barcarolle-like compound meter (9/8), bathed in a "nocturnal" and wistful atmosphere emphasizing clarinets, harps, and high violins, and conveyed through soft dynamics and prolific expressive markings—all these elements show Saint-Saëns's affinities with his eminent elder. The form is conventional (sonatina) but the key radical for a symphony in E-flat major: E major. (In his last symphony, the "Organ," Saint-Saëns will again set the slow movement in the Neapolitan key.)

Filled with ties and syncopations, *P*, for clarinets and muted violins, continuously strives upward, eventually reaching b'' and descending two octaves; the climax occurs near the bottom of the descent on c', the lowered sixth degree in E major. Another ascending motive, *T* (marked *lusingando* or "coaxing," m.24) modulates to the dominant. *1S* ("canto," m.43) pits scalar descents in thirds against the main clarinet melody, while the cellos sustain a pedal on B; another chromatic ascent sounds in *2S*, this time reaching f-sharp'''. Like the beginning of *T*, *K* moves in broken figures (m.69). A loud C-natural interrupts another chromatic climb and becomes the basis of an inverted A-minor chord. The harmony slips down a semitone to B Major (V/E), and the recapitulation begins; it is intensified in texture but otherwise straightforward (m.85). For whatever reason, Saint-Saëns now designates *S* "cantabile" instead of "canto." At the end of *K* (which serves as a coda), the violins and harps ascend to their highest point in the movement (e''''), requiring harmonics. The cellos guide us to the Finale, which follows without a pause.

For this last movement, Saint-Saëns enlarges the orchestra considerably, adding piccolo, bass clarinet, cornets, saxhorns, trombones, cymbals, and two more harps. (The use of the saxhorns, invented only eight years earlier, shows the composer's Berliozian interest in sonic innovation—another trait that will reappear in the "Organ" Symphony.) If the march in the second movement proved elusive, here the composer offers a ceremonious procession akin to those in the *Symphonie fantastique* and *Symphonie funèbre et triomphale,* and as such it presages the familiar *Marche militaire française* from his own *Suite algérienne* (1880). The dotted rhythms and dense chordal textures, especially in the harps, recall similar passages in Schumann, for example the second movement (also a march) of his Fantasy in C major Opus 17. Beginning with the march, the Finale culminates in a fugue, an unusual and not totally successful pairing made presumably to give the movement weight, since the march itself sounds more like a splashy characteristic ending to an orchestral suite. The key scheme remains relatively simple but has frequent surprises on the surface.

The march begins after an introduction for woodwinds and brass over a twenty-two-measure pedal point on the timpani. Its dual strains consist of two sections each. The opening strain states each idea twice, first in the woodwinds and upper brass and then in the strings and lower brass (*1a* begins at m.22, *1b* at m.38). The first half of the second strain (*2a*, m.53) is based on a gesture from *1a*, while *2b* (m.59), in dotted rhythm, climbs to f''. Winding down, the march gives way to a quiet interlude (m.68). In a Berliozian gesture, a sudden *fortissimo* chord dashes the prevailing mood; its resolution ushers in the fugue, the subject of which is *2a* (m.103). The fugue consists of an exposition, an episode in which the subject remains omnipresent (m.149), and a stretto (m.192) which also incorporates a gesture from mm.11–12 of the introduction. A coda, based on a new theme of similar character as *1a,* leads to a triumphant close for full ensemble.

The critics received the First Symphony with qualified praise. Many objected to the concealment of Saint-Saëns's name, describing it, naively, as an unnecessary stratagem. They liked the inner movements but found the outer ones impersonal and bombastic. Still, they concluded, the symphony represented a worthy and promising first effort (the critics of course could not have known of the A Major Symphony). The following reviews are typical: Henri Blanchard critiqued the premiere while Paul Scudo evaluated a subsequent performance, by which time Saint-Saëns's identity had been revealed:

Has the anonymous or pseudonymous one created a masterpiece? No. Has he produced a mediocre work? Not that either. The first movement is vague and lacks character especially in its thematic material—young composers today neglect this element much too much, or else they don't know how to find melodies which are free, original, [and] well designed. The *scherzo,* we hasten to add, is charming: it is a jewel of melody and order in the manner of Haydn. Its idea is clear and accompaniments lively, gay, witty. If the melodic thought is a little close to that of Berlioz's *Marche des Pélerins* [from *Harold in Italy*], one can't say that this nearness degenerates into a narrow liaison; it's only a vague reminiscence. The adagio or andante is of a very fine character. It is grandiose in melody and harmony: it is a hymn thoroughly imprinted with religious feeling. There you have two very remarkable movements in this symphony. The finale is not at the same high level. It is noisy, brilliant, in a fugal style, but backwards-looking. The composer aspired to achieve an effect in bringing two orchestras together and did not fulfill his goal, unless he was planning on making this piece serve as the overture to a play by Shakespeare, entitled *Much Ado About Nothing.*[47]

The first movement isn't very significant: the theme lacks relief and character. The second movement or *scherzo* is infinitely superior, both in terms of melodic idea and in what allowances the young *maestro* draws from it. The andante that follows, on the other hand, is totally remarkable: it announces a happily gifted imagination which has a solid understanding in the material aspect of art. The finale seemed to be weakly conceived and its theme too feeble to support the double orchestra of brass instruments with which M. Saint-Saëns burdened it. . . . While rendering justice to M. Saint-Saëns's remarkable debut, it is not pointless to add that three or four movements of instrumental music which follow each other without any connection other than numerical order do not constitute a symphony. . . . It is by the unity of the conception that one can recognize a work . . . and this unity is so rare, so difficult to obtain, that Mendelssohn himself did not always find it. Because of this lack of cohesion, the work of this master often leaves something to be desired.[48]

Saint-Saëns's composition favorably impressed two very prominent listeners, Berlioz and Gounod: he overheard them commending it at a rehearsal, when the work was still anonymous. His friendship with Berlioz dates from the performance of this symphony, and Gounod sent the young composer a warm congratulatory note, which Saint-Saëns cherished all his life:

My dear Camille,

I was officially informed yesterday that you are the author of the symphony which they played on Sunday. I suspected it; but now that I am sure, I want to tell you at once how pleased I was with it. You are beyond your years; always keep on—and remember that on Sunday, December 18, 1853, you obligated yourself to become a great master.

Your pleased and devoted friend,
Charles Gounod[49]

SYMPHONY IN F MAJOR "URBS ROMA" (RATNER 163)

Saint-Saëns wrote his next symphony in June–July 1856 for a composition contest sponsored by the Société Sainte-Cécile of Bordeaux.[50] His entry won and premiered in Paris on February 15, 1857, at a concert of the Société des Jeunes Artistes conducted by Jules Pasdeloup. The Bordeaux premiere took place on June 10 of that year under the composer's direction. The contest rules stipulated that submissions bear a subtitle or motto and, for reasons he did not explain, Saint-Saëns chose "Urbs Roma" ("The City of Rome") in honor of a locale he had not yet visited (he competed for but never won the Prix de Rome). As with the Symphony in A major, Saint-Saëns disowned "Urbs Roma," and an edition appeared only in 1974, the same year as the earlier symphony's first performance. In a letter to Durand in 1901, Saint-Saëns noted but did not lament its neglect:

> I really believe the people of Bordeaux have forgotten that work which they formerly honored, and I understand their humiliation. Not only this work, but also an overture [*Spartacus*], equally honored by them, have disappeared from my works. These masterpieces did not have a hard life: these meteors *burned brightly for an instant, to be extinguished forever*! Let us weep over their fate, but let's not revive them.[51]

"Urbs Roma" is Saint-Saëns's longest and most Germanic symphony. It provides abundant evidence of the composer's growing maturity as a symphonist and contains many rewarding moments, but as a whole the work does not represent Saint-Saëns at his best and he did well to suppress it. Some thematic material is feeble, especially in the Scherzo; in addition, each movement contains padding or extraneous repetition, as a result of which the symphony reaches an exorbitant length of forty-five minutes if one observes all repeats. The key scheme is less audacious than that of the First Symphony: F major, A minor, F minor, F major. As in the earlier works, Saint-Saëns pits strings against woodwinds; frequently he states a theme twice, once in each family.

Many moments in the first movement (Largo–Allegro) recall Schumann, though without his rhythmic ambiguity. The symphony opens with a grand introduction whose fanfarish motive appears three times, in F major, D minor, and B-flat major, respectively. A sequential passage leads to the flattened mediant, A-flat major. To close the introduction, the first half of the motive wanders throughout the orchestra.

1P (m.22), in 6/4, opens with hammerstroke chords and ascending arpeggios (*1Pa*) and continues with a passage in trochaic rhythm (*1Pb*); Saint-Saëns builds much of the movement from these two elements. *2P* (m.34) continues the asymmetrical motion of *1P*. *T* (m.45) remains strongly indebted to *1P*. *1S* (m.71) is a rather non-descript motive in A-flat major which reappears in C major after a short "development." *2S* (m.107) shifts abruptly to A minor; its arpeggiated motions and staccato quarter-note runs create a feeling of 3/2. *K* (m.115) converts the trochees of *1Pb* into iambs. The exposition repeats.

Another unexpected harmonic shift—this time to D-flat major, the lowered submediant—initiates a long and rambling development (m.142). Motives worked over include *2S* (m.153), *1K* (m.162)—both in D minor—and *1P* (m.178). The section culminates in a fugato covering various keys (m.222); at the end the dominant C major reasserts itself. The introduction returns in altered form as the retransition, in *alla breve* and 6/4 meter (m.235). The recapitulation (m.261) omits *T*. In the coda (m.352) the introductory theme makes a final statement, followed by *2Sb* and *1K*. The end comes quickly and somewhat hurriedly.

For the second movement, Saint-Saëns writes a lively Scherzo and Trio in A minor and *alla breve* meter. Excessive repetition and banal material disfigure this movement, despite its striking principal melody. *A* unfolds as a miniature five-part rondo alternating two themes.

The dramatic main theme (*1A*, m.11) appears over trills on the third degree; *2A* reinforces the tonic (m.29). Saint-Saëns colors every reprise of *1A* with a different accompaniment. *B* (m.78), consisting of three motives in E minor, is much less distinctive. *1A* rounds off the Scherzo (m.144).

The Trio decidedly lacks inspiration: in *1C* the winds merely proceed up and down an A-major scale in thirds, though in a sprightly rhythm (m.173). *2C,* in F major, begins like *1C* but goes off in a new direction (m.228). The introduction returns as a transition to the Scherzo (m.302). Both Scherzo and Trio repeat in full. The composer treats the coda (Più Presto, m.312) as a *précis* of the whole movement and ill-advisedly subjects his listeners to a second recapitulation: full statements of *1A* and *2A* give way to a final Prestissimo derived from *1C* (m.371), in which the melody goes across the bar line and Saint-Saëns emphasizes the weak beats of the measure. A fast chromatic ascent concludes the piece.

The F minor Moderato assai serioso is a funeral procession for which the march from the "Eroica" almost certainly served as a model. Despite the same tendency to long-windedness that mars the rest of the symphony, this movement is the most impressive. Two elements dominate the discourse: the opening march motive (*x*) followed by a chromatic slide in double-dotted and thirty-second notes (*y*). *A* features numerous repetitions of *x* and *y* in different instruments and accompaniments. The final *y* combines with another stately double-dotted pattern, enhancing the lugubrious character of the movement.

B (m.59) presents a short but contrasting lyrical melody in F major. A dramatic repetition of *A* (m.79) develops *x;* at the climax, the key moves to B-flat minor, and *x* and *y* combine in counterpoint. *B* returns, rescored and slightly extended, in C major (m.125). A long bridge based on the final portion of *B* brings back *A* one last time, in the tonic but slightly shorter (m.157).

Saint-Saëns closes "Urbs Roma" with a gentle theme and variations in F major (Poco Allegretto). Following custom, strict variations gradually give way to freer ones. The variations explore a wide variety of tempos and meters. Although presumably inspired by the Finale of the "Eroica," this movement has little of its prototype's dynamism; rather, it brings the symphony to a quiet and serene finish. The theme unfolds in 3/4 meter in an *a* :‖: *b a* :‖ structure; charming, if somewhat breathless, it is noteworthy for ties over the bar line in *a* and the momentary suggestion of A minor in *b*. The ensuing variations make much of the syncopations in the melody. Although the first five observe most repetitions, Saint-Saëns writes them out, since he changes the scoring or texture with each statement.

The first variation features arpeggiated sixteenth notes, possibly derived from the rhythm of the fanfare that opens the first movement (m.30).[52] In the Scherzo-like Variation Two (m.70), running eighth notes in 9/8 engulf the orchestra. Variation Three (Meno mosso, m.115) converts the theme to 2/4, producing a slightly offbeat effect; running eighth notes again dominate the texture. Variation Four (L'istesso tempo, m.155) serves as the obligatory *minore* section. Saint-Saëns preserves the 2/4 meter but changes the basic pulse to dotted rhythms. An extension and bridge lead from the tonic minor back to the major. For the fifth variation (m.220), the composer switches to a striking 5/4 meter. It acts as an interlude, consisting of one statement of *a* in a broken soft and staccato woodwind line. Variation Six (Andante con moto, m.232) returns to 3/4. Keeping the broken-line pattern at first, the theme sounds in the upper woodwinds against pedals in the lower woodwinds and thirty-second-note runs in the violins.

Regularity breaks down at this point: a bridge based on the thirty-second runs leads to two partial variations of *a* (m.270); Saint-Saëns seems at a loss about what to do next. In the first of these mini-variations the music slows down rhythmically, while in the second he presents the theme in a pseudo-military fashion. The coda is tranquil, consisting largely of upward flourishes against a sustained tonic pedal (m.298).

SYMPHONY NO. 2 IN A MINOR OPUS 55 (RATNER 164)

The composer wrote the last of his early symphonies from July to September 1859; Pasdeloup performed it with the Société des Jeunes Artistes the following March. Saint-Saëns expressed his gratitude by dedicating the new symphony to the conductor. Shortly thereafter Pasdeloup founded the Concerts Populaires and began to back away from his commitment to contemporary French music, and Saint-Saëns turned against him. After Pasdeloup's death (1887), Saint-Saëns dismissed the conductor as a "very ordinary musician" who banished young French symphonists from his programs with the admonition to "Write symphonies like Beethoven's and I'll play them!"[53] Although others confirmed Saint-Saëns's low estimate of Pasdeloup's technical skills (Bizet called him a "dreary" musician while Reyer quipped that Pasdeloup's orchestra conducted him well),[54] his characterization of Pasdeloup as an enemy of French music is not totally just. While unquestionably less willing to support native composers than before, Pasdeloup still offered occasional opportunities (as he did with Bizet's *Roma*) when few others would: in addition, his orchestra frequently gave public read-throughs of new works after the main rehearsal.[55]

If "Urbs Roma" is Saint-Saëns's most expansive symphony, the Second Symphony represents his most concise. Approximately twenty-five minutes in length, it economizes its material: the opening motive generates many themes throughout the work, and the Finale reprises passages from previous movements. In addition, the composer alters the traditional structure of each movement by compressing or omitting returns. In its cyclic unity and formal experimentations designed to avoid what Saint-Saëns termed "needless repetitions," the Second Symphony (like the First in its harmonies and scoring) anticipates the "Organ" Symphony. He scores the work for full orchestra plus piccolo and English horn.

The frugal construction manifests itself clearly in the first movement, where almost every theme derives from the first two motives of the introduction (see Table XVI/4). All four introductory motives in fact bear close resemblances. An opening iv–V hammerstroke for full orchestra leads to *1–O,* the principal germ motive—a row of descending and ascending thirds that alternately suggest minor, major, and diminished tonalities (Example XVI/6). Throughout the work Saint-Saëns takes advantage of the multifaceted tonal implications in this motive.

The composer repeats and extends the opening chords in cut time and a faster tempo; *1–O* also returns, transposed up a fourth and now accompanied by an undulating motive that moves in contrary motion to it (throughout this movement Saint-Saëns uses contrary motion to heighten tension or vary the texture). While not distinctive in itself, *2–O* inspires subsequent themes, especially *S.* Another statement of the opening chords leads to *3–O,* a derivative of *2–O* (m.26), and *4–O* (m.28), the first of many variants of *1–O* in which passing seconds fill in some or all of the thirds. The end of *4–O* emphasizes the lowered second, an interval we shall encounter again in the Scherzo. A cadential chorale-like woodwind passage concludes the introduction.

Saint-Saëns marks the ensuing Allegro appassionato in cut time, befitting the learned style of the exposition. Perhaps inspired by the Finale of Mozart's "Jupiter" Symphony—which, as we have seen, Saint-Saëns knew very well—the composer sets *P* as a fugal exposition of five entries, each in four-measure units (m.66). Based on *1–O* in dotted rhythm, the subject contains three subsections (*a b c*), as does the countersubject (*d e f*) (see Example XVI/7 for *Pa-Pc*). A continuation follows, the first subsection of which (*g*) appears frequently

TABLE XVI/4
Cyclic Derivations in Saint-Saëns's Symphony No. 2/1

Introduction

m.2	*1-O*	A minor
14	*2-O (1-O)*	D minor
26	*3-O (2-O)*	
28	*4-O (1-O)*	mod. to V pedal

Exposition

66	*P (1-O)*	A minor
97	*1T (P)*	
105	*2T (P)*	E minor
117	*3T (P)*	
128	*S (2-O, 3-O)*	F
140	*Sᵏ (Pa)*	
144	*K (Pg)*	

Development

156	*S/Pg*	F →
178	*Pa/Pg*	A →

Recapitulation

206	*P*	A minor
220	*Sb/Pb*	
228	*1-O/Pb*	

Trans.

248	*1-O/Sb*	

Coda

268	*Pa/Pb*	

in subsequent developments.[56] The three themes that make up *T* (m.97) all derive from *P,* especially *Pa.* Saint-Saëns places *S* (m.128) in the submediant F major. Its antecedent resembles *2–O* while the consequent features a stepwise descent; both halves of *S* use the dotted rhythm of *Pa. K* (m.144) is based on *Pg.*

The development contains two brief sections: the first combines *S* with *Pg* against continuous triadic descents (m.156), and the second, in D minor, pits *Pa* and *Pg* against inversions of themselves (m.178). Saint-Saëns reduces the recapitulation to *P* with *Pg* as countersubject (m.206); an expanded and syncopated *Sb* with a variant of *Pb;* and *1–O,* combined with *Pb* in normal form in a series of pyramids over a diatonic version of the descent of *Sb.* A short transition recalling the first section of the development (m.248) leads to a dramatic coda which sets *Pa* and *Pb* against each other in contrary motion (m.268), culminating in a unison statement of both motives (m.281).

The form of the brief and lyrical Adagio is somewhat elliptical: *A–B–A–C*–Coda. In

EXAMPLE XVI/6 Saint-Saëns. Symphony No. 2/1, mm.1–6.

EXAMPLE XVI/7   Saint-Saëns. Symphony No. 2/1, mm.66–69.

E major, it features light scoring with muted strings and moves almost entirely in balanced phrases, usually 8 + 8. In its brevity and charm, this slow piece resembles an interlude rather than a symphonic movement. *A* is a broken melody for strings in the tonic, *B* a flowing line for violins and English horn in C-sharp minor (m.17). The latter closes with a steady diatonic descent in trochaic rhythm that suggests either *I/1–O* (filled in) or *I/Sb*. The first half of *A* returns in the woodwinds (m.36). *C* (m.44) weaves a new theme out of the cadence of *A*, making it sound somewhat like an extension. The coda acts as another cadential elaboration (m.60).

Strongly articulated rhythms, *sforzandi* dynamics, and phrase elisions create a Beethovenian tension throughout the Scherzo (Presto, A minor). *1A* divides into three parts. The first emphasizes strong trochaic rhythms, the second features Schumannesque hemiolas, and the third consists of a chorale-like passage in the winds. Both *1Ax* and *1Az* circle the tonic with the leading tone and lowered second. *2A* (m.76) introduces a new motive, accompanied by the leading tone-lowered second pattern from the end of *1A*. The reprise of *P* (m.139) is shortened and intensified. Each section of the Scherzo ends with a filled-in derivative of *I/1–O*.

While the Scherzo projects a stormy mood, the A-major Trio (Un poco meno mosso, m.203) is much more relaxed, albeit highly syncopated. It features a new stepwise theme (*1B*), again in Schumannesque rhythm—trochaic rhythm in triple meter with the downbeat deflected to the third beat. *2B* maintains the rhythmic displacement against a filled-in version of *I/1–O* (m.241). The Trio closes with an intensified restatement of *1B*. Saint-Saëns suppresses the repeat of the Scherzo, so the movement assumes an unconventional *AB* form. The coda consists of chorale-like plagal motions and a broken version of *1B* (m.289).

One might best describe the Prestissimo Finale as a sonata-rondo in A major with truncated recapitulation (*A–B–A C A–B* Coda); during its course various themes from previous movements reappear. *A* contains two distinct themes. *1P* moves in staccato eighth notes in 6/8 meter, somewhat like the Finale of Haydn's Symphony No. 100—perhaps not coincidentally, considering the explicitly Haydnesque coda to come. *2P* (m.38) is another filled-in *I/1–O* (specifically *1–Oa*) in trochaic rhythm. A four-measure bridge changes the key to F-sharp minor.

Four themes emerge in *B*. *1S* (m.57) moves in a gallop while *2S* playfully mixes broken rhythms with trochaic stepwise descents and ascents (m.74). The more transitory *3S* features stretto imitations of the stepwise motions of *2S* as the key moves to D minor (m.91). In character, the climactic *4S* resembles the saltarello of Mendelssohn's "Italian" Symphony (m.107); Saint-Saëns bases it on *III/2A*, in diminution and accompanied by the "galloping" rhythm of *1S*. Again a *1–O*-derived descent closes the section.

As expected, *A* returns to the tonic (m.133). Unlike its counterpart in the first movement, the development (m.190) breaks down into numerous subsections, most concerned with *S*, principally *2S* and *4S*. Its principal keys are B minor, C minor, D minor (the main point of arrival), and A minor. *4S* also governs the retransition (m.336).

A returns with a new countermelody in the woodwinds (m.350). Saint-Saëns reduces *B* to *3S* and *4S* (mm.402, 419), the latter in A minor and also with a countermelody. A two-measure grand pause terminates the argument and introduces the coda (m.448). In the first section, Saint-Saëns breaks up *1P* with unexpected rests and slowing tempos; the passage recalls Haydnesque wit, for example the Finale of his "Joke" Quartet Opus 33/2. He then reprises the coda of the second movement, though with inverted scoring (Andantino, 3/8, m.469). In the final section, *1P* and a filled-in *I/1–O* bring about a buoyant conclusion (Tempo primo, 6/8, m.488).

The new symphony initially received a guarded response. Saint-Saëns recalled that many listeners found the presence of a fugue "scandalous," and the critical reactions solidified a growing perception of the young (age twenty-four) composer as an academic musician.[57] A writer for the *Revue et gazette musicale,* lamenting the score's "labored designs" and excessive "science" (i.e., processes more intellectual than inspired), advised Saint-Saëns to return to Haydn for lessons in "charm and melodic simplicity":

> M. Saint-Saëns is one of our most celebrated young musicians. When the Société Sainte-Cécile existed, he was already productive as a symphonist. He was very young at the time; today, when he has grown in age and talent, we find in him a little too much predilection for science, with which he reaches the most lofty summits. He excels in combining sounds and in confusing designs which, while not being completely impossible, are nonetheless strange and sometimes labored. We counsel him to study further the charm and melodic simplicity of which the father of the symphony, Haydn, will furnish him with such delightful examples.[58]

Writing forty years later (1902), Tiersot upheld the charge of academicism. Ignoring or dismissing the formal innovations in the work, he wrote,

> The principal reproach one can make against [this symphony] is that it turns a little too much toward the past and affects a preference for scholastic forms that is too exclusive. The modern soul of a master who is otherwise so modern in other areas of his output does not vibrate in these [early] symphonies.[59]

By this time, however, the Second Symphony—published in 1879 as Opus 55—had become popular and it received many performances throughout the composer's lifetime; he often conducted the work on foreign tours. Saint-Saëns always retained tender feelings for this symphony (unlike its predecessors) and took great satisfaction in its success.[60]

Between Saint-Saëns's Second and Third: The "Revival" of Instrumental Music after 1870

Saint-Saëns wrote his next and last symphony in 1885–1886, after a quarter-century hiatus; by then, momentous changes had taken place in French musical life as well as in national attitudes toward symphonic music. The disastrous Franco-Prussian War of 1870–1871, followed by the horrors of the Siege of Paris and the Commune, engendered a mood of sobriety and nationalism that had profound ramifications for French music. At least for a time, audiences repented of their patronage of Offenbachian operetta and other "frivolous" entertainments associated with the disgraced Second Empire and turned to the more "noble" art of concert music. To regenerate French music and pride through such "high" genres as the symphony became an official goal: as one parliamentary deputy stated, symphonists and like-minded artists represented "our hope, our vengeance, our future."[61]

The founding of the Société Nationale de Musique in 1871 provided a visible demonstration of the new mood. Adopting the motto *Ars gallica,* the Société Nationale, which initially comprised most of the prominent musicians in France, actively promoted non-operatic compositions—"serious musical works" that "reveal elevated and artistic aspirations," as the founding charter put it. Financial constraints restricted the Société Nationale to only one or two orchestral concerts per season, so the symphony benefited less from this organization than chamber music; nevertheless, symphonies (or excerpts thereof) by member composers were occasionally heard, sometimes in four-hand reduction.[62]

The so-called "revival" of concert music in France owes much to the Société Nationale, but of even greater moment for the symphony was the emergence of two new orchestras. In 1873 Édouard Colonne founded the Concerts Nationaux—soon renamed the Association Artistique but more popularly known as Concerts Colonne (Plate B19). Colonne adored Berlioz's music, and the works of that recently deceased composer became the cornerstone of his society. *La Damnation de Faust* proved especially fashionable: Concerts Colonne performed it in full over 100 times between 1873 and 1914. In 1881 Charles Lamoureux established the Société des Nouveaux Concerts or Concerts Lamoureux (Plate B20). Lamoureux's idol was Wagner, and many concerts included portions of his operas. The rival orchestras played opposite each other on Sunday afternoons. Both series became very popular, and the state awarded a sizeable annual subsidy to each, confident they would further its goal of fostering a new school of French orchestral music.

By the early 1880s, hopeful anticipation had given way to renewed despair. The voracious public appetite for Wagner, Berlioz, and past masters, coupled with the conductors' unwillingness to challenge their audiences, again left contemporary French artists in the wilderness, albeit to a lesser extent than before. As Ernest Chausson wrote to Vincent d'Indy in 1884, "There is no longer a place for the young at the Sunday concerts: Colonne and Lamoureux do not exist for us."[63] A few years later, the prominent critic Arthur Pougin lamented, "Our young composers . . . are singularly neglected today. . . . It is very well to play Wagner and Berlioz, but perhaps, while still playing them, . . . one could, from time to time, think of the young artists who need to be heard and become known."[64] Colonne, Lamoureux, and even the Société des Concerts du Conservatoire did program symphonies by living composers at times, but they did so much more rarely than either the composers or friendly critics wanted.[65] The Conservatoire itself remained as inhospitable as ever: urged in 1892 to add the study of symphonies to the curriculum, director Ambroise Thomas replied, "But what composer of value would want to debase himself to teach symphonic music?"[66]

Despite such discouragements, the symphony began to flourish during these years of resurgent nationalism. Throughout the 1870s and 1880s, composers such as Benjamin Godard (1849–1895), Louis Lacombe (1818–1884), Augusta Holmès (1847–1903), and Cécile Chaminade (1857–1944) continued the tradition of the "dramatic symphony" or "ode symphony" for soloists, chorus, and orchestra established by Berlioz and David. Godard's dramatic symphony *Le Tasse* ("Tasso," 1878) won a prestigious composition prize, the Prix de la Ville de Paris; another such work, the *Symphonie légendaire,* followed in 1886. A prolific composer, Godard also wrote five conventional symphonies, the last three with programmatic titles: *Symphonie gothique* (1883), *Symphonie orientale* (1884), and *Symphonie descriptive* (unpublished). Although extremely popular for a time, his music disappeared quickly after his death: his own contemporaries, including those ordinarily loath to criticize the music of their peers, dismissed it as insubstantial, and history has not as yet seen fit to challenge that judgment. Lacombe achieved renown for his dramatic symphony *Sapho,* composed in 1878 and performed that year at the Paris World Exposition.

Holmès, born in France of Irish parents, became a follower of Wagner and Franck. She captivated both Franck and Saint-Saëns: the latter unsuccessfully sought her hand in marriage, while Franck's impassioned Piano Quintet in F Minor supposedly reflects sublimated feelings for her (Mme Franck certainly thought so). Unusually for a female composer of this time, Holmès specialized in large-scale symphonic and theatrical works, many of them on classical or mythological themes. Her dramatic symphonies include *Orlando furioso* for orchestra (1877); *Lutèce,* also for orchestra alone (1878); *Les Argonautes* for soloists, chorus, and orchestra (1881); and *Ludus pro patria* for chorus and orchestra (1888). Holmès also composed symphonic poems. Known primarily for piano music, Chaminade created one dramatic symphony, *Les Amazones* (1888).

One of the best-known symphonies of the period, at least by reputation, is Claude Debussy's Symphony in B Minor, written during his student years in 1880–1881 and dedicated to Tchaikovsky's patroness Nadezhda von Meck, whom he briefly served as a house pianist. Debussy apparently never orchestrated the work and only one movement survives, in a two-piano version.[67] In this early piece, Debussy's individualistic approach is already evident. While ostensibly in sonata form, the composer deviates from conventional practice by putting *S* in the Neapolitan key, inserting a slow parenthetical passage that has no relation to the rest of the movement into the development, and replacing *S* with a new melody in the recapitulation.[68]

Gabriel Fauré completed two symphonies, in F major Opus 20 (1869–1873; also confusingly entitled *Suite d'orchestre*) and D minor Opus 40 (1884). The latter contained only three movements, an arrangement that would become popular with *franckiste* composers. Both symphonies appeared at the Société Nationale. In addition, Colonne programmed the D Minor, and Vincent d'Indy conducted it in Antwerp in 1885; the latter performance apparently did not go very well, for d'Indy complained that he was allowed only two rehearsals.[69] Dissatisfied with both works, Fauré destroyed them and recycled selected themes in subsequent compositions.[70] He published the first movement of the F Major as *Allegro symphonique* Opus 68 (1895), transcribed for two pianos by Léon Boëllmann; of the Symphony in D minor only two violin parts survive. Later in the 1880s Fauré seems to have considered writing another symphony, one which would be "austere."[71] His word choice is intriguing, as "austere" was a label most often associated with (or applied to) composers of *franckiste* leanings; it implied a non-programmatic symphony built with cyclic construction. Whether or not Fauré intended to create this kind of symphony, he evidently abandoned the project early on.

In the 1870s, Vincent d'Indy completed two unpublished symphonies, which we shall consider later. Victorin de Joncières's *Symphonie romantique* of 1873 achieved some popularity: the orchestras performed it (either in whole or part, especially the slow movement) several times in the following decades. In 1881 he wrote an *ode-symphonie* for chorus and orchestra entitled *La Mer;* Debussy knew this work, although the extent of its influence on his own is not clear.[72] At age twenty-two, André Messager wrote a four-movement symphony in A major (1875), which premiered at Concerts Colonne in 1878. Like Saint-Saëns's First Symphony, Messager's owes debts to Schumann: *II/P* recalls *III/P* of the "Rhenish" Symphony, the jerky Scherzo delights in rhythmic displacement, and dotted rhythms appear throughout the Finale.

Despite such flourishes of activity, the so-called "revival" of symphonic writing in France properly belongs to the years 1886–1889. By coincidence, three notable symphonies premiered in 1886: Saint-Saëns's "Organ" Symphony (in London), d'Indy's *Symphony on a French Mountain Air,* and Lalo's Symphony in G minor; a fourth, Franck's, followed three years later. It is to these landmark works—all still regularly performed except for Lalo's—that we now turn.

Camille Saint-Saëns (continued)
SYMPHONY NO. 3 "ORGAN" IN C MINOR OPUS 78 (RATNER 176)

Saint-Saëns composed his most famous symphony at the invitation of the Royal Philharmonic Society of London, which commissioned some of the most notable symphonies of the century, including Mendelssohn's "Italian" and Dvořák's Seventh.[73] Since completing his Second Symphony, Saint-Saëns had written a series of progressive works in a style associated with Liszt and the New German School; these compositions, especially his four symphonic poems of the 1870s, left their mark on his new symphony.

The gestation proved arduous and caused the composer much frustration, though he found that he could reflect upon his labors with humor. As he wrote to Francesco Berger, the secretary of the Royal Philharmonic Society,

> The symphony is well in the making. I forewarn you that it will be dreadful. . . . Unfortunately it will be difficult. I shall do all that I can to mitigate the difficulties. . . .
>
> This devil of a symphony has risen a half-tone: it did not want to remain in *B minor* [the original tonic]; it is now in *C minor.*
>
> It will be an occasion for me to conduct this symphony. Will it be an occasion for the others who listen? That is the question. It is you who wanted to have it, and I wash my hands of it.[74]

Once initial questions were resolved, though, work proceeded relatively quickly, from August 1885 to April 1886.

Philharmonic concerts included analytical notes by the house annotator, and since he could not guarantee that an advance copy of the score would be ready in time, Saint-Saëns provided his own discussion of the piece. It is a valuable resource, all the more because he rarely described his music in print. Table XVI/5 reprints the text as it appeared in the program note.[75]

Saint-Saëns's new symphony included a number of innovations, and he proudly pointed to some of them in his analysis. Striving, as he had in the Second Symphony, to minimize "the endless resumptions and repetitions" typical of earlier music, the composer compressed this symphony's four movements into two continuous divisions (1–2, 3–4), a plan he had used earlier in his Piano Concerto No. 4 in C minor (1875) and Violin Sonata No. 1 in D minor (1885). Second, "believing that symphonic works should now be allowed to benefit by the progress of modern instrumentation," his orchestra included valved and natural horns, valved and natural trumpets, piano (in place of the harps), and of course the organ, the addition of which Saint-Saëns regarded as his most far-reaching innovation. Through such experiments, the composer claimed to "renew" symphonic form, and for the rest of his life he took offense when he felt (as he often did) that his efforts did not receive due credit—especially if it went instead to Franck, whose music he detested.[76]

In the end, Saint-Saëns does not prove to be the most perceptive analyst of his own work, for few of the innovations he cites are as original as he would have us believe. As Daniel Fallon correctly points out, Schumann's Fourth Symphony follows an even more radical structure, compressing all four movements into one cyclically unified division.[77] Nor is Saint-Saëns the first to add the organ to the orchestral ensemble: Franz Liszt used it in his symphonic poem *Hunnenschlacht* ("Battle of the Huns") in 1857. His claim that the first and third movements serve merely as introductions to the second and fourth is questionable and

---

TABLE XVI/5
Saint-Saëns's Program Note for Symphony No. 3

New Symphony in C minor and major
(Written for the Philharmonic Society and Conducted by the Composer)

(The score of this work includes a four-handed pianoforte part, which has been kindly undertaken by M.H.R. Bird and Mr. Eaton Faning.)

The score of this work not being at hand for analysis in the usual course, Mr. Saint-Saëns has kindly forwarded some remarks of his own, in elucidation of its aim and structure. Here follows a close translation [by Joseph Bennett, the regular annotator]:

"This Symphony, like its author's fourth Pianoforte Concerto, and Sonata for Piano and Violin, is divided into two movements. Nevertheless, it contains, in principle, the four traditional movements; but the first, arrested in development, serves as an introduction to the *Adagio*, and the *Scherzo* is linked by the same process to the *Finale*. The composer has sought to avoid thus the endless resumptions and repetitions which more and more tend to disappear from instrumental music under the influence of increasingly developed musical culture.

"The composer, believing that symphonic works should now be allowed to benefit by the progress of modern instrumentation, has made up his orchestra in the manner following: 3 flutes, 2 oboes, 1 English horn, 2 clarinets, 1 bass clarinet, 2 bassoons, 1 double bassoon, 2 horns, 2 valve horns, 1 trumpet, 2 valve trumpets, 3 trombones, 1 tuba, 3 drums, organ, pianoforte (sometimes played by two hands, sometimes by four), 1 triangle, 1 pair cymbals, 1 bass drum, and the usual strings.

"After a slow introduction consisting of a few plaintive bars—

the initial theme, somber and agitated in character, is stated by the strings, in C minor—

A first transformation of this theme—

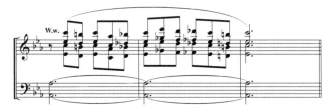

leads to a second subject—

TABLE XVI/5 (*continued*)

marked by a greater tranquility. This, after a short development presenting the two themes simultaneously, appears in a striking form—

which, however, is of brief duration. A second transformation of the initial theme follows—

Uncertain and restless in itself, it allows the plaintive notes of the introduction to be heard at intervals. Various episodes bring with them an increasing calm, and so lead to the

Adagio

in D-flat; the theme of which, extremely quiet and contemplative, is stated by the violins, violas, and celli, sustained by the chords of the organ—

This subject is next taken up by a clarinet, horn, and trombone, accompanied by the strings divided into a great many parts.

"After a variation (in arabesques) executed by the violins, the second transformation of the initial theme of the *Allegro* reappears, bringing back a vague feeling of unrest, augmented by dissonant harmonies—

which soon give place to the theme of the *Adagio*, this time played by a violin, viola, and violoncello *soli*, accompanied by the chords of the organ and the persistent rhythm in triplets of the preceding episode.

"The first movement ends with a *Coda*, mystical in sentiment, presenting in alternation the two chords of D-flat major and E minor, and resolving itself in the following manner—

"The second movement opens with an energetic figure, *Allegro moderato*—

TABLE XVI/5 (*continued*)

immediately followed by a third transformation of the initial theme of the first movement—

more agitated than its predecessors, and limited to a fantastic character which frankly declares itself in the *Presto*—

where appear from time to time, transient as lightning, the arpeggios and rapid scale passages of the pianoforte, accompanied by a syncopated rhythm in the orchestra, and occurring each time in a different key (F, E, E-flat, G). These playful flashes are interrupted by an expressive phrase—

To the repetition of the *Allegro moderato* succeeds a second *Presto,* which makes as though to repeat the first, but scarcely has it begun before there appears a new figure, calm, grave, austere—

and quite the opposite of fantastic in character. A conflict ensues, ending with the defeat of the agitated and fantastic element. The new idea soars aloft, as in the blue of a clear sky, to the heights of the orchestra, and after a vague reminiscence of the initial theme of the first movement—

TABLE XVI/5 (*continued*)

a *Maestoso* (C major) announces the ultimate triumph of the idea calm and elevated. The initial theme of the first movement, now completely transformed, is next stated by the strings (divided) and pianoforte (four hands)—

and taken up by the organ with all the forces of the orchestra. Development follows, almost entirely constructed, it should be observed, in three-bar rhythm—

TABLE XVI/5 (*continued*)

"An episode, quiet and somewhat pastoral in character, is twice repeated—

and a brilliant *Coda*, in which the initial theme, by a final transformation, takes the form of a violin passage—

and finishes the work; the three-bar rhythm here becoming, by natural logic, one vast measure in triple time, of a semibreve each, or twelve crotchets in the bar."

[Source: Fallon/SYMPHONIES, pp. 459–71.]

his statement that the first movement is "arrested in development" by sliding into the second plainly wrong, as the movement contains a truncated but definite recapitulation. Further, the symphony contains its share of repetitions, including a full and literal return of the Scherzo; it even experiments with unconventional reprises, such as the repeat of the development just before the coda in the Finale.

This does not mean that the "Organ" Symphony contains nothing original, for it features several significant innovations that Saint-Saëns does not mention. He relies heavily upon the Neapolitan key and other dominant substitutes, as reflected in the unusual tonal plan for the movements: C minor, D-flat major, C minor, and C major. Even more importantly, he unifies the symphony through the rigorous application of cyclic processes and thematic transformation, not just of one theme but four (Table XVI/6). Analysts and critics associated these processes more with program music than abstract symphonies and consequently many of them described this work as a merger of symphonic poem and symphony.

As the above shows, Saint-Saëns's good friend Liszt exerted a strong and conscious influence on this symphony. Ludwig Finscher has indicated other homages to the Hungarian composer. *III/3S* opens with an intonation formula found in many of Liszt's sacred works,

TABLE XVI/6
Cyclic Derivations in Saint-Saëns's Symphony No. 3

Note: the four cyclic motives—*1-O*, *2-O*, *I/1P*, and *III/3S*—are indicated in underlining

PART I

[*Movement I*]	Adagio-allegro	
Introduction [Adagio]		
1	*1-O*	D-flat
3	*2-O*	B dim.
Exposition [Allegro moderato]		
12	*1P* (*1-O*, *2-O*)	C minor
55	*2P*	
74	*3P* (opens with *2-O* in retrograde)	
84	*P^k* (variation of *1Pa*)	
90	*T* (*1Pa*)	
102	*S* (*1-O*, *2-O*, *2P*)	D-flat
114	*S^k* (*1Pa*, *1-O*-derived chromatic sequences)	
132	*1K* (*S*)	F
144	*2K*	
150	*3K*	
Development		
159	*1Pa* (transformed), *1-O*, *2-O*	F →
181	*3P*, *1Pa*	D-flat minor/major →
208	*3Pa*	
218	*3P*	V pedal
Recapitulation		
233	*1P* (in rhythm of *P^k*)	C minor
253	*2P*	
266	*3P*	
276	*P^k*	
282	*T*	
301	*S*	F—E
315	*3K*	E
Transition		
324	*1P* (transformed as in m.159)	
332	*1-O*, *2-O*	
[*Movement II*]	Poco adagio	
A		
350	*1A*	D-flat
366	*1A'*	
380	*2A* (continuation of *1A*)	
403	*1A"*	
B		
424	*B* (*I/1Pa*)	D-flat minor
A		
439	*1A'''*	D-flat
458	*Coda*	D-flat/E minor

PART II

[*Movement III*]		
Scherzo	Allegro moderato	
1	*1P* (*2-O*; similarities to *I/1P*)	C minor
17	*2P* (transformation of *I/1Pa*)	
26	*1P*	C/D-flat minor
47	*2P*	C/D-flat minor
59	*3P*	C minor
Trio	Presto	
71	*1S* (*2-O* in retrograde, perhaps *I/1Pa*)	C →
109	*2S* (*1-O* in accompaniment?)	A-flat, G
196	*1S*	G

TABLE XVI/6 *(continued)*			
Scherzo repeated			
207			C minor
Trio			
277	*1S*/*3S*		A-flat
Transition			
320	*III*/*3S*		A-flat
364	*I*/*1P*		V/C
[*Movement IV*]	Maestoso—Allegro		
Introduction	Maestoso		
376	*III*/*3S* (majestic transformation)		C
384	*I*/*1Pa* ("celestial" transformation)		
392	*I*/*1Pa* ("fanfarish" transformation)		
Exposition	Allegro		
400	P (transformation of *I*/*1P* from Movement III, m.17)		
419	T (*I*/*1Pa* at the end of each phrase)		
429	S		B—D
450	K (S)		G
Development			
462	*I*/*1Pa* (as in m.400), *III*/*3S*		G minor →
496	*retransition*		E-flat
Recapitulation			
504	P' (new transformation of *I*/*1Pa*)		E-flat—F
532	T		
547	S		E—G
568	K		C
Development			
580	a fourth higher		C minor—A-flat
Coda			
610	*I*/*1Pa* (3 simultaneous soundings)	*Sans presser*	C minor → C
640	*I*/*1Pa*	*Più allegro*	
651	T (*I*/*1Pa*)	*Pesante*	
665	*I*/*1Pa*	*Sans presser*	C

and the first transformation of *I*/*1P* in the Finale (m.384) closely resembles the opening of a popular Arcadelt *Ave Maria,* for which Liszt wrote an organ transcription.[78]

The first movement consists of a brief introduction and sonata conventional in all but key layout.[79] The introduction (Adagio) presents the first two cyclic motives. In *1–O,* the upper strings decorate the tonic with its upper and lower semitone neighbors: a D-flat triad "resolves" to a first-inversion B-diminished triad (mm.1–3; see [1] of Saint-Saëns's analysis, Table XVI/5). In *2–O,* an ascending motive in the oboes fills out the upper notes of a B-diminished seventh, thus outlining a tritone (D to A-flat, mm.3–4). Saint-Saëns repeats both motives, rescored and lowered an octave. The introduction concludes with variants of *1–O* and *2–O* in pizzicato cellos and woodwinds, respectively.

The Allegro moderato commences with the principal cyclic theme. *1P,* an agitated melody for upper strings, pivots around E-flat in a continuous sixteenth-note rhythm with each pitch repeated. *1P* divides into four sections, each of which incorporates either *1–O* or *2–O.* The beginning of *1Pa* (m.12) conspicuously recalls the opening of the *Dies irae* chant, while Saint-Saëns embeds *2–O* (now a perfect fifth) into the notes that follow (Example XVI/8). Because *1Pa* resembles the famous melody (Example XVI/9) and the composer inscribed the published score "to the memory of Franz Liszt," a legend arose that the symphony represents a requiem for his late friend and acts out a program of death and apotheosis. But

EXAMPLE XVI/8   Saint-Saëns. Symphony No. 3/1, mm.12–19.

Liszt died two months *after* the premiere, and Saint-Saëns added the commemorative motto only at the time of publication. He intended all along to dedicate the published work to Liszt, who responded with a note of appreciation:

> I am whole-heartedly grateful to you for your friendship. The success of your symphony in London gives me great pleasure. . . . For the purposes of the dedication I ask that you simply give my name.[80]

No reason exists for positing a "death program" for the "Organ" Symphony, still less for assigning titles such as "theme of resurrection" to various transformations of *1P* (as Baumann/ SAINT-SAËNS does). Still, as early as the premiere critics remarked upon the similarity

EXAMPLE XVI/9   *Dies irae* chant, opening.

Dí - es   í - rae,   dí - es   íl - la,

between *1Pa* and the *Dies irae;* Saint-Saëns said nothing about it, and what it meant for him, if anything, remains a mystery.[81]

Another figure looms strongly over the symphony: Franz Schubert (who also profoundly influenced Liszt). The rustling agitation of *1P* brings not only the *Dies irae* to mind but also the primary themes of the "Unfinished" Symphony and the equally unfinished C minor "Quartettsatz" (String Quartet No. 12) (Example XVI/10a-b). That Saint-Saëns originally conceived the symphony in B minor suggests that any allusions to the "Unfinished" may have been deliberate.[82] Further evidence of the Viennese master's influence on Saint-Saëns includes the strong emphasis upon the Neapolitan key (as in the "Quartettsatz" and the String Quintet in C major) as well as the use of three-key expositions in the first and last movements (C minor / D-flat major / F major, C major / B major / G major)—an exceptional procedure for French symphonists, including Saint-Saëns himself, before this point.

2–O appears more clearly in *1Pb* as an ascending woodwind pattern (m.18). In *1Pc*, *1–O* takes over in the winds and brass while the strings elaborate on it in a descending pattern (m.22). Finally, *1Pd* (m.28) features a steady descent in the strings against a dominant pedal; each measure includes the drop of a semitone. All four modules begin one eighth or sixteenth note after the downbeat, so that the rhythm takes on a Schumannesque ambiguity. Saint-Saëns repeats and rescores *1P* (m.34) but cuts off the end of *Pd* in order to launch into *2P* (m.55), which features a sequential two-octave ascent from g' to g'''.[83] *3P*—the opening four notes of which suggest *2–O* in retrograde—plummets from g''' to middle C (m.74). A variation of *1Pa* rounds off *P* (*Pᵏ*, m.84); here Saint-Saëns ties the repeated notes so that the motive moves in eighth notes while written as sixteenths.

Based on *1Pa*, *T* (m.90) shifts to A-flat major to prepare *S*. A lyrical theme in D-flat major for first violins, *S* combines the interval span of *2–O* (compressed to a perfect fourth) and the rhythm and contour of *2P* with *1–O* in woodwinds and the rhythm of *1P* in second violins and violas (m.102; [4] of Table XVI/5). *Sᵏ* (m.114), a short developmental passage, highlights the pseudo-*Dies irae* in the trombones and sets up the parallel subdominant key F major. *1K* (m.132) transforms *S* into a martial style, while *2K* (m.144) features trumpet fanfares as the bass sustains F major. With *3K* (m.150) the energy dissipates, setting the stage for the development.

The development is short and based almost entirely on various modules of *P* and *O*. In section one (m.159), *1Pa* becomes a broken staccato eighth-note theme played first in F major and then G minor (Saint-Saëns habitually states an idea twice, usually raising the second by a whole or half step and placing it in invertible counterpoint); *1–O* and *2–O* accompany both statements. The next section (m.181) features a sequence based on the descending pattern of *3P*; the sixteenth-note rhythm of *1P* returns in the violas and *1Pa* appears both in normal form in the violins and in augmentation in the low brass and woodwinds starting in m.196. The harmony is rooted in D-flat, then E-flat. Section three (m.208) sets *3P* in a shorter sequence. *3P* appears one last time in the retransition (m.218), over a dominant pedal.

Saint-Saëns intensifies the recapitulation (m.233) in a Beethovenian manner: *P* is sounded by full orchestra, *fortissimo* (*fff* at *3P*), with new countermotives. The articulation of *Pᵏ*

EXAMPLE XVI/10A   Schubert. Symphony No. 8/1, mm.8–10.

EXAMPLE XVI/10B   Schubert. String Quartet No. 12 ("Quartettsatz"), mm.1–4.

appears as it did before, with the repeated sixteenth notes again tied into eighths. Instead of the Neapolitan, *1S* begins in F major and shifts suddenly to E major (m.301); again Saint-Saëns has avoided the relative major. Staying in E, he jumps to *3K* (m.315). Still in E major, the transition to the second movement starts off like the development (m.324): the texture thins out, leaving only *1–O* and *2–O*. After a grand pause, the organ enters for the first time, playing a soft low A-flat, which resolves to the new tonic, the Neapolitan D-flat major. Throughout this movement, the organ performs a supportive and coloristic role—Daniel Fallon calls it "a meditative calm"[84]—rarely rising above *piano* and offering mostly harmonic support or counterpoint to the principal theme.

Saint-Saëns sets the Poco Adagio (m.350) in *A–B–A* form. *1A* consists of a miniature theme and variations, the theme being a lyrical melody for octave strings in three four-measure phrases ([7] of Table XVI/5); the organ provides a countermelody.[85] The melody closes with a two-measure tag, a filled-in descending tonic arpeggio. For the first variation, *1A* appears in the clarinet, horns, and trombones with counterpoint in the strings; the organ drops out (m.366).

What follows might best be understood as a continuation of *1A* (*2A*, m.380). The instruments that played in the preceding variation alternate with the strings over harmonic support in the organ as the key moves from A-flat major back to the tonic; the organ takes up the tag. A second variation of *1A* now appears, for strings and organ alone (m.403); the theme undergoes rhythmic displacements in a series of decorative hockets described by the composer as "arabesques." This variation remains in the tonic but omits the tag.

Turning to the tonic minor, *B* transforms *I/1Pa* in a manner similar to the development of the first movement (m.424): instead of broken eighth notes as before, however, the low strings play broken triplets pizzicato.[86] Three statements of *I/1Pa*, each a third higher, are separated by *1–O* in the woodwinds. Saint-Saëns returns to the tonic via a series of alternating major and augmented chords, the former of which create an ascending pattern in minor thirds:

C-flat – C aug. – D – E-flat aug. – F – B-flat aug. – A-flat → D-flat   (mm.433–39)

Saint-Saëns describes this passage as producing "a vague feeling of unrest."

EXAMPLE XVI/11   Saint-Saëns. Symphony No. 3/3, mm.1–9.

The reprise of *A* (m.439) features one more variation of *1A* in half of the first violins, violas, and cellos; the other strings continue the *I/1Pa*-derived pizzicato motion of the preceding section and the organ plays counterpoint. The latter part of *A* juxtaposes ascending chromatic patterns in the organ and woodwinds against a long syncopated descent from b''' to d'' in the strings. As at the end of *B,* the coda oscillates unrelated harmonies, this time D-flat major and E minor (mm.458–69). Saint-Saëns characterized this coda as "mystical in sentiment." An E-flat augmented triad leads back definitively to a final cadence in D-flat major.

The Scherzo (Allegro moderato) returns to the key and mood of the first movement. It has three themes. *1P,* in 6/8, adopts the agitated repeated notes and sixteenth-note motion of *I/1P,* now distributed as eighth note plus four sixteenths, the latter all on the same note; the contour loosely resembles *2–O* (Example XVI/11). *2P* (m.17) features another transformation of *I/1P* (Example XVI/12a). Saint-Saëns repeats *1P* in the woodwinds in C minor (m.26) and in the strings in D-flat minor. The Neapolitan relationship becomes more evident in the following bridge (m.47), set in D-flat major and reinforced by sharp punctuations of D-flat in the strings. The Scherzo closes with *3P* (m.59), a syncopated motive that leads back to C minor, accompanied by the rhythm of *1P.*

The stormy Scherzo suddenly gives way to a fleet Trio in C major (m.71, Presto), whose character Saint-Saëns describes as "fantastic." To help create the mood, the piano, triangle, and cymbals join the ensemble.[87] The Trio has two themes. *1S* begins with *2–O* in retrograde followed by allusions to *I/1P;* the quirky melody crosses over the bar line in fast triplets, creating another Schumannesque ambiguity. The piano engages in harp-like motions of upward arpeggios and scalar runs, described by the composer as "playful flashes" ([12] of Table XVI/5). Key movements are equally sportive. Beginning in C major, *1S* cadences in F major, followed by a two-measure tag in the strings based on the semitonal motion of *1–O.* Saint-Saëns repeats *1S* twice. The first time, it moves from C major to E major; he increases the rhythmic uncertainty by starting the triplets on an off-beat and adding two new notes. He extends the triplets further in the second repetition by inserting a fugato; this time *1S* starts in D major and cadences in E-flat.

As a counterbalance to the preceding hyperactivity, *2S* features an extended lyrical string theme in A-flat major accompanied by a decorated dominant pedal in the woodwinds (m.109, 2/4; [13] of Table XVI/5). The repetition of *2S* moves to the woodwinds in G major (m.158). The Trio closes with a final reprise of the piano flourishes from *1S* (still in G), followed by a rapid three-octave descent in the strings (g'''–g) and a *fortissimo* half-cadence (m.196).

Saint-Saëns writes out a full repeat of the Scherzo (m.207), changing only the end, when a deceptive cadence to A-flat major brings back the Trio, which mostly remains in that key (m.277). Upon an elongated *1S,* the composer superimposes a new theme (*3S*), a chorale

EXAMPLE XVI/12A   Saint-Saëns. Symphony No. 3/3, mm.17–21 (transformation of *I/1Pa*).

in canon at the octave appearing in the brass and bass instruments ([14] of Table XVI/5). Saint-Saëns portrays this passage as a conflict between "the fantastic element" and the chorale, though one may ask how much of a "battle" takes place since the chorale dominates from the start. After a final flourish in the piano, the orchestra begins another precipitous descent, but its progress is arrested by the return of the chorale, which begins the transition to the Finale.[88]

This passage recalls its counterpart in Schumann's Fourth Symphony. The first section features the chorale in another octave canon in the upper strings followed by a series of overlapping A-flat scale patterns (m.320)—a gesture which to Saint-Saëns denotes the defeat of the fantastic element. In the second section (m.364, Allegro moderato), another variant of *I/1Pa* appears in the lower strings, pizzicato; this time the theme is in straight unbroken triplets. A half cadence on G ends the transition.

Much of the Finale consists of progressively "victorious" transformations of *I/1P* and *III/3S* (the chorale), set loosely into sonata form. The introduction opens with an emphatic C major chord in the organ—its first *forte* in the symphony (m.376, Maestoso). A sharply articulated eighth-note transformation of *III/3S* follows in 6/4 meter. *I/1Pa* appears in a soothing "celestial" style in which divisi strings in high range state the melody in quarter notes (with longer notes at cadence points), accompanied by soft organ chords and rippling harp-like arpeggios in the piano, played four-hands (m.384; [16] of Table XVI/5). *I/1Pa* changes into a more regal style, sounded *fortissimo* in the organ and strings, with each phrase punctuated by brass fanfares (m.392). Daniel Fallon likens this passage to one in Liszt's *Hunnenschlacht,* which also features a chorale interrupted by trombones. As we have already seen, this symphonic poem adumbrates Saint-Saëns's symphony in uniting organ and orchestra, though Liszt's piece does not include a piano.[89] Saint-Saëns sets both transformations of *I/1Pa* in 9/4 with cadence points in 6/4.

As in the first movement of the Second Symphony, this sonata opens with a fugal exposition: the subject, *IV/1P* (Allegro, m.400), is the variant of *I/1P* heard in the third movement

EXAMPLE XVI/12B   Saint-Saëns. Symphony No. 3/4, mm.400–409 (*I/1Pa* as fugue subject).

(Example XVI/12b). The composer adopts what he calls "three-bar rhythm," meaning that the subject takes three bars of cut time but sounds like one continuous measure. The fugato ends at *T* (m.419), in which a thrice-stated sequence in the organ—with *I/1Pa* embedded in the end of the phrase—steers the harmony to B major, the key of *S*. Saint-Saëns thus again places the secondary key in a semitonal relationship with the tonic—now below, instead of above as in the first movement. Saint-Saëns describes this theme as "pastoral," gently moving

EXAMPLE XVI/12B *(continued)*

up and down the octave in another "three-bar rhythm" ([19] of Table XVI/5). Beginning in the woodwinds, the violins take over at m.439 and change the key to D major. *K* (m.450)—based on *S,* as in the first movement—appears in G major, the first time in this symphony that the composer assigns significant thematic material to the dominant.

The development is even shorter than that of the first movement; it deals with the fugue subject (especially its rhythm) and the chorale. Beginning in the cellos, *IV/P* works its way through the upper strings and lower woodwinds, answered by a chromatic ascent in the higher woodwinds (m.462). The chorale appears in three-part canon in the brass and winds while the strings continue to play with *IV/1P* (m.478). The retransition decorates a harmonic pedal on E-flat, as the winds and strings alternate the rhythm of *IV/1P* (m.496).

Instead of reprising *IV/1P,* the recapitulation introduces a noble transformation of *I/1P* (m.504): the theme twice appears in white notes, in E-flat major and F major; a large organ chord punctuates each phrase. The accompaniment retains the rhythm of the fugue subject. *S* (m.547), in E major, begins a fourth higher than before and moves to G major. *K* (m.568) appears in the tonic C major. Saint-Saëns then takes the uncommon step of repeating the development (m.580); he rescores it and moves it up a fourth like *S,* but otherwise the reprise is literal.

The coda consists of increasingly majestic transformations of *I/1Pa* as the tempo accelerates proportionally. The first section (*Sans presser,* m.610) combines three versions of *I/1P:* continuous sixteenth notes in tremolo in the violins ([20] of Table XVI/5; the composer likens this passage to a violin solo); a stentorian declaration of *I/1Pa* in the brass and low strings; and the same passage in the woodwinds sounded as an answer to the brass but in syncopation. This section proceeds in an ascending sequence from A-flat major to C major. A *stringendo* passage pits *I/1Pa* against a dominant pedal.

The second section (Più allegro, ♩=138; m.640) consists of a series of arpeggios in 3/1 time, where one measure equals three of the preceding section. The organ continues to hold a dominant pedal. Another *stringendo,* followed by four measures in syncopated rhythm (Molto Allegro, ○=88), leads to the next passage, marked Pesante (m.651); here *T* appears for full orchestra. Saint-Saëns makes a final proportional change: the ♩ now=100 and the meter changes to 3/2, but the tactus remains the same (m.655). These measures are based on the section of *T* derived from *I/1Pa.*

The final section (Sans presser, m.665) retains the tempo and beat of the previous passage but the meter changes again to 3/1—in Saint-Saëns's words, "one vast measure of triple time" ([21] of Table XVI/5, which notates the passage in 6/2). The strings and woodwinds engage in the kinds of "majestic" upward flourishes associated with the French Overture, while the double basses and bassoons play an active walking bass. The symphony ends brilliantly, with a large C major chord for full orchestra.

The Symphony in C minor premiered in London on May 19, 1886: the concert began with Saint-Saëns as soloist in Beethoven's Fourth Piano Concerto (with Arthur Sullivan conducting), and then the composer directed the symphony; afterward he was received by the Prince of Wales. The public responded enthusiastically, but most critics were lukewarm. The early movements went over well, especially the second, but they found the Finale inflated and empty. Many reviewers deplored the "profitless tinkle" of the piano; the organ bothered them less, although they felt its sound did not blend well with the orchestra.[90] They acknowledged the composer's prerogative to experiment with the traditional structures but felt that his use of cyclic form and thematic transformation placed the work outside the realm of the symphony. Many critics therefore described the Third Symphony as a rhapsody or fantasia ("there is a great deal to admire in this glowing Orchestral Rhapsody, but we distinctly decline to term it a 'Symphony' "); a few even described the cyclic melody as a leitmotif.[91] At a later performance in 1894, Bernard Shaw praised the scoring—"a model of elegant instrumentation"—but like his predecessors he condemned the "barren coda stuff" that to his ears disfigured the symphony.[92] The Philharmonic did not add the symphony to its regular repertory, which offended the composer: "[Henry Wood] played my symphony in C Minor. He avenges me for the neglect into which the London Philharmonic has let this symphony *written for it* fall, and I am very grateful to him."[93]

Paris first heard the "Organ" Symphony (accompanied by Saint-Saëns's analytical note) on January 9, 1887, with Jules Garcin conducting the Société des Concerts du Conservatoire. It was still relatively uncommon for contemporary music of any breadth to appear at the Conservatoire concerts, and so successful did this symphony prove that the orchestra performed it an unprecedented three times that season (because of limited seating in the hall, the Conservatoire customarily repeated each concert the following Sunday, but it rarely added an additional encore performance). Gounod pronounced Saint-Saëns "the French Beethoven," while Fauré wrote the composer that his symphony would long outlast both of them.[94] As in London, however, reviewers showed more reserve, at least at first. Johannès Weber, the influential critic for *Le Temps,* found the melodic material (which he also labeled *leitmotifs*) lacking in distinction:

> The themes of the symphony utterly lack originality. . . . If they don't have a distinctive enough appearance, the audience will be quite unable to recognize them under all the disguises they assume, at least without recourse to the "analytical program." . . . That is exactly what happened to me, which limits me from opening my ears to hear M. Saint-Saëns's symphony.[95]

But the symphony also had defenders. Camille Bellaigue, an equally important critic who wrote for the *Revue des deux mondes,* praised the symphony in rapturous terms:

> Nothing more beautiful in this genre has appeared since Mendelssohn and perhaps since Beethoven. . . . [Saint-Saëns] has demonstrated here all the characteristics of the great masters: imagination and reason, whim and order, profundity and clarity. This symphony is more symphonic than any other: I don't know of any, even among the most illustrious, that is treated with more rigor, in which the principal idea dominates to a greater degree and gathers around it elements that are more varied and docile at the same time.[96]

Unlike Weber, Bellaigue found the main idea "of a rare quality, and lovers of 'melody' can savor it without shame. . . . [It] is quite strong enough to sustain almost a whole symphony, firm enough that one can recognize it in its development and metamorphoses, either in whole or in fragments."[97] In sum, "It has been said that M. Saint-Saëns's symphony was the work of a musical chemist [i.e., one who composed by applying intellectual formulae]; so be it, but a chemist who knew how to make gold."[98]

Saint-Saëns had become very controversial by 1886. Reviled by conservatives in the 1860s and 1870s for his supposedly progressive tendencies, he earned the opprobrium of the French Wagnerians and the Franck circle during the 1880s by his vituperative attacks on both groups.[99] Period reviews of the symphony should be read with this in mind. For instance, Guy Ropartz's 1891 analysis of the four "core" symphonies of the mid-1880s—Saint-Saëns, Lalo, d'Indy, and Franck—was most likely colored by partisan feelings (Ropartz was one of Franck's most devoted pupils). Perhaps reflecting his Wagnerian leanings, most of Ropartz's analysis of the "Organ" Symphony consists of tracing the transformations of the cyclic motive. Like Weber, he found the thematic material insufficiently distinctive and occasionally banal, and he declared the four-in-two structure a failure, saying it made each part too long. On the other hand, he praised "the perfectly beautiful orchestration" without reservation and concluded by stating, somewhat neutrally, that the work as a whole deserved admiration, whatever its faults.[100]

Even when they knew better than to read a "death-and-transfiguration" program into it, analysts from the symphony's inception have assumed that Saint-Saëns attempted to work out a "darkness-to-light" or "defeat to victory" idea—a perception no doubt reinforced (consciously or not) by the composer himself when he set the symphony in the key of Beethoven's Fifth. In his study of the "Organ" Symphony in the *Cours de composition musicale* (a redaction of his lectures on music history and analysis at the Schola Cantorum), Vincent d'Indy declared that Saint-Saëns won "a true wager" by building a successful symphony upon such an idiosyncratic tonal plan. D'Indy's analysis for the classroom (*ca. 1899*) was admiring, if grudgingly so, but the judgment in his hagiographic biography of his teacher Franck (1906) took a different position. Ignoring any question of technical skill, he declared that the "Organ" Symphony foundered in its expressive mission: for all its veneer of triumph, at the end the victory rings hollow and "the final impression remains a feeling of doubt and sadness."[101]

Many later biographers, especially those in Great Britain, have taken d'Indy's conclusion for granted and depicted Saint-Saëns's work as a well-meaning but failed attempt to banish a spirit of pessimism.[102] Like Ropartz, though, d'Indy had an interest in finding fault with this symphony, for he could then oppose it to Franck's—"a constant ascent towards pure joy and life-giving light," as he informs us in the following sentence. Even if they agree with his opinion, modern writers should embrace d'Indy's verdict with caution. In terms of expressing victory through the metamorphosis of "negative" material into more "positive" substance, Saint-Saëns's symphony, *pace* d'Indy, is no less convincing in its final "triumph" than Franck's.

In Paris, the symphony quickly became popular, though performances remained limited because many concert venues lacked an organ. Nevertheless, by the end of the century the Symphony in C minor had entered the repertory of most societies. The composer himself understood this work, his longest and most ambitious instrumental composition, as a personal summation. As he told Alfred Bruneau, "the *Symphony in C* and [his oratorio] *Le Déluge* are my masterpieces"—and he henceforth renounced the genre: "In that work I gave all that I could give. . . . What I have done, therefore, I shall never do again."[103] Many years later, Saint-Saëns even agreed with his arch-nemesis Debussy that the symphony had run its course: "The *Symphony* . . . seems to have blossomed to the full; like the sonata, it no longer has much of anything to teach us."[104]

French Symphonies after 1885: Classical and Romantic Camps

By the 1890s, critics observed a dichotomy between two kinds of French symphonies—those of a "classical" bent, exemplified by Saint-Saëns's Third, and those with more "romantic" affinities, which took Franck's Symphony in D minor as their model. As Julien Tiersot wrote, "[The works by] Saint-Saëns and César Franck are the two types of the modern French symphony: they represent perfectly its double tendency. They have followed two different paths, but we can say that these paths remain the only ones explored."[105] (Tiersot personally preferred the classical path but accepted both as equally valid.) Until the 1920s, most French symphonists patterned their works to some degree after one or the other of these compositions; to Saint-Saëns's disgust, Franck's symphony proved the more influential.

The terminology requires explanation. One can easily see what makes Franck's work "romantic," but the "Organ" Symphony hardly exemplifies "classicism" in the traditional sense. It follows a clearly "romantic" dark-to-light program, sharing key and topic with Beethoven's Fifth Symphony, and its innovative devices—thematic transformation, audacious tonal relations, unusual orchestration—certainly distance it from classical models. In fact, if cyclic unity represents the distinguishing mark of symphonic romanticism, Saint-Saëns's symphony is arguably the more "romantic," for its use of transformation makes it more tightly unified than Franck's symphony, which relies primarily on thematic recall.

But aestheticians of the day did not measure "classicism" by technical criteria alone. For them, the essential distinction between classical and romantic works lay in the intended purpose of the composition. According to Tiersot, "classical" symphonies had a "lighter" character, reflected in a preference for Scherzo movements, and aimed primarily to entertain through the abstract manipulations of sound and form—art for art's sake. Saint-Saëns may have employed procedures associated with "romantic" works but, according to the analysts, he did so in order to create a satisfying work of "pure music" and not for any programmatic or didactic end.

Jules Combarieu summarized Saint-Saëns's accomplishment in this way:

> It is popular to treat [symphonies] like psychological documents and see in them an image of the passions that could have traveled through and excited an artist's soul, pushing it to a sort of irresistible confession. . . . Here it would be difficult: this Third Symphony, a little austere but so full and rich in form, is a monument of pure music in which the genius of the sound-architect triumphs. . . . To move freely and with an imagination which has pondered deeply in the world of melody and rhythm, to create something *large and grand,* to build counterpoint in joining clarity and elegance to the variety of forms—to be, in a word, a worker of art pushing the excellence of craft as far as possible—such is the goal that seems to have been sought for and achieved in this symphony.[106]

One expects that Combarieu's assessment would have pleased Saint-Saëns, who often expressed impatience with music that strove to express more than intrinsic beauty: "For me, Art is *Form* above all. . . . The artist who does not feel fully satisfied with elegant lines, harmonious colors, and a beautiful series of chords does not understand Art."[107]

Franckist symphonies, on the other hand, strove for something more: their "grave" and "austere" works sought to convey serious messages, whether psychological (as Combarieu indicated) or philosophical—compositions in which the creator sought to make "confessions" or "teach" the listener rather than simply give pleasure. What Gaston Carraud said of Albéric Magnard held true for many composers in Franck's orbit:

> Magnard is a thinker. . . . Solemn ideas dominate his music. . . . For him the true, the just, and the good are essential elements of beauty. . . . As well as a rhythm, a sound, a melodic line, and a harmonic substance, his music has a meaning, and it can no more do without this meaning than without any of the other elements. Thus as a musician his art is that of a poet—or rather a master of prose . . . —[and the creator] of an art that is more meaningful than evocative.[108]

Tiersot noted that *franckiste* composers frequently omitted Scherzo movements in their symphonies, perhaps to demonstrate their sobriety.[109] Paul-Marie Masson classified the camps in this way: the *franckistes* sought to create a *musique-discours* ("oration music") that spoke to and reasoned with the listener, while composers following Saint-Saëns's lead devoted themselves to *musique-contemplation* ("meditation music") in which the listener reveled in the sonic unfolding of the composer's thought.[110]

Before examining the works of the *franckistes,* let us consider another symphony widely categorized as "classical," the Symphony in G Minor of Édouard Lalo. As an avatar of classicism this work poses as many problems as Saint-Saëns's Third, owing to the theatrical origins and bearing of much of the music. Nevertheless, Lalo insisted that his symphony functioned purely as absolute music; and, considering the "lighter" touch of many parts of the composition, one could indeed describe it as "classical"—more so, in fact, than the "Organ" Symphony.

Édouard Lalo

Édouard Lalo (1823–1892) is an unfortunate figure in French music. Even more than Saint-Saëns, who ardently sought success in opera, Lalo's first allegiance lay with instrumental music, and as a result he suffered to a greater extent from the relative disinterest in such music during the Second Empire. The violist with the prestigious Armingaud Quartet, he spoke forthrightly about his Germanophilia, describing Germany as "my true musical homeland."[111] (By "German tradition" Lalo, like most Frenchmen, meant Viennese Classical and early Romantic composers through Schumann; he disliked contemporary German music, although he grudgingly praised Brahms's chamber music.) No surprise then that Lalo labored for many years with little success. He destroyed at least two symphonies written before 1870 because no one would play them; as he complained to Ferdinand Hiller, "The orchestras of Paris are closed to me because my music is *too German* and *not lively enough.*"[112] That Lalo always sought to season his adoption of Germanic idioms with Gallic flavor made no difference to many of his listeners.

Lalo's unhappy experience with his ballet *Namouna* (1882) reflects the prejudice that composers of instrumental music could encounter even late in the century. He gave the orchestra a more prominent role than normal for a French ballet, and his temerity earned him public failure and critical rebuke. Many reviewers blithely dismissed *Namouna* as the work of a "symphonist," by which they meant a composer more interested in developing motives than in writing hummable tunes. As Victorin de Joncières—himself a composer of symphonies—wrote,

> M. Lalo is a symphonist above all. . . . He excels at developing a motive; but the melodic fount finds him a bit lacking. The composer's very real imagination delights in the setting rather than in the imagination of the idea itself. That kind of temperament makes such a musician absolutely unsuited to writing a ballet.[113]

Lalo observed bitterly that to be a "symphonist" was "a word of praise in Germany [but] an insult in France. . . . Any composer who refuses to offer [theatrical audiences] suites of formulaic tunes is but a failure, boring, without ideas—*a symphonist!*"[114] To assuage his frustration, the composer extracted several suites from the ballet, and these quickly found a home in the concert hall. (*Namouna* did gain friends, among them the young Claude Debussy, who shouted his approval so forcefully that on one occasion the usher threw him out of the hall.)[115]

SYMPHONY IN G MINOR

Lalo's only extant symphony (Table XVI/7), dedicated "à mon ami Charles Lamoureux," has a tangled history that relates directly to the composer's travails on the stage and in the concert hall. He claimed he wrote it in four months in 1886, "knowing in advance that this genre interests only an infinitesimal minority."[116] Lalo exaggerated: he may have compiled and arranged the score in four months, but much of the content originated in earlier compositions. The Scherzo, for example, belonged to one of the discarded symphonies. Lalo recycled much of that work in an opera, *Fiesque* (1867–1868). To his dismay, the opera suffered the same fate as the symphony and remained unperformed. When he composed the G Minor Symphony, Lalo took back the Scherzo themes from *Fiesque* and put them into the new work. The Scherzo thus traveled a circuitous path from symphony to opera to symphony:

TABLE XVI/7

The Symphonies of Édouard Lalo

Key	Date	Title	Movements	Instrumentation	Comments
	by 1862				Two early symphonies completed and later destroyed. Jules Pasdeloup auditioned and rejected at least one of them.
G Minor	1886	Symphony in G Minor	1. Andante—Allegro non troppo 4/4 (201 m.) 2. Vivace 6/8—Quasi Andantino non troppo 4/4 (245 m.) E major/minor 3. Adagio 3/4 (109 m.) B-flat major 4. Allegro 12/8 (162 m.)	Grand + Picc., 2 Cornets	Many passages reworked from *Fiesque*, a discarded opera. Scherzo taken from one of the destroyed early symphonies. *IV/P* taken from the opera *Le roi d'Ys*. Dedicated to Charles Lamoureux. First performance: Paris, Concerts Lamoureux, conducted by Charles Lamoureux on February 13, 1887. Published in Paris: Heugel, 1887.

> I was very young when I presented my first symphony to Pasdeloup: the potentate de-
> clared it detestable—and the *scherzo* above all, since it was in quarter time, thus breaking
> with the classical conventions of the *scherzo;* he burst out laughing. I naively believed
> that the great man couldn't be wrong; I destroyed my symphony and transplanted all its
> themes into *Fiesque.* Only two years ago, when I wrote my Symphony in G [minor], I
> wanted to prove to *myself* that – I hadn't been wrong. I easily recovered all the elements
> of my first *scherzo* in *Fiesque,* I reconstructed them, and there you have the movement.[117]

The composer plundered the opera for other material as well: the cyclic theme and all of the
important material of the slow movement come from *Fiesque,* though not from the original
symphony.[118] In addition, Lalo took *IV/1P* from his more successful opera, *Le Roi d'Ys.*

Lalo unifies the diffuse elements of his symphony by several means. A cyclic theme (*O*)
dominates the first movement and makes cameo appearances in the third and fourth. The Finale recalls material from the first two movements, and *IV/S* derives from *I/S.* Finally, two
rhythmic gestures recur throughout the work: triplet motions and dotted or double-dotted
patterns. As befits its origins, much of the Symphony in G minor projects a passionate and
stormy character; other passages, however, recall the *entr'acte.* Lalo scores the symphony for
conventional orchestra, though the ensemble can sound fuller because of frequent *tutti* passages. His scoring favors the woodwinds. This "classical" work adheres to conventional symphonic form, although unusual structural features appear in each movement. As is his wont,
Lalo keeps counterpoint to a minimum and focuses on clever harmonic progressions.

The form of the opening movement is traditional, including an exposition repeat. The
Andante introduction begins with *O*. This motive, which comes from the introduction to
Act III of *Fiesque,* recurs with its signature triplet many times throughout the work, almost
always in prime form (Example XVI/13).[119] Harmonically the introduction consists of deco-
rations of the dominant chord. Lalo builds *1P* (Allegro non troppo, m.22) from three one-
measure cells, the first two of which permeate the entire movement: a stepwise cadential gesture ($\hat{3}$–$\hat{2}$–$\hat{1}$) in double-dotted rhythm, a sixteenth-note triplet gesture, and a tonic chord
declaimed by the full orchestra, also in double-dotted rhythm. *2P* (m.31) shifts to D major;
unlike *1P,* it forms an extended melody, combining the double-dotted rhythm of *1Pa* with the
triplet gestures of *1Pb* in the accompaniment. The horns, ascending in half notes, start on the
second beat of the measure, throwing everything off; such syncopations, as well as the dotted
rhythms, suggest the influence of Schumann, one of Lalo's favorite composers.

Dramatic flourishes herald *T* (m.42). Merging the gestures of *1Pa* and *1Pb,* it culminates
in an E-diminished seventh. A lyrical and expansive melody in F major, *S* adopts the dotted
pattern of *2P* with occasional suggestions of the triplet rhythm of *1Pb* (m.49). Moving to
B-flat major, *K* (m.63) features fanfarish syncopations produced by combining two double-
dotted patterns. In the exposition repeat, *1Pa* and *b* appear an octave higher.

The development (m.80) divides into three roughly symmetrical sections: each begins
with *1Pa* or *Sa,* continues with a new motive (*1N*) which uses the rhythm of *O,* and closes
with *O* itself in augmentation—the first two times in half notes and the last in double-dotted
rhythm. Sections one and two are largely in C minor. The harmony wanders in section three
(m.105). *1N* features a passage of quasi-Brucknerian quarter-note triplets (mm.118–21), leading to a final statement of *O* in double-dotted rhythm in the tonic. The recapitulation enters
without a retransition (m.126) and proceeds normally, but it omits *T. S* and *K* appear in the
dominant. The coda contains four sections. The first features *1N* (m.167) and the second
juxtaposes *1Pa* and *1Pb* (m.173). Section three presents a new motive, *2N,* followed by *O* in
half notes for full orchestra (m.179, *a tempo*). The movement concludes with *1Pa, 1Pb,* and

EXAMPLE XVI/13   Lalo. Symphony in G Minor/1, mm.1–6.

reiterated tonic chords, grandiloquently stated by the full orchestra in a relentless *fortissimo* (m.187).

The Scherzo (Vivace, 6/8)—which, one recalls, Lalo resurrected from the earlier symphony, by way of *Fiesque*—is in the third-related key of E major. An extroverted piece with unexpectedly somber moments, it announces its ambiguous character at the start with sharply reiterated F-sharp-diminished seventh chords that quickly slide to the tonic (recurring emphatic chords occur frequently in Lalo's music).[120] Three increasingly exuberant themes follow in quick succession. *1P* (m.9) is a playful romp for flutes and oboes, underpinned by a pedal E in the double basses. (In *Fiesque,* Lalo assigned this theme to a choral dance in Act I; other passages from this movement became choral interjections in an aria from the same act.)[121] The strings take over for *2P,* which moves in trochees against staccato interjections for full orchestra (m.33). *3P* unites strings and woodwinds in triplet motions enhanced by occasional duple divisions and syncopations (m.60). The colorful orchestration and fast-moving staccato triplets of all three parts of *P* recall both Mendelssohn and the *entr'acte.* In the last section of the Scherzo, ascending scale patterns in the strings and upper woodwinds give way to a minor-key descent in the clarinets, which conspicuously recalls the end of the first movement (m.76; compare I/187–90).

Instead of a conventional Trio, Lalo writes a slow section in quarter time (Quasi andantino non troppo) which alternates and combines two themes in E minor. (This passage, the one that provoked Pasdeloup's derision, became a lament in Act I of *Fiesque.*)[122] The first theme, *1S,* is a mournful quarter-note melody for woodwinds (m.98); the mode oscillates between minor and aeolian through the interchange of D-natural and D-flat. *2S* (m.106) is a dramatic motive for octave strings moving in the double-dotted rhythm of *II/1Pa.* Each reprise of these themes gains in strength. This section is about to culminate in a grand cadence in E minor when the Scherzo rhythm intervenes.

The return of the Scherzo (m.149) is shortened but intensified; it includes a new theme for full orchestra (*4P*), which leads toward a final tonic cadence. For the second time, Lalo halts the momentum by leaping into a new section (m.205). Opening with chromatic movements in dotted quarters in the lower timbres, upon which the composer superimposes regular triplet motion in the upper strings, the coda builds to a large cadence in E major. One expects the end at this point, but Lalo has a final surprise in store: he adds on five concluding measures in which the tempo slows down and the strings sound a *pianissimo* gesture reminiscent of the beginning of the plaintive *1S*. As in the first movement, then, the Scherzo closes with a dramatic gesture: a seemingly "happy" ending gives way to a quiet, sorrowful cadence in the minor.

Much of the Adagio (B-flat major) originated in *Fiesque,* specifically Act III, Scene 1;[123] but it is also the most obviously "Germanic" movement, filled with passionate string melodies marked by expressive appoggiaturas, high ranges, wide leaps, and 9–8 suspensions. The movement follows *A–B–A* form. *A* is monothematic, consisting of four varied statements of the opening theme; it reaches full bloom with the fourth presentation (m.30), which begins in the solo flute and moves to the violins.

B (m.43) contains three distinct parts unified by constant triplet rhythms in 3/4 time. The first subsection presents a triplet-based lyrical theme. The second treats a three-measure passage sequentially, reaching its pinnacle with a triumphal-sounding theme in G-flat major which incorporates the melody of *A* (m.68). Lalo heightens the reprise of *A* by adding a countermotive and retaining the triplet rhythm of *B* as accompaniment (m.83). At the climax, the strings, horns, trombones, and tuba interject *O* in an ominous and grandiose unison statement in B-flat minor (m.95). One finds no discernible rationale for this intrusion but, as we saw in the Scherzo, to disrupt a happy or triumphant mood is consistent with the "tragic" ethos of this symphony. After the interruption, the movement resumes its course and ends quietly by reiterating tonic harmonies in triplet rhythm.

The Finale (Allegro) is unusual in form and character: structurally it resembles a free sonata-rondo (*A–B–A–B–C–A–B* Coda) in 12/8 meter, and the style lies somewhere between a saltarello and a march. The opening and closing sections quote earlier material, converted into the new meter. The movement begins with *O* and the double-dotted *I/1Pa*, the latter extended into a five-note pattern. Lalo borrowed *IV/1P* (m.5) from the orchestral introduction to the women's chorus "Venez, l'heure presse!" in Act I, Scene 3, of his opera *Le Roi d'Ys*. As in the Scherzo, the woodwinds carry the burden of the argument in soft staccato triplets. This time, however, the minor key, rhythmic character (triplets with frequent sixteenth-note subdivisions), and loud punctuating chords give this march-like melody a "nervous, edgy" feel, as Ralph Locke aptly terms it (Example XVI/14).[124] *2P* (m.11) is even more agitated, with further sixteenth-note subdivisions in the triplets and trills in the woodwinds. A two-measure bridge brings back *1P* in the strings.

The tonality shifts to D major for *B* (m.23). *1S*, in the violas, begins with the same contour and intervallic content as *I/S; 1P* rhythms accompany in the winds. *2S* (m.30), a transitional passage with emphatic reiterated chords as in *1P,* returns to the tonic. Shortened repeats of portions of *A* and *B* follow, in their original keys. The latter ends with a new theme, *3S,* in D major (m.53): an extended string theme in dotted-quarter and duple-within-triple rhythms, its lyricism in some ways recalls Bizet.

As expected in a sonata-rondo, *C* (m.69) acts like a development: it first considers *1Sa* in A major and then all of *1S,* varied and transposed to F major. The retransition returns to G minor (m.83). *A* repeats in full (m.87). *B* begins with *1S* (m.105) but replaces *2S* with *II/1P,* in G major (m.112). *3S* and again *1S* follow in the same key. The section closes with a reprise of *I/2N,* also in 12/8 and G major (m.136). At the beginning of the coda, *1P* and *1S* alternate several times as if to symbolize a combat between the modes of G major and G minor (m.140). The latter wins out, and to close the work Lalo returns to the end of the first movement: the full orchestra in octaves declaims the double-dotted descent of *I/1Pa* (m.146), followed by *O* in the brass in dotted half notes; cadential gestures lead to a final invocation of *I/1Pa* for

EXAMPLE XVI/14   Lalo. Symphony in G Minor/4, mm.5–9.

all players except the high woodwinds. With a grandiose flourish of powerful and tragic-sounding tonic chords, the symphony comes to an end—a fine work of memorable lyricism and striking orchestration (especially for the woodwinds), marred at times by overwrought dramatics in the repeats of *O* and the closings of the first and last movements. Overall, the work effectively illustrates Lalo's goal of composing Germanic-style music with a French touch.

Lalo's symphony premiered on February 13, 1887, at Concerts Lamoureux. For once, the reception from both critics and public was largely favorable. Complaints generally centered on the theatricality of the music and the degree to which Lalo departed from classical norms. Even if they did not know about the borrowings from *Fiesque,* many reviewers sensed the dramatic aura of the themes. Adolphe Jullien, for example, asked why Lalo did not provide commentary to explain the work's seemingly obvious programmaticism.[125] Others complained about the cyclic organization, which they interpreted as a deviation from tradition:

> We heard M. Lalo's Symphony in G Minor with the greatest pleasure; it is a work of very elevated character. . . . But what has M. Lalo gained by turning aside from the traditional forms? Why this persistence in retaining the same themes? Why lose the benefit of this variety which pleases the listener and keeps one from depriving oneself of the [lessons of the] great masters? The work of M. Lalo is remarkable, lofty, but uniformly sad and tragic. . . . [In sum], M. Lalo's Symphony in G Minor is a beautiful and interesting work. Its success was lively and deserved.[126]

Guy Ropartz's 1890 analysis focused on the theatrical aspect. Consistent with his Wagnerian sympathies, Ropartz imagined Lalo's melodies as leitmotifs, and he created dramatic labels for the themes of the first movement: *O* became the "theme of fatality," *P* the "theme of revolt," and *S* the "motive of tenderness." Ropartz did not try to imagine a program beyond this, however.[127]

Some critics denied the work symphonic status because of its dramatic origins, but Vincent d'Indy among others stressed its fundamentally conservative idiom: "Lalo's Symphony in G Minor, very classical in its outline, is remarkable for the allurement of its chosen themes and even more for the charm and elegance of its rhythms and harmonies."[128] D'Indy implies that the work is essentially classical rather than romantic because its primary goal is to convey elegance and charm. In a concurring opinion, Tiersot placed the work squarely within the Saint-Saëns camp:

> This symphony is a work of complete refinement. In it let us not search for passion or impetuosity or sublimity; we would be disappointed. But in return let us admire a marvelously sculpted work of art. . . . This certainly is French music of the first rank.[129]

César Franck

The work that embodies the "romantic" pole of symphonic writing is probably the most popular and unquestionably the most controversial French symphony composed after Berlioz's time (Table XVI/8). During his life, and even more after his death, the music of César Franck (1822–1890) (Plate B21) inspired remarkable adulation and condemnation, both for its style and for what the beholder took it to represent. Debates could reach extravagant lengths. Since he was born in Liège to a German mother, many musicians, including Saint-Saëns and Debussy, dismissed him as Belgian and irrelevant to French musical history. Supporters like d'Indy responded that Franck embodied the Gallic spirit precisely *because* of his Walloonian heritage. Numerous publications argued one side or the other.[130] However picayune on the surface, this quarrel over Franck's birthright had serious implications, for it determined who belonged to the true French musical heritage; and if Franck's opponents could expel him as an outsider, they could also banish those composers who followed him.

An organ professor at the Conservatoire, Franck became the leader of an underground composition class for students who chafed at the officially sanctioned styles of writing and methods of advancement. Drawn both to Franck's progressive compositional style and to his personal aura of artistic integrity, they responded with an extraordinary loyalty that approached

TABLE XVI/8

The Symphonies of César Franck

Opus	Fauquet	Key	Date	Title	Movements	Instrumentation	Comments
13	125	G Major	1841	First Symphony for Grand Orchestra		Grand?	First performance: Société Philharmonique d'Orléans, probably on February 16, 1847. Not clear whether this was a public performance or private reading. See Fauquet/FRANCK, pp. 69, 251–52 for details. Unpublished. Manuscript lost.
48	130	D Minor	1887–88	Symphony in D Minor	1. Lento 4/4—Allegro non troppo ¢ (521 m.) 2. Allegretto 3/4 (262 m.) B-flat minor/major 3. Allegro non troppo ¢ (440 m.) D major	Grand + EH, Bclar., 2 Cornets, Harp	Dedicated to Henri Duparc. First performance: Paris, Société des Concerts du Conservatoire, conducted by Jules Garcin on February 17, 1889. Published in Paris: Hamelle, 1890 (four-hand reduction, Hamelle, 1888).

worship. The coterie—branded *La Bande à Franck* ("Franck's gang") by exasperated Conservatoire officials—included Henri Duparc, Ernest Chausson, Guy Ropartz, Augusta Holmès, Guillaume Lekeu, Pierre de Bréville, and Vincent d'Indy, who assumed the role of unofficial propagandist. The *franckistes,* as they were also known, typically came from higher social classes, including the nobility, and had the luxury to adopt an idealistic and non-pragmatic view of art. They glorified Franck (whom they nicknamed *Pater seraphicus*) as the disinterested artist *par excellence,* who sought to create pure and sublime works instead of merely entertaining the public. His music was said to proclaim the triumph of faith over doubt, integrity over expediency, good over evil. Ropartz, one of the most loyal members of the *bande,* wrote,

> Among the multitude of contemporary composers, M. César Franck appears to be a man from another time. They are skeptics, he is a believer; they are occupied with themselves, he works in silence; they seek glory, he awaits it; others make concessions and compromises—the basest even, the shameful steps towards easy fame—while he works quietly and firmly at what he has to do, without hesitation, without weakness, without calculation; he has given us the most beautiful example of artistic probity one could encounter.[131]

Franck also gave his pupils lessons in dealing with adversity, for his music aroused passionate opposition. Without meaning to, he developed a gift for attracting disharmony, and never more so than when the Symphony in D minor premiered. The *bande* was struck by his genuinely serene response to harsh antagonism. Some pupils made a virtue of his unpopularity, taking it as a sign that he was following the right path. The following letter from Henri Duparc to Ernest Chausson gives an idea of the idealistic and elitist attitudes common among the *franckistes:*

> You know with what profound and faithful passion I love my admirable Master; your letter moved me to tears because you told me [Franck's Symphony, dedicated to Duparc] is sublime. [Its bad reception] matters little to me: I would even say that a success at the Conservatoire would have disturbed me a bit—I will always refuse to admit that those people have the right to understand the things we love at first hearing. I would even say that if they understood them, we would have to look for another path without delay. But there is no danger, and we can with tranquility write as we think, without having to fear a compromising success.[132]

SYMPHONY IN D MINOR OPUS 48 (FAUQUET 130)[133]

For some time, the *franckistes* had lobbied their teacher to write a symphony, confident that in his maturity he would offer the world a compelling example (as a teenager he had composed a "Première Symphonie à Grand Orchestre," a true *oeuvre de jeunesse* in which the large orchestra plays *tutti* for almost the entire work).[134] Upset with his recent symphonic poems, which they found either unduly graphic (*Le Chasseur maudit,* 1882) or embarrassingly sensual (*Psyché,* 1887–1888), the students repeatedly pestered Franck to allow no extramusical elements into his new work.[135] They need not have worried: intrigued by the challenge of doing something innovative with abstract symphonic form, Franck had no interest in creating a program symphony.

His aspirations were stimulated by two recent works, the *Symphony on a French Mountain Air* by his pupil Vincent d'Indy and Saint-Saëns's "Organ" Symphony. Keen to deny any influence by the latter, d'Indy misrepresented the chronology of his teacher's symphony: he claimed that Franck finished the work before he ever heard the "Organ" Symphony (January 1887), when in fact he had not yet even begun it. Further, despite d'Indy's claims to the contrary, Franck admired his rival's composition and forbade his pupils to criticize it in his presence.[136] He sketched his own symphony in the fall of 1887 and finished the score in August 1888.

Like Saint-Saëns, Franck pointed with pride to the experiments he essayed in his symphony, such as the "double exposition" of the first movement, the embedding of the Scherzo within the slow movement, and the symbolic return of earlier material in the Finale. That he used cyclic procedures was to be expected, since they appeared consistently in his music since his early piano trios of the 1840s, and they were also central features of the symphonies of Saint-Saëns and d'Indy. The structural innovations, on the other hand, reflected Franck's determination to do something new. Perhaps inspired by Saint-Saëns's example, he provided an analytical note to explain these novelties (Table XVI/9 Part A) and privately reinforced these points to his students (Part B). To Pierre de Bréville he described the work as "in some ways the *Quintet* for orchestra," a reference to the Piano Quintet in F minor of 1878–1879.

The opening Lento (4/4, D minor) serves both as slow introduction and *1P*. It contains three subsections of two to four measures each (Franck also constructs *2P, 3P,* and *1S* in this manner). *1Pa* consists, famously, of a gesture found in three prominent works from earlier in the century: the "Muß es sein?" motive from the Finale of Beethoven's String Quartet in F major Opus 135; the opening of Liszt's *Les Préludes;* and the "Fate" motive from Wagner's *Die Walküre* (Example XVI/15a–d). *1Pb* sounds like an organ opening up the registers and *1Pc* leads chromatically to a half cadence. A tremolo passage leads to two repetitions of *1Pa* and *b* in the woodwinds. An ascending sequence growing in instrumentation and dynamic power culminates in a large half cadence.

The tempo changes to Allegro non troppo and the meter to cut time. *2Pa* (m.29) duplicates *1Pa* but *2Pb* goes off in a new direction. *2Pc* concludes the theme with a downward string pattern in double-dotted rhythm (see [2] of Franck's analysis, Table XVI/9, Part A). *3P* (m.39) exemplifies several Franckian characteristics such as chromaticism, twisted contours, and syncopated descending patterns; the cellos accompany with *2Pb* (Example XVI/16). An inversion of *2Pb* ends the *P* group on a minor dominant half cadence.

According to d'Indy, Franck conceived of his symphony as a struggle between the opposing "tonal poles" of D and F, culminating in the victory of the former; all the important harmonic areas in the work relate to one of these "poles." To establish the terms of the conflict, Franck takes the radical step of repeating everything heard to this point up a third, in F minor (m.49); only the final transition differs, an extension of *3Pc* for woodwind choir. The symphony became famous for this so-called "double exposition" (technically a misnomer since it involves only *P*).[137]

Without transition, Franck switches to F major for *S. 1S* is another tripartite melody (m.99; [5] of Table XVI/9, Part A). Based on *3Pc, 1Sa* features counterpoint among the strings while *1Sb* contains dotted-rhythm chromatic twists similar to but more conjunct than *3Pa; 1Sc* extends *1Sb*. Franck repeats *1Sa* and *b* in D-flat major but replaces *1Sc* with a new motive that leads to *2S,* the central melody of the movement. It emerges in the full orchestra in F major (m.129). Unlike the previous melodies, it breaks into only two smaller motifs. Like *3P,* this theme is very characteristic of its composer: *2Sa* centers around one pitch—A appears eight times in four measures—while *2Sb* features another descending chromatic pattern in syncopated rhythm ([6] of Table XVI/9, Part A). *S* closes with a short cadential passage (m.145). *K* juxtaposes *2Sa* in the horns and oboes against another cadential figure (m.175).

TABLE XVI/9
Franck's Comments on His Symphony in D Minor

Part A. Concert note by Franck [Source: Franck/NOTICE, reprinted in Fauquet/FRANCK, pp. 971–75].

First performance by the Société des Concerts in Paris: concerts of 17 and 24 February1889.

I.

Slow and somber introduction:

This phrase is developed for about thirty measures and leads to the Allegro, which has an energetic and animated character:

return of the introduction, but in F minor:

return of the exposition of the Allegro in F minor:

leading to a second phrase:

then to a third, which will be used a great deal in the development and which will reappear in the finale:

After the second part of the Allegro, very developed, a part of the introduction returns, but fortissimo and in canon:

return of the Allegro and conclusion of the first movement.

TABLE XVI/9 (*continued*)

II.

This movement begins with chords plucked by strings and harps, which do not outline the melodic phrase at first. This phrase, which has a sweet and melancholic character, is presented by the English horn:

The clarinet, horn, and flute complete this first period; then the violins state the following phrase:

after some modulations this phrase concludes in B-flat major.

The English horn and various wind instruments again take up some fragments of the first theme in B-flat minor; then we arrive at a section which is a complete movement (belonging to the scherzo genre), very light and very gentle. Here is the principal theme:

At the return of this motive, the initial expressive theme of the movement joins with it: once in G minor, once in C minor. Then the entire expressive melody, stated by the English horn, unites with the whole period of the scherzo, stated by the violins:

III.

This movement begins with a phrase in a clear and quasi-luminous key, thus contrasting with the rather somber and melancholy themes of the two preceding movements:

TABLE XVI/9 (*continued*)

This first theme fills 60 or so measures [actually 71] and leads to a theme in B major stated by the brass, alternating with the strings:

then another, more somber:

then the first theme of the second movement reappears, accompanied by a pattern in triplets:

Developments of the motives of this Finale.
Palpable slowing of the motion.
Fragment of the first motive of the second movement, alternating with fragments of the more somber motive of the Finale [K]—Return of the initial tempo; great crescendo leading to the recapitulation of the motive in D major with as much sound as possible.—Return of the expressive theme of the second movement with full sound.
The sound decreases, and then the third phrase of the first movement reappears:

leading to a coda formed from the principal themes of the first movement, mingled with the initial melody of the Finale.

Part B. Franck's explanation of his symphony to his students [Source: letter of Pierre de Bréville to Vincent d'Indy in *S.I.M.*, 1 November 1913, p. 45, quoted in Fauquet/FRANCK, pp. 723–24].

To some of us, our master explained his work: "It is a classical symphony. At the beginning of the first movement there is a reprise, like that which one did in earlier times to affirm the themes more strongly. But this one is in a different key. Then there is an andante and a scherzo which are tied to each other. I had wanted them to be built in such a way that each beat of the andante is equal to a bar of the scherzo, so that the latter, after a complete development of the two passages, could be superimposed upon the former. I succeeded in solving this problem."

"The finale, like that of [Beethoven's] *Ninth*, recalls all the themes. But they do not appear as mere citations—I do something with them, they take on the role of new elements. I think it's good. I think you will be happy." Certainly we were happy!

EXAMPLE XVI/15A   Franck. Symphony in D Minor/1, mm.1–8.

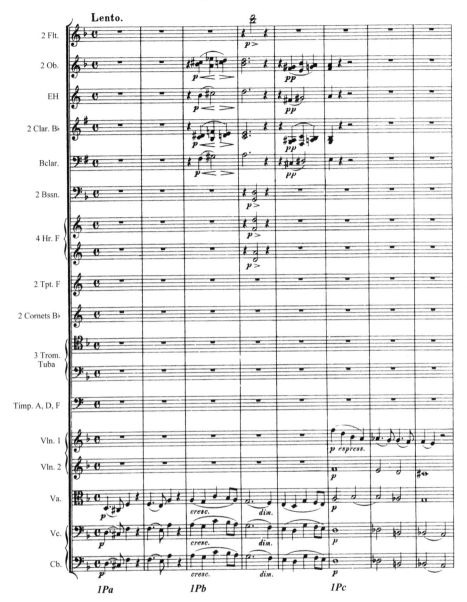

The development proceeds mostly by sequential motion: *1P, 2P, 2S*, and two new motives appear against a background of continuous and wide-ranging modulations. Most keys revolve around the "pole" of F; Franck gives particular attention to A-flat minor, altered mediant to F minor and tritone to D minor. The composer opens the development with a short bridge which passes *2Sa* around the strings (m.191). Section one features *2P* in A-flat minor and B major/minor (m.199). Section two introduces *1N*, which consists of descending

EXAMPLE XVI/15B Beethoven. String Quartet in F Major, Op. 135/4, introductory cipher and mm.1–5.

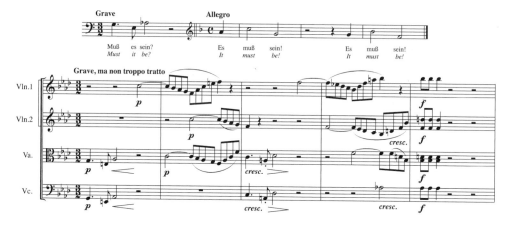

EXAMPLE XVI/15C Liszt. *Les Préludes*, mm.1–5.

EXAMPLE XVI/15D Wagner. *Die Walküre*, Act II/4, opening ("Annunciation of Death") motive.

EXAMPLE XVI/16   Franck. Symphony in D Minor/1, mm.39–46.

patterns repeated sequentially against a pedal on D (m.213); at the end, the key slips to D-flat major.

A-flat returns in section three, the heart of the development. Franck augments *1Pc* and treats it sequentially, beginning in A-flat minor (m.227). A second sequence combines *3Pc* with another new theme, *2N,* which he creates by merging transformations of *1Pa* and *2Pb* (m.245); this passage covers a circular tonal spectrum, from A-flat to E and back to A-flat. Meanwhile, the bass descends by semitones. Sequencing of *1Pc* resumes, each statement articulated by pseudo-Wagnerian surges in the violins at the end of each phrase (m.267). The extended retransition (m.285) pits the opening of *2Sa* against an augmented version of *1Pa*— a dialogue between "faith" and "doubt," perhaps, and a preview of what will come in the Finale.

The striking manner in which Franck intensifies the opening of the recapitulation (Lento, 4/4, m.331; [7] of Table XVI/9, Part A) shows his love of counterpoint. The composer transforms the introduction into an octave canon at the half-bar between the lower strings/trombones and the trumpets/cornets; after starting off with a tremolo pattern, the violins join in the canon. Franck mirrors the exposition "poles" of D and F by presenting *1Pa* and *b* in D minor and B minor. After a brilliant elision created by compressing *1P, 2P* enters in the very distant key of E-flat minor (Allegro, cut time, m.349); he omits *2Pb* and extends *2Pc* canonically to return to the tonic by way of G minor. *3P* (m.375) begins in the Neapolitan E-flat major but likewise turns back to D minor. As if to atone for the irregularities of *P, S* and *K* proceed normally in D minor, save for a brief journey to B-flat major in *1S. Franckiste* hermeneutics might have interpreted the stability of *S* and *K* as a statement that hope and faith remain no matter how much the outside world (symbolized by *P*) may change.

As in the other majestic D-minor symphonies, the Ninths of Beethoven and Bruckner (the latter appeared a few years after Franck's), the coda builds considerable tension. D'Indy considered it a second development, devoted this time to the pole of D.[138] The key returns to D via B-flat minor (m.473). Another new theme appears in the tonic, loosely reminiscent of the bridge to the recapitulation from m.323 and suggesting the rhythm and contour of *2Sa* (m.485). The orchestra builds to a forceful *tutti* featuring *1P*, augmented and canonic, and in Lento tempo (m.513); the movement ends with a plagal cadence in D minor with a Picardy third.

The Allegretto (3/4, B-flat minor) has always been the most admired movement, winning over even those who dislike the rest of the symphony; the critic Camille Bellaigue called it "the oasis in this desert."[139] Light and transparent scoring accompanies lyrical, long-breathed themes, much broader than those in the preceding movement. They break down almost invariably into architectonic units of four, eight, or sixteen measures. The form is innovative. Franck insisted that this modified *A–B–A* encapsulated both slow movement and Scherzo, *B* serving as the latter. Although new to the French symphony, Franck's innovation was not totally without precedent: Franz Berwald did the same in his *Symphonie singulière*, a work which Franck almost certainly did not know (written in 1845, it premiered only in 1905).[140] By implanting one movement into another, Franck claimed he preserved the conventional four-movement structure while doing something new with it. His experiment of embedding proved more audacious than Saint-Saëns's linking two movements together without a break, and it had a greater influence on succeeding generations of symphonists.

Franck sets this movement in the submediant minor. Sixteen measures of plucked strings and harp lay out the harmonic outline of *1P*, which these instruments accompany like a guitar in a serenade. *1P* itself is a lyrical and melancholy melody for the English horn. The first three notes duplicate *I/1Pa* in even quarter notes (Example XVI/17). When asked by his pupil Louis de Serres if the symphony had programmatic inspiration, Franck—presumably to Serres's relief—reportedly replied, "No! – It is music, simply music – However, in composing the Allegretto (especially the first melody), I thought, oh! very vaguely, of a sort of procession of olden times."[141] This is the composer's only recorded reference to extramusical thought in the work. Franck took great pride in this theme, telling critic Pierre Lalo with disarming candor: "Here, my dear child, a marvelous idea came to me—a celestial idea, a truly angelic idea."[142]

The composer repeats the first strain, adding a countermotive in contrary motion in the violas. The second strain also appears twice, first for clarinet and horn (m.33), then with flute joining the melody while cellos provide a countermotive. The final cadence shifts to B-flat major, the proper submediant for a symphony in D minor. Like *I/2S, 2P* moves in a narrow contour, oscillating between upper neighbor notes (m.49; [9] of Table XVI/9,

EXAMPLE XVI/17   Franck. Symphony in D Minor/2, mm.16–28.

Part A). Franck assigns the melody to first violins in counterpoint with the lower strings. The melody begins and ends in B-flat major but modulates within. A shortened form of *1P* closes this section (m.87). To elide to the following Scherzo, Franck places its first motive, *1S,* in dialogue with a fragment from *2P* (m.96); this transition contains numerous stops and starts.

1S (m.109; [10] of Table XVI/9, Part A) is a theme for violins in tremolo triplets set over the same harmonic pattern as that of *1P* but in G minor; the tempo remains the same. The melody recalls Mendelssohn in its use of sixteenth-note rhythms, minor mode, transparent scoring, and mostly quiet dynamics. Like both *P* themes, *2S,* the Trio, is presented contrapuntally: the theme in the clarinet, a countertheme in the lower strings (m.135). *2S* appears in E-flat major and then a third higher in G-flat major. Like *I/3P* and *I/2S, II/2S* has the typical Franckist sound: highly modulatory, with ascending and descending chromatic sequences in dotted rhythm, and laid out in eight bars. (For reasons he did not explain, d'Indy disliked the Trio, dismissing it briskly as "not the best part of the piece.")[143] The rhythm of *1S* continues in the second violins. Chromatic meanderings lead to a final statement of *2S* in E-flat major. *1S* returns in the violins (m.176), and upon it Franck superimposes the opening of *1P* in the English horn. Beginning in G minor, the theme moves down to C minor. More chromatic wanderings lead to the return of the Allegretto.

The reprise of *A* builds on the juxtaposition of *1P* and *1S* (m.200; [11] of Table XVI/9, Part A). The key returns to B-flat minor. After one statement, Franck moves to the Coda (m.222). In this final section, *2P* in the woodwinds trades off against *2S* in the strings. As the composer marks *2P* "poco più lento" and *2S* "Tempo 1," the tempo constantly fluctuates; the passage reminds one of an organ with shifting registers. Traveling through B major and F major, Franck arrives definitively at B-flat major and quietly ends the movement via a plagal cadence.

In the sonata form Finale (Allegro non troppo, cut time), Franck "resolves" the issues raised in the previous movements. Loud octave Ds in the strings followed by fast alternations of B-flat-seventh and D-major chords in the rest of the orchestra (perhaps to recall the key of the previous movement) produce a burst of that "pure joy and life-giving light" that d'Indy described as the hallmark of this symphony.[144] Unlike that of the first movement, this exposition follows a conventional outline. *P* (m.7) is one of the most famous melodies in French symphonic literature: long, syncopated, and spontaneous-sounding despite its layout in four-measure groups, it stays mostly in the tonic D major but touches briefly upon other areas (Example XVI/18; see also [12] of Table XVI/9, Part A). The signature contour of *II/1P* appears in the melody (as in *II/P*), at the beginning of the second strain (mm.19–20); this section promptly undergoes significant motivic stretching. The melody ends with another B-flat to D inflection.

T begins with a *tutti* statement of *P,* and then wanders afield (m.37). *S* consists of a brass chorale, followed by an effusive answer in the strings (m.72; [13] of Table XVI/9, Part A). Starting off in B major (another mediant relation), it modulates by ascending major thirds until again reaching B. At the point of return, however, Franck shifts to B minor for *K* (m.98; [14] of Table XVI/9, Part A). Brooding in nature, this *S*-derived theme appears twice, the second time with counterpoint. To conclude the exposition, Franck changes the meter to 3/4 while maintaining the same beat, i.e., $\mathsf{C}\ \! \mathord{\downarrow} = 3/4\ \mathord{\downarrow}$ and inserts a complete statement of *II/1P* in B minor (m.125; [15] of Table XVI/9, Part A); the composer noted this early example of "metric modulation" in his comments to his students about the symphony (see Table XVI/9, Part B). Except for a running triplet accompaniment in the violins and violas and harmonic support in the horns and upper woodwinds, the scoring remains the same as in the original. As in the second movement, the mode changes at the final cadence.

The development treats *P, S,* and *K* in succession. Maintaining the beat, the meter returns to cut time. The peaceful first section (m.140) trades *Pa* among various instruments in a descending sequence from B major to A-flat major. Section two (m.187) presents *S* in

EXAMPLE XVI/18 Franck. Symphony in D Minor/3, mm.1–20.

EXAMPLE XVI/18   (*continued*)

chromatic *tutti* statements; it ends on a dominant ninth chord over G, followed by a grand pause. The tempo slows for section three (Più lento, m.212), which features a dialogue in G minor between the opening of *K* in the strings and a fragmentary *II/1P* in the woodwinds. The original tempo (Allegro non troppo) returns at the retransition (m.228), a series of increasingly chromatic ascents and descents leading from G minor to the dominant of D major.

The recapitulation is short, limited to *P* and *II/1P* (m.268). *P* begins with an even greater burst than before, *Pa* appearing throughout most of the orchestra in octaves; the second half confines itself to the violins, as before. *II/1P* enters abruptly, in a *fortissimo* statement for full orchestra in D minor against sixteenth-note runs in the strings (m.300); again the meter changes but Franck preserves the initial beat. The change of mode to D major at the final cadence (mm.313–14) signals the decisive harmonic victory; never again will the music be so dark.

Now that he has tamed *II/1P,* Franck turns to the themes from the first movement. For the last time he returns to ¢ meter (directing, as always, that the beat remain the same). A transition (m.318) moves us to B-flat major, in which key *I/2S* appears quietly, alternating between the strings and the woodwinds (m.330). As the coda begins, the long-delayed confrontation ensues between the two themes that for *franckistes* represented the opposing poles of faith and doubt. *I/1P* ("doubt") appears in D major in "celestial" fashion—quiet, in augmentation, with murmuring harp arpeggios; *I/2S* ("faith") answers in E-flat major (m.354). Franck then repeats this exchange up a semitone.

However tempered by its quiescent "celestial" surroundings, *I/1P* remains a dark element; Franck thus expels the motive and replaces it with *III/P* ("joy," according to Ropartz), which engages in a short dialogue with *I/2S* (m.386). At the end, only *III/P* remains, given in a full and exuberant statement in D major. The symphony closes in "joy" with *III/Pa* in canon for the *tutti* orchestra, in the tonic. (Table XVI/10 provides an outline summary of the complete symphony.)

Franck's Symphony in D Minor faced intense opposition from the start. The composer wanted Charles Lamoureux to give the premiere, as his audience tended to be the most receptive to new works, but the conductor disliked Franck's music and told Chausson (asking on his teacher's behalf) to take the composition to the Société des Concerts du Conservatoire, which he called "the temple for the symphony."[145] The Conservatoire's programming committee accepted the work. The *franckistes* interpreted this pleasant turn of events as a sign of growing respect for their teacher, but it also disquieted them for they sensed trouble ahead. If d'Indy is to be believed—and his relentless determination to portray Franck as a martyr to the Conservatoire Philistines potentially renders his uncorroborated account suspect—the problems started right away: the orchestra hated the symphony, and only the insistence of conductor Jules Garcin allowed the premiere to proceed on February 17 and 24, 1889.[146]

As his students predicted, the notoriously conservative audience of the Société reacted coldly to Franck's work. Pierre de Bréville left an account:

> Among the subscribers only four or five of us [Franck's pupils] were able to slip in. They were almost alone in applauding, and even that greatly scandalized our neighbors. I can still see an old lady who, totally serious and with eyes fixed, spoke as if *ex cathedra* to everyone and to no one but in reality to me, and declared, "Why play this symphony here? Who is this Monsieur Franck? – a harmonium professor, I believe –."

TABLE XVI/10

César Franck. Symphony in D Minor: Structure

Movement I

Introduction: Lento C	*Exposition:* Allegro non troppo ¢		*Introduction:* Lento C	*Exposition:* Allegro non troppo ¢					
1P	2P (1P)	3P	1P	2P (1P)	3P	trans. ¢	1S	2S	K (2S)
D minor			F minor				F major		
1	29	39	49	77	87	95	99	129	175

Development

Part 1		*Part 2*	*Part 3*			*Part 4* (retransition)		
2Sa mod.	2P	1N	1Pc	3Pc+2N	1Pc	2Sa+1Pc	2Sa+1Pa	bridge
191	199	213	227	245	267	285	293	323

Recapitulation

Lento C		Allegro ¢		3P		1S	2S	K
1P	1Pe	2P ext.	2Pa+2Pc	3P	3Pc	1S	2S	K
D minor, B minor		E-flat minor		E-flat major → D minor		D major		
331	345	349	361	375	381	389	419	465

Coda

trans.	3N	Lento	
		1Pa	
D minor		D minor with Picardy third	
473	485	513	

Movement II

A | Slow movement, Allegretto 3/4

Introduction	2P	1P	trans.
1P	2P	1P	trans.
B-flat minor/major	B-flat major	B-flat minor/major	
17	49	87	96

TABLE XVI/10 (continued)

B   Scherzo and Trio

1S	2S (1S) Trio	1S+1P
G minor	E-flat major	G minor
109	135	176

A/B   Slow movement and Scherzo combined

1P+1S	*Coda*
B-flat minor	2P+2S
200	mod. to B-flat major
	222

Movement III

Exposition Allegro non troppo ¢
"blazing light"

P	T (P)	S	K (S)	II/P
D major	37	B major	B minor	125
1		72	98	

Development

P	S	K, II/P (altered)	
B major mod.	A-flat major mod.	G minor	retrans.
140	187	212	mod. to A
			228

Recapitulation   *Coda*

P	II/P	I/2S	II/P ("celestial" transformation)	I/2S + III/P	III/P in canon
D major	D minor/major	B-flat major	D major, E-flat major	E major, D major	D major
268	300	318	354	386	426

The next day the press remained silent. A small musical newspaper inserted an abusive article in which Delibes was accused of committing a great blunder because he applauded.[147]

Romain Rolland recorded a similar account in his diary:

An organ style. A regular development, powerful, stiff. Phrases chopped up harshly, shouted out by the brass. Dryness at times. Brusque passages without transitions, from *fff* to *ppp* (as in [Franck's oratorio] the *Béatitudes*). But there is grandeur, emotion, thoughts that recall the *Béatitudes*. A personality.

In the hall, three audiences: frenzied applause—very few; more numerous—"Hush! Hush!" (They are normally rare at the Conservatoire). These calls came mostly from the front boxes. During the performance, I saw some listeners pretending to stop up their ears. Finally, the mass of the public, indifferent.[148]

As part of their agenda to make Franck a victim, d'Indy and other pupils gleefully circulated comments attributed to the composer's uncomprehending colleagues. Charles Gounod allegedly (and enigmatically) condemned the symphony as "the affirmation of incompetence pushed to dogmatic lengths." Most biographies of Franck take the authenticity of this quip for granted, but in fact Gounod was not in Paris when the symphony premiered.[149] Ambroise Thomas was quoted as asking, "What is a symphony in D minor whose first theme is in D-flat at the ninth measure, C-flat at the tenth, F-sharp minor at the twenty-first, C minor at the twenty-sixth, E-flat at the thirty-ninth, and F minor at the forty-ninth?"[150] And d'Indy quoted an unnamed professor who famously asked him,

That, a symphony? But dear sir, who ever heard of writing a part for English horn in a symphony? Name one symphony by Haydn or Beethoven where you will find an English horn –. Well then, you see that this music of your Franck is all you would want it to be, but it will never be a symphony![151]

Contrary to Bréville's assertion that the press ignored the new work, critics lit into it. Johannès Weber of *Le Temps* criticized the analytical note as a distraction (he did the same with the "Organ" Symphony). Toward the music he was lukewarm at best:

M. Franck sins by an excess of enthusiasm: in wanting to do too much, he has made his work dull and has abused chromatic progressions to a singular degree.[152]

Camille Bellaigue, on the other hand, loathed the work and compared it very unfavorably to the "Organ" Symphony. His review provides a valuable appraisal of the merits of "classical" and "romantic" symphonies from the conservative perspective:

The other day I heard M. Franck's overzealous disciples comparing the symphony of their master with the latest symphony of M. Saint-Saëns—or should I say they were impudently immolating the latter. . . . Of these two symphonies, one is night and the other day: with the latter a person breathes with full lung capacity, with the former he chokes and dies. In M. Saint-Saëns's work, the structure appears and asserts itself right away; in M. Franck's it hides and steals away. One always follows M. Saint-Saëns's theme—it moves around, divides into a thousand clear and fruitful little streams, and then restores and reassembles itself; but M. Franck's themes are born only to be lost right away, without any flower springing up from their passing. Oh! This arid and drab music, without any touch of grace or charm, without a smile! The motives themselves most often lack interest: the first, a kind of musical question mark, is hardly above the level of those themes that students at the Conservatoire are given to develop. Another theme has more allure and daring, but the composer has not made the most of it.

The beginning of the second movement is the oasis in this desert. For an instant one feels refreshed by a beautiful song in the English horn, supported by the plucked chords of harps and strings. Perhaps sitting at his organ one evening, M. Franck found this almost religious inspiration—a religious feeling that is neither insipid nor mystically sensual. Why didn't he follow through on this theme? Why didn't he make a whole movement out of this happy theme, as the composer of the "Italian" Symphony did with an equally religious melody? Because M. Franck is not Mendelssohn; and we will not permit ourselves to be sorry if, the other day, one of his followers did not allow himself to rejoice over it.

The Finale of the *Symphony in D Minor* seemed especially painful. With a fury it brings back the motives of the preceding movements. Perhaps one mustn't abuse this [cyclic] system, which is much in favor today. Haydn used it (*adagio* and *presto* of the 58th Quartet) and Beethoven after him, but both used it reservedly. M. Saint-Saëns did the same, with much more insistence and in much larger proportions; but, in the finale of the Symphony in C Minor, the motives which are already familiar—and which are much more interesting in themselves than those of M. Franck—pass through rhythmic, harmonic, and instrumental metamorphoses that are so varied and unexpected that one always remains amazed. M. Franck is far from this abundance and brilliance, and what he takes to be unity and cohesion could well be nothing but aridity and poverty.[153]

As the above suggests, Franck's critics complained about the symphony's unorthodox structure, pervasive chromaticism, and simplistic thematic material. But others were offended less by supposed technical deficiencies than by the work's palpable emotionalism. More than Saint-Saëns's symphony, Franck's seemed to be *about* something. As we have seen, interpretations of its message mostly centered on a struggle between "darkness" (doubt, evil) and "light" (faith, goodness, joy), with the ultimate triumph of the latter. The *franckistes* responded strongly to this hermeneutic. Speaking for them, Camille Benoît praised the composition, using the quasi-ecstatic rhetoric with which Franck's pupils typically described music:

[Franck's symphony] introduced an element that was new, lively, young, and ardent into the midst of this coterie of enervated people. . . . For me, above all I love to see in this work the nobility and beauty of soul of a Master worthy of all veneration; alongside the virile sorrows of a lofty spirit, alongside the outbursts of a vigorous faith and an inexhaustible energy, I love to see in this composition the tendernesses and delicateness of a heart remaining young. . . . I love to find there . . . the courageous cheerfulness that can confront the baseness, tyrannies, and cruelties in the combat of life; the splendid folly of the martyr; the joyous disdain which good has for malice, which the high has for the low; the inevitable triumph of what is just.[154]

As he did for Lalo's symphony, Ropartz assigned affective titles to several themes, although his choice of motives to label was somewhat arbitrary. I/1S he called the "theme of hope," perhaps to underscore it as the first positive-sounding melody in the symphony, while I/2S became the "theme of faith," belief presumably being reflected in its tonal stability.

Curiously, he did not name any *P* themes or any melodies from the second movement. *III/P* he entitled the "theme of joy," *III/S* the "theme of triumph" (a dubious choice since the motive disappears after the development) and *III/K* the "theme of trouble."[155]

Franck's symphony gained friends outside the *bande,* sometimes from unexpected quarters. Emmanuel Chabrier and Jules Massenet voiced strong support; and Claude Debussy, who was not in the habit of praising symphonies, told his teacher Ernest Guiraud that "Father Franck's symphony is amazing. I would like less solid build [*carrure*]. But what stylish ideas!"[156]

And what was Franck's own response? Let Bréville tell us:

> At the exit, we trembled at the prospect of finding Father Franck saddened by the frigidity of the public.
>
> He was radiant! He had heard his music—a joy which he was rarely accorded—and it seemed to him that the symphony had pleased. – and he reckoned that it would please even more the following Sunday, since at this time the B series of subscribers had the reputation of being "more advanced" than Series A (I don't know why).[157]

If he really believed that his work had gone over well, Franck was mercifully oblivious; but his reaction seems to have been genuine and illustrates the engaging naiveté for which the composer was celebrated. According to Bréville, Franck regarded the performance as a joy and a lesson ("I received a precious one today on the manner of using the brass").[158] And Franck's son told d'Indy that on arriving home after the premiere, the composer informed his anxious family that the work "sounded well, like I thought it would!"[159]

Before long, the Symphony in D minor overcame its inauspicious debut, though not soon enough for the composer to enjoy it (he died the following year, in 1890). By 1900, the work had become the most popular French symphony; only Beethoven's symphonies and Berlioz's "dramatic legend" *La Damnation de Faust* rivaled it in public favor.[160] It had a decisive impact not only on composers in his circle but on anyone attracted to the Romantic pole of symphonic composition. Franck influenced later French composers in their melodic style (chromatic motives, sequential motions in dotted rhythms), choice of structure (embedding movements—though some, possibly misconstruing Franck's intentions, composed symphonies in three movements without embedding), and approach to the cyclic process (the "Organ" Symphony notwithstanding, thematic recall came to be associated primarily with Franck, especially when it did not involve thematic transformation). Franck exercised both a stylistic and aesthetic influence: the sense of emotional expression, a philosophical program of "darkness" yielding to "light"—these are also the legacies of Franck's symphony, however much they occur in earlier works, e.g., Beethoven's Fifth. Guy Ropartz summed up what the *franckistes* saw as their master's contribution:

> There are also "true philosophical thoughts" that M. César Franck has expressed in this symphony through the medium of sounds. As it is childish to try to paint objects of the outside world through sounds, so it is rational to choose the immaterial language of music to translate sensations, sentiments, the ideas of a high-minded philosophy. One can think in music the same as one can think in prose and in verse; M. César Franck thinks in music.[161]

The controversy over the Symphony in D minor continues into our day. Although in the twentieth century it became one of the most popular of all symphonies, the work has received scant analytical attention, and most writers content themselves with enumerating its strengths and weaknesses according to their perspective. Few symphonies, in fact, have elicited so much qualified praise or outright censure: typically, when analysts do not damn the piece, they adopt Norman Demuth's verdict that "never was there such magnificent music so badly written."[162]

Following the lead of Weber, Bellaigue, and others, Franck's critics have drawn up a sizeable bill of indictments against the workmanship, melodic style, and harmonic language of his symphony. The composition unfolds like an organ improvisation, full of distracting stops and starts, abrupt tempo changes, short phrases merely strung together, endless sequences and modulations, and so forth; I/1P is too short, while on the other hand I/1S repeats the same pitch excessively; the symphony moves in too many four-bar phrases; the cyclic treatment is forced, imposing reprises instead of allowing them to emerge naturally; the chromaticism becomes cloying; and the orchestration of the outer movements resembles an organist changing manuals, while the Finale, insisting immoderately on its victory, gives too much prominence to the brass. Finally, declare the naysayers, the work is ineptly titled: Franck's composition makes its effect (allegedly) by appeals to emotion rather than purely musical logic, and therefore the work should not be called a symphony.[163]

The outer movements receive most of the criticism, especially the first. Franck's melodic faults, his "abuse" of sequence and modulation, the slow (indeed ponderous) unfolding of material, the organ-like orchestration—all of these abound in that movement, according to the critics. At the same time, one could argue, they have overstated these supposed weaknesses. As with Bruckner, with whom Franck is often compared, elements that appear in isolation as structural or stylistic flaws cohere to powerful effect; further, they become of secondary importance if performers present the drama straightforwardly instead of trying to conceal it. But while they should not be apologetic about projecting the drama, neither ought they compound it by playing the work at a slower tempo than Franck indicates or inserting additional rhetoric through ritardandos and fermatas. Franck is often blamed for the sins of the conductor. Paradoxically, perhaps, the French understand this best; for all that they may have carped about surcharged emotionalism, the most successful performances of this symphony are often led by French or at least Francophile conductors and orchestras.

Ernest Chausson

Ernest Chausson (1855–1899), one of Franck's most illustrious pupils, enjoyed independent wealth and could devote extensive time and effort to composition (Plate B22). He found the process arduous and even torturous. Obsessed with creating works that were at once deeply passionate and technically flawless (a fixation shared by most of the *franckistes* except d'Indy), Chausson suffered perennial disappointment as he measured what he accomplished against his ideal. His letters bear ample witness to his frustration, as here in 1884:

> In spite of all I have told you about the perception of a work of art and the discouragement I feel at never being able to create one, I labor as if I thought completely differently at that moment. But once that warm feeling has passed, I erupt with rage at seeing how what I can do is so far from what I would like to do, from what I seem to hear in my head. And the next day I go back to work all the same.[164]

The composer never overcame his feelings of inadequacy. He wrote the following in 1889 as he struggled over his opera *Le Roi Arthus*:

I flounder, I growl, I believe I've found it, I erase it, I work like a wretch, and I barely make any progress, I go to sleep in despair and I wake up terrified; I would like to talk with friends and afterwards I'm afraid of what they could say to me; time goes on, frightful time; that's how I live.[165]

SYMPHONY IN B-FLAT MAJOR OPUS 20

Chausson's battles of self-doubt reached a climax as he worked on the Symphony in B-flat major, his first large-scale instrumental piece (Table XVI/11). The composer documented his inner torments in letters to his friend Paul Poujaud and his brother-in-law Henry Lerolle. The first movement seems to have gone fairly smoothly, but the middle movement caused problems. His anxieties peaked in the Finale when he labored unsuccessfully to resolve a single measure (not identified) on which he had been stuck for over a month. The letters tell a story of intense discouragement:

[October 31, 1889, to Lerolle:] I'm in too odious a mood to write. Here it's been more than a week that I've been stuck in the same place. Impossible to move forward, and I work like a wretch. I'm mad with rage.[166]

[November 1889, to Poujaud:] Imagine that since I've been here I work like a wretch and I'm still at the same measure! I've tried hard to stop; impossible. I return to my paper as to a vice. To do anything else, more impossible still. I cannot think and I can only think of that one measure; so I curse it, I insult myself, I throw punches at myself. As you can imagine, that does a lot of good. The most horrible thing is that what I am doing is very good. I don't tell you that very often about my music; this time, I sincerely believe it's good. . . . I play what I've done over and over, always hoping that a good inspiration will allow me to get past the fatal measure, and it's always the same thing: I start over and stop anew.[167]

[Later in November, again to Poujaud:] No, I haven't found it. And after this measure, there have been others that I haven't found any better. . . . You've said it well, I can attest that some moments of ease are necessary. For the moment I've plunged myself completely into *The Magic Flute*.[168]

[December 5, 1889, to Lerolle:] Mongrel, what a mess you've put me in! [a good-natured complaint; it was Lerolle who persuaded Chausson to try his hand at a symphony] . . . I've never been in this state for so long. . . . It's the Andante—I haven't been able to get it on its feet. Yet the components seem good to me, but the whole doesn't fit together well. . . . And this scoundrel of a Finale! . . . I remain like an idiot on the same measure. What I need is a phrase in C-sharp in 4/4.[169]

Eventually Chausson conquered all difficulties and completed the work. He was happy with the end result, all the more for it having been so hard-won. The composer had the further satisfaction of receiving Franck's blessing: Chausson played the symphony for his teacher shortly before Franck's death, and "he absolutely adored the first two movements. He found something to revise in the middle of the finale. All the same I believe that I will have to do hardly any retouching."[170] Chausson dedicated the symphony to Lerolle.

Among Franck's disciples, Chausson's music most closely resembles his, at least on the surface. Some analysts stress affinities between their symphonies to the point of portraying Chausson's as a clone.[171] Both works consist of three cyclically unified movements, both slow

TABLE XVI/11

The Symphonies of Ernest Chausson

Opus	Key	Date	Title	Movements	Instrumentation	Comments
20	B-flat Major	1889–90	Symphony in B-Flat Major	1. Lent (4/4)—Allegro vivo 3/4 (680 m.) 2. Très lent 4/4 (101 m.) D minor 3. Animé ¢ (510 m.) B-flat minor/major	Grand+Picc., EH, Bclar., Bssn., 2 Tpt., 2 Harps	Dedicated to Henry Lerolle. First performance: Paris, Société Nationale, conducted by Chausson on April 18, 1891. Published in Paris: Rouart, Lerolle, et Cie., 1908 (four-hand piano reduction: E. Bardoux, 1896).
W60		1899	Symphony No. 2 [?]	Fragment of first movement		Opening sketched shortly before Chausson's death.

movements have prominent solos for English horn, each features a climactic canonic passage (though in different movements), and the final movements represent a struggle between "light" and "darkness" that culminates in the victory of "light."

As usual with such comparisons, however, the differences are more numerous and striking. Chausson does not copy the unique structural features of Franck's symphony: the first movement has no double exposition, nor does the composer embed a Scherzo within the slow movement—his symphony divides unambiguously into three movements. The Finale recalls themes from the first movement (though not the second) but does not set them into conflict with motives from the Finale and change "darkness" into "light." While some themes follow *franckiste* two- and four-bar phrase construction, many are of longer breadth and not as chromatic. Similarly, Chausson creates a more transparent and varied orchestration, writing many passages for solo instruments; only the final coda resembles organ-like registrations and then by design, in order to reinforce the closing chorale. Finally, Chausson's work is not as dramatic in its overall ambiance as Franck's, though it certainly has its share of striking moments. More comprehensive comparisons of the two symphonies are available elsewhere.[172]

The interval of the third is central to each movement: I/O, II/A, III/P, and other themes feature it prominently, either as a leap or filled-in gesture, and many modulation patterns move by that interval. Other notable characteristics include sequences of short descending patterns, though Chausson does not rely as much as Franck on this process to generate momentum; hemiola rhythms or at least the illusion of same (e.g., II/P, III/S); and tripartite divisions of *P* and *S* in the outer movements. Both the orchestration and certain thematic constructions reflect the influence of Wagner as much as Franck, and sometimes more so.

The symphony opens with an extensive and dramatic introduction (Lent). The cyclic theme, *O*, appears at the outset in middle and low strings, first and fourth horns, and first clarinet: its nine measures divide into two phrases, *a* and *b*. The key is B-flat but the mode uncertain because Chausson employs both natural and flattened versions of the third degree (Example XVI/19). A descending pattern gives way to a rising one derived from *Oa*, supported by an ascending bass (m.23). The sequence culminates in a *fortissimo* statement of *Oa* for full orchestra in B minor and C-sharp minor (m.33). The introduction ends with a bridge featuring drooping ♭6–5 appoggiaturas over a dominant pedal. Chausson's emphasis on dark timbres, pervasive sequences, and descending semitonal appoggiaturas creates an atmosphere of ominous foreboding like that of Wagner's *Ring*. An upward flourish in the first violins and upper woodwinds suddenly clears the air and ushers in the sunny exposition.

P enters in the first horn and bassoon (Allegro vivo, m.48); a sixteen-bar melody divided into two equal phrases, it progresses in a hemiola-like pattern suggesting 6/4 or 3/2 instead of

EXAMPLE XVI/19   Chausson. Symphony in B-flat Major/1, mm.1–9. © by Editions Salabert.

EXAMPLE XVI/20   Chausson. Symphony in B-flat Major/1, mm.48–64. © by Editions Salabert.

the notated 3/4. *Pa* begins diatonically while *Pb* becomes more chromatic (Example XVI/20). Chausson repeats *P* with a new scoring (m.64). An unexpected G-sharp diminished seventh chord heralds a connecting bridge consisting of sequential repetitions of an ascending arpeggio (m.80). *P* closes with a varied restatement of the theme, accompanied by the full orchestra (Allegro molto, m.108): in place of *Pb* Chausson introduces a new module, *Pc*, which gives a strong sense of closure even though the key has already begun to stray from the tonic. The phrase construction changes from four to two bars.

T features a perky pyramid-shaped staccato phrase in solo woodwinds (*Ta*) against a short lyrical line in the violins (*Tb*) which presages *S* (m.146). Pentatonic in mode, *Ta* moves the harmony to C-sharp major. The opening of *S* (m.164) fulfills the expectations aroused by *Tb*. In F-sharp major (enharmonic third to B-flat) and scored for solo strings and winds, this theme, like *P*, subdivides into two smaller units; this time, however, the divisions are asymmetrical—12 (6 + 6) + 10. Again like *P*, *S* consists of three sections. High violins dominate the chromatic second section, accompanied by horns and winds (m.186). The hemiola rhythms of *P* return. For the last section, Chausson expands the reprise of *S*— 16 + 12 measures, all in four-bar units—with *Ta* filling in the space between the phrases (m.202). *S* ends with an embellished chromatic octave ascent in the cellos. A short bridge based on *Pa* connects the exposition to the development (Plus lent, m.246); a slower and subdued passage for oboe and flute in F-sharp major, it recalls the equivalent moment in the first movement of Franck's symphony, which is built upon the first phrase of *S* (cf. Franck, mm.175–89).

The development repeats *P*, *T*, and *O* in various colors and keys; most modulations take place by thirds. Like Franck's, Chausson's development includes many tempo variations. In section one (Allegro scherzando, m.261), pizzicato strings and staccato woodwinds bounce around a skeleton outline of *Pa* in B-flat minor and D minor. A syncopated ascending pattern faintly resembling *Pc* migrates throughout the orchestra, culminating in a four-octave harp flourish in D major. Section two centers on *T* (m.305). Beginning in G pentatonic, the repetitions rise by thirds. Chausson then concentrates only on *Ta*. The sequences reach a climax with a diminished seventh on G.

In the third section, *Pa* returns in varied form, followed by free material (Cédez un peu, m.346). A descending cadential gesture composed of two whole steps with a major third between (somewhat similar to *I/K* of d'Indy's *Symphony on a French Mountain Air*) eventually becomes a flute ostinato while two horns play a further adaptation of *Pa* in straight 3/4 meter in E-flat major (m.399). The oboe repeats *Pa* without the ostinato a half-step lower. The tempo picks up for a lengthy retransition (Allegro molto, m.417). *O* appears in augmentation in the brass, while portions of *T* accompany and separate the phrases. The modulations go through various flat keys, all minor; the section ends with a two-octave chromatic ascent in thirds in the clarinets, recalling the flourish that closes the introduction.

Unlike most of the symphonies we have examined thus far, the recapitulation of this one begins quietly, with the first horn and harp (taking the place of the bassoon) stating *P* over soft Wagnerian-style arpeggios in the violins and flutes (Allegro vivo, m.495). Chausson proceeds directly to *S* in the woodwinds in G major (m.559); the second statement of this theme receives the intensification we might have expected for *P*. Since he gave it to the wrong theme and an unstable key area (a modulatory D major), the composer follows *S* with a final statement of *Pa* for full orchestra in the tonic, thus providing a dynamic and timbral climax with the "proper" theme and key; to reinforce the sense of closure, he adds *Sa* as a countermelody (m.626). An animated coda ensues, based almost totally on *Pa* in cut time (Presto, m.642); the rhythm is "straightened out," without syncopation or hemiola.

The slow movement (Très lent), generally described as a lament, represents the emotional heart of the symphony and was the passage most commented upon by reviewers, favorably or otherwise. Composing it gave Chausson much trouble. He originally implanted a Scherzo into the middle *à la* Franck but expunged it, finding the passage ill-suited to the surrounding material:

> [November 9–13, 1889, to Lerolle:] Your scoundrel of a symphony has left me in a pretty state. Finally, I have left the andante behind, or just about, but by a violent means. . . . I have always had the pleasure of thinking I had finished with it. Then I played it all the way through. Then I saw very clearly that the middle was not only abominable—which doesn't surprise me—but also perfectly useless. I'm simply going to have to cut it out and make a skillful weld, if I can, and recast the ending.[173]

Chausson's instincts proved correct. In Franck the merger of the two movements works because the general ambiance is lyrical and relatively light; Chausson's movement, on the other hand, is brooding and intense, and a Scherzo interlude would not only have sounded out of place but would have diluted the mood. Chausson's refusal to mimic Franck shows that he was more concerned with letting his music follow its natural course than adhering to his teacher's model, regardless of what his critics said. Everything in this movement unfolds logically, and little trace remains of the composer's creative struggles.

In ternary form and D minor, the movement emphasizes expressive lyricism in which the interval of a third again plays an essential role. *A* opens with a plaintive theme to be played "with a grand intensity of expression." A filled-in third in the violins (*x*) is answered with another third in the violas and low woodwinds in syncopated rhythm (*y*), producing a minor-dominant harmony (Example XVI/21). Although notated in 4/4, the melody actually unfolds in 6/4, so that the downbeat regularly shifts from the first to third beats of the measure. A chromatic sequence leads to a subdominant cadence and an extension back to D minor. The whole passage suggests Grieg, specifically "Åse's Death" from *Peer Gynt;* the Norwegian composer enjoyed considerable popularity in Paris at the time Chausson wrote his symphony, so the familial resemblance may not be a coincidence.[174] The central section of *A* begins with another short motive built from thirds (m.19); the material that follows recalls Chausson's Arthurian tone poem *Viviane* (1882). *1A* returns rescored in A minor (m.33); runs of thirds and filled-in thirds accompany the theme, which achieves a final cadence in E minor. A short transition extending the final cadence moves the harmony to B-flat major.

EXAMPLE XVI/21 Chausson. Symphony in B-flat Major/2, mm.1–20. © by Editions Salabert.

A striking change of scoring announces *B* (Un peu plus vite, m.44): various string accompaniments of soft oscillating triplets, arpeggios, tremolos, and a pedal on B-flat (all marked ***ppp***) support a lyrical and expressive theme for English horn doubled by a solo cello in high register. (All three of the principal *franckiste* symphonies of the 1880s and early 1890s—Franck's, Chausson's, and d'Indy's *Mountain Air*—feature prominent solos for the English horn; it is not clear whether they inspired each other or were all influenced by earlier examples, especially Wagner's languorous passage in Act III of *Tristan.*) The melody begins in B-flat major but shifts quickly to the minor. The violins, cellos, and first horn repeat the theme as the winds play ascending arabesques.

Thirty-second runs in the woodwinds and strings underpin a motive that vaguely resembles *III/P* (m.65). A short quasi-*franckiste* canonic passage based on *1Ax* introduces an impassioned restatement of the complete *1A* in D minor (Un peu plus vite, m.75): the brass sound *x,* the strings and lower winds *y,* and the winds add oscillating thirds over the

EXAMPLE XVI/21   (*continued*)

cadential note of *y*. *2A* returns, equally intense, in brass and strings (m.83). The coda (Mouvement du commencement, m.92) faintly recalls *2Ay* at the beginning and ends with a broad assertion of *1A* in D major, bringing this turbulent movement to a close on a Picardy third.

Chausson also considered adding a Scherzo between the second and third movements to alleviate the dark mood created by placing two "heavy" and "somber" movements back to back. He abandoned this idea as well, in part because he could not decide on a shape for the movement: "I would not want a classical Scherzo. It has to go well with the rest of the symphony, and that would be difficult with the rhythm of a Scherzo."[175] Again Chausson displayed sound instincts, for the two movements need no mediation and a light-spirited passage would indeed have proved just as unsuitable here as within the slow movement.

The Finale has a reputation as the weak link in this symphony. Critics habitually blame Franck, supposing that Chausson patterned his movement after his teacher's and

EXAMPLE XVI/21 (*continued*)

copied its defects as well as its virtues. But the problems in Chausson's movement do not arise from an overreliance on Franck; in fact, the relationship between the two once more is exaggerated. Franck's finale supposedly portrays the defeat of darkness and the triumph of light by means of a "conflict" between the plaintive *III/A* and the affirmative *III/P,* as well as the "taming" of *I/1P* in the coda. Chausson, on the other hand, does not reprise material from the second movement. *I/P* returns in a Scherzoish transformation but its alternations with *III/P* do not suggest conflict, let alone a contest between darkness and light; he achieves "victory" by changing *I/O* into a brass chorale—one which moreover makes a stronger impact than Franck's. The snag is the development, which loses momentum and rambles as if the composer has lost his place. It is well to remember Chausson's travails in composing this movement; unlike the slow movement, the Finale bears the scars of his struggles.

From the outset, the mood changes from introspection to storm and stress: over a carpet of agitated and scurrying sixteenth notes in the strings (in cut time), the trumpet and middle woodwinds attempt to enunciate *III/P* but manage only the first phrase. Shifting down from B-flat minor to A-flat minor, the rescored ensemble tries again but this bid proves just as unsuccessful. As the exposition opens, the lower strings state *P* in a more extended but still incomplete version in B-flat minor (Très animé, m.29). Finally, the violins present a full statement of the theme: thirds, syncopations, dotted rhythms, and descending chromaticism all figure in it, thereby relating *III/P* to *I/O* and *II/1A,* though it does not derive from them. The theme begins symmetrically but breaks into uneven extensions which travel into the extreme high register of the violins. Like *I/P,* the full statement begins to wander tonally, so that it could almost serve simultaneously as a transitional function.

The actual *T* (m.77) is a two-bar motive which passes through various instruments, changing key as it does so: most striking is the unprepared shift to major mode (G-sharp major, mm.81–82). *T* then breaks down to one-bar units migrating among the woodwinds, after which the strings take over with a rising sequence that dissolves into a series of runs.

S (Encore plus animé, m.99), like *I/P* and *I/S,* falls into a tripartite structure. Section one is a chorale for full orchestra, stated homorhythmically in white notes in D major; notated in cut time, the theme moves as if in syncopated 4/2 bars. Section two (m.115) introduces a new motive based on *1S* in the oboe and clarinet, underpinned by cross-rhythms in the strings (eighth notes versus layers of eighth-note and quarter-note triplets). When *1S* returns in the strings, Chausson adjusts the rhythm, beginning the theme on a downbeat instead of an upbeat as before. A chromatic descending motive in the lower strings interrupts the chorale before it completes its thought (m.139).

As noted, the development poses the greatest problems, as it lacks tension, and that which exists seems arbitrary. The first section alternates variants of *III/Pa* and *I/Pa* (Très animé, m.151): *III/Pa* appears in a "straightened-out" rhythm, without the dotted gestures, while *I/Pa* answers as a Scherzo-like melody that recalls the playfulness of *I/Ta.* *I/Pa* migrates to various instruments, each time changing key, mostly in a pattern of ascending thirds (B major–E-flat major–F-sharp major–A minor–A-flat major).

1N, a pleasant violin theme, introduces the next section (m.194). A descending chromatic sequence follows, *franckiste* in sound but more dramatic than the context justifies (compare mm.208–14 with Franck's *I/364–74*). The sequence lengthens out into whole and half notes, producing six measures that strongly suggest the sound of Bruckner (mm.215–20). This gives way to another dramatic passage, based on an extension of *III/P* (cf. m.221–28 and mm.67–72).

The last section of the development (m.238) is the longest and least effective, featuring *1S* in several pastoral but static presentations, interspersed by variants of the theme. The key moves from B major to G-sharp major to D-flat major. *1S* plays in cut time but the accompaniment moves in triplets, creating another cross-rhythm. A bass ascent leads to a series of syncopated dominant-ninth chords that abruptly usher in the recapitulation.

The latter section begins with a forceful *P* (m.321). The first half of *T* follows, extended by one repetition (m.351). Another new theme takes over: the first half is in the strings with eighth-note punctuations in the woodwinds, while the second adds a flurry of trills, tremolos, and short pedals to the texture (m.360). The reprise of *S* (Un peu plus lent, m.384) begins in the solo horn in D major, to which the strings and woodwinds soon add their voices in G major. A diminished seventh on A intrudes, followed by a precipitous three-octave descent in the violins. *2S* (m.418) is sequentially extended and reaches high registers. The coda follows immediately.

Moving in a slow tempo, the coda (Grave, m.460) occupies almost a third of the movement. The trumpet states *I/O* in augmentation while the rest of the brass choir accompanies in conscious imitation of the organ. The chorale moves to the violins, supported by flute and clarinet; a variant of *III/P*, its ferocity gone, accompanies in the lower timbres and also appears between strophes of the chorale. Reiterated harmonies in the upper woodwinds suggest a "celestial style." The final moments feature a melodic line built from elements of *I/P* and *III/P* and conclude with a grand augmented statement of the first two bars of *I/O* against a sustained tonic chord. (Table XVI/12 summarizes the symphony in outline form.)

Chausson's symphony premiered on April 18, 1891, at the Société Nationale, under the composer's baton; Charles Lamoureux, who apparently thought as little of Chausson's music as he did of Franck's, was supposed to conduct but backed out at the last minute. By this time, the Société consisted largely of Franck's disciples and supporters, and the audience, thus favorably predisposed, responded accordingly. The symphony's "darkness to light" topos and solemn mood carried special resonance, for Franck had died five months earlier, while Chausson was orchestrating the work. D'Indy said that it "carries the imprint of a superior personality," and Paul Dukas declared that, while immature, Chausson's symphony displayed "the strongest vigor."[176] Raymond Bonheur spoke of the work as "one of the most beautiful and powerful efforts of the young French school in recent years—the andante especially having an almost elegiac sentiment which is so penetrating—illuminating brilliantly the lofty aspirations of a rare and exquisitely musical mind."[177] Most critics, however, were less charitable. The reviewer for *Le Figaro* congratulated the composer on making progress but others, including the writers for *Gazette de France, Le Guide musical,* and *Le Monde musical,* declared the symphony incomprehensible and excessively dependent on *franckiste* and *wagnériste* formulae.[178] Even at this late date, as Jean Gallois points out, conservative critics tended to react with knee-jerk mystification to any composition of vast proportions and serious import.[179] Some additionally found the emotions depressing.

Taking Chausson's symphony as the emblematic "grave and severe" French "romantic" symphony, Julien Tiersot illustrated the division between the two camps by comparing it to Lalo's "classical" work. Whereas the latter included two Scherzos (the second and last movements), the younger composer suppressed that movement, "as perhaps representing a futile element." Lalo's follows a fairly clear tonal plan but Chausson disrupts tonal equilibrium with his chromaticism and makes the expression even more brooding and despairing—a "heightened minor mode." Ordinarily an admirer of Chausson, this time

TABLE XVI/12

Ernest Chausson. Symphony in B-flat Major: Structure

Movement I

Introduction: Lent 4/4			*Exposition*: Allegro vivo 3/4			
O	Oa	trans.	P	T	S	trans. (*Pa*)
		V/B-flat	B-flat major		F-sharp major	
1	23	40	48	146	164	246

Development

Pa (Allegro scherzando)	T		*Pa* (Cédez un peu)	*N*/*Pa* (Moins vite)	*T + O* (Allegro molto)
B-flat minor, D minor	G major—B-flat major—		mod.		mod. to V
	D major → G°⁷				
261	305		346	378	417

Recapitulation

P (Allegro vivo)	S	*Pa*	*Coda*: Presto
			Pa
B-flat major	G major	B-flat major	
495	559	626	642

Movement II

A	Très lent 4/4			

1A	*2A*	*1A*	trans.
D minor		ends in E minor	B-flat major
1	19	33	41

B	Un peu plus vite

B		
B-flat minor	trans.	
44	65	

A	Un peu plus vite		*Coda* Mouvement du commencement

1A	*2A*	*2Ay*
D minor		ends in D major
75	83	92

Movement III

Introduction Animé ¢		*Exposition* Très animé			
Fragments of *P*		P	T	S (Encore plus animé)	trans.
		B-flat minor		D major	
1		29	77	99	139

Development Très animé

II/*Pa* + *III*/*Pa*	*1N*	new material + *Pb*	S	trans.
mod.				V⁹/B-flat
151	194	215	238	313

Recapitulation

P	*Ta*	*2N*	S (Un peu plus lent)	*Coda* Grave 4/4
				I/O
B-flat minor			G major mod.	B-flat major
321	351	360	384	460

Coda cont.

I/ O + III/P ("celestial style")	*I/P, III/P, I/O*
481	501

Tiersot found him stifled: "the effort he had to make to raise himself up to the heights of the symphony blocked the spontaneity of his inspiration, because this work does not rank with his best."[180]

The symphony received several more hearings in the composer's lifetime, mostly outside of France; it did not reappear in Paris until 1897, when the Berlin Philharmonic performed it during a tour of the French capital. Chausson started a second symphony in 1899 but completed only a few sketches before his death that June in a freak bicycle accident (he lost control going down a hill and crashed head-on into a wall). Like Franck's, Chausson's symphony became more popular in the years after 1900: appearing only sporadically before 1909, it then became a regular staple of Parisian concerts; d'Indy conducted the work on foreign tours to Belgium, Italy, and America. After a performance in 1913, the critic Jean d'Udine summarized the current attitude toward Chausson's work:

> Generally I care neither for the musical period nor the genre to which this composition belongs. There is in this symphony a search for the uncommon, a complexity of means, [and] a refinement of harmony which in my opinion really serves no useful purpose; its themes offer hardly any originality; the stylistic traits of other composers— notably Wagner, Franck, and M. d'Indy—abound in the work; [and] its orchestration is almost always heavy and at the same time quite hollow. All of this should make me hate this work; I love it immensely, because from one end to the other I find this one incomparable thing, the element which provides the only *raison d'être* for art and which alone suffices to legitimize it despite all prejudices and all deficiencies of form: emotion.
>
> Chausson's symphony is imbued with so much feeling, with a lyrical aspiration that is quite touching, and with such a strong need to love and realize itself musically that I wouldn't dream of reproaching the composer for his obvious lack of originality or the complications of his speech. By whatever means, he touches me, and I forget right away that I don't like his style so that I can profit from the excellence of his heart and the tender nobility of his soul. If I had to defend such an impression aesthetically, I would have a hard time doing so. But when someone pleases you, whether personally or in one of his works, all theories fail; you look at him, you listen to him, you smile at him and sympathy no longer leaves room for criticism.[181]

One assumes Chausson would not have appreciated d'Udine's remarks on his complexity and lack of originality (though he might well have agreed with them), but he no doubt would have been gratified to see his symphony succeed in that which mattered most— expressing and sharing his feelings.

Paul Dukas

Paul Dukas (1865–1935) was one of the finest musicians of his generation: a celebrated composer, critic (he wrote over 600 articles), and later professor of composition at the Conservatoire (Plate B23); his students included Olivier Messiaen. Like Gabriel Fauré, he mostly stayed above the rivalries that dominated *fin-de-siècle* musical life and maintained the friendship and respect of people on all sides of the political and artistic divides; these included Debussy, who disliked his music and criticized it both in private letters and public reviews, and the anti-Semitic d'Indy, who held the Jewish composer and his work in high esteem. Although not strictly speaking a *franckiste,* Dukas had strong sympathies with Franck's circle and shared many of its goals.

A consummate craftsman, Dukas left one masterful work in most of the major orchestral, dramatic, and solo genres—concert overture, symphony, symphonic poem, piano sonata, variations set, ballet, and opera—as well as a few shorter compositions. Like most of the *franckistes* (except d'Indy), Dukas sought to achieve both immaculate form and perfect expression, and he adopted unreasonably high standards to which he feared he never measured up. He wrote the following to his friend Pierre Lalo (Édouard's son) in 1901, expressing gratitude for the critic's favorable review of his Piano Sonata:

> Shall I confess to you that I would have loved to find some reservations alongside the praises you bestowed on me? . . . Because I'm a bit frightened by the obligations that such commendations impose: they compel me in some way to write from now on only things that have no weaknesses. That is quite terrifying – at my age, because musically I sound like a beginner who has but a glimpse of what I must do. . . .
>
> Let me say that I feel largely recompensed for my efforts by the approval that you and some others have given me. I won't need more to drive myself to work with yet more courage and confidence. You inspire me with faith that I can be good at something since you think I can add some words to the truths which true art has as its mission to make heard among all the lies of life – and of false art. I wish for the strength and will do everything in my power not to disappoint your expectation.[182]

Dukas probably never disappointed Lalo's expectations, but he did his own. Unlike Chausson, who despite his lack of confidence chose to let his works take their chances in the world, Dukas refused to release any major compositions after his ballet *La Péri* (1912). He began or completed many other pieces, including a violin sonata, a symphonic poem, a ballet, a theatrical work based on Shakespeare's *The Tempest,* and (most importantly for our purposes) another symphony. None saw the light of day, for the composer's crippling self-criticism drove him to burn them shortly before his death—an action all the more regrettable because there is no empirical reason to believe they fell below the high level of the works that survive, except in his own mind. That Dukas profoundly misjudged his gifts is demonstrated by the fact that he would have destroyed *La Péri*—by any measure one of the most exquisite works of the French school—but for the intervention of friends (including d'Indy, who called it the finest theatrical work since Wagner). Lamented the composer's friend Robert Brussel, who heard the composer play some of these ill-fated scores: "Anyone who knew these works and witnessed their beauty is really at a loss to discover the deep-seated motives behind such a sacrifice."[183]

SYMPHONY IN C MAJOR

Dukas's only surviving symphony, written in 1895–1896, belongs in some ways to both the conservative and romantic schools (Table XVI/13). Like those of Chausson and d'Indy (the *Mountain Air*), it unfolds in three movements without a Scherzo—a division to which the published score calls attention, for it entitles the work *Symphonie en trois parties* as well as *Symphonie en ut majeur.* Certain themes recall Franckist phrase structure: short chromatic motives in trochaic rhythms with a clear up-and-down contour, internal modulation, and sequential repetition (e.g., *III/1S,* Example XVI/22; also *I/S*). Others, however, such as *II/P* and *II/1P,* are expansive, usually triadic in outline and defined by incisive rhythms (a Dukas hallmark). This symphony contains even more tempo modifications than Franck's: accelerations and stringendos occur frequently as Dukas proceeds from one theme group to another, but they do not disturb the flow. As befits the composer of *L'Apprenti sorcier* and *La Péri,* this work abounds in colorful but transparent orchestration: he takes full advantage of the large but not Wagnerian-size ensemble (two instead of three woodwinds and no percussion except

TABLE XVI/13

The Symphonies of Paul Dukas

Key	Date	Title	Movements	Instrumentation	Comments
C major	1895–96	Symphony in C Major	1. Allegro non troppo vivace, ma con fuoco 6/8 (564 m.) 2. Andante espressivo e sostenuto 4/8 (178 m.) E minor 3. Allegro spiritoso 3/4, 9/8 (562 m.)	Grand, + Picc., EH, small Tpt.	Also known as *Symphonie en trois parties*. Dedicated to Paul Vidal. First performance: Paris, Concerts de l'Opéra, conducted by Paul Vidal on January 3, 1897. Published: Rouart, Lerolle, et Cie., 1908 (four-hand reduction: Rouart, 1896).
		Symphony No. 2 [?]			Apparently composed after 1912 and destroyed by the composer shortly before his death.

EXAMPLE XVI/22   Dukas. Symphony in C Major/3, mm.53–60 (*III/1S*). © by Editions Salabert.

tympani, though he does include a piccolo trumpet). The outer movements display lively spirits, while the expressive middle movement reaches profound depths.

The Symphony in C Major is not cyclic, but several themes share similar rhythmic traits, such as prominent subdivisions, often on the final beat of the phrase, and, as mentioned, a fondness for triplet and trochaic rhythms. Sonata form underlies each movement: the first two are sonata-allegros, the last a modified sonata-rondo. Critics often cited Beethoven as a model, in part because Dukas develops his themes by fragmentation instead of repetition, especially in the opening movement. Another Classical characteristic is the lucid tonal scheme: despite a fair amount of chromaticism and momentary modulation, the diatonic foundations remain clear. In sum, Dukas's symphony is characterized by keen rhythms, translucent orchestration, limpid structures, and a sunny and animated spirit balanced by introversion. Merging Classical form and style with *franckiste* expressiveness and thematic and harmonic processes, the work stands as one of the most memorable symphonies of the late-nineteenth-century French school.

For a composer in 1895 to write a symphony in C major—of all keys—struck critics as audacious. Moreover, unlike so many works of the period which announce their tonality only after a struggle, this one starts off with a forceful tonic chord played throughout the orchestra, followed by a drum pedal on C in the violins and violas (Allegro non troppo vivace, ma con fuoco, 6/8; Example XVI/23). In this respect the work resembles Sibelius's Seventh Symphony, which at an even later date (1924) also takes C major as its key and commences with an equally bold and unambiguous assertion (an ascending tonic scale). Having thus thrown down the gauntlet, as it were, Dukas plunges into the exposition.

P, a memorable violin melody, unfolds in three sections (mm.1, 9, 13); Dukas builds it—as well as much of the movement—from three modules heard at the beginning of *Pa: Pax, Pay, Paz* (Example XVI/23, mm.3–8). *T,* a more extended section, encompasses three separate themes. *1T* (m.23), derived from *Pax* and *Pay,* yields to *2T,* a lively syncopated motive stated twice by the brass, the second time a step lower (m.27). *3T* (m.37) starts off as three sequential statements of a four-measure chromatic motive—beginning on F, A, and C, respectively—and then splinters into smaller and uneven components. A short cadential passage sets up *S.*

A lyrical eight-bar theme in the relative key of A minor, *S* moves in trochaic rhythm in the strings (Calme, m.70). Dukas presents *S* twice, with a short digression between. He interrupts the second statement with an unexpected and somewhat awkward *ombra* intrusion consisting of sequences leading to *K* (m.94). Like *T, K* consists of three themes plus a closing section. *1K* is an energetic eight-bar motive for the brass in the subdominant F major (m.108); its assertive spirit makes this the most immediately memorable theme of the exposition. Again Dukas presents two statements of the theme, separating them with a brief tangent, this time to E-flat major. The second *1K* returns to F major but changes its character from a fanfare to a march. *2K* (m.132) begins like a variant of *1K* but becomes harmonically

EXAMPLE XVI/23 Dukas. Symphony in C Major/1, mm.1–12. © by Editions Salabert.

unstable as it prepares *3K,* an aggressive motive in violins and woodwinds more or less in G phrygian (m.144). In *K^k* (m.152), based on *3K,* the energy dissipates while Dukas maintains a pedal on G.

In this exposition, then, Dukas allots one theme to *P* and *S* while *T* and *K* each have three. As in the "Organ" Symphony, the section covers three keys, I, vi, and IV. (Because of the prominence of *1K* and its tonality, Ropartz and others analyzed this movement as ternary

EXAMPLE XVI/23 *(continued)*

Paz

rather than sonata-allegro, an indication of how rare three-key expositions were in French practice.)[184] But if the exposition bears evidence of Schubertian procedure, the next section distinctly recalls Beethoven.

Dukas devotes almost the entire development to *P.* It divides into eight segments distinguished by texture. Dukas focuses on the parallel minor, and within that circle the tonal bases remain fairly traditional. Section one (m.163) starts in C minor and alternates *P* and *3K.* Changing abruptly to A-flat major and then B-flat minor, section two combines the two themes contrapuntally (m.190). Section three (m.209), starting in F minor, devotes itself to *Paz.*

EXAMPLE XVI/23 (*continued*)

Dukas now begins in earnest to fragment *P* and play with the individual modules. The segments become increasingly abstract, with fewer recognizable themes, though one can clearly detect *Pax*, *Pay*, or *Paz* tossed about. Section four (m.221) commences with a new lyrical motive in F-sharp minor derived from *Pay* but it soon becomes disjointed; *Pax* also appears. The following section (m.235) is essentially transitional. Section six briefly digresses to *S* (m.265, G minor), its only appearance in the development. A few measures later, Dukas superimposes *Pax* and *Pay* onto *S* (m.274); *S* quickly drops out and *Pax* alternates with *Paz*. The retransition continues to oppose these two modules over an extended dominant pedal (m.294).

The recapitulation (m.310) proceeds normally, with *S* in C minor and *K* in C major. At 2*K* (m.439), Dukas begins to build a sequential "pre-coda" that accelerates into a fast passage based on *1K*. The movement could end satisfactorily at this point, but the tempo suddenly slows to make way for the "real" coda, which is less traditional than what preceded it. With an abrupt change of mood, dynamic, meter, and key (Modéré, m.496), Dukas creates a quiet and heady chromatic atmosphere in which *Pax* becomes a dotted theme and *1K* swirling arpeggios; for the first time, one detects the shade of Wagner. The composer notates the meter 12 / 16 = 2/4. The prevailing temper is one of mystery. Another accelerando leads out of the dark grotto into brightness (m.520), and *1Ka*, accompanied by *Pax*, repeats over and over in the tonic (m.532), save for one enigmatic invocation in C-sharp minor (mm.555–56). C major quickly returns and *1Ka* leads without further interruption to the exhilarating conclusion.

Most analysts single out the E-minor Andante espressivo e sostenuto (4/8) as the high point of the symphony. To Ropartz this movement typified Dukas's ability to straddle the classic and romantic camps. He couches his praise in the typically expansive (and not terribly precise) prose of the period:

> In this movement not only does Dukas master the difficulties of abstract musical language in the surest fashion but he imbues it with extraordinary emotion. It reveals his sensibility. A totally profound sensibility that does not pour out in grandiloquent expressions. There is obviously no romanticism in him, no need to bare his soul in some theatrical posture. Quite the contrary: Dukas's sensibility veils itself with modesty but, by forgetting the "me," it raises itself to a humanism that is appropriately classical. . . . At length you think you perceive this second part of the symphony (which is truly an admirable movement) as a deep landscape of the most delicate poetry. It is not without use to make note of this because Dukas has not been prodigal with impressions of nature in his works. Man, with his struggles and his victories, his joys and his pains—these preoccupy the composer infinitely more than the framework in which he moves.[185]

Although again in sonata form, the movement unfolds in a markedly different manner than its predecessor. The exposition takes up almost half its length, whereas the previous one occupied less than a third. *P* and *S* have three themes each, and *T* and *K* one; Dukas distinguishes *P, S,* and *K* not only by their themes but by the rhythms of their accompaniment patterns.

A four-measure introduction decorates a dominant chord over which the horns play a rhythmic gesture (*A*) that appears throughout *P*. *1P* is a lyrical theme for first violins which expresses, according to reviewer René de Castéra, "un beau caractère d'affliction";[186] *A* accompanies in the middle-to-lower timbres (Example XVI/24). Opening briefly in E-flat, *2P* shifts back to E minor and, adopting the rhythm of *A*, it rises to e''' over a tonic pedal. *2P* concludes with *A*-derived descending patterns that *3P* converts into a somewhat Brucknerian melody for first violins in E major (m.22). The accompaniment of *3P* also derives from *A*, as does a short *P*ᵏ in E major (m.30). A solitary c' in the third flute disrupts the closing harmony.

T features soft chromatic motions in tremolo strings against *A*-based turn figures in the flutes and clarinets as well as an arpeggiated motive in the first horn (m.37). *1S*, a tender theme for first violins (in octaves) and solo flute and oboe, begins in A-flat major and moves quickly to E-flat minor, courtesy of augmented triads. It introduces a new accompanimental

EXAMPLE XVI/24   Dukas. Symphony in C Major/2, mm.1–14. © by Editions Salabert.

EXAMPLE XVI/24   (*continued*)

figure, *1B*, a series of thirty-second-note sextuplets. Ropartz commented on the changing emotional meaning of the accompaniment pattern: for *1P* it represents "a sort of lamentation which adds to the melancholy of the theme"; now in *1S* "it is something luminous which combines admirably with everything it encloses with smiling clarity."[187] *2S* combines *1B* and a variant, *2B* (*1B* in a march style), with *1S* and the *A*-derived turn figure from *T* (m.56); it travels from E-flat major to G major. *3S* merges *1S* with both *B* patterns as well as a new pattern in continuous thirty-seconds (m.64). Dukas sets *K* for two solo cellos over a delicately scored layer of accompanimental patterns in cross-rhythms: sixteenths, thirty-seconds, thirty-second sextuplets, and others (m.71).

The development divides into two brief sections. Part one (m.82) opens with a new accompaniment figure, a syncopated gesture for *divisi* strings; against this, momentary citations from *P* and *A* appear, with several fluctuations of tempo. The second part consists of a chorale for brass choir and assorted woodwinds and strings in B major (Largo e maestoso, m.106). Even more than *3P*, this chorale brings Bruckner to mind. The resemblance seems to be by chance, as the Austrian composer was little played and less appreciated in France at the time Dukas wrote his symphony (though Lamoureux had conducted the Eighth in 1894); what he knew or thought of Bruckner, either then or later, is not recorded.

Dukas substantially rescores the recapitulation, intensifying the emotional impact of *1P* (Primo tempo, m.118): *A* becomes less prominent, while a new chromatic descending gesture appears in the oboe and English horn at the downbeat of every measure; meanwhile, the second violins move in continuous sixty-fourths. Dukas omits *3P*. Even more than in the exposition, the return of *S* is harmonically unstable, dancing around several keys. The tonic E minor returns in the Coda (m.165), based mostly on *Pa* and *A*.

The sprightly Finale (Allegro spiritoso, 3/4=9/8) is a kind of sonata rondo (*A–B–A–C–A–B* Coda). *A* comprises the *P* and *T* areas. *P* is a rhythmically incisive theme in 3/4 for horns, bassoons, and cellos in C major, accompanied by a violin countermotive in 9/8 and syncopated rhythm in the woodwinds in 3/4. Soon the whole orchestra joins in stating *P*. *T* consists of sequential statements of a descending motive opposite ascending sixteenth-note flourishes in the violins (m.38).

B (Plus modéré, m.53) has three themes. *1S* is a triadic violin melody accompanied by the rhythm of *T*; its repetitive structure and apparent tonal elasticity suggest affinities with Franck, though it merely follows the harmonic pattern V7/V–N/V–V–I (see Example XVI/22). *2S*, a sequential motive in low timbres, combines with a syncopated motive in the upper strings and a galloping rhythm in the horns and other strings (Tempo primo, m.79). *3S* extends *2S* through more sequences (m.95). Throughout *B* the tonality remains fluid. *A* returns in the tonic, with *P* in the lower strings (m.123). It becomes transitional, ending on the dominant of E major, the primary key of the following section.

The developmental *C* consists of four parts, each of which ends with an acceleration. In part one the first violins introduce *N*, another lyrical triadic melody (Molto meno vivace, m.177; Example XVI/25). Like *I/S*, this melody recalls Franck, this time through the use of small-range motives that decorate a single block of notes; although modulatory, the basic tonality remains E major. In part two *N* moves to the oboe and clarinet while a semitone gesture appears in hocket style between the flutes and violins; under this the lower strings and brass form a pedal on a C-sharp second-inversion seventh chord (m.197). *P* returns in the next section against the continuing hocket-like figure (m.213). The climax of *C* features *1S*, augmented and extended through modal repetitions and supported by a busier variant of the hocket figure—a continuous series of dropping and ascending semitones (m.229). The statement

EXAMPLE XVI/25   Dukas. Symphony in C Major/3, mm.177–84. © by Editions Salabert.

ends in E major. A Scherzo-like transformation of *P* in the woodwinds serves as the retransition (m.259).

At the reprise of *A, Pa* sounds throughout the orchestra (m.288). Dukas then sets off in a new direction, borrowing a rhythmic gesture from the retransition. *B* presents *1S* in a celestial style accompanied by soft tremolos, pedal points, and oscillating triadic notes (m.323). The section ends by recalling the modal extension of *S* heard in *C*. The tonality moves from F-sharp major to C major. Dukas ends his symphony with an extended coda in which fragments of *P, 1S,* and especially *N* appear in various combinations and keys (m.350). He combines *N* and *P* in a brief peroration. *N,* in augmentation, assumes the character of a chorale sounded throughout the orchestra, with *P* in normal form in lower timbres (m.450). Hints of *S* and *P* (in the rhythm of *S*) lead to the final section, devoted almost entirely to *N* in a brisk transformation, with *Sa* between strophes (Allegro molto, 6/8, m.504). The symphony ends as it began, in an ebullient and unambiguous C major.

Dukas's Symphony in C major received its premiere at a short-lived concert series sponsored by the Opéra; Paul Vidal, the conductor and dedicatee, performed the work on January 3 and 10, 1897 (other French symphonies performed at the Opéra included Widor's Third Symphony and Saint-Saëns's First).[188] The debut was not auspicious. The public consisted of subscribers to the Opéra rather than habitual concertgoers and, not being accustomed to abstract music, let alone works in "modern" style, they responded badly. Nor were the performers any kinder, as D.-E. Ingelbrecht, who played in the orchestra, recalled:

> Who could have thought that this work, which seems so clear to us today, stirred up protests at the time of its premiere, not only by the public on the day of the concert but even before then by the musicians of the orchestra? The jeers never stopped spreading around me during the rehearsals, and it must even be said that the players did not always refrain from trying to sabotage both the new work and the young conductor Paul Vidal, who had assumed the responsibility for directing it.[189]

The critics also raged against Dukas's symphony. Typical is this sarcastic review by Charles-Henry Hirsch:

> M. Paul Dukas opened the season at the Concerts de l'Opéra. Reviewers everywhere must take satisfaction from this, for to start things off the management of the Opéra has handed them a critic in person to devour. M. Dukas writes discerning and well-informed articles on music. The symphony he had played is the work of a critic. It's like a long assignment the composer inflicted on himself to prove to the musicians whose productions he decorticates that he, the critic, is not afraid to show them he is capable of doing the things he judges. And I well believe one will not find the least bit of incorrectness in this interminable symphony. But a grammar lesson must be brief. M. Dukas has attempted to demonstrate all his skill and knowledge, at the risk of being dry. He is that and more, for this symphony seems so well built that from one end to the other in each

movement, it prepares us for the arrival of something which might be less well constructed but better all the same because it's inspired—and this something never comes. This dense score lacks light. The first movement ends with an *accelerando,* which provides a happy diversion, and from an unexpected change of rhythm it takes on a quite personal character. The *Andante* (2nd movement) vaguely recalls the Prelude to *Tristan* in its manner of handling the strings; similarly, the prodigal distribution of the brass in the final *Allegro* recalls the Bruneau of the *Requiem.*—After all this, maybe I'm mistaken: what if, without realizing it, I have just spoken about a masterpiece?[190]

Debussy shared Hirsch's sentiments; with characteristic irony, he pronounced Dukas's symphony "a disappointment . . . something tiny, like a mixture of Beethoven and Charpentier."[191] Small wonder that in an autobiographical sketch of 1899 the composer laconically noted, "In 1897, for the concerts at the Opéra I gave a symphony in three parts and it provoked vigorous debate."[192]

In any event, the Symphony in C major was promptly overshadowed by the phenomenal success of *L'Apprenti sorcier* only four months later (the latter work soon entered the canon, an honor then quite rare for a young and relatively unknown composer). The symphony was performed again at Concerts Lamoureux in 1902, where it received a much warmer reception. The critics regarded it as immature compared to what came after (*L'Apprenti sorcier* and the large-scale Piano Sonata in E minor), but still found it full of riches. Pierre Lalo praised its "inner energy and the concentrated vehemence of feeling, the love of rhythm, the passionate taste for order and musical architecture, the acute sense of expression and instrumental color," concluding that the work revealed "such a wealth of music, such a richness of thought, such a strength of motion, such a clarity of ordering and development that, even to the public most hostile to novelty, it reveals itself as belonging to the same family as the masterpieces of the great composers."[193] Curiously, Hugues Imbert (another respected critic) found the symphony programmatic and rebuked Dukas for not telling the audience what it meant. As his review indicates, many French concert-goers, even informed musicians, continued to approach abstract compositions visually:

> The Symphony in C Major of M. Paul Dukas . . . is further removed from the classical form than César Franck's Symphony. Its audacious harmonies, very strange rhythms, unforeseen modulations, and somewhat harsh and thick scoring make us think of a pictorial *tableau,* the subject of which remains an enigma for the listener. After hearing the work, one of our colleagues told us, "We need a detailed program to follow the thread of the composer's ideas." This is obviously a criticism, since in a pure symphony the musical element is amply sufficient for understanding the work. . . . In constructing his symphony, M. Dukas has clearly used the same procedures he employed in writing *L'Apprenti sorcier.* But the orchestral plot which perfectly translates a very animated poem into music is no longer completely right for unfolding a symphony in an ample and clear manner without adding a program.

Despite this failing, Imbert concluded, the work is "of beautiful demeanor and ranks its composer among the best of the young symphonists of the French school."[194]

Tiersot noted that Dukas allied himself aesthetically with the *franckistes* but his symphony really belonged to the classical camp, and for that reason he preferred it to Chausson's. While chromaticism obscured and even disfigured the latter's symphony (according to Tiersot), the same presented no problems in Dukas's work because the underlying tonal foundations remained clear. Tiersot found his symphony too serious and austere—a charge frequently brought against works by *franckistes* and their supporters—but he declared that it had "a real and high value" all the same.[195]

In his article Tiersot raises an issue which has been much commented upon since and should be briefly noted here: the tendency for French *fin-de-siècle* composers, especially *franckistes,* to write only one symphony. Speaking of Franck, Lalo, Chausson, Dukas, and d'Indy, the author asks, "Why have our musicians always limited themselves to the composition of a single symphony, as almost all of them save M. Saint-Saëns have done? Does it require such a superhuman effort that it cannot be repeated?"[196] Many subsequent writers have reiterated Tiersot's question, often with concomitant speculations about the inability of French composers to express themselves profoundly more than once.

The facts, however, show this phenomenon to be exaggerated. Lalo wrote and destroyed two symphonies before the G Minor Symphony, so it was actually his third. Neither Chausson nor Dukas renounced the genre: Chausson had begun another symphony when he died and, as we have seen, a symphony (in whatever state of completion) figured among the scores Dukas consigned to the flames at the end of his life. Franck died the year after his symphony premiered (it was his last orchestral composition), and nothing indicates that he considered his business with the genre to be concluded. Unknown to Tiersot, d'Indy was at that moment writing his Second Symphony. Moreover, Saint-Saëns and d'Indy were not the only musicians to publish more than one symphony between 1885 and 1925: others include Albéric Magnard (four), Guy Ropartz (four; a fifth appeared many years later), Charles-Marie Widor (three; two others came earlier), Charles Tournemire (eight), Théodore Dubois (three), and Albert Roussel (two, with two more to follow), as well as lesser figures. The phenomenon of the single symphony is merely an accident of history and reflects nothing of French symphonic predilections or aptitudes.

Vincent d'Indy

Franck's most prominent pupil, d'Indy (1851–1931) enjoyed a multifaceted and successful career as composer, conductor, pedagogue, administrator, and writer (Plate B24). Despite his many achievements, his reputation today is generally low. An ardent defender of post-Wagnerian aesthetics and style, he (like his enemy Saint-Saëns) vociferously opposed Debussyism, Schoenberg, Stravinsky, Les Six, and other early-twentieth-century artistic trends and thereby gained an unflattering and not totally accurate image as a reactionary pedant. Much more damaging, however, has been d'Indy's widely publicized far-right and virulently anti-Semitic convictions. By all accounts a shy and self-effacing man who genuinely embraced colleagues of all backgrounds and convictions (including Jews, like Dukas), d'Indy's diffidence vanished when he expressed himself in print, often in the starkest manner possible. His combativeness has understandably aroused scholarly indignation: as Robert Orledge has aptly observed, "As a man he either fascinates or irritates in the extreme, and it is his least attractive qualities that have received the most publicity."[197] Not infrequently, negative feelings aroused by those least attractive qualities have strongly colored judgments of his artistic accomplishments.

His failings notwithstanding, d'Indy was in fact a very fine composer of orchestral, chamber, and operatic works modeled on the triumvirate of Beethoven, Wagner, and Franck. His influence on the music and culture of his nation from the 1880s to the 1920s was immense, arguably second only to Debussy's, and he enjoyed the sincere respect of most French musicians, even those who despised everything he stood for. A fanatical devotee of Art (which he often spelled thus to underline its stature), d'Indy believed ardently in the power of music to ennoble and edify, and he became one of the most important supporters of the symphony, that "loftiest" of genres.[198] Like Saint-Saëns, he wrote five, two of which he never published.

While on a tour of Italy in 1869, the eighteen-year-old composer, like Bizet before him, decided to record his memories in a symphonic panorama. As he wrote in his diary,

> I have in my head the grand canvas of a *Symphony,* and in it I am going to transmit my impressions during the trip. A melody will play the part of Ellie [MacSwinney, a young Scottish woman with whom d'Indy was infatuated] and, if it is not too bad, her name will be written on the first page. The first movement will be *Rome,* the *Andante* I don't know what, the *Scherzo* Naples and the *Finale* Venice.[199]

As work progressed, d'Indy switched the roles of some movements and (presumably without knowing it) duplicated the scheme Bizet adopted for *Roma:* Venice became the Andante, Florence the Scherzo, and Naples the Finale. The plan for Rome, however, took on extravagant dimensions Bizet never envisioned, as the Eternal City became for d'Indy the symbol of a philosophical drama. According to the composer's breathless description,

> [The first movement] will represent firmly the triumph of Christianity over Paganism: first the Andante *for four horns, piano,* will be the nascent Christian idea, then will come a melody which represents my thought for Ellie—because it's for her that I write it, I mustn't hide it—then the tutti *f* is ancient Rome, the Republic that seems to degenerate little by little, and the Christian idea little by little takes on more stability; then it shows itself in two phrases and smothers Paganism and everything ends with a religious march—perhaps the same as at the beginning, after my habit.
>
> To be sure, *no one will perceive all this,* but *it's my idea and that's enough.*[200]

He combined the descriptive and conceptual programs in a letter to his cousin:

> My *Symphony* is a personification of Italy: the finale, a saltarello, represents Naples, the light and lively scherzo Florence, the Andante will be Venice, and finally I want to paint Rome in the first movement and (you'll make fun of me for this, but that's all right) *portray the triumph of Christianity over Paganism*—in other words, set the *Coliseum into a fight with St. Peter.* Quite bold, no? And no one will see it, I'm convinced of that, but it's my idea and I want to follow it.[201]

At this point, d'Indy had not yet begun formal composition lessons—his studies with Franck started only after he had finished the symphony—making his project all the more audacious. Working intermittently, he finished it in 1872. The previous year, Pasdeloup's orchestra read the Scherzo; Bizet and Massenet attended the rehearsal and complemented the composer.[202] Pasdeloup read the entire symphony in 1873, which garnered d'Indy further praise from Massenet and Lalo. D'Indy himself pronounced the Finale weak but expressed satisfaction with the other movements, especially the Andante.[203] He decided not to revise the symphony (which became known as the *Symphonie italienne*) and left it unpublished. In terms of d'Indy's future development, the work is notable primarily for the philosophical motivation behind the first movement as well as the composer's indifference to making it public—an attitude we will encounter again in his mature symphonies.

In 1874, d'Indy began a programmatic symphony inspired by the fifteenth-century Hungarian hero János Hunyady, "a very beautiful subject—heroic, Christian, and patriotic all at the same time."[204] The composer later called this work—known variously as *Jean Hunyade* and the *Symphonie chevaleresque* or "Chivalrous Symphony"—his "first *true* Symphony," though he

TABLE XVI/14

The Symphonies of Vincent d'Indy

Opus	Key	Date	Title	Movements	Instrumentation	Comments
	A Major	1870–72	*Symphonie italienne*			A musical panorama of Italy with a philosophical program the composer did not intend to publicize. 1. Rome: the Triumph of Christianity over Paganism. 2. Venice (Andante). 3. Florence (Scherzo). 4. Naples (Finale). Public reading; Concerts Populaires, conducted by Jules Pasdeloup, 1873. Unpublished.
		1874–76	*Jean Hunyade (Symphonie chevaleresque)*			"János Hunyady" or "Chivalrous Symphony." First partial performance: two movements (Andante—Finale and Hymn) in Paris, Société Nationale, conducted by Édouard Colonne on April 1, 1876. First complete performance: Budapest, 1924. Unpublished.
25	G Major	1886	*Symphony on a French Mountain Air (Symphonie cévenole)*	1. Assez lent 9/8—Modérément animé 3/4 (268 m.) 2. Assez modéré, mais sans lenteur 3/4, 2/4, 4/4 (132 m.) B-flat major/minor 3. Animé 2/4, 3/4, 6/8 (612 m.)	Grand + Picc., Flt., Ob., EH, Bclar., Bssn., 2 Cornets, BD, Cym., Tri., Harp, Piano	*Symphonie sur un chant montagnard français.* Dedicated to Mme Bordes-Pène, the first soloist. First performance: Paris, Concerts Lamoureux, conducted by Charles Lamoureux on March 20, 1887. Published in Paris: Hamelle, 1887.

TABLE XVI/14 (*continued*)

Opus	Key	Date	Title	Movements	Instrumentation	Comments
57	B-flat (no mode specified)	1902–03	Symphony No. 2 in B-flat	1. Extrêmement lent 4/2—Très vif 3/4 (525 m.) 2. Modérément lent 6/4, 3/2 (144 m.) D-flat major 3. Modéré 2/4, 3/4, 3/8 (286 m.) D minor 4. Lent 4/4, 6/4, 3/2—Modéré et solennel 3/4—Assez vif 5/4—Lent 3/2 (373 m.)	Grand + Picc., Flt., EH, Bclar., Bssn., Small Tpt., Btrom., Tri., Cym., BD, 2 Harps	Dedicated to Paul Dukas. First performance: Paris, Concerts Lamoureux, conducted by Camille Chevillard on February 28, 1904. Published in Paris: Durand, 1904.
73	D Major	1916–18	Symphony No. 3 "Sinfonia brevis *de bello gallico*"	1. Lent et calme—Animé 4/4, 6/8, 3/4, 2/2, 2/4 (291 m.) 2. Assez vite 3/4, 5/4 (201 m.) G minor, E-flat major 3. Lent 4/4, 3/4 (125 m.) B major 4. Très animé 12/8, 4/4, 3/4, 2/2 (277 m.)	Grand + Picc., EH, Small Clar., Bclar., Bssn., Small Tpt., Tpt., Cornet, Contrabass, Trom., SD, Flat drum, BD, Cym., Xylophone, Celesta, 2 Harps	"Little Symphony *About the War in France.*" D'Indy's program as explained to Guy Ropartz (but not made public): 1. Mobilization, the Marne. 2. Scherzo: Gaiety at the Front. 3. Andante: Latin Art and Boche Art. 4. Finale: Victory with the Hymn of St. Michael as a Peroration. Dedicated to Commandant Édmond de Pampelonne. First performed: Paris, Société Nationale, May 1919. Published in Paris: Rouart, Lerolle, et Cie., 1919.

spoke little about it in his diary and letters.[205] The Société Nationale played the Andante and Finale in March 1876, and the first and only complete performance took place in Budapest in 1924.[206] D'Indy likewise consigned this work to the shelf and never published it. Strictly speaking, then, the *Symphonie sur un chant montagnard français* (Symphony on a French Mountain Air) is d'Indy's third symphony, but it is his first published one (see Table XVI/14).

SYMPHONY ON A FRENCH MOUNTAIN AIR (*SYMPHONIE CÉVENOLE*) OPUS 25

As a composer d'Indy lives principally by this evergreen work, also known as the *Symphonie cévenole.* It reflects several of d'Indy's interests: a musical connection to his ancestral land in the Ardèche district in Southern France, cyclic procedures, and innovative orchestration. The composer based the symphony on a shepherd's song he heard while walking in the Cévennes mountains in the Ardèche during the summer of 1885. He decided to create a fantasy for piano and orchestra upon this theme, probably in emulation of Franck's recent *Les Djinns* (1884) and *Variations symphoniques* (1885), both one-movement compositions for piano and orchestra. D'Indy soon expanded his plan to a symphony, which he finished by early autumn of 1886.

Even more than Franck, d'Indy committed himself to the principle of organic cyclic unity, citing late Beethoven as his authority; the composer regarded his "more rigorous application" of cyclic form as his contribution to the chain of tradition, taking what his elders had done and proceeding to the next step (see the first paragraph of Table XVI/15). In the case of the *Symphonie cévenole,* the mountain song (*O*) or transformations thereof dominate all three movements; a theme from the second movement also returns in the Finale. The modulatory nature of d'Indy's themes shows Franck's influence, though the melodies themselves bear little resemblance to those of the teacher's. D'Indy had a liking for supple rhythms and irregularly paced melodies that stretched over the bar line, and both can be found here: for example, *O* alternates 9/8 and 6/8, and d'Indy sets *III/S* in a meter of 2+3/4. As in the symphonies of Franck and Dukas, the tempo often fluctuates.

The orchestration garnered high praise from the critics and remains one of the most admired aspects of this symphony. The composer described the scoring as "Wagnerian," meaning that he called for three or four of each woodwind and brass. In his detailed analysis for the *Cours de composition musicale* (Table XVI/15), d'Indy insisted that the pianist not treat the work as a concerto; and indeed the soloist most often plays an obbligato role, supporting the ensemble with fast arpeggios and thirty-second-note runs. The symphony therefore follows in the tradition of Berlioz's *Harold en Italie,* though d'Indy most likely would have rejected the comparison (in the *Cours* he dismisses Berlioz as a composer of badly constructed symphonic poems that masquerade as symphonies; he ignores *Harold* altogether). Whereas Saint-Saëns employed the piano as a substitute for the harp, d'Indy includes both instruments. As a whole, the scoring of the *Symphonie cévenole* is luminescent and transparent, often conveyed through soft dynamics.

The introduction—which d'Indy somewhat enigmatically described as Haydnesque—opens with two statements of *O* in the English horn and flute, respectively. While Franck (perhaps inspired by his pupil's example) took criticism for featuring the English horn in his own symphony—assuming d'Indy's anecdote, cited earlier, is reliable[207]—no one complained about its prominence here. Perhaps this is because d'Indy's symphony premiered at Concerts Lamoureux, the patrons of which had the reputation of being the most receptive to new works (Lamoureux himself liked d'Indy's music much more than he did Franck's or Chausson's), while the deeply reactionary tastes of the Conservatoire subscribers undoubtedly had much to do with the failure of Franck's symphony there.

The wistful and melancholy Mountain Air divides into two phrases (*Oa, Ob*), both of which alternate between 9/8 and 6/8 (Example XVI/26). A short transition based on *Obx* and

TABLE XVI/15
D'Indy's Analysis of the *Symphony on a French Mountain Air*

As you can see, it is contemporaneous with the two symphonies of Franck and Saint-Saëns . . . We have seen why we must reject any notion of mutual influence between these two composers; the date at which Saint-Saëns's work came to be known (1887) also excludes any supposition of that sort where the present symphony is concerned.[i] But the composer of the *Symphony on a Mountain Air* has never had any thought of denying the influence of his revered master, who was preparing his magnificent Symphony in D Minor at the same time.[ii] Without pretending to make any innovations with regard to the methods of thematic and tonal construction inaugurated by Haydn and expanded by Beethoven, the Symphony in G Major marks above all a tendency to strengthen the *cyclic* character of the leading motifs, binding them more closely together, to the point of even unifying them at times—the natural consequence of a state of things created more or less consciously by Beethoven in his late period, then resolutely perfected by Franck and applied even more rigorously by those musicians for whom Franck was the model, whether they acknowledged his influence or not. Here one principal theme, the *Mountain Air* heard in the Cévennes—which is why this symphony sometimes has the subtitle *Symphonie cévenole*—governs the three movements by furnishing the thematic material for each of their opening ideas. It is the *cyclic theme* par excellence (*x*):

It is not the only theme having this character, however: we must also note the role of a second motive (*y*), which does not appear until the beginning of the slow movement:

Completely Classical in form (sonata-allegro), the first movement begins with an introduction like one would find back with Haydn. The [English] horn and then the flute play the cyclic theme (*x*) in turn. From this same theme comes the beginning of the *first idea* (A [= P]) derived from the animated section to which the Introduction leads:

The piano *accompanies* this first idea with some scalar passages and arpeggios [*traits et batteries*]. We cannot stress this point too much because the Symphony is in no way a "Piano Concerto," as too many performers have seemed to think.

A very short *bridge* (P [=T]), also drawn from the cyclic theme (*x*) follows Theme A:

The *second idea* (B) enters immediately afterwards:

This second idea, equally supported by the piano, is a phrase in *lied* form (*a b a*), laid out in the key of B. Its central section is modulatory and the key of B reappears only for the conclusion.

The *development* uses the last notes of the second theme, transposed to B-flat major, in order soon to reach the key of E major, which marks the culminating point of the development. Then the basses play the first idea while the trumpets, supported by the oboes and violas, recall the cyclic theme. In this manner we arrive at the key of C-sharp major and then the tonal march gets under way again: a short rest on F-sharp major, always in the rhythm of the first idea, precedes the *pedal* heralding the recapitulation. By a trick quite often used since, this pedal finds itself on the dominant of A-flat rather than G, and it is a simple chromatic slide from this dominant (E-flat) to its neighbor the true dominant (D), which marks the reentry of the *first idea* in all its power. The *recapitulation* makes hardly any changes except modifications in orchestration and the tonal adjustments necessary for the conclusion. We must note, though, that the *bridge*, leading no longer to B major (a distant key) but to G major (the tonic), is enriched with more complex modulations in order to lend interest to the tonic, in which key the *second idea* resides. A simple *coda* without a true final development recalls the Introduction, which combines with reminiscences of the second idea like a final résumé.

TABLE XVI/15 (continued)

We can assign the following tonal bases to this movement: G major, B major, E major, and G major, the development proceeding by modulations which are more and more clear—as long as we do not forget that keys *written* with *flats* for convenience's sake are but *heterography* for the eye and not *enharmony* for the ear.[iii]

The slow movement can be considered as a grand *Lied* [ternary form], consisting of *three* large double sections or six smaller ones. The first large section begins with the piano stating a modified form of the cyclic theme (*x*) in B-flat major:

We can subdivide this phrase into three small periods; it is followed by another, of similar structure, which presents the second cyclic motive (*y*) for the first time, in B-flat minor:

The second large section contains first a statement of the initial theme of the movement in G-flat major, with arpeggios in the piano; but this statement is suspended and while the theme continues in the low timbres, it modulates at the same time—from F major towards A major and then towards C major. A temporary recall of cyclic theme *x* in the horns in D-flat major, modulating brusquely, connects with cyclic motive *y* over a persistent pattern in the basses; meanwhile one hears fragments of motive *x* in a vast *crescendo* preparing for the definitive and forceful return of the theme [P] with which the third large section opens. This recapitulation, in G minor, the relative key of the tonic, moves aside little by little, while Theme *y* remains alone. Like the first time, an episode for the horns recalls the cyclic theme, but now it is in B-flat; we can call this the final half-section, which concludes with a reminiscence of *x* in the basses.

The tonal bases of this movement can be described thus:

1st section: B-flat (*major* and *minor*)
2nd section: G-flat (*darker*)
3rd section: B-flat (*brighter*)

The Finale of this Symphony consists of a sort of Sonata-Rondo founded on two very developed ideas. Three times the *refrain* appears in a persistent rhythm in the piano; its kinship with the cyclic theme is easily noticeable:

Immediately a first *couplet* forming a *second idea* in E major follows, without a *bridge*:

After this completely classical *exposition* comes the normal return of the *refrain*, but its rhythm is modified to 6/8; after a few measures, it is interrupted and gives way to a *development* in which first one hears the *refrain* in B-flat minor, then the *second theme* (or *couplet*) in D-flat minor (C-sharp minor by *enharmonic respelling*) and finally a combination of the two themes in E major accompanied by the cyclic pattern *y*, taken from the slow movement. This is the culminating point of the development and the moment of most clarity in the modulations. Despite its tonality, this passage takes the place of the third statement of the *refrain*; the recollections of the slow movement in the horns blur into darker and darker keys until reaching A-flat minor, at which point the development concludes by superimposing the two cyclic themes *x* and *y*. The *refrain* then appears for the fourth time but in the tonic and with more precision than in the third. Little by little, the bass pattern—proceeding as always from Theme *y*—seems to grow in strength, come closer, and finally burst out in a veritable explosion of all the orchestra in B minor. This theme then fades away, and we hear the primary theme of the slow movement return in the distant key of G-flat minor—as if it came, in reality, "from very far away." Here we find the fifth repetition of the *refrain*, in the tonic but in yet another rhythm, as if little by little it were trying to recapture the initial appearance of the *Mountain Air*:

First thus (in 2/4):

TABLE XVI/15 (*continued*)

Then thus (in 3/8):

The *second theme* then reappears in its normal place and in the tonic; and the *refrain* comes back for the sixth and last time, in a rhythm that approaches even more the rhythm of the cyclic theme:

It is followed by several concluding measures, forming a cadence.

The construction of this Finale is therefore quite simple and differs very little from that of a Beethovenian rondo except in the transformations of the *refrain*, presented "in miniature" as it repeats and is transposed (one time only) into another key.

The tonal bases rest on G major, E major, and G again; however, the modulations of the development proceed in the opposite direction of those from the first movement. That is, they move towards darker tonalities—B-flat minor, D-flat major, D-flat minor, F-flat major (E major in *enharmonic respelling*), then C major (which as a result becomes equivalent to D-double flat major), and A-flat major, leading thus to the reentry of G major with a maximum of brightness.

The orchestra is laid out in the so-called Wagnerian manner, three instruments per section. It has no special features other than a part for harp and the principal part for piano—a part which people have too often confused with that of a true Concerto.

Source: d'Indy/SYMPHONIE, pp. 170–74.

i. As we saw earlier (pp. 592–93), d'Indy falsified chronology to suggest that Franck owed nothing to Saint-Saëns. D'Indy also wrote his own symphony a few months after the "Organ" Symphony was completed but, as he implies, there is no evidence that he knew Saint-Saëns's work at the time.

ii. Another misrepresentation: Franck composed his work in 1887–88, after d'Indy's work had premiered. If anything, d'Indy's symphony influenced Franck, as we have seen.

iii. "Tonal bases" (*assises tonales*) refer to the central keys of a movement. D'Indy teaches that modulations should move in one direction, towards progressively brighter ("clearer") or darker keys. To justify his analyses, d'Indy often resorts to enharmonic respellings, which he calls *hétérographie*. For this symphony he states that the modulations in the first and last movements move to brighter and darker keys respectively.

Oax leads to the exposition. *P* enters in the lower strings and bassoons against rippling arpeggios in the piano (m.27). The opening measure of this double-dotted theme derives from *Oa* (Example XVI/27). *P* passes through several keys but begins and ends in the tonic G major. *1T* transfers *P* to the piano (m.39) while *2T* (m.49) trades *Oa* among various woodwinds with *Pa* in the piano and makes its way to the dominant of B major (III).

While *P* ascends one and a half octaves entirely in two-bar phrases, *S* features a steady octave-length descent in quarter notes which extends irregularly over the bar line (Un peu plus vite, m.64; see Theme [5] in d'Indy's analysis). Laid out as a miniature *a–b–a*, *S* also

EXAMPLE XVI/26   d'Indy. *Symphony on a French Mountain Air*/1, mm.2–11. Courtesy of Edwin F. Kalmus & Co.

EXAMPLE XVI/27   d'Indy. *Symphony on a French Mountain Air*/1, mm.27–30. Courtesy of Edwin F. Kalmus & Co.

modulates internally but begins and ends in B major. D'Indy scores *S* with great sensitivity, assigning *Sa* to the flute, harp, first horn, and piano (the latter with figural decoration), and *Sa'* to the violins and cellos, accompanied by arpeggios in the harp and piano and arabesques in the flute and clarinet. *K* serves as a short bridge built of a descending pattern derived from the closing measures of *S;* it elides into the development (m.104).

The development consists of sequential repetitions of *P, Oa,* and *K.* To begin, *K* in the piano shifts from B to B-flat major while the oboe plays *Oa* in augmentation (m.112). Section two opens in E major, which d'Indy identifies as the primary key of the development (m.124). In this brightly scored section, *P* appears in low timbres while *Oa,* still in augmentation, switches to the trumpet; descending woodwind runs are answered with ascending arpeggios in the harp and piano. In section three, d'Indy combines *P* in the piano with *Oa* in the strings in D-flat major (m.136); by the end, d'Indy respells D-flat as C-sharp and makes it the dominant of F-sharp, the key of section four. This part, the only one in which *Oa* does not appear, unites *K* and *Pa* (m.150). A further enharmonic change from F-sharp to G-flat allows d'Indy to move to E-flat for the retransition, concerned largely with *K* plus *Oa* in the horns (m.161); the lower strings undergird this passage with an ostinato that oscillates between E-flat and the dominant tone D.

The opening of the recapitulation is intense: *P* appears in the lower string, brass, and wind timbres while the other instruments provide a decorative background in a sustained *fortissimo* (the first truly loud music in the piece); piano and harp play flourishes between phrases (m.171). D'Indy jumps to *2T* as the dynamics soften again (m.187). *S* returns in the tonic in the strings and piano; the latter embellishes the melody with grace notes (m.199). The composer then starts the coda, in which *O* returns in prime form in the English horn against a backdrop of tremolos in muted strings (Assez lent, m.245). *S* follows in hymn-like block chords and brings the movement to a quiet close (m.254).

D'Indy calls the second movement (Assez modéré, mais sans lenteur) a *Lied,* a common French designation for *A–B–A* form. The key is B-flat major, mediant to G major. As in the first movement, the dynamic is mostly soft. The movement begins with *P,* derived from *I/O* and built from three antiphonal exchanges between the piano (*Pa*) and the strings, flutes, and bassoons (*Pb*). Like *I/O, P* moves in flexible meters, alternating between triple and duple divisions (Example XVI/28). Sequential statements of *Pb* form a short bridge linking *P* and *S* (m.12). For the latter d'Indy abruptly shifts to the parallel minor (m.18). Loosely related to *Pb,* it becomes the second cyclic theme of the symphony; its crucial gesture is the turn in the first measure, *Sax* (Example XVI/28, m.18). Set once again in a mini-ternary form—*a* (18), *b* (26), *a* (34)—*S* faintly resembles the principal theme of Franck's *Variations symphoniques.*

B demonstrates the modulation skills d'Indy learned from Franck. It opens with a tenderly rescored repeat of *P* in G-flat major, alternating strings with woodwinds and brass (m.41). D'Indy reprises *Pa* in A major, at which he arrives through more enharmonic respellings (Un peu plus vite, m.52). The texture thickens and leads by a Wagnerian 4–3 appoggiatura to an E-diminished harmony over a C pedal in the tympani. The third and fourth

EXAMPLE XVI/28   d'Indy. *Symphony on a French Mountain Air*/2, mm.1–21. Courtesy of Edwin F. Kalmus & Co.

EXAMPLE XVI/28   (*continued*)

horns "clear the air" by playing *Oa* in a hunting style in D-flat but still with the C pedal; over this the first horn outlines a D-augmented chord, creating a stopped sonority on the final A-sharp. To return to *A,* d'Indy juxtaposes the somber *Sax* in the piano and lower timbres with *Oa* in a fanfare style in the other instruments (m.68); a chromatic bass ascent out of the darker key regions moves back toward B-flat major.

As in the first movement, the return of *A* signals a dynamic and textural climax, as *P* sounds throughout the orchestra (m.86). The key at this point is somewhat more ambiguous than before: although d'Indy identifies it as G minor, one could also hear it as B-flat major. *S* appears in the flutes in D minor (m.104). The third and fourth horns again state *Oa,* this time in B-flat major; the upper horns outline a B major triad, once more with the top note stopped. This moment of uncertain tonality gives way to a coda solidly in B-flat (Au mouvement, m.119). A solo viola plays *Pa* against soft tremolos in other instruments, and the movement ends quietly on a sustained tonic chord with arpeggios in the piano.

The final movement (Animé) can be understood as a sonata-rondo in *A–B–A C A–D A–B–A* form; *A–D* acts as a recapitulation, so that the second *A–B–A* is actually the coda. This movement recalls earlier themes—*I/O* in the development and *II/P* and *II/S* in the recapitulation. Joyous in affect, set in a clear G major (with Franckian chromaticism in the melodies), and orchestrated in an even more sparkling manner than the previous movements, this Finale enjoyed the greatest success from the beginning, even among those critical of the rest of the work.

The refrain contains two motives. The piano plays *Pa,* an accompanimental gesture that transforms *Oa* into an arabesque ostinato in 2/4, over which other instruments superimpose *Pb,* an extroverted melody sharing the double-dotted rhythm and regular metric value of *I/P* (Example XVI/29). D'Indy adds a twist to the sonata-rondo by varying each return of the refrain, placing it in different meters and altering its character. In addition, he gradually expands *Pa* so that by the coda it becomes a theme in its own right. *T* begins with a tutti statement of *Pb* (m.77); the piano and harp play four-octave flourishes at the end of each phrase.

B introduces *S,* an extended lyrical theme in E major. It contains two large phrases, *Sa* in a solo clarinet (Plus modéré, m.113) and *Sb* in the violins (Un peu plus agité, m.129). D'Indy sets *S* in the unusual meter of 2+3/4, giving it an unpredictable contour even though it proceeds mostly in quarter notes (in this way *III/S* resembles *I/S,* also in a flexible meter). A chromatic bridge based on *S* (m.141) leads to the reprise of *A,* which contains a partial statement of *Pa* in the strings in E major (1er mouvement [original tempo], m.156). The motive now moves in steady eighth notes in 6/8, while the piano creates cross-rhythms by executing decorative sixteenth-note runs in 2/4.

D'Indy articulates each section within *C* (the development) by clear and striking changes of texture. It opens with three statements of *Pa* in various timbres and rhythms in G major and B-flat minor (m.172). The section continues with complete renditions of *S, P,* and *I/O. S* is in D-flat minor, the flattened minor dominant (m.226). For *P,* which d'Indy sets in the submediant E major, he again creates cross-rhythms by combining *Pa* in the piano in 6/8 with *Pb* in the woodwinds in 2/4; he calls this the third return of the refrain (m.258). Pairs of horns state *I/O* in gapped triplets (with the second note of the triplet silent), like a hunt motif; the key is C major (m.280). The retransition combines *Pa* in the woodwinds (also in gapped triplets) with a chromatic descent in the strings (m.292), which turns into an ostinato based on *II/Sax.*

In the "recapitulation," *Pa* appears in triplets in trumpets and cornets while the upper strings play *Pb* and the *II/Sax*-derived ostinato continues in the cellos and double basses (m.316). D'Indy follows this with an even more forceful statement of *Pb* (m.348). *P* drops

EXAMPLE XVI/29   d'Indy. *Symphony on a French Mountain Air/*3, mm.1–51. Courtesy of
Edwin F. Kalmus & Co.

EXAMPLE XVI/29   (*continued*)

EXAMPLE XVI/29 (*continued*)

out, leaving only the ostinato, which moves from triplets to eighth notes to a hocket-like texture. *II/S* itself appears in the violins and violas in B minor (m.386), followed by a recall of *II/P* in the horns (Mouvement du No. II, m.430); the latter is answered in turn by *II/Sax* in the violins and double basses.

For the coda, *Pa* transforms into an autonomous melody in G major: it appears dance-like in the piano in 2/4 (Très animé, m.456; Example XVI/30a) and then march-like in the woodwinds, trumpet, and harp in 3/8, with the cadence still in 2/4 (m.485; Example XVI/30b). *Pb,* no longer needed, disappears. A chorale-like statement of *S* intervenes, again in 2+3/4, played by the full orchestra except piano and harp (Plus modéré, m.518). The transformed *Pa* then resumes its course (Très vite, m.568; Example XVI/30c); for this last statement it assumes a majestic character in 3/4. Soon the entire ensemble plays in cross-rhythms—the piano, trumpets, and cornets in 3/4 and the remaining instruments in 2/4. After a few interjections of the flattened sixth degree (E-flat), the movement concludes with a tutti V-I cadence. So ends one of the most effervescent French symphonies, a singular work both in the Gallic repertory and d'Indy's own output. (Table XVI/16 provides an outline of the symphony.)

EXAMPLE XVI/30A   d'Indy. *Symphony on a French Mountain Air*/3, mm.456–61. Courtesy of Edwin F. Kalmus & Co.

EXAMPLE XVI/30B   d'Indy. *Symphony on a French Mountain Air*/3, mm.485–90.

EXAMPLE XVI/30C   d'Indy. *Symphony on a French Mountain Air*/3, mm.568–81.

TABLE XVI/16

Vincent d'Indy. *Symphony on a French Mountain Air:* Structure

---

Movement I

Introduction: Assez lent 9/8, 6/8   *Exposition* Modérément animé 3 [3/4]

O	trans. (O)	P (Oa)	IT (P)	2T (Oa, Pa)	S	S^k(Sb)	K
G major		G major			B major		
2	18	27	39	49	64	94	104

Development

K/Oa	P/Oa	P/Oa		K/Pa	retrans. (K/Oa)
B-flat major	E major	D-flat major mod.		F-sharp major mod.	E-flat major
112	124	136		150	161

Recapitulation   *Coda* Assez lent 6/8, 9/8

P	2T	S	S^k	O	S
G major mod.				G major	
171	187	199	228	245	254

Movement II Assez modéré, mais sans lenteur (3/4, 2/4)

A

P (O)	trans.	S
B-flat major		B-flat minor
1	12	18

B

P	Pa	Oa	Sax/Oa
G-flat major	A major mod.	D-flat major (with C pedal)	mod. to B-flat major
41	52	63	68

A

P	trans.	S	Oa
G minor, B-flat major		D minor	B-flat major, B major
86	98	104	113

Coda Au mouvement, un peu plus vite
P
B-flat major
119

Movement III Animé

Exposition

P(O)	T(Pb)	S	trans. (S)	Pa
G major		E major		E major
2/4	2+3/4			2/4

A		B		A
1	77	113	141	156

Development

Pa	S	P	O	retrans.
G major, B-flat minor	D-flat minor	E major	C major	
6/8	2+3/4	2/4	6/8 + 2/4	6/8

C
172	226	258	280	292

TABLE XVI/16 (*continued*)		
Recapitulation		
P + II/Sax	II/S	II/P + II/S
G major mod.	B minor	mod. to V/G
6/8, 2/4		
⟨A⟩	⟨D⟩	
316	386	430
Coda		
Pa	S	Pa
G major		
2/4, 3/8	2+3/4	3/4, 2/4
⟨A⟩	⟨B⟩	⟨A⟩
456	518	568

The *Symphony on a French Mountain Air* premiered at Concerts Lamoureux in March 1887. All praised the performance of the soloist, Mme Bordes-Pène, as did the composer, who dedicated the score to her in gratitude. The audience responded warmly, most critics less so. Camille Bellaigue, a representative of the conservative position, detested Franck's music, as we have seen:

> *Boredom in music*! Fine subject for an article on our times, and what a long article it would be! He would have his place in it, the composer of *Ruth* and *Les Béatitudes,* the person whom his zealous disciples call the French Bach, *the Master,* and who is at bottom nothing more than an excellent professor.[208]

As for the works of his pupils, Bellaigue found them full of "eccentricities and bizarreness," with half-baked melodies and poorly constructed forms built with harmonic "crudities." That said, he responded to d'Indy's symphony with relative sympathy—certainly with more than he did to the "excellent professor's" own symphony of two years later. Like many opponents of the *franckistes,* he criticized the cyclic process in general and especially in this symphony, because he did not find the theme distinctive enough to support repetition and variation over three movements:

> One can't listen to M. d'Indy's symphony without becoming fatigued, but this doesn't at all mean that one listens without interest. His symphony is built on a single melody, a mountain song from the Cévennes. This total unification of an entire symphony is acceptable in principle but hazardous in practice. Beethoven himself didn't dare draw on a single theme for more than one movement, and M. Saint-Saëns in [the "Organ" Symphony] gave the fundamental idea the first place among many but not all the places. M. d'Indy wanted to be more rigorous: this is a mistake. His theme is original; it gives . . . an impression of the countryside and open air . . . but it is not strong enough to sustain a whole symphony. It is too irresolute; its contour and rhythm neither reveal enough nor assert themselves enough. Same problem with the development of the theme as with the theme itself. One cannot follow M. d'Indy easily; walking behind him, we don't see where we are going, and we grope to take his hand. The result: a certain discomfort for the listener, exacerbated by mishaps on the road—interrupted cadences, bizarre resolutions, endless modulations, all of which help to break the tenuous thread of the labyrinth.[209]

Bellaigue described the first movement as "more a fantasy than a symphony" because d'Indy only varied the theme instead of developing it. The second movement he found incomprehensible, but he enjoyed the Finale: "its gaiety is infectious: one smiles, one laughs, almost audibly."[210] His final verdict: "Ah! If M. d'Indy would strive to search less, he perhaps would find more!"[211]

Other critics echoed Bellaigue's complaint that the work bore little structural resemblance to a symphony. Ernest Reyer described it as "quite simply a suite in three movements which are themselves only variations, or rather variants, of a French mountain air."[212] Ropartz agreed that the work lay somewhat outside symphonic boundaries—"it is rather a three-part symphonic suite on a single theme"—but, like Reyer, he thought highly of it. He lauded the notion of a symphony with obbligato instrument as a viable alternative to the concerto, which he (and many others at the time) found outmoded and compromised by its legacy of empty virtuosity.[213] As per his custom, Ropartz described d'Indy's symphony in poetic terms. Of the mountain theme he wrote the following:

> Some shepherd doubtless played it on his bagpipe, thus expressing his dreams—because shepherds dream, like sailors do, [and] because infinities suggest dreams, whether the infinity of the sea or the infinity of the mountains.

The second movement, which Ropartz described as a free form like a fantasia, evoked to him a night in the mountains; and the third movement suggested a raucous peasant dance.[214]

The *Symphonie cévenole* was popular from the start, and d'Indy conducted it frequently throughout Europe and the United States, almost always to enthusiastic acclaim.[215] It caught on more slowly in Paris, not appearing again until 1893 at Concerts Lamoureux. Reviewing that warmly received performance, Paul Dukas, like Ropartz and Reyer before him, found the form unconventional ("a single piece in three episodes") but he praised it highly. For Dukas, d'Indy's symphony represented not only a musical meditation on the songs of the mountain regions but also a translation of the natural elements themselves:

> His work is but an amplification of the expressive content of this melody, this voice by which the mountain itself speaks and lives. And it is in fact a "poem of the mountains" which M. d'Indy seems to have wanted to write for us: a poem of nature which reflects something of the lofty independence of the summits, a page of music where you feel you are breathing their perennial air, loaded with feral smells, [and] where you think you see the unchangeable whiteness of the peaks glisten under the varied plays of light.[216]

Tiersot regarded the work as a true symphony, built with solid classical procedures under its novel scoring and apparent formal and harmonic innovations; he commended it to his readers as "one of the most accomplished models of modern French music."[217] By then (1902), the *Symphonie cévenole* had become very popular, rivaling only the symphonies of Franck and Saint-Saëns (the "Organ") in public approval.

Between the *Mountain Air* and d'Indy's Second:
The Symphony at the Turn of the Century

As noted before, the Conservatoire maintained an official indifference to the symphony throughout the later nineteenth century. Individual composition teachers like Charles-Marie Widor included symphonies in their lessons, but the emphasis remained on teaching the fugue and dramatic cantata (a miniature oratorio for soloists and orchestra) since these were the only pathways for a student to obtain the all-important Prix de Rome. At century's end, the academic attitude began to change. In 1896, d'Indy became director of the Schola Cantorum, a recently founded school for religious music, and by 1900 he converted it into a rival to the Conservatoire. As part of the reaction against what he contemptuously called *enseignement officiel* ("academically approved instruction"), d'Indy crafted a program of *enseignement libre* ("independent instruction") which favored concert music over opera. The curriculum included a comprehensive survey of symphonic history, albeit from a chauvinistic perspective: d'Indy taught that all German symphonies after Beethoven were defective and only the French school—especially Franck and his followers—understood and applied the German master's "true lessons."[218] When Gabriel Fauré became director of the Conservatoire in 1905, that school followed d'Indy's lead and added the symphony to its curriculum, though opera retained most-favored status.

As the schools opened their doors to the symphony, the Third Republic took an interest in sponsoring the genre. As we observed earlier, politicians looked to the development of a distinguished French instrumental repertory as a matter of national pride. Deputies noted disapprovingly that Concerts Colonne and Concerts Lamoureux, both subsidized by the government, rarely programmed extended works by contemporary French composers, especially those who lacked established reputations. As early as 1886, aggrieved composers and their defenders petitioned the State to force the conductors to recognize symphonists of their own land and time:

> [I]t has become almost impossible for beginning composers to get a hearing. . . . One cannot believe that the State, which awards a subvention to several of our orchestras, wants its cash to encourage only performances of symphonies and concertos by classical masters and composers who are already famous. So, since they receive however-many-thousand francs by right of subsidy, why not require all the symphonic societies subventioned in Paris or the provinces to play so many new compositions by well-known and unknown composers? . . . If the concerts are going to keep turning to the same cycle of pieces *ad infinitum,* we might as well give up any notion of seeing a truly French school finally emerge.[219]

Eighteen years later, in 1904, the Ministry of Fine Arts passed such a regulation: it required Colonne and Camille Chevillard (Lamoureux's son-in-law and successor) henceforth to program each season at least three hours worth of premieres of works by living French composers as a condition for receiving their annual subvention (the Ministry had already passed a similar stricture for the theaters). At least four of the new pieces were to be "symphonic or lyric works lasting at least thirty minutes." According to a Ministry spokesman, the government hoped the promise of state support would "assure French symphonists that they would have an outlet for their works" and prompt them "to return to the symphony, the highest form of music."[220] At the same time, the Ministry established the Prix Cressent (also spelled Crescent), a contest for the writing of symphonies and works of similar breadth. By offering composers a financial incentive to compose symphonies and venues in which to play them, the government hoped they would rise to the challenge and create symphonies that could stand proudly alongside those from Germany.

From the moment d'Indy positioned the Schola Cantorum as a rival to the Conservatoire, the two schools engaged in open warfare, as the participants themselves described it. Politics compounded the quarrel, for the Conservatoire received financial support from the government, while right-wing opponents of the Republic lent their support to the Schola. Both institutions publicly aligned themselves with their benefactors, and most observers recognized the *guerre des écoles* as a proxy struggle between the opposing political forces.[221] To an extent, the continuing split between "classical" and "romantic" symphonies also reflected the divide, for composers at the Conservatoire created most of the former while the latter were by and large the work of members of the Schola or *franckiste* alumni of the Conservatoire who no longer belonged to that school. (Despite its affiliation with the Conservatoire, the government took no position on what kinds of symphonies to write.)

The politico-aesthetic conflicts at the beginning of the century left their mark on the music of the time, as composers began to state ideological positions through their art. Several prominent musicians, for instance, wrote pieces inspired by the recent Dreyfus Affair. Opera provided an obvious conduit—witness d'Indy's anti-Dreyfusard *La Légende de Saint-Christophe* (1908–1915), described by the composer as a *grand projet politique* (and more perniciously as a *drame anti-juif*)—but so did instrumental music, as d'Indy's pupil Albéric Magnard demonstrated with his resolutely pro-Dreyfus *Hymne à la justice* for orchestra in 1903.[222] With its tradition of the "grand statement," the symphony proved especially appealing as a means of expressing ideological and philosophical convictions.

As we have seen, French musicians (*franckistes* especially) typically interpreted modern symphonies in terms of a victorious progression from "darkness to light." In the nineteenth century, these referents usually remained generalized concepts for listeners to define as they wished; after 1900, however, composers began to write symphonies in which they assigned specific political, aesthetic, or religious labels to the "darkness" and "light." They considered the resulting "program" intrinsic to the symphony, not an afterthought. As Charles Tournemire began his Seventh Symphony, he wrote that "the themes exist [and] the plan is established; the philosophical substance, the emotive side have left my brain and heart, *volcanically*"; for Tournemire, the extramusical argument formed an integral component of the new symphony, as essential as the musical ideas.[223]

Aware that the "philosophical substance" of a symphony could not speak for itself, the composer explained his intentions to the audience by means of a concert note (written by himself or a surrogate), a text set in the work, or quotations of familiar and significative melodies. Such "message-symphonies," as we might call them, were not designed for casual listening: the composer expected the audience to follow the musical argument and apply whatever commentary he supplied. The listener did not have to understand the message in order to enjoy the music, but without that knowledge the full purpose of the composition remained hidden. To translate the message into music the composer employed conventions drawn both from the realms of program and absolute music. Cyclic form unified the piece and kept it "on topic"; thematic transformation depicted the metamorphosis of the "dark" element into "light"; and a closing peroration, usually symbolized by a triumphant chorale, announced the final defeat of the dark element. All of these elements can be found in symphonies that lack messages, but they are especially prominent and purposeful in the message-symphony.

Of course, conveying philosophical ideas in symphonies was nothing new, as we know from Beethoven's Ninth. To use Ropartz's phrase, non-French symphonists also "thought in music": Tchaikovsky in the "Pathétique," Nielsen in the Fourth and Fifth Symphonies, and Ives in his Fourth, not to mention Mahler. What sets the French message-symphony apart from its foreign cousins is the intentionally *polemic* nature of its ideas. While Mahler and Tchaikovsky externalized inner anxieties, and Beethoven, Ives, and Nielsen conveyed ideal visions of the world or made observations on the human spirit, many French composers treated the symphony as a salvo into the cultural and ideological quarrels of the day—a musical pamphlet as it were, similar to the literary publications which proliferated in the eighteenth century during the *guerre des bouffons* and the "war" between the Gluckists and Piccinnists. In his novel *Jean-Christophe,* Romain Rolland commented on the practice of making symphonies into manifestos:

> Besides [Debussy and the Impressionists], there were also the philosophers: they treated metaphysical problems in music; their symphonies were the struggle of abstract principles, the explanation of a symbol or a religion. . . . [Artists] of Christophe's day translated sociology into sixteenth notes. Zola, Nietzsche, Maeterlinck, Barrès, Jaurès, Mendès, the Gospels, and the Moulin Rouge all nourished the cistern to which composers of operas and symphonies came to draw their thoughts.[224]

Several of the following symphonies, such as d'Indy's Second (1904), Ropartz's Third (1906), Théodore Dubois's *Symphonie française* (1908), and several by Charles Tournemire, fall into the category of message-symphonies. By 1914, the message-symphony had become the most popular type of contemporary French symphony; though associated primarily with d'Indy and his circle, composers at the Conservatoire also made recourse to it, for their own ends.

Vincent d'Indy (continued)
SYMPHONY NO. 2 IN B-FLAT OPUS 57

D'Indy composed his Second Symphony in B-flat (he specified no mode) in 1902–1903, at the height of the *guerre des écoles.* At this moment, the government—a center-left coalition swept into power by the Dreyfus Affair—was acting to marginalize the political right and the Catholic Church, both sponsors of the Schola. In addition, Debussy's supporters, energized by the recent premiere of *Pelléas et Mélisande,* were beginning to mount opposition to d'Indy and his school (the quarrel between the so-called *d'indyste* and *debussyste* "chapels" became in some respects a microcosm of the *guerre des écoles,* as the *debussystes* supported the Conservatoire, especially after Fauré's accession in 1905). A committed anti-Dreyfusard, d'Indy did not hesitate to posit causal relationships between musical and social tendencies; in a 1902 letter to Ropartz, he denounced opponents of the symphony as "artistic Dreyfusards."[225] The composer began his Second Symphony the same year, and one is tempted to see the work as a riposte to those who would deny the legitimacy of the genre as well as those who challenged the values of his school. Certainly d'Indy's contemporaries understood the work as such: according to Léon Vallas, "[Its] unveiling was awaited with an impatience that was all the livelier because at that moment the *d'indystes* and *debussystes* were in full battle; the performance of the new work was to constitute an important episode in the little aesthetic war."[226]

D'Indy based the Second Symphony on two cyclic motives, which he labeled x and y (see Table XVI/17, Part A, for his analysis). He introduces both in the opening measures. X consists of an ascending minor third followed by a major third; together they span a tritone (Table XVI/18, [1]). Y features the expressive leap of a minor seventh (Table XVI/18, [5]). The symphony unfolds as a contest for priority between these motives as well as surrogate themes that they spawn; y emerges triumphant in the end (Table XVI/19 lists the derivations).

Such a scenario strongly suggested the presence of a motivating "plot," one perhaps involving symbols more concrete than "darkness" and "light." D'Indy kept the particulars to himself, though, giving at most generic hints to friends and pupils and nothing to the public.

Two months after the premiere, however, his student René de Castéra published a review in the anti-Dreyfusard journal *L'Occident* that appeared to offer a key to the meaning of the symphony. According to Castéra, d'Indy conceived of the battle between x and y as an

---

TABLE XVI/17
D'Indy's Analyses of His Symphony No. 2

[The musical examples appear in Table XVI/18.]

Part A. Analysis in the *Cours de composition musicale*
[Source: d'Indy/SYMPHONIE, pp. 175–76]

The Second Symphony, in B-flat, is in the traditional *four-movement* form. It is based on *two cyclic motives* (*x* and *y*), sketched out from the beginning of the Introduction. These motives serve in some ways as "antagonists."

The first-movement *Allegro* is in a totally regular structure [i.e., sonata form].

After a *development* in which Motive *x* reappears, the *recapitulation* proceeds normally save for a kind of false entry of Theme B [*S*] in G-flat major before arriving at the tonic. A short *terminal development* drawn from Theme *y* and the *bridge* [*1T*] completes the piece.

The slow movement forms a *Grand Lied* in *five* sections [*A–B–A–B–A*], based on a theme in D-flat major derived from Theme *y.*

The second and fourth sections have elements in common which contrast with the principal theme. The latter reappears in the fifth section with the modification of a *step* (that is to say, of its *employment* and not its *tonality*).

The very short *Scherzo* is in the form of a duple-meter *Intermezzo* with *two trios,* in the inverse direction of D minor. Its theme has the bearing of a *folk song.* (See Table XVI/18.)

The Finale, preceded by a recapitulatory Introduction in which all the principal themes of the work reappear—notably Motive *y* in fugal form—is a kind of Rondo whose *refrain* (in quintuple time) is drawn from this same Motive *y.*

A vast *crescendo* prepares the peroration in which the two guiding motives [*x* and *y*] combine in a sort of Chorale (Motive *y* is in the upper parts and Motive *x* in the bass), followed by an agogic conclusion.

Part B. Analysis given to composition students at the Schola Cantorum
[Source: Gabéaud/D'INDY, p. 26]

Here is his own analysis of his Second Symphony. This work places in opposition: an evil and adversarial idea, proceeding by major thirds and whole tones; and a loftier idea, an idea of goodness. After an ardent struggle, this latter theme descends from heaven in the Finale to triumph over the evil idea, which is finally pacified and subjected to discipline.

Part C. Analysis given to M.-D. Calvocoressi
[Source: Calvocoressi/MUSICIANS, pp. 114–15]
At the time when d'Indy had completed his Second Symphony, I was commissioned . . . to write an article on this work. Accordingly, I asked d'Indy if he could let me see the manuscript score and give me whatever information he saw fit. He agreed . . . [B]efore beginning to play the symphony at the piano, d'Indy explained to us its structure; and one of his first remarks was, "I call the first theme [*y*] the 'theme of good' and the second [*x*] the 'theme of evil': but these designations represent merely the play of my mind, and are not intended for publication."

---

emblematic contest between "traditional" and "modern" musics—that of "d'Indyists" and "Debussyists."

> The first [idea], sketching the interval of a tritone (*diabolus in musica*) by a set of alternating minor and major thirds, has a somber and menacing character that in the composer's mind vaguely symbolizes the modern element of bad influence. The second idea . . . responds to it like a sweet lament; it is the element of tradition, of good influence.[227]

TABLE XVI/18
Motives and Derivations in d'Indy's Symphony No. 2

TABLE XVI/19

Cyclic Derivations in d'Indy's Symphony No. 2

Measure	Theme and Direct Source	Ultimate Source
(Movement I)		
1	*x*	*x*
2	*y*	*y*
14	*P (y)*	*y*
67	*1T (Pb)*	—
97	*2T (x+1T)*	*x*
115	*3T (x+2T)*	*x*
135	*S (y)*	*y*
(Movement II)		
6	*P (I/S)*	*y*
35	*1S (II/2S of Franck's Symphony)*	—
44	*2S (x+1S)*	*x*
(Movement III)		
1	*A*	—
66	*1B (x+A)*	*x*
88	*2B (II/1S)*	—
100	*3B (1B)*	*x*
147	*4B (1B+2B)*	*x*
(Movement IV)		
	Introduction and Fugue	
1	*x, y, I/S, II/P, III/P, IV/2P*	*x, y*
31	*O (x, y)*	*x, y*
	Rondo	
100	*1P (Oc)*	*y*
107	*2P (II/Pb)*	*y*
122	*1S (2P, but not section based on y)*	—
127	*2S (1S)*	—
	Coda, Part I: Transition to Chorale	
246	*trans. (x+I/S)*	*x, y*
280	*x*	*x*
	Coda, Part II: Chorale	
329	*Strophes 1–2 (x, y, I/S, IV/1P)*	*x, y*
341	*Strophe 3 (y, II/P, III/P)*	*y*
353	*transition to close (I/Pa)*	*y*
370	*I/Sa (y)*	*y*

The subsequent victory of *y* demonstrated the message of the symphony: only art built upon "the traditional element" will survive.

D'Indy remained coy about the message of his symphony, conceding only that the combatant themes represented "good" and "evil" (Table XVI/17, Parts B–C). Nor does his analysis in the *Cours de composition musicale* mention any program. As a result, we cannot say whether Castéra's message truly reflected d'Indy's thoughts or whether the pupil drew his own ideologically charged conclusions about the meanings of "good" and "evil." Still, d'Indy plainly sanctioned the publication and dissemination of Castéra's interpretation, for it soon appeared in other venues. The same month that the article appeared, Jean Marnold wrote a review that referred to "the plan—premeditated, according to what I am told—of an antithesis between two ideas representing modern thought and that of the past."[228] Vallas mentioned the message in his biography of the composer, without any suggestion that it did not originate with d'Indy.[229] And the message began to appear in concert notes for subsequent performances. That d'Indy allowed Castéra's interpretation of his symphony to become the authorized explication suggests that at least it does not misrepresent his intentions.

As one might expect given its iconic status, the Second Symphony follows tradition in ways that the *Symphony on a French Mountain Air* did not. Consisting of four rather than three movements in the conventional structures, it borrows no folk themes; and d'Indy scores the work for a regular orchestra without piano, though he includes a prominent piccolo E-flat trumpet. The cyclic unity is even tighter: the two motives are cells, raw material out of which most of the thematic material evolves. Notably, the work contains a number of whole-tone passages and coloristic sonorities (augmented and extended tertian chords). While some of these "Debussyist moments" can be explained by the message—they often occur in conjunction with appearances of *x*, the "modern element"—others, such as conspicuous polytonal passages in the second and fourth movements, have little relation to it.

Other d'Indy compositions have even more Impressionistic passages, especially his symphonic triptych *Jour d'été à la montagne* ("Summer Day at the Mountain," 1905), a masterful evocation of morning, noon, and night in the Cévennes. D'Indy did not oppose all of Debussy's innovations, especially in the earlier works. He had considerable respect for *Prélude à l'après-midi d'un faune, Nocturnes,* and *Pelléas et Mélisande;* for the last he wrote a highly sympathetic and perceptive review.[230] (Debussy in turn warmly praised d'Indy's opera *L'Étranger.*) D'Indy reserved his disdain for Debussy's disciples, who according to him used ninth chords and whole-tone scales as ends in themselves, without regard for the more important elements of memorable melody, solid structure, and clear and conventional tonal foundations (d'Indy had such absolute respect for the latter that he criticized even Franck for allegedly straying in this area; see note 137). As he wrote in a letter to his friend Octave Maus in 1904, the year the Second Symphony premiered,

> I attach more and more importance to the theme in instrumental music [*musique symphonique*], and the further I go the more I believe that the purely decorative art . . . , which many people including Debussy himself now use in instrumental style, is a transitory art; it can be shimmering, pleasing for the moment, but it will fall into ruins very quickly for lack of solid foundations, . . . the *"pretty harmony"* having never replaced the *"theme"* in [symphonic] music.[231]

In the Second Symphony and other works, d'Indy practiced what we might call a conservative Impressionism, incorporating Debussyist passages but keeping them subordinate to classical bases.

D'Indy's symphony also has affinities with Chausson's, especially in the first movement, and some analysts have speculated that d'Indy conceived this work as a memorial to his friend. They cite these similarities: the key (B-flat); a dark introduction dispelled by a cheery *P* in the horn; and a jaunty, pentatonic *T* emphasizing woodwinds in fast staccato motion. In both symphonies the finale culminates in a chorale based upon the cyclic motive. At the same time, important structural differences remain, as d'Indy's symphony is in four movements and uses the cyclic process much more rigorously and systematically; moreover, if d'Indy composed the Second Symphony in Chausson's memory, he wrote it as a tribute rather than a lament, for nowhere can one detect an air of mourning.

The first movement is in sonata form with a slow introduction. As the symphony opens, (Extrêmement lent, B-flat minor), *x* and *y* engage each other three times. In the transition, the descending diminished fourth of *y* becomes a perfect fourth against a chromatically ascending bass and whole-tone flourishes in the violins, played in acceleration (like many *franckiste* symphonies, d'Indy's Second features numerous gradations of tempo). This dramatic passage suggests an arrival in the minor, but *P* enters suddenly in B-flat major.

P, a long-breathed melody in 3/4 played by the first horn (Très vif, m.14), has two components: *Pa,* the *y*-derived perfect fourth drop from the transition (Table XVI/18, [6]); and *Pb,* the filled-in ascent of an octave. Chromatic descents complete the theme. After a restatement by full orchestra, with added counterpoint and new modulations, *P* ends firmly in B-flat major. D'Indy follows the *y*-based *P* with an extensive *x*-derived *T. 1T* is a pentatonic rhythmic motive indebted to *Pb* and perhaps also to Chausson's *II/Ta* (m.67), but *x* dominates *2T* and *3T.* The former combines *x* with whole-tone patterns in the rhythm of *1T* (m.97) and *3T* sets a variant of *x* against the whole-tone patterns (m.115). Unstable "Debussyist" harmonies appear throughout this section. The meter changes to 3/2 for *S,* a lyrical transformation of *y* in F major and the central theme of the symphony (Un peu plus modéré, m.135; Table XVI/18, [7]); another expansive melody, it reaches a passionate climax. The exposition concludes without a *K.*

The development placidly works over *y*-derived material (m.166). In the first section, d'Indy subjects *Pa* to fragmentation and varied sequential repetition; its falling fourth gradually expands to a sixth (m.212). The next section alternates *Pa* and *1T,* concluding with a short whole-tone flourish (m.220). Like the exposition, the development culminates in a statement of *S* in 3/2, with *1T* superimposed onto it in 9/4 (m.258). After much wandering, the key settles on A minor. *X* returns in the retransition and again produces harmonic instability through whole-tone, tritonal, and extended tertian sonorities (Plus animé, m.273). In an attractive coloristic section, *x* sounds in the piccolo trumpet and trombones while harps and flutes play successive ninth chords on F-sharp and B-flat (m.291). As the meter returns to 3/4, *x* engages in accelerating sequences against ascending semitonal motions.

As at the end of the introduction, the sudden entrance of *P* (i.e., *y*) after a whole-tone harp flourish halts the ominous motion of *x* (Mvt. initial, m.327). D'Indy intensifies *P* and extends it through interjections in various solo instruments; although beginning and ending in B-flat major, it wanders internally. *1T* and *2T* become more ambiguous harmonically than before; *1T* in fact starts off on E, a tritone from the tonic (m.389). Like *P, S* (Un peu plus modéré, m.437) is lengthened and magnified as thematic fragments pass through a kaleidoscope of fast-changing colors; starting in G-flat major (the lowered submediant), it eventually modulates to the tonic. A bridge extends the second half of *S* (m.470).

The coda brings together all of the important material. Section one features a chorale-like peroration with *S* and *y* in a canon at the fourth (Mvt. initial, m.478). Section two joins *Pa* with the rhythm of *1T* (Assez animé, m.486), while *x* sounds prominently in the bass timbres. Most of the material in this movement, then, derives from the cyclic motives: *y* generates the main themes while *x* dominates transitional sections. By placing *x* in a subordinate position, d'Indy adumbrates the final outcome; but for the moment, the "modern element" remains a viable opponent.

The slow movement (Modérément lent, D-flat major), in *A–B–A–B–A* form, consists of more exchanges between themes derived from *x* and *y;* again, *y* dominates the principal sections while *x* takes the contrasting sections. The movement opens with a brief reminder of *II/Pa,* the central gesture of that movement. *II/P,* a long and expressive melody for strings and woodwinds in 6/4, stems from *I/S* and thus ultimately from *y* (m.6; Table XVI/18, [8]); highly chromatic, it features wide leaps but moves solidly in D-flat major. The melody ends on a half cadence, the resolution of which d'Indy defers for the moment.

For *B,* d'Indy switches to 3/2 (Plus animé, m.35). The only theme in this movement not indebted to *x* or *y*, *1S* is a stepwise processional moving in dotted rhythms in C-sharp dorian; curiously, it resembles *II/2S* of Franck's Symphony in D minor, a melody d'Indy disliked.[232] Above *1S*, the winds play *2S*, a lyrical variant of *x* in C-sharp minor (m.44); here the motive consists of two minor thirds that fill out a fifth (Table XVI/18, [2]). As in the first movement, whole-tone flourishes conclude this *x*-derived section.

In the second *A* (m.61), *Pa* returns in augmentation in the first violins against descending arpeggios in the first harp and a broken-octave pedal in the second violins; *Pb* resumes the normal rhythm. The key now is A major, the submediant of C-sharp minor. D'Indy also varies the return of *B*, placing *1S* in a straightforward C-sharp minor without modal inflections (m.83); at the end the theme pivots to B-flat minor for a brief statement of *2S*. A transition based on *P* leads to the final section. *P* returns to its original form, assigned to the flute and raised a step; the key, however, remains D-flat major, so d'Indy treats us to a moment of unexpected but discreet polytonality (Mvt. initial, m.103).

To end the movement, the orchestra tries three times to bring closure to the aborted cadence from mm.34–35. Whole-tone statements of *1S* frustrate its attempts twice; the third brings success, but the conspicuous intrusion of *x* in a solo trombone mitigates the effect (m.140). As in the first movement, then, *y* remains the dominant motive; but, by spoiling an otherwise solid resolution, *x* again denies it victory.

The third movement (Modéré) revisits the varied refrain structure of the *Symphonie cévenole* Finale. D'Indy combines Scherzo and Trio, theme and variation, and rondo into a hybrid form—*A–B–A'/B'–A''*. As in the *Cévenole*, each return of *A* constitutes a variation, increasing in tempo and surface rhythm. Just as the combining of two movements within one division (*à la* Franck or the "Organ" Symphony) became common practice in post-1900 French symphonies, so did d'Indy's structural cross-breeding.

We first hear *A* as a kind of intermezzo in 2/4. An original melody in D minor in the style of a *chant populaire*—simple, lyrical, and largely stepwise, with phrygian inflections and a lowered leading tone—it owes nothing to *x* or *y* (Example XVI/31a). The melody sounds twice; after the second statement, *x* appears in stopped horns as two major thirds forming a whole-tone pattern (Table XVI/18, [3]). An accelerando leads to the Trio.

D'Indy sets the Trio in the third-related key of B-flat major. It has three themes, all in woodwinds or brass. *1B* (Très animé, m.66) is based on the closing gesture of *A* while the violins accompany with variants of *x*; though rooted in B-flat, the passage proceeds largely in whole tones. *2B* reprises *II/1S* in whole tones (m.88), rooting its two statements on augmented triads on F-flat and F-natural, respectively. *3B* reprises *III/1B* in diminution but with more lyricism; this version, played by the piccolo trumpet, strengthens the B-flat tonality (Un peu plus calme, m.100). The Trio closes with chromatic flourishes.

The next section oscillates ambiguously between varied reprises of *A* and *B*. Reflecting the structural instability, the harmony consists mostly of augmented, diminished, and modal sonorities centered around A, with secondary emphasis on F and C. *A'* appears in A minor in 3/8, bouncing jauntily from one solo instrument to another (Assez vif, m.126; Example XVI/31b). It is interrupted by *4B*, a combination of *1B* and *2B* over an F-augmented triad (m.147). *A'* reasserts itself, faster and deformed by accidentals into an A-diminished pattern. After another intrusion by *4B*, it becomes a canon in A phrygian. The section closes with *1B* and *3B*, the former suggesting a C-augmented harmony (m.185) and the latter leading to an extended version of the chromatic flourishes that closed the Trio (Très animé, m.190).

The final section (Très vif, m.212) begins with *A''*, an even faster variation which moves in sixteenth notes in 2/8; highly modulatory, it alternates quickly between woodwinds and strings (Example XVI/31c). To bring peace, the second half of *A* returns more or less in original form

EXAMPLE XVI/31A   d'Indy. Symphony No. 2/3, mm.1–8.

EXAMPLE XVI/31B   d'Indy. Symphony No. 2/3, mm.126–35.

EXAMPLE XVI/31C   d'Indy. Symphony No. 2/3, mm.212–19.

and settles the key back in D minor (m.253). It dies away, and a sudden stretto of the opening of *A* closes the movement.

Most of the strife in this movement takes place between original themes, though *x* maintains a presence in transitions and *2B* alludes to the *x*-derived *II/2S*. Perhaps this Scherzo suggests a "dark" interlude before the final battle? The continually unstable harmonies as well as the progressive distortions of an innocent-sounding *A* lend support to such an interpretation.

The Finale has three distinct sections: introduction and fugue, rondo, and chorale coda. Almost everything stems from previous material. In the introduction (Lent), d'Indy, following Beethoven's Ninth, recalls a theme from each of the preceding movements—*III/A, II/P,* and *I/S* as well as *x*—and answers them with the incipient form of *IV/2P,* which originates with *II/Pb* and thus *y.*

The introduction gives way to a somber fugue in B-flat minor whose subject, *O,* is an altered form of *II/2S* (Modéré et solennel, m.31). *O* has three components: *O-a,* a statement of *x; O-b,* a falling dotted gesture; and *O-c,* which incorporates the semitonal motion and minor-seventh leap of *y* (Table XVI/18, [4]). By combining *x* and *y, O* adumbrates the union of the two motives which will take place in the final chorale; but here *x* dominates and *y* is submissive, implying perhaps that for the moment *y* is *subject* to the "darkness." The fugue progresses from darker to brighter timbres as it moves from the tonic minor to major. An extended transition combines *O-c* with chromatic ascents and descents over a large dominant prolongation on F with prominent G-flats (m.76).

The second portion of the Finale is an animated rondo in 5/4, a favorite d'Indy meter. The key returns to B-flat major. Arranged in *A–B–A'–B'–A''–B''* form, the rondo resembles a sonata if we accept *A'–B'* as a development and *A''–B''* as a thematic though not tonal recapitulation. The conflict between the cyclic motives returns: following the now-familiar pattern, *y* inspires the themes of the refrain while *x* inhabits the episodes. Like the preceding transition, *1P* is based on a diminution of *O-c* (Table XVI/18, [9]; Assez vif, m.100). As in the Finale of the *Symphonie cévenole*, it serves as accompaniment to *2P*; hinted at in the introduction, the latter theme now comes into its own as a speeded-up *II/Pb. B*, the second half of the "exposition," moves to G minor as a dominant substitute. *1S* is a dotted motive repeated sequentially in the violins (Un peu moins vite, m.122), while *2S* sounds in the woodwinds over repeating fragments of *1S* (Au mouvt., m.127).

In the "development," the key wanders liberally (m.144). *2P,* the makeup of which contains a hint of *II/2S,* is momentarily interrupted by a full statement of that earlier theme (m.152). *1S* appears twice in a polytonal canon (m.169); at the end of the development, *x*— now extended to a minor seventh—combines with *2S* (m.186). The "recapitulation" (*A''*) begins in D major (1er mouvement [original tempo], m.198). *1P* and *2P* appear in the full orchestra, *fortissimo. B''* continues the dynamic and textural intensification: *1S* leads to B-flat minor while *2S* ends on a dominant ninth on D-flat.

The transition to the coda begins with a tonal shift from six flats to no accidentals (m.246). *X* and *y* enter into combat for the final time: *x,* still extending to a seventh, appears both as itself and *O* in the lower and middle timbres; *y* answers in the form of *I/S* in extreme high ranges (solo violin and piccolo), suggesting a "celestial" style. *X* asserts itself repeatedly and threatens a sinister outcome; but in vain.

The Second Symphony culminates with a final transformation of the most important material in the form of a large three-strophe chorale for full orchestra. In strophes one and two, *x* and *y* appear simultaneously for the first time—*y* as *I/S* in the higher timbres, *x* in the lower (Example XVI/32 for strophe one); after each strophe the first violins play *IV/1P* and the horns sound the descending fourth of *I/Pa.* In the third strophe *x* drops out, replaced by the combination of *III/P* and the *y*-based *II/P* in augmentation against whole-tone flourishes in the upper strings. From this point on *y* has the field to itself and the key settles definitively in B-flat major. Numerous repetitions of *I/Pa* lead to a final climactic statement of *I/Sa,* with a prominent 9–8 appoggiatura.

The chorale can be interpreted in several ways: either *y* defeats *x* since the latter disappears by the end, or the motives reconcile because they join in the chorale and play equally important functions—*y* the melody and *x* the foundation (in the first two strophes). Castéra implied the former reading, but d'Indy's comment to Alice Gabéaud that *x* is "subjected to discipline" suggests it is tamed and domesticated, absorbed rather than obliterated (Table XVI/17 Part B). Albert Groz, a *scholiste* who reprinted the message in program notes for a 1912 performance, stated that "in this majestic peroration the two themes appear superimposed and narrowly intertwined, as if to tell us that in the composer's mind the only true art is that which knows how to unite the ardor for innovation with respect for tradition."[233] In other words, *x* is not stamped out but put in its place. So, depending on one's inclinations, the symphony could represent a rejection of modernism, an encouragement to use modernist procedures but temper them with deference to tradition, or a declaration that art must strive for a balance of the two elements.

As d'Indy implied by his reluctance to discuss the "message," one can enjoy the symphony without knowing the symbolic associations *x* and *y* supposedly carried. Indeed, assuming the authenticity of Castéra's interpretation, one can question whether the work conveys it effectively. *X*/modernism rarely rises above inferior status to mount a true challenge to *y*/tradition; instead of a mortal enemy, *x* appears like a nuisance—or, worse, simply as contrasting material. Possibly d'Indy wished to demonstrate that "modern" forces *a priori* had no chance against tradition? At any rate, despite some prosaic passages, the Second Symphony impresses through its finely varied orchestration, expressive themes (especially *II/P*),

EXAMPLE XVI/32   d'Indy. Symphony No. 2/4, mm.328–32 (Strophe 1 of chorale).

EXAMPLE XVI/32   (*continued*)

and beautiful impressionistic passages. The finely wrought Finale is especially effective because the composer prepares us carefully and logically for the final transformation. In sum, this work fully merits the high reputation it gained, and its absence from the concert hall is regrettable.

The Second Symphony premiered to great public and critical acclaim at Concerts Lamoureux in February 1904 (Plate B25). Pierre Lalo lauded the Finale, which he later declared "one of the most beautiful symphonic movements—perhaps the most beautiful—that anyone has written since Beethoven's time."[234] D'Indy's friend Paul Dukas, the dedicatee of the symphony, described it as "the logical result of the highest principles of [d'Indy's] teaching" and said it demonstrated that the symphonic genre remained a vibrant form: "contrary to the opinion of many critics and musicians, nothing seems to indicate that this form has evolved to its furthest limit."[235] Jean Chantavoine agreed that the Second Symphony represented a musical demonstration of *scholiste* instruction but found it an outsized textbook example rather than a living artwork:

> The Symphony in B-flat was written less by the composer than by the professor; it doesn't so much express a feeling as unveil a program; and this is why, having sought a confession in it, I found hardly more than a manifesto. . . . M. d'Indy wanted to compose a symphonic paradigm [*une symphonie-type*] which summarized, illustrated, and justified his aesthetic theories. Such was, I believe, his conscious or unconscious intent.[236]

Some reviewers found the symphony too dramatic: Jules Combarieu described it as "dramatic, pictorial, descriptive, parceled out in little spots of very fine and suggestive color, underlined by oppositions that . . . evoke situations in the theater," while Gaston Carraud concluded that it had "the appearance of a symphonic poem rather than a true symphony."[237] Complaints were also made about its "modernity" (Combarieu: "the work really abuses dissonances, and that *from the beginning*") and many foreign critics, including American reviewers, condemned the symphony—ironically, in light of its message—as a nadir of harmonic asperity and ugliness, rivaling that of Debussy and even Schoenberg.[238] Such responses confound the popularly held notion of d'Indy as a reactionary pedant.[239]

Somewhat surprisingly, no critic took on the supposed message of the work, even after it was made public. Anyone hoping for a fight would have been disappointed for, whatever their reservations, all the reviewers (including Combarieu, Carraud, and Chantavoine) praised the work in the end. Alfred Bruneau, the chief defender of Dreyfus among musicians and a harsh critic of d'Indy, delivered his verdict using significant rhetoric of the Dreyfusard camp: "For one to resist the fire [this symphony] produces is a matter of temperament; to deny its brilliance is the sin of injustice."[240] (Debussy apparently left no written comments about the symphony, if indeed he ever heard it.) Until the early 1930s, when the mature symphonies of Roussel and Honegger supplanted it, d'Indy's Second remained the most popular post-1900 French symphony, receiving numerous performances at home and abroad; the composer himself conducted it frequently in France as well as abroad, including in Boston. It might have received even more hearings had not difficulties in securing a piccolo trumpet—and paying the high fees charged by available performers—impeded orchestras from playing the work, especially after the war.

SYMPHONY NO. 3 "SINFONIA BREVIS DE BELLO GALLICO" OPUS 70

D'Indy wrote his last symphony during the summers of 1916–1918; he finished it on September 29, 1918, the Feast of St. Michael. This time, the composer planned from the outset to write a program symphony, although as usual he intended to keep the message to himself. With friends, however, he was more candid:

> I've started a Third Symphony, which is beginning well. The first movement is done (not yet orchestrated, but all the music is there). I'm happy with it. Obviously there's "some war" in it and more; but apart from a theme whose instrumental style (little drum and fifes) will be Boche [a derogatory epithet for Germans], I hope that no one will suspect the symphony's origin and that no one will call it the *Eroica* Symphony!
>
> I've carefully avoided all *Marseillaise,* all *Brabançonne* [the Belgian national anthem], all *Wacht am Rhein.* It's simply symphonic music in the most classical forms; it won't break any new ground, but I think it's "good music" all the same.
>
> And then (this will throw those who want to see only the war in it), there will be— after the first movement, which is very "Mobilization of 1914"—a disconcertingly tranquil Andante (you could entitle it: *the infantryman's dream!*)
>
> For that movement I found a theme which I think is really good. Nothing of *Pelléas, Scheherazade, Sacre du printemps* or even Strauss's new *Alpine Symphony* about it: it's a *very simple* melody, but I like it. I like it a lot and I think it will please you too. After this, a scherzo—with something Russian about it (but it's me)—and to close, a finale that I don't completely have hold of yet, but it will end with *the Alleluia of St. Michael* – which no one (except maybe for Gastoué – and a few others) will be able to recognize.[241]

For a while d'Indy stuck to his plan to keep the program hidden. As he wrote to his pupil Marcel Labey,

> I have plunged into a Symphony of which I've been able to finish the first three movements (in sketch). The Finale will be for next July. Although there's no hint of the *Marseillaise,* I have built this symphony on the war; but it's discreet, and moreover I won't be giving any explanation – people will see in it what they wish.[242]

To his friend Charles Legrand he wrote,

> I have composed a symphony in D with which I am quite happy. It is in four movements and *there is the war* within it – but I don't want anyone to suspect it and it will have no other title than *Third Symphony.*[243]

By 1918, however, the composer had amended his plans: he added the subtitle "Sinfonia brevis *de bello gallico*" (Little Symphony *about the War in France;* emphasis is d'Indy's) and reversed the placement of the Scherzo and Andante. To Ropartz, who made a four-hand transcription of the work, d'Indy gave a clear summation of its program:

> *First movement:* Mobilization, the Marne. *Scherzo:* Gaiety at the front. *Andante:* Latin art and Boche art. *Finale:* Victory with the Hymn of St. Michael as a Peroration.[244]

Finally, probably with the week-old Armistice in mind, he described the finished work to Octave Maus as the "Victory Symphony."[245] He dedicated the work to his cousin and brother-in-law "commandant É[dmond] de Pampalonne."

Perhaps mindful of his classroom admonitions that symphonies should not be programmatic, d'Indy continued to insist that his *bello gallico* symphony, its title notwithstanding, had no extramusical references. To the press he proclaimed it "a Haydn symphony" while he told Vallas (perhaps with some annoyance), "It is a symphony like all symphonies."[246] In the *Cours* he wrote merely the following: "Like the Second Symphony, the *Sinfonia brevis* in D Major is in four movements: but these movements are shorter and the Scherzo precedes the slow movement." The title seems to have been a satirical jibe in the spirit of Rossini's *Petite Messe Solenelle:* at 35 minutes, the *Sinfonia brevis* is indeed shorter than the Second Symphony—by seven minutes—but longer than the *Symphony on a French Mountain Air,* not to mention any symphony by Haydn.

D'Indy's final symphony features a larger orchestra than its predecessors: befitting the subject matter, he expands the brass (again using a piccolo trumpet) and especially the percussion, adding chromatic tympani, French parade drum, flat drum, bass drum, cymbals, xylophone, triangle, and celesta. Outwardly the work conforms to traditional symphonic form, though surprisingly it is not strongly cyclic. In the opening of the first movement (Lent et calme—Animé), chord streams, ninth chords, and whole-tone passages create a serene atmosphere redolent of the opening of *Jour d'été à la montagne.* An unexpected drum roll launches us into the sonata. Except for the modal and folk-like T, its themes lack distinction; aside from occasional passages in march style, the movement contains few obvious war references.

As with many of d'Indy's compositions (especially his chamber works), the Scherzo is the most captivating movement. Its principal theme, in G minor, features notably lydian C-sharp inflections. In addition to the folk-like melodies, one finds suggestions of folk dance. D'Indy sets the melody of the Trio, another rustic theme, in his favorite 5/4 meter. Short passages of military fanfares in the retransition remind us of the subject of this symphony.

D'Indy bases the slow movement on the extended melody in which he took so much pride in his letter to Poujaud; in its wide leaps and affective mien this theme recalls *II/P* from the Second Symphony. Against it d'Indy pits a bizarre and jerky chromatic motive which supposedly represents German art but in fact does nothing of the sort. Presumably he intended to contrast a contemplative Gallic soul with a neurotic Teutonic neighbor, but the total disparity in quality between the motives makes the comparison meaningless.

The Finale is the most obviously programmatic and least successful movement. It begins with combat music with fanfares in the brass and cannon fire in the bass drum. A short sonata ensues. At the end, over the orchestra the trumpet sounds a Gregorian melody from the Feast of St. Michael—the archangel who slays the (Teutonic) dragon—and the symphony comes to a triumphant if bombastic close.

The *Sinfonia brevis* premiered at the Société Nationale in May 1919 and repeated at Concerts Lamoureux in December. Its reception was much poorer than that of its predecessors. Though listeners sympathized with d'Indy's "act of anti-German polemics" (Vallas), the awkward mix of abstract form and plainly programmatic content made them uncomfortable.[247] As critic Jean Poueigh wrote, "M. d'Indy's personality is less evident in this new symphony than in its predecessors. . . . His subject constrained the composer to conceive his symphony in the style of a symphonic poem."[248] The general consensus from d'Indy's own time and since is that the *Sinfonia brevis,* however well intended, ultimately must be counted a failure. This verdict is at once fair and too harsh: unquestionably not d'Indy at his best (especially in the outer movements), the symphony still has memorable moments, particularly the introduction, the main theme of the slow movement, and the whole of the Scherzo.

Guy Ropartz

The longest-surviving member of the Franck circle, Joseph Guy Ropartz (1864–1955) was said to reflect his teacher's spiritual side most faithfully (Plate B26). Like many *franckistes,* he began on the regular composition track at the Conservatoire (studying with Massenet) but decided to switch to private lessons with Franck and forgo the Prix de Rome since only regularly enrolled composition students could compete. During his long life, Ropartz wrote almost 200 compositions—orchestral and chamber works, songs, choral pieces, and an opera set in his native Brittany—in which he forged a personal style built on the twin influences of Franck and Wagner. He directed the regional conservatories at Nancy (1894–1919) and Strasbourg (1919–1929), bringing *franckiste* ideals to the provinces. As a conductor Ropartz made these regions an important home for performances of modern French music. He succeeded Reynaldo Hahn in the Institut in 1949, at the advanced age of eighty-five.

Ropartz composed six symphonies (Table XVI/20). The first four were written in regular five- and six-year intervals, while the last two date from the 1940s. These works feature extended melodies, often in asymmetrical meters (*I/P* of the Third Symphony is a good example), and a compact and dense texture often described as "gray." Commentators routinely described Ropartz's music as "austere"—a label with unflattering implications, as he well understood:

> Among several others, there are two composers above all whose works are judged in advance: Vincent d'Indy and, much less importantly, myself. Whatever we do will always be "austere." Now, we know all about austerity, it's the name polite society gives to boredom.[249]

At times, he conceded that his voice was so idiosyncratic as to be hermetic: "It's not that what I write is very complicated, but I think that under its simplicity there is an interior life that only those who have lived close to me feel."[250] Nevertheless, as the Third Symphony demonstrates, his music can captivate. Its secrets involve religious faith, love of humanity, and adoration of nature.

Franck reportedly encouraged Ropartz to write a symphony, but he demurred, not yet feeling adequate to the task. Only in 1895, five years after his teacher's death, did the First Symphony, entitled *Symphonie en la mineur sur un choral breton* (Symphony in A Minor on a Breton Chorale) appear. Like Franck, Ropartz dedicated his symphony to Henri Duparc. Inspired perhaps by his friend Vincent d'Indy, Ropartz composed a cyclic symphony based on a folk melody from his native region. The composer modeled his structure on Franck's symphony, parsing the work into three divisions with the Scherzo embedded into the slow movement (the *B* section within an *A–B–A–B–A* form).

As one might expect, the symphony abounds with other echoes of his teacher (and perhaps Chausson as well) in its serpentine thematic contours, frequent tempo changes, and organ-like orchestration; but his work also has individual touches. Its most impressive section may be the opening—a slow, dramatic introduction featuring swelling tutti chords, between which the winds lay out the chorale phrase by phrase. The principal theme of the following sonata is derived from the folk hymn. The second movement is largely nostalgic in mood. Ropartz bases the exuberant Finale on a memorable folk-like theme of his own invention, but the original chorale returns in augmentation in the brass at the climax. Despite successful moments, Ropartz's first symphony betrays its beginner status in its prolixity (each movement rambles at points) and over-heavy scoring. In addition, in the Finale, the cyclic reprises of the Breton chorale fit in awkwardly with the surrounding material—a complaint heard frequently from reviewers of symphonies by Franck's pupils.

The First Symphony premiered at the Société Nationale. The Finale additionally figured on a program of French music heard at the Paris World Exhibition in 1900 (one of the few

TABLE XVI/20

The Symphonies of Guy Ropartz

Key	Date	Title	Movements	Instrumentation	Comments
A Minor	1894–95	Symphony No. 1	1. Lent et majestueux 4/4—Assez animé 2/2 (636 m.) 2. Lent 3/4—Vif 6/8 (253 m.) C-sharp minor 3. Pas très vite, mais joyeux 2/4 (517 m.) A major	Grand + Flt., Bclar., Tpt.	Subtitled "sur un choral breton" ("[based] on a Breton chorale"). Dedicated to Henri Duparc. First performance: Paris, Concerts d'Harcourt (concert of the Société Nationale), conducted by Ropartz on December 29, 1895. Published in Paris: A. Ponscarme, 1895.
F Minor	1900	Symphony No. 2	1. Adagio molto 3/4—Allegro 2/2 2. Molto vivace 3/4 G-sharp minor 3. Adagio 2/4 B-flat minor 4. Allegro molto 2/2 F minor	Grand + Flt.	Dedicated to Eugène Ysaÿe. First performance: Paris, Société Nationale, conducted by Pierre de Bréville on April 26, 1901. Published in Paris: Rouart, Lerolle, et Cie., n.d.
E Major	1905–06	Symphony No. 3 in E Major	1. Très lent 4/4—Animé 5/4 (313 m.) 2. Lent 4/4, 6/8, 5/4—Lent 3/4—Très vif 6/8 (686 m.) B minor, E minor 3. Assez lent—Très lent et calme—Lent—Assez animé 4/4, 5/4 (312 m.) D-flat major, E major	Grand + Flt., EH, Bclar., Bssn., Tpt., Btrom., 2 Harps SATB soli, SATB chorus	Sets the composer's own poem. Co-winner of Cressent competition for symphonies. First performance: Paris, Société des Concerts du Conservatoire, conducted by Georges Marty on November 11, 1906. Published in Paris: A. Joanin, 1909 (four-hand piano reduction: Joanin, 1906).
C Major	1910	Symphony No. 4	1. Allegro moderato 4/4 (232 m.) 2. Adagio 4/4—Allegretto 3/4 (206 m.) E minor/major 3. Allegro molto 3/4 (416 m.) C minor/major	Grand + Bclar., Btrom., Harp	Dedicated to Gaston Carraud. First performance: Paris, Concerts Lamoureux, conducted by Camille Chevillard on October 15, 1911. Published in Boston: Boston Music Company (Schirmer), 1914.
E-flat Major	1943	Little Symphony	1. Allegro 3/4 (241 m.) 2. Lento moderato 4/4 (79 m.) E minor, G minor/major 3. Presto 3/4 (414 m.)	Flt., Ob., 2 Clar., Bssn., 2 Hr., Tpt., Timp., Cym., Tri., Drum, Strings	*Petite Symphonie* for chamber orchestra. Dedicated to René Dommange. First performance: Angers, conducted by Jean Fournet during the 1945–46 season. Published in Paris: Durand et Cie., 1950.
G Major	1944–45	Symphony No. 5	1. Allegro assai 3/4 (508 m.) 2. Scherzo 3/8, 9/8 (271 m.) B minor/major 3. Largo 3/4, 4/4 (151 m.) E major 4. Finale 5/4 (163 m.)	Grand + Cym., Tri., Drum, Xylophone	First performance: Paris, Orchestre Nationale de la Radiodiffusion Française (Concerts de l'UNESCO), conducted by Charles Münch on November 14, 1946. Published in Paris: Durand et Cie., 1956.

Movement titles and instrumentation for the Second Symphony are found in Maillard/ROPARTZ, pp. 121–22.

symphonies accorded this honor), and Concerts Lamoureux performed the whole work in 1903. The symphony received a much cooler response than it had at the Société. Critics pronounced the work wanting in simplicity and spontaneity. Debussy credited Ropartz for trying to renew the supposedly tired symphonic structures but judged his efforts to be in vain:

> The [First Symphony] has many of the qualities that make Guy Ropartz an energetic and productive man. Why does he sometimes seem thwarted and even a bit paralyzed here? Would it not be because of this kind of fascination the word "symphony" exerts on today's musicians, in which the concern for form prevails over the freedom of ideas?
>
> By alternating fast and slow passages Guy Ropartz has rightly tried to shake off the heavy block of marble that a symphony represents; but right away this harms the unity of the composition—the first movement can take the place of the last and vice-versa, nothing distinguishing them very clearly.[251]

Presumably, Debussy's cryptic remark that the movements sound interchangeable means that to him the work lacks a sense of inevitable growth.

On the other hand, Paul Dukas praised Ropartz's symphony:

> This work of great importance and high musical quality is one of the most interesting we have heard for a long time. . . . M. Ropartz is one of those who seem to want to master the difficulties of abstract musical language with the greatest decisiveness. . . . Today, one can note the progress he is making in the path that he laid out for himself.[252]

Ropartz's Second Symphony, written in 1900 and premiered at the Société Nationale in May 1901, adopted a different tack. He based the entire work on a two-measure cell. The four movements consist of a sonata, a sonata-form Scherzo with Trio, an *A–B–A* slow movement, and a sonata-rondo that recalls material from previous movements. Jean Maillard describes the piece as "undoubtedly Ropartz's most *franckiste* symphony."[253] Most critics considered it an improvement over the First Symphony—simpler, clearer, and less dense. Paul Dukas, on the other hand, thought Ropartz compromised his naturally complex language by forcing it into a plainer style: the result demonstrated that "an artist always wins by not imposing any constraint upon himself, even in the name of the purest principles."[254] The symphony was heard again in 1911 at the short-lived Concerts Sechiari. The composer dedicated it to Eugène Ysaÿe.

SYMPHONY NO. 3 IN E MAJOR

Ropartz wrote his most celebrated symphony in 1905–1906. He submitted it to the first Cressent Competition, where it shared top prize with a much weaker symphony by a Conservatoire student, Eugène Cools. For Ropartz, the symphony represented "the supreme manifestation of the art of music . . . the essential expression of the idea by sounds";[255] reflecting his love of Wagnerian drama, he described its principal themes as "leitmotifs." The ideas which most concerned him were love of humanity and adoration of nature, and both appear in the Third Symphony. The Cressent competition considered symphonies, orchestral suites, and symphonic poems with voices, and Ropartz took the opportunity to compose a choral symphony to his own poetic text that explicated his social, religious, and political convictions. A utopian homily in praise of universal kinship, the composer contrasts the radiance of nature with the misery of humanity and exhorts his listeners to love each other and seek

---

TABLE XVI/21

Ropartz's Text for His Symphony No. 3

I

Night comes to an end – One after the other, the stars disappear into the breaking dawn – The mists waver, then fade away – And upon the Sea, and upon the Plain, and upon the Forest, the sky brightens, the Sun appears and its dazzling light ignites nature in joy.

II

Nature, Nature, in your joy, what does the distress of human hearts matter to you?

O calm Sea, your calm waves, like changing silk, brush the shore softly with their uncaring caress – And yet the frail vessels, rocked upon your tranquil waves, are bearers of human distress! –

O Plain, under your warm breezes you shiver with voluptuousness in your heads of corn that make the already ripened grain heavy – And yet in the hours of painful ploughing, human tears have fertilized your arid soil! –

O Forest, your joyous soul joyously beats and sings in the rustling leaves and in the song of the birds – And yet the shadow of your oaks stretches over the useless altars where man has called out to deaf Gods –

Sun, you shine! – But your light is powerless to pierce the darkness of our hearts!

Who will tell us the reason for living? – To suffer! – To suffer! in our bodies, in our hearts! – Why?

Man tramples man; endless battles drain us. Oppressed by laws imposed by those who are strongest, enslaved by kings, crushed by masters, we weep and no one consoles us; we cry out and no one listens to us; and our eyes are weary from looking to the heavens in the vain expectation and the vain hope that a God will finally show Himself.

III

Poor humans, wretched hearts, your illness is in you.

Each person groans about his own distress; each is in search of himself; each one loves himself and this love engenders only hate.

Love one another, and you will fathom life: love one another, this is the single law, here is all knowledge: love one another!

So that your suffering will be mild for you, ease the suffering of others. Let your freely accepted labor strive towards the happiness of your brethren, it will become light for you. Reclothe yourself in Love and Justice, open your soul to goodness.

Love one another!

- -

Divine Word, comforting Word! The darkness in which we have walked lights up; the veil of shadows is torn, and behold, in the evening of humanity a new dawn appears upon the world!

Let us love one another! Justice and truth, peace and goodness spread upon the earth.

Let us love one another! Transformed humanity rises towards the city of joy and ideal liberty where kings are no more, neither masters, where the single law of love has replaced those laws henceforth rendered useless!

O Nature, now be in celebration! O Nature, blend your joy with the immense joy of men!

O calm Sea, upon your calm waves balance the happy vessels that carry human gaiety!

O Plain, offer for the desire of men the splendor of your golden ears of corn that make the ripe grain heavy!

O Forest, let your soul sing, in the rustling leaves and in the song of the birds, to the glory of new altars!

And you, Sun, arise radiantly! Unite your dazzling light to the fires of the ideal sun of Truth, Justice, and Love!

This translation is taken from Hart/SYMPHONY, pp. 228–30, which includes the original French. The French text is also in Lamy/ROPARTZ, pp. 47–49.

---

beauty through upholding the social beauties of truth and justice (the text is reprinted in Table XVI/21).

Ropartz set the Third Symphony in four movements and three divisions, the last combining the slow movement and finale. The first three movements begin with the text, sung by SATB soloists and full chorus, and the following instrumental number comments upon the ideas stated by the voices; the Finale is texted throughout. To convey his ideas, Ropartz uses two kinds of "leitmotifs," as he would say: for the four elements of nature cited in the poem—sea, plain, forest, and sun—short motives appear every time the text invokes them (Table XVI/22, [1]);

TABLE XVI/22

Leitmotifs in Ropartz's Symphony No. 3

1. The Elements of Nature

Sea

Plains

Forest

Sun

2. "Suffering"

(Que nous____ di - ra la rai - son de viv - re?)

"Who will tell us the reason for living?"

3. "Love"

Ai - mez - vous les uns les aut - res

"Love one another"

those sections dealing with the human condition employ two themes representing the notions of suffering and redemption (Table XVI/22, [2]-[3]). These themes become the agents of the symbolic struggle and transformation that take place at the end of the symphony.

The text of the first movement praises the passing of night and the dawning of a new day. The final words "nature in joy" introduce an instrumental sonata which expresses the adoration of the earth through *P*, a long and exuberant violin theme in 5/4 (m.42; Example XVI/33

EXAMPLE XVI/33   Ropartz. Symphony No. 3/1, mm.42–46a. © by Editions Salabert.

shows the opening of this melody). The sonata unfolds in the normal manner, developing *P, S,* and the motives portraying the four nature elements. Despite some tonally adventurous passages, the movement remains in E major.

In the second movement, the mood turns from joy to sorrow as Ropartz contemplates spiritual darkness. Reflecting on nature's indifference and God's silence in the face of human misery, the composer despairs at the seeming meaninglessness of life. He accompanies the opening question, addressed by the chorus to nature ("What does the distress of human hearts matter to you?"), with a quote of the "Annunciation of Death" motive from Wagner's *Ring.* An instrumental fugue leads to a climactic choral exclamation, set to the fugue subject: "Who will tell us the reason for living? To suffer!" (Table XVI/22 [2]). This subject henceforth serves as the leitmotif for human suffering.

The text gives way to an agitated Scherzo in E minor in *A–B–A'–B'* form, an orchestral meditation upon suffering. *A* depicts despair in a *perpetuum mobile* of fast triplets (m.163): the principal melody contains a diminution of the fugue subject, making the topic of the instrumental section clear. The subject also appears in the brass at the climaxes of *B* and *B',* further linking this movement with its text. An anguished melody in long notes dominates *B;* Fernand Lamy (Ropartz's biographer) suggests that it symbolizes humanity's unanswered pleas for help (mm.321, 554).[256]

Darkness also pervades the opening of the last division, but the soloists soon pronounce the transforming imperative: "Love one another!" Its music becomes, in various harmonizations, the leitmotif of love (Table XVI/22 [3]). The somber mood brightens and the key emerges from ambiguity into the tonic E major. An expressive slow movement in a distant but mellow D-flat major invites the listener to reflect on love and the relief it gives to those who suffer (m.65). To make its thesis clear, Ropartz frames the movement with verbal statements of the love motive.

The Finale sets the motives of suffering and love into musical conflict. For seventy measures (mm.169–243), against ascending chromatic swells reminiscent of Tristan and Isolde's *Liebesnacht,* the motives alternate as if in wordless dialogue, with "suffering" asking, "What is the reason for living?" and "love" responding, "[to] love one another" (Example XVI/34). While this exchange takes place in the orchestra, the chorus envisions a happy future in which love replaces all kingdoms, national boundaries, and legal systems.

At the end of the musical dialogue, Ropartz transforms the "suffering" motive into *I/P,* "nature in joy" (m.243). Spiritual darkness is defeated. Ropartz adds a text to this formerly instrumental melody proclaiming that humans can appreciate the true brilliance of nature now that their souls are also alight. "Nature in joy" thus becomes a symbol not only of physical sunlight but also metaphysical enlightenment that manifests itself in the pursuit of "Truth, Justice, and Love." The symphony ends in splendor, with orchestral surges recalling the end of *Das Rheingold:* as Wagner's gods entered their new home, so (according to the poem) will humanity move into a new world built on love. Thus the symphony ends with a double transformation: the night of suffering gives way to the light of love, and the daylight of nature ascends to the brighter blaze of justice and truth.

EXAMPLE XVI/34 Ropartz. Symphony No. 3/4, mm.218–44. © by Editions Salabert.

EXAMPLE XVI/34   (*continued*)

"Suffering"   "Love"   "Suffering"
(Vc., Hr.)   (triadic descents)   (Vc., Trom., Hr.)

EXAMPLE XVI/34 *(continued)*

"Suffering"
(Flt., Tpt., Vln.)

"Love"
(Vln.)

"Suffering"
transformed to ⟶

EXAMPLE XVI/34   (*continued*)

"Nature in Joy"
(Orch. and Voices)

The voices of Wagner and Franck manifest themselves in various ways throughout this symphony. Presumably *Tristan* and the *Ring* loom large because of their emphasis upon nature, suffering, and renewal through love. In addition to leitmotifs, Ropartz employs Wagnerian harmonies—chromatic prolongations, extended tertian chords, and 4–3 suspensions. With Franck Ropartz shares not only the embedding process but also an emphasis upon counterpoint, continuous modulation, and a general spiritual ambiance. The contour and harmonization of certain themes additionally suggest the possible influence of d'Indy's Second Symphony. Finally, its dramatic merger of voices and orchestra place Ropartz's Third Symphony in the tradition of Berlioz's *Roméo et Juliette*.

While d'Indy and Ropartz both aspired to convey messages in their symphonies, they differed markedly in the means they chose to communicate them. Whereas d'Indy veiled the precise meaning of his message and allowed listeners to interpret it freely (while at the same time permitting the publication of a very specific exegesis), Ropartz made his message explicit with a sung text on which the symphony was wholly dependent. D'Indy's rival motives struggle for priority throughout his symphony, but in Ropartz the conflict of ideas manifests itself in the contrast between the second and third movements, and not until the Finale do the rival motives themselves enter into combat. In place of a victory chorale, the return of "nature in joy" serves as a peroration: the melody itself remains the same but the addition of text transforms it conceptually into an emblem of the twofold victory of light over material and spiritual darkness.

Even more striking than the technical distinctions between the two works is the dichotomy in the substance of their messages. Both symphonies are the work of Franck's pupils (and friends), but ideologically they come from opposite camps: d'Indy's upheld "Tradition," while Ropartz's defended the Dreyfusard values which were anathema to d'Indy and many of his supporters.

When the Third Symphony premiered in November 1906, the Dreyfus Affair remained a vivid memory and citizens were expressing concern about the growth of far-left movements; the French Socialist Party had just been formed the previous year, as Ropartz was writing the symphony. The Dreyfusard rhetoric of his poem—appeals to internationalism and anti-monarchism, hints of atheism (though the composer was a believer), and the exalting of truth, justice, and love as superior virtues to duty, honor, and authority—enchanted the left and antagonized the conservative center and the right. More than one reviewer interpreted the text as a socialist manifesto and praised or damned it accordingly. Not surprisingly, Alfred Bruneau figured prominently among the symphony's enthusiasts:

> A vast idea dominates and governs [the symphony], a literary and humane idea that engenders the musical idea and which is the glorification of truth, justice, goodness, peace, and love. The composer has fully, vigorously, and eloquently expressed all the nobility and all the magnificence of this idea; he has shown an uncommon strength, will, and talent in the conception and realization of this plan. His symphony . . . is a long and austere climb towards light, towards splendors.[257]

Bruneau's response incensed those on the other side. In one of the more intriguing reviews, Louis Régis specifically cited Bruneau's approval as confirmation of Ropartz's suspect loyalties:

> With its powerful orchestra, chorus, and solo quartet, the symphony is long and tiresome: the finale of the Ninth in my judgment constitutes neither a model nor an excuse for composers who introduce choirs into symphonic music. . . . The chorus and

soloists reveal to us the composer's philosophical and sociological opinions. . . . He inclines towards the egalitarian doctrines, and he has words that prove it to us:

"Transformed humanity rises towards the city of joy and ideal liberty where kings are no more, neither masters, where the single law of love has replaced those laws henceforth rendered useless."

All this is sung –.

The Symphony in E Major consists essentially of three large divisions, each containing a vocal part and an orchestral part; finally, it concludes with a choral section. The second part of Movement II, a kind of scherzo performed a bit ruggedly, is superior to the rest of the work, in my opinion.

"And you, Sun, arise radiantly! Unite your dazzling light to the fires of the ideal sun of Truth, Justice, and Love!" So ends the final chorus, and we know a certain epithet, evoking conflagrations—from which God preserve the Conservatoire hall on account of its narrow passageways and its torturous stairwells illuminated by candlelight!—an epithet quite fitting to M. Ropartz's style.

My neighbor seemed satisfied, he likes symphonies with lots of choirs. "At least," he says, "one doesn't have to exert any effort, one is sure of having understood." Poor me, who can't guess the verbal intentions of a piece of music! Therefore I've never "understood" anything! . . .

And naturally M. Alfred Bruneau, between the footraces and stock reports of the week, exults:

"A vast idea dominates and governs it, a literary and humane idea that engenders the musical idea and which is the glorification of truth, justice, goodness, peace, and love."

"His symphony . . . is a long and austere climb towards light, towards splendors." To press the point further would be cruel – for my readers. . . .

Our readers have learned in the daily papers everything else that remains to be said about the work of Guy Ropartz: they discovered (!) the influence of the master in the student, and this gave them a pretext to evoke the spirit, the soul, the breath of Franck hovering over the sails of the harmonies of the work that won the Crescent Prize.—Oh! the Symphony in D Minor![258]

Pierre Lalo, an anti-Dreyfusard who wrote for the centrist republican paper *Le Temps*, was much more positive toward the music but the text left him equally cold. He invoked the name of Dreyfus's best-known defender to condemn the style, and by implication the politics, of Ropartz's poem:

> The philosophy and literature are not the aspects of M. Ropartz's work that I prefer. In it the author presents a moral conception of the world and of life. . . . [His message] is undoubtedly highly commendable in feeling and intention; but one cannot find much originality, power, or depth in it. It is the Utopian candor, false dignity and superficial banality of those apotheoses that Zola gladly gave as the conclusion to his last thunderclaps; and it's nearly the same style.[259]

The critics generally spent much less time discussing the music, and while not as contentious they still divided over it. Like Régis, Lalo and Gaston Carraud objected to the chorus: if Ropartz insisted on using voices, they said, he should have followed Beethoven and reserved them for the Finale. Others found the symphony ostentatious: Jules Combarieu pronounced it "more substantial than moving," and the Cressent jury expressed similar sentiments.[260] Everyone found the Scherzo the most successful movement. But the fervency with which Ropartz expressed his convictions won over some critics, even when they did not share his beliefs. Jean d'Udine wrote of the emotional power this work held over him:

> I long to express all my affection for the 10th Symphony of M. Ropartz. People who believe that there is a good and a bad music are already asking me, "You understood this work, then?"—not without mockery for my mediocre musical "intelligence." Understood? Understood? Good grief, no! . . . [But] I love M. Ropartz's Third Symphony with all my heart, it touches me deeply. From one end to the other, I feel in it a humanity— I don't know what humanity—vibrate with a powerful tenderness, goodness, and generosity; and when the admirable Scherzo that closes the second part bursts forth with a unity, continuity, and abundance of motion which gives it so much classical grandeur and absolute pathos, I feel myself completely at one with the composer, I feel I am of his race and I love him for the intense joy he provides me.[261]

The premiere took place at a special concert at the Conservatoire devoted to Ropartz as a Cressent laureate. The audience responded with enthusiasm. Subsequent performances for the Conservatoire's regular subscribers were much less successful, eliciting at best a correct response—though a much better one, to be sure, than Franck's symphony had received seventeen years earlier. Nevertheless, owing to its status as a prizewinner, this work received more performances (four) than any symphony written between 1900 and 1918 save d'Indy's Second; in addition to the Conservatoire, the symphony also appeared at Concerts Colonne.[262] Although heard less after World War I, the work retained an appeal for later generations. Arthur Honegger loved it, and aspects of his own *Symphonie liturgique* (1946) are modeled on it; one could in fact describe the later work as a gloss on Ropartz's.[263]

Ropartz's Fourth Symphony in C major (1910), dedicated to Gaston Carraud, premiered at Concerts Lamoureux in October 1911. The form resembles his First Symphony: three cyclically unified movements, with the outer ones in sonata form and the Scherzo embedded into the slow movement (again as an *A–B–A–B–A* structure). Here, however, the movements synthesize into a single uninterrupted and integrated division, rather along the lines of Sibelius's Symphony No. 7 (1924), also in C major. In this symphony, then, Ropartz combines Saint-Saëns's practice of connecting movements with Franck's of embedding them.

Ropartz derives all the material for this symphony from a four-note cell, G–A–D–E. While less overtly indebted to Franck, the work retains his highly modulatory idiom. More concise than the First or Third Symphonies, it launches into the opening sonata without an introduction. The second movement is dominated by an extended melody in English horn—one more instance of the appeal of that instrument for *franckiste* composers—while the modal Scherzo centers around an original theme in Breton folk style. As in Chausson's Symphony, the last movement turns aggressive, suggesting a battle, before it ends peacefully in C major. To a greater degree than in his earlier symphonies, Ropartz scores his work with considerable variety and flexibility, using many colorful timbral combinations throughout.

Critics and public welcomed the new work; reviewers devoted most of their comments to the novelties of the form. Gaston Carraud, the dedicatee, wrote the following:

> When speaking of the rigorous forms in which members of the Franck school encase music, certain people reproach them as empty and mathematical death. To be sure, an empty form is nothing much—though perhaps better than emptiness without form— but when a strong thought fills and directs the form, one must admit that the form

makes the thought stronger. And thus it is that on the day precisely when M. Ropartz is most rigorous in his form, he proves to be the most spontaneously himself, in all the candor of his noble and sensitive nature; and never has he communicated more directly to his listeners, never has he been more "melodic" than in this Fourth Symphony.[264]

The composer himself expressed satisfaction with his work and the response to it:

> The audience reacted rather warmly, and the quasi-unanimity of the reviews that came out Monday was more than favorable. Personally, I wasn't displeased with myself: the work is much more powerful than I had thought—since I had been on the verge of entitling it *Sinfonietta* . . . and it doesn't give the impression of being a *little* symphony. I also think it did me good in people's minds.[265]

The last two symphonies date from much later in Ropartz's career. He wrote his *Petite Symphonie* in E-flat major in 1943 for a chamber orchestra of strings and selected winds, brass, and percussion. Its three short movements include an opening Allegro based on characteristically broad themes (*P* extends for eighteen measures), a gentle slow movement in A–B–B'–A form, and a Finale in sonata-rondo form.[266] The Fifth Symphony in G major (1944–1945) appeared two years later, when the composer was eighty. It consists of three movements: an opening sonata, a Scherzo in A–B–A'–B'–A form, an expressive slow movement said to reflect Ropartz's response to the Liberation, and a finale in 5/4 time. Neither symphony is cyclic.[267]

Charles Tournemire

Charles Tournemire (1870–1939) studied organ at the Conservatoire with Franck and his successor Charles-Marie Widor, taking first prize under the latter. He served as organist at Ste. Clothilde (Franck's church) from 1898 until his death, and starting in 1919 he also taught chamber music at the Conservatoire. Tournemire is best known today for *L'Orgue mystique,* a massive collection of fifty-one Office settings for that instrument, but he also composed eight symphonies between 1900 and 1924 (Table XVI/23), five of which qualify as message-symphonies. Appropriately for Franck's most mystic-minded pupil, the messages deal with faith and metaphysics rather than polemics. For each symphony except the Sixth, which sets a text, the composer wrote an extended poetic description to make the message—the "philosophical substance," as he called it—clear (these descriptions are reprinted in Table XVI/24).[268] None except the First adheres to conventional form.

The First and Second Symphonies (1900, 1908–1909) contain no messages but the composer gave them titles. For reasons that are not entirely clear, he named the first *Symphonie romantique;* premiering in Marseille in 1901, it appeared at the Société Nationale the following year. The second he called "Ouessant," after an island off Brittany. In the score, he attached the following note: "This work was inspired by the uncanny [landscape] of Ouessant. It leads to the glorification of the Eternal One." The symphony received its first hearing at Concerts Hasselmans (a smaller Parisian rival to Colonne and Lamoureux) in 1909.

The Third Symphony, "Moscou (1913)" (1912–1913), evokes the religious spirit Tournemire observed in Russia during a visit to that country—the spirit one suspects he wished to find among his own aggressively secular people. He modeled the structure on Saint-Saëns's "Organ" Symphony: four cyclically unified movements in two divisions. The score, suffused with chromaticism (as is Tournemire's wont), evokes the Slavic spirit through modal folk-like themes and suggestions of bells, especially at the opening of the third movement, "The Bells of Moscow." The symphony occasionally recalls Sibelius's sound world, especially in the dark colors of the first movement. It premiered in Amsterdam in 1913 and the first Parisian performance took place in 1919. The Fourth Symphony (1912–1913), Tournemire's last abstract one, consists of five sections within one continuous division. To acknowledge the unorthodox structure, Tournemire entitled the symphony *Pages symphoniques*. He wrote that it "exalts the poetry of Brittany."

Like Ropartz's Third, Tournemire's Fifth Symphony contrasts the glory of nature (in this case the Swiss Alps) with human distress, but here nature and humanity unite to praise God rather than seek temporal social justice. The work consists of two divisions, the second of which subdivides into two movements. The first division develops a chorale. Opening with a pastorale in hypolydian mode and changing compound meters, the second division concludes with an ecstatic peroration to which we are led by a theme derived from the chorale. Concerts Colonne-Lamoureux (the orchestras merged during the war) performed the first movement in 1918; the whole symphony premiered at The Hague in 1920 and Concerts Colonne performed it in 1923. Tournemire wrote his next symphony during the war (1915–1918). This expansive two-movement work begins with choral settings of anti-war texts from the Old Testament (Psalms, Jeremiah, Isaiah, and Hosea); at the climax of the second movement, a solo tenor intones Jesus's words from the Gospel of John promising peace in the midst of destruction. The composer thus directs the listener away from the darkness of violence and devastation toward the light of love.

The Seventh Symphony (1918–1922), the most ambitious and intriguing of the set, bears the title *Les Danses de la Vie* ("The Dances of Life"). This singular seventy-five-minute work for a 110-member orchestra contains five movements ("dances"), roughly fifteen minutes each. In this symphony Tournemire aspires to depict the search for God through consecutive ages of human history. According to the composer's program, the work begins with "primitive dances," when humanity lived in barbarism and inner darkness, seeking God without knowing for whom it searched. Christianity first appears in the "Gentile" or "pagan dances" and takes firm hold in the world in the "medieval dances." The sinful nature of humanity rises up, resulting in the "bloody dances" that extend from the Middle Ages to the present day (immediately after the war). The symphony concludes with the "future dances" in which humans finally attain the perfect knowledge of God; the music dissolves into a series of vague and unresolved progressions meant to suggest eternity, which by definition lacks closure. Unified by interconnecting motives and intervallic gestures, especially the tritone, the symphony skillfully blends chromatic *franckiste* harmonies, "pagan" Debussyist whole-tone scales and coloristic orchestration, "Christian" modality, and a propulsive rhythmic energy recalling Roussel. The result is a work of considerable originality. Tournemire sanctioned choreographic performances, though none took place.

The composer closed his symphonic corpus with his most personal work in the genre, the two-movement *La Symphonie du Triomphe de la Mort* ("The Symphony of the Triumph of Death," 1920–1924). This Eighth Symphony expresses the composer's grief over the loss of his wife: at first he sees death as an ending without hope, but he soon comes to understand it as only a temporary separation for the believer. An enigmatic composition, much of it is subdued—more disoriented than prostrate in its sorrow. Even the final triumph seems muted compared to his previous symphonies, which is not surprising since the composer's sorrow still weighs heavily upon him.

The ambitious length and programs of the later symphonies, their varied forms, and the expanded performing forces required all suggest the influence of Mahler, and indeed Tournemire studied the Austrian composer's works and appropriated some of his orchestral effects; he even inscribed footnotes into his scores citing specific borrowings from such compositions

TABLE XVI/23
The Symphonies of Charles Tournemire

Opus	Key	Date	Title	Movements	Instrumentation	Comments
18	A Major	1900	*Symphonie romantique* (Symphony No. 1)	1. Mouvement d'andante—Allegro moderato 2. Scherzo: Allegretto spiritoso 3. Largo (tempo de marcia funèbre) 4. Finale: Allegro energico	Grand + Flt., EH, Cbssn., 2 Cornets, Cym., BD, 2 Harps	Dedicated to Paul Viardot. First performance: Marseille, Orchestre des Concerts Classiques, conducted by Tournemire on March 10, 1901. Published in Paris: Max Eschig.
36	B Major	1908–09	Symphony No. 2 "Ouessant"	1. Prélude—Très modéré—Allegro moderato 2. Très calme 3. Choral—Allegro	Grand + Picc., EH, Bclar., Bssn., 2 offstage Hr., Picc. Tpt., 2 Harps	Named after an island off the coast of Brittany. Dedicated to the composer's wife. First performance: Paris, Concerts Hasselmans, conducted by Louis Hasselmans on April 3, 1909. Published in Paris: Max Eschig.
43	D Major	1912–13	Symphony No. 3 "Moscou (1913)"	A. 1. Bien modéré 2. Avec du mouvement B. 1. *Les cloches de Moscou* Lentement 2. Assez modéré—Avec assez de mouvement	Grand + Picc., EH, Bclar., offstage horn, Cym., BD, Cbssn., Tri., Bells, Celesta, Glockenspiel, Organ, 2 Harps	Dedicated to Evert Cornelis. First performance: Amsterdam, Concertgebouw, conducted by Evert Cornelis on October 19, 1913. Published in Paris: Max Eschig.
44	No key specified	1912–13	*Pages symphoniques* (Symphony No. 4)	Assez lent—Avec du mouvement—Modéré—Vif—Lent	Grand + Picc., EH, Bclar., Cbssn., BD, Tam-tam, Bell, Organ, 2 Harps	First performance: Paris, Concerts Colonne-Lamoureux, conducted by Camille Chevillard on March 12, 1916. Published in Paris: Max Eschig.
47	F Minor	1913–14	Symphony No. 5	I. Choral varié II a. Pastorale II b. *Vers la Lumière*	Grand + Picc., EH, Bclar., Cbssn., Cym., BD, Tri., Tam-tam, 2 Harps	Dedicated to the composer's wife. First partial performance (*Choral varié* only): Paris, Concerts Colonne-Lamoureux, conducted by Gabriel Pierné on January 20, 1918. First complete performance: The Hague, Residentie Orkest, conducted by Tournemire on March 10, 1920. Published in Paris: Max Eschig.

TABLE XVI/23 (*continued*)

Opus	Key	Date	Title	Movements	Instrumentation	Comments
48	E Major	1915–18	Symphony No. 6	1. Ad libitum—Lento—Allegro moderato—Energico 2. Largo—Allegro	Grand + 2 Picc., EH, Picc. Clar., Bclar., Cbssn., 2 Hr., 3 Tpt., Picc. Tpt., 1 Trom., Tuba, Bass Tuba, Cym., BD, Tri., Tam-tam, Bells, Celesta, Glockenspiel, Organ, 4 Harps, tenor soloist, chorus	Not performed in the composer's lifetime. First performance (for a recording): Liège, Orchestre Philharmonique de Liège et de la Communauté Française, conducted by Pierre Bartholomée in July and September 1995. Unpublished.
49	No key specified	1918–22	*Les Danses de la Vie* (Symphony No. 7)	1. Danses des Temps primitifs 2. Danses de la Gentilité 3. Danses médiévales 4. Danses sanglantes 5. Danses des Temps futurs	Grand + Picc., Ob. d'amore, EH, Picc. Clar., Bclar., Contrabass Clar., Sarrusophone, 2 Hr., 2 Tpt., Picc. Tpt., 1 Trom., Tuba, Bass Tuba, Cym., BD, Tri., Tam-tam, Lute, 2 Harps	"The Dances of Life." Expansive work with five movements or "dances." Composer sanctioned choreographic performances. Not performed in Tournemire's lifetime. First performance: Brussels, Orchestre Philharmonique de Liège et de la Communauté Française, conducted by Pierre Bartholomée on September 11, 1992. Unpublished.
51	B Minor	1920–24	*La Symphonie du Triomphe de la Mort* (Symphony No. 8)	1. Lento—Assez vif 2. Allegro—Lento	Grand + Picc., Ob. d'amore, EH, 1 Clar., Bclar., 1 Bssn., Sarrusophone, 2 Tpt., Tuba, Contrabass Tuba, 3 Saxophones, Cym., BD, Tri., Gong, Bells, Celesta, Lute, 2 Harps	"The Symphony of the Triumph of Death." Written in response to the death of the composer's wife; dedicated "to my wife, forever in the heights." Not performed in the composer's lifetime. First performance (for a recording): Liège, Orchestre Philharmonique de Liège et de la Communauté Française, conducted by Pierre Bartholomée on July 5 and 7, 1997. Unpublished.

Partially based on Fauquet/TOURNEMIRE, pp. 66–72, 90.

TABLE XVI/24
Charles Tournemire's Programs for His Symphonies Nos. 3, 5, 7, and 8

Symphony No. 3 in D Major, Op. 43 "Moscou (1913)"

Immense plains.

All beings, plunged into a deep darkness, roam in search of God the Savior – They sacrifice to the divinities Svarog and Dajbog, although fleeting glimmers penetrate their souls. They dance, they sing! – But now in Moscow the Holy the marvelous bells begin to sound with greater and greater gaiety: they announce an immense joy to the still-sleeping world!—the beings, suddenly awakened, look up and an unknown splendor offers itself to their astonished eyes; and from the plain a moving prayer arises, full of adoration and recognition of this cross which from the summits has just revealed to them the true path to happiness. And then while the bells sound, completely joyously, with a powerful and sonorous appeal, those who have seen the light slowly proceed towards It, climbing these steep paths on which they often fall and hurt themselves; but looking up they perceive the cross coming loose from the glistening peaks of purity, and voices sing to them with joy: "Come, rise up and come." And despite their injuries and weaknesses, they arise; and higher, always higher, hearing the bells of the Kingdom of the Heavens sound, they climb the roads, to the summits upon which they know they will find absolute happiness in the Peace of the Lord!

(For a performance in 1923, Tournemire added this disclaimer: This symphony—which has nothing in it of Bolshevism in the political sense of the word since it was written quite a bit before recent events—is inspired by the Russia that is believing and even fanatical. It exalts the grandeur and poetry of the endless plains and glorifies the divine Idea so dear to the hearts of Slavs –)

Symphony No. 5 in F Minor, Op. 47

I. *Choral varié* (Chorale with Variations)
In the Alps. Impressive gorges that include flowers and where the sun barely penetrates. Here and there some openings onto the sky. It is in such a frame that human anguish finds a powerful echo.
(Musically, the chorale, heard in *F minor*—the central key—and also in E-flat minor, in D minor, then anew in F minor, in which it concludes; its principal modulations are separated by grand symphonic variations.)

IIa. *Pastorale*
All the poetry of the mountain in its most intimate manifestations. Here the least flower is a world, it sings the glory of the Eternal. All is peace and the heart rouses itself to the noises of nature –
(Musically: a *lied*, very developed—affecting a mystical character.)

IIb. *Vers la Lumière* (Towards the Light)
From the high summits life is poured out upon the world in a beam of light.
All is joy and the soul combines with the precursor concert of the festivals of the On-High.
(Musically: a rondo that is joyful in the deep sense of the word.—The themes of the *Chorale* and *Pastorale* unite and mount towards the heights.)

Symphony No. 7, Les Danses de la Vie (The Dances of Life), Op. 49

Danses des Temps primitifs (Dances of Primitive Times)

Uncivilized nature. Grandiose boundaries. Humanity advances in the depths of the forests – In the thick forests men of the most remote times lived and tore one another to pieces – They were in search of a very wide clearing in order to glorify the All-Powerful by simple and vigorous dances.
After infinite gropings about, they finally arrived at an immense space in which a faint light took root in the shadows!
There the Dances of Primitive times began and ended.
Men searched for God.

Danses de la Gentilité (Dances of the Gentile Nations)

All around the gigantic temples of the Gentile nations, Humanity rendered homage to a multitude of gods –
These are the interminable rounds disengaged from the barbarity of the first ages, but into which the ineffable sweetness of the Xrist [Christ] has not yet penetrated.
Mankind has an Ideal but it is not pure –

TABLE XVI/24 (*continued*)

The gods share in the orgies of men – However the light always grows in intensity!!
Men always search for God! All while tearing each other to pieces –
In the central part, the Christian idea breaks through! All the poetry of the Gentiles becomes infuriated –
– Finally, paganism dies delightfully.

Danses médiévales (Medieval Dances)

The past seemed destined to exist no longer –
The very pale and very gentle face of the Xrist illuminated the temples of Christendom, yet the profane side did not lose its claims!
The profane dances became ethereal, forming impalpable processions of souls all around the innumerable cathedrals –
Men had finally found God! Suffering seemed to have disappeared. The Xrist spoke to men.

Danses sanglantes (Bloody Dances)

This *relative* blessedness of the medieval age came to an end, however!
And it is in a sea of blood that men revived the hours from the dawn of humanity, with an inconceivable mixture of the things of this world. Here the dances of Primitive Times, infuriated and in a struggle against the pale and gentle figure of the Xrist, unfolded in a terrifying manner – The temples of the Xrist collapsed. Satanic and deadly dances organized around these temples – Everything seemed to come to grief – Nature was red! Rivers flowed with blood – The sun was red!

Danses des Temps futurs (Dances of Future Times)

Souls leave the Earth for good in immense whirlwinds.
These are the eternal praises to Him who saved the World.
Dances a thousand times sacred.
These dances unite Earth to Heaven in immense scrolls of purified spirits who come without ceasing to enlarge the legions of Archangels populating the heights where all is Love.
Triumph of the cause of the Xrist.
Brightness without end. The harps sing the Glory of the Eternal –
Ascension of Humanity towards the God of gods, towards God!!
Light!!!

Symphony No. 8, La Symphonie du Triomphe de la Mort (The Symphony of the Triumph of Death), Op. 51

"—I was in the valley – I cried without ceasing – From the high mountains Heaven spoke to me and invited me to thoughts of the On-High – I did not resist – And here I am, dominating the valley, the valley of tears – understanding, from the summit of the mountain, the divine meaning of Sorrow, denying Death forever – I can finally read the spirit of her whom I no longer see, whom I no longer hear on earth! I lean out to her soul.

—Today, it's the great silence – The solemn minute which makes us understand the 'Beauty' of death – It is the beginning of the journey towards the marvelous comprehension of the 'Concert of Angels' which your beautiful soul—pure as the water of the high mountains, sweetly scented like the most fragrant of the flowers of the high summits—attends and takes part, in a great burst of gratitude towards God! My astonished soul also wants its part in the Concert – while awaiting the totality of the ineffable Joys that bathe in an eternal light the soul of my soul: your soul –"

Grande Chartreuse (Isère)
August 1920!"

Source: Fauquet/TOURNEMIRE, pp. 68–72.

as the "Resurrection" Symphony.[269] Also like Mahler (at first), Tournemire suffered neglect. The composer never heard the last three symphonies—they premiered only in the 1990s and remain unpublished—and the earlier ones did not appear much more frequently. Émile Vuillermoz, a fervent *debussyste* who normally opposed symphonies vehemently, lamented the absence of Tournemire's from the concert hall; in a jab at d'Indy, whom he detested, Vuillermoz saluted Tournemire for "making music and not musical politics."[270] (Despite their common bond as *franckistes,* Tournemire also seems to have had a low opinion of d'Indy; he told Felix Aprahamian in 1934 that "I don't much like this very cold musician!")[271] While none are regularly performed (though all have been recorded), Tournemire's highly imaginative symphonies reward closer investigation. In terms of mystic inspiration and comprehensive breadth, they form a direct link from Franck to Olivier Messiaen, who admired Tournemire and often heard him play at Ste. Clothilde.

Three Symphonists from the Conservatoire
THÉODORE DUBOIS

The message-symphony appealed primarily of course to composers of "romantic" symphonies, who were predisposed to treat them as conveyors of profound thought. Occasionally, however, it also enticed composers from the Conservatoire who had no use for *franckiste* or *d'indyste* aesthetics. Théodore Dubois (1837–1924), the director from 1896 to 1905 and d'Indy's principal antagonist in the *guerre des écoles,* wrote his First Symphony in 1908, after he had retired. For the man who directed the state school at a time when the symphony was still unwelcome there (and who ardently defended the school's pre-reform conservative policies) *himself* to turn to writing a symphony—and a message-symphony at that—reveals the degree to which d'Indyist attitudes had permeated *enseignement officiel* despite its most strident efforts.

Dubois aimed to create a patriotic work glorifying the nation, which he indicated by entitling the piece *Symphonie française* and featuring significant musical quotations in the work. The second movement is based on a folk-like theme, and the Finale culminates in a grand statement of the *Marseillaise* as a triumphant peroration. In this work, critics said, Dubois celebrated the nation and proclaimed its moral victory over Germany:

> What I prefer in the *Symphonie française* is its solemn opening. In all the rest of the work, M. Dubois has clearly set out to express the French character in all its diverse faces, though they are examined a bit superficially. He specifies his intention musically though the use of a folk theme and the *Marseillaise.* It seems to me that in the Finale our national anthem triumphed both over the Viennese waltz and a hollow Wagnerian Fafner.[272]

As the work of a composer closely identified with the Establishment and its state-supported institutions, the France that Dubois celebrated was naturally the nation in its republican embodiment. If d'Indy's symphony supposedly defended the values of the Right (which demanded an alternative to the Republic), and Ropartz's the Left (which demanded a less nationalistic Republic aggressively committed to individual rights), Dubois's symphony endorsed the centrist *status quo.* Charles-Marie Widor indicated as much when he wrote that the *Symphonie française* "seems to evoke all the Frances, from the majesty of the Reims Cathedral and the great figure of our Joan of Arc to the host of revolutionary *sans-culottes* marching against the enemy to the strains of the *Marseillaise.*"[273] Critics also remarked on the expanded scoring, which included a large percussion battery and prominent celesta. One wonders if Dubois reflected on the irony that some listeners ridiculed his use of the latter instrument quite as scornfully as they had Franck's employment of the English horn many years earlier.

Dubois's symphony received laudatory reviews (and some vitriolic ones), but many of them have a stilted and *pro forma* tone, as if the critic is dutifully paying respects to the composer's patriotic intentions and his stature as a member of the Institut instead of to the piece itself. This was not unusual for Dubois, whose works critics often pronounced "honest" or "honorable"—common faint-praise euphemisms for "correct, well-constructed, and utterly uninspired." (A reading of his symphonic scores tends to support their stern verdict.) Audiences, especially student listeners, responded much more bluntly, and Dubois's compositions regularly encountered unpleasantries at the *grands concerts.* Apparently the demonstrations were directed as much at the man and what he represented—the Conservatoire before Fauré's reforms—as at the music. Although the patriotic luster of the *Symphonie française* guaranteed it occasional performances, neither of Dubois's subsequent symphonies (1912, 1924) achieved success; indeed, the Second was soundly hissed at its premiere.

CHARLES-MARIE WIDOR

Another Conservatoire figure, Charles-Marie Widor (1844–1937), enjoyed more respect than Dubois but had equally checkered experiences with the symphony. Widor studied organ in Brussels, and in January 1870 (at age twenty-five) he became organist at Saint-Sulpice in Paris, where he served for nearly sixty-four years, retiring at the end of 1933. After Franck's death in 1890, Widor took over his organ class at the Conservatoire, and his pupils included Tournemire and Louis Vierne. When Dubois became director in 1896, Widor ascended to his composition chair and held the position for thirty-one years; he counted among his pupils Nadia Boulanger, Darius Milhaud, Arthur Honegger, and Edgard Varèse. Elected to the Institut in 1910, he became the *secrétaire perpetuel* ("perpetual secretary" or official recorder and administrative manager) of the Académie des Beaux-Arts four years later, an extremely prestigious position. When Widor died in 1937, he was a revered figure, the last survivor of the generation of Saint-Saëns, Bizet, Fauré, and d'Indy.

Remembered today almost exclusively for his ten symphonies for solo organ (especially the Fifth), Widor was in fact a compositional polymath, achieving success in opera, ballet, and various instrumental genres; he also published a widely respected update of Berlioz's orchestration treatise.[274] His works include six orchestral symphonies (Table XVI/25). The First and Second are for orchestra alone, the others include organ. The *Symphonie pour orgue et orchestre* Opus 42 is an arrangement of movements from the Second and Sixth Organ Symphonies; curiously, it bears the same opus number as the latter work.[275] Neither the First Symphony in F major Opus 16 (1872) nor the Second Symphony in A major Opus 52 (1882), both strongly influenced by Germanic models, made much impression. Both received polite reviews in Paris, but London critics gave the Second a withering reception in 1887; Bernard Shaw wrote, "Berlioz himself, in his most uninspired moments, could not have been more elaborately and intelligently dull."[276]

Quite different was the fate of the Third Symphony in E minor Opus 69: written to inaugurate the Victoria Hall in Geneva in 1893, it became Widor's most popular symphony and received numerous performances at home and abroad throughout his lifetime (usually with the composer either at the organ or conducting).[277] It has not remained in the repertory, and modern analysts tend to regard the work as a clone of Saint-Saëns's "Organ" Symphony: Widor replicates its four-in-two structure, with the organ appearing only in the second and fourth movements, and his themes, while not derived from Saint-Saëns's, faintly resemble

TABLE XVI/25

The Orchestral Symphonies of Charles-Marie Widor

Opus	Key	Date	Title	Movements	Instrumentation	Comments
16	F Major	1872	Symphony No. 1	1. Allegro con moto 2. Andante 3. Scherzo 4. Finale	Full	First partial performance (Movements II-III) in 1873. Published in Paris: Durand, Schoenenwerk, et Cie., 1873.
42 [*bis*]	G Minor	1882	Symphony for organ and orchestra	1. Allegro maestoso 4/4 (255 m.) 2. Andante 3/4 (183 m.) B-flat major 3. Final: Allegro 2/2 (254 m.) G major	Grand + 2 Cornets, Ophecleide, Cym., BD, Organ	Written for the Royal Albert Hall, London. A pastiche arrangement of three movements from his symphonies for solo organ: Movements 1 and 3 based on the first and fifth movements respectively of Organ Symphony VI in G Minor; Movement 2 drawn from the third movement of Symphony II in D Major. Widor gave this work the opus number 42, the same number as the set of Symphonies V–VIII; for clarity, editor John R. Near has amended it to 42 [*bis*]. First performance: Paris, concert at the Trocadéro on April 13, 1882. Published in Middleton, WI: A-R Editions, 2002.
54	A Major	1882	Symphony No. 2	1. Allegro vivace 3/4 (387 m.) 2. Moderato ₵ (179 m.) C-sharp minor 3. Andante con moto 3/4 (157 m.) D minor 4. Vivace—Scherzando—Moderato—Allegro con brio (373 m.) A major	Grand	First performance: London, Crystal Palace, conducted by August Manns in March 1887. Published in Paris: Heugel, 1886.
69	E Minor	1893	Symphony No. 3 for organ and orchestra	1a. Adagio 4/4—Allegro 6/8 (335 m.) 1b. Andante sostenuto 3/4 (139 m.) 2a. Vivace 6/8, 2/4 (333 m.) 2b. [Moderato] 3/4 (210 m.) E major	Grand + Organ	Commissioned for the first concert of the new Victoria Hall, Geneva. Dedicated to Sir Daniel Barton. First performance: Geneva, conducted by Widor on November 28, 1894. Published in Mainz: B. Schotts Söhne, 1895.
81	C Minor	1907	*Sinfonia sacra*	Adagio 12/8, 4/4 (116 m.)—Moderato 4/4 (58 m.) mod.—Andante con moto 3/4 (80 m.) mod.—Più vivo (44 m.) mod.—Allegro moderato 4/4 (169 m.)	Ob., Clar, Tpt., 3 Trom., Strings, Organ	Written to commemorate Widor's election to the Berlin Royal Academy of Fine Arts (Königliche Akademie der Schönen Künste). Dedicated to the Academy. Published in Paris: Hamelle, and Leipzig: June 1908.
83	D Minor	1911	*Symphonie antique*	1. Allegro moderato (Te Deum) 4/4 D minor 2. Adagio F-sharp major 3. Moderato—Allegro (Lauda Sion) B-flat major 4. Moderato: Te Deum laudamus 4/4 D major	Grand + Picc., EH, Bclar, Sarrusophone, 2 Tpt., Tuba, Tamb., Tri., Cym., BD, Tam-tam, Harp, Organ, SA soli, SATB chorus	Dedicated to Countess Renée de Béarn. First performance at the home of Countess de Béarn, conducted by Widor on March 22, 1911. First public performance: Paris, Concerts Colonne, conducted by Gabriel Pierné on December 24, 1911. Published in Paris: Heugel, 1911.

Partially based on Near/WIDOR.

them. In addition, both composers set their second movements in D-flat major, an even more remote key for Widor than for Saint-Saëns. A chorale operates as a cyclic theme throughout the work. Despite the obvious derivations, the symphony has many attractive passages and merits occasional revival. (Curiously, Parisian critics, usually so eager to condemn overt thematic and structural borrowings, seem to have ignored them here—as, apparently, did Saint-Saëns.)[278]

Widor's next major works, his ninth and tenth symphonies for organ, mark an important aesthetic change in his music. Having become convinced that music written to express the sacred should incorporate liturgical melodies, he based both works on plainchants (the first time such melodies appear in the organ symphonies). In the *Symphonie gothique* (1894), the Christmas Introit *Puer natus est nobis* appears only in the last two movements, but the *Symphonie romane* (1899) is a fully cyclic structure in which the Easter Gradual *Haec dies* saturates each movement except the third (which in turn quotes another chant, the familiar Easter sequence *Victimae paschali laudes*). With these compositions Widor declared his contribution to the organ symphony complete, but he continued to explore the use of sacred melodies in large-scale works in his two remaining orchestral symphonies.

At the suggestion of his friend and pupil Albert Schweitzer, Widor wrote the *Sinfonia sacra* (1907) in honor of his election to the Berlin Royal Academy of Fine Arts in 1906, and it premiered in Germany. An elaborate hybrid of symphony, symphonic poem, and fantasia upon the Lutheran Advent chorale *Nun komm, der Heiden Heiland,* this work adopts an innovative structure, one faintly reminiscent of Schumann's Fourth—a four-movement sonata cycle within one continuous division.[279]

In this work Widor's treatment of the sacred melody reaches a new stage of evolution. The composer grafts a different section of the chorale onto each movement, stating it in complete form only at the end. None of the movements follow conventional patterns. The opening, in C minor, alternates a syncopated theme with the first phrase of the chorale. The second movement, in C major, resembles a Scherzo in its toccata-like figuration for the organ; the oboe states the second phrase of the chorale. A through-composed Andante follows in F major with considerable modulation. The Finale opens with a chromatic fugue in C minor loosely based on a transformation of the theme from the first movement. This fugue leads to the full statement of the chorale in the winds and brass, after which the work ends triumphantly on a plagal cadence in C major. The unfolding suggests a progression from darkness to light, the latter symbolizing the Savior's appearance in the world; for much of the *Sinfonia sacra,* then, the orchestration emphasizes "dark" timbres. The organ acts as a partner with the orchestra rather than as a soloist, although the two bodies sometimes seem to exist on different planes.

After its premiere in Germany, the *Sinfonia sacra* appeared three times in Paris between 1908 and 1912 in performances by Concerts Sechiari and Concerts Hasselmans, two orchestras that were generally more innovative in their programming than Colonne or Lamoureux. Although the public responded favorably, only conservative critics welcomed the new work. By this time Widor, like Dubois and Saint-Saëns, was an outspoken (though less abrasive) reactionary whom more progressive figures regarded as a relic, a composer of intellect but no inspiration. Gaston Carraud's biting review is typical:

M. Widor probably knows all that one can know. But it seems that this knowledge has penetrated neither his imagination nor always even his writing. . . . The *Sinfonia sacra* borrows all its thematic elements from an old Gregorian chant [*sic*] and it is more consistent than certain pieces by M. Widor; but it does not present any less of the same mixture of rather dull clarities and endless complications.[280]

Such evaluations came as no news to Widor, who as far back as 1877 could read that he "is an intelligence rather than a heart. . . . One admires more than enjoys him."[281] In this case, at least, Carraud's judgment seems overly harsh, for the *Sinfonia sacra* is an effective work that deserves a better reputation.

Widor's last symphony, *Symphonie antique* (1911), was his largest and most ambitious. Like its predecessor, it is cyclically organized around liturgical melodies. The symphony also reflects a related interest: the supposed Greek origins of many Gregorian melodies. Widor advocated this notion in an article of 1895; now, a decade and a half later, he used this symphony to illustrate the point.[282]

According to the composer, the *Symphonie antique* dramatized the evolution of the *Te Deum* melody from its origin as a Greek war hymn to its ultimate form as a Catholic chant. As he explained in the program notes for the first performance,

> Legend attributes this melody to the improvisation of Sophocles on the evening of Salamine. The original words (Hymn that rendered thanks to the Gods of Victory) have not come down to us; the Latin text (*Te Deum laudamus*) was substituted for the Greek text by Saints Ambrose and Augustine.[283]

Taking Widor's epigraph as a point of departure, the program annotator (presumably with the composer's assistance) offered a detailed if somewhat convoluted interpretation of Widor's purpose:

> The primary idea that engendered this symphony is . . . pagan in origin. . . . Considering the lofty development the composer has given it here, would we be wrong to observe the double and grandiose evocation of two worlds throughout this work, both depicted with respect, one next to the other, in frescos of free and ample contour? . . . It seems that these pages reveal a philosophical vision of the world, proceeding from the thematic frame of the work and striving to realize a moral and universal synthesis.[284]

Considering the hostility the Third Republic bore toward the Church, it comes as no surprise that the "official" explication of the symphony implied equivalence between paganism and Christianity. Bruneau, however, took the position that the work "places pantheistic Greece in opposition to Christian Rome, expressing the historical struggle between the two worlds."[285] Those who supported this reading pointed out that Christianity triumphed in the end, via the *Te Deum*.

Widor's precise intentions remain obscure, but understanding the work as a conflict rather than reconciliation makes sense. The *Symphonie antique* gives much more weight to the "Christian" than the "pagan" version of the *Te Deum*. It supposedly follows the transformation of this chant from a "dark" song of war to a "light" song of praise. The first movement sonata in D minor accordingly takes on the character of a battle. The second movement, in F-sharp major, introduces the *Lauda Sion* sequence, which for unexplained reasons seems to compete for seniority with the *Te Deum* throughout the rest of the composition. The third movement is a Scherzo in B-flat major. Recalling previous themes, the Finale brings in the chorus and organ for a complete rendition of the *Te Deum* in D major, ending with a celestial apotheosis.

The *Symphonie antique* thus seems to express a clash between paganism and Christianity and assert the triumph of the latter—even if the notion of parity, appearing as it did in the concert notes, may have reflected his philosophy more accurately. Heard at Concerts Colonne at the end of 1911, the symphony, like its predecessor, found favor with the public but not the critics, who (once again save for the most conservative) found the texture dense, the polyphony labored, the plan unclear, and the orchestration overblown. As one reviewer dismissively stated, "Ch.-M. Widor's *Symphonie antique* could have been a noble and magnificent work. It is only an obscure and dull composition."[286] A second performance in 1929 made a more favorable impression.[287]

ANDRÉ GEDALGE

As Dubois and Widor demonstrate, composers from the Conservatoire occasionally yielded to the temptation to convey messages in symphonies. Not everyone, however: dissenters arose who, like Saint-Saëns, insisted that music should express only itself. The leading symphonist in this camp was André Gedalge (1856–1926) (Plate B27), a renowned counterpoint professor at the Conservatoire whose pupils included Ravel, Milhaud, and Nadia Boulanger.[288] Because of his stature as a pedagogue, the premiere of his Third Symphony in 1910 attracted considerable attention, all the more because Gedalge had never before released a major composition to the public (his First Symphony of 1893, dedicated to Saint-Saëns, was never performed, and he abandoned the Second of 1899–1902, although the success of the Third persuaded him to finish and release it in 1912).

Most critics found Gedalge's music a revelation, but what intrigued them most was the rubric he placed in the concert notes and score: "Ni littérature ni peinture" (Neither literature nor painting). The composer believed that music expressed strong but intangible emotions—undefinable even to him—and, instead of trying to identify them, the listener should simply enjoy the aural beauty produced in reaction to those emotions. Meaning must arise from the music and not from what the music supposedly represents.[289]

Gedalge explained his philosophy when his Second Symphony premiered. The concert notes included the following:

> It is the wish of M. Gédalge [*sic*] that his Symphony in C minor give no rise in these notes to any analysis, either technical or literary. These are his reasons:
>
> First, from the point of view of technique: if M. Gédalge does not in any way deny the importance of the role of the intellect and the will in the labor of composing, he does not ascribe any creative power to these faculties. He attributes all invention to the imagination alone. In other words, the form of a work of art is, in his view, absolutely inseparable from its essence; every musical idea naturally produces its own unfolding and determines the plan of the work to which it must give birth. Intellect and will do not have to begin by constructing empty frames which imagination undertakes to fill after the fact. And since the composer did not preconceive the general arrangement of the work, there is consequently nothing gained in revealing it in advance to the public, which can only let itself be led to wherever the inherent logic of the musical thought takes it.
>
> Besides, having taken "Neither literature nor painting" as his motto, M. Gédalge does not acknowledge that sounds necessarily have any power to evoke objects, feelings, or emotions. For him music is not a language, a system of signs for representing something other than itself; it is self-sufficient and does not need to translate scenes of material nature or dramas of interior life in order to move us.
>
> Therefore the listener will be sufficiently informed if he knows that M. Gédalge's Symphony in C minor is composed of the four traditional movements: an Allegro, an Adagio, a Scherzo, and a Finale; the Adagio is connected to the Scherzo.
>
> We will have completed our task of characterizing M. Gédalge's artistic tendencies if we say that, as the enemy of all excess, he has striven to avoid grandiloquence as well as preciosity, never to write anything that is not simple or natural.[290]

Gedalge's notion of music as unspecified emotion distinguished him from Saint-Saëns, who regarded artistic formalism as an end in itself.

The Third Symphony consists of the usual four movements without cyclic connections. Its high energy, dramatic motivic developments, and driving rhythms owe much to Beethoven; dotted rhythms and metric ambiguities, especially in the Scherzo, suggest affinities with Schumann as well. Gedalge's score abounds with expressive markings and extreme dynamic contrasts. The first movement sonata, in 6/4 meter (F major), is straightforward in form, with minimal chromaticism except in the development; its lively rhythms and joyful mood recall Dukas's symphony. Gedalge sets the warmly lyrical second movement in ternary form. The Scherzo (F major) is pastoral and somewhat folk-like, in a through-composed structure.

The final movement (F minor/major), another sonata, features a struggle between a violent theme outlining a chromatic scale and a lyrical folk-like melody. In the development, the conflict becomes so contentious that many critics—undoubtedly to Gedalge's consternation—assumed a hidden program lay behind it. One writer described the development as a "Homeric struggle": "one finds oneself in the presence of a well-arranged army and a well-ordered battle, and one is tempted to use military terms to replace the musical ones."[291] The closing chorale does not transform the violent theme into something more benign; it simply returns the symphony to its tonic F major. Like Beethoven's Ninth, the symphony ends with a short slow passage followed by a presto conclusion. Thus, although the Finale has characteristics associated with the message-symphony, namely dramatic thematic conflict (not merely dualism) and a peroration chorale, Gedalge uses them as abstract procedures and nowhere hints at any extramusical function. Perhaps he wished to demonstrate that he could employ these traits for their own sake, without making them *mean* anything.[292]

Most reviewers praised Gedalge's Third Symphony, especially its orchestration and treatment of form. The slow movement received the highest acclaim. Some critics like Lalo felt, though, that in his drive to expunge philosophy from the symphony, Gedalge also sacrificed personality:

> That his symphony has neither anecdote nor description is a marvel. But neither do I find a feeling, a thought, [or] a being, and that is unfortunate. It seems that the composer of this symphony wrote it to create music and not to express himself in writing it.[293]

Jean d'Udine, on the other hand, was profoundly affected: "It moved me to tears in more than one place. . . . What delights me most of all in M. Gédalge's [*sic*] masterpiece . . . is the perfect healthiness of the emotion, the perfect clarity of expression." He ranked the work with Saint-Saëns's Third and those of Franck and Lalo as the greatest symphonies of the French school. Whereas Saint-Saëns's composition offered "nobility and grandeur," Lalo's "color and life," and Franck's "anxiety and ecstasy," Gedalge's symphony contributed "good will and melancholy."[294]

Many symphonies appeared in the period between 1900 and 1920. Tables XVI/26 and 27 offer further details on some of these works; the first table lists message-symphonies and the second considers five prominent symphonies that do not belong to the message-symphony category.[295]

Albéric Magnard

We close this survey with the music of a composer virtually unknown outside his homeland and remembered within it primarily for the way he died—killed defending his estate against

---

TABLE XVI/26

Prominent "Message-Symphonies" Written Between 1900 and 1925

Vincent d'Indy: Symphony No. 2 in B-flat (1902–03)
Message (according to pupils and intimates of d'Indy): art founded upon "tradition" will triumph over "modern" art.

Guy Ropartz: Symphony No. 3 in E Major (1905–06)
Message: love one another and join with people of all nations to pursue truth, justice, and beauty.

Théodore Dubois: *Symphonie française* (Symphony No. 1, 1908)
Message: the glorification of the French Republic and, by implication, a proclamation of moral victory over Germany.

Charles-Marie Widor: *Symphonie antique* (1911)
Interpreted as a depiction of the struggle between pagan and Christian worlds (ending in the victory of the latter) or, conversely, as an assertion of equality between the two worlds.

Charles Tournemire: Symphony No. 3 in D Major "Moscou" (1911–13)
Evokes the religious spirit of the people of Tsarist Russia, as reflected in the sounds of their bells.

Charles Tournemire: Symphony No. 5 in F Major (1913–14)
Compares the majesty of nature with human misery; at the end, both nature and humanity unite in the Light of the Almighty.

Charles Tournemire: Symphony No. 6 (1915–18)
Written during World War I, this work sets Scripture to deplore war and proclaim Jesus' promise of peace.

Charles Tournemire: Symphony No. 7, *Les Danses de la Vie* ("The Dances of Life," 1918–22)
Depicts humanity's search for God through consecutive ages ("dances") of history.

Charles Tournemire: Symphony No. 8, *La Symphonie du Triomphe de la Mort* ("The Symphony of the Triumph of Death," 1920–24)
Traces the evolution of the composer's feelings from grief at the death of his wife to a renewal of hope as he realizes that this is only a temporary separation for the believer.

---

invading German soldiers in the first month of World War I. His so-called *mort heroïque* overshadowed his artistic accomplishments but, as increasing numbers of performances and recordings demonstrate, many of Magnard's twenty-one published works—symphonies, chamber works, and operas—are masterful compositions, revealing him as one of the most significant musical voices of his period.

Magnard (1865–1914) (see Plate B26) was notoriously irascible, even misanthropic; contemporaries spoke of his *caractère infernal*.[296] His frank manner earned him many enemies—conductors, critics, Establishment officials—which negatively impacted his career, at least in Paris. Fiercely independent and distrustful of publishers, Magnard printed his works himself but refused to advertise them, despite the means at his disposal (his father had edited *Le Figaro*). As a result, Magnard's music had considerably less exposure in his lifetime than it might have had otherwise.

Nevertheless, the composer had supporters. To Richard Strauss, Romain Rolland described Magnard as "the most original figure of young French music, along with Dukas and Debussy; and perhaps there is something more strong and rugged in him than in the two others."[297] After Magnard's death Darius Milhaud became an ardent defender, despite the unapologetically late Romantic language of his music:

> In my opinion, Magnard is one of the greatest French composers. His music is healthy and strong and his ideas always elevated and pure. When one analyzes an orchestral

---

TABLE XVI/27
Five Other Notable Symphonies of the 1900–1914 Period

Georges-Martin Witkowski: Symphony No. 1 in D Minor (1900)
A private pupil of d'Indy, Witkowski (1867–1943) based his cyclic three-movement symphony on a Breton song. It achieved considerable popularity in the years before World War I both in France and abroad (including America), but it is known best today as the subject of an often-quoted Debussy commentary on the "uselessness" of the symphony as a genre. Witkowski later wrote a second symphony (1909–10).

Albert Roussel: Symphony No. 1, *Le Poème de la forêt* ("The Poem of the Forest," 1904–06)
A member of the first graduating composition class at the Schola Cantorum, Roussel (1869–1937) became one of the most prominent composers in the generation between the world wars. According to the composer, the first of his four symphonies evokes his emotions observing the four seasons in the Forest of Fontainebleau. The work merges the structural and tonal qualities of *d'indyste* symphonies (such as cyclic organization) with *debussyste* language (whole-tone patterns, extended tertian chords, coloristic orchestration, etc.); many reviewers spoke approvingly of Roussel's skill at combining poetic imagination with traditional symphonic logic.

Sylvio Lazzari: Symphony in E-flat Major (1906?)
Lazzari (1857–1944) was best known in his day for a string quartet (1887), which may have influenced Franck's, and for the opera *La Lépreuse* (1899–1902; prem. 1912). His only symphony, a large cyclic work, embeds the Scherzo in the slow movement in the manner of Franck. This symphony has many expressive moments.

Paul Le Flem: Symphony No. 1 in A (1906–07)
A pupil of d'Indy and Roussel at the Schola Cantorum, Le Flem (1881–1984) wrote four symphonies, the last at age 91. Symphony No. 1 was performed piecemeal at various concerts between 1907 and 1914 and finally appeared complete in 1927, after which it enjoyed a brief popularity (Honegger praised it).

Louis Vierne: Symphony in A Minor (1907–08)
Vierne's only orchestral symphony, written during a crisis in his life. The composer quotes several despairing epigraphs from Verlaine in the score as if to suggest that the symphony expresses his misery.

---

score of Magnard, one cannot but be struck by the sobriety of his writing and the new and robust way it sounds. No extraneous notes, no string *divisi* which are made more for the eye than the ear.[298]

Again according to Milhaud, the generation of the 1920s, "certain members of which loved the music of Magnard with all their hearts, found in it a beneficial source of inspiration. This influence is very salutary: rhythmically it contributed to orienting the young people towards a livelier, airy, healthy, and virile music."[299] Milhaud also declared that Magnard's music "helped me find my own way."[300]

Magnard entered the Conservatoire in 1886 but left dissatisfied after two years. He turned to d'Indy and studied form, fugue, and instrumentation with him privately from 1888 to 1892. Despite their antipodal ideologies—Magnard was an outspoken defender of Dreyfus and atheist Republican, d'Indy an equally fervent anti-Dreyfusard and Catholic nationalist—teacher and pupil enjoyed a close relationship: Magnard said that "musically I owe everything to d'Indy," and the teacher fully reciprocated his student's admiration.[301]

Like most *franckistes,* Magnard set impossible standards for himself: weighing his work against Perfection, he always found it wanting. Gaston Carraud wrote that Magnard "seemed to live on the outskirts of his ideal."[302] We saw with Dukas how such obsessive self-criticism could lead to artistic catastrophe; fortunately Magnard pressed on, confident that the next work would bring him a step closer to his goal. As he stated (with typical directness) to his best friend Ropartz, "I continue to find what I write execrable, and if I don't stop myself from soiling the paper it is because I always harbor the naive hope of arriving finally at signing an impeccable work."[303] This continual sense of frustration and failure coupled with faith that improvement would follow gave Magnard a spirit of "enthusiastic pessimism"—a phrase he used in speaking of his friend Paul Poujaud and which Carraud turned back on him.[304] Magnard's music therefore tends to harbor dark strivings and emotional conflicts but ends with positive affirmation.

According to Carraud, Magnard considered the symphony to be "the perfect manifestation of music."[305] He composed four, which range in date from his student years to the end of his career (Table XVI/28). Each follows the traditional sonata-cycle plan, although Magnard experiments with the structure of individual movements. Carraud wrote that each adopted the same emotional pattern: "a great contest of will, then an escape into exterior joy followed by a deep meditation, from which is born true joy or definitive serenity in the triumph of action."[306] As Carraud's précis suggests, Magnard crafted a strikingly sober symphonic voice at one with the tradition of Beethoven. Of Debussy's most notable contemporaries, Magnard was perhaps the one least affected by his innovations: counterpoint rather than harmony forms the foundation of his work, and virtually no Debussian harmony appears in Magnard's compositions—whereas other *franckistes* routinely employed such passages, as d'Indy's Second Symphony attests.

The composer underlines the earnest nature of his discourse through such "learned" devices as *alla breve* meters, white-note passages, and fugatos; the latter in fact appear in almost every mature composition, particularly in development sections. Other traits include broad and expansive melodies that move in vigorous duple or triple-meter rhythms; allusions to rustic modal idioms and folk-fiddling; and long-range tonal stability, though within a movement the key may travel to distant regions. Although he avoided Impressionistic colorings, Magnard became a skilled orchestrator: partial to the strings, he provides striking passages for winds and brass as well, especially in the Fourth Symphony (only the First uses any percussion instruments besides the timpani).

The composer objected to programmatic interpretations of his symphonies and like Gedalge he discouraged printed analyses, wishing to let the music act with complete freedom on the listener's mind.[307] It follows that Magnard had little outward sympathy for the message-symphony, though he did on occasion write symphonic poems with messages; his *Hymne à la justice* in 1903 explicitly (by the title) salutes Dreyfusard values. Because of his emphasis on abstract symphonies that communicated generalized sentiments through standard forms suffused with rhythmic vitality and continuous variation, critics described Magnard (along with Dukas) as the modern embodiment of the Beethovenian ideal, the combination of expressive thought with sound formal and technical construction. Bach and Wagner also provided inspiration, the former in counterpoint and the latter in sound and harmony.

SYMPHONY NO. 1 IN C MINOR OPUS 4

Magnard wrote his First Symphony in C minor in 1889–1890, the years in which Franck's symphony premiered and Chausson finished his. He composed the work under the tutelage of d'Indy, to whom he dedicated it. His shortest symphony, it is also the most complicated and compact. The composition has its moments of technical inexperience—the consequence of dense scoring (it uses the largest orchestra of any Magnard symphony, including three saxophones), heavy counterpoint, and an overly rigorous application of the cyclic procedure. On the other hand, the melodies show great individuality: already Magnard speaks with a distinctive voice. The composer sets every movement except the second in the tonic.

TABLE XVI/28

The Symphonies of Albéric Magnard

Opus	Key	Date	Title	Movements	Instrumentation	Comments
4	C Minor	1889–90	Symphony No. 1	1. Strepitato 4/4 2. Religioso: Largo 3/2, 4/2 A-flat major 3. Scherzo: Presto 3/4 4. Finale: Molto energico 4/4	Grand + Picc., EH, Bclar., 2 Bssn., 2 Tpt., Trom., Tuba, 3 Saxophones, Cym., BD, Tri., 2 Harps	Dedicated "a mon maître et ami Vincent d'Indy." First partial performance (Movements I–II): Paris, Société Nationale, conducted by Gabriel Marie on April 18, 1891. First complete performance: Angers, Association Artistique d'Angers, conducted by P. Frémaux on March 12, 1893. Published (four-hand piano reduction only) in Paris: Baudoux, 1894.
6	E Major	1892–93, rev. 1896	Symphony No. 2	1. Ouverture: Assez animé 4/4, 3/4 2. Danses: Vif 2/4 A major 3. Chant varié: Très nuancé 4/4, 6/8, 9/8 F-sharp major 4. Final: Vif et gai ¢	Full + Trom., Harp	Dedicated to Jules Bordier. First performance (first version): Nancy, conducted by Guy Ropartz on February 9, 1896. Magnard revised the symphony, replacing the original second movement (*Fugue et danses*) with a new Scherzo (*Danses*). First performance of revised version: Paris, in a concert organized and conducted by Magnard on May 14, 1899. First version published (four-hand piano reduction only): Paris, Bardoux, ?1896. Revised version unpublished.
11	B-flat Minor	1895–96	Symphony No. 3	1. Introduction et Ouverture: Modéré 3/2—Vif 2/4 (446 m.) 2. Danses: Très vif 6/8, 2/4, 3/4 (371 m.) B-flat major 3. Pastorale: Modéré 3/4 (187 m.) F-sharp minor 4. Final: Vif ¢ (416 m.)	Grand	Dedicated to Estelle Fortier-Maire. First performance: Paris, in a concert organized and conducted by Magnard on May 14, 1899. Published in Paris privately by Magnard, 1902; later reprinted by Rouart, Lerolle, et Cie., n.d.
21	C-sharp Minor	1911–13	Symphony No. 4	1. Modéré ¢ (306 m.) 2. Vif 1/2, 3/4 (469 m.) F minor 3. Sans lenteur et nuancé 4/4 (172 m.) E major 4. Animé 3/2, 12/8 (242 m.) C-sharp minor, D-flat major	Grand + Picc., EH, Bclar., Harp	Dedicated to L'Union des Femmes Professeurs et Compositeurs de Musique. First performance: Paris, Orchestre de L'Union des Femmes Professeurs et Compositeurs de Musique, conducted by Magnard on April 2, 1914. Published in Paris: Rouart, Lerolle, et Cie, 1918.

Magnard marks the first movement *Strepitato* (noisily). *P,* the cyclic theme, like so many of the composer's melodies, is sharply profiled, featuring dotted rhythms and quarter-note triplets. *S,* in the remote key of B major, makes a gentle contrast. Complex polyphony appears in the development. Magnard marks the following movement *Religioso: Largo* (this is the only symphony in which the slow movement takes second position). It forms a five-part *Grand Lied, A–B–A'–B'–A.* The movement opens with a striking instrumental effect: a series of harmonies in the clarinets and saxophones simulate organ chords and lead into *A,* a chorale in A-flat major. The theme consists mostly of white notes in 3/2 and 4/2 meters. *B,* by contrast, is a more agitated section in F minor; the cyclic theme returns in *B'.* A fast and short movement (three-and-a-half minutes), the heavy material of the Scherzo offsets its light manner. The Trio is rustic in character. The cyclic theme intrudes in the retransition from the Trio to the Scherzo. The Finale, a rondo in *A–B–A–C–A* form, combines themes from the preceding movements contrapuntally, including the chorale from the second movement and of course the cyclic theme.[308]

The first two movements premiered at the Société Nationale in April 1891 and the whole work debuted in Angers in March 1893—the only complete performance in the composer's lifetime. Both renditions left critics underwhelmed; the reviewer of *Le Guide musical* admonished Magnard to write with "less technique, less empty knowledge, and more ideas."[309] Others, such as Emmanuel Chabrier, responded favorably. Ropartz provided perhaps the most balanced assessment: "The writing in this *First Symphony* is sometimes dense; the air does not circulate enough. The orchestration is often stiff as well, but there is in [this symphony] a great deal of music and the best kind."[310] The score was published in piano reduction in 1894.

SYMPHONY NO. 2 IN E MAJOR OPUS 6

Magnard's Second Symphony in E major (1892–1893; rev. 1896) shows significant advances. D'Indy did not oversee its composition, although he remained available for consultation. Ropartz conducted the premiere in Nancy in 1896. The audience reacted with hostility—one listener was heard to say, "You would need a logarithm table to initiate us to such music!"[311]— and even Ropartz found the symphony too long and complex. Magnard rewrote the second movement and shortened the third. The revised version received a much more favorable reception at its premiere in 1899, though it promptly fell under the shadow of the Third Symphony, which debuted on the same program. Magnard dedicated the work to Jules Bordier, founder of the Association Artistique of Angers.

Magnard's only symphony in a major key, and the longest (even after revision), the Second Symphony also stands apart in lacking cyclic unity. The first movement, *Ouverture* (E major), begins with a very long and animated *P:* as usual, *P* and *S* differ sharply, and the development is highly contrapuntal. The newly written Scherzo (*Danses,* A major), three years younger than the rest of the work, is a product of Magnard's maturity. It has three themes— the first a rustic modal motive, the second plaintive, and the third jaunty. The Trio is very tranquil, its theme somewhat reminiscent of Russian style, notably Borodin. The slow movement, *Chant varié,* presents an extended lyrical melody in F-sharp major with four variations and a coda; the first and third are miniature rondos, while the second and fourth resemble varied reprises. The *Final* is another sonata in which the principal themes contrast and the development continues in the coda. Like the First Symphony, the full score of the revised Second remains in manuscript, although a four-hand piano transcription did appear (the first version survives only in four-hand reduction). Both works deserve occasional hearings, the latter especially on account of its spry Scherzo and the tender lyricism of the *Chant varié.*

SYMPHONY NO. 3 IN B-FLAT MINOR OPUS 11

The Third Symphony in B-flat minor Opus 11 (1895–1896) was Magnard's first fully mature symphony and remains his best-known composition. He began it after a holiday in the Auvergne.[312] While in the country, Magnard observed a peasant girl singing and dancing to herself, and her song inspired the Scherzo; in addition, the quiet lyricism of the third movement, aided by its title *Pastorale,* recalled the countryside to many listeners. The poet René d'Avril nicknamed the symphony "Bucolique," but the designation did not take hold. Magnard dedicated the score to Mme Estelle Fortier-Maire, widow of a childhood friend.[313]

As usual with Magnard, the Third Symphony follows the traditional structure, with the Scherzo in second position. The opening chorale returns in the last movement but the composer does not derive material from it. Magnard reveals his admiration for Wagner in the chromaticism of the themes and the wide-ranging key relations: the first movement, in B-flat minor, begins its development in B minor; the Scherzo is in B-flat major, with the Trio predominantly in C major; the slow movement proceeds in the distant key of F-sharp minor (presumably an enharmonically respelled G-flat minor, submediant minor to B-flat minor); and the finale returns to B-flat major, though again with unusual internal progressions. Folk elements in the second movement suggest the sound of droned bagpipes or hurdy-gurdies as well as folk fiddling; in addition, *III/P* resembles a stylized folk melody with dorian inflections. Magnard favors the strings, especially the violins, which carry much of the principal material; further, the composer tends to treat families separately, with little blending. (Carraud and others reproached Magnard for overreliance on the strings; he agreed and gave the Fourth Symphony much more variety in its scoring.)[314] As in the symphonies of Franck and Dukas, many changes of tempo take place within movements.

Magnard entitles the first movement *Introduction et Ouverture* (Modéré). The introduction unfolds in *A–B–A–B–A* form and 3/2 meter. *1–O* (Example XVI/35a) is a quiet chorale in B-flat minor, a series of stately chords for woodwinds, brass, and double basses voiced to create organ-like sonorities; the harmonies are mostly perfect intervals, and the voice-leading features many plagal and modal progressions (Magnard is partial to plagal cadences as well as the lowered leading tone). *1–O* somewhat recalls the opening of d'Indy's then-popular symphonic poem *La Mort de Wallenstein* (1879), which Magnard surely knew; Harry Halbreich also postulates a connection to the Prologue of d'Indy's *Poèmes des montagnes* for piano (1881).[315] *1–O* is answered by *2–O* in the violas, cellos, and English horn (m.10; Example XVI/35b); expansive and rhythmically asymmetrical, this lyrical theme spans a wide contour. *1–O* returns and cadences a fifth higher in F minor, while *2–O* is altered to close on the major subdominant. The final *1–O* leads to the dominant, but the *Ouverture* interrupts before the chorale can finish its statement.

Magnard sets the *Ouverture* in sonata-allegro form (Vif, 2/4). *P* contains four themes set in alternating groupings of nine and eight bars; given entirely to the first violins, they form a continuous period in B-flat minor. The jaunty and jerky rhythm of *1P* is characteristic of Magnard (m.45; Example XVI/36a). He defines *2P* by its opening leap of a fifth, after which the motive wanders tonally (m.54; Example XVI/36b). *3P* has another signature opening, a repeated note (m.62; Example XVI/36c). *4P* derives from *1Pa* (m.71).

T consists of a sequential line in violas and lower woodwinds against a background of broken chords in the violins (Mouvement, m.79). *1S* is somewhat ambivalent: a twice-stated violin melody, it contains many Wagnerian gestures—chromaticism, 9–8 appoggiaturas, turn figures, and a wide range that reaches great heights (c-flat''''); although nominally in A-flat

EXAMPLE XVI/35A   Magnard. Symphony No. 3/1, mm.1–8.

EXAMPLE XVI/35B Magnard. Symphony No. 3/1, mm.9–17.

major, the key is unstable (Modéré sans lenteur, m.93). *2S,* a much lower melody in C minor, separates the two statements of *1S* (m.108). *K* (m.146) consists of a four-measure stepwise walking bass in A-flat minor. The principal keys of the exposition, therefore, are the remotely related B-flat minor and A-flat major/minor.

The development brings back most of the exposition material in the order it first appeared. Magnard develops by varied repetition instead of the fragmentation one might have expected of a symphony supposedly modeled on Beethoven. The development opens with *1P* (Vif, m.150) in B minor. A brief fugato on *2P* in E minor commences in the strings (Avec vigueur, m.165), with *3P* serving as episodes. *1P* repeats in G minor and B-flat major, and the fugato ends with a stretto of *2P* over a pedal on F-sharp (m.209). A change of texture announces *T* in the lower strings against a constant harmonic background of repeated chords in the wind choir (Plus animé; m.218). An intense varied statement of *S* in the first violins provides the climax of the development (Double plus lent; m.250); beginning weakly in D-flat major, it again becomes tonally ambiguous. An extended *K* in the lower strings and bassoons, combined with a new countertheme (*N*) in the first oboe and first violins, serves as retransition, in A minor/major (m.279). The obsessively repeating bass implies the dominant of D until the last two measures, when the other instruments obliquely set up the return to B-flat minor; still, the effect is of a semitone shift to the tonic.

EXAMPLE XVI/36A Magnard. Symphony No. 3/1, mm.45–51.

EXAMPLE XVI/36B Magnard. Symphony No. 3/1, mm.54–57.

EXAMPLE XVI/36C Magnard. Symphony No. 3/1, mm.62–65.

The recapitulation proceeds regularly (Vif, m.299); *S* appears in B-flat major, *K* in B-flat minor. The coda contains two large sections. The first reprises *1–O* and *2–O* in 3/2 (Mouvt. de l'Introduction, m.414). *1–O* appears an octave higher than before and with arpeggios in the violins and violas carried over from *K*. *2–O* follows in the violins with imitative counterpoint in the cellos (m.422). *T* functions as a bridge to section two, a placid cadential theme in B-flat major based in part on *N* (m.439); Magnard sets it in violins over a tonic pedal and harp-like arpeggios in the cellos—a moment of Wagnerian scoring. The movement closes with a plagal cadence.

The second movement, *Danses,* is a colorful and witty Scherzo and Trio featuring frequent and surprising shifts of meter, key, and timbre. Here the orchestration proves particularly deft: themes repeat frequently, each time with a new scoring. Magnard sets the Scherzo as a kind of sonatina in B-flat major. *P* has three ideas, each with a distinctive rhythm. *1P* begins with a drum bass on the tonic, followed by a syncopated motive in the first violins. Starting with repeated notes, *2P* (m.9) moves in trochaic motion in the violas and cellos. *3P* (m.15) features continuous triplets in the violins, progressively breaking down its measure groups as it modulates. *1P* returns in the flutes and closes the section in the tonic (m.32).

S also contains four subsections arrayed in the format *a–b–a–c* (as compared to *P*'s *a–b–c–a*). The dancelike *1S* interrupts *1P* and shifts gears to a new meter—7/4, barred 2/4+3/4+2/4—and new key, D major (m.42). Then a second abrupt contrast: a solo string quartet presents a new idea in G major which repeats in all the strings with a syncopated countermotive (*2S*, m.48). A triadic theme sounded over octave drones, it suggests pastoral folk music (Example XVI/37). *1S* returns in D major (m.64). The final idea, *3S*, features playful banter between the strings and woodwinds, one playing fast repeated notes and the other a chord with hairpin dynamics (m.70). The recapitulation opens with single statements of *1P* and *2P* (m.93). *1S* intrudes in B-flat major; *2S* shifts to A major; the syncopations are even stronger this time. *1S* returns in B-flat major, leading to a bridge that holds even more surprises: the meter reverts to 6/8, the key hints at E-flat minor, and a motive faintly reminiscent of *I/N* appears in the horns (m.143).

The Trio (Dédoublez; the dotted half note of the Scherzo now equals a half note) begins with yet another metric shift (2/2, m.155). Predominantly in C major, with excursions to F major and G minor, this section also invokes folk elements but of Slavic rather than Gallic provenance. Its tuneful melody, stated first in the clarinet and then the strings, has elements of pentatonicism and modality (lowered leading tone and supertonic) and, like many Russian themes, it emphasizes the fifth degree (Example XVI/38). Magnard repeats it in various timbres, recalling the Russian "changing background variations" technique; the melody in fact faintly resembles the English horn theme from Borodin's *In the Steppes of Central Asia.* Drone pedals underlie much of the section.

When the Scherzo returns (m.206), Magnard intensifies the scoring and adjusts the end of *3P* to lead into *S* without repeating *1P*. *1S* appears in G minor (m.239). The woodwinds take *2S* while the tympani and pizzicato strings provide a murky bass support, creating a sound akin to a Russian balalaika. Like *2S*, *3S* inverts the scoring of its first appearance (m.267). The recapitulation extends *1P* and shortens *3P* (B-flat major, m.290). *1S* is also in the tonic (m.318). In *2S*, the strings take the melody while the pseudo-balalaika accompaniment appears in the tympani and woodwinds. The coda begins with a bridge similar to that which led to the Trio (m.342); the correspondence to *I/N* seems even more pronounced. A final statement of *1Pa* in the tonic closes the movement.

The third movement, *Pastorale* (Modéré), unfolds in sonata form. The exposition contains three extended lyrical melodies; as he has done elsewhere, Magnard blurs the divisions

EXAMPLE XVI/37   Magnard. Symphony No. 3/2, mm.48–63.

so that one theme flows into the next. *P* is in F-sharp minor with Dorian inflections (Example XVI/39a shows the first two phrases). It divides into six four-bar measures with two irregularities: the fourth group interrupts the prevailing 3/4 meter with one bar of 2/4, and the fifth group is followed by a two-measure interruption, an ominous rumbling motion in the lower strings (henceforth designated *x*) outlining a diminished seventh on F-sharp (Example XVI/39b). The last four-bar group, marked "like an echo," serves as a close. The composer

EXAMPLE XVI/38   Magnard. Symphony No. 3/2, mm.155–63.

assigns this placid and melancholy modal theme to the oboe—one of the few times in this symphony he does not give essential thematic material to the strings—and the scoring enhances the gentle rustic atmosphere suggested by the title.

T (m.26), an equally plaintive but more chromatic and syncopated line for the violins, elides with *P. S* (m.41) continues the thought of *T.* This is a gentle melody, syncopated throughout (the downbeat falls on the second eighth note of the 3/4 measure), chromatic but firmly in D major although Magnard notates it with a key signature of three sharps and inserts further modal gestures. Again he assigns the melody to the violins, balancing it with a non-syncopated countermotive in the violas. The exposition ends with a three-measure bridge for the horns, the first non-melodic material in the movement.

The development devotes itself entirely to *P* and *x*. It begins with a variation of *P*—so identified in the score—again in the oboe (m.63); the key changes to A minor, again with dorian inflections, and a modified *x* appears in the last measure of every phrase. Magnard interrupts *P* in its third phrase to begin the heart of the development, an extended "storm and stress" passage subjecting *Pa* to changing background variations (Animé, m.76). Introduced by *x* in C-sharp minor, *Pa* in augmentation migrates between various timbres (flute and oboe, trombone, trumpet, first violins), each time over a new minor or diminished harmony. At the dramatic climax, *Pa* appears in B minor in the trumpet and woodwinds against precipitous descending patterns in the violins (m.100). A further repetition in F-sharp minor for the horns and bassoons (against a G-sharp major harmony) leads to a final appearance of the two motives telescoped into a single measure, followed by a bridge. Throughout the development, the meter alternates between 2/4 and 3/4.

EXAMPLE XVI/39A   Magnard. Symphony No. 3/3, mm.1–8.

EXAMPLE XVI/39B   Magnard. Symphony No. 3/3, mm.21–22.

For the recapitulation Magnard places *P* in the bassoons and first violins, converting the key to a mixolydian-inflected F-sharp major but omitting *x* and the final phrase (m.117). *T* roams among various timbres (m.137). *S,* also in F-sharp major, remains in the violins (m.151). The coda (m.173) begins with *Pa* once more in the oboe, initiating a sequence that leads to a 4–3 resolution in F-sharp major. A final appearance of *x* in the strings and bassoons hints at unrest, but all ends peacefully.

The *Final,* another sonata-allegro, is in B-flat major. Magnard does not transform earlier material in this movement, but *I/1–O* returns at strategic points. As in the first movement, the tonality of *P* remains relatively clear, while that of *S* is fraught with ambiguities. Like Franck, Magnard begins his finale with a burst of light. *1P,* a rhythmically high-spirited motive, dominates; of particular importance is *1Pa,* a tonic octave leap sounded antiphonally in the opening measures. When *P* appears in full—i.e., both *1P* and *2P*—the octave leap takes place on the tonic note; but when *1P* surfaces in isolation, as in the development, the leap tends to occur on the dominant degree, the tonic arriving only on the downbeat of the second measure. *2P* (m.9) is more ambiguous: the phrasing becomes irregular and the key tends toward the tonic minor by the end. *1P* returns, intensified and again in B-flat major (m.22).

Both *T* themes derive from *P* (m.30): *1T* continues its predecessor's bouncy character over trills in the upper woodwinds while *2T* shifts the key abruptly to A-flat major. *S* has three themes, all lyrical, highly chromatic (especially *2S*), and tonally ambivalent. *1S* and *3S* (mm.45, 76), both violin melodies, are primarily rooted around the dominant while *2S,* set for cellos with flute countermotive, travels to A minor (m.57). *K* (m.101), based on *1Pa,* disrupts F major with further chromatic decoration. The exposition repeats.

Much of the development concerns *1P* or *1Pa.* It opens with *1Pa* in a stepwise ascent from F-sharp to A-flat (m.109). The core of the section, however, belongs to *I/1–O,* which appears in three strophes in the first trombone as the violins exchange *1Pa* antiphonally (Dédoublez, m.134); the key centers around C minor. As he did in the second movement, Magnard enlarges the beat in the chorale: the measure fills a double whole note which is worth the value of two measures of the previous section. At the end of the first and second strophes, a dramatic buildup in strings and woodwinds leads to an emphatic statement of *1Pa* in augmentation in the trumpet and flute (for these passages Magnard returns to the standard beat of one whole note per measure). The third strophe is interrupted before it can move to the buildup; instead, a statement of *1Pa* in normal form (but outlining an F-sharp diminished chord) leads to an extended return of *2P* (m.199) followed by the retransition (m.210), which decorates a dominant pedal.

Magnard begins the recapitulation with a Beethovenian touch—a false start which brings back *1P* but in B major (Mouvement, m.219). He quickly slips down to the proper B-flat major. Most of *2P* is lowered a tone. Similarly, the composer displaces much of *1T* by an octave (m.254); *2T* moves to the dominant-seventh of B-flat. *1S* (m.269) remains harmonically ambiguous but suggests the tonic. The melody of *2S* appears in the flute and oboe, with second violins and violas providing an accompaniment of oscillating notes; the key centers around D. *3S* firmly establishes B-flat major. *K* remains disruptive as it leads to the coda (m.328).

The coda divides into two parts, the first featuring *I/1–O* and the second *1P*. The meter changes to 3/2 and the chorale appears as it did at the beginning, in woodwinds, brass, and lower strings while the violins and violas provide a new and continuously active accompaniment suggestive of a "celestial style" (m.336). Two soft and partial statements of the first strophe (G major, D major) lead to a full and expressive statement of the chorale, *forte,* in the tonic (m.360). A final harmonic surprise awaits: after *1Pa* returns (m.378), the trumpet loudly states the motive twice in B minor; but the orchestra quickly reclaims *1P* in the tonic, and the symphony comes to a joyful conclusion.

Magnard premiered the Third Symphony at a large concert he arranged at his own expense in May 1899: the program also included the revised Second Symphony, three songs, and two shorter orchestral pieces. The composer, as usual, refused to publicize the concert and answered for it with small audience attendance. Many musicians associated with the Société Nationale attended, including Ropartz, d'Indy, Chausson, Dukas, Isaac Albéniz, and critics Pierre Lalo and Henri Gauthier-Villars. All the compositions received a friendly response, but the Third Symphony aroused enthusiasm. D'Indy raved:

> I have just heard Magnard's Third Symphony. It's an *amazing* thing. I am absolutely overjoyed: the first two movements are beautiful in every respect; the first in particular is superb in its themes and form. It's a superior symphony. We haven't had beautiful symphonic music for a long time and it's refreshing to hear this work.[316]

Pierre de Bréville (another *franckiste*) concurred and declared, "Along with *Fervaal,* Magnard is Vincent d'Indy's most beautiful work."[317]

Despite Magnard's difficult relations with Parisian orchestras, Camille Chevillard conducted the symphony at Concerts Lamoureux in November 1904; the response was such that he repeated it in February 1905. Drawing a much larger audience than the concert of 1899, these performances received many more reviews. Both Dukas and Carraud (who had also reviewed the earlier concert) lauded the work's structural clarity, directness of expression, and depth of feeling; they felt that with this symphony Magnard took his place squarely in the classical tradition.[318] As Dukas wrote,

> M. Magnard's symphony . . . possesses above all a perfect clarity. . . . What distinguishes this symphony is only the natural effect of the power and rectitude of its conception, not the result of a feigned search for simplicity. . . . It is simple, as it is clear, only by virtue of its expression. And this expression is spontaneous and communicative to the highest degree, so that . . . it translates itself into melodic lines which are both lucid and flexible, and which render the meaning easily intelligible to all those who have learned to listen. In this way, as in many others, M. Magnard's art is profoundly classical. He joins the independence of feeling to the respect of form. . . . So boldly has he reinforced the architecture of his periods that one finds the powerful foundations of the Beethovenian symphony under their layout. And this is one more reason why his work is so imposing and

why it must impose itself at once upon any listener whose ear is oriented toward the grandiose order of the style of the masters.[319]

Louis Laloy described Magnard's work as "one of the leading compositions of the neo-classic school, perhaps its masterwork." His assessment, with its typical Gallic spin, resembled Dukas's:

> Quite modern in its compact and concise writing, it is at the same time—and above all—classical in the construction of the movements, in the nature of the ideas which express deep but general feelings, and finally in the color of the orchestra, which is solidly built upon the strings and disdains these timbral effects which have overrun symphonic music since Wagner. Through all these characteristics, the art of M. Magnard rejoins itself directly to Beethoven; and yet the style is quite French because it is precise, concentrated, compact within itself, and powerfully rhythmic.[320]

Laloy's good will toward Magnard's music soon evaporated. A close friend of Debussy, he became a fierce opponent of the symphony genre once the battle between the *debussystes* and *d'indystes* was joined; and as the putative emblematic composer of "neo-classic" (i.e., tradition-laden) music, Magnard became a choice target. (Debussy's disciples generally made little distinction between "classical" and "romantic" symphonies; although they preferred the former if pressed, they generally opposed the genre in all forms.) Some critics disliked the Third Symphony from the start. Amadée Boutarel complained about the "overzealous proselytes" who applauded Magnard's work, and he paid the composer a backhanded compliment which showed that conservative (non-*franckiste*) opposition to the symphony remained alive and well: "Magnard's symphony represents an earnest effort—which its success has repaid in full—to attain and realize polyphonic beauty in a genre that perhaps we must not encourage too much."[321] In 1902 the composer published the symphony at his own expense through a small communist printer.

The Société des Concerts du Conservatoire added the Third Symphony to its programs in January and November 1906, and again it received a positive reception. The symphony did not reappear in Paris until after Magnard's death, but it received numerous performances in other French venues (Nancy, Lyon, Bordeaux, Marseilles) as well as in Belgium (Brussels, Liège), the Netherlands (Amsterdam), and Switzerland (Lausanne, Neuchâtel). In 1905, at the invitation of Ferruccio Busoni, Magnard conducted the symphony in Berlin (to an unfavorable reception); he declined an offer to do the same in Moscow.

SYMPHONY NO. 4 IN C-SHARP MINOR OPUS 21

Magnard's last symphony ranks with the opera *Bérénice* (1911) as his masterpiece. Written between January 1912 and April 1913, it supposedly expressed "optimism" (without further elaboration), but the labor expended on its creation severely tested Magnard's spirits:

> Its optimism is repellent – and comical; no work gave me as much difficulty as this one or was conceived in a more completely depressed state. I thought I would never finish it.[322]

Carraud asserted that all of Magnard's mature compositions, and this one in particular, carried the implicit message of searching for artistic beauty, which symbolized a quest for the higher social beauties of truth and justice.[323] While Magnard did not express such a view himself, he certainly endorsed it in works by others—Ropartz's Third Symphony, for example ("a beautiful work, strongly original in conception and execution").[324]

The Fourth Symphony is more strongly cyclic than its predecessor, for Magnard writes it

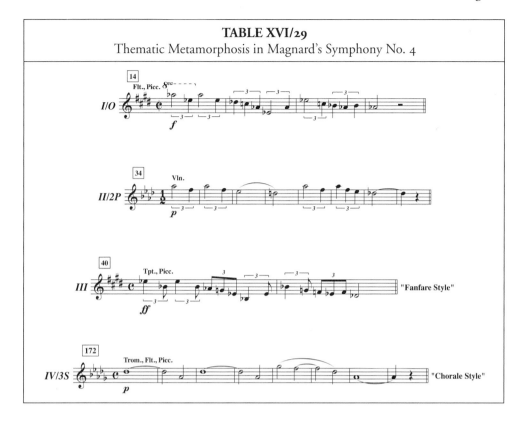

TABLE XVI/29
Thematic Metamorphosis in Magnard's Symphony No. 4

around a short motto apparently designed to convey optimism (Table XVI/29, [1]). Harmonically and melodically firm, it outlines a major triad and maintains that configuration in the midst of dark and occasionally violent passages, as if to assert the power of light over any situation. Magnard derives at least one theme in each movement from this motto. To unify the work further, the composer has the last three movements follow each other without interruption.

If, as Laloy and others said, Magnard's Third Symphony could trace its spiritual ancestry to Beethoven, the same holds true even more for the Fourth. As in Dukas's Symphony in C, the dramatic treatment of sonata-allegro form in the outer movements, vigorous motivic development, and intensified recapitulations with thematic expansions betray the influence of the Bonn master; other "Beethovenian" touches include the energetic and incisive rhythms at play throughout. As before, French folk idioms intermix with the prevailing Germanic language. One also finds traces of d'Indyist style: triplet rhythms, motivic "stretching," a preference for large upward leaps, and chromatic flourishes. Several melodies, especially *I/S* and *II/2P,* resemble themes from d'Indy's *La Mort de Wallenstein* (as did the cyclic chorale of the Third Symphony), though Magnard does not directly derive any material from d'Indy. Meters based on the breve, keys of multiple sharps or flats, continuous counterpoint, and a fugue in the Finale constitute the "learned" aspects of this piece.

Magnard sets his last two symphonies in hermetic keys—B-flat minor and C-sharp minor. In both cases, the underlying tonal foundations remain relatively stable, but in the

Fourth Magnard produces considerable foreground ambiguity through movements of steps and half-steps, constant modulation within themes, enharmonicism, abrupt shifts of mode, and harmonic borrowings from the parallel key. The bass often rides the fifth of the harmony or is dissonant to the prevailing key; for example, the opening motive of the symphony is in C-sharp minor while the bass remains on D-sharp (such passages also appear to a lesser extent in the Third Symphony). In addition, Magnard is partial to dominant substitutes, especially secondary dominants. He orchestrates with much more color and transparency than before; woodwinds and lower strings receive particularly sensitive treatment.

The Fourth Symphony opens with a concise sonata-allegro that features sharp dichotomies between dramatic and lyrical themes (Modéré, C-sharp minor); textures, tempi, and meters fluctuate constantly. A striking chromatic scalar flourish in middle and upper woodwinds leads to the first of three introductory motives (Plate B28). *X* appears in the strings against broken-chord sixteenths in the woodwinds and triplets in the horns. *Y,* a rising arpeggio, is given, Wagner-like, to the trombones and serves a modulatory function (m.8). Finally, the flute and piccolo introduce *O,* the cyclic motto, securely in the enharmonic dominant A-flat major (m.14). Varied repetitions of *x* and *y* lead to the exposition.

P, notated ¢ (12/8), derives from *x* (m.37). An extended and spirited theme in C-sharp minor moving in relentless triplet and trochaic patterns, it begins in the horns and lower woodwinds and ends in the strings (Example XVI/40). A short d'Indy-like motive in the trumpet, *T* sets up the secondary dominant D-sharp major (m.59). Instead of G-sharp, however, Magnard goes to the more conventional E major (III) for *S,* which enters abruptly in 3/2 meter (m.65). *K* returns to *alla breve.* Based on *P, 1K* is modulatory but *2K* returns to E major and closes the exposition without a repeat (mm.85, 91).

As in the Third Symphony, the development consists of restatements rather than fragmentation. *P* is heard in B minor and G minor (m.103). *T* proceeds in various timbres through the circle of fifths (E major–A minor–D minor) over the rhythm of *P* (m.122). *O* suddenly appears in the subdominant major (F-sharp major) against whole-tone flourishes and a pedal on G-sharp (m.139). *S* follows in the same key but without the whole tones (m.144). Modulatory reprises of *1K,* some in stretto with *y* (m.154), lead to the retransition, a series of intensified statements of *x* (m.171).

The recapitulation includes rescorings and new countermotives. *P* returns in the tonic C-sharp minor (m.195), *T* in the dominant, and *S* in the tonic major. *1K* again is modulatory but *2K,* in extended form, returns to the tonic major. The expressive coda remains in C-sharp major (Sonore, m.279): *x* sounds in augmentation over the propulsive rhythm of *P;* fragments of *S* lead to a quiet and peaceful statement of *O,* ending with a 6–5/4–3 appoggiatura. Having appeared at the beginning, midpoint, and conclusion, *O* thus forms a kind of arch within the movement.

The perpetual energy of the Scherzo (*Vif*), reflected by its unusual 1/2 meter (with occasional interjections of 3/4), recalls the rough spirit of the Scherzo of Beethoven's Ninth Symphony. The composer combines Scherzo and Trio with sonatina form: the first statement of both sections functions as the exposition (the Trio representing the secondary area), and he reprises both in the manner of a recapitulation. As is his habit, Magnard evokes popular rural idioms, especially in the Trio. The composer's gift at orchestration manifests itself particularly well in this movement.

The Scherzo contains four themes. *1P* moves skittishly through various timbres as it progresses from the tonic F minor to the minor dominant (throughout the movement, the dominant appears only in the minor). The next themes are tonally vague. *2P* turns *II/Oa* into a sustained violin melody, again of d'Indyist cast (m.34; Table XVI/29, [2]). A brief reprise of

EXAMPLE XVI/40   Magnard. Symphony No. 4/1, mm.38–41.

1P for the woodwind choir leads to *3P,* based on the rising thirds of *I/y* and featuring jerky tetrachord ascents in the strings (m.101). Finally, *4P* complements *2P* by transforming the second half of *I/O,* more or less in F major (m.148). Magnard bridges the Scherzo and Trio by trading an A-natural among various string and woodwind timbres in the manner of *Klang-farbenmelodie* (m.155; Example XVI/41a).

Borrowing its keys from the parallel major, the Trio returns us to the world of the French peasant. It has two closely connected themes. *1S* (m.171) is in A minor (mediant of F major) with inflections of A-phrygian. A solo violin plays in folk-fiddling style, alternating the notes of the theme with a pedal E; it is accompanied by drones and supporting patterns in a solo second violin and cello, *tutti* violas (pizzicato), and double basses, as well as by occasional interjections by solo bassoon and harp (Example XVI/41b). A playful motive, *2S* appears in a solo oboe in B-flat major (m.187). *1S* returns in the full string body and *2S,* following suit, appears in all the woodwinds; both themes retain their keys. An unexpected turn to C minor leads to the reprise of the Scherzo (m.254).

Magnard shortens the recapitulation of both sections and omits the *Klangfarben* transition, saving it for the end of the Trio. *1S* appears in straight quarter notes in F minor in a solo bassoon and horn, with drones in the other bassoons and horns and a solo string quartet (m.408). *2S* answers with the solo oboe over woodwind pedals. The *Klangfarben*-transition closes the Trio, this time on A-flat rather than A-natural; with this passage Magnard pivots into the next movement.

The slow movement (Sans lenteur et nuancé) is the emotional heart of the symphony. To achieve a cathartic transformation of mood from dark to light, Magnard calls upon the art of Wagner and Richard Strauss. He opens the movement with a striking passage in the strings that pits G-sharp against G-natural and produces a dissonance which, *Tristan*-like, achieves resolution only in the closing bars (Example XVI/42); and he devotes much of the movement to an expressive melody that conspicuously resembles (but is not related to) the "Transfiguration" theme of Strauss's *Tod und Verklärung.* Consistent with its rhetorical function, the movement abounds with nuances in scoring, phrasing, articulation, and dynamics. The form is a hybrid of arch form, variations, and rondo, best understood as *A–B–C–B'–A';* each section has a different texture and ends with a slow meditative transition (Table XVI/30). The transition sets up the key of the following section, but the section begins by switching to the parallel mode of that key. Until the final *A',* most themes remain tonally indefinite, sometimes suggesting several at once: the reprise of *I/O* in *B* and *B',* for instance, could be labeled in two different keys separated by a step. Despite interior uncertainties, the movement begins and ends solidly in E major.

After the opening dissonance (*1A*), the section continues with *2A,* an extended violin melody in the tonic; an incipient form of *3A* accompanies in the cellos (m.5). *3A,* the pseudo-Straussian theme, reaches full bloom in the clarinet in mediant key of G major (m.17; Example XVI/43a–b). A short transition to B major sets up the next section. Beginning ominously with a modal shift to B minor, *B* consists of a sharply drawn dotted-rhythm theme in the

EXAMPLE XVI/41A   Magnard. Symphony No. 4/2, mm.155–70.

lower strings and winds against a mosaic of scalar flourishes, whole-tone passages, trills, and oscillating figures (m.35). *I/O* bursts forth like a fanfare in the brass and upper woodwinds; Magnard alters pitches and accompaniment so that the motive dually implies E-flat major and D-flat major (m.40; Table XVI/29, [3]); runs continue in the other instruments. Another transition returns us to E major (m.47).

C (Chantant, m.57) both varies *A* and contrasts with it. The meter changes from the

EXAMPLE XVI/41B   Magnard. Symphony No. 4/2, mm.171–84.

previous 4/4 to 9/8 and the key (briefly) to E minor. The texture becomes a complex swirl of pointillistic woodwind trills and miniature runs or weak-beat interjections in other instruments; sustained but syncopated versions of *1A* and *2A* form a continuous line in the violas and cellos. *3A* (m.70) passes to the flutes in octaves; implying both E-flat major and C minor, it is underpinned by a bass pedal on G. The transition, based on *2A*, ends on G major (m.80).

For *B'* (which begins, as expected, in G minor), Magnard inverts the scoring, placing the theme in the woodwinds and the trills and oscillating chords in the strings (m.89). *I/O,* in the trombones, appears even more brilliantly with trumpet calls and scalar flourishes in

EXAMPLE XVI/42 Magnard. Symphony No. 4/3, mm.1–4 (strings only).

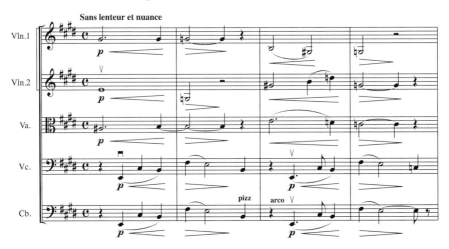

the strings (m.96); this time the key wavers between B major and A major. The transition features fragments of *3A* in E minor (m.103).

A' returns, firmly in E major (m.113). Magnard reorchestrates its themes and enriches the texture with frequent cross-rhythms and accompanimental gestures from *C*. Wagnerian-style surges lead to *I/O* in the woodwinds, followed by a passionate statement of *3A* (with an especially Straussian harmonization) in the violins over an E pedal (m.155). This climactic moment marks the triumph of "optimism." As if to affirm the victory, the closing measures (mm.167–72) resolve the harmonic dissonance introduced at the beginning of the movement, ending on a tonic chord with 9–8 suspension. The Finale follows immediately.

The Finale (Animé) possesses the frenetic vigor of the first movement but channels it into jovial and even witty fare. Another sonata-allegro, its themes reveal a progressive rhythmic lengthening: kinetic triplet energy characterizes *P* while *1S* moves mostly in eighth notes, *2S* in longer notes, and *3S* almost exclusively in white notes. Deepening the similitude between the two movements, the Finale opens with an ascending scalar flourish in the strings, reminiscent of the wind runs that began the symphony. *IV/P*, sharing the spirit of *II/P*, moves in jaunty rhythms of triplets and trochees marked in an unconventional meter of 3/2 18/8. The theme has three subsections: *Pa*, in C-sharp minor; *Pb* (m.5), in B major (V/III), marked by humorous grace notes; and *Pc* (m.9), back in C-sharp minor (Example XVI/44). Without transition, Magnard passes to *S:* where *P* is extroverted, *S* (in 2/2) becomes more introspective and lyrical. Like *P, S* divides threefold but this time the sections form distinct themes rooted around the third-related tonic A. *1S* conjures up a spirited and rather rustic-sounding mood in A major (m.16). *2S* switches to the parallel minor to present a more sober and expressive chorale-like melody accompanied by a chromatic ascending bass (m.25). *3S*, another augmented transformation of *I/O* in A major, approaches chorale style even more (m.45; Table XVI/29, [4]). Again omitting any transitional functions, Magnard proceeds to the development.

Save for one brief passage, the development (m.65) works exclusively with *P*. Its centerpiece is a whimsical fugue based on *Pb*. The subject retains the breezy spirit of the original motive—its opening octave leap, triplet motion, and ornamented repeated notes. The first

TABLE XVI/30
Albéric Magnard. Symphony No. 4/3: Structure

A							
1A			*2A*	*3A* ("Transfiguration")	trans.		
E minor (with harmonic dissonance)			E major	G major	mod. to B major		
1			5	17	32		

B							
B		*I/O*		trans.			
B minor → B-flat major		E-flat major, D-flat major		mod. to E major			
35		40		47			

C (variation of A)							
1A'	*2A'*	*3A'*		trans. (*2A*)			
E minor mod.	mod.	E-flat major, C minor		mod. to G major			
57	61	70		80			

B'							
B	*I/O*		trans. (*3A*)				
G minor	B major, A major		E minor				
89	96		103				

A'							
1A"	*2A"*	*3A"*	trans.	*I/O*	*3A* ("Transfiguration")	*1A* (opening dissonance resolved)	
E major							
113	117	125	134	148	155	167	

exposition, in C major, belongs to the strings (m.72). The modulatory first episode introduces an equally bouncy countersubject to be played *alla zingarese* (m.84). The second exposition continues the "gypsy style," with the subject in the horns and flutes (m.89). Episode two varies episode one (m.95). The final exposition places the subject in augmentation in the trumpets, which play it in F major (m.100). The fugue abruptly ends with the return of *Pc* in F minor (m.106). A brief modulatory transition leads to a stretto of *1Sa,* the part of *S* that most resembles *P* (m.112). A last statement of *Pbx* in augmentation in the trombones in D major (Neapolitan of C-sharp) leads to the retransition, an expansion of the flourish from the opening measure of the movement (m.123).

The recapitulation begins with *P* in the tonic (m.127); *Pb* is in the secondary dominant

EXAMPLE XVI/43A   Magnard. Symphony No. 4/3, mm.17–20.

EXAMPLE XVI/43B   Richard Strauss. *Tod und Verklärung,* mm.432–36 ("Transfiguration" theme).

D-sharp major against a pedal on C-sharp. *Pc* returns to the tonic, while *1S* switches to the parallel major (m.143). Beginning in a "celestial mode," *3S* (m. 172) swells into a grand peroration for full orchestra (m.186; Example XVI/45). Consisting almost entirely of white notes, this passage imitates the structure and harmonization of a Bach chorale; unlike d'Indy's Second and Magnard's own Third Symphonies, it neither recalls nor transforms cyclic material but simply fulfills the implications of this motive raised in the exposition. This effective peroration affirms definitively the victory wrought at the end of the previous movement. The tonic changes at this point from C-sharp major to the softer D-flat.

The symphony moves quickly to its end. The low trombones state *Pa* in augmentation, accompanied by itself in normal form in the violins and upper woodwinds (m.214). Over a G-flat pedal triad, a moving transformation of *2S* spiced with poignant accidentals reminds us that victory has come at a price (m.222). Finally the strings and woodwinds intone *I/O* in prime form in D-flat major, and the work ends serenely on a tonic cadence with an ascending 2–3 appoggiatura in the trombone (as opposed to the descending one at the end of the first movement). So ends one of the most effective and accomplished symphonies of the French school, a work that, like most of Magnard's music, deserves far wider exposure.

A committed feminist, Magnard dedicated the Fourth Symphony to a women's orchestra, the Union des Femmes Professeurs et Compositeurs, which premiered it under his direction in April 1914. The debut went badly: the orchestra struggled with the score, and the composer's baton inexperience betrayed him. Blaming the performers and ignoring his own failures, Magnard raged to Ropartz, who had been unable to attend:

> Thank you for your kind word. The first performance of my symphony was pitiful and I prefer it that you weren't there.
>
> Won over by the marvelous interpretation these ladies gave to the *Hymne à la justice* in 1911, I had promised them a more important work. I kept my promise. I was wrong. I won't make the same mistake again and this all proves once again that you mustn't dedicate music to instrumentalists.[325]

Despite Magnard's disgruntlement, the audience (which included d'Indy, Lalo, Carraud, and Milhaud) welcomed the new work. Carraud exulted: "Never has his rhythm been so incisive, his tone so energetically impassioned, his imagination so robust; never has he

EXAMPLE XVI/44   Magnard. Symphony No. 4/4, mm.2–4, 5–7, 9–10.

lifted himself so naturally to the summits."[326] Henri Quittard in *Le Figaro* pointed out Magnard's originality in daring to write a symphony that pretended that the nearly two-decade-old Debussyist revolution had not existed.[327] D'Indy, for his part, spoke glowingly of this "truly very beautiful music."[328]

The Société Nationale played the Fourth Symphony the following month under the noted conductor Rhené-Baton with much better aural results. The critical reaction, however, was more ambivalent: as before, many reviewers praised the work, but Debussyist protests also surfaced. Speaking on behalf of those voices Magnard supposedly ignored (according to Quittard), the critic for *Paris-Midi* damned Magnard's symphony and the entire culture of the Société Nationale in provocatively militant terms:

> We are in the atmosphere of a study hall where one labors over manuscript paper as if on a bench, where one works out compositions that have neither charm nor freedom, where imagination is suspect and where one seeks only two dimensions: loftiness and profundity. You know this type of so-called "lofty" music, which generally extends to the boundaries of boredom. . . . You know that state of mind of these young musicians who have been born reactionary and have thought as wise old men since they reached the age of reason. They are cautious, fearful, enemies of novelty and respecters of hierarchies. Instinctively, they assemble and form battalions. We have seen one of these squads in action this afternoon. It is led by an experienced veteran, a recruitment sergeant accompanies him, and soldiers of all ages mark time there.[329]

In a more tempered response, Charles Tenroc wrote that the work had many beauties, especially in the inner movements, and presented a satisfactory combination of virtue and fault: "The composer, whose sincere art encloses him in an ivory tower that merits all respect, possesses a majestic gift for sound, an intransigent will, a remarkable facility for associating ideas, an ampleness and a rhythmic fertility that compels attention—and sometimes also a grandiloquence that produces fatigue."[330] But most agreed with Ropartz's appraisal: "Never has his music so burst with ideas, rhythms, [and] expression; never has it sung with such inspiration, never clothed itself with such vibrant colors. This symphony remains the most accomplished of all his instrumental works."[331] Magnard's *mort heroïque* five months after the premiere renewed interest in his music, and the Fourth Symphony was heard with some regularity in the post-war years. Milhaud especially admired it: on at least one occasion, when a performance was to be broadcast on the radio, he invited friends to come and share the experience.[332]

EXAMPLE XVI/45   Magnard. Symphony No. 4/4, mm.186–201 (chorale).

Conclusion

We begin this conclusion with a few words about a major work not covered in this chapter—Debussy's *La Mer* (1905), which is occasionally described (usually to the detriment of the works studied here) as the greatest French symphony. Despite Debussy's oft-expressed disdain for the genre, his musical seascape employs procedures recognized by contemporary aestheticians as essentially symphonic: a unified structure, both in terms of cyclic organization and of oneness of character between the three movements; a relatively coherent tonal structure (loosely following the trajectory D-flat–E–D-flat, with E serving as a flattened mediant); and the Finale as the summation of the work.[333] To the joy of some and discomfiture of many

EXAMPLE XVI/45   *(continued)*

others, listeners found *La Mer* a more "developed" work than they expected from Debussy. His own thoughts on the work were characteristically elusive: he entitled *La Mer* "three symphonic sketches" but also spoke of it as "ma symphonie"; and he insisted that, unlike his earlier orchestral triptych *Nocturnes,* it should be performed only *in toto.*[334]

Despite its semblances to a symphony, aestheticians of Debussy's day most likely would have categorized *La Mer* as a *voisin-symphonie* or "pseudo-symphony"—Conservatoire theorist Albert Lavignac's term for works that strayed too far from structural and stylistic norms.[335] The thematic material is much "looser" than customary, consisting mostly of short motives and arabesques that continually evolve into other motives; and the movements do not follow traditional symphonic structures, though Debussy does allude to them as they help illustrate the movement titles. "De l'aube à midi sur la mer," described by some as an irregular sonata, proceeds by continual growth toward the climax, mirroring the progression from dawn to noon on the sea. The fast, continuous and unpredictable motivic evolutions in "Jeux de vagues," an even more irregular Scherzo, suggest the overlapping billows and constant mutations of the watery surface (and a Scherzo of course is appropriate for a piece depicting the *play* of waves). In the last movement, "Dialogue du vent et de la mer," a rondo-like alternation of two thematic blocks makes the exchanges between wind and sea musically apparent. Theorists defined a symphonic poem as a work in which the content determined the form, thus permitting the composer to omit recapitulations, create ambiguous forms, work with "unsymphonic" themes, and avoid traditional development with impunity. To that end, Debussy's friend Louis Laloy, in a reading the composer did not contest, described *La Mer* as a symphonic poem in the shape of a symphony.[336]

Whether or not one hears *La Mer* as a symphony is ultimately up to each listener to decide. But Laloy's description of the work as a multi-movement tone poem in symphonic form suggests a category worth considering. As we have seen, descriptive *suites d'orchestre* such as Saint-Saëns's *Suite algérienne,* Jules Massenet's *Scènes pittoresques,* and Gustave Charpentier's *Impressions d'Italie*—not to mention concert suites extracted from stage works like Bizet's *L'Arlésienne* and Lalo's *Namouna*—were popular with composers and audiences in nineteenth-century France (recall that Bizet's publisher first designated *Roma* as a *suite de concert* rather than the more austere *symphonie*). Toward the end of the century, musicians sought to create multi-movement works that avoided certain "demands" (especially structural) of symphonic convention yet embraced its possibilities of cohesiveness. They found a fruitful model in the "symphonic suite," a term coined by Rimsky-Korsakov for *Antar* and *Sheherazade.* This genre stands as a hybrid between symphony and picturesque concert suite: symphonic suites consisted of three or four *integrated and non-detachable* movements, whereas those of the suite generally eschewed standard symphonic forms and were unified only in their suggestive titles. Symphonic suites thus combined the descriptiveness and structural liberty of symphonic poems and suites with the unity and internal logic of a symphony— all of which *La Mer* possesses to various degrees. By this measure, then, we might consider *La Mer* the finest example of a *suite symphonique;* other noteworthy examples include d'Indy's *Jour d'été à la montagne* (1905) and Albert Roussel's *Évocations* (1911).[337]

Except for Bizet's youthful work, Franck's mature one, and Saint-Saëns's "Organ," none of the symphonies covered in this chapter are repertory staples, especially compared to *La Mer,* though Chausson's, Dukas's, and d'Indy's *Mountain Air* make occasional appearances. Recordings have rightly granted many symphonies, especially Magnard's, a new—or, in the case of Tournemire's later symphonies, a first—lease on life. Indeed, as of February 2006, most of the compositions considered in this study have been preserved on commercial disc. (Exceptions include the symphonies of Dubois and Gedalge, as well as Ropartz's Second and Fifth, although a recorded survey of the latter's complete symphonies is currently in progress.)

As this survey has demonstrated, the symphony occupied a prominent and vibrant role in French musical culture in the second half of the nineteenth century and first decades of the twentieth. Later writers, especially from Britain, have tended (following the Debussyists) to disparage French symphonists as incompetent creators of sterile works.[338] In truth, they created a wide variety of symphonies in various forms and styles; in no way was the French symphony merely a pale imitation of Germanic models. While most composers (Tournemire excepted) remained faithful to the traditional tenets of symphonic writing, they granted themselves considerable freedom to reinterpret the structure of the whole as well as of individual movements. Some followed Saint-Saëns and combined separate movements into a continuous division; others like Franck embedded one movement into another; and yet others like d'Indy and Magnard crafted hybrid movements which combined several different forms. Further, there is the preference among *franckistes* for symphonies of three movements. French composers of various camps explored the possibilities of cyclic unity with varying degrees of rigor. And after 1900, they even created a new and uniquely French symphony in which a composer could express his or her personal ideological convictions. By the beginning of World War I, composers like Magnard, and Dukas to a lesser extent, had become revolutionaries of a sort for stubbornly (and successfully) continuing to find new things to say in the Beethovenian symphony at a time when most of their colleagues had turned away from Romanticism toward Debussy, Stravinsky, and Schoenberg.

Bibliographic Overview

There are no comprehensive studies of the symphony in France. The most useful is Locke/FRENCH, a clear and concise introduction to the genre *ca.* 1830 to 1910, excluding Berlioz. Davies/SYMPHONY FRANCE encompasses a wider period (Gossec to Dutilleux) but is hobbled by factual errors and at times a patronizing attitude toward many of the works. Cooper/FRENCH provides a helpful overview in English for French music between 1870 and 1920, but also suffers from a Germanic bias. Dufourcq/MUSIQUE covers the entire history of French music so the discussions of individual composers and works are necessarily brief.

Cooper/RISE, Bernard/PASDELOUP, Strasser/ARS GALLICA, Fauser/ORCHESTER-GESANG, and Holoman/SOCIÉTÉ provide important information on the performing institutions in which the symphony flourished. Cooper considers the state of instrumental music in Paris before the Franco-Prussian War; Bernard the career of Jules Pasdeloup, the most prominent conductor of the Second Empire; Strasser the early years of the Société Nationale; and Fauser the concert societies at the turn of the century. Holoman's history of the long-lasting and influential Conservatoire orchestra (which gave the first performance of Franck's Symphony in D minor, among others) unfortunately appeared too recently to be consulted for this study. Ropartz/SYMPHONIES and Tiersot/SYMPHONIE are short but important articles that examine nineteenth-century French symphonies from a period perspective (1891, 1902). Servières/SYMPHONIE covers the same material at a slightly later date (1923).

Fulcher/CULTURAL examines the fierce aesthetic battles that in one way or another affected the work and reception of most composers and genres in the years between the end of the Dreyfus Affair and World War I (1900–1914). Hart/SYMPHONY focuses specifically on this genre during the same period from several perspectives: the ways in which it was taught, the arguments musicians advanced for and against the genre, the kinds of symphonies written, and government support for the symphony. Hart/WAGNER examines the influence that the German composer had on the development of the *franckiste* symphony, especially the message-symphony. Vuillermoz/SYMPHONIE provides an example of the "politicization" of the symphony in the early twentieth century, as the author discusses the genre and its composers from a Debussyist and republican perspective: he describes the symphony as "an acquiescence to social order" supported principally by "partisans of authority" (p. 324).

No composer has an entire book devoted to his symphonies; at most they rate a short article or a passage in a biography. Hughes/GOUNOD examines his two symphonies;

biographies, including the composer's autobiography, mention only their composition history and reception. Shanet/BIZET examines the correlations between Bizet's Symphony in C major and Gounod's First Symphony; Curtiss/BIZET and especially Dean/BIZET (excellent biographies both) consider the work in some detail. By far the most important source for Saint-Saëns's symphonies is Fallon/SYMPHONIES, a thorough analysis of each symphony and each symphonic poem; as an unpublished dissertation, its access is unfortunately limited. Baumann/SAINT-SAËNS of 1905 studies Saint-Saëns's works from a much more affective angle. None of the composer's biographies engage the works beyond generalities; the most important are Bonnerot/SAINT-SAËNS (essential because of the author's personal access to the composer) and, more recently, by Studd. Lalo/CORRESPONDANCE reveals this composer's frustrations pursuing instrumental music in a hostile environment. Servières/LALO discusses his Symphony in G minor; Macdonald/FIESQUE explains which parts of the symphony are recycled from a discarded opera. Macdonald/LALO provides the best introduction to the composer in English.

Despite its canonic status as one of the most performed of all French works, few worthwhile studies of Franck's Symphony in D minor exist. The best source, Fauquet/FRANCK, provides invaluable documentary information but does not include analyses. Fauquet's edition of Franck's correspondence reveals little about the composer's thoughts on his works, including the symphony. The biographies tend to concentrate on its performance history and gloss over the music with subjective comments: for example, Davies/FRANCK stresses its faults, while d'Indy/FRANCK exaggerates its virtues.

In contrast Vallas/D'INDY discusses every major work; a close friend of d'Indy, Vallas's two-volume life-and-works is the essential source on this composer. D'Indy/VIE, an extensive edition of the composer's diary and selected letters preserved at the family château Les Faugs, offers rich insights into the man but unfortunately very little on the symphonies except for the *Sinfonia brevis* and the unpublished *Symphonie italienne*. On the other hand, in d'Indy/SYMPHONIE the composer gives a detailed analysis of his *Symphony on a French Mountain Air* and a shorter analysis of his Second Symphony. Thomson/D'INDY makes important contributions to the composer's biography but the discussion of the music is perfunctory. Hart/D'INDY traces the composer's influence on the development of the symphony in France, through his own works and also those of his pupils Magnard, Roussel, and Honegger. Two forthcoming books, Schwartz/D'INDY and Michel/D'INDY, feature articles based on papers given at conferences commemorating d'Indy's sesquicentennial in 2001.

The principal biographies of Chausson—by Barricelli, Grover, and especially Gallois—all contribute vital information on the composer and his music. Chausson/ÉCRITS reveals much about the composer's creative struggles, including his frustrations over the composition of the Symphony in B-flat major. Georges Favre has done the most extensive research to date on Dukas: Favre/DUKAS is a short biography; Favre/OEUVRE is devoted to the music; and his edition of the composer's letters is found in Dukas/CORRESPONDANCE. Ropartz/DUKAS contributes additional insights from a contemporary. Dukas was a prominent critic in turn-of-the-century France, and selected articles are reprinted in Dukas/ÉCRITS, including reviews of some symphonies. The best and virtually only source on Dukas in English is Schwartz/DUKAS.

Carraud/VIE and Perret/MAGNARD are the definitive studies on Magnard; the latter includes analyses of each of the composer's works by Harry Halbreich. In addition, Magnard/CORRESPONDANCE provides a fascinating picture of the man himself.

Maillard/MAGNARD and Maillard/ROPARTZ offer brief sketches of each symphony of the two composers (with thematic incipits); Maillard's presentation formed part of a symposium on *fin-de-siècle* French musicians, and transcripts of the papers and round-table discussions appear throughout the volume, e.g., in Boursiac/ROMANTISME. The most important biographies of Ropartz are by Lamy and Kornprobst. Ropartz wrote poetry as well, and Djemil/ROPARTZ discusses his literary work as it relates to his music in works like the Third Symphony. The most extensive discussion of Charles Tournemire's symphonies appears in Petit/INTRODUCTION; the catalog in Fauquet/TOURNEMIRE reprints the poetic descriptions the composer wrote to explain the messages of his symphonies. By far the best source on Widor is Near/WIDOR, although its concern is biography rather than analysis.

Debussy's writings are collected in Debussy/CROCHE; the English version of this volume (*Debussy on Music*) sometimes has imprecise translations but includes material not in the original French edition. Debussy referred to the symphony many times in his articles and letters, almost always abusively. Hart/DEBUSSY summarizes the composer's attitude toward the genre and its influence on his own works, especially *La Mer.*

Appendix: The Symphonic Repertoire Volume III Part A Contents

Notes

XIV. THE SYMPHONY IN GREAT BRITAIN

1. Foster/PHILHARMONIC SOCIETY LONDON, p. 4.
2. Elkin/ROYAL PHILHARMONIC, p. 12.
3. Foster/PHILHARMONIC SOCIETY LONDON, p. 8.
4. Ehrlich/PHILHARMONIC SOCIETY LONDON, p. 4.
5. Foster/PHILHARMONIC SOCIETY LONDON.
6. See Craig/BEETHOVEN. Tables 2 and 3 document the number of Philharmonic Society performances of Beethoven's works.
7. Willetts/BEETHOVEN England, p. 47.
8. Foster/PHILHARMONIC SOCIETY LONDON, p. 73.
9. See Jacobs/SPOHR BATON.
10. Foster/PHILHARMONIC SOCIETY LONDON, pp. 45, 50, 109, 131, 159, 160, 173, 197, and 206.
11. Foster/PHILHARMONIC SOCIETY LONDON, p. 93.
12. See Cooper/ITALIAN and Cooper/ZWEIFEL.
13. Slonimsky/BAKER'S, p. 1513.
14. Mackeson/SOCIETY MUSICIANS, p. 492.
15. Scholes/MIRROR MUSIC I, p. 24; see also Bennett/STERNDALE BENNETT LIFE, p. 37, and Davison/MENDELSSOHN TO WAGNER, p. 56.
16. See Bennett/STERNDALE BENNETT LIFE, p. 37.
17. Slonimsky/BAKER'S, p. 269.
18. See Peter/POTTER II, pp. 218–19.
19. Anderson/BEETHOVEN LETTERS II, p. 759. The interchangeability of names beginning with B and P is a Germanic characteristic at this time period.
20. Reprinted in Peter/POTTER II, pp. 43–47.
21. Sainsbury/DICTIONARY II, pp. 304–05.
22. Reprinted in Peter/POTTER II, pp. 48–64; quote p. 48.
23. For examples, see Chopin's piano concertos and the version with orchestral accompaniment of the *Grand Polonaise Brillante* Opus 22, as well as some Rossini overtures.
24. *HARM* IV (July 1826), p. 151.
25. Peter/POTTER I, pp. 260–63.
26. See Brown/FIRST GOLDEN AGE, pp. 294–95.
27. *Athenaeum* No. 972 (June 13, 1846), p. 612.
28. Peter/POTTER I, pp. 262–63.
29. *HARM* VII (July 1829), p. 175.
30. Peter/POTTER II, pp. 102–03 and British Library Loan 4/374.
31. Rushton/POTTER 10.
32. *HARM* XI (July 1833), p. 154.
33. Wagner/MY LIFE, pp. 521–22. See also Wagner/CONDUCTING, pp. 24–25.
34. *MW* XXXIII/22 (June 2, 1855), p. 347.
35. Reprinted in Peter/POTTER II, pp. 242–44.
36. Peter/POTTER II, p. 240.

37. Peter/POTTER II, pp. 243–44.
38. Peter/POTTER II, pp. 244–45.
39. Reprinted in Peter/POTTER II, p. 244.
40. Peter/POTTER II, p. 244.
41. Peter/POTTER II, p. 244.
42. *MW* I/2 (March 25, 1836), p. 27.
43. *Athenaeum* No. 439 (March 26, 1836), p. 228.
44. Peter/POTTER II, p. 105.
45. Peter/POTTER II, p. 239.
46. Peter/POTTER II, p. 239.
47. Peter/POTTER II, p. 240.
48. See Stanford/INTERLUDES, pp. 20–21.
49. Peter/POTTER II, p. 240.
50. Peter/POTTER II, p. 241.
51. Peter/POTTER II, p. 241.
52. *MW* XIX/25 (June 20, 1844), p. 206.
53. *Athenaeum* No. 1174 (April 27, 1850), p. 457.
54. *MW* XXV/17 (April 27, 1850), pp. 254–55.
55. *MW* XIX/25 (June 20, 1844), p. 206.
56. Williamson/BENNETT CatalogUE.
57. Williamson/BENNETT CatalogUE, pp. 442–44.
58. Temperley/BENNETT SYMPHONIES, p. xix.
59. Bennett/STERNDALE BENNETT LIFE, p. 26.
60. Bennett/STERNDALE BENNETT LIFE, p. 25.
61. Bennett/STERNDALE BENNETT LIFE, p. 455.
62. Macfarren/POTTER, pp. 48–49.
63. Temperley/BENNETT SYMPHONIES, p. xx.
64. See Mendelssohn Symphony No. 1/1 and Spohr Symphony No. 2/1.
65. Temperley/BENNETT SYMPHONIES, p. xxii.
66. Temperley/BENNETT SYMPHONIES, p. xxii.
67. *Athenaeum* No. 337 (January 17, 1835), p. 58.
68. Bennett/STERNDALE BENNETT LIFE, pp. 34–35.
69. Temperley/BENNETT SYMPHONIES, p. xxiii.
70. Temperley/BENNETT SYMPHONIES, p. xxiii.
71. Temperley/BENNETT SYMPHONIES, pp. xxvi–xxvii.
72. *Athenaeum* No. 433 (February 13, 1836), p. 132.
73. Bennett/STERNDALE BENNETT LIFE, pp. 41–42.
74. See Dörffel/GEWANDHAUS II, p. 8.
75. Davison/MENDELSSOHN TO WAGNER, pp. 30–32.
76. Bennett/STERNDALE BENNETT LIFE, p. 334.
77. Bennett/STERNDALE BENNETT LIFE, pp. 333–34.
78. Temperley/BENNETT SYMPHONIES, p. xxv.
79. Bennett/STERNDALE BENNETT LIFE, p. 334.
80. See Sage & Hickman/ROMANCE.
81. *PMG* as reprinted in *MW* XLV/29 (July 20, 1867), p. 482.
82. *MW* XLV/28 (July 13, 1867), p. 466.
83. Temperley/BENNETT SYMPHONIES, p. xxvi.
84. Bennett/STERNDALE BENNETT LIFE, p. 334.

85. Temperley/BENNETT SYMPHONIES, p. xvii.

86. Bennett/STERNDALE BENNETT LIFE, p. 334.

87. *AMZ* III/3 (January 18, 1865), col. 53.

88. *NZfM* LXI/5 (January 27, 1865), p. 40.

89. *MW* XLIII/18 (May 6, 1865), p. 277.

90. Shaw/MUSIC I, pp. 73–74.

91. See Temperley/SCHUMANN & BENNETT.

92. Schumann/MUSIC I, pp. 142–43.

93. Goodwin/LONDON, p. 195.

94. Davison/MENDELSSOHN TO WAGNER, p. 130.

95. Fuller-Maitland/COWEN, p. 631.

96. Slonimsky/BAKER'S, p. 1452.

97. Legge/CLIFFE, p. 558.

98. See Pupils/STANFORD and Rodmell/STANFORD, pp. 341–73.

99. Pupils/STANFORD, p. 202.

100. *MT* XX/434 (April 1, 1879), p. 206.

101. *Athenaeum* No. 2861 (March 15, 1879), p. 354.

102. Fuller-Maitland/PARRY & STANFORD, p. 39.

103. Scholes/MIRROR MUSIC I, pp. 224–25.

104. *Athenaeum* No. 2837 (March 11, 1882), pp. 324–25.

105. *MT* XXIII/470 (April 1, 1882), p. 211.

106. Stanford/FOLK-SONG.

107. See Stanford/FOLK-SONG, pp. 239–40.

108. Stanford/FOLK-SONG, pp. 239–40.

109. Porte/STANFORD, p. 34.

110. Porte/STANFORD, p. 35.

111. *The Times* (London), July 1, 1887, p. 4.

112. *MT* XXIX/539 (January 1, 1888), pp. 21–22.

113. Shaw/MUSIC I, p. 515.

114. Shaw/MUSIC II, pp. 876–83.

115. C.A.B. [Charles Ainslie Barry], Crystal Palace Program for February 23, 1889, p. 335.

116. Porte/STANFORD, p. 37.

117. Fuller-Maitland/PARRY & STANFORD, p. 40.

118. *Börsen Courier* (Berlin), as trans. in *MT* XXX/553 (March 1, 1889), p. 153.

119. *Berliner Reichsbote,* as trans. in *MT* XXX/553 (March 1, 1889), pp. 153–54.

120. *MT* XXX/553 (March 1, 1889), pp. 151–52.

121. A more detailed attempt to connect almost every line of the Milton to Stanford's music is offered in Rodmell/STANFORD, pp. 222–27.

122. *Athenaeum* No. 3517 (March 23, 1895), pp. 385–86.

123. *MT* XXXVI/626 (April 1, 1895), p. 233.

124. Porte/STANFORD, p. 56.

125. Fuller-Maitland/PARRY & STANFORD, p. 47.

126. Rodmell/STANFORD reproduces Watts's associated representations in plates 6–9.

127. Foreman/STANFORD 6.

128. Foreman/STANFORD 6.

129. Norris/STANFORD, pp. 557–58.

130. Greene/STANFORD, p. 278.

131. *MT* XLVII/815 (February 1, 1906), p. 121.

132. *Athenaeum* No. 4083 (January 27, 1906), p. 114.

133. Hudson/CATALOGUE STANFORD REV, p. 115.

134. See Chapter IX in Part A, p. 631.

135. *MT* LIII/830 (April 1, 1912), p. 257.

136. Norris/STANFORD, p. 575.

137. See Dibble/PARRY, pp. 299–300, Benoliel/PARRY, pp. 61–68, and Shaw/MUSIC II, p. 869.

138. Dibble/PARRY, p. 436.

139. Dibble/PARRY, p. 458.

140. Dibble/PARRY, p. 435.

141. Dibble/PARRY, pp. 160–61.

142. See Benoliel/PARRY, p. 41.

143. For some idea of the Crystal Palace repertoire, see Musgrave/CRYSTAL PALACE, pp. 222–29.

144. Dibble/PARRY, p. 201.

145. Dibble/PARRY, p. 201.

146. Benoliel/PARRY, pp. 44–45, and Dibble/PARRY, p. 202.

147. Benoliel/PARRY, pp. 44–45.

148. Dibble/PARRY, p. 201.

149. *Athenaeum* No. 2863 (September 9, 1882), p. 347.

150. *MT* XXIII/476 (October 1, 1882), pp. 536–37.

151. See the various reviews in *The Athenaeum* and *MT.*

152. *Athenaeum* No. 3111 (June 11, 1887), pp. 776–77.

153. Dibble/PARRY, p. 209.

154. See Dibble/PARRY, p. 212, and Brown/SECOND GOLDEN AGE, pp. 63–64.

155. Dibble/PARRY, p. 209.

156. *MT* XXIV/485 (July 1, 1883), p. 383.

157. *Athenaeum* No. 2904 (June 23, 1883), pp. 806–07.

158. *MT* XXVIII/533 (July 1, 1887), p. 409.

159. *Athenaeum* No. 3111 (June 11, 1887), pp. 776–77.

160. Dibble/PARRY, p. 276.

161. Dibble/PARRY, p. 276.

162. Dibble/PARRY, p. 515.

163. Fuller-Maitland/PARRY & STANFORD, p. 41.

164. *Athenaeum* No. 3214 (June 1, 1889), p. 703.

165. Benoliel/PARRY, p. 48.

166. Dibble/PARRY, p. 278.

167. Dibble/PARRY, p. 278, and Benoliel/PARRY, p. 48.

168. Benoliel/PARRY, p. 48.

169. Shaw/MUSIC I, p. 638.

170. *Athenaeum* No. 3214 (June 1, 1889), pp. 703–04.

171. Dibble/PARRY, pp. 279–80, 434–35.

172. Dibble/PARRY, p. 435.

173. Dibble/PARRY, p. 435.

174. *MT* XXX/558 (August 1, 1889), p. 473.

175. Dibble/PARRY, pp. 436–37.

176. Dibble/PARRY, pp. 436–37.

177. Dibble/PARRY, pp. 436–37.

178. Dibble/PARRY, p. 439.

179. Dibble/PARRY, p. 439.

180. See Russell/England II, pp. 227–29.

181. Dibble/PARRY, p. 440.

182. Dibble/PARRY, p. 440.

183. *Athenaeum* No. 3219 (July 6, 1889), p. 41.

184. *MMR* No. XIX/224 (August 1, 1889), p. 184, and *MT* XXX/558 (August 1, 1889), p. 473.

185. *MT* LI/805 (March 1, 1910), p. 167.

186. *Athenaeum* No. 4295 (February 19, 1910), p. 226.

187. Dibble/PARRY, p. 343.

188. Tovey/ESSAYS II, pp. 142–45.

189. Dibble/PARRY, p. 455.

190. *MT* LIV/839 (January 1, 1913), p. 38.

191. Dibble/PARRY, p. 466.

192. *MT* LIV/839 (January 1, 1913), p. 38.

193. *Athenaeum* No. 4442 (December 14, 1912), p. 738.

194. Parry/SYMPHONY, p.795.

195. Waite/ELGAR, PARRY, STANFORD, p. 178.

196. See Brown/GROVE.

197. Moore/ELGAR, pp. 60 and 80.

198. Moore/ELGAR, p. 480.

199. *MT* XL/673 (March 1, 1899), p. 161.

200. Moore/ELGAR, pp. 119–20.

201. Moore/ELGAR, p. 247.

202. Kennedy/ELGAR ORCHESTRAL, p. 53.

203. Reed/ELGAR, p. 97.

204. See Brown/SECOND GOLDEN AGE, pp. 10–11.

205. Young/ELGAR, pp. 191–92.

206. Anderson/ELGAR MANUSCRIPT, p. 97.

207. Reed/ELGAR KNEW, pp. 140–41.

208. Kennedy/ELGAR ORCHESTRAL, p. 54.

209. Moore/ELGAR, p. 532.

210. Kennedy/ELGAR ORCHESTRAL, p. 54.

211. Moore/ELGAR, p. 536.

212. Moore/ELGAR, p. 530.

213. Moore/ELGAR, p. 531.

214. Reed/ELGAR KNEW, pp. 140–41.

215. Dennison/ELGAR'S APPRENTICESHIP, pp. 32–33.

216. Anderson/ELGAR MANUSCRIPT, p. 97.

217. Moore/ELGAR, p. 538.

218. *Athenaeum* No. 4232 (December 5, 1908), p. 729, and see also No. 4233 (December 12, 1908), p. 769.

219. *MT* L/791 (January 1, 1909), p. 25.

220. *The Times* (London) December 8, 1908, p. 12.

221. *MT* XLIX/790 (December 1, 1908), pp. 778–80.

222. Reed/ELGAR, p. 105.

223. Kennedy/ELGAR, p. 200.
224. See Brown/FIRST GOLDEN AGE, p. 460.
225. See Tovey/ESSAYS II, p. 117.
226. Moore/ELGAR, p. 604.
227. Moore/ELGAR, p. 599.
228. Anderson/ELGAR MANUSCRIPT, p. 104.
229. Moore/ELGAR, p. 606.
230. Gimbel/ELGAR 2, p. 239.
231. Moore/ELGAR, p. 608.
232. See Gimbel/ELGAR 2, Kent/ELGAR 2, and Moore/ELGAR, pp. 594–617.
233. Tovey/ESSAYS II, pp. 114–21.
234. Anderson/ELGAR MANUSCRIPT, p. 107.
235. Moore/ELGAR, p. 606.
236. Reed/ELGAR KNEW, p. 107.
237. Anderson/ELGAR MANUSCRIPT, p. 107.
238. See Tennyson's poem "Maud."
239. Moore/ELGAR, p. 608. For the full quotation, p. 328.
240. Kent/ELGAR 2, p. 57.
241. Kent/ELGAR 2, p. 58.
242. Gimbel/ELGAR 2, p. 239.
243. *Athenaeum* No. 4361 (May 27, 1911), p. 610.
244. *The Times* (London), May 25, 1911, p. 10.
245. *MT* LII/820 (June 1, 1911), p. 381.
246. Moore/WINDFLOWER LETTERS, p. 63.
247. The documents below are based on Moore/ELGAR, pp. 795–818. Specific page numbers are cited for each quote in the text.
248. Moore/ELGAR, p. 819.
249. Payne/ELGAR 3, p. 13.
250. Moore/ELGAR, pp. 819–20.
251. Moore/ELGAR, p. 821.
252. Reed/ELGAR KNEW, p. 170.
253. Payne/ELGAR 3, p. 15.
254. Reed/ELGAR'S THIRD.
255. Payne/ELGAR 3, p. 3.
256. Payne/ELGAR 3, pp. 5, 25.
257. Payne/ELGAR 3, p. 35.
258. http://www.elgar.org/3symph3b.htm as of June 2003.

XV. THE SYMPHONY IN RUSSIA

1. For research on the music societies and the structure of public musical life in the first half of the nineteenth century, see in particular Petrovskaia/KONTSERTNAIA and Petrovskaia/MUZYKAL'NOE.
2. See Leonard/RUSSIAN MUSIC, pp. 28–32. For a more thorough treatment of this aspect, see Ritzarev & Porfireva/ITALIAN IN RUSSIA.
3. Abraham/USSR IX/i–iii, p. 381.
4. Druskin/LENINGRAD, p. 660.
5. Ridenour/19C RUSSIAN MUSIC, pp. 25–108.
6. Ridenour/19C RUSSIAN MUSIC, pp. 25–64.

7. See Taruskin/KUCHKA.

8. See Garden/BALAKIREV and Garden/BALAKIREV PERSONALITY.

9. See Ridenour/19C RUSSIAN MUSIC.

10. Ridenour/19C RUSSIAN MUSIC, pp. 33–34.

11. Tchaikovsky/LIFE & LETTERS I, pp. 250–53.

12. Morgenstern/COMPOSERS, p. 278.

13. Calvocoressi/MUSSORGSKY, pp. 26, 207.

14. Ridenour/19C RUSSIAN MUSIC, p. 126.

15. See Garden/BALAKIREV, pp. 89–121.

16. Tchaikovsky/LIFE & LETTERS II, p. 564.

17. For further on *Kamarinskaya,* see Taruskin/ACORN.

18. The citation of the origins of the themes is from Downes/GUIDE SYMPHONY, p. 361.

19. According to the works list in Brown/NG GLINKA, pp. 33–40.

20. Abraham/ARAB MELODIES.

21. See Abraham/RIMSKY SELF-CRITIC.

22. Rimsky-Korsakov/MUSICAL LIFE, pp. 34–35.

23. Griffiths/RIMSKY-KORSAKOV, p. 46.

24. Taruskin/RIMSKY-KORSAKOV SYMPHONIES, p. 6.

25. Rimsky-Korsakov/MUSICAL LIFE, p. 22.

26. Griffiths/RIMSKY-KORSAKOV, p. 47.

27. Rimsky-Korsakov/MUSICAL LIFE, p. 35.

28. Campbell/RUSSIAN MUSIC 1830–1880, pp. 181–83.

29. Abraham/ARAB MELODIES, pp. 93–96.

30. Rimsky-Korsakov/MUSICAL LIFE, p. 96.

31. Abraham/RIMSKY SELF-CRITIC, pp. 198–99.

32. Rimsky-Korsakov/MUSICAL LIFE, p. 92.

33. Rimsky-Korsakov/MUSICAL LIFE, pp. 92–93.

34. Taruskin/RIMSKY-KORSAKOV SYMPHONIES, p. 9.

35. Rimsky-Korsakov/MUSICAL LIFE, p. 93.

36. Rimsky-Korsakov/MUSICAL LIFE, p. 93.

37. For a survey of its use, see Taruskin/CHERNOMOR.

38. Rimsky-Korsakov/MUSICAL LIFE, p. 289.

39. Rimsky-Korsakov/MUSICAL LIFE, pp. 93–94.

40. Rimsky-Korsakov/MUSICAL LIFE, p. 45.

41. Campbell/RUSSIAN MUSIC 1830–1880, pp. 193–95. Originally published in *Sankt-Peterburgskie vedomosti,* "Muzykal'nye zametki: kontsert bezplatnoi muzykal'noi shkoly; kontserty Russkogo Muzykal'nogo Obshchestva (7-i i 8-i)," March 20, 1869.

42. *Golos,* December 29, 1871.

43. *SPb Vedomosti,* January 11, 1872.

44. Rostislav [F. Tolstoi], "Petersburg Letters: *Antar,* the Second Symphony of Mr. Rimsky-Korsakov," *Moskovskie vedomosti,* January 18, 1876.

45. Rimsky-Korsakov/MUSICAL LIFE, p. 133.

46. Rimsky-Korsakov/MUSICAL LIFE, pp. 133–34.

47. Taruskin/RIMSKY-KORSAKOV SYMPHONIES, p. 11.

48. Additionally, according to Griffiths/RIMSKY-KORSAKOV, p. 147, the Finale's coda recalls material from the first movement and Trio.

49. Taruskin/RIMSKY-KORSAKOV SYMPHONIES, p. 11.

50. Orlova/TCHAIKOVSKY, p. 41

51. "Piatoe simfonicheskoe sobranie. –Vtoraia kvartetnaia seriia.—Ital'ianskaia opera," in Tchaikovsky/CRITICISM, 195–201. Originally published in *Russkie vedomosti*, January 3, 1875.

52. [M. Ivanov], "Muzykal'noe obozrenie." *Nuvellist*, 1886, no. 8, December, *Muzykal'no-teatral'naia gazeta: 1–4.*

53. Seaman/RIMSKY GUIDE, p. 20.

54. English translation of the "Program" is from the first Dover edition (Dover Publications, 1984).

55. Rimsky-Korsakov/MUSICAL LIFE, p. 294.

56. See Yastrebtsev/RIMSKY-KORSAKOV, p. 31, and Abraham/PROGRAMME SCHEHERAZADE, pp. 141–42.

57. "Muzykal'noe obozrenie," *Nuvellist*, 1888, no. 7, November, *Muzykal'no-teatral'naia gazeta: 1–3.*

58. Ts. K. [César Cui], "Russkie simfonicheskie kontserty," *Muzykal'noe obozrenie*, no. 22, October 27, 1888, 171–72.

59. Rimsky-Korsakov/MUSICAL LIFE, pp. 57–58.

60. Abraham & Lloyd-Jones/NG BORODIN, pp. 55–61.

61. Lloyd-Jones/BORODIN 1, p. 95.

62. Dianin/BORODIN, pp. 201, 203.

63. "3-i kontsert Russkogo Muzykal'nogo Obshchestva," *Vest'*, 1869, no. 9.

64. Morgenstern/COMPOSERS, pp. 217–18.

65. W., "Chetvertoe simofinicheskoe sobranie Russkogo Muzykal'nogo Obshchestva," *Muzykal'noe obozrenie*, no. 15, January 16, 1886: 114–15.

66. Abraham/BORODIN SYMPHONIST, pp. 117–18.

67. Lloyd-Jones/EDITION BORODIN, pp. 83–86.

68. See Dianin/BORODIN, pp. 207–08.

69. Rimsky-Korsakov/MUSICAL LIFE, p. 188.

70. Dianin/BORODIN, pp. 207–09.

71. [César Cui], "Obshchedostupnyi russkii simfonicheskii kontsert," *Muzykal'noe obozrenie*, no. 11, December 5, 1885: 81–82. Comments on the first performance were published in *Muzykal'nyi svet*, but were not substantive enough to include.

72. As trans. from Kuhn/BORODIN, pp. 310–11.

73. Lloyd-Jones/BORODIN 3, p. 101.

74. "Pervyi russkii simfonicheskii kontsert," *Muzykal'noe obozrenie*, no. 21, October 29, 1887: 44–45.

75. "Muzykal'noe obozrenie," *Nuvellist*, 1887, no. 7, November, *Muzykal'no-teatral'naia gazeta: 1–3.*

76. Abraham/TCHAIKOVSKY MANFRED, p. 633.

77. Tchaikovsky, Symphony No. 7, Philadelphia Orchestra, conducted by Eugene Ormandy, Columbia Masterworks MS 6349, 1962.

78. Melodiya USSR/EMI Records Ltd.

79. Ts. Kiui [César Cui], "Muzykal'nye zametki: Konservatorskie solisty I kompozitor," *Sankt Peterburgskie vedomosti*, March 24, 1866.

80. Brown/TCHAIKOVSKY I, p. 103.

81. Lloyd-Jones/TCHAIKOVSKY 1, p. 655.

82. Lloyd-Jones/TCHAIKOVSKY 1, p. 655.

83. Lloyd-Jones/TCHAIKOVSKY 1, p. 655.

84. "Vtoroi russkii simfonicheskii kontsert," *Muzykal'noe obozrenie,* no. 6, October 30, 1886: 41–42.

85. Abraham/TCHAIKOVSKY 2, p. 656.

86. Abraham/TCHAIKOVSKY 2, p. 659.

87. Abraham/TCHAIKOVSKY 2, p. 656.

88. Abraham/TCHAIKOVSKY 2, p. 657.

89. See Brown/FIRST GOLDEN AGE, pp. 632–33.

90. Brown/TCHAIKOVSKY I, pp. 256–57.

91. Brown/TCHAIKOVSKY I, pp. 257–58.

92. This passage also served as a model for Wagner's Symphony in C; see Chapter II in Part A, p. 46.

93. Campbell/RUSSIAN MUSIC 1830–1880, pp. 257–58. Originally published in Larosh [Laroche], "Novaia russkaia simfoniia," *Moskovskie vedomosti,* February 7, 1873, no. 33.

94. Abraham/TCHAIKOVSKY 3, p. 660.

95. Brown/TCHAIKOVSKY II, p. 47.

96. "5-i kontsert Russkogo Muzykal'nogo Obshchestva 24 ianvaria," *Golos,* January 28, 1876. Reprinted in Laroche/TCHAIKOVSKY, pp. 79–82.

97. [N. F.] Solov'ev, "Muzykal'noe obozrenie," *Novoe vremia,* January 30/February 11, 1876.

98. *NYT,* February 9, 1879.

99. Tchaikovsky/LIFE & LETTERS I, pp. 274–75.

100. Mazo/LVOV & PRACH, p. 440.

101. Keller/TCHAIKOVSKY SYMPHONIES, pp. 349–50.

102. Brown/TCHAIKOVSKY II, p. 168, Brown/RUSSIA SYMPHONY, pp. 273–74, and Garden/TCHAIKOVSKY, pp. 81–82.

103. Tchaikovsky/LIFE & LETTERS I, pp. 271–72.

104. "Muzykal'nye ocherki. 4,5,6-i kontserty Muzykal'nogo obshchestva," *Golos,* December 7, 1878. Reprinted in Laroche/TCHAIKOVSKY, pp. 101–02.

105. M. Ivanov, "Kontsertnoe i teatral'noe obozrenie," *Nuvellist,* 1879, no. 1, January, *Muzykal'no-Teatral'naia gazeta:* 1–2.

106. Tchaikovsky/LIFE & LETTERS I, pp. 292–93.

107. Tchaikovsky/LIFE & LETTERS I, pp. 293–95.

108. Minibayeva/TCHAIKOVSKY FIRST SUITE, p. 174.

109. Abraham/TCHAIKOVSKY MANFRED, p. 634.

110. Abraham/TCHAIKOVSKY MANFRED, p. 636.

111. Abraham/TCHAIKOVSKY MANFRED, p. 636.

112. Abraham/TCHAIKOVSKY MANFRED, p. 636.

113. Byron/LETTERS & JOURNALS, p. 170.

114. Byron/LETTERS & JOURNALS, p. 170.

115. Abraham/TCHAIKOVSKY MANFRED, p. 638.

116. Byron as quoted in Parsons/CSO MANFRED, p. 25.

117. Yastrebtsev/RIMSKY-KORSAKOV, p. 166.

118. "Muzykal'noe obozrenie," *Russkii vestnik,* 1886, no. 10 (October). Reprinted in Laroche/TCHAIKOVSKY, pp. 122–24.

119. [V. Baskin], "Muzykal'noe obozrenie." *Nuvellist,* 1887, no. 2, February, *Muzykal'no-teatral'naia gazeta:* 1–4.

120. Tchaikovsky/LIFE & LETTERS II, p. 497.

121. Tchaikovsky/LIFE & LETTERS II, p. 498.

122. Orlova/TCHAIKOVSKY, p. 290.

123. Orlova/TCHAIKOVSKY, p. 291.

124. Tchaikovsky/LIFE & LETTERS II, p. 560.

125. Seibert/TCHAIKOVSKY 5 PROGRAMME, p. 43.

126. Seibert/TCHAIKOVSKY 5 PROGRAMME, p. 43.

127. Seibert/TCHAIKOVSKY 5 PROGRAMME, p. 43.

128. Tchaikovsky/LIFE & LETTERS II, p. 561.

129. Seibert/TCHAIKOVSKY 5 PROGRAMME, p. 43.

130. Seibert/TCHAIKOVSKY 5 PROGRAMME, p. 44.

131. Tchaikovsky/LIFE & LETTERS II, p. 566.

132. Tchaikovsky/LIFE & LETTERS II, p. 566.

133. As quoted in Burk/BSO TCHAIKOVSKY 5, p. 469.

134. Seibert/TCHAIKOVSKY 5 PROGRAMME.

135. Brown/TCHAIKOVSKY IV, pp. 148–49.

136. Orlova/TCHAIKOVSKY, p. 119.

137. Tchaikovsky/LIFE & LETTERS I, p. 294.

138. Brown/TCHAIKOVSKY IV, p. 154, and Garden/TCHAIKOVSKY, p. 120.

139. Orlova/TCHAIKOVSKY, pp. 111–12.

140. Tovey/TCHAIKOVSKY 5, p. 60.

141. Blume/CLASSIC & ROMANTIC, p. 157.

142. Tovey/TCHAIKOVSKY 5, p. 59.

143. Tovey/TCHAIKOVSKY 5, p. 65.

144. Lloyd-Jones/TCHAIKOVSKY 5, p. 667.

145. Orlova/TCHAIKOVSKY, pp. 349–50.

146. "Muzykal'noe obozrenie," *Nuvellist,* 1888, no. 8, December, *Muzykal'no-teatral'naia gazeta:* 2–4.

147. Ts. Kiui [César Cui], "Kontsert Filarmonicheskogo Obshchestva," *Muzykal'noe obozrenie,* no. 25, November 17, 1888: 195–96.

148. Brown/TCHAIKOVSKY IV, Evans/TCHAIKOVSKY, p. 45, and Garden/TCHAIKOVSKY, p. 107.

149. Tchaikovsky/LIFE & LETTERS II, pp. 702–03.

150. Tchaikovsky/LIFE & LETTERS II, p. 714.

151. Tchaikovsky/LIFE & LETTERS II, p. 714.

152. Tchaikovsky/LIFE & LETTERS II, p. 718.

153. Tchaikovsky/LIFE & LETTERS II, p. 721.

154. Abraham/PROGRAMME PATHÉTIQUE, p. 145.

155. Abraham/TCHAIKOVSKY REFLECTIONS, pp. 113–15, and Zajaczkowski/TCHAIKOVSKY PATHÉTIQUE, p. 562.

156. See also Becker/SPOHR RUSSISCHE, pp. 117–18, 123–29.

157. Kohlhase/EINFÜHRUNGEN ČAJKOVSKIJS, p. 119.

158. Jackson/TCHAIKOVSKY 6, pp. 4–5.

159. Norris/STANFORD, p. 398.

160. Cooper/TCHAIKOVSKY SYMPHONIES, p. 270.

161. Keller/TCHAIKOVSKY SYMPHONIES, p. 353.

162. Warrack/TCHAIKOVSKY SYMPHONIES, p. 36.

163. Garden/TCHAIKOVSKY, p. 145.

164. Brown/NG TCHAIKOVSKY, p. 223.

165. Kohlhase/EINFÜHRUNGEN ČAJKOVSKIJS, p. 93.

166. Kraus/TCHAIKOVSKY [SYMPHONIES], p. 322.

167. Tovey/TCHAIKOVSKY PATHETIC, p. 88.

168. Kohlhase/EINFÜHRUNGEN ČAJKOVSKIJS, pp. 109–10.

169. *Novoe vremia* (St. Petersburg), October 18/30, 1893.

170. Larosh, "Muzykal'naia khronika," *Teatral'naia gazeta*, no. 18, 1893: 3–4.

171. V. Baskin, "Muzykal'noe obozrenie, " *Nuvellist*, 1893, no. 8, December, *Muzykal'no-teatral'naia gazeta*: 1–3.

172. Hanslick/CRITICISM, p. 303.

173. Bauer-Lechner/RECOLLECTIONS, p. 166.

174. Rimsky-Korsakov/MUSICAL LIFE, p. 27.

175. Abraham/BALAKIREV'S SYMPHONIES, pp. 184–85.

176. Garden/BALAKIREV, p. 202.

177. Abraham/BALAKIREV'S SYMPHONIES, p. 187.

178. Rimsky-Korsakov/MUSICAL LIFE, p. 63.

179. Abraham/BALAKIREV'S SYMPHONIES, p. 188.

180. Abraham/BALAKIREV'S SYMPHONIES, p. 189, and Garden/BALAKIREV, pp. 205–06.

181. L., "Concert of the Free Music School," *Russian Musical Gazette*, 1898, nos. 5–6: 462–64.

182. Abraham/BALAKIREV'S SYMPHONIES, p. 191, and Garden/BALAKIREV, pp. 213–15.

183. See Abraham/BALAKIREV'S SYMPHONIES, p. 191, and Garden/BALAKIREV, p. 213.

184. Abraham/BALAKIREV'S SYMPHONIES, p. 191.

185. Garden/BALAKIREV, p. 214.

186. Iu. E., "Theater and Music," *Russkie vedomosti*, no. 66, March 21, 1909.

187. "S.-Petersburg: Concerts," *Russian Musical Gazette*, 1909, no. 16: 440–42.

188. See Seaman/KALINNIKOV, p. 291, and Spencer/KALINNIKOV, p. 776.

189. Seaman/KALINNIKOV, p. 290.

190. Nest'ev/PROKOFIEV, p. 172. This was not the first time Prokofiev was compared to Kalinnikov; see also p. 58.

191. "Music in the Provinces: Kiev," *Russian Musical Gazette*, March 1897: 503–06.

192. Iv. Lipaev, "Musical Life of Moscow," *Russian Musical Gazette*, 1898, no. 1: 94–95.

193. Asafiev/RUSSIAN MUSIC, p. 163.

194. "Kiev," *Russian Musical Gazette*, 1898, no. 3: 324.

195. Iv. Lipaev, "From Moscow," *Russian Musical Gazette*, 1899, no. 12: 378–79.

196. Cannata/RACHMANINOFF SYMPHONY, p. 25.

197. Norris/RACHMANINOFF, pp. 97–100.

198. Swan/RACHMANINOFF, p. 185.

199. See Cannata/RACHMANINOFF SYMPHONY, p. 74, n. 16.

200. Piggott/RACHMANINOFF, p. 25.

201. Riesemann/RACHMANINOFF, pp. 97–98.

202. Riesemann/RACHMANINOFF, p. 98.

203. As trans. in Slonimsky/LEXICON, p. 137.

204. As trans. in Norris/RACHMANINOFF, p. 97.

205. Nik[olai] F[indeizen], "3rd and 4th Russian Symphonic Concerts and the 6th Russian Quartet Evening," *Russian Musical Gazette*, April 1897: 650–53.

206. Simpson/RACHMANINOFF SYMPHONIES, p. 129.

50. For details on this organization and its prize, see Fallon/SYMPHONIES, pp. 120–30, as well as his "Saint-Saëns and the *Concours de composition musicale* in Bordeaux," *JAMS* (Summer 1978), pp. 309–25.

51. Reprinted in Ratner/SAINT-SAËNS, p. 268.

52. Fallon/SYMPHONIES, p. 150.

53. Saint-Saëns/MEMORIES, p. 199; HARMONIE, p. 209; and PORTRAITS, p. 124.

54. Curtiss/BIZET, pp. 231–32.

55. For a full account of Pasdeloup's achievements for French music, see Bernard/PASDELOUP.

56. The subsection divisions are Fallon's, who notes the familial similarity of *Pg* with *I/P* of Schumann's Fourth Symphony. The cyclic unity of that work may have served as an additional model for Saint-Saëns. See Fallon/SYMPHONIES, pp. 171–72.

57. Saint-Saëns/IDÉES, p. 34.

58. Anonymous, *Revue et gazette musicale* 27, (April 8, 1860); translated in Fallon/SYMPHONIES, pp. 160–61.

59. Tiersot/SYMPHONIE, p. 397.

60. Ratner/SAINT-SAËNS, pp. 271–73.

61. Deputy Charles Beulé, reprinted in *Journal officiel* (March 21, 1874); quoted and translated in Strasser/ARS GALLICA, p. 115. Chapter II of Strasser provides a detailed discussion of the new mood that swept France in the aftermath of the so-called *année terrible.*

62. See Strasser/ARS GALLICA for a thorough consideration of this organization during its first twenty years and the artistic and social context in which it flourished.

63. Quoted in Strasser/ARS GALLICA, p. 562.

64. "Revue des grands concerts," *Le Ménestrel* 57/1 (January 4, 1891), pp. 4–5; quoted and translated in Strasser/ARS GALLICA, p. 522.

65. For details, see Chapters VI and XII of Strasser/ARS GALLICA.

66. Lalo/RÉFORMES. The quote also appears in Vallas/D'INDY II, pp. 26–27, where it is attributed to Émile Réty, the general secretary for the school.

67. The score, published in Moscow in 1933, is reprinted in the appendix of Rodman/DEBUSSY, pp. 324–43. The surviving movement is presumably the first; the others were entitled Andante, Air de Ballet, and Final.

68. Rodman analyzes the movement as follows: Exposition (mm. 1–63), Development (mm. 64–91), interpolated ternary section (mm. 92–146), Development resumed (mm. 147–96), and Recapitulation (mm. 197–249); see Rodman/DEBUSSY, p. 120.

69. Letter to his wife, October 15, 1885; d'Indy/VIE, p. 389.

70. For details see Orledge/FAURÉ, pp. 327–28.

71. See his letter to Vicomtesse Greffulhe in Orledge/FAURÉ, p. 71.

72. Simon Trezise discusses sea-settings by Joncières and Paul Gilson as well as other possible prototypes for Debussy in Trezise/MER, pp. 32–35.

73. The correspondence between the composer and the Philharmonic Society is reprinted in Fallon/SYMPHONIES (pp. 361–64, 449–58) and Ratner/SAINT-SAËNS (pp. 312–13).

74. Translated in Fallon/SYMPHONIES, pp. 456–57. Saint-Saëns writes "That is the question" in English.

75. Fallon reprints the note in full in Fallon/SYMPHONIES, Appendix III, pp. 459–71.

76. See for example his complaint to Pierre Aguétant in Aguétant/SAINT-SAËNS, p. 41.

77. Fallon/SYMPHONIES, p. 426.

78. Finscher/SAINT-SAËNS, pp. 108–11.

79. The most detailed analysis of the "Organ" Symphony is Fallon's, to which this study is greatly indebted. A few points of disagreement are noted below. Appendix One of Finscher/SAINT-SAËNS includes a useful table of transformations of the four cyclic themes.

80. Ratner/SAINT-SAËNS, pp. 313–14. The letter is dated June 19, 1886.

81. Fallon contends that Saint-Saëns was unaware of the similarity, which seems unlikely (SYMPHONIES, p. 375); Brian Rees says, equally speculatively, that the composer may have been referring to his own recent recovery from a serious illness (SAINT-SAËNS, p. 263).

82. For more on the original key of B minor, see Fallon/SYMPHONIES, p. 367 and Appendix II, p. 456 (not p. 467, as the footnote on p. 367 indicates).

83. Fallon regards this segment as the beginning of *T,* but Saint-Saëns does not leave the tonic area until m. 90.

84. Fallon/SYMPHONIES, p. 392.

85. *A* bears no relation to any material in the first movement. Finscher says it adumbrates the chorale first heard at the end of the Scherzo [*III/3S*], but I see little thematic relation between the two.

86. Fallon begins *B* with the arabesque variation but I prefer to mark it here because what follows is a complete contrast to *A* in key and theme.

87. Fallon suggests (SYMPHONIES, p. 404) that Saint-Saëns's work on *Carnival of the Animals,* which he composed simultaneously with the symphony, may have inspired this scoring.

88. Fallon marks the first entrance of the chorale (m. 280) as the beginning of the transition; I prefer to wait until this point, however, when all vestiges of the Trio have disappeared and only the chorale is left.

89. Fallon/SYMPHONIES, p. 417.

90. The quote is from the *Daily Telegraph,* reprinted in Studd/SAINT-SAËNS, p. 153.

91. The quote comes from an anonymous review, "Philharmonic Society," *MT* XXVII (June 1, 1886), p. 335, and the "leitmotif" connection from two anonymous reviews in May 1886 ("Philharmonic Society," *The Times,* May 22, 1886, and "Philharmonic Society," *MW,* May 29, 1886, p. 349).

92. *The World,* June 13, 1894, reprinted in Shaw/MUSIC, pp. 240–41.

93. Letter to Benno Hollander, February 13, 1910; Ratner/SAINT-SAËNS, p. 315.

94. Ratner/SAINT-SAËNS, p. 314; for a translation of the complete letter see Nectoux/CORRESPONDENCE, p. 46.

95. Johannès Weber, "Concert spirituel de la Société du Conservatoire: la 3e symphonie de M. Saint-Saëns et la symphonie de l'avenir," *Le Temps,* April 9, 1888.

96. Bellaigue/CONCERTS, pp. 458–59.

97. Bellaigue/CONCERTS, p. 459.

98. Bellaigue/CONCERTS, p. 461.

99. See Strasser/ARS GALLICA, pp. 419–43, for a detailed consideration of Saint-Saëns's aesthetic shift from a youthful "radical" to ardent anti-Wagnerian.

100. Ropartz/SYMPHONIES, pp. 191–97.

101. D'Indy/SYMPHONIES, p. 167; d'Indy/FRANCK, p. 153; English version, p. 172.

102. For example, Harding/SAINT-SAËNS, p. 173; Rees/SAINT-SAËNS, p. 264; Studd/SAINT-SAËNS, pp. 154–55. All three cite d'Indy as the ultimate authority on the work.

103. The comment to Bruneau is in Ratner/SAINT-SAËNS, p. 314; the disavowal appears in Bonnerot/SAINT-SAËNS, p. 120.

104. Saint-Saëns/IDÉES, p. 41.

105. Tiersot/SYMPHONIE, p. 399.

106. Combarieu/HISTOIRE, pp. 423–25.

107. Saint-Saëns/IDÉES, p. 7.

108. Carraud/VIE, pp. 116, 118, 119, 144.

109. Tiersot/SYMPHONIE, p. 400.

110. Masson/RAPPORT, pp. 10–14.

111. From a letter to Ferdinand Hiller, October 27, 1862; Lalo/CORRESPONDANCE, p. 77.

112. From the same letter to Hiller; Lalo/CORRESPONDANCE, p. 77.

113. *La Liberté,* March 13, 1882; reprinted in Lalo/CORRESPONDANCE, p. 239.

114. Letter to Georges Servières, February 19, 1883; reprinted in Lalo/CORRESPON-DANCE, p. 250, as well as Servières/LALO, p. 56.

115. Debussy referred to this incident in an article for *Gil Blas,* January 19, 1907; see Debussy/CROCHE, p. 77, as well as Debussy/LETTERS, p. 116. For more on the genesis and reception of *Namouna*—an important precursor to the twentieth-century "symphonic ballets" made up of a continuous orchestral narrative instead of a series of discrete dances—see Huebner/OPERA, pp. 231–34.

116. Letter to Adolphe Jullien, March 7, 1887; Lalo/CORRESPONDANCE, p. 169.

117. Letter to A. B. Marcel, May 1889; see Lalo/CORRESPONDANCE, p. 302. Throughout this chapter, single-space "suspension points" ("that... I hadn't been wrong"—a common French rhetorical strategy) that appear in the original are rendered as en dashes preceded and followed by spaces ("that – I hadn't been wrong").

118. Lalo also reused parts of *Fiesque* in other works. See Macdonald/FIESQUE for details. According to Macdonald, Lalo frequently resorted to self-borrowing in later years, apparently owing to failing health.

119. Macdonald/FIESQUE, p. 178.

120. Macdonald/LALO, p. 389.

121. Macdonald/FIESQUE, pp. 169, 171.

122. Macdonald/FIESQUE, pp. 171–72.

123. Macdonald/FIESQUE, p. 182.

124. Locke/FRENCH, p. 181.

125. Servières/LALO, p. 115n.

126. H. Barbadette, "Concert Lamoureux," *Le Ménestrel* LIII (December 18, 1887), p. 899. I am indebted to Michael Strasser for calling my attention to this review.

127. Ropartz/SYMPHONIES, p. 174.

128. D'Indy/FRANCK, p. 153; English version, p. 172.

129. Tiersot/SYMPHONIE, p. 399.

130. See for example Closson/ORIGINES.

131. Ropartz/SYMPHONIES, p. 181.

132. "Lettres d'Henri Duparc à Ernest Chausson," *Revue de musicologie,* December 1956, p. 130, quoted in Fauquet/FRANCK, pp. 726–27.

133. The latter number reflects Joël-Marie Fauquet's chronological numbering system for Franck's complete works; see Fauquet/FRANCK for details.

134. Tiersot/OEUVRES, pp. 111–12. Since Tiersot's time, the manuscript to this unpublished symphony has been lost.

135. Fauquet/FRANCK, p. 718.

136. Fauquet/FRANCK, p. 718. For d'Indy's revisionist chronology see d'Indy/FRANCK, p. 154n; English version, p. 173n.

137. In the *Cours de composition musicale,* d'Indy criticized Franck's experiment on the grounds that assigning parity to two different keys upset the tonal balance of the work. D'Indy/SYMPHONIE, p. 161.

138. D'Indy/SYMPHONIE, p. 163.

139. Camille Bellaigue, "Revue musicale," *Revue des deux mondes* XCII (March 15, 1889), p. 460.

140. See Chapter VI.

141. Louis de Serres, "Quelques souvenirs sur le père Franck, mon maître," *L'Art musical* (1935), quoted in Fauquet/FRANCK, p. 718.

142. Pierre Lalo, "César Franck," *De Rameau à Ravel* (Paris, 1947), p. 68, quoted in Fauquet/FRANCK, p. 719.

143. D'Indy/SYMPHONIE, p. 164.

144. D'Indy/FRANCK, p. 153; English, pp. 172–73.

145. Fauquet/FRANCK, p. 721.

146. D'Indy/FRANCK, p. 29; English, p. 54.

147. Quoted in Fauquet/FRANCK, p. 724.

148. Rolland, *Mémoires* (Paris, 1952), p. 171, quoted in Fauquet/FRANCK, p. 725.

149. Fauquet/FRANCK, pp. 727–28. Vallas also doubted that Gounod made the remark, in this case because he simply found it implausible (Vallas/FRANCK, p. 266; English, p. 212).

150. Fauquet/FRANCK, p. 728.

151. D'Indy/FRANCK, p. 30; English, p. 54. Franck was not the first to feature the English horn prominently in a symphony; d'Indy had already done so in his *Symphony on a French Mountain Air* and, the professor's observation notwithstanding, Joseph Haydn used English horns in place of oboes in his Symphony No. 22 ("The Philosopher," 1764).

152. Johannès Weber, "Concerts du Conservatoire: la symphonie de M. César Franck," *Le Temps,* March 4, 1889.

153. Camille Bellaigue, "Revue musicale," *Revue des deux mondes* XCII (March 15, 1889), pp. 460–61. Excerpts appear in Vallas/FRANCK, pp. 269–70; English, p. 215.

154. Quoted in Vallas/FRANCK, p. 268; English, pp. 213–14.

155. Ropartz/SYMPHONIES, pp. 184–88.

156. Debussy made this remark to Guiraud in 1889 or 1890. See Maurice Emmanuel, *César Franck: Étude critique* (Paris, 1930), p. 120, quoted in Fauquet/FRANCK, p. 727. In later years Debussy maintained his admiration for the work and its "innumerable beauties" (Debussy/CROCHE, p. 145).

157. Quoted in Fauquet/FRANCK, p. 724.

158. Quoted in Fauquet/FRANCK, p. 728.

159. D'Indy/FRANCK, pp. 30–31; English, p. 55.

160. For details of symphonies in concert programs in Paris between 1900 and 1914, see Hart/SYMPHONY, pp. 324–32.

161. Ropartz/SYMPHONIES, p. 190.

162. Demuth/FRANCK, p. 84.

163. Many older British writers, including Tovey, take this rather debatable last point for granted. For example, according to Martin Cooper, Franck's symphony "is one only in name and, loosely, in form. . . . [T]he very beauty and subtlety of the middle movement, for example, its weird and melancholy atmosphere, remove it from the symphonic class" (Cooper/FRENCH, pp. 49–50).

164. Letter to Paul Poujaud, 1884; Chausson/ÉCRITS, p. 172.

165. Letter to Paul Poujaud, June 1889; Chausson/ÉCRITS, p. 216.

166. Chausson/ÉCRITS, p. 230.

167. Chausson/ÉCRITS, p. 227.

168. Chausson/ÉCRITS, pp. 228–29.

169. Chausson/ÉCRITS, pp. 233–34. Excerpts of these letters can also be found in Barricelli/CHAUSSON, pp. 41–46.

170. Letter to Lerolle, September 28, 1890; Chausson/ÉCRITS, p. 243.

171. See for example Cooper/FRENCH, pp. 65–66, and Demuth/FRANCK, p. 191.

172. For such lists, see Barricelli/CHAUSSON, pp. 173–74, Gallois/CHAUSSON, pp. 255–58, and especially Grover/CHAUSSON, pp. 130–45. The last-named insists too strongly that Chausson's work is not only different from Franck's but infinitely superior.

173. Chausson/ÉCRITS, p. 232.

174. See Strasser/ARS GALLICA, pp. 491–98.

175. Letter to Lerolle, November 9, 1889; Chausson/ÉCRITS, pp. 231–32.

176. Gallois/CHAUSSON, p. 257.

177. Raymond Bonheur, "Petites notes de musique," *Mercure de France* III (July 1891), p. 57.

178. See excerpts of selected reviews in Barricelli/CHAUSSON, p. 48, and Gallois/CHAUSSON, pp. 248–49.

179. Gallois/CHAUSSON, p. 249.

180. Tiersot/SYMPHONIE, p. 400.

181. Jean d'Udine, "Concerts-Colonne et Lamoureux," *Le Courrier musical* XVI (January 1, 1913), p. 16.

182. Letter to Pierre Lalo, May 24, 1901; Dukas/CORRESPONDANCE, pp. 40–41.

183. Favre/OEUVRE, p. 28.

184. Ropartz/DUKAS, p. 63.

185. Ropartz/DUKAS, pp. 63–64.

186. René de Castéra, "La Symphonie en *ut* majeur de Paul Dukas," *L'Occident* (February 1902), p. 171.

187. Ropartz/DUKAS, pp. 63–64.

188. For more on this series, which lasted from 1895 to 1897, see Olin/CONCERTS.

189. D.-E. Ingelbrecht, *Mouvement contraire* (Paris, 1946), quoted in Favre/OEUVRE, p. 36.

190. Charles-Henry Hirsch, "Musique," *Mercure de France* XXI (February 1897), p. 425. Alfred Bruneau (1857–1934) was a notable composer of operas at the turn of the century, several in collaboration with his close friend Émile Zola. His Requiem, influenced by Berlioz's, dates from the 1880s.

191. Letter to Pierre Louÿs (February 9, 1897); Debussy/LETTERS, p. 89.

192. Dukas/AUTOBIOGRAPHIE, p. 748, reprinted in Dukas/CORRESPONDANCE, p. 30.

193. Pierre Lalo, *Le Temps* (January 28, 1902), quoted in Favre/OEUVRE, pp. 36–37.

194. Hugues Imbert, "Concerts Lamoureux," *Le Guide musical* XLVIII (January 26, 1902), pp. 79–80.

195. Tiersot/SYMPHONIE, pp. 400–01.

196. Tiersot/SYMPHONIE, p. 402.

197. Orledge/D'INDY, p. 222.

198. Hart/D'INDY discusses the composer's impact on the symphony through his work as teacher, composer, and apologist.

199. Diary entry, November 30, 1869; d'Indy/VIE, p. 76.

200. Diary entry, December 25, 1869; d'Indy/VIE, pp. 85–86.

201. Letter to his cousin Édmond de Pampelonne, January 5, 1872; d'Indy/VIE, p. 155.

202. Letter to his cousin Cécile d'Indy, November 6, 1871; d'Indy/VIE, pp. 150–51.

203. Letter to Édmond de Pampelonne, June 4, 1873; d'Indy/VIE, p. 202.

204. Letter to his cousin Roger de Pampelonne, April 9, 1874; d'Indy/VIE, p. 269.

205. Diary entry, August 11, 1875; D'Indy/VIE, p. 287.

206. Vallas/D'INDY I, pp. 203, 207–08.

207. See p. 608 above.

208. Bellaigue/CONCERTS, p. 458.

209. Bellaigue/CONCERTS, p. 457.

210. Bellaigue/CONCERTS, p. 457.

211. Bellaigue/CONCERTS, p. 458.

212. Ernest Reyer, *Journal des Débats,* March 27, 1887, quoted in Vallas/D'INDY II, p. 230.

213. Ropartz/SYMPHONIES, pp. 199, 200–01.

214. Ropartz/SYMPHONIES, pp. 200, 204–05.

215. D'Indy/VIE documents performances the composer led in Belgium, the Netherlands, Germany, Russia, Italy, and Spain.

216. Dukas/D'INDY, pp. 627, 628–29.

217. Tiersot/SYMPHONIES, p. 401.

218. See d'Indy/SYMPHONIE, especially pp. 147–77.

219. Fourcaud/MUSIQUE, pp. 244–45.

220. See Mangeot/AVENIR, which Carlo Caballero graciously called to my attention. Muret/RAPPORT expresses similar sentiments, and I am indebted to Michael Strasser for providing a transcript. For more on this "three-hour rule," see Fauser/ORCHESTERGESANG, Chapter IV; Chimènes/BUDGET; and Hart/SYMPHONY, pp. 299–314.

221. Hart/SYMPHONY, Chapter I, deals with the *guerre des écoles* as it impacted the symphony.

222. For a detailed study of the impact of the Affair on French musicians and musical life, see Fulcher/CULTURAL.

223. Letter to Pierre Garanger, 1918, quoted in Petit/INTRODUCTION, p. 116.

224. Rolland/CHRISTOPHE, p. 689.

225. Vincent d'Indy, letter to Guy Ropartz, October 10, 1902 (*Lettres autographes,* Bibliothèque Nationale). Michael Strasser and Catrina Flint de Médicis both provided to me a copy of this letter.

226. Vallas/D'INDY II, p. 246.

227. René de Castéra, "La Symphonie en *si* bémol de Vincent d'Indy," *L'Occident* (April 1904), pp. 174–75.

228. Jean Marnold, "Une *Symphonie* de Vincent d'Indy," *Mercure de France* L (1904), p. 249.

229. Vallas/D'INDY II, p. 247.

230. "A propos de *Pelléas et Mélisande,*" *L'Occident* (June 1902), pp. 374–81.

231. Letter to Octave Maus, September 14, 1904; d'Indy/VIE, p. 666.

232. See above, p. 602.

233. Albert Groz, "2e Symphonie de Vincent d'Indy," *Le Guide du concert* III (1912), p. 401.

234. Pierre Lalo, "La Musique," *Le Temps,* March 26, 1912.

235. Paul Dukas, "La Deuxième Symphonie de Vincent d'Indy," *Chronique des arts et de la curiosité* (March 1904); repr. in Dukas/ÉCRITS, pp. 609–10.

236. Jean Chantavoine, "Chronique musicale: La Symphonie en si bémol de M. Vincent d'Indy," *La Revue hebdomadaire* XIII (September 1904), pp. 212, 217.

237. Jules Combarieu, "La 2ᵉ Symphonie de M. Vincent d'Indy aux Concerts Lamoureux," *La Revue musicale* IV (November 15, 1904), p. 552; Gaston Carraud, "Les Concerts," *La Liberté,* March 8, 1904.

238. See Slonimsky/LEXICON, pp. 108–09.

239. Vallas/D'INDY II, p. 53.

240. Alfred Bruneau, "Les Concerts," *Le Matin,* February 29, 1904.

241. Letter to Paul Poujaud, August 5, 1916; d'Indy/VIE, p. 759. Amédée Gastoué (1873–1943) was a *scholiste*-trained musicologist who specialized in Gregorian chant.

242. Letter to Marcel Labey, December 1, 1916; d'Indy/VIE, p. 760.

243. Letter to Charles Legrand, August 22, 1917; d'Indy/VIE, p. 765.

244. Letter to Guy Ropartz, January 4, 1918, quoted in Vallas/D'INDY II, p. 261.

245. Letter to Octave Maus, November 19, 1918; d'Indy/VIE, p. 771.

246. Vallas/D'INDY II, p. 262.

247. Vallas/D'INDY II, p. 264.

248. Jean Poueigh, "Musique," *Comoedia,* January 5, 1920.

249. Boucher/ROPARTZ, p. 200. French sources give the composer's name variously as Guy Ropartz, Joseph Guy Ropartz, J. Guy Ropartz, Joseph-Guy Ropartz, and Guy-Ropartz.

250. Lamy/ROPARTZ, p. 28.

251. "Au Concerts Lamoureux," *Gil Blas,* February 23, 1903; Debussy/CROCHE, pp. 104–05.

252. Ferey & Menut/ROPARTZ, p. 12.

253. Maillard/ROPARTZ, p. 121.

254. Paul Dukas, "Les Concerts," *La Revue hebdomadaire* (1901); repr. in Dukas/ÉCRITS, p. 551.

255. Ropartz/SYMPHONIES, p. 166.

256. Lamy/ROPARTZ, p. 50.

257. Alfred Bruneau, "Les Concerts," *Le Matin,* November 12, 1906.

258. Régis/MUSIQUE, pp. 415–16.

259. Pierre Lalo, "Concours Cressent–M. Guy Ropartz," *Le Temps,* February 10, 1907.

260. Combarieu/HISTOIRE, p. 483.

261. Jean d'Udine, "Concerts Colonne et Lamoureux," *Le Courrier musical* XIV (December 15, 1911), p. 752. "10th Symphony" obviously refers to Hans von Bülow's famous description of the First Symphony of Brahms (whose music was not respected by most French musicians of this time).

262. Hart/SYMPHONY gives an account of the Cressent competition (p. 336); pp. 425–26 discuss Cools's work, which departed into oblivion after its first hearing.

263. For more, see Hart/SYMPHONY, p. 414.

264. Maillard/ROPARTZ, p. 127.

265. Ferey & Menut/ROPARTZ, pp. 6–7. Translation by author.

266. Maillard/ROPARTZ, pp. 127–28.

267. Maillard/ROPARTZ, pp. 128–30.

268. See p. 656 above for the source of the quote.

269. Mercier/TOURNEMIRE, p. 10.

270. Vuillermoz/SYMPHONIE, p. 339.

271. Reprinted in Thomson/WIDOR, p. 102 n38.

272. Gaston Carraud, "Les Concerts," *La Liberté,* March 8, 1910.

273. Widor/FONDATIONS, p. 192.

274. *Technique de l'orchestre moderne* (Paris: H. Lemoine, 1904). Ravel among others had high praise for Widor's treatise.

275. Opus 42 designates Widor's second set of Organ Symphonies (Nos.5–8). Why he gave the same number to the *Symphonie pour orgue et orchestre* is not clear. In his edition, John R. Near renumbers the work Opus 42 [*bis*] to alleviate confusion. See Near/WIDOR OPUS 42 [BIS], pp. ix–xv.

276. Thomson/WIDOR, p. 41.

277. The symphony figured in a concert at Saint-Sulpice in April 1934, given to honor Widor's retirement. The ninety-year-old composer insisted on conducting the symphony, but his strength failed during the performance and he finished only with great difficulty. See Near/WIDOR, pp. 297–99.

278. Widor had a cordial relationship with Saint-Saëns (who helped launch his career), though it was undoubtedly affected by Widor's increasingly unfriendly rivalry with Saint-Saëns's former student and intimate friend, Fauré.

279. Widor and Schweitzer chose the melody together. Thomson/WIDOR, p. 72.

280. Gaston Carraud, "Concert Sechiari—*Sinfonia sacra* de M. Widor," *La Liberté*, January 14, 1908.

281. From the *Revue et gazette musicale*, 1877; reprinted in Near/WIDOR, pp. 98–99.

282. "La Musique grecque et les Chants de l'église latine," *Revue des deux mondes* 131 (1895), pp. 694–706. Widor was inspired by the newly published writings of Peter Wagner and François Gevaert.

283. "*Symphonie antique*, Ch.-M. Widor," *Le Guide du concert* III (December 23, 1911), p. 189. Widor's note is also reprinted in the score.

284. "*Symphonie antique*, Ch.-M. Widor," *Le Guide du concert* III (December 23, 1911), p. 189.

285. Alfred Bruneau, "Les Concerts," *Le Matin*, December 25, 1911.

286. André-Lamette, "Concerts Colonne [Widor *Symphonie antique*]," *Le Guide musical* (December 31, 1911), p. 828.

287. Near/WIDOR, p. 258.

288. French sources variously spell his name as Gedalge and Gédalge; the family, however, uses the former.

289. Jean Laporte, "Symphonie en ut mineur de A. Gédalge" [*sic*] *S.I.M.* VIII (April 15, 1912), p. 58.

290. Jean d'Udine, "Concerts Colonne et Lamoureux," *Le Courrier musical* XV (March 15, 1912), pp. 169–70.

291. "*Troisième symphonie*, A. Gédalge [*sic*]," *Le Guide du concert* V (January 30, 1914), p. 245.

292. I am grateful to M. André Gedalge, the composer's grandson, for providing a copy of a privately owned recording of the symphony.

293. Pierre Lalo, "Au Châtelet: première audition d'une symphonie de M. André Gédalge [*sic*]," *Le Temps*, March 1, 1910.

294. Jean d'Udine, "Concerts Colonne et Lamoureux," *Le Courrier musical* XII (April 1, 1910), pp. 266–68.

295. For more discussion of these and other works not covered in the present chapter, see Chapters IV and VII and Appendix II of Hart/SYMPHONY. The first of Albert Roussel's four symphonies dates from this period (see Table XVI/27); at the time of writing, his works are slated to be examined in Volume V of this series.

296. Carraud/VIE, pp. 51–52.

297. Perret/MAGNARD, p. 209.

298. Perret/MAGNARD, p. 125.

299. Bardet/MAGNARD, pp. 1–2.

300. Perret/MAGNARD, p. 125.

301. Letter to Guy Ropartz, August 26, 1893; Magnard/CORRESPONDANCE, p. 94.

302. Carraud/VIE, p. 54.

303. Letter of August 19, 1903; Magnard/CORRESPONDANCE, pp. 205–06.

304. Letter to Paul Poujaud, July 8, 1905; cited in Carraud/VIE, p. 124. A lawyer by profession, Poujaud (1856–1936) enjoyed the close friendship of virtually every major French composer at the turn of the century, including both *franckistes* and Debussy.

305. Carraud/VIE, p. 35.

306. Carraud/VIE, p. 203.

307. Perret/MAGNARD, p. 227.

308. The analyses of the First and Second Symphonies are partially based on Harry Halbreich's study in Perret/MAGNARD, pp. 414–33, supplemented by my comments. Maillard/MAGNARD, pp. 91–97, also provides summary descriptions.

309. Perret/MAGNARD, p. 67.

310. Perret/MAGNARD, p. 69.

311. Perret/MAGNARD, p. 133.

312. Perret/MAGNARD, p. 434.

313. Magnard/CORRESPONDANCE, p. 188n.

314. Letter to Gaston Carraud, November 12, 1904; Magnard/CORRESPONDANCE, p. 223.

315. Perret/MAGNARD, p. 435.

316. Letter to Guy Ropartz, May 15, 1899; quoted in Vallas/D'INDY II, pp. 41–42, and in Magnard/CORRESPONDANCE, p. 195n.

317. Perret/MAGNARD, p. 157. *Fervaal,* d'Indy's first opera, premiered in Brussels to great acclaim in 1897.

318. Both reviews are reprinted in the Appendix of Magnard/CORRESPONDANCE, pp. 355–58. Carraud's appeared in *La Liberté,* November 8, 1904, and Dukas's in "La Troisième Symphonie d'Albéric Magnard" in *Chronique des arts et de la curiosité* (November 12, 1904; reprinted in Dukas/ÉCRITS, pp. 614–16).

319. Magnard/CORRESPONDANCE, pp. 357–58; Dukas/ÉCRITS, pp. 615–16.

320. Louis Laloy, "Concerts Chevillard," *La Revue musicale* IV (November 15, 1904), p. 557.

321. Amédée Boutarel, "Concerts Lamoureux [Magnard Third Symphony]," *Le Ménestrel* XVII (November 1904); reprinted in Magnard/CORRESPONDANCE, p. 221n.

322. Letter to Gaston Vallin, May 30, 1914, quoted in Carraud/VIE, p. 78.

323. Carraud/VIE, p. 119.

324. Letter to Ropartz, November 25, 1906; Magnard/CORRESPONDANCE, p. 256.

325. Letter of April 4, 1914; Magnard/CORRESPONDANCE, p. 348. The reference in the last phrase is to Eugène Ysaÿe, who had infuriated the composer by refusing to play the violin sonata Magnard wrote for him following a poor reception at its premiere.

326. Gaston Carraud, "Une symphonie nouvelle d'Albéric Magnard," *La Liberté,* April 7, 1914.

327. Perret/MAGNARD, p. 351.

328. Perret/MAGNARD, p. 353.

329. Perret/MAGNARD, p. 354. The "experienced veteran" is d'Indy, then in charge of the Société Nationale.

330. Tenroc/SOCIÉTÉ, p. 453.

331. Perret/MAGNARD, p. 342.

332. Boursiac/ROMANTISME, p. 27.

333. Analyses of *La Mer* vary widely: they rarely agree, for example, on the forms of the movements, especially "Jeux de vagues." Notable studies include Simon Trezise, *Debussy: La Mer* (Cambridge: Cambridge University Press, 1994), Chapters VI and VII; Marie Rolf, "*La Mer:* A Critical Analysis in the Light of Early Sketches and Editions" (Ph.D. diss., University of Rochester, 1976); Wolfgang Dömling, *Claude Debussy: La Mer* (Munich: Wilhelm Fink, 1976); and Jean Barraqué, "*La Mer* de Debussy, ou la naissance des formes ouvertes," *Analyse musicale* 12 (June 1988), pp. 15–62. Hart/DEBUSSY considers the connections between *La Mer* and the symphony in more detail.

334. For Debussy's comment about his "symphonie," see Debussy/CROCHE, p. 310. An ambiguous term, *symphonie* can signify either "symphony" or "symphonic work," and which one Debussy intended is not entirely clear. For the composer's insistence that *La Mer* be played complete, see Debussy/LETTERS, p. 185.

335. Lavignac/MUSIQUE, p. 408.

336. Laloy/NOUVELLE, p. 533; a translation of the full article can be found in *Louis Laloy (1874–1944) on Debussy, Ravel, and Stravinsky,* trans. and ed. by Deborah Priest (Brookfield, VT: Ashgate Press, 1999), pp. 195–204. Debussy's silence (at least in print) regarding Laloy's description is potentially significant because he often challenged reviews with which he disagreed; for instance, he later rebuked Laloy for praising Ravel's *Histoire naturelles.*

337. For more on *La Mer* and the symphonic suite, see Hart/SYMPHONY, pp. 358–78.

338. For example: "The history of the symphony in France is quickly told, for there are remarkably few notable symphonies by Frenchmen. . . . French composers who did write symphonies were either too heavily influenced by models from across the Rhine or simply lacked the essential qualities for the task. This certainly applies to Chausson, Dukas, Lalo and Saint-Saëns, to the young Bizet and, in a lesser degree, to Franck and d'Indy." Manduell/ROUSSEL, p. 104.

Bibliography of Works Cited

Abel/SINFONISCHEN RUSSLAND

Abel, Jörg Michael. *Die Enstehung der sinfonischen Musik in Russland.* Berlin: Ernst Kuhn, 1996.

Abraham/ARAB MELODIES

Abraham, Gerald. "Arab Melodies in Rimsky-Korsakov and Borodin." Abraham/RUSSIAN & EAST European, pp. 93–98.

Abraham/BALAKIREV

Abraham, Gerald. "Balakirev: A Flawed Genius." Abraham/STUDIES RUSSIAN MUSIC, pp. 311–33.

Abraham/BALAKIREV'S SYMPHONIES

Abraham, Gerald. "Balakirev's Symphonies." Abraham/RUSSIAN MUSIC, pp. 179–92.

Abraham/BORODIN

Abraham, Gerald. *Borodin: The Composer & His Music.* London: Reeves, 1927.

Abraham/BORODIN 2

Abraham, Gerald. "Borodin, Symphony No. 2 in B Minor." Field/MUSICIANS GUIDE, pp. 97–99.

Abraham/BORODIN SYMPHONIST

Abraham, Gerald. "Borodin as a Symphonist." Abraham/STUDIES RUSSIAN MUSIC, pp. 102–18.

Abraham/LISZT & HANDFUL

Abraham, Gerald. "Liszt's Influence on the 'Mighty Handful.'" Abraham/RUSSIAN MUSIC, pp. 81–90.

Abraham/MUSIC TCHAIKOVSKY

Abraham, Gerald, ed. *The Music of Tchaikovsky.* New York: Norton, 1974 [1946].

Abraham/NG MUSORGSKY

Abraham, Gerald. "Modest Musorgsky." NG RUSSIAN MASTERS 1, pp. 109–142.

Abraham/NG RIMSKY-KORSAKOV

Abraham, Gerald. "Nikolay Rimsky-Korsakov." NG RUSSIAN MASTERS 2, pp. 1–47.

Abraham/PROGRAMME PATHÉTIQUE

Abraham, Gerald. "The Programme of the 'Pathétique' Symphony." Abraham/RUSSIAN MUSIC, pp. 143–46.

Abraham/PROGRAMME SCHEHERAZADE

Abraham, Gerald. "The Programme of 'Scheherazade.'" Abraham/RUSSIAN MUSIC, pp. 138–43.

Abraham/RIMSKY SELF-CRITIC

Abraham, Gerald. "Rimsky-Korsakov as Self-Critic." Abraham/SLAVONIC & ROMANTIC, pp. 195–201.

Abraham/RUSSIAN & EAST European

Abraham, Gerald. *Essays on Russian and East European Music.* Oxford: Clarendon Press, 1985.

Abraham/RUSSIAN MUSIC

Abraham, Gerald. *On Russian Music.* London: Reeves, 1939.

Abraham/SLAVONIC & ROMANTIC

Abraham, Gerald. *Slavonic and Romantic Music: Essays and Studies.* New York: St. Martin's Press, 1968.

Abraham/STUDIES RUSSIAN MUSIC

Abraham, Gerald. *Studies in Russian Music.* London: Reeves, 1935.

Abraham/TCHAIKOVSKY 2

Abraham, Gerald. "Tchaikovsky. Symphony No. 2 in C Minor." Field/MUSICIANS GUIDE, pp. 656–59.

Bibliography of Works Cited

Abraham/TCHAIKOVSKY 3	Abraham, Gerald. "Tchaikovsky. Symphony No. 3 in D, Op. 29." Field/MUSICIANS GUIDE, pp. 660–61.
Abraham/TCHAIKOVSKY MANFRED	Abraham, Gerald. "Tchaikovsky. Manfred Symphony, Op. 58." Field/MUSICIANS GUIDE, pp. 633–38.
Abraham/TCHAIKOVSKY REFLECTIONS	Abraham, Gerald. "Tchaikovsky: Some Centennial Reflections." *ML* XXI (1940), 110.
Abraham/USSR IX/i–iii	Abraham, Gerald. "Union of Soviet Socialist Republics." IX/i–iii. *NG* XIX, pp. 380–84.
Abraham & Garden/NG BALAKIREV	Abraham, Gerald, and Garden, Edward. "Mily Balakirev." NG RUSSIAN MASTERS 1, pp. 77–106.
Abraham & Lloyd-Jones/NG BORODIN	Abraham, Gerald, and Lloyd-Jones, David. "Alexander Borodin." NG RUSSIAN MASTERS 1, pp. 45–74.
ABS	American Brahms Society
AfMw	*Archiv für Musikwissenschaft*
Aguétant/SAINT-SAËNS	Aguétant, Pierre. *Saint-Saëns par lui-même, d'après des letters reçues et commentées.* Paris: Éditions 'Alsatia,' 1938.
ALSJ	*American Liszt Society Journal*
Ambros/MUSIK & POESIE	Ambros, August Wilhelm. *Die Gränzen der Musik und Poesie; Eine Studie zur Aesthetik der Tonkunst.* Prag: H. Mercy, 1856.
AMZ	*Allgemeine Musikalische Zeitung* (Leipzig)
Anderson/BEETHOVEN LETTERS	Anderson, Emily. *The Letters of Beethoven.* 3 vols. London: Macmillan, 1961.
Anderson/ELGAR MANUSCRIPT	Anderson, Robert. *Elgar in Manuscript.* Portland: Amadeus Press, 1990.
Apel/HARVARD DICTIONARY 1969	Apel, Willi. *Harvard Dictionary of Music.* Cambridge: Harvard University Press, 1969.
Apel/ORCHESTRAS	Apel, Willi. "Orchestras." Apel/HARVARD DICTIONARY 1969, pp. 606–07.
Art Conducting	*The Art of Conducting: Great Conductors of the Past.* Produced by Stephany Marks and Mark Pickering. Directed by Sue Knussen. 117 min. Hamburg: Teldec Video, 1994. Videocassette.
Asafiev/RUSSIAN MUSIC	Asafiev, Boris Vladimirovich. *Russian Music from the Beginning of the Nineteenth Century.* Trans. by Alfred J. Swan. Ann Arbor: J.W. Edwards, 1953.
Bardet/MAGNARD	Bardet, Bernard, ed. *Albéric Magnard, 1865–1914.* Paris: Bibliothèque Nationale, 1966.
Barricelli/CHAUSSON	Barricelli, Jean-Pierre, and Weinstein, Leo. *Ernest Chausson.* Norman: University of Oklahoma Press, 1955.
Bauer-Lechner/RECOLLECTIONS	Bauer-Lechner, Natalie. *Recollections of Gustav Mahler.* Trans. by Dika Newlin. Ed. by Peter Franklin. Cambridge: Cambridge University Press, 1980.
Baumann/SAINT-SAËNS	Baumann, Émile. *Les Grandes formes de la musique: l'oeuvre de Camille Saint-Saëns.* Paris: Société d'éditions littéraires et artistiques, 1905.
BBS	*Bulletin of the Berlioz Society*

Becker/SPOHR RUSSISCHE	Becker, Hartmut. "Spohr und die russische Musik." Becker & Krempien/SPOHR FESTSCHRIFT, pp. 117–32.
Becker & Krempien/SPOHR FESTSCHRIFT	Becker, Hartmut, and Krempien, Ranier (eds.). *Louis Spohr: Festschrift und Ausstellungskatalogzum 200. Geburtstag*. Kassel: Wenderoth, 1984.
Bellaigue/CONCERTS	Bellaigue, Camille. "Les Concerts: Symphonies de MM. Victorin Joncières, Benjamin Godard, d'Indy et Saint-Saëns." *Revue des deux mondes* LXXXII (July 15, 1887):454–64.
Bennett/STERNDALE BENNETT LIFE	Bennett, J. R. Sterndale. *The Life of William Sterndale Bennett*. Cambridge: University Press, 1907.
Benoliel/PARRY	Benoliel, Bernard. *Parry before Jerusalem: Studies of his Life and Music with Excerpts from his Published Writings*. Aldershot: Ashgate, 1997.
Bernard/PASDELOUP	Bernard, Elisabeth. "Jules Pasdeloup et les Concerts Populaires." *Revue de musicologie* LVII (1971):150–78.
Billroth/MUSIKALISCH	Billroth, Theodor. *Wer ist musikalisch?* Preface by Eduard Hanslick. Berlin: Gebruder Paetel, 1898.
Blom/EARLY TCHAIKOVSKY SYM	Blom, E. W. "The Early Tchaikovsky Symphonies." In *Stepchildren of Music*. London: G. T. Foulis, [1925]. Reprint, Freeport, NY: Books for Libraries Press, 1967.
Bloom/PARIS 1830S	Bloom, Peter, ed. *Music in Paris in the Eighteen-Thirties*. Stuyvesant, NY: Pendragon Press, 1987.
Blume/CLASSIC & ROMANTIC	Blume, Friedrich. *Classic and Romantic Music: A Comprehensive Survey*. Trans. by M. D. Herter Norton. New York: Norton, 1970.
Bonds/AFTER BEETHOVEN	Bonds, Mark Evan. *After Beethoven: Imperatives of Originality in the Symphony*. Cambridge: Harvard University Press, 1996.
Bonnerot/SAINT-SAËNS	Bonnerot, Jean. *Camille Saint-Saëns: sa vie et son oeuvre*. Paris: Durand, 1914.
Boucher/ROPARTZ	Boucher, Maurice. "Guy Ropartz." *La Revue musicale* V (June 1, 1924):199–208.
Boult/NIKISCH	Boult, Adrian C. "Nikisch and Method in Rehearsal." *MR* XI/2 (May 1950):122–25.
Boursiac/ROMANTISME	Boursiac, Marcel. "Devenir de la musique française du romantisme à l'aube du XXᵉ siècle." Langevin/MUSICIENS, pp. 13–28.
Boyden/CONCERTO	Boyden, David. "When is a Concerto not a Concerto?" *MQ* XLIII/2 (April 1957):220–32.
BPLC	Boston Public Library Collection
Brook/SYMPHONY 1720–1840	Brook, Barry S., ed. in chief. *The Symphony, 1720–1840*. New York: Garland, 1979–1985.
Brown/FIRST GOLDEN AGE	Brown, A. Peter. *The Symphonic Repertoire*. Vol. II, *The First Golden Age of the Viennese Symphony: Haydn, Mozart, Beethoven, and Schubert*. Bloomington: Indiana University Press, 2001.

Brown/GLINKA — Brown, David. *Mikhail Glinka. A Biographical and Critical Study.* London: Oxford University Press, 1974.

Brown/GROVE — Brown, A. Peter. "Walking Through Different Grove's with Sir George." *American Scholar* LXIV/4 (Autumn 1995):579–89.

Brown/NG GLINKA — Brown, David. "Mikhail Glinka." NG RUSSIAN MASTERS 1, pp. 1–42.

Brown/NG TCHAIKOVSKY — Brown, David. "Pytor Il'yich Tchaikovsky." NG RUSSIAN MASTERS 1, pp. 145–250.

Brown/RUSSIA SYMPHONY — Brown, David. "Russia before the Revolution." Layton/SYMPHONY, pp. 262–91.

Brown/SECOND GOLDEN AGE — Brown, A. Peter. *The Symphonic Repertoire.* Vol. IV, *The Second Golden Age of the Viennese Symphony: Brahms, Bruckner, Dvořák, Mahler, and Selected Contemporaries.* Bloomington: Indiana University Press, 2003.

Brown/SIBELIUS EARLY SYMPHONIES RUSSIAN — Brown, Malcolm H. "Perspectives on the Early Symphonies: The Russian Connection Redux." Tarasti/SIBELIUS CONFERENCE 1990, pp. 21–30.

Brown/TCHAIKOVSKY I — Brown, David. *Tchaikovsky: A Biographical and Critical Study, Volume I: The Early Years (1840–1874).* New York and London: Norton, 1978.

Brown/TCHAIKOVSKY II — Brown, David. *Tchaikovsky: A Biographical and Critical Study, Volume II: The Crisis Years (1874–1878).* New York and London: Norton, 1982.

Brown/TCHAIKOVSKY III — Brown, David. *Tchaikovsky: A Biographical and Critical Study, Volume III: The Years of Wandering (1878–1885).* New York and London: Norton, 1986.

Brown/TCHAIKOVSKY IV — Brown, David. *Tchaikovsky: A Biographical and Critical Study, Volume IV: The Final Years (1885–1893).* New York and London: Norton, 1986.

Brown/TCHAIKOVSKY REMEMBERED — Brown, David. *Tchaikovsky Remembered.* London: Faber and Faber, 1993.

Brown & Wiley/SLAVONIC WESTERN — Brown, Malcolm Hamrick, and Wiley, Roland John (eds.). *Slavonic and Western Music: Essays for Gerald Abraham.* Ann Arbor: UMI Research Press, 1985.

BSBS — *Barry S. Brook Symphony;* see Brook/SYMPHONY 1720–1840.

Burk/BSO TCHAIKOVSKY 5 — Burk, John N. Program notes for the 57th season of the Boston Symphony Orchestra. "Tchaikovsky. Symphony No. 5 in E minor, Op. 64." December 24, 25, 1937, pp. 463–70.

Bush/BENNETT — Bush, Geoffrey. "Sterndale Bennett and the Orchestra." *MT* CXXVII/1719 (June 1986):322–24.

Busoni/BRIEFE FRAU — Busoni, Ferruccio. *Briefe an seine Frau.* Ed. by Friedrich Schnapp. Zurich: Rotaptel-Verlag, 1935.

Byron/LETTERS & JOURNALS — Byron, [George Gordon Lord]. *"So late into the night": Byron's Letters and Journals.* Vol. 5 1816–1817. Ed. by Leslie A. Marchand. Cambridge: Harvard University Press, 1976.

BzMw
Beiträge zur Musikwissenschaft

Calvocoressi/MUSICIANS
Calvocoressi, Michel-Dmitri. *Musicians Gallery: Music and Ballet in Paris and London.* London: Faber and Faber, 1933.

Calvocoressi/MUSSORGSKY
Calvocoressi, Michel-Dmitri. *Mussorgsky.* New York: Collier Books, 1962.

Campbell/RUSSIAN MUSIC 1830–1880
Campbell, Stuart, ed. and trans. *Russians on Russian Music, 1830–1880: An Anthology.* Cambridge: Cambridge University Press, 1994.

Cannata/RACHMANINOFF SYMPHONY
Cannata, David Butler. *Rachmaninoff and the Symphony.* Innsbruck-Vienna: Studien Verlag, 1999.

Carner/BEETHOVEN MVT
Carner, Mosco. "A Beethoven Movement and Its Successors." *ML* XX/3 (July 1939):281–91.

Carragan/WAGNERIAN SYMPHONY
Carragan, William, ed. *The Wagnerian Symphony.* Poughkeepsie, NY: The Bruckner Archive, forthcoming.

Carraud/HISTOIRE
Carraud, Gaston. "L'Histoire de la Symphonie au Concerts-Lamoureux—un membre amputé d'une symphonie de M. Roussel." *La Liberté,* November 12, 1907.

Carraud/VIE
Carraud, Gaston. *La Vie, l'oeuvre, et la mort d'Albéric Magnard.* Paris: Rouart, Lerolle, and Cie., 1921.

Charlton/HOFFMANN
Hoffmann, Ernst Theodor Amadeus. *E.T.A. Hoffmann's Musical Writings: "Kreisleriana," "The Poet and Composer," Music Criticism.* Ed. by David Charlton. Trans. by Martyn Clarke. Cambridge: Cambridge University Press, 1989.

Chausson/ÉCRITS
Chausson, Ernest. *Écrits inédits: Journaux intimes, roman de jeunesse, correspondance.* Ed. and annotated by Jean Gallois and Isabelle Bretaudeau. Monaco: Éditions du Rocher, 1999.

Chimènes/BUDGET
Chimènes, Myriam. "Le Budget de la musique sous la IIIᵉ République." Dufort & Fauquet/MUSIQUE, pp. 261–312.

Closson/ORIGINES
Closson, Ernest. "Les Origines germaniques de César Franck." *S.I.M.* VIII (April 15, 1913):24–30.

CM
Current Musicology

CMS
College Music Society

Cole/RONDO
Cole, Malcolm S. "The Development of the Instrumental Rondo Finale from 1750 to 1800." Ph.D. diss., Princeton University, 1964.

Colles/ELGAR 1
Colles, Henry Cope. "Sir Edward Elgar's Symphony." *MT* XLIX (December 1, 1908):778–80.

Colles/SYMPHONY & DRAMA
Colles, H. C. *Symphony and Drama 1850–1900.* Oxford History of Music Vol. VII. London: Oxford University Press, 1934.

Collins/GERM GUFF
Collins, M. Stuart. "Germ Motives and Guff." *MR* XXIII (August 1962):238–43.

Collins/RAKHMANINOV
Collins, Dana Livingston. "Form, Harmony, and Tonality in S. Rakhmaninov's Three Symphonies." Ph.D. diss., University of Arizona, 1988.

Combarieu/HISTOIRE — Combarieu, Jules. *Histoire de la musique III*. Paris: Armand Colin, 1919.

Cone/FANTASTIC — Cone, Edward T. *Berlioz. Fantastic Symphony*. (Norton Critical Score). New York: Norton, 1971.

Cooper/FRENCH — Cooper, Martin. *French Music from the Death of Berlioz to the Death of Fauré*. London: Oxford University Press, 1969.

Cooper/ITALIAN — Cooper, John Michael. *Felix Mendelssohn Bartholdy and the "Italian Symphony": Historical, Musical and Extramusical Perspectives*. Ph.D. diss., Duke University, 1994.

Cooper/RISE — Cooper, Jeffrey. *The Rise of Instrumental Music and Concert Series in Paris, 1828–1871*. Ann Arbor: UMI Research Press, 1983.

Cooper/TCHAIKOVSKY SYMPHONIES — Cooper, Martin. "The Symphonies." Abraham/MUSIC TCHAIKOVSKY, pp. 24–46.

Cooper/ZWEIFEL — Cooper, John Michael. " 'Aber eben dieser Zweifel': A New Look at Mendelssohn's 'Italian' Symphony." *19CM* XV/3 (Spring 1992), pp. 169–87.

Copland/NEW MUSIC — Copland, Aaron. *The New Music, 1900–1960*. Rev. and enlarged ed. New York: Norton, 1968.

Cowen/ART & FRIENDS — Cowen, Sir Frederic H. *My Art and My Friends*. London: Arnold, 1913.

Cox/ELGAR SYMPHONIES — Cox, David. "Edward Elgar (1857–1934)." Simpson/SYMPHONY, Vol. 2, pp. 15–28.

Craig/BEETHOVEN — Craig, Kenneth M. Jr. "The Beethoven Symphony in London: Initial Decades." *College Music Symposium* 25 (1985):73–91.

Culshaw/RACHMANINOV — Culshaw, John. *Sergei Rachmaninov*. London: Dobson, 1949.

Curtiss/BIZET — Curtiss, Mina. *Bizet and His World*. London: Secker & Warburg, 1959.

Dahlhaus/19CM — Dahlhaus, Carl. *Nineteenth-Century Music*. Trans. by J. Bradford Robinson. Berkeley: University of California Press, 1989.

Dahlhaus/ROMANTISCHEN SYMPHONIEN — Dahlhaus, Carl. "Studien zu romantischen Symphonien." *Jahrbuch des Staatlichen Instituts für Musikforschung, Preussischer Kulturbesitz* (Berlin, 1972): 104–19.

Dammann/TCHAIKOVSKY 4 — Dammann, Susanne. "An Examination of Problem History in Tchaikovsky's Fourth Symphony." Kearney/TCHAIKOVSKY WORLD, pp. 197–215.

Davies/FRANCK — Davies, Laurence. *César Franck and His Circle*. Boston: Houghton Mifflin Co., 1970.

Davies/PATHS MODERN — Davies, Laurence. *Paths to Modern Music: Aspects of Music from Wagner to the Present Day*. New York: Charles Scribner's Sons, 1971.

Davies/SYMPHONY FRANCE — Davies, Laurence. "The Symphony in France." Davies/PATHS MODERN, pp. 139–52.

Davison/MENDELSSOHN TO WAGNER   Davison, J. W. *Music during the Victorian Era: From Mendelssohn to Wagner.* Ed. by Henry Davison. London: Reeves, 1912.

Dean/BIZET   Dean, Winton. *Bizet.* The Master Musician Series. London: J. M. Dent & Sons, 1975.

Deane/ROUSSEL   Deane, Basil. *Albert Roussel.* London: Barrie and Rockliff, 1961.

Debussy/CROCHE   Debussy, Claude. *Monsieur Croche et autres écrits,* introduced with notes by François Lesure. Rev. and aug. ed. Paris: Gallimard, 1987.

Debussy/LETTERS   Debussy, Claude. *Debussy Letters.* Sel. and ed. by François Lesure and Roger Nichols, trans. by Roger Nichols. Cambridge, MA: Harvard University Press, 1987.

Deldevez/SOCIÉTÉ   Deldevez, Édouard. *La Société des Concerts, 1860 à 1885 (Conservatoire National de Musique).* Paris: Firmin-Didor, 1887; new ed., ed. and annotated by Gérard Streletski. Heilbronn: Lucie Galland, 1998.

Demuth/FRANCK   Demuth, Norman. *César Franck.* London: Dennis Dobson, 1949.

Dennison/ELGAR'S APPRENTICESHIP   Dennison, Peter. "Elgar's Musical Apprenticeship." Monk/ELGAR STUDIES, pp. 1–34.

DGG   *Deutsche Grammophon Gesellschaft*

Dianin/BORODIN   Dianin, Serge. *Borodin.* Trans. by Robert Lord. London: Oxford University Press, 1963.

Dibble/PARRY   Dibble, Jeremy. *C. Hubert H. Parry: His Life and Music.* Oxford: Clarendon Press, 1992.

Dibble/PARRY & ELGAR   Dibble, Jeremy. "Parry and Elgar: A New Perspective." *MT* CXXV/1701 (November 1984):639–43.

Dibble/PARRY, STANFORD, BRITISH SYMPHONY   Dibble, Jeremy. "Parry, Stanford and the Pursuit of the British Symphony 1880–1910." *Brio* XXXII/1 (Spring/Summer 1995):3–19.

Dibble/STANFORD   Dibble, Jeremy. *Charles Villiers Stanford: Man and Musician.* Oxford: Oxford University Press, 2002.

DJbMw   *Deutsches Jahrbuch des Musikwissenschaft*

Djemil/ROPARTZ   Djemil, Enyss. *J. Guy Ropartz ou la Recherche d'une vocation: l'oeuvre littéraire du maître et ses résonances musicales.* Le Mans: J. Vilaire, 1967.

Dörffel/GEWANDHAUS   Dörffel, Alfred. *Die Gewandhaus-Konzerte zu Leipzig, 1781–1881.* 2 Vols. Leipzig: VEB Deutscher Verlag für Musik, 1980 (reprint).

Downes/GUIDE SYMPHONY   Downes, Edward. *The New York Philharmonic Guide to the Symphony.* New York: Walker, 1976.

Druskin/LENINGRAD   Druskin, Mikhail. "Leningrad." *NG* X, pp. 659–65.

Dufort & Fauquet/MUSIQUE   Dufort, Hugues, and Fauquet, Joël-Marie (eds.). *La Musique: du théorique au politique.* Paris: Klincksieck, 1991.

Dufourcq/MUSIQUE   Dufourcq, Norbert. *La musique française.* Paris: A. and J. Picard, 1970.

Dukas/AUTOBIOGRAPHIE

Dukas, Paul. "Une autobiographie de M. Paul Dukas." *Revue musicale de Lyon* (March 27, 1910):746–49.

Dukas/CORRESPONDANCE

Dukas, Paul. *Correspondance de Paul Dukas.* Letters sel. and ed. by Georges Favre. Paris: Durand, 1971.

Dukas/ÉCRITS

Dukas, Paul. *Les Écrits de Paul Dukas sur la musique.* Paris: Société d'Éditions françaises et internationales, 1948.

Dukas/D'INDY

Dukas, Paul. "Concerts Lamoureux: La *Symphonie sur un thème montagnard français* de M. Vincent d'Indy." *La Revue hebdomadaire* (December 2, 1893):626–31.

Dunhill/STANFORD

Dunhill, Thomas F. "Charles Villiers Stanford: Some Aspects of his Work and Influence." *PRMA* LIII (1926–1927):41–65.

EcS

Eighteenth-century Studies

Eddins/ROUSSEL

Eddins, John. "The Symphonic Music of Albert Roussel." Ph.D. diss., Florida State University, 1966.

Ehrlich/PHILHARMONIC SOCIETY LONDON

Ehrlich, Cyril. *First Philharmonic: A History of the Royal Philharmonic Society.* Oxford: Oxford University Press, 1995.

Einstein/ROMANTIC

Einstein, Alfred. *Music in the Romantic Era.* New York: Norton, 1947.

Eisen/MOZART STUDIES [I]

Eisen, Cliff. *Mozart Studies [I].* Oxford: Clarendon Press, 1991.

Elkin/ROYAL PHILHARMONIC

Elkin, Robert. *Royal Philharmonic: The Annals of the Royal Philharmonic Society.* London: Rider, 1947.

Ellis/CRITICISM 19C FRANCE

Ellis, Katharine. *Music Criticism in Nineteenth-Century France: La Revue et Gazette musicale de Paris, 1834–80.* Cambridge: Cambridge University Press, 1995.

Elwart/SOCIÉTÉ

Elwart, A. *Histoire de la Société des concerts du Conservatoire impérial de musique.* Paris: A. Castel, 1860, expanded ed., 1864.

Evans/TCHAIKOVSKY

Evans, Edwin. *Tchaikovsky.* Rev. by Gerald Abraham. New York: Collier, 1963 [1935].

Fallon/SYMPHONIES

Fallon, Daniel Martin. "The Symphonies and Symphonic Poems of Camille Saint-Saëns." Ph.D. diss., Yale University, 1973.

Fauquet/FRANCK

Fauquet, Joël-Marie. *César Franck.* Paris: Fayard, 1999.

Fauquet/TOURNEMIRE

Fauquet, Joël-Marie. *Catalogue de l'oeuvre de Charles Tournemire.* Geneva: Minkoff, 1979.

Fauser/ORCHESTERGESANG

Fauser, Annegret. *Der Orchestergesang in Frankreich zwischen 1870 und 1920.* Freiburg: Laaber, 1994.

Fauser & Schwartz/WAGNÉRISME

Fauser, Annegret, and Schwartz, Manuela (eds.). *Von Wagner zum 'wagnérisme': Musik, Literatur, Kunst, Politik.* Deutsch-Französische Kulturbibliothek, Band 12. Leipzig: Universitätsverlag, 1999.

Favre/DUKAS   Favre, Georges. *Paul Dukas*. Paris: La Colombe, 1948.

Favre/OEUVRE   Favre, Georges. *L'Oeuvre de Paul Dukas*. Paris: Durand, 1969.

Fellinger/PERIODICALS   Fellinger, Imogen. "Periodicals." *NG* XIV, pp. 407–32.

Ferey & Menut/ROPARTZ   Ferey, Mathieu, and Menut, Benoît. "Fascinantes Symphonies–" Liner notes to Guy Ropartz, Symphony Nos. 1 and 4. Trans. by John Tyler Tuttle. Orchestre Symphonique et Lyrique de Nancy/Sebastian Lang-Lessing (Timpani 1C1093, 2006).

FESTSCHRIFT CONRADIN   Kalisch, Volker. *Festschrift Han Conradin zum 70. Geburtstag*. Berg: Haupt, 1983.

FESTSCHRIFT DAVISON   *Essays on Music in Honor of Archibald Thompson Davison*. Cambridge: Department of Music, Harvard University, 1957.

FESTSCHRIFT FORCHERT   Allroggen, Gerhard, and Altenberg, Detlef (eds.). *Festschrift Arno Forchert zum 60. Geburtstag am 29. Dezember 1985*. Kassel: Bärenreiter, 1986.

FESTSCHRIFT MUSIKFORENINGENS   Ravn, V. C., and Hammerich, Angul. *Festskrift: Anledning af Musikforeningens Halvhundredaarsdag*. Copenhagen: Udgivet af Musikforeningen, 1886.

FESTSCHRIFT ROSENTHAL   Elvers, Rudolf, ed. *Festschrift Albi Rosenthal*. Tutzing: Hans Schneider, 1984.

FESTSCHRIFT SCHIØRRING   *Til Professor, Dr.phil. Nils Schiørring pa hans tres ars fodselsdag den 8.april 1970. En samling kortere musikhistoriske og teoretiske bidrag*. Copenhagen: Musikvidenskabeligt Inst., Copenhagen University, 1970.

FESTSCHRIFT WIORA   Finscher, Ludwig, and Mahling, Christoph-Hellmut. *Festschrift Wiora*. Kassel: Bärenreiter, 1967.

Fétis/CURIOSITÉS   Fétis, François-Joseph. *Curiosités historiques de la musique*. Paris: Janet et Cotelle, 1830.

Fétis/FANTASTIQUE   Fétis, François-Joseph. "Analyse critique: Épisode de la Vie d'un Artiste. Grande Symphonie Fantastique par H. Berlioz." *RM* II/15 (February 1, 1835):33–35. Trans. in Cone/FANTASTIC, pp. 215–20.

Fidler & James/INTERNATIONAL MUSIC JOURNALS   Fidler, Linda, and James, Richard S. *International Music Journals*. New York: Greenwood Press, 1990.

Field/MUSICIANS GUIDE   Field, Corey. *The Musician's Guide to Symphonic Music: Essays from the Eulenburg Scores*. Mainz: Schott, 1997.

Finscher/SAINT-SAËNS   Finscher, Ludwig. "The Symphony and the Artist's Creed: Camille Saint-Saëns and His Third Symphony." Knowles/CRITICA MUSICA, pp. 97–124.

Floros/BEETHOVENS EROICA   Floros, Constantin. *Beethovens Eroica und Prometheus-Musik: Sujet-Studien*. Wilhelmshaven: Heinrichshofen, 1978.

Floros/MAHLER III   Floros, Constantin. *Gustav Mahler III: Die Symphonien*. Wiesbaden: Breitkopf & Härtel, 1985.

Forbes/BEETHOVEN 5

Forbes, Elliot, ed. *Beethoven Symphony No.5.* New York: Norton, 1971.

Foreman/MUSIC HAZELL'S ANNUAL

Foreman, Lewis, ed. *Music in England, 1885–1920: As Recounted in Hazell's Annual.* London: Thames, 1994.

Foreman/STANFORD 6

Foreman, Lewis. Liner notes to Sir Charles Villiers Stanford, Symphony No. 6 in E-flat major, Op. 94. Ulster Orchestra/Vernon Handley (Colchester, England: Chandos Records Ltd., 1988).

Foster/PHILHARMONIC SOCIETY LONDON

Foster, Myles Birket. *The History of the Philharmonic Society of London: 1813–1912.* London: John Lane, 1912.

Fourcaud/MUSIQUE

Fourcaud, Louis. "Musique." *La Revue indépendante,* nouvelle série, Tome I (December 1886):238–45.

Franck/CORRESPONDANCE

Franck, César. *Correspondance.* Ed. and annotated by Joël-Marie Fauquet. Sprimont, Belgium: Pierre Mardaga, 1999.

Franck/NOTICE

Franck, César. *Notice analytique et thématique de la* Symphonie en ré mineur *de César Franck.* Paris: J. Hamelle, 1896; repr. in Léon Vallas, "La Symphonie de César Franck." *Nouvelle revue musicale* (March 25, 1906):696–702 and Fauquet/FRANCK.

Friedland/FARRENC

Friedland, Bea. *Louise Farrenc, 1804–1875: Composer, Performer, Scholar.* Ann Arbor: UMI Research Press, 1980.

Fulcher/CULTURAL

Fulcher, Jane F. *French Cultural Politics and Music from the Dreyfus Affair to the First World War.* New York: Oxford University Press, 1999.

Fulcher/DEBUSSY

Fulcher, Jane, ed. *Debussy and His World.* Princeton: Princeton University Press, 2001.

Fuller-Maitland/COWEN

Fuller-Maitland, J. A. "Cowen, Frederic Hymen." Grove 2/I, pp. 630–31.

Fuller-Maitland/ENGLISH MUSIC 19th

Fuller-Maitland, J. A. *English Music in the XIXth Century.* New York: Dutton, 1902.

Fuller-Maitland/LIE

Fuller-Maitland, J. A. "Lie, Sigurd." Grove 2/II, p. 724.

Fuller-Maitland/PARRY & STANFORD

Fuller-Maitland, J. A. *The Music of Parry and Stanford: An Essay in Comparative Criticism.* Cambridge: Heffer & Sons, 1934.

Gabéaud/D'INDY

Gabéaud, Alice. *Auprès du maître Vincent d'Indy: souvenirs des cours de composition.* Paris: Éditions de la Schola Cantorum, 1933.

Gallois/CHAUSSON

Gallois, Jean. *Ernest Chausson.* Paris: Fayard, 1994.

Gallois/CHAUSSON 1967

Gallois, Jean. *Ernest Chausson: L'homme et son oeuvre.* Paris: Seghers, 1967.

Garden/BALAKIREV

Garden, Edward. *Balakirev: A Critical Study of His Life and Music.* London: Faber & Faber, 1967.

Garden/BALAKIREV PERSONALITY

Garden. Edward. "Balakirev's Personality." *PRMA* XCVI (1969–1970):43–55.

Garden/BALAKIREV & TCHAIKOVSKY

Garden, Edward. "The Influence of Balakirev on Tchaikovsky." *PRMA* CVII (1980–1981):86–100.

Garden/SIBELIUS & BALAKIREV

Garden, Edward. "Sibelius and Balakirev." Brown & Wiley/SLAVONIC WESTERN, pp. 215–18.

Garden/TCHAIKOVSKY

Garden, Edward. *Tchaikovsky.* London: Dent, 1973.

Garlington/LESUEUR, OSSIAN

Garlington, Aubrey S. "Lesueur, Ossian, and a 'Synthesis of the Arts.'" *CMS* XVIII (Winter 1964): 352–56.

Garlington/LESUEUR, OSSIAN, BERLIOZ

Garlington, Aubrey S. "Lesueur, 'Ossian,' and Berlioz." *JAMS* XVII/2 (Summer 1964):206–08.

George/TONALITY

George, Graham. *Tonality and Musical Structure.* New York: Praeger, 1970.

Gérard/DUPARC

Gérard, Yves. "Lettres d'Henri Duparc à Ernest Chausson." *Revue de musicologie* (December 1956):125–46.

Gimbel/ELGAR 2

Gimbel, Allen. "Elgar's Prize Song: Quotation and Allusion in the Second Symphony." *19CM* XII/3 (Spring 1989):231–40.

Glinka/MEMOIRS

Glinka, Mikhail Ivanovich. *Memoirs.* Trans. by Richard B. Mudge. Norman: University of Oklahoma Press, 1963.

Goepp/SYMPHONIES MEANING

Goepp, Philip Henry. *Symphonies and their Meaning.* Ser. I-III. Philadelphia & London: J. B. Lippincott Company, 1897–1913.

Goodwin/LONDON

Goodwin, Nöel. "London (VI: 2, 6: iii)." *NG* XI, pp. 182–88, 210–11.

Göthel/SWV

Göthel, Folker. *Thematisch-Bibliographisches Verzeichnis der Werke von Louis Spohr.* Tutzing: Schneider, 1981.

Gounod/AUTOBIOGRAPHICAL

Gounod, Charles. *Autobiographical Reminiscences.* Trans. by W. Hely Hutchinson. London: William Heinemann, 1896.

Graves/PARRY

Graves, Charles C. *Hubert Parry: His Life and Works.* 2 Vols. London: Macmillan, 1926.

Gray/SIBELIUS RECEPTION ENGLISH SYMPHONIC THEORY

Gray, Laura J. "'The Symphony in the Mind of God': Sibelius Reception and English Symphonic Theory." Murtomäki, Kilpeläinen & Väisänen/SIBELIUS CONFERENCE 1995, pp. 62–72.

Greenawalt/RUSSIAN SYMPHONY

Greenawalt, Terrence Lee. "A Study of the Symphony in Russia from Glinka to the Early Twentieth Century." Ph.D. diss., Eastman School of Music, 1972.

Greene/STANFORD

Greene, Harry Plunket. *Charles Villiers Stanford.* London: Arnold, 1935.

Greyerz/RÖSELIGARTE

Greyerz, Otto Aimé Alphons von, and Bohnenblust, Gottfried. *Im Röseligarte, schweizerische Volkslieder.* Bern: A. Francke, 1914.

Griffiths/RIMSKY-KORSAKOV

Griffiths, Steven. *A Critical Study of the Music of Rimsky-Korsakov, 1844–1890.* New York: Garland, 1989.

[Grove]/CRYSTAL PALACE CATALOGUE	[Grove, George?]. *Crystal Palace: Catalogue of the Principal Instrumental and Vocal Works Performed at the Saturday Concerts from 1855–1872.* London: Burt, 1872.
Grove/MENDELSSOHN	Grove, Sir George. *Beethoven, Schubert, Mendelssohn.* London: Macmillan & Co., 1951.
GROVE 2	*The Grove Dictionaries of Music and Musicians.* 2nd ed. Ed. by J. A. Fuller-Maitland. London: Macmillan, 1910.
GROVE 5	*The Grove Dictionaries of Music and Musicians.* 5th ed. Ed. by Eric Blom. London: Macmillan, 1954; New York: St. Martin's Press, 1970.
Grover/CHAUSSON	Grover, Ralph Scott. *Ernest Chausson.* London: Associated University Presses, 1980.
Hadow/PARRY	Hadow, William Henry. "Sir Hubert Parry." *PRMA* XLV (1918–1919):135–47.
Halbreich/TOURNEMIRE	Halbreich, Harry. Liner notes to Charles Tournemire, Symphonies Nos. 5 and 8. L'Orchestre philharmonique de Liège et de la communauté française/Pierre Bartholomée (Auvidis Valois 4793, 1997).
Hamburger/LISZT & SAINT-SAËNS	Hamburger, Klára. "Three Unpublished Letters by Liszt to Saint-Saëns." *NHQ* XXIX/III (Autumn 1988):222–29.
Hanslick/BEAUTIFUL	Hanslick, Eduard. *The Beautiful in Music.* Trans. by Gustav Cohen. Ed. by Morris Weitz. Indianapolis: Bobbs-Merrill, 1957.
Hanslick/CONCERTE 1870–1885	Hanslick, Eduard. *Concerte, Componisten und Virtuosen der lezten Jahre, 1870–1885.* 3rd ed. Berlin: Allgemeiner Verein für Deutsche Litteratur, 1896.
Hanslick/CRITICISM	Hanslick, Eduard. *Hanslick's Music Criticisms.* Trans. and ed. by Henry Pleasants. New York: Dover, 1988 [1950].
Hanslick/TAGEBUCHE	Hanslick, Eduard. *Aus dem Tagebuche eines Musikers.* 3rd ed. Berlin: Allgemeiner Verein für Deutsche Litteratur, 1892.
Harding/SAINT-SAËNS	Harding, James. *Saint-Saëns and His Circle.* London: Chapman & Hall, 1965.
HARM	*The Harmonicon*
Hart/DEBUSSY	Hart, Brian. "The Symphony in Debussy's World: A Context for His Criticisms of the Genre and Early Interpretations of *La Mer.*" Fulcher/DEBUSSY, pp. 181–201.
Hart/D'INDY	Hart, Brian. "Vincent d'Indy and the Development of the French Symphony." *ML* 87 (May 2006), pp. 237–61.
Hart/D'INDY & ROPARTZ	Hart, Brian. "Two French Responses to the Wagnerian Symphony: d'Indy's Second and Ropartz's Third." Carragan/WAGNERIAN SYMPHONY.

Hart/NATIONAL	Hart, Brian. "The Symphony and Questions of National Identity in Early Twentieth-Century France." In *Music, Culture, and National Identity in France (1870–1939),* ed. Barbara Kelly. Eastman Studies in Music, ed. Ralph P. Locke. Rochester: University of Rochester Press, forthcoming.
Hart/SYMPHONY	Hart, Brian J. "The Symphony in Theory and Practice in France, 1900–1914." Ph.D. diss., Indiana University, 1994.
Hart/WAGNER	Hart, Brian J. "Wagner and the *franckiste* 'Message-Symphony' in Early Twentieth-Century France." Fauser & Schwartz/WAGNÉRISME, pp. 315–37.
Hascher/SCHUBERT	Hascher, Xavier. "Schubert's Reception in France: A Chronology (1828–1928)." In *The Cambridge Companion to Schubert,* ed. Christopher H. Gibbs. Cambridge: Cambridge University Press, 1997, pp. 263–69.
Heartz/HUNTING CHORUS	Heartz, Daniel. "The Hunting Chorus in Haydn's *Jahreszeiten* and the 'Air the Chasses' in the *Encyclopédie.*" *EcS* IX/4 (Summer 1976):523–39.
Hepokoski/ELGAR [SYMPHONIES]	Hepokoski, James. "Elgar [Symphonies]." Holoman/19C SYM, pp. 327–44.
Hill/SYMPHONY	Hill, Ralph, ed. *The Symphony.* London: Penguin Books, 1949.
Hoffmann/MUSIC CRITICISM	Hoffmann, E. T. A. *E. T. A. Hoffmann's Musical Writings: Kreisleriana, the Poet and the Composer, Music Criticism.* Ed., annotated, and introduced by David Charlton. Trans. by Martyn Clarke. Cambridge: Cambridge University Press, 1989.
Holoman/19C SYM	Holoman, D. Kern, ed. *The Nineteenth-Century Symphony.* New York: Schirmer Books, 1997.
Holoman/SOCIÉTÉ	Holoman, D. Kern. *The Société des Concerts du Conservatoire 1828–1967.* Berkeley: University of California Press, 2004.
Howes/MUSICAL RENAISSANCE	Howes, Frank. *The English Musical Renaissance.* New York: Stein and Day, 1966.
Hudson/CATALOGUE STANFORD REV	Hudson, Frederick. "A Revised and Extended Catalogue of the Works of Charles Villiers Stanford (1852–1924)." *MR* XXXVII/2 (May 1976): 106–29.
Hudson/RUBATO	Hudson, Richard. *Stolen Time: The History of Tempo Rubato.* Oxford: Clarendon Press, 1994.
Huebner/GOUNOD	Huebner, Steven. "Charles Gounod." *NG 2* X, pp. 215–36.
Huebner/OPERA	Huebner, Steven. *French Opera at the* Fin de siècle: *Wagnerism, Nationalism, and Style.* New York: Oxford University Press, 1999.

Hueffer/MUSIC ENGLAND 1837–1887 — Hueffer, Francis. *Half a Century of Music in England, 1837–1887: Essays Towards a History.* London: Chapman and Hall, 1889.

Hughes/GOUNOD — Hughes, Gervaise. "Gounod's Symphonies." *Sidelights on a Century of Music: 1825–1924.* London: Macdonald, 1969, pp. 9–13.

Hull/RACHMANINOV — Hull, Robin. "Sergei Rachmaninov (1873–1943)." Hill/SYMPHONY, pp. 390–401.

Hume/OLSEN — Hume, Duncan. "Olsen, Ole." Grove 2/III, p. 433.

Hume/SINDING — Hume, Duncan. "Sinding, Christian." Grove 2/IV, p. 458.

d'Indy/COURS COMPOSITION — d'Indy Vincent. *Cours de composition musicale.* Ed. by Auguste Sérieyx. Vol. 3: IIe livre. 2e partie. Paris: Durand, 1933.

d'Indy/ÉCOLE — d'Indy, Vincent. "Une école d'art répondant aux besoins modernes." *La Tribune de Saint-Gervais* VI (November 1900):303–14.

d'Indy/FRANCK — d'Indy, Vincent. *César Franck.* Paris: Felix Alcan, 1906. Trans. by Rosa Newmarch as *César Franck.* New York: Dover, 1965.

d'Indy/MUSIQUE — d'Indy, Vincent. "Musique française et musique allemande." *La Renaissance politique, littéraire, et artistique* III (June 12, 1915):1–8.

d'Indy/SYMPHONIE — d'Indy, Vincent. "La Symphonie proprement dite." d'Indy/COURS COMPOSITION, pp. 99–177.

d'Indy/VIE — d'Indy, Vincent. *Ma vie: Journal de jeunesse, correspondance familiale et intime.* Ed. and annotated by Marie d'Indy. Paris: Séguier, 2001.

Jackson/TCHAIKOVSKY 6 — Jackson, Timothy L. *Tchaikovsky. Symphony No. 6 (Pathétique).* Cambridge: Cambridge University Press, 1999.

Jacobs/SPOHR BATON — Jacobs, Arthur. "Spohr and the Baton." *ML* XXXI/4 (October 1950), pp. 307–17.

JALS — *Journal of the American Liszt Society*

JAMS — *Journal of the American Musicological Society*

JbSIMfPK — *Jahrbuch des Staatlichen Instituts für Musikforschung Preussischer Kulturbesitz*

Jenkins & Visocchi/MENDELSSOHN SCOTLAND — Jenkins, David, and Visocchi, Mark. *Mendelssohn in Scotland.* London: Chappell, 1978.

JM — *Journal of Musicology*

JMR — *Journal of Musicological Research*

JMT — *Journal of Music Theory*

Karr/ROMÉO — Karr, Alphonse. Les guêpes. (1^{re}Année) 2e livraison. Décembre. Paris, Au Bureau de Figaro, p. 96.

Kastner/ROMÉO — Kastner, Georges. "Roméo et Juliette." *AMZ* XLII/2 (January 8, 1840), cols. 17–20.

Kaufmann/FAUST — Goethe, Johann Wolfgang von. *Faust.* Trans. and intro. by Walter Kaufmann. Garden City, NY: Doubleday, 1961. Reprint, New York: Anchor Books, 1989.

Kearney/TCHAIKOVSKY WORLD — Kearney, Leslie, ed. *Tchaikovsky and His World.* Princeton: Princeton University Press, 1998.

Keller/TCHAIKOVSKY SYMPHONIES — Keller, Hans. "Peter Ilyich Tchaikovsky (1840–93)." Simpson/SYMPHONY Vol. 1, pp. 342–353.

Kelly/FAUST — Kelly, James William. *The Faust Legend in Music.* Detroit: Information Coordinators, 1976.

Kelly/FIRST NIGHTS — Kelly, Thomas Forest. *First Nights: Five Musical Premieres.* New Haven: Yale University Press, 2000.

Kennedy/ELGAR — Kennedy, Michael. *Portrait of Elgar.* London: Oxford University Press, 1968.

Kennedy/ELGAR ORCHESTRAL — Kennedy, Michael. *Elgar Orchestral Music.* London: BBC, 1970.

Kent/ELGAR 2 — Kent, Christopher. "A View of Elgar's Method of Composition through the Sketches of the Symphony No. 2 in Eb (Op. 63)." *PRMA* CIII (1976–1977):41–60.

King/MOUNTAINS, MUSIC, MUSICIANS — King, A. Hyatt. "Mountains, Music, and Musicians." *MQ* XXXI/4 (October 1945):395–419.

Kirkendale/CICERONIANS VS ARISTOTELIANS — Kirkendale, Warren. "Ciceronians versus Aristotelians on the Ricercar as Exordium, from Bembo to Bach." *JAMS* XXXII/1 (Spring 1979):1–44.

Kirkendale/FUGUE — Kirkendale, Warren. *Fugue and Fugato in Rococo and Classical Chamber Music.* 2nd ed. trans. by Margaret Bent and the Author. Durham, NC: Duke University Press, 1979.

Kirnberger/STRICT COMPOSITION — Kirnberger, Johann Philipp. *The Art of Strict Musical Composition.* Trans. by David Beach and Jürgen Thym. Introduction and explanatory notes by David Beach. New Haven: Yale University Press, 1982.

Knight/CAMBRIDGE MUSIC — Knight, Frida. *Cambridge Music: From the Middle Ages to Modern Times.* Cambridge: Oleander Press, 1980.

Knowles/CRITICA MUSICA — Knowles, John, ed. *Critica Musica: Essays in Honor of Paul Brainard.* New York: Gordon and Breach, 1996.

Kohlhase/EINFÜHRUNGEN ČAJKOVSKIJS — Kohlhase, Thomas. *Einführungen in ausgewählte Werke Petr Il'ičajkovskijs.* Mainz: Schott, 1996.

Kornprobst/ROPARTZ — Kornprobst, Louis. *J. Guy Ropartz: étude biographique et musicale.* Strasbourg: Éditions musicales d'Alsace, 1949.

Kramer/CULTURAL PRACTICE — Kramer, Lawrence. *Music as Cultural Practice, 1800–1900.* Berkeley: University of California Press, 1990.

Kraus/SIBELIUS 1 & RUSSIAN INFLUENCE — Kraus, Joseph. "The 'Russian' Influence in the First Symphony of Jean Sibelius: Chance Intersection or Profound Integration?" Murtomäki, Kilpeläinen, & Väisänen/SIBELIUS CONFERENCE 1995, pp. 142–52.

Kraus/TCHAIKOVSKY 5 — Kraus, Joseph C. "Tonal Plan and Narrative Plot in Tchaikovsky's Symphony No. 5 in E Minor." *MTS* XIII/1 (Spring 1991):21–47.

Kraus/TCHAIKOVSKY [SYMPHONIES] — Kraus, Joseph Charles. "Tchaikovsky [Symphonies]." Holoman/19C SYM, pp. 299–326.

Kross/SYMPHONISCHEN TRADITION

Kross, Siegfried, ed. *Probleme der Symphonischen Tradition im 19.Jahrhundert.* Kongressbericht Bonn 1989. Tutzing: Schneider, 1990.

Krummel & Sadie/MUSIC PRINTING & PUBLISHING

Krummel, Donald, and Sadie, Stanley. *Music Printing and Publishing.* New York: Norton, 1980.

Kuhn/BORODIN

Kuhn, Ernst, ed. *Alexander Borodin: Sein Leben, seine Musik, seine Schriften.* Berlin: Ernst Kuhn, 1992.

Lalo/CORRESPONDANCE

Lalo, Édouard. *Correspondance.* Coll. and ed. by Joël-Marie Fauquet. Paris: Aux Amateurs de Livres, 1989.

Lalo/ÉVOLUTIONS

Lalo, Pierre. "De quelques évolutions récentes de la musique française." *Le Courier musical* XII (1909):302–306.

Lalo/MORCELLEMENT

Lalo, Pierre. "Aux Concerts Lamoureux . . . le morcelle-ment des symphonies." *Le Temps,* 19 November 1907.

Lalo/RÉFORMES

Lalo, Pierre. "Au Conservatoire—la grande commis-sion de réformes de 1892." *Le Temps,* August 8, 1901.

Laloy/NOUVELLE

Laloy, Louis. "La Nouvelle manière de Claude De-bussy." *La Grande Revue* 47 (February 10, 1908):530–35.

Lambert/MUSIC HO!

Lambert, Constant. *Music Ho! A Study of Music in Decline.* New York: Scribner's Sons, 1934.

Lamy/ROPARTZ

Lamy, Fernand. *J. Guy Ropartz: L'homme et l'oeuvre.* Paris: Durand et Cie., 1948.

Langevin/MUSICIENS

Langevin, Paul-Gilbert, ed. *Musiciens de France: la génération des grands symphonistes.* Paris: La Revue Musicale (Éditions Richard-Masse), 1979.

Laroche/TCHAIKOVSKY

Larosh [Laroche], G. A. *Izbrannye stat'i.* Vyp. 2, *P. I. Chaikovskii.* Leningrad: Muzyka, Leningrad Otd-nie, 1974.

LaRue/BIFOCAL

LaRue, Jan. "Bifocal Tonality: An Explanation for Ambiguous Baroque Cadences." *FESTSCHRIFT DAVISON,* pp. 173–84.

LaRue/GUIDELINES

LaRue, Jan. *Guidelines for Style Analysis,* 2nd ed. Warren, MI: Harmonie Park Press, 1992.

Lavignac/MUSIQUE

Lavignac, Albert. *La musique et les musicians.* Paris: Delagrave, 1924.

Lawson/NIELSEN GREAT BRITAIN

Lawson, Jack. "Carl Nielsen—as Seen from Great Britain." *MD* XLII/1 (1990):2–5.

Layton/SYMPHONY

Layton, Robert, ed. *A Guide to the Symphony.* Oxford: Oxford University Press, 1993.

Legge/CLIFFE

Legge, Robin H. "Cliffe, Frederick." Grove 2/I, p. 588.

Leonard/RUSSIAN MUSIC

Leonard, Richard Anthony. *A History of Russian Music.* New York: Funk & Wagnalls, 1968 [1956].

Little/SALTARELLO

Little, Meredith Ellis. "Saltarello." *NG* XVI, pp. 430–32.

Lloyd-Jones/BORODIN 1

Lloyd-Jones, David. "Borodin, Symphony No. 1 in E flat Major." Field/MUSICIANS GUIDE, pp. 95–96.

Lloyd-Jones/BORODIN 3

Lloyd-Jones, David. "Borodin, Symphony No. 3 in A Minor (Unfinished)." Field/MUSICIANS GUIDE, pp. 100–101.

Lloyd-Jones/EDITION BORODIN — Lloyd-Jones, David. "Towards a Scholarly Edition of Borodin's Symphonies." *Soundings* VI (1977):81–87.

Lloyd-Jones/SCHEHERAZADE — Lloyd-Jones, David. "Rimsky-Korsakov, Scheherazade." Field/MUSICIANS GUIDE, pp, 463–64.

Lloyd-Jones/TCHAIKOVSKY 1 — Lloyd-Jones, David. "Tchaikovsky, Symphony No. 1 in G Minor, Op. 13 (Winter Reveries)." Field/MUSICIANS GUIDE, pp. 654–55.

Lloyd-Jones/TCHAIKOVSKY 4 — Lloyd-Jones, David. "Tchaikovsky, Symphony No. 4 in F Minor, Op. 36." Field/MUSICIANS GUIDE, pp. 662–65.

Lloyd-Jones/TCHAIKOVSKY 5 — Lloyd-Jones, David. "Tchaikovsky, Symphony No. 5 in E Minor, Op. 64." Field/MUSICIANS GUIDE, pp. 666–68.

Lloyd-Jones/TCHAIKOVSKY 6 — Lloyd-Jones, David. "Tchaikovsky, Symphony No. 6 in B Minor, Op. 74 'Pathétique.'" Field/MUSICIANS GUIDE, pp. 669–71.

Locke/FRENCH — Locke, Ralph. "The French Symphony: David, Gounod, and Bizet to Saint-Saëns, Franck, and Their Followers." Holoman/19C SYM, pp. 163–94.

Lockspeiser/DEBUSSY — Lockspeiser, Edward. *Debussy: His Life and Mind.* 2 Vols. New York: Macmillan, 1962.

Longyear/RIMSKY-KORSAKOV 3 — Longyear, Rey. M. "Communication [Rimsky-Korsakov Symphony No.3]." *JAMS* XXXIX/1 (Spring 1986), p. 216.

LS — *Liszt-Studien*

LSJ — *Liszt Society Journal*

Lvov & Prach/RUSSIAN FOLK SONGS — Lvov, Nikolai, and Prach, Ivan. *A Collection of Russian Folk Songs.* Ed. by Malcolm Hamrick Brown. Ann Arbor: UMI Research Press, 1987.

MA — *Music Analysis*

Macdonald/FIESQUE — Macdonald, Hugh. "A Fiasco Remembered: *Fiesque* Dismembered." Brown & Wiley/SLAVONIC WESTERN, pp. 163–85.

Macdonald/LALO — Macdonald, Hugh. "Édouard Lalo." *NG* X, pp. 387–89.

Macfarren/MEMORIES — Macfarren, Walter. *Memories: An Autobiography.* London: Scott, 1905.

Macfarren/POTTER — Macfarren, George. "Cipriani Potter: His Life and Work." *PRMA* X (1884):41–56.

Mackeson/SOCIETY MUSICIANS — Mackeson, Charles. "Society of British Musicians, The." Grove 2/V, pp. 492–93.

Maes/RUSSIAN MUSIC — Maes, Francis. *A History of Russian Music From Kamarinskaya to Babi Yar.* Trans. by Arnold J. Pomerans and Erica Pomerans. Berkeley: University of California Press, 2002.

Magnard/CORRESPONDANCE — Magnard, Albéric. *Correspondance (1888–1914).* Ed. with notes by Claire Vlach. Paris: Publications de la Société française de musicologie (Deuxième Série, Tome XVI), 1997.

Mahling/ÜBER SYMPHONIEN

Mahling, Christoph Hellmut, ed. *Über Symphonien: Beiträge zu einer musikalischen Gattung.* Tutzing: Hans Schneider, 1979.

Maillard/MAGNARD

Maillard, Jean. "Albéric Magnard: les quatre symphonies, étude analytique." Langevin/MUSICIENS, pp. 89–104.

Maillard/ROPARTZ

Maillard, Jean. "Guy Ropartz: les six symphonies, étude analytique." Langevin/MUSICIENS, pp. 118–32.

Maine/ELGAR

Maine, Basil. *Elgar: His Life and Works.* 2 Vols. London: Bell & Sons, 1933.

Manduell/ROUSSEL

Manduell, John. "Albert Roussel." Simpson/SYMPHONY, vol. 2, pp. 104–14.

Mangeot/AVENIR

Mangeot, A. "Un nouvel avenir pour la musique symphonique française." *Le Monde musical* (February 15, 1904):34.

Masson/RAPPORT

Masson, Paul-Marie, ed. *Rapport sur la musique française contemporaine.* Rome: Armani and Stein, 1913.

Mazo/LVOV & PRACH

Mazo, Margarita. Introduction and Appendixes to Lvov & Prach/RUSSIAN FOLK SONGS, pp. xi–xv, 3–82, 414–78.

McVeagh/ELGAR

McVeagh, Diana M. *Edward Elgar: His Life and Music.* London: Dent & Sons, 1955.

MD

Musical Denmark

Mendelssohn/SOUCHAY LETTER 1842

Mendelssohn, Felix. Letter to Marc-André Souchay, Berlin, October 15, 1842. In *Felix Mendelssohn-Bartholdy, Letters,* ed. Gisella Selden-Goth (New York: Pantheon, 1945), p. 313.

Mercier/TOURNEMIRE

Mercier, Philippe. "Charles Tournemire, compositeur oublié." Liner notes to Charles Tournemire, Symphonies Nos. 3 and 7. L'Orchestre philharmonique de Liège et de la communauté française/Pierre Bartholomée (ADDA AD 284, 1992).

Mf

Musikforschung

MGG

Die Musik in Geschichte und Gegenwart

Michel/D'INDY

Michel, Fabien, ed. *Nouveaux regards sur Vincent d'Indy.* Lyon: Éditions Symétrie, forthcoming.

Minibayeva/TCHAIKOVSKY FIRST SUITE

Minibayeva, Natalia. "*Per Aspera ad Astra:* Symphonic Tradition in Tchaikovsky's First Suite for Orchestra." Kearney/TCHAIKOVSKY WORLD, pp. 163–96.

MK

Musik-Konzepte

ML

Music and Letters

MLA

Music Library Association

MM

Master Musicians

MMR

The Monthly Musical Record

MN

Musical Newsletter

Mof

Musik og forskning

Monk/ELGAR STUDIES

Monk, Raymond, ed. *Elgar Studies.* Aldershot: Scolar Press, 1990.

Moore/ELGAR — Moore, Jerrold Northrop. *Edward Elgar: A Creative Life.* Oxford: Oxford University Press, 1984.

Moore/ELGAR LETTERS LIFE — Moore, Jerrold Northrop. *Edward Elgar: Letters of a Lifetime.* Oxford: Clarendon Press, 1990.

Moore/ELGAR PUBLISHER LETTERS — Moore, Jerrold Northrop. *Elgar and his Publishers: Letters of a Creative Life.* 2 Vols. Oxford: Clarendon Press, 1987.

Moore/ELGAR RECORD — Moore, Jerrold Northrop. *Elgar on Record: The Composer and the Gramophone.* London: Oxford University Press, 1974.

Moore/WINDFLOWER LETTERS — Moore, Jerrold Northrop. *Edward Elgar: The Windflower Letters. Correspondence with Alice Caroline Stuart Wortley and her Family.* Oxford: Clarendon Press, 1989.

Morley-Pegge & Fitzpatrick/DAUPRAT — Morley-Pegge, Reginald, and Fitzpatrick, Horace. "Dauprat, Louis François." *NG* V, p. 255.

Morgenstern/COMPOSERS — Morgenstern, Sam, ed. *Composers on Music: An Anthology of Composers' Writings from Palestrina to Copland.* [New York]: Pantheon, 1956.

MQ — *Musical Quarterly*

MR — *Music Review*

MS — *Music Survey*

MT — *Musical Times*

MTS — *Music Theory Spectrum*

Müller-Reuter/LEXIKON — Müller-Reuter, Theodor. *Lexikon der deutschen Konzertliteratur.* Leipzig: Kahnt, 1909.

Muret/RAPPORT — Muret, Henry. "Rapport sur le budget des dépenses de 1904." *Journal officiel de la République française: Assemblée Nationale #1953.*

Murtomäki/RUSSIAN INFLUENCE SIBELIUS — Murtomäki, Veijo. "Russian Influence on Sibelius." Murtomäki, Kilpeläinen, & Väisänen/SIBELIUS CONFERENCE 1995, pp. 153–61.

Murtomäki, Kilpeläinen, & Väisänen/ SIBELIUS CONFERENCE 1995 — Murtomäki, Veijo, Kilpeläinen, Kari, and Väisänen, Risto. *Proceedings from the Second International Jean Sibelius Conference, Helsinki, November 25–29, 1995.* Helsinki: Sibelius Academy, 1998.

Musa/PORTABLE DANTE — Musa, Mark, ed. *The Portable Dante.* New York: Penguin, 1995.

Musgrave/CRYSTAL PALACE — Musgrave, Michael. *The Musical Life of the Crystal Palace.* Cambridge: Cambridge University Press, 1995.

MW — *Musical World*

Near/WIDOR — Near, John Richard. "The Life and Work of Charles-Marie Widor." DMA diss., Boston University, 1985.

Near/WIDOR OPUS 42 [BIS] — Near, John Richard. Introduction to his edition of Charles-Marie Widor, *Symphonie pour orgue et orchestre opus 42 [bis].* Middleton, WI: A-R Editions, Inc., 2002.

Nectoux/CORRESPONDENCE   Nectoux, Jean-Michel, ed. *The Correspondence of Camille Saint-Saëns and Gabriel Fauré: Sixty Years of Friendship.* Trans. with an introduction by J. Barrie Jones. Burlington, VT: Ashgate, 2004.

Nectoux/FAURÉ   Nectoux, Jean-Michel. *Gabriel Fauré: A Musical Life.* Trans. by Roger Nichols. Cambridge: Cambridge University Press, 1991.

Neef/RUSSISCHEN FÜNF   Neef, Sigfrid. *Die Russischen Fünf: Balakirew—Borodin—Cui—Mussorgski—Rimsky-Korsakow. Monographien—Dokumente—Briefe—Programme-Werke.* Berlin: E. Kuhn, 1992.

Nest'ev/PROKOFIEV   Nest'ev, Izrail' V. *Prokofiev: His Musical Life.* Trans. by Rose Prokofieva. New York: Knopf, 1946.

NG   *The New Grove Dictionary of Music and Musicians.* Ed. by Stanley Sadie. London: Macmillan; Washington, D. C.: Grove's Dictionaries of Music, 1980.

NG 2   *The New Grove Dictionary of Music and Musicians.* 2nd ed. Ed. by Stanley Sadie. London: Macmillan; Washington, D. C.: Grove's Dictionaries of Music, 2001.

NG RUSSIAN MASTERS 1   *The New Grove Russian Masters 1: Glinka, Borodin, Balakirev, Musorgsky, Tchaikovsky.* New York: Norton, 1986.

NG RUSSIAN MASTERS 2   *The New Grove Russian Masters 2: Rimsky-Korsakov, Rakhmaninov, Skryabin, Prokofiev, Shostakovich.* New York: Norton, 1986.

NHQ   *New Hungarian Quarterly*

Nichols/DEBUSSY   Nichols, Roger. *Debussy Remembered.* London: Faber & Faber, 1992.

19CM   *Nineteenth Century Music*

NM-Z   *Neue Musik-Zeitung*

Norris/NG2 RACHMANINOFF   Norris, Goeffrey. "Serge Rachmaninoff." *NG 2* XX, pp. 707–18.

Norris/NG RAKHMANINOV   Norris, Geoffrey. "Sergey Rakhmaninov." NG RUSSIAN MASTERS 2, pp. 75–105.

Norris/RAKHMANINOV   Norris, Geoffrey. *Rakhmaninov.* London: Dent, 1976.

Norris/STANFORD   Norris, Gerald. *Stanford, The Cambridge Jubilee, and Tchaikovsky.* Newton Abbot: David & Charles, 1980.

NYT   *New York Times*

NY TRB   *New York Tribune*

NZfM   *Neue Zeitschrift für Musik*

Oechsle/SYMPHONIK   Oechsle, Sigfried. *Symphonik nach Beethoven: Studien zu Schubert, Schumann, Mendelssohn und Gade.* Kassel, Germany: Bärenreiter, 1992.

Olin/CONCERTS   Olin, Elinor. "The Concerts de L'Opéra 1895–97: New Music at the Monument Garnier." *19CM* XVI (Spring 1993):253–66.

ÖMZ	*Österreichische Musikzeitschrift*
Orledge/FAURÉ	Orledge, Robert. *Gabriel Fauré.* London: Eulenberg, 1979.
Orledge/D'INDY	Orledge, Robert. "Vincent d'Indy." *NG* 9, pp. 220–225.
Orlova/TCHAIKOVSKY	Orlova, Alexandra. *Tchaikovsky: A Self-Portrait.* Trans. by R. M. Davison. Oxford: Oxford University Press, 1990.
Palmieri/GUIDE	Palmieri, Robert, ed. *Sergei Vasil'evich Rachmaninoff: A Guide to Research.* New York and London: Garland Publishing, 1985.
Parry/EVOLUTION MUSIC	Parry, C. Hubert H. *The Evolution of the Art of Music.* New York: D. Appleton, 1930.
Parry/SYMPHONY	Parry, C. Hubert H. "Symphony (SINFONIA, SINFONIE, SYMPHONIE)." Grove 2/III, pp. 763–97.
Parsons/CSO MANFRED	Parsons, Arrand. Program notes for the 78th season of the Chicago Symphony Orchestra. "Tchaikovsky. Symphony on Byron's *Manfred,* Op. 58." December 5–7, 1968, pp. 21–29.
Payne/ELGAR 3	Payne, Anthony. *Elgar's Third Symphony: The Story of the Reconstruction.* London: Faber & Faber, 1998.
Perret/MAGNARD	Perret, Simon-Pierre, and Halbreich, Harry. *Albéric Magnard.* Paris: Fayard, 2001.
Peter/POTTER	Peter, Philip Henry. "The Life and Work of Cipriani Potter (1792–1871)." Ph.D. diss., Northwestern University, 1972.
Petit/INTRODUCTION	Petit, Raymond. "Introduction à l'étude de l'oeuvre de Charles Tournemire." *L'Orgue* CXV (July-August-September 1965):111–37.
Petrovskaia/KONSERTNAIA	Petrovskaia, I. F. *Konsertnaia zhizn' Peterburga: muzyka v obshchestvennom i domashnem bytu, 1801–1859 gody.* St. Petersburg: Petrovskii Fond, 2000.
Petrovskaia/MUZYKAL'NOE	Petrovskaia, I. F. *Muzykal'noe obrazovanie i muzykal'nye obshchestvennye organizatsii v Peterburge, 1801–1917.* St. Petersburg: Petrovskii Fond, 1999.
Piggott/RACHMANINOV	Piggott, Patrick. *Rachmaninov.* London: Faber & Faber, 1978.
Piggott/RACHMANINOV ORCHESTRAL	Piggott, Patrick. *Rachmaninov Orchestral Music.* London: BBC, 1974.
Pirie/MUSICAL RENAISSANCE	Pirie, Peter J. *The English Musical Renaissance.* New York: St. Martin's Press, 1979.
PMG	*Pall Mall Gazette*
Porte/STANFORD	Porte, John F. *Sir Charles V. Stanford.* London: Kegan Paul, 1921.
Poznansky/TCHAIKOVSKY QUEST	Poznansky, Alexander. *Tchaikovsky: The Quest for the Inner Man.* New York: Schirmer Books, 1991.
Poznansky/TCHAIKOVSKY RECONSIDERED	Poznansky, Alexander. "Tchaikovsky: A Life Reconsidered." Kearney/TCHAIKOVSKY WORLD, pp. 3–54.

Poznansky & Langston/TCHAIKOVSKY HANDBOOK — Poznansky, Alexander, and Langston, Brett. *The Tchaikovsky Handbook: A Guide to the Man and His Music.* 2 Vols. Bloomington: Indiana University Press, 2002.

Preminger/POETRY & POETICS — Preminger, Alex, ed. *Princeton Encyclopedia of Poetry and Poetics.* Princeton: Princeton University Press, 1974.

PRMA — *Proceedings of the Royal Musical Association*

Prod'homme/BERLIOZ, MUSSET, DE QUINCEY — Prod'homme, J.-G. "Berlioz, Musset, and Thomas de Quincey." *MQ* XXXII/1 (January 1946):98–106.

Prod'homme/GOUNOD — Prod'homme, J.-G., and Dandelot, A. *Gounod: sa vie et ses oeuvres.* Vols. 1–2. Geneva: Minkoff, 1973 [Delagrave, 1911].

Pupils/STANFORD — His Pupils. "Charles Villiers Stanford." *ML* V/3 (July 1924):193–207.

Rachmaninoff Sym 3/FOREWORD — Foreword to *Sergei Rachmaninoff, Third Symphony in A minor, Op. 44.* Centennial Edition. Bryn Mawr, PA: Theodore Presser, 1972.

Ratner/SAINT-SAËNS — Ratner, Sabina Teller. *Camille Saint-Saëns 1835–1921: A Thematic Catalogue of His Complete Works.* Volume 1: *The Instrumental Works.* New York: Oxford University Press, 2002.

Rauchhaupt/SYMPHONY — Rauchhaupt, Ursula von, ed. *The Symphony.* London: Thames and Hudson, 1973.

Redwood/ELGAR COMPANION — Redwood, Christopher, ed. *An Elgar Companion.* Derbyshire: Sequoia & Moorland, 1982.

Reed/ELGAR — Reed, William. H. *Elgar.* London: Dent, 1939.

Reed/ELGAR KNEW — Reed, William H. *Elgar as I knew Him.* Oxford, Oxford University Press, 1936.

Reed/ELGAR'S THIRD — Reed, William H. "Elgar's Third Symphony." *The Listener.* Supplement no. 24, XIV, no. 346 (Aug. 28, 1935):1–16.

Rees/SAINT-SAËNS — Rees, Brian. *Camille Saint-Saëns: A Life.* London: Chatto & Windus, 1998.

Régis/MUSIQUE — Régis, Louis. "Musique moderne: Conservatoire-oeuvres de M. Guy Ropartz." *Le Mercure musical* II (December 15, 1906):414–16.

Rellstab/SCHRIFTEN — Rellstab, Ludwig. *Gesammelte Schriften.* Leipzig: F.A. Brockhaus, 1843, 1846.

Rellstab/ÜBERBLICK — Rellstab, Ludwig. "Überblick der Ereignisse." *Iris im Gebiete der Tonkunst* III/47 (November 23, 1832): 187–88.

Ridenour/19C RUSSIAN MUSIC — Ridenour, Robert C. *Nationalism, Modernism, and Personal Rivalry in Nineteenth-Century Russian Music.* Ann Arbor: UMI Research Press, 1981.

Riesemann/RACHMANINOFF — Rachmaninoff, Sergei. *Rachmaninoff's Recollections, Told to Oskar von Riesemann.* New York: Macmillan, 1934.

Rimsky-Korsakov/MUSICAL LIFE — Rimsky-Korsakov, Nikolay Andreyevich. *My Musical Life*. Trans. from the 5th rev. Russian ed. by Judah A. Joffe. Intro. by Carl van Vechten. New York: Knopf, 1942.

Rimsky-Korsakov/ORCHESTRATION — Rimsky-Korsakov, Nikolay. *Principles of Orchestration, with Musical Examples Drawn from His Own Works*. Ed. by Maximilian Steinberg. Trans. by Edward Agate. New York: Dover, 1964.

Ritzarev & Porfireva/ITALIAN IN RUSSIA — Ritzarev (Rytsareva), Marina, and Porferiva, Anna. "The Italian Diaspora in Eighteenth-Century Russia." Strohm/DIASPORA ITALIAN, pp. 211–54.

RM — *La Revue Musicale*

RMZ — *Rheinische Musikzeitung für Kunstfreunde und Künstler*

Rodman/DEBUSSY — Rodman, Ronald W. "Thematic and Tonal Processes in the Development-Reprise Forms of Claude Debussy, 1880–1905." Ph.D. diss., Indiana University, 1992.

Rodmell/STANFORD — Rodmell, Paul. *Charles Villiers Stanford*. Aldershot: Ashgate, 2002.

Rohozinski/MUSIQUE FRANÇAISE — Rohozinski, Ladislas, ed. *Cinquante ans de musique française (1874–1925)*. 2 Vols. Paris: Les Éditions Musicales de la Librairie de France, 1925.

Rolland/CHRISTOPHE — Rolland, Romain. *Jean-Christophe: La Foire sur la place*. Édition définitive. Paris: Albin Michel, 1948.

Rolland/MUSICIENS — Rolland, Romain. *Musiciens d'aujourd'hui*. Paris: Hachette et Cie., 1908. Trans. by Mary Blaiklock as *Musicians of Today*. New York: Henry Holt, 1915.

Ropartz/DUKAS — Ropartz, Guy. "Les Oeuvres symphoniques de Paul Dukas." *La Revue musicale*, numéro spéciale: Paul Dukas (May-June 1936):61–68.

Ropartz/SYMPHONIES — Ropartz, Guy. "A propos de quelques symphonies modernes." *Notations artistiques*. Paris: Lemerre, 1891, pp. 163–208.

Rosand/DESCENDING TETRACHORD — Rosand, Ellen. "The Descending Tetrachord: An Emblem of Lament." *MQ* LXV/3 (July 1979):346–59.

Rosen/ROMANTIC — Rosen, Charles. *The Romantic Generation*. Cambridge: Harvard University Press, 1995.

Roth/BUSINESS MUSIC — Roth, Ernst. *The Business of Music*. New York: Oxford University Press, 1969.

Rousseau/DICTIONARY — Rousseau, Jean-Jacques. *A Complete Dictionary of Music*. Trans. by William Waring, 2nd ed. New York: AMS Press, 1975.

Roussel/LETTRES — Roussel, Albert. *Lettres et écrits*. Ed. with notes by Nicole Labelle. Paris: Flammarion, 1987.

Rushton/POTTER 10 — Rushton, Julian. "Introduction" to *Cipriani Potter. Symphony in G Minor (1832)*. Musica Britannica LXXVII. London: Stainer and Bell, 2001.

Russell/ENGLAND II

Russell, Iian. "England (i) II: Traditional Music." *NG 2* VIII, pp. 227–39.

Sage & Hickman/ROMANCE

Sage, Jack, and Hickman, Roger. "Romance." *NG* XVI, pp. 121–26.

Sainsbury/DICTIONARY

Sainsbury, John S. *A Dictionary of Musicians from the Earliest Ages to the Present Time.* London: Printed for Sainsbury and Co., 1824.

Saint-Saëns/HARMONIE

Saint-Saëns, Camille. *Harmonie et mélodie.* Paris: Calmann-Lévy, 1885.

Saint-Saëns/IDÉES

Saint-Saëns, Camille. *Les Idées de M. Vincent d'Indy.* Paris: Pierre Lafitte, 1919.

Saint-Saëns/MEMORIES

Saint-Saëns, Camille. *Musical Memories.* Trans. by Edwin Gile Rich. Boston: Small, Maynard & Co., 1919.

Saint-Saëns/PORTRAITS

Saint-Saëns, Camille. *Portraits et souvenirs.* Paris: Société d'Édition Artistique, 1900.

Samson/LATE ROMANTIC

Samson, Jim, ed. *The Late Romantic Era: From the Mid-19th Century to World War I.* London: Macmillan, 1991.

Saremba/ELGAR, BRITTEN & CO.

Saremba, Meinhard. *Elgar, Britten & Co.: Eine Geschichte der britischen Musik in zwölf Portraits.* Zürich: M & T Verlag, 1994.

Schnepel/GREAT AMERICAN SYMPHONY

Schnepel, Julie. "The Critical Pursuit of the Great American Symphony, 1893–1950." Ph.D. diss., Indiana University, 1995.

Schoenberg/STYLE & IDEA

Schoenberg, Arnold. *Style and Idea: Selected Writings.* Ed. by Leonard Stein, trans. by Leo Black. Berkeley: University of California Press, 1985.

Scholes/MIRROR MUSIC

Scholes, Percy A. *The Mirror of Music, 1844–1944: A Century of Musical Life in Britain as Reflected in the Pages of the Musical Times.* 2 Vols. London: Novello and Oxford University Press, 1947.

Schönzeler/NIKISCH

Schönzeler, Hans-Hubert. "Nikisch, Arthur." *NG* XIII, pp. 244–45.

Schulz/SYMPHONY

Churgin, Bathia. "The Symphony as Described by J. A. P. Schulz (1774): A Commentary and Translation." *CM* XXIX (1980):7–16.

Schumann/MUSIC

Schumann, Robert. *Music and Musicians: Essays and Criticisms.* 2 Vols. Trans., ed., and annotated by Fanny Ritter. 8th ed. London: New Temple Press, [n.d.].

Schumann/MUSICAL WORLD

Schumann, Robert. *The Musical World of Robert Schumann: A Selection from His Own Writings.* Trans., ed., and annotated by Henry Pleasants. New York: St. Martin's Press, 1965.

Schumann/ON MUSIC

Schumann, Robert. *On Music and Musicians.* Ed. by Konrad Wolff. Trans. by Paul Rosenfeld. New York: Pantheon, 1946.

SCHUMANN ROMANTISCHES ERBE   *Robert Schumann: Ein romantisches Erbe in neuer Forschung: acht Studien.* Herausgegeben von der Robert-Schumann-Gesellschaft Düsseldorf. Mainz; New York: Schott, ca. 1984.

Schwandt/TARANTELLA   Schwandt, Erich. "Tarantella." *NG* XVIII, pp. 575–76.

Schwartz/DUKAS   Schwartz, Manuela, with G. W. Hopkins. "Paul Dukas." *NG 2* VII, pp. 670–74.

Schwartz/D'INDY   Schwartz, Manuela, ed. *Vincent d'Indy et son temps.* Liège: Mardaga, 2006.

Seaman/KALINNIKOV   Seaman, Gerald. "V. S. Kalinnikov (1866–1900)." *MR* XXVIII/4 (November 1967):289–99.

Seaman/RIMSKY GUIDE   Seaman, Gerald R. *Nikolai Andreevich Rimsky-Korsakov: A Guide to Research.* New York: Garland, 1988.

Seibert/TCHAIKOVSKY 5 PROGRAMME   Seibert, Donald C. "The Tchaikovsky Fifth: A Symphony without a Programme." *MR* LI/1 (February 1990):36–45.

Seroff/PROKOFIEV   Seroff, Victor. *Sergei Prokofiev: A Soviet Tragedy.* London: Frewin, 1969.

Seroff/RACHMANINOFF   Seroff, Victor I. *Rachmaninoff.* New York: Simon and Schuster, 1950.

Servières/LALO   Servières, Georges. *Édouard Lalo.* Paris: H. Laurens, 1925.

Servières/SYMPHONIE   Servières, Georges. "La Symphonie en France au XIXᵉ siècle (avant 1870)." *Le ménestrel* LXXXV (September 28, 1923):397–400; (October 5, 1923):405–07; (October 19, 1923):425–27.

Shanet/BIZET   Shanet, Howard. "Bizet's Suppressed Symphony." *MQ* XLIV (1958):461–76.

Shaw/MUSIC   Shaw, Bernard. *Shaw's Music: The Complete Musical Criticism.* 3 Vols. Ed. by Dan H. Laurence. New York: Dodd, Mead, & Co., 1981.

Shera/ELGAR INSTRUMENTAL   Shera, F. H. *Elgar: Instrumental Works.* London: Oxford University Press, 1931.

Sietz/REINECKE   Sietz, Reinhold. "Reinecke, Carl." *NG* XV, pp. 718–19.

SIGNALE   *Signale für das musikalische Welt*

S.I.M.   *Société Internationale de Musique*

Simpson/RACHMANINOFF SYMPHONIES   Simpson, Robert. "Sergei Rachmaninoff (1873–1943)." Simpson/SYMPHONY vol. 2, pp. 128–131.

Simpson/SYMPHONY   Simpson, Robert, ed. *The Symphony.* 2 Vols. London: Penguin Books, 1966–1967.

Slonimsky/BAKER'S   Slonimsky, Nicolas. *Baker's Biographical Dictionary of Musicians.* 8th ed. New York: Schirmer Books, 1992.

Slonimsky/LEXICON   Slonimsky, Nicolas. *Lexicon of Musical Invective: Critical Assaults on Composers since Beethoven's Time.* Seattle: University of Washington Press, 1953; rev. 1969.

Smith/PARRY — Smith, A. E. Brent. "Charles Hubert Hastings Parry." *ML* VII/3 (July 1926):221–28.

Solomon/ROCHLITZ & MOZART — Solomon, Maynard. "The Rochlitz Anecdotes: Issues of Authenticity in Early Mozart Biography." Eisen/MOZART STUDIES [I], pp. 1–60.

Southgate/SAINT-SAËNS — Southgate, T. L. "Musical Intelligence: The Philharmonic Society and M. Saint-Saëns's New Symphony." *The Musical Standard* XXIX (May 1886): 334–35.

Spencer/KALINNIKOV — Spencer, Jennifer. "Kalinnikov, Vasily Sergeyevich." *NG 2*, IX, pp. 776–78.

SR — *Studies in Romanticism*

Stanford/BENNETT — Stanford, Charles Villiers. "William Sterndale Bennett, 1816–1875." *MQ* II/4 (October 1916):628–57.

Stanford/FOLK-SONG — Stanford, Charles Villiers. "Some Thoughts Concerning Folk-Song and Nationality." *MQ* I/2 (April 1915):232–45.

Stanford/INTERLUDES — Stanford, Charles V. *Interludes: Records and Reflections*. London: John Murray, 1922.

Stanford/STUDIES MEMORIES — Stanford, C. V. *Studies and Memories*. London: Archibald Constable, 1908.

Stanford/UNWRITTEN DIARY — Stanford, Charles Villiers. *Pages from an Unwritten Diary*. London: Arnold, 1914.

Stasov/ESSAYS — Stasov, Vladimir Vasilevich. *Selected Essays on Music*. Trans. by Florence Jonas. London: Barrie & Rockliff, 1968.

Stendhal (Beyle)/RED AND BLACK — Stendhal (Marie-Henri Beyle). *The Red and the Black*. Trans. By C. K. Scott Moncrieff. New York: Modern Library, 1926.

StM — *Studia Musicologica*

Strasser/ARS GALLICA — Strasser, Michael C. "Ars Gallica: The Société Nationale de Musique and its Role in French Musical Life, 1871–1891." Ph.D. diss., University of Illinois, 1998.

Strohm/DIASPORA ITALIAN — Strohm, Reinhard, ed. *The Eighteenth-Century Diaspora of Italian Music and Musicians*. Turnhout: Brepols, 2001.

Studd/SAINT-SAËNS — Studd, Stephen. *Saint-Saëns: A Critical Biography*. London: Cygnus Arts, 1998.

Swan/RACHMANINOFF — Swan, A. J. and Katherine. "Rachmaninoff: Personal Reminiscences." *MQ* XXX/1 (January 1944):1–19; XXX/2 (April 1944):174–91.

Tarasti/SIBELIUS CONFERENCE 1990 — Tarasti, Eero. *Proceedings from the First International Jean Sibelius Conference, Helsinki, August 1990*. Helsinki: Sibelius Academy, 1995.

Taruskin/ACORN — Taruskin, Richard. "How the Acorn Took Root: A Tale of Russia." *19CM* VI/3 (Spring 1983):189–212.

Taruskin/CHERNOMOR

Taruskin, Richard. "Chernomor to Kashchei: Harmonic Sorcery; or, Stravinsky's 'Angle.'" *JAMS* XXXVIII/1 (Spring 1985):72–142.

Taruskin/DEFINING RUSSIA

Taruskin, Richard. *Defining Russia Musically: Historical and Hermeneutical Essays.* Princeton: Princeton University Press, 1997.

Taruskin/KUCHKA

Taruskin, Richard. "What is a Kuchka?" Taruskin/ MUSORGSKY, pp. xxxiii–xxxiv.

Taruskin/MUSORGSKY

Taruskin, Richard. *Musorgsky: Eight Essays and an Epilogue.* Princeton: Princeton University Press, 1993.

Taruskin/RIMSKY-KORSAKOV SYMPHONIES

Taruskin, Richard. Liner notes to Nikolay Rimsky-Korsakov, Three Symphonies. Gothenburg Symphony Orchestra/Neeme Järvi (Deutsche Grammophon 423 604–2).

Taruskin/STRAVINSKY

Taruskin, Richard. *Stravinsky and the Russian Traditions: A Biography of the Works Through Mavra.* 2 Vols. Berkeley: University of California Press, 1996.

Tchaikovsky/CRITICISM

Tchaikovsky, Piotr Ilyich. *Muzykal'no-kriticheskie stat'i.* Leningrad: Muzyka, 1986.

Tchaikovsky/LETTERS FAMILY

Tchaikovsky, Piotr Ilyich. *Letters to His Family: An Autobiography.* Trans. by Galina von Meck with additional annotations by Percy M. Young. New York: Stein and Day, 1981.

Tchaikovsky/LIFE & LETTERS

Tchaikovsky, Modeste. *The Life and Letters of Peter Ilich Tchaikovsky.* Ed. and intro. by Rosa Newmarch. 2 Vols. New York: Vienna House, 1973 [1906].

Temperley/BENNETT SYMPHONIES

Temperley, Nicholas, ed. *William Sterndale Bennett 1816–1875: Three Symphonies 3,4,5.* BSBS E/VII.

Temperley/SCHUMANN & BENNETT

Temperley, Nicholas. "Schumann and Sterndale Bennett." *19CM* XII/3 (Spring 1989):207–20.

Temperley et al./LONDON NG

Nicholas Temperley et al. "London." *NG* XI, pp. 142–217.

Tenroc/SOCIÉTÉ

Tenroc, Charles, "Société Nationale de Musique." *Le Guide musical* LX (June 7–14, 1914), 453.

Thayer-Forbes/BEETHOVEN

Thayer, Alexander Wheelock. *Thayer's Life of Beethoven.* 2 Vols. Ed. by Elliot Forbes. Princeton: Princeton University Press, 1970.

Thomas/MEMOIRS THOMAS

Thomas, Rose Fay. *Memoirs of Theodore Thomas.* New York: Moffat, Yard & Co., 1911.

Thomson/D'INDY

Thomson, Andrew. *Vincent d'Indy and His World.* Oxford: Clarendon Press, 1996.

Thomson/MUSICAL SCENE

Thomson, Virgil. *The Musical Scene.* New York: Knopf, 1947.

Thomson/WIDOR

Thomson, Andrew. *Widor: The Life and Times of Charles-Marie Widor.* Oxford: Oxford University Press, 1987.

Threlfall & Norris/RACHMANINOFF CATALOGUE

Threlfall, Robert, and Norris, Geoffrey. *A Catalogue of the Compositions of S. Rachmaninoff.* London: Scolar Press, 1982.

Tiersot/OEUVRES

Tiersot, Julien. "Les Oeuvres inédites de César Franck." *La Revue musicale* III (December 1, 1922): 97–138.

Tiersot/SYMPHONIE

Tiersot, Julien. "La Symphonie en France." *Zeitschrift der Internationalen Musikgesellschaft* X (1902): 391–402.

TLS

Times Literary Supplement

Tovey/ELGAR 2

Tovey, Donald Francis. "Elgar. LVI. Symphony in E-flat, No. 2, Op. 63." Tovey/ESSAYS II, pp. 114–21.

Tovey/ESSAYS

Tovey, Donald Francis. *Essays in Musical Analysis.* Vols. 1–6. London: Oxford University Press, 1935–1939.

Tovey/PARRY VARIATIONS

Tovey, Donald Francis. "C. Hubert H. Parry. LXIII. Symphonic Variations for Orchestra." Tovey/ESSAYS II, pp. 142–45.

Tovey/TCHAIKOVSKY 5

Tovey, Donald Francis. "Tchaikovsky. L. Symphony in E Minor, No. 5, Op. 64." Tovey/ESSAYS VI, pp. 58–65.

Tovey/TCHAIKOVSKY PATHETIC

Tovey, Donald Francis. "Tchaikovsky. CCXLI. Pathetic Symphony in B Minor, No. 6, Op. 74." Tovey/ESSAYS II, pp. 84–89.

Trezise/MER

Trezise, Simon. *Debussy: La Mer.* Cambridge Music Handbooks. Cambridge: Cambridge University Press, 1994.

Tyler/MUSIC DEPARTMENT STORES

Tyler, Linda. "'Commerce and Poetry Hand in Hand': Music in American Department Stores, 1880–1930." *JAMS* XLV/1 (Spring 1992):75–120.

Vallas/FRANCK

Vallas, Léon. *La véritable histoire de César Franck (1822–1890).* Paris: Flammarion, 1955. Trans. by Hubert Foss as *César Franck.* New York: Oxford University Press, 1951.

Vallas/d'INDY I

Vallas, Léon. *Vincent d'Indy. Vol. 1: La Jeunesse (1851–1886).* Paris: Albin Michel, 1946.

Vallas/d'INDY II

Vallas, Léon. *Vincent d'Indy. Vol. 2: La Maturité, la vieillesse (1886–1931).* Paris: Albin Michel, 1950.

VERZEICHNIS TSCHAIKOWSKY

Tschaikowsky—Studio Institut International, ed. Systematisches Verzeichnis der Werke von Pjotr Iljitsch Tschaikowsky: Ein Handbuch für die Musikpraxis. Hamburg: Sikorski, 1973.

Vuillermoz/SYMPHONIE

Vuillermoz, Émile. "La Symphonie." Rohozinski/ MUSIQUE FRANÇAISE, Vol. 1, pp. 323–88.

Wagner/CONDUCTING

Wagner, Richard. *Wagner on Conducting.* Trans. by Edward Dannreuther. New York: Dover, 1989.

Wagner/MY LIFE

Wagner, Richard. *My Life.* Trans. by Andrew Gray. Ed. by Mary Whittal. Cambridge: Cambridge University Press, 1983.

Waite/ELGAR, PARRY, STANFORD   Waite, Vincent. "Elgar, Parry and Stanford." Redwood/ELGAR COMPANION, pp. 178–88.

Walker/MUSIC ENGLAND   Walker, Ernest. *A History of Music in England.* 3rd ed. Rev. and enlarged by J. A. Westrup. Oxford: Clarendon Press, 1952.

Warrack/MANFRED LINER NOTES   Warrack, John. Liner notes to Tchaikovsky, *Manfred* Symphony. Philadelphia Orchestra/Eugene Ormandy (RCA Records ARL1-2945, 1979).

Warrack/TCHAIKOVSKY   Warrack, John. *Tchaikovsky.* New York: Scribner's, 1973.

Warrack/TCHAIKOVSKY BALLET   Warrack, John. *Tchaikovsky Ballet Music.* London: BBC, 1979.

Warrack/TCHAIKOVSKY SYMPHONIES   Warrack, John. *Tchaikovsky. Symphonies and Concertos.* London: BBC, 1969.

Weber/MUSIC MIDDLE CLASS   Weber, William. *Music and the Middle Class: The Social Structure of Concert Life in London, Paris, and Vienna.* London: Croom Helm, 1975.

Weingartner/RATSCHLÄGE   Weingartner, Felix. *Ratschläge für Aufführungen klassischer Symphonien, Vol. 2, Schubert und Schumann.* Leipzig: Breitkopf & Härtel, 1918. Trans. by Theodore Albrecht as "On the Performance of the Symphonies of Schubert and Schumann." *Journal of the Conductor's Guild* 7 (Winter 1986):2–24; (Spring 1986): 55–75; (Summer/Fall 1986):78–95.

Weingartner/SYMPHONY   Weingartner, Felix. *The Symphony since Beethoven.* Trans. from the 2nd German ed. by Maude Barrows Dutton. Boston: Oliver Ditson Co., 1904.

Whittall/MUSIC SINCE WWI   Whittall, Arnold. *Music Since the First World War.* New York: St. Martin's Press, 1977.

Widor/FONDATIONS   Widor, Charles-Marie. *Académie des Beaux-Arts: Fondations-Portraits de Massenet á Paladilhe.* Paris: Durand, 1927.

Wiley/TCHAIKOVSKY   Wiley, Roland John. "Tchaikovsky, Pyotr Il'yich." *NG 2* XXV, pp. 144–83.

Willetts/BEETHOVEN ENGLAND   Willetts, Pamela J. *Beethoven and England: An Account of Sources in the British Museum.* London: British Museum, 1970.

Williamson/BENNETT CATALOGUE   Williamson, Rosemary. *William Sterndale Bennett: A Descriptive Thematic Catalogue.* Oxford: Clarendon Press, 1996.

Wood/ORCHESTRAL WORKS TCHAIKOVSKY   Wood, Ralph W. "Miscellaneous Orchestral Works." Abraham/MUSIC TCHAIKOVSKY, pp. 74–103.

Wright/GOUNOD   Wright, Lesley A. "Gounod and Bizet: A Study in Musical Paternity." *JMR* XIII (1993):31–48.

Wyndham/MANNS   Wyndham, H. Saxe. *August Manns and the Saturday Concerts: A Memoir and a Retrospect.* London: Scott, 1909.

Yampolsky/MOSCOW   Yampolsky, I. M. "Moscow." *NG* XII, pp. 600–08.

Yasser/RACHMANINOFF CONCERTO 3 — Yasser, Joseph. "The Opening Theme of Rachmaninoff's Third Piano Concerto and its Liturgical Prototype." *MQ* LV/3 (July 1969):313–28.

Yastrebtsev/RIMSKY-KORSAKOV — Yastrebtsev, V. V. *Reminiscences of Rimsky-Korsakov.* Ed and trans. by Florence Jonas. New York: Columbia University Press, 1985.

YMC — *Your Musical Cue*

Young/ELGAR — Young, Percy M. *Elgar O. M.: A Study of a Musician.* London: Purnell, 1973.

Young/ELGAR LETTERS — Young, Percy M., ed. *Letters of Edward Elgar and Other Writings.* London: G. Bles, 1956.

Zajaczkowski/OBSESSIVE TCHAIKOVSKY — Zajaczkowski, Henry. "The Function of Obsessive Elements in Tchaikovsky's Style." *MR* XLIII/1 (February 1982):24–30.

Zajaczkowski/TCHAIKOVSKY 4 — Zajaczkowski, Henry. "Tchaikovsky's Fourth Symphony." *MR* XLV/3–4 (August-November 1984):265–76.

Zajaczkowski/TCHAIKOVSKY PATHÉTIQUE — Zajaczkowski, Henry. "Not to be Born Were Best . . ." *MT* CXXXIV/1808 (October 1993):561–66.

Zajaczkowski/TCHAIKOVSKY'S STYLE — Zajaczkowski, Henry. *Tchaikovsky's Musical Style.* Ann Arbor: UMI Research Press, 1987.

Index

References to tables and musical examples are italicized.

Index of Works

References to tables and musical examples are italicized.

A. Peter Brown (1943–2003) was born in Chicago, where he was inspired as a youth by the Chicago Symphony Orchestra performances conducted by Fritz Reiner. He studied French horn with Philip Farkas and Christopher Leube and received his B.M.E. (1965), M.M. (1966), and Ph.D. (1970) degrees from Northwestern University. He was a participant in Pierre Monteux's Domaine School for Conductors and Orchestral Players and did postdoctoral studies with Jan LaRue at New York University. After teaching at the University of Hawai'i, in 1974 he joined the musicology faculty of the Indiana University School of Music where he was professor of musicology and department chair at the time of his death. He was a Guggenheim Fellow and a Fellow of the American Council of Learned Societies, as well as a member of the National Academy of Recording Arts and Sciences.

As an eighteenth- and nineteenth-century music scholar, he was author of more than eighty published articles and reviews, but was especially known for his articles and books on Joseph Haydn, among them *Performing Haydn's* The Creation: *Reconstructing the Earliest Renditions* and *Joseph Haydn's Keyboard Music: Sources and Style* (both published by Indiana University Press, 1986). His performance edition of Haydn's *The Creation* has been conducted and recorded by Georg Solti, Christopher Hogwood, John Eliot Gardiner, and others. At the time of his death in March 2003, he had completed volumes 2, 3, and 4 of *The Symphonic Repertoire* series. He is survived by his wife, Carol Vanderbilt Brown, and one daughter, Heidi Elizabeth Vanderbilt-Brown.

Brian Hart is Associate Professor of Music History at Northern Illinois University. He received his Ph.D. in musicology in 1994 from Indiana University, where A. Peter Brown was among his teachers and mentors. He has written articles and papers on various aspects of the late romantic French symphony, including its place in Parisian concert life, the use of the symphony to communicate socio-political philosophies, Debussy's attitude toward the symphony, Vincent d'Indy's contributions to French symphonic development, and the organ symphonies of Charles-Marie Widor and Louis Vierne.